WORLD HISTORY
People & Nations
✦ MODERN WORLD ✦

WORLD HISTORY
People & Nations
✦ MODERN WORLD ✦

HOLT, RINEHART AND WINSTON

A Harcourt Classroom Education Company

Austin · New York · Orlando · Atlanta · San Francisco · Boston · Dallas · Toronto · London

Staff Credits

Editorial
Sue Miller, *Director*
Robert Wehnke, *Managing Editor*
Rhonda Haynes, *Senior Editor*
Christopher J. Parker, *Associate Editor*

Editorial Permissions
Janet Harrington

Art, Design, and Photo
Book and Media Design
Joe Melomo, *Art Director*

Cover Design
Joe Melomo, *Art Director*
Angela Austin, *Designer*

Photo Research
Peggy Cooper, *Photo Research Manager*
Tim Taylor, *Senior Photo Researcher*
Kristin Hay, *Assistant Photo Researcher*
Stephanie Friedman, *Assistant Photo Researcher*

Image Services
Elaine Tate, *Art Buyer Supervisor*
CoCo Weir, *Art Buyer*

New Media Design
Susan Michael, *Art Director*

Design and Page Production
The Quarasan Group, Inc.
ShoeHorn, Inc.

New Media
Kate Bennett, *Associate Director*
Armin Gutzmer, *Manager Training
    and Technical Support*
Cathy Kuhles, *Technical Assistant*
Nina Degollado, *Intern*

Production
Gene Rumann, *Production Manager*
Leanna Ford, *Production Assistant*

Media Production
Kim Anderson-Scott, *Media Production Manager*
Nancy Hargis, *Production Supervisor*
Adriana Bardin, *Production Coordinator*

Manufacturing
Shirley Cantrell, *Manufacturing Coordinator*

For acknowledgments, see page R59, which is an extension of the copyright page.

Printed in the United States of America

ISBN 0-03-053528-X

1 2 3 4 5 6 7 8 9   61   01 00 99 98

Content Reviewers

Dr. Pierre Cagniart
Southwest Texas State University
Ancient history

Dr. Laurel Carrington
St. Olaf College
Medieval, early modern Europe, intellectual

Dr. Robert Divine
University of Texas
American diplomatic

Dr. Roberta Ann Dunbar
University of North Carolina
 at Chapel Hill
African, Afro-American studies

Dr. Michael Hall
University of Texas
Colonial America

Professor Robin Higham, Emeritus
Kansas State University
Military, aviation, technology

Dr. Julian Martin
University of Alberta
Science and medicine, early modern Britain

Dr. Alida Metcalf
Trinity University
Latin America, Brazil

Dr. Gail Minault
University of Texas
India

Dr. Mark Parillo
Kansas State University
United States military,
diplomatic, Japan

Dr. E. Bruce Reynolds
San Jose State University
Japan, China, Southeast Asia

Dr. Richard Saller
University of Chicago
Ancient, early Roman Empire

Dr. Robert Mark Spaulding
University of North Carolina
at Wilmington
Modern German, modern Europe

Dr. Peter Stearns
Carnegie Mellon University
Comparative social, aging, emotions

Dr. Lynn Struve
Indiana University
Premodern China, Chinese
political and intellectual history

Educational Reviewers

James Allocco
Dumont High School
Dumont, New Jersey

Linda Crockford
St. Brendan High School
Miami, Florida

Mary H. Naylor
Deep Creek High School
Chesapeake, Virginia

David Olson
Angola High School
Angola, Indiana

Elizabeth Silva
Dartmouth High School
Dartmouth, Massachusetts

Laura Watkins
Acton Boxborough Regional High School
Acton, Massachusetts

Scott Whitlow
Round Rock High School
Round Rock, Texas

Contents

UNIT 1 — The Emergence of Modern Nations   42

CHAPTER 1

UNIT ②

Industrialism and Nationalism
206

Reference Section

Maps

Atlas

Charts and Graphs

Geography and World History: An Introduction

World History: People and Nations tells the story of the world's people from the very earliest times to the present. History describes the events that make up this story, while geography describes the places in which the events take place. History, then, represents the unfolding drama of people and events through the ages. Geography describes the stage on which this drama is played out. History and geography are so intertwined that to separate them would leave the story only partially told.

Time and Space
Even though history and geography are closely related, they are still two distinct subjects. The basic difference between them may be stated quite simply. As you study history, you acquire an orientation to time; as you study geography, you acquire an orientation to space. Geographers organize their thoughts with respect to spatial arrangements and distributions over Earth's surface. Historians, on the other hand, organize their ideas with respect to time.

Although history is mostly concerned with time, and geography mostly with space, each subject employs aspects of the other as analytical tools. Historians know full well that events occur in places as well as in time. Events, like people, are widely distributed across Earth. In other words, events have a spatial, or geographic, dimension. And geographers, in examining distributions and arrangements throughout the world today, find that they often must look back to a period in time in order to explain these current patterns.

World History: People and Nations tells the story of the world's history. Geography helps to bring this story into focus. Therefore, understanding the special themes and tools of geography will be of great value to you as you read and think about the great personalities and events of the past.

The Five Basic Themes in Geography
Modern geography focuses on five basic themes, or topics: location, place, human-environment interaction, movement, and regions. Each of these five basic themes helps to clarify the relationship between the world's physical landscape and its human occupants. These relationships, of course, have a time span as well as a spatial context.

Location. The first theme, location, has two aspects. Absolute location deals with the exact, or precise, spot on Earth that a place occupies. Relative location, on the other hand, describes the position of a particular place in relation to other places.

The latitude and longitude of a place best describes its absolute location. To calculate latitude and longitude, geographers use a grid formed by a series of imaginary lines drawn around Earth. (See globe on this page.) The equator, an imaginary line that circles Earth halfway between the North and South Poles, divides Earth into two halves, or hemispheres. Geographers call these hemispheres the Northern Hemisphere and the Southern Hemisphere. Several shorter imaginary lines called parallels, or lines of latitude, circle Earth, parallel to the equator.

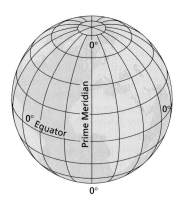

Geographers identify the parallels through a special numbering system based on degrees. In the Northern Hemisphere, the parallels number from zero degrees (0°) at the equator to ninety degrees north (90°N) at the North Pole. Similarly, in the Southern Hemisphere, they run from 0° at the equator to 90° S at the South Pole.

Another set of imaginary lines—called meridians, or lines of longitude—is used to measure Earth east and west. The prime meridian—which runs from pole to pole through the Royal Observatory in Greenwich, England—serves as 0° longitude. The meridian directly opposite the prime meridian, on the other side of the globe, is the 180° meridian. The prime meridian and the 180° meridian together divide Earth into the Eastern and Western Hemispheres. The Eastern Hemisphere is the half of Earth that extends east of the prime meridian to the 180° meridian. The Western Hemisphere is the half of Earth west of the prime meridian to the 180° meridian.

Together, parallels and meridians form an imaginary grid over Earth. Since each degree of latitude and longitude can be broken into 60′ (60 minutes), and each minute can be broken into 60" (60 seconds), the grid fixes the precise location of any place on Earth's surface. For example, the absolute location of Santa Fe, New Mexico, is 35°41' north and 105°57' west. No other place on Earth is located at exactly this same place.

The relative location of a place is often described in terms of direction and distance from another place. Santa Fe's relative location, for example, might be expressed as 58 miles northeast of Albuquerque. Other ways of describing relative location include nearness to resources and accessibility to trade routes.

Place. Place has to do with a location's physical and human characteristics. Every location on Earth has its own unique, or distinctive, physical and human characteristics. Physical characteristics include the shape of the land, climate, soils, vegetation, and animal life. Land use, street layout, architecture, and population distribution are a location's human characteristics. Physically, Santa Fe is in the foothills of the southern Rocky Mountains. Its human characteristics include its traditional Pueblo and Spanish architecture. Together, the physical and human characteristics make up a location's place identity. This identity changes through time and is therefore very important to an understanding of history.

Human-Environment Interaction. Throughout time, people have adapted their way of life to accommodate to their environment. For example, people who live in hot, dry climates such as in Sante Fe and other parts of the American Southwest have built houses of adobe, or sun-dried clay bricks. Even in extreme heat, the adobe helps to keep the house cool.

People also have made changes to their physical environment. For instance, they have cleared forests, dug irrigation ditches, and built huge cities. Geographers consider all the ways in which people interact with their natural environment.

The theme of human-environment interaction is of great importance to historians, for it concerns not only the ways in which people interact with their physical surroundings but also the consequences of such interactions. For example, the decision to mine and use fossil fuels to produce energy had the negative consequence of polluting the environment. This consequence, in turn, gave rise to people acting together to protect their environment. Such actions are of great interest to historians.

Tea fields in Sri Lanka

Movement. The fourth theme of modern geography, movement, concerns the interactions of people with one another as they travel, communicate, and exchange goods and services on a worldwide basis. Through much of its history, for example, Santa Fe has been a trading center for ranchers, farmers, and American Indians. Movement also includes an examination of the spread of ideas and the great human migrations that have occurred through the centuries—two vital issues in the study of history.

Regions. In order to better study and understand Earth, geographers think of it in units called regions. A region is an area having a specific characteristic or characteristics. The characterisics used to define a region may be physical features such as climate, vegetation, and landforms, or they may be cultural features such as a dominant religion or language. The particular features that characterize a region set it apart from other regions. Since there are different kinds of regions, any given area might be part of several regions. For example, Sante Fe is the state capital of New Mexico (a political region), at the foot of the Sangre de Cristo Range of the Rocky Mountains (a climate region), and it has a large Spanish-American population (a cultural region).

The Tools of Geography
To develop these five basic themes, geographers use a wide

Skyline of Houston, Texas

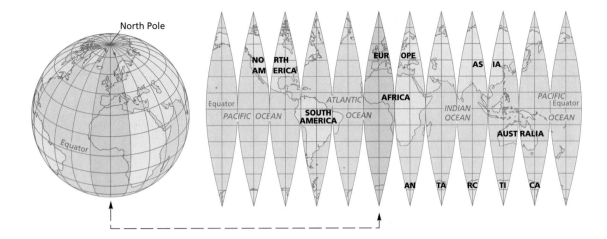

variety of tools. These tools include such modern and sophisticated items as aerial photographs, satellite images, and extremely intricate computer programs. However, a geographer's most basic and essential tools—globes and maps—have been used for centuries. Globes and maps, of course, are very familiar objects. You have seen them in your classroom or in the school library, and perhaps also in your home. Globes and maps are essential to the study of geography because they provide fairly accurate representations of Earth. However, globes and maps are not perfect models of Earth, and, therefore, each has advantages and disadvantages as a geographical tool.

The most important advantage of a globe is its shape. It is the only model of Earth that is spherical. Because a globe's shape follows the shape of Earth, the landmasses and bodies of water shown on it are correct in terms of shape and relative area. A globe also accurately shows distance and direction from one place to another.

In spite of its accuracy, the globe has some limitations. To begin with, a globe is bulky and awkward to carry. In addition, a globe does not allow you to see the entire Earth at once. For example, if you look at South

America, Australia is hidden from your view. When you turn the globe to find Australia, South America is not visible. A globe's greatest problem, however, is that it lacks detail. Even the largest globes could not show the detailed features of the ancient Nile Valley. There would be no way to indicate the location of each of the 35 major pyramids that stand near the Nile River, the huge stone figure of the Sphinx, or the numerous irrigation channels and reservoirs used by the farmers of the region.

In contrast, the intricate details shown on maps make them useful to geographers. Through the use of symbols and colors, a huge range of information can be shown clearly on a map. By comparing maps, geographers can see movements, the effects of human-environment interactions, and the locations of various physical and cultural regions. In addition, maps are far more manageable than globes. They can be rolled or folded, and therefore they are easy to carry.

Still, maps do have one serious drawback: they are never totally accurate. Regardless of the skill of the cartographer, or mapmaker, no map can accurately show the qualities of shape, area,

distance, and direction at the same time because mapmaking involves recording on a flat surface what is curved on Earth's surface. (See map on this page.)

To appreciate the problems faced by cartographers, place a piece of paper directly over one of the Great Lakes of North America on a globe. Now trace the outline of the lake onto your paper. You should be able to trace its outline accurately without once bending or twisting your paper. Next, try tracing the outline of the entire North American continent. You can see immediately that some cutting or folding of the paper is required. Otherwise, you will drastically distort the outline of the continent. On the other hand, in cutting or folding the map, you create other distortions.

Distortion, then, is a major problem for cartographers when depicting large areas of Earth's curved surface on a flat map. Since maps cannot accurately show all four kinds of map information—shape, area, distance, and direction—at the same time, cartographers must decide which information they want their maps to distort least. Cartographers use a variety of projections—methods by which Earth's surface is recorded, or projected, onto paper to create flat maps.

Map Projections

Literally thousands of map projections exist. Each one distorts one or more of the four major map attributes. The projection that a cartographer chooses depends on the size and location of the area to be projected and on the purpose of the map.

Cartographers often choose the Robinson projection. (See map at right.) This projection is unique because it is a compromise projection. It maintains no single property but minimizes overall distortion.

If true shape is the most important objective of the cartographer, he or she will select a conformal projection, such as the Mercator projection. (See map below.) On a map that uses such a projection, land masses are shown in their true shapes. Size relationships, however, are distorted. If the purpose of the map is to show

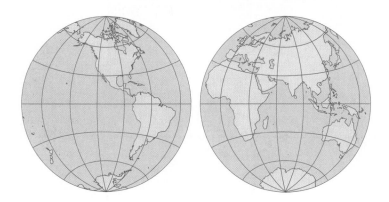

correct relative size, an equal-area projection, such as the Molleweide projection or the Peters projection, will be used. (See maps on this page.) Maps whose projections show correct distances between places are called equidistant maps. Equidistant maps work well for projecting areas of limited size, such as a city or a state. A map of the entire world could never be equidistant, however, because it is impossible to show the lengths of lines of latitude and longitude on a flat map as accurately as they appear on a globe. Finally, maps that show true distances and direction measurements from a central point on the map are called azimuthal maps. (See map at the bottom of this page.) These maps are often used to show the polar regions.

Each kind of projection has its strengths and weaknesses. On a conformal map, for example, angles and directions are correct, but size relationships are quite distorted. Compare, for example, the relative sizes of Africa and Greenland on the Mercator projection with their relative size on the Molleweide or Peters projection or on a globe.

Equal-area maps, on the other hand, are especially useful for comparing factors that may be affected by an area's size, such as temperature patterns, population size, or mineral production. The greatest drawback of equal-area maps is that they distort the shapes of the areas shown.

Equidistant projections are used for road maps because they allow the driver to get a clear and accurate picture of the distances to be traveled. Certain types of azimuthal maps, in contrast, are especially useful to pilots because they show the shortest distance between two places on Earth as a straight line.

In spite of their drawbacks, then, there is indeed a map projection to meet every need. In studying maps, however, always remember to note the type of projection that was used so that you will be aware of how it is different from a globe, the one precise model of Earth. To aid you in this task, each of the maps in this book identifies the map projection used.

Ancient World

TIME

c.* 3,700,000 B.C.–1500 A.D.

3,700,000 B.C.–1500 A.D.

3.7 million B.C. | 4000 B.C. | A.D. 2100

*c. stands for *circa* and means "about."

PLACE

Africa, Asia, Europe, the
Americas, and Australia

**Ruins of the Parthenon,
Acropolis, Athens**

Significance

Because we have no written record of prehistoric times, many events of our remote past remain cloaked in mystery. Nevertheless, we know that prehistoric people invented tools, produced beautiful art, built cities, and developed governments. They gradually created what we call **civilizations**—highly organized societies with complex institutions and attitudes that link a large number of people together.

Civilizations first appeared in four great river valleys—the Nile, the Tigris-Euphrates, the Indus, and the Huang He. It is here that our main story begins.

Terms to Define

civilizations	tyrants
division of labor	direct democracy
cultural diffusion	patriarchs
polytheism	pope
monotheism	icons
cuneiform	feudalism
ziggurats	sacraments
ethical monotheism	canon law
dharma	Inquisition
caste system	common law
stupa	Great Schism
Mandate of Heaven	kami
the Five Classics	adobe
polis	*quipu*

People to Identify

Hammurabi	Constantine
Brahma	Justinian
the Buddha	Muhammad
Confucius	Ottomans
Pericles	Charlemagne
Alexander the Great	Habsburgs
Jesus	Kublai Khan

Places to Locate

Nile River	China
Tigris River	Athens
Euphrates River	Sparta
Indus River	Rome
Huang He	Kiev
Egypt	Mali
Mohenjo-Daro	Songhay

In 1979 in a remote, almost inaccessible region of northern Tanzania, the scientist Mary Leakey made a remarkable discovery. As she stared down into the rugged terrain, she was amazed to see that a simple series of footprints lay imbedded in the volcanic rock. What fascinated her was that these footprints had not been left earlier that day or even earlier that week. Instead, she found that they were millions of years old. Made in the soft ash of a volcanic eruption, the prints had been preserved as the ash had hardened.

Although we will never know exactly who made these prints, Leakey believes that they belonged to a hominid, one of the humanlike creatures who, scientists theorize, preceded us on Earth.

“Following the path produces, at least for me, a kind of poignant time wrench. At one point, and you need not be an expert tracker to discern this, the traveler stops, pauses, turns to the left to glance at some possible threat or irregularity, then continues to the north. This motion, so intensely human, transcends time. Three million seven hundred thousand years ago, a remote ancestor—just as you or I—experienced a moment of doubt.”

Leakey is only one of many dedicated scholars who have tried to piece together the distant past.

Section 1

The First Civilizations

Focus Questions

- **What important developments occurred during the Middle and New Stone Ages?**
- **Where did the first civilizations develop?**
- **What were the great achievements of the first civilizations?**

The Emergence of Civilization

“In the beginning human history is a great darkness.” This observation, made twenty-five years ago by a leading world historian, is still true today. Despite great efforts by archaeologists—the scientists who study ancient fossils, settlements, and artifacts—and other researchers, over the years, we are still forced to reconstruct the story of early human beings before the development of writing from very little evidence. It is a story that depends upon little more than a basketful of human bones, fossils, and artifacts. Yet despite these limitations, through research and new scientific techniques scholars have been able to unearth a great deal of information about the emergence and early development of civilization. Most scholars refer to this period before the invention of writing as prehistory.

Prehistoric peoples. Archaeologists have found evidence that humanlike creatures first appeared on Earth millions of years ago. At some point, probably between 300,000 and 200,000 years ago, the species known as *Homo sapiens*, which includes Neanderthal and Cro-Magnon people as well as all people living today, appeared in Africa. Over thousands of years, the first prehistoric people migrated to many parts of the world.

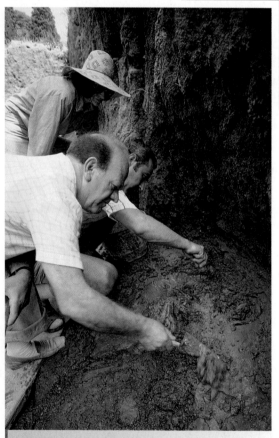

Archaeologists study past cultures by analyzing human remains and artifacts.

Scientists today often classify the stages of human development according to the kinds of tools people used. The Stone Age, the period in which people used tools made primarily of stone, is divided into three parts: the Old Stone Age, or Paleolithic Age; the Middle Stone Age, or Mesolithic Age; and the New Stone Age, or Neolithic Age. These periods lasted different lengths of time in different parts of the world, depending on when people developed newer and better stone tools. In general, however, the Old Stone Age lasted from about 2 million years ago until about 12,000 years ago. The Middle Stone Age lasted from about 12,000 to about 10,000 years ago, and the New Stone Age lasted from about 10,000 to about 5,000 years ago.

At first, early humans were nomads, moving from place to place in search of food. These early peoples seem to have been greatly affected by climatic changes, particularly the long periods of extremely cold weather known collectively as the Ice Age. During the Ice Age, Neanderthals and later Cro-Magnons learned to use fire and to make warm clothing, which helped them survive in colder regions. During the Ice Age the sea level dropped because so much water was frozen in the icecaps. As the sea level fell, land bridges emerged between the continents. People and animals crossed the land bridges into new territories. In this way, humans spread into all parts of the world.

As people adapted to the changes in their environment, they discovered new ways of living. During the Middle Stone Age, for example, they tamed the dog, and invented the bow and arrow, fishhooks, fish spears, and harpoons made from bones and antlers. More important changes occurred during the New Stone Age. During this period, some Neolithic peoples began settling in permanent villages. Some people learned to grow their own plants, which led to the development of agriculture, and to domesticate, or tame, herd animals such as cattle, goats, sheep, and pigs. Depending on local conditions, some people became primarily farmers, while others survived by herding animals.

Agriculture and the domestication of animals changed the basic way people lived. While farmers had to settle in one area, herders often remained partly nomadic, moving with their herds in search of grazing land. In addition, the kind of agriculture people practiced varied from region to region as different plant species were domesticated in different parts of the world. Wheat and barley, for example, originated in Southwest Asia and rice developed in South Asia.

Archaeologists have discovered the remains of mud-brick houses and shrines at Çatalhüyük.

Corn was first cultivated in the Americas, bananas in Southeast Asia, and potatoes in South America. The shift from food gathering to food producing is often called the Neolithic Revolution.

The foundations of civilization. As people learned to farm and began to settle down, they also began to establish towns, such as Çatalhüyük in Turkey. Eventually, where conditions were right, people organized themselves on an even larger scale into what we today call civilizations. Most civilizations have at least three characteristics: (1) People have been able to produce surplus food. (2) People have created large towns or cities with some form of government. (3) A **division of labor** exists, in which different people perform different jobs, instead of each person doing all kinds of work. Some historians also consider the development of a calendar or some form of writing to be characteristic of civilization.

Meanwhile, people were also improving their tools. In particular, they learned to use metals. With the discovery of copper and bronze, some people moved into the Bronze Age. People in the Nile and Tigris-Euphrates River valleys knew how to make bronze jewelry and weapons as early as 5,000 years ago. By about 3,200 years ago, people in southwestern Asia had learned to make iron and to craft tools from it, thereby launching the Iron Age.

Improved farming, made possible by techniques such as irrigation and better tools, caused a surplus of higher quality food and therefore a healthier and more comfortable life for each person. Improvements in agriculture also led to an increase in population, and some of the early village communities grew to become cities. The large number of people living in cities provided the labor to create great palaces, temples, and other public buildings.

The development of agriculture had significant consequences for family life in early human settlements. At first, women did much of the farming, both planting and harvesting crops. With steady food supplies from agriculture, men hunted less. As women became responsible for much of the food supply, their authority and independence seems to have increased. When the plow was invented, however, men again became the primary food providers and assumed their former dominance in the family.

As farming methods improved, fewer people had to work in the fields in order to produce enough food for all. Some could specialize in other kinds of work. Those skilled in making tools and weapons, for example, could devote all their time to such work, trading their products for the food they needed. Thus a skilled class of craft workers called artisans appeared. Other people became traders and merchants. Traders not only transported goods for sale, but also passed along ideas. We call the spread of aspects of culture from one area to another **cultural diffusion.** People in the river valleys also developed calendars early in their histories, as they sought to know when to plant and harvest their crops. Writing too developed as civilizations expanded their trade and discovered the need to keep records. By developing written language, the early river valley civilizations created a record of their culture and society— the era of recorded history had begun.

The first civilizations that we know of developed in or around four great river valleys: the Nile Valley in Africa; the Tigris-Euphrates Valley in southwest Asia; the Indus Valley in south Asia; and the Huang He, or Yellow River Valley in east Asia. Farming in these river valleys depended on irrigation. Farmers had to get water from the rivers to their fields during the dry season. They had to control floods, so that their crops were not washed away. Building large irrigation and flood control projects required a high level of cooperation. Governments may have developed gradually as a result of such cooperation. To work together effectively, people made rules to govern their behavior and to plan, direct, and regulate their work.

Kingdoms of the Nile

The ancient Greek historian Herodotus once observed that all Egypt was "the gift of the Nile." Each year rain caused the river to flood, bringing rich silts down from the Ethiopian Highlands and depositing them over the lower parts of the river valley. From the earliest times, Egyptian farmers planned their work around the flood, not only taking advantage of the richness of the soil it left behind, but also using its waters for irrigation.

Over the centuries, strong leaders united early Egyptian farming settlements to create two kingdoms, Lower Egypt in the north, and Upper Egypt in the south. Then, sometime after 3200 B.C., a king of Upper Egypt, known as Menes (MEE•neez), united the two kingdoms. He and his successors eventually took the title pharaoh. They crushed rebellions, gained new territory, regulated irrigation, and encouraged trade, bringing increased prosperity. From the time of Menes to almost 300 B.C., about 30 Egyptian dynasties, or families of rulers, rose and fell. Historians divide this time span into three kingdoms: the Old Kingdom, which lasted from about 2650 to 2180 B.C.; the Middle Kingdom, from about 2040 to 1780 B.C.; and the New Kingdom, which was established about 1570 B.C. The periods between the kingdoms are referred to as intermediate periods.

During the second intermediate period, about 1650, much of Egypt fell under the control of an Asiatic people—the Hyksos (HIK•sohs)—whose horse-drawn chariots overwhelmed the Egyptians. Eventually, a new leader emerged in the city of Thebes who drove the Hyksos out of Egypt and proclaimed the New Kingdom under his own dynasty. Adopting the battle techniques of the Hyksos, the pharaohs of the New Kingdom conquered new territories in Nubia and along the eastern Mediterranean coast, in the process establishing an empire.

From about 1380 to 1362 B.C., Egypt was ruled by the pharaoh Amenhotep (ahm•uhn•HOH•tep) IV. Amenhotep IV tried to replace the traditional Egyptian belief in many gods, a practice known as **polytheism,** with his own belief in only one god, a practice known as **monotheism.** The new god was symbolized by the disk of the Sun, called the Aton, and Amenhotep even changed his name to Akhenaton (ahk•NAHT•uhn), or "he who is pleasing to Aton." Akhenaton's religious revolution stirred up resentment and the end of his reign was marked by strife between the pharaoh and the priests of the old religious cults. After Akhenaton's death, the priests regained power and, under the boy-king Tutankhamen (too•tang•KAHM•uhn), they restored the old polytheistic religion in Egypt.

After Akhenaton, few strong pharaohs ruled Egypt. Perhaps the most important exception was Ramses II, sometimes called Ramses the Great, who ruled from about 1279 to 1213 B.C. Ramses' successors could not hold the empire together, however, and eventually Egyptian power declined.

With the prosperity provided by the Nile's bounty and protected for the most part from invaders by its geographical location, Egyptian civilization was remarkably stable over the course of its long history.

Egypt: The New Kingdom, c. 1450 B.C.

Learning from Maps The New Kingdom extended Egypt's borders.

? Location Approximately how many miles is it from the northernmost point to the southernmost point of the New Kingdom?

Anxious to keep track of the Nile floods, the Egyptians developed a remarkably accurate calendar based on the rising and setting of the star Sirius. They also developed a number system based on 10, remarkably similar to the decimal system we use today. They used geometry to calculate how to restore the boundaries of fields after floods, and also to build the pyramids. Egyptian architects and engineers ranked among the best of the ancient world. The Egyptians also learned a great deal about the human body and used this knowledge to treat illnesses and to preserve the bodies of the dead.

At the heart of Egyptian civilization was the Egyptians' concern with religion. Egyptians believed in many gods, including the idea that the pharaoh himself was a god. The most important of these gods was Amon, or Amon-Re, the king of the gods. They also came to believe in an afterlife and the possibility of achieving immortality after death by preserving the body of someone who had died. To do this, they developed a process known as mummification, which involved removing internal organs and treating the body with chemicals so that it would remain preserved for centuries. Although at first only the pharaoh was treated in this fashion, eventually even ordinary Egyptians hoped to survive after physical death. In later periods, they included copies of the Book of the Dead—hymns, prayers, and spells that acted as a kind of guide to the afterlife—in people's tombs. It was largely in an effort to preserve bodies and to safeguard all the articles with which they were buried for the needs of the afterlife that Egyptians spent so much time constructing elaborate tombs like the pyramids. Much of Egyptian art was also devoted to religious themes and to decorating the tombs in which people expected to spend eternity.

The Fertile Crescent, c. 2900 B.C.

Learning from Maps The Fertile Crescent arcs from the Isthmus of Suez through Mesopotamia to the Persian Gulf.

? Location Near what Sumerian city do the Tigris and Euphrates Rivers come within 20 miles of each other?

Kingdoms of the Tigris-Euphrates

The ancient Egyptians developed a civilization that reflected the generally bountiful nature of the Nile. In the Tigris-Euphrates Valley—sometimes called Mesopotamia, after the later Greek term for "land between the rivers," or the Fertile Crescent—civilization developed along rather different lines. The Tigris and Euphrates Rivers begin in the hills of modern Turkey and flow south to the Persian Gulf. The flooding of the Tigris and Euphrates, unlike that of the Nile, cannot be easily predicted. Not only is the exact time of year unpredictable, but the extent of the flood cannot be estimated. Not surprisingly, the people of the valley viewed nature and the gods as angry and unreasonable. Even so, the two rivers provided water and rich soils for agriculture, particularly in Sumer in the southern region.

Sumerian civilization. In Sumer, Neolithic people settled, grew crops, and over time created what we call Sumerian culture in a number of small city-states. A city-state included not only the city itself but also the land and fields around it. By 3000 B.C., the Sumerians knew how to use metal and had developed a new form of wedge-shaped writing, known as **cuneiform** from the Latin word for wedge.

The ancient Sumerians established many of the patterns of civilization that would be adopted by later civilizations in the Tigris-Euphrates region. They built their houses and other buildings from sun-dried clay bricks. They may have also invented several important architectural designs, including the arch. The most striking buildings were temples, known as **ziggurats,** which formed the central feature of a city-state. Ziggurats were built up like a layered wedding cake, with each story a bit smaller than the one on which it sat. At the top was a shrine to one of the Sumerian gods.

In addition to their architectural advances, the Sumerians also made many other important discoveries. Some scholars think they were the first to develop and use the wheel. In mathematics they used a number system based on 60, and divided the circle into 360 degrees, with each degree made up of 60 minutes, and each minute further subdivided into 60 seconds.

Religion was at the heart of Sumerian civilization. Like the ancient Egyptians, the Sumerians were polytheists, believing in many gods. They believed that each city was the property of a god or goddess, who were also associated with the forces of nature and with heavenly bodies like the moon and the Sun. Unlike the Egyptians, however, the Sumerians viewed their gods as unpredictable and cruel—rather like the natural environment around them. Consequently, they had little conception of an elaborate afterlife. Indeed, competition among the city-states over water rights along the rivers was often interpreted as a battle between the gods of the respective city-states.

Empires of the Fertile Crescent. The lack of unity among the Sumerian city-states made them vulnerable to attack not only by rival cities, but also by surrounding nomadic peoples who were attracted by the relative wealth of the cities. As these nomadic peoples interacted with the settled communities of the cities, they soon began to learn the skills of civilization. Combining this new knowledge with their own warlike skills, some began to conquer the cities of the Tigris-Euphrates and to create the first empires.

Some time around 2330 B.C., the Akkadians, a people who also lived in Mesopotamia, conquered the Sumerians. The most powerful of the Akkadian kings, Sargon, who ruled from about 2350 to 2300 B.C., established a great empire that extended as far west as the Mediterranean Sea. Although it only lasted about a hundred years, the Akkadian Empire was the first of many to take control of the area.

Around 1792 B.C., a powerful ruler named Hammurabi (ham•uh•RAUB•ee) came to power in the city of Babylon and conquered most of the upper Tigris-Euphrates Valley. More than just an outstand-

The Eastern Mediterranean, c. 1200 B.C.–1000 B.C.

Learning from Maps Because of their location along the Mediterranean, many of the region's peoples turned to the sea for commercial activity.

? Region Which mountain range created a natural boundary between Phoenicia and the Kingdom of Israel?

ing military leader, Hammurabi was an outstanding political leader as well. He is best known for the Code of Hammurabi, a collection of laws compiled under his direction. Like the Akkadians, the Babylonians copied many aspects of Sumerian culture, including their religious beliefs.

Sometime in the 1600s B.C., yet another group of warlike peoples, an Indo-European speaking group known as the Hittites, invaded the Tigris-Euphrates Valley from Asia Minor. The Hittites were among the first to use iron weapons. They also introduced a new, more reasonable set of laws than the harsher ones laid down in Hammurabi's code. Yet, while they conquered Babylon, the Hittites were unable to hold the region for long and eventually withdrew to their new home base in Asia Minor.

After a prolonged period of further invasions by migrating peoples, about 900 B.C. the Assyrians, a Semitic-speaking people, began to expand their rule throughout the Fertile Crescent. Eventually, they conquered a vast empire that stretched from Egypt to the Iranian Plateau.

The Assyrians excelled in warfare. They were the first to make extensive use of cavalry—units of soldiers mounted on horses. They also waged war ferociously, frequently killing their war captives and sometimes massacring the inhabitants of cities they conquered to instill terror in others. They ruled their empire through an efficient system of imperial bureaucracy. Governors ruled conquered territories and made regular reports to the king. To ensure loyalty, secret inspectors checked up on the governors and reported on their activities to the king directly. Like other conquerors before them, the Assyrians were influenced by the earlier patterns of Sumerian civilization. In fact, it was while excavating the great library of the Assyrian capital of Nineveh that modern archaeologists found a copy of the ancient Sumerian *Epic of Gilgamesh*, one of the oldest works of literature known.

The Assyrians' tactics won them many enemies. Finally, in 612 B.C., an alliance of their foes, led by the Medes and the Chaldeans, captured and totally destroyed the Assyrian capital of Nineveh and put an end once and for all to Assyrian power.

Under the leadership of king Nebuchadnezzar (neb•uh•kuhd•NEZ•uhr), the Chaldeans conquered most of the Fertile Crescent. Babylon, their capital, once again became a large and rich city. After Nebuchadnezzar's death, however, this brief revival of Babylonian power faltered and in 539 Babylon fell to yet another Indo-European speaking people from the Iranian Plateau, the Persians. Under their great rulers, Cyrus the Great and Darius I, the Persians created the largest empire yet seen, ruling the peoples of southwest Asia and Egypt with an efficient and generally tolerant imperial bureaucracy.

The Phoenicians, Lydians, and Hebrews

The peoples who lived in the western end of the Fertile Crescent and in western Asia Minor did not create large empires, but they had great influence on the modern world.

Phoenicia consisted of a loose union of city-states, each governed by a different king. The Phoenicians turned to the sea and to commerce for their living and became the greatest traders in the ancient Mediterranean world. Perhaps most important, the Phoenicians developed the alphabet on which our own alphabet is patterned.

The Lydians of Asia Minor are remembered as the first people in history to use coined money, beginning in about 600 B.C. Through trade, they passed on the idea of a money economy to the Greeks and Persians.

As in the eastern part of the Fertile Crescent, a series of peoples inhabited Canaan, which lay south of Phoenicia along the land bridge between Asia and Africa. The Semitic-speaking Hebrews, the ancestors

Darius I is shown here in a stone carving receiving homage in his palace at Persepolis.

of modern Jews, had a great influence on this region and on all of history.

The Hebrews worshiped one god, Yahweh. They thought of their god not as a glorified human being, but as the one true god, the creator of the universe. The Torah, part of the Hebrew scriptures, outlines the Hebrew code of laws. This code set a higher value on human life than had earlier law codes. Because of its emphasis on ethics, or right conduct, Judaism, the Hebrew form of monotheism is often called **ethical monotheism**. It ranks as the Hebrews' most important contribution to Western civilization.

Section 1 Review

1. **Define** civilizations, division of labor, cultural diffusion, polytheism, monotheism, cuneiform, ziggurats, ethical monotheism
2. **Identify** Hammurabi
3. **Locate and Explain the Significance** Nile River, Tigris River, Euphrates River, Egypt
4. **Identifying Ideas** Describe the advances made in the Middle and New Stone Ages in the way people lived.
5. **Understanding Ideas** What are the three characteristics of a civilization, and where did the first civilizations develop?
6. **Summarizing Ideas** Briefly describe some of the achievements of the civilizations of the Nile, Fertile Crescent, and western Asia Minor.

Section 2

Ancient India and China

Focus Questions

- What were the characteristics of early Indo-Aryan society?
- What are the basic teachings of Hinduism and Buddhism?
- What were the major accomplishments of the Qin and Han dynasties in China that impacted later dynasties?

As civilization was becoming complex in southwest Asia and northeastern Africa, so too peoples in ancient India and China learned the techniques of agriculture, built cities, and began to develop more and more complex civilizations of their own.

Ancient Indian Civilization

As far as scholars can tell, the first civilization in India developed about 4500 years ago, in the valley of the Indus River. This was several hundred years after Egypt and Sumer developed civilizations. Although our knowledge of this civilization is incomplete, the ruins of two cities, Mohenjo-Daro and Harappa, provide us with the best evidence. Scholars often refer to this civilization as the Harappan civilization because it was in Harappa that archaeologists first discovered its artifacts.

Harappan civilization. Both Harappa and Mohenjo-Daro show evidence of extremely sophisticated city planning and design. Both cities, for example, had wide streets laid out on a grid pattern, as well as extensive public water works, including public baths and a covered brick sewer system for private homes. The early Indus Valley people also developed their own written language, though modern scholars have not yet learned to decipher it. Scholars disagree about why this civilization declined. Some have suggested that the course of the Indus River changed dramatically, with devastating consequences for agriculture in the valley and flooding in the cities. Others have suggested invasion by migrating tribes led to the conquest and downfall of the civilization. Still others have argued that the region was subject to major earthquakes. The real reasons remain a mystery.

Indo-Aryan migrants. What is certain, however, is that sometime around 1750 B.C., new groups of Indo-European speaking peoples, whose original homeland was probably somewhere north of the Black and Caspian Seas, began to move south through the mountain passes

Harappan seals show examples of the picture writing of the Harappans

into northern India. Although they called themselves Aryans, scholars today refer to them as Indo-Aryans, to distinguish them from those Aryan tribes who remained in what is now Iran. The nomadic Indo-Aryans herded sheep and cows. Skillful fighters, the Indo-Aryans eventually conquered the Indus Valley and then gradually moved eastward along the great Ganges River, until after several centuries they controlled the entire Gangetic plain of northern India.

Most of what we know about early Indo-Aryan society comes from the Vedas, the great literature of the Indo-Aryan religion. Eventually, Indo-Aryan settlements joined to form small city-states, each ruled by a raja—a prince or king. Differences between the Indo-Aryans and the earlier inhabitants of India led to the development over time of a complex social system, with warriors and later priests at the top, followed by merchants, traders, farmers, and servants at the bottom.

Less influenced by the influx of the Indo-Aryans, southern India at first developed somewhat differently from the north. Separated from the Indo-Gangetic plain in the north by the forest-covered mountains of the Vindhya Range, the people of the south were able to resist conquest by the Indo-Aryans for centuries. They remained linguistically, ethnically, and culturally distinct from the populations of the north. The southern part of India is quite hilly, and this too worked against political or cultural unification. As a result, southern India remained fragmented into many different groups. Some lived as farmers, others as hunter-gatherers. Those living along the coast often turned to trade and commerce for a living and, through coastal ports, southern Indians eventually made contact with other civilizations in southeast Asia.

Hinduism and Buddhism. Two of the world's great religions developed in ancient India—Hinduism and Buddhism. According to Hinduism, the world known to our senses is an illusion called maya, which betrays people, giving them sorrow and pain. People can be delivered from their suffering if they learn to identify maya. Because this learning takes lifetimes of experience, reincarnation—the rebirth of the soul—occurs to make it possible. According to Hinduism, the soul does not die with the body, but is reincarnated, or reborn, in the body of another being, either human or animal, and thus lives again. Ultimately, Hindus hope to end the repeated reincarnations and enable their souls to reunite with the universal spirit, Brahma.

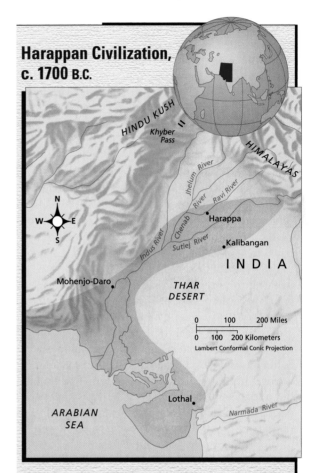

Harappan Civilization, c. 1700 B.C.

Learning from Maps Rivers formed natural highways that encouraged exchange as well as unity in the Harappan civilization.

? Location Which two Harappan cities are connected by rivers?

Two major events in the theory in reincarnation are known as dharma and karma. **Dharma** is fulfillment of one's moral duty in this life so that the soul can make progress toward deliverance from punishment in the next life. Karma is the positive or negative force generated by a person's actions, which will determine that person's status in the next life.

According to Hinduism, people who fulfill their dharma are rewarded with good karma and are reborn into a higher social group. People who do not live moral lives are reborn into a lower social group or even into the bodies of animals or insects.

The other great religion of India, Buddhism, was founded by Siddhartha Gautama, who became known as the Buddha, or "the Enlightened One."

The Buddha accepted the Hindu belief that the progress of the soul depends on how one leads one's life. He taught that salvation comes from knowing the Four Noble Truths and following the Eightfold Path. The Four Noble Truths are (1) that all human life involves suffering and sorrow, (2) that the desire for a life of pleasure and material gain causes suffering and sorrow, (3) that renouncing desire frees people from suffering and helps their souls attain nirvana, the perfect peace, which releases the soul from the endless cycle of reincarnation, and (4) that the Eightfold Path leads to renunciation, or denial, of desire. The Eightfold Path consists of (1) right views, or seeing life as it truly is, (2) right intentions, (3) right speech, (4) right action, (5) right living, (6) right effort, or working to prevent evil, (7) right mindfulness, or constant awareness of one's self, and (8) right concentration to direct the mind in meditation.

The Buddha's teachings stressed ethics, a code of morals and conduct, rather than ceremonies. He believed that desire caused suffering, and consequently he stressed the denial of self. The Buddha did not accept the Hindu gods, and he taught that priests should live peaceful and highly moral lives of poverty.

Opposed by the powerful Brahmins, or Hindu priests, Buddhism flourished briefly in India but then went into decline. However, even as it declined in India, Buddhism spread along the trade routes to other parts of Asia. Sometime between 200 B.C. and A.D. 200 the movement split into two branches—Theraveda Buddhism, which viewed the Buddha himself simply as an outstanding spiritual teacher and guide, and Mahayana Buddhism, which saw the Buddha as a god and savior. Mahayana Buddhism in particular greatly influenced peoples in China, Japan, and Korea. Theraveda Buddhism was more influential in southeast Asia.

Ancient Indian dynasties and empires. The first great Indian empire was established by a young adventurer named Chandragupta Maurya. Under Chadragupta Maurya and his grandson, Asoka, the Mauryan Empire united all of India except the southern tip for almost 150 years before it collapsed in 184 B.C.

In the aftermath of the fall of the Mauryan Empire, parts of northern India fell under foreign rulers, while the rest splintered back into local kingdoms. Eventually, however, in A.D. 320 a new

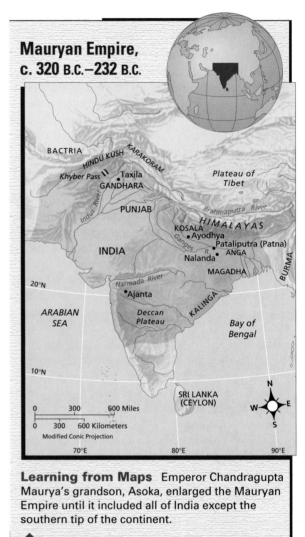

Mauryan Empire, c. 320 B.C.–232 B.C.

Learning from Maps Emperor Chandragupta Maurya's grandson, Asoka, enlarged the Mauryan Empire until it included all of India except the southern tip of the continent.

? **Location** Which mountain ranges form the northern boundary of the Mauryan Empire?

dynasty emerged to reunite most of northern India. This new dynasty—the Guptas—presided over what has been called a golden age of Indian history. Both society and the arts prospered under their rule. It was also under the patronage of the Guptas that Hinduism finally prevailed over Buddhism as the dominant religious system in India. Gupta rule finally ended, however, by about A.D. 550. Waves of invaders had begun to enter northern India in the late A.D. 400s. These invaders eventually gained control of the area.

Ancient Indian life and culture. The ancient Indian societies established the basic social and cultural patterns of Indian civilization and left the world a rich legacy in art, literature, mathematics, and science. Under the Indo-Aryan influence, four distinct varna, or social classes, emerged in Indian society: the Brahmins, or priests; the Kshatriyas, or warriors; the Vaisya, which included farmers, traders, and merchants; and the Sudras, or peasants. A fifth group, known as Pariahs "untouchables," stood at the bottom of society as virtual outcasts. As time passed, these four great varnas further subdivided into hereditary groups known as *jati,* each with its own fixed social position and rules about eating, marriage, labor, and worship. Westerners would later refer to this division of society as the **caste system**.

The social divisions of Indian society were reinforced by religious teachings. So too was the position of women, which was subordinate to that of men. Polygyny, the marriage of a man to more than one woman, for example, was accepted in Indo-Aryan society and became more widespread during the Gupta period. Another practice that became more common under Gupta rule, especially among the upper castes, was suttee, which required a widow to commit suicide by throwing herself on her husband's funeral pyre.

Religion, in fact, was a central feature of Indian life. In addition to the Vedas, over the centuries other religious writings became important. Sometime after 700 b.c., for example, religious thinkers began to question the authority of the Brahmins. Wandering and teaching their message among the forests of the Ganges plain, these thinkers produced a new body of religious literature known as the *Upanishads,* complex explanations of the Vedic religion. Ordinary people, however, preferred the two great epics of Indian poetry, the *Mahabharata* and *Ramayana,* which taught the doctrines of Hinduism through historical and religious stories. The last part of the *Mahabharata,* known as the *Baghavad Gita,* or "Song of the Lord," was especially popular. Its main teachings were devotion to God and that one should conduct oneself according to one's dharma, or moral duty in life, so that the soul could progress toward deliverance from the cycle of reincarnation. Under the Guptas, Indians also enjoyed the *Panchatantra,* a series of fables that included the story of Sinbad the Sailor, which later found its way into the Persian tale of *The Thousand and One Nights.*

Art and architecture also developed, particularly under the Guptas, as did mural paintings in caves. These paintings are a valuable source of information about the daily life of the Indian people at that time. Buddhist architecture developed its own distinctive style in the **stupa**—the dome-shaped shrines that held artifacts and objects associated with the Buddha.

Perhaps the most significant developments came in the sciences. Indian mathematicians understood abstract numbers and negative numbers, as well as the concepts of zero and infinity. Indians probably invented the numbers we call "Arabic": the digits 1 through 9. Indian astronomers also understood the rotation of Earth on its axis and could accurately predict eclipses of the Sun and moon. Indian physicians understood the importance of the spinal column and invented the technique of inoculation—infecting a person with a mild form of a disease so that he or she will not fall ill with the more serious form. They also practiced bone-setting and plastic surgery, and some understood the importance of disinfecting wounds and practicing strict cleanliness to avoid infection. By the time of the Guptas, such knowledge was passed on through the great university at Nalanda, a Buddhist institution that offered a free education to as many as 10,000 students.

In this relief from Gandhara, two young Brahmins raise their right hands to perform the *abhaya mudra,* a gesture of benediction.

Ancient Chinese Civilization

Unlike civilizations further west, Chinese civilization developed in relative isolation from outside influences. This was because China was cut off by its great distance from other centers of civilization, as well as by geographical barriers such as the Gobi desert and the towering mountains of Central Asia.

Their lack of contact with foreigners helped give the Chinese a strong sense of identity and superiority. They regarded their land as the only civilized land and called it *Zhongguo*, the "Middle Kingdom." To the Chinese it represented the center of world.

Geographical and cultural influences. As elsewhere, the development of civilization in China was greatly affected by its geography. The heartland of China stretches from the coast up the valleys of the Huang He, Chang Jiang, and Xi Jiang rivers. The valley of the Huang He is particularly fertile due to the rich yellow soil known as loess. So much of this soil washes into the Huang He that it is sometimes called the Yellow River. The river is also prone to flooding, which in turn has led to another nickname, "China's Sorrow." In addition to being isolated by mountains and deserts, China itself is divided by the Qinling (CHIN•LING) Shandi, a range of mountains that separates north and south China. These mountains also mark the boundary between two different types of agriculture—in the north, wheat was the principal crop, while in the south Chinese farmers primarily grew rice.

This heartland region, sometimes called China Proper, is surrounded by a number of outlying regions: Tibet, Xinjiang (SHIN•JYAHNG), Mongolia, Manchuria, and Korea. From these more forbidding areas, the heartland of China has sometimes been attacked by nomadic or semi-nomadic peoples. Historically, the Chinese have tried to control these areas, either to protect themselves from attack or to gain valuable trade routes. In the process of unifying or controlling all these areas, the Chinese developed a tradition of imperial rule.

The Shang dynasty. China's first historic dynasty, the Shang, began along the Huang He sometime between 1750 B.C. and 1500 B.C. During the Shang period, many elements of later Chinese civilization began to develop, notably a writing system, and a religious tradition that combined animism—a belief that spirits inhabit everything—with ancestor worship. The Chinese worshiped gods of the wind, Sun, clouds, and moon. They also believed that the principal god, Shang Ti, was responsible for their destiny and controlled the forces of nature. Shang rulers tried to appeal to Shang Ti through their ancestors.

The Zhou, Qin, and Han dynasties. In 1122 B.C., the Shang were conquered by the Zhou (JOH), a powerful tribe from the northwest frontier. The Zhou claimed that their right to rule was divinely granted because Shang Ti had withdrawn his favor from the Shang dynasty. Instead, the **Mandate of Heaven**, as they began to call it, had passed to them. Future rulers of China would also argue that they ruled because they had this mandate, and if a dynasty lost the throne it was because they had lost the Mandate of Heaven.

Although they ruled China for about 900 years, the Zhou did not impose a centralized form of government. Instead they granted territories to members of the royal family and their allies to rule as they liked, so long as they provided the Zhou monarch with military service and tribute. Eventually, Zhou power declined and a number of warring states emerged to struggle for control of the country. One of these warring states, the Qin (CHIN), emerged victorious in 221 B.C. and founded a new dynasty.

Although the Qin dynasty only lasted a short time, until 206 B.C., it united China under a strong, central government for the first time in history. The first Qin ruler took the title Shi Huangdi, meaning "first emperor." The Qin established the first real Chinese empire. They also standardized weights, measures, and coinage; established a uniform system of writing; and imposed a single system of taxation throughout the country. In order to maintain their rule, however, the Qin were harsh in their methods. Discontent soon grew, and in 202 B.C. Liu Bang, a commoner, raised a revolt that overthrew the Qin and established a new dynasty, the Han.

Like the Qin, the Han dynasty maintained a strong centralized government, but it ruled less harshly and more wisely. The Han improved the Qin bureaucracy and built a centralized civil service system, eventually based on an examination system for prospective officials, to run the empire. They also increased trade, expanded and defended the frontiers, and generally tried to improve the economy of China. Under their rule, China prospered and many new tools and luxury goods became available—including paper, a Chinese invention that later spread to the West. Eventually, however, the quality of emperors declined and in A.D. 220 the Han dynasty fell. For hundreds of years, nomadic tribes swept across northern China. Not until A.D. 589 did a Chinese general once again unify China and restore the imperial tradition.

Chinese life and culture. In the uncertain times of the late Zhou period, Chinese philosophers laid the

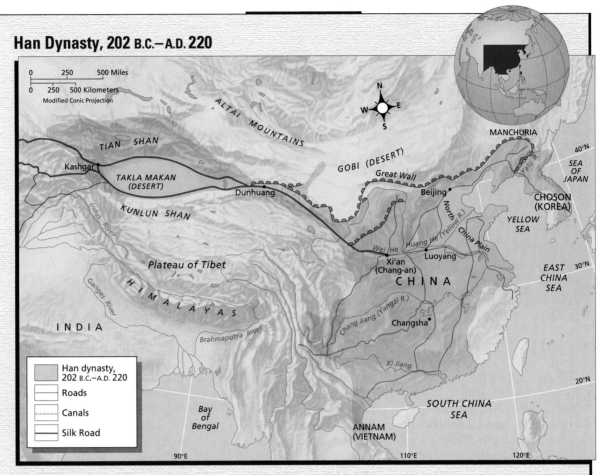

Han Dynasty, 202 B.C.–A.D. 220

0   250   500 Miles
0   250   500 Kilometers
Modified Conic Projection

Legend:
- Han dynasty, 202 B.C.–A.D. 220
- Roads
- Canals
- Silk Road

ALTAI MOUNTAINS
TIAN SHAN
Kashgar
TAKLA MAKAN (DESERT)
KUNLUN SHAN
Indus River
Ganges River
Plateau of Tibet
HIMALAYAS
INDIA
Brahmaputra River
Bay of Bengal
Dunhuang
GOBI (DESERT)
Great Wall
Beijing
North China Plain
Wei He
Huang He (Yellow R.)
Xi'an (Chang-an)
Luoyang
CHINA
Chang Jiang (Yangzi R.)
Changsha
Xi Jiang
ANNAM (VIETNAM)
SOUTH CHINA SEA
MANCHURIA
Yalu R.
CHOSON (KOREA)
YELLOW SEA
SEA OF JAPAN
EAST CHINA SEA
40°N
30°N
20°N
90°E   110°E   120°E

Learning from Maps During the Han dynasty, trade prospered throughout Central Asia to the Mediterranean region.

? Movement Name two cities through which a merchant would have to pass while traveling along the Silk Road.

groundwork for the basic philosophical schools that would be influential in later Chinese history. One of their basic ideas was the dualism, or two-sidedness, of nature. They taught that everything in the world results from a balancing of complimentary forces, called yin and yang. Through the balancing of yin and yang, people could achieve harmony. Perhaps the most influential scholar to offer a practical guide to achieving this harmony was Kongzi, known in the West as Confucius. Confucius taught about the importance of family, respect for one's elders, and reverence for the past. These three concepts formed the basis of Confucian philosophy.

Other philosophies and religious teachings offered other ideas about China's problems. Daoism, for exam-

ple, took its name from its central idea, the Dao, or Way of Nature. Daoists believed that people should withdraw and contemplate the natural harmony of the world in order to learn from it and allow it to govern human affairs. Daosim and Confucianism eventually came to complement one another.

Legalism, on the other hand, was a school of philosophy that taught that people were basically selfish and untrustworthy and had to be controlled with harsh measures. The Legalists believed in power, not virtue, and in the importance of having harsh laws. It was in part their adherence to Legalist views that made the Qin under Shi Huangdi so unpopular. The Han, on the other hand, followed a Confucian model in their approach to government.

The imperial tomb of Shi Huangdi contained more than 6,000 life-sized terra-cotta figures of soldiers and horses.

The family, not the individual, was the most important unit of Chinese society. The father ruled the family and women were subordinate to men—although Chinese society also taught great respect for mothers and mothers-in-law. Within the household, these women held considerable power. Until she had born a son, on the other hand, a new wife might be treated almost like a servant in her husband's family. Respect for one's aged parents, and especially for one's father, was an important virtue.

As civilization prospered in China, the Chinese also developed skills in the arts and sciences. The most important works of Chinese literature were **the Five Classics:** the *Book of History;* the *Book of Poetry;* the *Book of Divination;* the *Spring and Autumn Annals;* and the *Book of Rites.* The Five Classics became the basis on which all Chinese scholars were educated. We do not know who wrote these works or when they were written. *The Analects* of Confucius were also essential reading for all properly brought up young men. Indeed, these works became the mainstay of the imperial civil service examinations and did much to maintain the unity of imperial culture throughout the various regions of China. Most of all, the use of these texts in Chinese education emphasized respect for tradition and knowledge of the past.

In science, Chinese astronomers early on computed the year to be 365¼ days long. In 28 B.C.,

Chinese astronomers first observed sunspots and sometime before A.D. 100 they were building special instruments to observe the movement of planets. Another scientific invention was a primitive seismograph that could detect even the faintest earthquakes. The Chinese developed paper, as well as such things as the sundial, the water clock, and a process of printing.

Section 2 Review

1. **Define** caste system, dharma, stupa, Mandate of Heaven, the Five Classics
2. **Identify** Indo-Aryans, Brahma, the Buddha, Confucius
3. **Locate and Explain the Significance** Mohenjo-Daro, Harappan, China
4. **Summarizing Ideas** How was Indo-Aryan society structured?
5. **Analyzing Ideas (a)** What are the basic beliefs of Hinduism? **(b)** What was the Hindu belief that the Buddha accepted? **(c)** Explain the Four Noble Truths and the principles of the Eightfold Path.
6. **Interpreting Ideas (a)** What were some of the accomplishments of the Shang, Zhou, Qin, and Han dynasties? **(b)** What role did Confucianism and other philosophies play in Chinese society?

Civilizations of the Mediterranean World

Focus Questions

- **How and why did the government of the Greek city-states change over time?**
- **How did Roman expansion affect the government of the Roman Republic?**
- **What role did Christianity play in the Roman world?**

While China developed in relative isolation in eastern Asia, far to the west new civilizations began to develop around the shores of the Mediterranean Sea. These civilizations were the beneficiaries of earlier developments in Mesopotamia and Egypt.

The Greek City-States

In the area in and around the Aegean Sea, an Indo-European speaking people, known as the Greeks, established themselves in small city-states sometime after 2000 B.C. The Greeks eventually created a brilliant civilization that became one of the foundations of modern Western civilization.

Early Greeks and the rise of city-states. Even before the Greeks appeared in the Aegean, an earlier people had established a powerful civilization on the island of Crete. The Greeks remembered this earlier civilization in their myths. Around A.D. 1900, archaeologists began to unearth evidence that proved the stories had a basis in fact. They named the people the Minoan civilization, after the fabled King Minos of Greek myths. Scholars believe that the civilization was already well established by 2000 B.C.

The Minoans were great seafarers and traders. They built magnificent palaces and homes for nobles decorated with beautiful frescoes and complete with running water. Sometime around 1500 B.C., however, a volcanic eruption on a nearby island sent great tidal waves crashing across Crete, causing enormous destruction. Although the Minoans rebuilt after the disaster, their civilization never fully recovered. Their last great palace at Knossos was destroyed around 1400 B.C., probably by Greek-speaking Indo-Europeans known as Mycenaeans, who had migrated to Greece after 2000 B.C.

The Mycenaeans built fortified cities in the southern part of Greece. By about 1200 B.C., however, most of their cities had been destroyed and a more primitive Greek people, the Dorians, had moved into the peninsula. Eventually, all these Greek-speaking peoples, influenced by the geography of the terrain and their own tribal organization, established city-states in the 800s and 700s B.C.

The Greek word for city-state is **polis**. All Greek city-states shared certain features. They tended to be small in area as well as in population—though the two most important city-states, Athens and Sparta, were exceptions to this rule. Most city-states were organized around hilltops, known as an acropolis, where temples and other public buildings were located alongside a fort that could provide protection. In addition, each city-state had a market place, which could also be used as a public meeting place, as well as surrounding lands for agriculture and herding.

Greek government and society. According to tradition, the poet Homer gathered and wove together an earlier oral tradition into the two greatest Greek epics, the *Iliad* and the *Odyssey*. The *Iliad* told of the Trojan War, between the Mycenaeans and their Greek allies, and the city of Troy in Asia Minor. The *Odyssey* was the story of the homeward voyage of one of the Greek princes, Odysseus. Scholars often refer to the era of these epics as the Homeric Age. Through these poems we are able to get a glimpse of what early Greek society was like. The early city-states were tribal kingdoms that constantly waged war on each other.

During the Homeric Age, the Greeks developed religious ideas that focused on explaining the natural world and human actions rather than on moral issues and life after death. Their gods had many human characteristics. Believing that the gods delighted in displays of strength and courage, the Greeks held athletic contests in their honor—the most famous of these were the games at Olympia, held every four years in honor of Zeus, the king of the gods.

Over time, the early kingships gave way to rule by the chief landowners, or aristocrats. The power of these nobles was in part due to the fact that they were the only ones who could afford the weapons and armor of warfare. But by 600 B.C., wealthy nonaristocrats could afford some weaponry of their own. A new class of nonaristocratic foot soldiers, known as hoplites, emerged. As the hoplites took on a larger and larger role in defending the city-states, the nonaristocrats began to demand more say in the government.

Ancient Greece, c. 750 B.C.–450 B.C.

The Greek Heartland

Colony
City-state
Trade route

Learning from Maps Greek culture spread throughout the Mediterranean region as city-states were established on islands across the Black, Aegean, and Mediterranean Seas.

? Region What Black Sea colony exported grain, timber, and slaves?

Some leaders took advantage of popular discontent to establish themselves as **tyrants**. The tyrants seized power unlawfully, but they ruled with the people's support. Over time, however, they became harsh and unjust, and the word *tyrant* took on its present meaning of a ruler who exercises absolute power brutally and oppressively. Eventually, many city-states ousted their tyrants and adopted the idea that people could and should rule themselves. This led to the form of government called democracy—a government in which all people take part.

Sparta and Athens. The differences that existed among the Greek city-states is perhaps best illustrated by Sparta and Athens. Spartan society developed primarily out of the need for security. The Dorian invaders who

established Sparta had conquered and enslaved the surrounding peoples. Eventually, three social groups emerged in Sparta. The first group, known as the equals, was composed of all adult male descendants of the original Dorian invaders who had established Sparta. All land in the state was divided equally among these citizens and their families. Along with each allotment of land went state slaves, called helots, to work it. The second group was made up of so-called half-citizens, free men who paid taxes and might even serve in the army, but who had no political power. The third group consisted of the helots.

The helots greatly outnumbered the Spartans who lived in constant fear of a helot revolt. Consequently, the Spartans developed a rigid military social structure to guard against such a revolt. All Spartan males were trained from birth to be soldiers and Spartan females were raised to be wives and mothers of soldiers. The strict discipline of Sparta did lead to efficient government and an almost unconquerable army, but the Spartans paid a heavy price for this military might by sacrificing individual freedoms for the state. Furthermore, they produced little in the way of art, science, literature, or philosophy.

Athens on the other hand developed very differently. In Athens, as elsewhere in Greece, social standing and political power were closely linked. At the top stood the citizens—consisting of all adult males born in the polis. Athenian women were also citizens but could not vote and were legally considered minors. People born outside Athens were noncitizens. Called metics, they worked as merchants or artisans, but could not own land or take part in politics. At the bottom of society stood the slaves who comprised more than half the population during Athens's greatest period.

Initially a monarchy, Athens made the transition to an aristocratic form of government early on. By the late 600s, however, social discontent among nonaristocratic citizens led to reforms and the creation of Athens's first written law code. About 594 B.C. the aristocratic leader Solon instituted further reforms, cancelling debts and outlawing the practice of enslaving people for debt. Still, unrest continued and around 546 B.C. a wealthy aristocrat named Peisistratus seized power as a tyrant. Finally, around 508 B.C., Cleisthenes overthrew the tyrannical government and established a **direct democracy** in Athens, in which all citizens played an equal role in making decisions for the state.

The Expansion of Greece. During the aristocratic period in Greek development, many cities sent out colonists to settle throughout the eastern and central Mediterranean world, even as far as the shores of the

Black Sea. Both the Greek city-states and these colonies developed for a long time without interference from the empires of Southwest Asia. In 546 B.C., however, the Persian king, Cyrus the Great, conquered Lydia in Asia Minor and acquired the Greek city-states along the western coast of the Aegean Sea. After a series of revolts among these Greek cities, aided by Athens, both Darius I and his son Xerxes I sent huge armies to conquer mainland Greece. In 479 B.C., however, the Athenians and Spartans combined to defeat the Persians at the battle of Plataea.

After these Persian Wars, Athens used diplomacy to create the Delian League, an alliance with some 140 city-states. By the 450s B.C., however, the Delian League had become little more than an Athenian empire. Ironically, even as the League was being turned into an empire, under the Athenian leader Pericles, democracy was reaching its height in Athens. Pericles hoped to unite all Greece under Athenian leadership. Other city-states increasingly resented Athens's domination, and in 431 B.C. the devastating Peloponnesian War broke out, with Sparta leading a coalition of states against Athens. After almost a generation of warfare, Athens finally had to surrender to Sparta in 404 B.C.

Greece's Golden and Hellenistic Ages

Despite the failure of political unity in the Greek world, during the 400s B.C. Greek culture reached new heights. It was a period so magnificent that it is often called Greece's golden age.

Greek art. Greek art reflected the way in which Greeks viewed themselves and the world. The pride people took in their city-states was perhaps most effectively displayed in the great temples and public buildings the Greeks built to adorn their cities.

What If?

The Persian Wars

The Greek victory over Persia ensured the survival of Greek civilization. As a result, the Greek ideal of democracy, rather than the Persian concept of rule by an absolute monarch, was passed on to the Western world. How do you think a Persian victory would have affected the course of world history?

Structures such as the magnificent Parthenon, an engineering masterpiece in its own right, were decorated with the finest sculptures the Greeks could produce. The golden age in Greece produced some of the finest sculptors who have ever lived—men like Myron, who created the famous *Discus Thrower;* Phidias, who created the statue of Zeus at the Temple of Olympia; and Praxiteles, renowned for his delicate, lifelike, and often life-sized figures. In addition to sculpture, the Greeks also painted—their best preserved paintings are found on vases. Vase paintings illustrated everyday life as well as myths.

Thinkers and writers of the golden age. Even before the golden age, the Greeks displayed a keen

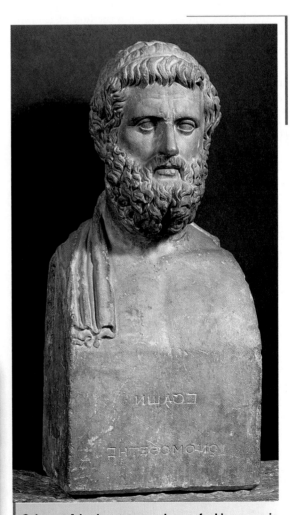

Solon, an Athenian statesman known for his economic and political reforms, was Athens' first poet and was later named one of the Seven Wise Men of Greece.

interest in the things of the mind—philosophy, mathematics, science, and literature. As they investigated the natural world, Greek thinkers moved away from the myths of the past and sought natural explanations for the phenomena around them. In the 500s B.C., for example, before the golden age began, the philosopher Pythagoras wrote that everything could be explained or expressed through numbers and the relationships, or ratios, between them. Hippocrates, considered the founder of modern medicine, taught that disease comes from natural causes, not as punishment from the gods.

During the golden age itself, Greek philosophers increasingly turned their attention to human nature and the human mind. Socrates, for example, who lived in Athens from 470 to 399 B.C., wanted people to think for themselves and established a method of learning through questioning. Today we call this the Socratic method. In this way, he believed, people might acquire wisdom. Accused of corrupting the minds of the youth and for showing irreverence for the gods, he was condemned to death by his enemies in Athens. His pupil,

Plato, founded the Academy, a school devoted to teaching philosophy. Plato was interested in discovering the true nature of things, which he expressed in his theory of forms—the idea that everything physical is but an imperfect expression of a perfect universal form, or idea. Plato was also interested in politics and wrote the *Republic*, outlining his idea that society should be organized so that the best and brightest might govern it—a meritocracy in which all people would do the work for which they were best suited.

One of Plato's students at the Academy was Aristotle, who was determined to apply philosophical reasoning and logic to every branch of human knowledge. Aristotle concluded that the Greek ideal of style in the arts—balance, order, and restraint—also represented the highest ideal in terms of human behavior—an ideal that was most likely to bring people the greatest happiness. Applying his reasoning skills to politics, Aristotle concluded that the best form of government was one that combined certain elements of monarchy, aristocracy, and democracy into a kind of limited democracy in the hands of the middle class.

This mosaic depicts Plato's Academy, founded around 387 B.C. as an institute to instruct students in the systematic pursuit of philosophical knowledge and scientific research.

The Greeks also applied this method of logical reasoning to human affairs, particularly to the writing of history. Herodotus and especially Thucydides, who wrote the *History of the Peloponnesian War*, were the first great historians of the Western world. Combining reason with beauty, however, they also saw history as a branch of literature. Another branch was drama. Greek playwrights explored the conflicts of human existence in terms of both tragedy, in which the major characters struggle unsuccessfully against their fate, and comedy, in which they succeed in solving their problems.

Alexander the Great. So long as the Greeks remained disunited, to a considerable extent the achievements of their civilization also remained relatively limited in their impact on other peoples and civilizations. In 359 B.C. this changed when Phillip II became king of Macedonia and began to unite Greece under his own rule by conquering the Greek city-states. The process of Greek unification and expansion was taken even further by Phillip's son, Alexander the Great. Alexander the Great was one of the greatest military leaders in world history. Picking up where his father had left off, Alexander not only completed the conquest and unification of the Greek world, but also set out to conquer the rest of the known world. By 331 B.C., he had conquered Asia Minor, Syria, Egypt, Mesopotamia, and the rest of the Persian Empire and was attempting to conquer the plains of northern India. After a long campaign in India, however, he was forced by his men to turn back home. In 323 B.C., he died in Babylon. He was not yet 33 years old. In his short life, he had laid the foundations of an empire that would spread Greek ideas to other parts of the world and in turn expose Greek civilization to new influences and ideas from outside its borders. A new civilization, often called Hellenistic, meaning Greek-like, emerged in those areas ruled by Alexander and his successors.

The spread of Hellenistic culture. After Alexander's death, his generals murdered his family and divided his short-lived empire among themselves into a number of kingdoms, including Macedonia, Egypt, and Syria. Despite this political division, Hellenistic society continued to spread through trade and the exchange of ideas among scholars in many lands, who could all communicate in Greek. Trade routes now connected the entire Mediterranean world and reached as far as India. The growth of trade in turn led to the growth of a middle class, a middle class that fostered a rise in education and levels of literacy. The decline of the old Greek ideals of the polis also led to new developments in religion and philosophy.

This mosaic shows the death of Archimedes, c. 212 B.C. Archimedes is considered the greatest Greek scientist of the Hellenistic period.

Some people adopted the practice of ruler-worship. Others sought to counter the feelings that they had lost control over their own destinies by turning to new mystery religions that promised immortality after death. Still others turned to philosophy.

Hellenistic philosophers were more concerned with ethics than with basic questions of reality and human existence. Four chief schools of philosophy emerged: Cynicism, Skepticism, Stoicism, and Epicureanism. Cynics believed that people should live according to nature, scorning pleasure, wealth, and social position. Skeptics philosophized that no definite knowledge is possible because everything is always changing. Stoics believed that divine reason directs the world, and that only by trying to follow the path laid down by the divine spark within every person could one find true happiness. Epicureans taught that the aim of life is to seek pleasure and avoid pain—and that one of the ways to achieve this was by limiting one's desires, rather than trying to fulfill all of them.

While people grappled with the problems brought on by living within a more complex and sophisticated world, Hellenistic scientists were also learning more and more about how the world around them functioned. Many advances were made in mathematics. The Greek mathematician Euclid further systematized geometry. Archimedes, considered the greatest scientist and inventor of the Hellenistic period, applied geometry to measure spheres, cones, and cylinders and to advance developments in mechanics. Other scientists used mathematics to calculate the daily positions of the planets and stars, and even to calculate the circumference of Earth with amazing accuracy. Hellenistic physicians learned much about the human body and greatly increased medical knowledge by dissecting human bodies.

The Roman World

The spread of Hellenistic and Greek culture occurred not only in the eastern Mediterranean, but also in the west, where it had a great influence on the a new power in the Italian peninsula, the city of Rome.

The founding of the Roman Republic. Many peoples had inhabited Italy since ancient times. Sometime around the mid-700s B.C., a group of people called Latins built villages along the Tiber River. Located near a shallow river crossing, the Latins had settled in the middle of important trade routes that spread out in all directions. Eventually, these villages united to form the city-state of Rome. In the late 600s B.C., Rome came under the control of the Etruscans, from whom the Romans learned many of the arts of civilization. Rome was also influenced by Greek settlements in Sicily and southern Italy.

Latins, Etruscans, and other peoples living around Rome gradually came to be called Romans. In 509 B.C., the Roman aristocracy overthrew the last Etruscan monarch and set up a republic, a form of government in which voters elect their leaders. Only

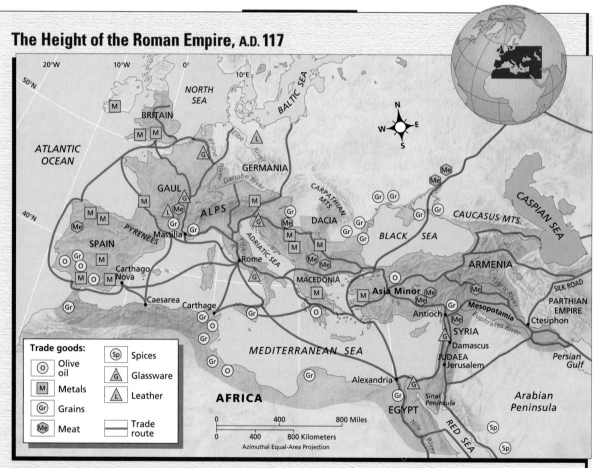

The Height of the Roman Empire, A.D. 117

Trade goods:
- Olive oil
- Metals
- Grains
- Meat
- Spices
- Glassware
- Leather
- Trade route

Learning from Maps During the time of the Pax Romana, trade thrived throughout the entire Roman Empire as a result of an improved system of roads.

? Region What two areas were large producers of glassware and leather?

adult male citizens who owned land could vote. Three groups of citizens helped govern Rome: the Senate, various popular assemblies, and officials known as magistrates. After the end of the monarchy, Roman society was also split between the powerful aristocratic class, known as patricians, and the nonaristocrats known as plebeians. Over time, the plebeians successfully forced the patricians to grant them greater political participation. By about 300 B.C., wealthy plebeians had even joined with the patricians to form a new Roman nobility that soon controlled the state.

For more than 200 years after the founding of the republic, the Romans fought many wars against neighboring peoples in Italy. By 265 B.C., the Romans controlled all of Italy south of the Rubicon River on the northeast coast. Both military organization, based upon legions made up of Roman citizen-soldiers, and wise policies that gradually granted full or partial citizenship to the inhabitants of other Italian cities, helped the Romans achieve their victories.

Roman expansion. As Roman power grew, the Romans came into conflict with Carthage, a powerful city located on the coast of North Africa. In a series of three wars, called the Punic Wars, the Romans completely destroyed their rivals and took over their colonies around the Mediterranean. At the same time, they also began to conquer the eastern parts of the Mediterranean world. As the Roman Republic created this vast new empire, the role of the citizen-farmer and the traditional values of earlier Roman society weakened. As land and slaves became more expensive, and military service kept many citizen-farmers away from their farms, many lost their lands and moved to the cities, where they joined the unemployed masses. In addition, the pressures of ruling such a large empire placed strains on a government that had been designed to rule a small city-state.

The Roman Empire. By 133 B.C. the Roman Republic faced many problems. Although several leaders attempted reforms, their programs angered many senators, and as a result some leaders were violently overthrown. Expansion of the empire brought changes in the army, and eroded the old reliance on citizen-farmers as the backbone of the legions. As the values of the old republic began to break down, many new leaders struggled for power. Emerging from such a power struggle, in 44 B.C. Julius Caesar became dictator for life. He proved to be an able politician. He granted citizenship to many people in the provinces and gave land to veterans and grain to the poor in Rome. His new position angered conservative Roman families and on the Ides of March (March 15), 44 B.C., conspirators

This sculpture demonstrates the new Roman concept of divine ruler. Augustus' body is idealized and heroic in form.

stabbed Caesar to death in the Senate Chambers.

Caesar's death soon led to a division of the Roman world between his heir, Octavian, and his friend and ally, Marc Antony. As Octavian built up his power in Rome and the western half of the empire, Marc Antony allied himself with Queen Cleopatra of Egypt and made his base in the eastern part of the empire. Eventually, civil war between the two split the empire. Finally, in 31 B.C., Octavian defeated Antony and Cleopatra at the great naval battle of Actium and became master of the Roman world. In 27 B.C. the Senate proclaimed him Augustus Caesar, or Augustus "the revered one." Historians agree that Augustus was the first real Roman emperor and they mark his reign as the end of the old republic and the beginning of the Roman Empire.

Augustus and his successors established Roman power throughout the Mediterranean world and imposed what became known as the Pax Romana, or Roman Peace. Law, military organization, and widespread trade and transportation held the empire together and brought about peace and economic prosperity for more than 200 years.

Roman society and culture. The Pax Romana meant prosperity to many people, but the wealth was not evenly distributed. Rich citizens usually had both a country home and a city home. Such houses were often equipped with modern conveniences like running water and baths. The average Roman on the other hand lived in a poorly constructed apartment building with very little furniture. Most residents of the city of Rome were farmers or artisans who barely made a living. To divert their attention from their problems, the Roman government provided free grain to residents of the capital, as well as public entertainment. Romans were fond of the theater, especially satires and comedies. Their favorite pastimes, however, were more brutal sports—such as chariot racing in the huge Circus Maximus racetrack in Rome, where spectacular crashes might occur. They also enjoyed gladiatorial combats between humans or beasts—or sometimes both—in the Colosseum, Rome's great amphitheater. So important were such entertainments in Roman society that the poet Juvenal once observed that only two things interested the Roman masses: "bread and circuses."

The practical Romans applied the scientific knowledge they gained from the Greeks in planning cities, building water and sewage systems, and improving farming and livestock breeding. Roman engineers surpassed all ancient peoples in their ability to construct roads, bridges, aqueducts, amphitheaters, and public buildings. Perhaps the most important contribution of Roman architects was the use of concrete, which made large buildings possible in terms of both cost and engineering. The Romans often based their buildings on Greek models. Unlike the Greeks, however, they also knew how to build the arch and vaulted domes, and emphasized size as well as pleasing proportions.

Greek influence was also strong in the arts, though a number of Romans produced works of great originality, especially in literature. Virgil, a contemporary of Augustus, was one of the greatest Roman poets and author of the *Aeneid*—an epic poem that told the story of a Trojan prince named Aeneas, a legendary ancestor of the Latins. The poet Ovid wrote love lyrics and the *Metamorphoses*, a collection of myths written in verse. Another poet, Horace, wrote of human emotions in his odes, satires, and letters. The Romans also valued works of history, such as the *Annals*, a history of Rome under Augustus and his immediate successors, written by Tacitus.

The rise of Christianity. One of the world's major religions, Christianity, originated during the Roman Empire in the Roman-controlled territory of Judaea. It was founded by a Jewish teacher known as Jesus of Nazareth. Roman histories say very little about Jesus. Our knowledge of Jesus comes mainly from the Gospels of Matthew, Mark, Luke, and John—the first four books of the New Testament of the Christian Bible.

According to these accounts, Jesus was born in Bethlehem, grew up in Nazareth, worked for a time as a carpenter, and began preaching as an adult. The teachings of Jesus have become one of the greatest influences on the Western world. He accepted the Hebrew Ten Commandments as guides to right living, but he gave them added meaning. He summarized the Ten Commandments in two great rules: people must love God above all else, and they must love others as they love themselves.

Both the conservative Jewish hierarchy in Jerusalem and the Roman authorities felt threatened by Jesus' message. Eventually the Romans put Jesus to death by crucifixion, a common form of execution for criminals in the Roman world. According to the Gospels, however, Jesus arose from the dead, remained on Earth another 40 days, and then ascended into heaven. His followers believed that his resurrection and ascension proved that Jesus was the Messiah, the savior of mankind sent by God, and they called him Jesus Christ after the Greek word for Messiah—Christos. His followers began to preach that through the death of Jesus Christ, the son of God who had died for the sins of the human race, all people could achieve redemption.

Believing that the day of God's final judgment was close at hand, Jesus' disciples set out to spread his message. At first they worked mainly in the Jewish communities of Palestine. Eventually, however, the Christian message was spread into the Greek and Roman world by a new convert, a Jew named Saul of Tarsus who took the name Paul after becoming a Christian. It was Paul who emphasized that Christianity was for everyone, not just Jews. He journeyed throughout the eastern Mediterranean establishing Christian churches and encouraging them through his Epistles, or letters which still form an important part of the New Testament. According to tradition, he was eventually put to death while visiting Rome. His message continued, however, and within 400 years, Christianity had spread to all parts of the huge Roman Empire. The true success of the church was marked when the emperor Constantine proclaimed himself a Christian in A.D. 312. After A.D. 391, when the emperor Theodosius banned the old pagan religion of Rome, Christianity became the sole official religion of the entire empire.

During the later years of the Roman Empire, Christianity developed a definitive church organization. Priests conducted services and performed baptisms and marriages. Above the priests were the bishops, who headed the church in each city. The bishops of Rome, Constantinople, Alexandria, Antioch, and Jerusalem, the most important administrative centers of the church, were called **patriarchs**. Over time, the bishop of Rome assumed the title of **pope**, from a Latin word for father, and claimed supremacy over the church.

The fall of the Roman Empire in the west. The success of Christianity within the empire was in part due to a growing sense of insecurity among many people. During most of the A.D. 200s, the empire experienced dreadful confusion, civil war, and barbarian invasions. If not for the efforts of two emperors, Diocletian and Constantine, the empire probably would have collapsed. Their reforms and reorganization of the empire postponed final collapse for about 200 years. Diocletian divided the empire administratively and appointed a co-emperor to help govern the vast territory more efficiently. Constantine continued these reforms and established a second capital at Constantinople, from which the eastern provinces of the empire could be more efficiently administered. After Constantine's death, however, the administrative division eventually became a permanent division into what ultimately became to two separate empires.

This relief sculpture shows a Roman legionary and an attacking barbarian.

As the two parts of the empire drifted apart, both came under increasing pressure from invading barbarian tribes like the Huns. The wealthier and more populous eastern half was able to defend itself better than the relatively poor, agrarian western half. Weakened within as well as by attacks from outside, eventually the western half of the empire collapsed in A.D. 476, when Romulus Augustulus, the last emperor of Rome in the west, was defeated and killed by invading barbarians. Actually, no such thing as a single fall occurred, but instead the empire gradually disintegrated. Despite this "fall" of the Roman Empire in the west, the eastern empire, usually called the Byzantine Empire, continued to exist for nearly another thousand years. Roman imperial traditions were preserved even after the collapse of the western empire through the continuance of the Roman Church, the only imperial institution to survive relatively intact. Through the church, Roman ideas and civilization remained an important base on which a new civilization would eventually be built in western Europe.

Section 3 Review

1. **Define** polis, tyrants, direct democracy, patriarchs, pope
2. **Identify** Pericles, Alexander the Great, Jesus, Constantine
3. **Locate and Explain the Significance** Athens, Sparta, Rome
4. **Interpreting Ideas (a)** How did the nobles win power in Greece? **(b)** Why did they lose power? **(c)** What part did tyrants play in the process?
5. **Determining Cause and Effect** How did the government and social structure of Rome change as a result of the conquest of new territories?
6. **Analyzing Ideas** Why were the early Christians persecuted in the Roman Empire?
7. **Integrating Ideas** What factors contributed to the collapse of the Roman Empire in the West?

Europe in Transition

Focus Questions

- How did the Byzantine Empire perpetuate the heritage of the old Roman world?
- What are the major beliefs of Islam?
- What role did Christianity play in Europe after the fall of the Roman Empire?
- What factors strengthened the central governments of England, France and Spain?

After the fall of the western Roman Empire, civilization in the Mediterranean region came under severe attack from outside invaders. In the east, the Byzantine Empire preserved and expanded Greek and Roman influences, while in the west, the remnants of Roman civilization were transformed by contact with Germanic invaders who began to settle in western Europe. Meanwhile, the rise of a new religion, Islam, soon created a distinct civilization of its own in Southwest Asia and North Africa.

The Byzantine Empire, Kievan Russia, and the Mongols

While barbarians plundered the western part of the Roman Empire in the A.D. 400s and 500s, the Byzantine Empire continued to thrive. Although surrounded by enemies, the Byzantine Empire maintained its independence and even expanded its influence to the north.

The Byzantine Empire. By the early 500s, the Western Roman Empire had broken down into a group of Germanic tribal kingdoms. The Eastern Roman Empire, on the other hand, had defeated the barbarians and was primed for a great political, economic, intellectual, and artistic revival. Emperor Justinian, who ruled from 527 to 565, led this revival. In addition to recovering some of the old Roman territories in Italy and the Mediterranean, Justinian proved a capable ruler who preserved and further codified Roman law. During the Middle Ages, the Justinianic Code became the basis of many European legal systems and its influence continues today.

After Justinian's death, however, the empire suffered from both internal civil wars and conflicts with the Persians to the east and Slavic and Germanic tribes to the north and west. During the 600s, a new power also emerged in the south, from the deserts of Arabia, inspired by the religious faith of Islam. Muslim armies

Early Christian/Byzantine wall mosaic

soon overran major parts of the Byzantine Empire in North Africa and the Fertile Crescent. Under such blows, after 650 the Byzantine Empire was reduced to little more than Asia Minor, the southern Balkan peninsula, parts of Italy, and nearby islands of the eastern Mediterranean and the Aegean.

In addition to preserving Roman law, the Byzantine Empire also protected and perpetuated its own brand of Christianity, sometimes called Orthodox Christianity. Because religion was so closely bound up with the state, Byzantine leaders saw controversies over religious doctrines and rituals as important matters of state. Such attitudes often involved the state in major controversies. One of the most important, for example, was the debate over the use of **icons**—holy portraits of Jesus, the Virgin Mary, and the saints—in the 700s and early 800s. Those who favored their use in worship fought the iconoclasts, who thought of icons as idols and wished to suppress their use. Eventually, the iconoclasts lost the debate, but in the meantime the state had been seriously disrupted. Despite such debates, Christianity remained one of the most important aspects of Byzantine society and proved instrumental in expanding Byzantine influence among the Slavic tribes that threatened the northern borders of the empire.

The rise of Russia. The expansion of Orthodox Christianity from Constantinople also affected the emergence of new civilization to the north, where, beginning in the A.D. 200s, Slavic tribes settled in much of eastern Europe. Other peoples, like the Huns, Avars, and Magyars, often invaded the region and for a time made the Slavs their subjects. During the 800s, Vikings from Scandinavia also swept into eastern Europe. The Vikings came more as traders than conquerors, however, and several cities sprang up along the Viking trade routes.

Two such cities were Novgorod, south of Lake Ladoga, and Kiev, on the Dnieper River. In 862, a people called the Rus, under their war leader Rurik, took control of Novgorod and established a dynasty. Eventually the Rus, whose name is probably the origin of the name Russia, also took control of Kiev and several other principalities. By the 800s, they had come to rule over all the Slavic tribes along the Dnieper River. Kiev especially prospered because of its location along

Peoples of Europe, 600–1000

Learning from Maps Muslims, Slavs, Magyars, and Vikings invaded central Europe in the 800s.

❔ **Movement** Across which bodies of water did the Vikings travel to settle in England and eastern Europe?

the rich trade route that extended north from Constantinople to the Baltic Sea. Kiev grew to become the most important principality in Kievan Russia.

Despite the Kievan prince's predominant position, a centralized government never fully developed. Instead, the rulers of other principalities simply paid tribute to Kiev and largely ran their own affairs as they liked. At times, the princes of the cities of Kievan Russia ruled with the advice of councils of boyars, or nobles. Another important institution widely used in both Kiev and Novgorod was the town meeting, where the heads of all households gathered at the command of the prince to consider such matters as war, disputes among princes, and special measures to deal with emergencies.

As the Kievan state developed, it came increasingly under the influence of Constantinople to the south. In 988, the Kievan ruler Vladimir I converted to Orthodox Christianity, partly out of a desire to marry the Byzantine emperor's sister, Anna. Thereafter, the Byzantine Church became increasingly important in Kievan Russia. The patriarch of Constantinople chose the chief bishop, or metropolitan, of the Kievan Church. New monasteries in the region soon became centers for social services, education, and artistic expression.

The rise of the Mongols. After the death of Prince Yaroslav the Wise, in 1054, Kiev declined in power and wealth. Disputes among Kievan princes as well as raids on the state's trade by Turkish peoples to the south weakened the state. After groups of princes sacked Kiev in 1169 and again in 1203, the city's prosperity was ruined. As the princes continued to fight among themselves, new invaders from Central Asia took advantage of Kiev's weakness. These invaders, the Mongols, came from the Asian steppe east of the Ural mountains. By 1240, the new invaders had conquered and burned almost every city in Kievan Russia.

The Mongols did not try to impose their way of life on the Slavic peoples whom they conquered. They wanted only to collect wealth from the region. In time, Mongol power weakened and the princes of the region grew more independent. During the early 1300s, Moscow, or Muscovy, became the strongest principality, partly because its ruler, Prince Ivan I, cooperated with the Mongols. In return for his cooperation, the Mongols granted Ivan the title of Grand Prince. By the time of Ivan III, also called the Great, who ruled from 1462 to 1505, Moscow had become so powerful that Ivan was finally able to overthrow Mongol rule altogether in 1480. Uniting the principalities and con-

quering more territory to the west, he became the first ruler of the independent state of Russia.

The Islamic Empire

While the Byzantine Empire spread Christianity to the north, in the south Arab armies inspired by a new religion, Islam, swept out of the Arabian peninsula and overran much of the old Byzantine territory.

Muhammad and Islam. In the A.D. 600s, the prophet Muhammad began preaching Islam, today the world's second largest religion. The central message of Islam is that there is only one God. The holy book of Islam is the Qur'an, which according to Muslims is the word of God revealed to Muhammad through a series of revelations. The Qur'an presents God's laws and teachings and outlines what is expected of all good Muslims. According to the Qur'an, Muslims must meet five important obligations known as the Five Pillars of Islam: (1) Recite the profession of faith, "...there is no deity except Allah [God] and Muhammad is His Servant and Messenger." (2) Pray five times a day facing Mecca, the holy city of Islam. (3) Give alms—money or food—to the poor. (4) Fast from first light to sunset during the month of Ramadan. (5) If possible, make a pilgrimage to Mecca at least once in a lifetime.

Muhammad also emphasized the importance of the jihad, or struggle to defend the faith. Anyone who died in this struggle, Muhammad said, was a martyr who would receive God's blessings and rewards in heaven.

Islamic civilization. Under Muhammad's successors, known as caliphs, Islam spread throughout Southwest Asia and North Africa, and even into Spain and northern India. Although an elected office at first, eventually the position of caliph became hereditary. However, disputes over the succession led to political and religious divisions within the Islamic world, the most important being that between Sunni Islam and Shi'ah Islam. At one point, three claimants to the caliphate ruled from three different parts of the Muslim world: Baghdad in present-day Iraq, Cairo in Egypt, and Córdoba in Spain. Despite these political divisions, Islamic civilization remained remarkably unified culturally. Trade flourished partly because Islam had developed in a region that dominated the most important trade routes between Europe, Asia, and Africa. Manufacturing increased because of the demands of trade. The empire produced silk, cotton, and woolen textiles, as well as tapestries and carpets. Luxuries such as jewelry, perfumes, and spices were in great demand.

Building History Study Skills

READ
WRITE
INTERPRET
CONNECT
THINK

Reading About History: Understanding Sequence

A sequence is the order in which things happen in time. Sequencing events, then, is arranging these events in the order in which they occurred. Sequencing helps you to organize information. From the pattern of the data, you can determine how events are related to each other. The relationship among these events can help you identify other important ideas such as cause and effect and historical significance.

How to Sequence Information
To sequence information, follow these steps:
1. Identify what you hope to learn by sequencing the information being studied.
2. Look for calendar references, clue words, and time periods. Calendar references include centuries, years, and dates. Clue words include *first, second, after, before, meanwhile, and later.*
3. Determine whether there is an implied sequence or a cause-and-effect relationship. For example, could one event have happened without the other taking place?
4. List the events in sequence.
5. Make a statement about the relationship between the items, actions, or events. What is the significance of the pattern of data?

Developing the Skill
You can better understand the expansion of Islam by organizing significant events sequentially. The following statements about the spread of Islam are not listed in the order that they occurred. As you read the list, try to determine the proper sequence.
1. Muhammad's preaching was opposed, and in 622 he fled to Yathrib (Al-Madínah).
2. By 632, when Muhammad died, a large part of Arabia had accepted Islam.
3. Muhammad's successors pursued a policy aimed at conquering non-Muslim territory.
4. Muhammad considered himself a prophet and a teacher and believed that there is only one God.
5. Muhammad became the leader of the community in Yathrib (Al-Madínah).
6. The Muslims usually allowed conquered peoples to choose either to accept Islam or to pay a tribute.

Persian miniature illustrating "the arrival of the prophet"

7. In 732 the Franks defeated the Moors at the Battle of Tours.
8. Less than a century after the death of Muhammad, his followers had conquered Arabia, Palestine, Syria, Mesopotamia, Persia, part of India, and all of North Africa.

The correct sequence of events would be 4, 1, 5, 2, 3, 8, 6, and 7. The first statement (4) establishes Muhammad as the leader. Muhammad's beliefs are an implied part of the sequence. Muhammad has to be preaching something in order to be expelled from Mecca (1). Muhammad then became the leader of the Al-Madínah community (5). The date 632 completes Muhammad's lifetime (2). His successors (3) would have to follow after his death. They conquered neighboring territories and then went to India and North Africa (8). Their conquering policy (6) is then explained as an implied part of the sequence. The defeat at Tours marks the limit of Muslim expansion into other parts of Europe in 732 (7).

Practicing the Skill
Using the guidelines for sequencing information, make a list of important events at your school, and arrange them in sequence. Include events such as special assemblies, school-sponsored club activities, and sports competitions.

To apply this skill, see Applying History Study Skills on page 41.

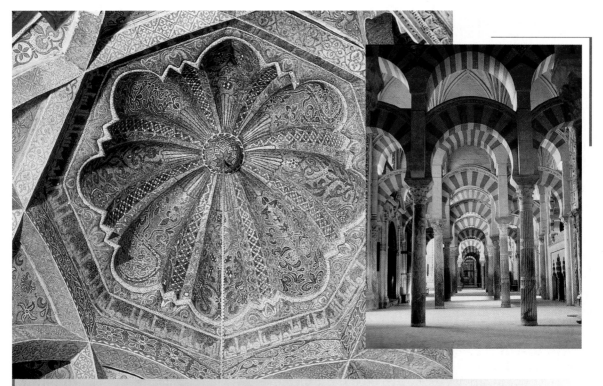

The Great Mosque of Córdoba took more than 200 years to complete and is considered a masterpiece of Islamic architecture. [Ceiling work (left) and pillars (right) at the Mosque of Córdoba.]

In Islamic families, the father acted as the head of the household. The family provided both economic security and physical protection to its members. Women had a clearly defined position in Islamic society giving them similar rights to men but not placing them above men.

Influenced by the more sophisticated civilizations into which they expanded, the Arabs adopted the best ideas, customs, and institutions they found. They combined and preserved the scientific and philosophical ideas of Greece, Rome, and Asia in their culture. As Islam drew more and more converts among non-Arab peoples, the initial dominance of the Arabs in the Islamic world gradually diminished and soon a truly Islamic culture emerged. Muslim scientists from Spain to Persia wrote books and encyclopedias on many subjects. Muslim geographers and navigators perfected the astrolabe and learned the art of making paper from the Chinese. Muslim physicians added to the store of medical knowledge and passed it on to other parts of the world. Muslim mathematicians adopted the numbering system invented in India and transmitted it to western Europe, where it became known as Arabic numerals. Particularly through

Muslim Spain and Sicily, the knowledge of the ancient world was preserved and passed on to Christian and Jewish scholars, who in turn carried it to the rest of Europe.

Islamic and Mughal rulers in India. While the Arabs first carried Islam to the rest of the world, by the late 1000s power in the Islamic world was shifting to new peoples coming out of Central Asia, the Turks. As Turkish tribes came into contact with Islam, they too were inspired and soon began to spread the faith. During the first half of the 1300s, a group of Turks known as the Ottomans began to build a great Islamic empire of their own. Eventually, they conquered the last remnants of the old Byzantine Empire and established their own Ottoman Empire, with its capital at Constantinople, eventually renamed Istanbul.

Meanwhile, Turkish Muslims had also begun to establish Islamic rule in India. In 997, for example, Turks began to raid northern India. Over time, the small states of the Rajput princes, which had emerged after the fall of the Gupta Empire in the 500s, fell to the Turkish invaders. In 1193, Muslim armies captured the city of Delhi and by the early 1200s they controlled most of northern India in what became

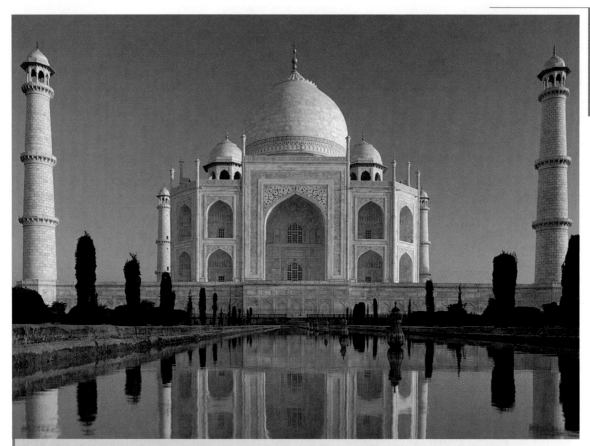

The glorious Taj Mahal stands on a north-south axis and is flanked on either side by symmetric minarets.

known as the Delhi sultanate. The new rulers introduced not only their religion of Islam into India, but also a new language, Urdu.

Civil wars and the devastating onslaught of the Turko-Mongol leader, Timur, weakened the Delhi sultanate and provided an opening for the Rajputs to challenge Muslim control again. Eventually, this weakness was used by yet another Turko-Mongol leader, Babur the Tiger, a descendant of Timur, to overthrow the Delhi sultanate and establish his own dynasty, the Mughals. Under Babur and his successors, the Mughals unified much of the Indian subcontinent and presided over a great flowering of Islamic culture and civilization. Under the Mughals, particularly Akbar the Great, who ruled from 1556 to 1605, a synthesis of Hindu and Muslim cultures occurred. Out of this synthesis emerged a brilliant civilization that produced such masterpieces of architecture as the Taj Mahal, a great tomb built by Shah Jahan for his beloved wife Mumtaz Mahal in the mid-1600s.

The Rise of the Middle Ages

While the Islamic Empire was expanding in Southwest Asia and North Africa, in western Europe a new civilization soon began to emerge from the ruins of the old Roman Empire. The period of western European history following the collapse of the western empire, from about A.D. 500 until about 1500 is often called the Middle Ages.

The rise of the Franks. After the Roman Empire in the west collapsed, many Germanic tribes, including the Visigoths, the Vandals, the Burgundians, and the Ostrogoths, plundered Europe. Some established kingdoms. Of all the Germanic tribes, however, it was probably the Franks, who settled in what is now northwestern France, who played the greatest role in European history. Sometime around A.D. 500 one of the Frankish dynasties, the Merovingians, converted to Christianity. They also began to conquer the other Frankish tribes and eventually came to control all of northern Gaul (the old Roman province in what is now France). In the 700s, the Franks continued to expand their power under the new Carolingian dynasty. The Carolingian monarch, Pepin III (also known as Pepin the Short), defended the pope against the Lombards, a Germanic tribe invading Italy, and an alliance began between the Franks and the pope that greatly strengthened both sides.

On Christmas Day 800, the pope crowned Pepin's son, Charles the Great, or Charlemagne, "Emperor of the Romans." The new title signified that Charlemagne, who had united much of Europe for the first time in 400 years, was regarded as the successor to the emperors of Rome. Charlemagne did his best to revive the old Roman Empire—although his empire was more German and Christian than Roman, and its capital was in the northwestern European city of Aix-la-Chapelle. After his death, the empire was divided among his sons and never reunited. But the unifying ideal of the Roman Empire remained strong in the new civilization of the Middle Ages in western Europe.

Feudalism and the manorial system. Charlemagne's empire disintegrated not only because of internal feuds among his heirs but also because new invaders—Muslims, Slavs, Vikings, and Magyars—swarmed into the empire from every direction. In the face of this military threat, the Franks developed a governmental and military system that today we call **feudalism**. Feudalism was a system in which kings and powerful nobles granted land to other nobles in return for loyalty, military assistance, and other services. The land grant was usually in the form of a manor, a large estate that included a village. The estate included peasants, many of whom were serfs bound to the land and forbidden to leave it. The peasants did the work necessary to grow food and keep the estate as self-sufficient as possible. This new economic organization became know as the manor system. The purpose of this system was to provide a base of support for mounted warriors, called knights, as well as foot soldiers, who could be called on to fight when necessary.

The Church. After Charlemagne's death, central governments in medieval Europe were weak or did not exist at all. Consequently, the church performed many of the functions of modern governments. Members of the clergy were organized in ranks according to their power and responsibilities. The levels of this hierarchy, starting at the bottom, were the parish priest, the bishop, the archbishop, and the pope and his curia, or council. Cardinals, the most important members of the curia, advised the pope on legal and spiritual matters, and beginning in 1059 it was also the cardinals who elected each new pope. Although the lowest in rank, the parish priest was enormously important, for it was he who administered the **sacraments**, a set of special ceremonies established by the church as the means by which participants could receive the direct favor, or grace, of God and thereby ward off the consequences of sin.

A second group of clergy was the monastics—monks and nuns—who believed that they could best serve God by withdrawing from the world and practicing prayer, fasting, and self-denial. In the early years of Christianity, some monks and nuns went to extreme lengths to practice such devotion to God, in many cases inflicting physical suffering on themselves

Charlemagne, a patron of learning, encouraged the development of art, science, and literature during a period known as the Carolingian Renaissance.

Magna Carta

foundations of the Christian religion. Those who did so were considered guilty of heresy—the crime of questioning the church's principles or preaching unauthorized doctrines—and risked eternal damnation. In the mid-1200s, the church ordered the monastic order known as the Dominicans to seek out heretics and eliminate heresy, thereby launching the **Inquisition**.

The struggle for power in England and France. The feudal system often led to struggles for power between kings and their more powerful nobles. In some parts of Europe, strong kingdoms gradually emerged from such struggles, as the kings' authority became more powerful than that of the nobles.

In 1066, for example, Duke William of Normandy invaded and conquered England. He laid the foundation for a centralized government by requiring each of his feudal lords to swear allegiance directly to him. Kings after William, especially Henry II, strengthened the central government. However, one of Henry's sons, King John, brought on a revolt among the nobles when he tried to force them to pay taxes they considered unjust. In 1215, the nobles forced John to accept Magna Carta, or "great charter," which protected the liberties of the nobles, as well as dealing with the rights of England's ordinary people. Magna Carta meant that the king was not above the law—he had to obey the law just as his subjects did, or they would be free to rebel against him.

In the century after Magna Carta, the two most important developments in England were the evolution of Parliament and the growth of common law. In the 1260s, nobles led by Simon de Montfort revolted and demanded changes in the king's Great Council that would increase the nobles' representation. De Montfort called on the middle classes as well as the nobles to support the reforms and the result was a broadening of the Great Council into what we know today as Parliament, a body representative of commoners as well as nobles. Although unable at first to pass any laws, Parliament did have the power to refuse to agree to any new taxes—a power it used over the years to gain further power and influence in the affairs of the kingdom.

As Parliamentary power and representation were broadening, so too was the application of a single legal system throughout England. As royal courts provided justice for everyone throughout the kingdom, their decisions became precedents for future cases. This type of law, based on judges' decisions rather than on a code of statutes like Roman law, became known as **common law**, because it was common to all people in England.

to test their souls. Eventually, however, the church stopped such practices and encouraged monastics to live in groups in monasteries and convents (hence the term monastic—those who practiced monasticism). In the early 500s, a young Roman noble named Benedict established a set of rules to govern life in the monastery he established at Monte Cassino in Italy. The Benedictine Rule, as it was known, became a model for other monastic orders as well.

With such a large organization to regulate, the church had its own code of law, known as **canon law**, and its own courts, where members of the clergy were tried for offenses. This separate treatment of the clergy, however, sometimes caused friction between the religious authorities and the secular authorities of the kings and nobles. In fact, the enormous wealth and power of the church soon generated a number of problems between religious and secular authorities.

One of the most important problems concerned lay investiture, or the question of who should appoint bishops and abbots—kings and nobles or the church itself? Such controversies could be especially difficult since the church did not allow anyone to question its basic principles or doctrines, which it regarded as the

Meanwhile, in France the kings also struggled with their nobles, particularly after Hugh Capet was chosen king in 987. The Capetian dynasty, as his successors are known, ruled for over 300 years and gradually increased their own power at the expense of the nobles, as well as gaining control over the clergy. In order to gain popular support for his efforts to control the clergy in France, Philip the Fair, who ruled from 1285 to 1314, convened the Estates General as an advisory body in 1302. Members of the Estates General were drawn from the three major classes of French society—the clergy, the nobles, and the commoners. After many ups and downs in the struggle for power, by the early 1300s the power of the king was greater than that of the nobles in France. However, in 1328, the long line of the Capetians ended.

The clash over Italy and Germany. While the struggle for power produced strong kingdoms in England and France, during the A.D. 1000s a similar struggle emerged in the Holy Roman Empire between the emperors and the popes concerning lay investiture. The issue was finally settled in 1122 when an assembly of church leaders, nobles, and representatives of the Holy Roman Empire reached an agreement known as the Concordat of Worms (named for the city where it was signed). The concordat, or agreement, provided that only church officials could elect bishops and grant them their spiritual powers, though the emperor could grant church officials lands and secular powers. Even then the struggle for power between popes and emperors did not end and the result was that neither Italy nor Germany were able to develop strong, centrally governed states, but remained internally fragmented.

The High Middle Ages

During the Middle Ages in Europe, town life gradually revived and cities became powerful centers of social and political change. In part this was due to the revival of long-distance trade, which had declined with the fall of the Roman Empire in the West. In part too it was due to new influences from the east, as Europeans began to look outward once again, away from Europe. New technologies adapted from other civilizations contributed to the process of recovery and development in the new civilization that was emerging in Europe during the Middle Ages.

The Crusades. During the A.D. 1000s, the Saljuq Turks, nomadic warriors from Central Asia who had converted to Islam, conquered Palestine and attacked Asia Minor, a part of the Byzantine Empire. When

Crusader siege of Jerusalem

the Turks threatened Constantinople, the Byzantine emperor appealed to the pope in Rome for help. In 1095, Pope Urban II urged the powerful nobles and kings of Europe to join in one great war to recover the Holy Land, as Christians called Palestine because it was where Christ had lived. The expeditions to regain the Holy Land are called the Crusades.

The first Crusade succeeded, and Christian forces from Europe took control of the Holy Land. The victory did not last long, however, and Muslim forces under Salah al-Din recaptured Jerusalem in 1187. Eventually, all of Palestine once again fell under Muslim control and the Crusades ultimately ended in military failure.

Despite the military failure, however, the Crusades had important consequences and lessons for Europe.

Europeans learned about new weapons, such as the crossbow, as well as new siege tactics for taking fortified cities. They may even have learned about gunpowder from Muslims, who probably obtained such knowledge from the Chinese. In addition, the drain of so many nobles to fight in the Holy Land strengthened monarchs at home and may have hastened the decline of feudalism and the rise of strong, centrally organized kingdoms in Europe. Meanwhile, Europeans were influenced by the exchange of ideas among crusaders from different countries and between crusaders and the other cultures they encountered. Commercial changes also occurred. Italian cities benefitted from transporting crusaders and the products with which they had become familiar in the Holy Land. Thanks to the Crusades, Europeans now demanded rice, sugar, lemons, apricots, melons, and many other things.

The growth of trade and towns. The growing trade with the East was part of a larger revival of trade throughout Europe. This revival began in Italy, where neither trade nor town life had declined as much as elsewhere in Europe after the end of the Roman Empire. Moreover, Italy was geographically located between northern Europe and Southwest Asia. The Italians consequently became the great European distributors, acting as go-betweens for traders from Asia and traders from central and northern Europe.

Meanwhile, trade also revived in northern Europe along trade routes that led across France, down the Rhine River in Germany, across the English Channel from England, and south from the coasts of the Baltic Sea. These routes all connected in Flanders, today a part of Belgium and northern France, where great trade fairs began to take place. Flanders was also important as a source of fine woolen cloth, which was the region's chief product. Further north, Hamburg, Bremen, and Lubeck became the most important commercial cities as trade flourished along the shores of the North and Baltic Seas. These cities and others formed the powerful Hanseatic League, with permanent trading posts in Flanders, Scandinavia, England, and Russia.

By far the most profitable trade for medieval merchants was in luxury goods from eastern and southwestern Asia—spices, medicines, perfumes, dyes, silks, cotton, and linen fabrics, and of course gold and silver, among other things. Europe offered a variety of goods for exchange, including furs, timber, and fish from the Baltic region; wine, oil, leather, weapons, and armor from Spain; metal goods and glassware from Venice; and fine woolen cloth from England and Flanders. Out of all this trade activity, three important developments occurred in Europe—a manufacturing system, a banking system, and the practice of investing capital, which is the wealth earned, saved, and invested to make profits. These three developments laid the foundation for the emergence of a market economy, an economy in which land, labor, and capital are controlled by individuals.

The growth of towns accompanied the revival of trade. As the number of towns increased and their populations grew, a new class of merchants, master workers, and skilled workers also emerged in medieval society. Townspeople did not fit well into the manorial system and soon began to want to control their own governments. Some were granted charters, written statements of their liberties, from their lords. Within the towns themselves, merchants and artisans established associations, or guilds, that regulated their activities and acted as charitable organizations for their members.

The rise of towns also led to a decline in serfdom, since serfs might escape to a town and become free. Moreover, the growing demand for food from the towns meant that the serfs could sell the food they produced for money, and then use that money instead of their own labor to pay for the land they used from their lords. Changes in agriculture, which made it more efficient and required less serfs to produce the same amount of food, also led to a decline in serfdom, as did the Black Death—or bubonic plague—which swept into Europe in the 1300s and killed millions.

Bruges, one of the chief Hanseatic cities, known as the "City of Bridges," became a commercial center in the 1300s. This is a map of Bruges during the 1300s.

Scene from *The Canterbury Tales*

Life and culture in the Middle Ages. As towns and trade revived, so did the cultural and intellectual life of Europe. Two writers, Dante and Chaucer, represent the flowering of medieval literature. Dante Alighieri was born in Italy in 1265. His greatest work is *The Divine Comedy*. Geoffrey Chaucer of England wrote *The Canterbury Tales*, in the form of a series of stories told by a group of religious pilgrims. The later Middle Ages also witnessed the growth of universities. By the 1300s, universities could be found throughout northern and central Europe. Art also flourished, mostly in religious architecture, as Europeans built great soaring cathedrals, first in the rather low, heavy Romanesque style and then in the graceful, upward soaring Gothic style. Other art forms were used to beautify churches, as most medieval artists dedicated themselves to glorifying God.

Unification and monarchy. As feudalism declined, kings began to build their kingdoms into organized nations. This movement was often aided by developments in warfare. The military strength of a professional army and the support of townspeople strengthened the king's position against the feudal lords. The use of new weapons also weakened feudalism. During the Hundred Years War with France, for example, the English use of the longbow, which could penetrate armor, allowed English foot soldiers to defeat French feudal cavalry at Agincourt in 1415. Both French and English troops also began to use gunpowder during the war. Cannons, however, could also be used by a king to blast down the castle walls of his feudal nobles.

The Hundred Years' War increased the power of the English Parliament at the expense of the king's power. Angry over the course of the war, the House of Commons demanded the right to consider tax legislation before it was considered by the lords. Moreover, the general English failure in the war discredited the monarchy and led to a devastating civil war, known as the War of the Roses, as rivals struggled for the throne. Eventually, the War of the Roses ended when Henry Tudor established a new dynasty as Henry VII. The English people, tired of war and disorder, willingly accepted the strong government that Henry VII established.

Meanwhile, the Hundred Years' War strengthened the monarchy in France. During the war, Joan of Arc, a French peasant girl, had participated in the defense of the city of Orléans and helped the heir to the French throne take the crown as Charles VII. Her actions inspired French feelings of patriotism. Such feelings were only reinforced when she was captured by English allies and burned at the stake in 1430.

Warfare also aided the unification of Spain into a single nation. King Ferdinand of Aragon and Queen Isabella of Castile married in 1469, uniting two of the four kingdoms in Spain. They then fought a war against the last of the Muslim kingdoms, Granada, which they conquered in 1492. In the 1500s, they united Castile and Aragon to form the new nation of Spain and added the kingdom of Navarre to its territories. Ferdinand and Isabella made Spain a strong monarchy, taking powers away from both the church courts and the nobles.

While Spain, France, and England were becoming strong unified national kingdoms, a different pattern developed in Germany and Italy. In 1273, a member of the Habsburg family from a small state in what is now Switzerland became Holy Roman emperor. After 1537 the emperor was nearly always a Habsburg. Through clever marriages, they eventually became the most powerful family in Europe. Nevertheless, in the face of strong opposition from local German princes as well as the popes in Rome, they never had enough power to unify the empire or even the regions within it into a single strong, centrally governed state. Not until the 1800s would such national states emerge in Germany and Italy.

Challenges to church power. While monarchs in western Europe were unifying their kingdoms, the church was experiencing new challenges to its power. For a time, in the early 1300s, French kings gained enough power to name the popes and to force them to move from Rome to Avignon in southeastern France.

This period of papal history—from 1309 to 1377—is known as the Babylonian Captivity. The situation worsened after 1378 when two rival popes, one French and the other Italian, claimed power during the period known as the **Great Schism.** The Babylonian Captivity and the Great Schism weakened the authority and prestige of the papacy.

Section 4 Review

1. **Define** icons, feudalism, sacraments, canon law, Inquisition, common law, Great Schism
2. **Identify** Justinian, Muhammad, Ottomans, Charlemagne, Habsburgs
3. **Locate and Explain the Significance** Kiev
4. **Analyzing Ideas** How and why was the Byzantine Empire able to survive and prosper?
5. **Understanding Ideas** List the five chief duties of a Muslim.
6. **Interpreting Ideas** How did the Catholic Church affect political, economic, and social life in the Middle Ages?
7. **Analyzing Ideas** What led to the strengthening of central governments after the One Hundred Year's War.

Section 5

Asia, Africa, and the Americas

Focus Questions

- **How did civilizations in East Asia develop after A.D. 500?**
- **What factors affected the development of kingdoms in Sub-Saharan Africa?**
- **What were the most important civilizations to develop in Mesoamerica and South America, and what were some of their achievements?**

From about A.D. 552 to 1573, great civilizations flourished in East Asia. The Chinese and Japanese established complex patterns of government, society, and culture. Great civilizations also developed in Africa and the Americas. In Africa, trade played an important role in the growth of kingdoms. In the Americas, on the other hand, civilizations developed in isolation from the rest of the world.

The Civilizations of East Asia

In Europe the Western Roman Empire never recovered after its collapse in the late 400s. In China the Han dynasty collapsed about the same time. However, the Hun and other nomadic invaders from Tibet and Mongolia eventually settled down, established kingdoms, and adopted Chinese customs. In the late 500s, a unified empire was re-established in China.

China under the Sui, Tang, and Song dynasties. The short-lived Sui dynasty reunited China in 589. During their brief period in power, Sui rulers began building the Grand Canal, an engineering marvel that connected northern and southern China for the first time in history. When the Sui tried to conquer new territory in Manchuria and Korea, however, they were defeated by invading Turks. In 618 an uprising ended and the Sui dynasty and ushered in a new dynasty—the Tang. Although also relatively short-lived, the Tang dynasty, like the Han dynasty, began a golden age of steady cultural development in Chinese history. The Tang dyanasty reached its height in about 750, and then gradually declined until it was overthrown in 907. In 960, the Song dynasty came to power.

Although numerous foreign invaders threatened northern China, eventually even forcing the Song to move their capital south to Hangzhou, trade, the arts, and technological development flourished. Hangzhou and Guangzhou became major bases for overseas commerce. Exports included gold, silver, copper, and "cash"—strings of copper coins. Porcelain, a fine translucent pottery, became one of China's most valuable exports. Song artisans perfected the art of making porcelain, while Song artists, partly inspired by the Daoist love of nature, produced beautiful landscape paintings.

The Song further improved the civil service system that produced administrators for the empire. In technology, they developed such innovations as moveable type, though it was not widely used in China because of the number of characters in the Chinese language. The use of gunpowder as an explosive for war, appeared under the Song. Under both the Tang and the Song, technological improvements in agriculture, particularly extensive water control projects, as well as the introduction of new strains of quick-ripening rice from Southeast Asia, improved food supplies. Also, a new crop, tea, began to be cultivated.

Mongol warriors demonstrated amazing horsemanship; they exhibited such skill by shooting arrows while riding at top speeds. This manuscript from the 1200s illustrates a battle between Mongol tribes.

The Mongol Empire. While China continued to develop and become prosperous, to the north a new power emerged in the form of the Mongols, a fierce nomadic people who had adapted to life in the great steppes of Mongolia. Under a new leader, who became known as Genghis Khan, or "Universal Ruler," the Mongols created a vast empire that eventually stretched from Europe to China and the borders of India. In the early 1200s, the Mongols captured the city now called Beijing in northern China. Under Kublai Khan, one of Genghis Khan's grandsons, the Mongols completed their conquest of China and Kublai Khan proclaimed the beginning of his own Yuan dynasty in 1271.

Over a century of warfare and invasion the population of China had declined from about 100 million to about 60 million, but after the consolidation of Mongol rule, China once again began to prosper in many ways. The population began to increase again, and Kublai Khan extended the Grand Canal all the way to Beijing. The Mongols also linked China to India and Persia by new roads, and encouraged trade throughout their vast empire. During Mongol rule, contacts between China and Europe increased, as Christian missionaries and merchants like Marco Polo travelled to China and back. Despite such benefits, however, the Chinese always regarded the Mongols as invaders and in 1368 the Chinese overthrew the last Mongol emperor and established a new Chinese dynasty, the Ming, on the throne.

Japan, Korea, and Southeast Asia. Chinese civilization also greatly influenced surrounding peoples. Civilization in Japan was largely inspired by contacts with China, and the Japanese initially developed a centralized imperial political system modeled in many

ways on that of China. Chinese Buddhism also heavily influenced the Japanese, many of whom accepted it side by side with their own native religion, now called Shinto, which was based on a belief in gods or nature spirits called **kami.** The Japanese also adopted the Chinese style of writing, as well as such things as artistic designs, road engineering, medical knowledge, and even styles of clothing.

While imperial rule was usually centralized in China, a different pattern developed in Japan after about 800. Although the emperor remained an important spiritual symbol, power gradually shifted to great war lords. Eventually a decentralized kind of political system developed that resembled feudalism in Europe. Under the theoretical authority of the emperor, a shogun, or supreme military commander, ruled loosely over powerful local lords, who were in turn supported by warriors known as samurai. Eventually, the most powerful lords, known as daimyo, or "great names," fought among themselves for power, while the emperor and the shoguns were relatively powerless.

Chinese influence was even more pronounced in Korea, the rugged, mountainous peninsula south of Manchuria on the east coast of Asia. China had conquered Korea under the Han dynasty. After the fall of the Han, three kingdoms emerged in Korea, which struggled for control of the peninsula. Eventually, the strongest, Silla, united Korea under its own rule. Thereafter, apart from conquest by the Mongols, Korea retained its political independence, but continued to be heavily influenced by Chinese culture. Koreans adopted the Chinese civil service system, for example. Korean scholars also studied the Confucian Classics. Chinese Buddhism, especially Zen Buddhism, became extremely influential in Korea. Nevertheless, the Koreans retained their own sense of identity, expressed in such things as their own language and their native dress.

Chinese influence even penetrated to Southeast Asia, where the modern-day countries of Cambodia, Laos, Vietnam, Myanmar, Malaysia, and Thailand (formerly Siam) are found. China controlled northern Vietnam, for example, a region then known as Nam Viet, for much of its history. Other parts of Southeast Asia, on the other hand, such as Cambodia, were heavily influenced by contacts with Indian civilization and Hinduism, as well as Indian versions of Buddhism.

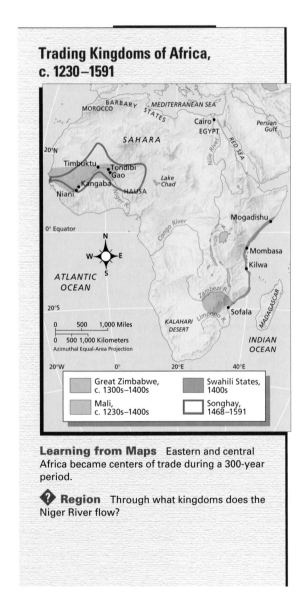

Trading Kingdoms of Africa, c. 1230–1591

Learning from Maps Eastern and central Africa became centers of trade during a 300-year period.

? Region Through what kingdoms does the Niger River flow?

Africa and the Americas

The civilizations of Europe, Southwest Asia, and East Asia were all in contact with each other. Consequently, developments in one often found their way to the others and often had great influence. In Sub-Saharan Africa and especially the Americas, however, such early contact with other regions of the world was minimal or non-existent. Consequently, these civilizations developed in unique ways.

Africa's early history. Scholars rely on many methods to understand the history of Africa. Linguists study the development and spread of language groups like Bantu, for example, to understand the spread of African peoples throughout the continent. Oral traditions—poems, songs, or stories passed from one generation to the next—have also been a major source of information about specific African clans, villages, and dynasties. Scholars believe that most Africans lived in small, independent villages and were farmers, herders, or fishers. Relationships established by kinship and age provided the ties that bound the different societies together. Religion was an important part of life in many African societies. Elders usually exercised authority over the village. Life in African villages was closely bound to the agricultural cycles of planting and harvesting. Through the rise and fall of numerous kingdoms, the village survived as the basic unit of society and the economy.

African city-states and kingdoms. While some African peoples lived happily without developing state structures, others came together to establish small city-states, kingdoms, and even empires. These states were as diverse as the African geography and peoples that created them.

Along the Nile River, south of the major centers of ancient Egypt, arose a powerful kingdom known as Kush. At first, Kush maintained close cultural and economic ties with Egypt. Beginning in about 1300 B.C., however, Kush started to become more independent. Then in about 710 B.C. it conquered Upper Egypt. For about 40 years a Kush dynasty ruled a unified Egypt. Then the Assyrians, who were armed with iron weapons, invaded in 671 B.C. With the Assyrian invasion the kingdom of Kush weakened. Later, the kingdom of Aksum arose in the Ethiopian Highlands. As Kush declined, Aksum became a major competitor for control of trade in this area.

No large kingdoms such as Kush and Aksum emerged on the coast of East Africa. Instead, a series of city-states emerged and dominated coastal trade in the Indian Ocean. The growth of Indian Ocean trade after the A.D. 900s dramatically increased the demand for gold. The Shona people, who immigrated onto the plateau land of what is today Zimbabwe, achieved control over local peoples and mining activities. The spread of Islam also created favorable conditions for trade and gave rise to a new society along the coast that merged African, Arabic, and even Persian elements—as the language it produced, Swahili, testifies.

In West Africa, between Lake Chad and the Atlantic Ocean, several important African societies and empires flourished. They included the empires of Ghana, Mali, and Songhay. The wealth and strength of these kingdoms depended on control of the trade routes across the Sahara Desert. At the desert's edge, traders exchanged gold, extracted from mines south of the desert region, for salt, which was mined in the Sahara itself. The spread of Islam in the region was often an important factor in the creation of great empires. Mali and Songhay both, for example, were Muslim states.

The earliest Americans. The first people in the Americas lived by hunting and gathering. Gradually, a new way of life emerged—farming. In what are now the United States and Canada, many different cultures and societies thrived. The cultures of these peoples often depended on the geography of the region they inhabited. In the dry, desert-like conditions of the Southwest, for example, farmers lived in permanent settlements made up of communal houses, rather like apartment buildings, built out of **adobe**—a sun-dried brick. On the northwest coast of North America, on the other hand, people relied primarily on fishing and carved great totem poles with their family histories from the enormous trees that forested the region. On the Great Plains, tribal peoples survived by hunting buffalo, following the herds wherever they went. More sophisticated cultures developed in the diverse environment of the Eastern Woodlands. The Hopewell Culture, for example, left many mounds, presumably burial sites, as well as the foundations of buildings, which archaeologists have recently uncovered.

The empires of Mexico and Peru. In Central and South America a variety of cultures also developed. Early cultures in Mesoamerica included the Olmecs in Mexico and the Maya in the Yucatan Peninsula. The Maya were farmers who were also skilled architects and engineers. They built steep pyramid-shaped temples to their gods and invented the only writing system in the Americas. Despite the brilliance of their civilization, however, which was scattered among many city-states throughout the Yucatan region and into present-day El Salvador, about A.D. 900 they suddenly abandoned their ceremonial centers.

Meanwhile, further north, other civilizations had also developed in central Mexico. About A.D. 650 a people called the Toltec invaded central Mexico from the north. Ruled by a military class, the Toltec soon spread their influence as far south as the Yucatan. Around 1200 A.D. other peoples from the north also invaded central Mexico. One of these peoples, the Aztecs, soon emerged as the strongest. The Aztecs incorporated into their culture the inventions of peoples they conquered or with whom they traded. They also made and acquired the use of the calendar and mathematics. To sustain their gods, they practiced human sacrifice.

At about the same time that Aztec civilization was at its height, another civilization was expanding in the Andes Mountains of South America. These people—the Inca—based their religion on worship of the Sun and moon. Their name meant "children of the Sun." By the late 1400s, the Inca Empire extended along most of the west coast of South America and far into the Andes, covering much of the present-day nations of Peru, Ecuador, Bolivia, and Chile. The Inca built fortresses and irrigation systems and laid roads, many of them paved. The rulers of the empire prevented local famines by maintaining storehouses and distributing food supplies when crops failed. After conquering their neighbors, the Inca sought to eliminate regional diversity in their empire. They established an educational system, particularly for the children of the nobility, that taught the imperial language, Inca religion, and history. Although the Inca did not have a writing system, they kept records by means of the **quipu**, a kind of knotted string used to assist the memory. They were also quite advanced in the practice of medicine, using anesthetics and even performing operations on the brain.

Section 5 Review

1. **Define** kami, adobe, *quipu*
2. **Identify** Kublai Khan
3. **Locate and Explain the Significance** Mali, Songhay
4. **Identifying Ideas** What important changes occurred in government and society in East Asia after A.D. 500?
5. **Synthesizing Ideas** What conclusions have scholars reached about the role of trade in the development of kingdoms in Sub-Saharan Africa?
6. **Summarizing Ideas** What were some of the achievements of the empires of the Americas?

Prologue Chapter Review

c. 1000-700 B.C.
Phoenicia improves metal working and glassblowing.

8000 B.C.   2000 B.C.   1500 B.C.   1000 B.C.

c. 8000 B.C.
Ice Age ends.

c. 2500 B.C.
Harappan civilization develops in Indus River Valley.

c. 800 B.C.
Sparta and Athens develop into powerful city-states.

Prologue Summary

The following list contains the key concepts you have learned about the ancient civilizations, civilizations of the Mediterranean world, and the world in transition.

1. Scholars believe that people lived on Earth long before the development of writing, during the period known as prehistory. Although unable to write, prehistoric people made significant discoveries and advances.
2. Civilizations first appeared along the Nile, Tigris–Euphrates, Indus, and Huang He Rivers.
3. In ancient India, people learned how to farm, developed a written language and calendars, and created a complex civilization.
4. China developed and retained its own distinctive culture in relative isolation.
5. On the southern end of the mountainous Balkan Peninsula, as well as in Asia Minor and on the nearby islands, the Greek civilization—one of the greatest the world has ever known—developed.
6. Greek culture reached new heights during the 400s B.C.—a period so magnificent that it is often called Greece's golden age.
7. The date 146 B.C. is often given as the end of the Hellenistic Age because by that year the Romans had extended their power over a large part of the eastern Mediterranean area.

8. The collapse of the Roman Empire in the west resulted in the disappearance of strong governments. However, the Roman Empire in the east—the Byzantine Empire—maintained its traditions and kept out barbarian invaders.
9. In the A.D. 600s the prophet Muhammad began preaching Islam, today the world's second largest religion.
10. The period in western European history following the collapse of the Roman Empire, from about A.D. 500 to about 1500, is called the Middle Ages.
11. During the Middle Ages cities became powerful centers of social and political change. Trade revived as people began to look outward, away from Europe.
12. From about A.D. 552 to 1573 great civilizations flourished in East Asia.
13. Successive waves of immigrants from Asia settled the Americas. Many crossed the land bridge that linked Asia and the Americas.
14. Civilizations developed in unique ways in Africa and in the Americas. Trade was an important factor in how various kingdoms and empires developed in Africa south of the Sahara. In isolation from contact with other parts of the world, complex civilizations grew up in the Andes and Mesoamerica.

Reviewing Important Terms

On a separate sheet of paper, supply the term that correctly completes each statement.

1. _____ _____ _____ is a system in which different people perform different jobs, instead of each person having to do all kinds of work.
2. _____ was a custom in which a widow would commit suicide by throwing herself on top of her husband's flaming funeral pyre.
3. A bishop of one of the five most important early Christian cities was called a _____.
4. Holy pictures of Jesus, the Virgin Mary, and the saints, typically used in devotions, are called _____.
5. A _____ is a kind of knotted string developed by the Inca to assist the memory.

Developing Critical Thinking Skills

1. **Understanding Ideas** What advances were made by the people of the earliest civilizations?
2. **Explaining Ideas** Describe the development of democracy in ancient Greece.
3. **Summarizing Ideas** What were the basic principles of feudalism and the manorial system?
4. **Classifying Ideas** How did different types of cultures develop in different parts of Africa?

Relating Geography to History

The earliest civilizations developed in four great river valleys—the Huang He, the Nile, the Indus, and the Tigris-Euphrates. Many other civilizations also originally developed in river valleys. What advantages did rivers provide to the people of early civilizations?

c. A.D. 1040
Chinese employ movable type for printing.

A.D. 1   A.D. 500   A.D. 1000   A.D. 1500

335 B.C.
Aristotle founds school in Athens.

A.D. 528
Compilation of Justianic Code begins.

A.D. 1215
Signing of Magna Carta.

Relating Past to Present

1. The Roman Republic had a citizen army rather than a professional army. (a) What kind of army do we have in the United States today? (b) What are the advantages and disadvantages of each type of army?
2. Many English words have roots in Latin American cultures. Use a dictionary to find the origin of these words: chocolate, hammock, potato, quinine, tapioca, tobacco, tomato, avocado.

Applying History Study Skills

Before completing this activity, review Building History Study Skills on page 28.

All Muslims are expected, if possible, to make at least one pilgrimage to Mecca during their lifetime. The following selection describes the events that occur during this pilgrimage. Read the selection. Then list the events in sequence.

"Scarcely had the first smile of morning beamed . . . when we arose, bathed, and proceeded in our pilgrim-garb to the Sanctuary [the Ka'bah]. We entered by the principal . . . northern door, descended two long flights of steps, traversed the cloister, and stood in the sight of the Bayt Allah [House of God]. . . . We proceeded to the . . . open pavement . . . where we performed the usual two-bow prayer in honour of the Mosque. This was followed by a cup of holy water and a present to the . . . carriers, who for the consideration distributed, in my name, a large earthen vaseful to poor pilgrims.

We then advanced towards the eastern angle of the [Ka'bah], in which is inserted the Black Stone; and, standing about ten yards from it, repeated with upraised hands, 'There is no God but Allah alone, Whose covenant is Truth, and Whose Servant is Victorious'. . . . After which we approached as close as we could to the stone. . . .

Then commenced the ceremony of Tawáf, or circumambulation [a circling on foot], our route being the . . . low oval of polished granite immediately surrounding the [Ka'bah]. . . .

At the conclusion of the Tawáf, it was deemed advisable to kiss the stone. . . .

In the evening, . . . I again . . . repaired to the [Ka'bah]."

internet connect

Search the Internet through the HRW Web site for information on the Black Death in Europe in the 1300s. Find as many details as you can about the course of the disease and its effects on communities and individuals. Then write a newspaper article about the plague as if you were living at the time.

GO TO: go.hrw.com
KEYWORD: SCØ Black Death

Building Your Portfolio

1. **Reporting on Technology** The pyramids are among the most impressive structures left by any civilization. Research and write a report on techniques of ancient Egyptian building. You might use the following books as sources: William Fix's *Pyramid Odyssey* (Mercury Media, 1984) and Zaui A. Hawass's *The Pyramids of Ancient Egypt* (Carnegie Museum of Natural History, 1990). Place the report in your portfolio.
2. **Constructing a Model** Use resources in your school or public library to find more information about medieval manors. Then construct a scale model of a typical manor. Be sure to label all the structures and areas on your model. Place a sketch of the model in your portfolio.
3. **Writing a Report** In January 1997, several archaeologists and anthropologists visited the site of Monte Verde in Chile. These scientists now believe that this site pushes back the date of the migrations to the Americas. Research (using magazines, the Internet, etc.) the excavation and studies of Monte Verde. Then write a report on the findings of the scientists. Place the report in your portfolio.

POLITICS AND GOVERNMENT

1375	1425	1475	1525

1347
Black Death strikes Europe

1368
Ming dynasty established in China

1492
Christopher Columbus reaches the Americas

Ivory statue of a Daoist figure carved during the Ming dynasty

SOCIETY AND CULTURE

1375	1425	1475	1525

1508
Michelangelo begins painting Sistine Chapel

1509
Erasmus's *The Praise of Folly*

1513
Machiavelli's *The Prince*

SCIENCE AND TECHNOLOGY

1375	1425	1475	1525

c.1450
Johannes Gutenberg begins using movable type to print books

Latin version of the Gutenburg Bible, 1456

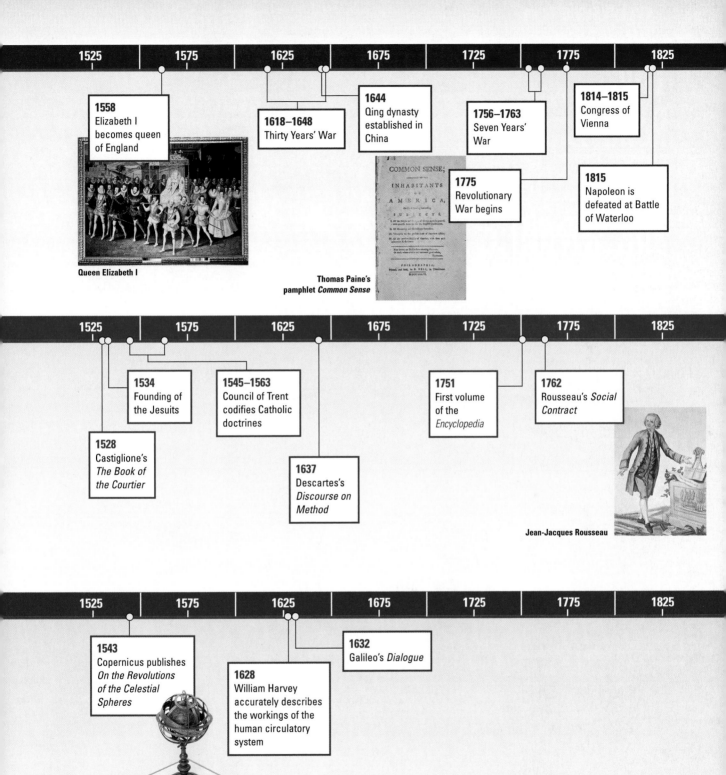

Timeline 1

1525 — 1575 — 1625 — 1675 — 1725 — 1775 — 1825

1558
Elizabeth I becomes queen of England

1618–1648
Thirty Years' War

1644
Qing dynasty established in China

1756–1763
Seven Years' War

1814–1815
Congress of Vienna

1775
Revolutionary War begins

1815
Napoleon is defeated at Battle of Waterloo

Queen Elizabeth I

Thomas Paine's pamphlet *Common Sense*

COMMON SENSE;
INHABITANTS
OF
AMERICA,

Timeline 2

1525 — 1575 — 1625 — 1675 — 1725 — 1775 — 1825

1534
Founding of the Jesuits

1545–1563
Council of Trent codifies Catholic doctrines

1751
First volume of the *Encyclopedia*

1762
Rousseau's *Social Contract*

1528
Castiglione's *The Book of the Courtier*

1637
Descartes's *Discourse on Method*

Jean-Jacques Rousseau

Timeline 3

1525 — 1575 — 1625 — 1675 — 1725 — 1775 — 1825

1543
Copernicus publishes *On the Revolutions of the Celestial Spheres*

1632
Galileo's *Dialogue*

1628
William Harvey accurately describes the workings of the human circulatory system

Caspar Vopell's manuscript globe of Earth, 1543

The Renaissance, Reformation, and Scientific Revolution

TIME

A.D. 1350–1700

| 3.7 million B.C. | 4000 B.C. | A.D. 1350–1700 | | A.D. 2100 |

PLACE

Europe

Europe

ARCTIC OCEAN

NORTH AMERICA

EUROPE

ASIA

PACIFIC OCEAN

AFRICA

Equator

AUSTRALIA

SOUTH AMERICA

ATLANTIC OCEAN

INDIAN OCEAN

PACIFIC OCEAN

ANTARCTICA

The Medici Family Palazzo, Florence

Significance

If you were to think about the differences between medieval and modern times, you would probably think first of the great difference in the material goods available. Today we have CD players, microwave ovens, and conveniences that medieval people never dreamed of. However, another and perhaps even greater difference exists: a difference in attitudes. Beginning in the 1300s, people gradually began to look for new ways to explain why and how things happened in the world.

Many historians believe that the changes in attitude that altered how people viewed themselves and their world grew out of a philosophical and artistic movement that began in Italy in the early 1300s. Because it centered on a revival of interest in the classical learning of Greece and Rome, we call this movement the **Renaissance** (REN·uh·sahnts), a French word meaning "rebirth."

Terms to Define

Renaissance	Counter-Reformation
humanists	broadsides
perspective	almanacs
Reformation	standard of living
indulgences	inflation
95 theses	Scientific Revolution
sects	scientific method
predestination	geocentric theory
theocracy	heliocentric theory

People to Identify

Niccolò Machiavelli	Martin Luther
Leonardo da Vinci	John Calvin
Michelangelo	Ignatius de Loyola
Johannes Gutenberg	Nicolaus Copernicus
William Shakespeare	Galileo

Places to Locate

Florence	Zurich
Venice	Geneva
Wittenberg	

Chapter Theme Questions

- **The Arts** How might the influx of new ideas affect the arts?
- **Religion** What factors might have led to major shifts in religious thought?
- **Science** How might a change in methods of investigation lead to an entirely new way of viewing the world?

On November 4, 1966, newscasts across the world carried reports of a staggering natural disaster. In northern Italy the Arno River had burst over its banks, sending torrents of swirling floodwaters cascading through the museums, cathedrals, and libraries of Florence. When the waters receded, they left layer upon layer of sewage and muck. Within days, hundreds of people converged on the water-logged city to help with the massive cleanup.

Why would news of a flood in northern Italy electrify people across the world? Quite simply because that city contained the world's greatest store of Renaissance art and literature. One reporter noted:

❝It is fair to say that much of what we know today of painting and sculpture, of architecture and political science, of scientific method and economic theory, we owe to the artists, politicians, statesmen, bankers, and merchants of the Renaissance—that explosion of intellectual and artistic energy in Italy between 1300 and 1600. And Florentines stood at the turbulent center of the Renaissance.❞

The outpouring of creativity that was the Renaissance changed the course of Western civilization.

Section 1

Renaissance Writers and Artists

Focus Questions

- **What led to the Italian Renaissance?**
- **What were the characteristics of Italian Renaissance art?**
- **What were the characteristics of the Northern Renaissance in terms of humanist thought, literature, and art?**

Scholars use the term *Renaissance* to refer not only to a philosophical and artistic movement but also to the period during which it flourished. The

Renaissance was a time of many developments, including the invention of the printing press, advances in science, and a new emphasis on reason.

The Origins of the Italian Renaissance

A renewed interest in Greek and Roman literature and life characterized the Renaissance. In many ways it was natural that this interest would reawaken in Italy. Ruins of the mighty Roman Empire served as constant reminders of Roman glory. The tradition of Rome as the capital city of a vast empire lived on in the popes, who made Rome the seat of the Roman Catholic Church. The Crusades and trade with Africa and Southwest Asia introduced new ideas and brought Italians into contact with the Byzantine civilization, whose scholars had preserved much learning from classical Greece and Rome. Arab and African developments in such disciplines as medicine and science fired the curiosity of many Italian scholars.

Italian cities such as Florence, Rome, Venice, Milan, and Naples had grown rich through trade and industry. Their citizens included many educated, wealthy merchants. In Florence, for example, the Medici (MED·ee·chee) family grew wealthy first as bankers and then as rulers of the city-state. As leader of Florence, Lorenzo Medici became a great patron of the arts and influenced Florence's artistic awakening.

The Humanities

Beginning in the 1300s, a number of Italian scholars developed a lively interest in classical Greek and Roman literature. Medieval scholars who had studied ancient history had tried to bring everything they learned into harmony with Christian doctrine. By contrast, the Italian scholars studied the ancient world to explore its great achievements.

These Italian scholars stressed the study of grammar, rhetoric, history, and poetry, using classical texts. We call these studies the *humanities*; people who specialized in the humanities were called **humanists.** Humanists searched out manuscripts written in Greek and Latin. Often they would find more than one copy of a work. If the copies differed, humanists compared the different versions to try to determine which was most authentic. In doing so they displayed a critical approach to learning that had been lacking.

As humanists studied classical manuscripts, they came to believe that it was important to know how things worked. This belief led them to emphasize education. However, they also felt that a person should lead a meaningful life. Humanists became convinced that a person had to become actively involved in practical affairs such as patronage of the arts.

Humanists viewed existence not only as a preparation for life after death but also as a joy in itself. Along with a belief in individual dignity came an admiration for individual achievement. Many individuals of this period displayed a variety of talents, such as being both poet and scientist.

Writers of the Italian Renaissance

One of the first humanists, the Italian Francesco Petrarch (PEE·trahrk), lived from 1304 to 1374. Like many of the humanists, Petrarch became famous as a scholar and as a teacher. He also wrote poetry, and his sonnets to Laura, an imaginary ideal

Renaissance Italy, c. 1500

Learning from Maps During the Renaissance, Italy was a patchwork of small states.

❓ **Place** To what republic did the island of Corsica belong?

Machiavelli: Lessons in Statecraft

Niccolò Machiavelli is considered one of the most influential political writers of the Renaissance. While the political theorists of the Middle Ages wrote about politics in an idealistic way, Machiavelli strived to present the realistic side of politics in his work. His ideas were based on his perception of human nature from a historical context.

According to Machiavelli, an essential link existed between the condition of the state and the condition of the people. The state, he wrote, must be unified and efficient. If the state were divided and inefficient, drastic measures might be required to regain control.

Machiavelli's most well-known work, *The Prince*, was essentially a handbook on how to be a great ruler. Machiavelli believed that a ruler did not have to abide by traditional customs and morals but instead should be concerned only with power and success in political ventures. As an example of this new type of ruler, Machiavelli cited Cesare Borgia, who achieved political power through cruel and ruthless means. *The Prince* has often been considered a justification of the type of tyrannical leadership practiced by rulers such as Borgia.

In his essay, Machiavelli advised rulers to maintain the safety of their states by whatever means they thought necessary and not to let considerations of honesty, justice, or honor hamper them. Today we use the word Machiavellian to describe people who use deceit and who have little regard for morality in their effort to get what they want. In this excerpt from *The Prince,* Machiavelli discusses power and the need to inspire fear in one's subjects: "A controversy has arisen about this: whether it is better to be loved than feared, or vice versa. My view is that it is desirable to be both loved and feared; but it is difficult to achieve both and, if one of them has to be lacking, it is much safer to be feared than loved.

"For this may be said of men generally: they are ungrateful, fickle, feigners [liars] and dissemblers [deceivers], avoiders of danger, eager for gain. While you benefit them they are all devoted to you: they would shed their blood for you; they offer their possessions, their lives, and their sons . . . when the need to do so is far off. But when you are hard pressed, they turn away. A ruler who has relied completely on their promises and has neglected to prepare other defences, will be ruined, because friendships that are acquired with money, and not through greatness and nobility of character, are paid for but not secured, and prove unreliable just when they are needed.

"Men are less hesitant about offending or harming a ruler who makes himself less loved than one who inspires fear. For love is sustained by a bond of gratitude which, because men are excessively self-interested, is broken whenever they see a chance to benefit themselves. But fear is sustained by a dread of punishment that is always effective."

Machiavelli

Title page from *The Prince*

woman, are considered some of the greatest love poems in literature.

Petrarch's main influence, however, grew out of his desire for continuity with classical writers, whom he believed were committed to virtue in both public and private life. Petrarch thought these individuals could best be imitated if one studied their writings. The study of the writings of the ancient Greeks and Romans came to be called *classical education*. A command of classical languages, as they had been used by the ancient Greeks and Romans, became the mark of an educated person.

The humanists remained deeply committed to Christian teachings. For that reason, they sometimes felt a tension between their commitment to the study of the ancients and their commitment to Christianity. Petrarch, for instance, agonized over his lust for fame (a common Roman ambition) because he feared it would hurt his chances for salvation. Like most Italian humanists, Petrarch thought it important to lead a full and active life here on earth, even if that meant devoting less time to spiritual concerns.

Niccolò Machiavelli (mahk·yah·VEL·lee) of Florence, a diplomat and historian who lived from 1469 to 1527, ranks as one of the most illustrious of the many Renaissance writers. In 1513 he wrote a famous essay, *The Prince*, which described government not in terms of lofty ideals but as Machiavelli felt government actually worked.

Machiavelli can be considered a humanist because he looked to the ancient Romans for models and because such matters as the workings of politics interested him. However, the lack of concern for morality that he wrote about in *The Prince* set him apart from other humanists, who considered virtue their main aim.

Baldassare Castiglione (kahs·teel·YOH·nay) was an Italian diplomat and writer who lived from 1478 to 1529. In 1528 he published what was probably the most famous book of the Renaissance, *The Book of the Courtier*. Castiglione's work is a book on courtesy as well as an explanation of the role of the refined courtier as opposed to that of the coarse knight of the Middle Ages. As nobles lost their military role, Castiglione gave them a new idea of refined behavior. The setting for the book is the court at Urbino, an Italian city-state where the author lived many happy years. Castiglione's characters are real people who reflect in fictional conversations on how gentlemen and gentlewomen ought to act in polite society.

The Italian writer Baldassare Castiglione used the literary device of a dialogue between friends to discuss proper manners for ladies and gentlemen at Renaissance courts.

Italian Renaissance Artists

Art in addition to literature flourished in Italy during the Renaissance. In an outburst of creativity, Italian artists produced some of the world's most exquisite masterpieces.

Medieval paintings stressed the world beyond everyday life—a world associated with religious subjects—and depicted formal and stylized figures. The most noticeable characteristic of Renaissance painting, on the other hand, is its realism. Renaissance painters depicted realistic and lifelike human figures in their paintings. Even the backgrounds of these paintings differed from those of medieval paintings. Earlier artists had portrayed the Holy Land. Renaissance painters showed the rugged countryside that they knew.

The success of many female Renaissance artists, such as Sofonisba Anguissola, was accepted only as a pursuit of "womanly virtue." Anguissola is best known for her self-portraits and for her portrait of Philip II.

Realism and Perspective

In the Middle Ages, paintings did not look particularly realistic. Almost all art was religious, and artists were not interested in drawing attention to the human nature of, for example, Jesus and Mary. Instead, artists tried to visually represent spiritual aspects of their subjects. For example, the relative size of figures or objects often showed their importance in a spiritual hierarchy.

With the Renaissance came a new interest in accurately depicting the beauty of the human form and the natural world. To be realistic, a painting had to create the illusion of distance and depth on a flat surface. In the early 1400s, a Renaissance architect named Filippo Brunelleschi performed a series of optical experiments to devise mathematical formulas for achieving perspective. Brunelleschi discovered the laws of linear perspective, which explain how the human eye perceives distant objects as

smaller than close ones. Renaissance painters soon began to use Brunelleschi's rules of perspective in their works.

In *The School of Athens* (above), Raphael used precise mathematical measurements and perspective techniques to render the architectural setting and the people within it. In this scene, which appears on a wall in the Vatican Palace in Rome, Plato and Aristotle are surrounded by other famous Greek philosophers.

Renaissance painters could make their works lifelike because they had learned a very important technique of painting called **perspective.** By making distant objects smaller than those in the foreground, and by arranging objects in certain ways, an artist could create the illusion of depth on a flat canvas.

Giotto (JAWT·oh), who lived from 1276 to 1337, and Masaccio (mah·ZAHT·choh), who lived from 1401 to 1428, were important realist painters. According to legend, a fly in one of Giotto's paintings looked so lifelike that an observer tried to brush it off. Masaccio used light and shadows to give the effect of depth to objects.

The late 1400s and early 1500s are often referred to as the High Renaissance. Among the many great painters of this period, four made particularly outstanding contributions to the arts.

Leonardo da Vinci (dah·VEEN·chee)—painter, sculptor, engineer, architect, and scientist—lived from 1452 to 1519. Da Vinci used his experiments in science to enhance his painting. Studies of anatomy helped him draw the human figure, and mathematics helped him organize the space in his paintings. People throughout the world still marvel at his mural *The Last Supper.* Probably his most famous painting is the portrait called *Mona Lisa.*

Another master of Renaissance art, Michelangelo Buonarroti (mee·kay·LAHN·jay·loh bwaw·nahr·RAW·tee), lived from 1475 to 1564. Millions of people have visited the Sistine Chapel of the Vatican, the residence of the pope in Rome, and looked with wonder at the frescoes Michelangelo painted on the ceiling.

Although he was a brilliant painter, Michelangelo preferred sculpture. Both his paintings and his stone carvings of such biblical figures as David and Moses suggest a massive dignity. Almost as versatile as da Vinci, Michelangelo also wrote poetry and worked as an architect, helping design St. Peter's Basilica in Rome.

Raphael (RAF·ee·el), who lived from 1483 to 1520, became so popular in Florence that the pope hired him to help beautify the Vatican by painting frescoes in the papal chambers. Raphael also painted exquisite madonnas, representations of the Virgin Mary.

Titian (TISH·uhn), who lived from about 1488 to 1576, spent most of his life in his native Venice. His works, such as *The Assumption of the Virgin*, portray a vivid sense of drama and are noted for their rich colors. The Holy Roman Emperor sponsored many of Titian's works, and he became one of the first painters to obtain wealth for his paintings.

Dozens of other artists prospered in Italy in the 1400s and 1500s. Princes supported many of these artists. The princes thought they would achieve lasting fame if they became patrons of the arts. Thus the patrons helped foster the enormous creativity of the period.

The Northern Renaissance

Humanist thought spread beyond Italy. Numerous mountain passes, such as the Brenner and the Great Saint Bernard, pierced the rugged Alps and allowed people—and ideas—to pass from Italy to northern Europe. The Danube, Rhône, and Rhine rivers provided even easier routes. New ideas, often carried by northern European students who had studied in Italy, soon traveled to Germany, the Netherlands, France, and England.

Printing. A remarkable new process—printing—also helped ideas spread. Hundreds of years earlier, the Chinese had learned how to create a wooden block into which writing or pictures could be etched. Printers applied ink to the block and pressed the block onto paper. Then the block was reinked. In this way the writing or pictures could be reproduced many times. The Chinese had also learned how to assemble the block from separate pieces, or type, that could be used again and again—movable type. The European invention of printing, however, appears to have been completely independent of the Chinese process.

Scholars believe that in about 1450, Johannes Gutenberg of Mainz, Germany, became the first European to use movable type to print books.

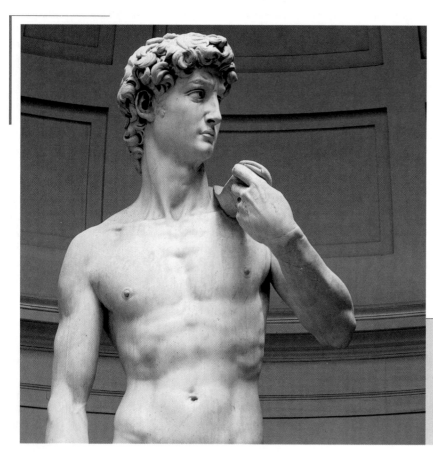

Michelangelo was commissioned to create his sculpture *David* in 1501. Standing in front of the Palazzo Vecchio, Florence, it embodies the power and beauty of Michelangelo's style.

Building History Study Skills

READ
WRITE
INTERPRET
CONNECT
THINK

Making Connections with History: Using Art to Understand Values

In 1508 Pope Julius II commissioned Michelangelo to paint the ceiling of the Sistine Chapel in Rome. Perched atop a new type of scaffolding that he had designed for the project, Michelangelo worked until 1512 to complete the commission. The result of his work has often been called the best example of Renaissance art in the world.

By studying the works of art produced during a specific period in history, we can learn much about the values of the people who created the art. Much of the art of the Middle Ages in western Europe, for example, reflects the religious nature of the society. The backgrounds of paintings focus not on real scenery but on heavenly backdrops, symbols, or gold reflections. People's faces reflect piety rather than individuality, and the figures themselves do not appear three-dimensional. Renaissance art retains religious themes while reflecting the humanistic and secular values of the time.

How to Use Art to Understand Values

To use art for understanding values, follow these steps.

1. Identify when the artwork was produced. What historical period does the artwork represent?
2. Explain what major theme the artist is attempting to illustrate. Does the artwork depict a religious theme? Does it show daily life?
3. Identify the subject of the work of art and note the details.
4. Use the theme and the subject to help explain the values of the historical period in which the work was created.

Developing the Skill

The illustration at the top of this page shows a detail from Michelangelo's *The Creation of Adam* on the ceiling of the Sistine Chapel in Rome. The painting reflects the values of the southern Renaissance.

The painting has a religious theme, similar to paintings of the Middle Ages. The subject is God's creation of Adam; however, the focus is on the humanity of Adam. Michelangelo captures Adam at the very moment that God holds out his hand to give life to his creation. Michelangelo portrays Adam as weak—barely able to lift his arm to receive the gift of life from God. God, on the other hand, appears supremely powerful.

Based on the painting, what conclusions can you draw about values during the Renaissance? The painting shows the concern with religious themes, as does medieval art. Michelangelo, however, depicts figures as intensely human and realistic. The painting captures the beauty of Adam's face, his reflection of God's power and glory, and the heroic individualism at the beginning of life. The painting shows that during the Renaissance people were intensely religious. At the same time, they believed in the dignity of human beings.

Practicing the Skill

Find and study an illustration of a modern work of art. Explain how this artwork reflects the values of modern society.

To apply this skill, see Applying History Study Skills on page 73.

Gutenberg developed a printing press on which he printed a number of copies of the Bible between 1453 and 1455. Other publishers adopted the printing press, and books soon helped spread new ideas to a large audience.

The most influential humanist of northern Europe was Desiderius Erasmus (i·RAZ·muhs), who was a Dutch scholar. He learned about the ideas of the Italian humanists from printed books. Erasmus, who lived from around 1466 to 1536, entered a monastery as a young man. After his ordination into the priesthood, though, he left the monastery so that he could pursue his studies of the classics.

Unlike the Italian humanists, Erasmus and other northern humanists were interested in the early Christian period as well as in early Roman and Greek culture. Erasmus believed that in its early years, Christianity had existed in harmony with classical civilization. He applied to his study of the Bible the critical method that the Italian humanists had developed, and he argued for a return to the original, simple message of Jesus. Erasmus was saddened that the medieval scholars had made Christian faith less spiritual and more complicated and ceremonial. He published stinging criticisms of the church's lack of spirituality, as did other northern humanists.

Erasmus's most famous book, *The Praise of Folly*, ridiculed ignorance, superstition, and vice among Christians. Erasmus criticized fasting, pilgrimages to religious shrines, and even the church's interpretation of parts of the Bible.

Erasmus's friend Thomas More, the English humanist, took a similar view. In 1516 More published *Utopia*, a book in which he criticized the society of his day by describing an imaginary, ideal society. Here citizens lived together harmoniously. All citizens were equal, and everyone worked to support the society. More's Utopia became so popular that today *utopia* means "an ideal place or society."

English literature. Renaissance literature in England reached its peak in the late 1500s and early 1600s. William Shakespeare (1564–1616) stands out as the most prominent English literary figure of this period. Like many other playwrights, Shakespeare used familiar plots, but he built masterpieces of poetic drama around them.

Shakespeare portrayed personality and human emotions with a skill that few writers have ever matched. The moody Hamlet, the young lovers Romeo and Juliet, and the tragic Macbeth seem as real today as when Shakespeare first created them.

Northern Renaissance Artists

The dynamic new painting techniques of Italian artists inspired artists outside of Italy. Northern European merchants carried Italian paintings home, and painters from northern Europe studied with Italian masters.

In Flanders, a group of painters developed their own distinct style. The painters became known as the Flemish School. They are credited with perfecting the technique of painting in oils on canvas. The brothers Hubert and Jan van Eyck, who lived in Flanders until the mid-1400s, paid great attention to detail in works such as *The Adoration of the Lamb*, the altarpiece of the cathedral at Ghent.

One of the most famous Flemish artists, Pieter Brueghel (BROO·guhl) the Elder, painted in the mid-1500s. Brueghel loved the countryside and the peasants of his native Flanders and painted lively scenes of village festivals and dances. He also used his paintings as a means to criticize the intolerance and cruelty he saw around him.

The German artist Albrecht Dürer (DYUR·uhr), who lived from 1471 to 1528, was famous for his

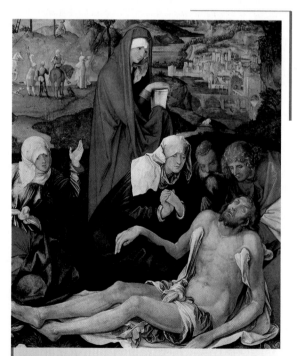

Albrecht Dürer, a renowned German printmaker and painter of the Renaissance, depicted various biblical scenes in his works. This image shows the deposition, or removal, of Christ from the cross.

copper engravings and woodcuts. Advances in printing technology had already made mass production of books possible. Dürer became one of the first to see the possibilities of printed illustrations in books.

Although a German, Hans Holbein the Younger (c.1497-1543), did most of his work in other countries. Holbein traveled throughout Europe to paint portraits of famous people such as Erasmus, Thomas More, and King Henry VIII of England. This emphasis on portrait painting reflected the Renaissance interest in the individual.

Section 1 Review

1. **Define** Renaissance, humanists, perspective
2. **Identify** Niccolò Machiavelli, Leonardo da Vinci, Michelangelo, Johannes Gutenberg, William Shakespeare, Pieter Brueghel, Albrecht Dürer, Hans Holbein the Younger
3. **Locate and Explain the Significance** Florence, Venice
4. **Analyzing Ideas** What impact did humanist ideas have on the Italian Renaissance?
5. **Understanding Ideas** Describe the realism of Italian Renaissance art as related to the work of one Italian Renaissance artist.
6. **Contrasting Ideas** Contrast the Northern Renaissance with the Italian Renaissance in terms of humanist thought, literature, and art.

Section 2

The Protestant Reformation

Focus Questions

- **What circumstances made Germany vulnerable to major religious change?**
- **Who was Martin Luther and what were the reforms that he proposed?**
- **How and why did Protestantism spread beyond the country of Germany?**

In about 1500, several northern humanists suggested that the Roman Catholic Church had lost sight of the spiritual mission proclaimed by Jesus. Instead of setting an example of moral leadership, they said, popes acted as political leaders and warriors. Instead of encouraging inner piety, priests engaged in vice and misconduct. The humanists claimed that the church as a whole seemed more interested in its income than in saving souls. The northern humanists sought a new emphasis on personal faith and spirituality. When the Catholic Church ignored their concerns, a new generation of reformers urged believers who were unhappy with traditional religion to withdraw from the church and gather together with like-minded people. This religious revolution, which split the church in western Europe and created several new churches, is called the **Reformation.**

The Origins of the Reformation

The first break with the Roman Catholic Church occurred in Germany, where the political situation of the time helped lay the foundation for the Reformation. Unlike some countries during the early 1500s, Germany lacked a strong central government. Although Germany formed the core of the Holy Roman Empire, the empire included about 300 independent states. The weak emperor could not control independent ideas about religion within the German states or prevent abuses of power by the pope.

Pope Leo X continued the rebuilding of St. Peter's Basilica in Rome. An enthusiastic monk named Johann Tetzel was sent to raise funds in northern Germany. Using a technique that had become accepted in the church, Tetzel asked people to buy **indulgences,** or pardons from punishment for sin.

Indulgences, part of the sacrament of penance, had originally been a reward for exceptionally pious deeds, such as helping a poor person go on a Crusade. Renaissance popes, however, sold indulgences simply to raise money.

This misuse of indulgences appalled the northern humanists, who wanted the church to become more spiritual. The concern grew especially strong in Germany, where many political leaders gave sellers of indulgences great freedom of movement. One unhappy observer, Martin Luther, protested Tetzel's behavior in 1517.

Martin Luther's Protest

Martin Luther was born in 1483 to a moderately prosperous peasant family in the small mining community of Eisleben in Saxony. Luther's family made sure he received a good education. Although he planned to become a lawyer, as a young man Luther considered

Although Martin Luther studied law at the University of Erfurt, he subsequently joined the Augustinian order and received a doctorate in theology.

himself a terrible sinner, and he worried desperately about the salvation of his soul. One summer day as he walked home, a sudden storm overtook him. A blinding bolt of lightning struck close by. Luther cried out, "Saint Anne, help! I will become a monk!" He gave up studying law to enter a monastery and spend his life in search of salvation.

Luther found that the church's methods for overcoming sin gave him no comfort. He did all the things required of him, including making a trip to holy places in Rome. Nothing, however, relieved his feeling of damnation.

Through his biblical studies, a revelation, or new understanding, came to Luther. He came to believe that all the ceremonies and good deeds made no difference in saving a sinner. The only thing that counted, Luther felt, was an inner faith in God. As long as people did not rely on their own actions, but believed God would save them, they could receive salvation by God's grace.

On the basis of this new insight, he developed beliefs that later became known as Lutheranism. Luther believed that a simple faith could lead everyone to salvation. He also believed Tetzel committed a grave theological error by asking poor people to give up their money for false promises of forgiveness.

In 1517 Luther challenged Tetzel by posting on the church door at Wittenberg **95 theses,** or statements, about indulgences. Sales of indulgences began to decline. The news quickly spread across Europe that a monk had publicly challenged the selling of indulgences.

Luther clearly considered himself a reformer within the main tradition of the church. He was surprised at the widespread impact of his ideas, and had no wish to break with the church. But because he dared to challenge church practices, church leaders denounced him.

Luther's Break with the Medieval Church

By 1520 Luther openly disagreed with many church doctrines. The sole religious authority, he said, was the Bible. Popes and bishops should not tell a person what to believe. Luther believed that ceremonies did not counteract sins and that priests had no special role in helping people to salvation. He felt that God viewed all people with faith equally. Luther considered his church a "priesthood of all believers."

Taking advantage of the power of the printed word to spread ideas, in 1520 Luther wrote three publications that outlined his doctrines, attacked the pope, and called on all Germans to support his views. In 1521 Pope Leo X declared Luther a heretic and excommunicated him.

To put Luther's punishment into effect, the Holy Roman Emperor Charles V summoned Luther to the Imperial Diet, a special meeting of the rulers of the empire, at the city of Worms (VOHRMZ). Luther was commanded to renounce his ideas. When he refused, the Diet of Worms banished him from the empire and prohibited the sale or printing of his works. Luther was now considered an outlaw. Because Germany lacked a strong government, however, the emperor could not enforce the Diet's ruling. The Elector of Saxony, Frederick the Wise, protected Luther and provided a place for him to hide while the uproar caused by the confrontation at the Diet of Worms died down.

In 1522, while under the protection of Frederick the Wise, Luther translated the New Testament of the Bible into German. By 1534 he had translated the entire Bible from Hebrew and Greek. Now all literate Christians that lived in Germany could read the Bible themselves.

Emperor Charles V continued to oppose Luther's doctrines and did what he could to keep Lutheranism from spreading. The princes who supported Luther protested the emperor's treatment of Lutheranism. Because of the protest, the followers of Luther and all later reformers came to be called "Protestants."

Luther's works continued to circulate, and his ideas continued to spread. In time he established a new church called the Lutheran Church. Luther kept the organization of the new church as simple as possible. Lutheran clergy, called ministers, had no special powers; they served merely to guide their congregations to the true faith. Ministers also had less importance than Catholic priests had, because Luther permitted only the two sacraments mentioned in the Bible—baptism and communion—rather than the seven sacraments practiced in the Roman Catholic Church.

The Spread of Protestantism

Luther had touched a very deep desire among the people of Europe for a simpler, more direct faith. Within a short time after he took his stand, many rulers in the German states established the Lutheran Church within their domains. In addition, dozens of other reformers appeared who were dissatisfied with both the Roman Catholic Church and the Lutheran Church.

Charles V attempted to stop the spread of Protestantism, but for about 10 years he was too busy fighting the Ottoman Turks and the French. Then in 1546 he sent his armies against the Protestant princes in Germany for both religious and political reasons. The emperor won most of his battles with the princes, but in the end he could not defeat them or the Lutheran Church. Charles V finally reached a compromise with the princes with the signing of the Peace of Augsburg in 1555.

One of the provisions of the Peace of Augsburg stated that each German ruler had the right to choose the religion for his state. His subjects had to accept the ruler's decision or move away. Almost all the princes of northern Germany accepted Luther's faith.

The sects. Hundreds of new religious groups emerged throughout Germany and Switzerland in the 1520s and 1530s. These groups, known as **sects,** did not form organized churches with clear-cut rules, authority, discipline, and membership. The sects were societies of a few people gathered together, usually with a preacher as their leader.

Most of the sects later died out. The Anabaptists are somewhat of an exception. This sect believed that infants should not receive baptism because they could not understand the significance of the ceremony. Instead, they believed baptism should be offered only to adults who accepted the Anabaptist faith. The beliefs of this sect survive today in Mennonite and Hutterite religious communities.

The Anglican Church. In England the Protestant Reformation came about by entirely different means than in Germany. True, some Protestant ideas had filtered into England by the 1520s. The English also had a tradition of resistance to the popes that went back to John Wycliffe in the 1300s. However, King Henry VIII caused the break between England and the Roman Catholic Church between 1529 and 1536. The break was a political move that had little to do

This manuscript page illustrates the restoration of a statue of Mary that had been destroyed by violence during the Reformation.

with religious doctrine. In fact, before 1529 Henry VIII had defended the church so well against Martin Luther's ideas that the pope had granted Henry the title of "Defender of the Faith"—a title that the present monarch of England still bears.

England's break with Rome took place because Henry VIII wanted to divorce his wife, Catherine of Aragon, for not producing a male heir to the throne. The king believed that a continuing strong monarchy depended on having a son to succeed him. The royal couple had a daughter, Mary, but England had no tradition of a ruling queen. Furthermore, Henry wanted to be rid of Catherine and to marry Anne Boleyn, a lady-in-waiting at the court.

Although the Catholic Church forbade divorce, the pope could make exceptions. Pope Clement VII, however, refused to dissolve Henry's marriage. Clement made his decision in part because troops led by Catherine of Aragon's nephew, the Holy Roman Emperor Charles V, had captured and sacked Rome in 1527.

Pope Clement's refusal to grant the divorce infuriated Henry, who withdrew England from the Catholic Church and created a new church. In a series of laws, Parliament created the Church of England with the king as its head. Although the Church of England, or Anglican Church, slowly acquired some Protestant doctrines, it kept the organization and many of the ceremonial features of the Catholic Church.

Of course, Henry VIII's church granted his divorce. The king eventually married six times in all. He finally fathered a son, the future Edward VI, although not by Anne Boleyn. More important historically, by creating the Anglican Church he opened the way for the Protestant Reformation in England.

Section 2 Review

1. **Define** Reformation, indulgences, 95 theses, sects
2. **Identify** Martin Luther
3. **Locate and Explain the Significance** Wittenberg
4. **Understanding Ideas** What specific issue sparked the Reformation in Germany?
5. **Contrasting Ideas** What were the main differences between Luther's ideas and those of the Roman Catholic Church?
6. **Summarizing Ideas** Describe how Protestantism spread beyond Germany.

The Catholic Reformation

Focus Questions
- **Who was John Calvin? What role did he play in the Reformation?**
- **What steps did the Catholic Church take to respond to Protestant reform?**
- **What was the approach used by the Jesuits to Catholic reform?**

Although areas of northern Europe became Protestant during the Reformation, millions of Europeans remained faithful to the Roman Catholic Church. Change and challenge continued, however, even in countries such as France, where the Catholic faith remained strong. After 1550 the religious conflict in Europe was dominated by the followers of a French-born reformer named John Calvin and a remarkable Catholic revival known as the Counter-Reformation.

Calvin and Calvinism
Huldrych Zwingli (TSVING·lee), the vicar at the cathedral in Zurich in the early 1500s, was greatly influenced by the humanist writings of Erasmus. Zwingli was stirring up religious reform in Switzerland when he heard about Luther's 95 theses. Zwingli and Luther met and discovered that they agreed, more or less, on doctrine but disagreed about forms of worship and the use of images. Zwingli's supporters, for example, covered up wall decorations in churches.

In 1531 Zwingli died in a battle between Catholics and Protestants, but the French Protestant John Calvin carried on the work of the Reformation in Switzerland. Calvin founded a Protestant church that had a strong following. He formulated a complete and clear set of beliefs, the *Institutes of the Christian Religion*, published in 1536. This work laid down exactly what the faithful ought to believe on every major question of religion. Calvin thus provided his followers—Calvinists—with a code that united them and strengthened them against opposition and persecution.

In 1536 Calvin settled in the city of Geneva, where Calvinism became the official religion. Calvin retained Luther's reliance on faith and on the Bible. He also placed added emphasis on the belief, common among Protestant theologians during the 1500s, that God had decided, at the beginning of time, who would be saved—a belief known as **predestination.** Those predestined (or chosen beforehand) for salvation were called "the elect." They formed a special community of people who were expected to follow the highest moral standards. These standards placed great emphasis on devoutness and self-discipline and frowned on frivolity. The individual was to possess a complete dedication to God's wishes.

Calvin became very influential in Geneva. The city became a **theocracy,** or a government ruled by a clergy claiming God's authority. By attaching such great importance to righteous living, the lives of the citizens were regulated down to the smallest detail. Laws prohibited dancing, card playing, showy dress, and profane language. Violation of these laws resulted in severe punishment.

Calvinism soon spread to France, where its converts became known as Huguenots (HYOO·guh·nahts). Although France remained primarily Catholic, Calvinists controlled nearly one third of the country at one point. Many high-ranking nobles as well as townspeople adopted the Calvinist doctrines. The Catholic French monarchs considered the Huguenots a threat to national unity.

Beginning in 1562 the Huguenots defended themselves in a series of bloody civil wars with the Catholics. In 1598 King Henry IV issued the Edict of Nantes (NANTS), which gave the Huguenots freedom of worship and some political rights.

Calvinist minorities also existed in Poland and Hungary in eastern Europe. The Calvinists met with the most success, however, in Scotland, in the northern Netherlands, and in some parts of Germany. In these countries the strength of the Calvinists among the people persuaded rulers to change their views. In a form called *Puritanism,* Calvinism would play a vital role in England and in its North American colonies. By 1600 the Calvinist churches were among the strongest of the many Protestant churches established in Europe.

1. S. Gervais.	4. La Porte de la Monoye.	7. S. Germain.	10. La Porte de Treille.	13. Bouleverd du Pin.	16. La Porte Neufue.	19. Moulins.
2. Le Chasteau Vieux.	5. Le Lac Leman.	8. Maison de Ville.	11. Prisons.	14. Bouleverd de S. Legier.	17. Bouleverd de Loije.	
3. La Tour de L'Isle.	6. La Porte de la Tartace.	9. S. Pierre.	12. Hospitale.	15. Porte de S. Legier.	18. L'Hospitale.	

From 1536 until his death in 1564, John Calvin was instrumental in the foundation of Protestantism in Geneva. This is a map of Geneva during the time of Calvin.

The Counter-Reformation

It took some time for the Catholic Church to recognize that Protestantism posed a serious threat. The pope at first dismissed Luther's criticisms. A number of people within the Catholic Church, including Erasmus, had called for internal reforms even before Luther appeared. As the breakup of the church continued, these reformers eventually convinced the pope of the drastic need for change.

In the 1530s a major reform effort known as the **Counter-Reformation,** or the Catholic Reformation, began in the Catholic Church. Initially created to foster a more spiritual outlook in the Catholic Church, the Counter-Reformation also clarified the doctrines of the church and pursued an aggressive campaign against Protestantism.

Pope Paul III commissioned the Venetian painter Titian to record the Council of Trent in session.

Counter-Reformation tactics. Pope Paul III, who reigned as pope from 1534 to 1549, began a deliberate policy of reviving a more spiritual outlook in the Catholic Church. To accomplish this, he appointed devout and learned men as bishops and cardinals.

Pope Paul III also brought the medieval Inquisition to Rome. Spanish authorities had been trying and punishing so-called heretics since 1478. The Inquisition borrowed its cruel punishments, such as burning at the stake, from governments, which had used such methods against the worst criminals and traitors. The leaders of the Inquisition did not see themselves primarily as punishing Protestants but rather as keeping Catholics within the church.

In 1559 Pope Paul IV introduced another method of combating heresy. He established the *Index of Forbidden Books,* which forbade Catholics to read certain books that were considered harmful to faith or morals. The Index was a recognition of the role printing had played in spreading the Reformation. Before the printing press, the church could easily find and burn manuscripts of heretical works. After printing was developed, it became far easier to forbid people to read certain books than to burn the books. The Catholic Church maintained the Index until 1966, when the Second Vatican Council finally abandoned it.

The Council of Trent. Pope Paul III knew that no counterattack against Protestantism would be possible unless Catholic doctrines were well defined. Church authorities often disagreed about complicated doctrines, which made it difficult to take a stand against opposition. In 1545 Paul summoned church leaders to the Italian city of Trent. The Council of Trent, which met in three sessions from 1545 to 1563, defined official church doctrine with the same precision Calvin had used to define his faith.

The Council of Trent banned the sale of indulgences and tightened discipline for the clergy. In most cases, however, the council reaffirmed the importance of those doctrines that Protestants rejected. It emphasized the need for ceremonies, arguing that God ought to be worshiped with pomp and splendor. It noted that people must depend on priests because God granted forgiveness only through the church. The council stressed that although everyone enjoyed free will, a person's fate after death depended not only on his or her faith, as Luther claimed, but on ceremonial church actions as well.

The decisions made at the Council of Trent were effective for the Catholic Church. Many people found Protestantism's simplicity and austerity appealing, but many others took comfort from ancient ceremonies, beautifully decorated churches, the authority of priests, and the idea that one could perform good works to gain salvation.

Soldiers of the Counter-Reformation

A new aggressiveness on the part of the Catholic Church became a major reason for the success of the Counter-Reformation. This aggressiveness took many forms. Better-educated priests worked more forcefully for the church. The old religious orders reformed their rules, while new religious orders such as the Society of Jesus, known as the Jesuits, formed.

Ignatius de Loyola founded the Jesuits in 1534. Loyola was a Spanish soldier whose leg had been shattered fighting for Charles V against the French. Loyola's long period of recovery from his injury gave him time to read about the lives of Jesus and the saints. Like Martin Luther, Loyola wondered how he could attain salvation despite his sins. The answer came to him in a vision that he recorded in his book *Spiritual Exercises*. According to Loyola, salvation could be achieved by self-discipline and by doing good deeds—in other words, by one's own actions. Loyola convinced six fellow students at the University of Paris to take religious vows of poverty, chastity, and obedience to the pope and to follow him. Less than 10 years after Loyola founded his group, Pope Paul III recognized it as an official order of the Catholic Church.

Loyola organized the Jesuits like a military body, with discipline and strict obedience. He was the general of the order; the members were his soldiers. The Jesuits quickly became the most effective agents in spreading Catholicism. By 1556 the order had about 1,000 members. Their missions took them as far away as China and Japan. In Europe their preaching and their hearing of confessions slowed the spread of Protestantism in Poland, Germany, and France.

The Jesuits stressed education. They founded some of the best colleges in Europe, combining humanist values with theology to turn out learned, fervent supporters of the church.

Although some people had cherished hopes that the Reformation would bring about a new spirit of tolerance, the period from the 1530s through the mid-1600s was a time of devastating religious wars, sometimes interrupted by long truces, in Germany, Switzerland, France, and the Netherlands. Not until the mid-1600s, when the wars ended, could the

Ignatius de Loyola received approval from Pope Paul III to found a new Catholic order, that of the Society of Jesus, or Jesuits, through which he organized a system of schools and universities.

results of the Reformation and the Counter-Reformation be fully seen.

Results of the Religious Upheaval

The most striking result of the religious struggle of the 1500s was the emergence of many different churches in western Europe. In Italy, although Protestantism never made much headway, interest in church reform remained strong. Most of the people of southern and eastern Europe and the native population of Ireland remained firmly Catholic. France and the Netherlands had large numbers of Protestants. In Switzerland, northern Germany, England, Scotland, Norway, Denmark, and Sweden, various Protestant faiths became the established church, backed by the central government (see map on page 60).

Another far-reaching result of the Reformation and Counter-Reformation was a new interest in education. Many new universities had appeared in the 1400s and 1500s because of the humanists' concern for learning. After the mid-1500s enrollments in

European Religions, 1600

Lutheran		Roman Catholic	
Calvinist		Orthodox	
Anglican		Muslim	
Roman Catholic with Protestant minorities		Boundary of Holy Roman Empire	

Learning from Maps Although the Reformation gained many converts in northern Europe, southern Italy remained predominantly Catholic.

Region What religions were dominant in Scotland? Norway? England?

these universities increased dramatically; religious reformers supported this trend.

Protestants believed that people could find their way to Christian faith by studying the Bible. As a result, reading became increasingly important. In their schools the Jesuits and other new religious orders worked to strengthen the faith of the Catholics. Education did not mean tolerance of new ideas, however. Neither the Protestant nor the Catholic authorities permitted views that differed from their own.

The Reformation led to an increase in power of national governments and a decrease in power of the pope. In Protestant regions each government took responsibility for the leadership of the official church. In Catholic areas, rulers loyal to the pope often obtained considerable control over their churches.

1. **Define** predestination, theocracy, Counter-Reformation
2. **Identify** John Calvin, Ignatius de Loyola
3. **Locate and Explain the Significance** Zurich, Geneva
4. **Understanding Ideas** What were the main ideas of John Calvin and how were they expressed in the government of Geneva?
5. **Summarizing Ideas** Describe how the Catholic Church responded to the Reformation, including the role of the Council of Trent.
6. **Analyzing Ideas** Why were Ignatius de Loyola's efforts to strengthen the Catholic Church successful?

Section 4

Culture and Daily Life

Focus Questions

- **What were the characteristics of village life in Europe during the period of time known as the Renaissance and Reformation?**
- **How did villagers learn about the world outside their villages?**
- **What changes in daily life occurred in the 1500s and 1600s?**

The ideas that shaped the Renaissance, the Reformation, and the Counter-Reformation involved relatively few people. Ordinary people had their own views about themselves and the world around them.

Magic and Witchcraft

Most Europeans lived in or near small villages and spent their entire lives combating nature to raise food. People close to the land could never predict what life would bring. They never knew when a cow might suddenly fall ill, when lightning might burn down a cottage, or when churning would fail to turn milk into butter.

The world of spirits. Since people considered God to be a distant, unknowable force, they thought spirits populated the world. Although good spirits abounded, demons, or devils, made life difficult. Because of this belief in spirits, nothing was considered an accident.

If lightning struck a house, a demon had caused it. If a pitcher of milk spilled, the evil work of a demon was the cause. Many "superstitions," such as the belief that walking under a ladder might bring bad luck, began during this period.

Village priests usually accepted these beliefs or at least pretended to ignore them. To the ordinary villager, the priest's explanation that the misfortune was God's will or God's punishment for sin was not very satisfying. Nevertheless, villagers believed that the priest's actions could have positive effects. For example, every spring in a special ceremony, the priest would go out to the fields to bless the earth and pray for good crops. His blessing of a husband and wife at a wedding supposedly gave the couple a good start in life, and baptism was thought to safeguard a newborn child.

The priest, however, was not the only person to whom the villagers turned in times of trouble. They also looked to a so-called "wise" or "cunning" man or woman. This person, usually an older village member, was thought to have a special understanding of the way the world operated. Ordinary people would explain their problem—a lost ring, a cruel husband, a sick pig, or even an ominous sign—to these "wise" folk. Since people believed nothing happened by accident, anything unusual, such as a frog jumping into a fishing boat, was taken as a warning. The wise man or woman would explain what the warning meant and would sometimes recommend a remedy to ward off evil. The remedy might include wearing a good-luck charm, chanting a strange spell, or drinking a special potion.

The belief in witchcraft. Wise people were often called "good witches." However, if their relationship with their neighbors turned sour, wise people might be accused of being "bad witches." In many cases the person accused of witchcraft would be an elderly widow. Perhaps too weak to work, with no husband or family to support her, she would be the most defenseless person in the community and an easy target for attack.

Stories about witches became more sensational as they spread throughout the countryside. Outrageous accusations were made. A person might be accused of flying on a broomstick, sticking pins into dolls, or dancing with the devil in the woods at night. If the majority of people believed an accusation, a priest might be asked to hold a ceremony to exorcise, or drive out, a demon that was thought to have taken over the witch's body. In other cases, the accused person might be dragged to a bonfire, tied to a stake, and burned, perhaps with the approval of the local lord.

An enormous outburst of "witch hunting" occurred in Europe in the mid-1500s and lasted for more than 100 years. Both religious and secular leaders were ready to see the existence of witches as an acceptable explanation for the problems in the world around them. Eventually, however, as the religious wars came to an end and people experienced greater security in their lives, fewer cases of witchcraft were reported.

Forms of Recreation

For most people, daylight meant work and night meant sleep. Because manual farming methods were slow, people needed all their daylight hours for raising food. Evening activities were limited because the farmers were exhausted from working all day and because they could not afford the candles needed for light. Still, they did find time for relaxation.

Every village had a gathering place where people came together to drink, sew, do simple chores, and tell stories. Some people played games such as skittles (a form of bowling). Occasionally, traveling companies of actors passed through a village and put on a simple show. The year contained many special days. The church decreed some holidays. Others honored a local saint or tradition. During some holidays, the villagers donned costumes and would often put on their own ceremonies.

A favorite ceremony poked fun at the familiar sights and scenes of village life. In different parts of Europe, this ceremony had different names. Whether it was called "rough music," "charivari," or "abbeys of misrule," the basic ceremony was much the same. The young men of the village formed a procession and marched along, ridiculing accepted customs or the foolish people of the village. For example, two young men might impersonate a couple known to everyone because the wife beat the husband. The impersonators would be pulled along in a cart and, as they passed by, the other villagers would jeer and hoot at them.

Sometimes the marchers had more serious targets; they might want to show how things would look if the poor or the weak had power. They would dress a fool like a bishop, or they would put the poorest man on a throne. At this point, the jokes lost their lightheartedness and symbolized the resentment the villagers felt about the privileges of those who ruled them.

Pieter Brueghel the Elder is known for his depictions of peasant life. *The Peasant Wedding,* painted in the 1560s, shows a group of guests seated at a table as food is being prepared.

Games

People throughout the ages have played games for amusement and diversion. In some cultures, games were a way for children to learn skills that would be useful to them in later life. In addition, games provided relief and relaxation from the routine of hard work in the home or the fields.

Dice have been found in Egyptian tombs. The modern game of backgammon developed from a board game played in Mesopotamia, and chess probably was first played in India.

More than 400 years ago, the Flemish artist Pieter Brueghel painted the large picture shown here (above). The picture is almost an encyclopedia of the games played by children of Brueghel's time. Brueghel loved to show the activities of peasants and working people. This painting depicts at least 80 games, including everything from marbles to hockey to ring-around-the-rosy and hoop rolling.

Many games are played by adults as well as by children. Baseball, for example, can be a pickup game in a neighborhood park or a schoolyard, or a competition among professional athletes. In recent years people of all ages have been fascinated by the new games and twists on old games that electronics and the computer have made possible.

The wide appeal of games to people of all ages may account for a feature of Brueghel's painting that has never been explained. Some people think that all the people playing games in his paintings look like adults. Perhaps Brueghel wanted to suggest that adult activities are no different from the games that children play. However, we cannot know for sure. What we do know is that many of these games and activities are still amusements today (center), for children as well as for grownups throughout the world.

Violence and Protest in the Village

Villagers lived in close-knit communities. Anyone who seemed to upset their traditions or their sense of proper behavior was treated harshly. The strain of hardship or famine could cause villagers to respond, sometimes violently.

The women of the village often led these protests. Because women were responsible for feeding their families, they especially felt the impact of taxes or food shortages. If the women suspected, for example, that a baker hoarded bread or sent it elsewhere for higher profits, they might ransack the baker's shop.

On the other hand, people of this time tended to identify closely with other members of their community. In large communities, such as towns, this might mean members of one's profession. In smaller villages, whole communities tended to work and make decisions together.

Printing and the Spread of Knowledge

In the 1500s the world beyond the village began to affect village life. Printed works and, in some areas, traveling preachers, inspired the changes.

Few ordinary villagers could read. Often even the village priest could not read. Nevertheless, soon after the invention of movable type, publishers started selling popular works. Single printed sheets known as **broadsides** began to appear. A broadside might include a royal decree or news of some sensational crime or other event. Books and broadsides arrived in the village, carried by peddlers who brought goods from the outside world. When the villagers gathered together, they might enjoy listening to someone read the latest broadside.

While romances and epics of the classical age appealed to the nobility, publishers quickly found subjects that appealed to country folk and produced cheap books for this new market. The most common books were **almanacs,** the ancestors of *The Old Farmer's Almanac* of today. In the almanacs were predictions about the weather and the prospects for growing crops. Almanacs also contained calendars, maps, and medical advice. The books were best-sellers because they spoke to the beliefs and concerns of the ordinary people.

Soon after Luther's break with the church in 1521, new religious ideas reached the villages. Sometimes preachers came to visit. Books might come out of the peddlers' packs. Perhaps people heard stories that attacked the church read in the village gathering place. Certainly the messages of Luther and Calvin traveled in this way, as did translations of the Bible.

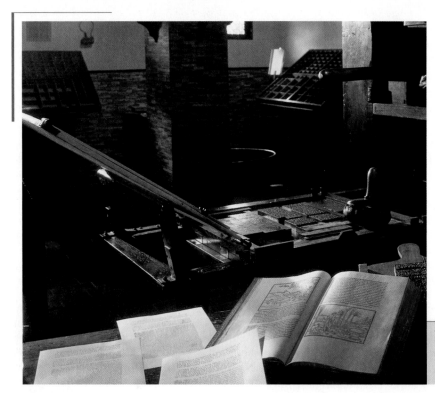

This photograph shows the printing press invented by Johannes Gutenberg.

As Protestants and Catholics battled for the loyalties of ordinary people, leaders of both sides encouraged the founding of primary schools in the villages and towns. Both Protestant and Catholic leaders believed that knowledge would lead a person to support the faith. In spite of this common concern for education, the followers of the differing religions struggled to coexist peacefully. Neither side, unfortunately, included tolerance in its teachings.

Changes in Daily Life

In addition to undergoing religious and political changes, Europeans experienced economic changes as well. The measure of the quality of life of a people or a country is called the **standard of living.** The standard of living is not strictly limited to income or economic output; it also includes working conditions, home life, the environment, health, and leisure.

Population and inflation. After the Black Death of the 1300s cut Europe's population by at least one third, some peasants prospered. There were fewer people to cultivate the land, so their labor was in demand. This often resulted in higher wages.

By 1550, when the religious wars had begun to ravage Europe, conditions changed. The population was growing rapidly. With the growth of the population came **inflation,** a rise in prices for goods. After 1550 wages could not keep up with the rise in prices, especially of farm products.

Diet. During this period, white bread made from wheat was a rarity. Meat was scarce and expensive, and fish only a little less so. Salt, needed to preserve fish and meats, had long been an important item of trade in Europe, but was still costly. Cheese and eggs, cheap sources of protein, were an important part of the diet everywhere. Butter was not widely used outside northern Europe until the 1700s.

The spices that had earlier come to Europe from the East had been largely luxury items. By the 1500s and 1600s, however, the importation of spices had become highly competitive. In the 1500s traders began introducing Europeans not only to new vegetables— asparagus, spinach, lettuce, green beans, tomatoes, and melons—but also to the luxuries of coffee, tea, and chocolate.

Not everyone had access to the new and varied diets. Wealthy people still lived better than most of the peasants and the urban poor, who for the most part ate the same simple meals they had eaten for centuries.

The table settings and customs that we know today were not common in the early Renaissance period. People ate mostly with their fingers, picking what they wanted from a large common dish. In some areas people ate from wooden plates. Guests brought their own knives; individual forks did not come into use until the 1500s, and spoons not until a century after that.

Housing. Brick and stone became more common construction materials in the growing cities of Europe after the 1500s. In the countryside, however, peasants continued to live in thatched-roof cottages as they had in the Middle Ages. Most rural houses were small. Because glass was expensive and sometimes not available even for the wealthy, most houses had shutters rather than glass windows.

Peasants' houses boasted only the necessities of rural life—a large cooking pot, a table, a bench, and a few tools. Those who were fortunate had a bed; others slept on sacks filled with straw. Entrenched in poverty, with little hope of escaping their fate, many peasants sought refuge in the cities.

The Decline of Traditional Culture

The migration from countryside to city further altered traditional popular culture. In the city, food came from a shop rather than directly from a field. Local governments helped out when disaster occurred. If famine struck, authorities distributed bread. If plagues broke out, the government would set up hospitals and quarantines.

Gradually, more sophisticated attitudes began to take hold among the residents of towns and cities. In particular, people's understanding of how things happened in the world began to change. Demons and spirits no longer dominated views of daily life. People sought rational explanations for day-to-day events, and there now seemed less need for magic and "wise" folk. This development has been referred to as the "disenchantment" of the world—the removal of "enchantment," or magic, from nature. One of the most important influences on the growth of this new attitude was the cultivation of modern science.

1. **Define** broadsides, almanacs, standard of living, inflation
2. **Determining Cause and Effect** How did a belief in spirits lead to the witch hunts of the 1600s?
3. **Analyzing Ideas** Describe the importance of printing in the spread of knowledge.
4. **Interpreting Ideas** What economic and cultural changes occurred in the lives of people living in the 1500s and 1600s?

Section 5

The Scientific Revolution

Focus Questions

- What factors contributed to the birth of the Scientific Revolution?
- How did Copernicus, Kepler, and Galileo challenge traditionally held views?
- How did Descartes, Bacon, and Newton help to shape the scientific method?
- What were some of the discoveries made during the Scientific Revolution?

Unlikely though it may seem, belief in magic helped create the revolution in thinking that led to modern science. In the 1500s it was not only ordinary people who thought hidden forces controlled the world; the early scientists also hoped to discover what they called the secrets of nature. Alchemists were people who used spells and magic formulas to try to change one substance into another—for example, lead into gold. Astrologers believed that the position of the stars in the sky affected human life.

What made the early scientists more than just alchemists or astrologers was that they had very general interests. They wanted to find out why stones fall, why the stars seem to move, or what function the heart serves. They attempted to uncover the invisible structure of the universe by performing experiments and using mathematics—two methods that proved more effective than chants or spells.

The success of these early investigators in solving ancient problems in astronomy, physics, and anatomy created a new way of thinking that no longer relied on magic. This new way of pursuing

knowledge is now called science. Before the 1600s the word science meant "knowledge." After the 1600s the sense of the word evolved into the narrower meaning it has today.

Experiments and Mathematics

The Europeans' ideas about the universe had come to them from the ancient Greeks and Romans. People considered Aristotle and Galen to be absolute authorities who knew the truth. However, as the humanists unearthed more classical manuscripts, they found that even the respected ancient writers did not agree with each other. As people began to examine the world around them, they made observations that did not correspond to ancient beliefs.

As a result, people in the 1500s began to question traditional opinions. They began to observe and experiment for themselves. Most importantly, they described nature without any reference to previous beliefs. The foundation of this approach was the principle of doubt; nothing was to be believed unless it could be proved by experiment or mathematics. The transformation in thinking that occurred during the 1500s and 1600s as a result of this new system of investigation is known as the **Scientific Revolution.**

The new approach relied heavily on the scientists' ability to conduct scientific experiments. Scientists had access to newly invented instruments, such as the barometer, the microscope, and the thermometer, which improved their ability to observe and measure. At the same time, improved mathematical calculations became essential to investigations of nature. The method of inquiry that includes carefully conducted experiments and mathematical calculations—to verify the results of these repeatable experiments—is called the **scientific method.** The scientific method also involves making logical deductions from self-evident principles.

Astronomy, Physics, and Anatomy

New frontiers in science attracted people with interests in different fields of study. Five Europeans in particular—Copernicus, Kepler, Galileo, Vesalius, and Harvey—became pioneers of modern astronomy, physics, and anatomy.

Copernicus. For centuries astronomers had believed in the theory Ptolemy put forth in about A.D. 100: Earth was the center of the universe and the other planets and the Sun moved around it. Ptolemy's theory is called the **geocentric** ("Earth-centered") **theory,** from the Greek words *geo,* meaning "Earth," and *kentron,* meaning "center."

In the early 1500s, a Polish scientist named Nicolaus Copernicus discovered ancient writings arguing that the Sun was the center of the universe. Copernicus's theory developed as the **heliocentric theory,** from the Greek word *helios*, meaning "sun." After a long period of study and observation, Copernicus became convinced that the heliocentric theory best explained all the known facts of astronomy of his time. In 1543 Copernicus published his conclusions in a book titled *On the Revolutions of the Celestial Spheres.*

The book caused little stir at the time. Few people believed in the heliocentric theory because it seemed to contradict the evidence of the senses. Anyone could "see" that the Sun and planets moved around Earth. Anyone could "feel" that solid Earth did not move.

Copernicus could not test and prove the heliocentric theory with the instruments or the mathematics available to him. Proof had to wait for the work of two later scientists, a German named Kepler and an Italian named Galileo.

Kepler and Galileo. Johannes Kepler, who was a brilliant mathematician who lived in the late 1500s and early 1600s, used mathematics to test the heliocentric theory of Copernicus. At first Kepler could not make the theory fit the observed facts. It is said that he calculated the problem many times before he discovered the solution. Copernicus had written that Earth and other planets went around the Sun in orbits, or paths in space, that were exact circles. Kepler discovered that the orbits were not exact circles, they were ovals called ellipses. Now other facts made sense. The heliocentric theory of the universe *could* be supported mathematically.

Because Kepler's proof could not be seen or observed, only mathematicians understood it. An Italian professor of mathematics and astronomer, Galileo Galilei, provided concrete evidence that Earth revolves around the Sun.

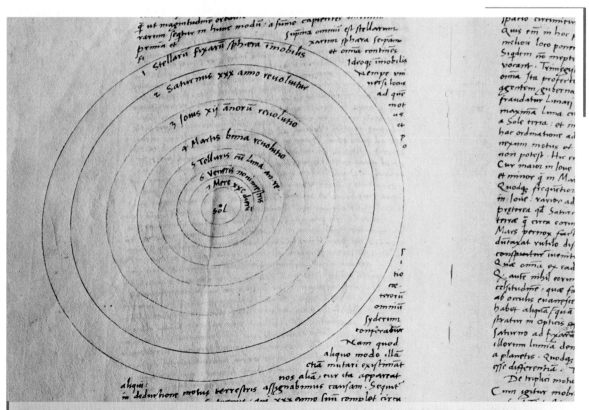

Nicolaus Copernicus published his support of the heliocentric theory of the universe in 1543. This 16th-century manuscript shows the Copernican (heliocentric) system of the universe with the Sun at the center and the planets orbiting the Sun.

Galileo had read of a Dutch eyeglass-maker who put two glass lenses together in a tube to make a telescope. By looking through the telescope, a person could see distant objects more clearly. Galileo made a telescope for himself. By modern standards Galileo's telescope was only a small one, but it allowed him to see more of the heavens than anyone had ever seen. He could see the mountains and valleys of the moon and the rings around the planet Saturn. He observed sunspots. He proved that Earth rotated on its axis. His discovery that the moons of Jupiter revolve around the planet helped disprove the geocentric theory of Ptolemy by showing that not every heavenly body revolves around Earth.

Galileo published his findings in 1632 in a work called *Dialogue on the Two Great Systems of the World.*

His work, unlike that of Copernicus, caused an uproar. Many people now wanted telescopes. Many others believed telescopes to be the devil's work and refused to have anything to do with them. Scholars who accepted the authority of Ptolemy refused to believe the heliocentric theory. The church disapproved because the theory seemed to contradict the Bible. The church further insisted upon its right to condemn any scientific explanations that differed from scripture. In 1633 the Inquisition summoned Galileo to Rome, where it ordered him to renounce his belief that Earth moves around the Sun. Galileo did as he was asked, but legend tells us that as he rose from his knees before the Inquisitors he muttered, "Yet the earth *does* move." The new ideas continued to advance.

The Italian astronomer Galileo was called before the Inquisition and forced to deny his observations.

The Microscope and the Telescope

Repeated experimentation and careful measurement—so vital to the scientific method—were greatly aided by the development of new technology. Two of the technological innovations of the Renaissance—the microscope and the telescope—expanded human sight in amazing ways. One allowed scientists to look inward at the minute structures of the human body. The other opened the door to the universe beyond.

Engravers, workers in fine detail, are thought to have been the first to capture water in glass globes and gaze through it as a magnification aid. Lenses appeared in the late 1200s. It is not surprising therefore that three spectacle-makers, Zacharias Janssen, his father Hans, and Hans Lippershey, have been credited with developing an early microscope with simple lenses in the final decade of the 1500s. Less than 100 years later, in the 1670s, Anton van Leeuwenhoek

had devised a microscope that allowed him to see bacteria of only 2 to 3 micrometers in diameter.

Galileo, in 1609, was the first to use the compound lenses of a telescope to view the skies. The telescopes that he built were larger and more powerful than any that had been built before. What he observed with his telescope confirmed Galileo's belief in the heliocentric views of Copernicus. Both these inventions, developed within twenty years of each other, were to open the eyes of science for centuries to come.

TVBVM OPTICVM VIDES GALILAEI INVENTVM ET OPVS, QVO SOLIS MACVLAS ET EXTIMOS LVNAE MONTES, ET IOVIS SATELLITES, ET NOVAM QVASI RERVM VNIVERSITATE PRIMVS DISPEXIT A. MDCIX.

Galileo was interested in physics as well as astronomy. Perhaps the most remarkable of his discoveries disproved the popular belief that heavier bodies fall faster than lighter ones. Galileo proved mathematically that, in the absence of air friction, all objects fall at the same speed regardless of their weight. This discovery laid the foundation for the modern science of mechanics, the study of matter in motion.

Vesalius and Harvey. Andreas Vesalius, a Flemish scientist, pioneered the study of anatomy. Vesalius refused to accept the descriptions of human muscles and tissues that Galen had written 1,400 years earlier. Vesalius conducted his own investigations to see how the human body was constructed. In 1543, the same year that Copernicus published his book, Vesalius published a landmark work in the history of medicine called *On the Fabric of the Human Body.*

Equally important was the work of William Harvey, an English physician. Using laboratory experiments, Harvey described the circulation of the blood through veins and arteries, the working of the body's most important muscle—the heart, and the function of the blood vessels.

The Triumph of Science

The effects of these discoveries were felt throughout Europe. So much had been accomplished. Knowledge had advanced so far that the scientists' methods became examples for everyone.

Just as new religious orders of the Counter-Reformation spread the revived faith in the church, scientific "orders" helped spread developments of the Scientific Revolution. In Rome there was the Accademia dei Lincei, founded in 1603. King Charles II granted a charter to the Royal Society in London in 1662, and Louis XIV established the French Academy of Sciences in 1666. The printing press helped the scientists just as it had the religious reformers. Most societies published journals so that scientists everywhere could read of work being done throughout Europe.

Descartes. One of the most influential advocates of science was René Descartes (day·KAHRT), a French philosopher and scientist who lived from 1596 to 1650. Educated at a Jesuit college, Descartes decided to become a soldier in order to learn more about the world around him. He saw little fighting as a soldier and thus had ample time to think.

Descartes believed that one should question all assumptions before accepting them. He decided to start fresh with a new philosophy based on his own reason. In his *Discourse on Method* (1637), he argued that everything had to be proved, except basic ideas that were true beyond all doubt. For example, Descartes believed that the fact that he could think proved that he existed: "I think, therefore I am," he wrote. This was his first truth. From this basic truth, Descartes established a method of inquiry in which all

René Descartes published his *Discourse on Method* anonymously in 1637.

thoughts would follow the clear, orderly progression of scientific reasoning.

Bacon. Descartes's contemporary, the English philosopher Francis Bacon, took a somewhat stronger line concerning how conclusions should be reached. Bacon rejected deducing knowledge from self-evident principles and instead argued that only through observation and repeatable experiments could theories be built. Bacon thus relied on proofs that could be demonstrated physically, not through deductive logic. He believed that the pursuit of scientific knowledge would enrich human life immeasurably.

Newton. In 1687 Isaac Newton published his *The Mathematical Principles of Natural Philosophy*. It combined and related the contributions of Copernicus, Kepler, and Galileo. These early scientists had shown that the planets, including Earth, revolve around the Sun. But they had not been able to explain *why* the planets moved as they did.

Newton's book contained his laws of motion and universal gravitation, which explained the movements of objects on Earth as well as of the planets. His law of universal gravitation states that all bodies attract each other with a force that can be measured. This force holds the whole system of sun and planets together by keeping them in their orbits.

Newton's work had a tremendous influence on the thinking of his own era and on all later scientific thought. The English poet Alexander Pope described Newton's impact: "Nature and Nature's laws lay hid in night; God said, 'Let Newton be!,' and all was light."

Other scientific discoveries. New discoveries were made elsewhere in Europe. Working independently of each other, both Newton and Gottfried Wilhelm Leibniz (LYP·nits), a German philosopher and mathematician, developed calculus, a branch of mathematics that studies continuously changing quantities. A Dutch scientist, Antoni van Leeuwenhoek (LAY·vuhn·hook), used the microscope, an invention of the late 1500s, to discover bacteria. The microscope enabled him to study a whole new world of life that could not normally be seen by the human eye.

Robert Hooke of England, who lived from 1635 to 1703, also worked with the microscope. The first person to identify cells in living matter, Hooke examined a thin slice of cork and noticed that it consisted of small rectangular "rooms." He called these "rooms" cells because they looked like the *cells* in which bees store their honey.

The Anglo-Irish scientist Robert Boyle is known as the founder of modern chemistry, the study of the

This painting, which hangs in the palace at Versailles, shows the establishment of the French Academy of Sciences in 1666.

composition of materials and the changes they undergo. Another English chemist, Joseph Priestley, discovered the element later called oxygen. (Elements are the fundamental substances that make up matter.)

A French scientist, Antoine Lavoisier (luhv·WAHZ·ee·ay), named oxygen. Lavoisier showed that fire was not an element, as many had believed. He proved that fire was the result of the rapid combination of oxygen with another substance. Lavoisier also demonstrated that matter is indestructible; it can be changed from one form into another, but it cannot be created or destroyed. For example, when water boils, it does not disappear. It forms steam, which combines with the air. The water's form has changed, but the water has not disappeared. Lavoisier's discovery is known as the law of the conservation of matter.

By the time Priestley and Lavoisier made their discoveries, the scientific point of view dominated European thought. The people of the 1700s spoke of their changing times as an "Age of Enlightenment."

Section 5 Review

1. **Define** Scientific Revolution, scientific method, geocentric theory, heliocentric theory

2. **Identify** Nicolaus Copernicus, Galileo

3. **Analyzing Ideas (a)** Define "Scientific Revolution." **(b)** Describe the factors that led to the birth of the Scientific Revolution.

4. **Summarizing Ideas** Explain how Copernicus, Kepler, and Galileo challenged traditionally held views and developed the heliocentric theory.

5. **Interpreting Ideas** Why were the ideas of Descartes, Bacon, and Newton significant to the scientific method?

6. **Evaluating Ideas** Choose three discoveries of the Renaissance and Reformation era and evaluate their importance.

Chapter 1 Review

A.D. 1516
More publishes *Utopia*.

A.D. 1521
Diet of Worms is held.

A.D. 1300 | A.D. 1400 | A.D. 1500 | A.D. 1510 | A.D. 1520

C. A.D. 1300
Italian Renaissance begins.

C. A.D. 1450
Gutenberg develops printing press with movable type.

A.D. 1509
Erasmus publishes *The Praise of Folly*.

A.D. 1513
Machiavelli publishes *The Prince*.

A.D. 1517
Luther posts 95 theses.

Chapter Summary
The following list contains the key concepts you have learned about the Renaissance and the Reformation.
1. Beginning in the early 1300s, a literary and artistic movement known as the Renaissance swept Italy and then spread to northern Europe.
2. The humanists, such as Petrarch, Erasmus, and More, emphasized a renewed interest in classical learning, a critical spirit, and enthusiasm for life in this world.
3. The Renaissance also inspired masterpieces in painting and sculpture.
4. In Germany, Martin Luther broke away from the Roman Catholic Church and began the Protestant Reformation. The doctrines he developed, known today as Lutheranism, spread throughout northern Europe.
5. In England the Anglican Church was founded under Henry VIII.
6. John Calvin's teachings spread from Switzerland to much of Europe.
7. In the 1530s the Roman Catholic Church began the Counter-Reformation. At the Council of Trent, church leaders defined official doctrines. The church used the Inquisition and the *Index of Forbidden Books* to combat heresy. New religious orders, such as the Jesuits, tried to halt the spread of Protestantism.
8. The development of the printing press and the religious changes of the Reformation brought new ideas to the lives of ordinary people. New attitudes toward nature and toward the community took hold.
9. The Scientific Revolution transformed the methods and understanding of astronomy, physics, and anatomy. Europeans made important technological and scientific achievements. The new scientific attitude would dominate future European thought.

Reviewing Important Terms
On a separate sheet of paper, supply the term that correctly completes each statement.
1. The creative movement that began in Italy in the 1300s and included a revival of interest in the classical learning of ancient Greece and Rome is called the _____.
2. People who used classical texts to study grammar, rhetoric, history, and poetry were called _____.
3. The painting technique in which painters make distant objects smaller than those in the foreground and arrange the objects in certain ways to make them appear more realistic is called _____.
4. The religious revolution, which split the church in western Europe and created several new churches, is called the _____.
5. The sale of _____ by the church in Germany sparked the Reformation.
6. Calvin made Geneva a _____ in which the government was ruled by a clergy claiming God's authority.
7. The _____ _____ marked the development of a new way of thinking about the world.
8. Nicolaus Copernicus caused controversy with the _____ _____, which contradicted what most people believed about the relationship between Earth and the Sun.

Developing Critical Thinking Skills
1. **Evaluating Ideas** Identify what each of the following people contributed to the humanist movement. Which person do you think made the greatest contribution? Why? **(a)** Petrarch; **(b)** Machiavelli; **(c)** Erasmus; **(d)** Shakespeare?
2. **Summarizing Ideas** Describe what Martin Luther's ideas were on each of the following: **(a)** salvation; **(b)** the sacraments; **(c)** the clergy.

A.D. 1534
Loyola founds the Jesuit order.

A.D. 1543
Copernicus publishes *On the Revolutions of the Celestial Spheres.*

A.D. 1555
Peace of Augsburg is signed.

A.D. 1687
Newton publishes *Mathematical Principles of Natural Philosophy.*

A.D. 1530 | A.D. 1540 | A.D. 1550 | A.D. 1600 | A.D. 1700

C. A.D. 1530
Counter-Reformation begins.

A.D. 1536
Calvin publishes *Institutes of the Christian Religion.*

A.D. 1545-1563
Council of Trent meets.

A.D. 1632
Galileo publishes *Dialogue on the Two Great Systems of the World.*

A.D. 1637
Descartes publishes *Discourse on Method.*

3. **Interpreting Ideas** (a) What was the Counter-Reformation? (b) What did it try to accomplish? (c) How successful was it?
4. **Understanding Ideas** During the time of the Reformation, most people in Europe lived in small villages. Describe how villagers explained the natural events that occurred in their lives.
5. **Analyzing Ideas** How did the Scientific Revolution change the way people viewed themselves and their world?

Relating Geography to History

Study the map of the world on pages R4 and R5 in the Atlas. (a) Why was Italy ideally suited to establish trade with Southwest Asia? (b) How did the ideas of the Italian Renaissance spread to northern Europe?

Relating Past to Present

1. A Renaissance person is defined as one who is knowledgeable in both science and art. (a) Give an example of someone in today's world who might be called a Renaissance person. (b) What are the advantages and disadvantages of this combination of knowledge for an educated person?
2. (a) How did the invention of printing revolutionize the spread of knowledge and ideas in Europe during the time of the Reformation? (b) Describe how radio and television have changed our understanding of the world.

Applying History
Study Skills

Before completing this activity, review Building History Study Skills on page 51.

Look again at Michelangelo's *The Creation of Adam* on page 51. Then look at the statue of Hermes by Praxiteles in column two on this page.
1. How do these works of art show similarities between the values of Greek and Renaissance societies?
2. How do they show differences?

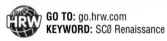
internetconnect

Search the Internet through the HRW Web site for more information on one of the Renaissance writers that you read about in this chapter. Present an oral report about that person. Be certain that your biography discusses the person's major achievements.

HRW **GO TO:** go.hrw.com
KEYWORD: SCØ Renaissance

Building
Your Portfolio

1. **Writing a Report** Leonardo da Vinci was one of the greatest geniuses of the Renaissance. Prepare a written report on Leonardo's talents and achievements and place a copy in your portfolio. You may use the following sources: "The Scope of Genius" in John Hale's *The Renaissance* (Time-Life Books) and "Leonardo da Vinci" in *Horizon Book of the Renaissance* (American Heritage).
2. **Writing a Monologue** Do research to find out additional information about what it was like to be a European villager during some part of the period from 1300 to 1700. Write a monologue about a typical day or week in your life, or about a special occasion such as a holiday or feast. Begin with a description of the time and place when you lived. Place a copy of the monologue in your portfolio.

CHAPTER 2

European Exploration, Expansion, and Absolutism

TIME

A.D. 1400–1800

A.D. 1400–1800

3.7 million B.C. | 4000 B.C. | A.D. 2100

PLACE

Europe, Asia, North and South America

Europe

ARCTIC OCEAN
NORTH AMERICA
EUROPE
ASIA
PACIFIC OCEAN
AFRICA
Equator
SOUTH AMERICA
ATLANTIC OCEAN
INDIAN OCEAN
AUSTRALIA
PACIFIC OCEAN
ANTARCTICA

North and South America

Asia

King Louis XIV of France

CHAPTER FOCUS

Significance

European expansion between 1400 and 1800 occurred only after technological, economic, and political changes had taken place in Europe. By the 1600s, a system of government called **absolute monarchy** (where the ruler has total control of the state without needing to consult other leaders or representatives of the people) had become dominant in Europe.

Terms to Define

absolute monarchy	subsidies
compass	Treaty of Tordesillas
astrolabe	triangular trade
latitude	Middle Passage
galleys	viceroys
Commercial Revolution	guerrilla warfare
joint-stock company	tax farming
mercantilism	intendants
favorable balance of trade	divine right of kings
tariffs	balance of power

People to Identify

Prince Henry the Navigator	Marie de Medici
Bartholomeu Dias	Cardinal Richelieu
Vasco da Gama	Cardinal Mazarin
Amerigo Vespucci	Jean-Baptiste Colbert
Vasco Núñez de Balboa	Jacques Cartier
Ferdinand Magellan	René-Robert de La Salle
Juan Sebastián de Elcano	Peter the Great
Juan Ponce de Léon	Catherine the Great
Hernán Cortés	Maria Theresa
Moctezuma	the Great Elector
Francisco Pizarro	Frederick William I
Charles V	Frederick the Great
Philip II	

Places to Locate

Cape of Good Hope	Moscow
Brazil	Sea of Azov
Isthmus of Panama	Black Sea
Philippine Islands	St. Petersburg
Tenochtitlán	Siberia
Versailles	

Chapter Theme Questions

- **Economic Organization** What factors might lead nations to venture into the unknown?
- **Politics and Government** How might a vast colonial empire affect a nation's health at home?
- **War and Diplomacy** What might happen when countries expand their borders rather than seek colonies overseas?

Archaeologists believe recently discovered ruins on Haiti's north shore may be those of the first Spanish settlement in North America—Christopher Columbus's lost colony, La Navidad. Archaeologist Kathleen A. Deagan, confident that her search for the colony had ended, wrote:

❝ *Just before midnight on Christmas Eve, 1492, a sleepy helmsman gave the tiller of Christopher Columbus's flagship,* Santa María, *to the ship's boy. . . . The hapless lad promptly ran the ship onto a coral reef off the north coast of Haiti . . . Attempts to free the vessel failed, the planking opened, and the Admiral abandoned her for* Niña. *. . .*

Columbus appealed for help to Guacanagari, the Indian . . . chief, whose village was about four miles from the wreck. The Indians helped unload supplies, . . . dismantle the ship's timbers and boards, and carry them . . . to the village. . . . Thus the tiny settlement—named for the infant child of Christmas, La Navidad—was established. . . .

We can only speculate upon what happened next. When Columbus returned 11 months later, he found the settlement burned and all his men dead. . . .

The site was forgotten for nearly 500 years. Now . . . our team . . . believes we have found it again. ❞

Christopher Columbus was only one of many Europeans who spread Western civilization throughout the world.

Section 1

The Foundations of European Exploration

Focus Questions

- **What technological advances helped make the great European explorations possible?**
- **What was the Commercial Revolution?**
- **What was mercantilism, and what role did colonies play in it?**

Before the 1400s, Europeans had little contact with other parts of the world. Marco Polo traveled to

China, the Crusaders tried to capture the Holy Land from the Arabs, and Europeans engaged in the spice trade. Nevertheless, in general Europeans had neither the interest nor the ability to explore foreign lands. By the late 1400s, however, technology, economics, politics, and society as a whole had changed significantly. These changes sparked European interest in the world beyond Europe and provided the opportunity to explore them. Soon adventurous Europeans discovered new routes to many foreign places. These discoveries opened up an era of exploration that lasted for the next 400 years.

Technological Advances

Since the time of the Crusades, Europeans had known about the riches of Asia—spices, silks, and jewels. Early European explorers sought to acquire these goods, which were very valuable trading items, even in small amounts. Spices, silks, and jewels came mainly from India, China, and the islands of Southeast Asia. To reach these distant places safely

In his paintings, Jan Vermeer frequently gives the viewer a glimpse of a figure in the midst of an activity. "The Astronomer" illustrates research and work related to mapmaking.

and to compete successfully with powerful Arab and local traders, Europeans began to focus on finding new sea routes to the East. To do this, Europeans needed better maps, navigation instruments, ships, and guns—in short, Europeans needed a more advanced technology.

Mapmaking. Mapmaking improved during the Renaissance because of the Europeans' growing interest in the writings of ancient geographers and their desire for pictorial accuracy. Most scholars knew—as Ptolemy's maps had shown—that the world was round. Renaissance mapmakers added information about Africa and Asia but not yet, of course, about North and South America. It seemed possible that the distance from Europe to Asia would be shorter going west—across the Atlantic Ocean—than going east. Inspired by the new maps, daring sea captains soon set out on their travels, opening up new worlds scarcely dreamed of before.

Navigation instruments. Just as important as maps were the navigation instruments that helped make it possible for ships to sail out of the sight of land without losing their bearings. One such navigation instrument was the **compass**. As early as the 1100s, European navigators had learned that an iron needle rubbed against a piece of lodestone—a kind of magnetic rock—would become magnetized and turn toward the north if they floated it in water on a stick or through a straw. In the 1300s, by fixing the needle to a card marked with directions, these European navigators created a true compass.

Another important navigation instrument, the **astrolabe**, applied astronomy and geometry to navigation and allowed sailors to determine the relative apparent height of stars and planets. Using this information, they could calculate a ship's **latitude**, its distance north or south of the equator.

New ships. Long-distance exploration also required improvements in ships. Before and even during the 1400s, long ships called **galleys** carried most European coastal trade. Slaves or prisoners of war strained at the 50 or 60 oars that propelled the galley. In deep ocean waters, traders used sailing ships. Until the late 1400s, these clumsy sailing vessels could travel only in the direction in which the wind blew.

In the late 1400s, ship designers in Portugal and Spain made important improvements. They reduced the width of ships in proportion to their length, made smaller and different-shaped sails, and moved the location of the rudder—a device used for steering— from the side to the rear, or stern, of the ship.

A Mariner's Astrolabe

The process of determining a vehicle's position and directing its movement is called navigation. The word *navigation* comes from two Latin words—*navis*, meaning "ship," and *agere*, meaning "to drive."

The explorers of the 1500s sailed with only a few simple technological aids to guide them. However, with these, along with the stars and the Sun, they navigated the oceans of the world. They could plot and hold a course, measure their progress, and estimate their position in relation to land.

Astrolabes, usually made of brass or iron, were widely used in the Middle Ages by astronomers to plot the position of the Sun and other celestial bodies. In the 1400s, sailors began using the technology of astrolabes to determine the latitude of their ships.

A sailor would sight a star along the bar shown in the photograph. Then, by aligning the bar with markings engraved on the disk of the astrolabe, he could determine the latitude.

The astrolabe became obsolete with the invention of the sextant, an instrument navigators use to measure the angular distance between two points such as the horizon and the Sun.

These improvements allowed ships to sail against the wind, to travel quickly, and to be steered with reasonable accuracy.

The cannon. Europeans first used cannons in war during the 1400s. Until then naval warfare had consisted of ramming and boarding an enemy vessel. Shipboard cannons and the handguns carried by sailors now helped Europeans defeat the navies of their enemies.

Economic Changes

The development of improved ways of doing business also played an important part in the new exploration. In some cases, developments that had already begun, such as the use of money and the services provided by banks, simply changed to accommodate the needs of exploration. In other cases, the old methods of doing business became inadequate, and Europeans worked out new ones. The changes in the European economy were so extensive that some historians have referred to the period from 1400 to 1750 as the **Commercial Revolution**.

Standardized money. Before the 1400s, the value of money had not been standardized. That is, the value of certain coins might change, depending on the amount of precious metal used to make them. The scarcity of precious metals from which coins were made, the great variety of coins in use, and the lack of a fixed value for money handicapped Europeans.

During the 1400s, however, Europeans developed standard systems of money. The Italian cities led the way in minting coins that had a fixed value. The value of the gold florin of Florence and the ducat (DUHK·uht) of Venice became very dependable. Later the Spanish kings used silver and gold shipped from the New World to pay debts owed their bankers. These payments helped relieve the shortage of precious metals in Europe.

The standardization of money made economic transactions much more reliable. Anyone who accepted a florin in payment for goods or services knew that the money was worth a certain amount and could be used to buy other goods or services. This in turn encouraged the growth of international trade and banking. The large sums that banks now accumulated made it possible for them to lend money to governments and major trading companies who financed large overseas expeditions.

Joint-stock companies. Individual merchants often combined their resources in a new type of business organization called a **joint-stock company**. Such a company raised money by selling stock, or shares, in the company to investors. These shareholders became co-owners. Shareholders divided profits according to the numbers of shares of stock they owned. Joint-stock companies raised large amounts of money from people willing to invest in their activities.

With the standardization of money, monarchs financed overseas trade and the settlement of colonies.

Political Changes

Technological and commercial advances alone could not have made successful explorations possible. Money provided by the stronger and more ambitious monarchies that emerged in Europe in the 1400s and 1500s financed these expeditions. By then dynastic ambitions and rivalries between countries often made the central governments enthusiastic supporters of new exploration and colonization. Gaining riches from overseas exploration was one way a country could become more powerful than its rivals.

Despite the contributions of the Italian city-states to the Commercial Revolution and the growth of capitalism, they had not financed explorations or established overseas colonies. As the age of exploration began, trade that previously had been concentrated in the Mediterranean area and southern Germany now moved to the Atlantic nations. In Portugal, Spain, and France, monarchs and their advisers not only financed voyages but also controlled exploration and the building of overseas empires.

Mercantilism

The economic and political changes associated with overseas expansion also contributed to a new economic theory called **mercantilism**. According to this theory, a country's government should do all it could to increase the country's wealth. A country's wealth was measured by how much gold and silver it possessed. Because according to this belief the world contained only a fixed amount of such wealth, to increase its own wealth, a country had to take wealth away from another country.

Balance of trade. Mercantilists thought a nation could gain wealth by mining gold and silver at home or by acquiring colonies that were rich in those precious metals. It could also get wealth by selling more goods than it bought in foreign countries, thus creating a **favorable balance of trade**. By bringing money into a country, a favorable balance of trade strengthened the country itself and weakened its foreign rivals, who ultimately paid in gold and silver for the goods they bought, thus depleting their supplies of those metals.

To gain a favorable balance of trade, a nation could take several measures. It could reduce the amount of goods imported into the country by imposing **tariffs**, or import taxes, on foreign goods. The importer paid the tax and added that amount to the selling price of the goods. The higher price discouraged people from buying foreign goods. A nation could also try to

The Growth of Banking Families

One of the outgrowths of the Commercial Revolution was the formation of powerful families in Europe that handled trading and banking concerns. Such families thrived as the economic life of the Middle Ages began to change and long-distance trade became more common.

Although a local guild leader could handle trade in his area, he did not have the capital, the time, or the knowledge to run a worldwide operation. A new kind of businessman emerged to fill the gap. Usually such a man began as a merchant of a specific type and ended as a banker. The Medici family of Italy followed this path. So did the Fuggers (FOOG´uhrz) in the area that is now Germany.

The Fuggers began their rise in the early 1400s, when Hans (or Johann) Fugger gained control of the weaver's guild in Augsburg. He began to deal in a new type of cloth, thereby extending his base of trade. As family members traveled to Venice, the business began to encompass spices, silks, and other Eastern goods. The Fuggers invested their profits in non-textile concerns, including mining. By the 1500s, they had enough extra capital to lend money to the popes, to Charles V (who spent it to gain the title Holy Roman emperor), and later to both the German and Spanish ruling families. Jakob II (called the Rich) Fugger, grandson of Hans, is shown above with his chief accountant.

The Fuggers continued to be a force through the end of the 1500s, declining only after 1600 as trade in the Atlantic became more important and the Dutch took control of the mouth of the Rhine River for their own profit.

---

increase the value of its exports. Manufactured goods were the most valuable kind of exports because they sold for more money than raw materials; woolen cloth, for instance, brought more than raw wool. Therefore, mercantilist nations encouraged manufacturers, exporters of manufactured goods, and shipbuilders. In many cases, governments made grants of money called **subsidies** to help establish new industries and build ships. A nation could also try to make itself self-sufficient by producing everything it needed, plus a surplus of goods for export. The self-sufficient nation did not have to depend on foreign countries, which were always rivals and might at any time become active enemies. The desire for self-sufficiency helped stimulate the race to acquire overseas colonies.

The role of colonies. Colonies played an important part in mercantilism. Those that produced gold and silver were the most desirable. Next best were those that produced raw materials that could not be produced at home. By buying these materials in its colonies, a nation could avoid buying from a foreign rival. Thus money did not leave the nation or empire, which maintained complete control over its wealth.

Finally, mercantilist theory put a high value on colonies as markets for the manufactured goods of the home country. Governments passed strict laws to prevent colonists from buying foreign manufactured goods or selling their raw materials anywhere except the home country. In this way, the home country kept strict economic control of its colonies. In addition, home countries might ban colonies from manufacturing their own goods, forcing the colonists to buy such goods from the home country.

Social Change

Government policies by themselves did not create a willingness to explore and settle overseas. Certain changes in society also made exploration and resettlement abroad attractive to many people.

After 1500 Europe experienced a population increase. Some urban areas became very crowded. Adventurous people hoped that despite harsh living conditions in the colonies, settling overseas would give them a fresh start and a better life.

Some people went to the colonies hoping to reap quick profits. Tales of gold and jewels, of fabulous cities such as the legendary El Dorado in South America, as well as of fertile soil persuaded thousands that easy wealth lay overseas.

Others—such as the French Huguenots and the English Puritans—went overseas to escape religious or political persecution at home. Some went to spread Christianity. Often a combination of reasons caused people to resettle in new lands.

Section 1 Review

1. **Define** absolute monarchy, compass, astrolabe, latitude, galleys, Commercial Revolution, joint-stock company, mercantilism, favorable balance of trade, tariffs, subsidies
2. **Summarizing Ideas** Describe the improvements in navigational aids and ship construction that made long-range exploration possible.
3. **Understanding Ideas** Explain the importance of the Commercial Revolution.
4. **Interpreting Ideas** What role did colonies play in mercantilism?

Section 2

Voyages of Portugal and Spain

Focus Questions

- **What were the accomplishments of Prince Henry the Navigator, Bartholomeu Dias, and Vasco da Gama?**
- **What was the impact of the voyages of Christopher Columbus?**
- **What were the characteristics of the Atlantic slave trade, and why did it prosper?**

Explorers sailing under the flags of Portugal and Spain made the first European voyages into unknown waters. These explorers were driven by curiosity and by religious and economic aims and backed by their governments. The voyages of these courageous men served as the foundation for future empires.

Portugal and Prince Henry

Perched at the southwestern corner of Europe, the small nation of Portugal was one of the first to become strongly interested in exploration. Prince Henry (often called the Navigator), a member of the Portuguese royal family, was largely responsible for this interest. Henry hoped to acquire gold for Portugal. He also hoped to start a Crusade against the Muslims in Africa, where he thought he might even find and join forces with a legendary priest and king known as Prester John.

To help accomplish his goals, Prince Henry is thought to have founded a school of sailing and navigation at Sagres. (Some historians dispute the existence of this school.) By 1418 his navigators began a series of explorations westward into the Atlantic and southward along the west coast of Africa. Henry's explorers claimed for Portugal several islands, including the Azores in the Atlantic Ocean. On the African coast, the Portuguese began to trade for slaves, gold, and ivory.

Further explorations brought the Portuguese even greater gains. In 1488 Bartholomeu Dias sailed around the Cape of Good Hope at the southern tip of Africa. Although Dias had to turn back, he had found the route to the Indian Ocean. Building on this knowledge in 1497, Vasco da Gama sailed beyond the Cape of Good Hope eastward across the Indian Ocean, landing in India in 1498. (See map on pages 82 and 83.) From a second voyage a few years later, he returned home with a fabulous cargo of spices and jewels.

Da Gama's successful voyages represented a tremendous stroke of good fortune for the Portuguese. Their ships could now sail to India and the East Indies and bring back rich cargoes of Asian goods. The direct ocean route saved the Portuguese money because they could buy goods directly from Asia rather than from Arab traders or Italian merchants, who charged very high prices. Ships could carry goods for long distances more cheaply than could wagons or animals traveling overland. In addition, ships did not have to pay the tolls that frequently were levied on overland transportation.

Christopher Columbus

Spain, too, became interested in the search for new trade routes. Its rulers, King Ferdinand and Queen Isabella, decided to finance a voyage by Christopher Columbus, a Genoan navigator. Inspired by the writings of Marco Polo and influenced by Ptolemy's description of the round Earth, Columbus believed he could reach Asia quickly by sailing westward instead of making the long trip around the tip of Africa.

In August 1492, Columbus set sail from Palos, Spain, with three small ships—the *Ninã*, the *Pinta*,

Pictured is a woodcut illustration of Columbus's flagship *Santa Maria*.

and the *Santa Maria*—across the Atlantic. On October 12, 1492, his small fleet landed at a tiny island that Columbus named San Salvador. (See map on pages 82 and 83.)

After exploring other islands in the area, he returned triumphantly to Spain early in 1493 to report his discoveries. Because he believed the islands lay off the east coast of India, Columbus called them the Indies and their inhabitants Indians. In fact, he had discovered the islands in the Americas that were later to be known as the West Indies. Columbus made three more voyages to the "Indies" between 1493 and 1504. For the rest of his life he believed he had landed off the coast of Asia.

The Impact of Columbus's Voyages

In the years after Columbus's voyages, a massive interaction between the so-called New World and the Old World took place. This interaction, often referred to as the Columbian Exchange, involved the movement of products, plants, animals, and even diseases between the Western and Eastern Hemispheres. For example, gold and silver mined in South America were shipped eastward to Spain. American precious metals helped Spain become a world power.

The interchange between the Americas and the Old World affected the way people lived. The diet of Europeans changed markedly after American foods such as potatoes, tomatoes, beans, and corn were introduced in Europe. Horses and cattle, brought to the Americas by the Spanish, greatly altered the lives of Native Americans, especially in what today is Mexico and the southwestern United States. Other exchanges were less beneficial.

European Explorations, 1487–1682

Learning from Maps European explorers set out to the east and west to discover new lands.

Portuguese exploration
Spanish exploration
French exploration
English exploration
Dutch exploration

Arctic Circle

60°N

EUROPE

ASIA

JAPAN

30°N

Tropic of Cancer

PACIFIC OCEAN

CHINA

Hormuz

Arabian Peninsula

INDIA

Diu

DA GAMA, 1497–1499

Calicut
Cochin

Strait of Malacca

CEYLON

PHILIPPINES

AFRICA

CABRAL, 1500–1501

Malacca

BORNEO

MOLUCCAS (SPICE ISLANDS)

DRAKE, 1577–1580

0° Equator

MAGELLAN, 1519–1521

Malindi
Mombasa

INDIAN OCEAN

SUMATRA

EAST INDIES

TASMAN, 1642–1643

Luanda

JAVA

TASMAN, 1642–1643

Batavia

TASMAN, 1644

Tropic of Capricorn

DRAKE, 1577–1580

1497–1499

Cape of Good Hope

ELCANO, 1521–1522

AUSTRALIA

30°S

DA GAMA,

TASMAN, 1642–1643

Treaty of Tordesillas Line of Demarcation, 1494

60°S

? **Movement** Around what continent did Drake sail between 1577 and 1580?

EUROPEAN EXPLORATION, EXPANSION, AND ABSOLUTISM 83

The Columbian Exchange

Today computer and communication technologies enable people all over the world to exchange information and goods and services, making the world seem a smaller place. What we call the Columbian Exchange, an equally important kind of exchange between the Americas and the rest of the world, began in 1492, when Columbus sailed from Spain across the Atlantic Ocean. With their arrival in the Americas, Columbus and the Europeans who came after him initiated contact between peoples and civilizations that had not been in contact for 9,000 years. Along with the exchange of people came a variety of other exchanges. We are still experiencing today both the positive and negative impacts of this contact.

This Aztec drawing shows the stages of smallpox, ending with death.

The exchange of crops across the Atlantic caused landscapes to change and populations to grow. White potatoes, originally grown and domesticated in the Andes, today feed millions of people in northern Europe, Russia, and China. Wheat, on the other hand, was not grown in the Americas until it was brought there by Europeans. American corn, or maize, first domesticated by Native Americans, is now an essential crop in many nations, including Romania, Egypt, South Africa, and China. The tomato originated not in Italy but in the Americas.

Many animals were also introduced to the Americas by Columbus and other Europeans. Horses, cattle, goats, sheep, chickens, and house cats crossed the Atlantic Ocean with European travelers. North America, in exchange, gave Europe and Asia the turkey, gray squirrel, and muskrat.

Of course, there were also negative consequences of the Columbian Exchange. The most devastating imports from Europe and elsewhere to the Americas were diseases: measles, typhus, plague, and smallpox. Native American populations had never experienced these diseases before and had no immunity to them. They were thus extremely vulnerable to such diseases, and millions died from them.

Smallpox and other diseases carried westward by Europeans nearly destroyed the native population of Spanish America.

Dividing the New Lands

In the late 1400s, Spain and Portugal often claimed the same newly discovered lands. To resolve their conflicts, in 1493 Pope Alexander VI issued an edict that drew on a world map a line of demarcation down the middle of the Atlantic Ocean. He granted Spain the rights to all newly discovered lands west of the line. Portugal could claim all those to the east of the line. Neither country, however, was to occupy lands already claimed by a Christian ruler.

A year later, the **Treaty of Tordesillas** between Spain and Portugal moved the line farther west. (See map on pages 82 and 83.) A Portuguese captain, Pedro Cabral, reached the east coast of South America by accident in 1500. He had sailed for India but had been blown off course and reached Brazil. He was able to claim this region for Portugal under the Treaty of Tordesillas.

Eventually, Spain took control of most of Central and South America, along with the Philippines. (See map on pages 90 and 91.) Portugal had the territory on the Brazilian coast as well as territory on both the eastern and western coasts of Africa and in Asia and the East Indies.

Vespucci, Balboa, and Magellan

Other explorers followed Columbus westward. Between 1497 and 1503, Amerigo Vespucci, a navigator from Florence, took part in several Spanish and Portuguese expeditions across the Atlantic. Unlike other explorers, Vespucci was convinced that the land he saw was not part of Asia but was instead what he called a New World. After reading Vespucci's writings describing this new land, a German mapmaker called it America after Vespucci, whose first name, in Latin, is *Americus*.

In 1513 a Spaniard named Vasco Núñez de Balboa crossed the Isthmus of Panama and reached a vast ocean. Balboa called it the South Sea and claimed it for Spain. It now seemed clear that the so-called New World really was a distinct landmass, separate from Asia.

Ferdinand Magellan, a Portuguese navigator sailing for Spain, proved it. In 1519, with five ships, Magellan set out from Spain, crossed the Atlantic to South America, and sailed along its eastern shore until he reached the southernmost tip. After passing through the strait now named for him, Magellan found himself in a great ocean. Because it appeared to be very calm, he named it the Pacific Ocean, from the Latin word *pacificus*, meaning "peaceful." This was the same ocean Balboa had named the South Sea.

Magellan sailed westward across the Pacific and reached the Philippine Islands, claiming them for Spain. There in 1521 he died in a fight with the islanders. His crew, led by Juan Sebastián de Elcano, sailed on. Eventually, one ship and 18 crew members made it back to Spain in 1522, completing this first round-the-world voyage.

Portuguese Expansion

After the voyages of Dias and da Gama, the Portuguese pursued the dream of dominating trade with Asia.

Around 1510 the Portuguese conquered part of the southwest coast of India, making the port of

Magellan (shown here) and Elcano's circumnavigation of the globe between 1519 and 1522 provided the first indisputable proof that Earth was round.

Goa (GOH·uh) their administrative center. From India they moved on to the East Indies. (See map on pages 82 and 83.) They conquered Malacca (muh·LAK·uh), on the southwest coast of the Malay Peninsula. Then they moved east to take the Moluccas (muh·LUKH·uhz), a group of islands. Europeans called them the Spice Islands because spices grew there in abundance.

The Portuguese then turned their attention to the island of Ceylon (now Sri Lanka), off the southeast coast of India, adding it to their chain of trading bases. With its key location between Goa and Malacca and its tea and spices, Ceylon helped the Portuguese dominate trade with the East Indies. The Portuguese also gained footholds in China and Japan, and established several fortified trading posts on the East African coast.

Portugal's colonies in Asia and around the Indian Ocean, though important, were small trading bases. In the Americas, however, the Portuguese founded a much larger colony in Brazil. There they established enormous agricultural estates on which they grew sugar for export.

The Slave Trade

As they did in Asia, the Portuguese went to Africa to trade. At first the Portuguese, largely at the request of Christian missionaries who wanted to convert the continent's inhabitants, maintained friendly relations with the Africans. The Portuguese treated the monarch of the African kingdom of Kongo as a legitimate and "brother" king to the Portuguese ruler. In turn, the king of the Kongo welcomed the newcomers and accepted baptism. Envoys from the Kongo traveled to Europe. The cordial relations, however, soon collapsed when the economic interests of Portuguese traders became evident.

Portuguese economic interests in Africa centered largely on slavery, which had been practiced for thousands of years. Europeans themselves had been slaves in the Byzantine Empire and in the Arab and Turkish Empires. During the 1500s, however, the new European overseas empires began to require slave labor.

The slave trade grew very gradually, beginning in earnest when the Portuguese set up sugar plantations on the islands of Príncipe and São Tomé off the coast of west-central Africa. To operate efficiently and profitably, these plantations required large numbers of slaves. Plantation owners acquired their slaves from the African mainland. As plantation agriculture spread to Brazil and the Caribbean islands, the demand for slaves increased. By the early 1600s, the slave trade served as the chief purpose of European relations with Africa.

Spain annexed Portugal in 1580. At around the same time, the Dutch emerged as the leading naval power and became active in the slave trade. The Dutch also took over some of Portugal's colonies, most notably the East Indies. Later the English and the French also became involved in the slave trade.

Triangular trade. The Atlantic slave trade was one aspect of a system known as the **triangular trade**. In the first stage of the system, merchants shipped cotton goods, weapons, and liquor to Africa in exchange for slaves or gold. The second stage—called the **Middle Passage**—was the shipment of slaves across the Atlantic to the Americas. There the traders sold the slaves for produce from the plantations. To complete the triangle, merchants sent the plantations' products to Europe, where they were used to buy manufactured products to be sold in the Americas. Some products from plantations, such as tobacco, were traded in Africa for more slaves.

Middle Passage. The Middle Passage had a brutal and dehumanizing effect on all involved. The traders chained the slaves in the overcrowded hold of the ship to prevent them from jumping overboard or organizing a rebellion aboard ship. In the hold, slaves had little food or water and no provision for sanitation. Many died before they ever reached their destination.

At the height of the trade, between 1741 and 1810, European slave ships carried an average of about 60,000 slaves each year. Recent estimates indicate that between 1451 and 1870 some 10 million Africans survived the horrendous journey to become slaves in the Americas. Perhaps another 1.5 million died during the Middle Passage. Many others died even earlier, during the process of enslavement by fellow Africans and on the hard trip from the interior of Africa to the coast. This tragic loss meant that Africa's population did not increase between 1650 and 1800, when Europe's population was growing rapidly.

African kingdoms and slavery. Beginning in the 1400s and 1500s, strong states began to emerge in West Africa. Over the next centuries, groups such as the Asante and kingdoms such as Benin and Dahomey became powerful. Many of these states profited from the slave trade.

Although not all Africans participated in the slave trade with Europeans, many African societies had practiced slavery well before the arrival of the Europeans. Slaves were usually obtained through war or in raids.

This 1800s sketch shows the horribly crowded conditions aboard a slave ship.

African slavery differed in some respects from that in the Americas, however. African slave owners preferred women and children for labor and sometimes killed males because they were likely to cause trouble or try to escape. Europeans, on the other hand, were more interested in male slaves to do manual work on colonial plantations. African societies generally allowed slaves to buy back their freedom, and they treated slaves as people with a role in society. Europeans, on the other hand, generally considered slaves as property to be bought or sold for profit.

Because Europeans rarely ventured beyond Africa's coast, they needed the help of Africans in gathering and transporting slaves. Some African societies and individuals willingly joined in the slave trade to obtain arms and other goods from Europe. In turn neighboring groups either had to participate in the trade or become its victims. The demand for slaves led to increased slave raiding, which had a disastrous effect on the future of the continent.

Weaknesses of the Portuguese Empire

Portugal rapidly acquired wealth and a vast empire, but that empire declined almost as swiftly as it rose. Several factors hastened the decline. First, the Portuguese government, with a shaky financial base, had overextended its empire.

Second, the sea voyages to the distant colonies, and the governing of them, proved to be a drain on Portugal's population. Many Portuguese men went to sea, never to return. Thousands of soldiers and sailors were needed to sustain the overseas empire. While Portuguese ships made enormous profits in trade, frequent mishaps from shipwrecks and encounters with enemies reduced both monetary gains and the number of men who were able to return home.

Because Portugal had a small population to begin with, the losses could not easily be replaced.

Third, Spain annexed Portugal in 1580, and Portugal did not regain its independence until 1640. In the meantime, Spain limited Portuguese trade and also neglected the colonies that the Portuguese had established overseas.

Taking advantage of these weaknesses, the Dutch and English captured much of the Asian trade from the Portuguese during the 1600s. However, small Portuguese colonies survived in Africa, India, and China, but they no longer served as sources of great wealth. Only Brazil and Angola continued to serve as major Portuguese colonies.

Section 2 Review

1. **Define** Treaty of Tordesillas, triangular trade, Middle Passage
2. **Identify** Prince Henry the Navigator, Bartholomeu Dias, Vasco da Gama, Amerigo Vespucci, Vasco Núñez de Balboa, Ferdinand Magellan, Juan Sebastián de Elcano
3. **Locate and Explain the Significance** Cape of Good Hope, Brazil, Isthmus of Panama, Philippine Islands
4. **Summarizing Ideas** Briefly state the major accomplishments of each of the following people: Prince Henry the Navigator, Bartholomeu Dias, and Vasco da Gama.
5. **Evaluating Ideas** Why were the voyages of Christopher Columbus important?
6. **Understanding Ideas** Describe how the Atlantic slave trade worked and what led to its success.

The Spanish and Dutch Empires

Focus Questions

- **How did Spain extend its power abroad and at home?**
- **Why were the Dutch successful in the 1600s?**
- **Why did the Spanish Empire decline?**

Throughout the 1500s, Spain was the most powerful nation in Europe and had the largest overseas empire. Within just 150 years, however, Spain's power declined. The reasons for the rise and rapid decline of the Spanish Empire are woven through an intricate network of historical events.

Spain's Colonial Empire

Portugal's main interests, with the exception of Brazil, lay in Africa and Asia. Spain, on the other hand, turned most of its energies to the Americas. In Asia only the Philippine Islands held great interest to Spain as a colony.

Beginning with the expeditions of Columbus, Spaniards explored the West Indies, Central America, and parts of the mainland of North and South America. (See map on pages 82 and 83.) They failed to find the spices they sought and soon learned that the land they explored was not the East Indies. However, America's abundant natural resources offered them other opportunities.

Starting in the Caribbean, Spanish exploration and colonization moved to the American mainland. Leaving Puerto Rico, Juan Ponce de León sailed northward in 1513 and explored what today is the state of Florida. A later expedition to Florida, under Pánfilo de Narváez, ended in disaster in 1528. A handful of survivors, led by Alvar Núñez Cabeza de Vaca, traveled through what is now the southwestern United States and Mexico for seven years.

Conquests. Other explorers went to the Yucatán in Mexico and learned of the great Maya and Aztec civilizations. In 1519, with 11 ships and about 600 men, Hernán Cortés invaded Mexico. After seizing the Aztec ruler Moctezuma (MAWK·tay·soo·muh), Cortés captured and destroyed the great Aztec city of Tenochtitlán—on the ruins of which the Spanish built Mexico City—and eventually conquered the entire Aztec Empire. Horses and guns, unknown in the Americas, helped the small Spanish force overcome the Aztec armies.

The Spaniards also heard of a great and rich civilization in South America. In early 1530, Francisco Pizarro led an expedition of 180 men and 37 horses from the Isthmus of Panama to the Inca Empire in what is now Peru and in 1532 seized it for Spain.

In time Spain controlled a vast empire in the West Indies, Central America, southern and western North America, and much of South America. (See map on pages 90 and 91.) The Spaniards became colonizers in the true sense of the word. Unlike the Europeans in Africa and Asia, who became mainly traders, the Spaniards in the Americas established settlements.

Government and society. Spain developed a centralized form of government for its colonies. **Viceroys**, representatives of the monarch, reported to the Council of the Indies in Spain. The council planned and directed the development of Spain's empire.

For a time, Spain grew enormously rich from its colonies' valuable silver mines in the regions that are now Bolivia and northern Mexico. Although agriculture and trade remained important, mineral resources became the Spanish Empire's main asset.

The native inhabitants had no immunity to diseases that the Spanish brought with them. The societies conquered by Cortés and Pizarro had already been weakened by European diseases. Massive epidemics of smallpox, typhus, and measles killed millions. In an area covering Mexico, the southwestern United States, and much of Central America, the native population is estimated to have declined from between 11 and 25 million in 1492 to 1.25 million by 1625. Because the Spaniards needed workers for mines and farms, they imported slaves from Africa to compensate for the loss of Indian labor.

Spain's Colonial Rivals

The Spanish government made every effort to keep the wealth of the Americas for Spain alone. It kept foreigners out of the Spanish colonies and decreed that silver and gold from the Americas could be carried only in Spanish ships and only to the Spanish port of Seville.

Making rules, however, proved easier than enforcing them. Spain's colonial rivals—the French, Dutch, and English—envied Spain's American wealth and used various means to capture a share of it. They traded in Spain's American ports and encouraged pirates to attack Spanish ships.

Shortly after arriving in Peru, Francisco Pizarro's group met the Inca emperor Atahualpa (shown kneeling). When he refused to acquiesce to either Christianity or the Spanish Crown, they captured and killed him.

Spain's rivals also attempted to establish colonies in the Americas, paying no attention to the pope's line of demarcation. Some inroads were made on Spanish territory; for example, England, Holland, and France acquired islands in the West Indies. However, the Spanish Empire in the Americas remained otherwise largely intact until the early 1800s.

Charles V

While Spanish explorers were creating a great empire outside Europe, Spanish kings expanded their authority in Spain itself. One of the greatest of these kings was Charles V, a member of the Habsburg family.

The Habsburgs were an old German family that often succeeded in increasing its land and power through marriages. A series of such marriages brought Charles to the Spanish throne in 1516. Three years later, he was elected Holy Roman emperor. Although he was the first king named Charles to rule Spain, he was the fifth Charles with the title Holy Roman emperor and is known in history as Charles V.

With Charles's titles and power came great responsibilities and conflicts. Born in Flanders, Charles, according to one historian, "spoke Flemish by choice, Spanish, French, and Italian to his officials, and German to his horse." As king of Spain, he needed to acquire a Spanish viewpoint. As Holy Roman emperor, however, he would be expected to support German aims. Charles was embroiled in religious conflicts in Germany; it was he who called Martin Luther to Worms in 1521. Moreover, as the secular leader of Christian Europe, Charles had to assume responsibility for defending Europe against the Ottoman Turks. The Ottoman Turks were invading central Europe and attacking European ships as they sailed in the Mediterranean.

Charles V halted the Turkish penetration of central Europe by driving the Turks away from Vienna in 1529. Religious wars between Catholics and Lutherans in Germany were temporarily settled by the 1555 Peace of Augsburg. Yet the nearly continuous wars drained Spain's human and financial resources.

European Overseas Empires, 1700

Learning from Maps European countries governed territories across the globe.

ENMARK

EUROPE

ASIA

60°N

AFRICA

ARABIA

CHINA

JAPAN

30°N

HIMALAYAS

INDIA

Ft. Williams
(Calcutta)

FORMOSA
(TAIWAN)

Macao

PACIFIC
OCEAN

Bombay

Madras

Goa

Pondicherry

Manila

PHILIPPINES

Cochin

CEYLON

Strait of
Malacca

SUMATRA

Malacca

BORNEO

MOLUCCAS
(SPICE ISLANDS)

Equator   0°

uanda

Malindi
Mombasa
Kilwa

NGOLA

Mozambique

MADAGASCAR

INDIAN
OCEAN

Batavia
(Jakarta)

JAVA

TIMOR

NEW GUINEA

MAURITIUS
BOURBON (RÉUNION)

AUSTRALIA
(NEW HOLLAND)

30°S

ape
wn

Cape of
Good Hope

NEW
ZEALAND

TASMANIA

60°S

	Spanish territory		Dutch territory
	Portuguese territory		French territory
	English territory		

30°E

60°E

90°E

120°E

150°E

180°

ANTARCTICA

❓ **Region** What countries controlled port cities in India?

In this scene, Charles V observes the ladies taking their turn at the hunt.

Charles V himself retired to a monastery, where he continued to take an interest in political affairs. He died in 1558.

Philip II

Unlike his father Charles V, Philip II was born and educated in Spain. He ruled until his death in 1598. Philip had such a dedicated sense of responsibility that he had almost no private life and worked long hours at the business of being king. He wanted to make Spain stronger at home so that it might continue as Europe's leading power. He made the central government responsible only to the king.

Philip built a new royal residence, El Escorial, 25 miles from Madrid. From there, surrounded by mounds of government papers, he drew the reins of the government so tightly that he almost paralyzed the administration. Philip II also saw himself as the leader of the Counter-Reformation. A very devout Catholic, he ordered the Spanish Inquisition to redouble its efforts to find and stamp out heresy at home. Abroad Philip became involved in wars to defend Catholicism and advance Spain's glory. These wars further drained the Spanish treasury. As taxes never kept up with expenses and bankers charged more and more interest on loans they made to Spain, the government's financial problems grew worse.

Philip found it impossible to subdue all the enemies of Spanish power and of Catholicism. He defeated the Ottoman Empire in the Mediterranean, but an attempted invasion of England in 1588 by a huge fleet, the Spanish Armada, ended in disaster. An attempt to invade France to prevent a Protestant from becoming king also proved an expensive failure. The most costly disaster of all resulted from Philip's policy toward the Netherlands.

The Rise of the Dutch

The provinces of the Netherlands that Philip II inherited had been a great trading center and one of Europe's richest areas since the Middle Ages. The people of these provinces had a proud tradition of independence. By the 1550s, Calvinism was already making headway in the area. Philip II's harsh treatment of his subjects in the Netherlands led to catastrophe for Spain.

The people of the Netherlands strongly distrusted Philip, who turned this distrust into outright rebellion by making three fundamental errors. First, he ignored the long tradition of self-rule in the Netherlands and insisted that he, not the local nobles, held all authority. Second, he taxed the Netherlands' trade heavily

Spain lacked industries, and the government did little to encourage them. It also had difficulty feeding its people because so much land was devoted to raising sheep for wool. Food prices quintupled between 1500 and the mid-1600s. Charles's government, although tightly controlled by him, could not operate efficiently over a realm that included lands scattered throughout Europe as well as colonies overseas in the Americas.

Charles V realized that this scattered empire had become too large for any one monarch to rule. In 1556 he gave up his throne and divided his vast lands between members of his family. Charles's son Philip II received Spain and its possessions, and his branch of the family became known as the Spanish Habsburgs. Charles's brother Ferdinand I, king of Hungary and Bohemia, became Holy Roman emperor and head of the Austrian branch of the Habsburg family.

Young Woman with a Water Jug

What does this young woman see as she gazes through the window? On the wall behind her is a map, and perhaps it has led her thoughts to faraway places. The window lets light in on her starched linen headdress, and the Sun sparkles on the metal pitcher and tray, defining the pattern on the Asian tablecloth. The cloth is an example of the varied goods that overseas trade brought to the Dutch people after they had won their independence from Spain.

In the 1600s, Dutch merchants grew rich enough to buy handsome silks and linens for their wives and to commission artists to paint for them. Artists flourished in the prosperous economy of the Netherlands, and Jan Vermeer, who painted this picture, was one of the finest. His painting gives us a close look at daily Dutch life.

The Metropolitan Museum of Art, Marquand Collection, Gift of Henry G. Marquand, 1889. (89.15.21). Photograph © 1993 The Metropolitan Museum of Art.

Vermeer's *Young Woman with a Water Jug*

to finance Spanish wars. Third, he persecuted the Calvinists.

In 1568 a revolt led by William the Silent, the prince of Orange, grew so strong that Philip could not stop it. The people of the Calvinist northern provinces lived on land that was below sea level, protected by large dikes. They opened the dikes, flooding the countryside and leaving Philip's army helpless. William relied on swift raids by bands of soldiers to keep the Spanish army off balance. Today we call this military technique **guerrilla warfare**.

In 1579, under William the Silent's leadership, the northern provinces declared their independence from Spain and became known as the United Provinces of the Netherlands. Today we refer to this area as simply the Netherlands.

William was assassinated in 1584, but his sons continued the struggle against Spain. The war continued, interrupted by a 12-year truce from 1609 to 1621, until 1648, when the northern provinces won their independence. Spain did manage to win back the loyalty of the heavily Catholic southern provinces of the Netherlands, partly because Philip

promised them greater self-rule. The southern region remained under the rule of Spain and was known as the Spanish Netherlands. (See map on page 106.) In 1713, when the Austrian Habsburgs took possession, it became known as the Austrian Netherlands. Since 1830 it has been the independent country of Belgium.

Dutch society. The people of the northern provinces of the Netherlands—the Dutch—created one of Europe's most remarkable societies. The Netherlands lay on the North Sea, and the Dutch, a seafaring people, built very efficient ships and became excellent sailors. Primarily traders, they dominated European commerce throughout the 1600s. Their ships carried most of Europe's trade. The city of Amsterdam became a world financial center. Dutch banks, trading companies, manufacturing enterprises—especially shipbuilding—and overseas colonies became models of efficiency.

The Dutch had a relatively open society. Calvinists did become the dominant religious group, and only Calvinists could hold political offices. The Dutch generally, however, moved toward a policy of religious toleration.

Amsterdam also became a lively cultural center. The philosopher René Descartes, the scholar of international law and freedom of the seas Hugo Grotius, and the painter Rembrandt thrived in this comfortable and inspiring setting.

The Dutch colonial empire. In the age of exploration, Dutch merchants set up a number of companies to trade in various parts of the world. In 1602 the Dutch combined several of their trading companies into one powerful organization, the Dutch East India Company. The Dutch government gave this company the sole right to carry on trade between the Netherlands and Africa and the East Indies.

The Dutch established their first colony in Asia in 1619 on the island of Java. From Java they expanded westward to take the island of Sumatra and eastward to seize the valuable Spice Islands from the Portuguese. Next came Malacca and the island of Ceylon, as well as Cochin on the southwest coast of India. In 1652 the Dutch founded a colony at the Cape of Good Hope, which helped them supply and protect their trade routes to Asia and along the African coast.

The Portuguese had held only strategic points along the coasts in order to control the sea-lanes. The Dutch, however, realized that a successful empire required much more extensive control, both on the land and over the people. They did not stop with establishing a trading post at Batavia (now Jakarta) on the island of Java, for example, but instead took over the entire island with its crops of sugar, tea, coffee, and spices.

The Dutch even gained some commercial influence in Japan. Because they had not come as missionaries, the shogun—the Japanese military ruler—allowed the Dutch to trade in Japan and to operate a trading post at Nagasaki.

In the Western Hemisphere, the Dutch founded colonies in three areas—the West Indies, South America, and North America. In 1626 they purchased Manhattan Island from the Indians. There they founded New Amsterdam, which later became known as New York City.

The colonial empire that the Dutch established differed significantly from that of the Spanish. At no time did the Dutch try to convert the people they conquered to Christianity or force them to speak Dutch or to live under the laws of the Netherlands. The Dutch came as traders, with the intention of making money. In this sense, the overseas empire of the Netherlands reflected the businesslike society of the home country.

Decline of the Spanish Empire

The revolt of the Netherlands against Spanish rule in 1579 marked the beginning of the decline of the mighty Spanish Empire. A number of factors led to this decline. One factor was a steadily growing population—more people needed to be fed, clothed, and housed. At the same time, gold and silver flowed into Spain from the colonies. As a result of this gold and silver flowing into Spain, the increase in the amount of money drove up prices in Spain. Because it cost more to produce goods in Spain than in other countries, Spanish industry declined.

An enterprising middle class might have helped Spanish industries develop despite these obstacles. Many Spanish nobles, however, preferred military careers. Some of the ablest individuals chose careers in the church rather than in secular life. In addition, Spain expelled first the Jews and later the Moriscos—Moorish converts to Christianity who were suspected of secretly practicing Islam. Unfortunately for the Spanish economy, many Moriscos were skilled farmers and able artisans. The expulsion of the Jews and the Moriscos may have contributed to the weakening of Spain's economy.

Much of the wealth from its empire simply passed through Spain because it was used to buy goods from other nations. In contrast, with the gold and silver they received for goods they sold to Spain, Spain's enemies—France, England, and the Netherlands—developed their own industries and grew strong at Spain's expense.

At home, high taxation and inflation brought on economic discontent. This discontent, along with agricultural failures, caused many country people to leave their homes and eventually led to their emigration from Spain.

Section 3 Review

1. **Define** viceroys, guerrilla warfare
2. **Identify** Juan Ponce de Léon, Hernán Cortés, Moctezuma, Francisco Pizarro, Charles V, Philip II
3. **Locate and Explain the Significance** Tenochtitlán
4. **Understanding Ideas** Describe the growth of the Spanish colonial empire.
5. **Contrasting Ideas** How did the Dutch colonial empire differ from the Spanish colonial empire?
6. **Interpreting Ideas** Why did Spanish power decline in the late 1500s?

France in the Age of Absolutism

Focus Questions

- **How did Henry IV and Cardinal Richelieu strengthen France?**
- **What was the Thirty Years' War?**
- **How was central authority strengthened during the reign of Louis XIV?**

Following Spain's slow decline, France, under King Louis XIV, emerged as the leading European power. It had recovered rapidly from the religious wars of the 1500s, thanks to the policies of Henry IV, the first monarch of a new royal house in France, the Bourbons. Assisted by two shrewd Roman Catholic cardinals, the Bourbons would make the monarchy absolute in France.

Henry IV

Henry IV was from Navarre—a tiny kingdom that straddled the Pyrenees between France and Spain. He ruled France from 1589 to 1610. Henry had been a Huguenot, but he realized he could not rule France successfully as a member of a religious minority. Wanting to rule a strong, united, and peaceful kingdom, he converted to Catholicism, reportedly remarking, "Paris is well worth a mass!" To protect the Huguenots, however, he issued a special order, the Edict of Nantes, which guaranteed freedom of worship and political rights. The edict defused the religious conflict and ended the civil wars.

Henry also attempted to resolve other major problems. Powerful nobles had undermined royal authority in the 1500s, and Henry worked to restore the power of the central government. He also attempted to discipline the army and rebuild the infrastructure of the country. France's financial difficulties, however, defied easy solutions. The French system of taxation was inefficient, corrupt, and unjust. As in the Roman Empire, **tax farming**, selling the right to collect taxes to private individuals called tax farmers, was common. These tax farmers paid the government a fixed sum, collected all they could, and kept any surplus. Many became rich. Furthermore, because the nobles and clergy did not pay the direct tax, called the taille (TY),

and had few other taxes to pay, the tax burden fell most heavily on the peasants.

Henry chose the able Duke of Sully as minister in charge of finances. Even Sully, however, could not make the system truly fair. Nobles and clergy continued to be largely free from taxation. Nevertheless, Sully abolished some unnecessary public offices and stopped certain tax collection abuses. As a result, the treasury showed a sizable surplus, which provided funds to finance trade and industry.

Cardinal Richelieu's Program for France

Henry IV's son and successor, Louis XIII, was only eight years old when a fanatical monk stabbed his father to death in 1610. The boy's mother, Marie de Medici, became regent—the ruler of France until Louis came of age.

Louis XIII came of age in 1614, but his mother continued to rule for three years thereafter. Louis's health was poor and he suffered from a lack of concentration, but he quickly learned to select good advisers who provided firm leadership. Louis chose as his chief

In addition to supporting the arts and the University of Paris, Cardinal Richelieu founded the French Academy, which continues to reflect literary standards today.

minister Cardinal Richelieu (RISH·uhl·oo), who ran the government of France from 1624 until 1642.

A political genius, Richelieu had a keen understanding of the possibilities of politics and diplomacy. He wanted to make the king supreme in France, and France supreme in Europe. To accomplish the first aim, he set out to destroy the power of the nobles and the remaining political independence of the Huguenots, which had been protected by the Edict of Nantes. In addition, he wanted to strengthen France economically by continuing Sully's policy of encouraging trade and industry. To make France supreme in Europe, Richelieu planned to reduce the power of the Spanish and Austrian Habsburgs.

Huguenots. Richelieu believed that the provisions of the Edict of Nantes allowing the Huguenots to control fortified cities were politically dangerous. The Huguenot cities, which were like states within a state, made strong centralized government impossible. In 1627 Richelieu himself, temporarily trading his cardinal's hat for a military helmet, directed the attacks on the Huguenot seaport of La Rochelle and other fortified towns. The next year, after stubborn but futile resistance, the Huguenots asked for peace. Richelieu took away their special rights in fortified cities, but he allowed the Huguenots to continue to worship freely, hold public office, and attend schools and colleges.

Nobles. The cardinal next turned to the problem of the nobles to finish the work that Henry IV had begun. To crush the nobles' military power, he ordered that any of their fortified castles not necessary for the defense of France be leveled. Then he reduced their political power. With the king's consent, the cardinal appointed as governors of provinces only well-educated professionals who favored a strong monarchy. He also strengthened the power of the regional administrators known as **intendants**. To hold these positions, he chose middle-class people who had no interest in advancing the power of the nobles. Richelieu gave the intendants strong administrative powers and made them directly responsible to the king, who appointed them and could remove them.

The Thirty Years' War

Richelieu's foreign policy was as determined and calculating as his policy at home. He did not allow his position as a Catholic cardinal to interfere with his primary goal of strengthening France at the expense of the Habsburgs. The Thirty Years' War (1618–1648) offered a golden opportunity to achieve this goal.

The Thirty Years' War actually consisted of stretches of fighting interrupted by intervals of peace. It began because the religious conflicts between Protestants and Catholics in Germany had never completely died down following the Peace of Augsburg in 1555. Constant rivalry continued among the more than 300 German princes, who also wanted to be independent of the Holy Roman emperor. In addition, France, Denmark, and Sweden were all looking for opportunities to diminish the power of the Habsburgs and the Holy Roman Empire.

The war began in 1618 in Prague, when Protestant rebels threw two emissaries of the Holy Roman emperor from a castle window. The incident erupted into a rebellion, which the emperor sent troops to suppress. Protestant German princes and Protestant Danes went to war against him. The emperor defeated the king of Denmark, who had to promise not to interfere in German affairs. Sweden then took up arms.

Cardinal Richelieu favored the Swedes over the Catholic Habsburgs, but he believed that it was in France's interest to prolong the war without involving France directly. The other nations would become weak from fighting, while France remained strong. Most of the battles of the Thirty Years' War took place in Germany, much of which became a wasteland through fire, disease, and plundering by soldiers. France eventually joined the war against the Habsburgs. By 1648 the French and their allies had achieved many of their aims.

The participants in the Thirty Years' War, many exhausted after the years of fighting, signed the Treaty of Westphalia in 1648. (See map on page 99.) France was strengthened by receiving Alsace, a valuable territory along the Rhine River. The Treaty of Westphalia recognized the Netherlands and Switzerland as independent nations, which weakened the Habsburgs. The Habsburgs suffered further blows because the peace made the princes in Germany virtually independent of the Holy Roman emperor.

Because the Austrian Habsburgs no longer exercised any real authority in Germany, they began to look eastward rather than westward. They paid more attention to their own possessions—Austria, Bohemia, and Hungary—and eventually created a new empire centered along the Danube River instead of in Germany.

The Fronde. Although France emerged more powerful from the Peace of Westphalia, a series of rebellions erupted in the country between 1648 and 1652. These rebellions were known as the Fronde, from the French word for "sling." The term compared the rebels—Frondeurs—to mischievous schoolboys who use slingshots when the teacher looks away. Nobles led the rebellions, but many peasants and the citizens of Paris also supported them. The Fronde threatened the centralized royal power that Richelieu and Cardinal Mazarin, his successor, had built up. The Frondeurs wanted to revive the independence of localities and the power of the nobility. Mazarin crushed the Fronde, although with some difficulty, and no major attempts to restrict the French royal power were made for more than 135 years.

The Sun King

Louis XIV, whose 72-year reign from 1643 to 1715 was the longest in French history, benefited from the strengthening of central authority. While a boy, Louis had witnessed the rebellion of the Fronde in Paris. It may have been the dangers and humiliation he faced during that time that made him determined to allow no opposition and to make his power absolute.

Versailles. As a way to help accomplish these goals, Louis built an enormous palace at Versailles (ver·SY), a few miles outside of Paris. There he established his court and moved the French government. The elaborate palace cost an immense sum that strained the French economy. Louis was denounced as being too extravagant and was even accused of trying to ruin the nation financially.

The palace emphasized the grandeur and power of Louis XIV and France. Louis believed in the **divine right of kings**, meaning that God had ordained him to govern France. "L'état, c'est moi" ("I am the state"), he proclaimed.

To increase royal authority over the nobility, Louis insisted that the most important nobles of France live at Versailles. There they had to serve him, helping him dress in the morning, joining him in the hunt—a passion with the Bourbons—performing the ceremonies of the court, and handing him his nightshirt when he went to bed. In this way, Louis could keep his eye on them. Instead of trying to gain power by fighting the monarchy, the nobility now could advance only by getting royal favors and offices.

Versailles and its absolute monarch became the ideal of European royalty. European nobility adopted the language and customs of France. Louis XIV adopted as his personal emblem the Sun, whose rays symbolized the extent of his power and influence. He looked like a king, lived like a king, and behaved like a king.

The policies of Louis XIV. Louis chose competent advisers, although he made most important decisions himself. One of his most outstanding advisers was

Louis XIV (shown on the horse above the crowd in this painting) encouraged improvements in most realms of French society, from art and literature to transportation.

Jean-Baptiste Colbert (kawl·BAIR), an expert in finance. Colbert, a member of the middle class, followed Sully's ideas in promoting economic development. He tried to bolster French industry at home and French trade abroad. He granted government subsidies to private companies to build new industries or strengthen existing ones. He placed high tariffs on foreign imports and improved transportation. Colbert encouraged French companies to establish colonies and carry on trade with Canada, the West Indies, and East Asia.

Like Sully, Colbert also tried to eliminate corruption and waste in the tax-farming system. His efforts resulted for a time in the accumulation of enough money to pay for economic improvements, a large army, and exploration abroad.

Louis XIV was concerned about religious disunity in France. The Huguenots, he believed, disturbed the unity of the country and weakened the central authority. Consequently, in 1685 he revoked the Edict of Nantes, ending the policy of toleration for Protestants.

More than 200,000 productive Protestant citizens fled France rather than become Catholics, a development that weakened France in the long run.

The Wars of Louis XIV

Louis chose as his secretary of state for war the Marquis de Louvois (loov·WAH), a military genius who completely reorganized the army. Officers and soldiers received extensive training and followed strict discipline. The officer responsible for this training, General Jean Martinet, furnished a word to the language: anyone who is a strict disciplinarian is called a martinet. By the early 1700s, the French had a force of 400,000 well-trained soldiers, an army larger and more powerful than Europe had ever seen.

Why did Louis XIV need such a large army? He had territorial ambitions and was convinced that France's security depended on the country having natural frontiers. The Alps, the Mediterranean Sea, the Pyrenees, the Atlantic Ocean, and the English Channel already protected France in the southeast, south, southwest, and northwest. Like Richelieu, Louis wanted to make France even safer by extending its territory to the Rhine River, its natural frontier on the northeast and east. To gain his ends, Louis fought four wars between 1667 and 1713. (See map on opposite page.)

Louis's goals alarmed the other European countries, which united to counteract the great power of France. At various times, the Netherlands, England, and Spain, as well as Austria, Brandenburg, and other German states, formed alliances to amass enough power to equal or surpass that of France. The maintenance of an equilibrium in international politics is known as the **balance of power**.

The wars took a tremendous toll on France's resources. By the end of Louis's third war, in 1697, France was under tremendous financial strain. Louis even melted down the royal silver to help pay for his wars.

War of the Spanish Succession. The War of the Spanish Succession was Louis XIV's last war. It was fought over the question of who should succeed to the throne of Spain. The last Spanish Habsburg king had died in 1700, leaving the throne to a French prince, Philip of Anjou, Louis's grandson.

The other European nations feared the prospect of Bourbon rulers in both Spain and France. Dreading the possibility of the two nations under one monarch, the nations of Europe went to war with Louis. Battles raged throughout Europe, on the high seas, and in America.

French armies and fleets met defeats everywhere, and Louis finally agreed to a settlement in 1713.

The European settlement in 1713. The Treaty of Utrecht, which ended the War of the Spanish Succession, became important in the history of both Europe and America. It recognized Louis XIV's grandson as King Philip V of Spain but provided that the French and Spanish crowns were never to be united. Great Britain became France's chief enemy because the treaty gave it lands in North America at the expense of France.

The French Colonial Empire

The empire that France began to lose after the War of the Spanish Succession had begun in the early 1500s. French explorers such as Jacques Cartier (kahr·TYAY) made several voyages to North America. Cartier's voyage up the St. Lawrence River as far as Montreal in 1535 to 1536 gave the French a claim to much of eastern Canada. Not until 1608, however, when Samuel de Champlain founded Quebec, did they make a permanent settlement.

France then established several other settlements in the St. Lawrence Valley and in the Great Lakes region. The French developed a profitable fur trade with the Indians and engaged in fishing cod off Newfoundland and Nova Scotia.

Between 1679 and 1682, René-Robert de La Salle sailed down the Mississippi River to the Gulf of Mexico and claimed the entire inland region of North America for France. He named the region Louisiana in honor of Louis XIV. French settlement in North America grew very slowly, however. Elsewhere in the Americas, the French occupied Haiti and the sugar producing islands of Guadeloupe and Martinique in the West Indies.

The French also established colonies in Asia. On the southeast coast of India, the French East India Company established a trading post at Pondicherry in 1674 and controlled part of India through the 1700s.

The Legacy of Louis XIV

Louis XIV died in 1715. His endless wars in which so many lives were lost and so much money was spent had exhausted the French people. Nevertheless, despite his defeats, the Sun King had in fact made France a very powerful nation. While Great Britain became the strongest colonial power, within Europe France remained the largest, the richest, and the most influential nation.

After Louis's death, the nobles won back many of the powers they had been deprived of under his rule. For the next 50 years, the French government seemed stable. Beneath this appearance of stability, however, lay a decline in royal authority that led to revolution. Louis XIV's great-grandson and successor, Louis XV, proved to be an ineffectual ruler partly because of his lack of self-confidence. During his reign (1715–1774), a succession of ministers ran the country.

The Growth of France Under Louis XIV, 1643–1715

Learning from Maps Louis XIV made France a large and powerful nation, extending its territory in three directions.

Place What city in southeastern France remained outside Louis XIV's control?

Eastern and Central Europe in the Age of Absolutism

Focus Questions

- Why was Russia isolated from western Europe?
- What changes did Peter the Great and Catherine the Great bring to Russia?
- What problems faced the Habsburgs and the Hohenzollerns in eastern Europe, and what conflicts resulted from them?

While in the countries of western Europe national governments were strengthened at the expense of local authorities and the nobility, the new empires of Russia, Prussia, and Austria developed in eastern and central Europe.

Russian Isolation

After more than 200 years of Mongol rule, Russia became an independent country in 1480. By this time, the rulers of Moscow had become the most important in Russia, and they continued to expand their power and territory by conquests, marriages, and alliances.

Building History Study Skills

READ
WRITE
INTERPRET
CONNECT
THINK

Reading About History: Making Inferences

As you study history, you often read a source to understand the facts of an event or events the author is explaining. For example, read the following description of Versailles.

"The palace of Versailles cost 5 million livres out of a total state budget of 120 million livres.... In 1682, 22,000 workers were laboring on it; the next year, there were 36,000. In 230 acres of gardens, 1,400 fountains were installed, and 25,000 full-grown trees were transplanted in one year so that Louis XIV would not have to wait for saplings to grow."

The facts of the quotation are obvious. Thousands of people worked on the palace at Versailles (shown in photo), and the construction cost a great deal of money. By "reading between the lines," however, you can find information that is only implied—for example, that Louis XIV possessed great power.

When you read between the lines, you are using your reasoning ability to discover new meanings. In this way, you can identify something that the writer does not actually state. Your identifications are called inferences.

How to Make Inferences
To make inferences, follow these steps.
1. Select the main idea or literal interpretation.
2. Look for clues that suggest, or imply, additional meaning, such as key phrases or emotional words.
3. Add the clues to the original interpretation.
4. Create a revised meaning based on the connection between the stated ideas and the implied ideas.

Developing the Skill
In the following selection from *A Description of East India Company,* Peter Van Dam, an officer of the company, describes how the Dutch government stimulated and promoted trade by establishing the Dutch East India Company. What inferences can you make about the key to the company's success?

"The Company's charter authorized it to make alliances with princes and potentates east of the Cape of Good Hope and beyond the Straits of Magellan, to make contracts, build fortresses and strongholds, name governors, raise troops, appoint officers of justice, and perform other necessary services for the advancement of trade. ...The Company after the date of this charter has made great progress in the Indies. It has captured a number of fortresses from the Spaniards and the Portuguese...and has established trading posts at several places. It was decided as a consequence that it was desirable to establish a formal government in the Indies."

The selection states that the company could make treaties and set up governments. The key phrases "made great progress" and "as a consequence" are clues that can help you "read between the lines." These phrases indicate that although the company was set up for trade, it had many political successes. One inference that you can make is that the company owed its economic success to the political powers that it enjoyed. Control of certain political rights was linked to the development of trade. The Dutch East India Company was a political as well as an economic organization.

Practicing the Skill
Read a political article in the newspaper or listen to a televised news program that focuses on a political issue. Then list several facts and any inferences you can make from the article or program.

To apply this skill, see Applying History Study Skills on page 111.

Moscow's rulers differed widely in their abilities, but a few had the qualities needed to build a large and powerful state.

Several factors—both cultural and physical—tended to separate Russia from western Europe. One factor was an Asian influence resulting from Mongol domination. Another factor was that Western civilization had reached Russia from Constantinople and the Byzantine Empire, not from western Europe. Russia's religion was Eastern Orthodox rather than Roman Catholic or Protestant. Russia's use of the Cyrillic alphabet posed a barrier to communication for Russia with the rest of Europe, which used the Roman alphabet.

Most importantly, Russia's geography isolated the country from the rest of Europe. The country was almost entirely landlocked. The stronger kingdoms of Sweden and Poland blocked Russia from the Baltic Sea. To the south, the Ottoman Turks held the coast of the Black Sea. To the west, the vast plains of Poland and eastern Europe hindered commercial contacts. Russia's many navigable rivers did not flow into the great oceans and seas of commerce.

A new dynasty. Some 20 years after the death of Ivan the Terrible in 1584, Russia underwent a period of unrest. Nobles fought for power, various claimants sought the throne, and Russia's neighbors invaded. Then in 1613 a national assembly elected as czar Michael Romanov, the first of the Romanov dynasty, which would rule Russia for 300 years.

In the mid-1600s, the response of the Romanov rulers to events in Russia strengthened the monarchy. Representative institutions were restrained. The government repressed religious dissenters called Old Believers, who opposed reforms decreed by the patriarch of Moscow. It established mutually beneficial relations with Cossacks, peasants who had fled from Polish serfdom and settled on Russia's southern frontier. Moreover, the Romanovs established serfdom more firmly during this time.

In this way, the czars continued and reinforced the Russian form of absolutism created by Ivan the Terrible. In 1682 Peter I became czar at the age of 10, co-ruling with his half brother and half sister. He became the sole ruler of Russia in 1689. A leader of remarkable vision, Czar Peter I used his power to change Russia in important ways.

Peter the Great

Czar Peter I ruled Russia until 1725. An energetic giant of a man—more than six and a half feet tall—he had dark hair and eyes, a swarthy complexion, and a prominent nose. Peter also had a violent temper and was capable of great cruelty. His suspicions that his son Alexis was disloyal led to Alexis's death in prison. This strong-willed and ruthless czar decided that Russia's future lay toward Europe.

One of Peter's major goals was to enable Russia to end its landlocked situation and acquire warm-water ports on the Sea of Azov and the Black Sea. The Ottoman Empire, which controlled all the land between the Black Sea and the Mediterranean Sea, blocked that ambition. Peter realized that to defeat the Turks he would need two things: help from western Europe and a stronger, more efficient Russia.

Peter's foreign mission. In 1697 Peter, who often disguised himself as a private citizen, went with a Russian delegation to several countries in western Europe to negotiate an alliance against the Turks. The mission failed in that purpose, but it was of great importance because the czar learned about the West. He met leaders in many fields of activity and learned from scientists and artisans. He even worked as a carpenter in a Dutch East India Company shipyard to learn ship construction.

Westernization. Peter decided to remodel Russia along western European lines. Influenced by the example of France, he reorganized his army and equipped it with better weapons. He then engaged the army in a long war (1700–1721) with Sweden, which resulted in Russia gaining territory with access to the Baltic Sea. The war also ended Sweden's short-lived role as a great power in Europe.

In this new territory on the eastern coast of the Gulf of Finland, Peter built a completely new city, St. Petersburg. (See map on page 103.) In 1703 he moved the capital from Moscow to St. Petersburg, bringing the center of Russian government closer to the nations of western Europe. As Russia's "window to the West," St. Petersburg came to symbolize the new Russian policy of westernization.

Westernization meant many things. Women abandoned some of their former isolation and took a greater part in community life. The czar forced the nobles to give up their long robes—suitable for Russia's long, bitterly cold winters—and wear European-style short coats. Peter also forced men to shave off their long beards.

Much more important, however, were Peter's changes in Russian trade, finance, industry, and government. Armies and navies cost money to operate; to obtain this money, Peter imposed taxes on nearly everything. He also encouraged the development of foreign trade and manufacturing.

In government Peter followed the absolutist ideas of Louis XIV of France. The czar had complete control of a highly centralized administration, and the nobles were merely his agents. As in France, the monarchy controlled local governments. The Orthodox Church, too, fell under Peter's control.

The nobility. Peter created a new service nobility, whose rank and privileges depended on the amount of government service performed rather than on family status. In return for government service, Peter granted the nobles large estates with thousands of serfs. His changes not only increased the number of serfs but also worsened their condition. At a time when serfdom was declining rapidly throughout western Europe, the czar began a policy of binding the Russian serfs to their lords as well as to the land. When the serfs rebelled, they were brutally crushed.

Although Peter failed to westernize Russian society completely, under his leadership Russia became a great power. Few individuals in history have made so strong a personal mark on their time.

Catherine the Great

Peter was succeeded by his second wife, Catherine I, who ruled for two years. She was followed by several other Romanov rulers. Peter's daughter Elizabeth

Peter the Great built the city of St. Petersburg to be the capital of his empire.

undercurrent of discontent that finally exploded in revolution in Russia in the 1900s.

It was Catherine's foreign policy—a continuation of the expansionist policies of Peter the Great—that made her great. Russia still sought warm-water ports through the control of the Sea of Azov and the Black Sea. In a successful war against the Turks, Catherine won control of most of the northern shore of the Black Sea and a protectorate over the Crimea.

This painting shows Peter the Great disguised as a Dutch shipbuilder. He toured western Europe to familiarize himself with advances in European technology.

then ruled from 1741 to 1762 and paved the way for Catherine II, later known as Catherine the Great.

A princess from a small German state, Catherine had married the heir to the Russian throne, Elizabeth's nephew and Peter the Great's grandson. However, her unpopular husband, who became Peter III, preferred Prussians and Prussia to anything Russian. Peter III ruled for only six months in 1762 and then was murdered by powerful nobles who supported Catherine. She ruled from that time until 1796.

Domestic and foreign policy. Catherine II did not earn her title "the Great" from her domestic policy. Her support of art, science, literature, and the theater had little meaning or value to most Russians, who lived in deep ignorance and poverty. She extended serfdom into the new lands she acquired, and the masses—the common people—lived much as they had before. Under Catherine II, the nobility, however, became more westernized. They spoke French and lost touch with most of the Russian people. The vast gap between rulers and ruled helps explain the

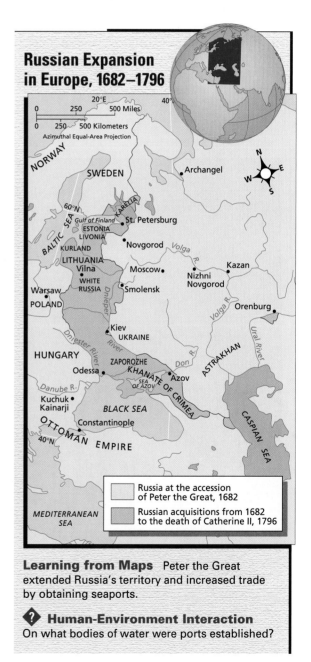

Russian Expansion in Europe, 1682–1796

| | Russia at the accession of Peter the Great, 1682 |
| | Russian acquisitions from 1682 to the death of Catherine II, 1796 |

Learning from Maps Peter the Great extended Russia's territory and increased trade by obtaining seaports.

❓ Human-Environment Interaction
On what bodies of water were ports established?

The Polish question. Catherine also made great territorial gains to the west. There the kingdom of Poland was large but weak. Its kings were elected by the nobles. The election campaigns to determine who would be king invited domestic and international troubles. Prussia, Austria, France, and Russia each repeatedly plotted to put its favorite on the Polish throne.

In Poland's legislature, only nobles were represented. The legislature rarely accomplished anything because any one member could veto any legislation being considered.

Poland contained large minority groups of various nationalities and religions. Most Poles were Roman Catholic, and they and their leaders often discriminated against and oppressed minority groups. Sometimes the oppressed groups appealed to Prussia, Austria, or Russia for help.

In 1772 these three powers decided to take advantage of Poland's weak condition and seize slices of Polish territory for themselves. This action is known as the First Partition of Poland. (See map on opposite page.)

The Poles were unable to resist the partition. In 1791 they tried to reform and strengthen their nation by adopting a new constitution. This constitution would have established a hereditary monarchy and abolished the veto privileges in the legislature. However, in 1793 Russia and Prussia took another helping of Polish lands with the Second Partition. In the Third Partition by Austria, Prussia, and Russia in 1795, Poland disappeared from the map of Europe until 1919.

Catherine the Great had not only wrested control of the Black Sea from the Turks but had also acquired the largest share of Poland. She had added more than

Catherine the Great supported art and literature, favored the education of women, and built hospitals.

The Partitions of Poland, 1772–1795

1772
SWEDEN
BALTIC SEA
WEST PRUSSIA
PRUSSIA
Danzig
Königsberg
EAST PRUSSIA
Riga
RUSSIAN EMPIRE
W. Dvina River
Neman River
Dnieper River
Vistula River
Warsaw
Kraków
SILESIA
GALICIA
Kiev
Dniester River
Vienna
AUSTRIA
Budapest
OTTOMAN EMPIRE
N W E S

1793
SWEDEN
BALTIC SEA
PRUSSIA
Danzig
Königsberg
Riga
RUSSIAN EMPIRE
W. Dvina River
Neman River
Dnieper River
Vistula River
Warsaw
Kraków
SILESIA
GALICIA
Kiev
Dniester River
Vienna
AUSTRIA
Budapest
OTTOMAN EMPIRE

1795
SWEDEN
BALTIC SEA
PRUSSIA
Danzig
Königsberg
Riga
RUSSIAN EMPIRE
W. Dvina River
Neman River
Dnieper River
Vistula River
Warsaw
Kraków
SILESIA
GALICIA
Kiev
Dniester River
Vienna
AUSTRIA
Budapest
OTTOMAN EMPIRE

Boundary of Poland before the partitions
Poland
Territory acquired by Russia
Territory acquired by Austria
Territory acquired by Prussia

0   150   300 Miles
0   150   300 Kilometers
Azimuthal Equal-Area Projection

Learning from Maps Catherine the Great acquired Poland through a series of partitions.

? Region By 1795 what countries had received sections of territory previously held by Poland?

200,000 square miles of territory to her empire. Russia's borders now extended well into central Europe, and Russia became a force to consider in the European balance of power.

Russian Expansion

Russia's expansion differed from that of the western European countries. Instead of expanding overseas, Russia expanded overland. In addition to the political expansion south and west, Russian settlers, spear-

headed by the freedom-loving Cossacks, moved eastward. In 1581 the Cossacks conquered the remnants of the Mongol Golden Horde and captured their capital city of Sibir. With that, the way lay open to the vast, sparsely populated region east of the Urals known as Siberia.

This region's rich fur trade drew many people. Much like the pioneers of the American West, the early Russian settlers built small posts for trade and defense. These grew into the towns and cities of Siberia. At the Amur River, Russians came in contact with the Chinese, who resisted Russian expansion into their country. In 1689 the Russians and Chinese signed a treaty that fixed the boundary between them north of the Amur River and provided for Chinese-Russian trade. By 1741 the Russians had crossed the Bering Strait and established a colony in Alaska in North America. Later Russian trading posts expanded southward.

What If?

Russian Expansion
Instead of colonizing lands across the seas as several European countries did, Russia expanded overland to its east through Siberia and colonized Alaska. If the Russians had colonized all of what is now Canada as well as Alaska, how might the history of the United States have been different?

Habsburg Austria

The Austrian Habsburgs lost much territory in the Thirty Years' War. In the 100 years after the war,

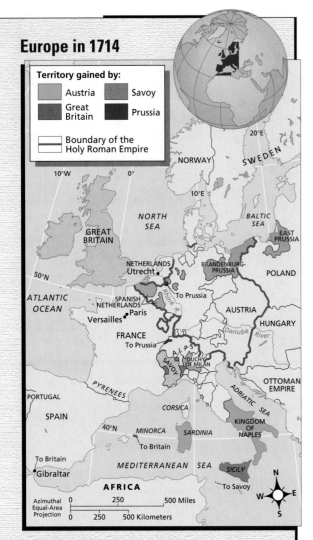

Europe in 1714

Territory gained by:
- Austria
- Savoy
- Great Britain
- Prussia
- Boundary of the Holy Roman Empire

20°E

NORWAY

SWEDEN

10°W   0°

10°E

NORTH SEA

BALTIC SEA

GREAT BRITAIN

EAST PRUSSIA

NETHERLANDS
Utrecht

BRANDENBURG-PRUSSIA

POLAND

50°N

ATLANTIC OCEAN

SPANISH NETHERLANDS

To Prussia

AUSTRIA

Versailles Paris

HUNGARY

FRANCE
To Prussia

Danube River

Rhine R.

ALPS

DUCHY OF MILAN

SAVOY

OTTOMAN EMPIRE

PORTUGAL

PYRENEES

ADRIATIC SEA

CORSICA

SPAIN

KINGDOM OF NAPLES

40°N   MINORCA   SARDINIA

To Britain

To Britain
Gibraltar

MEDITERRANEAN SEA

SICILY

To Savoy

AFRICA

N
W   E
S

Azimuthal Equal-Area Projection

0   250   500 Miles
0   250   500 Kilometers

Learning from Maps The governance of many European territories was redistributed by 1714.

? Region What four areas did Austria acquire?

however, Austria won new lands. These gains came in central Europe and the Balkans at the expense of the Turks and in territories received as a result of the Treaty of Utrecht. The Habsburgs now had an empire that extended into Hungary, the Balkans, and the Italian Peninsula.

In 1740 Holy Roman Emperor Charles VI died, leaving no sons and only his 23-year-old daughter, Maria Theresa, to inherit Austria and the other Habsburg lands. Charles had spent most of his reign (1711–1740) trying to persuade other European rulers to accept a statement called the Pragmatic Sanction.

By it, the rulers of Europe would promise to allow Maria Theresa to inherit the Habsburg lands intact, even though the law in some lands required that the inheritance go to a male.

The laws of the Holy Roman Empire also prevented Maria Theresa from being elected empress. She became Holy Roman empress in 1745, however, when her husband Francis was elected emperor.

Maria Theresa inherited a patchwork of territories and peoples: Germans, Hungarians, Italians, Belgians, Romanians, Poles, Bohemians, Serbs, Croatians, and Slovenes. This great variety led to many conflicts of language, religion, and nationality within the empire.

Several German states envied Habsburg power. For example, Bavaria, which is located in southern Germany, jealously guarded its lands and independence. They did this sometimes by forming alliances with France against the Habsburgs. Austria's chief rival was Brandenburg-Prussia, a small north German state that in 1740 did not even have a common boundary with Austria.

The Rise of the Hohenzollerns

During the Middle Ages, the Hohenzollerns had ruled only a small territory in southern Germany. The ambitious family wanted to increase its power, influence, and landholdings. Near the end of the Middle Ages, one branch of the family settled in Brandenburg, in northern Germany. The ruler of Brandenburg eventually became an elector of the Holy Roman Empire.

During the Reformation, the Protestant Hohenzollerns seized lands belonging to the Catholic Church in their territories. By the end of the Thirty Years' War in 1648, they ruled several widely scattered territories in Germany, including Prussia, which bordered the Baltic Sea.

The Hohenzollerns

1640–1688	Frederick William, the Great Elector
1688–1713	Frederick I
1713–1740	Frederick William I
1740–1786	Frederick II (the Great)

Maria Theresa (standing next to her husband, Francis) made improvements in education, medicine, and military affairs. Among her 16 children was Marie Antoinette, the future queen of France.

One of the greatest of the Hohenzollerns, Frederick William, called the Great Elector, guided his state through the difficult last years of the Thirty Years' War. After the Thirty Years' War ended, he then turned to the rebuilding and further strengthening of Brandenburg-Prussia. The Great Elector reorganized the armies of all his lands into one strong force. In addition to reorganizing his armies, he also improved the tax collection system and encouraged agriculture, industry, and transportation.

All the Hohenzollern possessions in northern Germany were called Prussia beginning with the reign of Frederick I (1688–1713), the Great Elector's successor and the first king of Prussia.* The original duchy of Prussia became known as East Prussia. (See map on opposite page.)

*As a reward for supporting the Habsburgs in the War of the Spanish Succession, the Holy Roman emperor granted Frederick I the title King of Prussia in 1701.

Frederick William I. Frederick I, one of the many European rulers who tried to imitate Louis XIV of France, maintained a large, lavish court. His son and successor, Frederick William I, disliked French ways intensely and got rid of much of this luxury when he became king in 1713.

Frederick William used the money he saved to strengthen Prussia. He doubled the size of the Prussian army and made it the most efficient fighting force in Europe. One of Frederick William's few extravagances was going to great expense to obtain tall soldiers, men between six and seven feet in height, from countries all over Europe, to form a regiment of giants.

In addition to strengthening the army, Frederick William created an efficient governmental bureaucracy. Tax collecting and government spending were carefully planned. Frederick William also encouraged trade and the development of new industries. Convinced that all children should have a primary education, he required that all parents send their children to school.

Europe in 1786

Legend:
- Possessions of the Austrian Habsburgs
- Possessions of the Hohenzollerns
- Boundary of Holy Roman Empire

0   250   500 Miles
0   250   500 Kilometers
Azimuthal Equal-Area Projection

Learning from Maps By 1763 the Habsburgs and Hohenzollerns both controlled vast lands in Europe.

Location What two cities stand on opposite sides of the Danube River?

Frederick the Great. Frederick William I worried that his son and successor, Frederick, showed little interest in either military life or government service. Instead, the youth wrote poetry, played the flute, and read philosophy. The king used the harshest methods, even imprisonment, to force his heir to become the kind of son he desired. Frederick and a companion tried to escape the country, but they were both caught. King Frederick William I forced his son to watch as his friend was executed.

Frederick William I need not have worried about his son's ability to lead his country. Frederick II— or Frederick the Great—proved to be an even stronger ruler than his father. He became king in

1740, the same year that Maria Theresa became ruler of Austria. Frederick II was highly intelligent, and he was also dedicated to expanding the territory and prestige of Prussia.

Conflict Between Prussia and Austria

Frederick William I had signed the Pragmatic Sanction guaranteeing Maria Theresa her Habsburg possessions. Shortly after becoming king, however, Frederick II marched the strong army his father had created into Silesia, one of Maria Theresa's most valuable provinces. Prussia had no legal claim to Silesia; the province had rich farmlands and iron deposits, however, and possessing it would add greatly to Prussia. Frederick seized it easily.

The conquest of Silesia marked the beginning of the first of two major European wars—the War of the Austrian Succession, which lasted from 1740 to 1748. In this war, Austria, Great Britain, the Netherlands, and eventually Russia were allied against Prussia, Bavaria, Spain, and France. Austria and its allies lost the war, and Silesia was ceded to Prussia.

The Diplomatic Revolution and the Seven Years' War. Several years after the War of the Austrian Succession there was a major "reversal of alliances," known as the Diplomatic Revolution, in Europe. Austria and Great Britain had since the time of Louis XIV been allied against the French. In 1756, however, Great Britain allied itself with powerful Prussia in an attempt to gain greater security; France, in an attempt to curb Prussia's power, allied itself with Austria and Russia. For many years afterward, France and Austria continued steadfastly to oppose Great Britain and Prussia.

These rivalries led to the Seven Years' War, which lasted from 1756 to 1763. Like the War of the Austrian Succession, the Seven Years' War involved almost all of Europe at one time or another. Because European countries had colonies overseas, the fighting was not limited to Europe. Battles were also fought between Great Britain and France in India and North America. In America the Seven Years' War is known as the French and Indian War. In fact, the fighting of the Seven Years' War actually began in North America.

At one point in the Seven Years' War, Prussia was opposed by virtually all the European powers except Britain and seemed on the brink of total defeat. Fighting against great odds, Frederick dashed from one front to another to direct his troops in holding off the invaders. Prussia was aided by the death of Empress Elizabeth of Russia, a bitter opponent. Her successor, Czar Peter III of Russia, admired Frederick and made peace with Prussia.

By the Treaty of Hubertusburg in 1763, Prussia kept Silesia. By the Treaty of Paris, which was signed in the same year, France lost most of its colonies in North America. The British gained control of Canada and of Louisiana east of the Mississippi River, and they remained dominant in India. The Seven Years' War ended, however, with no clear victor.

The years of peace. Frederick the Great spent the first 23 years of his reign at war. He spent the last 23 years of his reign showing that he also had a genius for organization and administration. He expanded and further improved public education and the already excellent Prussian civil service system. He made legal and court reforms and encouraged trade and manufacturing. He was committed to religious tolerance, although he had no interest in granting self-government to national or ethnic minorities under Prussian rule. Through Frederick's hard work and wise direction, the expanded state of Prussia recovered the prosperity it had lost during the long years of war. (See map on opposite page.)

Prussia also continued to make territorial gains. Frederick the Great helped to bring about the First Partition of Poland in 1772. By taking Polish territory along the Baltic coast, he linked Prussia and East Prussia. When he died in 1786, Frederick left a greatly enlarged and prosperous nation. Prussia had become a formidable rival of Austria for control of the German states and a first-class power in Europe.

Section 5 Review

1. **Identify** Peter the Great, Catherine the Great, Maria Theresa, the Great Elector, Frederick William I, Frederick the Great

2. **Locate and Explain the Significance** Moscow, Sea of Azov, Black Sea, St. Petersburg

3. **Understanding Ideas** What factors separated Russia from western Europe?

4. **Interpreting Ideas (a)** Describe how Peter the Great tried to westernize Russia both culturally and politically. **(b)** How did Catherine the Great continue Peter's foreign policy?

5. **Analyzing Ideas** How did Frederick the Great contribute to the growth of Prussia?

Chapter 2 Review

A.D. 1497–1498
Vasco da Gama makes his first voyage to India.

A.D. 1519–1522
Magellan-Elcano expedition sails around the world.

A.D. 1400

A.D. 1450

A.D. 1500

A.D. 1550

A.D. 1600

A.D. 1418
Portuguese explorations begin.

A.D. 1492
Columbus makes his first voyage.

A.D. 1516–1556
Charles V rules Spain.

A.D. 1613
Michael Romanov is elected czar.

A.D. 1556–1598
Philip II rules Spain.

Chapter Summary

The following list contains the key concepts you have learned about European expansion and the formation of strong, centralized monarchies in Europe from about 1400 to about 1800.

1. Europeans were able to expand overseas because they developed or improved techniques to be used in mapmaking, navigation, ship design, and weaponry.
2. The development of new economic policies and the Commercial Revolution that began in 1400 also enabled Europeans to begin large-scale overseas expansion.
3. The political and economic changes associated with overseas expansion contributed to a new economic theory called mercantilism.
4. Portuguese and Spanish explorers took the lead in discovering new lands and trade routes. Sometimes these countries came into conflict over their possessions.
5. Beginning with Portugal, European countries became involved in the slave trade in Africa.
6. Spain established a vast colonial empire and became the greatest power on the European continent until the mid-1600s. It lost this superiority, however, because of its foreign and domestic policies.
7. After the Dutch declared their independence from Spain, they created a large overseas empire. They dominated European commerce throughout the 1600s.
8. Cardinal Richelieu and Louis XIV weakened the Habsburgs and made France an absolute monarchy. Their ambition to expand to France's natural frontiers, territory reaching the Rhine River, brought France into a series of wars.
9. During the 1700s Peter the Great and Catherine the Great extended both the powers of the central government and the boundaries of Russia.
10. Conflict between the rising power of Hohenzollern Prussia and the Habsburgs of Austria brought most of Europe into wars fought in Europe, North America, and India.

Reviewing Important Terms

On a separate sheet of paper, supply the term that correctly completes each statement.

1. In a(n) _____ _____, the ruler determines policy without needing to consult other authorities or the people's representatives and has complete power.
2. The captain of a ship at sea can determine latitude by means of an instrument called the _____.
3. The changes in the European economy were so considerable that some historians have referred to the period from 1400 to 1750 as the _____ _____.
4. A(n) ____ ____ ____ raised money by selling shares in the company to investors.
5. An economic theory called _____ maintained that governments should try to increase their nations' wealth and that the world contained only a fixed amount of wealth.
6. By selling more goods in foreign countries than it buys, a country creates a(n) ____ ____ ____ ____.
7. A(n) _____ is an import tax on foreign goods.
8. Government grants of money called _____ helped establish new industries and build ships.
9. ____ ____ was a term for selling the right to collect taxes to private individuals.
10. In France Cardinal Richelieu strengthened the power of regional administrators known as _____.
11. The _____ _____ was the shipment of slaves across the Atlantic Ocean to the West Indies or the southern colonies of British North America.
12. The principal of maintaining an equilibrium in international politics is known as the ____ ____ ____.

Developing Critical Thinking Skills

1. **Interpreting Ideas** What were the changes in technology that made it possible for Europeans to explore foreign lands?
2. **Summarizing Ideas** What social changes in Europe created a willingness to explore and settle overseas?
3. **Evaluating Ideas** Why was Dutch society considered one of Europe's most remarkable societies?
4. **Comparing Ideas** How was Spanish and Dutch colonization different from Portuguese colonization?
5. **Understanding Ideas** (a) How did the Thirty Years' War weaken the Austrian Habsburgs? (b) How did

| A.D. 1624–1642 Richelieu is powerful figure in France. | | A.D. 1682–1725 Peter the Great rules Russia. | | A.D. 1740–1786 Frederick the Great rules Prussia. | A.D. 1772 First Partition of Poland takes place. |

| A.D. 1625 | A.D. 1650 | A.D. 1675 | A.D. 1700 | A.D. 1725 | A.D. 1750 | A.D. 1775 | A.D. 1800 |

A.D. 1618–1648 Thirty Years' War is fought.

A.D. 1643–1715 Louis XIV rules France.

A.D. 1740–1780 Maria Theresa rules Austria.

A.D. 1762–1796 Catherine the Great rules Russia.

Austria benefit in the 100 years after the war? **(c)** What country benefited most from the Thirty Years' War?

6. **Contrasting Ideas** Compare the reigns of Peter the Great and Catherine the Great. **(a)** How were they different? **(b)** What were the important accomplishments of each?

7. **Synthesizing Ideas** Explain how Cardinal Richelieu and Louis XIV strengthened the central government in France over local, religious, and class interests.

8. **Analyzing Ideas** What factors enabled Prussia to create a strong, centralized government and become a great European power by the mid-1700s?

Relating Geography to History

During the period of the great European overseas explorations, certain geographical areas were important to navigation, exploration, and trade routes. Using the map on pages 82 and 83 and information in your textbook, explain the geographical importance of the following: **(a)** Cape of Good Hope; **(b)** Strait of Magellan; **(c)** African coast.

Relating Past to Present

1. It has been said that Louis XIV's control of a large and well-trained army gave him the desire to use it. Does the existence of great armies today lead to the same result? Explain your answer.

2. The 1600s are often called the French century. Is there a nation you think the 1900s will be named after? Give reasons for your answer.

Applying History Study Skills

Before completing this activity, review Building History Study Skills on page 100.

Queen Elizabeth I of England addressed her military forces on August 9, 1588, as they prepared to fight the Spanish Armada sent by Philip II. From the following selection, what inferences can you make about Queen Elizabeth?

"Let tyrants fear; I have always so behaved myself that, under God, I have placed my chiefest strength and safeguard in the loyal hearts and good will of my subjects. And therefore I am come amongst you at this time, not for my recreation or sport, but being resolved, in the

midst and heat of the battle, to live or die amongst you all; to lay down, for my God, and for my kingdom, and for my people, my honour and my blood...

I know I have but the body of a weak and feeble woman; but I have the heart of a king, and of a king of England too; and think foul scorn that Parma or Spain, or any prince of Europe, should dare to invade the borders of my realms: to which, rather that my dishonour should grow by me, I myself will take up arms."

1. Why is Elizabeth making the speech?
2. What does the speech tell you about Elizabeth's relationship to her people?
3. What does Elizabeth mean by "I have the body of a weak and feeble woman; but I have the heart of a king"?
4. What inferences can you make about Elizabeth's role as a ruler? About Elizabeth as a person?

internet connect

Search the Internet through the HRW Web site to find information on the Atlantic slave trade. Prepare an oral report that includes information that you researched from these Web sites. **GO TO:** go.hrw.com **KEYWORD:** SC0 Slave Trade

Building Your Portfolio

1. **Relating Literature to History** The novels of Alexander Dumas deal with France during the reign of Louis XIV. Read one of these novels to discover more about life in France during this period. *The Three Musketeers* or *The Man in the Iron Mask* might be especially appropriate. Write a brief book report. Place your report in your portfolio.

2. **Conducting Research** St. Petersburg (for many years known as Leningrad), founded by Peter the Great, became a symbol of the new Russian policy of westernization. Using books in your library, prepare a short report on St. Petersburg, concentrating mainly on its founding. Place your report in your portfolio.

Revolution and Change in England

TIME

A.D. **1485–1760**

A.D. **1485–1760**

3.7 million B.C. | 4000 B.C. | A.D. **2100**

PLACE

The British Isles, North America, India

British Isles

North America

ARCTIC OCEAN

NORTH AMERICA

EUROPE

ASIA

AFRICA

Equator

AUSTRALIA

PACIFIC OCEAN

SOUTH AMERICA

ATLANTIC OCEAN

INDIAN OCEAN

ANTARCTICA

India

English victory over the Spanish Armada in 1588

Significance

England experienced religious and political turmoil from the end of the 1400s to the middle of the 1700s. In addition to problems at home, rebellions in Ireland and Scotland also troubled English rulers. England, however, moved toward a stronger parliamentary government and emerged with one of the world's most powerful empires.

Terms to Define

revolution	Toleration Act
gentry	cabinet
burgesses	prime minister
covenant	limited constitutional
Long Parliament	monarchy
constitution	sea dogs
habeas corpus	

People to Identify

Mary I	Charles II
Philip II	Tories
Elizabeth I	Whigs
Mary Queen of Scots	James II
James I	William III
Charles I	Mary II
Cavaliers	Thomas Hobbes
Roundheads	John Locke
Oliver Cromwell	John Cabot
New Model Army	Sir Francis Drake
Rump Parliament	Henry Hudson

Places to Locate

English Channel	Jamestown
Ulster	Plymouth
Bombay	Barbados
Hudson Bay	

Chapter Theme Questions

- **Religion** How might religious conflict lead to political conflict?
- **Politics and Law** What kinds of struggles might occur as a nation moves toward a representative form of government?
- **Geography** How might an island nation expand its empire?

I n the following passage, the author Lytton Strachey gives us a glimpse of Queen Elizabeth I, who ruled England from 1558 to 1603.

❝ *While the Spanish ambassador declared that ten thousand devils possessed her, the ordinary Englishman saw in King Hal's full-blooded daughter a Queen after his own heart. She swore; she spat; she struck with her fist when she was angry; she roared with laughter when she was amused. And she was often amused. A radiant atmosphere of humour coloured and softened the harsh lines of her destiny, and buoyed her up along the zigzags of her dreadful path. Her response to every stimulus was immediate and rich: to the folly of the moment, to the clash and horror of great events, her soul leapt out with a vivacity, an abandonment, a complete awareness of the situation, which made her, which makes her still, a fascinating spectacle.* ❞

Elizabeth I, one of England's strongest monarchs, led her country successfully through a very turbulent time in its history.

Section 1

The Tudors and the Stuarts

Focus Questions

- **How did Tudor and Stuart rulers handle conflicts between central government and local authority in their monarchies?**
- **What role did religious intolerance play in the growing struggle between Parliament and royalty?**
- **How did financial pressures become the source of conflict between monarchs and Parliament?**

Chapter 2 described the struggle between central governments and local authorities for control in

European countries. In these countries, the central governments usually won, and the most extreme form of central government—absolute monarchy—became common in most of these European countries. Of all the revolts in the mid-1600s, the most severe took place in England. The clash there led in the 1640s and 1650s to civil war and **revolution**—a radical attempt to change the very structure of a country's government. Although a more limited monarchy was eventually restored, this period of conflict influenced both English history and political ideas throughout Europe.

The Reign of Mary Tudor

In the late 1400s, a new royal family, the Tudors, became England's rulers. The Tudors made efforts to strengthen their powers as rulers in a way similar to those made by rulers of France and Spain. Following the turbulence of the Wars of the Roses, the first Tudor king, Henry VII, brought stability and prosperity to England. Of the five Tudor monarchs, Henry VIII, who reigned from 1509 to 1547, and his daughter Elizabeth I, who reigned from 1558 to 1603, had the greatest success as rulers over England. During his reign, Henry VIII established a new official English church, the Anglican Church.

Elizabeth I's life was full of conflict; her half sister Mary I imprisoned her in the Tower of London for two months for what Mary deemed suspicious activity.

After the short reign of sickly Edward VI, Mary I, the oldest daughter of Henry VIII, ascended the throne in 1553 to become the first reigning queen of England. Her personal unhappiness and her devotion to Catholicism shaped her reign. Though she did not lack courage or kindness, she had a fierce determination to make England a Catholic nation again. Mary's unpopular marriage to Philip II of Spain, a leader of the Counter-Reformation, outraged her Protestant subjects. Determined to rid England of clergy who would not conform to the laws of the Catholic Church, Mary had nearly 300 people burned at the stake, including Thomas Cranmer, archbishop of Canterbury. These persecutions earned her the nickname "Bloody Mary" and provoked rebellion, but they completely failed to destroy Protestantism.

The Reign of Elizabeth I

When Mary I died in 1558, her Protestant half sister Elizabeth became queen. Adept at politics, Elizabeth used parliamentary acts to prevent conflict and strengthen Protestantism. For example, people who did not attend the Anglican Church had to pay fines.

Mary Queen of Scots. Religion also entered into the question of who should succeed Elizabeth. In a monarchy, the oldest child usually inherits the throne. Elizabeth did not marry, however, and had no children. Her closest relative and heir—Mary Stuart, queen of Scotland, or Mary Queen of Scots as she is more commonly known—was Catholic.

The prospect of Mary Queen of Scots becoming queen of England horrified English Protestants. However, it also delayed the plans of Philip II of Spain to invade England and force a Catholic ruler on the English people.

In 1568, to escape problems in Scotland, the headstrong Mary fled to England, only to be imprisoned by Elizabeth. Later Mary foolishly plotted with Philip II's ambassadors in England to kill Elizabeth and seize the English throne. After some hesitation, Elizabeth signed the Scottish queen's death warrant, and in 1587 Mary was beheaded. King Philip II, angered by English raiders at sea and Elizabeth's aid to Protestants in his realm, planned an invasion of England.

The Spanish Armada. In 1588 Philip sent a fleet of 130 ships, called the Invincible Armada, north toward the English Channel. The English summoned all their ships to intercept the Spanish Armada. The smaller English ships were swifter and more maneuverable, and their guns fired faster and from a longer range than the guns on the Spanish ships.

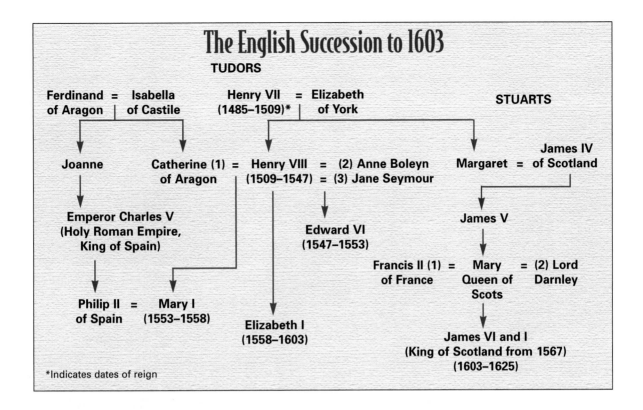

The English Succession to 1603

TUDORS

Ferdinand = Isabella   Henry VII = Elizabeth
of Aragon | of Castile   (1485–1509)* | of York   **STUARTS**

Joanne   Catherine (1) = Henry VIII = (2) Anne Boleyn   Margaret = James IV
        of Aragon   (1509–1547) = (3) Jane Seymour   of Scotland

Emperor Charles V   James V
(Holy Roman Empire,   Edward VI
King of Spain)   (1547–1553)

Philip II = Mary I   Francis II (1) = Mary = (2) Lord
of Spain (1553–1558)   of France   Queen of   Darnley
            Elizabeth I   Scots
            (1558–1603)

James VI and I
(King of Scotland from 1567)
(1603–1625)

*Indicates dates of reign

The English broke the huge Spanish formation, then damaged and sank some of the lumbering vessels. The Spaniards attempted to escape to the North Sea and then northwest around all the British Isles. Autumn storms, navigation errors, and lack of supplies proved deadly. Some of the Spanish ships reached the open sea and limped home, but many foundered on the rocky, desolate coasts of Scotland and Ireland. Only about half of the Invincible Armada straggled back to Spain. The combination of skilled English seafaring and bad weather had been disastrous for King Philip's enormous fleet and his overseas ambitions. Even with Spain's external threat destroyed and Elizabeth's Protestant rule secure, Elizabeth's government still faced two major problems at home.

The religious problem. Religious issues in England were unsettled. The monarchy under Henry VIII had broken with the pope and established Anglicanism as England's religion, but many people believed that the change had not gone far enough. They wanted to "purify" the English church even more. These people, called Puritans, objected to the continuation of many Catholic practices. Although the Anglican Church had abolished the Mass, it still had bishops. Priests still dressed in elaborate robes for religious services, and the congregation still knelt during services.

The Puritans thought these customs too Catholic and wanted to abolish them.

Like many monarchs, the Protestant Tudors thought religious disunity threatened stability. They wanted to unite their subjects in the Anglican faith. Therefore, they persecuted both remaining Catholics and non-Anglican Protestants such as Puritans. Not only did they fail to end dissent, but they made dangerous enemies of non-Anglican Protestants.

The Puritans became increasingly unhappy about the Anglican Church and the quality of the clergy. Queen Elizabeth, however, refused to allow further changes in the church. Her religious policies were tolerant compared to those of other rulers, but they were objectionable to Catholics on one side and Puritans on the other. Eventually, these same objections would contribute to rebellion against the monarchy itself.

Elizabeth I and Parliament. In England, Parliament, the body of representatives from the whole country, had the right to approve all taxes and pass laws. Parliament gained power and prestige in the 1530s, when Henry VIII used it to pass laws that made England a Protestant nation. Moreover, people looked to Parliament as a restraint on the monarchy because it represented the wishes of people outside the central government.

Theater

Ruins of a Roman theater with a 3,500 seating capacity

New Shakespeare Globe Theater in London

Interior of the new Shakespeare Globe Theater

People have enjoyed going to see plays as a form of entertainment since the earliest times. In ancient Greece and Rome, performances were given in great open-air arenas (above). In ancient Japan, the Noh plays were popular forms of entertainment.

During the Middle Ages, sacred stories and plays with Christian themes, called morality plays, were performed in or near churches. By the time of the Renaissance, special buildings were built for dramatic performances. These buildings came to be known as theaters.

Perhaps the most famous theater in history was the Globe. This octagon-shaped theater was built in the late 1500s on the south bank of the Thames River, across from London. Most of William Shakespeare's plays had their earliest performances in the Globe. A reconstructed Globe Theater now stands near the site of the original theater.

Londoners flocked to see the latest comedies and tragedies of writers such as Shakespeare, Christopher Marlowe, and Ben Jonson. Often drawing on the models of classical Greece and Rome, these writers created dramas beyond mere morality plays; they were works full of romance, humor, violence, and despair.

Plays were performed in the daytime, when there was enough natural light to illuminate the stage. The center of the theater was open to the sky. Ordinary tradespeople sat or stood in this open area, ready to be rained upon if the weather turned bad. Nobles and rich merchants sat in boxes around the sides of the theater. The stage itself was covered by an overhanging roof.

The human emotions explored by the plays of the Elizabethan and Restoration periods are so universal that many of the plays continue to be performed. Love, ambition, madness, and revenge have been themes of drama since ancient times. The same themes are still used by modern playwrights. Our enjoyment of the theater is one way in which we are linked with our ancestors.

Parliament had two houses. The House of Lords consisted of nobles and higher clergy. The House of Commons represented two classes: gentry and burgesses. The **gentry**, though without titles, had social position and owned land. Occasionally, younger sons of nobles, who could not inherit their fathers' titles or positions, settled into the gentry. Merchants and professional people from towns and cities made up the **burgesses**.

Although England maintained distinct classes, lines between the gentry and burgesses could and sometimes did become blurred. Class lines, for example, might be crossed for economic reasons. Rich merchants who owned land might be considered gentry. Younger sons of nobles might enter professions and come to be regarded as burgesses. Together the two groups had considerable power that commanded the respect of the monarch.

Elizabeth I summoned Parliaments often during her reign and gave the appearance of heeding them. She managed Parliament cleverly, obtaining the taxes she needed without letting members influence her policy too directly. Although annoyed at petitions urging her to marry, Elizabeth generally refrained from curtailing freedom of speech in Parliament. Despite her skill at managing Parliament, Elizabeth found it increasingly difficult to prevent its members, particularly Puritans, from questioning government policies. During the reigns of her successors, Parliament's questions became ever more challenging. In time members of Parliament would begin a revolution when a monarch refused to hear their views.

The Roots of the English Revolution

Between 1603, when Elizabeth died, and 1640, relations between the monarchy and its subjects deteriorated. The main stages in that deterioration suggest how and why it happened.

James I. The first problem arose almost immediately. Elizabeth I had never married and left no heir. King James VI of Scotland, a member of the Stuart family and the son of Mary Queen of Scots, succeeded Elizabeth to the English throne as James I of England.* At age 39, he had thin brown hair, a straggly beard, and spindly legs. The gangly king also had rough manners, at least according to his English political opponents. However, James had a taste for learning and was a man of considerable intelligence. A writer in his youth, he was an experienced ruler when he came south to

---

*From this time on, England and Scotland were ruled by the same monarch.

England. Even so, he lacked common sense in financial matters and in diplomacy. According to Henry IV of France, he was "the wisest fool in Christendom."

James had managed to rule Scotland by balancing one faction with another and keeping the church in Scotland under control. His English subjects, however, suspected that, as a foreigner, he did not really understand how their parliamentary system worked. At his first Parliament, James, who strongly believed in the divine right of kings, intervened in a House of Commons matter over membership. A few insulted members drew up a document called *The Form of Apology and Satisfaction* to define the role of the House of Commons for the king.

Finance and foreign policy occupied James's attention during much of his reign. He was a strong supporter of the Anglican Church and had little tolerance for the Puritans' demands for reform. Although James did agree to a new translation of the Bible into English, the King James Version, he refused other changes to church doctrine. (This Bible, also known as the Authorized Version, is still one of the most widely used English translations.) It was during James's reign that some Puritans began to leave England, including one group that fled to Holland and later sailed to America in the *Mayflower*.

The main opposition to James I came from Parliament, in which the Puritans were strongly represented. His reign saw rising inflation and growing government activity. James could never collect enough money in taxes to finance his policies. When taxes passed by Parliament proved insufficient, he raised money by selling titles of nobility, granting monopoly rights to private companies, and increasing customs duties. Parliament objected to these methods. It also objected to James's attempt to create an alliance with England's old enemy, Spain. The negotiations finally broke down, and the two nations went to war.

Charles I. At the time of his death in 1625, James I and his subjects had an uneasy relationship. The tension between the monarchy and the people exploded during the reign of his son Charles I, who ruled from 1625 to 1649. Brave but personally shy, Charles believed in the divine right of kings as firmly as his father had. These qualities kept him out of touch with people and political realities. Charles married a French Catholic princess, Henrietta Maria, an unpopular choice that further isolated him from the people.

When Charles I could not get funds from the Puritan-dominated Parliament, he tried to force people to lend him money and imprisoned some who

History Through the Arts

The Authorized Version of the Bible (The King James Bible)

In January 1604, James I of England held the Hampton Court Conference near London. At this conference, James responded to demands of the Puritans that included reforms to church government and changes in *The Book of Common Prayer*. The king rejected many of the Puritans' demands but agreed to one that had a powerful effect on religious practice as well as English literature and speech for centuries to come: a new translation of the Bible.

James approved a committee of 54 scholars for the translation task, but the finished work was that of only 47 of these scholars. They worked in six groups at three locations—Westminster, Oxford, and Cambridge—with each group assigned a section of the text. The labor took seven years to complete, and the new translation was published in 1611. The scholars worked with both existing English translations and texts available in the original languages of Hebrew and Greek. The result was a translation that became the standard Bible in English for nearly three centuries. It quickly became the most popular book in English.

Although later translators had access to more accurate texts as well as a better understanding of Greek and Hebrew, the King James Version of the Bible is a masterpiece of the English language of the time—the language of great English writers such as Shakespeare, Ben Jonson, and John Donne. Its grandeur and simplicity had an influence on English prose and poetic style for many years to come.

---

refused. Confrontation with Parliament during 1628 led members to present Charles with the Petition of Right, which reasserted four ancient liberties. Charles signed the Petition of Right, hoping Parliament would release funds. He agreed not to levy taxes without consent of Parliament, not to declare martial law, not to quarter soldiers in private homes in peacetime, and not to imprison people without specific charge. Charles did, however, continue to levy taxes. When members of the House of Commons vehemently objected, he dissolved Parliament.

For the next 11 years, Charles refused to call Parliament into session, hoping to govern without opposition. During these years, he used drastic means to collect money and revived long-ignored royal fees and fines. The economy improved, but resentment grew.

Charles took his title as head of the Anglican Church seriously. He favored a formal and ceremonial faith, which seemed Catholic and offensive to Puritans. Many left the country for a new life in America during the 1630s, following those who had been leaving since the early 1600s. Those who stayed became determined opponents of the king.

These Puritans increasingly dominated the House of Commons, joining others in Parliament who thought the king's rule was growing tyrannical. Charles began to use royal courts against his enemies. The once popular royal courts, though, did not guarantee civil liberties, a fact exploited by the king. Decisions were made in secret by judges, not by juries. Lawyers of common-law courts resented these rivals to their system, especially because they believed the king controlled the judges. One court, the Court of Star Chamber—named for the wall and ceiling designs in the room where it met—severely prosecuted Puritans and critics of government. Members of the gentry, who would have been exempt from corporal punishment in civil courts, and other commoners who opposed Charles hated the Star Chamber. It seemed to many English people that Charles was increasingly imposing an absolute rule.

The Scots. When Charles tried to impose a liturgy, or prescribed form of ritual, based on the Anglican *Book of Common Prayer*, on Scotland, rebellion broke out. The state religion of Scotland was Presbyterianism, a Protestant denomination modeled on Calvinism.

Anthony Van Dyck, Charles I's court painter from 1632 to 1641, painted this hunting portrait of the king in 1635.

Elders known as presbyters, rather than bishops, ruled the Presbyterian Church, and Presbyterians had their own liturgy. Moreover, the changes appeared to Scots to move toward hated Catholicism. In 1638 many responded to Charles's attempt to Anglicanize the Presbyterian service by signing a National Covenant. In this **covenant**, or solemn agreement, Scots swore that changes in the church in Scotland violated both their religion and acts of the Scottish Parliament. To Scottish Presbyterians, loyalty to their church—the Kirk—came before loyalty to the king. The Scots raised an army, and Charles took troops to Scotland, but he was easily outmaneuvered. Seeking more funds to put down the rebellion, he called Parliament into session, then dismissed it when it insisted on airing its grievances first. A second defeat—this time in England itself—gravely disturbed Charles. Realizing he could not defend England without new taxation, he again called Parliament into session in November 1640.

Civil War and Revolution

Focus Questions

- How did rebellion in Ireland trigger the English Civil War?
- What was Cromwell's commonwealth, and how did it govern after the war?
- Why was the monarchy restored in England?

The Parliament of 1640—known as the **Long Parliament**—reconvened periodically for 20 years. The Puritans who controlled the House of Commons took actions to limit the monarchy. They abolished the king's power to dissolve Parliament and passed a law requiring that Parliament meet at least once every three years. They declared illegal or amended many of the king's tax levies. Parliament abolished the Court of Star Chamber and forced the execution of two of the king's advisers for treason. When radical Puritans in Parliament tried to effect sweeping changes in the church, public support began to move toward the king.

The Irish Problem

While the Long Parliament worked at reducing the king's authority, trouble broke out in Ireland. England had ruled parts of Ireland since the late 1100s but had never brought the Irish completely under control. The English conquerors historically had seized land belonging to Irish owners and given it to English settlers. Under James I, the English settlers who went to Ireland were mostly Anglican. These landowning Anglo-Irish became the upper class and controlled most of the country's wealth. Later, Scottish Presbyterians settled in the northern region called Ulster. Mostly farmers and merchants, they became the middle class. The majority of native Irish remained Roman Catholic and worked as tenant farmers and laborers. They formed the lowest social and economic class and were often brutally repressed. In 1641 a bloody rebellion led primarily by Irish Catholics began against England, heightening Protestant fears of Catholics.

The rebellion in Ireland brought crisis. Parliament knew it needed a huge army to put down the Irish rebellion, but it did not trust Charles to control it. A complete list of grievances against the king, the Grand Remonstrance, was passed. Bills were proposed to put the military under Parliament's control.

"By God, not for an hour," replied Charles. Charles heard rumors that the queen might be impeached and led troops to the House of Commons to arrest some of his opponents. Neither side compromised, and a civil war began in 1642.

English Civil War

The citizenry was divided. Generally, the king's supporters, called royalists or Cavaliers, after the king's cavalry, included Anglicans, Roman Catholics, nobles, and those who opposed the changes that Parliament wanted. Those citizens who believed that royal power should be curbed, including Puritans and other non-Anglican Protestants, supported the parliamentary opposition. They were sometimes called Roundheads, after the close haircuts that the Puritan soldiers wore.

Oliver Cromwell, a rising Puritan leader, organized his troops into a powerful army that had great success against the royalists. Cromwell's New Model Army, which was formed in 1645, was drilled, disciplined, and zealous. After a defeat at Naseby in 1645, Charles fled to the Scots. Oxford, the Royalist headquarters, surrendered to the New Model Army in June 1646, bringing an end to the first stage of the civil war. After negotiations failed between Charles and the Scots, they turned him over to Parliament.

Various political and religious groups struggled for control. Chief among these groups were the Presbyterians, a majority in Parliament, and the Independents, supported by the army. Cromwell conducted negotiations with the king, hoping he would agree to become a figurehead. Then, in November 1647, Charles escaped and organized his Scottish supporters to fight again. Cromwell's army crushed them and hardened its attitude. Troops moved on the House of Commons, preventing Anglican and Presbyterian members from entering, leaving approximately 60 Independents loyal to the army. This remnant of the Long Parliament became known as the Rump Parliament.

Death of the king. The Rump Parliament abolished both the monarchy and the House of Lords. It proclaimed England a commonwealth, a term used at the time to mean a republic, and appointed a special court to try Charles for treason and other crimes. Charles refused to plead to a court he considered illegal. The court condemned Charles, and he was beheaded in front of the palace at Whitehall in 1649. Charles I faced death bravely and was regarded by many people as a martyr. His courage and the citizens' desire for stability would make it easier for his son, who fled to France after his father's death, to return later as king. Meanwhile, Oliver Cromwell took control of England.

Cromwell's Commonwealth

Oliver Cromwell was a pious and honest Puritan who possessed the qualities of a powerful orator and skilled leader. However, he also believed that he had been placed in power by divine providence. Therefore, when he felt moved to suppress dissent, such as in Ireland, he could be harsh. He was privately tolerant in religious matters, though fervent Puritan followers sometimes forced his hand.

Although Cromwell held considerable power, he was a reluctant dictator. He preferred a parliamentary, republican government and made several attempts to create one amid the chaos. He tried twice to establish a **constitution**—a document outlining the fundamental laws and principles that govern a nation. The Instrument of Government in 1653 was the first written constitution of a major European nation. It gave Cromwell the title lord protector and provided that landowners would elect members of Parliament. Cromwell was lord protector until 1658, an era often called the Protectorate.

Discontent never subsided. Cromwell's government might have been overthrown except for three factors: (1) It had enough money from taxes and the sale of confiscated royalist lands to support itself and its army. (2) Its army was disciplined and powerful, discouraging other groups from making attempts against it. (3) Its enemies, the Irish and the royalists, had no organized army. Cromwell repressed the Irish so brutally that his name inspires hatred even today, and the royalists never posed a serious threat.

Cromwell's foreign policy related to his domestic policy, that of encouraging manufacturing and trade. During the civil war in England, Dutch merchants and shipowners had established a profitable trade

Oliver Cromwell led parliamentary forces in battles at Naseby and Oxford. Following the execution of Charles I in 1649, Cromwell ruled England as lord protector from 1653 to 1658.

transporting goods. Cromwell challenged the Dutch by having Parliament pass the Navigation Act of 1651, requiring that all imports be shipped in English ships or ships of the country producing the goods.

Cromwell's policies led to a war with the Dutch from 1652 to 1654. Because the Dutch transported so much of the world's trade, they realized that the freedom of the seas was at stake. Although the war ended indecisively, the English navy gained prestige, and Cromwell demonstrated that the English government would use its growing power to aid English commerce.

The End of the Revolution

The experiment with republican government failed. Cromwell quarreled almost as much with Parliament as had the Stuart kings, and parliamentary resentment of central power resurfaced. Before his death in 1658, Cromwell, like Charles I whom he had replaced as king, dissolved Parliament and ruled alone. After Cromwell's death, his son Richard was named lord protector, but his weak leadership lost the support of the army.

By 1660 the English people, too, had undergone a change of feelings. Though some had favored the execution of Charles I, Cromwell's commonwealth had neither settled the nation nor solved its problems. After some hesitation, the Parliament of 1660, with the support of the army, invited Charles II, the son of Charles I, to return to England. Wildly cheering crowds greeted him in London. Some historians call the period from 1642 to 1660 the English Revolution. This includes the years of civil war from 1642 to 1649, together with the changes in society and government that continued until the return of a monarch in 1660. Although the country seemed to have weathered its troubles, another 30 years would pass before the monarchy and Parliament would achieve a workable balance.

Section 3

England's Constitutional Monarchy

Focus Questions

- **What happened during the Restoration?**
- **What was the Glorious Revolution?**
- **How did a constitutional monarchy come into being in England?**

The struggles between king and Parliament did not end in 1660. An echo of the crisis occurred in the 1680s. After that uncertainty passed, however, the English created a more stable government that linked monarch and Parliament in a workable partnership.

Charles II and the Restoration

The reign of Charles II is called the Restoration because monarchy was restored in England. Literature and music of the time are referred to as Restoration works, and the arts prospered under Charles II.

Unlike his father, this Charles was a tall, striking figure. He had dark brown hair and eyes, and he resembled his Medici and Bourbon ancestors. Charles was well-mannered, but because he also loved entertainment and pleasure, people dubbed him the "Merry Monarch." Charles removed restrictions on the theater and other forms of entertainment that the stern Puritans of the commonwealth era had legislated.

The period following the fall of Cromwell's commonwealth in 1660 is known as the Restoration because the monarchy was restored to England with Charles II (shown here as a small boy).

Contrary to his nickname, the "Merry Monarch," however, Charles II had learned much from his years in exile after his father's death. Cynical and cautious, he deferred to Parliament when his policies met opposition, although he often used roundabout methods to gain his ends. Charles continued Cromwell's commercial policy, which eventually led to wars with the Dutch. During these wars, England seized the Dutch settlement of New Amsterdam in North America and renamed it New York. Charles also explored an alliance with France, partly in secret, but public protest forced him away from close relations with that nation. Charles's decision not to ally his country with France marked the beginning of 150 years of rivalry between England and France for mastery of the sea and for colonial power.

Charles II tolerated Catholicism and hoped to lift some of the legal restrictions on the faith during his reign. However, attempts to do so met with such strong parliamentary opposition that he abandoned the effort.

Political Parties Develop

Because Charles II and his Portuguese queen, Catherine of Braganza, had no children, it seemed clear that Charles's younger brother James, a Roman Catholic, would succeed him. The two political parties that were developing at this time held opposing ideas about royal succession.

The two groups, of almost equal strength—Tories and Whigs—had begun to develop in Parliament. Like the terms *Cavalier* and *Roundhead*, the terms *Tory* and *Whig* were originally unflattering nicknames. *Tory* was an Irish word that suggested a Catholic outlaw. It was applied to people who supported the hereditary right of James to rule. Although Tories strongly supported the Anglican Church, they were willing to accept a Roman Catholic ruler. The term *Whig* originally meant "horse thief" and later was applied to Scottish Presbyterians. It suggested a group that was rebellious. The Whigs claimed the right to deny the throne to James and wanted a strong Parliament. They vigorously opposed the idea of a Catholic ruler.

James II and the Glorious Revolution

Charles II died in 1685, and his younger brother did come to the throne, as James II. The humorless James was less flexible than his older brother. As a Catholic and an ardent believer in royal absolutism, James antagonized both Whigs and Tories. Many of his actions, intended to ease life for Catholics, frightened and roused Protestants to greater resistance.

One of the issues of James's reign once again involved succession to the throne. James's daughters, Mary and Anne, were both raised as Protestants at Charles II's insistence, and both married Protestant princes. However, James's first wife died, and he married again, this time to a Catholic princess, Mary of Modena. In 1688 she gave birth to a son, who would by law succeed his father before his older half sisters. Because the boy was a Catholic like his parents, English Protestants feared a whole line of Catholic rulers on the throne of England.

Now all the groups who opposed James combined to bring about the event known as the Glorious Revolution. Whigs and Tories, united in fear of Catholicism, agreed that James must abdicate. A number of leading nobles invited James's daughter Mary and her Dutch husband William of Orange to take the throne of England. Although William landed in England with an army in 1688, armed force was hardly necessary. James, unable to rally anyone to his support and fearful of assassination, fled to France. Parliament gave the crown to William and Mary as the joint rulers William III and Mary II.

New Ideas About Government

The English civil war and the events that followed led not only to changes in government but also to new ideas about government. The English philosopher Thomas Hobbes lived through the civil war and was disturbed by the chaos it created. He set forth his political philosophy in a book called *Leviathan*, published in 1651.

Hobbes explained that groups of people first lived in anarchy, what he considered a state of nature.

Although Mary II's parents were Catholic, they raised their daughter as a Protestant. Mary I's marriage to her Protestant cousin William III led to five years of joint Protestant rule.

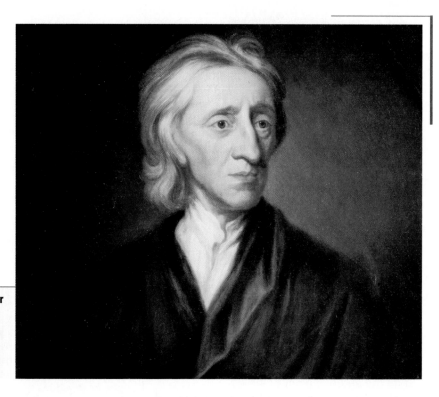

John Locke, an English writer of philosophy and political thought, believed that people have certain rights that the state should protect.

Life was violent and dangerous under these circumstances, so people chose a leader to rule them. To maintain a stable society, people made an unwritten social contract or "covenant." Under this contract, argued Hobbes, people must give the monarch absolute power, or anarchy results. The people retain only the right to protect their own lives.

John Locke, another English philosopher, considered these ideas but interpreted them differently. Locke supported Parliament in the struggles with James II. He articulated the principles on which supporters of the Glorious Revolution acted in 1688, publishing them in his *Two Treatises of Government* in 1690.

Like Hobbes, Locke believed that people had first lived individually and then made a social contract. However, he believed that people had given up only some of their individual rights and had kept others. The rights they kept included the right to live, to enjoy liberty, and to own property, and they could expect rulers to preserve these rights.

According to Locke, a ruler who violated these rights violated natural law and broke the unwritten social contract. The people had the right to overthrow such a ruler and replace him with one who pledged to observe and protect their rights. Locke thus defended the actions of those who had forced James II to leave the throne, and provided a justification for offering the crown to William and Mary. Locke's ideas would influence later revolutions in America and France as well.

Safeguards Against Absolute Rule

Parliament passed laws attempting to safeguard against arbitrary rule as early as the reign of Charles II. In 1679 it passed an important measure, the Habeas Corpus Act. This act provided that anyone who was arrested could obtain a writ, or order, demanding to be brought before a judge within a specified period of time. The judge would decide whether the prisoner should be released or charged and tried for a crime. The writ itself was called **habeas corpus**, Latin for "you shall have the body." The Habeas Corpus Act protected individuals against arbitrary arrest and imprisonment.

A document called the Declaration of Rights was read to William and Mary before their ascent to the throne in 1689. That year, Parliament formalized the Declaration of Rights as the Bill of Rights. The Bill of Rights declared that Parliament would choose the ruler, who as an official would be subject to parliamentary laws. The ruler could not proclaim or suspend any law.

Building History Study Skills

READ
WRITE
INTERPRET
CONNECT
THINK

Reading About History: Identifying a Point of View

A point of view presents a person's outlook on a subject or an event. It is important to know the author's point of view in order to determine the accuracy of the information presented. By understanding the author's viewpoint, you can tell what facts have been ignored or what data have been exaggerated. You can also evaluate how reliable the information is.

How to Identify a Point of View
Follow these guidelines to identify a point of view.
1. State the author's topic.
2. Identify the main idea.
3. Determine how and why emphasis has been placed on the main idea.
4. Select words and phrases that signal an opinion, emotion, or exaggeration.
5. Indicate ideas or facts about the subject that the author did not include.
6. State the author's point of view.

Developing the Skill
The issue of how and why government is organized was an integral part of the English civil war and the Glorious Revolution. Thomas Hobbes in *Leviathan* and John Locke in *Two Treatises of Government* contributed their thoughts to the discussion. Read the selections from their works. What are their points of view? How are their ideas similar? How are they different?

❝In the first place, I put for a general inclination of all mankind, a perpetual and restless desire of power after power, that ceaseth only in death. . . .

During the time men live without a common power to keep them all in awe, they are in that condition which is called war; . . . as is of every man, against every man. . . .

In such condition, there is no place for industry . . . and consequently no culture of the earth; no navigation; . . . no commodious building; . . . no arts; no letters; no society; and which is worst of all, continual fear, and danger of violent death; and the life of man, solitary, poor, nasty, brutish, and short. . . .

The only way . . . they may nourish themselves and live contentedly is to confer all their power and strength upon one man, or upon one assembly of men, that may reduce all their wills . . .

unto one will. . . . This is more than consent, or concord; it is a real unity of them all, in one and the same person, made by covenant of every man with every man. . . . This done, the multitude so united in one person, is called a commonwealth.❞

(Thomas Hobbes, *Leviathan*)

❝Political power is that power which every man having in the state of nature has given up into the hands of the society. . . . And this power has its original only from compact and agreement, and the mutual consent of those who make up the community. . . .

The reason why men enter into society is the preservation of their property; and the end why they choose and authorize a legislative is that there may be laws made and rules set as guards and fences to the properties of all the members of the society. . . . Whenever the legislators endeavor to take away and destroy the property of the people, or to reduce them to slavery under arbitrary power, they put themselves into a state of war with the people who are thereupon absolved from any further obedience.❞

(John Locke, *The Second Treatise of Government*)

Both men discuss how governments are formed. Hobbes claims that man in a state of nature is in constant disorder. He forms a government to insure protection, prosperity, and order for himself. Man gives up his individual will to a ruler. Revolution is not justified because the ruler protects the common good. The signal words are fear, danger, brutish, concord, unity, and consent.

Locke believes that man in a state of nature has political power and forms a society to protect property. Government is a contract between the ruler and the governed. The government's purpose is to protect individual rights. Locke says that the contract can be broken if the ruler does not protect property. The signal words are arbitrary and slavery.

Practicing the Skill
Choose a current political article from a periodical and identify the point of view.

To apply this skill, see Applying History Study Skills on page 133.

The ruler could not impose any tax or maintain an army in peacetime without Parliament's consent. Parliament had to meet frequently, and the monarch could not interfere with the elections of its members. The Bill of Rights guaranteed the right of the members of Parliament to express themselves freely.

The Bill of Rights also protected private citizens. All citizens had the right to petition the government for relief of injustice. In addition, no one could be required to pay excessive bail or be subjected to cruel and unusual punishment.

In 1689 Parliament also passed the **Toleration Act**. This act granted freedom of conscience and the right of public worship to those Protestants (now called Dissenters) who were not members of the Anglican Church. It did not, however, bring about complete religious freedom. For example, Roman Catholics and Jews lived under heavy restrictions, and Dissenters could not hold public office.

In 1701 Parliament passed the Act of Settlement, designed to keep Catholics from the English throne. The act provided that if William III should die with no heir, Mary's sister, Anne, would inherit the throne. If Anne had no children, the throne would go to another Protestant granddaughter of James I, Sophia, the electress of Hanover in Germany.

Parliament Rules England
The Bill of Rights and the Act of Settlement marked the end of the long struggle between monarch and Parliament to determine who would rule the country. By 1700, although England remained a monarchy, Parliament held the power. However, Parliament did not represent all the people. Hereditary nobles and higher clergy made up the House of Lords. Even the House of Commons, which was gradually becoming the more powerful of the two houses, was not particularly representative. Only the male gentry who were landowners and the powerful commercial people had the right to vote for members of the House of Commons.

In the 50 years following 1689, Parliament continued to gain importance as the real power in the governing of England. During this time, the organization and institutions characteristic of today's British government gradually emerged.

For centuries English monarchs had met with advisers to discuss government problems. After the revolution and Restoration, parliamentary leaders had the power to accomplish goals, and William III chose his officers of state from among them. These ministers, or heads of government departments, became known as the **cabinet**.

At first the cabinet included both Whigs and Tories. However, during the reign of William III, it became clear that the government ran more smoothly when most of the cabinet ministers belonged to the majority party in the House of Commons. Sometimes rulers accepted those whom they did not prefer merely to make working with Parliament possible. Additional changes increased parliamentary control of the English government during and following the reign of William III. Among these changes, Parliament gained the right to declare war, and the monarch stopped vetoing acts of Parliament.

Act of Union
In 1707 the parliaments of England and Scotland passed the Act of Union, uniting England and Scotland. At the end of William's reign, impending war with France made the union a strategic and political asset. Scottish resentment of wealthy England might otherwise have led the Scots to take the side of France again. The Act of Union merged the two countries into one kingdom, known as Great Britain. (See map on page 128.) The act abolished Scotland's parliament and gave the Scots seats in the English House of Lords and House of Commons.

Some people opposed the union at first, particularly some in Scotland, but the union proved beneficial. By removing trade barriers, it encouraged commerce and brought prosperity to both England and Scotland. The Scottish city of Glasgow grew from a fishing village into a great port. The Universities of Edinburgh and Glasgow became major centers of learning in Europe during the 1700s.

Queen Anne, who ruled from 1702 to 1714, had 17 children, but none survived her. When she died, her designated successor, Sophia, electress of Hanover, had already died. Thus Sophia's son George became George I, the first of the Hanoverian dynasty of Great Britain. Both he and his son George II were born in Germany and were unfamiliar with British government and customs. George I, who ruled until 1727, spoke no English. George II, who was king until 1760, spoke fluent English but depended on ministers such as Sir Robert Walpole to manage the administration. Although the details of British government interested both kings, neither understood the larger issues. As a result, the cabinet became increasingly important in the British system of government.

The British Isles, 1707

0   100   200 Miles

0   100   200 Kilometers
Azimuthal Equal-Area Projection

60°N

ORKNEY
ISLANDS

THE HEBRIDES

57°N

SCOTLAND

GRAMPIANS

Firth of Forth
•Edinburgh
Glasgow

NORTH
SEA

Cheviots

Londonderry•
•Ulster

54°N

IRELAND

ISLE
OF
MAN

THE PENNINES

York

IRISH SEA
Liverpool•

River
Humber

The Wash

Shannon R.

Dublin•

Trent R.

ENGLAND

Norwich

St. George's Channel

WALES

Stratford-
upon-Avon

Cambridge

Oxford
•London

51°N

Bristol Channel

Bristol Thames R. Canterbury

Exeter•

ISLE OF
WIGHT

ATLANTIC
OCEAN

•Plymouth

English   Channel   0°

9°W   6°W   3°W

FRANCE

Learning from Maps In 1707 Parliament united Scotland and England as the Kingdom of Great Britain.

? Place What islands lie off the coast of Scotland?

A Constitutional Monarchy

For more than 20 years—from 1721 to 1742—the Whigs controlled the House of Commons. Their recognized leader, Sir Robert Walpole, was a minister under two kings. Walpole had strong leadership capabilities and was regarded as the **prime minister**, the first minister, although early prime ministers usually carried the title of first lord of the treasury. Under the rule of the Hanoverians, the prime minister became the real head of the government, and Great Britain became a **limited constitutional monarchy**. It was a monarchy in that a king or queen was the

head of state. The monarchy was limited, however, in that a constitution restricted the monarch's powers and the monarch was required to consult Parliament.

The British constitution is not a single written document such as that of the United States. It consists partly of great documents that include among others the Magna Carta, the Petition of Right, the Habeas Corpus Act, the Bill of Rights, and the Act of Settlement. It also includes acts of Parliament, which any succeeding Parliament may change. Several features of the British governmental system have never been written down; for example, the powers of the prime minister and the functions of the cabinet are based largely on tradition. The prime minister rather than the monarch selects the other members of the cabinet. Together the prime minister and the cabinet plan and carry out policies of the government.

Great Britain is one of the world's oldest constitutional governments. Its limited monarchy became a model for governments of other nations that wanted to end absolute monarchies.

Section 3 Review

1. **Define** habeas corpus, Toleration Act, cabinet, prime minister, limited constitutional monarchy
2. **Identify** Charles II, Tories, Whigs, James II, William III, Mary II, Thomas Hobbes, John Locke
3. **Understanding Ideas** How did the Restoration renew religious discord within Parliament?
4. **Analyzing Ideas** What role did attitudes toward Catholicism play in the Glorious Revolution?
5. **Interpreting Ideas** (a) How did the English Bill of Rights limit the powers of the monarch? (b) How did it protect private citizens?

Section 4

English Colonial Expansion

Focus Questions

- How did British naval exploits strengthen the empire?
- How did mercantilism affect colonial policy?

Spain and Portugal established vast overseas empires during the 1500s, while England remained preoccupied with problems at home. Even though these problems persisted during the 1600s, English mariners began explorations that allowed the English to claim lands in the Americas and Asia. English merchants founded companies to trade in these new lands, in addition to the English companies that traded in Russia and in the Baltic. By the mid-1600s, English naval power had become a major force, and in the 1700s, Europe began to recognize British naval supremacy on the high seas. At the same time, the British merchant shipping fleet had replaced the Dutch fleet as leader in mercantile shipping. By the 1760s, Great Britain's colonial empire had no serious mercantile competition in North America or India.

Explorers and Sea Dogs

Shortly after Columbus landed in the Western Hemisphere in 1492, King Henry VII commissioned a Venetian captain named John Cabot to sail to North America. In 1497 and 1498, Cabot explored the coasts of Newfoundland, Nova Scotia, and possibly New England. Although Cabot's voyages gave the English a claim in North America, it was not until almost a century later that the English took steps to develop this territory in North America.

During the reign of Queen Elizabeth I, in the second half of the 1500s, an adventurous group of sea captains appeared in England. The English called this group of traders and pirates **sea dogs**. These men—Sir John Hawkins, Sir Francis Drake, and Sir Walter Raleigh, among others—challenged Portuguese and Spanish monopolies of overseas trade. They also made important voyages of exploration. Sir Francis Drake, for example, sailed westward from North America across the Pacific Ocean, around the southern tip of Africa, and north to England. In 1580 he became the first English sea captain to sail around the globe.

However, the English sea dogs were better known for plundering foreign shipping. They stole from Spanish ships not protected by convoys, and they seized slaves that were being shipped from Africa and sold them in Spanish colonies. These repeated raids greatly angered King Philip II of Spain. He protested to Queen Elizabeth, who claimed that she was helpless in the matter. Secretly though, Queen Elizabeth supported the sea dogs and shared what they had stolen. Pirates and patriots, the sea dogs played a part in England's defeat of the Spanish Armada in 1588, and they strengthened the seafaring tradition of the island nation.

Upon Francis Drake's return from his three-year circumnavigation of the world, Queen Elizabeth I knighted him for his discoveries.

The English in India

The defeat of the Spanish Armada encouraged the English to establish colonies overseas. In 1600 Queen Elizabeth I granted a charter to a trading company called the British East India Company.

This company set up trading posts at Bombay, Calcutta, and Madras in India. The company dealt mainly with local rulers because the Mughal Empire had declined in power. To gain the support of these rulers, the company helped those who were weak, used force without hesitation against those who opposed the company, and extended generous gifts to those who might be swayed by bribery.

The British East India Company eventually set up a few trading posts in Malaya and the East Indies, but India remained its headquarters and chief source of trade and wealth. The company became extremely wealthy and powerful and virtually ruled India into the 1800s.

This is a painted wood model from the first half of the nineteenth century depicting an Indian court (called the Cutcherry) which was presided over by an English East India Company officer.

The English in the Americas

England was slow to establish colonies in North America. Initially, the English explored the continent in order to find the so-called Northwest Passage to Asia—a non-existent water route through the Americas to the north and west. The Spanish dominated the southern route around Cape Horn in South America.

Henry Hudson searched extensively and unsuccessfully for the Northwest Passage. In 1609, on a voyage for the Dutch, he charted much of the coast of eastern North America and explored the river that now carries his name. On a voyage for the English one year later, he explored Hudson Bay in northern Canada.

As the search for a Northwest Passage to India continued, the English began to establish colonies along North America's eastern coast. The first of these colonies were founded by private companies or individuals. The English established the first permanent settlement at Jamestown, Virginia, in 1607. In 1620 they founded the second settlement, Plymouth, in what is now the state of Massachusetts.

Many of the settlements were founded for commercial purposes. Investors hoped that the settlers would raise products that would make the home country more self-sufficient. However, the first North American colonies proved to be an economic disappointment. Few of the original investors made a profit or even got their money back. Many colonists had reasons other than profit for settling in North America. These people hoped to find greater political and religious freedom and to make better lives for their families.

As in other colonial empires, the English used slavery in their colonies, especially those in southern North America and the West Indies. Settlements on the Caribbean islands, such as Barbados, were commercially successful largely because of slave labor.

Self-government set England's empire apart from other European colonial empires. Most English colonies had some form of representative assembly, or governing body, although official control remained firmly in the hands of the home country.

In his expeditions for the Dutch and the English, Henry Hudson explored a river and a bay that were later given his name. This image shows the landing of Henry Hudson on Manhattan Island.

Mercantilism and the British Colonies

The British government did intervene in colonial economies in attempts to make them more profitable. The policy of mercantilism maintained that colonies existed for the benefit of the home country. Colonies supplied needed raw materials and furnished a market for Britain's manufactured products.

The British government passed a number of mercantilist regulations that affected its North American colonies, beginning in the 1650s. One regulation required that certain colonial products could be sold only in Britain, even though higher prices might be obtainable in another country. Other regulations discouraged colonists from manufacturing. For example, the British government forbade colonists to ship woolen cloth that they had manufactured to places outside their own colony.

These trade regulations aroused resentment, and colonists found many ways to evade them. Colonists avoided paying taxes whenever and however they could. Smuggling became a respectable occupation and was difficult to prevent because the long American coastline had many harbors and inlets. Until the mid-1700s, however, the British government only loosely enforced its trade restrictions.

Section 4 Review

1. **Define** sea dogs
2. **Identify** John Cabot, Sir Francis Drake, Henry Hudson
3. **Locate and Explain the Significance** Bombay, Hudson Bay, Jamestown, Plymouth, Barbados
4. **Understanding Ideas** What was the significance of the English sea dogs?
5. **Analyzing Ideas** What were the results of British mercantilist policy?

Chapter 3 Review

A.D. **1558–1603**
Elizabeth I reigns.

A.D. **1603**
Stuart dynasty is established in England.

A.D. **1500** A.D. **1550** A.D. **1600**

A.D. **1485–1603**
Tudor monarchs reign.

A.D. **1588**
Spanish Armada is defeated.

Chapter Summary

The following list contains the key concepts you have learned about England, the evolution of its monarchy, and the growth of its empire.

1. Elizabeth I faced threats from Spain abroad and from Catholics and Puritans at home. She established a strong central government while respecting the rights of members of Parliament.
2. The Stuarts believed in the divine right of kings. Their reigns were characterized by quarrels with Parliament over taxation and a wide variety of other issues.
3. Oliver Cromwell and the Puritans executed King Charles I and established a republic called a commonwealth. Cromwell made England strong, but his experiment in republican government failed. After his death, the English restored the monarchy under Charles II.
4. Under the later Stuarts, England feared the prospect of Catholic succession to the throne. Developing political parties called Whigs and Tories united to create a permanent Protestant succession. Parliament passed the Act of Settlement, which was designed to keep Catholics from the English throne.
5. Thomas Hobbes and John Locke each formed a theory of government based on a social contract between rulers and ruled. Locke's idea that the people had the right to overthrow a ruler who violated the contract expressed the English and later American and French justification for revolution.
6. In the first half of the 1700s, Britain established an empire in North America and India that was largely unchallenged. Mercantilism, the idea that colonies exist for the benefit of the home country, was the governing philosophy of the empire.

Reviewing Important Terms

On a separate sheet of paper, supply the term that correctly completes each statement.

1. Members of the House of Commons came from the _____, who represented the landowning classes, and the _____, who represented the urban merchants and professional people.
2. A(n) _____ is a document outlining the fundamental laws and principles that govern a nation.
3. The _____ _____ _____ protected individuals against arbitrary arrest and imprisonment.
4. The _____ is a small group of advisers or ministers who deal with government policy and issues.
5. English traders and pirates who challenged overseas trade monopolies were called _____ _____.
6. A radical attempt to change the very structure of a country's government is called a(n) _____.
7. England developed a(n) _____ _____ _____, or government in which a constitution limits the powers of the monarch and a prime minister is the real head of the government.

Developing Critical Thinking Skills

1. **Understanding Ideas** (a) Why did James I and Charles I quarrel with Parliament? (b) What issues led to a civil war in the 1640s?
2. **Explaining Ideas** (a) Why did Catholicism cause fear among many English people during the 1500s and 1600s? (b) What did Parliament do in 1701 to prevent Catholics from becoming kings and queens of England?
3. **Comparing Ideas** Compare the strengths and weaknesses of Parliament and monarchs during the reigns of Elizabeth I, Charles I, and William and Mary.
4. **Applying Ideas** (a) How did the view of English monarchs differ from the view of members of Parliament on the role and succession of royalty? (b) What other issues lay behind the divisions among people, Parliament, and rulers as they struggled to govern their country?
5. **Evaluating Ideas** Do you think the conflict between the monarchy and Parliament was more about control of government or more about religious issues? Explain.

Relating Geography to History

Use the map of the British Isles on page 128 to answer the following questions. (a) What geographical advantages did the Scots have over Charles I in the rebellion over the imposition of Anglican liturgy? (b) How did geography contribute to the difference between English attitudes toward the Scots and toward the Irish?

A.D. 1625–1649
Charles I reigns.

A.D. 1660
Monarchy is restored.

A.D. 1679
Parliament passes the Habeas Corpus Act.

A.D. 1688–1689
Glorious Revolution occurs.

A.D. 1701
Parliament passes the Act of Settlement.

A.D. 1727–1760
George II reigns.

A.D. 1650   A.D. 1700   A.D. 1750

A.D. 1628
Petition of Right is signed by Charles I.

A.D. 1642–1660
English Revolution occurs.

A.D. 1689
Parliament formalizes the Bill of Rights.

A.D. 1707
England and Scotland are united.

A.D. 1714
Hanoverian dynasty is established in England.

Relating Past to Present

1. The Petition of Right, the Habeas Corpus Act, the English Bill of Rights, and the Toleration Act covered many important rights of individual citizens. List the rights protected by these measures. Use American civics or government books to find out how many of these rights are protected today by the United States Constitution.

2. The British monarchy today has little power, yet the monarchy as an institution is generally respected and supported in Great Britain. The monarch still serves certain functions in Great Britain and what is today known as the Commonwealth of Nations. Examine textbooks that discuss comparative government or articles about British life today, and list some important functions that the monarch still performs. You might want to compare the political role of Queen Elizabeth II with that of Elizabeth I, listing the powers that belonged to the earlier queen that do not belong to the current queen.

Applying History Study Skills

Before completing this activity, review Building History Study Skills on page 126.

During the English Civil War, the victorious Parliamentarians and their generals sought to devise a new government for England. A small party of radicals, called the Levelers, demanded a radical change for the government of England. Their point of view is represented in the Putney Debates, from which the following selection is taken. Read the excerpt below, and try to identify the point of view presented.

"I do hear nothing at all that can convince me why any man that is born in England ought not to have his voice in election of burgesses. It is said that if a man have not a permanent interest, he can have no claim; and we must be no freer than the laws will let us to be . . . and I do think that the main cause why Almighty God gave men reason, it was that they should make use of that reason, and that they should improve it for that end and purpose that God gave it [to] them. . . . I do not find anything in the law of God, that a lord shall choose twenty burgesses, and a gentleman but two, or a poor man shall choose none: I find no such thing in the law of

nature, nor in the law of nations . . . and am still of the same opinion, that every man born in England cannot, ought not, neither by the law of God nor the law of nature, to be exempted from the choice of those who are to make laws and for him to live under, and for him (for aught I know) to lose his life under."

1. (a) What is the main idea? (b) How is the main idea repeated and emphasized?
2. What are the signal words?
3. Which ideas has the speaker neglected to mention?
4. Why are the speaker's ideas considered radical?
5. What is the speaker's point of view about men and their relationship to their government?

📑 internet**connect**

Sir Walter Raleigh did not limit his activities to the high seas. In addition to being a favorite of Elizabeth I, he was also a prolific writer. Search the Internet through the HRW Web site to find and print out examples of his writing. Discuss what you have found in class.

HRW
GO TO: go.hrw.com
KEYWORD: SC0 Sir Walter Raleigh

Building Your Portfolio

1. **Writing a Report** Prepare a report about the Spanish Armada. Answer the following questions in your report. (a) What was the background of the Spanish-English conflict? (b) Why did Philip II want to conquer England? (c) How was religion a factor? (d) How was Elizabeth I regarded by other European monarchs? (e) How was the Spanish fleet defeated? (f) What was the significance of the English victory? You might use encyclopedias and Garrett Mattingly's *Armada* (Houghton Mifflin). Place your report in your portfolio.

2. **Presenting an Oral Report** Rulers such as Queen Isabella of Spain and Queen Elizabeth I of England supported voyages of exploration. Find out more about these rulers and why they supported these adventures. Include examples of voyages of exploration in your research. Present an oral report to the class. Place your notes in your portfolio.

CHAPTER 4

The American and French Revolutions

TIME
A.D. 1715–1829

A.D. 1715–1829

| 3.7 million B.C. | 4000 B.C. | A.D. 2100 |

PLACE
North America, France, and the rest of Europe

Europe

North America

France

A 1789 painting illustrating the day after the storming of the Bastille

Significance

The idea that people should have a voice in government greatly influenced French political writers of the 1700s. In addition, the American Revolution, with its central theme of the freedom and dignity of human beings, helped inspire the French people to overthrow the existing government and establish a government based on these ideas.

Terms to Define

Enlightenment	conservatives
rationalism	radicals
philosophes	moderates
salons	universal manhood
popular sovereignty	suffrage
enlightened despotism	conscription
Patriots	counterrevolution
Loyalists	coup d'état
federal system of	plebiscite
government	Concordat
executive branch	nationalism
legislative branch	scorched-earth policy
judicial branch	legitimacy
Bill of Rights	indemnity
bourgeoisie	reaction
tithe	reactionaries
émigrés	liberalism
departments	

People to Identify

Denis Diderot	Maximilien
Baron de Montesquieu	Robespierre
Voltaire	Napoleon Bonaparte
Jean-Jacques Rousseau	Horatio Nelson
Lord North	Duke of Wellington
Louis XV	Czar Alexander I
Louis XVI	Louis XVIII
Emmanuel Joseph Sieyès	Castlereagh
Olympe de Gouges	Talleyrand
Georges-Jacques Danton	Metternich

Places to Locate

Concord	Kingdom of the
Yorktown	Netherlands
Elba	Saxony
Waterloo	Grand Duchy of
St. Helena	Warsaw

Chapter Theme Questions

- **Philosophy** How might applying logic and reason to politics change people's political views?
- **War and Diplomacy** How might a colonial society react to mistreatment by the home country?
- **Politics and Law** What conditions might lead to revolution, and how might revolution open the door to new political systems?

Although Baroness Emmuska Orczy wrote the novel *The Scarlet Pimpernel* years after the French Revolution, in it she captured the spirit of an age that transformed the social order, as this excerpt shows.

❝ *During the greater part of the day, the guillotine had been kept busy at its ghastly work; all that France had boasted of in the past centuries of ancient names and blue blood had paid toll to her desire for liberty and for fraternity. . . .*

But this was as it should be. Were not the people now the rulers of France? Every aristocrat was a traitor; . . . for two hundred years now, the people had sweated and toiled and starved to keep a lustful court in lavish extravagance. Now the descendants of those who had helped to make those courts brilliant had to hide for their lives—to fly, if they wished to avoid the tardy vengeance of the people. **❞**

Like many revolutions, the French Revolution traced its roots to early political writers.

Section 1

The Enlightenment

Focus Questions

- **What changing worldviews characterized the Age of Enlightenment?**
- **What qualities of government did philosophes praise and promote?**
- **How were the ideas of Diderot, Montesquieu, Voltaire, and Rousseau similar? How were their ideas different?**

Some people who lived during the 1700s thought of their century as an Age of Enlightenment. Spurred by Descartes's methodology for understanding the truth and by Newton's explanation of the working of the universe, researchers had made great advances in the physical sciences. During the **Enlightenment** philosophers believed they could apply the scientific method and use reason to logically explain human nature.

Characteristics of the Enlightenment

During the 1700s, an increasing number of people began to believe that every natural phenomenon had both a cause and an effect. The thinkers of the Enlightenment attempted to test everything by observation and to determine the cause-and-effect relationships between natural events.

Another characteristic of the Enlightenment was **rationalism**, the belief that truth can be arrived at solely by reason, or rational, logical thinking. Because of this central belief, historians also refer to the Age of Enlightenment as the Age of Reason.

Thinkers during the Enlightenment also believed in natural law—that objects in nature behaved in ways that humans could understand and predict. The discoveries of Newton and other scientists seemed to support the idea of an orderly universe. Many individuals came to feel that laws of nature governed the universe and all its creatures. These beliefs formed the foundation of modern natural sciences.

God, they believed, had created the world and made rules for all living things. Just as the law of gravity governed the physical movement of planets, so other laws governed human behavior. To live in harmony, people had to live according to this natural law. Thus the thinkers of the Enlightenment became convinced that progress could always take place.

Crusaders of the Enlightenment

Their contemporaries called the thinkers of the Enlightenment **philosophes** (fee·luh·ZAWFS); *philosophe* is the French word for "philosopher." The philosophes were not only philosophers, however, but also critics of society. They wrote to one another, and they published their ideas in books, plays, pamphlets, newspapers, and "encyclopedias." Before and during the Reformation, the humanists and religious reformers had used the printing press effectively. Now the philosophes used the printed word to spread the ideas of the Enlightenment.

The *Encyclopedia.* Although Britain and its allies curbed Louis XIV's expansion of French rule and maintained the balance of power, France remained both the strongest political power and the dominant cultural influence in Europe. Educated people throughout Europe spoke and wrote French. They read the *Encyclopedia*, a handbook or reference book on the Enlightenment, which became the most famous publication of the period.

The philosophe Denis Diderot (dee·DROH) edited the *Encyclopedia*. He and his co-editor, Jean d'Alembert, published the first edition of the *Encyclopedia* in 28 volumes between 1751 and 1772.

The leading philosophes all contributed articles to the *Encyclopedia*. Their writings criticized the church, the government, the slave trade, torture, taxes, and war. They covered nearly every subject—many of them technical in nature—in the rational, questioning style of the Enlightenment.

The French authorities frowned on critical writings, however, and they imprisoned Diderot and several other philosophes. Nevertheless, people throughout Europe purchased editions of the *Encyclopedia*, read it, and adopted its ideas.

Salons. Philosophes gravitated to France, particularly to Paris. There famous hostesses set up **salons**, or gatherings of the social, political, and cultural elite. One such hostess, Marie-Thérèse Geoffrin, subsidized the *Encyclopedia*. Amid lavish entertainment and witty and intelligent conversation, the philosophes could meet and discuss their ideas.

Political Criticism

The philosophes critically examined the political and social institutions of their day. They tried to learn how these institutions had developed. They analyzed the power of kings, the special position of the church, and the privileges of clergy and nobles. Several philosophes attacked the idea of privileged classes. They thought that political and social institutions should be changed to benefit everyone instead of just certain groups.

Montesquieu. A number of French philosophes adopted the ideas of John Locke, about whom you read in Chapter 3. In 1748 Baron de Montesquieu (MOHN·tes·kyoo) published *The Spirit of the Laws*, in which he tried to describe what he considered a perfect government. After studying all existing governments, Montesquieu concluded that the British had the most nearly perfect form. He wrote that its greatest strength lay in the fact that power was divided equally among the three branches of government: the legislative, which made the laws; the executive, which administered them; and the judicial, which interpreted and applied them. Each branch balanced and checked the power of the others.

Montesquieu's high opinion of the British form of government was based on a misunderstanding of it. As you know from reading Chapter 3, the legislative and executive powers were largely combined in the House of Commons rather than organized into

Marie-Thérèse Geoffrin's salon in the Hôtel Rambouillet provided an opportunity for others to meet artists on Mondays and writers on Wednesdays.

separate branches of government. Nevertheless, Montesquieu's ideas carried great weight in the formation of limited monarchies in Europe. In the United States, his concept of checks and balances influenced the framers of the Constitution in 1787.

Voltaire. The French writer François-Marie Arouet, known as Voltaire, exemplified the spirit of the Enlightenment. After serving two sentences in the Bastille (Paris's prison), Voltaire fled for a time to Britain. He commented on the political system of Britain and British customs in *Philosophical Letters* (1734), which helped popularize British ideas in France.

When he returned to France, Voltaire attacked everything he considered sham or superstition. He wrote a variety of works, including plays, histories, essays, poems, and books. His novel *Candide* is a satire that ridicules everything from oppressive government to prejudice and bigotry. Voltaire was a prominent public figure, and he fought against intolerance and injustice, particularly in cases involving religious prejudice. He is credited with a famous statement on

freedom of speech: "I disapprove of what you say, but I will defend to the death your right to say it."

Rousseau. Jean-Jacques Rousseau (roo·SOH) first gained attention in 1749 by writing that history repeats itself in cycles of decay and that we have only to look at Egypt, Greece, Rome, and Byzantium for examples. In his most famous book, *The Social Contract,* published in 1762, Rousseau wrote that people are born good but that environment, education, and laws corrupt them. The free and good state into which people are born can be preserved only if they live under a government that they have chosen and can control. In other words, just laws and wise governments must be based on **popular sovereignty**—that is, created by and subject to the will of the people. This idea of Rousseau's had enormous influence, extending even to the colonial revolutionaries in North America.

In some ways, Rousseau belongs outside the Enlightenment. In an age of reason, he distrusted reason, believing that it brought corruption and misery. Rousseau preferred a kind of pastoral state, free of complicated institutions. By the 1780s, many people who had tired of rationalism accepted Rousseau's philosophy. His influence was greatest in the later years of the Enlightenment.

His work foreshadows romanticism, which became significant during the first half of the 1800s.

Enlightened Despotism

The philosophes argued and worked to make a better world based on reason. They did not criticize religion and people's faith, as it might have appeared. Rather, they fought superstition, the institution of the church, and the ignorance of some of the clergy. They recognized the role of monarchy, but they disliked absolute monarchy. Most philosophes favored **enlightened despotism**—a system of government in which absolute monarchs ruled according to the principles of the Enlightenment.

In countries with absolute monarchies and strong censorship, rulers and clergy fought the ideas of the philosophes. They prohibited the publishing of books by philosophes, or they censored the books, removing any material unflattering to public officials or the church. The clergy preached against the philosophes, whom they accused of undermining the church.

Faced with this unfavorable attention, the philosophes became cautious. Some, such as Voltaire, moved to other countries, out of the reach of the French authorities. Later, other people not content merely to discuss such ideas preferred instead to act on them. By the late 1700s, both North America and France, the home of the Enlightenment, were settings for major political and social revolutions.

Section 1 Review

1. **Define** Enlightenment, rationalism, philosophes, salons, popular sovereignty, enlightened despotism
2. **Identify** Denis Diderot, Baron de Montesquieu, Voltaire, Jean-Jacques Rousseau
3. **Understanding Ideas** What were the main characteristics of Enlightenment thinking?
4. **Summarizing Ideas** Describe three examples of systems of government that philosophes found to be praiseworthy.
5. **Contrasting Ideas** Compare and contrast the ideas of the following philosophes: Diderot, Montesquieu, Voltaire, and Rousseau.

The American Revolution

Focus Questions
- How did the colonists' attitudes toward Britain change during the early and mid-1700s?
- Why were the Articles of Confederation considered to be inadequate?
- What system of government did the Constitution establish?

New ideas were not confined to Europe in the 1700s. In North America, the British colonists' new way of life and their distance from Britain began to create new attitudes about their relationship with the home country. Their immediate concerns had to do with British trade regulations and how they affected the colonists' quality of life. The colonists also disliked the French along their borders. After defeating the French, however, the North American colonists struggled increasingly with the British and finally declared their independence.

British-French Rivalry

While the British established colonies along the Atlantic coast of North America, the French developed settlements to the north and west in what was called New France. In the 1700s, as American settlers moved westward across the Appalachian Mountains, conflict with the French was inevitable.

The French and British governments had struggled for decades for dominance in Europe. The conflicts between these two powers were also acted out in North America, mostly in the form of frontier skirmishes. The colonies counted on British assistance for defense against the French, and both sides recruited Native Americans to fight with them.

The decisive conflict that settled the British-French imperial rivalry in North America was the French and Indian War (1754–1763), known in Europe as the Seven Years' War. The Treaty of Paris in 1763 confirmed the sweeping British victories not only in North America but in many other parts of the world as well. The British now controlled land from the Atlantic Ocean to the Mississippi River and from the Gulf of Mexico almost to the Arctic Ocean. British power and worldwide prestige had reached a new height.

Increased Control over the Colonies

The British built up a large debt while waging war against the French on three continents between 1754 and 1763. Because the British had helped the colonists, they felt justified in asking the colonists to help repay this debt.

At the same time, British governments during the 1760s lacked a consistent policy toward their greatly expanded North American empire. In 1763, following an American Indian uprising, the British forbade any colonists to settle in the land west of the Appalachian Mountains. Great Britain also attempted to bring its colonies under closer economic control by enforcing mercantilist trade regulations. The Sugar Act of 1764 imposed new taxes on sugar and many other items imported into North America from non-British colonies. The colonists came to believe that the British intended to curb their liberties.

In 1765 Parliament passed the Stamp Act. This law required that the colonists pay a tax—in the form of special stamps—on wills, mortgages, contracts, newspapers, pamphlets, calendars, playing cards, and almanacs. The colonists unified in opposition to the Stamp Act. They began to think as a single people instead of as people from 13 separate colonies. They boycotted British products. Their refusal to buy British goods exerted economic pressure on British merchants, who complained to Parliament. As a result, the British repealed the Stamp Act in 1766.

With each new law, the colonists increased their resistance. Some laws were repealed; others were not. The colonists argued that they had no representatives in the British Parliament and that "taxation without representation" constituted tyranny. Between 1763 and 1775, relations between the British government and the American colonies grew steadily worse.

Intensified Conflict

King George III, who reigned from 1760 to 1820, was the first Hanoverian monarch to be born in England and the first to place England's interests over those of his German possession of Hanover.

George believed that Parliament had too much power in the constitutional system governing Great Britain. He was determined to select his own ministers from the "King's Friends" in Parliament. The political world became extremely unsettled. Six prime ministers came to power during an eight-year period. Against this confusion, the crises leading to the final break with the American colonies unfolded. As the

The Stamp Act required stamps such as this one to be placed on all the colonists' commercial and legal papers.

colonists hardened their resistance to British policy, George III became equally determined to coerce them. By 1770 he found a prime minister who was willing to carry out this objective—Lord North.

The colonists were by no means united for independence. However, more and more came to believe that breaking away from British rule was the only way to guarantee their rights. About one third of the colonists were **Patriots**, who actively favored independence. Another third were **Loyalists** (also known as Tories), who strongly opposed independence. The remainder of the colonists did not take sides.

In 1773 Lord North's government allowed the British East India Company to ship tea directly to the colonies. Angry colonists, upset at the prospect of a monopoly, threw the tea into the Boston harbor (the "Boston Tea Party"). The British government responded to the Boston Tea Party by closing the port of Boston to all shipping. Colonists called this act and a series of other laws passed in 1774 the Intolerable Acts.

The Patriots took action. In the fall of 1774, delegates from 12 of the 13 colonies—Georgia did not attend—met in Philadelphia in the First Continental Congress. The delegates demanded that the colonists be granted the full rights of British citizens. The delegates also pledged to support each other in the future and agreed to meet the following year if Great Britain did not repeal the Intolerable Acts.

The Battles of Lexington and Concord (shown above) marked the beginning of the American Revolution.

In April 1775, British troops, feeling threatened, marched from Boston to seize colonial guns and gunpowder stored nearby. At the towns of Lexington and Concord, the British fought skirmishes with groups of armed colonists, who forced them to retreat to Boston. The American Revolution had begun.

The Declaration of Independence

When delegates to a Second Continental Congress met in Philadelphia in May 1775, many still hoped for reconciliation. Then news of the fighting at Lexington spread, and attitudes changed. The delegates took steps to prepare for war. A little more than a year later, the delegates voted to declare their freedom from Great Britain. On July 4, 1776, they adopted the Declaration of Independence, which established the United States of America as an independent nation. Thomas Jefferson, the declaration's principal author, expressed American sentiments with nobility and grandeur.

The Declaration of Independence shows the influence of Enlightenment philosophers such as John Locke. It states that all men are created equal and have certain "unalienable Rights." Among these rights are "Life, Liberty, and the pursuit of Happiness." This idea—the right to equal opportunity and equal justice—is the foundation of our democratic ideal. Although the ideal was not stated to include women or

slaves, the demand for a broader equality and justice concerned many people.

The declaration also stated that all powers of government come from the people. No government can exist without the consent of its citizens because citizens create governments to protect individual rights. If a government fails to protect or attempts to destroy rights, the people have the right "to alter or to abolish" the government and to set up a new government that will safeguard their rights.

These were extreme ideas. It is one thing to reject absolute monarchy. It is quite another to give people the right to abolish a government that does not uphold the rights of the citizens.

The War for Independence

Each side had advantages and weaknesses as the American Revolutionary War began. The Americans were defending their own homes in well-known territory. The British had to cross an ocean, bringing with them most of their military supplies and equipment.

The war against the colonists was not popular in Great Britain. Some British even sympathized with the Americans. The British had not favored large standing armies since the English civil war in the late 1600s. In addition, Britain had no allies against the colonists. Therefore, King George III had to hire mercenaries, many of them German. Nevertheless, Great Britain's strength lay in the organization of its army and navy. British troops were well trained, and the British fleet was the strongest in the world.

The lack of unity among the colonies helped the British. The colonies voluntarily sent representatives to the Continental Congress, but progress was slow because the proposals of the Continental Congress had to be almost unanimously passed. Moreover, to meet the immediate need of financing the war, the Continental Congress borrowed money and printed its own paper money. However, because it had no way of paying its debts, its credit was poor.

The weaknesses of the American government made it difficult to build a strong army. At first the American forces were mostly poorly trained and undisciplined volunteers. The American troops could seldom successfully oppose the well-trained British army in large-scale battle. Nevertheless, the Americans had good leaders, including General George Washington, who served as commander of the American forces. In addition, other nations offered military officers, troops, ships, and money to the colonists' cause.

The fighting. Most of the fighting took place between 1776 and 1781. (See map on this page.) A major turning point came when the Americans defeated a British force under General John Burgoyne at Saratoga, New York, in October 1777. Now the colonists seemed to have a chance of winning. The French government, eager to weaken the British empire, agreed to an alliance with the United States. Spain and the Netherlands also joined the colonists' efforts. In 1781 the Americans and their French allies trapped the main British army at Yorktown, Virginia. (See map on page 142.) With this victory, the Americans had effectively won the war.

Ending the war. In 1783, after two years of negotiation, with Benjamin Franklin as the shrewd and persuasive chief American negotiator, the British and the Americans and their allies signed the Treaty of Paris. The Americans won not only independence but also a territory much larger than the original thirteen colonies. (See map on page 143.)

Military Campaigns of the American Revolution, 1775–1783

3 Captured by Americans, Nov. 12, 1775.

Lake Superior

QUEBEC

Montreal

Ft. Ticonderoga May 10–12, 1775

1 War begins, April 19, 1775.

ME (MA)

NH

Bunker Hill

4 First great American victory, Oct. 17, 1777.

Saratoga

Lexington and Concord

Boston

MA

2 British defeat Americans, June 17, 1775.

Lake Michigan

Lake Huron

Lake Erie

NY

CT

RI

St. Lawrence River

60° W

40° N

PA

Germantown, Oct. 4, 1777

Valley Forge

Brandywine, Sept. 11, 1777

New York

NJ

5 Campaign of Sept. 1777 to June 1778. Washington spends terrible winter at Valley Forge.

6 George Rogers Clark defeats British along Ohio River, 1778–1779.

Philadelphia

Vincennes Feb. 25, 1779

Ohio River

MD

DE

VA

10 French blockade, Sept. 1781.

ATLANTIC OCEAN

SPANISH LOUISIANA

APPALACHIAN MOUNTAINS

Yorktown

Guilford Courthouse March 15, 1781

NC

11 General Cornwallis surrenders to Washington, Oct. 19, 1781.

Kings Mountain Oct. 7, 1780

Mississippi River

9 French forces join Washington's army, July 1781–Sept. 1781.

Wilmington

N W E S

Camden Aug. 16, 1780

SC

GA

Charleston

7 Controlled by British, Feb. 1781–Nov. 1781.

8 Occupied by British, May 12, 1780. Recaptured by American general Nathanael Greene, Dec. 14, 1782.

30° N

	American campaign
	British campaign
☼	American victory
☼	British victory
▲▲▲	Blockade

0   125   250 Miles
0   125   250 Kilometers
Albers Equal-Area Projection

Gulf of Mexico

90° W

80° W

70° W

Learning from Maps Saratoga marked the first great American victory.

? Place In what state was the Battle of Saratoga fought?

The Articles of Confederation

In 1781 the American states ratified, or accepted, the Articles of Confederation, a plan of government the Second Continental Congress had adopted in 1777. The Articles of Confederation provided for a central government, with a one-house Congress in which each state had a single vote. Congress had the authority to declare war, make peace, conduct foreign relations, and settle disputes between the states.

The government under the Articles of Confederation lasted from 1781 to 1789. The great weakness of the Articles was that Congress had no power to enforce its measures. The government had no power to tax, to coin money, or to regulate trade with foreign countries or among the states. Laws required the approval of at least nine of the states. The Articles provided for no chief executive officer, and the only courts were state courts.

The Constitution

Americans soon realized that the Articles of Confederation provided inadequate government. In 1787 delegates from the states met again in Philadelphia to revise the Articles. It soon became apparent, however, that what was needed was more than just a revision of the Articles; the delegates needed to write a constitution that would provide the framework for a new, stronger government.

After unanimously electing George Washington as the presiding officer, the delegates to the Constitutional Convention turned to the issue at hand—to create a central government strong enough to act on matters that concerned all the states. At the same time, they wanted to leave the states *some* freedom to act for themselves. To solve this problem, the delegates decided to adopt the **federal system of government.** The resulting Constitution divided governmental powers between the central, or federal, government and the individual states. It gave the federal government the power to declare war, make treaties, coin money, raise armies, and regulate trade with foreign countries. All other powers belonged to or were shared by the states and the people.

The framers of the Constitution created three branches of the federal government. The **executive branch** (the president) enforced the laws, the **legislative branch** (Congress) made the laws, and the **judicial branch** (the federal courts) interpreted and applied the laws. The framers gave each branch certain powers and specified in the Constitution how each branch of government acted as a check on the others.

Some Americans were concerned that the Constitution did not offer enough protection and freedom to individuals. They wanted to be sure of what rights they did or did not have. The first 10 amendments of the Constitution, added in 1791, are known collectively as the **Bill of Rights.** They specifically guarantee certain basic rights of every United States citizen. These rights include freedom of religion, speech, press, assembly, and petition. The Bill of Rights also guarantees freedom from illegal search and seizure and the right to a jury trial.

The Siege of Yorktown, September 28–October 19, 1781

York River

Gloucester

British ships

French ships

Yorktown

To Williamsburg

Swamp

Surrender field

Swamp

N
W E
S

0   1 Mile
0   1 Kilometer
Polyconic Projection

American forces
French forces
British forces

■ Building
Road
Fortification

Learning from Maps The British were trapped with their backs to the sea during the siege of Yorktown.

? Movment What country provided the Americans with aid at sea?

The United States in 1783

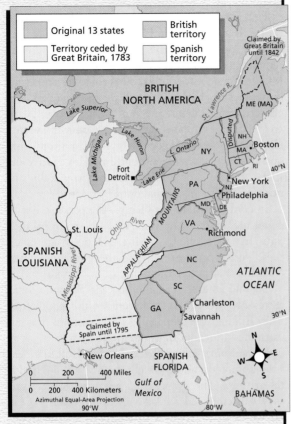

Legend:
- Original 13 states
- Territory ceded by Great Britain, 1783
- British territory
- Spanish territory
- Claimed by Great Britain until 1842

BRITISH NORTH AMERICA

Lake Superior, Lake Michigan, Lake Huron, Fort Detroit, Lake Erie, L. Ontario, St. Lawrence R.

ME (MA), NH, MA, Boston, NY, CT, RI, 40°N, New York, PA, NJ, Philadelphia, MD, DE, VA, Richmond, NC, SC, Charleston, GA, Savannah, 30°N

Disputed, MOUNTAINS, APPALACHIAN, Ohio River

St. Louis

SPANISH LOUISIANA, Mississippi R.

Claimed by Spain until 1795

New Orleans, SPANISH FLORIDA, Gulf of Mexico, BAHAMAS, ATLANTIC OCEAN

0   200   400 Miles
0   200   400 Kilometers
Azimuthal Equal-Area Projection
90°W   80°W

Learning from Maps The Treaty of Paris gave the United States additional territory to the west of the original 13 colonies.

? Region What was the western border of the new nation?

Effects of American Independence

The American Revolution put into practice the ideas of John Locke and other political philosophers of the Enlightenment. The American experience gave encouragement to people everywhere who opposed domination by absolute monarchy and privileged classes. The adoption of democratic ideals of government was a landmark in world history.

The democracy that the Americans achieved in 1789, however, was very different from democracy today. In 1789, the states restricted voting to adult, free, property-owning males. Also in 1789, women could not vote, and the large black slave population had no political rights at all.

Clearly, many liberties still had to be won. Nonetheless, from the American Revolution, there emerged a new kind of government and a new relationship among citizens. Its final form may not have been what most American patriots intended when the Revolution began. However, their common beliefs and the economic and political needs of the new nation created a country that inspired loyalty.

Section 2 Review

1. **Define** Patriots, Loyalists, federal system of government, executive branch, legislative branch, judicial branch, Bill of Rights
2. **Identify** Lord North
3. **Locate and Explain the Significance** Concord, Yorktown
4. **Interpreting Ideas** How did mercantilism affect the British colonies in North America?
5. **Analyzing Ideas** Why were the Articles of Confederation ineffective?
6. **Summarizing Ideas** Describe the government created by the Constitution.

Section 3

The French Revolution

Focus Questions

- What conditions in France in the early and mid-1700s contributed to the movement there toward revolution?
- What did the National Assembly accomplish?
- What type of government did the Constitution of 1791 establish?
- What occurred after the Constitution of 1791 went into effect?

At almost the same time that revolution was brewing in the British colonies, disturbing events were also occurring in France. When the French Revolution began in 1789, the rest of Europe watched in horrified astonishment. For more than 100 years, France had been the largest and most powerful European nation. Within a few months, however, the king lost his power to make laws, and eventually

While paintings such as this one seem to idealize peasant life, in reality members of the Third Estate lived under harsh and oppressive conditions that were anything but idyllic.

The First and Second Estates had the fewest people, but these estates also had the most wealth, power, and privilege.

First Estate. The First Estate consisted of the clergy of the Roman Catholic Church and constituted less than 1 percent of the population. The church retained many of the privileges it had held since the Middle Ages. Only church courts could try priests and bishops. The clergy did not have to pay taxes. The church owned about one tenth of all French land and received enormous amounts of money from rents, taxes, and fees. The higher clergy—archbishops, bishops, and abbots—held most of this wealth. As a result, some of these people had become lazy, worldly, and neglectful of their spiritual duties.

In contrast, the lower clergy—the parish priests—performed most of the work and received very little pay. In addition to giving religious guidance, these parish priests tended to the problems of and educated their parishioners.

Second Estate. The nobility, the Second Estate, represented less than 2 percent of the population. They still had special privileges and customs that had originated in feudal times: the right to wear a sword; primogeniture, or the right of the eldest son to inherit titles and lands; and the right to function as "lord of the manor." The nobles paid few taxes, if any, and they still collected feudal dues from peasants. Only nobles held the highest positions in the army and government. Although some cared about the welfare of France, as a class the nobility were thoughtless, irresponsible, and extravagant.

Third Estate. The rest of the people of France—approximately 97 percent—belonged to the Third Estate. This Third Estate was itself subdivided into three groups.

At the top stood the **bourgeoisie**—the city-dwelling middle class—made up of merchants, manufacturers, and professional people such as doctors and lawyers. Many of them possessed wealth and education. Below the bourgeoisie came the laborers and artisans of the cities. The peasants ranked at the bottom of the Third Estate and often led miserable lives. By the 1700s, most peasants still owed feudal dues and services such as working on roads. They paid rent for the land they worked, the heaviest taxes, and one tenth of their income—the **tithe**—to the church. They worked long and hard, but they had no voice in making or changing the laws that kept them under the absolute control of their landlords and the king.

the people's elected representatives voted for his execution. These new rulers wrote a constitution and reformed many laws. The radical change made people feel that they were living in a new era. They began to refer to the period before 1789 as the Old Regime.

The Old Regime

How did the French Revolution happen? To answer that question, we must look first at the Old Regime. You will recall from earlier chapters that the French kings constructed an absolute monarchy in which the king's will was law. You will remember, too, that the French organized their society into three estates. Great inequality existed among these estates.

Growing Discontent

Around the mid-1700s, discontent in France began to grow. Several factors explain this discontent. The first resulted from the growth of the French population. Families had more children to support, and they needed more food and money.

Changing economic conditions in France also spurred discontent. The nobles, clergy, and some of the bourgeoisie who owned land pressed the peasants for higher rents. In the cities, laborers found food prices rising higher and higher, but wages were not going up as quickly. The artisans and peasants resented the rich, who collected their rents, lived in big houses, and had plenty to eat. The poor blamed the king for allowing prices to get so high. They loathed having to pay taxes when the nobles and clergy did not. Sometimes the poor took to the streets and rioted against these higher prices and taxes. The worsening economic conditions also reinforced the determination of the first two estates to protect their most important privilege: freedom from taxation.

Although the bourgeoisie prospered during the 1700s, they too experienced discontent. They wanted political power equal to their economic strength. Rich merchants and manufacturers resented paying taxes when the nobles and clergy did not. The bourgeoisie wanted to be able to conduct business without any interference from government. They also wanted their sons to have important positions in the church, army, and government. However, only nobles could hold such positions.

Discontent simmered among the First and Second Estates too. For a century or more, the nobility and upper clergy had disliked the increasing concentration of power in the hands of French kings. France became larger and its kings more powerful, with larger armies at their disposal. The nobles did not profit from this trend; instead, they lost much of their influence.

Mutual discontent. The various groups in French society had different kinds of grievances, but they shared the same ideas and used the same words to express them. They all talked of "liberty" and "equality" as their natural rights. Even though they meant different things to different people, these ideas of liberty and equality more or less unified France's various groups in a major challenge to the king's power in 1789.

The Financial Crisis

The crisis that now paralyzed France stemmed from many years of conflict. The wars of Louis XIV had left France saddled with a huge debt. In 1715 a new king, Louis XV, had begun his reign, and for nearly two decades France had enjoyed peace. However, the national debt had continued to grow. Wise rulers might have averted this financial crisis, which ultimately toppled the monarchy, but the Bourbons had apparently lacked that wisdom.

Louis XV. King Louis XV's reign, one of the longest in French history, lasted 59 years—from 1715 to 1774. Only 5 years old when he came to the throne, he began his reign backed by the goodwill of the French people, who called him Louis the Well-Beloved. The intelligent Louis XV might have become a great king, but in later years his laziness, personal vices, and intrigues exhausted the country's goodwill.

When taxes did not produce enough money to meet expenses, Louis borrowed more and more from the bankers. He refused to economize. Warned that his actions endangered France, he supposedly remarked, "It will survive for my time. After me, the deluge."

Louis XVI. In 1774 Louis XVI succeeded Louis XV as the ruler of France. His wife, Marie Antoinette, the daughter of the Austrian empress Maria Theresa, served as the target for all people determined to undermine the monarchy. To begin with, her marriage to Louis was part of an unpopular alliance between Austria and France. She had beauty, grace, and charm, but she chose her friends unwisely and allowed their ideas to influence her unwelcome involvement with politics. In time the French people came to hate her.

King at the age of 19, Louis XVI cared more for hunting than governing his country. However, France's worsening debt, which had grown rapidly because of French assistance to the United States during the American Revolution, forced him to tackle his governmental tasks.

Louis sought help from financial experts. They all gave him the same advice: tax the first two estates. Each time new taxes were proposed, however, the nobles protested and refused to cooperate. Sometimes they led riots that the king found difficult to put down. By 1787 the country had exhausted its credit, and bankers refused to lend the government more money. France faced financial disaster.

Reluctantly, Louis XVI decided to convene the Estates General at Versailles in May 1789. He hoped that by calling together the representatives of all three estates, not just of the nobility, he could get approval for his plan to tax the wealthy.

The Meeting of the Estates General

At the time the king called the meeting of the Estates General, France was suffering from crippling inflation in addition to the government's financial crisis. Moreover, the harvest of 1788 had been poor; because food was in short supply, it was extremely expensive. Peasants and urban laborers found they had to spend half their income just for bread.

The planned meeting of the Estates General created feelings of excitement and expectation among the people. Emmanuel Joseph Sieyès (syay·YES), a clergyman who would become a leading revolutionary, expressed the grievances of the Third Estate:

> "What then is the Third Estate? All. But an 'all' that is fettered [chained] and oppressed. What would it be without the privileged order? It would be all; but free and flourishing. Nothing will go well without the Third Estate; everything would go considerably better without the two others."

The French people hoped the meeting of the Estates General would solve their problems. However, no one knew exactly what powers and rules the Estates General had, because it had not met for 175 years. Many people felt that if it had power only to advise the king and not to make and carry out laws, the meeting would be useless. They also argued about the rules. In the past, the three estates had met separately, and each estate had cast one vote. This procedure had always allowed the clergy and nobles of the First and Second Estates to outvote the Third Estate.

Some representatives of the Third Estate were acquainted with the ideas of Montesquieu and Voltaire. A few nobles, such as Count de Mirabeau, also consented to represent the Third Estate. As the representatives of the majority of the people, they insisted on having a real voice in decisions without being automatically outvoted by the other two estates. The Third Estate had as many representatives as the First and Second Estates combined. Therefore, the Third Estate wanted the three estates to meet together, with representatives voting as individuals.

The Estates General assembled first in a combined meeting on May 5, 1789. Louis XVI then instructed the delegates to follow the old custom of each estate meeting separately and voting as one body. The representatives of the Third Estate refused to meet separately. They claimed that the Estates General represented the French people, not the three classes. Therefore, all the representatives should meet together and vote as individuals.

Always hesitant, Louis failed to take action. As a result, on June 17, 1789, the Third Estate proclaimed itself the National Assembly. The French Revolution had begun. The rebellious representatives then invited the delegates of the other two estates to join them in working for the welfare of France. When the king had the representatives of the Third Estate locked out of their meeting place, they met at a nearby indoor tennis court. There, on June 20, they made a pledge called the Tennis Court Oath. The representatives declared that they would not stop meeting until they had written a constitution for France and had seen it adopted. Finally, the king gave in and ordered the three estates to meet together.

The Third Estate stood relentless in its desire for all the estates to meet together. Locked out of their usual meeting hall, they gathered at a nearby tennis court, pledging to continue their efforts until France adopted a constitution.

The Spread of the Revolution

Now Louis XVI tried to do secretly what he had dared not do openly. He began to bring troops to Paris and to Versailles, where the representatives were meeting. Fearing that he planned to drive out the National Assembly by force, the people of Paris took action. On July 14, 1789, they stormed and captured the Bastille, the hated prison-fortress, in search of weapons. They planned to use the weapons to defend the National Assembly against the royal troops.

The outbreak of violence by the people of Paris led to the formation of a new government for the city.

Independence Days

Most modern nations celebrate a day in honor of their heritage each year. For many this takes the form of an independence day, marking the date when the nation became a distinct political unit.

Perhaps the oldest independence day is August 1 in Switzerland. It marks the day in 1291 when three Swiss cantons, or states, agreed to form a union. Switzerland has now grown to 26 cantons, and they all celebrate independence on August 1.

After World War II, many colonies of European nations gained independence. Each year some hold festivals celebrating their freedom, such as the ones in India (below left) and in Mexico (below right).

Even nations so ancient that they cannot record an independence date have established a national festive day. For example, in England there are fireworks on Guy Fawkes Day, November 5, to commemorate the day in 1605 when the British government uncovered and foiled a plot to blow up Parliament.

A number of nations consider themselves to be creations of revolutions. The French observe

Bastille Day every July 14. It marks the day in 1789 on which a Paris mob stormed the dreaded royal prison, the Bastille. The French people regard this event as the beginning of their freedom.

In the United States, Americans observe a holiday on July 4, the day in 1776 on which the Declaration of Independence was adopted. Americans celebrate the day with parades, speeches, and fireworks (above).

During the War of 1812 between the United States and Great Britain, the British attacked coastal strongholds from the sea with cannons and rockets. After the British bombarded Fort McHenry, in Baltimore, Maryland, in this way, an American lawyer named Francis Scott Key wrote a poem describing the battle that he had witnessed. Later his poem, set to music, became the American national anthem. Today, as Americans watch "the rockets' red glare" during Independence Day fireworks displays, they are reminded of the link between the beauty of the celebration and the seriousness of battle.

Under General Lafayette, the French hero who had fought in the American Revolution, a people's army, the National Guard, was formed. The tricolor—a flag bearing vertical red, white, and blue stripes, which has remained the flag of France—replaced the white flag of the Bourbons with its fleur-de-lis (lily) symbols.

The events in Paris were repeated throughout France. In July and August, a "Great Fear" swept across the land. The peasants believed rumors that the nobles planned to send bandits into the countryside to crush them and the French Revolution. They feared that the nobles would hoard grain and starve the peasants into submission. Eager to take revenge for old wrongs, the peasants attacked and often destroyed monasteries and manor houses. They burned the hated documents that recorded rents, feudal dues, and other obligations. These actions showed how widespread people's hatred of the social system of the Old Regime had become.

The End of the Old Regime

Many members of the National Assembly felt that they could deal with revolutionary violence only by removing the oppression and injustice that produced it. In a little more than a month, they took several important steps in this direction.

As of August 4, 1789, the National Assembly abolished the last remnants of feudalism in France. Delegates repealed the tithe and canceled all feudal dues and services owed by the peasants. They also did away with the special privileges of the First and Second Estates.

Following these reforms, on August 27, 1789, the assembly adopted the Declaration of the Rights of Man and of the Citizen. The English Bill of Rights, the writings of Rousseau and other philosophes, and the American Declaration of Independence strongly influenced this document.

The Declaration of the Rights of Man stated that men are born equal and remain equal before the law. It proclaimed freedom of speech, of the press, and of religion. It guaranteed men the right to take part in their government and to resist oppression and declared that all citizens had an equal right to hold public office. It also assured the right to personal liberty, which men could lose only after a fair trial and conviction. The declaration stated and defined the principles that became the slogan of the French Revolution: "liberty, equality, fraternity."

These rights, however, were not extended to women. During the French Revolution a group of women led by a Parisian playwright, Olympe de Gouges, wrote the *Declaration of the Rights of Women and Citizenesses*, but the National Assembly rejected it. The leaders of the Revolution believed in equality for men, but they did not believe that women were the equals of men.

Although the National Assembly swept away the remains of feudalism in France, the Old Regime died hard. Many nobles fled to Great Britain, to Italy, and to Germany. There they plotted continuously to overturn the Revolution. These **émigrés**—French for "emigrants"—became a constant source of trouble for France in the years to come.

Some nobles remained at Versailles with the king. Their opposition to some of his policies had helped start the Revolution. Now they sided with the king in favor of a return to the Old Regime. This was made clear at a banquet at which the king and queen were greeted with loud applause, royalist tunes were played, and insults were shouted at the National Assembly. When news of this banquet reached the people several days later, a crowd led by women stormed into the palace and forced Louis XVI, Marie Antoinette, and their family to return to Paris with them. The National Assembly accompanied the royal family to Paris.

Reforms in Government

The abolition of feudalism and the issuing of the Declaration of the Rights of Man established the guiding principles of the French Revolution. The National Assembly then began to work out the details. Between 1789 and 1791, it passed many laws aimed at correcting abuses and setting up a new government.

The National Assembly reformed France's administrative structure, abolished the old provinces, and divided France into 83 equal districts called **departments.** It also called for the election of all local officials.

The National Assembly, in addition, assumed the burden of the national debt. In 1789 the assembly seized land that belonged to the Catholic Church and offered it for sale to the public. The proceeds from the sale would then be used to pay off the national debt. The wealthier peasants, who had been renting this land, bought a good portion of it.

In 1790 the assembly issued the Civil Constitution of the Clergy. This law stated that people in the parishes and dioceses would elect their clergy. The government—as a compensation for seizing church lands—would pay the salaries of priests and bishops. The pope refused to allow the clergy to accept this arrangement, and most obeyed him.

This engraving depicts a mob of angry Parisian women on October 5, 1789, marching to Versailles. They blamed Louis XVI for the nationwide food shortage.

The Constitution of 1791

In 1791 the National Assembly finally finished writing a constitution for France. This constitution limited the authority of the king and set up a government that was divided into three branches—executive, legislative, and judicial.

The constitution greatly reduced the powers of the king. He could not proclaim laws or block laws passed by the legislature. Tax-paying male voters elected the members of the one-house legislature, the Legislative Assembly. The National Assembly was dissolved, and no one who had been a member could run for election to the Legislative Assembly. Despite the guarantees of equal rights and powers, wealthy men held most of the political power under France's new constitution.

Louis XVI reluctantly consented to the limitations imposed on him. At the same time, he secretly encouraged the émigrés to plot with foreign governments. The king hoped that such plots would lead to the overthrow of the new government and a return to the Old Regime.

Some of the king's advisers urged him to flee and seek help directly from nations friendly to the monarchy. On June 20–21, 1791, Louis XVI and his family did attempt to escape to the country. In spite of a disguise, Louis was recognized. The revolutionaries arrested him and his family and sent them back to Paris.

People hoped that under the new constitutional monarchy, France could recover without further revolutionary disturbances. Instead, the king's attempted escape marked a fatal turning point. People no longer trusted Louis, and they publicly discussed creating a republic.

The Legislative Assembly and War

The new government provided for by the Constitution of 1791 went into effect in October, but it lasted less than a year. The revolutionaries had not

Two Declarations of Freedom

In the last decades of the 1700s, revolutions shook both sides of the Atlantic. In 1776 the 13 British colonies of North America declared their independence. In 1789 the French people overturned the absolute power of King Louis XVI and established a limited monarchy.

In both of these revolutions, important documents marked political change: the Declaration of Independence in the United States in 1776 and the Declaration of the Rights of Man and of the Citizen in France in 1789. The two share many features and ideas.

The French undoubtedly were inspired by the American example. However, the common elements are not just due to imitation. The documents resemble each other because both drew on similar ideas.

It was the time of the Enlightenment, also called the Age of Reason. People were beginning to question old institutions.

They no longer accepted, for example, that monarchies were the natural order of things. In this climate of critical evaluation, the two declarations were born. Both claimed the sanction of God. The Americans wrote in 1776 that men "are endowed by their Creator with certain unalienable Rights." The French in 1789 proclaimed the rights of man "under the auspices of the Supreme Being."

Both documents drew on the political ideas of John Locke, who had brilliantly defended the Glorious Revolution of 1688. Locke had maintained that men are "by nature, all free, equal, and independent." Governments, he said, were established by people and could be changed by people—if necessary by force.

There are two other striking parallels between the American and French declarations. First, each presented ideas in general terms; *all* mankind, in *all* societies, had the same rights the Americans and the French claimed. Second, each carefully avoided a clear statement on the issue of slavery. Neither explained how slavery could or should be reconciled with universal freedom.

There were also major differences between the two documents; the documents came out of different societies. The Declaration of Independence was written when the American colonies were at war. The government in London refused to negotiate with the colonies in a state of rebellion. Early battles such as Bunker Hill resolved little except to strengthen the determination of the American patriots. State assemblies were setting up governments to replace British officials who had fled or been thrown out. Many nations, including France, sympathized with the colonies.

Thus certain features of the Declaration of Independence can be placed in perspective. Written largely by Thomas Jefferson, the Declaration of Independence was carefully composed and elegantly written. It took pains to explain American actions to the outside world. It went from general principles to a lengthy set of charges against George III. The king, it said, had proved himself a tyrant "unfit to be the ruler of a free people." The document vividly invited other oppressed peoples to follow the American lead. When governments become despotic, people must respond: "It is their right, it is their duty, to throw off such Government."

In contrast, the Declaration of the Rights of Man was written when France was experiencing a time of relative—though also uneasy—peace. The French had just recently overcome an unjust division into three estates: the clergy, the nobles, and the commoners. The commoners had chafed under the injustice of this division. They were the most numerous and the most heavily taxed. Why, then, should they have so little voice in the government? They had successfully rebelled and formed a national assembly. Now they prepared to write a constitution. The Declaration of the Rights of Man was composed to guide those who were drafting the constitution.

The Declaration of the Rights of Man lacked the organization and the brilliant force of its American counterpart, but its purpose was clear: to remind France's citizens of "the natural, unalienable and sacred rights of man."

Starting with a statement of general principles, the Declaration of the Rights of Man followed with the listing of 17 specific claims. In this document, there was no direct attack on the king, nor was there a direct call for other peoples to follow the French in overturning an unjust government.

Instead, the document took aim at specific abuses of the Old Regime. No one, it said, should be persecuted for religious beliefs. Those who are taxed should have a say in its proportion, collection, and duration. Public offices should be open to all.

While the American Declaration of Independence was a war cry for a society under attack, the French Declaration of the Rights of Man was intended to stabilize the new order. Yet it failed. The turmoil in France was not over. The king balked at his diminished role. Some revolutionaries wanted to spread the new order beyond the borders of France, plunging the nation into war with its neighbors. France then fell under a dictatorship that limited some of the very rights the document so eloquently guaranteed. Thus, to some extent the Declaration of the Rights of Man was overwhelmed by events, whereas the Declaration of Independence led Americans to victory and freedom.

Page 150: Thomas Jefferson (top), Signing the Declaration of Independence (bottom). Page 151: Revolution in Paris (top), John Locke (middle), Declaration of the Rights of Man (below).

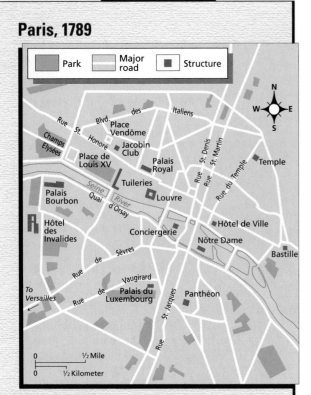

Paris, 1789

Park	Major road	Structure

Rue St. Honoré
Champs Elysées
Blvd. des Italiens
Place Vendôme
Jacobin Club
Place de Louis XV
Palais Royal
Tuileries
Seine River
Quai d'Orsay
Palais Bourbon
Louvre
Rue St. Denis
Rue St. Martin
Rue du Temple
Temple
Hôtel des Invalides
Conciergerie
Hôtel de Ville
Nôtre Dame
Bastille
Rue de Sèvres
Rue de Vaugirard
Palais du Luxembourg
To Versailles
Rue St. Jacques
Panthéon
Rue

0 ½ Mile
0 ½ Kilometer

Learning from Maps Louis XVI and his family were imprisoned in the Temple.

Location In which direction is the Temple from the Tuileries?

Revolution, the terms *right*, *center*, and *left* have referred to conservative, moderate, and radical political opinions, respectively.

The Legislative Assembly frequently deadlocked on domestic issues, but it united in facing a foreign threat. Before the Legislative Assembly first met, Marie Antoinette's brother Emperor Leopold II of Austria and King Frederick William II of Prussia had issued the Declaration of Pillnitz. This declaration invited European rulers to help Louis XVI restore the French monarchy.

The fear of foreign invasion electrified the Legislative Assembly. Each group in the assembly hoped that a successful foreign war would increase its own influence. Louis XVI favored war because he hoped that foreign armies would defeat the French army and restore his authority. Only a few people feared that war would lead to dictatorship. With only a few members opposed, in April 1792, the Legislative Assembly voted to declare war on Austria. It hoped to keep Prussia and the other German states out of the war, but it failed in that objective. Soon afterward an army of Austrian and Prussian troops invaded France.

The End of the Monarchy

The invasion of France by Austrian and Prussian armies touched off mass uprisings in Paris. A group of radicals seized control of the city government and set up an organization called the Commune.*

When the Prussian commander, the Duke of Brunswick, vowed to destroy Paris and punish the revolutionaries if any harm came to the royal family, members of the Commune threatened the Legislative Assembly with violence unless it abolished the monarchy. The Commune accurately accused Louis XVI of plotting with foreign monarchs to overthrow the Constitution of 1791. Revolutionary troops arrived from Marseilles to defend Paris, singing their marching song—"La Marseillaise"—which became France's national anthem.

---

*People called *sans-culottes* offered the greatest support to the Commune. The term *sans-culottes* means "without knee breeches"—the craftworkers, artisans, apprentices, and small shopkeepers of Paris who belonged to the *sans-culottes* wore long pants, while the nobility and rich bourgeoisie wore knee breeches. It became unfashionable to dress like the nobles and the wealthy, so in this way, revolution and social class influenced fashion. In the 1800s and 1900s, all men in the West began wearing long pants.

created a sound government to replace the Old Regime. They had set up a weak executive and a powerful but inexperienced legislature elected by a minority of the population.

Three factions, or groups of people with differing attitudes, sat in the Legislative Assembly. One group believed that the Revolution had gone far enough. They considered the ideal form of government to be one in which the king had limited authority. They were the **conservatives**—that is, they did not want to change existing conditions. Another group, called the **radicals**, wanted to get rid of the king, set up a republic, and institute far-reaching changes. A third group, the **moderates**, had no extreme views. They sided with either conservatives or radicals depending on the issues at hand.

In the hall where the Legislative Assembly met, conservatives sat on the right, moderates in the center, and radicals on the left. Since the French

Thinking About History:
Examining How Perspective Influences Viewpoints

A person's perspective often influences how he or she views events. Many factors, including education, social class, religion, age, gender, ethnic group, and personality, shape a person's perspective and influence his or her viewpoint. For example, a wealthy man might feel that only people who own property should be allowed to vote because they have a material stake in the society. In this case, the man's social class influences his viewpoint on voting rights. You can understand events in history more clearly if you can determine the way different groups of people interpret the meanings of these events.

How to Examine
How Perspective Influences Viewpoints
To examine how perspective influences viewpoints, follow these steps.
1. Identify the goal or purpose of your analysis.
2. Determine what factors help to shape the person's perspective.
3. Identify how the person views specific events in history.
4. Determine how the person's perspective influences his or her viewpoint.

Developing the Skill
Olympe de Gouges was from the lower middle class in Paris during the French Revolution. The following excerpt is from her Declaration of the Rights of Women and Citizenesses. Determine how her perspective would influence her viewpoint on the Declaration of the Rights of Man and of the Citizen and on the Constitution of 1791.

❝Woman is born free and her rights are the same as those of man. Social distinctions can be based only on the common good . . . The law must be an expression of the general will; all citizens, men and women alike . . . must be equally eligible for all public offices, positions, and jobs, according to their capacity and without any other criteria than those of their virtues and talents. [Women] . . . have the right to go to the scaffold; they must also have the right to go to parliament. . . .

Women, wake up . . . recognize your rights. Man, the slave, has multiplied his strength. . . .

A patriotic women's club at the time of the French Revolution

What advantages have you got from the Revolution?❞

The goal is to determine whether Olympe de Gouges would view the events of the French Revolution as steps toward liberty. Her words show her concern for political justice and rights for women. She believes that if women can fight and die for the Revolution, they are entitled to its benefits. Her perspective as a woman influences her viewpoint.

The Declaration of the Rights of Man made no mention of women. Olympe de Gouges wrote her declaration in response to this omission. She asserts that people who "go to the scaffold" (the platform on which beheadings took place) also have the right "to go to parliament."

Olympe de Gouges would condemn the Constitution of 1791 as a denial of liberty. It reinforced property rights for upper-class men. People had to own property to have the right to vote. Women could not own property, so they could not vote. Olympe de Gouges's perspective leads her to the view that the French Revolution was not over because it had not gone far enough in guaranteeing liberty for all people.

Practicing the Skill
How might the perspective of a wealthy factory owner and that of an unemployed laborer influence their viewpoints on a new law lowering taxes and canceling unemployment insurance?

To apply this skill, see Applying History Study Skills on page 171.

On August 10, 1792, the Legislative Assembly, coerced by the Commune, suspended the office of king. Armed Parisians marched on the Tuileries Palace, massacred many of the king's guards, and imprisoned Louis and his family in the Temple. (See map on page 152.) The Commune now ruled Paris, and the Legislative Assembly tried to govern France.

With the monarchy suspended, France needed a new constitution. The Legislative Assembly voted itself out of existence and set a date for the election of delegates to a National Convention to draw up another constitution for France. In late 1792, in the midst of great danger, with a foreign war and political turmoil at home, France faced both a national election and a complete change of government.

Section 3 Review

1. **Define** bourgeoisie, tithe, émigrés, departments, conservatives, radicals, moderates
2. **Identify** Louis XV, Louis XVI, Emmanuel Joseph Sieyès, Olympe de Gouges
3. **Explaining Ideas** Describe the social structure of France during the Old Regime.
4. **Interpreting Ideas** Why did discontent grow in France during the mid-1700s?
5. **Understanding Ideas** Describe the accomplishments of the National Assembly.
6. **Summarizing Ideas** For what kind of government did the Constitution of 1791 provide?
7. **Analyzing Ideas** Why did the Legislative Assembly exist for so short a period of time?

Section 4

The French Republic

Focus Questions

- How did the National Convention govern France from 1792 to 1793?
- Why did the Reign of Terror occur, and what did its supporters hope to accomplish?
- In what ways did Napoleon Bonaparte distinguish himself prior to 1799?

The delegates to the National Convention were elected by **universal manhood suffrage**. This meant that every adult male could vote, whether he owned property or not.

The National Convention

The National Convention held its first meeting in September 1792. The delegates, like those in the Legislative Assembly, were divided into three main groups. This time, however, no one supported the king. The Girondists, so called because many of them came from the department of the Gironde in southwestern France, were republicans who represented the middle class and feared the domination of France by Paris. The Jacobins, members of a radical political club of that name, were republicans who favored domination by Paris. Among the most powerful Jacobins were Georges-Jacques Danton and Maximilien Robespierre. The third group consisted of delegates who had no definite views. Later most of these delegates came to favor the Jacobins. The National Convention also included some Jacobins who were extreme radicals and wanted reforms that would benefit all classes in society, including the *sans-culottes*. Jean-Paul Marat, a doctor from Paris, led these radicals.

The National Convention governed France for three years. As soon as it met, it proclaimed the end of the monarchy and the beginning of a republic. Besides drawing up a new constitution, it had to suppress disorder and revolt at home and fight a war against foreign invaders.

The National Convention tried Louis XVI on charges of plotting against the security of the nation. The National Convention found Louis XVI guilty and sentenced him to death. On January 21, 1793, Louis was beheaded by the guillotine, a new device believed by its inventor to allow for quick and more humane executions. The trial and execution of a monarch was shocking to the rest of Europe. Even in the United States, many people were disturbed by the increasing radicalism of the French government.

What If?

Louis XVI
Louis XVI was a weak monarch who was more interested in hunting than in governing France. How do you think world history would have been different if Louis XVI had been a strong king such as Louis XIV?

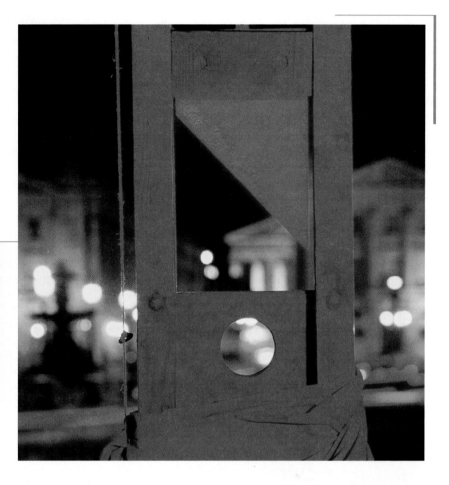

The National Convention sentenced Louis XVI to death. He was beheaded on January 21, 1793, by the guillotine, a device that had been introduced in France the year before. Shown here is a museum photo of a restored guillotine.

Exporting the Revolution

Even before Louis XVI's execution, the National Convention had heard encouraging news. They were told that the French army had defeated the Austrian and Prussian forces and stopped the invasion. The French followed up their military victories by invading the Austrian Netherlands.

The decision to export the ideas of the French Revolution by force of arms alarmed the monarchs of Europe. Great Britain, the Netherlands, Spain, and the kingdom of Sardinia joined Austria and Prussia to form an alliance (later called the First Coalition) against France. For a time, the enemies of France succeeded in driving French troops out of the Austrian Netherlands, and they invaded France again.

In 1793 the National Convention took extreme steps to meet these challenges from outside France. It set up the Committee of Public Safety, one of whose jobs was to direct the army in crushing foreign invaders. It also established a court called the Revolutionary Tribunal to try "enemies of the Revolution."

To meet the danger of invasion, the Committee of Public Safety adopted **conscription**—the draft. All unmarried, able-bodied men between 18 and 25 were liable for military service. As a force of loyal, patriotic young men, the French army took on a new, nationalistic spirit. In this "new" army, men of all classes who proved their ability and daring could serve as officers. For the first time, a country called upon the talents and abilities of its entire population to fight a war. During the 1800s conscription became common in Europe.

There were armed uprisings against the revolutionary government. In western France, particularly in the department of the Vendée, the "Royal and Catholic army" fought against the French revolutionary army. The term that describes their activities is **counterrevolution**, because it was aimed counter to, or against, the Revolution. In short, counterrevolutionaries supported the Old Regime.

Jacobins, including Danton and Robespierre, controlled the National Convention. They arrested many Girondist delegates who opposed their policies.

Charlotte Corday, a young woman from Normandy influenced by Girondist propaganda, journeyed to Paris and assassinated Marat. The Revolutionary Tribunal sent her to the guillotine for her crime.

The Reign of Terror

To meet the danger of opposition and revolt within France, the National Convention started systematically suppressing all opposition. The Reign of Terror, as it became known, lasted from September 1793 to July 1794. Robespierre wrote: "It is necessary to annihilate both the internal and external enemies of the republic or perish with its fall."

The Revolutionary Tribunal arrested, tried, and executed many people on mere suspicion. Marie Antoinette became an early victim of the Reign of Terror. The Jacobins directed the Reign of Terror not only against the nobility, however. The guillotine was used to behead people suspected of disloyalty regardless of their class. The revolutionaries executed twice as many people from the bourgeoisie as nobles and clergy, and nearly three times as many peasants and laborers as people from all other classes. Danton and Robespierre sent their Girondist opponents and Olympe de Gouges to the scaffold.

In the spring of 1794, Danton made it known that he felt the Reign of Terror had accomplished its purpose and should be relaxed. In contrast Robespierre became even more fanatical and accused Danton of disloyalty to the Revolution. He had Danton and his followers put to death.

For several months, Robespierre carried out a policy of extreme suppression, convinced that only he could protect the Revolution from its enemies.

Bust of Robespierre. Jacobins, including Danton and Robespierre, controlled the French National Convention.

The Death of Marat

It is hardly surprising that the art of France reflected the shattering changes brought about by the French Revolution. In subject, in mood, and in technique, these changes are evident in this work by Jacques-Louis David. His painting illustrates the Jacobin leader Jean-Paul Marat who was stabbed to death by Charlotte Corday as he was bathing. (Marat suffered from a painful skin disease caught while he was hiding in the sewers, and he could only find relief by sitting in a warm bath.) Corday sympathized with the Girondists, who felt that Marat was a cruel tyrant.

Because of its bizarre circumstances, Marat's assassination was not a conventional subject for a painting. But David—himself a revolutionary who at one time presided over the National Convention—was a celebrated artist and succeeded in creating a moving and forceful painting. In Marat's hand is a letter from his assassin. The knife that she plunged into his

chest lies on the floor. The painting's stark drama is highlighted by David's simple inscription, "To Marat."

Finally, a few members of the National Convention called a halt. In July 1794, they arrested Robespierre and guillotined him. The Reign of Terror was over.

Work of the National Convention

Despite the dangers and difficulties of the time, the National Convention made many reforms, affecting every level of French society. It provided for a national system of public education, and it abolished slavery in the French colonies.

In addition, the National Convention adopted the metric system of weights and measures. Today most parts of the world use the metric system. The National Convention also adopted a new calendar with colorful names that reflected the seasons, such as

Thermidor for the time of heat (roughly July) and *Ventôse* for the time of wind (roughly March). This calendar did not survive, however, perhaps because it also increased the number of days in a week from 7 to 10—an arrangement that met with little support among working people!

Meanwhile, the citizen army swept to victory. By 1795 the French had driven invaders from French soil and conquered territory as far as the Rhine River in Germany. Even more important, the First Coalition began to break up. A new militaristic spirit swept the country. The National Convention used the army to quell opposition even at home. It crushed an uprising in Paris in October 1795, demonstrating that the new government would not accept any opposition.

The Directory

In 1795 the National Convention drafted another constitution. Universal manhood suffrage disappeared and only male property owners could vote. The wealthy controlled the government, as they had under the rule of the National Assembly. The new constitution established an executive branch of five directors. The directors gave their name to the government that was created by the Constitution of 1795: the Directory.

Although the Directory governed France for four years, it pleased neither the radicals nor the conservatives. Prices skyrocketed out of control, and the peasants, *sans-culottes*, and all the poor people suffered. Weak, corrupt, and selfish, the five directors quarreled among themselves and were ineffective problem solvers. The economic situation got worse. When crowds protested, the directors used the army to put down the unrest. A worker in Paris summed up his feelings this way:

> **"**Under Robespierre blood was spilled and we had bread. Now blood is no longer spilled, and we have no bread. Perhaps we must spill some blood in order to have bread.**"**

The Directory soon became as unpopular as the Old Regime. It repeated history by going bankrupt, and it paved the way for military dictatorship.

Napoleon Bonaparte

Under the guidance of the Directory, the continuing war with Great Britain, Austria, and Sardinia provided opportunities for able military leaders. During this period, from 1795 to 1799, a relatively unknown general named Napoleon Bonaparte came to the public's attention. As a general at age 26, he had suppressed the uprising in Paris aimed at preventing the establishment of the Directory.

Born in 1769 on the French island of Corsica, Napoleon Bonaparte attended military school in France and graduated as an artillery officer. He might have remained there had the Revolution not given him the opportunity to rise to the rank of general.

Napoleon bundled extraordinary energy into a five-foot-two-inch frame. He combined overwhelming ambition with a vain and domineering personality. He also proved to be a superb organizer and administrator in both political and military affairs. Above all, Napoleon had military genius.

Napoleon Bonaparte is considered to rank among the great generals of all time. Because of the dominant

Napoleon attended three different military academies during his youth.

role that he played beginning in 1796, the wars that the French fought from then until 1815 are generally known as the Napoleonic Wars.

Napoleon's genius lay in his ability to move troops rapidly and to mass forces at critical points on the battlefield. These techniques gave him an advantage over his opponents' older, slower tactics.

In Italy Napoleon quickly showed his ability. He took a small, weak, and poorly equipped French army and within weeks so organized and inspired it that he forced the Sardinians to make peace. Napoleon defeated the Austrians four times, and in 1797 he forced them to sign a humiliating peace treaty that gave France control of all of northern Italy.

The Directory worried that the popular Napoleon might seize power. Napoleon, on the other hand, continually sought new conquests to keep his name before the French people. He proposed to weaken the British in a military campaign in Egypt that would cut off their trade with India. The Directory quickly agreed because such a campaign would keep him out of Paris.

In 1798 Napoleon launched the military campaign in Egypt. It ended in disaster. The British destroyed the French fleet near Alexandria, thus cutting the French army's supply lines. Napoleon left his army to its fate and returned to France. He concealed the true situation in Egypt and made exaggerated claims of victories.

Although Napoleon became the popular hero of the time, France faced a truly dangerous situation. The British had organized a Second Coalition against France that included Austria and Russia. Coalition forces drove French armies out of Italy, and French control over the other conquered states slipped.

Napoleon's Seizure of Power

As conditions worsened, Napoleon's supporters believed that only he could win victory abroad and restore order at home. Fearing that royalists might seize control, these supporters organized a plot to overthrow the government and place Napoleon in power. The plotters wanted stability in France to ensure that they could keep the nationalized property they had bought and the power they had acquired. In 1799 the legislature ousted four of the directors, leaving the way open for change. Troops with bayonets surrounded the legislature and forced most of its members to leave. Those who remained turned the government over to Napoleon and his fellow plotters.

A seizure of power by force is called a **coup d'état** (koo day·TAH), meaning literally a "stroke of state." Napoleon himself said later, "I found the crown of France lying on the ground, and I picked it up with my sword."

Section 4 Review

1. **Define** universal manhood suffrage, conscription, counterrevolution, coup d'état
2. **Identify** Georges-Jacques Danton, Maximilien Robespierre, Napoleon Bonaparte
3. **Understanding Ideas** Describe the three main groups that made up the National Convention.
4. **Summarizing Ideas (a)** What was the Reign of Terror? **(b)** What kinds of people were among its victims?
5. **Analyzing Ideas** Explain the circumstances that made Napoleon's coup d'état possible.

Section 5

The Napoleonic Era

Focus Questions

- **What course did Napoleon's career take between 1799 and 1804? What powers did he hold?**
- **What effect did Napoleon have on the rest of Europe, and what conflicts emerged?**
- **How was Napoleon defeated?**

Although Napoleon's government kept the form of a republic, the coup d'état of 1799 had made him dictator of France. From 1799 until 1814, Napoleon influenced events in France and the rest of Europe to such a great extent that this period is known as the Napoleonic Era, or the Age of Napoleon.

The people of France accepted Napoleon's dictatorship. Some, weary of the long period of chaos, wanted stability. Others were afraid to protest because they feared arrest. Instead of trying to abolish the changes brought on by the Revolution, Napoleon supported many of them. He respected most of the ideals of the Declaration of the Rights of Man and did not restore serfdom and feudal privileges. He reassured the peasants that the land they owned would remain theirs.

However, liberty under Napoleon meant only freedom of opportunity. It was not liberty from control because Napoleon believed that the people should obey orders given by a leader.

Napoleon and the Consulate

Napoleon reorganized and centralized the administration of France to give himself unlimited power. The executive branch, made up of three consuls, gave its name to the first five years of Napoleon's rule—the Consulate. Napoleon took the title First Consul, the title used in the Roman Republic.

As First Consul, Napoleon commanded the army and navy. He also had the right to appoint and dismiss all officials and to propose all new laws. None of the Consulate's legislative bodies had any real power; they merely rubber-stamped Napoleon's decrees.

Napoleon submitted the constitution of his new government to the people for a vote, a procedure known as a **plebiscite**. Under this procedure, people could vote only yes or no and could not make any changes. Even with these limitations, a vast majority of French voters approved the new constitution.

People usually remember Napoleon for his military leadership. However, his work in government had more importance and a more lasting effect. Under Napoleon's direction, scholars completed the revision and organization of all French law into a system called the Napoleonic Code.

Napoleon established the Bank of France, a central financial institution. His government also established the public education system planned by the National Convention. This system included elementary schools, high schools, universities, and technical schools. A central agency called the University of France supervised and directed the nation's schools.

The Civil Constitution of the Clergy of 1790 had ruptured relations between the Roman Catholic Church and the French government. Napoleon ended the conflict by reaching an agreement called the **Concordat** with the pope in 1801. The Concordat acknowledged Catholicism as the religion of most French citizens, but it did not abolish the religious toleration guaranteed by the Declaration of the Rights of Man. Most important, the church gave up claims to the property the government had seized and sold during the Revolution.

In a display of shrewd and skillful diplomacy, Napoleon destroyed the Second Coalition. Russia deserted the coalition in 1799. By 1801 Austria asked France for peace, and in 1802 Great Britain and France signed a peace treaty. For a time, it looked as though Napoleon would keep his promise to the French people: peace won by military victory, firm and steady government, and economic prosperity.

Napoleon as Emperor

In France Napoleon's supporters moved to increase his power by making it permanent and hereditary. In another plebiscite in 1804, the French people voted to declare France an empire. First Consul Napoleon Bonaparte became Emperor Napoleon I.

The coronation of Napoleon in the Cathedral of Notre Dame in Paris inaugurated the empire. One part of the elaborate ceremony was especially significant. The pope had come to Paris to crown the new emperor. However, when the time came for him to place the crown on Napoleon's head, Napoleon seized the crown and placed it on his head himself. Thus he demonstrated that the power and authority that he held were not given to him by anyone but himself.

The empire expanded far beyond France's old boundaries. Throughout Europe, however, people wanted to destroy Napoleon's empire. The British became his most determined adversaries once they realized that his ambition threatened their commerce, their empire, and their control of the seas. Great Britain renewed the war against France and in 1805 organized the Third Coalition. Austria, Russia, and Sweden allied themselves with Great Britain; Spain was allied with France. Napoleon planned to defeat the British navy and then invade Great Britain.

However, in 1805 a British fleet led by Admiral Horatio Nelson defeated a combined French and Spanish fleet near Trafalgar off the southern coast of Spain. Nelson was killed in the battle, but not before he had destroyed the French and Spanish fleet. Britain was no longer in danger of invasion. Napoleon succeeded spectacularly, however, in land battles against Austria and Russia.

The Continental System

Napoleon had nothing but contempt for the British, calling them "a nation of shopkeepers." He believed that if the British lost their foreign trade and its profits, they would be willing to make peace on his terms. Therefore, he ordered a blockade of the British Isles and forbade anyone in the French Empire or its allied states to trade with the British. This blockade was called the Continental System because Napoleon controlled so much of the continent of Europe.

The British responded with a blockade of their own against the French. They ordered ships of neutral countries to stop at British ports to get a license before trading with France or its allies. Napoleon in turn ordered the French navy to seize any neutral ship that obeyed the British order.

This conflict placed neutral nations in an awkward position. The Continental System and the British blockade hit the United States especially hard. Both France and Great Britain stopped American ships, but British ships did the most damage to American trade. This conflict helped bring about the War of 1812 between Great Britain and the United States.

Although the British blockade hurt France, Napoleon continued to win battles against the powers in the Third Coalition. In December 1805, he smashed the combined forces of Russia and Austria at Austerlitz, a town north of Vienna. Shortly thereafter, the Third Coalition collapsed.

The Reorganization of Europe

By 1808 Napoleon completely dominated Europe. (See map on page 162.) He forced Austria and Prussia to sign humiliating peace treaties, and Czar

As emperor, Napoleon established several institutions similar to those of the old monarchy. For example, this painting by Jacques-Louis David shows Napoleon crowning his wife, Josephine, empress on December 2, 1804, in Notre Dame Cathedral.

Alexander I allied Russia with France. Napoleon ruled the Austrian and Dutch Netherlands and Spain and forced Denmark and the Papal States into alliances.

Napoleon organized the most important of the German states into the Confederation of the Rhine, with himself as protector. He abolished the Holy Roman Empire in 1806, with its emperor taking the lesser title of emperor of Austria. He unified all the small northern Italian states into the kingdom of Italy and made them dependencies of France. He also placed members of his large family on the thrones of the countries he had conquered.

Napoleon did not limit the changes he made in Europe to enlarging his empire and reorganizing the conquered territories. On the contrary, he instituted far-reaching changes. Wherever the French army went, it put the Napoleonic Code into effect, abolished feudalism and serfdom, and introduced its modern military techniques.

Without intending to, the French also helped awaken in the people they conquered a spirit of **nationalism**, or love of one's country rather than of one's native region. In France the events of the Revolution and the stirring words of the Declaration of the Rights of Man had made people think of themselves as French, with a country and ideals worth fighting for. Now these same feelings of loyalty and patriotism for their homelands appeared among the conquered peoples, and they wanted to rid themselves of French rule.

In 1808 Napoleon ruled Europe, but time worked on the side of his enemies. The coalitions reassembled, and his opponents' armies grew stronger. The military leaders who opposed him copied his methods of moving and massing troops quickly.

The Peninsular War

To the south of France, on the Iberian Peninsula, lay Spain and Portugal. In 1807 Portugal refused to observe the Continental System because the nation's prosperity depended on trade with Great Britain. In retaliation the French army occupied Portugal and drove its king into exile.

Napoleon then decided to conquer Spain. After forcing the Spanish king to abdicate, Napoleon made his brother Joseph the king of Spain. Resenting a foreign king, the Spanish people revolted in 1808. The British sent an army under Arthur Wellesley, the future Duke of Wellington, to help the Spanish and Portuguese drive out the French. In spite of Napoleon's attempts, he failed to suppress the Spanish uprising and defeat the British.

The Peninsular War, as this war was called, lasted from 1808 to 1814. Napoleon continued to control Spain's government, but the campaign drained French military resources.

In 1814 the Spanish, with British help, drove out Joseph Bonaparte. They then drew up a new constitution that provided for a limited monarchy. The Spanish revolt and the new constitution illustrated the tremendous influence of the ideals of the French Revolution. It also showed the rising spirit of nationalism as well as general opposition to Napoleon.

Catastrophe in Russia

Czar Alexander I of Russia, who reigned from 1801 to 1825, viewed Napoleon's domination of Europe with alarm and distrust. The French Continental System had disrupted a long-established exchange of Russian raw materials for British manufactured goods. Gradually, the czar relaxed his enforcement of the Continental System in Russia, and in 1812 he announced the resumption of trade with Great Britain.

Inefficient as it was, the blockade continued to be Napoleon's only way of striking at the British.

The Napoleonic Empire, 1805–1815

Learning from Maps Napoleon gained control over most of western Europe through a series of conquests and alliances.

? Region What area was neutral in 1812?

He found it intolerable for Russia, a French ally, to openly ignore it. Napoleon decided to invade Russia, and he exerted pressure on all parts of his empire to supply soldiers.

When finally assembled, Napoleon's Grand Army totaled 600,000 soldiers. However, this huge force differed greatly from the enthusiastic, loyal, and patriotic armies of the early French Empire. Fewer than half the soldiers were French. The majority of the Grand Army consisted of soldiers from Napoleon's conquered states or from countries he forced to be his allies. The soldiers had little heart for this war.

In the spring of 1812, Napoleon's army began its march eastward toward Russia. (See map on opposite page.) Instead of battling the French on the vast plains of western Russia, the Russian army retreated slowly, drawing Napoleon's army deeper into the country. As the Russians retreated, they practiced a **scorched-earth policy**, the tactic of burning or destroying crops and everything else that might be of value to the invaders.

In autumn the French captured Moscow, but it was a hollow victory. As soon as the French entered the city, the Russians set it afire so that nothing would be left for their enemies. The fire destroyed so many buildings that the French troops had no housing. To make matters worse, the harsh Russian winter lay ahead, and Russian troops lurked in the countryside, endangering the Grand Army's long supply line from France. Napoleon had already lost many soldiers to disease, cold, and hunger, in addition to those killed in battle. Faced with further hardships, he ordered a retreat to France on October 19, 1812.

Napoleon's retreat from Moscow ranks as one of the greatest military disasters of all time. In addition to the snow and bitter cold, the French troops had to pass through devastated countryside, constantly under attack from Russians. Napoleon left his army to fend for itself and hurried to France to raise new forces to defend his empire. When the Grand Army reached Prussia in December, it had lost more than two thirds of its troops. The Russian army followed the retreating French and invaded Napoleon's empire.

Final Defeat

Everywhere in western Europe, monarchs broke their alliances with Napoleon. Prussia, Austria, and Great Britain joined Russia in a new and final alliance to crush France. Napoleon faced overwhelming odds.

Napoleon tried his old strategy of striking before his enemies could unite, but this time he was too late.

In October 1813, Napoleon's forces and the army of the new alliance met at Leipzig, in Saxony. The allies beat the French decisively, and Napoleon retreated into France. A series of brilliant military maneuvers by Napoleon did not prevent the allies from capturing Paris in March 1814.

Napoleon agreed to give up all claims to the throne for himself and his family. The allies granted him a pension and allowed him to retire to the small island of Elba off the west coast of Italy.

The victorious allies wanted to make peace with France and to make sure the country could never again disrupt European affairs. They agreed that France could keep the boundaries of 1792. They also restored the Bourbon monarchy to the throne in the person of Louis XVIII, brother of executed Louis XVI.*

The Hundred Days

During 1814 and early 1815, the restored Bourbons made many enemies among the French people. Learning of the discontent in France, Napoleon plotted his return. He escaped from Elba and landed in France on March 1, 1815.

When Louis XVIII sent troops to capture Napoleon, Napoleon faced the soldiers, saying, "If there be one among you who wishes to kill his Emperor, he can. I come to offer myself to your assaults." Resistance quickly crumbled, and Napoleon led a triumphant army into Paris on March 20, beginning a period called the Hundred Days. A frightened Louis XVIII had fled into exile; Napoleon once again ruled France.

Napoleon hoped that disputes among his opponents over the division of territory in Europe would keep them from opposing his return, but he was mistaken. The combined armies of Prussia, Great Britain, and the Netherlands moved toward France. Napoleon once more assembled a French army to battle them.

On June 18, 1815, the allied and French armies met in battle at Waterloo, where the British, under the command of the Duke of Wellington, and their Prussian allies dealt Napoleon a final defeat. Napoleon abdicated again, and the Bourbons returned once more.

Napoleon surrendered to the British, asking at first to be allowed to go to the United States. Instead, the British sent the defeated emperor to live under constant guard on the lonely, dismal island of St. Helena in the South Atlantic. There Napoleon died in 1821.

---

*Royalists referred to the young son of Louis XVI and Marie Antoinette as King Louis XVII. He is believed to have died in prison in 1795.

Government of France, 1774–1814

Year	Event
1774	Louis XVI became king.
1789	Third Estate, as National Assembly, assumed power.
1791	Legislative Assembly, with Louis XVI as constitutional monarch, began rule.
1792	Monarchy was suspended and National Convention began governing.
1795	Directory took control.
1799	Consulate was established, with Napoleon as First Consul.
1804	Napoleon was crowned emperor.
1814	Napoleon was overthrown and Bourbon monarchy was restored.

As the years passed, Napoleon's legend grew. People forgot the war and his failures and remembered only his glories and achievements. Literature and art celebrating Napoleon and his achievements multiplied. In 1840 the British allowed the French to take his remains back to Paris, where they lie to this day under the dome of the Invalides, the magnificent home for disabled soldiers.

Section 5 Review

1. **Define** plebiscite, Concordat, nationalism, scorched-earth policy
2. **Identify** Horatio Nelson, Duke of Wellington, Czar Alexander I, Louis XVIII
3. **Locate and Explain the Significance** Elba, Waterloo, St. Helena
4. **Summarizing Ideas** Describe Napoleon's career from the coup d'etat through 1804.
5. **Analyzing Ideas** How did Napoleon's actions affect other parts of Europe?
6. **Synthesizing Ideas** Explain the circumstances that led to Napoleon's defeat.

A Return to Peace

Focus Questions

- **What were the guiding principles at the Congress of Vienna?**
- **What steps did European powers take to maintain order and stability in the years following the Congress of Vienna?**
- **What effect did Metternich and liberalism have on Europe?**

With the final defeat of Napoleon in 1815, Europe reached an important turning point. For more than 25 years, the most powerful political influence on the continent had been the French Revolution. Even though Napoleon did not always uphold the ideals of the Revolution—liberty, equality, and fraternity—he did carry its influence throughout Europe.

As long as Napoleon ruled France, the governments of other nations feared that France would export political unrest or rebellion and challenge their authority. Once they defeated Napoleon, the major European powers were determined to restore order, keep peace, and squelch the ideas of the Revolution. After 1815 they followed policies designed to maintain stability and to suppress any danger of political upheaval.

The Congress of Vienna

Stability could be achieved only by settling political and territorial questions arising from the Napoleonic Wars. The Congress of Vienna, a conference held in the Austrian capital, undertook the settling of these questions. The congress began in September 1814, while Napoleon was in exile on Elba. Napoleon's return from exile interrupted the congress in 1815, but after his final defeat at Waterloo, it resumed its work.

Despite the presence of hundreds of statesmen and diplomats, only a few people made the real decisions at the Congress of Vienna. Great Britain, Austria, Russia, and Prussia had done the most to defeat Napoleon. Their four representatives were Viscount Castlereagh, foreign secretary of Great Britain; Prince Klemens von Metternich, foreign minister of Austria and chairman of the conference; Czar Alexander I of Russia; and King Frederick William III of Prussia.

Two of the most influential diplomats at the Congress of Vienna were Talleyrand of France and Metternich of Austria. This painting by Jean-Baptiste Isabey shows the Congress of Vienna in session.

Surprisingly, the representative of defeated France, Charles-Maurice de Talleyrand, played an important part at the Congress of Vienna. A shrewd negotiator, Talleyrand wielded great influence as the representative of Louis XVIII.

The Principles of the Congress of Vienna

Three principles guided the decisions of the Congress of Vienna. (1) The countries that suffered most at the hands of Napoleon—especially the four great powers—had to be compensated for their losses. (2) The balance of power had to be restored in Europe. This meant that the nations of Europe had to keep any one nation from becoming too powerful. (3) All decisions would follow the rule of **legitimacy**, which meant that all former ruling families should be restored to their thrones.

Compensation. The Netherlands, one of Napoleon's early conquests, received the Austrian Netherlands and became the single Kingdom of the Netherlands. As compensation for this loss, the Austrians gained the northern Italian states of Venetia and Lombardy. Austrian Habsburgs also became rulers of the northern Italian states of Parma, Modena, and Tuscany.

Because Sweden had fought against Napoleon, it received Norway, formerly a Danish possession. This territorial adjustment punished Denmark for cooperating with Napoleon. Prussia received an area along the Rhine River.

Although Great Britain did not receive any territory in continental Europe, it did gain possessions overseas—several islands in the French West Indies and the Mediterranean island of Malta. From the Danish, the British gained Helgoland, an island in the North Sea. British possession of Cape Colony in Africa was also confirmed.

However, the winning powers soon quarreled over the division of spoils. The two most difficult problems concerned Poland and the German state of Saxony. From Prussia's Polish territory, Napoleon had created the Grand Duchy of Warsaw, which he had given to his faithful ally, the king of Saxony. Russia now demanded this territory. Prussia agreed to this provided that it gain possession of Saxony.

Balance of power. The proposed arrangement between Prussia and Russia for the territories of Saxony and the Grand Duchy of Warsaw also threatened the balance of power that the Congress of Vienna was trying to create. Both Great Britain and Austria opposed the arrangement. Great Britain did not want to see Russia become too strong. Austria feared that the addition of Saxony might make Prussia too powerful in German affairs. For a time, the threat of war loomed. Then Talleyrand suggested a compromise that settled the argument. Most of what had been the Grand Duchy of Warsaw went to Russia. Prussia got the rest of it, along with part of Saxony. (See map on this page.)

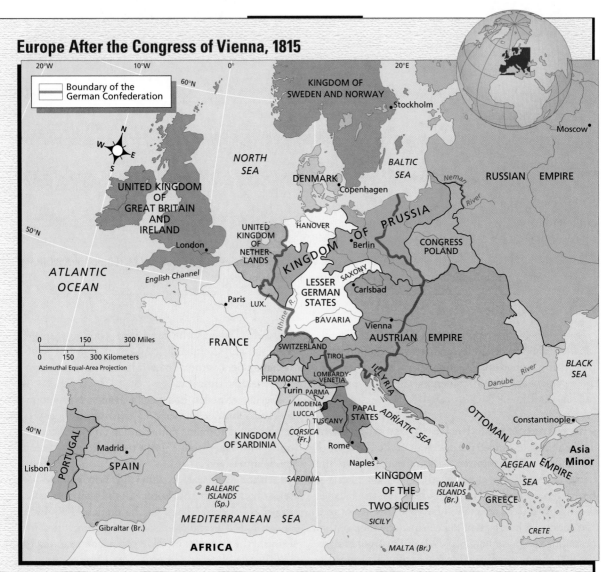

Europe After the Congress of Vienna, 1815

Learning from Maps The Congress of Vienna attempted to settle political and territorial questions arising from the Napoleonic Wars.

? Place France's territory was greatly reduced after the Congress of Vienna; what island remained under the French crown?

All of this territorial reshuffling set up a ring of strong states around France so that it could not again threaten the peace of Europe. France was stripped of its conquests, and its boundaries were returned to where they had been in 1792. In addition, it had to pay a large **indemnity**—a compensation to other nations for damages it had inflicted on them. France also had to pay for forts that the victorious nations now maintained on the French borders.

However, consideration for the balance of power prevented a much harsher punishment, which some delegates wanted to impose on France. Most European leaders realized that, for example, dividing France up among the victorious powers would cause instability in the future. Besides, Britain and Austria, concerned about the rising military strength of Prussia and Russia, wanted France to serve as a counterbalance.

Legitimacy. At Talleyrand's urging, the Congress of Vienna made settlements based on the principle of legitimacy. The Bourbon monarchy, already restored in France, also returned to power in Spain and in the kingdom of the Two Sicilies. This principle was not followed everywhere, however. The Austrian Habsburgs, for example, now dominated Italy through their new Italian territorial gains.

Reaction, Absolutism, and Nationalism

A time of **reaction** followed the first few years after the Napoleonic Era. In other words, those in authority wanted to return to the conditions of an earlier period. **Reactionaries** are extremists who not only oppose change but generally would like to turn the clock back to the time before certain changes occurred. After 1815 the victors in Europe attempted to restore a balance of power, or stability, and to emphasize a conservative view toward all things political.

In Spain and the Two Sicilies, the reinstated rulers abolished the constitutions that had been adopted during Napoleon's rule. They returned to absolutism almost as if nothing had ever happened. Switzerland alone retained its constitutional government but had to promise to remain neutral in European wars. The European powers guaranteed this neutrality.

Napoleon's conquests had resulted in the spread of new political ideas and the rise of nationalism. Groups that shared a common language, history, and culture now wanted to be united under their own governments. The reactionary powers considered this movement dangerous and tried to stamp it out. For a while they succeeded, and the Congress of Vienna left

nationalist groups disappointed. Some Italians, for example, had hoped for a united Italy. Their hope went unfulfilled. To make matters worse, many Italian states were placed under a hated foreign rule. The major powers also blocked the desire of the Polish people for national independence.

The German desire for national unity came closer to fulfillment. Napoleon had consolidated many of the German states into the Confederation of the Rhine. Now more states, including Prussia, formed the German Confederation, which had 39 members. Austria dominated this confederation because an Austrian delegate always presided over its assembly.

Alliances Among the Great Powers

The idea of revolution still haunted the governments of Europe. As a result, they believed that a special watch had to be kept for the lurking dangers that might upset the peace they had so painstakingly created.

The Quadruple Alliance. The four allies that had finally defeated Napoleon—Great Britain, Austria, Russia, and Prussia—agreed in 1815 to continue their alliance. The chief purpose of the Quadruple Alliance was to discuss common interests and help maintain peace. Members of the alliance agreed to hold periodic conferences to keep the major powers in agreement on matters that concerned them all.

The Holy Alliance. Czar Alexander I of Russia held strong religious ideals. He believed that Christian moral principles and a strong sense of duty should guide monarchs. He also firmly believed in absolute monarchy. Shortly before joining the Quadruple Alliance, he urged that all rulers pledge themselves to rule as Christian princes by signing an agreement called the Holy Alliance. All the rulers of Europe signed it except the British king; the Turkish sultan, who was not a Christian; and the pope, who refused to be instructed in Christian principles by the Orthodox czar. Historians view the document as a major symbol of the conservatism that existed during this period. Metternich and Castlereagh personally viewed the agreement as an insignificant document and a meaningless event.

The Concert of Europe. Out of the more practical Quadruple Alliance grew what was called the Concert of Europe—a form of international government by concert, or agreement. It was aimed at maintaining peace and the status quo (a Latin phrase meaning roughly "the condition in which things exist"). In this case, the status quo meant maintaining the balance of power established by the Congress of Vienna.

The first of the periodic conferences provided for by the Quadruple Alliance met in 1818. France, having fulfilled the terms of the peace settlements, returned to the European family of nations and was admitted to the Quadruple Alliance, making it the Quintuple Alliance. The Concert of Europe succeeded in peacefully solving several international disputes, setting a precedent for future international organizations. The Concert of Europe continued to be effective until 1848.

The Age of Metternich

For 30 years after the Congress of Vienna, Prince Metternich influenced Europe so strongly that the period is sometimes known as the Age of Metternich.

---

* Today, liberalism is identified with government programs that seek to protect the individual, such as Social Security.

A reactionary, Metternich believed strongly in absolute monarchy. He looked with fear and horror at liberalism. The movement known as **liberalism*** extended the principles of the American and French Revolutions with their ideals of individual rights and the rule of law. Metternich believed in suppressing such ideas as freedom of speech and of the press.

Metternich aimed to prevent war or revolution and to preserve absolutism. He had little difficulty achieving these goals in Austria. To meet these ends, he set up an efficient secret police system to spy on revolutionary organizations and individuals.

Because Austria controlled the German Confederation, Metternich persuaded the rulers of most German states to adopt the same methods. In France, King Louis XVIII moved cautiously in domestic affairs. However, he willingly joined in suppressing revolutions elsewhere.

Metternich (shown in painting) was instrumental in the reorganization of Europe after the Napoleonic Era.

Political Liberalism

The ideas of liberals greatly influenced politics during the 1800s. These ideas could be seen in the internal political conflicts of Great Britain, France, Italy, Germany, and the United States. Liberalism took many different forms in these countries, but certain key ideas remained identical. These included a belief in the importance of individual liberties, such as freedom of thought, religion, and economic opportunity. Above all, liberals hated the tyranny of absolute rule. Thus they worked to secure constitutions and other legal safeguards to limit governmental authority and protect civil liberties. On the other hand, most liberals during this period did not believe that all people should have the right to vote. Instead, most liberals believed that voting should be limited to men with property.

Reaction to Metternich

Liberals reacted strongly to the decisions of the Congress of Vienna and to Metternich's actions. A number of uprisings occurred in Europe, and Metternich turned the Concert of Europe into an instrument of suppression. Whenever a threat to the status quo arose, representatives of the five powers gathered to discuss ways of handling it. Austria, Russia, and Prussia, in particular, were zealous in their efforts to thwart revolutions.

Great Britain, however, had no desire to intervene in other nations' affairs. It opposed interfering in the attempts of liberal popular movements to overthrow absolute rulers. Great Britain itself had a representative government. The British people as a whole sympathized with liberal popular movements in their struggles to institute similar governments. Furthermore, Great Britain had national interests that were different from those of other European nations. Great Britain withdrew from the Quintuple Alliance in 1822, and under the influence of a new foreign secretary, George Canning, increasingly turned away from the autocratic states of the continent.

The Metternich System in Operation

For a time, the Metternich system operated successfully. When discontent flared up among German university students in 1819, Metternich called together the leaders of the larger states of the German Confederation at Carlsbad in Bohemia. At his insistence, they adopted measures known as the Carlsbad Decrees. The decrees placed students and faculty members under strict watch. They censored newspapers and periodicals and authorized an organization to search for secret revolutionary activities. These measures prohibited political reforms that conflicted with absolute monarchy.

As repression increased, several underground movements that opposed the status quo were initiated. In 1820 a revolt in Spain forced King Ferdinand VII to restore the constitution he had abolished. This alarmed the four continental members of the Quintuple Alliance. Despite British protests, they sent a French army to Spain. In 1823 they restored Ferdinand to power, brutally crushing the revolt and its leaders.

The Spanish revolt inspired other uprisings in the 1820s. In the kingdom of the Two Sicilies, revolutionaries forced the ruler to grant a constitution. An Austrian army put down this revolt.

In 1821 nationalism upset the international order when the Greeks revolted against the Ottoman Turks. Influenced by Metternich, European rulers ignored Greek pleas for aid. However, many individuals supported the Greeks, either as volunteers or by sending arms. One volunteer was Lord Byron, the British poet, who died of a fever in Greece in 1824.

Finally, Russia, Great Britain, and France brought pressure on the Ottoman sultan. By the Treaty of Adrianople in 1829, Greece became an independent state. Greek independence demonstrated the first real failure of the Metternich system in Europe. This successful attempt at independence showed that the sense of nationalism encouraged by the French Revolution could not be suppressed forever.

Section 6 Review

1. **Define** legitimacy, indemnity, reaction, reactionaries, liberalism
2. **Identify** Castlereagh, Talleyrand, Metternich
3. **Locate and Explain the Significance** Kingdom of the Netherlands, Saxony, Grand Duchy of Warsaw
4. **Understanding Ideas** Describe the guiding principles at the Congress of Vienna.
5. **Summarizing Ideas** Describe the alliances made by the European powers in the years after Napoleon.
6. **Synthesizing Ideas** Explain the interplay between Metternich and liberalism in Europe.

Chapter 4 Review

A.D. 1762 Rousseau publishes *The Social Contract.*

A.D. **1710** | A.D. **1720** | A.D. **1730** | A.D. **1740** | A.D. **1750** | A.D. **1760**

A.D. 1715 Louis XV begins his reign.

A.D. 1734 Voltaire publishes *Philosophical Letters.*

A.D. 1748 Montesquieu publishes *The Spirit of the Laws.*

A.D. 1765 Stamp Act is passed.

Chapter Summary

The following list contains the key concepts you have learned about the American Revolution, the French Revolution, and the Napoleonic Era.

1. During the Enlightenment, thinkers began to criticize the established political institutions.
2. The philosophes included Diderot, Montesquieu, Voltaire, and Rousseau.
3. Great Britain had been involved in worldwide conflicts from 1754 to 1763. This left the British heavily in debt. However, when they attempted to tax their North American colonies, they met opposition.
4. The American colonists disagreed with the way the British governed them. Unable to change British policy, the thirteen colonies chose independence.
5. Discontent that existed in France and Louis XVI's failure to solve the government's continuing financial crisis were the direct causes of the French Revolution.
6. In 1789 Louis XVI summoned a meeting of the Estates General in an attempt to solve the financial crisis of the monarchy. When he insisted on following old procedures, the Third Estate met separately and proclaimed itself the National Assembly.
7. The National Assembly wrote the Constitution of 1791, creating a limited constitutional

monarchy. Invasion by Austrian and Prussian troops touched off riots that led to the end of the monarchy in 1792.

8. The National Convention proclaimed a republic and executed the king. Threatened by new invasions, an army was drafted to defend the nation while the Reign of Terror suppressed opposition at home.
9. The inefficient and corrupt Directory followed the National Convention.
10. In 1799 Napoleon Bonaparte took over the government in a coup d'état. Napoleon ruled France as a military dictator and expanded French control throughout Europe.
11. Napoleon became emperor. In response to French invasion, feelings of nationalism were ignited through most of Europe.
12. After several military defeats, Napoleon abdicated and went into exile on Elba in 1814. Napoleon soon escaped, only to be defeated again at Waterloo.
13. The Congress of Vienna and alliances that were established later attempted to restore the status quo in Europe.
14. The ideals of liberalism and nationalism could not be suppressed. In the 1820s, rebellions against reactionary policies broke out in several European countries.

Reviewing Important Terms

On a separate sheet of paper, match each of the following terms with the correct definition below.

a. Enlightenment
b. scorched-earth policy
c. federal system of government
d. popular sovereignty
e. department
f. conscription
g. coup d'état
h. conservatives
i. bourgeoisie
j. executive branch

_____ 1. Movement stressing the use of reason to explain human nature logically
_____ 2. City-dwelling middle class in France
_____ 3. One of 83 administrative districts in France
_____ 4. People who do not want to change conditions as they exist
_____ 5. Government in which power is divided between the central government and states
_____ 6. Government policy requiring people to serve in the army
_____ 7. Burning or destroying crops and everything else that might be of value to the enemy

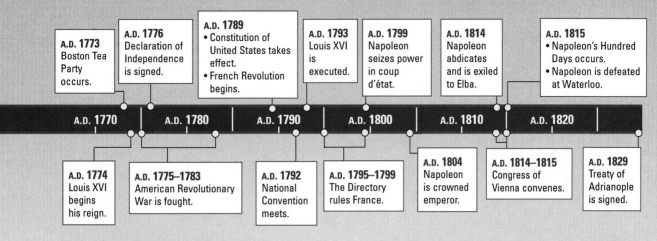

A.D. 1773 Boston Tea Party occurs.

A.D. 1776 Declaration of Independence is signed.

A.D. 1789
• Constitution of United States takes effect.
• French Revolution begins.

A.D. 1793 Louis XVI is executed.

A.D. 1799 Napoleon seizes power in coup d'état.

A.D. 1814 Napoleon abdicates and is exiled to Elba.

A.D. 1815
• Napoleon's Hundred Days occurs.
• Napoleon is defeated at Waterloo.

A.D. 1770 | **A.D. 1780** | **A.D. 1790** | **A.D. 1800** | **A.D. 1810** | **A.D. 1820**

A.D. 1774 Louis XVI begins his reign.

A.D. 1775–1783 American Revolutionary War is fought.

A.D. 1792 National Convention meets.

A.D. 1795–1799 The Directory rules France.

A.D. 1804 Napoleon is crowned emperor.

A.D. 1814–1815 Congress of Vienna convenes.

A.D. 1829 Treaty of Adrianople is signed.

_____ 8. Seizure of power by force
_____ 9. Government by free choice of the people
_____ 10. Division of American government that enforces the laws

Developing Critical Thinking Skills

1. **Understanding Ideas (a)** What were the major ideas of the Enlightenment? **(b)** How did Diderot help spread these ideas?
2. **Evaluating Ideas** The Declaration of Independence and the U.S. Constitution have been called documents for the ages. Do you agree with this description? Explain.
3. **Analyzing Ideas (a)** What were the lasting social, political, and cultural effects of the French Revolution? **(b)** Given these effects, do you think the French Revolution was successful? Why or why not?
4. **Synthesizing Ideas** Who do you think had a greater impact on Europe in the 1800s—Metternich or Napoleon? Supply evidence from this chapter.

Relating Geography to History

Compare the map of Napoleonic Europe on page 162 with the map of Europe after the Congress of Vienna on page 166. Then write a paragraph describing the resulting boundary changes.

Relating Past to Present

1. The French Revolution completely altered the political structure of Europe. **(a)** What effects are revolutions having on life in today's world? **(b)** Where are revolutions currently taking place?
2. Compared to the disciplined methods of the British soldiers, the North American colonists' techniques were guerrilla warfare. **(a)** How is guerrilla warfare conducted? **(b)** Why has this type of warfare often been effective against trained, disciplined armies?

Applying History Study Skills

Before completing this activity, review Building History Study Skills on page 153.

Edmund Burke was a member of the British Parliament during the American and French Revolutions. During the unrest leading up to the American Revolution, he urged Parliament to compromise with the colonists' demands. In 1790 he published his *Reflections on the Revolution in France.* Read the excerpt below and explain how his perspective influences the way in which he views the events of the French Revolution.

"The fresh ruins of France, which shock our feelings wherever we can turn our eyes, are not the devastation of civil war; they are the sad but instructive monuments of rash and ignorant counsel in time of profound peace…Whilst they are possessed of these notions, it is vain to talk to them of the practice of their ancestors, the fundamental laws of their country, the fixed form of a constitution, whose merits are confirmed by the solid test of long experience…

They have the 'rights of men.'…But to form a free government; that is, to temper together these opposite elements of liberty and restraint in one consistent work, requires much thought, deep reflection, . . . [a] powerful and combining mind. This I do not find in those who take the lead in the National Assembly."

internet **connect**

Search the Internet through the HRW Web site for information on one of the major battles of the American Revolution. (There are several military history sites on the Internet.) Focus on the battle's significance.

GO TO: go.hrw.com
KEYWORD: SC0
American Revolution

Building Your Portfolio

1. **Preparing a Book Report** Read *A Tale of Two Cities* by Charles Dickens. Describe how the French Revolution affected the lives of the main characters. Place the book report in your portfolio.
2. **Writing an Essay** Describe how the ideas of Montesquieu and Rousseau were reflected in the Declaration of the Rights of Man and the French constitutional monarchy set up by the National Assembly in 1791. Place the essay in your portfolio.

Asia in Transition

The Imperial Palace in the Forbidden City (Beijing, China)

Significance

Between 1400 and the mid-1800s, many of the major countries in Asia reached a political and cultural peak and then began to decline. In China and Japan, following centuries of remarkable political and technological achievement, rulers attempted to keep their countries stable and orderly and to prevent change by limiting contact with the outside world. This policy, however, had a price. Although China and Japan had built civilizations at least as sophisticated as those in Europe, these civilizations gradually slowed their courses of progress without ideas and innovations from other countries.

The Ottoman, Mughal, and Persian Safavid Empires reached the zenith of their political and cultural power in the 1500s and 1600s. Then decline also overtook these three empires.

Terms to Define

junks	extraterritoriality
queue	consulates
philology	sepoys
free trade	

People to Identify

Nurhachi	Selim III
Kangxi	Safavids
Oda Nobunaga	Shah 'Abbas I
Toyotomi Hideyoshi	Nadir Shah
Tokugawa Ieyasu	Robert Clive
Matthew Perry	Charles Cornwallis
Süleyman the Magnificent	

Places to Locate

Beijing	Nagasaki
Manchuria	Lepanto
Guangzhou	Black Sea
Shanghai	Sea of Azov
Macao	Isfahan
Hong Kong	Tehran
Kyoto	Delhi
Edo	Bengal

Chapter Theme Questions

- **Cross-Cultural Interaction** Why might a country want to limit its contacts with other countries?
- **Politics and Law** What are possible advantages of centralized power?
- **Religion** What might be the positive and negative effects of close ties between the religion and government of a country?

One of the greatest contributions of the Japanese to the literary world is a form of poetry called haiku, which means "comic" or "lighthearted." A highly popular form of poetry, haiku are very short verses—usually 17 syllables—that convey ideas and achieve subtle effects. The following examples of these charming verses are from the Japanese poet Matsuo Basho, who wrote in the 1600s.

"There goes my best hat
as down comes rain on my bald
*   pate, plop! plop! Oh well. . ."*

"Low clouds are shattered
into small distant fragments
*   of moonlit mountains."*

"Swallows, spare those bees
humming westward at evening
*   laden with honey."*

"Scattered on the sand
like jewels, seashells tangled
*   in kelp and rubbish. . ."*

"The best I have to
offer you is the small size
*   of the mosquitoes."*

"On a journey, ill,
and over fields all withered, dreams
*   go wandering still."*

Asian civilizations had long fascinated Europeans. Asian rulers, however, did not always consider contact with Europeans desirable.

Section 1

The Ming and Qing Dynasties

Focus Questions

- **How did the Ming relate to the outside world?**
- **What were the achievements and problems of the Qing?**
- **How was Chinese culture affected by the arrival of Europeans?**

In 1368 Zhu Yuanzhang (joo yoo·en·jahng), who was a former Buddhist monk, overthrew the Mongol

Yuan dynasty of China. Calling himself the Hongwu, or "Vastly Martial," emperor, he established the Ming, or "Brilliant," dynasty, which remained in power until 1636, when the Qing (ching), or "Pure," dynasty replaced it.

Ming Policy Toward the Outside World

During the early Ming period, the Chinese were probably the most skillful sailors in the world. They built large, sturdy ships known as **junks**, some of which were over 400 feet long. Since the early 1100s, the Chinese had used the compass—which they probably invented—in navigation. Under the Ming dynasty, in 1405, the emperor financed a Chinese fleet that sailed all the way around Southeast Asia to India. Another Chinese fleet crossed the Indian Ocean and reached Aden, on the southern coast of the Arabian Peninsula, in 1415.

The Ming Empire, 1424

Learning from Maps Ming rulers moved the imperial capital from Nanjing to Beijing.

? Movement Along which waterway could a traveler journey from Hangzhou to Beijing?

These and other voyages occurred almost 100 years before Vasco da Gama sailed from Portugal to India by going around the tip of Africa. The Chinese clearly had the ability to become a great seafaring power, as several European countries later did. However, the naval expeditions of the early Ming period did not continue for very long. The later Ming emperors—unlike, for example, Prince Henry the Navigator in Portugal or Queen Elizabeth I in England—had little interest in sea power or in foreign trade. They stopped financing naval expeditions and for a time outlawed overseas trade. Both Confucian attitudes toward trade and concern for the security of the land frontier between China and Central Asia prompted this policy.

Confucian Attitudes Toward Trade

After defeating the Mongols in 1368, the Ming emperors tried to rid China of all Mongol influences. They looked to the great ages in China's past for inspiration and tried to re-create the grandeur of the Han, Tang, and Song dynasties. As part of that effort, the Ming emperors restored Confucianism—to which the Mongols had paid only lip service—as the official philosophy of the government.

Confucian philosophy divided society into four classes. First in order of importance were the scholar-gentry, who governed the country for the emperor. Next came the peasants, who produced food and paid the taxes that supported the empire. Artisans, who made useful and beautiful objects, came third. At the bottom of the social order were the merchants. The Chinese tended to regard merchants as parasites who made profits from selling goods that the peasants and artisans had produced. The Chinese saw trade as a necessary evil, not as a desirable pursuit.

As followers of Confucius, the Ming emperors tried to keep trade with other countries to a minimum. Unlike European monarchs, who were influenced by mercantilism, the emperors of China did not believe that foreign trade benefited the country, which they saw as self-sufficient. Trade, therefore, was seen as beneficial to the other party, not to China. Government revenue came from land taxes, not taxes on trade. The emperors received tribute from governments in Korea, Japan, and Tibet. In return they gave the rulers of these nations lavish presents. The emperors did not intend these exchanges to increase China's wealth—they designed the tribute system to enhance China's prestige and security.

The Northern Frontier

After their victory over the Mongols, the Ming emperors wanted to make sure that no Central Asian people ever again conquered China. They therefore concentrated their efforts on securing the long northern land frontier. Defense of the frontier required constant attention, and it cost a great deal of money.

To protect that frontier, the Ming strengthened the Great Wall of China. They encouraged soldiers to move with their families into the frontier zone, offering the soldiers free land there in exchange for protection of the strategic mountain passes. Peasants and city dwellers were also encouraged to move. In 1421 the Ming moved the imperial capital from Nanjing, in central China, to Beijing, in the north. (See map on opposite page.) Beijing was only 40 miles south of the Great Wall.

The Ming emperors tried to prevent the nomadic tribes of the north from uniting to create a powerful fighting force. Individual tribes that submitted to the Ming sent yearly tribute to Beijing and exchanged gifts with the emperor. In return for their loyalty, the Ming rulers gave the nomadic chiefs titles, money, and honors. In addition, the emperors had to entertain and present lavish gifts to the hundreds of nomads who came to Beijing on yearly tribute missions.

The overseas expeditions had been extremely expensive. The Ming emperors did not have the financial resources to encourage overseas expeditions in addition to financing their domestic expenses. To save money for frontier defense, among other reasons, the Ming emperors ended the long-range overseas expeditions of the early 1400s.

The Founding of the Qing Dynasty

Throughout most of the Ming period, the northern frontier remained secure. Occasionally, small bands of nomads seeking greater riches than they could obtain through the tribute system crossed the frontier, but the Chinese always succeeded in driving them away.

In the early 1600s, however, a new and very serious threat emerged in Manchuria, to the northeast of China. (See map on page 176.) There a chieftain named Nurhachi unified the many tribes into a single people—the Manchu. After taking over Korea and Inner Mongolia, Nurhachi's son and successor, Abahai, proclaimed the Qing dynasty. The Manchu captured Beijing in 1644 with the help of a Chinese general. The Qing dynasty ruled China from this time until 1911. Once again, despite all the efforts of the

Ming, barbarians (outsiders) had conquered China and established their own dynasty.

Even though the Qing dynasty was non-Chinese, it actually became one of the most characteristically Chinese in outlook. The Qing emperors adopted the culture of the Chinese and governed the country with traditional Chinese techniques.

One such ruler was Emperor Kangxi (KAHNG·SHEE), who ruled from 1661 to 1722. Kangxi knew the Chinese classics well and sponsored many important literary and educational projects. He actively presided over the civil service examination system. He supervised efforts to control flooding on China's major rivers and to build grain storehouses in case of famine. He reduced expenditures at his court and exempted many people from taxes. Kangxi ruled in accordance with the teachings of Confucius, just as the Ming emperors had done.

At the same time, Kangxi and the other Qing emperors tried to preserve distinctions between the Manchu—who were a minority in the empire—and the Chinese people. All Manchu had to study the Manchu language and Manchu cultural traditions. The Qing forbade the Chinese people to marry Manchu or to settle in Manchuria. The dynasty maintained this region as a tribal homeland for the Manchu. Finally, the Qing required all Chinese men to wear their hair in a single braid, called a **queue** (tail). The queue distinguished the Chinese from the Manchu and signified Chinese submission to Manchu rule.

The Ming and Qing Economies

The Qing emperors, like the Ming, considered agriculture to be the basis of China's wealth. They maintained traditional political institutions and generally supported traditional Chinese ideas and values. Neither the Ming nor the Qing emperors showed great interest in change. Nevertheless, change occurred.

The Qing Empire, 1760

Learning from Maps Under the Qing dynasty, China's borders expanded to the north and to the west.

 Place Which mountain range lies on China's southwest border?

New patterns of commerce and trade began to appear. The growth of cities begun during the Song dynasty continued under the rule of the Ming and Qing emperors. Peace and urban growth contributed to the expansion of trade within China. While the Chinese looked down on merchants in theory, in practice they needed them to supply the urban population with food, textiles for clothing, and other essential goods.

Certain regions of the country began to specialize in the production of particular products. For example, Guangzhou (GWANG·JOH) in the south, formerly called Canton by English-speakers, became a center for the manufacture of woks—the shallow iron cooking pans that the Chinese still use today. The region inland from Shanghai, in central China, became a center for the weaving of cotton cloth. Traders transported goods from these manufacturing centers by barge and junk along the rivers, canals, and coastal waters. The goods came to Beijing, the new and growing capital city, and to other large urban centers such as Guangzhou and Shanghai.

Father Matteo Ricci, who was an Italian missionary to China in the late 1500s, gives a fascinating description of the Grand Canal and the hazards of traveling on it.

"So great is the number of boats that frequently many days are lost in transit by crowding each other, particularly when water is low in the canals. To prevent this, the water is held back at stated places by wooden locks, which also serve as bridges. ... At times it happens that the rush of water is so high and strong, at the exit from one lock or at the entrance to another, that the boats are capsized and the whole crew is drowned. The boats of the Magistrates and of other Government dignitaries are drawn up the stream, against the current, by wooden devices on the shore, and the expense for such hauling is paid by the Government.**”**

The Chinese shipped such goods as tea and silk by caravan to Central Asia and Russia. In addition, some Chinese ships continued to sail to Southeast Asia and India to trade, despite the government's disapproval of such voyages.

While cities grew, the vast majority of China's people continued to live in the countryside, where they increased the amount of land under cultivation. New crops—such as sweet potatoes, peanuts, and tobacco—were introduced from the Americas. The sweet potato became known as "the poor man's food" in southern China because it thrived in soils unsuited to the growing of rice. It also provided more basic nutritional value than most other food crops.

The Growth of Popular Culture

As in Europe, the growth of cities and the increasing wealth of urban merchants and artisans in China encouraged the rise of popular culture. As early as the Yuan dynasty in the 1300s, city people read novels and plays in the common everyday language rather than in the literary language. During the Ming and Qing dynasties, these popular novels and plays increased in number. Old tales about bandits and corrupt officials, which had once been recited by storytellers in the streets, now appeared in novels written by professional authors. The writings of this period realistically portrayed Chinese society and family life.

Scholarship also flourished under the rule of the Ming and Qing emperors. Under Kangxi especially, Chinese scholars wrote long and detailed histories of earlier dynasties as well as essays on Confucian ethics. As the humanists had done in Europe during the Renaissance, Chinese scholars applied intensive study to ancient writings. In the 1700s, Chinese scholars began to compile a great manuscript library that included rare works of the past. Eventually the library contained 36,000 volumes. During the Qing dynasty also, scholars studied **philology**, the history of literature and language. A few scholars, mostly Daoists, conducted studies of plants and animals.

This picture scroll shows a street scene during the Ming dynasty.

Qing Society

Qing society continued to be based on the family—a unit of people related to each other by blood, marriage, or adoption. Daughters, when they married, would go to live with their new husbands' families. The wives of a family's sons would join the sons' household.

The male head of the family had considerable power to direct the activities of each member for the good of the family as a whole. The family, like the state, reflected the hierarchies of Confucian thought.

The Decline of the Qing Dynasty

By about 1800 the Qing dynasty had begun to decline. After more than a century of peace, the soldiers of the Manchu army had lost much of their discipline and skill as warriors.

Under the rule of the Qing, government services for the people also deteriorated. China's population had grown rapidly. Between 1750 and 1850, for example, the population more than doubled, increasing to 430 million people. Peace and increases in agricultural output contributed significantly to this population growth. Chinese peasants raised larger crops, making it possible to feed more people. The increase in population, however, was not matched by growth in either the number or the efficiency of government officials.

As in the past, local officials relied on powerful local rural families, the gentry, to make the political system work. These local officials collected taxes from the peasants, sending the revenue to the government.

These Chinese silk weavers are working on a manual loom during the Qing dynasty.

In return, the emperor permitted them to keep a small portion of the taxes they collected.

This system functioned fairly smoothly for many years and made it possible for a relatively small number of officials to administer the affairs of a large country. During the late Qing period, however, corruption among government officials caused serious problems. High-ranking bureaucrats began to use their positions in the emperor's service to acquire great personal fortunes. They pressured local officials throughout China to give them money and expensive gifts.

Those local officials, forced to pay bribes or lose their jobs, pressured the gentry for more tax revenues. The gentry in turn demanded more taxes from the peasants. Less and less of the money collected went to provide necessary services such as flood control and road repairs. Instead, the money ended up in the hands of the emperor's officials.

Discontent and Rebellion

In 1796, discontent over increased taxes and decreased services erupted into a great peasant rebellion, the White Lotus Rebellion. Members of the White Lotus Society, a Buddhist cult that had been active in the late Yuan and Ming periods, led the revolt. The government succeeded in restoring peace in 1804, after a difficult struggle. The dynasty had been seriously weakened, however, and in subsequent years it weakened further. The basic causes of discontent remained, and other uprisings and rebellions occurred frequently after 1850.

The Qing dynasty seemed to be following in the footsteps of previous Chinese dynasties. It had claimed the Mandate of Heaven after victories in battle and had achieved great heights. Now a discontented people challenged the dynasty. If the pattern of past Chinese history had repeated itself, eventually a powerful rival to the Qing emperor would have emerged, defeated the Qing army in battle, and claimed the Mandate of Heaven for himself. The new emperor would then have established a new and more vigorous dynasty.

Chinese history did not follow that traditional pattern now, however, because new influences appeared from abroad. Just as the Qing dynasty started its decline, new peoples appeared in China—the Europeans. Before very long, an unprecedented series of crises developed in China.

The Portuguese in China

Around 1514, the first Portuguese ships reached the southeastern coast of China. After years of negotiation, the Chinese allowed the Portuguese to establish a trading station at Macao in 1557.

Portugal's impact, however, was not limited to trade. The Jesuit missionaries who arrived on Portuguese ships enjoyed considerable success in China. They used their knowledge of astronomy to gain admission to the emperor's circle. By helping to revise the Chinese calendar, they proved themselves useful to the emperor, whose duties still included predicting eclipses and the timing of the seasons. The emperor appointed the Jesuit missionaries to official positions in his palace, giving them the opportunity to convert a number of high-ranking Chinese officials to Christianity.

In the 1700s, however, the Qing emperors turned against the Jesuits, claiming that they had become too much involved in Chinese politics. The emperors denounced Christianity as a subversive, anti-Confucian sect. After that, the number of converts to Christianity dwindled.

The British in China

In the early 1700s, British ships began arriving frequently at Guangzhou, where the British had established a trading post in the late 1600s. The British came to China to buy silk and tea, which the Dutch had introduced to Europe in the 1600s. Great Britain was rapidly becoming a land of tea drinkers, and the British regarded Chinese teas as the best in the world.

The British East India Company monopolized the new trade in Chinese teas. The company agreed to accept Chinese restrictions on its activities in order to get adequate supplies of tea. The Chinese allowed company ships to dock only at Guangzhou and to trade only with a small number of officially licensed Chinese merchants. These Chinese merchants in turn paid large fees to the Chinese government. Only a few representatives of the British East India Company were permitted to stay in Guangzhou,

This early map of Nanking, China, indicates the location of Jesuit missions there.

where they lived in a special foreign settlement outside the city walls.

For a time the Chinese government succeeded in isolating the British with these trading and housing restrictions. They kept contact between the British and the Chinese to a minimum. In the late 1700s, however, two new developments led to a deterioration in British-Chinese relations and eventually resulted in war between these two countries.

Free trade ideas. The first development was the spread of **free trade** ideas from the West. The concept of free trade, which developed as a reaction against mercantilism, meant that government should not restrict or interfere in international trade. Not all British traders worked for the British East India Company. Those who tried to operate independently in Asia resented the monopolies enjoyed by the British company.

The British government also wanted to secure additional overseas markets for the products of British industry. It sent official missions to Beijing in 1793 and again in 1816 to request that the Chinese open several more ports to British ships. Both missions failed.

In 1834 the British government took a decisive step in initiating a free trade policy. It abolished the British East India Company's monopoly on trade with China. The British government sent an official to Guangzhou for trade talks, but the Chinese rebuffed this official's efforts.

The opium trade. The other development that led to war between China and Great Britain involved the steady expansion of the tea trade. The British East India Company had paid for its purchases of Chinese tea with cotton from India, which was used to supply the many weavers in central China. There was a limit to the Chinese demand for this cotton, however, and the Chinese showed little interest in other European trade goods. The British demand for tea, on the other hand, continued to increase. The company had to find some new product to exchange for tea. The product they chose was opium, an addictive narcotic.

British India produced opium and exported it to China in increasing quantities from the late 1700s onward. Opium addiction spread among the Chinese people, and the Chinese government grew alarmed—especially since much of China's silver supply was being used to help pay for the ever-growing volume of imported opium. Chinese authorities demanded that opium sales be stopped and that all opium cargoes be turned over to them.

The Metropolitan Museum of Art. Purchase, The Lucille and Robert H. Gries Charity Fund. 1970. (1970.220.1). Photograph © 1998 The Metropolitan Museum of Art.

One Chinese product prized by Europeans was porcelain like this decorative plate.

The Opium War. When the Chinese tried to suppress the opium traffic in South China and insisted on maintaining the traditional merchant tribute system, a war broke out between China and Great Britain. This conflict, known as the Opium War, lasted from 1839 to 1842.

During the Opium War, the Chinese army and naval forces proved to be no match for the better-armed and better-trained British. A small British naval force, which included iron-hulled steamships, moved up the coast from Guangzhou, defeating Chinese resistance with relative ease. In 1842 the British secured control of a region near Nanjing, a population center strategically located close to the Grand Canal. At that point the Qing officials agreed to negotiate on British terms.

The 1842 Treaty of Nanjing ended the Opium War. This treaty compelled China to give the island of Hong Kong to the British and to open five ports to British trade. These ports became the first Chinese treaty ports. Only a fixed, low tariff could be charged on British goods entering the country by these ports. A further provision of the treaty stated that British subjects in these ports would be governed by British, not Chinese, laws and would be tried in British courts. This exemption of foreigners from the laws of the country in which they live or do business is called **extraterritoriality**.

The Opium War broke out when the Chinese government tried to control the British opium trade between India and China. This painting from Britain's National Maritime Museum illustrates the British merchant steamer *Nemesis* attacking and destroying 11 Chinese junks at Chuenpez Canton, China.

Great Britain could not hold its privileged trade monopoly in China for long. France and other Western powers, including the United States, soon demanded and received similar trade treaties with provisions for extraterritoriality. Forced to sign them, the Chinese called them "unequal" treaties. They were unequal in that the Chinese received no benefits from them; all gains were made by the other countries who insisted on the treaties.

The Taiping and Other Rebellions

An event that occurred within China made the intrusion of the Western powers easier. In the mid-1800s, southern and central China were torn by a great rebellion that threatened to overthrow the Qing. The leader of this revolt was a southern Chinese man named Hong Xiuquan (hoohng shee·oo·choo·ahn), who had been influenced by Christian teachings. He claimed to be the younger brother of Jesus and that his mission was to establish a new dynasty—the Taiping, meaning "Heavenly Peace." His ideas attracted many followers among the Chinese.

The Taiping Rebellion lasted from 1850 to 1864 and caused terrible destruction in southern China and the Chang Jiang valley. Millions of people were killed, and cities and agricultural resources were destroyed. At the same time, the Qing faced rebellions by Muslims in central and western China who wanted to create their own independent states. After a long struggle, the Qing finally put down these rebellions in the late 1870s.

The Taiping Rebellion and the other revolts seriously weakened both the Qing dynasty and China as a whole. To raise money, the government established a system of internal tariffs. Administered locally, the tariffs tended to weaken the central government even more. Then foreigners took over the collection of customs duties in Chinese ports, weakening China's control over its revenues still further.

More "unequal" treaties. In 1856, war with Great Britain again broke out over a trade dispute. British forces, with French aid, again defeated the Chinese. The Chinese were forced to sign another "unequal" treaty, which opened additional treaty ports on the coast and along the Chang Jiang. The Chinese had to allow the British to open an embassy in Beijing, the Qing capital. Other foreign powers soon followed Great Britain's example by opening their embassies in Beijing.

Building History Study Skills

READ
WRITE
INTERPRET
CONNECT
THINK

Thinking About History: Analyzing Consequences

Every human action and decision produces a consequence, or result. For example, if you stayed up last night until about 2:00 A.M. and had to get up at 6:00 A.M. today, the consequence would be that you are tired today. If you decided to work very hard to prepare for a test, the result would probably be a good grade on the test. Since history deals with human actions, analyzing the consequences of these actions will help you gain new insight into historic events. Knowing the consequences helps you understand the impact of historic changes. Consequences can be immediate or long-range, positive or negative.

How to Analyze Consequences

To analyze consequences, follow these steps.
1. Identify the purpose or goal of the action or decision that you are studying. Ask: What did the person or persons hope to achieve?
2. Identify the immediate and long-range consequences of the action or decision.
3. State the positive and/or negative consequences of the action or decision.
4. Draw a conclusion by asking: Did the action or decision help to achieve the purpose or goal?

Developing the Skill

The excerpt below describes the civil service examinations in China. As you read, consider what consequences the examinations had for the government of China.

"A much-debated issue about Chinese history is the extent to which the examination system was vigorously applied and whether it brought a significant flow of new blood into Chinese ruling circles. . . .

. . . The system was on the whole highly competitive, and it certainly succeeded in impressing upon most people the idea that they were being ruled by their . . . superiors. . . . In traditional China the sons of mandarins obviously had . . . advantages because they were brought up in a home environment in which education and the achievement of official status were stressed. . . .

However, few families had more than two generations in office. . . . On balance, it would seem

that there was more mobility throughout most of Chinese history than in even eighteenth- and nineteenth-century England."

The purpose of your study is to analyze the consequences of the civil service examination system for Chinese government and society. The statement discusses the positive outcomes of the system. The examinations contributed to social mobility. Anyone could take them, and the examinations had a performance requirement rather than a class requirement. People from all classes could be chosen for positions by scoring well. Therefore, the system provided for competent leadership by the ablest people. Other positive consequences included an emphasis on education, since education was the best means of securing a position in the civil service. It was also a movement away from the traditional pattern of heredity determining ability.

What were the overall consequences of the civil service examination system for Chinese government and society? The civil service examination system rewarded talent, not birth, and promoted education and efficient government.

Practicing the Skill

In a local newspaper, read an article that deals with a government decision or policy. Then analyze the consequences that this decision or policy might have.

To apply this skill, see Applying History Study Skills on page 197.

Chinese scholars collating classic texts

In addition, Great Britain took possession of a small section of the Chinese mainland that was located opposite of Hong Kong, and the Chinese government had to pledge to protect Christian missionaries and their converts.

In separate treaties, Russia gained even more than trade privileges and extraterritoriality. It received territory north of the Amur River and east of the Ussuri River, bordering on the Sea of Japan. In the southern part of this newly gained territory, the Russians founded the port of Vladivostok.

Section 1 Review

1. **Define** junks, queue, philology, free trade, extraterritoriality
2. **Identify** Nurhachi, Kangxi, Hong Xiuquan
3. **Locate and Explain the Significance** Beijing, Manchuria, Guangzhou, Macao
4. **Understanding Ideas** Why did foreign trade and overseas explorations decline during the Ming dynasty?
5. **Interpreting Ideas** (a) What cultural developments took place during the Ming and Qing dynasties? (b) What led to the decline of the Qing dynasty?
6. **Analyzing Ideas** Analyze the impact that contact with Europeans had on China.

Section 2

The Tokugawa Shoguns in Japan

Focus Questions

- **What were the strengths of the Tokugawa shoguns in Japan?**
- **What was society like under the rule of the Tokugawa shoguns?**
- **How did Japan's isolation end?**

China's culture influenced that of early Japan. Until the late 1500s, however, feudal Japan followed a course of political development more like that of Europe than of China.

In the late 1400s, the Japanese local lords—daimyo—began to fight among themselves for survival and supremacy. The struggle among the daimyo resulted in the creation of a political system that was a cross between feudalism and centralized monarchy. The Japanese established this hybrid system during the Tokugawa (TOH·KOOHG·AH·WAH) shogunate, in 1603. It survived until 1868.

Founding of the Tokugawa Shogunate

In 1467, rival branches of the Ashikaga family in Japan became involved in a dispute over the selection of the next shogun. This conflict marked the beginning of 100 years of almost constant warfare in Japan. A number of local daimyo, sensing the weakness of the Ashikaga, fought for control of the country. A series of three daimyo emerged in the late 1500s as victors in this long struggle. They succeeded in establishing themselves as overlords of the other daimyo, and they created a centralized feudal system.

Oda Nobunaga. The first of these overlords, Oda Nobunaga (ohd·ah noh·boo·NAH·gah), began his career as a minor daimyo. He succeeded, by means of conquest and alliances, in capturing the city of Kyoto in 1568. Nobunaga ended the Ashikaga shogunate in 1573 and then started to consolidate his power in central Japan. Before he could defeat his remaining rivals, however, one of his own vassals killed him in 1582.

Toyotomi Hideyoshi. Another vassal, Toyotomi (toh·yoh·toh·mee) Hideyoshi, leader of Nobunaga's army, assumed Nobunaga's position as overlord after he was murdered. Born in 1536 to a humble peasant family, Hideyoshi had risen to a high position—from warrior to general—in Nobunaga's army. In the 1580s Hideyoshi defeated several powerful daimyo in battle, and by threats and diplomacy he forced the others to pledge their loyalty to him.

Hideyoshi did not totally destroy the defeated daimyo, but he weakened them by reducing the size of their territories so that they could not threaten him again. He also carried out a "sword hunt" to disarm the peasants. Thereafter, peasants could no longer rise to become warriors. Only men born into warrior families could become warriors.

In 1592, and again in 1597, the ambitious Hideyoshi sent his army to invade Korea. He wanted to build an extensive empire and give Japanese warriors an opportunity to do battle. At first the Japanese invasion force succeeded. As the battles continued, however, a Chinese army that was aiding the Koreans pushed the Japanese invaders back to the coast.

Japanese warriors regularly exercised and meditated to keep fit for battle.

When Hideyoshi died in 1598, the Japanese withdrew to their homeland.

Tokugawa Ieyasu. Hideyoshi's most powerful vassal, Tokugawa Ieyasu, succeeded him as overlord. Ieyasu established his capital at Edo (AY·doh), the city that is now Tokyo. (See map on page 185.) Other daimyo resisted Ieyasu, but he defeated them in 1600. Then, in 1603, he became shogun. The Tokugawa family retained the title of shogun for more than 250 years, establishing a government known as the Tokugawa shogunate.

Tokugawa Ieyasu crushed his defeated rivals. He took away much of their land and made them swear oaths of loyalty to him and his family. He allowed other daimyo, who then numbered about 260, to keep possession of their private domains. However, he reserved for himself the right to expand or reduce the size of their territories in the future.

Within his own domain, each daimyo governed almost as an absolute ruler. The local peasants paid taxes that the daimyo used to support both himself and those in his service, such as the samurai. The Tokugawa family had its own very large domain, which comprised about one fourth of the productive land in Japan. Thus, the Tokugawa did not rule the entire country directly, nor did they personally tax the entire population. In this way Japan maintained a degree of political and economic decentralization.

Tokugawa Power

As overlords the Tokugawa did have considerable influence over the behavior of the daimyo. Behind this influence lay the Tokugawa wealth and military power. The Tokugawa shoguns prohibited daimyo alliances. Most daimyo had to spend every other year in Edo, the shogun's capital, and they left their families there as hostages when they returned to their own domains. The expense of maintaining two grand residences—one in Edo and one in the provinces—and of traveling to and from Edo in elaborate processions drained the financial resources of the daimyo. Living in Edo also tended to transform them from warriors into courtiers. In this manner the Tokugawa shoguns maintained control over the daimyo.

The Tokugawa shogunate shaped Japanese life in several ways. By establishing a strong central government, the shoguns brought more than two centuries of stability to Japan. Their control of the daimyo helped to keep peace in the countryside. In addition, by setting trade restrictions and limiting contact with foreigners, they achieved almost complete isolation from Europe by 1650. This was a response to the growing contact with foreigners that had occurred over the previous centuries.

Japan and Foreign Contacts

Japanese sailors and traders had traveled overseas since the 1000s. In the early 1400s, during the Ashikaga shogunate, Japanese ships had sailed to Korea and China, seeking profitable trade. Sometimes the Japanese had resorted to piracy, seizing whatever they could from the local inhabitants.

These Japanese traders sailed mostly from those ports in western Japan that were closest to the Asian mainland. They carried sulfur, copper-painted folding fans, scrolls, and swords as exports, and they imported silks, porcelains, books, paintings, and copper coins.

The Portuguese in Japan. In the mid-1500s, the daimyo found another source of wealth: trade with the Portuguese, whose ships began to appear in Japanese waters. Portuguese traders introduced two influences in Japan that the Tokugawa shoguns later considered undesirable: the musket and Christianity. Oda Nobunaga had used troops armed with muskets during his military campaigns. However, the Tokugawa shoguns considered the musket an unwelcome invention. This new weapon went against the traditional samurai ethic, an ethic based on skill. With strict limits placed on their manufacture, the technology of firearms in Japan made no advances and may have even declined after 1650. Christianity was undesirable because it taught loyalty to a power other than the Tokugawa shogun.

Christian missionaries. In the wake of Portuguese traders came Christian missionaries. Chief among them were the Jesuits, who had achieved notable success during the Counter-Reformation in Europe. The Jesuits concentrated their efforts on converting the daimyo to Christianity. They had discovered that it was easier to convert a daimyo first and then build churches and seek converts in the domain that he controlled. By the early 1600s, the missionaries had converted as many as 500,000 Japanese to Christianity.

Closing the country. The success of the Jesuits alarmed the Tokugawa shoguns. They saw Christianity as a subversive force that might undermine their authority. They also feared that the missionaries might bring European armies to conquer Japan. Early in the 1600s, the shoguns forced Portuguese traders and missionaries to leave Japan.

By this time the Portuguese faced stiff competition from the Dutch, both in Japan and in the spice trade in the islands off the coast of Southeast Asia. The Dutch had accepted a strictly controlled trading relationship with the Tokugawa shogunate. The shoguns allowed only a few Dutch merchants to live near Nagasaki, a port city on the Japanese island of Kyushu. In addition, the shoguns themselves controlled the small amount of trade Japan conducted with the Dutch.

These Dutch merchants were the only Europeans allowed to trade in Japan after the Tokugawa closed the country in the 1630s. The Tokugawa prohibited the building of oceangoing ships, banned travel abroad by Japanese, and killed foreign sailors who had been shipwrecked in Japan. Like China, Japan now concentrated on domestic affairs and tried to ignore the outside world. As an island country without any land frontiers across which people might slip unnoticed, Japan achieved more complete isolation than did China.

Society Under the Tokugawa

The Tokugawa shoguns, like most of the emperors of China, did not promote change. Stability was a much more important ideal. Confucian ideas and institutions borrowed from China supported this ideal.

First, the Tokugawa shoguns adopted—with some modifications—the Confucian ideal of social classes.

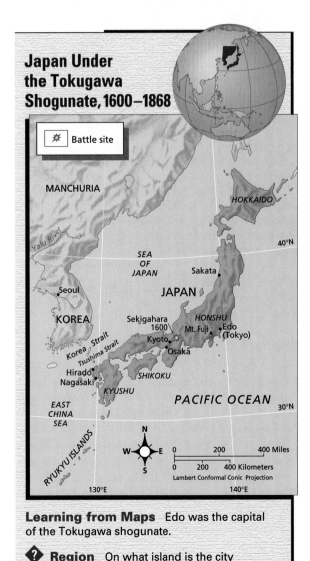

Japan Under the Tokugawa Shogunate, 1600–1868

Battle site

MANCHURIA

HOKKAIDO

Yalu River

SEA OF JAPAN

40°N

Sakata

JAPAN

Seoul

KOREA

Sekigahara 1600

HONSHU

Mt. Fuji

Edo (Tokyo)

Korea Strait

Kyoto

Tsushima Strait

Osaka

Hirado

Nagasaki

SHIKOKU

KYUSHU

PACIFIC OCEAN

EAST CHINA SEA

30°N

RYUKYU ISLANDS

N
W   E
S

0   200   400 Miles
0   200   400 Kilometers
Lambert Conformal Conic Projection

130°E

140°E

Learning from Maps Edo was the capital of the Tokugawa shogunate.

Region On what island is the city of Edo located?

PRINTING

Evening Squall at Ohashi

The emergence of popular culture in Tokugawa Japan was reflected in the subjects of woodblock prints. Recreational and theatrical scenes, as well as scenes of such commonplace activities as fishing and farming, were captured by the gifted artists and printmakers of the 1600s, 1700s, and 1800s.

In this woodblock print by Ando Hiroshige, people are opening umbrellas over their heads to protect themselves from the rain as they hurry over a wooden bridge. The artist shows a single moment caught in time. As we look at the picture, we can almost sense the suddenness of the storm and feel the sensation of the rain on our skin.

Prints such as this were the result of a collaboration of skilled artists and craftspeople. A publisher suggested the subject and directed the production of the print. The artist then made the first drawing, which the engraver cut into a series of wooden blocks. Finally, the printer chose the colors and applied one color to each block. Specially made papers were pressed onto each of the blocks in succession, and the accumulation of color produced the total picture. The blocks could be used repeatedly, and the resulting prints were sold in the publisher's shop.

Woodblock prints were first utilized as illustrations in popular books. However, when many people showed interest in the prints themselves, publishers began producing them separately. As the technique became more popular, it began to reflect the tastes of people in the growing middle class. They were the chief buyers of the prints, which they used for decoration in place of more expensive paintings.

They ranked warriors, who fulfilled roughly the same role as scholar-gentry in China, first. Peasants, artisans, and merchants followed in descending order of importance.

In Japan, people belonged to these classes by birth. Sons followed the occupations of their fathers. For example, a person born into an artisan family in the city of Osaka remained a member of the artisan class in Osaka for life.

Second, the Tokugawa shoguns encouraged education in the Confucian classics for members of the warrior class. The shoguns established schools in the various domains to prepare young warriors for their new peacetime role as government officials. The shoguns, however, did not adopt the Chinese civil service examination system. In Japan, warriors became officials by heredity alone. Males born into low-ranking warrior families worked as low-ranking officials in their domains. Those born into high-ranking families served as high-ranking officials.

As a further means of maintaining control, the shoguns usually required a warrior to live in the castle town of his daimyo. Instead of living on the income of their own estates in the countryside, warriors now received salaries. This policy deprived them of the opportunity to develop independent sources of wealth or power. It also eliminated any opportunity to revolt against their lords.

Change and Culture in Tokugawa Japan

As in China, the rulers of Japan could not prevent social, economic, and political change within their country. Much of the change that took place in Japan resembled that which occurred in China. Cities grew in both size and importance. Internal trade expanded, and various regions of the country began to specialize in certain crops and handicrafts. The growth of cities and the increasing wealth of merchants and artisans led to the rise of a popular culture. By the early 1700s, new forms of literature, theater, and art had taken root. Many of these new forms catered to the tastes and lifestyles of ordinary city residents.

The End of Japan's Isolation

As part of the Tokugawa plan for keeping Japan isolated, the government refused to give shelter to ships of other nations during storms and, in fact, treated shipwrecked sailors harshly. Such treatment of American whaling and merchant ships angered westerners. Western nations wanted Japan to follow China's lead and end its isolation.

At last, in 1853, United States President Millard Fillmore sent a naval force to Japan under Commodore Matthew Perry. Commodore Perry had orders to negotiate a diplomatic and commercial treaty that would guarantee the safety of American sailors and also open Japanese ports to American trade. He presented a letter from President Fillmore—a letter strongly urging the Japanese to agree to such a treaty—and promised to return for an answer the following year.

The American visit to Japan sparked controversy within Japan. Some powerful leaders favored military resistance and continued isolation. Others, however, believed that Japan could not hold out, and the views of this group prevailed. The shogun, influenced by the threat of naval bombardment by the Americans, reluctantly agreed to negotiate when Commodore Perry returned in 1854.

The negotiations between Commodore Perry and the shogun led to the Treaty of Kanagawa (kah·NAH·gah·wah) in 1854, which was a turning point in Japanese history. The Japanese opened two ports to let Americans obtain shelter, fuel, and supplies, opening the door to trade. Within two years Japan signed similar treaties with Great Britain, Russia, and the Netherlands. As part of the

Typical instrumentation of a trio from the Tokugawa period included a singer, a lute player, and a flutist.

agreements with these countries, the foreign nations were allowed to establish **consulates**—diplomatic offices headed by consuls.

Japanese opponents of the Tokugawa shogunate criticized the government for agreeing to the treaties that had been signed with these foreign nations. Nevertheless, in 1858 the governments of Japan and the United States agreed to exchange ministers. The new treaty between these two countries also allowed foreign residence in Edo and Osaka, international trade, and extraterritorial privileges. In addition, the Japanese now opened more treaty ports to the United States. Similar agreements with other nations soon followed.

The Decision to Modernize

As Japan confronted challenges from the outside world, the Japanese recognized the need to modernize their country if they were to maintain their independence. The question was, on what basis would the modernization take place?

The Tokugawa shoguns hoped to maintain their own position by preserving the traditional political institutions of the shogunate. Their inability to resist Western demands, however, undermined their right to rule in the minds of many samurai. A growing number of opponents of the shogunate began to complain about its weakness abroad and autocracy at home. In the 1860s, civil war broke out between the Tokugawa and anti-Tokugawa forces in Japan. Calling for major political reforms, the anti-Tokugawa forces overthrew the shogunate in 1868. Restoring the power of the emperor, they moved Japan towards a more centralized government. The emperor, a teenager, named his reign Meiji, meaning "Enlightened Rule."

Section 2 Review

1. **Define** consulates
2. **Identify** Oda Nobunaga, Toyotomi Hideyoshi, Tokugawa Ieyasu, Matthew Perry
3. **Locate and Explain the Significance** Kyoto, Edo, Nagasaki
4. **Understanding Ideas** What benefits did the Tokugawa shoguns bring to Japan?
5. **Summarizing Ideas** What was society like under the Tokugawa shogunate?
6. **Analyzing Ideas** How did the isolation of Japan end?

The Islamic Empires of Asia

Focus Questions

- **What problems did the Ottoman and Safavid empires face?**
- **What factors weakened the Mughal Empire?**
- **How did the British expand their control over the country of India?**

In the 1500s, Islam was the dominant religion from the Iberian Peninsula to the East Indies. Three large Islamic empires existed in that vast area: the Ottoman, the Persian, and the Mughal.

The rulers of these Muslim states set up strong central governments. They also faced religious divisions among their people with continuing quarrels between the Shi'ah and the Sunnis.

During the Tokugawa period, artists made miniature sculptures called netsukes. These small figures were often inlaid with shells and ivory and worn as jewelry.

This painting illustrates the Turkish sultan Süleyman the Magnificent at the Battle of Mohács in Hungary.

The Ottoman Empire

After the Ottoman Turks conquered Constantinople in 1453, they continued to expand overland while European nations expanded overseas. Led by Süleyman the Magnificent (called by his people Süleyman the Lawgiver), the Turks conquered Hungary and nearly captured the Habsburg capital of Vienna in 1529. By the middle of the 1500s, the Ottomans ruled most of eastern Europe, western Asia, and North Africa. (See map on page 190.)

Later in the century, however, the Ottomans began to suffer reverses. In 1571 a fleet composed of ships from several European powers, led by Philip II of Spain, defeated the Turks at the Battle of Lepanto, near Greece. In 1683, troops led by the Polish king John Sobieski again halted them outside Vienna.

The Ottoman Empire's capital was Constantinople. From there the sultans and their grand viziers (vuh·ZIRZ)—whose duties were similar to a prime minister's—ruled the empire's diverse population. Turks lived in the heart of the empire in Asia Minor. Christians of various ethnic groups inhabited the Balkans, and Muslim Arabs lived in the Fertile Crescent and along the Mediterranean shore of North Africa.

Decline begins. Süleyman the Magnificent died in 1566. In the 1600s the empire began its slow decline. The economy suffered because the empire had lost its control of both the silk and the spice trades when the new sea routes to Asia were opened up by Europeans. The empire was weakened by poor government, conflicts over the succession to the sultanate, corruption, an enormous bureaucracy, and rebellions among the Janissaries, the elite slave troops. The Ottomans lost the Crimean Peninsula and lands around the Black Sea and the Sea of Azov to the Russians in the late 1700s. Napoleon invaded Egypt, an Ottoman possession, in 1798. Later, territories in the Balkans were also lost.

Attempts at reform. Sultan Selim III, who ruled the empire from 1789 to 1807, attempted reforms in administration, taxation, and the military. However, conservatives and Janissaries who were opposed to change overthrew him.

Another ruler, Mahmud II, had more success with reform. Mahmud ruled from 1808 to 1839. Although Great Britain, France, and Russia forced him to recognize Greece's independence in 1829, Mahmud destroyed the Janissaries and modernized the government through autocratic reforms. The Ottoman Empire continued to decline, however. A constitution that provided for representative government was adopted in 1876 but then ignored. In the late 1800s, more lands in the Balkans, the Mediterranean, and North Africa were lost. Rebellions, such as one attempted by the Armenians, were harshly suppressed. By the early 1900s, the Ottoman Empire had become so weak that it was known as the "Sick Man of Europe." The empire finally came to an end in 1923, when a republic was established in Turkey.

Persia

The peoples of Persia, the land lying between the Ottoman Empire and the Mughal Empire of India, had become Muslim early in Islamic history, in the 600s. In 1501 a Turkic dynasty called the Safavids (sah·FAH·vidz) established a very strong central government, with its first capital city at Tabriz, in northwestern Persia.

The Safavids, especially under the rule of Shah 'Abbas I (from 1588 to 1629), brought Persian society to great heights in the 1500s and early 1600s. Isfahan,

The Ottoman Empire, 1453–1683

Legend:
- Ottoman Empire, 1453
- Territory added, 1454–1519
- Territory added, 1520–1566
- ✹ Battle site

0 250 500 Miles
0 250 500 Kilometers
Robinson Projection

Learning from Maps At its zenith under Suleyman, the Ottoman Empire included parts of eastern Europe, western Asia, and northern Africa.

❓ **Location** Which two battle sites are found around the 38°N parallel?

Shah 'Abbas I strengthened the Safavid dynasty by forcing Uzbek and Ottoman forces out of Persia.

which became the new capital in 1598, had a brilliant court and was considered one of the great cities of the Muslim world. Shah 'Abbas's reign saw a flowering of literature—especially poetry—and the arts. Persian calligraphy, textiles, and carpet weaving became renowned. The economy thrived.

The Safavids followed the Shi'ah element of Islam, and they ruthlessly forced Shi'ism upon the Persian population as the state religion. Shi'ism made a very important contribution to later Iranian nationalism. Shi'ah helped give the Persians—today's Iranians—a separate identity from the greater number of Sunnis—Turks and Arabs—who lived around them. This nationalism would have important consequences for Iran in the 1900s.

The rulers who succeeded 'Abbas proved increasingly inept, and in 1736 the Safavid dynasty ended. The Persian nobles then chose a brilliant military leader, Nadir Shah, as their new monarch. Nadir Shah began a campaign of conquest that brought the lands as far west as Delhi under Persian control. He also seized part of the Ottoman Empire. After Nadir Shah's assassination in 1747, however, Persia lost those lands. Persia then split into a number of small states. At the end of the 1700s, the Qajar—another Turkic people—established a Persian dynasty with its capital at Tehran.

The Mughal Empire in India

The wealth and resources of India and its position along the sea routes to Southeast Asia attracted European traders. India had impressive quantities of jewels and gold. European travelers observed that India's rulers enjoyed luxurious lives, unmatched by those of any European monarchs. India's great cities, such as Agra and Delhi, seemed much larger than any in Europe. Agriculture flourished on the subcontinent, where the monsoon season allowed more than one harvest a year.

Nevertheless, the Mughal Empire had become the weakest of the three Muslim empires by the 1700s. Since the mid-1600s, Mughal rulers had faced financial difficulties that weakened the central government. The Mughals maintained huge and expensive armies which they believed were necessary to hold their empire together. In addition, the court became increasingly luxurious and expensive to support. To pay for these expenses, the Mughal emperors increased taxes.

The Mercator Projection: A Map for Navigators

When people look at a map, they usually have no idea of which projection cartographers used to construct that map. However, almost everyone has heard of or seen the most frequently used projection—the Mercator—developed by Gerardus Mercator in 1569. It was the map projection used by European navigators in their voyages of exploration and empire building in the years that followed.

In his projection Mercator drew the lines of latitude and longitude as straight lines that crossed each other at right angles so that navigators could draw straight lines to plot their courses. This meant that the distance between parallels, or lines of latitude, increased as latitude increased. If Mercator had drawn the parallels with even spacing, as they are shown on a globe, straight lines plotted on them would not represent true compass bearings.

The actual mathematical computations that Mercator used to develop his projection were complex, but the idea behind his projection was quite simple. Picture a spherical balloon inside a hollow cylinder. Then, imagine that the balloon has lines of latitude and longitude marked on it and that the line marking the equator just touches the wall of the cylinder. Now imagine blowing up the balloon. As the balloon stretches, the lines of longitude lie as straight lines along the walls of the cylinder and the lines of latitude are stretched apart in proportion. As a result, the farther away from the equator and towards the poles you look, the greater the distortion in scale. Also, although land shapes appear correct, the areas of the landmasses are greatly distorted. Nevertheless, for every point on the map, the angles shown are uniform in every direction. This allows a navigator to plot a straight line course, because a line connecting any two points follows a single compass direction.

The Mercator projection is a valuable navigational tool. It is convenient to use because the shapes of the continents are correct and are easily recognized. But as a result of frequently seeing the Mercator projection, many people have no idea of the proper size of the continents in relation to one another.

On the Mercator projection, landmasses retain their true shape, although their scale becomes more distorted as distance from the equator increases.

As a result of his two governorships in Bengal, Robert Clive laid the foundation for the expansion of the British Empire in India.

Sometimes one third or more of the crops that the peasants raised had to be paid as taxes. As a result, the peasants' levels of production and prosperity declined, reducing the revenue base.

With the empire weakened, the powerful new Persian ruler Nadir Shah delivered the final blow to Mughal power in India. In 1739 Nadir Shah sacked Delhi and confiscated the jewel-encrusted Peacock Throne of the Mughals. The Mughals lost their wealth, their prestige, their army, and much of their territory. Although an emperor remained on the throne in Delhi until the 1850s, during the remainder of the 1700s the Marathas, Sikhs from the Punjab, and Afghan Muslim invaders fought for control of the country. An India torn by dissension was much easier for Europeans to conquer.

Europeans in India

The Mughal Empire was the least successful of the major Muslim empires in confronting European power. To the east, the Chinese and Japanese managed to keep Europeans out altogether for a long time. In India, however, the Mughal emperors could not dislodge the Portuguese in the 1500s. Nor could they resist the English, who by the 1600s had begun to replace the Portuguese as the major European presence in India. Over the years this presence grew.

The British East India Company, founded in 1600, controlled England's trade with India. By the 1700s the company's chief rival was the French East India Company. Both the English and the French trading companies desired commercial profits, not Indian colonies, since few of their citizens lived there.

In 1756 the Seven Years' War began in Europe, with England and France on opposing sides. Hostilities between the two countries occurred in India as well as elsewhere around the world. At this time the Mughal Empire lacked a strong central power, and local leaders struggled for advantage. Taking advantage of the chaos, the British and the French formed alliances with rival Indian rulers.

The British trading post at Calcutta lay within the important Indian state of Bengal, whose ruler was allied with the French. In 1756, Bengali troops captured Calcutta and imprisoned many British citizens, locking them up overnight in a small jail cell that became known as the Black Hole of Calcutta. By morning, dozens of the prisoners had suffocated.

The British East India Company and its Indian allies, who were under military leader Robert Clive,

India, 1835–1858

Learning from Maps The British acquired a large amount of territory in India during the early to mid-1800s.

? Human-Environment Interaction Around which physical features did the British settle by 1856?

fought back vigorously. In a series of decisive victories, Clive crushed the French and their Indian allies. The Treaty of Paris in 1763, which ended the Seven Years' War and its related conflicts around the world, left the French with only a few tiny footholds in India along the coast and gave the British a free hand in the rest of the subcontinent.

Expansion of British Authority

The British East India Company now governed a huge realm. The responsibility soon strained the company's resources, and some of its officials engaged in corrupt practices. As a result the British government began to regulate the company's activities. In the late 1700s, the British government assumed the right to appoint the company's highest official, the governor-general. However, the company remained free to earn profits and to use its officials and troops as it chose.

In the late 1780s, the British government named Charles Cornwallis—the same General Cornwallis who had surrendered to George Washington at Yorktown in 1781—governor-general of the British East India Company in India. One of his first actions was to clean up the widespread corruption among company officials. Blaming some of the corruption on Indian employees, Cornwallis ordered them excluded from all important company positions. Indian resentment over this discrimination lasted for years.

Rivalries and even warfare continued among various Indian states. The British took advantage of these conflicts to expand their control over additional Indian territory. Religious hatred between Hindus and Muslims helped the British, as did the caste system (which was discussed in Chapter 3), which prevented Indians from uniting against the foreigners. The British did not even always need to employ their own troops in actual fighting. Often they could make use of local Indian troops—called **sepoys** (SEE·poyz)—who were trained and led by British officers.

By 1857 the British East India Company ruled about three fifths of the Indian subcontinent directly. This company ruled most of the rest of the Indian subcontinent indirectly through its control of local princes. Great Britain also controlled the island of Ceylon (now named Sri Lanka), which it had seized from the Dutch between 1795 and 1796.

Until about 1825 the British made no attempt to impose their own way of life on India. In the 1830s, however, English became the language of instruction in Indian schools, and Indian pupils studied Western literature, history, and science.

Like their Mughal predecessors, the British in India tried to prohibit slavery, the killing of infant girls, and the ritual suicide of widows (which is known as suttee). The British also tried to suppress thuggee, which involved ritual murders and robberies committed by members of a secret religious cult. From this practice we get our word *thug*.

The Indian Revolt

India in the mid-1800s was a huge piece of land, with millions of people and an ancient civilization, controlled by a foreign commercial corporation. The British population in India had grown rapidly and now included the wives and families of British men.

Indians resented the British and their increasing tendency to impose Western ways of life upon India. The sepoys were particularly dissatisfied because they had been forced to fight for the British in numerous campaigns in Afghanistan and Burma. In 1857 they revolted.

The immediate cause of the Indian Mutiny, or Sepoy Rebellion, involved a new kind of rifle that the British East India Company had issued in 1857. In order to load his rifle, the sepoy had to bite off part of the cartridge. A false rumor spread that these cartridges had been greased with the fat of cows and pigs to make the bullets slide more easily through the barrel. The sepoys included both Hindus and Muslims; Hindus regard cows as sacred, and Muslims are forbidden to eat pork. This rumor, therefore, struck at the religious sensibilities of both groups.

Agitators whipped up existing resentments by claiming that the company had purposely insulted the two religions. With help from Indian civilians, the sepoys staged a widespread and violent mutiny against their British masters. (See map on opposite page.)

The Indian Mutiny nearly drove the British out of India, but troops sent from Great Britain finally suppressed the rebellion. To discourage future uprisings, the British took several steps. Leading sepoys were executed. In 1858 the British Parliament, concerned over the administration of India by the British East India Company, dissolved the company and transferred its power in India to the British government.

In 1876 Britain's Queen Victoria was proclaimed empress of India. Great Britain now formally filled the void left by the passing of the Mughals.

Section 3 Review

1. **Define** sepoys
2. **Identify** Süleyman the Magnificent, Selim III, Mahmud II, Safavids, Shah 'Abbas I, Nadir Shah, Robert Clive, Charles Cornwallis
3. **Locate and Explain the Significance** Black Sea, Sea of Azov, Delhi, Bengal
4. **Contrasting Ideas** In what ways were the problems of the Ottoman and Safavid Empires similar and different?
5. **Summarizing Ideas** What weaknesses led to the end of the Mughal Empire?
6. **Analyzing Ideas** How did the British expand their authority over India?

During the 1857 massacre at Cawnpore (Kanpur), a town in northern India, rebelling sepoys killed British women and children.

Chapter 5 Review

c. A.D. 1514 First Portuguese ships reach China.

A.D. 1566 Süleyman the Magnificent dies.

Early 1600s Jesuits are banned from Japan.

A.D. 1400   A.D. 1450   A.D. 1500   A.D. 1550   A.D. 1600

A.D. 1368 Ming dynasty is established in China.

A.D. 1501–1736 Safavid dynasty rules Persia.

A.D. 1592 First Japanese invasion of Korea occurs.

Chapter Summary

The following list contains the key concepts you have learned about China, Japan, Southwest Asia, and India in the era of European expansion.

1. The rulers of the Ming and Qing dynasties tried to isolate China by prohibiting Chinese merchants from trading overseas and by restricting foreign merchants to special settlements inside China.
2. The Ming and Qing emperors brought peace to China, but by the late 1700s, corruption among officials, increased taxes, and decreased services led to discontent and rebellion. China's defeat by Great Britain in the Opium War forced the nation to deal with the outside world. Chinese weakness enabled foreigners to obtain special privileges in China.
3. The Japanese struggled over who was to be supreme—the central government run by the shoguns or the local lords called daimyo.
4. The Tokugawa shoguns established internal peace and in the 1630s closed Japan to foreign missionaries and merchants. In 1853 the United States sent a naval force to Japan to negotiate a diplomatic and commercial treaty to guarantee the safety of American sailors. These negotiations led to the Treaty of Kanagawa in 1854, which opened Japan. Similar agreements followed.
5. The Ottoman Empire remained a threat to central and eastern Europe until the late 1600s, after which it began a gradual decline. In the early 1800s, Mahmud II introduced reforms, but the Ottoman Empire continued to decline until it was replaced by a Turkish republic in 1923.
6. The Safavid dynasty brought Persia to great cultural and political heights. After the Safavid dynasty fell, Nadir Shah assumed power. Through a campaign of military conquest, Nadir Shah greatly extended Persia's boundaries. After his assassination, however, Persia lost these lands and split into smaller states.
7. The Mughal emperors could not keep European traders out of India. The Seven Years' War between Great Britain and France helped to cement British domination in India.
8. India was governed by the British East India Company. In 1857 the Indians rebelled against the British in what is known as the Sepoy Rebellion. The British put down the rebellion and dissolved the British East India Company. They transferred the rule of India to the British government. Some years later, Queen Victoria was proclaimed Empress of India.

Reviewing Important Terms

On a separate sheet of paper, supply the term that correctly completes each statement.

1. Early Chinese ships were called _____.
2. The Manchu emperors forced Chinese men to wear a long braid called a _____ to symbolize submission.
3. Chinese scholars during the Qing dynasty became interested in _____, the study of the history of literature and language.
4. Under _____ _____, the government does not restrict or interfere in international trade.
5. Diplomatic offices headed by consuls are called _____.
6. _____ were native Indian troops trained by British officers.
7. _____ exempts foreigners from the laws of the country in which they live or do business.

Developing Critical Thinking Skills

1. **Summarizing Ideas** List the actions taken by the Ming dynasty to protect China's northern frontier.
2. **Explaining Ideas** How did the Tokugawa shogunate maintain a long period of peace within Japan?
3. **Analyzing Ideas** What issues were of concern to the Japanese in deciding whether to modernize their country, and what was the outcome?
4. **Interpreting Ideas** Explain the ways in which the decline of the Ottoman Empire and the decline of the Persian Safavid Empire were similar.
5. **Comparing Ideas** Compare the way the British established trade in China with the way in which they established it in India.
6. **Understanding Relationships** Describe the results of European contact with each of the following: **(a)** China; **(b)** Japan; **(c)** India.

A.D. 1683
John Sobieski turns back Turks at Vienna.

A.D. 1603–1868
Tokugawa shogunate rules Japan.

A.D. 1650 | A.D. 1700 | A.D. 1750 | A.D. 1800 | A.D. 1850

A.D. 1644
Qing dynasty is established in China.

C. A.D. 1699
British establish trading post at Guangzhou.

A.D. 1796
White Lotus Rebellion begins in China.

A.D. 1808–1839
Mahmud II rules Ottoman Empire.

Relating Geography to History

Turn to the map of India on page 194, and answer the following questions: (a) Why did British control of India begin along the coast and move gradually inland? (b) When you look at British acquisitions from 1835 to 1858, what geographic pattern do they seem to follow? (c) Why might the British have had more difficulty controlling some areas than others?

Relating Past to Present

1. Review the military problems that the Ming dynasty had along its land borders with central and northern Asia. Then ask your librarian to help you find source materials on the tensions between China and the former Soviet Union, China and India, or China and Vietnam, since the 1950s. What are the reasons for the tensions between these countries?

2. Europeans transmitted their culture to the areas of the world that came under their domination. Choose an area of the world today that is experiencing the influence of Western ideas and culture. Describe some of these influences. What impact might they have on the traditional way of life in that area?

3. The British excluded the Indians from any important positions in the British East India Company. Naturally, the Indians developed a deep resentment of this policy of exclusion. How do you think this superior attitude that colonial rulers had over their subjected people has affected the relationship between the former colonial power and its former colonies?

Applying History Study Skills

Before completing this activity, review Building History Study Skills on page 182.

Read the following selection from a 1636 Tokugawa edict banning contact with foreigners. Then answer the questions that follow.

"No Japanese ships may leave for foreign countries. . . . No Japanese may go abroad secretly. If anyone tries to do this, he will be killed, and the ship and owner(s) will be placed under arrest while higher authority is informed. . . . No offspring of Southern Barbarians [Europeans] will be allowed to remain. Anyone

violating this order will be killed and all his relatives punished according to the gravity of the offense."

1. What consequences did people face if they ignored the decree?

2. What do you think were the positive and negative long-term consequences of the decree?

internet connect

Search the Internet through the HRW Web site to gather information on the history of Japan's samurai warriors. Imagine that you are a samurai. Write a journal entry describing the issues you face.

HRW GO TO: go.hrw.com
KEYWORD: SC0 Samurai Warriors

Building Your Portfolio

1. **Writing a Report** As you have read, the art form of woodblock printing became popular in Japan during the Tokugawa period. Use books in your library to write a report in which you answer the following questions: Why was this art form popular? What was its subject matter? How did Japanese woodblock prints change in the 1800s? One source for your research might be Seiichiro Takahashi's *Traditional Woodblock Prints of Japan* (Weatherhill). Place the report in your portfolio.

2. **Writing an Essay** The opium trade became a major source of conflict between Great Britain and China. Write an essay describing the dilemma of the Chinese officials in attempting to stop the opium traffic. Also, describe how the British used the Opium War to place demands on the Chinese. Place the essay in your portfolio.

3. **Presenting an Oral Report** Prepare an oral report to describe how the Indians reacted to British rule. Be sure to include details of the Sepoy Rebellion. Place the notes and research materials for your report in your portfolio.

Unit Summary

The following list contains the key concepts you have learned about the emergence of modern nations.

1. Beginning in the 1300s a revival of interest in the classical learning of Greece and Rome, known as the Renaissance, swept Italy and later the rest of Europe.

2. In Germany, Martin Luther began a reform movement within the Roman Catholic Church but ended by breaking with the church. The result was the Protestant Reformation. The doctrines he developed, known today as Lutheranism, spread throughout northern Europe. Later, churches in many parts of Europe broke away from the Roman Catholic Church.

3. The Scientific Revolution of the 1500s and 1600s transformed methods and understanding of astronomy, physics, and anatomy.

4. In the 1400s and 1500s, Europeans expanded overseas. Portuguese and Spanish explorers took the lead in discovering new lands and trade routes that paved the way for Europe's domination of most of the world.

5. The rulers of Europe centralized government in their own hands, and by the mid-1600s they had established absolute monarchies in France, Russia, Prussia, and Austria.

6. In England monarchs and Parliament clashed throughout the 1600s. Finally, Parliament emerged the winner and launched Great Britain on the road to democratic government.

7. During the Enlightenment, thinkers began to criticize the established political institutions.

8. In the 1700s the British colonists in what is today the United States won their independence.

9. Growing discontent in France, and Louis XVI's failure to solve the government's continuing financial crisis, led to the French Revolution in 1789.

10. Through a series of steps France became first a republic and then an empire under Napoleon Bonaparte. When Napoleon was defeated in 1815, the European powers attempted to restore the old regimes, but the principles of the revolution could not be suppressed.

11. China and Japan tried to protect their cultures from outside influences. However, they were unsuccessful as European powers made major inroads into both of these countries by the 1800s.

12. The Ottoman, Persian, and Mughal Empires declined in the 1700s. India then became a target for European colonialism. Great Britain began taking control of the Indian subcontinent in the late 1700s.

Reviewing Concepts

On a separate sheet of paper, match each of the following people with the appropriate description from the list that follows:

a. Leonardo da Vinci
b. Peter I
c. Prince Henry
d. Louis XVI
e. Bartholomeu Dias
f. Michelangelo
g. Tokugawa Ieyasu

h. Machiavelli
i. Petrarch
j. Charles V
k. Oliver Cromwell
l. Catherine II
m. Henry VIII
n. Copernicus

_____1. Built a new capital in Russia that would be a "window to the West"

_____2. Painter, sculptor, and engineer, architect, and scientist who painted the *Mona Lisa*

_____3. Polish scientist who concluded that the Sun was the center of the universe

_____4. English king who broke with the Roman Catholic Church

_____5. Powerful overlord who established a long-lasting shogunate

_____6. Sailed around the southern tip of Africa

_____7. Italian poet who was one of the first humanists

_____8. Led the revolt against Charles I in England

_____9. Russian ruler whose expansionism gained control of the northern shore of the Black Sea

_____10. Supported Portugal's interest in exploration

_____11. King of France, who was executed

_____12. Artist who painted the frescoes on the ceiling of the Sistine Chapel

_____13. Italian Renaissance thinker who wrote about politics and government

_____14. Habsburg who was king of Spain and Holy Roman emperor

Applying Critical Thinking Skills

1. **Interpreting Ideas** In what ways did European art of the 1500s and 1600s reflect the new ideas and attitudes of the Renaissance?

2. **Analyzing Ideas** How did the ideas of humanism and the Scientific Revolution change Europe?

3. **Understanding Ideas** (a) According to the theory of mercantilism, what benefits did European nations hope to gain from colonial empires? (b) How did the building of empires affect the people of the colonies?

4. **Classifying Ideas** List the powers that Parliament gained at the expense of the English monarch between 1603 and 1714.

5. **Describing Ideas** (a) Describe the changes that occurred in China during the Ming and Qing dynasties. (b) How were they similar to the changes that took place under the Tokugawa shogunate?

6. **Comparing Ideas** Compare the goals and achievements of the French and American Revolutions.

Relating Geography to History

How did the relative locations of China and Japan make it easier for the governments in those countries to shun contact with foreigners, while the relative location of the Ottoman Empire made such isolation more difficult?

Writing About History

1. Use resources in your school or public library to find information on Japanese and Chinese painting in the 1700s and 1800s. Then find sources that explain how Japanese and Chinese artists influenced European and American artists. Present your findings in a written report.
2. Work with two or three of your classmates to develop a comparative essay explaining the unique features of Japanese, Chinese, European, Indian, Persian, and Ottoman cultures in the 1700s and 1800s.

Further Readings

Bainton, Roland H. *Here I Stand: A Life of Martin Luther.* NAL/Dutton, 1995. Recounts major events of Luther's life.

Dickens, Charles. *A Tale of Two Cities.* Bantam, 1989. Fictional account of events in London and Paris at the time of the French Revolution.

Ferguson, Wallace K. *The Renaissance.* Paperbook Press, Inc., 1991. Analyzes the causes of the Renaissance and compares the Italian Renaissance with the Northern Renaissance.

UNIT 1 CHRONOLOGY

Date	Politics	Science and Technology	Society and Culture
1300–1450	Ming Dynasty established **5** Growth of Italian cities **1***	Prince Henry the Navigator **2** Printing press **1**	Humanism **1** Italian Renaissance **1**
1450–1550	Columbus **2** Treaty of Tordesillas **2** Da Gama **2** Cortés **2** Magellan **2** Beginnings of Safavid dynasty **5** Henry VIII **1**	Copernicus **1** Vesalius **1**	Northern Renaissance **1** Da Vinci **1** *The Prince* **1** *Utopia* **1** Michelangelo **1** Luther **1** Diet of Worms **1** Counter-Reformation **1** Council of Trent **1**
1550–1650	Peace of Augsburg **1** Süleyman the Magnificent **5** Spanish Armada **2** Elizabeth I **3** Edict of Nantes **1** Tokugawa shogunate established **5** Michael Romanov **2** Richelieu **2** Thirty Years' War **2** Qing dynasty established **5**	European shipbuilding **2** Microscope **1** Kepler **1** Galileo **1** Telescope **1**	Shakespeare **1** King James Version of the Bible **3** Rembrandt **2**
1650–1750	Louis XIV **2** Glorious Revolution **4** Peter I **2** Act of Union **3** Maria Theresa **2** Frederick the Great **2**	Versailles **2** Newton **1**	*Leviathan* **3** *Two Treatises of Government* **3** Enlightenment **4** Voltaire **4** Rousseau **4**
1750–1850	Catherine II **2** Partitioning of Poland **2** American Revolution **4** French Revolution **4** Napoleon **4** Congress of Vienna **4**		*Encyclopedia* **4** *The Social Contract* **4**

*Indicates chapter in which development is discussed

The Emergence of Modern Nations

CHAPTER 1

The Renaissance, Reformation, and Scientific Revolution

A great burst of creativity began in Italy in the early 1300s. Because this movement centered on a revival of interest in the classical learning of Greece and Rome, we call it the Renaissance, a French word meaning "rebirth."

Renaissance Writers and Artists

Beginning around the 1300s, a number of Italian scholars, such as Francesco Petrarch (PEE·trahrk) and Baldassare Castiglione (kahs·teel·YOH·nay), developed a lively interest in classical Greek and Roman literature. Using classical texts, these Italian scholars stressed the study of grammar, rhetoric, history, and poetry. These studies were called the humanities, and people who specialized in the humanities were called humanists. A Renaissance diplomat and historian, Niccolò Machiavelli (mahk·yah·VEL·lee), wrote his famous book *The Prince*, in which he described government not in terms of lofty ideas but as he believed that government actually worked.

Art as well as literature flourished during the Renaissance. The most noticeable characteristic of Renaissance painting is realism, as shown in the works of Giotto (JAWT·oh), Masaccio, Leonardo da Vinci, Michelangelo Buonarroti (mee·kay·LAHN·jay·loh   bwaw·nahr·RAW·tee), Raphael, and Titian (TISH·uhn).

Over time, humanist thought spread beyond Italy into northern Europe. Northern humanist writers, such as Erasmus and Thomas More, were interested in the early Christian period as well as in Greek and Roman culture. Expanding trade and the invention of the printing press helped ideas to spread during the Renaissance.

The Protestant Reformation

In about 1500, several northern humanists suggested that the Roman Catholic Church had lost sight of its spiritual mission. When the Catholic Church ignored their concerns, a new generation of reformers spurred a religious revolution. This revolution, which split the church and created several new churches, is called the Reformation.

The first break with the Roman Catholic Church occurred in Germany, where many humanists opposed the church's policy of selling indulgences, or pardons from punishment for sin. One of these critics was Martin Luther, a German monk. Although his original intent was to bring reforms to the Roman Catholic Church, Luther was denounced, and his actions resulted in the founding of the Lutheran Church. Other religious groups, called Protestant because their founders protested Catholic Church policies, also sprang up.

The Catholic Reformation

Although areas of northern Europe became Protestant during the Reformation, millions of Europeans remained faithful to the Roman Catholic Church. After 1550, religious conflicts arose between followers of the reformer John Calvin and supporters of a Catholic revival known as the Counter-Reformation.

John Calvin founded a theocracy—a government ruled by clergy claiming God's authority—in Geneva, Switzerland. Calvinism spread to France and to other parts of Europe. The Calvinists and other reform groups posed a threat to the Catholic Church. In

The Medici Family Palazzo, Florence

response, the papacy initiated reforms to foster a more spiritual outlook, to clarify doctrines, and to lead an aggressive campaign against heresy. During this time Ignatius de Loyola founded the Society of Jesus, or the Jesuits.

The religious struggles of the 1500s had a number of results, including the emergence of many different churches in western Europe, a new interest in education, an increase in the power of national governments, and a decrease in the power of the pope.

Culture and Daily Life

At the time of the Renaissance and the Reformation, most Europeans lived in small villages. Over time, people left the countryside in search of a better life in growing towns and cities. Gradually, more sophisticated attitudes began to take hold among these urban residents, and people's understanding of the world began to change. People sought rational explanations for day-to-day events through science.

The Scientific Revolution

Science changed as early investigators began to question traditional opinions and to perform new experiments. Most important, they described nature without any reference to previous beliefs. The foundation of this approach was the principle of doubt; nothing was to be believed unless it could be proved by observation, experiment, or mathematics. The transformation in thinking that occurred during the 1500s and 1600s as a result of these new attitudes and methods is known as the Scientific Revolution. Advances occurred in the fields of astronomy, physics, anatomy, biology, and chemistry. Five Europeans in particular—Copernicus, Kepler, Galileo, Vesalius, and Harvey—became pioneers of modern science. Descartes, Bacon, and Newton advanced the philosophical and scientific thinking of the time.

CHAPTER 2

European Exploration, Expansion, and Absolutism

In 1400 Europe's monarchs lacked the wealth and power of the strongest rulers of China, India, Africa, the Americas, and Europe's neighbor, the Ottoman Empire. Less than 400 years later, however, Europe had become the dominant civilization on Earth, and European nations had colonies all around the world.

Foundations of Exploration

Several factors encouraged Europeans to explore the world. First, technological advances—such as improved mapmaking, better navigation instruments, advanced ship design, and new weapons—made long voyages possible. Second, the development of new economic policies and improved ways of doing business, including the standardization of money and the creation of joint-stock companies, played an important part in exploration. Third, strong and ambitious monarchies supported exploration and colonization. Finally, social changes such as overcrowding in Europe and religious zeal stimulated exploration.

Voyages of Portugal and Spain

Explorers sailing under the flags of Portugal and Spain made the first European voyages into unknown waters. The Portuguese sailed along the west coast of Africa, around the Cape of Good Hope, and across the Indian Ocean to India. Likewise, the Spanish became interested in the search for new trade routes; they sent expeditions across the Atlantic to the Americas. A tragic aspect of the building of these empires was the slave trade. As Spain and Portugal established colonies across the globe, they imported African slaves to work the lands.

Although Portugal rapidly acquired wealth and a vast empire, that empire declined almost as swiftly as it rose. Three main factors hastened the decline. First, the Portuguese government, with an insecure financial base, had overextended its empire. Second, the empire proved to be a drain on Portugal's population. Third, Spain annexed Portugal in 1580, and until Portugal won independence in 1640, Spain limited Portuguese trade and neglected its colonies.

The Spanish and Dutch Empires

Spain turned most of its colonial energies towards the Americas—the West Indies, Central America, North America, and South America. Spain developed a centralized form of government for its colonies. Representatives of the monarch, called viceroys, reported to the Council of the Indies in Spain.

While explorers were creating a great empire outside Europe, kings expanded the authority of Spain itself. Such a king was Charles V, who was also the Holy Roman emperor. He halted the Turkish penetration of central Europe and, with the Peace of Augsburg, for a time settled religious wars between the Catholics and the Lutherans in Germany. Continuous war, however, drained Spain's human and financial resources. Spain also lacked industries, and land was not used efficiently for food production.

Charles V realized that this scattered empire had become too large for any one monarch to rule. In 1556 he gave up his throne and divided his vast lands between his son, who became Philip II of Spain, and his brother, who became Holy Roman emperor Ferdinand I.

The people of the Dutch provinces that were inherited by Philip II, however, strongly distrusted the Spanish crown. Philip had ignored the authority of the local nobles, taxed Dutch trade heavily, and persecuted the Calvinists. In 1579 the Dutch declared their independence from Spain.

Throughout the 1600s, the Dutch dominated European commerce. They built efficient ships and were excellent sailors. The city of Amsterdam became a world financial center. Dutch banks, trading companies, manufacturing enterprises, and overseas colonies became models of efficiency.

After the Dutch revolt, the Spanish Empire declined. Population growth, inflation, the lack of an enterprising middle class, and undeveloped industry were all contributing factors. Discontent caused many people to emigrate from Spain.

France
After Spain's decline, France emerged as a leading European power under Louis XIV. It had recovered rapidly from the religious wars of the 1500s, thanks to the policies of Henry IV, the first Bourbon monarch. The Bourbon kings would make the monarchy absolute in France.

The Thirty Years' War strengthened France and weakened the Habsburgs' rule in Austria. Louis XIV increased royal authority and engaged in wars that extended France's territory. Besides claiming territory to the northeast, Louis XIV claimed Canadian territory in North America.

Eastern and Central Europe
The empires of Russia, Prussia, and Austria developed in eastern and central Europe. In the 1600s, Russian czars dealt successfully with many internal problems and created a form of absolutism. Peter I, called Peter the Great, acquired ports on the Black Sea, claimed new territories, and established closer ties with the West. Catherine I, called Catherine the Great, further strengthened Russian culture and foreign policy. Russia's expansion differed from that of the western European countries; instead of expanding overseas, Russia expanded overland.

CHAPTER 3

Revolution and Change in England

While nations of the continent of Europe were establishing absolute monarchies, England was developing a constitutional form of government.

The Tudors and the Stuarts
In the late 1400s a new royal family, the Tudors, became rulers in England. They brought stability and prosperity to England. Parliament gained power and prestige during the reign of Elizabeth I. However, when the throne passed to the Stuarts, the relationship between Parliament and the monarchs deteriorated. The reign of James I was characterized by financial difficulties. Although Charles I, his successor, tried to rule without calling Parliament, he assembled the legislative body in 1640 because he was in need of funds.

Civil War and Revolution
The Parliament of 1640, controlled by the Puritans, took actions to limit the monarchy. A rebellion in Ireland sent the monarchy into crisis and provoked a violent civil war in 1642. As a result of this conflict the Puritan Oliver Cromwell came to power, establishing a republican form of government. Charles I was executed.

The experiment with republican government failed, however; Parliament and Cromwell quarreled nearly as much as the legislature had with previous rulers. By 1660 the English people had undergone a

English (shown in painting) victory over the Spanish Armada in 1588

change of sentiment. Although some had favored the execution of Charles I, Cromwell's commonwealth had neither settled the nation nor solved its problems. After some hesitation, the Parliament of 1660 invited Charles II, the son of Charles I, to return to England.

England's Constitutional Monarchy

Having learned from his years in exile, Charles II cooperated with Parliament. However, the next king was his brother, James II, who clashed with the legislative body. When James's Catholic wife gave birth to a son, both of England's political parties opposed the idea of a Catholic ruler and forced James to abdicate. A number of leading nobles invited James's Protestant daughter, Mary, and her husband, William of Orange, to take the throne of England. Thus Parliament gave the crown to William and Mary as joint rulers.

Over time, many safeguards were instituted against absolute monarchy in England. For example, in 1679 Parliament passed the Habeas Corpus Act, which made provisions for arrested people to appear before a judge. Before granting the throne to William and Mary, Parliament required them to accept the Bill of Rights. This document declared that Parliament would choose the ruler, who would be subject to parliamentary laws. In addition, the ruler could not proclaim or suspend laws, impose taxes, maintain an army in peacetime without Parliament's consent, or interfere with the elections of Parliament's members.

Although England remained a monarchy in 1700, Parliament held the power. In 1707 the parliaments of England and Scotland passed the Act of Union, uniting the two countries into one kingdom known as Great Britain.

English Colonial Expansion

While Spain and Portugal established vast overseas empires during the 1500s, England remained preoccupied with problems at home. Even though these problems persisted during the 1600s, English mariners began explorations that allowed England to claim lands in the Americas and Asia. By the 1760s the British empire had no real mercantile competition in North America or in India. The English East India Company set up trading posts in India, Malaya, and the East Indies. In search of a Northwest Passage to India, the English also established colonies along North America's eastern coast.

CHAPTER 4

The American and French Revolutions

The idea that the people should have a voice in government greatly influenced French politics of the 1700s. The American Revolution, with its central theme of freedom and dignity of human beings, helped to inspire the French Revolution.

The Enlightenment

Some people of the 1700s thought of their century as an Age of Enlightenment. Thinkers of the Enlightenment believed that they could apply the scientific method and logically explain human nature. The philosophes, such as Denis Diderot (dee·DROH), Baron de Montesquieu (MOHN·tes·kyoo), Voltaire, and Jean-Jacques Rousseau (roo·SOH) were not only philosophers, however, but also critics of society and politics.

The American Revolution

New ideas were not confined to Europe in the 1700s. The British colonists' new way of life in North

America and their distance from Britain began to create new attitudes about their relationship with the home country. Their immediate concerns were British trade regulations and the presence of the French along their borders. Colonists struggled increasingly with the British and finally declared their independence.

The new nation attempted government under the Articles of Confederation. However, when it became evident that the articles did not give the central government enough power, the nation adopted the Constitution with provisions for a stronger federal government. To guarantee the rights of American citizens, the Bill of Rights was added to the Constitution.

The French Revolution

Simultaneous with revolution in the British colonies, disturbing events were occurring in France. The French rulers had constructed an absolute monarchy based upon the division of society into three groups, or estates. The First and Second Estates, including the clergy and the nobility, had the fewest people but the most wealth, power, and privilege. The Third Estate, which included more than 90 percent of the people, consisted mostly of peasants and had very little power.

Discontent in France began to grow in the mid-1700s. Several factors explain this dissatisfaction. The population was growing, and French families needed more food and money. The middle and poorer classes loathed having to pay taxes when the nobles and clergy did not. Finally, both the nobles and the clergy disliked the increasing concentration of power in the hands of the king.

When Louis XVI called a meeting of the Estates-General in 1789, discontented groups throughout France hoped for reforms. The people did not want to follow the old custom of each estate meeting separately and voting as one body. They claimed that all the estates should meet and vote. When Louis failed to take action, members of the Third Estate boldly proclaimed themselves the National Assembly, thus beginning the French Revolution.

Hearing that the king had ordered troops to Paris and Versailles, the French people took action. On July 14, 1789, they stormed and captured the prison-fortress known as the Bastille in search of weapons to defend themselves.

Quite rapidly, the National Assembly became the government of France and enacted reforms to abolish the last remnants of feudalism in France. The assembly adopted the Declaration of the Rights of Man and of the Citizen, guaranteeing basic human rights. Likewise, the assembly passed laws aimed at correcting abuses and organizing a new government. In 1791 the assembly finished writing a constitution that limited the powers of the king and established a constitutional monarchy.

When Austria and Prussia invaded France, a group of radicals seized control of the Paris government and established the Commune. The Commune accused Louis XVI of plotting with foreign monarchs to overthrow the Constitution of 1791. Subsequently, the Legislative Assembly voted to suspend the French monarchy.

The French Republic

A new legislative body, the National Convention, met in 1792 to proclaim the end of the monarchy and the beginning of a republic. The convention also tried Louis XIV on charges of plotting against the security of the nation and ordered his execution.

In spite of the dangers and difficulties of the time, the National Convention made many reforms in France. It provided for a national system of public education, and it abolished slavery in the French colonies.

In 1795 the directors of the National Convention drafted another constitution, under which an executive

A 1789 painting illustrating the day after the storming of the Bastille body called the Directory controlled France. Although the Directory governed for four years, it pleased neither the radicals nor the conservatives. Finally, in 1799, Napoleon Bonaparte took over the government.

The Napoleonic Era

Although Napoleon's government kept the form of a republic, he became dictator and emperor of France. The French army conquered most of Europe under his rule. However, Great Britain, Austria, Prussia, and Russia soon united against the French. Napoleon was decisively defeated at the Battle of Waterloo in 1815 and exiled to the island of St. Helena, where he died in 1821.

A Return to Peace

After the final defeat of Napoleon in 1815, European leaders met at the Congress of Vienna to redraw the map of Europe. Three principles guided the decisions of the Congress of Vienna. First, the countries that suffered most at the hands of Napoleon—especially the four great powers—had to be compensated for their losses. Second, the balance of power had to be restored in Europe. This meant that the nations of Europe had to keep any one nation from becoming too powerful. Third, legitimacy, which meant that all former ruling families should be restored to their thrones, had to be upheld.

CHAPTER 5

Asia in Transition

Between 1400 and the mid-1800s, many of the countries in Asia reached a political and cultural peak and then began to decline.

China

During the Ming and Qing dynasties, peace and urban growth contributed to the expansion of trade in China. The growth of cities and the increasing wealth of urban merchants and artisans in China encouraged the rise of popular culture. Scholarship also flourished under the rule of the Ming and Qing emperors.

Just as the Qing dynasty started its decline, Europeans appeared in China. The Portuguese, the British, and the Russians claimed trading privileges in China—often with disastrous effects for the Chinese people.

Japan

In the late 1400s the Japanese daimyo began to fight among themselves for survival and supremacy. The struggle among the daimyo resulted in the creation of a political system that was a cross between feudalism and centralized monarchy. The Japanese established this hybrid system, known as the Tokugawa (TOH·KOOHG·AH·WAH) shogunate, in 1603.

The Tokugawa shogunate shaped Japanese life in several ways. By establishing a strong central government, the shoguns brought more than two centuries of stability to Japan. In setting trade restrictions and limiting contact with foreigners, they achieved almost complete isolation from Europe by 1650. Internal trade expanded, and various regions began to specialize in particular crops and handicrafts.

The Islamic Empires

In the 1500s three large Islamic empires existed: the Ottoman, the Persian, and the Mughal. The rulers of these Muslim states set up strong central governments. However, the Mughal Empire in India, financially weak, had little success when it confronted a European power. The British East India Company steadily increased its control until India became an official part of the British Empire in 1876.

Synthesis Review

1. **Understanding Ideas** Why did Martin Luther and John Calvin criticize the Roman Catholic Church?

2. **Summarizing Ideas** What factors encouraged European exploration and expansion?

3. **Determining Cause and Effect** In what ways did wars and revolutions in England encourage the growth of constitutional government?

4. **Seeing Relationships** How did discontent in France and America lead to the French and American Revolutions?

5. **Analyzing Ideas** How did Britain gain power and influence throughout India?

6. **Synthesizing Ideas** In what ways did revolutions in England and America influence the French Revolution?

POLITICS AND GOVERNMENT

| 1700 | 1725 | 1750 | 1775 |

1789
French Revolution topples monarchy

1791
Revolution breaks out in Haiti against France

SOCIETY AND CULTURE

| 1700 | 1725 | 1750 | 1775 |

c. 1700
Enclosure movement continues in England

1770
Composer Ludwig von Beethoven born in Germany

1776
Adam Smith publishes *The Wealth of Nations*

Title page from *The Wealth of Nations*

Adam Smith

SCIENCE AND TECHNOLOGY

| 1700 | 1725 | 1750 | 1775 |

1712
Thomas Newcomen devises first successful steam engine

1733
Flying shuttle rapidly increases weaving rate

1769
James Watt patents modern steam engine

1793
American Eli Whitney invents the cotton gin

Thomas Newcomen's steam engine

1800   **1825**   **1850**   **1875**   **1900**   **1925**

1822
Brazil declares independence from Portugal

1823
Monroe Doctrine proclaimed

1837
Queen Victoria begins her reign

1854
Crimean War begins

1867
Canada becomes a self-governing dominion

1870
• Franco-Prussian War results in German Empire
• Italy united

1898
Spanish American War occurs

1905
• Japan wins Russo-Japanese War
• Czar puts down revolt in Russia

Theodore Roosevelt and the Rough Riders

1800   **1825**   **1850**   **1875**   **1900**   **1925**

1829
Robert Peel organizes London police force

1833
Factory Act in Britain aims to stem child labor abuse

1848
• Women's rights conference in Seneca Falls, New York, occurs
• Engels and Marx publish the *Communist Manifesto*

1874
Impressionist artists hold first exhibition in France

1868
Meiji era begins in Japan

1863
Lincoln issues Emancipation Proclamation

c. 1890
• Mass emigration continues from Europe to America
• Frazer's *The Golden Bough*, landmark in anthropology, published

Children working in a factory in England during the 1800's

The Terrace at Sainte-Adresse by Claude Monet

1800   **1825**   **1850**   **1875**   **1900**   **1925**

1796
Edward Jenner experiments with smallpox vaccination

1844
Samuel Morse's telegraph becomes a practical communications device

1850s
Bessemer process for steelmaking developed

1866
Transatlantic telegraph cable laid

1879
Thomas Edison develops electric lights

1893
First gasoline-powered automobile developed

1901
Wireless message crosses Atlantic Ocean

1903
Successful powered flight by Wright brothers

Wright Brothers airplane

CHAPTER 6

The Industrial Revolution

TIME

A.D. 1600–1901

A.D. 1600–1901

3.7 million B.C. | 4000 B.C. | A.D. 2100

PLACE

Great Britain, the United States, France, and Germany

Germany

United States

ARCTIC OCEAN

NORTH AMERICA

EUROPE

ASIA

PACIFIC OCEAN

AFRICA

EQUATOR

SOUTH AMERICA

INDIAN OCEAN

AUSTRALIA

PACIFIC OCEAN

ATLANTIC OCEAN

ANTARCTICA

British Isles

France

Steam locomotive

CHAPTER FOCUS

Significance

A revolution began in the 1700s, when power-driven machines began to perform much of the work that people had done before. This shift is referred to as the **Industrial Revolution**. It led to so many significant changes in the way goods were produced and in the way people lived that it completely transformed the world.

Terms to Define

Industrial Revolution	monopoly
enclosure movement	cartels
crop rotation	business cycle
factors of production	depression
mechanization	free enterprise
domestic system	laissez-faire
factory system	utilitarianism
Bessemer process	strike
capitalism	unions
commercial capitalism	collective bargaining
industrial capitalism	socialism
division of labor	utopian socialists
interchangeable parts	bourgeoisie
mass production	proletariat
sole proprietorship	authoritarian socialism
partnership	communism
corporation	democratic socialism

People to Identify

James Hargreaves	Adam Smith
Richard Arkwright	Thomas Malthus
Eli Whitney	David Ricardo
James Watt	Charles Dickens
Henry Bessemer	Jeremy Bentham
John McAdam	John Stuart Mill
Robert Fulton	Sir Thomas More
Samuel Morse	Robert Owen
Cyrus Field	Karl Marx

Places to Locate

Manchester	Silesia
Lyons	

Chapter Theme Questions

- **Technology** What effect might new machines and inventions have on how people work and how they view their work?
- **Social Relations** How might the shift from an agricultural society to an industrial society change people's social relationships?
- **Economic Organization** What new ideas about working and business might arise from worker discontent and rapid industrial growth?

I magine an American farmer of English and German heritage talking to his granddaughter about his life. He sits on a porch looking out over land that he and his ancestors have tilled for three generations. The old man tells his granddaughter about the stories he heard when he was a boy in the 1890s—stories of how his ancestors had left the old country and migrated to America.

They farmed and ranched, making a hard living from the land. They had no tractors, planters, or harvesters. They traveled by horse and buggy and planned parties for nights when the moon was full so that travelers could find their way back to their homes over unlit roads. They wore handstitched clothes, which they washed by hand and hung on a line to dry. They could not watch television, go to the movies, surf the Internet, or drive a car on paved roads to buy frozen foods at supermarkets.

As a young man at the turn of the century, the grandfather saw more changes within a few years than generations of old folks had seen in a lifetime. Now he speaks to his granddaughter about seeing the promise of modern technology fulfilled, making a better life for the generations to come.

The rapid changes the old man began witnessing in the early part of the twentieth century were the product of the Industrial Revolution, which changed the way goods were produced and the way people lived.

Section 1

The Origins of the Industrial Revolution

Focus Questions

- **Why did the Industrial Revolution originate in Great Britain?**
- **How did new inventions in the textile industry spur the development of other new inventions?**
- **What developments in transportation and communication helped speed and spread the Industrial Revolution?**

Significant changes in agricultural methods, though gradual, preceded and made possible the

Industrial Revolution. These changes, known as the Agricultural Revolution, began with farming changes made in the Netherlands, which were then copied and developed by the British. The Agricultural Revolution's results helped bring about the Industrial Revolution that originated in Great Britain.

The Agricultural Revolution

Before the 1600s, most European villagers were allotted a plot or strip of land for cultivating their own food. In addition to this land for individual use, there were open, common lands used jointly by the villagers for grazing sheep and cattle. In the 1600s, English farmers accelerated the process of fencing off, or enclosing, common lands into individual holdings, largely for the benefit of the already wealthy landholders. This **enclosure movement** continued into the 1700s. Farmers combined small strips of land to form larger holdings that were more efficient for large-scale farming. The enclosure movement reached its height in the early 1800s in Great Britain, when a growing population increased demand and raised prices for agricultural products. The need to feed its own people during the Napoleonic Wars also made it necessary for Britain to increase its food production.

The enclosure movement had significant consequences. As large landowners added to their holdings, they forced owners of small plots to either become tenant farmers or give up farming and move to the cities. Also, because land did not have to be farmed in common, farmers could experiment with their new methods of farming without having to seek the consent of the other villagers.

Among the first who experimented in the early 1700s were so-called gentlemen farmers such as Jethro Tull. Concerned about the wasteful practice of scattering seeds by hand over a wide area, Tull invented a seed drill, which made it possible to plant seeds in the soil in regular rows.

While visiting France and Italy, Tull saw that grape farmers had good results from uprooting the weeds between the rows and breaking up the soil. Tull developed a horse-drawn hoe to do this work on his own fields in England.

Another English gentleman farmer, Viscount Charles "Turnip" Townshend, a former British ambassador to the Netherlands, began to use a Dutch technique to avoid another wasteful practice. Traditionally, farmers left some of their fields unplanted, or fallow, each year to allow nutrients to replenish the soil. By means of repeated experiments, Townshend learned that alternating different kinds of crops would preserve soil fertility. For example, he would plant grain crops such as wheat and barley one year and root crops such as turnips the next. This system, called **crop rotation**, has become a basic principle of modern farming.

Additional improvements in machinery increased production and made farm labor easier. For example, iron plows replaced wooden ones. An American inventor, Jethro Wood, invented an iron plow with standard parts so that a farmer could replace a broken part at low cost rather than having to buy a whole new plow every time one part broke.

Some of the new agricultural techniques and machines were expensive. Farmers who could afford them made large profits, but many farmers with small holdings could not afford additional equipment.

By the 1800s, improvements in agriculture had decreased the demand for farm laborers. People who might have worked on farms chose instead to look for work in the cities, where they created a large labor force.

Factors of Production

The more intense phase of technological development known as the Industrial Revolution that followed the Agricultural Revolution began in Great Britain because a certain combination of conditions existed there. Great Britain had what economists call the **factors of production**, or the basic resources necessary for industrialization: land, capital, and labor. When economists speak of land, they are referring to all natural resources, of which Great Britain had an abundant supply—particularly of coal and iron ore. Furthermore, Britain's excellent harbors facilitated trade, and its many rivers provided waterpower and inland transportation.

Great Britain also had access to capital. Capital includes money and goods such as tools, machinery, equipment, and inventory that are used in the production process. Many Britons had grown rich in the 1700s and now wanted to invest in new businesses.

In addition to land and capital, Great Britain had an abundant supply of labor, in this case, industrial workers. A growing population and migration into the cities fueled this supply.

Several other conditions help explain why the Industrial Revolution began in Great Britain. The British Isles and overseas colonies represented huge markets that created a large demand for British goods. Additional trade opportunities also existed in many other parts of the world, which could be reached by the British navy and merchant fleet, the best in the world. Equally important was the British government's concern for commercial interests. Parliament passed laws that protected businesses and helped them expand.

The Textile Industry

The cotton textile industry was the first industry in Great Britain to undergo **mechanization**, the use of automatic machinery to increase production. England had imported cotton cloth since the late Middle Ages, but in the 1600s, businesses began importing raw cotton and employing spinners and weavers to make it into cloth. This industry was an example of the **domestic system**, a system in which men and women work in their homes. The work was done by hand, and England could not produce enough cotton cloth to meet demand.

New inventions. The first step toward mechanization came with the improvement of the loom for weaving cloth. A loom is set up with a series of threads, called the warp, strung from top to bottom. The loom operator pushes a shuttle containing the woof (now called the weft), or the thread running crosswise to the warp, back and forth across the loom in a very time-consuming process. In 1733 an engineer named John Kay invented the flying shuttle, a cord mechanism that moved the woof thread more rapidly through the loom. Now weavers could weave faster than the spinners could produce thread on their simple spinning wheels. The demand for thread rose dramatically—a better spinning machine was needed.

James Hargreaves, a poor English weaver, came up with a machine in the 1760s that he named the spinning "jenny," probably for a member of his family. This machine could produce eight times as much thread as a single spinning wheel. Several years later, Richard Arkwright made further improvements with a machine called the water frame, which was a machine driven by waterpower.

Workers could use the jenny and the small, hand-operated, and relatively inexpensive flying shuttle in their homes. However, most people who worked at home could not make use of the expensive water frame, which required waterpower and a good deal of space. For this reason, Arkwright opened a spinning mill, bringing workers and machines together in one place to make goods. Employees worked a set number of hours for a certain amount of money. By 1784 Arkwright employed several hundred workers. This spinning mill marked the beginning of the modern **factory system**.

In 1779 Samuel Crompton combined the best features of the spinning jenny and the water frame in another machine, the spinning mule. Now weavers could get plenty of fine-quality thread. However, even with the flying shuttle, the weavers failed to meet the demand for cloth.

In 1785 an English minister, Edmund Cartwright, met the need for a faster weaving process with his invention of a loom which was powered by using water.

This print published circa 1835 illustrates a carding engine (left) delivering the cotton in a single sliver. The machines are driven by belts from the overhead shafts, which could be powered by water or steam.

The Story Behind the Industrial Revolution

Historians consider the Industrial Revolution to be one of the two most important changes that have taken place in the history of the world. Just as the start of agriculture did 10,000 years ago, the Industrial Revolution marks a turning point in history.

The Industrial Revolution is, of course, a more recent change. Just 300 years ago, people could do work or produce goods only by using their own muscles, the muscles of animals, or unreliable sources of power such as wind (in windmills) or water (in water mills). As a result, production was limited.

The Industrial Revolution made

it possible to do more work and produce goods in abundance. Now people could use machines driven by fuels such as coal and oil, and the supply of these fuels seemed unlimited.

This remarkable change in production began at a particular time, the late 1700s, and in a particular country, Great Britain. Why did this change in production start then and there? Historians suggest that all of the pieces of the puzzle, as it were, happened to exist in Britain, and only in Britain.

For one thing, after the mid-1700s, the demand for manufactured goods such as cloth grew rapidly and outran the capacity of individual, rural spinners and weavers, who often worked in their own homes. In addition, the population grew faster than the

Top: Trade Emblem of the Amalgamated Society of Engineers, Machinists, Millwrights, Smiths and Pattern Makers
Bottom: James Ward painting of a farm family before the Industrial Revolution

American chemical plant, 1920

Lacking an empire, there were no instant markets that would create demand for French-made products.

Britain was a country with limited government, enthusiasm for change, and a stimulating contact with the outside world. By the 1780s, the Industrial Revolution had begun to transform the textile industry. Developments in that industry spurred other advances.

More than any other invention, the steam engine drove the Industrial Revolution forward by providing a source of power that did not depend on human muscle or the power of the wind or moving water. The increase in power now available to produce goods was remarkable.

supply of goods. Moreover, if Britain could produce goods quickly and cheaply, it had existing markets, both at home and overseas. Britain's empire included parts of North and South America, Asia, and Africa. The demand was there. The problem was how to satisfy it. Here Britain had an advantage over its European neighbors. Because of advances in agriculture, Britain had better farm machinery and more scientific methods of cultivation than most of Europe. The process of consolidating small landholdings into larger, more productive farms was already well under way. This paved the way for industry because fewer farmworkers were needed, and more workers were available for other jobs.

If labor is one necessary resource, raw materials are equally important resources. As it happened, Britain's plentiful underground supplies of coal became the key to Britain being able to support its own new industries. Another piece of the puzzle fell into place.

Already wealthy because of trade with the outside world, Britain could afford to invest in new ventures. In addition, the British government safeguarded property against seizure by the government. Both these facts provided a perfect climate for individual and industrial innovation. Thus, a talented inventor such as James Watt, who devised an efficient steam engine, found himself richly rewarded—in a country where such wealth was secure.

The other wealthy countries of western Europe could not match Britain's advantages—they did not have all the pieces of the puzzle. For example, France, by 1763, had lost much of its empire to Britain.

Industrial change spread in two important ways. First, new industries sprang up as people applied the steam engine to new uses. Second, the Industrial Revolution crossed from Britain to other countries. Between 1815 and the 1850s, steam engines, factories, and railroads began to appear in parts of France, Belgium, the Netherlands, Germany, and northern Italy.

After 1870 the Industrial Revolution entered still another phase. It is the period that extends to the present; some historians call it the Second Industrial Revolution. Electric power and the internal combustion engine joined the steam engine. Many products of industry—telephones, automobiles, radios, and television sets—became available to most citizens of industrialized countries. The great industrial transformation that had begun in the special conditions of Great Britain soon encircled the globe.

First auto show, Madison Square Garden, 1900

Using this power loom, one person could weave as much cloth as 200 hand-loom operators.

This series of spinning and weaving innovations illustrates the cascading effect of invention. The flying shuttle created a need for more thread. The resulting faster method of spinning caused the price of cloth to go down, and the demand went up, creating a need for improved weaving machines. The power loom filled that need. Each invention went on to create a new need, and human ingenuity filled each new gap with a new invention.

Effects of mechanization. With all these improvements, cotton cloth became cheaper to produce and sell. As the price went down, the demand increased and so did the need for more raw cotton. In 1761 England imported 4 million pounds of cotton. In 1815 it imported 100 million pounds.

Most of the imported raw cotton came from the southern United States. At first, cotton cultivation had not been profitable there because it was difficult to remove the seeds from the cotton fibers to prepare the cotton for market. Cleaning the cotton was slow manual work. In 1793 Eli Whitney invented the cotton gin, a machine that could do this job much more quickly and efficiently than by hand. Equipped with Whitney's invention, the southern United States met the demands of the British textile manufacturers and became the cotton-producing center of the world. At the same time, by making cotton production more profitable, the cotton gin helped perpetuate slavery in the United States.

Steam Engines

Waterpower drove the early machines of the Industrial Revolution. Although waterpower represented a great improvement over human, animal, and wind power, it did have drawbacks. A factory had to be located beside a stream or river, preferably near a natural waterfall or a place where a dam could be built. Often this location was not near transportation, raw materials, a labor supply, or markets. A second drawback was that the water flow could vary greatly with the seasons. People began to look for a continuous, dependable, and portable power source; they found it in steam.

People had observed the power contained in steam since ancient times. It was not until 1712, however, that Thomas Newcomen, who was an English engineer, produced the first successful steam engine. Initially, workers used Newcomen engines to pump water from mines. These crude machines were more

What If?

The Cotton Gin
What if the cotton gin had not been invented? How might the history of the American South have been different?

powerful and dependable than water wheels, however, they were expensive to operate.

In the 1760s, James Watt, a Scottish instrument maker and engineer, studied the Newcomen engine. He invented several improvements and in 1769 patented the modern steam engine. Industry quickly adapted the Watt engine to drive the new spinning and weaving machines. As a result of Watt's invention, steam replaced water as industry's major power source.

Iron and Steel

The invention and availability of more and more machines produced a great demand for iron to make them. From early times, people in the British Isles had produced iron, using wood or charcoal to fuel the forges needed to separate the element from its ore. Then it was discovered that coal worked even better than wood or charcoal. As the Industrial Revolution continued, iron and coal became the two major raw materials of modern industry. Great Britain had an enormous advantage over other countries because it had large amounts of these two resources.

Many early steam engines exploded because the iron used to build them could not withstand the high pressure of steam. Industry needed a stronger, harder metal. Suppliers met this need with steel, which is iron with certain impurities removed. In the 1800s, the process for making steel was slow and expensive. However, during the 1850s, an American, William Kelly, and an Englishman, Henry Bessemer, developed a cheap and efficient method of making steel. It involved forcing air through the molten metal to burn out carbon and other impurities that made the metal brittle. This procedure is known today as the **Bessemer process**.

Industrialization in Other Fields

Using steam engines and iron and steel, British manufacturers quickly introduced power-driven machinery in many industries. The production of shoes, clothing, ammunition, and furniture became mechanized, as did printing and papermaking. People used machines to cut and finish lumber, to process foods, and to make other machines.

Some new inventions and innovative processes had important by-products. These by-products often developed into separate industries. For example, iron smelteries used coke, a by-product of coal, to improve the smelting process. Then someone discovered that the gases that coal released during the coke-making process could be burned to give light. During the 1810s, London became one of the first cities to pipe in gas to burn in street lamps. By the 1850s, hundreds of cities throughout the Western world used gas to light streets and homes.

Improvements in the production of rubber expanded the use of this raw material during the 1800s. Rubber was first used to make waterproof shoes and coats, but they became sticky in warm weather. In 1839, after years of experimenting, Charles Goodyear of the United States discovered a process of "curing" rubber to make it more elastic and usable. He mixed raw rubber with sulfur and then heated the mixture. Goodyear's method, called vulcanizing, became the basis of the modern rubber industry.

The oil industry developed around the mid-1800s, when people discovered how to use crude oil, or petroleum, to produce paraffin for candles, lubricating oil for machinery, and kerosene for lighting and heating.

Transportation

The Industrial Revolution also transformed transportation. When the revolution first began, land transportation was almost the same as it had been during the Middle Ages. Roads were little more than trails blurred with thick dust in dry weather and buried in deep, slippery mud when it rained.

A passenger in a stagecoach could travel perhaps 50 miles in one long day, barring unforeseen delays. Pack horses and clumsy wagons carrying heavy goods made even less progress in a day's journey.

Roads and canals. Industrialization made improved transportation necessary. Factories required delivery of raw materials, and finished products had to be transported to markets as quickly as possible. A Scottish engineer, John McAdam, worked out a new way of building roads that improved travel conditions. Layers of carefully selected smaller stones topped a roadbed of large stones. These roads, called macadam roads, served as a model for engineers in

This photo, taken in a steel works plant in Homestead, Pennsylvania, shows a huge Bessemer converter that converts iron into steel in 15 minutes.

later times. Today road builders use asphalt to bind the smaller stones together.

Great Britain and other countries of western Europe also had extensive networks of rivers that served as water highways. Some canals connected them, but workers constructed many more canals after engineers began using locks—gates that regulate the level and flow of water. Many canals were built between 1760 and 1850. However, although canals were cheaper and slightly faster than roads, new forms of transportation soon began to compete with the canals.

Railroads and steamboats. Watt's steam engine offered many possibilities for new means of transportation. In 1814 George Stephenson, an English engineer, perfected a steam-propelled moving engine, or locomotive, that ran on rails. In 1829 Stephenson's famous locomotive, the *Rocket*, pulled a line of cars from Liverpool to Manchester, reaching for a short time the amazing speed of 30 miles per hour. Networks of railroads soon connected much of the Western world. Continuous improvements, such as steel rails, air brakes, and comfortable coaches made railroad transportation fast, safe, and affordable.

Many people tried adapting the steam engine for use on ships. Robert Fulton, an American engineer and inventor, was the first to succeed at this.

This scene of steamboats on the Mississippi River was prepared by the nineteenth-century lithograph firm Currier & Ives. Their hand-colored prints recorded local social history.

He established the first regular inland steamboat service that produced a profit. His boat, the *Clermont*, was launched on the Hudson River in 1807. One year later, after improvements to the boat, the *Clermont* began regular trips between New York City and Albany. Steamboats soon appeared on many of the rivers and lakes of the world.

In 1838 the *Great Western*, a ship operated only by steam, crossed the Atlantic Ocean in 15 days, less than half the time it took a sailing ship. Samuel Cunard of Great Britain, who founded the Cunard Line shipping company in 1839, provided regular steamboat service across the Atlantic. Soon ships built of iron and steel instead of wood moved goods all over the world in less time and for less money than ever before.

The Communications Revolution

Scientific research played only a small role in the invention of textile machinery, the steam engine, the locomotive, and the steamship. All of these inventions represented the work of amateur inventors and engineers. These inventions did not come from scientists' laboratories. In communications, however, scientific research played a more significant role in the development of technology.

For centuries people had observed electricity and its connection with magnetism, but they had put their knowledge to little practical use. For one thing, no one had found a way to provide a steady flow of electric current. Around 1800 an Italian, Alessandro Volta, built the first battery, a device that provided a steady current of electricity. In the 1820s, André Ampère of France worked out principles governing the magnetic effect of an electric current.

Samuel Morse of the United States put the work of Volta and Ampère to practical use. Morse sent an electrical current over a wire to a machine at the other end of the wire. Each time electricity passed along the wire, the machine clicked. By 1838 Morse had worked out a system of dots and dashes—the Morse code—by which these clicks could be translated into letters of the alphabet. By 1844 Morse's invention, the telegraph, had become a practical communication instrument. Soon telegraph wires, stretched across continents, transmitted ideas at the speed of electricity.

People also found a way to carry electricity under the sea by using cables—heavily insulated telegraph wires. Early in the 1850s, a cable across the English Channel connected Great Britain with the European continent.

However, spanning the great distance of the Atlantic Ocean presented enormous difficulties. Not until 1866 did Cyrus Field and a group of Americans lay a cable across the Atlantic Ocean. Soon afterward cables connected all continents of the world.

The Spread of Industry

For various reasons, the rapid changes in agriculture, industry, transportation, and communications had little effect on the European continent for several years. Many European countries did not have raw materials or large, accessible markets for their products. In addition, the wars of the French Revolution and the Napoleonic Era slowed Europe's industrial development.

France, however, did develop some industry, especially textiles, iron, and mining. The French government helped this development in two ways. First, it imposed high tariffs to keep out foreign manufactured goods. Second, it encouraged the construction of railroads. However, in the 1800s France remained largely an agricultural country. Most of France's working population at this time was still made up of farmers and peasants.

Industry grew more slowly in the German states than in Great Britain because Germany had no efficient central government to aid industrial growth. Still, Germany held its own as an industrial power. By the time the German states were unified in the 1870s, the pace of Germany's industrialization was approaching that of Great Britain.

The United States eagerly adopted British inventions and methods. The United States had everything it needed for industrial development—national unity and a vast country with rich natural resources. It also had a rapidly increasing population, inventive genius, and a willingness to adopt, to adapt, and to take the risks involved in business.

A network of canals and railroads crept across the United States during the 1800s, and industry moved west as transportation developed. The steel industry grew in Pittsburgh and the Great Lakes region, and machinery was manufactured in Chicago. By 1869 a railroad connected the East Coast with the West Coast of the United States. Before the end of the century, the United States had surpassed Great Britain in the production of iron and steel.

Along with the growth of American industry came significant changes in farming. Eli Whitney's cotton gin enabled the southern states to supply cotton to the British textile industry. Another invention was a machine for harvesting grain, patented by Cyrus McCormick in 1834. The McCormick reaper, which was drawn by horses, freed many farmers from the slow, backbreaking work of cutting grain with sickles or scythes. Other inventions, such as the mechanical thresher for separating the grains of wheat from their stalks and hulls, followed.

Section 1 Review

1. **Define** Industrial Revolution, enclosure movement, crop rotation, factors of production, mechanization, domestic system, factory system, Bessemer process
2. **Identify** James Hargreaves, Richard Arkwright, Eli Whitney, James Watt, Henry Bessemer, John McAdam, Robert Fulton, Samuel Morse, Cyrus Field
3. **Determining Cause and Effect** (a) What was the enclosure movement, and how did this movement lead to changes in agriculture? (b) What were the principal effects of the Agricultural Revolution?
4. **Analyzing Ideas** Why did the Industrial Revolution begin in Great Britain?
5. **Synthesizing Ideas** Describe the importance and results of inventions in the textile industry.
6. **Evaluating Ideas** What were four important developments in transportation and communication during the Industrial Revolution?

Section 2

The Factory System

Focus Questions

- In what ways did the increased use of machinery affect workers and working conditions?
- What caused the middle class to expand, and in what ways was the middle class distinct from the working class?
- How did the lives of women change during the Industrial Revolution?

For centuries skilled artisans produced goods of all kinds in their homes or in small shops. The artisan controlled the training of apprentices, the quality and price of goods, and the pace of each workday. During the 1700s, the opportunity for a higher standard of living lured thousands of English farm workers to the city to work in the factories spawned by the Industrial Revolution. The emergence of these factories was only one of the many changes the Industrial Revolution created.

The Effect of Machines on Work

The introduction of steam-powered machinery made work easier to do. Instead of spending several years as an apprentice learning a trade, a person could learn to perform a task or operate a machine in a few days.

Employers wanted people who could learn a few simple tasks and soon discovered that women and children could operate machines as efficiently as men. Employers preferred to hire young men and women rather than older, skilled people. Young people did not have set working habits and did not expect high wages. Women and children would work for lower wages than men. Consequently, the early textile factories employed mainly children and young women.

As machines became more widely used, older, skilled workers often found themselves unemployed. Factories no longer needed their abilities as weavers or spinners and would not hire them for simpler work. To make up for their lost income, many of these people sent their children to work in textile factories while they looked for odd jobs in cities or on farms.

The Wage System

The factory system differed significantly from the domestic system. Under the domestic system, workers usually worked unsupervised in their homes. They turned over finished products, such as thread or cloth, perhaps once a week, and were paid for the number of items completed. In factories, instead of working on a product from beginning to end, each worker performed only a small part of the entire job. Under the factory system, dozens or hundreds of workers toiled in the same room under the watchful eyes of supervisors. Everyone was employed by the factory owners. Factory owners paid their workers wages based on the number of hours worked or the amount of goods produced.

Several factors determined factory workers' wages. First, employers wanted to produce goods as cheaply as possible. Thus, factory owners set wages in relation to other costs of production. For example, if the cost of land or capital increased, the owners lowered wages.

Second, an oversupply of workers lowered wages. On the other hand, wages rose when there were not enough workers to do a particular job.

Third, wages often depended on what people could earn at other kinds of work. For example, early employers in textile factories wanted to attract young women as workers. The employers therefore paid young women more than they could earn as household servants.

Fourth, wages were higher for men than for women. For example, in cotton mills and the London clothing trades in Great Britain, men earned as much as twice what women earned. Women were thought to be adding "a little something" to a family's income, even if in reality a woman was the only wage earner for her family.

Factory workers acquired skills and were paid accordingly, but they had little else to show for their work. They did not own their tools or equipment, as domestic workers had, and there were few opportunities for advancement within the factory.

Factory Rules and Regulations

Factory work changed working people's work habits. Workers had many rules to follow. They had to arrive at the factory for work promptly. They could eat meals and take breaks only at set times, and they could leave only with permission. They worked whether it was hot or cold, winter or summer, day or night. Breaking the rules or missing work for any reason could result in heavy fines, pay cuts, or job loss.

In the early factories, workers spent 14 hours a day, six days a week, on the job. Instead of the work being adjusted to the seasons, as it was under the domestic system or on farms, factory workers had to adjust their lives to the demands of machines, and the machines never needed to rest. Some workers even complained that people in authority expected them to become machines themselves.

Factories were uncomfortable places; they were noisy, dirty, and poorly ventilated. The air was hot and steamy in summer and cold and damp in winter. Sanitary facilities were primitive. Early machines had no safety devices, and serious injuries occurred frequently. Employers provided no accident insurance or other form of compensation for injury.

One of the most alarming features of early industrialization—in light of twentieth-century attitudes—was child labor. Five-year-old children were commonly employed in cotton mills and in mines. Conditions were particularly bad in coal mines, where women and children pulled carts through tunnels that were too low to allow a donkey or a grown man to pass through.

Thonet Rocker

Some inventions, such as the steam engine, affected people the world over. Others were less universal in their impact, though no less significant in terms of their ingenuity. Michael Thonet, a German cabinetmaker living in Austria, invented a process that revolutionized furniture making. He used this process in the mid-1860s to craft the bentwood rocker shown here. Thonet's patent consisted of bending solid wood by steaming it and then clamping a thin strip of steel along one side. The process eliminated complex jointing and carving. The simple process allowed Thonet to hire local people rather than expensive artisans for his European factories.

Many years before the Industrial Revolution had any impact on the rest of the furniture industry, Thonet's chairs, hat stands, and other pieces were being mass-produced. By 1870 Thonet's company was making about 1,300 pieces of furniture a day. In other words, with a six-day workweek, his factory produced 400,000 pieces annually—an early triumph in mass production.

Abusive situations in factories soon scandalized Great Britain. In 1832 a parliamentary committee investigated working conditions of children in textile mills. As a result of this investigation, Parliament passed the Factory Act of 1833, which allowed for factory inspection and enforcement of child labor laws. The following exchange between the parliamentary committee and 23-year-old Elizabeth Bently, who began to work in a flax mill when she was 6 years old, illustrates the committee's findings:

"What were your hours of labor?—From five in the morning till nine at night, when they were thronged. . . .
Suppose you flagged a little, or were too late, what would they do?—Strap us.
Girls as well as boys?—Yes.
Have you ever been strapped?—Yes, severely. . . .

You are considerably deformed in your person in consequence of this labor?—Yes, I am.
At what time did it come on?—I was about thirteen years old when it began coming, and it has got worse since."

Living Conditions of Workers

Life in the mines and factories was hard and monotonous, and life in the workers' homes was not much better. Working people lived in cramped and poorly maintained apartment houses called tenements. As many as a dozen people might dwell in a single room. One bed might have been shared by half a dozen children at one time. As late as 1840, 40,000 to 50,000 working-class people in Manchester, England, lived in cellars. The illness, death, or unemployment of a working father or mother could send a family to the brink of starvation.

Although the working classes suffered during the Industrial Revolution, their living standard improved considerably when inexpensive consumer goods produced in the factories became available to them. In time, workers' wages increased somewhat, increasing the buying power of the large working sector of the population.

Conditions in industrial cities during the Industrial Revolution were shocking when evaluated by today's standards. However, the lower economic classes, whether peasants or artisans, had always worked long and hard. They had always suffered from periodic famines and epidemics. Moreover, women and children had always worked hard, especially in rural areas.

The Development of the Middle Class

During the Industrial Revolution, the balance of economic and political power shifted from agriculture to manufacturing. As the two trends of industrialization and urbanization continued and the industrial society expanded and became more complicated, a middle class grew. It consisted of bankers, manufacturers, merchants, lawyers, doctors, engineers, professors, and their families.

The life of the middle and upper tiers of the middle class contrasted markedly with that of the working class. The groups lived apart, workers in crowded slums and middle-class people in larger houses in more spacious neighborhoods. The two groups dressed differently. Workers wore work shirts; lawyers and merchants wore suits. Working-class women dressed in plain skirts and blouses; most women of the middle class wore lace and frills. The lower tier of the middle class, however, would have been largely indistinguishable from the working-class people.

The laboring poor who worked on farms or in factories continued to struggle economically as had their parents and grandparents. The middle class, however, gained prestige and political recognition. Members of the middle and upper tiers of the middle class could afford to own property, hire servants, eat well, and enjoy some comfort. Affluent middle-class parents sent their children to school to receive training for good jobs. Often the younger generation inherited money and social position from their parents.

Aristocratic government leaders sought the advice of middle-class economists. Soon government leaders became as concerned about the future of industry as they were about the future of agriculture.

The Effect of Industrialization on Women's Lives

The Industrial Revolution affected women of different classes in different ways. In the past, in addition to working in the fields, women had spun yarn, woven cloth, made clothing, and prepared meals. They manufactured goods for sale and assisted their husbands in craft shops or small family businesses. However, the Industrial Revolution moved most manufacturing into factories and many working families into the cities. All classes of city-dwelling people purchased food and clothing at large markets instead of making these products at home. As city dwellers, many women no longer had the resources or the need to do the important work of growing food or making cloth for clothing.

Working-class women. The early textile mills hired women to tend machines that spun cotton into thread. Women could perform this task efficiently and were paid less than men. Thus industrialization changed the location of work for working-class women, but it did not raise their status.

While some working-class women took factory jobs, many others continued to work at what was a traditional job for women, domestic service. For centuries young, single women had been hired as maids, cooks, and nannies in other people's homes. Many men had worked as grooms, gardeners, footmen, valets, and butlers. After industrialization more middle-class families could afford to hire servants. As a result, more jobs for servants became available.

As the number of farms declined during the Industrial Revolution, rural areas offered fewer jobs. Daughters of farm families now took jobs as servants in the city. For many country women, domestic service represented a first step into city life. Working as a servant called for the skills that most girls would have been taught anyway, such as cleaning, cooking, and caring for young children. Servants lived with the families for whom they worked. Thus a girl moving from the country had a place to live and food to eat. After living for a while in the city as a servant, a young woman might take a job in a shop or factory.

Middle-class women. The Industrial Revolution brought new wealth and greater luxury to middle-class women, who could hire servants to assist them in cooking, cleaning, and taking care of their children. While their husbands went to work each day, middle-class wives stayed home. Middle-class people placed increasing emphasis on the idea that women belonged at home and men belonged in the working

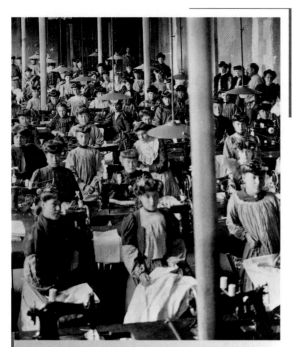

During the Industrial Revolution, many young girls, such as those seen here, took jobs in garment factories.

world. According to some writers of the day, woman's nature equipped her only for raising children and caring for the home. More and more people considered earning money as a corruption of "true womanhood." Some women accepted and enjoyed this role, but others began to express a very different attitude.

In the mid-1800s, some middle-class women began voicing their need for roles outside the home. For some, a life outside the home meant a measure of freedom. For others, especially those who were single, this meant paid work, which was a financial necessity, not just charity work. The issue of a woman's right to work was hotly debated throughout the 1800s. Gradually, the idea gained some acceptance.

During the late 1800s, more jobs became available and acceptable for women. The demand for public health care created a need for nurses and social workers, greatly increasing opportunities for women. In addition, the call for secretaries and telephone and telegraph operators opened up other avenues for women who needed or wanted to work.

Demands also arose for improvements in education. College courses were opened to women, and special women's colleges were established. As public education spread in the 1870s and 1880s in France

and Great Britain, the need for teachers increased. Women began to enter the teaching field. By the end of the 1800s, elementary school teaching had become largely a female profession.

Section 2 Review

1. **Locate and Explain the Significance** Manchester
2. **Understanding Ideas** How did machines change the way work was done?
3. **Summarizing Ideas** What four factors determined the wages of a factory worker?
4. **Analyzing Ideas** Tell how the middle class expanded and gained in importance.
5. **Synthesizing Ideas** (a) What jobs were open to women in the 1800s? (b) How did these jobs affect their lives?

Section 3

New Methods and Business Organizations

Focus Questions

- How did methods of production change during the Industrial Revolution?
- Why did corporations emerge, and how did they affect the way business was done?
- What is the business cycle, and how does it affect society?

Throughout the 1800s, inventions, new sales methods, and new methods of production and distribution of goods caused rapid growth in industry. This growth brought many changes to the factory system and to the organization of businesses. Some of these changes date to the early Industrial Revolution. Other changes came after about 1870 as a result of scientific developments.

The factory system also introduced a new phase in the development of **capitalism**—the economic system in which individuals rather than governments control the factors of production. Before the Industrial Revolution, most capitalists were merchants who bought, sold, and exchanged goods. We refer to this type of capitalism as **commercial capitalism**. However, the capitalists of the Industrial Revolution became more involved in producing and manufacturing goods themselves. Furthermore, the methods used for production were largely mechanized and industrialized. For these reasons, this type of capitalism is referred to as **industrial capitalism**.

Division of Labor

As we have seen, industrialization changed the methods of production. Factory owners hired large numbers of unskilled laborers, divided the manufacturing process into a series of steps, and then assigned a step to each worker. This was a form of **division of labor**. Because a large number of items could be produced in a given length of time, the cost of the items diminished. The use of machinery helped the division of labor because machines performed many of the steps.

Interchangeable Parts

The American inventor Eli Whitney used division of labor and **interchangeable parts** to make muskets in the late 1700s. In Whitney's factory, some people worked on musket barrels, others on trigger mecha-

nisms, and still others on the wooden stocks or handles.

The use of interchangeable parts for his firearms became an essential part of Whitney's system. Previously, firearms had been handmade by skilled artisans. Each gun was slightly different. Whitney designed machinery that unskilled workers could operate. This machinery turned out identical, interchangeable parts. This development made division of labor possible in a product composed of several parts that had to fit together. Whitney's system resulted in the speedy production of a large number of inexpensive muskets that could be easily repaired. Other manufacturers, realizing the usefulness of interchangeable parts, quickly adopted the idea.

The Assembly Line

Division of labor and the use of interchangeable parts are two essential elements of mass production. **Mass production** is the system of manufacturing large numbers of identical items.

A third element of mass production is the assembly line. Until the late 1800s, each of the various parts of a manufactured object was transported to a central point, where workers assembled the object. Then

In 1913 Henry Ford's main plant was located in the Detroit suburb of Highland Park.

manufacturers devised the assembly line. A conveyor belt carried unfinished products from worker to worker. As each item passed, each worker performed a certain task. The assembly line saved time and energy and increased the number of times per hour a worker could perform his or her assigned task.

Henry Ford saw great potential in the mass-production system. By applying it to the production of automobiles, he founded one of the largest industries in the United States. A conveyor belt carried the automobile frame from one worker to the next. Each worker made a small contribution by adding one or more of the thousands of interchangeable parts that composed the Model T Ford. Mass production lowered the price of automobiles, making them accessible to most American families.

American and European industrialists began to mass-produce clothing, furniture, and machinery. Because mass production usually lowered the cost of an item, more people could buy more and more goods and enjoy a higher standard of living.

Rise of the Corporation

Before the Industrial Revolution, most businesses were either sole proprietorships or partnerships. A business owned and controlled by one person is a **sole proprietorship**; a **partnership** is a business owned and controlled by two or more people. Although both types of businesses give their owners considerable freedom to make economic decisions, both types have disadvantages. For example, both sole proprietors and partners are responsible for all debts even if the debts exceed the original amount of investment. In addition, sole proprietorships and partnerships usually remain small. Small companies with few workers typically cannot afford mass-production methods or the machinery necessary for large-scale production.

As the scale of business grew during the 1800s, so too did the **corporation**. A corporation is a business organization in which individuals buy shares of stock, elect directors to decide policies and hire managers, and receive dividends according to the number of shares they own. Unlike sole proprietors and partners, a shareholder's financial responsibility is limited to the amount that he or she invests. For this reason, corporations are attractive to investors.

In the late 1800s, corporations increased greatly in terms of the amount of capital invested and in terms of size. In 1901 American financier J. P. Morgan and his associates formed the United States Steel Company, the first of many billion-dollar corporations.

Banks and other financial institutions played an increasingly important role in forming and operating these large corporations.

Increasing the size of a corporation did not always increase its profits. A large manufacturing enterprise could generally produce goods at a lower cost than a small one. To get lower costs, however, the factory had to operate at full capacity, turning out as many goods as possible. Sometimes a factory produced so many goods that selling them all became a problem.

When a number of corporations were producing the same products, competition became very keen. The smaller and less efficient businesses suffered if they tried to sell their products by cutting prices. Often these smaller firms had to sell out to larger firms.

As a result, although the size of individual corporations increased steadily, the number of individual corporations in some industries decreased. Sometimes a corporation would buy so many smaller companies that it would create a **monopoly**. A monopoly is the complete control of the production or sale of a good or service by a single firm. In the United States, corporations such as Standard Oil and United States Steel created monopolies.

By 1900 a number of giant corporations in Germany had combined to control entire industries. These combinations of corporations were known as **cartels**. For example, a cartel might own coal and iron mines, steel mills, and factories that used steel to build machines, thus controlling all aspects of an industry.

Business Cycles

As industrial production became more and more important, it influenced a country's entire economy. The Industrial Revolution brought alternating periods of prosperity and decline—a pattern known as the **business cycle**.

When one industry did well, other industries also prospered. If, for example, there was a great demand for machines, there would also be a demand for the coal and iron needed to make them. If, on the other hand, a large firm reduced its orders of iron and laid off workers, other companies would also be affected. The iron suppliers might have to cut down production and lay off workers as well. The laid-off workers would not be able to pay their rent or buy food. These workers would have to apply for other jobs. When there were many workers available for just a few jobs, employers reduced wages, knowing that they could find workers who would agree to low pay. In some cases, the effects would go on spreading to other industries, until the entire economy was in a **depression**, the lowest point of a business cycle.

These economic fluctuations affected the lives of all the people in an industrialized country, even those people who did not work in factories. In addition, events in one country could affect the economy of another country. During the American Civil War, for example, the Confederacy could not ship cotton to Great Britain. The shortage of cotton contributed to a depression in the British textile industry.

Section 3 Review
---

1. **Define** capitalism, commercial capitalism, industrial capitalism, division of labor, interchangeable parts, mass production, sole proprietorship, partnership, corporation, monopoly, cartels, business cycle, depression
2. **Evaluating Ideas (a)** What is the chief advantage of mass production? **(b)** What three elements are needed to make mass production possible?
3. **Comparing Ideas** What advantages did corporations have over sole proprietorships and partnerships?
4. **Analyzing Ideas** Why might monopolies and cartels be harmful to a nation's economy?
5. **Synthesizing Ideas** How did the Industrial Revolution bring about the business cycle?

Section 4

Living and Working Conditions

Focus Questions

- What were Adam Smith's ideas, and how did they affect people's views of industrialism?
- Why did reform movements arise, and what issues did reformers take on?
- How did workers themselves try to improve their situations?

As the Industrial Revolution progressed, the interests of employers often conflicted with the interests of workers. Employers needed workers who would come to work on time, do their jobs quickly and well, follow factory rules, and accept relatively low wages.

Workers, on the other hand, needed wages high enough to support their families even through difficulties. They wanted some control over their work hours, the conditions in the factories, and the conditions in the towns where they lived. However, society in general was influenced by certain economic theories that had become widespread as the Industrial Revolution progressed, and workers' demands went unanswered.

Adam Smith

During the Enlightenment of the 1700s, a group of economists, called Physiocrats, attacked the ideas of mercantilism. Mercantilism was the economic theory based on the belief that the world contained only a fixed amount of wealth, and, in order to increase its wealth, a country had to take some wealth from another country. These economists believed that natural laws should be left to govern economic life. Any attempt to interfere with these natural economic laws was certain to bring disaster. Adam Smith, a Scot who accepted some of the ideas of the Physiocrats, stated his views in his book *The Wealth of Nations*, which was published in 1776.

Smith reasoned that two natural laws—the law of supply and demand and the law of competition—regulate all business and economic activity. In any business, Smith believed, prices—and therefore profits—will be fixed by the relationship of supply to demand. If an article is scarce and in great demand, people will pay a high price for it. Thus profits from its sales will rise. The makers of the product will then invest their money to produce more of the scarce article. Soon the supply of the article will exceed the demand for it.

Now each manufacturer will face competition. To get people to buy a product, the manufacturer will have to reduce the price or improve the quality or both. If too many manufacturers produce the same article, the price of the item will go down so far that some manufacturers will not make enough money to cover their costs. The least efficient businesses may be forced out of business. When such manufacturers quit producing the article, the supply of the article will decrease and the price will go up. Then the capable, efficient, and well-organized producers will make a reasonable profit.

Adam Smith wrote that every person should have the freedom to start any business of their choice.

Interpreting Visuals: Determining Cause and Effect

Understanding history requires that you identify the causes of historical events and determine their effect on history. A cause is the reason that something else happened. An effect is the result or consequence of an action or a situation. Usually an event, an idea, or a situation results from several causes. In history causes can be divided into two types. Underlying causes are long term. Immediate causes lead directly to an event. For example, practicing a sport may lead to a championship. The immediate cause of that victory, however, is the winning game.

How to Determine Cause and Effect

To determine cause and effect, follow these steps.
1. Identify the focal point of your study.
2. Determine the underlying causes. For example, did new ideas cause people to act in a certain way?
3. Identify the immediate cause. For example, did a political candidate seeking an office win or lose the election because bad weather resulted in a low voter turnout?
4. Formulate a conclusion about the significance of the causes and effects of a historical event.

Developing the Skill

Economists often wonder why industrialization suddenly "takes off" at a certain time in a particular place. Walter Rostow, a twentieth-century economic historian, has advanced the theory that every society develops according to a dynamic production pattern that consists of five stages. The chart below explains the five stages of Rostow's theory.

The chart shows that in stage one, the economy is based on agriculture. Traditional values prevail. The underlying causes for the Industrial Revolution are economic, political, social, and intellectual. Economically, there needs to be an agricultural surplus that generates capital. The traditional social structure declines with the rise of a commercial class. A centralized national government encourages economic modernization. Ideas about the benefits of profit are praised rather than degraded. The immediate cause originates from a surge of production and the rapid expansion in one industry, which serves as the basis for modernization. The significance of the process is that in order for the Industrial Revolution to occur, a social, political, and intellectual change must take place. The economic system is intertwined with the culture and the value system.

Practicing the Skill

Use the characteristics of society on the chart as the basis for your own chart on the development of the space industry.

To apply this skill, see Applying History Study Skills on page 233.

Rostow's Theory of Industrial Development

Characteristics	Stage One: *Traditional Society*	Stage Two: *Preconditions for Take-Off*	Stage Three: *Take-Off*	Stage Four: *Drive to Maturity*	Stage Five: *Age of Mass Consumption*
Economy	• agricultural • limited production	• agricultural surplus • surplus capital • expansion of trade	• surge of technology • rapid expansion of industry	• technology extended to all sectors	• increased production and use of durable goods
Society	• hierarchical social structure	• beginning of a commercial class	• entrepreneurial class more dominant	• urbanization • increase in skilled and professional workers	• rise of a new middle class • shift to suburbs
Political Power	• regionally based power in the hands of landowners	• centralized national government	• groups in power encourage economic modernization	• industrial leaders highly influential	• social welfare • more resources for military
Values	• belief that change will not occur	• spirit of progress	• investment of capital for profit becomes important	• emphasis on technology • expectation of progress	• acquisition of consumer goods important

He also believed that a person's business should be operated for the greatest advantage. The result, Smith said, would benefit everyone. Laborers would have jobs, investors and owners would make profits, and buyers would receive better goods at lower prices. Smith's system was one of complete **free enterprise**.

Smith's ideas appealed to industrialists because the forces he outlined supposedly worked automatically. Smith argued that if anything interfered with the absolutely free working of supply and demand and competition, the system could not work well. Laws and regulations, such as those imposed under mercantilism, were thought of as interfering with the workings of natural law or natural economic forces.

Thomas Malthus and David Ricardo

Smith's ideas received strong support from Thomas Malthus and David Ricardo. Malthus was an Anglican clergyman who became a professor of economics. In his book *An Essay on the Principle of Population*, published in 1798, he wrote that population increases present the greatest obstacle to human progress. People, he said, multiply more rapidly than the food supply increases, despite such checks as famines, epidemics, and wars. He believed that human misery and poverty are inevitable.

David Ricardo was an English businessman who amassed a large fortune early in life and then was elected to the House of Commons. He, too, wrote that working-class poverty is inevitable. In his book *Principles of Political Economy and Taxation*, published in 1817, Ricardo stated that supply and demand determine wages. When labor is plentiful, wages remain low. When labor is scarce, wages soar. As population grows, Ricardo wrote, more and more workers become available, and wages inevitably drop. Ricardo's idea became known as the iron law of wages.

Malthus and Ricardo painted a grim picture of workers as inevitably poor and suffering. Understandably, the new social science of economics became known as the "dismal science."

Laissez-Faire

The writings of economists such as Smith, Malthus, and Ricardo supported industrialists who wanted to buy labor, like any other commodity, as cheaply as possible. Their economic theories also indicated that governments should not interfere with the operations of business. This attitude was summed up in the French phrase **laissez-faire** (le·say-FAR), meaning "let do" or leave things alone.

The British put the theory of laissez-faire into practice. Formerly, either the government or the guilds had regulated the quantity and quality of goods and the hours and wages of workers. Starting in the 1840s, most regulations were discontinued. Tariffs, which had regulated foreign trade, were abolished. Trade was almost completely unregulated. Other European countries and the United States adopted features of laissez-faire economics, although not as completely as did Britain.

Growing Interest in Reform

At the same time, more and more people were realizing that things could not be left entirely alone. Humanitarians—people who work to improve the conditions of others—urged reforms. Ministers preached against what they considered the unchristian selfishness of businesspeople.

Influential writers made the public aware of the terrible conditions in mines and factories. The great English writer Charles Dickens used his novels *Dombey and Son* and *Hard Times* to attack selfish business leaders. In *David Copperfield*, Dickens drew on his own wretched childhood experiences as a worker in a warehouse. Essayists and critics such as Thomas Carlyle and John Ruskin denounced the materialism—the obsession with money and the neglect of spiritual values—of their times.

Many people began to feel that government needed to regulate work hours and set minimal standards for wages and working conditions. These people argued that such laws would not interfere with the natural workings of the economy.

In Great Britain, some reformers adopted the ideas of philosopher Jeremy Bentham. In his 1789 book, *An Introduction to the Principles of Morals and Legislation*, Bentham argued that every act of a society should be judged in terms of its utility, or usefulness. His theory was thus known as **utilitarianism**. A law was useful, and therefore good, said Bentham, if it led to "the greatest happiness of the greatest number" of people. Bentham believed that people needed education so they could better determine what things were good for them or made them happy.

Bentham and his followers advocated reform of the prison system; they advocated education as well as legal reform. They thought that government should create conditions to enable as many people as possible to find happiness.

Hard Times

English novelist Charles Dickens (1812–1870) achieved lasting fame for his portrayal of British society during the early Industrial Revolution. These excerpts from the novel *Hard Times* describe Coketown, a town spawned by the Industrial Revolution.*

"It was a town of red brick, or of brick that would have been red if the smoke and ashes had allowed it; but as matters stood it was a town of unnatural red and black like the painted face of a savage. It was a town of machinery and tall chimneys, out of which interminable serpents of smoke trailed themselves for ever and ever, and never got uncoiled. It had a black canal in it, and a river that ran purple with ill-smelling dye, and vast piles of buildings full of windows where there was a rattling and a trembling all day long, and where the piston of the steam-engine worked monotonously up and down like the head of an elephant in a state of melancholy madness. It contained several large streets all very like one another, and many small streets still more like one another, inhabited by people equally like one another, who all went in and out at the same hours, with the same sound upon the same pavements, to do the same work, and to whom every day was the same as yesterday and tomorrow, and every year the counterpart of the last and the next. . . .

Seen from a distance . . . Coketown lay shrouded in a haze of its own, which appeared impervious to the sun's rays. You only knew the town was there, because you knew there could have been no such sulky blotch upon the prospect without a town. A blur of soot and smoke, now confusedly tending this way, now that way, now aspiring to the vault of Heaven, now murkily creeping along

The Bessemer works at Sheffield, England

the earth, as the wind rose and fell, or changed its quarter: a dense formless jumble, with sheets of cross light in it, that showed nothing but masses of darkness:—Coketown in the distance was suggestive of itself, though not a brick of it could be seen. . . .

The streets were hot and dusty on the summer day. . . . Stokers emerged from low underground doorways into factory yards, and sat on steps, and posts, and palings, wiping their swarthy visages, and contemplating coals. The whole town seemed to be frying in oil. There was a stifling smell of hot oil everywhere. The steam-engines shone with it, the dresses of the Hands were soiled with it, the mills throughout their many stories oozed and trickled it."

*Coke is the residue left after distillation of coal or other materials such as petroleum. Coke was often used as fuel.

John Stuart Mill

Philosopher John Stuart Mill, although a believer in laissez-faire, criticized what he considered the economic injustices and inequalities of British society. Mill's father had taught his son Bentham's principles of utilitarianism. Mill also believed government should work for the well-being of all its citizens. He could not accept an economic system that left the working classes trapped in miserable poverty. Mill believed government should intervene to protect working children and improve housing and factory conditions. He advocated not only full democracy but also complete equality in all respects between men and women. In 1861 he wrote, "All human beings have the same interest in good government; the welfare of all is alike affected by it, and they have equal need of a voice in it to secure their share of its benefits."

In Mill's view individual liberty, which included the liberty to think as one pleased and to express one's views, was a basic human right. Mill believed governments should guarantee that liberty.

Early Reform Laws

Great Britain made early attempts to improve working conditions through legislation. Britain's initial laws dealt with the employment of women and children. Working conditions for these two groups in particular scandalized many people.

Beginning in 1819, Parliament attempted to legislate hours and conditions for children working in cotton mills. The first of these laws, the Factory Act of 1819, proved ineffective because it included no means of enforcement. The Factory Act of 1833 allowed for investigation and enforcement of the previous act's measures and extended them to all textile factories. Under the terms of these laws, textile mills were prohibited from employing children under 9 years of age. Children between the ages of 9 and 13 could work no more than 8 hours daily, six days a week. Children between ages 13 and 18 could work no more than 12 hours a day.

Nine years later another law prohibited the employment in coal mines of all women and of children under 10. A great advance came in 1847 with the passage of the Ten Hours Act. This law established a 10-hour working day for women and for children under the age of 18 in textile factories. Because it was not profitable to keep the factories running when the women and children were gone, textile factories adopted the 10-hour workday for all workers.

Despite these reform laws, the conditions under which many workers labored remained harsh. Factory reform laws often were not strictly enforced, and these laws did not solve all of the workers' problems. For example, the factory reform laws did not deal with wages. Eventually, workers would achieve improved working conditions through better organization and government legislation.

Worker Strikes

One way that workers could protest working conditions and low wages was for a group of them to refuse to work. A group of miners, for example, who believed they were being paid too little for their work would refuse to enter the mines. When an entire group of workers refused to work, they were said to be on **strike**. Workers often made a list of their demands and told the employer they would not work until these demands were met. Employers sometimes

Young people made up a considerable portion of the American labor force. Strikes became common throughout the late 1800s and into the 1900s.

agreed to give the strikers what they wanted. At other times, the employers either fired all the strikers and hired new workers or simply waited until the strikers returned to work.

Hundreds of strikes took place in industrial countries during the 1800s. The strikers usually made two kinds of demands—higher wages for workers and more control over working conditions. Sometimes strikes began as demands for higher wages but became protests against general working and living conditions of the working class. Strike leaders demanded a reorganization of society to end the differences between rich and poor, employers and workers.

Large protest movements occurred in northern England in 1811 and 1812; in the silk-weaving city of Lyons, France, in 1831; and in the mining towns of Silesia, in eastern Europe, in 1844. These demonstrations ended when the governments sent troops to arrest protesting workers.

The Union Movement

To strengthen their position, workers sought ways to organize permanently. They felt their efforts would be more successful if they belonged to associations of workers. These associations would collect dues and use the money to pay workers while they were on strike. The associations could plan actions and coordinate the demands of different types of workers in the same factory. These associations came to be called **unions**.

Organizing unions was not easy. British, French, and German law, for instance, regarded workers' associations as illegal. When British workers tried to unite anyway, employers persuaded Parliament to pass laws against them. The Combination Acts of 1799 and 1800 stated that people who united with others to demand higher wages, shorter hours, or better working conditions could be imprisoned.

Eventually, however, the workers began to make some progress. In 1824 Parliament repealed the Combination Acts, permitting laborers to meet to agree on wages and hours. Finally, in the 1870s Parliament passed laws legalizing strikes.

When workers gained the legal rights to form unions and to strike, they gained power. Gradually, factory owners recognized unions as a single voice of all the member workers. Union and management representatives met to negotiate wages, hours, and working conditions. If the bargainers could agree, they wrote their agreements into a contract that would last for a fixed period of time. This process of negotiation is called **collective bargaining**.

Section 4 Review

1. **Define** free enterprise, laissez-faire, utilitarianism, strike, unions, collective bargaining
2. **Identify** Adam Smith, Thomas Malthus, David Ricardo, Charles Dickens, Jeremy Bentham, John Stuart Mill
3. **Locate and Explain the Significance** Lyons, Silesia
4. **Understanding Ideas (a)** According to Adam Smith, how did the law of supply and demand and the law of competition work? **(b)** What conclusion did Smith draw from these laws?
5. **Interpreting Ideas** How was the theory of utilitarianism applied to social reform?
6. **Evaluating Ideas** Were unions necessary, or could workers have found other ways to protect themselves? Explain your answer.

Section 5

Calls for Reform

Focus Questions
- **What type of society did early socialists want to establish?**
- **How did Robert Owen put his socialist beliefs into action?**
- **What did Karl Marx believe would happen to the capitalist world of the 1800s?**

In the economy that resulted from the Industrial Revolution, a few people became enormously rich, while most remained poor. The uneven distribution of wealth disturbed many people. Some reformers became convinced that laissez-faire capitalism was not the best economic system. They argued that laws could not do enough to remedy inequalities. The only way to distribute wealth more evenly, they thought, was to change the ownership and operation of the means of production. The means of production include the capital and equipment used to produce and exchange goods—for example, land, railroads, mines, factories, stores, banks, and machines.

Socialism

Some reformers of the 1800s advocated a political and economic system called **socialism.** In this system, governments own the means of production and operate them for the welfare of all people.

Socialists wanted to establish an economic system that would abolish the profit motive and competition. They believed everyone, not just capitalists and owners, had a right to share in the profits.

The early socialists believed that people could live at peace with each other if they lived in small cooperative settlements, owning all the means of production in common and sharing the products. The socialists tried to work out detailed plans for model communities and then tried to persuade people to set up the communities. Sir Thomas More, an English humanist, described such a model community in 1516 in his *Utopia*. Thus these early socialists were sometimes called **utopian socialists**.

In Great Britain, the most influential utopian socialist was Robert Owen, who lived from 1771 to 1858. Owen quit school at age 10 and went to work. By the age of 19, he managed a large cotton mill. In just a year or so, he was able to purchase, along with his partners, a spinning mill in New Lanark, Scotland. Owen ran the mill for decades, in spite of switching partners. In 1814 Owen entered into partnership with Jeremy Bentham.

Owen believed that if people lived in a good environment, they would cease to act selfishly. As a factory owner, Owen felt responsible for his workers and devoted much time and money to making their lives happier and more secure. He built good homes for them, established a store where they could buy inexpensive food and clothing, and set up schools for their children.

Owen believed, however, that workers should not be completely dependent on their employers. He encouraged workers to form unions. He also established cooperative communities in Great Britain and in the United States.

The Theories of Karl Marx

Some thinkers grew impatient with early socialism, which they regarded as impractical. They felt the entire capitalist system should be changed. Karl Marx, a journalist and the most important of these critics, was born in Prussia in 1818. Marx's radical political views made him unpopular in his own country. Forced to leave, he eventually settled in London, where he lived until his death in 1883.

Marx believed that all the great changes in history came from changes in economic conditions. In 1848, with a fellow German, Friedrich Engels, Marx published the *Communist Manifesto*, a pamphlet outlining his ideas. Marx and Engels summed up their view of human history in one sentence: "The history of all hitherto existing society is the history of class struggles." They then went on to support their view.

"Free man and slave, patrician and plebeian, lord and serf, guild master and journeyman, in a word, oppressor and oppressed, stood in constant opposition to one another, carried on an uninterrupted, now hidden, now open fight, a fight that each time ended either in a revolutionary reconstitution of society at large or in the common ruin of the contending classes."

Marx stated that each stage of history involved inequality, and therefore struggle, between those who owned property and those who did not. In the capitalist stage of the 1800s, for example, the struggle existed between the owners, or **bourgeoisie**, and the working class, or **proletariat**.

Marx argued that all wealth is created by labor. Under capitalism, he said, labor receives only a small fraction of the wealth it creates. Most of the wealth goes to the owners in the form of profits, which Marx called surplus value. As a result of this unequal distribution of wealth, he thought the time would soon come when capitalist society would divide into two classes—a few capitalists and a vast mass of workers, or proletariat. The proletariat, concentrated in cities, would suffer poverty and unemployment.

Marx predicted that the capitalists would continue to amass wealth while driving the proletariat deeper and deeper into poverty. In these circumstances, the proletariat in the most advanced and industrialized nations would unite, seize power in a revolution, and establish socialism. Because many people would not readily accept socialism, initially the workers would have to control the government. Marx referred to this phase as the "dictatorship of the proletariat." After a period of education, people would become experienced in working together cooperatively. Force would no longer be needed, and the state would "wither away." This last stage, characterized by a truly classless society, Marx called *pure communism*.

Marx believed that pure communism was the inevitable outcome of human history. Each person, Marx also believed, would contribute what he or she could and would receive what he or she needed. Marx said, "From each according to his abilities, to each according to his needs."

In Marx's time, the terms *communism* and *socialism* were used in many different ways. To Marx and Engels, a communist was one who believed that people would live cooperatively without being forced to do so.

Marx called his variety of socialism "scientific socialism" because he thought he was describing objective laws of historical development—laws that would work inevitably. Marx published many of his ideas in *Das Kapital* (German for "capital"), a book that analyzed capitalism in detail.

Variations of Socialism

In the mid-1800s, socialists in several European countries began forming political parties to put their ideas into practice. The ideas of Marx and Engels influenced many of these parties. Marxist, or radical, socialists generally believed in the necessity of revolution to overthrow the capitalist system. They wanted to establish a system in which government owned almost all means of production and controlled economic planning. Today we call this economic and political system—which ignores basic human rights—**authoritarian socialism**, or **communism**.

Another group of socialists, though influenced by Marx, believed that socialism could develop gradually through education and democratic forms of government. These moderate socialists believed that when enough people became educated about socialism, they would elect socialist representatives to their government. Then government would take over the means of production peacefully. The owners would be paid for their property, and government would operate the means of production in the interest of all people. Today we call this type of socialism **democratic socialism**. Under democratic socialism, unlike under authoritarian socialism, the people retain basic human rights and partial control over economic planning through the election of government officials. Individuals may own private property, but the government controls at least some of the means of production.

Marx believed that workers had to unite in order to fight capitalism successfully. In 1864 he helped establish the International Working Men's Association, called the First International. This organization disbanded, however, in 1876. A Second International was formed in 1889, after Marx's death. Torn by disagreements between moderate and radical socialists, the Second International survived only into the early 1900s. Elsewhere, particularly in Russia, Marx's ideas would have profound effects.

Karl Marx analyzed capitalism in *Das Kapital*. He did not foresee how collective bargaining would result in better working conditions, avoiding a worldwide socialist revolution.

Section 5 Review

1. **Define** socialism, utopian socialists, bourgeoisie, proletariat, authoritarian socialism, communism, democratic socialism
2. **Identify** Sir Thomas More, Robert Owen, Karl Marx
3. **Understanding Ideas** What were the important ideas contained in socialism?
4. **Summarizing Ideas** What kinds of reforms did Robert Owen suggest?
5. **Synthesizing Ideas** (a) According to Karl Marx, what causes conflict within a society? (b) What would inevitably happen within a capitalist society, and how would the conflict be resolved?

Chapter 6 Review

A.D. **1733**
John Kay invents
the flying shuttle.

A.D. **1776**
Adam Smith publishes
The Wealth of Nations.

A.D. **1600** | A.D. **1650** | A.D. **1700** | A.D. **1750**

A.D. **1600**
Enclosure movement
in England accelerates.

A.D. **1712**
Thomas Newcomen
invents the steam engine.

A.D. **1769**
James Watt produces the
modern steam engine.

Chapter Summary
The following list contains the key concepts that you have learned in this chapter about the Industrial Revolution and the resulting changes in political and economic thought.
1. The Industrial Revolution—changes brought about by the introduction of power-driven machinery—originated in Great Britain. In time, the Industrial Revolution transformed the world.
2. The Industrial Revolution was preceded by the Agricultural Revolution.
3. The replacement of waterpower by steam power was basic to the Industrial Revolution. Almost as important was the development of the Bessemer process, a new method of making steel that made steel readily available to the newly founded industries.
4. Transportation improved with better roads, networks of canals and railroads, and the use of steam power in ships. The wireless telegraph made rapid communication possible.
5. By gathering workers together in factories, the Industrial Revolution brought an end to the traditional practices of artisans who had worked in their homes or in small shops.
6. Factory workers became dependent on wages and no longer controlled the pace of their work because they had to do what they were told.
7. Living and working conditions were often poor during the early Industrial Revolution.
8. A series of innovations in business practices accompanied the Industrial Revolution. Mass production—based on the division of labor, interchangeable parts, and the assembly line—transformed several industries and permitted the growth of enormous corporations.
9. Workers began to protest harsh working conditions and low wages. The first labor unions were organized to seek improvements in working conditions and to obtain higher wages.
10. Socialists such as Karl Marx believed that a more fundamental transformation of politics and society was necessary.

Reviewing Important Terms
On a separate sheet of paper, supply the term that correctly completes each statement.
1. The changes industrial technology brought about affected manufacturing so deeply that they are referred to as the _____ _____.
2. The basic resources necessary for industrialization (land, labor, and capital) are called the _____ _____ _____.
3. Alternating crops to replenish nutrients in the soil is called _____ _____.
4. The use of _____ _____ allowed Eli Whitney to speed up the production of muskets.
5. The _____ _____ involved burning impurities such as carbon out of iron with a blast of air forced through molten metal.
6. A(n) _____ occurs at the lowest point in the business cycle.
7. A(n) _____ occurs when a group of workers refuse to work.
8. The idea that government should not interfere with the operation of business is called _____.
9. _____ is an economic system in which individuals control the factors of production.
10. A(n) _____ is the control of the total production or sale of a good or service by a single firm.
11. A(n) _____ is a business organization in which individuals buy shares of stock, elect directors to decide policies and hire managers, and receive dividends according to the number of shares they own.

Developing Critical Thinking Skills
1. **Determining Cause and Effect** How did the Industrial Revolution change the relationship between workers and employers that existed in the Middle Ages?
2. **Using Primary Sources** Laws regulating child labor did not exist in the 1700s. The following excerpt from Elizabeth Barrett Browning's poem "The Cry of the Children" describes the life of working-class children.

"'For oh,' say the children, 'we are weary,
    And we cannot run or leap. . . .
For all day, we drag our burden tiring
    Through the coal-dark, underground;
Or, all day, we drive the wheels of iron
    In the factories, round and round.'"

A.D. **1779**
James Crompton invents the spinning mule.

A.D. **1784**
The factory system begins.

A.D. **1814**
George Stephenson invents the locomotive.

A.D. **1839**
Charles Goodyear invents a rubber-curing process.

A.D. **1901**
United States Steel Company forms.

A.D. **1800**   A.D. **1850**   A.D. **1900**   A.D. **1950**

A.D. **1785**
Edmund Cartwright invents the power loom.

A.D. **1793**
Eli Whitney invents the cotton gin.

A.D. **1808**
Robert Fulton begins inland steam service.

A.D. **1848**
Karl Marx publishes the *Communist Manifesto*.

A.D. **1866**
Transatlantic cable is laid.

(a) How did Browning view working conditions in Great Britain? (b) What evidence in the poem supports your answer? (c) Based on information in this chapter, how were working conditions gradually improved?

3. **Analyzing Ideas** How did industrialization affect the lives of women?

4. **Summarizing Ideas** (a) What problems did workers face during the Industrial Revolution? (b) What problems did employers encounter?

5. **Understanding Ideas** (a) Why did Adam Smith's ideas appeal to industrialists? (b) Why did industrialists oppose the ideas of Karl Marx?

Relating Geography to History

Using information in this chapter, write a short essay on the relationship between geography and the Industrial Revolution. For example, how might working conditions have been different if the geography of Great Britain and the United States had not been suited to producing coal or growing cotton?

Relating Past to Present

1. During the Industrial Revolution, many countries held exhibitions to showcase the latest technological developments. Investigate some of the important technological achievements of the 1990s. Use this information to design a poster for a similar exposition in the near future.

2. Use resources in your school or public library to construct a chart showing how long it took to travel from New York to California in 1850, 1900, 1930, and 1990. Your chart should include what form of transportation most people used in each of the years listed.

Applying History Study Skills

Before completing this activity, review Building History Study Skills on page 225.

In the following excerpt from *The Stages of Economic Growth*, W. W. Rostow suggests why the Industrial Revolution began in England. Read the excerpt. Then answer the questions that follow.

"Now, why Britain? Why not France? . . . The French . . . were too rough with their Protestants. They were politically and socially too inflexible, caught up . . . in . . . a

caste society. The best minds and spirits of eighteenth-century France . . . had to think about political, social and religious revolution rather than economic revolution. Moreover the French were committed heavily to ground warfare in Europe; and they cheated on shipping and naval strength . . . when ships mattered greatly. . . .

Britain alone was in a position to weave together cotton manufacture, coal and iron technology, the steam-engine, and ample foreign trade to pull it off."

1. What question is Rostow posing?
2. What were the underlying causes for France's inability to industrialize?
3. What were the underlying causes for Great Britain industrializing first?

internet connect

In 1836, Robert Southey, the poet laureate of Great Britain, wrote Charlotte Brontë: "Literature cannot be the business of a woman's life, and it ought not to be." Search the Internet through the HRW Web site to find information on some of the female writers of the Victorian Age. Then write a short report describing the problems they faced and some of the ways they overcame them.

 GO TO: go.hrw.com
KEYWORD: SCØ
Victorian Writers

Building Your Portfolio

1. **Practicing Map Skills** By the 1850s, iron and coal had become the two major raw materials of modern industry. Using an atlas, draw an outline map of the world showing the global distribution of these resources today. Place the map in your portfolio.

2. **Relating Literature to History** Read the chapter entitled "No Way Out" in *Hard Times* by Charles Dickens. As you read, consider the differences between the worker (or "hand") and the owner of the factory. (a) How does Dickens portray industrial society in the 1800s? (b) What aspects of that society does he seem to be criticizing? Explain. Place your answers in your portfolio.

Life in the Industrial Age

TIME

A.D. **1800–1928**

A.D. **1800–1928**

3.7 million B.C. 4000 B.C. A.D. 2100

PLACE

The United States and Europe

Europe

United States

ARCTIC OCEAN

NORTH AMERICA

PACIFIC OCEAN

EUROPE

ASIA

AFRICA

Equator

AUSTRALIA

PACIFIC OCEAN

SOUTH AMERICA

ATLANTIC OCEAN

INDIAN OCEAN

ANTARCTICA

Joseph Nash lithograph of Machinery Hall in British section of Great Exhibition, 1851

CHAPTER FOCUS

Significance

In addition to changing economies and societies, the Industrial Revolution had a profound effect on science, art, music, and literature.

Terms to Define

dynamo	social sciences
aerodynamics	social Darwinism
biological sciences	psychoanalysis
physical sciences	psychiatry
evolution	emigrations
genetics	"bobbies"
pasteurization	suburbs
antisepsis	romanticism
radioactivity	realism
quantum	regionalism
quantum theory	naturalists
special theory of	impressionists
relativity	

People to Identify

Michael Faraday	Ivan Pavlov
Thomas Edison	Sigmund Freud
Alexander Graham Bell	Sir Robert Peel
Guglielmo Marconi	Walter Camp
Wilbur and Orville Wright	Sir Walter Scott
Charles Darwin	the Grimm brothers
Robert Koch	Johann Wolfgang von
Sir Alexander Fleming	Goethe
John Dalton	James Fenimore Cooper
Dmitry Mendeleyev	Ludwig van Beethoven
Wilhelm Röntgen	Pyotr Ilich Tchaikovsky
Pierre and Marie Curie	Giuseppe Verdi
Max Planck	Gustave Flaubert
Albert Einstein	Mark Twain
E. B. Tylor	Émile Zola
James George Frazer	Paul Cézanne
Auguste Comte	Auguste Rodin
Herbert Spencer	

Places to Locate

New York	Berlin
Paris	London

Chapter Theme Questions

- **Science and Technology** What might be the relationship between scientific discoveries and technological breakthroughs?
- **Social Relations** In what ways might industrialization alter society's institutions and change the way people live?
- **The Arts** How might social and economic developments influence artistic expression?

People's lives were altered greatly as a result of the Industrial Revolution. The era produced changes in the way people worked, but it also made changes to the way they lived and thought. The inventions that followed the initial wave of the Industrial Revolution were also significant. One of the greatest transformations of the 1800s and early 1900s was the advent of new ways to communicate.

In 1901 the Italian Guglielmo Marconi sent the first radio transmission across the Atlantic. This is how Marconi later described the event:

❝Shortly before mid-day I placed the single earphone to my ear and started listening. . . . The answer came at 12:30 when I heard, faintly but distinctly, pip-pip-pip. . . . The result meant much more to me than the mere successful realization of an experiment. . . . I now felt for the first time absolutely certain that the day would come when mankind would be able to send messages without wires not only across the Atlantic but between the farthermost ends of the earth.❞

Marconi glimpsed the future in a moment, a future of communication between nations, continents, and even the vast reaches of outer space.

Section 1

Advances in Technology and Communication

Focus Questions

- **How did the development of new sources of power lead to technological advances?**
- **What inventions improved communications in the late 1800s?**
- **What was the importance of the internal combustion engine?**

Beginning in the early 1800s, manufacturers increasingly applied the findings of science to their businesses, thus generating new industrial growth.

Paris Exposition Poster

In 1889 the French held a spectacular exposition in Paris to celebrate the hundredth anniversary of the French Revolution. In its many buildings, the exposition featured examples of the tremendous industrial progress that had been made during the 1800s. To celebrate the exposition, the French newspaper *Le Figaro* published a special supplement, using this poster as its cover. The famous Eiffel Tower soars in the background. At the time, the tower was the tallest structure in the world. It stands as a monument to the engineering skills and achievements of the 1880s.

The 1889 exposition made extensive use of electric lighting, then a great novelty. At night the lower part of the Eiffel Tower and the surrounding fountains were lit, creating a spectacular show. People from all over the world traveled to Paris to see the splendor of the exposition.

The exposition contained thousands of exhibits. The Gallery of Machines housed an exhibit of 16,000 machines developed during the Industrial Revolution. The exposition provided a preview of the technology that would be increasingly important in everyday life in the 1900s.

Today people continue to flock to world's fairs and other shows that, like the 1889 exposition, highlight technological advances.

The application of scientific solutions to industrial problems resulted in (1) the development and use of new sources of power, (2) inventions that provided rapid communications over long distances, and (3) the creation of new products and materials and the improvement of old ones.

Electricity

As industry grew during the 1800s, manufacturers continued to search for new and better power sources. In the 1870s, a tremendous new source of power—electricity—was developed.

The English scientist Michael Faraday made key discoveries about electricity in the 1820s and 1830s. From the work of André Ampère and other scientists, Faraday knew that electricity could produce magnetism. He wanted to find out whether magnetism could produce electricity. He found that by moving a magnet through a coil of wire he could generate an electric current in the wire.

Faraday concentrated primarily on exploring the nature of electricity. Others used his discovery to develop the **dynamo,** or electric generator. Driven either by a steam engine or by waterpower, the dynamo transformed mechanical power into electrical energy. This energy in turn could generate power to run machinery in factories.

English and American inventors worked on making practical use of another property of electricity that had been discovered. It was known that a current passing through certain kinds of wire caused the wire to glow. Here was a promising new source of light for streets, homes, and factories. Electric lightbulbs were first produced in the 1840s, but they burned out in a matter of minutes. In 1879 American inventor Thomas Edison made a bulb that glowed for two days before burning out. After further improvements, electric lighting gradually replaced other methods of illumination over the next several decades.

To make electricity practical, it had to be transmitted efficiently from the place it was generated to the place it would be used. After much work on the problem, Edison developed a successful central powerhouse and transmission system that was put into operation in 1882 in New York City and London and soon in a variety of other places.

The electrical industry grew rapidly. Waterfalls, such as Niagara Falls, were used to run huge dynamos, whose hydroelectric power was sent long distances through wires. Dams were built in many countries to provide artificial sources of waterpower.

As the large-scale production and transmission of electricity became a reality in the late 1800s, electric motors replaced steam engines in factories. Where hydroelectric power was either unavailable or too expensive, steam engines turned the generators at central powerhouses.

Communications

The development of electrical power spurred the growth of other inventions. A significant advance in the communications field occurred in the 1870s, when Alexander Graham Bell sent the human voice over a long distance by means of an electrical circuit. Bell, an American, patented his telephone in 1876. Then in 1895 the Italian inventor Guglielmo Marconi developed a way to send messages through space without wires.

Marconi's invention was based on the work of two earlier scientists, James Clerk Maxwell of Great Britain and Heinrich Rudolph Hertz of Germany. Maxwell had made a mathematical study of electricity and magnetism. In 1873 he asserted the existence of invisible electromagnetic waves that travel through space at the speed of light. In the 1880s, Hertz proved that such waves existed by transmitting and receiving them, and he also measured their length and speed.

Marconi invented instruments for sending and receiving these radio waves, as they came to be called. His wireless telegraph soon proved itself valuable for ship-to-ship and ship-to-shore communication. In 1901 he sent the first wireless message across the Atlantic Ocean.

The Internal Combustion Engine

Electricity was not the only type of power that became significant in the 1800s. The electric motor, although useful, had one significant limitation: it had to be connected to its power supply. This made it impractical as a means of moving vehicles.

Automobiles. In the late 1800s, several European inventors worked on engines that used a portable fuel supply of oil or gasoline to propel vehicles. The device was called the internal combustion engine because the combustion, or burning, of fuel took place inside a closed cylinder. (In the steam engine, combustion takes place outside the cylinder.) Pioneers in this field included Gottlieb Daimler and Karl Benz of Germany and Etienne Lenoir of France. In 1893 Charles and Frank Duryea built the first successful gasoline-driven automobile in the United States. Fifteen years later the American inventor Henry Ford produced his first commercially successful automobile, the Model T.

Airplanes. Since the 1700s, people had used balloons filled with gases lighter than air to float above

A French aviator, Louis Blériot, became famous in 1909 for making the first flight across the English Channel.

the ground. Beginning in the 1800s, inventors tried to devise a heavier-than-air machine that would actually fly. The first people to succeed in flying a powered airplane in sustained, controlled flight were Wilbur and Orville Wright of the United States. They achieved this feat at Kitty Hawk, North Carolina, in 1903.

The Wright brothers' achievement was another example of the combination of science and technology. The Wrights succeeded where others had failed because they had studied **aerodynamics**—the principles governing the movement of air around objects—and used the internal combustion engine to propel their plane through the air.

Section 1 Review

1. **Define** dynamo, aerodynamics
2. **Identify** Michael Faraday, Thomas Edison, Alexander Graham Bell, Guglielmo Marconi, Wilbur and Orville Wright
3. **Understanding Ideas** How does developing new sources of power spur the development of other types of inventions?
4. **Summarizing Ideas** Explain the importance of the telephone and the wireless telegraph.
5. **Analyzing Ideas** Why was the internal combustion engine superior to electricity for powering vehicles?

Petroleum and the Industrial Age

Petroleum—crude oil—and its products have been in use for thousands of years. Ancient Egyptians used pitch, a thick, sticky form of petroleum, to coat mummies as they prepared them for burial. Ancient Babylonians used pitch to build walls and pave streets.

Yet it took two inventions of the 1800s—the kerosene lamp and, to a much greater extent, the internal combustion engine—to create the enormous demand that has made petroleum such a crucial commodity today.

The petroleum industry is one of the world's largest. It experienced its first boom in 1859, when a retired train conductor in Pennsylvania powered a well drill with an old steam engine and struck oil. (See early wooden derrick oil field in photo.) The growth of this industry is an excellent example, however, of the interplay between technology and industry. At first kerosene was the chief product of the petroleum industry. Gasoline was seen as a useless by-product of the process and was even dumped in creeks and rivers. Around 1900, however, electric lights began to replace kerosene lamps, reducing the demand for this petroleum product. At the same time, the use of automobiles began to increase. With that development, the petroleum industry expanded rapidly.

Today petroleum powers automobiles, farm equipment, airplanes, trucks, trains, and ships, and it generates heat and electricity. Yet it is used for much more than fuel—petroleum products include detergents, carpeting, cosmetics, plastic, and fabrics.

Advances in Science and Medicine

Focus Questions

- **What progress was made in the area of biological sciences?**
- **How did advances in medicine benefit society?**
- **What advances were made in the study of atomic theory?**

The **biological sciences**—biology and genetics—deal with living organisms, as does medicine. The **physical sciences** are concerned with the properties of energy and inanimate, or nonliving, matter.

Physical sciences include astronomy, geology, physics, and chemistry. During the 1800s and early 1900s, significant advances were made in both branches of science and in medicine.

Cell Theory in Biology

Scientists of the 1800s were as interested in explaining the nature of life as they were in exploring the nature of nonliving matter. Biologists had long been familiar with the idea of cells, the tiny units of living matter. Scientists in the 1600s examined living matter under their microscopes and saw what we now know to be plant and animal cells. Those early observers noticed that the cells of different species are of different shapes and sizes, but they did not draw any general conclusions about them.

In the 1850s, the work of the German scientist Rudolf Virchow expanded cell theory. Virchow showed that disease in living organisms was caused by changes in cells, or their destruction, as a result of some outside force or agent. From his study of cells, Virchow also concluded that every new cell must come from some older cell and that only living matter can produce new living matter. Thus by the late 1800s, scientists generally accepted the cell as the basic unit of living matter.

Lamarck's Theory of Inheritance

Cell theory did not account for the rich variety of plants and animals on Earth. Until the mid-1800s, most people believed that all the different kinds of plants and animals had been created at one time. The religious beliefs of many cultures hold divine beings responsible for creating all things on Earth.

One group of scientists, however, offered a different theory. They argued that the thousands of kinds of modern plants and animals had evolved, or developed, from common ancestors long ago. This kind of development through change is called **evolution.**

In science new theories often raise new questions. Those who believed in evolution now had to explain how plants and animals had evolved. In the early 1800s, Jean-Baptiste Lamarck, a French biologist, suggested that living things changed their form in response to their environment. A giraffe, for example, acquired a long neck because it always had to stretch to eat leaves high up in trees. Such changes were then passed on by inheritance to its descendants. Conversely, other characteristics might gradually disappear if they were never used. Lamarck thought that these kinds of change, continuing from generation to generation for millions of years, could have produced present-day plants and animals out of the first bits of living matter.

Lamarck's theory did not become a part of modern biology because it was later largely disproved. However, it influenced other scientists, among them a British biologist named Charles Darwin.

Darwin's Theory of Evolution

Charles Darwin had spent nearly 30 years studying plant and animal life. In 1859 he published his theory of evolution in a book called *On the Origin of Species by Means of Natural Selection.*

Darwin began with a well-known biological fact: no two creatures are exactly alike, not even offspring and their parents. He combined this fact with the ideas of Thomas Malthus. Malthus believed that as a result of natural dangers and constraints, including a limited food supply, there were always more creatures born than could survive. Therefore, Darwin

Charles Darwin gathered most of the material for his theory of evolution during a 5-year surveying expedition off the coast of South America and the Pacific Islands. Upon his return to England, he spent 20 years writing his theory of evolution.

reasoned, in any generation some creatures will survive and some will perish. Those who survive will, in general, be those whose characteristics are best adapted to the existing environment. This idea is often called the survival of the fittest, or natural selection. The strongest survivors will live to produce offspring, who will then repeat the process and tend to possess the advantageous traits of their parents. In this way, Darwin theorized, one could explain the evolution of all forms of life from earlier forms.

Darwin's theory inspired a great deal of scientific activity. It motivated other scientists to gather evidence to try to either prove or disprove it. They looked for evidence in fossils as well as in the study of living organisms. The theory of natural selection was especially controversial, however, for two reasons. First, it stated that human beings developed from other animals, an idea many found offensive. Second, many people thought that it contradicted the story of Creation in the Bible.

Genetics

Darwin left an important question unanswered: Why were the offspring not exactly like their parents? Unknown to Darwin, Gregor Mendel, a monk in Austria, had been gathering evidence that would answer this question. Mendel founded **genetics**—the study of the ways in which the inborn characteristics of plants and animals are inherited by their descendants. He did much of his research in the 1850s and 1860s, although other scientists did not learn about it until later.

Mendel worked in a quiet monastery garden, where he bred pea plants. He mated tall plants with short plants, which produced not medium-sized pea plants but all tall plants. Then Mendel fertilized these tall offspring with their own pollen and was surprised to find that they produced a mixed generation of both short and tall plants. In some way, the characteristic of shortness had been hidden in the tall plants.

From his experiments, Mendel concluded that inborn characteristics were not necessarily blended or mixed together. Instead, he believed, they were all inherited as if they were separate particles. In some cases a trait could be carried but not expressed. For example, tall plants could carry and pass on to the next generation the particles that would cause shortness.

The Fight Against Disease

Remarkable breakthroughs in medicine accompanied the advances in science and helped prolong human life. Until the late 1800s, as many as 50 percent of the people born died within the first five years after birth. Disease killed more people than did wars, famines, or natural disasters. Little was known about the causes of disease. Scientists had seen bacteria under the microscope as early as the 1600s but had not suspected their connection with disease.

Edward Jenner. Smallpox was one of the most dreaded diseases of the time. Periodically, it swept through cities in epidemics. Edward Jenner, an English physician, made a thorough investigation of smallpox in the late 1700s in the hope of finding a way to prevent it. He learned that milkmaids who had once had cowpox (a disease similar to smallpox but much milder) did not get smallpox even during an epidemic. After years of experimenting, Jenner developed a safe technique for vaccinating people to prevent smallpox. (The principle of inoculation was very old—it had been known in India many centuries earlier. However, as practiced in Europe at the time, it involved inoculating people with human smallpox

What If?

Vaccines
In 1796 Edward Jenner developed a vaccine effective against smallpox. If the smallpox vaccine and vaccines effective against other diseases had been available earlier, society might be different in what ways?

bacilli. The procedure was dangerous and sometimes even fatal.) In 1796 Jenner made a vaccine from the fluid in cowpox sores and scratched it into the skin of a boy's arm. The boy developed a mild case of cowpox but quickly recovered. When the boy was later exposed to smallpox, he did not contract it.

Louis Pasteur. Jenner had developed a method of preventing smallpox through vaccination, but he did not know the scientific principle that made it work. This principle came to light in the late 1800s through the work of the French chemist Louis Pasteur. He identified small microorganisms called bacteria.

Louis Pasteur became known for discovering the process called pasteurization, which involves heating liquids and foods to high temperatures to kill bacteria.

Science Fiction

Storytellers since the time of the ancient Greeks have enjoyed imagining that people are capable of breaking the laws of nature and gaining fantastic strength or powers. They have also imagined amazing machines and mythical figures with magical abilities. In a sense, the spirit of discovery expressed in the scientific and industrial ages—and in new theories about the structure of the universe—was reflected as well in a type of literature that we today call science fiction.

Since the time of the Scientific Revolution, literary fantasies have often taken a special form inspired by the achievements of science. A favorite subject of science fiction has been space travel. The great scientist Johannes Kepler, who played a major part in the revolution in astronomy during the 1600s, wrote a book called *The Dream*. In it Kepler imagined his mother flying to the moon on a broomstick. This book created problems for his mother, for it was used as evidence that she was a witch. Although not strictly within the realm of science fiction, Kepler's work is an extremely imaginative description of life in space.

Stories similar to today's science fiction were popular in the 1700s and 1800s. The French philosopher Voltaire imagined a visit to Earth by an enormous native of the star Sirius. The English novelist Mary Wollstonecraft Shelley imagined a medical student named Victor Frankenstein, who created a living monster out of a corpse. In the late 1800s, the French writer Jules Verne wrote a series of stories about incredible journeys—in a balloon, on a rocket, and in a submarine. In the late 1800s, the English novelist H. G. Wells imagined a machine that could stop time. He also imagined Martians invading Earth.

In more recent times, much of science fiction—in films as well as books—has dealt with life on other worlds in space. However, the basic theme has remained the same: fantastic people or creatures who can do things that normally are impossible. By showing us the impossible, science fiction tries to teach us something about the limits of our lives.

Jules Verne illustration: "A Trip From the Earth to the Moon" (1865)

Still from "War of the Worlds"

The Museum of Modern Art/Film Stills Archives

Satellite circling Earth

Until Pasteur's time scientists believed that certain living things, including bacteria, sprang to life out of nonliving matter. This process was called spontaneous generation. Pasteur's experiments showed that bacteria reproduce like other living things and travel from place to place in the air, on people's hands, and in other ways.

Pasteur learned that bacteria are responsible for many phenomena. For example, some bacteria cause fermentation, turning grape juice into wine or making milk sour. In the 1860s, Pasteur developed a process of heating liquids to kill bacteria and prevent fermentation—a process that was named **pasteurization** in his honor. He also determined that some bacteria cause diseases in animals and also in humans. These harmful bacteria are called germs or microbes.

During the 1870s, Pasteur experimented with the germ that causes anthrax, a disease which is often fatal to both animals and humans. He produced a vaccine containing weakened anthrax germs, which he injected into animals. The vaccine prevented them from catching the disease. Pasteur determined that when weakened germs enter the body, the system builds up substances called antibodies to fight them. These antibodies remain in the body and are strong enough to kill the more deadly germs if exposure to them occurs. Thus Pasteur showed why Jenner's smallpox vaccine had been effective.

Pasteur used this same technique in fighting rabies, a fatal disease communicated to humans by dogs or other animals infected with a certain virus (a minute organism smaller than bacteria). In the 1880s, Pasteur found a way to weaken the rabies virus. He injected the vaccine he produced into a boy who had been bitten by a rabid dog, and the boy survived.

The Development of Surgery

Through the centuries, surgery had been a desperate measure, always painful and often fatal. Surgeons usually performed only operations that could be completed in a few minutes, such as tooth extractions and limb amputations. Sometimes more complicated procedures were attempted. Patients had to be forcibly held down or their senses dulled with liquor or opium.

In the 1840s, it was discovered that ether and chloroform would cause unconsciousness or deaden sensation and thus eliminate pain. Such anesthetics both relieved the patients' suffering and made longer operations possible.

Opium and rum were used for deadening pain until physicians of the 1800s discovered anesthetics such as nitrous oxide, ether, and chloroform.

Even after anesthetics came into use, however, many patients survived the surgeon's knife only to die from infection soon afterward. Pasteur's discoveries about germs helped remedy this situation. Joseph Lister, an English surgeon, studied Pasteur's work and developed **antisepsis**—the process of killing disease-causing germs. Lister used carbolic acid as an antiseptic; milder chemicals later came into use for this purpose. Although the general use of antiseptics was adopted slowly, it eventually helped reduce bacterial infection not only in surgery but also in childbirth and in the treatment of battle wounds.

Other Medical Advances

Robert Koch, a German physician, made discoveries that reinforced those of Pasteur. In 1882 Koch isolated the germ that causes tuberculosis. He also identified the germ responsible for Asiatic cholera and developed sanitary measures, such as water filtration, to prevent disease.

The discoveries of Pasteur, Lister, and Koch were the starting point of an international fight against disease. Knowing the nature and role of bacteria and viruses, scientists could now isolate the causes of many diseases and develop vaccines for inoculation against them.

Scientists traced some epidemic diseases, including malaria and yellow fever, to germs carried in the bodies of mosquitoes and transmitted by their bite. Thus the battle against disease was extended to the mosquitoes that carried it. Bubonic plague, found to be carried by fleas on rats, was brought under control in Western countries through rat-extermination campaigns.

Scientists developed and tested many new medicines. Aspirin, which became available in the 1890s, reduced pain and fever. Insulin, developed in the 1920s, saved diabetics from certain death and enabled them to lead normal lives. Other medicines were used to treat bacterial infections. For example, Sir Alexander Fleming of Great Britain discovered penicillin in 1928. The sulfonamides, or sulfa drugs, were developed in Germany in the 1930s. Neither penicillin nor the sulfas, however, came into wide use until the 1940s.

Atomic Theory

According to modern atomic theory, all matter in the universe consists of very small particles called atoms. The arrangement and structure of these atoms and their chemical combinations with each other account for the different characteristics of the materials that make up our world.

We can trace the beginnings of atomic theory, as we can many other scientific ideas, back to ancient Greek philosophers such as Democritus. For many centuries, however, this was only one of several philosophical theories about physical reality. During the Scientific Revolution of the 1500s and 1600s, people began to accept atomic theory as part of science, although neither experimental proof nor mathematical demonstration yet supported it.

John Dalton, an English chemist and schoolteacher, was the first scientist to obtain convincing experimental data about the atom. In 1803 he outlined a method for "weighing" atoms. After studying the ratios of elements in various gases, Dalton assigned an arbitrary weight of 1 to the lightest element, which is hydrogen. Dalton then expressed the weights of all of the other known elements in proportion to it.

During the 1800s, many scientists explored the paths opened up by Dalton, learning much about the atom. In 1869 the Russian chemist Dmitry Mendeleyev (men·duh·LAY·uhf) produced the first workable classification of the elements. Somewhat modified, Mendeleyev's periodic table is a familiar feature of today's chemistry textbooks.

Modern atomic theory originated in the study of chemistry. However, it soon became part of physics—the science of matter and energy—when scientists studying heat and gases explained their findings with a new theory about atoms in motion. In the 1800s, some scientists began to think of heat as the result of the motion of a substance's atomic particles. In a cold substance—ice, for example—the atoms move relatively slowly. In a hot substance—such as scalding water—the atoms move much more vigorously, even colliding with one another. When water boils, the atoms move extremely fast, and the water turns into a gas—water vapor.

The Structure of the Atom

In 1895 the German physicist Wilhelm C. Röntgen (RENT·guhn) was sending electricity through a vacuum inside a glass tube. He noticed that a fluorescent substance on a table nearby glowed brightly when the electric current was switched on in the tube. Röntgen immediately concluded that the tube was sending out a new form of ray. Soon he discovered that the rays penetrated many substances, including human skin and tissue, and could leave an image on a photographic plate. Because he did not know what caused this powerful penetrating radiation, Röntgen named the rays X rays. X rays became an important diagnostic tool in medicine, and their existence raised new questions about the physical world.

The English physicist J. J. Thomson probed further into the nature of matter. In 1897 he discovered the electron, a tiny particle that has a negative electrical charge. Thomson found that an electron was more than 1,000 times lighter than the smallest known atom, and he theorized that all atoms contained electrons. Therefore, subatomic particles (that is, particles inside atoms), rather than the atoms themselves, must be the true building blocks of all matter in the universe.

While most physicists reluctantly accepted the electron's existence, Pierre and Marie Curie, a French husband-and-wife team of chemists, provided new evidence that atoms were not the simple, indivisible particles pictured by earlier scientists. The Curies experimented with the elements uranium and radium. They found that the atoms of these elements constantly disintegrated and released energy on their own. This process is called **radioactivity.** Elements that disintegrate and release energy in this way are called radioactive elements.

Ernest Rutherford of Great Britain combined Thomson's ideas about electrons with the Curies' discovery of disintegrating atoms in a new theory of the atom. Rutherford maintained that at the center of the atom lay an extremely small and relatively heavy core, or nucleus. Electrons whirled in circular orbits around the nucleus. When Rutherford bombarded the nucleus with heavy particles from radioactive elements, he found that it was made up of positively-charged particles, which he called protons. With the discoveries of Thomson, the Curies, and Rutherford, scientists no longer thought of the atom as a solid piece of matter.

Later scientists modified Rutherford's description of the atom. Rutherford had thought in terms of two subatomic particles—electrons and protons. However, his successors discovered first another particle in the nucleus of atoms, the neutron, and eventually discovered many more elementary sub-atomic particles.

Planck and Einstein

In 1900 the German physicist Max Planck disproved the then-common belief that energy was continuous and that it could be divided into any number of smaller units. Planck proved that energy could be released only in definite "packages," which he called *quanta* (the plural of **quantum,** the Latin word for "how much"). Planck's **quantum theory** formed the basis for a completely new approach to the study of matter and energy.

In 1905 Albert Einstein, an extraordinary young German scientist, published four papers that revolutionized physics. In his first paper, Einstein examined some of the basic concepts of mechanics and tried to prove the existence of atoms. An earlier scientist had observed that pollen dust suspended in water moved in seemingly inexplicable ways. Einstein found that the movement of the pollen dust could be explained as the result of atoms hitting it.

In his second paper, Einstein extended Planck's quantum theory to describe the nature of light. Planck believed that light was a continuous wavelike phenomenon. Einstein used mathematics to show that light can also be described as a cascade of minute particles of energy.

In his third paper, Einstein developed the **special theory of relativity**. He concluded first that no particles of matter can move faster than the speed of light. He also maintained that motion can be measured only relative to some particular observer. From

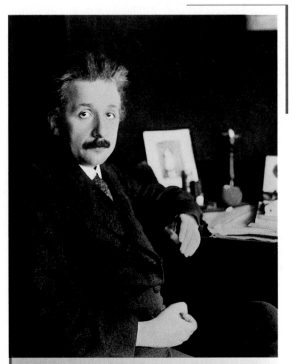

Albert Einstein, who had been a professor of physics at universities in Switzerland, Prague, and Germany in the early 1900s, was invited to join the Institute for Advanced Study in Princeton, New Jersey, in 1933.

this he claimed it does not make sense to speak of absolute motion, space, or time.

A brief fourth paper by Einstein developed the equation $E = mc^2$. According to this equation, E (energy) equals m (mass) multiplied by c^2 (the speed of light squared). This formula means that a small amount of mass can be transformed into a tremendous amount of energy.

Einstein's theories overturned long-held ideas. Isaac Newton and the scientists who followed him had thought of the universe in terms of three dimensions: length, breadth, and depth. They believed that gravity forced all particles of matter to move toward one another. Now Einstein's theory of relativity declared that all events occur not only in the three dimensions of space but also in a fourth dimension—time. This four-dimensional system Einstein called the space-time continuum. Gravity, he said, is not a property of matter but rather a property of the space-time continuum.

The theories of Max Planck and Albert Einstein paved the way for other important work. For example,

Niels Bohr, a student of J. J. Thomson, applied quantum theory to the study of the structure of atoms. He discovered that the behavior of atoms revealed information about their structure.

Section 2 Review

1. **Define** biological sciences, physical sciences, evolution, genetics, pasteurization, antisepsis, radioactivity, quantum, quantum theory, special theory of relativity
2. **Identify** Charles Darwin, Robert Koch, Sir Alexander Fleming, John Dalton Dmitry Mendeleyev, Wilhelm Röntgen, Pierre and Marie Curie, Max Planck, Albert Einstein
3. **Contrasting Ideas** Explain how Lamarck's theory of evolution differed from that proposed by Darwin.
4. **Evaluating Ideas** In what ways did Gregor Mendel's research strengthen the theories of Charles Darwin?
5. **Analyzing Ideas** How did the research of Edward Jenner, Louis Pasteur, and Joseph Lister benefit society?
6. **Summarizing Ideas** What were Einstein's major contributions to physics?

Section 3

Social Sciences in the Industrial Age

Focus Questions

- **What social sciences developed in the 1800s?**
- **What new ideas were introduced in the study of human behavior?**

During the 1800s, interest in a new field of study, the **social sciences**, grew rapidly. The social sciences are those branches of knowledge that scientifically study people as members of society. The social sciences deal with many subjects—economics, political institutions, history, and relations among people. The idea of making the study of these subjects objective and factual—of treating them like sciences—was new in the 1800s.

Political Science and Economics

The study of politics dates back to the Greek philosophers Plato and Aristotle. Later it was the subject of such thinkers as Machiavelli, Locke, and Rousseau. In the 1800s, the study of politics became known as political science, and writers tried to study law and government in the scientific manner of physicists and biologists.

Another social science, economics, had already been well developed in the work of Adam Smith and others. However, not until the later 1800s did economists begin to follow the practice of scientists by collecting and arranging statistics in order to test their theories.

History

Like political science, the study of history dates back to the Greeks. Views of history, however, also underwent change in the 1800s. Influenced by nationalism, many scholars wrote histories detailing the accomplishments and glories of their native countries. In addition, historians increasingly based their writings on the systematic study of original materials and the careful organization of facts. They began a massive search for evidence of the past in documents, diaries, letters, and other sources. New interpretations of history began to emerge.

One new trend in history was the study of all the people in a society. Here a writer of the 1700s proved influential—the French philosopher Voltaire, who was noted for his attention to social and intellectual history. His works inspired many historians to concentrate less on wars and great leaders and more on the study of ordinary people and how they lived. Another trend, influenced by Darwin, was the interpretation of historical events in terms of evolution.

Archaeology and Anthropology

Archaeology, the scientific study of human culture through the artifacts left behind, became a separate field of study in the mid-1800s. It was in the 1800s that scientists learned how old Earth was and how long humans had lived on it. Archaeologists found prehistoric cave paintings in Spain and France. They found remains of Egyptian, Sumerian, and Assyrian cultures and used excavation techniques to determine the sequence of cultural developments in such ancient cities as Troy and Mycenae.

Anthropology is the study of different societies, both of the past and of the present. Anthropologists in the 1800s began to explore the continuities in the attitudes of human societies and in the way people relate to one another. The British anthropologist E. B. Tylor adopted the German term *kultur* to describe the set of beliefs and behaviors that a society shares. Tylor discussed this concept in his book *Primitive Culture* (1871), in which he looked at religion as it evolved in all human cultures.

James George Frazer, another British anthropologist, took this approach further in his book *The Golden Bough* (first published in 1890). Frazer compared the customs of different societies and tried to show links between those societies in magical beliefs, religion, and attitudes toward authority. The study of similarities and differences among various societies has remained a major interest of anthropologists.

Sociology

Sociology—the study of human relationships in society—also first appeared in the 1800s. The writings of the French philosopher Auguste Comte greatly influenced this branch of the social sciences. Comte argued that the study of society should follow scientific methods by using objective facts and avoiding personal interpretations.

Photography by Egyptian Expedition, The Metropolitan Museum of Art

Tutankhamen's tomb remained preserved for more than 3,000 years, until Howard Carter excavated it in 1922. A room in the tomb with treasures is shown here.

In the 1800s, sociologists became particularly interested in adopting the theories of the biological sciences. Herbert Spencer, for example, used the concept of evolution as the basis for studying human communities. As you have read, Darwin claimed that nature "selected" certain individuals—those most fit to survive—and allowed others to die. In his works *Social Statics* (1851) and *Principles of Sociology* (1876, 1882, 1896), Spencer applied this theory of natural selection to society, coining the phrase "survival of the fittest."

Spencer thought that human society, like the plant and animal worlds, had evolved from lower to higher forms through natural selection.

"The individuals best adapted to the conditions of their existence," he wrote, "shall prosper most, and the individuals least adapted to the conditions of their existence shall prosper least. . . . Pervading all Nature we may see at work a stern discipline which is often a little cruel that it may be very kind."

The application of Darwin's theory to society came to be known as **social Darwinism**. It led to the conclusion that those who had acquired wealth and social standing had done so because of their superior abilities. Poverty, on the other hand, supposedly proved that people or groups were unfit. This view came to be seen as simplistic, however, as social problems grew more severe and society became more complex. Consequently, social Darwinism lost much influence.

Psychology

Psychology, another new science of the 1800s, studies the human mind—how it works and how it affects behavior. Psychology's origins can be traced back to the works of Greek thinkers. Because psychology did not involve experimentation, most people considered it a branch of philosophy. However, in the mid-1800s, a number of scientists began to approach psychology as an experimental science like biology.

Pavlov. Darwin's theory of evolution had a strong impact on the new science of psychology. Among other things, it influenced psychologists to study animal behavior and to apply their findings to humans. Perhaps the most famous of these early experimenters was the Russian physiologist Ivan Pavlov.

In the 1890s, Pavlov discovered the conditioned reflex. Psychologists had long known that certain behavior was automatic. A child does not have to be taught to pull his or her hand away from fire but removes it automatically. In the same way, a dog does not have to be taught to salivate, or water at the mouth, when eating food. Psychologists call this kind of involuntary response a reflex action.

By experimenting with dogs, however, Pavlov proved that an animal could be conditioned, or taught, to have certain reflex actions. First, he offered food to a dog. The dog salivated. Second, he rang a bell each time the food was presented to the dog. The animal salivated, evidently associating the sound of the bell with food. After many repetitions, Pavlov offered no food to the dog but rang the bell. The dog salivated. It had been conditioned to salivate when it heard the bell. As a result of his research, Pavlov believed that all habits, even mental activity, constitute a series of connected conditioned reflexes.

Freud. In the early 1900s, Austrian physician Sigmund Freud (FROID) developed a revolutionary explanation of human behavior. Freud introduced the concept of the unconscious—the mental processes of which a person is unaware—as a determining factor in human behavior.

Freud had hypnotized certain mentally disturbed patients. He found that under hypnosis the patients could remember past experiences that they otherwise could not recall. Freud believed that these early experiences had led to their illness. He treated his patients by gradually bringing the disturbing memories, fears, and conflicts back to the level of consciousness. To do this, he studied their dreams and encouraged them to talk about whatever came into their minds. Then he interpreted these dreams and thoughts to show what lay beneath them in the unconscious mind.

Freud believed that troubled patients had unknowingly forced unpleasant experiences into the unconscious. To cure such patients, it was necessary to make them aware of these experiences again. Freud called this process of revealing and analyzing the unconscious **psychoanalysis**. He discussed his theory fully in the book titled *A General Introduction to Psychoanalysis*, published in 1910.

Some psychologists challenged aspects of Freud's theories. However, much of his basic theory and method forms the foundation of modern **psychiatry**—the study and treatment of mental illness.

Freud's concepts were also extremely influential on several of the other social sciences. Sociologists, anthropologists, and political scientists adopted aspects of the Freudian perspective, seeing certain

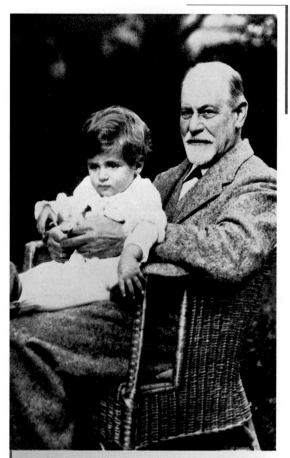

Sigmund Freud's pioneering work in psychoanalysis had a great influence on art, literature, and education.

social behaviors, cultural attitudes, and structures of authority as generated by unconscious psychological needs and motivations.

Section 3 Review

1. **Define** social sciences, social Darwinism, psychoanalysis, psychiatry
2. **Identify** E. B. Tylor, James George Frazer, Auguste Comte, Herbert Spencer, Ivan Pavlov, Sigmund Freud
3. **Analyzing Ideas** How did the study of politics, economics, and history change in the 1800s?
4. **Summarizing Ideas** What did the studies of anthropologists show?
5. **Understanding Ideas** What contributions did Pavlov and Freud make to the understanding of the human mind?

Society and Culture in the Industrial Age

Focus Questions

- **What factors led to the rapid growth of population in the 1800s?**
- **What were the causes and effects of the growth of public education?**
- **What new leisure and cultural activities developed during the 1800s?**

During the 1800s, improvements in medicine, sanitation, and food storage and distribution led to an increase in population. For example, Europe's population grew from about 200 million in 1800 to double that number by 1900. In the United States and Europe, the rate of population growth was highest in the regions where industrialization advanced most rapidly. At the same time, education became available to more than wealthy and middle-class children, and more people engaged in cultural and leisure activities.

Emigration

As the population in Europe grew, it also became more mobile. Large numbers of people moved across national boundaries and oceans to foreign lands. Such movements of people away from their homelands are called **emigrations.** The largest emigrations were from Europe to North and South America, Africa, Australia, and New Zealand.

Like so many other changes, these movements to other lands intensified after 1870. Between 1870 and 1900, more than 10 million people left Europe for the United States alone. This was one of the greatest mass movements of people in human history.

Many people fled from countries with poor economic conditions, such as Ireland and Italy. Other people, such as Jews, Armenians, and Slavs, fled oppression and discrimination.

Within Europe itself, large numbers of people moved to the areas of greatest industrialization in northern and western Europe, where rapid industrialization had created a great demand for factory labor. Higher wages in these countries attracted people, and steamships and trains made travel safer and more affordable.

The Shift to the Cities

As the population increased, changes in agriculture, industry, and transportation produced another striking result—the rapid growth of cities. While employment opportunities on farms declined, the developing industries located in or near cities offered new jobs. The factory system became the greatest spur to city growth.

Many early factories were located in already established cities, which then grew tremendously. The population of Manchester, England, for example, expanded from 18,000 in 1772 to 303,000 in 1851. When factories were built in rural areas, cities grew up around them. City living became the way of life for more and more people.

Before the Industrial Revolution, the vast majority of people lived in rural areas or in small villages. By 1900, however, in many nations, more people lived in or near cities than in the countryside. In Great Britain, about 10 percent of the population lived in cities in 1800. By 1921 that figure had grown to 80 percent. Similar changes took place in other countries. In 1800 not a single city in the Western world had a population of 1 million. Yet only 100 years later, cities such as New York, Paris, Berlin, and London each had more than a million inhabitants.

Sanitation and Public Order

European and American cities of the 1800s differed significantly from cities today. People got their daily water supply from public fountains because houses did not have running water inside. The water in fountains came from polluted rivers, which no one knew how to purify.

Until very late in the century, cities did not have sewers. Neither public nor private garbage collection companies existed, so people dumped garbage on the streets. In cities, smoke from the factories added to the bad smells from sewage and garbage. Thus large cities were foul-smelling, disease-ridden places.

After the 1870s, the situation began to change. Technological advances made possible many improvements such as iron pipes, flush toilets, and water systems. Cities installed closed public sewers and piped water into homes. City governments passed laws requiring better heating systems and better construction of buildings. Governments also installed street lights and paved roads.

The governments of the growing cities also found they needed a new kind of law enforcement. Police officers had to patrol streets to prevent robberies,

Ellis Island in New York Harbor served as a major immigration station, receiving approximately 17 million people into the United States between 1892 and 1943.

direct crowds safely, and protect the lives and property of city dwellers.

In 1829 Sir Robert Peel, a leader of the House of Commons, organized a permanent police force for the city of London. This force was responsible for maintaining order and making sure that people obeyed the law. The London police were nicknamed **"bobbies"** after Peel's first name, Robert, and are still called that today. Other major cities soon followed London's lead and established police forces.

The Development of Suburbs

As cities grew and became more crowded, their boundaries expanded to include surrounding areas. In addition, people moved outside cities to new areas called **suburbs**—residential areas on the outskirts of cities. In the United States, suburbs connected to the city by streetcar and ferry transportation began to develop in the early 1800s. Later in the century, they developed along railroad and horse-drawn bus lines. Families lived in the suburbs, where there was less crowding, noise, and dirt, but their working members journeyed each day to jobs in the city.

Suburbs began to spread quickly during the mid-to-late 1800s, as more and more cities established public transportation systems. At first ordinary working people could not afford the fares of trains and horse-drawn buses. Only employers, managers, merchants, and professionals enjoyed these transportation luxuries. They could afford to live fairly long distances from work, in the new suburbs, while factory workers had to live within walking distance of their jobs. In time, however, lower fares made it possible for more people to ride trolleys or other public transportation to work.

Improvements in Diet and Food Storage

Science and technology combined to produce better methods of preserving and transporting food. Pasteurization was one important step. So was refrigeration, which also retards the growth of bacteria. Refrigerators appeared in the late 1800s. They later became an indispensable household feature in many industrialized countries. Refrigerated railroad cars were first used around 1850 to transport meats, fruits, and vegetables. These developments helped make a balanced diet available year-round.

Scientists also learned more about the relationship of food to health. In the early 1900s, biologists discovered the importance of vitamins and minerals in the diet. Diseases resulting from vitamin deficiencies, such as beriberi and rickets, were soon wiped out in the more industrialized regions of the world. Life expectancy as well as population increased.

Growth of Public Education

To many people, the ideas of the American and French Revolutions about liberty, equality, and representative government made it important to provide education for all citizens. In the years following these events, both France and the United States took steps to establish public school systems.

There was some resistance to this idea from people who believed that the cost of education would result in increased taxes. As the years went by, however, other factors encouraged the development of free public education, schooling free of charge for all, regardless of social class. Industrialists wanted literate workers as well as more engineers, scientists, and skilled technicians. Other people believed that state-sponsored schools, rather than private ones, were necessary to develop patriotic citizens. Military leaders wanted educated soldiers for their armies. Many ordinary people believed that education would improve their children's chances for a better life.

After 1870 governments in western Europe and the United States began to pass laws making some form of education both universal—available to all children—and compulsory. In some countries, the government provided only elementary education. In others the government also funded secondary, or high school public education. In the United States, many public school systems were expanded to include kindergarten for young children and state universities for advanced study. New subjects, especially the sciences, were added to the existing curricula, and vocational and technical training were also introduced. Teachers had to take special courses that prepared them to teach new subjects.

In European nations, the central governments established and controlled schools. In the United States, where local governments were stronger, the individual states established schools and set standards. Local school districts administered schools and levied taxes to support them.

For the most part, children of the lower classes attended school only as long as the law required them to attend. Then they went to work to earn money to help support their families. Middle-class children, on the other hand, went on to secondary school and often went on to college.

Education for Women

During the 1800s, a great deal of debate focused on education for women. Some people argued that most educational courses were either unsuitable or unnecessary for women. Others insisted that education for women was important because it made them better wives and mothers. Still others said that women should have equal opportunity in every area of life, including training for careers outside the home.

Toward the end of the 1800s, elementary education for girls was included in the provisions many countries passed guaranteeing education for all. However, opportunities for secondary education were limited. In the United States, Great Britain, and France, high schools for girls emphasized foreign languages, literature, history, and home economics. Boys, on the other hand, studied sciences, mathematics, and philosophy as well as classics, history, and literature.

Some people objected to these differences. The Englishwoman Emily Davies, for example, urged her government to improve women's education sufficiently to allow women to attend the universities. In 1865 she said:

"We are not encumbered [burdened] by theories about equality and inequality of mental power in the sexes. All we claim is that the intelligence of women, be it great or small, shall have full and free development. And we claim it not specially in the interest of women, but as essential to the growth of the human race."

Few colleges admitted women as students during the 1800s. Consequently, people who believed that women should have the opportunity to receive a university education opened colleges for women. In the United States, Mary Lyon founded the Mount Holyoke Female Seminary in 1837. This school later became Mount Holyoke College. In Great Britain, Girton College opened in 1869, and Newnham College opened in 1871. Today these colleges are part of Cambridge University.

The Effects of Education

The spread of education had many positive results. People became better informed about current issues and took an active interest in a variety of government activities. Because more people could read, greater quantities of newspapers, magazines, and books were published for people of all ages.

Newspapers, which were not widely read before 1800, became especially popular and important. During the 1800s, they expanded their coverage to include politics, foreign affairs, and art and science. To attract readers, the editors also included weekly stories by famous authors, such as Émile Zola and Charles Dickens.

Some newspapers advocated a particular political position. They supported or criticized the policies of one political party or one government figure or another and often featured humorous political cartoons.

To expand circulation, newspapers lowered prices. Publishers used advertising as a way of increasing income, attracting readers, and keeping prices low. New technology, such as the linotype, which set type by machine instead of by hand, and the electric-powered rotary press, improved printing processes. The invention of the telegraph made it possible for reporters to convey news quickly. Newspapers could send reporters to distant places and have them transmit stories to their home offices.

As newspapers grew, so did the number of job opportunities for journalists and editors. In the past, writing had been something that people did in addition to other work. It was not a full-time profession. Over time, however, journalism became an accepted and respected occupation. People began to view it as an opportunity for an exciting career.

Leisure and Cultural Activities

Many of today's popular forms of entertainment first developed during the 1800s. Before that time, of course, people also enjoyed concerts, plays, games, and sports. As the populations of cities grew during the industrial age, however, the numbers and variety of these activities increased. Large audiences now paid to hear professional musicians perform or to watch professional athletes compete.

Sports. People had participated in athletic events for many centuries. The rich hunted wild animals and even played a form of tennis. The poor may have organized informal games on the village common. In

Education for women was changing during the 1800s. The women in this classroom are studying subjects such as geography and science.

Winslow Homer painted this scene of a croquet game in the park in 1866. He began his career at the age of 19 as a freelance magazine illustrator.

fact, we can trace the origins of soccer, rugby, and football to a game played by villagers using an inflated pig's bladder as a ball.

During the 1800s, many games became more organized. In Great Britain, "football" (known as soccer in the United States) was among the first games to change from an informal community activity to a professional spectator sport. Rugby and American football evolved from this early kicking game.

According to legend, in 1823 during a "football" game, a young student at Rugby School in England caught a kicked ball and ran toward the goal. Although the boy had violated the rules of the game, the idea of running with the ball eventually won favor and in time led to rugby.

In the 1860s, the London Football Association drew up official rules for games called soccer and rugby, and in 1871 the association established a national competition among football clubs. By the mid-1880s in England, many soccer and rugby players were full-time athletes. Football clubs for working-class

people were created in the 1870s. By that time, in England laws granted factory workers Saturday afternoon and Sunday as rest days.

In the 1880s an American named Walter Camp (the "father of football") adapted rugby into an early form of the game known as football in the United States. Professional football leagues were established in the United States by 1920. Soccer, rugby, and football were now three sports played by amateurs and professionals and watched by paying spectators.

A sport that experienced a great boom in the 1890s in the United States was bicycling. By 1896 there were more than 500 manufacturers of bicycles. These manufacturers, like automobile manufacturers several decades later, had machine technology and assembly-line systems. A traffic code introduced in New York City in 1897 to regulate bicycle and horse traffic also anticipated codes later established for automobiles.

Baseball also became popular in the late 1800s in the United States. English children's games using a bat and ball appear to date back to the 1700s, but it was in 1845 that a written set of rules gave baseball its modern form. The game became a popular pastime for troops in the Civil War, and in the late 1860s the first professional baseball team, the Cincinnati Red Stockings, was formed. Baseball quickly grew in popularity at both the amateur and professional levels.

Concert halls, museums, and libraries. Before the 1800s, individuals and private groups sponsored most cultural activities. Musicians performed concerts in the homes of the rich or as part of religious services. Wealthy individuals and families who wanted to commemorate a family or personal event commissioned paintings and sculptures. Religious or civic organizations also commissioned artworks for display in churches or clubs.

During the 1800s, art and music became available to more people. Popular entertainment had been available in taverns in England for many years. As the urban population grew in the 1800s, however, and there was a greater demand, music and concert halls began to spring up. Music halls offered a combination of musical and comic entertainment. In the latter part of the century in the United States, a type of light entertainment known as vaudeville became popular in frontier settlements as well as urban centers. [Vaudeville, named after a valley town

La Scala, the prominent Milanese opera house, opened in 1778. It can seat more than 2,000 people.

in France where satirical songs were performed, consisted of light, often comical theatrical performances that frequently combined dialogue, dancing, pantomime, and singing.]

During the 1800s, some art collections originally displayed in private homes and churches were moved to public museums. The Louvre museum in Paris, for instance, had contained the art collections of the kings of France. In 1793, as a consequence of the French Revolution, it became a public museum. Later the museum was enlarged and acquired major works of art from all over the world.

Public libraries were opened, including the great Bibliothèque Nationale in Paris and the reading-room of the British Museum in London. In the United States, the wealthy industrialist Andrew Carnegie sponsored free public libraries in many cities.

Public parks and urban planning. Crowded cities had few places for outdoor recreation. When railroads were built, people often rode trains to the countryside. They could spend the day there, away from the congestion, noise, and dirt of city streets. Some people demanded, in addition, that city governments provide parks within cities for recreation.

By the end of the 1800s, many cities had playgrounds for children. Private lands were donated or purchased by city governments and given to the people as public parks. Large areas inside city limits—for example, the Bois de Boulogne (BWA duh boo·LOHN) in Paris and Central Park in New York City—were set aside as public parks.

Section 4 Review

1. **Define** emigrations, "bobbies," suburbs
2. **Identify** Sir Robert Peel, Walter Camp
3. **Locate and Explain the Significance** New York, Paris, Berlin, London
4. **Summarizing Ideas** Explain the improvements in city life that were made possible by new technological advances.
5. **Interpreting Ideas** Describe how changes in diet and food storage helped the population grow.
6. **Analyzing Ideas** (a) List some of the reasons for the growth of public education. (b) What positive results occurred as a result of the spread of education?
7. **Classifying Ideas** What new forms of leisure and cultural activities developed in the 1800s?

Literature, Music, and Art in the Industrial Age

Focus Questions
- **What ideas were part of the romantic movement?**
- **Who were some of the great writers, musicians, and artists of the romantic movement?**
- **How does realism differ from romanticism?**
- **What other artistic movements emerged during this time?**

Literature, music, and art reflected the dramatic social and economic developments of the industrial age. Even in their most personal statements, artists often revealed in their works a sense of the rapidly changing times and the influence of revolutionary scientific ideas.

Romanticism

Many writers of the early 1800s belonged to the artistic movement known as **romanticism,** or the romantic movement. The work of such artists appealed to sentiment and imagination and dealt with the "romance" of life—life as they thought it should be rather than as it actually was. The romantic movement was partly a reaction to the Enlightenment, the movement in the 1700s that had emphasized reason and progress. Romantics glorified emotion and instinct. They idealized nature and the golden past.

The romantic movement was also a product of the revolutions of the 1700s and 1800s. Political revolution in France had overturned the old order of society in the names of liberty and equality. So, too, romanticism overturned the formal structures that had governed literature and art in the 1700s and released a spirit of creativity and individuality.

In Great Britain, the most famous romantics were a group of young poets whose works were filled with emotion and a strong love for beauty and nature. The works of William Wordsworth, Percy Bysshe Shelley, John Keats, Lord Byron, Samuel Taylor Coleridge, and others are among the classics of literature.

Many romantic writers glorified the past, especially the Middle Ages with its castles, ladies, and chivalrous knights. For example, in *Ivanhoe*, the Scottish novelist Sir Walter Scott wrote about the days of knighthood. *The Hunchback of Notre Dame*, by French author Victor Hugo, was also set in medieval times. Alexandre Dumas told the tale of *The Three Musketeers*, who roamed France in the days of Cardinal Richelieu.

Interest in the past was related to the growing nationalism of the times. Many writers turned to folklore, songs, and the history of their own countries for their subject matter. Germany was not yet a unified nation in the early 1800s, but a great national literature arose there. The Grimm brothers collected the famous fairy tales that bear their name. This collection remains a favorite of children even today. Friedrich von Schiller wrote of liberty in *William Tell*, a drama about a Swiss hero. Johann Wolfgang von Goethe (GUHR·tuh), one of the greatest German masters of poetry, drama, and the novel, also wrote during this period. The drama *Faust*, the story of a man's bargain with the devil, is the most famous of Goethe's works.

Romanticism also influenced American writers of the early 1800s. For example, James Fenimore Cooper wrote adventure stories that idealized the American Indian and the frontier. Washington Irving produced romantic stories that were set in New York's Hudson River valley.

Romantic Music

In music, as in literature, the 1800s began with a shift to romanticism. One of the leaders of this transition was the German composer Ludwig van Beethoven (BAYT·hoh·vuhn). Beethoven brought to music some of the same aims that the British poets of his time brought to literature. He expressed his love of nature in the *Pastoral Symphony*. A call for liberty and freedom dominates his one opera, *Fidelio*, as well as the final movement of his ninth, and last, symphony. Beethoven's music arouses powerful and passionate emotions.

The romantic movement produced a great outpouring of musical composition, especially in Austria and Germany. Johannes Brahms composed powerful symphonies and concertos. Although they are classical in form, they surge with rich, intensely emotional music. Franz Schubert, Robert Schumann, and Felix Mendelssohn brought to their music the lyric quality of romantic poetry. Schubert and Schumann are especially remembered for their melodic songs, or *lieder*.

Frédéric François Chopin (SHOH·pan), a Polish-born composer who lived in France, wrote expressive and beautiful piano works. Franz Liszt of Hungary used gypsy songs and dances in some of his compositions. He also developed the tone poem, a symphonic piece based on a literary or philosophical theme that was often taken from romantic literature.

In Russia, Pyotr Ilich Tchaikovsky (chy·KAHF·skee) wrote highly emotional and melodic operas, ballet music, symphonies, and other orchestral works. Often his compositions were built around stories. Examples are the fairy tale ballet *The Sleeping Beauty*, the overture fantasy *Romeo and Juliet*, and the *1812 Overture*, which commemorates Napoleon's defeat in Russia. Tchaikovsky and, even more, other Russian composers, especially Modest Mussorgsky—known for his opera *Boris Godunov*—developed nationalistic music that emphasized Russian folk themes. As in literature, strong national feeling was an essential part of the romantic movement in music.

Perhaps the greatest Italian operatic composer of the 1800s was Giuseppe Verdi. His best works, such as *Othello* and *Aïda*, contain some of the most beautiful and dramatic music ever written for the human voice. In keeping with the spirit of his times, the stories and themes of many of his early operas were highly nationalistic. Verdi's operas inspired a generation of Italians who were not yet politically united.

In Germany the best-known operatic composer of the 1800s was Richard Wagner (VAHG·nuhr). He referred to his operas as music dramas, and in them he combined singing, music, dancing, costumes, and scenery to create intensely dramatic spectacles.

A child prodigy, Frédéric Chopin began playing the piano at the age of six.

Mary Ann Evans wrote realistic novels under the name George Eliot.

romantic interest in nature. Their work had intense color and vitality, partly because they often painted outdoors instead of working in their studios.

Romanticism in architecture expressed itself first in the so-called Gothic revival of the mid-1800s. This was an attempt to re-create the great architectural style of the Middle Ages. The British houses of Parliament as well as many American churches, college buildings, and other public structures of the time were designed in the Gothic style.

Photography
The age of photography was born when Louis-Jacques-Mandé Daguerre introduced his daguerreotype, an early type of photograph, in 1839. Photography subsequently has had a significant impact on society. In the 1800s, photographs brought the world into people's hands and showed it to them in new ways. Photographs taken by William Jackson influenced Congress to vote to make Yellowstone the first national park. Mathew Brady's Civil War photographs depicted war's grim realities. Like the novels of Charles Dickens, the photographs of Jacob Riis and others showed the lives of poor people in dramatic ways. The camera's ability to capture such scenes helped give rise to realism.

The Rise of Realism
The subject matter of much romantic literature and art had little to do with the lives of ordinary people. In the mid-1800s, writers and artists began to take a new approach. Dealing with the realities of everyday life and expressing a keen observation of social settings, this approach is called **realism.** One of the most important realists was Gustave Flaubert (floh·BAIR) of France. His novel *Madame Bovary* (1857) described with extraordinary attention to detail the life of an ordinary woman. In Great Britain, Mary Ann Evans wrote realistic novels under the name George Eliot. In *Middlemarch* (1871–1872), considered her masterpiece, describes various classes in Victorian society.

Often the realists made social and economic conditions their theme. The Russian Leo Tolstoy in his monumental novel *War and Peace* (published in parts during the latter half of the 1860s) portrayed war not as a romantic adventure but as a vast confusion of misery and death. The Norwegian dramatist Henrik Ibsen brought human problems onto the stage. His play *A Doll's House* (1879) advocated the equality of husband and wife in marriage.

Like his contemporaries, Wagner was an intense nationalist. He based many of his operas on Germanic myths.

Other composers of the late 1800s followed in the general tradition of romantic music. Gustav Mahler of Austria, for example, wrote his lengthy symphonies for huge orchestras and choruses. Other composers, however, developed new styles. Claude Debussy (deb·YOO·see) of France employed unusual harmonies and rhythms in creating musical impressions of clouds, the sea, and other aspects of nature.

Romantic Painting and Architecture
Although Germans, Austrians, Russians, and Italians dominated the music world in the 1800s, many outstanding painters and sculptors were French, Spanish, and British.

In the 1820s and 1830s, romantic painters, like romantic writers, chose subjects from the past and depicted scenes bursting with action and drama. One such painter was Eugène Delacroix (del·uh·KRWAH) of France. Landscape painters John Constable and J. M. W. Turner of Great Britain reflected the

Building History Study Skills

READ
WRITE
INTERPRET
CONNECT
THINK

Interpreting Visuals: Using Art as a Historical Document

Works of art are usually not created in isolation from society. They often reflect not only the values of the artist but those of his or her society as well. The artist may be criticizing social conventions or political practices or reflecting the values of the historical period. In such cases, by paying attention to the details and themes that the artist depicts, you can gain a better understanding of the historical period. Asking questions, such as the ones below, is an important part of viewing a work of art and helps you understand its significance.

- What is the painting telling about the politics, the society, or the people of the historical period?
- To what extent is the artist reflecting or criticizing the society?
- To what extent is the painting a document?

How to Use Art as a Historical Document

To use art as a historical document, follow these steps.

1. Identify the historical period in which the work of art was created.
2. Determine the theme of the painting.
3. Connect the theme to the historical period.
4. Indicate whether the artwork reflects or criticizes the society, and explain how it does so.

Developing the Skill

Study Honoré Daumier's painting, *The Washer-woman* (right). What is it saying about working-class people and the kinds of lives that they lead?

Daumier rebelled against the romantic tradition in art and sympathized with the working class. Instead of imagining the past or musing about nature, Daumier's art reflects social realities. The Industrial Revolution created an urban working class that labored long and hard. The theme of *The Washerwoman* is the dignity and humanity of working people. The painting sensitively portrays poor, working people as having strength and dignity; harsh working or living conditions do not prevent their humanity from showing through.

Is there a message in this painting? Daumier's painting is telling us about the social effects of the Industrial Revolution. Daumier is realistically portraying hardship and struggle by showing the heavy bundle the woman carries and the posture of both figures. These are not people to pity, however. Instead, the artist portrays the individual humanity and strength of his subjects.

Practicing the Skill

Visit a local art museum or look in an art history book to find a modern painting. Study the painting carefully so that you can interpret what the artist is saying. Using the steps above, try to determine how the work of art could be used as a historical document.

To apply this skill, see Applying History Study Skills on page 261.

With *Le Moulin de la Galette,* Pierre-Auguste Renoir gives us a fleeting glimpse of people dancing and talking during a concert at an outdoor café in 1876.

In the United States, one form of realism was **regionalism**—the portrayal of everyday life with attention to how it was lived in particular locales. Examples are Mark Twain's novels *The Adventures of Tom Sawyer* (1876) and *The Adventures of Huckleberry Finn* (1884), with their earthy and humorous depictions of life along the Mississippi River.

Toward the end of the 1800s, a number of writers called **naturalists** carried realism even further. They described the ugly and sordid aspects of everyday life, attempting to screen emotion and opinion from their writings. The French novelist Émile Zola was a leader of this approach. He wrote as if he were a scientist objectively studying and carefully recording all human activities. Although people objected to his frankness, his exposure of shocking conditions of, for example, miners in his novel *Germinal* helped bring reform. Another realist was the British novelist Charles Dickens, who often wrote about the poor people of London.

In painting, the kind of realism that portrayed people and everyday life in the industrial age characterized the works of the French artists Gustave Courbet (koor·BAY) and Honoré Daumier (dohm·YAY). Another kind of "realism" was attempted by a group of painters who are known as **impressionists**.

Impressionist painting flourished first during the 1860s and 1870s in France. Impressionist painters tried to give vivid impressions of people and places as they appeared at a particular moment and in a particular light. To do this, the impressionists carefully studied light and color. They stopped motion and showed subjects from unusual, new perspectives. They experimented with small patches of different colors placed side by side to create shimmering effects. Claude Monet (moh·NAY) and Pierre-Auguste Renoir (ren·WAHR) were leading impressionist painters. Schools of impressionism also flourished in the United States and England.

The Metropolitan Museum of Art, H. O. Havemeyer Collection, Bequest of Mrs. H. O. Havemeyer, 1929. (29.100.370) Photograph © 1981 The Metropolitan Museum of Art

Edgar Degas, best known for his works of dancers, admired the human form and produced faithful renderings of it in oils, pastels, and bronze. Shown is Degas's "Little Fourteen-Year-Old Dancer."

Experiments in Art Forms

Like writers and musicians, painters and sculptors often rebelled against the materialism and mechanization of an industrial world. There was less nationalism in art than in literature or music. In painting and sculpture, there was much intensely individualistic experimentation. In the late 1800s, for example, there was the aesthetic movement in England. With a belief in "art for art's sake," this movement did not require art to be religious, political, or educational.

Paul Cézanne's landscapes and still lifes emphasized the forms and shapes of his subjects. He began to move beyond surface appearances to explore the abstract qualities of color and design. This shift away from showing recognizable, realistic scenes, introduced by Cézanne, influenced other artists who are often collectively termed postimpressionists.

One such artist was Paul Gauguin (goh·GAN). Gauguin, who left Europe to live in Tahiti, stressed color and simple, flat shapes in his paintings. Henri Matisse painted many decorative scenes of southern France. He, too, emphasized color design at the expense of realism. The Dutch painter Vincent van Gogh (van GOH) expressed intense emotions in his work by means of thick brush strokes of pure color and distorted perspectives. Edgar Degas (deh·GAH), Henri Toulouse-Lautrec (too·LOOZ·loh·TREK), and Édouard Manet (ma·NAY) all painted scenes of Parisian life in highly personal styles.

The French sculptor Auguste Rodin (roh·DAN) also broke with tradition. Some of his statues included unworked portions of the marble from which they were carved, giving his work a deliberately unfinished quality. Like many of the artists of the time, Rodin rejected expectations that art should show people, objects, and scenes as they appear in real life. The growing interest of many artists in abstract forms marked the end of the emotional strivings of romanticism and pointed the way toward the new artistic interests of the 1900s.

Section 5 Review

1. **Define** romanticism, realism, regionalism, naturalists, impressionists
2. **Identify** Sir Walter Scott, the Grimm brothers, Johann Wolfgang von Goethe, James Fenimore Cooper, Ludwig van Beethoven, Pyotr Ilich Tchaikovsky, Giuseppe Verdi, Gustave Flaubert, Mark Twain, Émile Zola, Paul Cézanne, Auguste Rodin
3. **Summarizing Ideas** Briefly explain the romantic movement of the early 1800s and give examples of romanticism in each of the following: literature, music, art, and architecture.
4. **Contrasting Ideas** How did the ideas and works of realists differ from those of the romantics?
5. **Analyzing Ideas** How did the work of Cézanne, Gauguin, and Rodin show individualism?

Chapter 7 Review

A.D. 1869
Dmitry Mendeleyev develops first workable classification of the elements.

A.D. 1800 | A.D. 1810 | A.D. 1820 | A.D. 1830 | A.D. 1840 | A.D. 1850 | A.D. 1860 | A.D. 1870

A.D. 1803
John Dalton outlines method of "weighing" atoms.

A.D. 1831
Michael Faraday produces electric current in wire.

A.D. 1859
Charles Darwin publishes *On the Origin of Species by Means of Natural Selection.*

Chapter Summary

The following list contains the key concepts you have learned about advances in technology, science, education, and the arts between 1800 and 1928.

1. In the late 1800s, the use of electricity became widespread. New inventions, such as the telephone and wireless telegraph, made rapid communication possible, and the development of the internal combustion engine helped to improve transportation.

2. Science developed rapidly during this period. In the biological sciences, knowledge of the cell, the basic unit of living matter, deepened. The theory of evolution proposed by Darwin had an enormous impact. The new science of genetics, founded by Mendel, answered many questions about biological inheritance.

3. Significant progress also was made in the physical sciences. Atomic theory became the basis for understanding matter. The brilliant work of Albert Einstein revolutionized the study of energy and matter.

4. Pasteur, Lister, Koch, and Fleming made advances in medicine. New drugs and medical techniques, such as surgery with anesthesia, were developed.

5. Those who studied the behavior of people as members of societies began to use scientific methods. Their fields of study came to be known as the social sciences and included new techniques for understanding history, politics, and economics. New social sciences included anthropology, sociology, and psychology.

6. Improvements in diet and food storage improved people's lives, while immigration to the cities changed population patterns.

7. Public education won gradual acceptance in western Europe and the United States in the late 1800s. More and more people learned to read and write. This educated audience spawned the publication of books, magazines, and newspapers.

8. The arts reflected the social and economic changes of the industrial age. In the early 1800s, many writers, musicians, and artists were caught up in the romantic movement, which emphasized emotion, nature, and often nationalism.

9. In the late 1800s, romanticism gradually gave way to realism. In painting and sculpture, romanticism and realism were followed by experimental, highly personal styles.

Reviewing Important Terms

On a separate sheet of paper, match each of the following terms with the correct definition below.

a. physical sciences
b. special theory of relativity
c. social science
d. romanticism
e. biological science
f. realism
g. regionalism
h. impressionists

_____ 1. The portrayal of everyday life with special attention to how it was lived in different locales

_____ 2. Artists who painted people and places as they appeared at a particular moment and who experimented with light and color

_____ 3. Art movement dealing with the realities of everyday life

_____ 4. Area of study dealing with living organisms

_____ 5. Area of study dealing with people as members of society

_____ 6. Artistic movement that emphasized sentiment and imagination

_____ 7. Theory that motion could be measured only relative to a particular observer

_____ 8. Area of study dealing with the properties of energy and nonliving aspects of nature

Developing Critical Thinking Skills

1. **Summarizing Ideas** List and describe four of the technological advances made during the last half of the 1800s.

2. **Understanding Ideas** What medical advances saved lives in the late 1800s and early 1900s?

3. **Determining Cause and Effect** What effects did population growth have on the growth of cities, and what effects did urbanization in turn have on people's lives?

A.D. 1884
Mark Twain publishes *The Adventures of Huckleberry Finn.*

A.D. 1895
Wilhelm Röntgen discovers X rays.

A.D. 1900
Max Planck develops quantum theory.

A.D. 1905
Albert Einstein develops the special theory of relativity.

A.D. 1880   A.D. 1890   A.D. 1900   A.D. 1910   A.D. 1920   A.D. 1930

A.D. 1876
• Alexander Graham Bell patents the telephone.
• Mark Twain publishes *The Adventures of Tom Sawyer.*

A.D. 1893
The first successful gasoline-driven automobile is built in the United States.

A.D. 1897
J. J. Thomson discovers the electron.

A.D. 1903
The Wright brothers make first successful airplane flight.

A.D. 1928
Alexander Fleming discovers penicillin.

---

4. **Classifying Ideas** Identify the name of the author or composer of each of the following literary or musical works: (a) *Madame Bovary;* (b) *Middlemarch;* (c) *A Doll's House;* (d) *The Adventures of Tom Sawyer;* (e) *Fidelio;* (f) *War and Peace;* (g) *Aïda.*

5. **Analyzing Ideas** How might each of the following be considered a response to industrialization: (a) romanticism; (b) realism; (c) compulsory education.

Relating Geography to History

Select a particular author, composer, or artist discussed in this chapter. Use encyclopedias or other references to find out about the area where this person lived and whether he or she traveled extensively. Then write a short summary explaining how that person's environment and the extent of his or her travel may have affected his or her contributions to literature, music, or art.

Relating Past to Present

1. To investigate medical progress during the 1900s, interview a physician, nurse, pharmacist, or public health official in your community. You may wish to include the following questions. (a) In your field, how have medical advances made during the 1800s been improved upon? (b) What do you feel has been the most significant medical breakthrough in recent years? Share the responses you receive with your classmates in a class discussion.

2. Newspapers and magazines experienced great growth during the late 1800s. Find two newspapers or magazines existing today that originated before 1928. Ask your librarian about the availability of early issues. Notice the kinds of articles and advertisements that ran when the magazine or newspaper first appeared. How do they compare with those printed today? What do the advertisements suggest about changes in society over a period of time?

Applying History Study Skills

Before completing this activity, review Building History Study Skills on page 257.

Several historical themes of the first half of the 1800s are combined in *Le Moulin de la Galette* by French painter Pierre-Auguste Renoir, shown on page 258. Renoir was an impressionist, and in this painting

he shows people at a popular café in a French city. Study the painting and answer the following questions.

1. (a) How would you define impressionism? (b) How is it portrayed in *Le Moulin de la Galette*?
2. What class of people does the painting show?
3. How does Renoir use light and color in this painting?
4. Compare *Le Moulin de la Galette* to Daumier's *The Washerwoman.* What are similarities? Differences?

internet**connect**

Section 4 of this chapter discussed the emigration of Europeans that intensified after 1870. Search the Internet through the HRW Web site for information on New York's Ellis Island. Focus on one aspect of the material, such as what immigrants experienced on their arrival, and write a short report on what you find.

GO TO: go.hrw.com
KEYWORD: SC0 Ellis Island

Building Your Portfolio

1. **Presenting an Oral Report** Using books on the history of art, such as Helen Gardner's *Art Through the Ages* (Harcourt Brace Jovanovich) or H. W. Janson's *History of Art* (Prentice-Hall), examine paintings from the romantic period. Choose one or more paintings by a particular artist. What is the subject of each painting? What do you think the artist was trying to convey? What techniques did he or she use to create the painting? In what way does this artist represent romanticism? Place your notes from your report in your portfolio.

2. **Preparing a Book Report** Writers of the early 1800s turned to nature and the past for inspiration, and their stories were often filled with adventure, romance, and heroism. Read one of the following novels and explain how it reflects the ideas of the romantic movement: Sir Walter Scott's *Ivanhoe* (Pocket Books); Rafael Sabatini's *Scaramouche* (Houghton Mifflin); Baroness Emmuska Orczy's *The Scarlet Pimpernel* (Macmillan). Place your book report in your portfolio.

The Age of Reform

TIME

A.D. **1791–1911**

A.D. **1791–1911**

3.7 million B.C.   4000 B.C.   A.D. 2100

PLACE

The British Empire, the United States, France, and Latin America

France

United States

Latin America

British Empire

Detail of painting by Everett Shinn, "The Eviction" (1904)

Significance

As the Industrial Revolution swept through Europe and the United States, an upper middle class emerged. Many members of this class believed in **liberalism***, a political philosophy grounded in the Enlightenment and the French Revolution. This philosophy advocated representative government to protect individual freedoms.

Terms to Define

liberalism	anarchists
suffrage	coalitions
Chartists	*haciendas*
home rule	*peninsulares*
suffragettes	creoles
Northwest Ordinance	*mestizos*
sectionalism	mulattoes
secede	Monroe Doctrine
total war	*caudillos*

People to Identify

Queen Victoria	Louis XVIII
Benjamin Disraeli	Charles X
William Gladstone	Louis Philippe
Fabian Society	Florence Nightingale
Lord Durham	Archduke Maximilian
Aborigines	Alfred Dreyfus
Maori	Toussaint-Louverture
the Grimké sisters	José de San Martín
Elizabeth Cady Stanton	Simón Bolívar
Lucretia Mott	Bernardo O'Higgins

Places to Locate

Ontario	Rio de Janeiro
Quebec	Haiti
Australia	Gran Colombia
New Zealand	

Chapter Theme Questions

- **Politics and Law** What might motivate people to reform society?
- **War and Diplomacy** What might happen when a nation experiences a civil war?
- **Social Relations** What factors might lead people to strive for independence?

---

*Liberalism in the 1800s differed greatly from liberalism today. For example, in the 1800s, a liberal policy might extend the vote only to educated male property owners.

F lorence Nightingale was a heroic Englishwoman who fought long-standing prejudices to make nursing more professional. During the Crimean War, under terrible conditions, she reorganized inept military hospitals into efficient, sanitary places for saving lives. The following excerpt from Cecil Woodham Smith's biography *Florence Nightingale* describes the admiration and respect she earned from the doctors and fighting men who observed her during the war.

❝*In January, 1855 there were 12,000 men in hospital and only 11,000 in the camp before Sebastopol; and still the shiploads came pouring down. It was, Miss Nightingale wrote, 'calamity unparalleled in the history of calamity.'*

In this emergency she became supreme. She was the rock to which everyone clung...

Her calmness, her resource, her power to take action raised her to the position of a goddess. The men adored her...The doctors came to be absolutely dependent on her.❞

The voices of women struggling for recognition of their rights through political reform began to be heard in the 1800s.

Liberal Reforms in Great Britain and Its Empire

Focus Questions

- **What types of reforms were instituted in Great Britain in the 1800s and 1900s?**
- **What were the achievements of Benjamin Disraeli and William Gladstone?**
- **How did Great Britain respond to the desire of its colonies for greater self-government?**

During the 1800s, individuals who believed in liberalism were very active in politics. In Great Britain and in other parts of the British Empire, for example, liberals helped enact a number of reforms aimed at protecting political and civil liberties. Some reforms extended the right to vote to working men and eventually to women. Another abolished slavery, which had denied human and civil rights to people of African descent.

British Reforms of the 1800s

Great Britain was one of the first European nations to sharply limit the power of the monarchy. The Glorious Revolution of 1688 made Parliament the real ruler of the country. (See Chapter 3.) Great Britain became a limited constitutional monarchy with executive power vested in a cabinet headed by the prime minister.

Voting restrictions. Theoretically, the House of Commons represented all British people. The voters of each borough, or local district, elected members of the House of Commons. However, the right to vote and the right to hold public office were severely restricted in several ways: (1) Only property owners and a few other privileged men could vote. (2) People voted in the open rather than in private. Unscrupulous people could ensure "cooperation" by bribing or intimidating voters. (3) In some boroughs, nobles, already members of the House of Lords, controlled the choice of a representative. (4) Antiquated boundaries of boroughs, or election districts, did not reflect population distribution at all. (5) Only men who owned substantial property could be elected to the House of Commons. (6) Catholics, Jews, and Dissenters (non-Anglican Protestants) could not hold political office.

The Reform Bill of 1832. As time went on, the middle class and the workers began to demand reforms. At first the upper classes resisted, not only because they wanted to retain power but also because they feared political change might bring about a reign of terror as it had during the French Revolution. Then, from 1793 to 1815, British involvement in wars with France delayed action on reform.

After Napoleon's defeat, Britain, like continental Europe, experienced a period of reaction that threatened even long-established civil liberties such as the right of *habeas corpus*. Reformers who once might have tried to gain the king's support could find no help because of George III's instability and George IV's inattention. However, in 1829, near the end of George IV's reign, one piece of reform legislation passed. The Catholic Emancipation Act permitted the election of Roman Catholics to Parliament if they recognized the Protestant monarch as the legitimate ruler of Great Britain.

By 1830 the middle class and laborers demanded more extensive reforms. Several times the House of Commons passed bills that gave more people the right to vote and reapportioned election districts more fairly. Each time, the House of Lords refused to pass the bill. When the Whigs came to power in 1830, Prime Minister Charles Grey recommended to William IV that he create as many new lords as necessary to give the bill a majority in the House of Lords. William at first refused, but he gave in when governmental chaos loomed. To avoid the threat of a new majority of lords with reformist intentions, the House of Lords grudgingly passed the bill in 1832.

The Reform Bill of 1832 took seats in the House of Commons away from the less populated boroughs and gave seats to the new industrial cities. It also lowered property qualifications for voting. Although no real change in the composition of the House of Commons resulted, the middle class created by the Industrial Revolution now had a voice in government, and this new class gained parliamentary power.

The Whig Party, which had forced passage of the Reform Bill of 1832, had the support of these new voters. Joining with some Radicals and more liberal members of the Tories, the party became the Liberal Party. The Tory Party of the large landowners, who had opposed the reforms of 1832 and hesitated to go farther, became known as the Conservative Party.

Social and economic change. Vital social and economic developments took place after 1832. In 1833 Parliament passed an act that provided for the abolition of slavery in British colonies. Now freedom from slavery was law throughout the British Empire.

The Liberal Party soon forced the adoption of other reforms. A modest first step toward free public education was taken in 1833, giving financial support to private and church schools.

The Liberal Party also helped repeal the unpopular Corn Laws. For many years, the Corn Laws had set high tariffs on imported grain. By raising prices on imports, the Corn Laws protected expensive British grain against competition from cheaper foreign crops. British landowners benefited because they could sell their grain at high prices. High prices, however, harmed British workers, who had to buy grain products or starve. In 1846, after a bitter fight, Parliament repealed the Corn Laws. Grain could be imported into Britain free of tax. The repeal of the Corn Laws represented Britain's first step toward free trade.

Chartism. Beginning in the 1830s, a group known as the London Workingmen's Association began its

Building History Study Skills

READ
WRITE
INTERPRET
CONNECT
THINK

Reading About History: Understanding Ideology

An ideology is a body of ideas on which a particular system is based. In the 1800s in Europe, the two conflicting ideologies were liberalism and conservatism. Liberalism was based on the political philosophy of the French Revolution and the Enlightenment. Those who followed the ideology of political liberalism believed in a constitution that protected individual rights. The role of the government was to protect these rights. An economic liberal believed in the freedom of the individual to pursue economic gain without government interference.

On the other hand, conservatism was the ideology of the old order that was hostile to the French Revolution and the Enlightenment. Those who followed the ideology of political conservatism believed in a traditional government system that upheld the privileges of the upper classes. Economic conservatives believed in the government's role to manage the economy so that the state would prosper.

Understanding an ideology helps you determine the extent to which a person's position is based on his or her belief in an ideology rather than specific facts. For example, to what extent is a newspaper's support for a presidential candidate determined by ideology?

How to Understand Ideology

To understand an ideology, follow these steps.
1. Define the ideology. Find out what a person's ideology is by determining how he or she views change and the role of government.
2. Make connections. How does the ideology affect the person's viewpoint or the development of the person's argument?
3. Categorize the ideology. Is it economic or is it political?

Developing the Skill

The cartoons on the right were printed during the debate over the extension of suffrage to the workingman in 1867 in Great Britain. The argument sharply divided liberals and conservatives. Study the cartoons to determine the ideology of each of the cartoonists.

The political cartoon at the top reflected the liberal ideology. The cartoonist depicted the workingman as an angel carrying his tools, while

drinking holy water from a font in a church. The cartoonist probably favored change and supported the government's extension of the right to vote because he drew the worker in such a positive way.

The political cartoon at the bottom expressed the conservative ideology. In this cartoon, the workingman was portrayed as a slovenly drunkard. This cartoonist's sympathy with the conservative ideology is apparent by the negative way in which he depicted the workingman. The cartoonist apparently opposed change because he would not have wanted the government to extend voting rights to the undeserving worker.

Practicing the Skill

Find a political cartoon in your local newspaper. By using the skills listed above, attempt to determine the political ideology of the cartoonist.

To apply this skill, see Applying History Study Skills on page 291.

Queen Victoria's reign, the longest in British history, was marked by industrial progress at home and colonial expansion abroad.

Disraeli and Gladstone

King William IV died in 1837 with no male heirs, so his 18-year-old niece, Victoria, became queen. She was interested in government but interfered little, allowing her prime ministers a free hand. Victoria reigned from June 1837 until January 1901, a 63-year period so distinguished in British history that it is known as the Victorian Age.

Two notable prime ministers—Benjamin Disraeli and William Gladstone—dominated the political arena between 1868 and 1894. Disraeli led the Conservative Party and served twice as prime minister. In addition to enthusiasm and a mastery of politics, Disraeli had an intense interest in foreign affairs and expansion of the British Empire.

Disraeli's first term as prime minister lasted only a few months. He first became prime minister when the Earl of Derby resigned in February 1868, but his party was defeated by the Liberals in a general election that was held that year. During his second ministry, from 1874 to 1880, Britain gained control of the Suez Canal, and Queen Victoria became the empress of India.

William Gladstone led the Liberal Party and served four terms as prime minister. He was devout, cautious, and formal. Gladstone concerned himself first with British domestic and financial matters. Under his leadership, Parliament attempted additional reforms, many of which went into effect.

reform work. Reforms such as universal male **suffrage**, or voting rights; the secret ballot; and payment for members of Parliament, so that even workingmen could afford to enter politics, were proposed by this group in a document called the People's Charter. Those who advocated these reforms became known as **Chartists**.

The Chartists presented petitions to Parliament in 1839, 1842, and 1848. The Chartists' popularity was based on very real grievances from the working class, but Chartists could not agree on aims and tactics. Many people believed such movements threatened the very foundations of society, and in 1848 British authorities worried that revolution might occur in Great Britain, as it had elsewhere. The economy improved, however, and unrest subsided.

Despite the failure of the Chartist movement, Parliament eventually adopted most of the reforms its members advocated. Workers continued to seek voting rights, and more and more who favored an increasingly democratic government joined them.

In 1867 Parliament passed a second reform bill with more sweeping reforms than the first. It almost doubled the number of those who could vote. By lowering property qualifications, the second reform bill extended the vote to most urban industrial workers. However, vast numbers of people in the lower classes, such as agricultural workers, could not yet vote, nor could women.

Benjamin Disraeli, Queen Victoria's favorite prime minister, served two terms, the first in 1868 and the second from 1874 to 1880.

Gladstone became prime minister in 1868. One of his achievements as prime minister was the passage of the Education Act of 1870, which created a national elementary education system. This act allowed children of the working classes to receive an elementary education for a small fee. Elementary education became free in England in 1891.

In 1872, under Gladstone's leadership, Britain adopted the secret ballot. Now a man could vote as he chose without fearing consequences because someone disapproved of his politics. The secret ballot also reduced bribery, which had been common, and protected workers in cities from intimidation by bosses.

In 1884 Gladstone and the Liberals pushed through Parliament the third reform bill, which gave the vote to most agricultural workers. In the following year, 1885, the Redistribution Bill divided Britain into electoral districts approximately equal in population. Although the bill did not achieve complete equality in representation, it was an important step in this direction.

The Irish Question

One area in which Liberals proved unsuccessful concerned the "Irish question," whether Ireland should rule itself or be ruled by England. Liberals favored **home rule** for Ireland. Conservatives were determined not to yield power. In 1801 the Act of Union had joined Ireland and Great Britain to form the United Kingdom of Great Britain and Ireland. The Act of Union disbanded Ireland's Parliament, leaving the Irish with little representation in the British Parliament. In addition to resenting scant parliamentary representation, the Irish people—mostly Catholic—resented their taxes supporting the Anglican Church.

The Irish hated British rule, especially absentee landlords, who owned much of the land. Policies designed to help British industry hurt Irish agriculture, and the poor suffered. In the mid-1800s, the potato crop failed and famine swept Ireland. Those who could fled to the United States. Gladstone tried unsuccessfully to get home rule bills passed. After much turbulence, Conservatives, in order to "kill Home Rule with kindness," agreed to some land reforms in the 1890s, and tension temporarily eased.

British Reforms of the Early 1900s

Social reform accompanied political reform. During the late 1800s and early 1900s, the labor union movement grew stronger in Great Britain. Socialism, too, attracted many followers.

Social reforms. In 1884 a group of intellectuals founded the Fabian Society, an organization aimed at improving society through socialist ideas and education. The Fabians, whose members included playwright George Bernard Shaw, began working through established political parties. In 1906 they helped workers, frustrated by both Liberals and Conservatives, found the British Labour Party.

In 1905 the Liberal Party returned to power. Under Herbert Asquith, who was the prime minister from 1908 to 1916, Liberals adopted extensive social welfare legislation. Laws provided for old-age pensions, health and unemployment insurance, and efforts to reduce unemployment. To pay for these benefits, Parliament raised taxes.

Changes within Parliament. The budget of 1909 increased taxes for the wealthy. The enraged House of Lords opposed the budget, and Liberals took steps to decrease the power of the lords. The Parliament Act of 1911 took away the lords' powers to veto tax and appropriation bills and allowed them only to delay

---

Reforming the British Parliamentary System

1829	Catholic Emancipation Act permitted Roman Catholics to be elected to Parliament.
1832	Reform Bill of 1832 redistributed seats in Parliament and lowered property qualifications for voting.
1867	Reform Bill of 1867 further lowered property qualifications, almost doubling electorate.
1872	Secret ballot was adopted.
1884	Reform Bill of 1884 gave vote to most farmworkers.
1885	Redistribution Bill divided Britain into approximately equal electoral districts.
1911	Parliament Act of 1911 took away power of House of Lords to veto parliamentary bills.
1928	All British women over age of 21 were granted voting rights.

Hunger and Despair: The Irish Potato Famine

One of the most wrenching changes of the 1800s was not the result of a reform movement. A terrible famine devastated Ireland in the 1840s. Millions left the country, an emigration that changed the social fabric of Ireland and the United States forever.

In 1845 a previously unknown fungus struck the potato crop, the mainstay of Irish agriculture. Plants that looked fine one day wilted the next or yielded potatoes that quickly rotted. The blight returned, year after year, and in the wretchedly poor country, hunger led to weakness, which led to epidemic and starvation. Unable to work or to pay their landlords, thousands of Irish families were evicted from their homes to die in the streets and countryside. Children, as in all famines, suffered most: "their limbs fleshless…their faces bloated yet wrinkled and of a pale greenish hue." Famine and disease probably killed between 1.1 and 1.5 million people.

Few in the British government cared. Some charitable efforts were made, and Sir Robert Peel urged policies to help the Irish, but relief was often too late. Distrust was so deep that some Irish refused British corn, fearing that the unknown food was poisonous.

Those who were able to do so left Ireland. More than 2 million people left between 1845 and

Irish immigrants sail to the United States, c.1848

1855, doing anything they could to raise the money needed for passage.

In America life was hard. Starving, often without skills, and facing both religious and cultural prejudice, the Irish were treated poorly. Exploited by employers and slumlords, women often became servants, and men became laborers.

Nevertheless, the Irish eventually became a potent force in American labor and politics. Many saw themselves as involuntary exiles and vowed to return to Ireland someday. Though they had left their native country they never abandoned their love of it, and pride in the ancestral homeland endures today.

---

passage of other bills. Many nobles bitterly opposed the act, and the House of Lords passed it only after George V, who had become king in 1910, threatened to create enough new Liberal lords to pass it.

Within a month after the passage of the Parliament Act of 1911 a law was passed that gave members of the House of Commons a salary of 400 pounds a year, which was a good salary for the time. It meant that a person without an independent income could afford to serve in Parliament.

Women's voting rights. Since the late 1880s, many women in Great Britain had demanded the right to vote. Led by energetic and outspoken women such as Emmeline Pankhurst and her daughter, Christabel, they were called **suffragettes** because they wanted suffrage for women. Suffragettes petitioned Parliament

and demonstrated, becoming increasingly disruptive and determined. Many people thought that compromise might be reached earlier, but woman suffrage was delayed until after World War I.*

Changes Within the British Empire

As Great Britain instituted social and political reforms, changes occurred within other parts of the British Empire as well. Settlers in the British colonies of Canada, Australia, and New Zealand benefited from the liberal policies being enacted in Great Britain.

---

*In 1918 a bill gave the right to vote to women over the age of 30 if they or their husbands owned property. In 1928 another bill granted all British women over the age of 21 the right to vote.

Canada

Canadians were dissatisfied with British rule in the early 1800s. British settlers in Upper Canada (part of what is now Ontario) wanted more self-government, and French Canadians in Lower Canada (part of what is now Quebec) resented British control.

During the 1830s, a business depression, unemployment, and crop failures led to uprisings in both Lower and Upper Canada. French Canadians tried to establish an independent French republic, and British Canadians sought greater freedom from British officials. Both revolts failed.

The Durham Report. In 1838 the British government sent a new governor-general, Lord Durham, to Canada to try to settle disagreements between English- and French-speaking Canadians. A member of the Liberal Party, Durham was given broad powers to reform Canada's government.

The Growth of Canada, 1791–1912

Learning from Maps In 1869 and 1870, Canada purchased many provinces and territories from the Hudson's Bay Company.

Movement What cities did the Canadian Pacific Railway connect?

This photograph shows Victoria, the capital of British Columbia. Founded in 1843, the territory was named after Queen Victoria and has remained quite British in character.

What If?

Great Britain and the American Revolution
What if Great Britain had not experienced the American Revolution? How might its policies have been different with regard to governing other colonies?

In 1839 Lord Durham submitted a report to Parliament with basic recommendations that governed later British colonial policy. Britain was anxious not to repeat in Canada the mistake that had cost it the American colonies. Remote government had failed to treat colonists as full citizens and was too far away to grasp unique circumstances or enforce central authority. Lord Durham suggested that if Great Britain granted self-government to colonies such as Canada, the colonies would remain in the empire.

Lord Durham also recommended that Canada be united. In 1840 the British Parliament did this with the passage of the Act of Union. Effective in 1841, British Upper Canada and French Lower Canada were united. A parliament was created in which French and British regions had equal representation. Between 1846 and 1848, the British expanded the power of Canada's Parliament and granted self-government to the Canadian people.

The British North America Act. The union of Upper and Lower Canada did not work well in any respect. Each region was suspicious of the other, and their equal strength in Parliament resulted in deadlock. A solution came in 1864, however, when the eastern colonies of New Brunswick, Nova Scotia, and Prince Edward Island considered forming a federal union. Delegates from Canada and the colonies met in the city of Quebec. They recommended a plan of federation, which the British Parliament approved as the British North America Act of 1867. The act created the Dominion of Canada with the provinces of Ontario, Quebec, Nova Scotia, and New Brunswick.

By the terms of the British North America Act, each province had a legislature to deal with local affairs. The federal Parliament, which dealt with national issues, met at the Dominion capital, Ottawa, Ontario. This government, far more powerful than the provincial legislatures, was a parliamentary democracy with a cabinet based on the British model. Liberal and Conservative political parties in Canada resembled those in Great Britain. The party in power appointed the prime minister, who had much the same role as the British counterpart.

In 1869 and 1870, Canada purchased huge areas of land, including the present Northwest Territories, from the Hudson's Bay Company, a private trading company. Some residents, a multiracial group called métis, resisted, arguing that the Hudson's Bay Company did not own the land to sell. As a concession to the métis, Canada created the province of Manitoba in the southeast portion of the area. This also served to strengthen Canadian control of the area, reducing the worry that the United States might attempt to annex the region. British Columbia and Prince Edward Island also became provinces during the 1870s, bringing the total number of provinces in the Dominion to seven.

Canada continued to expand westward, much as the United States was doing. The completion of the Canadian Pacific Railway opened western Canada to immigration. (See map on page 269.) As a result, two more provinces—Alberta and Saskatchewan—joined the Dominion in 1905.*

*In 1949 Newfoundland and its dependency, Labrador, became the tenth province of the Dominion of Canada.

The discovery of gold in the Klondike region led to the development of northwestern Canada. During the late 1890s, thousands of prospectors rushed to the area. The Klondike gold rush brought so many people that the Yukon Territory was organized in 1898.

Australia

Australia is a huge island, a continent in itself. Yet for centuries it remained unknown to the Western world. European explorers who sailed into the Pacific Ocean in the 1500s missed it entirely. The Dutch sighted the continent in the early 1600s and named it New Holland but considered it too poor to colonize. Captain James Cook, a British sailor on a scientific expedition for the navy, sailed along Australia's eastern shore in 1770. He named the region New South Wales, because of its resemblance to southern Wales, and claimed it for Great Britain.

Before the American Revolution, Great Britain often sent prisoners to North America. After the loss of the American colonies, the British began sending convicts to Australia. The first shiploads arrived in New South Wales in 1788, and soon the convicts founded the town of Sydney on the southeast coast. Free settlers with land grants arrived shortly afterward. Convicts who served their sentences and gained freedom could stay in Australia and own land. However, these two groups did not always get along.

The early 1800s became a lawless period in Australia. Clashes among immigrants, ex-convicts, and gangs of escaped convicts called bushrangers occurred often. The original Australian people, the Aborigines, were pushed into the interior.

In 1829 the British claimed the entire continent of Australia. By 1836 the colonies of Tasmania, Western Australia, and South Australia had been organized.

Australia and New Zealand, c. 1800s

Learning from Maps Britain established colonies across the Australian continent.

? Place What island did the British settle off one part of the southern coast of Australia between the 140°E and 160°E lines of longitude?

Kapunda Coppermine in South Australia

The colony of Victoria was formed in 1851, and the discovery of gold that year brought a flood of immigrants. Queensland was formed in 1859. (See map on this page.)

The Australian colonies developed independently of each other. They modeled their legislatures after the British Parliament, except that members of both the upper and lower houses were elected. (In New South Wales, members of the upper house were appointed.) In the 1890s, the colonies began to consider forming a federal union to protect against territorial expansion by European nations. The colonies united in 1901 to create the Commonwealth of Australia, a self-governing part of the British Empire.

The native Aborigine population was dramatically reduced by the settlement of Europeans. Many Aborigines died as the result of new diseases introduced to the area. Ideas of racial superiority also led to brutal violence against native peoples, and many whites wanted the Aborigines to simply die out. Similar attitudes shaped immigration policy, which prohibited immigration by non-Europeans. This "white Australia policy" antagonized many nations, particularly those in Asia.

As Australia's economy grew, trade unions and the Labor Party influenced Parliament to adopt social legislation. Parliament passed bills establishing old-age pensions, compulsory arbitration of labor disputes, and wage-fixing boards, among others.

New Zealand

Dutch sailors, and later Captain Cook, sighted the islands of New Zealand, southeast of Australia. Private companies developed the islands in the 1820s and 1830s. In 1840 a treaty with Maori (MOW·ree) chieftains, the native rulers of the islands, established British control. In 1852 Britain's Parliament gave New Zealand a constitution, and the islands became a self-governing colony.

Disputes over land brought British settlers into conflict with native inhabitants, and several Maori wars took place in the 1860s and early 1870s. In other respects, the development of New Zealand resembled that of Australia. The settlement of Europeans caused a decline in the Maori population—from both disease and warfare—as it had in the Australian Aborigine population. Gold was discovered in 1861, bringing new waves of immigrants. In 1893 New Zealand became the first country in the world to grant the vote to women. In 1907 New Zealand joined the British Empire as a dominion.

Section 1 Review

1. **Define** liberalism, suffrage, Chartists, home rule, suffragettes
2. **Identify** Queen Victoria, Benjamin Disraeli, William Gladstone, Fabian Society, Lord Durham, Aborigines, Maori
3. **Locate and Explain the Significance** Ontario, Quebec, Australia, New Zealand
4. **Understanding Cause and Effect (a)** Why was the Reform Bill of 1832 necessary in Great Britain? **(b)** How did the bill affect the British government?
5. **Comparing Ideas** Compare the views and achievements of British prime ministers Benjamin Disraeli and William Gladstone.
6. **Analyzing Ideas** In what ways did Great Britain influence the reform movement in its colonies?

Expansion and Reform in the United States

Focus Questions
- How did the United States expand its territory across the North American continent?
- What issues contributed to the Civil War, and what were its effects?
- How did the United States change in the period after the Civil War?

When the United States ratified its Constitution in 1788, the new nation consisted of 13 states along the Atlantic coast and additional territories that extended to the Mississippi River. The country's population was about 4 million people, most of whom lived in farming communities in the eastern part of the nation.

The nation was born during a time of European turmoil, and most Americans wanted to avoid European affairs and develop their country. They did this so successfully that, during the next 100 years, the territory of the United States grew to almost four times its original size, and its population increased to about 60 million. By 1900 the United States took its place among the great nations of the world.

Territorial Growth

By the mid-1800s, the United States had completed its territorial expansion across the North American continent to the Pacific Ocean. By the end of the century, it had also become an imperial power, acquiring territory in the Pacific and Caribbean regions.

The Northwest Territory. The land bounded by the Appalachian Mountains, the Ohio and Mississippi Rivers, and the Great Lakes was known as the Northwest Territory. States that had originally claimed this area turned the land over to the United States when they ratified the Articles of Confederation. Once the nation had won independence, hundreds of settlers pushed across the mountains into the Northwest Territory. In 1787 Congress passed the **Northwest Ordinance** to provide some form of government for the settlers.

The Northwest Ordinance of 1787 guaranteed that people who lived in territories would have rights equal to those who lived in the original 13 states. It

---

provided that the Northwest Territory would be divided into states and admitted into the Union on an equal basis with existing states. When a territory had 5,000 adult males, it could form a legislature to govern the territory. Then, when a territory had 60,000 inhabitants, it could adopt a constitution and apply for statehood.

Many people left their homes on the Atlantic seaboard to settle the Northwest Territory. These settlers knew that the territories would be admitted to the Union as states. Of the 10 new states that were added to the United States between 1791 and 1836, 6 were part of the Northwest Territory.

Completing the expansion. Many of the principles of the Northwest Ordinance were applied to new lands as the nation continued to expand. In 1803 Napoleon sold the vast territory of Louisiana (which Spain had ceded to France) to the United States. Extending westward from the Mississippi River roughly to the Rocky Mountains, the Louisiana

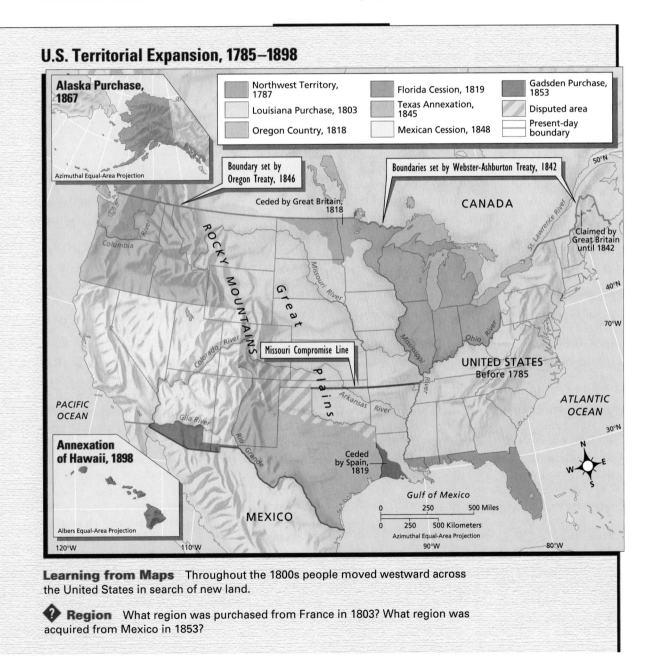

U.S. Territorial Expansion, 1785–1898

Alaska Purchase, 1867

Azimuthal Equal-Area Projection

Northwest Territory, 1787	Florida Cession, 1819	Gadsden Purchase, 1853
Louisiana Purchase, 1803	Texas Annexation, 1845	Disputed area
Oregon Country, 1818	Mexican Cession, 1848	Present-day boundary

Boundary set by Oregon Treaty, 1846

Boundaries set by Webster-Ashburton Treaty, 1842

Ceded by Great Britain, 1818

CANADA

Claimed by Great Britain until 1842

Columbia River

ROCKY MOUNTAINS

Great Plains

Missouri River

St. Lawrence River

Missouri Compromise Line

Colorado River

Ohio River

Mississippi River

UNITED STATES Before 1785

PACIFIC OCEAN

ATLANTIC OCEAN

Gila River

Arkansas River

Annexation of Hawaii, 1898

Rio Grande

Ceded by Spain, 1819

Albers Equal-Area Projection

MEXICO

Gulf of Mexico

0   250   500 Miles
0   250   500 Kilometers
Azimuthal Equal-Area Projection

120°W   110°W   90°W   80°W

50°N   40°N   70°W   30°N

N E W S

Learning from Maps Throughout the 1800s people moved westward across the United States in search of new land.

? Region What region was purchased from France in 1803? What region was acquired from Mexico in 1853?

Purchase almost doubled the territory of the United States. The United States also purchased Florida from Spain in 1819. (See map on page 273.)

In 1836 American settlers in Mexican territory south of the Louisiana Purchase declared themselves independent and established the Republic of Texas. The United States annexed Texas by treaty in 1845, and war with Mexico resulted. American victory in the Mexican War gained the Mexican Cession, a huge region that eventually became the states of Utah, Nevada, California, and parts of Arizona, Colorado, New Mexico, and Wyoming.

In 1846 a treaty with Great Britain gave the United States the Oregon Country. The states of Oregon, Washington, Idaho, and parts of Montana and Wyoming were created from this land. In 1853 the United States made the Gadsden Purchase, buying from Mexico a strip of land in what is now southern New Mexico and Arizona.

Thus by the 1850s, the young nation stretched from coast to coast and from Mexico to Canada. During the next 50 years, settlement caught up with territorial acquisition. Discovery of gold in California in 1848 led to the California gold rush and great westward migration. Cattle ranchers, farmers, and miners settled in the plains and mountains of the western United States.

Political Growth

In the early days of the United States, some states had allowed only white male property owners to vote. New states farther west imposed few property requirements. In time eastern states dropped property qualifications for male voters.

In the 1820s and 1830s, many other changes occurred. Public education became more widespread. An increasing number of political offices became elective instead of being appointive. Political candidates came to be chosen by party conventions rather than by small groups of legislators. Although voters had little say in who was nominated, more voters than ever before decided elections.

The Issue of Slavery

Although the United States had a unified federal government, **sectionalism**—rivalry among various sections of the country—plagued the young nation. During the early 1800s, three major sections emerged: the Northeast, a region of growing cities and industry; the South, an agricultural area with many farms, including large cotton and tobacco plantations;

and the West, a frontier region of small, independent farms that were located between the Appalachians and the Mississippi River.

With such different ways of life, it is not surprising that people from these sections held differing views on such subjects as federal financing of improvements, tariffs, banking and currency, and public lands. However, the issue of slavery soon became the greatest issue dividing the country.

Slavery had existed in the American colonies almost from the beginning. The United States Constitution accepted slavery but left its regulation up to the states. Each state had the power to preserve or abolish the institution of slavery.

Some people in the South believed they needed slaves to harvest cotton and tobacco, which grew well in the climate of the southern states and required intensive labor to cultivate. Thus slavery grew in the South, especially after the invention of the cotton gin made cotton a profitable crop.

A question soon arose: Should slavery be permitted in new territories? Southerners argued that Congress did not have the power to prohibit slavery in the new territories; Northerners argued that Congress did have this power. A growing number of people came to advocate the abolition of slavery altogether. Southerners were determined to preserve enough votes in the Senate to block abolition at the federal level.

Secession and Civil War

Arguments about slavery, as well as about states' rights versus the rights of the federal government, led to bitter sectional quarrels throughout the early 1800s. Southern states threatened many times to **secede**, or withdraw from the Union. Each time, compromises staved off secession. Then in 1860 Abraham Lincoln was elected president. Lincoln headed the newly formed Republican Party, which had pledged to prevent the spread of slavery into the territories.

Shortly after the election, South Carolina seceded from the Union and other southern states followed. They formed the Confederate States of America, with Jefferson Davis as president. Eventually 11 southern states joined the Confederacy.

President Lincoln, arguing that states had no constitutional right to secede, declared that the Southerners had rebelled. The United States government, he proclaimed, had a duty to suppress this rebellion. Efforts at compromise failed, and in 1861 the Union and the Confederacy began a bloody war that would last four years.

Major Civil War Battles

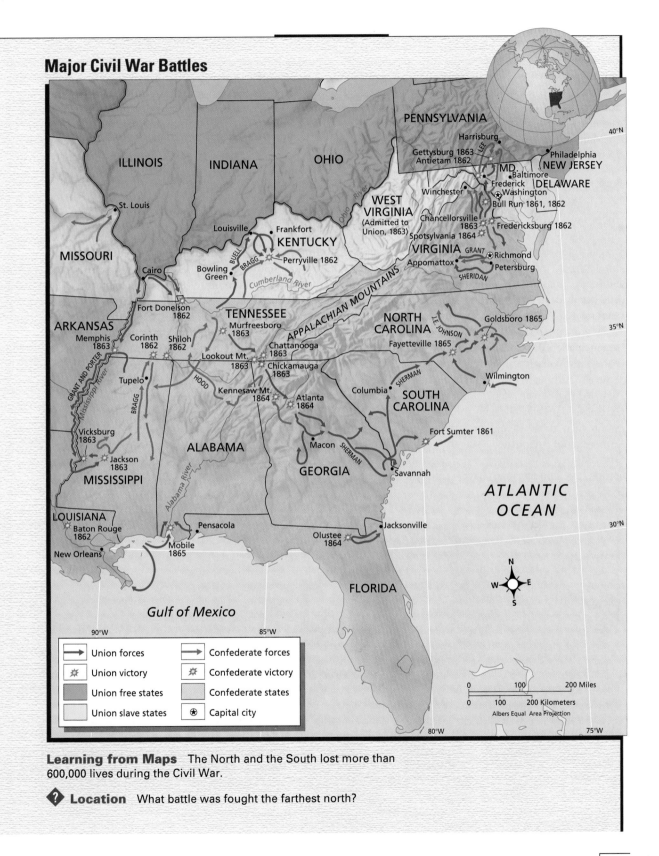

Learning from Maps The North and the South lost more than 600,000 lives during the Civil War.

❓ **Location** What battle was fought the farthest north?

The Civil War was the most costly conflict in which the United States has ever been involved. In many ways, it was also the first modern war. It introduced new and lethal devices such as the explosive shell and the Gatling gun. New strategies such as **total war**—targeting the enemy's military *and* civilian resources—were used. (See map on page 275.)

Many European nations favored the Confederacy. Industrial and commercial interests hoped the war would weaken their business competitors in the Northeast. The British needed cotton from the South and frequently aided Confederate ships by letting them use British ports. Napoleon III of France took advantage of the conflict to intervene in Mexico.

As time went on, it became clear that the agricultural South lacked the manpower, industries, and railroads necessary to defeat the North's armies. The end finally came in April 1865, when the Confederacy surrendered. The Union was preserved.

In January 1863 President Lincoln had issued the Emancipation Proclamation, freeing slaves in those parts of the country still "in rebellion against the United States." Although it had little immediate effect, it signaled that slavery would end everywhere at the end of the Civil War. Following the war, Congress passed three amendments to the Constitution. The Thirteenth Amendment abolished slavery, the Fourteenth Amendment gave former slaves citizenship and equal protection under the law, and the Fifteenth Amendment provided that the right to vote would not be denied "on account of race, color, or previous condition of servitude." Although in some areas of the country these laws were not well observed, the amendments strengthened the principle of equality before the law.

The price of preserving the Union was tragically high. The North and South together lost more than 600,000 people. Families were torn apart and the ideals of the republic damaged. Nor did freedom ease the lives of former slaves. Bitterness endured, for the war left wounds that the nation felt well into the 1900s.

A Changing Nation

The United States experienced phenomenal growth from 1865 to 1900 primarily as a result of industrialization. Cities doubled and tripled in size, and a network of railroads crisscrossed the country.

Immigration. Another important factor in this growth was immigration. For many decades people had come to the United States from England and Scotland. In the mid-1800s, a heavy wave of immigration came from two other regions: Ireland, which suffered severe potato famines, and Germany, where many people fled from revolutions in 1848.

In the late 1800s, immigration increased from southern and eastern Europe, especially Italy, Russia, and Austria-Hungary. Another great wave of immigration including people from Latin America occurred at the turn of the century.

At the Seneca Falls Convention in 1848, Elizabeth Cady Stanton (shown holding child in photo) and Lucretia Mott asked women to organize themselves and assert their rights. Their efforts launched the suffrage movement that won women the right to vote in 1920.

Woman suffrage. Many women campaigned for the abolition of slavery. Some of these abolitionists, such as the sisters Sarah Moore Grimké and Angelina Emily Grimké, began publicly to address the status of women. They insisted that equality be extended to women as well as men.

In 1848 a women's rights conference, organized by Elizabeth Cady Stanton and Lucretia Mott, was held in Seneca Falls, New York. Delegates drew up a list of demands, including suffrage for women.

In the 1890s and early 1900s, many women renewed the campaign for suffrage, skillfully employing both public opinion and the political system. In 1920, with the ratification of the Nineteenth Amendment to the Constitution, women won the right to vote.

Section 2 Review

1. **Define** Northwest Ordinance, sectionalism, secede, total war
2. **Identify** the Grimké sisters, Elizabeth Cady Stanton, Lucretia Mott
3. **Organizing Ideas** List the steps in the territorial expansion of the United States from 1787 to 1853.
4. **Analyzing Ideas** What were the issues that led up to the Civil War?
5. **Interpreting Ideas** How did immigration and the struggle for voting rights change life in the United States after the Civil War?

Revolution and Reform in France

Focus Questions

- In what ways did governmental change in France differ from reform in Great Britain during the 1800s and early 1900s?
- Who was Louis Napoleon, and how did he increase his own power in France?
- What problems faced republican France after the reign of Louis Napoleon?

The Congress of Vienna restored the Bourbon monarch, King Louis XVIII, to the throne of France following Napoleon's exiles in 1814 and 1815. Louis, who was glad to be king and unwilling to upset the situation, carried on many of the reforms established between 1789 and 1815. He accepted a constitution that limited his power, and he also established a legislature to assist in governing the country. Louis spent the nine years of his reign balancing between extremists who were determined to restore an absolute monarchy and reformers who were equally determined to further transform France into a true republic.

Charles X

When Louis XVIII died in 1824, his brother, Charles X—an ardent believer in absolute monarchy—succeeded him. As soon as Charles became king, he antagonized his subjects. First, he pledged that the government would reimburse the émigrés whose estates had been seized and sold to the peasants. This unpopular policy meant taxing all the people for the benefit of emigrant nobles, who had opposed reform or democracy in France. Second, Charles abolished most of the liberal provisions of the weak constitution his brother had accepted and tried to restore many features of the Old Regime.

Had Charles or his advisers shown any flexibility, revolution might have been avoided. However, they did not, and in July 1830, revolt spread throughout the country. Surprised by the growing hostility and unprepared to defend his regime, Charles X was forced to abdicate the throne.

The successful rebellion inspired revolutions elsewhere. In December 1830, for example, Belgians declared independence from their Dutch rulers.

Louis Philippe, the "Citizen King"

Leaders of the French revolution of 1830 wanted to be rid of Charles X, but they could not agree on the nature of government after his departure. Those favoring a republic lacked the strength to create one. Finally, all groups agreed on the choice of another king. They selected Louis Philippe, duke of Orléans, who belonged to a branch of the Bourbon family but had a record of liberal beliefs.

Louis Philippe was in a delicate position. He was a king, but an elected king. Having seen the fate of Charles X, Louis Philippe knew that he needed the support of the majority of the French people. He tried to please the people and called himself the citizen king, though he wanted more than merely a symbolic role.

The upper middle class benefited more than any other class during the reign of Louis Philippe. After the revolt of 1830, the voting population was expanded from 90,000 to 200,000 by lowering the voting age and the tax that qualified one to vote. Nevertheless, control was still firmly in the hands of the class of merchants and industrialists. Workers could not organize, and the government outlawed labor unions. High tariffs placed on imported goods benefited owners of industries because they kept foreign-made goods out of France. However, tariffs resulted in higher prices for domestic goods.

While the upper middle class generally favored Louis Philippe, he faced opposition from both monarchists and republicans. One group of monarchists wanted a direct descendant of Charles X to be king, while another group, the Bonapartists, wanted to revive Napoleon's empire. Napoleon's nephew attempted twice to take power, failed, and was sentenced to prison for life. He escaped to England.

At the other end of the political spectrum stood the republicans, who believed that France should become a republic, institute political rights, and make changes to benefit all the people. Most French workers agreed. Their lot had improved little, and they were increasingly attracted to the wealth of socialist ideas circulating at the time. Food shortages and widespread unemployment heightened discontent between 1846 and 1848.

The Revolutions of 1848

In 1848 opposition to the regime of Louis Philippe erupted into violence. Trouble began over the principle of free speech. In February opponents of the government organized "banquets" to criticize official policy (political meetings were forbidden). Louis Philippe issued a decree prohibiting the final "banquet" in Paris.

The decree sparked rioting. The disorder did not seem serious until the National Guard, summoned to restore order, joined the rioters. Although still in control of the army, Louis Philippe had a choice between violence or abdication. He, too, abdicated and left for England.

The people of Paris established a temporary government and proclaimed the Second French Republic in 1848. (The First Republic had lasted from 1792 until 1804, when Napoleon became emperor.) The most active group in the new government consisted of the urban working class, whose leaders believed in socialism. Because economic depression and widespread unemployment paralyzed France, socialist members of the government established "national workshops" to give people work.

This action marked an early instance of a modern government taking responsibility to remedy chronic unemployment in their country.

Adopting universal manhood suffrage, the Second Republic held elections for a National Assembly to write a constitution for a permanent government. When the new National Assembly met in June, conservative members in the majority voted to end the program of national workshops.

This action led to violent rioting in Paris. Fearing a widespread revolution, the National Assembly allowed army officers to assume power. For three days, Paris became a battlefield. The army crushed the rebellion and imprisoned, exiled, or executed its socialist leaders. Karl Marx, the founder of modern socialism, was among those expelled from France.

Louis Napoleon

The new constitution written by the National Assembly provided for a republican form of government, with an elected president. The president would serve a four-year term and would not be eligible for a second term. The National Assembly would be a single legislative body, consisting of representatives elected by universal manhood suffrage.

In December 1848, the Republic held its first elections. Instead of electing as president someone who had helped create the Second Republic, however, the voters overwhelmingly chose Louis Napoleon Bonaparte, Napoleon's nephew.

Louis Napoleon wanted to be more than president. He began to work for the support of various groups in France. Like his uncle, he did everything he could to gain the backing of the army. To win support from French Catholics, he helped the pope suppress an attempt in Italy to set up a republic in Rome. He assisted the Catholic Church in gaining more control over education.

The constitution of the Second Republic, however, limited the president to a single four-year term. Louis Napoleon hoped that an amendment could be passed that would allow him to run for a second term. When it became clear in 1851 that he lacked sufficient votes in the National Assembly to get the amendment, he acted on his second choice, a coup d'état. In December, 70 members of the National Assembly were arrested. Street rioting followed. Promising a vote and a new constitution, Louis Napoleon represented himself as a defender of order. He followed through with the plebiscite, a yes-or-no vote on his actions, which his uncle had employed so successfully.

The Gleaners

Artists convey messages through their choice of subject as well as their artistic style. Jean-François Millet not only rejected the popular romanticized style of his day—the 1850s and 1860s—but also used peasants and workers as his subjects.

Millet, a peasant himself, worked on the land until the age of 20, when he began studying with another artist. Understandably, then, he identified heavily with the peasant class.

Gleaners are the poorest peasants, who gather the leavings from a field after reaping. In this painting, Millet makes them appear graceful and dignified. That *The Gleaners* seems sentimental and idealized today is evidence of constantly changing tastes and values in art.

Believing in Louis Napoleon's famous name and that he actually stood for order, the people voted almost 12 to 1 in his favor.

The Second French Empire

The new constitution extended Louis Napoleon's term as president to 10 years. Although this gave him greater power, his real ambition appears to have been to restore the empire of his uncle Napoleon I.

In 1852 there was another plebiscite for yet another constitution. Following a Senate resolution to restore the empire, Louis Napoleon was elected Emperor Napoleon III. (Napoleon I had a son, who would have been Napoleon II, but he never reigned and died in 1832.)

Though Napoleon III posed as a champion of democratic rights, he limited criticism of his actions through strict censorship and exile of his critics. On the surface, the Second French Empire looked like a democracy. It allowed for a constitution and a legislature elected by universal manhood suffrage. In practice, however, the early reign of Napoleon III was a new style of absolutism. The legislature could pass only those laws proposed by the emperor. Civil liberties were reduced. Political opposition was stifled. Newspapers were censored. The government warned that any paper

criticizing the emperor or his government would be warned twice, then shut down. Freedom of speech did not exist. Some liberal professors in universities lost their jobs. For years it was impossible to organize opposition to the government.

As Napoleon III, Louis Napoleon tried to develop his empire through modernization. He helped the middle class by encouraging the development of manufacturing and railroads. At the same time, he tried to keep the favor of lower classes by setting up programs of public works that gave jobs to many people. Domestic affairs stabilized.

Problems in the Crimea and Mexico

To achieve recognition from other European rulers and to improve relations with Britain, Napoleon III involved France in a dispute with the Ottoman Empire.

Because of earlier agreements, Russia claimed the right to protect Orthodox Christians living under the rule of the Ottoman Turks. Similarly, France protected Catholics. In the 1850s, both Russia and France claimed jurisdiction over certain holy places in Palestine, then part of the Ottoman Empire. The Ottomans granted privileges to Catholics but did not do the same for Orthodox Christians. The czar demanded the same privileges for Orthodox

Florence Nightingale organized professional nursing of the wounded during the Crimean War. After the war, she was instrumental in the foundation of the Army Medical School and the Nightingale School for Nurses.

Into the valley of Death
  Rode the six hundred. . .
Cannon to right of them,
Cannon to left of them,
Cannon in front of them
  Volley'd and thunder'd;
Storm'd at with shot and shell,
Boldly they rode and well,
Into the jaws of Death,
Into the mouth of hell,
  Rode the six hundred. **"**

It took two years of fighting, with huge losses on both sides from battle and disease, for the allies to defeat Russia. France won glory but little else. Despite the dreadful carnage, the war had two constructive results. First, modern field hospitals to care for the wounded came into use. Second, Florence Nightingale established professional nursing of the wounded.

Napoleon III now turned to building the French colonial empire. In North Africa, he took advantage of a native revolt to strengthen French rule over Algeria, which had begun in 1830. In 1859 French engineers began constructing the Suez Canal in Egypt. In Asia Napoleon established French control over Cambodia, thus beginning a move into Indochina. He also tried unsuccessfully to intervene in Mexico. Beginning in 1863, French troops supported the regime of Archduke Maximilian of Austria, whom Napoleon III had installed as Mexico's emperor. Mexicans, led by Benito Juárez, overthrew and executed Maximilian in 1867.

Shortly thereafter Napoleon faced mounting pressure in France. Although he had relaxed controls on the press and the public in 1859 (over the objections of his advisers), and had undertaken other reforms, elections in 1869 showed the growing strength of the government's opponents.

The Franco-Prussian War

Napoleon III had to choose between more liberalization or more authoritarianism. He tried to liberalize, and voters approved. Meanwhile, a crisis with Prussia loomed. Prussia was working to unite all German states under its leadership. (See Chapter 22.) Napoleon opposed this unification, as did nearly all the French people, because they distrusted Prussian ambition.

Napoleon tried to prepare for a war by proposing to draft troops, but he was unsuccessful. Otto von Bismarck, head of the Prussian government, had decided that war with France would help achieve

Christians. Napoleon III opposed the Russian demand, forming an alliance with Great Britain, which feared Russian expansion toward the Mediterranean Sea.

The Ottoman Turks, backed by France and Great Britain, resisted Russian claims in the Palestine dispute. The three allies declared war in March 1854, and full-scale fighting began six months later, mostly in the Crimea, a peninsula of southern Russia.

The Crimean War has been called the most unnecessary war in history. The hostilities were marked by inefficiency and waste. The famous poem "The Charge of the Light Brigade" by Alfred, Lord Tennyson described one tragic event of the war. Some 600 English horsemen stormed needlessly across a valley and were cut to pieces by enemy fire. The following are two verses from the poem.

"Half a league, half a league,
  Half a league onward,
    All in the valley of Death
      Rode the six hundred.
  'Forward the Light Brigade!
  Charge for the guns!' he said.

German unification under Prussian leadership. To this end, Bismarck made a series of clever diplomatic maneuvers that insulted the French. In July 1870 France declared war on Prussia just as Bismarck had hoped that they would.

French defeat. From the start of the Franco-Prussian War, the French suffered disastrous defeats. Napoleon III took command of the army and was captured at Sedan. His regime could not survive.

Immediately after Napoleon's capture, the Legislative Assembly proclaimed the fall of the Second French Empire and the establishment of the Third Republic. The new government tried to defend the nation, but after a siege, Paris fell to the Prussians in January 1871, signaling the end of the war.

France Under German Domination

Bismarck drew up the Treaty of Frankfurt, dictating harsh terms to France. The treaty forced France to give up Alsace and the eastern part of Lorraine on the French-German border. France also had to pay a huge indemnity to Germany, and German troops were to occupy northern France until the indemnity was paid.

A provision of the armistice permitted the election of a National Assembly to decide whether France wanted to sign the peace treaty or to resume the war. The republicans urged renewal of the war. The monarchists took the position that France had already suffered defeat and should negotiate with the conquerors. Most of the elected delegates were monarchists—not because the French people favored monarchy but because they overwhelmingly wanted peace. The National Assembly voted to surrender.

As in the revolution of 1848, the people of Paris were strongly republican. They had fought almost alone to defend the besieged city against the Prussians and were angered by the peace terms.

In March socialists and radical republicans in Paris, supported by the National Guard, set up a municipal council to govern the city. It was called the Commune, like the Paris government established in 1792 during the French Revolution. The Communards, members of the Commune, proposed to change France. Their plans included decentralization—the shift of power from the central government to regional and local governments—separation of church and state, and other ideas consistent with socialist reform.

The French government, now in Versailles, thought it wise to disarm the Parisians. Troops sent by the National Assembly entered Paris and fought street to street against the Communards, finally destroying them in May 1871. Retreating Communards executed hostages, and government troops eventually killed or executed almost 20,000 of the Communards. The French government borrowed the money to pay the indemnity specified in the treaty, and the German soldiers left France in 1873.

Many famous buildings, such as the Tuileries royal palace shown in this photo burning, were destroyed by the Communards in the fighting of 1871 in Paris.

The Third Republic

After the fall of Napoleon III, quarreling factions in the National Assembly were unable to agree on a constitution until 1875. Finally, the assembly passed a group of laws known as the Constitution of 1875, which officially made France a republic.

The Third Republic included a president, elected by the legislature for a term of seven years. The legislature consisted of the Senate and the Chamber of Deputies. Members of the Senate were elected by an indirect system, whereas members of the Chamber of Deputies were elected by universal manhood suffrage. In many ways, the government functioned as a limited constitutional monarchy, with the legislature and a cabinet responsible for policy. Although there were many changes of government, the Constitution of 1875 stood for nearly 70 years.

During the late 1800s, France faced problems aggravated by the strongly held opinions of various factions in the legislature. One group wanted to make war on Germany in revenge for the Franco-Prussian War. Another group was hostile to Catholics. Still another backed French expansion overseas, along the lines begun by Napoleon III. The conservative republicans managed to steer a course that avoided extremes. Legislation encouraged education and legalized trade unions, but it did not really move the country toward socialism.

In the 1890s, a financial scandal rocked France. The crisis stemmed from the failure of the Panama Company, which had been formed to build a canal across the Isthmus of Panama. Ferdinand de Lesseps, the man responsible for building the Suez Canal, had been president of the company, and thousands of French people had invested in the venture. The effort failed because of misjudgment of the difficulty involved in building the canal, disease, and improper financing. Accusations of bribery against a number of legislators endangered the government.

Another threat to the Third Republic came from extremists of the labor movement; boycotts, sabotage, and strikes disrupted the economy. **Anarchists**, who believed in the abolition of all governments, waged a terrorist campaign in France and throughout Europe.

The Dreyfus case. Another serious danger to the Third Republic arose in 1894. An attempt to betray French military secrets to Germany was uncovered. A court accused and convicted Captain Alfred Dreyfus, a Jewish officer, of the crime and sentenced him to life imprisonment. However, evidence soon came to light indicating that Dreyfus had been falsely convicted.

Even so, the French army command would permit no criticism of its actions. Monarchists, many Catholics, and anti-Semites—people who dislike Jews—supported the army.

The real traitor was discovered, but the army cleared him. Then Émile Zola, a famous French novelist, wrote an open letter, "J'accuse" (I accuse), which was published in a newspaper. In the letter, Zola blamed the army command and its supporters for covering up the truth. Although many individuals responsible for the false charges against Dreyfus confessed, his name was not cleared until 1906.

The Dreyfus case led to alienation between those who had condemned Dreyfus and supported the army, and those who had supported Dreyfus's cause. The result of this case was widespread cynicism about the Third Republic.

Reform and coalition. After the Dreyfus case, French republicans planned several reforms. They took steps to end the favored position that Napoleon I had given the Catholic Church in France in 1801. The church and the state were officially separated in 1905, and France had complete religious freedom.

Rivalries among the many different political factions caused a great deal of political friction during this era. Groups ranged from monarchists on the far right to radical socialists on the far left. Major parties contained a number of "splinter groups," or smaller divisions. No one party ever completely controlled the French government. In order to get anything done, parties temporarily united to form **coalitions**, or political groups organized in support of a common cause. These coalitions, shifting and varying, nevertheless gave France a period of relative political stability between 1899 and 1905.

Section 3 Review

1. **Define** anarchist, coalition
2. **Identify** Louis XVIII, Charles X, Louis Philippe, Florence Nightingale, Archduke Maximilian, Alfred Dreyfus
3. **Contrasting Ideas** Compare the changes that took place in Great Britain and in France during the first half of the 1800s.
4. **Analyzing Ideas** How did the power of Louis Napoleon grow during his rule?
5. **Explaining Ideas** Describe France's internal political problems in the late 1800s and early 1900s.

Independence Movements in Latin America

Focus Questions

- **What was the relationship of Spain and Portugal to their colonies before 1800?**
- **How did class distinctions contribute to revolutions in Latin America?**
- **What difficulties did new countries in Latin America face after winning their independence?**

By the early 1800s, the ideologies behind the American and French Revolutions affected the political and social thinking of many Europeans. People in the Latin American colonies of Spain and Portugal were also influenced by these upheavals. In time strong movements for independence swept the whole region, from Mexico to the tip of South America.

Colonial Economy

Both the Spanish and Portuguese followed mercantilist principles in organizing their colonies. They believed they gained wealth and power at the expense of other countries and by amassing gold and silver, which they would then use to buy other goods they needed. Spain and Portugal took gold and silver from their colonies and used the colonies as markets for their own goods, cutting them off from trade with other countries. (See map on page 285.)

A system called *encomienda* (en·koh·mee·EN·dah) was introduced in Spanish colonies. Monarchs granted enormous estates to some colonists, or *encomenderos*—conquistadors, or conquerors, and court favorites. Huge land grants dotted Spanish-controlled America, from what today is California in the north to the modern-day nations of Chile and Argentina in the south. On the land, colonists formed large, self-sufficient farming estates, called **haciendas** (hah·see·EN·duhz) in Spanish America and *fazendas* in Brazil. A variety of goods were produced on these estates, such as cattle ranches, where meat and hides were produced, and sugar plantations.

As part of the *encomienda* system, American Indians were used as farm laborers, miners, or servants. The system had disastrous effects on the Indians, who were overworked and mistreated. European diseases also

Africans were imported by the Spanish and Portuguese to work as slaves on their estates, such as on this sugar plantation.

wiped out whole Indian settlements and led to a population decline of more than 90 percent in some areas. As a result of this decline and the increasing demand for labor, the Spanish and Portuguese began to import thousands of Africans as slaves.

Spanish wealth grew in the colonies. Mexico City, Lima, and other cities became centers of commerce, with imposing public buildings, cathedrals, and palaces. The colonial governments built immense fortresses, such as San Cristóbal guarding San Juan in Puerto Rico, to protect the cities from pirates and sea dogs.

Colonial Society

Social classes based on privilege marked colonial society. The highest ranks of society consisted of royal officials, owners of large estates, and mine owners, many of whom were titled nobility. An enormous social gap existed between these classes and town workers, peasants, and slaves.

Racial discrimination was always a fact of colonial life. Europeans, called **peninsulares** because they were born in Spain or Portugal on the Iberian Peninsula, ruled colonial society. Whites born in the colonies—called **creoles**—suffered social snobbery and job discrimination from the *peninsulares,* though some enjoyed great wealth and privilege. American Indians and African slaves shared the bottom of the social pyramid. Furthermore, laws upheld racial distinctions.

By the 1700s, people of mixed ancestry became a majority in Latin American society. **Mestizos** were of American Indian and European background, and **mulattoes** were of African and European ancestry. *Mestizos* and mulattoes usually faced social and racial barriers but had more opportunities than Africans or Indians. *Mestizos* and mulattoes lived and worked everywhere in Latin America, although more *mestizos* lived in Mexico than in Brazil, where mulattoes played a larger role. In the Andes, southern Mexico, and parts of Central America, American Indians remained the largest group.

The Catholic Church. The Catholic Church wielded great power and enormous influence in the Spanish and Portuguese colonies. Missionaries who accompanied explorers and conquistadors to Latin America immediately began converting American Indians to Catholicism. Contributions were made by some missionaries to the exploitation of Indians. Others took an interest in the native culture and tried to prevent the government and individual colonists from abusing the Indians. Bartolomé de Las Casas was an outspoken advocate for the Indians. He spent his life writing books, letters, and petitions decrying the oppression of the Indians.

Social life. A code of honor brought from Spain to Latin America governed all social interactions and served to maintain distance between social classes. For example, unruly or rebellious servants or slaves brought a man dishonor and could therefore be punished. Individual and family honor had to be protected. To accomplish this, women were secluded, chaperoned, and restricted. They could, however, inherit, bequeath, or own property.

In Indian cultures, women had a high status because they controlled food production and gave birth to and cared for children. However, the ruling classes considered all Indians, women and men, subordinate.

Growing Discontent

During the 1600s and 1700s, Spain had relaxed its control over its colonies. This allowed creoles to become more powerful. They began to fill many upper-level positions in the colonial government and owned and operated mines and *haciendas.* In the mid-1700s, in an effort to reassert control, King Charles III of Spain instituted certain changes.

Some of these changes that were introduced by King Charles were viewed unfavorably by the colonists.

For example, Charles sent *peninsulares* to take over the top jobs and tightened control over the Catholic Church in the colonies. The Jesuits had become extremely powerful and rich through the ownership of *haciendas,* town property, mines, and thousands of slaves. During the mid-1700s, both the Spanish and Portuguese kings dissolved the Jesuit order in their kingdoms and seized all their colonial property.

Spain's economic policies also angered creoles. Charles III began to relax stiff mercantilist restrictions, and open trade had the potential to harm the interests of creole merchants. In addition, the colonists increasingly resented paying taxes to finance Spain's European wars.

Other factors that led to independence movements were growing feelings of nationalism and interest in the revolutionary events in British North America and France. Patriotism led the creole revolutionary Simón Bolívar (boh·LEE·vahr) to say in 1815, "The hatred that the Peninsula has inspired in us is greater than the ocean between us."

Haiti's Slave Revolution

By the early 1800s, Spain's American colonies were ripe for revolution. The first successful revolt, however, took place in the French colony of Saint Domingue, which is located on the western half of the island of Hispaniola in the West Indies.

In Saint Domingue, a small number of French planters owned plantations tended by African slaves. When the French Revolution broke out, the free mulattoes demanded the same rights as French settlers. In 1791 the slave population rebelled. Mulattoes and blacks united under the leadership of Toussaint-Louverture (TOO·san·LOO·ver·toor), a freed slave, and won control of Saint Domingue in the only successful revolution led by slaves anywhere in the world.

Napoleon I sent an army to try to reestablish slavery and French authority. The French captured Toussaint-Louverture, who died a prisoner in France. However, in 1804 a rebel army defeated the French, and Saint Domingue proclaimed its independence under the ancient name of Haiti, becoming the first independent country in Latin America.

Mexico and Central America

Napoleon's conquest of Spain in 1808 and the Spanish revolt that followed gave colonists in the New World a golden opportunity to declare their

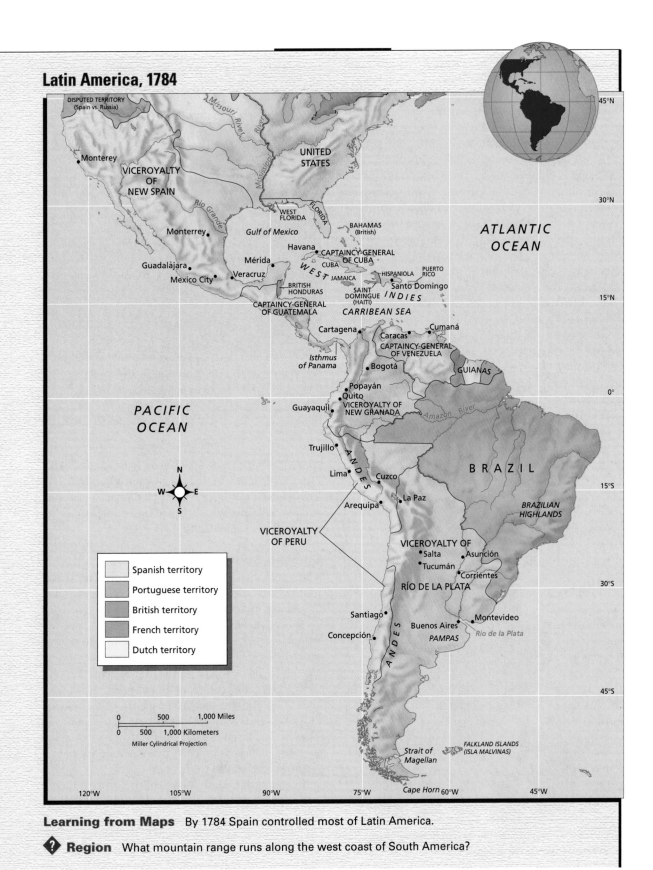

Latin America, 1784

DISPUTED TERRITORY
(Spain vs. Russia)

Missouri River

UNITED STATES

45°N

30°N

Monterey

VICEROYALTY OF NEW SPAIN

Rio Grande

Mississippi

WEST FLORIDA

FLORIDA

BAHAMAS (British)

ATLANTIC OCEAN

Monterrey

Gulf of Mexico

Havana

CAPTAINCY-GENERAL OF CUBA

CUBA

HISPANIOLA

PUERTO RICO

Guadalàjara

Mérida

Veracruz

JAMAICA

SAINT DOMINGUE (HAITI)

Santo Domingo

Mexico City

BRITISH HONDURAS

WEST INDIES

15°N

CAPTAINCY-GENERAL OF GUATEMALA

CARIBBEAN SEA

Cartagena

Cumaná

Caracas

CAPTAINCY-GENERAL OF VENEZUELA

Isthmus of Panama

Bogotá

GUIANAS

PACIFIC OCEAN

Popayán

Quito

Guayaquil

VICEROYALTY OF NEW GRANADA

Amazon River

0°

Trujillo

A N D E S

B R A Z I L

Lima

Cuzco

15°S

Arequipa

La Paz

BRAZILIAN HIGHLANDS

VICEROYALTY OF PERU

N
W E
S

VICEROYALTY OF

Salta

Asunción

Tucumán

Corrientes

RÍO DE LA PLATA

30°S

	Spanish territory
	Portuguese territory
	British territory
	French territory
	Dutch territory

Santiago

A N D E S

Buenos Aires

Montevideo

Concepción

PAMPAS

Rio de la Plata

45°S

0   500   1,000 Miles
0   500   1,000 Kilometers
Miller Cylindrical Projection

Strait of Magellan

FALKLAND ISLANDS (ISLA MALVINAS)

Cape Horn

120°W   105°W   90°W   75°W   60°W   45°W

Learning from Maps By 1784 Spain controlled most of Latin America.

❓ **Region** What mountain range runs along the west coast of South America?

independence. In Mexico, creoles, *mestizos*, and American Indians all participated in revolutionary activities. In 1810 a priest named Miguel Hidalgo y Costilla initiated an independence movement in Mexico. He led an army of Indian peasants against Spanish *peninsulares* and creoles.

After Hidalgo's forces achieved some early victories, the Spanish captured and executed him and dispersed his peasant army in 1811. Another priest, José María Morelos y Pavón, who wanted independence, land reform, and the abolition of slavery, assumed leadership of the rebels. Upper-class Mexican creoles feared Morelos and remained loyal to Spain. In 1815 authorities captured and shot him.

In 1814 the absolutist Ferdinand VII regained the throne of Spain. Mexican creoles looked favorably on Ferdinand. However, in 1820 liberal army rebels in Spain stripped the king of some of his powers. The rebellion caused upper-class Mexicans to fear that the new Spanish government would apply liberal reforms in the colonies. Therefore, in 1821 they carried out an independence movement of their own. A militia general named Agustín de Iturbide (ee·toor·BEE·day) proclaimed himself Emperor Agustín I, but his unpopular dictatorial rule did not last long. In 1823 Mexican generals overthrew him, and Mexico became a republic.

José de San Martín (left), an Argentine general, led independence movements in Argentina, Chile, and Peru between 1812 and 1821.

Central America was briefly part of Iturbide's Mexican empire. In 1823, however, representatives from Guatemala, El Salvador, Honduras, Nicaragua, and Costa Rica met to form a federal union called the United Provinces of Central America.

Spanish South America

Three great South American leaders—Simón Bolívar, José de San Martín, and Bernardo O'Higgins—had traveled or studied in North America or Europe. They knew well the ideas of the Enlightenment and the French Revolution. One of the first revolts against Spain took place in 1810 in the southernmost viceroyalty of La Plata. Creole rebels deposed the Spanish viceroy and seized control of the government. Six years later, they declared the independence of the United Provinces of the Rio de la Plata, later named Argentina. Meanwhile, Paraguay, another part of the viceroyalty of La Plata, achieved its independence from Spain in a bloodless rebellion in 1811.

In the rest of South America, the struggle turned into a long and bloody civil war led by Simón Bolívar, "the Liberator." Bolívar started the revolt in his native city of Caracas in 1810. He did not succeed in destroying Spain's power in Venezuela until 1821 at the battle of Carabobo. In the meantime, he raised

Toussaint-Louverture led the Haitian independence movement against Napoleon.

another army and defeated the Spanish in New Granada in 1819 at the battle of Boyacá.

Bolívar became president, with almost absolute power, of a new nation called Gran Colombia. The new nation included the present-day countries of Colombia, Venezuela, Ecuador, and Panama.

Meanwhile, Argentine general San Martín gathered another army and made a difficult crossing of the Andes into the region known as Chile. He joined forces with Chileans led by Bernardo O'Higgins and overcame Spanish resistance there in 1818.

From Chile, San Martín's forces sailed north to capture the city of Lima in Peru. The Spanish government fled, and San Martín declared the independence of Peru in 1821. Royalist forces, however, remained in parts of Peru. Internal squabbling among the independence leaders led some Peruvians to invite Bolívar to help them defeat the Spanish. San Martín then withdrew, turning leadership over to the ambitious Bolívar.

In August 1824 Bolívar won a major victory over Spanish forces at Junín (hoo·NEEN) in Peru. By December of that year, the revolutionaries gained their final victory in Peru at Ayacucho (eye·ah·KOO·choh). Peru was free from Spanish rule. In 1825 the northern territory of Upper Peru became a separate republic, named Bolivia in honor of Bolívar.

Brazil

When Napoleon's army invaded Portugal in 1807, the prince regent Dom João, his royal court, and his family fled to Brazil. There the prince regent's rule benefited Brazil, as he opened ports to trade, founded a national bank, and encouraged industry. After the overthrow of Napoleon, Dom João—now King John VI, a dual monarch of Brazil and Portugal—remained in Brazil. In 1820, however, a revolt broke out in Portugal, and the Portuguese insisted that Dom João return home.

The Portuguese then tried to reassert control over Brazil from overseas. Angered Brazilians urged Dom Pedro, Dom João's son who had stayed in Brazil, to declare independence, which he did in 1822. Dom Pedro ruled as emperor until 1831, when he was forced to abdicate. His son, Dom Pedro II, became emperor in 1831 and ruled until 1889.

The new nations of Brazil and Argentina struggled over territory that lay between them. Patriots in this disputed territory gained independence in 1825, calling their country Uruguay.

Almost all of Latin America had thus become independent by 1825. Portugal lost its entire Latin American empire. The Spanish lost all their colonies

Simón Bolívar, nicknamed the Liberator, led revolutions against the Spanish in Venezuela, Colombia, Ecuador, Peru, and Bolivia.

except Cuba and Puerto Rico. Elsewhere in the region, only a few Caribbean islands, parts of Central America, the Guianas, and the Falkland Islands remained under colonial rule. (See map on page 288.)

Foreign Reactions to Independence

Independence opened Latin American markets to trade with countries other than Spain and Portugal. The British hoped to benefit. They were eager to increase commerce with the region, and they viewed the Latin Americans as potential allies against continental Europe, which was growing more conservative.

Preoccupied first with the War of 1812 against Britain and then expansionism, including difficult negotiations with Spain over Florida, the United States paid little attention to Latin America. Even after Spain ceded Florida in 1819, the United States had no established Latin American policy until late in the administration of President James Monroe. Like the British, however, Americans saw Latin America as a new market and were concerned when Spain tried to regain its colonies in the 1820s.

In 1823 President James Monroe sent a dramatic message to Congress. This message is known as the **Monroe Doctrine**. It declared that the United

States would not intervene in Europe's affairs or interfere in any of Europe's remaining colonies in the Western Hemisphere. At the same time, the United States would oppose any attempt by European nations to reestablish their lost colonies, to form new colonies, or to interfere with any government in the Western Hemisphere.

Although European leaders denounced the Monroe Doctrine, no nation seriously tested it. The United States was too weak to enforce the doctrine at the time, but British naval might and political unrest in many nations on the European continent prevented much involvement by European powers in Latin American affairs.

Latin American Unity

Enormous distances, geographical barriers, and regional rivalries prevented unity among the new Latin American countries. Of the former Spanish and Portuguese territories, only Brazil managed to maintain

Latin America, 1830

Learning from Maps Within 50 years, the huge Spanish empire in Latin America broke into many independent nations.

❓ Place What islands remained under Spanish or British rule in 1830?

national unity. Ecuador and Venezuela broke away from Gran Colombia. The United Provinces of Central America crumbled into five separate countries, and Argentina was threatened with divisions within its own country.

In 1826 Bolívar called a congress of Latin American nations to meet in Panama to promote unification. Only Colombia, Peru, Central America, and Mexico attended the Panama Congress. Although the Panama Congress failed, many Latin Americans cherished the ideal of unity.

Internal Problems

Despite problems in the new countries of Latin America, the removal of European authority did have some positive consequences for these countries. For example, some groups began to enjoy greater social mobility. *Mestizos*, in particular, found they were more able to advance socially. International trade also expanded once it was freed from the restrictions of the former colonial powers. In addition, tribute payments by Indians were abolished, and slavery was abolished in most countries by the 1850s, and throughout Latin America by 1888.

Although creoles eventually abolished slavery everywhere, it remained an unresolved issue in some Latin American countries. For example, the slave economy was integral in Brazil throughout the early and middle 1800s. In general though, the creoles attempted to take over the positions of power in the new Latin American nations. Creoles also battled to take over communal lands belonging to the American Indian population, claiming that they needed the lands for economic progress. Moreover, the *haciendas* continued to grow.

Conflict between liberals and conservatives kept many countries in a state of turmoil. The conflict tended to follow class lines, with upper-class creoles espousing conservative values and *mestizos* embracing a liberal philosophy. Conservatives favored retaining as much as possible from their European heritage. They wanted a strong Catholic Church, a monarchy or powerful executive, and government control of the economy. Liberals advocated the separation of church and state, the formation of democratic republics, and a laissez-faire economy.

These internal disagreements prevented the establishment of governments based on an orderly rule of law. Latin American governments came to power as often by rebellion as they did by election. During colonial times, strong central governments merged with upper-class economic interests to hold the countries together. Brazil, in fact, retained an emperor until 1889, working in concert with an assembly, and was comparatively stable. However, in many countries, creoles retreated to their *haciendas*, while **caudillos**, ambitious *mestizo* military leaders who ruled by personal power, became presidents. These governments headed by the *caudillos* often provided stability but not freedom and tended to last only as long as the dictator did.

Liberals and conservatives also battled over the role of the Catholic Church. Republican governments often took positions against the church. However, educational systems that had been run by the church were neglected, and there was scant public education to replace them. Conservatives, who still constituted the upper class, opposed the loss of church power, and the lower classes remained staunchly Catholic in faith. The result was a jumble of disunity.

With all these conflicts, the first 50 or 60 years of independence proved difficult in many of the Latin American countries. However, in the latter part of the 1800s, growing industry and expanding trade began to bring a somewhat broader distribution of wealth to these countries. Development was rapid, and cities grew, thus bringing social change. Political unrest was frequent; however, many Latin American countries began to achieve stability and economic growth.

Section 4 Review

1. **Define** *haciendas, peninsulares,* creoles, *mestizos,* mulattoes, Monroe Doctrine, *caudillos*
2. **Identify** Toussaint-Louverture, José de San Martín, Simón Bolívar, Bernardo O'Higgins
3. **Locate and Explain the Significance** Rio de Janeiro, Haiti, Gran Colombia
4. **Explaining Ideas** What aspects of Spanish and Portuguese rule in Latin America led to discontent?
5. **Summarizing Ideas (a)** What were the goals of the revolutions that took place in Mexico and Central America? **(b)** What were the results of these revolutions?
6. **Relating Ideas (a)** What economic and social problems faced the creoles in Latin America on the eve of their independence? **(b)** What problems were evident for the creoles after their independence?

Chapter 8 Review

A.D. 1818
Spanish rule ends in Chile.

A.D. 1823
Monroe Doctrine is proclaimed.

A.D. 1854–1856
Crimean War occurs.

A.D. 1790 | A.D. 1800 | A.D. 1810 | A.D. 1820 | A.D. 1830 | A.D. 1850

A.D. 1791
Haiti revolts.

A.D. 1801
British Parliament passes the Act of Union.

A.D. 1804
Haiti proclaims independence.

A.D. 1810
La Plata (Argentina) revolts against Spain.

A.D. 1819
Bolívar becomes president of Gran Colombia.

A.D. 1832
Great Britain enacts Reform Bill of 1832.

A.D. 1852
Napoleon III founds Second French Empire.

Chapter Summary

The following list contains the key concepts you have learned about political changes in the British Empire, the United States, France, and Latin America during the 1800s and early 1900s.

1. Many reforms occurred in Great Britain in the 1800s and early 1900s. With the Reform Bill of 1832 and agitation from people such as the Chartists, voting rights were greatly broadened in Britain. In the early 1900s, women finally gained the right to vote.

2. Queen Victoria gave her prime ministers a great deal of power. Two dominant prime ministers of the Victorian Era were Benjamin Disraeli, leader of the Conservative Party, and William Gladstone, leader of the Liberal Party.

3. The labor union movement and socialism grew in Great Britain in the late 1800s and early 1900s. This movement led to the rise of the Labour Party. When the Liberal Party came to power in 1905, Great Britain adopted extensive welfare legislation.

4. Britain's social and political reforms also extended to colonies within the British Empire, such as Canada, Australia, and New Zealand, which were allowed self-government.

5. Territorial growth and sectionalism in the United States led to war over the issue of slavery.

6. Following the Civil War, Congress passed the Thirteenth, Fourteenth, and Fifteenth Amendments to the Constitution. These amendments abolished slavery, made former slaves citizens, and gave African American men the right to vote. Women in the United States were given the right to vote in 1920, by the Nineteenth Amendment.

7. France experienced a series of upheavals in 1830, 1848, and 1871 that rekindled the revolutionary spirit of the 1790s. Each time, politics soon returned to a more stable form. The monarchy was eventually abolished, as was the position of emperor that Napoleon III created for himself. By the early 1900s, France was a republic, governed by coalitions of parties that represented monarchist, liberal, and socialist beliefs.

8. In the early part of the 1800s, revolutions took place throughout Latin America. Following their independence from Spain, most Latin American countries set up democratic governments.

9. The peoples of Latin America had many regional, economic, ethnic, and social differences. For these reasons, they did not unite but split into many nations after their wars for independence in the early 1800s. Only Brazil managed to maintain stability.

Reviewing Important Terms

On a separate sheet of paper, supply the term that correctly completes each statement.

1. _____ was a movement whose followers believed that people ought to be free to think and work as they please.
2. _____ _____ is a term for self-government.
3. _____ were women who wanted voting rights for all women.
4. _____ is a rivalry among the parts of a country.
5. A(n) _____ believes in the abolition of all government.
6. A(n) _____ is formed by political groups organized in support of a common cause.

Developing Critical Thinking Skills

1. **Analyzing Ideas** (a) What were the aims of the Chartists? (b) How did they contribute to the growth of democracy in Great Britain?
2. **Explaining Ideas** Why did Great Britain allow Canada, Australia, and New Zealand to develop their own governments?
3. **Interpreting Ideas** Describe the actions of Louis Napoleon Bonaparte as liberal or reactionary.
4. **Summarizing Ideas** (a) What was the Monroe Doctrine? (b) Why was it issued?
5. **Explaining Ideas** How did the geography of Latin America prevent unity among its countries?

A.D. **1863** President Lincoln issues Emancipation Proclamation.

A.D. **1870–1871** Franco-Prussian War occurs.

A.D. **1875** Third French Republic is established.

A.D. **1884** Great Britain enacts Reform Bill of 1884.

A.D. **1901** Commonwealth of Australia is created.

A.D. **1860** | A.D. **1870** | A.D. **1880** | A.D. **1890** | A.D. **1900** | A.D. **1910**

A.D. **1861–1865** Civil War in the United States occurs.

A.D. **1867**
• Dominion of Canada is created.
• Great Britain enacts Reform Bill of 1867.

A.D. **1872** Great Britain adopts secret ballot.

A.D. **1894–1906** Dreyfus case divides France.

A.D. **1907** Dominion of New Zealand is formed.

A.D. **1911** Great Britain enacts Parliament Act of 1911.

Relating Geography to History

Turn to the map on page 273 and answer the following questions. **(a)** After 1783, how did the United States acquire most of its territory? **(b)** Was the land in your state part of the United States before the 1800s? **(c)** If not, when was it acquired? **(d)** How long did it take for the United States to expand its borders from the Mississippi River to the Pacific Ocean? **(e)** Why might such rapid growth encourage the development of liberalism and nationalism?

Relating Past to Present

1. Before taking office, William Gladstone pledged, "My mission is to pacify Ireland." Review the events that prompted Gladstone to make this remark. Then investigate the situation in Ireland today. Which of the problems faced in the 1880s have lingered into the present? How has the British government dealt with the problems in the 1990s?
2. How did the spread of liberalism inspire the start of the woman's suffrage movement in Great Britain and the United States? Even though women now have the vote, some people are still working to extend the rights of women. What are some of the reforms that women have called for during the last decade?

Applying History Study Skills

Before completing this activity, review Building History Study Skills on page 265.

Read the following selection from William Gladstone's speech to Parliament on April 8, 1886, supporting home rule for Ireland.

"Our intention is, Sir, to propose to the House of Commons that which, as we think,...will liberate Parliament from the restraints under which of late years it has ineffectually struggled to perform the Business of the country; [that is, to] obtain an answer...to the question whether it is or is not possible to establish good and harmonious relations between Great Britain and Ireland on the footing of those free institutions to which Englishmen, Scotchmen, and Irishmen are alike unalterably attached...

...in point of fact, law is discredited...in Ireland upon this ground especially—that it comes to the people of

that country with a foreign aspect, and in a foreign garb. These Coercion Bills of ours...are stiffly resisted by the Members who represent Ireland in Parliament. The English mind...is estranged from the Irish people and the Irish mind is estranged from the people of England and Scotland."

1. How does Gladstone defend his view of home rule for Ireland?
2. Does Gladstone's position, as represented in this selection, represent a liberal or conservative ideology? Explain how you know this.
3. Is Gladstone's ideology economic or political? Write a response to Gladstone from another ideology. How did you determine what would be included in your response?

---

internetconnect

Search the Internet through the HRW Web site for letters and diary entries from soldiers who served in the U.S. Civil War. Use the documents to explain how the people who served felt about the war and its goals. Be sure to note for which side each of the soldiers fought, and examine how this may have affected his views.

 GO TO: go.hrw.com
KEYWORD: SC0 Civil War

Building Your Portfolio

1. **Presenting an Oral Report** Use encyclopedias to learn more about the ministries in Great Britain of Benjamin Disraeli and William Gladstone. Give an oral report on the types of programs each prime minister supported and how they influenced the direction of Great Britain's domestic and foreign policy. Place your notes in your portfolio.
2. **Writing a Report** During the revolutions of 1848, the people of Paris set up a provisional government and proclaimed the Second French Republic. Using available sources, prepare a report explaining the form that this republic was to take. Place the report in your portfolio.

Nationalism in Europe

TIME

A.D. 1806–1913

A.D. 1806–1913

3.7 million B.C. | 4000 B.C. | A.D. 2100

PLACE

Europe

Europe

Portrait of Giuseppe Garibaldi in 1849

Significance

In the 1800s, growing nationalism created political change in Europe. Drives to unify peoples and states transformed the continent. These changes brought forward forces that would also have profound impact in the twentieth century.

Terms to Define

risorgimento	Pan-Slavism
Young Italy movement	Emancipation Edict
Zollverein	People's Will
Treaty of Prague	terrorism
kaiser	pogroms
Bundesrat	Social Democratic
Reichstag	Labor Party
Kulturkampf	Duma
Social Democratic Party	Treaty of San Stefano
autocrat	Balkan League
Russification	

People to Identify

Carbonari	William I
Giuseppe Mazzini	Iron Chancellor
Victor Emmanuel II	William II
Camillo Benso di Cavour	nihilists
Napoleon III	Magyars
Junkers	Francis Joseph I

Places to Locate

Lombardy	Holstein
Venetia	Bavaria
the kingdom	Württemberg
of Sardinia	Romania
kingdom of the	Budapest
Two Sicilies	Serbia
Tuscany	Montenegro
Modena	Bulgaria
Parma	Bosnia
Papal States	Herzegovina
Saxony	Cyprus
Schleswig	Rhodes

Chapter Theme Questions

- **Politics and Law** What factors might contribute to a desire for national unification?
- **War and Diplomacy** How can war be a force in unifying a country?
- **Social Relations** What might happen when there is great resistance to reform movements by countries?

Giuseppe Mazzini, who lived from 1805 to 1872, was one of the three rulers of a republic set up in Rome during the ill-fated revolution of 1848–1849. He expresses his anger and sadness at the worsening military situation in the following excerpt from a letter he wrote to an English friend in 1849.

“*Terror now reigns in Rome; the prisons are choked with men who have been arrested and detained without trial; . . . the citizens best known for their moderation are exiled; the army is almost entirely dissolved, the city disarmed, and the 'factious' sent away even to the last man; and yet France dares not consult in a legal manner the will of the population, but re-establishes the papal authority by military decree. I do not believe that since the dismemberment of Poland there has been committed a more atrocious injustice, a more gross violation of the eternal right which God has implanted in the peoples, that of appreciating and defining for themselves their own life, and governing themselves in accordance with their own appreciation of it. And I cannot believe that it is well for you or for Europe that such things can be accomplished in the eyes of the world, without one nation arising out of its immobility to protest in the name of universal justice.*”

The upheaval in Rome was only one of many that erupted in Europe in the mid-1800s.

Section 1

The Unification of Italy

Focus Questions

- **What events led to nationalistic movements for unification in Italy?**
- **Who were the important leaders in the fight for the unification of Italy?**
- **What problems did Italy face after unification?**

Many Italians had been inspired by the liberal and nationalistic ideals of the French Revolution in the

1790s, and revolutionary movements formed against several rulers of the Italian states. Then, conquest by Napoleon I gave the Italian Peninsula something resembling unity for a few years. However, following Napoleon's defeat and the Congress of Vienna in 1815, Italy was again divided. Austria annexed the rich territories of Lombardy and Venetia. The rest of Italy was fragmented into several large and small states. These states were either dominated by Austria or ruled by reactionary monarchs who tried to undo any advances made during Napoleon's time. (See map on page 297.)

Early Movements Toward Unification

Italian nationalism became a strong force in the early 1800s when many thinkers and writers tried to revive interest in Italy's traditions. This nationalistic movement, with its goal of liberation and unification, became known as the **risorgimento**—the Italian word for "resurgence." Because nationalists could not support their cause openly, they formed secret societies. An early group of this sort was the *Carbonari*, Italian for "charcoal-burners."

One of its most famous members, Giuseppe Mazzini, envisioned a united Italy, and he devoted his entire life to this goal. Born in 1805, Mazzini was both imprisoned and exiled for his revolutionary activities. In 1831 he called for all Italian patriots to join a new movement, known as the **Young Italy movement**, to spread the ideals of the risorgimento. The first Italian democratic movement open to all classes, Young Italy insisted that "neither pope nor king," but rather a republic, should rule Italy.

In 1848 liberals and nationalists led revolts in several Italian states. These rebellions overthrew Austrian rule in Lombardy and Venetia, and forced the rulers of the kingdom of Sardinia, the kingdom of the Two Sicilies, and Tuscany to grant constitutions to their subjects. Revolutionaries seized Rome in 1849 and set up a republic that Mazzini and two other leaders governed. However, all but one of these revolutionary movements soon failed. The Austrian army succeeded in recapturing some of its former possessions in northern Italy during the summer of 1849. Former rulers returned to power, revoking constitutions and filling prisons. Only the kingdom of Sardinia, with its mainland capital of Turin, remained an independent kingdom.

After the failure of the revolts of 1848 and 1849, Italian liberals continued their efforts with little success. Disagreeing among themselves, and with the church opposed to them, liberals began to see their movement fall apart. Many Italians, especially the Catholic clergy, wanted a federation of Italian states headed by the pope. Liberals, however, wanted a republic. They opposed federation, partly because the papacy had withdrawn support from the revolt in 1849. Still others wanted a constitutional monarchy under King Victor Emmanuel II of the kingdom of Sardinia.

Only in the kingdom of Sardinia was there hope for progress. Although King Victor Emmanuel II was not especially sympathetic to the liberals and was motivated mainly by a wish to expand Sardinian territory, his parliament and his chief minister, Camillo Benso di Cavour (kahv·OOHR), a liberal and an Italian patriot, supported the goals of the liberals.

Cavour in Sardinia

The chief minister or premier, Count Camillo Benso di Cavour, and not Victor Emmanuel, actually governed the kingdom of Sardinia. Born in 1810, Cavour was a well-educated and widely traveled aristocrat. He edited a nationalist newspaper, *Il Risorgimento*, in 1847, took part in the revolutions of 1848, and in 1852 became premier of the kingdom of Sardinia.

Cavour disliked absolutism and admired the British system of parliamentary government. He wanted Italy to be both united and industrialized under Sardinia's leadership.

Cavour reorganized and strengthened the army. He helped to establish banks, factories, and railroads, encouraged shipbuilding, and negotiated treaties with other countries to increase trade. Believing in the separation of church and state, he tried to reduce the political influence of the church, and he attempted to expel the politically powerful Jesuit order from the country. He also brought the kingdom of Sardinia to prominence through alliance with France and Great Britain in the Crimean War and in the peace conference at Paris in 1856 that ended that war.

Napoleon III and War with Austria

Cavour saw Austria as the greatest obstacle to Italian unification because of its control of part of northern Italy. He proposed an alliance of France and Sardinia against Austria. Napoleon III sought ways to increase French influence, and he hoped that with Austria driven out of Italy, France could dominate a weak confederation of Italian states. Cavour, on the other hand, believed that with Austria out of Italy, other Italian states would join the kingdom of Sardinia in a strong alliance against both France and Austria.

Cavour sought an alliance with Napoleon III in 1858 to evict the Austrians and to unify Italy under the kingdom of Sardinia.

In 1858 Cavour and Napoleon III met secretly to plan strategy against Austria. Napoleon III agreed that if Austria could be provoked into declaring war on the kingdom of Sardinia, France would send troops to help drive the Austrians out of Lombardy and Venetia. In return for this help, Cavour promised to give the French-speaking regions of Nice and Savoy—then Sardinia's possessions—to France. In 1859 Cavour began military preparations for war. Austria demanded that the military buildup in the kingdom of Sardinia be stopped within three days. When this ultimatum was rejected, Austria, as Cavour had hoped, declared war.

At first the war went according to Cavour's plan. Combined forces from the kingdom of Sardinia and France quickly drove the Austrians out of Lombardy and marched on into Venetia. Italian patriots in Tuscany, Modena, and Parma overthrew their Austrian rulers and asked to be annexed to the kingdom of Sardinia.

Napoleon III had not expected Italians to consolidate in this way. He did not want a strong, united Italy, and feared that Prussia, in its own interest, might help Austria. Napoleon III had no desire to get involved in a war against both Austria and Prussia and wished to do nothing to unite the two. In July 1859, only three months after the war began,

Napoleon III signed a secret armistice with Austria. According to its terms, the kingdom of Sardinia received Lombardy, but Austria kept Venetia. The agreement also returned Austrian rulers to Tuscany, Modena, and Parma.

This armistice marked a severe setback for Cavour and the Italian nationalists. Napoleon III had delivered only half of his side of the bargain—control of Lombardy to the kingdom of Sardinia. However, he insisted on collecting his full price—Nice and Savoy. Afraid of losing even the partial victory, King Victor Emmanuel II agreed to the French terms.

The Italian people, however, refused to abandon the idea of unity. Popular feeling ran far ahead of governmental caution. Rebellions in Parma, Modena, and Tuscany again expelled the Austrian rulers and set up temporary governments. The people of Romagna, a province in the Papal States, also revolted. When each of these areas held a plebiscite, or direct vote on the issue, voters overwhelmingly favored joining the kingdom of Sardinia.

Garibaldi and the Thousand

The southern half of the Italian Peninsula, together with the island of Sicily, made up the kingdom of the Two Sicilies. Earlier revolts against harsh Bourbon rule of the kingdom had failed, but it now became the target of the Italian nationalists. Giuseppe Garibaldi, a man devoted to Italian freedom, led the way.

Born in Nice in 1807, Garibaldi joined Mazzini's Young Italy movement when he was in his twenties. In 1834, after being involved in a revolutionary plot in Piedmont, Garibaldi fled for his life to Latin America. Returning to Italy, he fought in the revolutions of 1848. Forced to flee again, he lived in North Africa, the United States, and Peru, before Cavour arranged his return to Italy in 1854.

With Cavour's approval, Garibaldi recruited an army of nearly 1,100 soldiers. They were called Red Shirts because of the colorful uniforms they wore into battle. In the spring of 1860, Garibaldi and his "Expedition of the Thousand" invaded and took Sicily. Crossing to Italy's mainland, Garibaldi and his growing forces seized Naples, the capital city, and drove Francis II and his troops north to the border of the Papal States. Celebrated as a patriot and military genius, Garibaldi became a national and international hero.

Garibaldi planned to continue north to capture Rome and then Venetia. But Cavour, afraid that Garibaldi might set up a republic or that his fame might displace Victor Emmanuel II as Italy's leader, sent an army south to stop Garibaldi's advance. In the process, the kingdom of Sardinia annexed most of the territory of the Papal States.

In the fall of 1860, Garibaldi and Cavour met in Naples. Garibaldi agreed to support the establishment of the kingdom of Italy, with Victor Emmanuel II as king. Garibaldi asked only to serve as governor of Naples. The king and Cavour, fearing his huge popularity, refused his request.

Unification

During 1860 plebiscites were held everywhere in Italy except in Venetia and Rome. The people voted overwhelmingly for national unity under the king of the kingdom of Sardinia. Representatives of the various states met in Turin, the capital of the kingdom of Sardinia, in February 1861, where they confirmed Victor Emmanuel II as king of Italy, and proclaimed his inauguration on March 17.

The new kingdom included nearly all of Italy except Venetia, which still belonged to Austria, and the western part of the Papal States around the city of Rome, ruled by the pope. (See map on opposite page.)

European governments were left with two choices—either recognize the new state or fight it. Outmaneuvered by Cavour, Napoleon III stopped short of war with Italy but did send French troops to protect the papacy and to prevent Italian nationalists from seizing Rome.

Unification was furthered when Italy gained Venetia in the Seven Weeks' War of 1866. When the Franco-Prussian War broke out in 1870, Napoleon III recalled his troops from Rome. The Italians entered the city, over the objections of the pope. The citizens of Rome voted for union with Italy, and later that year Rome was proclaimed the capital of the kingdom of Italy.

Problems of a United Italy

Although politically united, Italy still faced many problems. Few Italians had experience with self-government, and scandals frequently rocked the young nation. The various regions of the country remained divided by cultural traditions and independence. Tensions grew between the industrialized north and the agricultural south. In Sicily local

Giuseppe Garibaldi and his supporters, known as Red Shirts, conquered the Kingdom of the Two Sicilies in 1860, adding this area to the kingdom of Italy.

Unification of Italy, 1858–1870

Legend:
- Kingdom of Sardinia, 1858
- Austrian territory annexed by Sardinia, 1859
- Territory annexed by Sardinia to form kingdom of Italy, 1860
- Austrian territory annexed by Italy, 1866
- Territory annexed by Italy, 1870

FRANCE
Vienna
SWITZERLAND
AUSTRIA-HUNGARY
Danube River
SAVOY (to France in 1860)
LOMBARDY
Milan
VENETIA
Turin
Po R.
Venice
NICE (to France in 1860)
Genoa
PARMA
MODENA
SAN MARINO
OTTOMAN EMPIRE
MONACO
Florence
TUSCANY
PAPAL STATES
KINGDOM
ADRIATIC SEA
KINGDOM OF SARDINIA
CORSICA (French)
OF
PAPAL STATES
Tiber R.
Rome
ITALY
40°N
SARDINIA
Naples
KINGDOM OF THE TWO SICILIES
TYRRHENIAN SEA
MEDITERRANEAN SEA
10°E
SICILY
0   100   200 Miles
0   100   200 Kilometers
Azimuthal Equal-Area Projection
15°E

Learning from Maps Italy was united into a single kingdom over a 12-year period.

? Region What territories did Italy cede to France in 1860?

Ottoman Empire in 1911 brought little material return. The conquest of Libya in 1912 strengthened Italy's position in the Mediterranean region but divided the nation. Although geographically unified, Italy had not achieved political stability.

Section 1 Review

1. **Define** risorgimento, Young Italy movement
2. **Identify** *Carbonari*, Giuseppe Mazzini, Victor Emmanuel II, Camillo Benso di Cavour, Napoleon III
3. **Locate and Explain the Significance** Lombardy, Venetia, the kingdom of Sardinia, kingdom of the Two Sicilies, Tuscany, Modena, Parma, Papal States
4. **Explaining Ideas** Describe the early nationalistic movements toward unification in Italy.
5. **Summarizing Ideas** Explain the contributions of Mazzini, Garibaldi, and Cavour in the Italian unification process.
6. **Analyzing Ideas** Were the problems that Italy faced after its unification in 1870 the result of earlier disunity? Explain your answer.

Section 2

The Unification of Germany

Focus Questions

- How did Prussia replace Austria as the leading German state in Europe?
- In what ways did German unification differ from Italian unification?
- What changes in German government occurred as a result of unification?

That the German people did not form an enduring union before the late 1800s is somewhat surprising. Germans shared a common language and history. Several times, vigorous, intelligent rulers nearly achieved a strong central government, but all of them failed. In the mid-1800s Germany remained what it had been for centuries—a patchwork of independent states. Each one had its own laws, currency, and

---

leaders organized a secret society known as the Mafia, a kind of state within the state that the central government was powerless to control.

Modernization was slow after a brief period of expansion, impeded by political crises and changing government policies. The standard of living remained low for most Italians, and labor problems arose.

Some of Italy's leaders admired the military strength of Germany and hoped to follow a similar course. Attempting to build a colonial empire, Italy engaged in several ventures in Africa in the 1870s and 1880s. A brief, expensive war against the rulers. In the late 1800s, Prussia led the fight for unification of these states.

Prussia as Leader

Prussia built a strong and prosperous state in the 1700s during the reigns of Frederick William I and his son Frederick the Great. But Napoleon I defeated Prussian armies in 1806 and dominated Prussia for seven years. He seized Prussian lands to form new states and gave them to relatives and allies. To prevent a military threat, he limited the size of Prussia's army and levied a large indemnity. He forced Prussia to support an occupation army within its territory and to contribute soldiers to French armies.

The Prussians, however, found ways around Napoleon's restrictions. For example, Prussia's strength had been based on its army, which the French had now restricted in size. But the Prussians drafted all able-bodied men and required them to serve only short terms, during which they received intensive military training. They then went into the reserves, and a new group of men was drafted into the regular army. Thus trained men, not counted as part of the regular army, could be called into active service when needed. Technically Prussia observed the limits that the French had placed on its standing army but still kept available a large force of trained men.

The revived Prussian state played a major part in the final struggle against Napoleon. Prussian armies defeated the French at Leipzig in 1813 and fought at Waterloo in 1815. Prussia was one of the four great powers represented at the Congress of Vienna. It also joined the Quadruple Alliance.

In 1815 the Congress of Vienna turned Napoleon's Confederation of the Rhine into the German Confederation with additional members that included Prussia. The Congress of Vienna gave Prussia much important territory, including two thirds of Saxony and an area along the lower Rhine River. Prussian lands now stretched almost unbroken from Russia to the Rhine and beyond. Prussia integrated these territories into its efficient government and strong economy.

These territorial changes worked in Prussia's favor. Austria was Prussia's strongest rival for leadership of the German states. An Austrian Habsburg had held the position of Holy Roman emperor since the 1400s, thus giving Austria a vague claim over German states. Napoleon abolished the Holy Roman Empire, and it was not restored by the Congress of Vienna.

In addition, Napoleon's rule had stimulated nationalism in the German states as it had throughout Europe. Some of Germany's greatest thinkers and writers were active during the period of the French Revolution. Although Frederick the Great despised the German language and had usually written and spoken French, Germans now began to appreciate their language, their past, and their traditions.

German nationalism favored Prussia more than Austria. The population of Prussia was mostly German. In Austria, although Germans ruled, there were many other nationalities, including Hungarians, Romanians, Italians, and Slavs. Territorial shifts after the Congress of Vienna moved the focus of Austrian attention south and east, toward Italy and the Balkans.

The *Zollverein*

The first major step toward German unity after the Congress of Vienna concerned the economy. Tariffs levied by each German state made movement of goods from one state to another costly, increasing the price of goods and reducing the amount sold. Prussians even placed tariffs on items shipped from one Prussian possession to another.

The Junkers (YOOHNG·kuhrz), a class of aristocratic landowners, complained that tariffs were hurting sales of farm products. Tradespeople, intellectuals, financiers, and manufacturers began a campaign for freer movement of goods. In 1818 they persuaded the king of Prussia to abolish tariffs within his territories. Beginning in 1820 German states began to make treaties that in 1834 resulted in a customs union called the **Zollverein** (TSOHL·fer·yn). By 1854, the *Zollverein* included most of the German states, except, most notably, Austria.

The *Zollverein* benefited its members by making prices both lower and more uniform. It also led to the spread of industrialization in the German states by providing wide, free markets for German goods and by offering tariff protection against foreign competition. The German states adopted uniform systems of weights, measures, and currency. Manufacturers produced and sold more goods, and the German economy moved toward unification.

The establishment of the *Zollverein* did not bring about immediate political unity. Each of the various states in the German Confederation continued to act independently of the other states. However, by making member states economically dependent on one another, the *Zollverein* paved the way for later political unification.

In the years after the Congress of Vienna, strong nationalistic and democratic movements emerged within the states of the German Confederation. In

1848 uprisings broke out in France. Within weeks, demands for liberal reforms had brought revolutions to almost all the German states. Agitation was intense for a while, and elections were held for representatives to a National Assembly in Frankfurt to try to unify Germany. The constitution drafted by the National Assembly provided for a hereditary monarch, with powers limited by a popularly elected legislature. However, the demands of liberals for representative government were eventually thwarted, leaving an essentially absolutist system in place. German unification was to be accomplished instead by a king and the plans of his powerful chancellor.

Bismarck and Prussian Strength

William I became king of Prussia in 1861. The next year he appointed Otto von Bismarck, who was a conservative Junker politician, to head the Prussian cabinet. Bismarck built the Prussian army into a powerful war machine.

Bismarck opposed democracy and the idea of a parliament. His vision of a state that maintained authority by rewarding the obedient left little room at first for compromise or reform. Bismarck had great contempt for idealists, regarding them as mere talkers, not people of action. He also believed strongly in Prussian destiny to lead the German people to unification. Realizing that unification would come one way or another, his goal was to ensure Prussian dominance of the future German state. He once said that Prussian policy could be carried out "not . . . by speeches and majority decisions . . . but by iron and blood."

Bismarck and William I wanted to strengthen central authority and the Prussian military, but they faced a challenge from the Prussian parliament.

When the parliament refused to approve money for a military expansion program, Bismarck simply collected the taxes without parliamentary authorization. He claimed that the government had to keep functioning

Otto von Bismarck's effective diplomatic alliances and military policies became assets during his unification of Germany into a single empire.

Nationalism

In the early 1800s, Germans began to take a new interest in their national traditions, language, and customs. This nationalistic spirit, inspired in part by the French Revolution, began to be expressed in art, literature, and music in the form of the romantic movement. Romanticism, in turn, helped inspire the political steps toward the unification of Germany.

Inspired by thinkers such as Giuseppe Mazzini, many Germans believed that nationalism was inseparable from liberalism, and that representative government and individual freedoms would advance together with the principles of nationality. However, German unification took a very different direction. Under the direction of Otto von Bismarck and his king, William I of Prussia, Germany's nationalism was conservative

King William I of Prussia

and authoritarian. For these leaders, German nationalism was primarily a tool to help advance Prussian control over the rest of Germany.

An obstacle to Prussian ambition appeared to be the liberals in parliament, who were reluctant to fund the expanding Prussian military. Bismarck had no desire to make concessions to liberals and the lower classes. However, he knew that he had no choice but to make some compromises with the liberals dominating parliament.

However, Bismarck also realized that successful military campaigns, appealing to nationalist enthusiasm, could win support from liberals in Germany. The military victories in 1864, 1866, and 1871 helped to convince many liberals to support the Prussian state.

even without agreement. In so doing, he ignored the constitution and the outrage of the liberals. As protests grew, Bismarck hoped that successful foreign policy would calm an increasingly hostile people.

Unification Through War

To increase the power and size of Prussia, Bismarck had to overcome two major obstacles. First, Prussia had to drive Austria from its position of leadership in the German Confederation. Second, Prussia had to overcome Austria's influence over the southern German states, which opposed Prussian leadership. He accomplished these objectives in three wars—the Danish War, the Seven Weeks' War, and the Franco-Prussian War.

The Danish War. On the border between Denmark and Germany lay two small states—the duchies of Schleswig and Holstein. (See map on page 304.) The population of Holstein, which had been part of the German Confederation since 1815, was entirely German. Schleswig's population included a mix of Germans and Danes. The Danish king ruled the two

duchies under a constitution that provided separation from Denmark. In 1863 King Christian IX came to the Danish throne. At the insistence of many Danes, he proclaimed a new constitution under which he tried to annex Schleswig to Denmark.

Both Prussia and Austria protested the new Danish constitution. Together they demanded that it be revoked. When Denmark refused, Prussia and Austria declared war on Denmark. Denmark hoped for help from France and Great Britain; however, neither country acted. In 1864, after three months of fighting, Denmark surrendered.

The peace treaty gave the two duchies to Prussia and Austria jointly. That arrangement brought conflict between Austria and Prussia. Austria wanted the two duchies to form a single independent state within the German Confederation. Prussia opposed the idea. After a bitter quarrel, Prussian and Austrian leaders decided that Prussia would administer Schleswig, and Austria would administer Holstein.

The Seven Weeks' War. As Prussian influence expanded, Bismarck moved to confront Austria. He prepared for conflict by means of skillful diplomatic actions, ensuring that no one would aid Austria. First, he persuaded Napoleon III of France to remain neutral if war broke out between Prussia and Austria. In return for neutrality, France expected territory from the German Confederation. Bismarck left Napoleon III with the mistaken idea he might gain some territory on the Rhine, although none was ever ceded.

Bismarck next formed an alliance with the new nation of Italy. In return for support against Austria, Italy would receive the Austrian territory of Venetia. Then, using the ongoing dispute over Schleswig and Holstein, Bismarck provoked Austria into declaring war on Prussia in 1866.

Austria did not anticipate the superb training and preparation of the Prussian army. In fact, Prussia's efficient conduct of the war startled the whole world. Prussian forces took advantage of technology— moving by train, communicating via the telegraph, and using modern weaponry. They defeated the once-powerful Austrians in only seven weeks. The balance of European power dramatically changed.

The **Treaty of Prague** ended the so-called Seven Weeks' War in the summer of 1866. Under its lenient terms Austria approved the dissolution of the German Confederation and surrendered Holstein to Prussia. The Italians gained Venetia.

In 1867 several north German states united with Prussia to form the North German Confederation. Each state had self-government, but the king of Prussia was hereditary president of the Confederation. As the largest state, with the most powerful industry and army, and with the greatest number of representatives, Prussia dominated the legislature of the new confederation.

Only the three southern states of Bavaria, Baden, and Württemberg and the southern part of Hesse-Darmstadt remained outside Prussia's influence. If they could be persuaded to join Prussia, German unity would be complete.

The Franco-Prussian War. Bismarck decided that the way to unite the southern states with the rest of Germany was to provoke a war with France. His opportunity came in 1870 when Spain sought a new ruler. Spain offered the throne to Prince Leopold, cousin of the king of Prussia. France objected to the appointment because it meant that the Hohenzollern family would rule both Prussia and Spain, encircling France. Alarmed by Prussian ambition and angered that Bismarck had "tried to cheat" him after the Seven Weeks' War, Napoleon III demanded of Prussia and Spain that Leopold turn down the offer.

Leopold did withdraw, but the French also insisted that King William I of Prussia pledge publicly that no member of the Hohenzollern family would ever be a candidate for the Spanish throne.

The French ambassador delivered the French demand to King William at a resort known as Ems. The king replied vaguely but politely and declined to discuss such a pledge further at Ems.

Bismarck received a detailed dispatch from the king, summarizing the meeting with the French ambassador. Bismarck edited the dispatch, altering and omitting details. He made it seem as though the French had tried to humiliate the Prussian king, and that William had dismissed the ambassador offensively and contemptuously. Then Bismarck released the so-called Ems telegram to the newspapers.

Outraged at the Ems telegram, France declared war on Prussia in July 1870. Bismarck reasoned correctly that the southern German states would unite against a perceived French threat. He thus converted the states from rivals into allies against France.

The Franco-Prussian War was short but decisive. No outside nation came to the aid of France. Well trained, well equipped, and ably led, the Prussian army defeated the French in hard fighting within a few months. Napoleon III himself surrendered in September, and his government fell. Guerrilla fighting continued until Paris surrendered in January 1871 after a bitter siege. A treaty was concluded in May.

Bismarck had been lenient with Austria following its defeat because he did not want its large German population as enemies, nor did he wish to invite French intervention. He had no such reservations after the Franco-Prussian war, however. France was occupied by German troops, lost Alsace and part of Lorraine, and had to pay a huge indemnity.

Formation of the German Empire

For Germany the peace was not as important as an event that took place before the signing of the treaty. On January 18, 1871, representatives of the allied German states met in the Hall of Mirrors of the palace of Versailles near Paris. There they issued a proclamation declaring the formation of the German Empire, which included all German states except Austria. (See map on page 304.) Berlin, the Prussian capital, became the capital of the empire. King William I of Prussia was proclaimed German emperor. The position of chancellor—or chief minister—was created for Bismarck, who retained his post of prime minister of Prussia as well.

As much as he disliked constitutions, Bismarck, who was nicknamed the "Iron Chancellor" for his policy of "iron and blood," accepted a constitution that united the 25 German states in a federal form of government. This constitution, though it reflected Bismarck's tendency toward authoritarian government, also allowed for rights for individual states because of the rural nature of the region. Each state had its own ruler as well as the right to handle its own domestic matters, including education, law enforcement, and local taxation. Southern states had some special rights, such as Bavaria's right to control its military.

The federal government controlled all common matters, such as national defense, foreign affairs, and commerce. The emperor, called the **kaiser**, headed the government. The kaiser held tremendous power. He appointed the chancellor, and he commanded the army and navy. The kaiser could declare a defensive war on his own, and he could order an offensive war with the agreement of the upper house of the legislature.

The legislative branch of the government consisted of two houses. The **Bundesrat**, or upper house, was a federal council, which consisted of 58 appointed members. The **Reichstag**, or legislative assembly, made up the German legislature's lower house. Its nearly 400 members were elected by universal male suffrage. Theoretically a representative body, the Reichstag, however, had limited powers. It could approve military budgets only once every seven years and saw only those bills that the Bundesrat had already approved. This combination of restrictions made it almost impossible for the Reichstag to effect any liberal democratic change that the Bundesrat or emperor might not support.

The German constitution strongly favored the interests of Prussia. The king of Prussia was also the kaiser of Germany. Prussia had the most delegates in the Bundesrat and, because it was the most populous German state, it also had the largest representation in the Reichstag.

This painting depicts the ceremony in which King William I of Prussia was crowned emperor of Germany.

Building History Study Skills

READ
WRITE
INTERPRET
CONNECT
THINK

Writing About History: Writing a Comparison Essay

To make comparisons is to identify both similarities and differences. Writing a comparison essay helps us to see relationships, make connections between conflicting ideas, and analyze the similarities and differences between these ideas.

How to Write a Comparison Essay

To write a comparison essay, follow these steps.

1. State the topic for comparison.
2. On a separate sheet of paper, write the categories for comparison. The categories should be broad points under which similarities and differences on the topic can be listed.
3. List the similarities and differences under each category. Then begin writing the essay, further explaining these similarities and differences that have been listed under each category.
4. In the last paragraph, form a conclusion that synthesizes the information in your essay. The conclusion should be more than a summary. It should be an analytical statement of comparison, using the categories that you have already developed in the body of the essay.

Developing the Skill

If you were to write an essay comparing Italian and German unification, you might establish the categories of comparison as leadership, methods, and results. Study the following essay and identify the categories.

A caricature of Bismarck

"A renewed spirit of nationalism marked the late 1800s in Europe. Nationalism triumphed in both Italy and Germany. The unification of these nations was accomplished because of the leadership of Cavour and Garibaldi in Italy, and of Bismarck in Germany.

Cavour's skill lay in his ability to direct political events to his own grand scheme. After he started a war with Austria in 1859, France entered on the side of Italy. Cavour also succeeded in getting Lombardy and some of the central states annexed to Italy.

Garibaldi led his republican army in rebellion in the kingdom of Two Sicilies and, in a compromise with Cavour, made them part of the kingdom of Italy.

German unification did not have the multiple leadership and republican elements that existed in Italian unification. However, the manipulation of Austria and the provoking of war were similar characteristics. Bismarck manipulated events and took advantage of opportunities. He united the southern part of Germany with the rest of the country when he stirred up nationalistic and emotional feelings against France after provoking a war with that nation. Republicanism and liberalism were not part of the German unification process.

Italian unification, although it did involve war, incorporated the ideals of republicanism and nationalism and had two leaders, Cavour and Garibaldi. The unification of Germany included nationalism but came about through Bismarck's policies of 'iron and blood'."

Notice that the first paragraph identified the topic and stated the categories. The second, third, and fourth paragraphs developed the categories of leadership, methods, and results. The concluding paragraph synthesized the categories of comparison by showing the different methods of unification.

Practicing the Skill

After reading current newspaper or magazine articles, write a comparison essay on the views of any two political candidates.

To apply this skill, see Applying History Study Skills on page 317.

Unification of Germany, 1865–1871

Learning from Maps As a result of Germany's three wars against Denmark, Austria, and France, Bismarck completed the unification of Germany in 1871.

? Place Which battles were fought within the boundary of the German Empire? outside the empire?

Section 2 Review

1. **Define** *Zollverein*, Treaty of Prague, kaiser, Bundesrat, Reichstag
2. **Identify** Junkers, William I, Iron Chancellor
3. **Locate and Explain the Significance** Saxony, Schleswig, Holstein, Bavaria, Württemberg
4. **Analyzing Ideas** Explain how the Seven Weeks' War served to display Prussia's superiority over Austria.
5. **Contrasting Ideas** Compare and contrast the different roads that were taken to unification by Italy and Germany.
6. **Summarizing Ideas** Describe the type of government that Germany had after the unification of the German states.

Section 3

Opposition to Bismarck

Focus Questions

- **What problems did Bismarck face as chancellor of the German Empire?**
- **How did Germany become industrialized under Bismarck's leadership?**
- **What factors led to the waning of Bismarck's power as chancellor?**

Because the constitution did not give Bismarck the absolute monarchy he wanted, he tried to achieve it in other ways. However, in the years after formation of the German Empire, he had to accept compromises to make the political system work. Although the constitution gave the people little voice, the government was increasingly forced to attend to their demands.

Problems for the Empire

In spite of rigid control by aristocratic Prussians, the new German federal government soon encountered problems. Dissatisfied groups formed political parties that opposed Bismarck's policies. Some wanted the government to be more liberal and democratic and to enact social reforms. Others feared Bismarck's military policy and the ever-growing army.

Representatives in the legislative assemblies from Prussia were conservative, elected by a special system that gave more representation to voters from the upper class, but politicians from other areas of the empire were more likely to oppose Bismarck. Increasing power of other political groups in the rest of the empire thus increased tension between Prussia and the other German states.

Relations with the Catholic Church presented special problems for Bismarck. He was a Protestant and did not trust the church. A doctrine of papal infallibility announced by the Vatican Council in 1870 added to his distrust of Catholic loyalty to the empire. Many Catholics were also members of the Centre Party, a party he regarded as an enemy.

Bismarck initiated the anti-Catholic program of **Kulturkampf**—German for "culture struggle"—in which Germany passed strict laws to control Catholic clergy and Catholic schools. The laws expelled Jesuits, forbade political expression from the pulpit, and required that all Catholic clergy be Germans who had been educated in German schools. Diplomatic relations with the Vatican were broken as part of *Kulturkampf*, and even more restrictive laws went into effect, establishing civil marriage and eventually confiscating church property.

These policies stirred opposition. The Centre Party doubled in size. Many non-Catholic liberals also joined the opposition. By 1878 Bismarck began to modify the *Kulturkampf* because he needed the support of the Centre Party against a growing socialist presence. He reestablished diplomatic relations with the papacy and had laws against Catholics eased or repealed. The *Kulturkampf* ended in failure by 1887.

Industrial Development Under Bismarck

Bismarck transformed Prussia into an industrial giant. Germany contained a rich store of natural resources, including great coal and iron deposits in the Ruhr Valley and Silesia. The German government managed railroads to promote industrial development, and a system of canals provided cheaper transportation.

Industrialization came later in Germany than in Great Britain and France, which proved to be an advantage for Germany. German industries could use the best methods and most advanced machinery that had been developed elsewhere. German scientists then worked out further changes and improvements.

As chancellor of the German Empire, Bismarck initiated several industrial reforms such as the standardization of money and the centralization of transportation. This photo shows the German industrial city of Dresden in 1875.

Under Bismarck's leadership, the government helped industry in many ways. It standardized money and banking laws throughout the empire. Postal and telegraph services—the means of communication by which so much business was conducted—were centralized. The government encouraged German industrialists to form cartels to control prices, and adopted a high-tariff policy to protect industries from foreign competition. Germany rapidly became an industrial power rivaling Great Britain and France.

Socialism in Germany

With the growth of German industry, cities grew rapidly, and a class of factory workers appeared. German laborers, like those in other nations, wanted decent working conditions. Some people believed that the action of the cartels led to lower wages for workers and higher prices for consumers. Many people thought that these problems required government action. They wanted the government to pass laws that would benefit workers and regulate industry.

As in other European nations, socialist reformers went further, advocating government ownership of major industries. German socialists banded together in 1869 to form what would become the **Social Democratic Party** (SDP). The party grew quickly, with most of its members coming from the ranks of urban workers. By 1877 the Social Democratic Party had elected 12 members to the Reichstag.

Even if the SDP had gained a much greater representation, it would have accomplished very little. The Reichstag could not pass any laws that the Bundesrat opposed. Because the Bundesrat represented aristocratic hereditary rulers, there was little chance that it would propose or pass the laws that socialists wanted. The Reichstag, however, served as a limited public forum in which socialist members could express grievances and make proposals of what they would do if they were given the power.

Bismarck's Antisocialist Campaign

Every gain in socialist voting strength—and every new demand for reform—alarmed Bismarck. When the Social Democrats won more than 490,000 votes in an election in 1877, the chancellor decided to use all of his power to fight them. His opportunity came in 1878, when two attempts to assassinate the emperor occurred. Neither of the would-be assassins had any connection with socialism, and Bismarck knew this. However, he took advantage of public concern to accuse the Social Democrats of plotting

the assassination attempts. The emperor and the Bundesrat dissolved the Reichstag and then called for new elections. A widespread campaign against socialists and their ideas followed.

The election did not change the strength of the Social Democrats in the Reichstag. Bismarck, however, pushed through a number of laws aimed at repressing the socialists. The new laws prohibited newspapers, books, or pamphlets from spreading socialist ideas and banned public meetings of socialists.

Despite such restrictive laws, socialists continued their efforts and the Social Democrats increased their support with each election. As he had done in the *Kulturkampf*, Bismarck changed his tactics to try to retain control against growing opposition.

Since repression had failed, the Iron Chancellor was forced to try another approach. He decided to grant many of the reforms the socialists proposed. If the government granted reforms, Bismarck believed, fewer people would have reason to support the socialists, and the party would lose strength.

Beginning in 1883, he endorsed several far-reaching reforms. First came insurance against sickness, then insurance against accidents—both paid for by employers. Other laws limited working hours, provided for certain holidays from work, and guaranteed pensions for disabled and retired workers.

Germany thus adopted a pioneering program of government-directed social reforms. The reforms did not end socialism in Germany, but they did diminish some of the workers' grievances. Many other industrial nations later adopted similar programs of government-directed social reforms.

The Resignation of Bismarck

Emperor William I died in 1888. His son, Frederick III, reigned for only a few months before he, too, died and was succeeded by his son, William II.

What If?

Bismarck
What if Bismarck had not initiated a program of social reform in Germany in the 1880s? How might the history of Germany and other industrial nations have been different?

The young monarch and the old chancellor soon disagreed deeply. William II felt that Bismarck was too powerful. Bismarck resented the way that the young emperor reduced powers the chancellor had wielded effectively for years. When the socialists scored huge gains in the 1890 elections, Bismarck considered convening the aristocrats to come up with a new constitution.

William II realized that this would create governmental havoc at the outset of his reign. He asked Bismarck to resign, which Bismarck did with a great deal of bitterness. Bismarck criticized his successors for the rest of his life, and though elected to the Reichstag, he refused to serve.

With Bismarck gone, William II set out to expand Germany's influence in the world. He increased the size and strength of the German army even further and began to expand the German navy. This move brought Germany into competition with Great Britain, at that time the world's leading naval power. William signed new agreements with neighboring nations, and by the early 1900s Germany was stronger than ever before.

Shortly after his ascent to Germany's throne, William II (left) forced Bismarck to resign as chancellor.

Section 3 Review

1. **Define** *Kulturkampf,* Social Democratic Party
2. **Identify** William II
3. **Understanding Ideas** What were two problems faced by the German Empire in the 1870s and 1880s?
4. **Analyzing Ideas** What were the major factors responsible for Germany's rapid industrial development under Bismarck?
5. **Interpreting Ideas** What factors combined to decrease Bismarck's power?

Section 4

Reform and Revolution in Russia

Focus Questions

- **What geographical and cultural factors made Russia different from the rest of Europe?**
- **What were the characteristics of Russian domestic and foreign policies?**
- **What types of reform movements occurred in Russia, and what were their results?**

By the mid-1800s Russia had the largest territory and population of any European nation. Yet industrial development, which so strengthened the West, lagged in Russia. Most of the country's extensive natural resources lay undeveloped. Ports were blocked by ice for much of the year, or exits from the seas were controlled by other countries, leaving Russia virtually landlocked. This situation had led to many Russian attempts to win access to the Mediterranean, past Constantinople and the Ottoman-controlled Dardanelles. However, these efforts led to conflicts with the Ottoman Empire.

Unlike Great Britain or France, Russia lacked a homogeneous population. The huge Russian Empire included a great variety of peoples and national groups. Although the largest ethnic groups in the European part of Russia—the Belorussian or White Russian group in the west, the Ukrainians in the agricultural south, and the Great Russians in north and central Russia—were related groups descended from Slavic ancestors, each had their own language, customs, and history. These main Slavic groups were also divided by vast geography. Scattered throughout the empire were numerous racial, national, and religious minorities speaking many languages. Many of these groups, such as the Poles and Finns, had been conquered by the Russians and disliked Russian rule.

Russian Domestic and Foreign Policies

The liberal movement that influenced other European nations so strongly in the 1800s made little progress in Russia. The czar ruled the huge Russian Empire as an **autocrat**, one who holds absolute power. Although the czars tried to maintain autocracy, liberal political developments in Europe affected Russia.

Russia had struggled with the influence of the West from before the time of Peter the Great a century earlier. Nationalistic ideas appealed to the Russian minorities, especially to the strongly patriotic Poles and Finns. By the early 1800s, liberalism began to attract some of the educated members of the Russian aristocracy.

Faced with problems caused by liberal ideas and restless nationalities, the czars took harsh measures. To counteract liberalism the government strictly censored speech and the press and rejected all demands for a constitution. In the 1830s Czar Nicholas I began a program of "**Russification**." This program forced non-Russian peoples in the empire to use the Russian language, accept the Orthodox religion, and adopt Russian customs.

Russian foreign policy had two primary features. (1) In the Balkans, Russia promoted **Pan-Slavism**—the union of all Slavic peoples under Russian leadership. (2) Elsewhere, Russia sought to continue expansion, begun under the first czars, east into Asia and south toward the Ottoman Empire. Expansion southward, however, was halted with a defeat in the Crimean War in the 1850s. Russia lost crucial border territory.

Alexander II and Reforms

Alexander II became czar in 1855. Although basically conservative and autocratic, Alexander cared about public opinion, and he responded, though cautiously, to the movement for freedom for all serfs. His actions were the first steps toward modernization for a country that realized its backwardness with its defeat in the Crimea.

Serfdom had taken a different form in Russia than it had in the rest of Europe. After the time of Peter the Great, serfs were bound to persons and not to the land. They could not leave their villages or masters' homes unless permitted to do so by their owners or ordered to do so by government officials. Although unable to move freely, and largely under the control of their masters, serfs still held a few civil rights such as the right to sue in court.

Toward the middle of the 1800s, reform of serfdom became clearly necessary. Serfdom obstructed development by restricting the labor pool. Factory owners would benefit if the serfs were freed. The industrialists did not believe in liberal ideas; they simply needed workers for their factories. Some nobles who felt a great nation should not sanction the ownership of people also began to support a campaign against serfdom. Another group of government officials, most notably in the ministry of the interior, sought reform for the serfs and convinced Alexander II to consider abolishing this institution.

In 1861 Alexander II issued the **Emancipation Edict,** which freed all serfs. The czar had concluded "it is better to abolish serfdom from above than to wait until the serfs begin to liberate themselves from below." The terms of the edict compensated nobles for land, which peasants could buy in small tracts from the government.

Emancipation did not really improve conditions for the former serfs. Some of the land they had previously farmed was sold to them in tiny plots at high prices. Most freed serfs could not afford to buy enough land to earn the payments for the land, pay taxes, and still make a living. Therefore, they had to rent more land from their former owners—and rents were high. Some former serfs, unable to either buy or rent land, moved to growing towns and cities, where they became cheap sources of labor for factories.

Alexander II attempted other liberal reforms, looking to modernize his nation. Beginning in 1864 he allowed rural districts to elect *zemstvos*. These were councils, at the provincial and county levels, which were elected by all classes, including peasants. *Zemstvos* could levy taxes and controlled programs such as public health, education, assistance for the poor, local crafts, and some public works programs.

Alexander also reformed the courts. Civil and criminal courts were modeled after their European counterparts, and appeals courts were instituted, as were local justices of the peace. Delay and corruption declined in the court system. However, the ministry of the interior still had power beyond the reach of the courts in political cases.

Fabergé Egg

This unusual piece of art is an enameled gold egg containing a completely accurate model of the Gatchina Palace near St. Petersburg. Only five inches high, it even includes a tiny flag flying from the palace tower. It is decorated with pearls and diamonds. Historians think this egg was given to the mother of Czar Nicholas II on Easter morning, 1902. It was customary for the Russian royal family to exchange eggs like this one every Easter. An egg is an ancient symbol of rebirth or renewed life, expressed in Christianity as the resurrection of Jesus at Easter.

The Gatchina egg, as it is called, was created in the jewelry firm of Carl Fabergé in St. Petersburg. Founded in 1842, this company employed the finest jewelers and goldsmiths in all of Europe. These artisans also designed magnificent boxes, clocks, tableware, and jewelry. It was the series of eggs, however, that secured Fabergé's reputation. Most of the eggs were signed by Michael Perchin, who was one of the few native Russians employed by Fabergé.

The famed House of Fabergé was closed in 1918 by officials of the new government. In order to raise money, the government sold all but 10 of the eggs. Today, many of these priceless eggs are housed in private collections and museums.

The policies of reform did not please everyone. Conservatives opposed them and tried to convince the czar that such actions endangered the position of the ruler and the nobles, and thus the stability of the nation. Liberals considered Alexander's reforms to be mere first steps and pointed out the need for further changes. Radicals criticized Alexander even more strongly.

Radicals and Government Reaction

Several groups carried on radical political activity in Russia. Many middle and upper-class intellectuals became nihilists—from the Latin word *nihil*, meaning "nothing"—in the 1860s. They believed a just society could be created only by abolishing the existing political, economic, and social structures and building a completely new Russia.

In the 1870s another group, the Populists, urged their followers to live among peasants as teachers and doctors. Some believed that the large estates of the nobles should be seized and the land divided among the peasants. After the government arrested many Populists, some Russian radicals turned to violent action, splitting off to a movement called **People's Will**. These radicals used **terrorism**—bombings and assassinations by political groups—to try to force the government to grant their demands.

Radical activity gradually made Alexander II more conservative. The first attempt on his life was made in 1866, and after this attempt, he turned to repressive measures. Still, reforms continued. In 1870, major cities were granted limited elected government and in 1874 military reforms were instituted. After repeated assassination attempts, which Alexander faced with great courage, he was killed by a bomb attack by People's Will in 1881.

The assassination of Alexander II ended liberal reform and led to an era of intensive repression. Alexander III and his successor, Nicholas II, used every available means to stamp out liberalism—censorship, control of the church and of education, spies and informers, even imprisonment and exile. They revived and intensified Russification in heavy-handed discrimination against minority groups, and sponsored massacres of Jews in riots called **pogroms** (POH·gruhmz). Many of the reforms of Alexander II were overturned, and Nicholas labeled liberal goals "senseless dreams."

The attempt to preserve the old order met with much opposition—both overt and covert. The development of industry in Russia had produced a class of city workers who wanted the right to form unions and to strike. Liberals and radicals, more determined than ever to gain reforms, found an audience in these often-exploited workers.

The attempts of the Russian government to block all change produced an explosive situation. Terrorism increased. Socialists, who in 1898 had founded the **Social Democratic Labor Party** in imitation of the German Social Democratic Party, grew increasingly radical. The government's repression backfired.

The Revolution of 1905

In 1904 and 1905, Russia went to war with Japan over territories in China and Korea. To the surprise of the world, the Japanese dealt the Russians a humiliating defeat. Russia's loss exposed a government that was corrupt and inefficient, as well as autocratic and oppressive. The defeat spurred discontented groups in the country to action.

On January 22, 1905, "Bloody Sunday," the czar's troops shot at a group of unarmed strikers on their way to deliver a petition to him. The incident triggered the Revolution of 1905. Workers struck and held demonstrations. The street fighting that broke out was especially violent in non-Russian areas, and there were mutinies in the army and navy. Czar

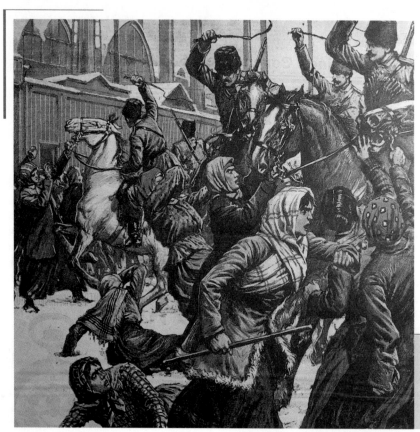

On Bloody Sunday, January 22, 1905, Russian troops fired shots at a group of peaceful demonstrators, thus beginning the Revolution of 1905.

Nicholas II faced a crisis. Russian autocracy had to yield or perish. He reluctantly decided to yield.

The czar issued a decree called the October Manifesto, which promised individual liberties and provided for the election of a parliament called the **Duma**. After more bloody fighting, severe repression and executions stilled the revolution.

Because of its weakness after the Russo-Japanese War, the government had to confront its critics. But autocracy continued. The czar dismissed two sessions of the Duma because members insisted that the czar's ministers be responsible to the Duma. A 1907 electoral law increased the representation of large landowners and restricted the voting of others. The result was a more conservative Duma and one more cooperative with the czar.

The revolutionary movement of 1905 failed to overthrow the czar for three main reasons: (1) The army remained loyal and thus would not end the czar's regime. (2) The French, bound to Russia by military alliance, lent money to the government. (3) The many revolutionary groups were divided in their goals. Moderates feared radical demands and radicals disagreed among themselves.

The reactionaries learned nothing from the Revolution of 1905. The government often treated people with contempt, and bureaucrats openly broke laws that they were supposed to enforce. Using extreme repressive measures as before, the autocracy tried vainly to resist change and to preserve the thousand-year-old monarchy.

Section 4 Review

1. **Define** autocrat, Russification, Pan-Slavism, Emancipation Edict, People's Will, terrorism, pogroms, Social Democratic Labor Party, Duma
2. **Identify** nihilists
3. **Interpreting Ideas** How did Russia's geography and culture make its situation different from Britain and France?
4. **Summarizing Ideas** (a) Explain how liberalism affected Russia's domestic policy. (b) Describe the two features of Russia's foreign policy.
5. **Organizing Ideas** (a) List the liberal reforms that Alexander II accomplished in Russia. (b) What did he do with regard to the serfs?
6. **Analyzing Ideas** (a) Why did the Revolution of 1905 fail to overthrow the monarchy? (b) How did Nicholas II respond to the Revolution of 1905?

Unrest in Austria-Hungary

Focus Questions

- **What led to the formation of the Dual Monarchy, and what problems did it face?**
- **How did the decline of the Ottoman Empire affect European politics?**
- **How did ethnic clashes in southern Europe set the stage for a showdown among major powers?**

"When France sneezes, all Europe catches cold," the Austrian minister Metternich said in 1848. He was referring to the fact that uprisings in France had set off revolts in almost every other European nation. The Austrian Empire proved no exception.

In Vienna demonstrators and the army clashed. A frightened Emperor Ferdinand ordered Metternich, his chief minister, to resign. After having dominated European affairs for over 30 years, Metternich fled the country. Later in 1848 Ferdinand himself abdicated, and the throne went to 18-year-old Francis Joseph I.

Uprisings also occurred in Hungary. The people of this region—one of the largest parts of the Austrian Empire—chafed under Austrian rule. Most of them were Magyars—descendants of a nomadic warrior group that had migrated to Hungary from Russia and Romania in the 900s. The Magyars spoke a language unlike other European languages and maintained a distinct culture. A strong nationalist movement centered on making the Magyars dominant in Hungary and freeing the region from Austrian domination.

Hungarian patriot Lajos Kossuth led a revolt in 1848. For a time it looked as though Hungary would gain independence, and in 1849 Kossuth was elected "responsible governor president" by the Hungarian Diet. However, Austria, with Russia's assistance, soon ousted the revolutionaries. Czar Nicholas I sent troops because he feared that revolution might spread to Russian-controlled Poland. Kossuth fled to Turkey, temporarily ending Hungarian attempts at independence.

Formation of the Dual Monarchy

For almost 20 years after the Revolution of 1848, Austria managed to keep liberalism and nationalism

Ethnic Groups in Austria-Hungary, 1867

PRUSSIA

Elbe River

Oder River

RUSSIAN EMPIRE

Vistula River

• Prague

BOHEMIA

CZECHS

MORAVIA
• Brno

BAVARIA

GALICIA

Kraków •

SLOVAKS

Danube River

Vienna •

• Salzburg

AUSTRIA-HUNGARY

Buda • Pest

Tisza River

• Innsbruck

TIROL

Drava River

CARNIOLA

• Trieste

CROATS

TRANSYLVANIA

LOMBARDY

Po River

CROATIA-SLAVONIA

CROATS

SERBS

BOSNIA

SERBS

SERBIA

ROMANIA

KINGDOM OF ITALY

DALMATIA

ADRIATIC SEA

Sarajevo •

HERZE-GOVINA

OTTOMAN EMPIRE

• MONTENEGRO

42°N

Slavs:	Others:
Croats and Serbs	Germans
Czechs and Slovaks	Magyars
Poles	Romanians
Slovenes	Italians
Ukrainians	

0   100   200 Miles
0   100   200 Kilometers
Lambert Conformal Conic Projection

12°E   18°E

Learning from Maps While Austria and Hungary joined together under the Dual Monarchy, they retained separate parliaments and languages.

? Human-Environment Interaction Which non-Slavic peoples settled throughout Austria-Hungary?

---

from wrecking its empire. However, after Austria's defeat by Prussia in 1866, Hungarians demanded more freedom. Austria responded in 1867 by forming the Dual Monarchy—also called Austria-Hungary—in which Hungarians shared power with Austrians.

The Dual Monarchy had a common ruler, Francis Joseph I, whose title was Emperor of Austria and King of Hungary. Although three ministries—war, finance, and foreign affairs—conducted government business for the whole empire, Austria and Hungary each had its own parliament. The Austrian parliament met

in Vienna; the Hungarian one met in what became the city of Budapest.

The Dual Monarchy proved to be a practical economic arrangement. Hungary, chiefly agricultural, furnished raw materials and food. Austria, strongly industrial, produced manufactured goods. Each provided markets for the other.

Many problems existed, however. Because of its manufacturing interests, Austria wanted high protective tariffs. As a farming region, Hungary favored low tariffs and freer trade.

Moreover, the formation of the Dual Monarchy did not solve the problem of nationalities. The Austrian Germans and the Hungarian Magyars dominated the population in each of their separate national states. The Austrians spoke German. The Hungarians spoke Magyar, or Hungarian, which had been declared the official language of Hungary. National minorities—the Czechs, Serbs, Croats, Romanians, Poles, Slovenes, Ukrainians, and Italians—existed in both Austria and Hungary. (See map on opposite page.) These people benefited very little from the Dual Monarchy and continued to agitate for self-government.

A disastrous and stunning defeat by Prussia in the Seven Weeks' War in 1866 forced Austria from positions of power in Germany and Italy and its leadership of Europe. To compensate for this setback, and hoping to gain influence and territory, the Dual Monarchy turned toward the Balkans, a region to the southeast controlled chiefly by the Ottoman Empire.

The Ottoman Empire

By the 1800s the Ottoman Empire had declined substantially. At its peak in the 1500s, the empire had stretched around the Mediterranean Sea from Algeria through Egypt and the Arabian Peninsula, through Asia Minor, Mesopotamia, Greece, and into southern Europe as far as Austria. But economic problems and the vast size of the empire made it hard to govern. Military defeats in the 1700s diminished the empire's size, and the rise of local rulers weakened central authority. A rising population was difficult to feed on poor lands. Slow modernization, for economic and cultural reasons, also contributed to the decline of the once-strong and disciplined empire.

Economic and social problems. The subject peoples of the Ottoman Turks did not regard their rulers favorably. Ottoman rulers in the 1800s could not afford many improvements in agriculture or public works projects such as roads and hospitals. The tax system often favored foreign interests at the expense of Ottoman subjects. Many of the people living in the empire were Christians or Jews. In religious and cultural matters, the Turks granted toleration and self-control to non-Muslims under their own religious leaders. However, there was no pretense of equality in Ottoman society or governmental affairs.

Discontent in the Balkans

In the early 1800s, the rise of nationalism increased discontent in the Balkan area of the Ottoman Empire. The Balkan region contained several different peoples—Serbs, Bulgarians, Romanians, Albanians, and Greeks, for example—all of whom wanted to govern themselves.

The Turks tried to suppress nationalistic movements. During the 1820s Greeks and Serbs revolted. Aided by outside powers, Greece gained independence in 1829, and Serbia achieved a degree of self-rule. Encouraged by these successes and by the evident weakness of the Turks, Serbia and Greece tried to gain more territory.

Foreign countries intervened to promote their own interests in struggles between the Turks and these nationalist groups. Russia supported Balkan nationalists for several reasons. The Russians were Slavs like the Bulgarians and Serbs. In addition, like many of the discontented Balkan groups, the Russians were Orthodox Christians. Strategically, if the Ottoman Empire collapsed, Russia might be able to control the water route from the Black Sea to the Mediterranean Sea.

The Russian drive toward the eastern Mediterranean caused the British to support the crumbling Ottoman Empire. Great Britain did not want the Russians in the Mediterranean, where they might challenge British sea power.

It was a curious alignment of nations. The autocratic Russian government promoted the independence of the Balkan peoples. Democratic Great Britain supported the Turks in suppressing self-rule.

The Congress of Berlin and the Balkan Wars

In 1875 revolts broke out in several Turkish provinces in the Balkans. Two years later Russia chose to support the rebels and declared war on the Ottoman Empire. The Turks were defeated and forced to sign the **Treaty of San Stefano** in 1878. The treaty granted independence to Romania, Serbia, and Montenegro. It also created an autonomous Bulgaria, which Russian troops then occupied for some years. The new boundaries of Bulgaria extended to the Aegean Sea in the eastern Mediterranean.

The sudden increase of Russian influence in the Balkans alarmed other European powers. Before the Treaty of San Stefano went into effect, a group of nations led by Great Britain and Austria forced Russia to consent to an international conference.

All the major European powers met at the Congress of Berlin in 1878. The Congress dealt with several territorial issues. Serbia, Montenegro, and Romania retained their independence. Bulgaria was granted self-government, but its area was divided and reduced in size, and it was kept within the Ottoman Empire—thus removing Russia's access to the Aegean Sea. Austria continued to govern Bosnia and Herzegovina but was not permitted to annex them.

The British were given the right to occupy and administer the island of Cyprus, long held by the Turks. The Turkish sultan still officially ruled the island, but Great Britain actually took over. The use of Cyprus as a naval base increased Great Britain's power in the eastern Mediterranean and kept Russia out of the region.

Other nations continued to reduce the size and power of the Ottoman Empire. France, Great Britain, and Italy each seized parts of its African territory. In 1908 Bulgaria became completely independent. In the same year, Austria broke the agreement of the Congress of Berlin by annexing Bosnia and Herzegovina outright. In 1912 Italy seized several islands in the southeastern Aegean Sea, including Rhodes. The island of Crete revolted in 1896 and 1905, resulting first in a degree of self-government and then annexation by Greece in 1913.

Decline of the Ottoman Empire, 1699–1913

Legend:
- Territory lost, 1699–1913
- Ottoman Empire in 1913
- ✷ National capital
- • Other city

Dates on the map indicate independence or acquisition by another country.

Learning from Maps Throughout the 1800s and early 1900s many territories of the Ottoman Empire became independent or were annexed by other countries.

? Location What are the approximate latitude and longitude coordinates for the capital of the Ottoman Empire?

As a result of the two Balkan Wars, the Ottoman Empire lost a considerable amount of territory. This Balkan Wars illustration is taken from the cover of a 1913 *Le Petit Journal* supplement.

In 1912 and 1913, two wars between independent Balkan nations and the Ottomans further altered national boundaries and increased international tensions. Bulgaria, Serbia, Greece, and Montenegro, known as the **Balkan League**, declared war on the Ottoman Empire and won. The Balkan League wanted to divide among themselves the Balkan territories of the Ottoman Empire. However, they could not agree on the partition of the Turkish territories, and hostilities broke out again in 1913. This time, Serbia, Greece, Montenegro, Romania, and the Ottoman Empire fought against and defeated Bulgaria.

As a result of the first war, Serbia gained a seaport on the Adriatic, and Albania became independent. Bulgaria claimed considerable territory in the central Balkans and along the Aegean Sea. As a result of the second war, however, Bulgaria suffered humiliating territorial losses and was left with only a small outlet on the Aegean.

By the end of 1913, the territory of the Ottoman Empire in Europe had shrunk dramatically. It included only the city of Constantinople and a small region that gave it control of the vital water route from the Black Sea to the Mediterranean. (See map on opposite page.)

Everywhere in Europe, tension, aggression, and expansion marked the behavior of new nations and old in the early 1900s. Internal and international hostilities began to rise to dangerous levels. War clouds gathered on the horizons of major imperial European powers.

Section 5 Review

1. **Define** Treaty of San Stefano, Balkan League
2. **Identify** Magyars, Francis Joseph I
3. **Locate and Explain the Significance** Romania, Budapest, Serbia, Montenegro, Bulgaria, Bosnia, Herzegovina, Cyprus, Rhodes
4. **Summarizing Ideas** (a) When was the Dual Monarchy formed? (b) What were its strengths and weaknesses?
5. **Organizing Ideas** (a) How was the Ottoman Empire reduced in size between 1878 and 1913? (b) How did this decline of the Ottoman Empire affect European politics?
6. **Interpreting Ideas** (a) Why did the Western nations fear Russian influence in the Balkans? (b) What prompted the Congress of Berlin?

Chapter 9 Review

A.D. 1848
Revolts take place in Italy, Germany, and the Austrian Empire.

A.D. 1810

A.D. 1830

A.D. 1850

A.D. 1806–1813
Napoleon I dominates Prussia.

A.D. 1820–1854
Organization and expansion of *Zollverein* occurs.

Chapter Summary
The following list contains the key concepts you have learned about the unification of Italy and Germany and about conflicts that arose in other European nations in the late 1800s and early 1900s.
1. Italy was unified in 1870 due to the efforts of Mazzini, Garibaldi, and Cavour. A kingdom was established, and the capital of this kingdom was Rome.
2. The kingdom of Prussia led the German unification under the leadership of Otto von Bismarck.
3. In Germany, aggressive behavior brought about unification. The Germans used three victorious wars to crush their rivals and to strengthen German nationalism.
4. Bismarck ran into opposition from various political groups. He at first tried to repress the socialists and then endorsed certain reforms. A clash with the new emperor, William II, forced Bismarck's resignation in 1890.
5. Under Bismarck's leadership, Germany industrialized rapidly and became one of the strongest powers in Europe.
6. In Russia the czar maintained autocratic control over the country, despite such reforms as the emancipation of the serfs.
7. Discontent and rebellion continued to occur in the Austrian Empire even after the Dual Monarchy, also called Austria-Hungary, was created. Holding its various nationalities together in unity was a major problem of the Dual Monarchy.
8. As the Ottoman Empire declined, discontent in its Balkan territories led to two Balkan Wars in 1912 and 1913. International tensions increased as a result.

Reviewing Important Terms
On a separate sheet of paper, supply the term that correctly completes each statement.
1. The nationalistic movement in Italy, with its goals of liberation and unification, was called the _____.
2. The emperor of united Germany was called the _____.
3. A(n) _____ is someone who holds absolute power.
4. Bombings and assassinations of high officials by political groups are called _____.
5. The massacres of the Jews in czarist Russia were called _____.

Reviewing Critical Thinking Skills
1. **Comparing Ideas** What were the similarities and differences between the processes of unification in Italy and Germany?
2. **Analyzing Ideas** Otto von Bismarck once remarked, "Politics is the art of the possible." How did Bismarck's actions in forming the German Empire demonstrate his belief in this statement?
3. **Interpreting Ideas** (a) Why did the liberal movement make little progress in Russia during the 1800s? (b) Explain how Russian radicals attempted to bring about change.
4. **Understanding Relationships** Why might each of the following events be considered a response to the rise of nationalism? (a) Unification of Italy and Germany; (b) Start of the Russification program; (c) Establishment of the Dual Monarchy; (d) Further decline of the Ottoman Empire.

Relating Geography to History
In Chapter 2 you read about the rivalry between Prussia and Austria to dominate central Europe. To study the outcome of this struggle for domination, compare the two maps on pages 108 and 304. How did the balance of power change during the period from 1786 to 1871? Using the information in this chapter and in Chapter 2, briefly explain how Prussia came to rule the German Empire.

Relating Past to Present
1. The *Zollverein* was a major step toward German unity. (a) Who belonged to this customs union? (b) How did the various member states benefit from economic cooperation? (c) Using American history or civics books, find out about the laws regulating

A.D. 1861	A.D. 1870	A.D. 1862–1890	A.D. 1905
Serfs are emancipated in Russia.	Final unification of Italy occurs.	Bismarck is prime minister of Prussia.	Revolution of 1905 occurs in Russia.

A.D. 1870　　　A.D. 1890　　　A.D. 1910

A.D. 1867	A.D. 1861–1888	A.D. 1878	A.D. 1912–1913
Austrian Empire forms the Dual Monarchy.	William I rules Prussia.	Congress of Berlin takes place.	Balkan wars take place.

trade among the states in the United States. Can the states impose or collect tariffs? **(d)** Can the federal government grant special trade concessions to any one state or region? **(e)** What evidence of trade among the states can you find in your home?

2. Review the problems facing Russia's economic development during the 1800s. Then clip newspaper and magazine articles that illustrate economic issues facing the region today. Compare the issues of the 1800s with those of the present day. What seem to be the similarities and differences?

Applying History Study Skills

Before completing this activity, review Building History Study Skills on page 303.

Read the following statements. The first is from a speech by Otto von Bismarck on his view of the unification of Germany. The other is from a letter by Giuseppe Garibaldi on his conquest of Naples. How are their views of unification different? How are they similar?

"Germany does not look to Prussia's liberalism, but to its power. Bavaria, Württemburg, and Baden [the south German states] would like to turn to liberalism, but they shall not assume Prussia's role. Prussia must collect its forces for the favorable occasion, which has several times been neglected; Prussia's borders are not favorable to a healthy national life. Not by speeches and decisions of majorities will the greatest problems of the time be decided—that was the mistake of 1848–1849—but by iron and blood."
(Speech to the Prussian Diet, September 1862)

"Having reached the strait, it became necessary to cross it. To have reinstated Sicily in the great Italian family was certainly a glorious achievement. But what then? Were we, in compliance with diplomacy, to leave our country incomplete and maimed? What of the two Calabrias, and Naples, awaiting us with open arms? And the rest of Italy still enslaved by the foreigner and the priest? . . .

I entered Naples with the whole of the southern army as yet a long way off in the direction of the Straits of Messina, the King of Naples having, on the previous day, quitted his palace to retire to Capua.

At Naples, as in all places we had passed through since crossing the strait, the populace were sublime in

their enthusiastic patriotism, and the resolute tone assumed by them certainly had no small share in the brilliant results obtained."
(Garibaldi's Report on the Conquest of Naples)

1. How did Bismarck feel about liberalism?
2. **(a)** How did Garibaldi feel about the role of the people in uniting Italy? **(b)** How did his opinion differ from Bismarck's?
3. What does Bismarck mean by the expression "iron and blood"?
4. **(a)** How was Garibaldi greeted in Naples? **(b)** What might Bismarck have said about this greeting?
5. What was the primary difference between Garibaldi's and Bismarck's approaches to unification?

---

internet**connect**

Search the Internet through the HRW Web site for information on the emancipation of the serfs in Russia in 1861. You might, for example, locate a copy of the Emancipation Manifesto of March 3, 1861, or find information about Alexander II. Print out what you find and be prepared to give an oral report.

HRW　**GO TO:** go.hrw.com
KEYWORD: SCØ
　　　　　Alexander II

Building Your Portfolio

1. **Presenting an Oral Report** Read Garibaldi's "Proclamation to the Italians," and Bismarck's "iron and blood" speech. Present an oral report explaining why each of these documents might be considered an expression of nationalism. Discuss which one is more idealistic than the other and explain why you feel this way. Place your notes in your portfolio.

2. **Writing a Report** Garibaldi and his comparatively small army succeeded in conquering the Kingdom of the Two Sicilies, which later became part of a united Italy. Prepare a written report on Garibaldi's exploits in Sicily. Place the report in your portfolio.

The Age of Imperialism

TIME

A.D. **1830–1917**

A.D. **1830–1917**

|3.7 million B.C. | 4000 B.C. | A.D. 2100 |

PLACE

Africa, Asia, the Pacific, and Latin America

Latin America

ARCTIC OCEAN

NORTH AMERICA · EUROPE · ASIA

PACIFIC OCEAN

Equator

AFRICA

AUSTRALIA · PACIFIC OCEAN · SOUTH AMERICA · ATLANTIC OCEAN · INDIAN OCEAN

ANTARCTICA

Asia and the Pacific

Africa

The first voyage through the Suez Canal on November 17, 1869

Significance

By the early 1800s, European expansion continued as waves of immigrants flowed into the new nations of the Americas or established new settlement colonies in Africa and the Pacific.

Where once they had exercised informal influence over other peoples, after 1870 the empire-builders began to establish new **dependent colonies**, in which non-European majorities were ruled by relatively few European colonial officials. By 1914 the great industrial powers of Europe, the United States, and Japan controlled practically the entire world.

Terms to Define

dependent colonies	paternalism
imperialism	assimilation
"White Man's Burden"	Muslim League
colony	Treaty of Shimonoseki
protectorate	Chinese Eastern Railway
condominium	*Maine*
sphere of influence	Platt Amendment
Fashoda crisis	Roosevelt Corollary

People to Identify

Henry Stanley	Porfirio Díaz
Leopold II	Victoriano Huerta
Cecil Rhodes	Venustiano Carranza
Emilio Aguinaldo	Pancho Villa

Places to Locate

Algiers	Singapore
Tunis	Samoa Islands
Suez Canal	British Guiana
Formosa	Puerto Rico
Liaodong Peninsula	Panama Canal

Chapter Theme Questions

- **Economic Organization** What economic factors might lead a nation to seek relationships with overseas nations or establish overseas colonies?
- **Cross-Cultural Interaction** How might imperialism affect the flow of ideas among peoples?
- **Politics and Law** How might domination by an imperialist nation affect the government and organization of a state, both during foreign dominance and after regaining independence?

I n 1869 the *New York Herald* hired journalist Henry Stanley to locate Dr. David Livingstone, who had disappeared in Africa. In 1871 Stanley finally located Livingstone and wrote of their meeting.

> ❝So I did that which I thought was most dignified. I pushed back the crowds, and, passing from the rear, walked down a living avenue of people, until I came in front of the semicircle of Arabs, in front of which stood the white man with the gray beard. As I advanced slowly toward him I noticed he was pale, looked wearied...I would have run to him, only I was a coward in the presence of such a mob... So I did what cowardice and false pride suggested was the best thing—walked deliberately to him, took off my hat, and said, 'Dr. Livingstone, I presume?'
>
> 'Yes,' said he, with a kind smile, lifting his cap slightly.❞

Stanley's highly publicized trip did much to spark European interest in Africa.

Section 1

The Roots of Imperialism

Focus Questions

- **Why did Europeans look outside their own countries for raw materials and markets?**
- **What reasons, other than industrialization, led Europeans to establish colonies and expand their empires?**
- **How did imperialism develop, and what different types of colonial relationships existed?**

Imperialism—the ambition of a powerful nation to dominate the political, economic, and cultural affairs of another nation or region—arose out of a complex mixture of political, economic, and social forces. Historians do not agree on which influences were most important.

Desire for Self-Sufficiency

After 1850 the Industrial Revolution accelerated as new sources of power, new machinery, and new industries were developed. Increased industrial production spurred the demand for traditional raw materials such as iron and coal. In addition, the new industries needed other raw materials, such as manganese and tungsten for making steel alloys, copper for the electrical industry, and rubber for a variety of uses. Industrialization also brought rising standards of living in Europe and the United States and increased the demand for products such as coffee, tea, and spices.

None of the industrialized nations wanted to depend on other nations for raw materials. Government leaders feared that in the event of war their countries would be at the mercy of an enemy. Thus the leaders of the industrial nations sought ways to become self-sufficient by gaining control of the sources of the raw materials they needed.

Need for New Markets

After 1870 new technology made it possible to produce goods in enormous quantities. When the new and expensive industrial machinery was used to full capacity, it could pay for itself and generate profits for its owners. If the machinery was not used to full capacity, owners lost money.

Even with their rising standards of living, people in Europe and the United States could not buy all the goods on the market. To market their goods and to continue to increase their profits, industrialists began to look for new markets in nonindustrialized regions, especially in Asia, Africa, and Latin America.

Imperialists believed that if people in nonindustrialized areas were aware of manufactured goods and if the goods were available, they would buy them. Imperialists even argued that the customs of these people might be remolded to create new markets. Advocates of imperialism wrote articles describing how busy European and American factories would be and how much profit they could earn if only the people of central Africa could be persuaded to wear shirts and ties.

Many Europeans believed that industrialized nations should control their new markets abroad, just as they controlled the colonial sources of their raw materials. Industrialists wanted their governments to guarantee them exclusive rights to sell in these markets. At the same time, they demanded protective tariffs to ensure that they would not lose their home markets to foreign competition.

Nationalism

Nationalism, a strong force throughout the 1800s, became particularly powerful between 1870 and 1914. Many nationalists now argued that having colonies added to their nations' strength and prestige. The recently unified nations of Germany and Italy felt that they had to build up colonial empires to compete with longtime colonial powers such as Great Britain, France, and the Netherlands. However, it is notable that the British, who already had a large empire, entered the imperialistic race for colonies as enthusiastically as did the Germans or Italians.

Imperialists also viewed colonies as sources of troops for the rapidly growing armies of the day. Gurkhas, soldiers from Nepal, joined Australians and New Zealanders to strengthen British armies. Senegalese troops from West Africa fought for the French.

A large navy was even more necessary than a large army to protect widely scattered colonies and far-ranging merchant ships. For many years, steam-powered ships burned coal, and the range of a steamship was "from coal to coal." Thus the coaling station, a place where warships and merchant ships could refuel, became highly important for military and commercial purposes. Tiny islands with nothing to offer except their strategic locations became coaling stations or naval bases. Often these islands became objects of fierce competition among naval powers.

Outlets for Population

Rapid population growth accompanied industrialization. Some historians estimate that the world's population doubled between 1800 and 1900. Industrial development created many jobs, but in Europe there was not enough work to employ all the new job seekers. Displaced farmers and farm laborers, in particular, found it either preferable or necessary to go elsewhere. As a result, Europeans left their home countries in record numbers in the 1880s.

For some countries, such as Britain, Germany, and France, overseas migration was not a new phenomenon. However, for other countries, such as Italy, Spain, and Austria-Hungary, the wave of emigration in the 1880s marked the first mass movement of their peoples. The populations of North America, South America, and Australia swelled as the Europeans established themselves within their borders.

Missionary Motives

The urge to spread the Christian religion influenced colonial expansion during the 1500s and 1600s.

Although Roman Catholic missionaries had continued their work since that time, they increased their activities during the period of imperialism. Growing numbers of Protestant missionaries also attempted to convert people in the colonies to Christianity.

Missionaries did other work as well. Education became a regular missionary activity. Trained medical missionaries went out from Europe and the United States. Consequently, knowledge of medicine, hygiene, and sanitation spread with Christianity.

Cultural Motives

Closely related to the missionary motive was the idea that the people of industrialized Western nations had a duty to transmit Western ideas and knowledge across the globe. People were considered lacking if their religion or their culture differed from that of the West.

The idea of Western superiority was expressed by British poet Rudyard Kipling. The phrase Kipling used as the title of the poem **"The White Man's Burden"** has often been used to identify the attitude that Europeans had toward people in non-Western, nonindustrialized nations. Many Europeans felt an obligation to carry Western civilization to those that they considered less fortunate than themselves. These judgments, however inaccurate, motivated Europeans to alter the way of life of countless peoples, all under the guise of "helping" or "improving" them. Europeans also used the idea of their "burden" to justify imposing their own values and cultural ideas on other peoples.

The British were not the only Europeans who had these attitudes. The French also spoke of their "civilizing mission." The people of each industrial nation considered their civilization and culture to be the highest and therefore the one most suited for enlightening other, less industrialized peoples on Earth.

Opponents of imperialism claimed that the only burden the white man wanted to take up was the burden of colonial wealth, which he wanted to carry back home as fast as possible. Such opponents, however, formed a minority with little influence in their countries.

The Nature of Imperialism

Imperialism created bitter rivalries among the imperial powers and hatred among the colonized peoples. Rivalries led to the building of larger armies and navies and eventually to world conflict.

In the beginning, European governments did not actively plan imperialism. Often it began with the work of individuals such as merchants, explorers, or missionaries. Sometimes these Europeans met with resistance or violence from the local inhabitants. Then European soldiers appeared, followed by government officials to protect the interests of their citizens. Builders, engineers, and technicians who opened mines, built roads, and improved other means of transportation often followed the soldiers and officials. Then the

This photo shows a missionary classroom in the Philippines. In addition to establishing Christianity during the age of imperialism, missionaries also spread their knowledge of education and medicine.

LITERATURE

The Voice of Rudyard Kipling

Rudyard Kipling, who lived from 1865 to 1936, is often considered the poet of British imperialism. One of his best-known poems, "The White Man's Burden," was actually written to address the United States's involvement in the Philippines. The first stanza of the poem follows.

> "Take up the White Man's burden—
> Send forth the best ye breed—
> Go bind your sons to exile
> To serve your captives' need;
> To wait in heavy harness,
> On fluttered folk and wild—
> Your new-caught, sullen peoples,
> Half devil and half child."

This poem supplied the phrase "The White Man's Burden," which is often used to sum up the imperialist motive to protect and civilize groups of people who were considered by Europeans to be "primitive"—in Kipling's words, "half devil and half child." Of course, those groups often had rich and highly complex cultures, and coming under European "protection" usually meant conquest and exploitation for them.

Kipling's work reflects many of the troubling and conflicting impulses of imperialism. He did believe that British civilization should be the model for everyone. Yet he was not the shallow racist he is often misunderstood to be. In fact, he strongly believed in the moral worth of all human beings. The words of "The White Man's Burden" dwell on the responsibilities and costs of imperialism, and some of his other

poems criticize a failure to live up to the ideals of imperialism.

Kipling was born in Bombay, India, where he learned the Hindi language from Indian servants. At the age of five or six, he was sent to England and spent much of the rest of his life in England and the United States. He did return to India as a journalist in 1882, spending seven years there. In 1900 he went to South Africa to report on the Boer War. In 1901 he completed his first major novel, *Kim,* which is set in India, as are many of his other novels and stories. In 1907 he won the Nobel Prize for literature.

region would be developed for the benefit of the developers. The local population had very little, if any, say in this process.

One of the things that prompted imperialism was the fact that the newly industrialized Europeans had surplus cash. They were looking for new ideas and new places in which to invest. Loans to local rulers often provided the initial wedge of imperialism. Economic involvement in a country often led to political involvement and eventually to control.

Europeans often used this process as a means of gaining control of an area or region.

Several terms used in connection with imperialism need explanation. Originally, a colony was a settlement established in another region by citizens of a country. Early examples of colonies include the Greek colonies throughout the Mediterranean and the British colonies in North America. During the imperialistic era, however, a **colony** was an area in which a foreign nation gained complete control over a given region and its local population. A colony was first gained by settlement or conquest and then annexed, becoming a part of the foreign nation's empire.

In a **protectorate**, the local ruler kept his title, but officials of the foreign power actually controlled the region. The "protecting" power kept out other foreign nations. In a **condominium**, two nations ruled a region as partners. A concession was the grant of economic rights and privileges in a given area. Concessions were given by local rulers to foreign merchants or capitalists who wanted to trade, to build railroads, or to develop mineral deposits and other natural resources. A **sphere of influence** was a region in which one nation had special, sometimes exclusive, economic and political privileges that were recognized by other nations.

Section 1 Review

1. **Define** dependent colonies, imperialism, "White Man's Burden," colony, protectorate, condominium, sphere of influence
2. **Understanding Ideas** Why did European countries seek raw materials and markets outside their own countries?
3. **Summarizing Ideas** Describe four motives behind imperialism that are not related to raw materials or markets.
4. **Comparing Ideas** How might life have differed under the different types of imperialism?

Section 2

European Claims in North Africa and the Sudan

Focus Questions

- **What motives did European nations have for establishing colonies or spheres of influence in North Africa?**
- **What type of control did France exercise over Algiers and Tunis?**
- **What interests did Britain have in Egypt and in the Sudan?**
- **How did Italy gain control of Libya?**

Throughout history many conquerors, including the Romans, the Byzantines, and the Arabs, imposed their rule on North Africa. In the 1800s, most of the region belonged to the Ottoman Empire, although Ottoman control was weak.

The French in North Africa

For a long time, expert Muslim seafarers known as the Barbary pirates operated off the coast of North Africa, preying on Mediterranean shipping. The term *Barbary* means "of the Berbers"—a people of North Africa who had converted to Islam during the 600s. Four Muslim states—Morocco, Algiers, Tunis, and Tripoli—made up the so-called Barbary States. The countries of Morocco, Algeria, Tunisia, and Libya now occupy the area of the former Barbary States.

The operations of the Barbary pirates gave the French an excuse to intervene in North Africa. A French representative went to the governor of Algiers to discuss the Barbary pirates in 1827. The governor allegedly insulted the French representative by striking him with a flyswatter. By 1830 a French force occupied the city of Algiers. For more than 40 years, the French fought against almost continuous local rebellions.

Economically, however, Algiers was worth the trouble. Many French people and other Europeans moved in. The French officials appropriated, or claimed ownership of, land on which to settle colonists.

Seizure of Tunis. East of Algiers lay the small state of Tunis. Tunis belonged to the Ottoman Empire, though in fact it operated independently. Tunisians were relieved by the French takeover of Algiers in 1830; Algiers had long sought to assert its influence over Tunis. The bey (the Turkish provincial governor) of Tunis at that time was open to Western ideas. He accepted military advice from French advisers and allowed economic assistance to flow from French banks.

The bey imposed higher taxes to pay back the French banks. This was too much of a burden for the still poor population to bear, and there was widespread unrest. By 1869 Tunis was bankrupt. A financial commission was established to restore order and to reorganize Tunis's finances. The commission included British, French, and Italian representatives.

In a complicated series of negotiations, France and Great Britain reached an agreement that was announced in 1878 at the Congress of Berlin. The French were to have a free hand in Tunis, and the British could occupy the island of Cyprus. Italy—which also had aspirations for Tunis—was new, poor, and inexperienced at the diplomatic game and as a result was ignored.

In 1881 France completed the process of exerting its control over Tunis by finding a weak excuse to stage a military action. The result was a protectorate in which the bey remained ruler in name, but the senior French official in Tunis wielded the power. Under the protectorate, public order was maintained, schools and industries were developed, and Tunis's finances were stabilized. However, religious differences and a rising spirit of nationalism inspired many Tunisians to work for independence.

Rivalry over Morocco. After acquiring Algiers and Tunis, it seemed only natural to the French that they continue to expand their influence. Morocco's strategic location along the Strait of Gibraltar made it an appealing prize. Many other European countries also recognized Morocco's importance. France, Spain, Britain, Italy, and Germany all had hopes of acquiring at least some interest in Morocco.

In 1904 France took advantage of Morocco's internal instability by making agreements with Britain, Spain, and Italy. France assumed control of Morocco and promised not to hinder Britain's plans for Egypt or Italy's plans for Libya. Moreover, Spain was allowed to maintain a sphere of influence (for trading purposes) in northern Morocco. Whatever claims Germany made for involvement in North Africa were ignored.

For eight years, the French allowed Morocco's sultans to remain on the throne. The sultan who assumed the title in 1908 proved unable to balance the various factions and European influences in the country. Threatened with utter disorder, he had to resort to asking the French to rescue him. In return, they forced him to sign a treaty by which Morocco became a protectorate in 1912.

The British in Egypt

Egypt had been part of the Ottoman Empire for centuries. However, by the mid-1800s, this empire was crumbling. The Ottoman viceroy in Egypt, called the khedive (kuh·DEEV), had become nearly independent. The khedive still paid some tribute to the Ottoman sultan, but he ruled Egypt with absolute authority.

France held Tunis (now Tunisia) as a protectorate from 1881 until granting it independence in 1956. This illustration shows the French troops storming Tunis in 1881.

In 1854 a French company headed by Ferdinand de Lesseps gained a concession to build a canal through the Isthmus of Suez. The Egyptian government bought almost half of the stock in the company. Individual French citizens bought most of the remaining shares.

Isma'il, the khedive when the canal was completed in 1869, not only inherited a significant debt but was also extravagant and unwise in his own decisions about spending money. Between 1869 and 1879, he increased the foreign debt of his government by more than 2,000 percent.

One of Isma'il's attempts to avoid bankruptcy was to sell Egypt's stock in the Suez Canal. This action provided an opportunity for the British, who wanted to control the canal because it was a vital link in the trade and communication route between Great Britain and India, Australia, and New Zealand. In 1875 the British government bought the Egyptian stock and became the largest single stockholder. Because the British now owned so much of the stock and the rest was so widely scattered among private investors, the British gained virtual control of the canal.

Near the end of Isma'il's reign, an international committee had been established to manage Egypt's huge debt. Having lost favor, Isma'il was deposed in 1879. His successor was challenged by a nationalist group whose members resented increased European control. The nationalists mounted a rebellion in 1882. A British fleet bombarded Alexandria to put down the rioting. Britain then sent troops to suppress another pocket of rebellion near the Suez Canal and then to occupy Cairo. The Egyptian government remained outwardly independent during this period of British occupation, but the British actually ruled Egypt.

Anglo-Egyptian Sudan

The Sudan, a vast region of savannas south of the Sahara, stretches from the Atlantic Ocean to the Nile River valley and beyond. In the imperialistic era, the term *Sudan* also referred to a specific eastern part of this region south of Egypt. Arabs and various local groups inhabited the area, which Egypt claimed.

After Great Britain established control over Egypt in 1882, the Sudan became important to the British. Because the upper Nile flows through the Sudan, control of the region would afford a chance to build dams to store water for irrigation and to control the flow of water in the lower Nile. France also wanted the Sudan; it held possessions farther west, and it already

had a toehold on the Red Sea (French Somaliland) and wanted to extend its territory inland.

In 1881 Muhammed Ahmad, proclaiming himself the Mahdi, a title meaning "expected one," became a leader of Muslims discontented with the Sudan's religious and administrative state. Revolutionary forces, inspired by the Mahdi, gained control of several major cities. In early 1885, they captured Khartoum and ruled from there until 1898. In that year, Great Britain invaded the Sudan, intending to prevent the French from gaining control. Under General Herbert Kitchener, British troops quickly and soundly defeated a large Mahdist army.

In June 1896, the French had sent an expedition to Africa under Captain Jean-Baptiste Marchand. The goal was to gain control of the upper Nile at Fashoda. Starting from the French Congo, Marchand and his small force of Senegalese soldiers made a daring, 3,000-mile journey through tropical Africa. In July 1898, Marchand reached Fashoda. British forces arrived two months later. Marchand and Kitchener waited for orders from their respective rulers, while both countries prepared for war. Recognizing that neither its army nor its navy could dominate, France yielded Fashoda to Britain.

The outcome of the **Fashoda crisis** was that France recognized the British as masters of the Sudan. In return, Britain recognized France's claims in French West Africa. Great Britain and Egypt established a condominium in the area, which became known as the Anglo-Egyptian Sudan. The arrangement was an unequal partnership, to say the least, and Britain held the upper hand in all matters.

The Italians in Tripoli

Desert covered most of Tripoli, the Barbary state to the west of Egypt. It, too, was Ottoman. Though Tripoli had little economic value, Italy pursued its imperial interests there. Italy was unable to compete with the larger European imperialist powers, so it had to settle for the crumbs, as it were, of those nations.

In 1911 Italy invaded Tripoli, claiming that some previous trade agreements had been violated. Although the local Turks showed surprisingly strong resistance, the Italians defeated them.

Italy took Tripoli as a colony and renamed it Libya. It was a profitless victory. Except for a narrow strip along the coast, the land was barren. The small population violently opposed Italian rule, and the expense of maintaining troops in Libya proved a drain on the Italian economy.

Section 2 Review

---

1. **Define** Fashoda crisis
2. **Locate and Explain the Significance** Algiers, Tunis, Suez Canal
3. **Understanding Ideas** How did imperialism in North Africa threaten world peace?
4. **Summarizing Ideas** Describe the French presence in North Africa.
5. **Integrating Ideas** Why did the British want to take control of Egypt and the Sudan?
6. **Interpreting Ideas** What does the statement "Italy ate the crumbs of imperialism" mean?

Section 3

European Claims in Sub-Saharan Africa

Focus Questions

- **What features of West Africa particularly appealed to French and British imperialists?**
- **What European claims were made in Central and East Africa?**
- **Why was South Africa so valuable?**
- **How did European imperialism affect Africa?**

In the 1500s and 1600s, considered to be the first great period of European colonization, several nations established trading posts on the east and west coasts of Sub-Saharan Africa. Interest in this vast portion of Africa was rekindled during the imperialism of the late 1800s.

Competition for West Africa

West Africa had been a major center of the slave trade. First the Portuguese and Dutch and later the British and French had established trading posts along the coast. When most European countries abolished the slave trade in the early 1800s, these former slaving centers turned to other types of commerce. They traded in palm oil, feathers, ivory, rubber, and other products from the interior. Eager to control this trade, Europeans began to push inland.

European countries sought to link their coastal possessions with new inland holdings. In the bulge of

western Africa, the French claimed the ancient city of Timbuktu. They also increased the number of commercial settlements in the coastal areas of Senegal, French Guinea, the Ivory Coast (present-day Côte d'Ivoire), and Dahomey. By 1900 France had claimed a vast area called French West Africa. (See map on page 327.)

In many cases, the French as well as other Europeans met with fierce resistance in their drive to colonize Africa. In what is today Senegal, for example, Samory Touré fought the French on and off from 1883 until he was captured in 1898. In another instance of heroic resistance, the king of Dahomey resisted the French until 1893.

The British competed with the French throughout West Africa. They, too, sought to connect their coastal settlements by means of interior expansion. The Gold Coast (modern Ghana) particularly interested them. Moving inland from coastal bases there, the British came up against the powerful African kingdom of Ashanti. By 1901, however, Britain had annexed all the territory of Ashanti and made the Gold Coast a colony.

The British also expanded into Nigeria, a territory to the east of the Gold Coast that took its name from the Niger, one of the great rivers of Africa. Control of the Niger River ensured control of a huge region rich in resources. In 1861 the British annexed the port city of Lagos and then pushed steadily inland. The Africans resisted the British, but British military forces crushed all resistance and brought Nigeria under colonial rule.

By the early 1900s, France, Britain, Germany, Spain, and Portugal had claimed all of West Africa except Liberia. (See map on page 327.) Settled by freed slaves from the United States, Liberia had become an independent republic in 1847.

Although economically and militarily weak, Liberia maintained its independence. It no doubt would have become the protectorate of an ambitious European power if not for its special relationship to the United States. American diplomatic pressure discouraged European attempts to take over the small republic.

Competition for Central Africa

Henry Stanley's successful search for Dr. David Livingstone did much to publicize the possibilities for imperialistic development in central Africa. Stanley tried but failed to interest the British government in the vast area that he had explored. He then turned to King Leopold II of Belgium, who did want the region.

Africa in 1914

Territory:
- German
- Portuguese
- Belgian
- Italian
- British
- French
- Spanish
- Independent

0   500   1,000 Miles
0   500   1,000 Kilometers
Azimuthal Equal-Area Projection

Learning from Maps By 1914, most of the major European countries had established colonies throughout Africa.

❓ **Region** What two African nations remained independent?

After much national and international maneuvering, Leopold, acting as a private citizen, carved out a personal empire of 900,000 square miles.

Leopold's rule of the Congo provides an example of the worst aspects of imperialism. His only interest was in extracting as much wealth as possible from the colony. Forming a corporation, he sold concessions to speculators who shared his interest in a quick profit. Their exploitation of the Congo's supply of natural rubber became an international scandal. Leopold, who never visited Africa, established trading monopolies and introduced a system of forced labor. Thousands of Africans died in Leopold's "service." Finally, faced with international criticism of conditions in the Congo, Leopold transferred ownership of his private colony to the Belgian government in 1908.

North of Leopold's Congo, Pierre de Brazza traveled to the lower Congo River in 1880 and signed treaties establishing a French protectorate. The affected region officially became the French Congo in 1891. The French extended their claims to the northeast, gaining control of a large region north of the Congo and adjoining French West Africa. Combined with the French Congo, this region formed French Equatorial Africa. (See map on page 327.)

Competition for East Africa

On the east coast of Africa, Portugal strengthened and extended its control over Mozambique. To the north of Mozambique, Great Britain and Germany competed for territorial domination. The slave trade had been only marginally active in East Africa before the late 1700s, but it began to increase after about 1780. During this period of more active slave trading, the efforts of missionaries to end the slave trade focused public attention on the area and helped justify European intervention in the area.

The European nations rapidly carved the rest of East Africa into colonies. (See map on page 327.) The only exception was the ancient empire of Ethiopia. Although Italy invaded Ethiopia, the Ethiopian army defeated the Italians at Adowa in 1896, thus ensuring their country's freedom from foreign domination.

Another factor that made it easier for Europeans to colonize East Africa was an ecological disaster in the 1890s. Domestic cattle, introduced to Africa by Europeans, carried a fatal disease known as rinderpest. Rinderpest decimated the East African herds, leading to widespread starvation. The people, thus weakened and besieged by troubles, lacked the ability to resist European colonization.

Competition for Southern Africa

European settlement in South Africa began in 1652, when Dutch settlers founded Cape Town as a resupplying station for ships sailing to the East Indies. The Dutch settlement grew into a large colony called Cape Colony. During the Napoleonic Wars of the early 1800s, the British seized Cape Colony, which then became a British possession.

As British administration became established, many people left the colony and moved to the north and east in a mass migration known as the Great Trek. These people—descendants of the original Dutch settlers—were Boers, and they spoke their own language, known as Afrikaans. In the new territories, the Boers carved out three colonies—Natal (nuh·TAHL), on the southeast coast, the Orange Free State to the west, and the Transvaal to the north.

As the Boers moved into the new territories, they came in contact with the Zulu who lived in the region. Under the great leader Shaka, the Zulu had created a thriving empire with a strong army. For years this army fought the Boers for control of the region. In 1879 the British joined in the war, defeating the Zulu and destroying their empire.

The discovery of diamonds in the Orange Free State and gold in the Transvaal soon intensified the competition in southern Africa. Germany, hoping to find rich mineral reserves, declared a protectorate over the territory of South-West Africa in 1884. In the same year, Great Britain began moving into the interior section of Africa from the south, greatly increasing its holdings. Closely associated with these territorial acquisitions was one individual, Cecil Rhodes, a British speculator.

Rhodes and his influence. Rhodes, a sickly young man who hoped that the climate would improve his health, arrived in Cape Colony in 1870. Moving to the diamond fields in the Boer-controlled Orange Free State, he soon demonstrated a talent for business and a genius for organization. Within 20 years of his arrival, he completely controlled South African diamond production.

Rhodes later organized the colonization of a huge territory farther north. This territory was named Rhodesia after him. Throughout his career, Rhodes displayed creative ideas with regard to both politics and business. One of his greatest hopes was to see British possessions extending from the Cape Colony in the southern part of Africa to Cairo in the north.

In 1895 a colleague of Rhodes tried to topple the Transvaal government, which had resisted European

The Berlin Conference: Making a New Map of Africa

In the mid-1800s, much of the continent of Africa was still completely unknown to Europeans. Despite a history of European contact and involvement in Africa that dated back to Roman times and even earlier, European maps showed the interior of Africa as a blank space—unexplored territory. Trading posts and a few colonies located on the coasts were the extent of Europe's presence in Africa.

However, before the end of the century Europeans had explored and then conquered nearly the entire continent. This remarkable rush to seize territory is often called "The Scramble for Africa." No single event exemplifies this phenomenon as well as the Berlin Conference in 1884.

Otto von Bismarck, the German imperial chancellor, called the Berlin Conference at a time of tension between the nations that were vying for African territory: Portugal, France, Great Britain, Spain, Italy, Belgium, and Germany. Representatives of each of these powers attended the conference, along with delegates from the United States and the Ottoman Empire. No African leaders were invited to attend this conference.

The purpose of the conference was to resolve potential conflicts over colonies. As European leaders' claims to pieces of territories began to overlap, it seemed very possible that the scramble might set off a war in Europe. The conference was called to head off such a war by establishing boundaries that all European powers would respect.

At the time of the Berlin Conference, many Africans were still living under their own governments. With absolutely no regard for those local boundaries, the representatives carved up the continent among themselves. These representatives argued over, drew, erased, and redrew the boundary lines of their new

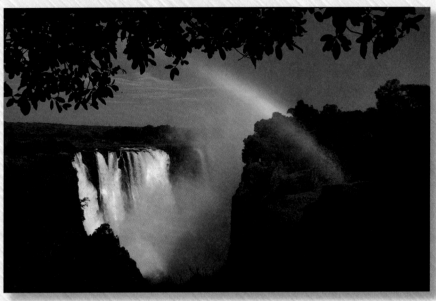

Victoria Falls, on the Zambia-Zimbabwe border

colonies. Huge parcels of land changed hands, sometimes simply at the whim of one representative. Often people from the same ethnic group found themselves separated and ruled by different colonial powers. Conversely, the new boundaries frequently threw together ethnic groups hostile to one another. Also, in drawing boundary lines the representatives ignored such natural boundaries as rivers and mountain ranges. Ignorant of the continent's geography, the representatives had no idea of the location of such natural dividing lines. (See photo above.)

The decisions made at the Berlin Conference still plague Africa today. Much of Africa secured independence after 1950, but the colonial boundaries established by the Berlin Conference had acquired the legitimacy of time. Even though many of these boundaries were arbitrary and a possible cause of future trouble, the leaders of the new African nations feared that drawing new boundaries might result in complete chaos. Yet at the same time these leaders found it almost impossible to make the old boundary lines function. For many Africans, loyalty to their ethnic group still had far greater meaning than national identity. Conflicting loyalties had disastrous consequences in many countries.

attempts to establish mining operations. The attempt failed, but Great Britain's apparent support of it made relations between the Boers and the British openly hostile. In 1899 war broke out. After three years of costly fighting, the British defeated the Boers and imposed a settlement that favored mining interests.

To ensure Boer support of the peace, the British allowed the Boers to continue using the Afrikaans language in their schools and courts. The British also provided funds for Boers—though not for Africans—to rebuild their destroyed farms. In 1910 a federal constitution united the Cape Colony, Natal, the Transvaal, and the Orange Free State into the Union of South Africa, which was a British dominion. The constitution made it virtually impossible for nonwhites to be given voting rights. The settlement of the South African War, or Boer War, thus laid the basis for the later development of a system of complete racial segregation.

European Government in Africa

The European powers that established empires in Africa generally used one of two forms of government in their territories. France, Germany, Belgium, and Portugal practiced direct rule. Great Britain practiced indirect rule.

The British fought the Boers for three years to gain control of South Africa. This photo shows Boer guerrillas in South Africa.

Direct rule. In colonies with direct rule, the imperial power controlled all levels of government and appointed its own officials to govern the colonies. The Europeans based this type of government on their belief that the Africans were not capable of ruling themselves. As a result of this belief, the Europeans practiced what we refer to as **paternalism**, the system of governing colonies in much the same way that parents guide their children.

European nations practiced various forms of direct rule. For example, the French encouraged **assimilation**, in which the people of the colonies abandoned their local cultures and adopted all aspects of French culture.

Indirect rule. Under the British system of indirect rule, a British governor and a council of advisers made colonial laws, but local rulers exerted some authority. The British chose indirect rule largely because they lacked enough workers to staff all the governments of the vast British Empire, which by then covered almost one fourth of the earth's land surface.

Costs and Benefits of Imperialism

Imperialism was a harsh experience for the entire continent of Africa. The costs and benefits resulting from European expansion were unevenly distributed across the continent.

Some individuals and groups in African society did benefit. New agricultural techniques were introduced in many areas. For example, in Uganda, British support of cotton cultivation gave rise to a relatively stable economy in which cotton still plays an important part. Europeans introduced medicines to help people live longer and healthier lives. They also constructed roads and railroads. These means of transportation were used mostly to connect areas of European settlement with the coast and to move goods to and from European industries. They also served to make African products available for the world market. In the long run, however, the world did not clamor for African products, much to the disappointment of the imperialists.

In spite of decades of intervention or control, most Africans would not and did not adopt European customs or culture. Perhaps this is not so surprising because the European industries and institutions were established largely for the benefit of the Europeans, not for the Africans, who were deemed unworthy of the same treatment as Europeans. The majority of Africans continued to live largely by traditional means, as subsistence farmers or migrant workers.

Thinking About History: Determining Relevancy

As you do historical research, you often must sift through mountains of information to find what you need. As you do so, you need to be able to distinguish between relevant and irrelevant information. Relevant information includes facts that apply to your topic. For example, if you are researching how the Japanese resisted European imperialism, the shogun's response to Commodore Perry's ultimatum would be relevant. A description of the beauty of Kyoto, which is the emperor's residence, would not be relevant information because it would not help you explain the resistance to imperialism.

How to Determine Relevancy

To determine relevancy, follow these steps.

1. State the topic that you are researching.
2. Identify categories that will help you organize the research topic.
3. Look for definitions, descriptions, details, and evidence on your topic.
4. Examine each piece of information and relate it to the topic. Use the categories you have devised, and discard all information that has no bearing on them.

Developing the Skill

If you were researching the impact that imperialism had on European economies, you might use two categories: costs and benefits. Read the following two selections and determine whether either would be relevant in your research. The first excerpt is from a speech by the British member of parliament Joseph Chamberlain. The second is from the writings of Lord Frederick Lugard, a long-time British colonial administrator.

[1] "We have suffered much in this country from depression of trade. We know how many of our

Political cartoon of Cecil Rhodes astride Africa

fellow-subjects are at this moment unemployed. Is there any man in his senses who believes that the crowded population of these islands [the British Isles] could exist for a single day if we were to cut adrift from us the great dependencies which now look to us for protection and assistance, and which are the natural markets for our trade?...If tomorrow it were possible, as some people apparently desire, to reduce by a stroke of the pen the British Empire to the dimensions of the United Kingdom, half at least of our population would be starved."

[2] "By railways and roads, by reclamation of swamps and irrigation of deserts, and by a system of fair trade and competition, we have added to the prosperity and wealth of these lands [in Africa], and checked famine and disease...We are endeavouring to teach the native races to conduct their own affairs with justice and humanity, and to educate them alike in letters and in industry."

In the first excerpt, Chamberlain discusses one of the major benefits of imperialism. It provides trade outlets and also helps feed the many people of Great Britain. It would be relevant in your research of the costs and benefits of imperialism.

The second excerpt, however, would not be relevant to your topic. This excerpt describes the author's view of the benefits of imperialism for the *colonized* nation, not for the *imperial* nation which you are researching.

Practicing the Skill

Read the Rudyard Kipling excerpt on page 322. Then determine whether it would provide relevant information about the costs and benefits of imperialism.

To apply this skill, see Applying History Study Skills on page 347.

Section 4

European Expansion in South and East Asia

Focus Questions
- How did Britain's rule of India contribute to the growth of Indian nationalism?
- What happened in Japan under the Meiji government, and how did Japan respond to Western imperialism?
- Why did Western nations compete for lands in East Asia, and what lands did they claim as their own?

The strong forces of imperialism that swept Africa in the 1800s also brought important and fateful changes to South and East Asia. In these regions, however, the changes were not as abrupt as they were in so many parts of Africa.

British Imperialism in India
As you read earlier, the British government ruled India directly after the Sepoy Rebellion in 1857. However, British control of the subcontinent remained essentially the same as it had been under the British East India Company. British India still made up about three fifths of the subcontinent. The rest consisted of more than 550 states, headed by local princes. The British government, through its viceroy, controlled the local princes' rights to make treaties and declare war, either with foreign countries or with one another. Great Britain also regulated Indian internal affairs when it seemed necessary.

To control both British India and Indian states, the British government used the old Roman method of divide and rule. It granted favors to those princes who cooperated with British rule and dealt harshly with those who did not. It treated Hindus and Muslims equally but did little to ease religious hatred between them.

The British were interested chiefly in profitable trade in India. To achieve it, they maintained public order by ending the many local wars and massacres. They set up an efficient governmental administration that built roads, bridges, railroads, factories, hospitals, and schools. They tried to improve agricultural methods, public health, and sanitation.

Many of these improvements helped the Indians, but other effects of British rule were harmful. The Indian handicraft industry almost disappeared. British cotton mills made cloth so cheaply that it could be transported to India and sold for less than handwoven Indian products. Local artisans thus found themselves without a means of support.

During the late 1800s and early 1900s, British rule in India had created a situation in which the peoples of two very different cultures lived side by side with almost no contact. The British had imposed themselves above Indian society as a superior race, a sort of supercaste. The British formed exclusive social circles, open to any European but closed to any Indian, no matter how distinguished. For generations Indians were treated with contempt regardless of their social status, education, or abilities.

The Rise of Indian Nationalism
Although the British did not mingle socially with the Indians, Western civilization had a powerful impact on India. For one thing, it led to a serious conflict of values.

Both Hinduism and Islam stressed age-old customs and respect for tradition. Western culture, on the other hand, emphasized material progress and political change. Indians regarded Europeans as materialists who cared little for the higher values of mind, soul, and spirit. To many Indians, it was impossible to separate religious values and ideas from other parts of their lives. Their religion dictated how they behaved in public, how they conducted business, and so on. The Europeans' ability to separate religion from other aspects of their lives was incomprehensible to traditional Hindus and Muslims.

British education had a profound effect on India. Under the guidance of Viceroy Curzon, who assumed his post in 1899, the British administration actively pursued widespread establishment of schools of all levels. British-provided education was usually in English to further westernize these subjects of the British Crown. In the schools, students also learned about Western ideas such as democracy. Many Indians also came to learn about and believe in the ideas of socialism.

A movement for Indian self-rule began in the late 1800s. Not all Indian nationalists supported the same approach. Some, especially those who had been educated in British schools and universities, wanted to advance toward independence gradually and by democratic methods. They also wanted to keep certain aspects of Western culture and industry that they thought could benefit India. The Indian National Congress, a political party founded in 1885, advocated this moderate approach.

Other people wanted to break all ties with Great Britain in an effort to sweep away all Western influence. The Hindus, particularly, wished to revolt not only against Western culture but also against Islam. The views of this second group alarmed Indian Muslims, who were a minority in the land. British rule protected them from violence, and they feared that if British rule were removed, their future might be in danger. The Muslims were therefore much less enthusiastic about driving out the British than were the Hindus. In 1906 Muslims formed the **Muslim League** to protect their interests. The independence movement in India gathered strength very slowly, and the British kept the country under a tight rein.

The Meiji Restoration in Japan

While imperialism remained firmly entrenched in India, it took a different course in Japan. Although European influence in Japan became strong after the overthrow of the Tokugawa shogunate in 1868, Europeans did not dominate Japan as they did India. Rather, the Japanese under the rule of the Meiji emperor controlled their own affairs and began to industrialize their country.

Real power in the Meiji government was exercised not by the emperor but by samurai from several domains in western Japan. These samurai had grown impatient under the strict, hereditary system of the Tokugawa period, in which birth, not ability, counted. They persuaded the emperor that Japan must take the road toward modernization. Even though the samurai were members of Japan's traditional ruling class, they advocated and carried out radical changes in Japan.

This cartoon shows the residents of Bombay welcoming Prince Edward during his 1875 tour of India. When his mother, Queen Victoria, died in 1901, he became Edward VII, king of Great Britain and emperor of India.

The Meiji Restoration, as the change in 1868 from the Tokugawa shogunate to imperial government is called, was really a social, political, and economic revolution. It corresponded in scope to the revolutions in Western nations during the 1700s.

The old system of social classes was abolished, and all Japanese became free to choose the occupations they wished to pursue. The government established universal compulsory education and almost wiped out illiteracy.

A centralized government replaced the political system of the Tokugawa period. The city of Edo, renamed Tokyo, became the new imperial capital, and the domains came under the control of government officials. The central government encouraged feelings of nationalism and unity by forming a national army and adopting universal conscription.

During the 1880s, an appointed commission wrote a constitution, which the emperor accepted and proclaimed in 1889. The constitution had two major purposes: to impress Western governments with Japan's progress and to provide the Japanese people with a voice, though limited, in national affairs.

The leaders of the Meiji government were monarchists who did not believe in democracy. However, they knew from their study of Western cultures that political absolutism led to popular discontent. Although the new constitution gave the emperor supreme power, he did not exercise it. The constitution established a two-house national assembly, called the Diet, one house of which was elected. Initially, only those Japanese who owned a substantial amount of property had the right to vote, and the elected house of the Diet had very limited powers. In practice, a small group of leaders, acting in the name of the emperor, held the real power in Japan.

The new constitution and the Diet satisfied most Japanese. The government, for its part, was able to concentrate its energies and resources on promoting industrialization and economic development. Japanese leaders believed that their nation had to either catch up with Western nations in technology and wealth or face the humiliation of foreign domination.

Industrialization

Fortunately, Japan was in a position to make rapid economic and industrial progress. Its traditional agricultural economy had created surpluses that could be used to finance industrialization. The government also used factory machinery purchased from several Western countries and enacted a new commercial policy to encourage private investment in industrial enterprises.

By 1900 Japan had acquired the foundations of an industrial economy. Railroads, the telegraph, and telephones linked Japanese cities. Light manufacturing, especially of textiles, was well developed, and Japan had begun exporting machine-made cotton cloth and silk to other countries. The money that these exports earned helped pay for imports of industrial raw materials such as iron ore and petroleum, of which Japan had only limited quantities. The Japanese then used these raw materials in steel production and shipbuilding. Although Japan's economy remained smaller and weaker than that of Western nations, the gap between these nations gradually narrowed as Japan became the first country in Asia to industrialize.

Nevertheless, Japan's leaders continued to feel threatened by imperialist expansion in Asia. This fear motivated the Japanese to embark on a course of imperialist expansion themselves.

The Sino-Japanese War

The territory that most interested Japan was the nearby Korean Peninsula, long a dependency of China. Korean authorities had to refer all matters involving foreign relations to the Chinese emperor. No foreigners were allowed into the country. However, Russia, France, and the United States were all interested in gaining trading privileges there. Fearing that a Western-controlled Korea might threaten its safety, Japan began to demand privileges on the Korean peninsula.

Japan maintained that Korea was independent, while China still claimed Korea as a dependency. In 1876, out of this confusion, Japan secured a treaty that opened three Korean ports to Japanese trade. China then allowed the Koreans to sign treaties of trade and friendship with five Western nations.

In 1894 a rebellion calling for popular liberation broke out in Korea. Both Japan and China sent armed forces to end it. It was a turbulent situation that exploded into the brief Sino-Japanese War, in which Japan defeated China. (*Sino* means "Chinese.")

In addition to trade privileges, the Japanese wanted territory. The **Treaty of Shimonoseki** in 1895 forced China to recognize the complete independence of Korea. China also had to give to Japan the island of Formosa and the nearby islands, the Pescadores. In another provision, China gave Japan the strategic Liaodong Peninsula on the southern coast of Manchuria. At the tip of the Liaodong Peninsula,

This was the scene at Yokohama in 1871 as Prince Iwakura left on Japan's foreign mission to learn about Western countries.

which juts into the Yellow Sea, lay the excellent harbor of Port Arthur. (See map on page 336.) Finally, China also had to pay Japan an indemnity equivalent to $150 million.

Russia and the East Asian Mainland

The Treaty of Shimonoseki displeased the Russians, who had long yearned to expand to the south. Russia had wanted to build a railroad across Manchuria and the Liaodong Peninsula to Port Arthur.

With these plans in the process of development, Russia was more than willing to help China keep Japan away from the Asian mainland. France, which had recently signed an alliance with Russia, was also willing to assist its ally. Germany, which was eager to improve its relationship with Russia, also offered its services. Thus, in a joint note, Russia, France, and Germany advised the Japanese government to withdraw from the Liaodong Peninsula.

The Japanese were furious, but they were not able to resist such powerful forces. They gave the Liaodong Peninsula back to China in return for a larger indemnity. The peninsula was regained by Japan in 1905 and annexed in 1910.

The Price of European Aid

China had to pay a price for the help it received. Its indebtedness to foreign powers led to a flurry of foreign demands. France demanded and received special trading privileges and the right to develop mineral resources in southern China. It also leased the territory of Kwangchowan and acquired permission to build a railroad linking southern China with the French protectorate in Indochina.

Germany leased Qingdao (CHING·DOW) port and surrounding territory on the south shore of the Shandong Peninsula. Germany also received mining rights and permission to build a railway in Shandong.

Great Britain would not be left out. It negotiated for more trading privileges in the Chang Jiang valley and the right to build a naval base at Weihai on the north shore of the Shandong Peninsula to balance the German base at Qingdao.

Russia demanded and received the right to build a railroad across Manchuria—to be called the **Chinese Eastern Railway**. It also received permission to police the Manchurian route as well as certain other extraterritorial privileges.

These privileges greatly angered the Japanese. Western powers had forced them to give up the spoils of their victory. Both China and Japan recalled these events during the next 50 years as they strove for power in East Asia.

Section 4 Review

1. **Define** Muslim League, Treaty of Shimonoseki, Chinese Eastern Railway
2. **Locate and Explain the Significance** Formosa, Liaodong Peninsula
3. **Evaluating Ideas** What were the British methods of government and control in India, and how did they affect the rise of nationalism?
4. **Analyzing Ideas (a)** What governmental and social changes did the Meiji Restoration bring about? **(b)** What role did Western ideas play in these changes?
5. **Determining Cause and Effect** Describe the causes and results of the Sino-Japanese War.

Imperialism in East Asia to 1914

Territory Claimed by:
- France
- Germany
- Great Britain
- Japan
- Netherlands
- United States
- ⊙ Chinese treaty port
- • Other city

RUSSIAN EMPIRE

TRANS-SIBERIAN RAILWAY

CHINESE EASTERN RAILWAY

SAKHALIN

MONGOLIA

Manchuria

Harbin

45°N

Vladivostok

Lüshun (Port Arthur)

Beijing

KOREA

SEA OF JAPAN

JAPAN

Tianjin

Liaodong Pen.

WEIHAI (Br.)

Seoul

Edo (Tokyo)

Shandong Peninsula

Yokohama

QINGDAO (German)

YELLOW SEA

Huang He

CHINA

Nanjing

Nagasaki

30°N

Chongqing

Hankou

Shanghai

Chang Jiang

Hangzhou

Ningbo

AFGHANISTAN

Fuzhou

Wenzhou

PERSIA

Indus River

NEPAL

Guangzhou (Canton)

Xiamen

PESCADORES IS. (Japanese)

RYUKYU IS.

Ganges River

BHUTAN

Xi Jiang

HONG KONG (Br.)

FORMOSA (TAIWAN)

PACIFIC OCEAN

BRITISH INDIA

BURMA

MACAO (Port.)

ZHANJIANG (Fr.)

DIU (Port.)

DAMAN (Port.)

HAINAN

MARIANA ISLANDS (German)

15°N

YANAON (Fr.)

Bay of Bengal

SIAM

FRENCH INDOCHINA

Manila

PHILIPPINES

GUAM (U.S.)

GOA (Port.)

ANDAMAN IS. (Br.)

SOUTH CHINA SEA

ARABIAN SEA

MAHÉ (Fr.)

PONDICHERRY (Fr.)

KARIKAL (Fr.)

CEYLON

NICOBAR IS. (Br.)

Mekong River

BRITISH NORTH BORNEO

CAROLINE ISLANDS (German)

MALDIVES (Br.)

Strait of Malacca

MALAY STATES

Singapore

SARAWAK

BORNEO

Equator 0°

SUMATRA

CELEBES

BISMARCK ARCH.

NEW GUINEA

N
W—E
S

NETHERLANDS EAST INDIES

JAVA

TIMOR (Port.)

135°E

INDIAN OCEAN

15°S

0   500   1,000 Miles
0 500 1,000 Kilometers
Miller Cylindrical Projection

120°E

150°E

75°E   90°E   105°E

AUSTRALIA

Learning from Maps By 1914, much of East Asia was controlled by various foreign powers.

? Place Although the British government ruled India, which other European countries controlled Indian cities?

Chinese porcelain was imported to Europe where it was considered quite valuable. This punch bowl design depicts trading centers at Canton.

Foreign Influence in Southeast Asia and the Pacific

Focus Questions
- Where in Southeast Asia did each of the major imperial nations extend its influence?
- Why were European nations interested in the Pacific islands?
- Which nations ended up acquiring or controlling the Pacific islands?

The tide of imperialism did not stop in South Asia and East Asia. It affected Southeast Asia and the islands of the Pacific.

Imperialism in Southeast Asia
In the late 1400s and early 1500s, European traders explored the East Indies. In the seaports of these islands and on the nearby mainland, Portuguese and Dutch merchants enjoyed a rich and active trade until the early 1800s.

In the 1800s and early 1900s, European imperialism made its way to Southeast Asia as it did to nearby India and China. The area became an important source not only of spices but also of the world's tea. Later valuable products such as tin and oil came from this area.

British successes. It was natural that the British should take an interest in the kingdom of Burma, on the eastern border of India. By 1886 all of Burma had come under British control.

The island of Singapore, on the tip of the Malay Peninsula, guards the entrance to the Strait of Malacca—one of the most vital trade routes in the world. Britain's first recorded contact with Singapore was by a representative of the East India Company. In 1819 a company ship landed at Singapore. Informed that there were only a few residents and no Dutch among them, the company decided to purchase land for a factory site. It created a city at Singapore, which became an important naval base in the British Empire.

French gains. The eastern part of the mainland of Southeast Asia contained several small nations that struggled with internal instability and were at times also under the influence of Siam. In the late 1800s, French imperialists, by means of assertive economic measures and military intervention, laid claims to the area, and the French became the dominant power in what became known as French Indochina. The original three nations eventually regained their independence and today are the nations of Laos, Cambodia, and Vietnam.

Siam. The kingdom of Siam was better organized than were other parts of Southeast Asia. The British on the Malay Peninsula and the French in Indochina nibbled at the borders of Siam. To maintain their independence, Siamese rulers skillfully maneuvered British interests against French interests. The British and French finally agreed that an independent Siam was a useful buffer state between their possessions. A buffer state, located between two hostile powers, is a small country that serves to decrease the possibility of conflict between them.

The Dutch East Indies. The Dutch East India Company, formed in 1602 to protect Dutch trading interests in the Indian Ocean, succeeded for many years.

By the late 1700s, however, it had become corrupt and inefficient. In 1799 the government of the Netherlands revoked the company's charter and took over the administration of the Netherlands East Indies. By the late 1800s, several local revolts convinced the government of the Netherlands to make basic reforms in the administration of its richest imperial possession.

Interest in the Pacific Islands

Only a few of the islands and island groups in the Pacific were economically attractive to imperialist powers. Europeans were at first interested in acquiring valuable raw materials, such as sandalwood or pearl shell, from the islands. Some of the areas had fertile soil that could support rich plantations. Other islands had minerals to be mined. Imperialism in most of the Pacific islands, however, was based on another motive—the need for coaling stations and naval bases. Because the imperialist powers competed in the Pacific, as elsewhere, none was willing to trust the others for its coal supplies and naval repairs. Each of the powers therefore sought out its own Pacific islands. By 1900 imperialist nations controlled almost all the islands. (See map on page 339.)

The Samoa Islands. In the late 1800s, a serious rivalry over territory in the Pacific involved the Samoa Islands. Here the United States played a major role. American interests in the area had been developing for a number of years. During the 1870s Americans gained the right to use the harbor city of Pago Pago (PAHNG·oh PAHNG·oh) on the island of Tutuila (too·too·WEE·luh), as a trading post, coaling station, and naval base. Great Britain and Germany secured similar rights in other parts of the Samoa Islands.

For a number of years, rivalry among the three foreign nations for control of the Samoa Islands simmered until they teetered on the brink of war. To prevent further trouble, the three nations set up a system of joint control, but it was not to last.

In 1899 the rivals signed a treaty ending the dispute. Great Britain, preoccupied with the South African War, withdrew its interests. The United States established firm control over Tutuila and six other small islands whose combined area was only about 75 square miles. Together these possessions became known as American Samoa. Germany gained control of all the other islands in the Samoan group, which eventually became known as Western Samoa.

The Hawaiian Islands. Far more important to the United States than its Samoan possessions were the Hawaiian Islands. (See map on page 339.) This group of islands had fertile soil, good rainfall, and a mild climate. Foreign traders and missionaries, including Americans, had begun settling there in the 1820s but interfered little with the government and economy of the local people. After 1865, however, businesses from the United States and other foreign nations began to develop sugarcane and pineapple plantations on the islands.

The queen of the Hawaiian Islands resented foreign influence and tried to overturn or bring an end to treaties created by the previous two rulers. Her antiforeign feelings were in turn resented by the resident foreign business leaders. A combination of influential businessmen and their political supporters brought an end to the queen's reign. After several years of turmoil, the queen officially abdicated in 1895 to avoid bloodshed between her supporters and her opponents. The United States annexed the islands in 1898.

The Philippines, Guam, and Wake Island. Since the 1500s and 1600s, the Philippine Islands and Guam in the western Pacific Ocean had been parts of Spain's far-flung empire. In 1898 the United States and Spain went to war. Most of the fighting occurred in Cuba and Puerto Rico, but the first United States military action against Spain took place in the Pacific.

When war erupted, United States naval forces were ordered into action. A squadron of six ships under the command of Commodore George Dewey steamed from the British port of Hong Kong and moved quickly into the harbor of Manila, the capital of the Philippine Islands. Early on the morning of May 1, Dewey's forces attacked the decrepit Spanish fleet. By noon the Spanish ships were completely destroyed, and the city of Manila was at Dewey's mercy. Not a single American sailor was killed in the battle. Within a few months, American land forces, supported by local revolutionaries, defeated the Spanish forces in Manila. With the collapse of

What If?

Imperialism
In the late 1800s and early 1900s, European countries carved out empires in Africa, Asia, and the Pacific. How do you think world history would have been different if the Europeans had not established these empires?

Spanish power at Manila, the entire Philippine Islands came under the control of the United States. At about this time, American forces also occupied Guam, which was a small Spanish-held island east of the Philippines.

Some Filipinos welcomed the Americans and even fought with them against the Spaniards. Most of the local population had suffered under Spanish rule for centuries. Yet many saw little advantage in changing one foreign master for another. Led by Emilio Aguinaldo, Filipino locals fought for independence for three years against American troops. The Filipinos used guerrilla warfare against the better-equipped United States army but were finally defeated in 1901.

Besides acquiring the Philippine Islands and Guam, the United States also took possession of Wake Island in the central Pacific. Thus the United States acquired another link in a chain of island possessions running from its west coast across the vast distances of the Pacific Ocean all the way to East Asia.

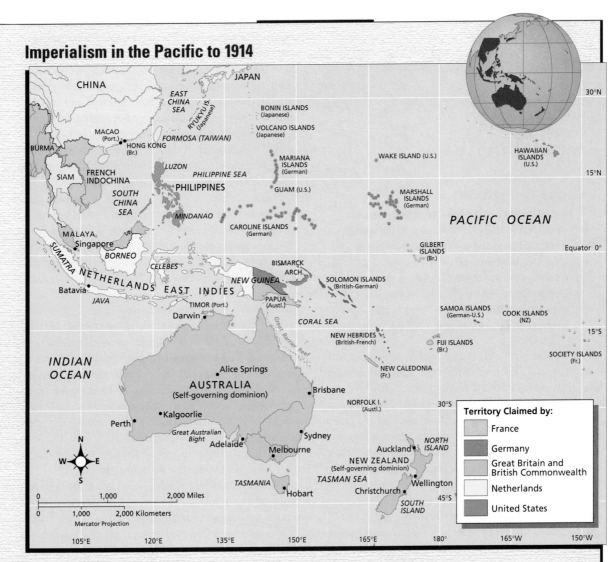

Imperialism in the Pacific to 1914

Learning from Maps As a result of the 1898 war with Spain, the United States gained territories in the Pacific.

? Location What islands in the Pacific were claimed by the United States?

1. **Identify** Emilio Aguinaldo
2. **Locate and Explain the Significance** Singapore, Samoan Islands
3. **Analyzing Maps** Using the map on page 339, list the Southeast Asian possessions that colonial powers had acquired by 1914.
4. **Analyzing Ideas** Why were the Pacific islands important possessions?
5. **Summarizing Ideas** Which Pacific islands did the United States control?

Section 6

Imperialism in Latin America

Focus Questions

- In what ways was imperialism different in Latin America than it was in other parts of the world?
- What conditions led to foreign intervention in Latin American nations?
- What was the Roosevelt Corollary to the Monroe Doctrine?
- How and why did the United States further intervene in Latin America through the 1930s?

Imperialism in Latin America differed from imperialism in the Pacific. Although Latin American countries were weak, the Monroe Doctrine of the United States, Great Britain's commercial interests and powerful navy, and European attention to other matters prevented attempts to recolonize Latin America. Nevertheless, economic interference in Latin American nations became common as they increasingly attracted European and American investments.

New Opportunities for Trade

As the pace of the Industrial Revolution quickened in Europe and the United States, more agricultural products and raw materials came from Latin American countries. Americans, for example, acquired a taste for bananas, which were imported largely from Central America, and for coffee, which came mostly from Brazil. They bought sugar which was made from sugarcane grown in Cuba, and they smoked cigars made from Cuban tobacco.

The British purchased large quantities of wool, which their factories needed, as well as wheat, beef, and mutton from Argentina and Uruguay. Chile mined nitrates from natural deposits in its northern deserts and sold them to industrial countries for production of fertilizers and explosives. Brazil exported natural rubber from its vast Amazon forests.

Railroads were built to bring these goods to Latin American port cities. The ports were also improved to ease loading of newly perfected steamships. All these developments brought more prosperity to those countries of Latin America that had the opportunity to engage in trade. Argentina especially benefited from these developments. However, some Latin American countries, such as Bolivia and Paraguay, hardly participated in this trade at all. Ruinous internal and external military struggles and ineffective government administration and policy limited their economic growth.

As had occurred in the United States, a few of the Latin American countries—most notably Argentina, Brazil, and Uruguay—attracted a large number of immigrants from Europe. In those countries with successful export trade, industries also began to develop. Foreign investors built factories such as sugar mills to process export goods. Other new factories—textile mills, flour mills, and metalworking shops—produced goods for local markets.

Economic Imperialism

Foreign investors, particularly from Great Britain, owned many of the new railroads, ranches, plantations, and mines in Latin America. Foreign banks financed large-scale commercial agriculture. Central governments allowed foreign capital to enter their countries without much regulation in the hope that foreigners would develop the economy by establishing new businesses there. However, investors usually sent profits from these businesses and interest payments from loans back to their own countries.

Foreign banks lent funds for public improvements. Some of this money went to strengthening armies and navies, making it easier to suppress internal rebellions. However, revolutions sometimes toppled governments that had borrowed money, and new governments would refuse to pay the old debts or pay for foreign property. In addition, most of the development was concentrated in the hands of a few people in cities, so distribution of wealth was uneven, leading to further instability.

Unpaid loans led to intervention by foreign powers. European banking and business leaders persuaded their governments to pressure Latin American governments for payment. Sometimes ships and troops were sent to compel payment. For example, to secure repayment of a debt that the Mexican government under Juarez had refused to pay, France attacked Mexico, set up a government in Mexico City, and made a Habsburg prince, Maximilian, emperor from 1864 to 1867.

American Intervention

Late in the nineteenth century, as the United States became an industrial power, it began to challenge Great Britain, its main rival for dominance of the Western Hemisphere. In the early 1800s, a weak United States made no attempt to enforce the Monroe Doctrine when the offender was Great Britain. For example, the British ousted Argentina from the Falkland Islands (Islas Malvinas), near the tip of South America, in 1833. Although Argentina protested, the United States did not oppose the British action, having had its own difficulties several years before with the Argentines over detainment of shipping in the area.

In 1895, however, the United States did intervene in a dispute between Great Britain and Venezuela. Great Britain had acquired British Guiana (gee·AH·nuh), on the northern coast of South America early in the 1800s. On a number of occasions, Great Britain had tried to extend the boundary of British Guiana westward into territory claimed by Venezuela. The discovery of gold in the disputed area made the crisis more urgent.

Great Britain refused Venezuela's requests to submit the border dispute to arbitration—negotiation for a settlement of the dispute by a party agreed upon by all sides. Venezuela appealed for American help, and President Grover Cleveland pressed Britain. Finally, preoccupied with the South African War, Great Britain submitted the dispute to arbitration for settlement. The United States had successfully championed the cause of a weak Latin American nation against powerful European interests. Perhaps, however, the United States had its own motives for helping Venezuela—the gold in the region was now more accessible to American investors.

The Spanish-American War

In 1898 the United States became even more deeply involved in Latin American affairs. Its involvement grew out of disputes with Spain.

Many railroads in Latin America were funded by Britain and the United States. This railroad runs through a banana plantation in Costa Rica.

The main cause of tension between Spain and the United States was Cuba, a Spanish colony in the Caribbean. (See map on page 344.) For many years, Cubans had been unhappy under Spanish rule. Nationalists, such as the poet-lawyer José Martí, attempted to overthrow the government in the Ten Years' War (1868–1878). However, this military stalemate, and a later failed rebellion in 1895—in which Martí was killed—elevated tension to a high level. The unrest alarmed Americans who had growing investments in Cuba.

Concern for American property was only one reason for tension between the United States and Spain. Many Americans felt sympathy toward Cuba's desire for independence. Anti-Spanish speeches and writings by Cubans who lived in the United States and sensational stories in American newspapers of Spanish atrocities in Cuba stirred hostile feelings.

Anger boiled in 1898 when an American battleship, the *Maine*, exploded in Havana harbor, killing 260 Americans. The *Maine* had been sent to Cuba to protect American citizens and their property. No one knew the cause of the explosion, but many in the United States assumed that Spaniards were to blame. American newspapers played on this assumption, encouraging rising popular sentiment in the United States for war with Spain.

Spain was willing to make concessions to avoid war, but it would not withdraw from Cuba or grant it independence. President McKinley, like his predecessor Cleveland, did not want war. American leaders felt unable to resist mounting popular demand, however, and declared war in April 1898. To pacify members who opposed growing American imperialism, Congress declared that the United States was fighting only on behalf of Cuban independence and had no intention of taking the island for itself.

The war, which had begun with the defeat of the Spanish in the Philippines (see pages 338–339), was a lopsided victory for the United States. In Cuba, American troops, including Theodore Roosevelt and his Rough Riders, landed east of Santiago in June. With Cuban help, American troops pushed to the city. Trying to flee Santiago Harbor, Spanish ships came under heavy fire. All ships were damaged or set ablaze and run aground. After these defeats, Spain sought peace. The Treaty of Paris was signed in December 1898.

By the terms of the peace treaty, Spain surrendered its claim to Cuba. It also ceded its colony Puerto Rico in the Caribbean and the Pacific island of Guam to the United States. In addition, Spain sold the Philippines to the United States for $20 million.

Following the war, United States troops occupied Cuba. The American military disbanded the Cuban army and at first sought to keep Cubans from governing, but it also established schools, built roads, provided sanitation, and worked to wipe out yellow fever. Finally, the United States recognized Cuba's independence, and an elected government led by President Tomás Estrada Palma took office in 1902. Although the United States permitted a Cuban assembly to draw up a constitution, it insisted that the Cuban constitution include the so-called **Platt Amendment**. This amendment forbade any transfer of land except to the United States and gave the United States the right to intervene in Cuba whenever it thought orderly government was endangered. The United States also insisted on having a permanent naval base in Cuba at Guantánamo Bay.

The Panama Canal

In addition to governing its new and far-flung possessions, the United States suddenly had to prepare to defend them. An example of the problem of defense occurred during the Spanish-American War.

Before the war, the American battleship *Oregon* had been stationed on the Pacific coast of the United States. When war became likely, the *Oregon* was summoned to the Caribbean Sea. The battleship had to race around the entire South American continent, a distance of almost 13,000 miles, to reach the Caribbean. The United States realized that it would either have to build two complete navies or find an easier and quicker way to move warships between the Atlantic and Pacific Oceans.

A canal across the Isthmus of Panama had long been considered. The French company that built the Suez Canal had tried unsuccessfully to build a canal across Panama. In the late 1800s, the United States began negotiating for permission and a right-of-way to build a canal. It asked Colombia for a lease to a strip of land across the Isthmus of Panama, then a Colombian province. (See map on page 344.)

Theodore Roosevelt and his regiment of cavalry volunteers known as the Rough Riders fought against the Spanish in Cuba.

After negotiations the Colombian senate rejected the request, a move that angered people in the United States and some in the province of Panama who wanted the canal because it would create great benefits for them. When negotiations seemingly broke down, some Panamanian business leaders and American residents of Panama proclaimed a revolution to gain independence from Colombia.

American warships stationed at Panama prevented Colombian troops from moving in reinforcements to suppress the revolt. The revolution succeeded, and the United States recognized the independence of Panama. In 1903 the new government gave the United States all rights necessary to build a canal across Panama.

The Panama Canal, one of the world's great engineering achievements, opened in 1914. It might have been impossible to build without newly invented power shovels and other new machines. Medical science, too, played a vital part. A Cuban doctor, Carlos Juan Finlay, discovered that mosquitoes carry yellow fever, a disease that had decimated workers attempting to build the canal. By destroying the mosquitoes, scientists controlled the spread of the disease, thus enabling construction crews to work in the Panamanian jungles.

The new canal shortened the sea route from New York to San Francisco by about 8,000 miles. Fleets in the Atlantic and Pacific Oceans could be shifted quickly. Merchant ships of all nations paid a toll to use the canal, but the vastly shortened route saved time and operating costs.

The Panama Canal also had an important effect on the countries of Central and South America that bordered the Caribbean Sea. Formerly a poor and unsettled region in frequent chaos, Central America became a crossroads of trade.

The Roosevelt Corollary

Long before the completion of the Panama Canal, the United States recognized that any strong European power with a foothold in the Caribbean region could threaten the canal or the sea-lanes leading to it. Therefore, the United States adopted a new policy regarding foreign influence in Latin America.

In 1904 President Theodore Roosevelt extended the ideas of the Monroe Doctrine. Roosevelt said that if any situation threatened the independence of any country in the Western Hemisphere, the United States would act as an international police power to prevent a foreign country from intervening. Further, the United States guaranteed that Latin American nations

Passing through a series of locks and lakes over a 15- to 20-hour period, ships move from the Atlantic Ocean to the Pacific Ocean through the Panama Canal.

would meet their international obligations. This policy became known as the **Roosevelt Corollary** to the Monroe Doctrine. It was regarded as a natural consequence of the earlier policy, and it would be called into use several times in the coming years.

Although European and American investors stood to benefit from the Roosevelt Corollary, Latin Americans were enraged at the implication that they could not manage their own affairs. Latin American nations supported a statement made by Luis Drago, foreign minister of Argentina. He vehemently denied the European or American right to use military intervention to collect foreign debts—a declaration known as the Drago Doctrine.

Further United States Expansion

Because of political disturbances and defaults on loans, the United States continued to expand its influence in Central America and the Caribbean. The United States created military governments in Nicaragua from 1912 to 1933, Haiti from 1915 to 1934, and the Dominican Republic from 1916 to 1924. Cuba once again was subjected to an occupation government from 1906 to 1909, and United States troops intervened in Cuba again in 1912.

The United States intervened in these countries for several reasons. During the early 1900s, the economies of several nations in the area almost collapsed. The United States feared that its sizeable investments would be destroyed by anarchy or that governments might fall into the hands of leaders who would refuse to pay debts owed to foreign banks. European nations might have used a refusal to pay debts as a pretext for large-scale intervention in the region.

In 1917 the United States purchased from Denmark three of the Virgin Islands east of Puerto Rico. With this purchase, the United States added another base to ensure control over the Caribbean. At the same time, Puerto Ricans became United States citizens and received the right of self-government to guarantee their loyalty in dangerous times.

Mexico's Revolution

The greatest upheaval in Latin America during the age of imperialism was the Mexican Revolution. For 35 years, one dictator, Porfirio Díaz, had dominated Mexico. He had permitted foreign companies to develop many of Mexico's natural resources and had allowed major landowners to buy much of the country's land from poor peasants. In 1910, when the aging Díaz jailed Francisco Madero, his opponent for the presidency, rebellion broke out.

Madero escaped and hoped for a general uprising that did not materialize. A guerrilla war broadened, though, and eventually put Madero in power in 1911. Counterrevolution followed, and in 1913 Victoriano Huerta, a government general, betrayed Madero and seized control of the government. Madero was taken prisoner and shot. A rebellion led by constitutionalist Venustiano Carranza against Huerta began and eventually developed into intense and prolonged civil war among various factions. Warfare dragged on for a decade and approximately 1 million lives were lost.

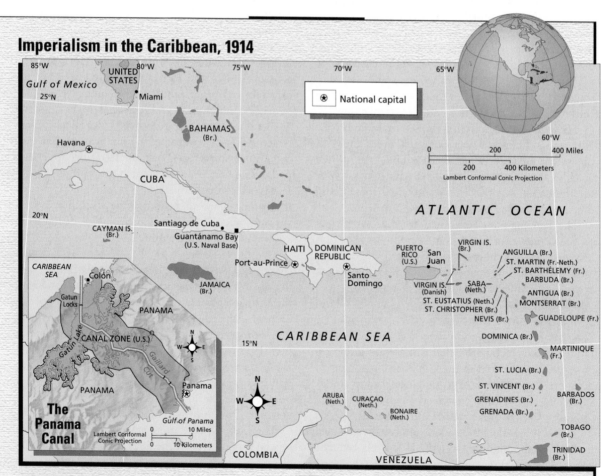

Imperialism in the Caribbean, 1914

Learning from Maps The Caribbean islands, like other countries and territories in East Asia and in the Pacific, were dominated by foreign nations.

? Movement How many miles would a person travel between Miami and San Juan?

Pancho Villa (shown seated in the Presidential Chair) and Emiliano Zapata (seated to Villa's left) were both Mexican revolutionary and guerrilla leaders.

Underlying these struggles were widespread calls for rights to the land. The peasant leader Emiliano Zapata (sah·PAH·tah) voiced these demands.

The violence and unrest frightened American investors and the thousands of Americans who lived in Mexico. President Woodrow Wilson refused to recognize Huerta's government and openly supported Carranza. The idealistic Wilson opposed the Huerta regime because it had deposed Madero, whose movement Wilson had admired. However, Wilson was at first reluctant to send troops into Mexico to protect American lives and property, deciding instead to wait and see what developed. In 1914, though, after the arrest of American soldiers, United States marines occupied the port at Veracruz, cutting off supplies and money to Huerta. Carranza's revolt succeeded, but Pancho Villa (VEE·yah), another revolutionary leader and rival, continued skirmishes with Carranza's government. Two years later, the United States sent troops into Mexico to capture Villa, who had raided a border town in New Mexico, killing several Americans. As American troops went deeper into Mexico, Carranza's government became more upset. Tensions mounted, and for a time there was a threat of war. In 1917 the United States withdrew its troops from Mexico and focused on the world war that was taking place in Europe.

Section 6 Review

1. **Define** *Maine*, Platt Amendment, Roosevelt Corollary

2. **Identify** Porfirio Díaz, Victoriano Huerta, Venustiano Carranza, Pancho Villa

3. **Locate and Explain the Significance** Puerto Rico, Panama Canal

4. **Summarizing Ideas** Describe the nature of imperialism in Latin America.

5. **Analyzing Ideas** For what reasons did foreign powers intervene in Latin American nations?

6. **Understanding Ideas (a)** Explain how the United States applied the Monroe Doctrine in the 1890s. **(b)** What was the Roosevelt Corollary to the Monroe Doctrine?

7. **Analyzing Ideas** Why did the United States intervene in several Latin American countries, including Mexico, in the early decades of the 1900s?

Chapter 10 Review

A.D. **1882**
British occupy Egypt.

A.D. **1885**
Indian National Congress is founded.

A.D. **1894–1895**
Sino-Japanese War is fought.

A.D. **1899**
Agreement over Samoa is reached.

A.D. **1830**   A.D. **1850**   A.D. **1870**   A.D. **1880**   A.D. **1890**   A.D. **1900**

A.D. **1830**
France occupies Algiers.

A.D. **1847**
Liberia becomes independent.

A.D. **1869**
Suez Canal is completed.

A.D. **1881**
Tunisia becomes French protectorate.

A.D. **1898**
• Spanish-American War occurs.
• Fashoda incident occurs.
• United States annexes Hawaii.

Chapter Summary

The following list contains the key concepts you have learned about imperialism in the late 1800s and early 1900s.

1. In the late 1800s, European nations became involved in a new kind of empire building, imperialism, that arose from the need for self-sufficiency, new markets, and places in which an ever-growing population could settle.
2. European nations divided up almost all of Africa in the late 1800s. Communication and transportation improved, and the slave trade was abolished. For the most part, Africa and Africans were exploited, and tensions developed that would lead to further struggles later in the 1900s.
3. In India the British government assumed direct control. The British established themselves as a caste superior to the native population.
4. After a civil war in Japan, the emperor was restored to power in 1868. The Japanese then began a successful process of industrialization.

5. Although foreign powers helped China resist the Japanese, the Chinese had to make concessions for receiving this European assistance.
6. Imperialism was also a strong force in Southeast Asia and in the Pacific. By the late 1800s, the kingdom of Siam was the only area of Southeast Asia that remained free from foreign rule.
7. The Pacific islands became valuable as coaling stations and naval bases.
8. The countries of Latin America were weak and vulnerable to economic imperialism. The United States sought to extend its influence and to protect Latin America from the influence of powerful European nations.
9. The relatively easy American victory in the Spanish-American War dramatized the growing strength of the United States. In the early 1900s, the United States became increasingly involved in Latin American affairs, often invoking the Roosevelt Corollary.

Reviewing Important Terms

On a separate sheet of paper, match each of the following terms with the correct definition below.

a. paternalism
b. assimilation
c. arbitration
d. direct rule
e. protectorate
f. sphere of influence
g. buffer state
h. colony
i. concession
j. indirect rule
k. condominium

___ 1. System of colonial government in which the local ruler kept his title but officials of the foreign power actually controlled the region
___ 2. System in which the people of the colonies abandoned their local cultures and adopted all aspects of the colonial power's culture
___ 3. Settlement of a dispute by a party agreed upon by all sides
___ 4. System of colonial government in which the imperialist power controlled all levels of government and appointed its own officials to govern the colony

___ 5. Small country located between two hostile powers and whose presence decreased the possibility of conflict between them
___ 6. Region in which one foreign nation had special, sometimes exclusive, economic and political privileges that were recognized by other nations
___ 7. System of governing colonies just as parents guide their children
___ 8. A system of colonial government under which the governor and a council of advisers developed laws for the colony but local rulers were given the opportunity to exert some degree of authority
___ 9. Grant of economic rights and privileges in a particular area usually given to foreign merchants or capitalists
___ 10. System whereby two nations ruled a region as partners
___ 11. Area in which a foreign nation gained complete control over a given region and the region's local population

A.D. **1904**
Roosevelt
Corollary
is adopted.

A.D. **1906**
Muslim League
is formed in India.

A.D. **1905**   A.D. **1910**   A.D. **1915**   A.D. **1920**

A.D. **1899–1902**
Boer War
(South African
War) is fought.

A.D. **1910**
Mexican
Revolution begins.

A.D. **1914**
Panama
Canal opens.

A.D. **1917**
American troops
withdraw from Mexico.

Developing Critical Thinking Skills

1. **Classifying Ideas** Name the imperialist nation that claimed each of the following territories: **(a)** Libya; **(b)** Nigeria; **(c)** Algeria; **(d)** Gold Coast; **(e)** Morocco.
2. **Contrasting Ideas (a)** How does economic imperialism differ from political imperialism? **(b)** Why did one often lead to the other during the late 1800s?
3. **Summarizing Ideas** Tell how each of the following nations was able to preserve its independence: **(a)** Liberia; **(b)** Ethiopia; **(c)** Japan; **(d)** Siam.
4. **Contrasting Ideas** In what ways did the colonial policy of the United States differ from that of other nations?
5. **Evaluating Ideas** What were the positive and negative effects of imperialism in Africa and in India?
6. **Analyzing Primary Sources** Reread the lines from the Rudyard Kipling poem "The White Man's Burden" on page 322. **(a)** What does Kipling mean by the phrase "white man's burden"? **(b)** How does he characterize the people who must be "served"? **(c)** Based on what you have learned about early African, Asian, and Indian civilizations, what arguments might you use to prove Kipling wrong?

Relating Geography to History
Use the maps in the Atlas section of your textbook to answer the following questions: **(a)** If the Suez Canal did not exist, what would be the shortest water route between London and Bombay? **(b)** If the Panama Canal did not exist, what would be the shortest water route between New York and Hawaii?

Relating Past to Present

1. Using a world atlas, prepare a map showing the distribution of natural resources in Africa. Compare this map with the map on page 327. **(a)** What resources did each imperialist nation stand to gain through its possession of African colonies? **(b)** Which of these resources are most important to industrial nations today?
2. Review the reasons for the United States government's decision to build a canal across the Isthmus of Panama. Then research what has occurred with the canal during the past decade and its status today.

Applying History Study Skills
Before completing this activity, review Building History Study Skills on page 331.

Your topic is "How did the Meiji Restoration speed the industrialization of Japan?" Which of the following items would be relevant to your topic?
1. A new government was located in Tokyo.
2. A system of universal education was set up in Japan.
3. Treaties that gave foreign powers economic advantages were revised.
4. One of the first acts of the new government was to form a national army.
5. Former feudal class privileges were eliminated during the Meiji Restoration.
6. Government policy was primarily decided by a group of young samurai.

Use the Internet through the HRW Web site to search for information on the British East India Company. Write a newspaper article describing the key players and telling how the company changed over time.

GO TO: go.hrw.com
KEYWORD: SC0 East India

Building Your Portfolio

1. **Conducting a Debate** Work with several of your classmates to find information on European imperialism in Africa. Then prepare a debate on the following topic: Resolved: The Europeans exploited Africa and severely damaged indigenous cultures. Place your notes and other research in your portfolio.
2. **Writing a Report** Imperialism arose out of a complex mixture of political, economic, and social forces. One of these was the missionary motive. Using books in your library, prepare a report on missionary activities in colonial areas. Place the report in your portfolio.

Unit Summary

The following list contains the key concepts you have learned about the development of industrial society.

1. The Industrial Revolution—the production of goods by power-driven machinery in factories—began in Great Britain and changed the world. Both steam power and the Bessemer process were extremely important to the early Industrial Revolution.

2. Workers began to protest harsh working conditions and low wages. The first labor unions were organized to seek improvements in working conditions.

3. Socialists such as Karl Marx believed that a more fundamental transformation of politics and society was necessary and would resolve human problems.

4. In the 1800s and early 1900s new inventions, scientific discoveries, compulsory public education, and an interest in the arts improved the quality of life.

5. Many social and political reforms occurred in Great Britain and the British Empire in the 1800s and early 1900s.

6. Territorial growth and sectionalism in the United States eventually led to conflict over the issue of slavery. Eventually the North and South fought a bitter civil war.

7. France experienced political instability in the 1800s. By the early 1900s, France was a republic governed by coalitions of parties that represented monarchist, liberal, and socialist beliefs.

8. The peoples of Latin America gained their independence in the 1800s but did not unite.

9. Due to the efforts of Mazzini, Garibaldi, and Cavour, Italy was unified by 1870. In Germany, Prussia led the movement toward unification.

10. In Russia the czar maintained autocratic control, while discontent and rebellion in the Austrian Empire led to the formation of the Dual Monarchy.

11. In the late 1800s, European nations became involved in a new kind of empire building—imperialism. Europeans established colonies in Africa, Asia, and the Pacific. In most of Latin America, imperialism was economic rather than political.

Reviewing Concepts

On a separate sheet of paper, match each of the following individuals with the correct concept in column two.

a. Mazzini
b. Bismarck
c. Spencer
d. Smith
e. Marx
f. Daumier
g. Beethoven
h. Pankhurst
i. Bentham
j. Monet
k. Einstein
l. Owen
m. Kipling
n. Freud

1. romanticism in music
2. psychoanalysis
3. utilitarianism
4. relativity
5. utopian socialism
6. impressionism
7. risorgimento
8. "White Man's Burden"
9. pure communism
10. *Kulturkampf*
11. realism in art
12. social Darwinism
13. laissez–faire
14. woman suffrage

Applying Critical Thinking Skills

1. **Interpreting Ideas (a)** How did the agricultural revolution help to create a large labor force in the cities? **(b)** Why was this necessary for the development of an industrial economy?

2. **Determining Cause and Effect** What effect did the Industrial Revolution have on each of the following: **(a)** living conditions; **(b)** women's lives; **(c)** family size; **(d)** use of leisure time.

3. **Classifying Ideas** Identify the accomplishments of each of the following: **(a)** John Dalton; **(b)** Marie Curie; **(c)** Albert Einstein; **(d)** Charles Darwin; **(e)** Edward Jenner; **(f)** Louis Pasteur; **(g)** Joseph Lister; **(h)** Sigmund Freud

4. **Understanding Ideas** During the 1800s liberalism emerged as a vital force in Europe. **(a)** What were some of the political ideas associated with liberalism? **(b)** In what nations did liberalism make the greatest progress? **(c)** the least progress?

5. **Analyzing Primary Sources** Metternich once commented, "When France sneezes, all Europe catches cold." **(a)** What do you think he meant by this remark? **(b)** In light of the actions taken by Napoleon III, would you agree or disagree with Metternich? Why or why not?

6. **Evaluating Ideas (a)** What conditions encouraged the growth of nationalism in Europe? **(b)** How did the spirit of nationalism affect the development of Italy? **(c)** of Germany? **(d)** of Austria-Hungary? **(e)** of Russia?

7. **Synthesizing Ideas (a)** How did the Industrial Revolution and the rise of nationalism rekindle the desire for colonies? **(b)** What other factors promoted the renewed interest in empire building? **(c)** How did the imperialism of the late 1800s differ from the colonization of the 1500s and 1600s?

Relating Geography to History

Turn to the map of Africa on page R16. **(a)** How many independent nations exist in present-day Africa? **(b)** How does this number compare with the number of nations shown on the map on page 327? **(c)** Which imperialist power gave up the most territory? **(d)** the least territory?

Writing About History

1. Choose one of the scientists discussed in Chapter 7. Then use resources in your school or public library to find what recent discoveries have advanced the work of this scientist. Write a report detailing your findings.
2. Write a newspaper article dated October 25, 1876, that is written to convince readers that European countries should establish colonies.

Further Readings

Cary, Joyce. *Mister Johnson*. New Directions, 1989. Account of the author's experiences in the British colonial service in Nigeria from 1913–1919.

Morris, James. *Pax Britannica: The Climax of an Empire*. HarBrace, 1980. Well-written and colorful account of the British Empire at its height, at the time of Queen Victoria's Diamond Jubilee.

Mosse, W.E. *Alexander II and the Modernization of Russia*. St. Martin, 1992. Comprehensive biography of Alexander II of Russia that analyzes his impact on Russian society, particularly the peasant classes.

Sinclair, Upton. *The Jungle*. NAL-Dutton, 1960. Reprint of famous social critique of the Industrial Revolution in the United States, including graphic descriptions of abuses of workers.

Twain, Mark. *The Adventures of Huckleberry Finn*. NAL-Dutton, 1997. One of many reprintings of the famous American novel about life on the Mississippi during the early nineteenth century.

UNIT 2 CHRONOLOGY

Date	Politics	Science and Technology	Society and Culture
1750–1800	French and British anti-union laws 6* Haiti revolt 8 Commercial capitalism 6	Watt's steam engine 6 Factory system 6 Cartwright's power loom 6 Whitney's cotton gin 6 Jenner and smallpox 7	*The Wealth of Nations* 6 Beethoven 7 *An Essay on the Principle of Population* 6
1800–1850	British industrial reform 6 Latin American independence 8 Chartist movement 8 *Zollverein* 9 Laissez-faire economics 6 Continuous decline of Ottoman Empire 9 Revolutions of 1848 8, 9 Imperialism in China 10	Fulton's *Clermont* 6 Stephenson's locomotive 6 McCormick's reaper 6 Goodyear's vulcanized rubber 6 Morse's telegraph 6	Romanticism 7 Tchaikovsky, Wagner, and Verdi 7 Brothers Grimm, Goethe, Cooper, and Irving 7 *Communist Manifesto* 6 Victorian Age 8 Utopians 6
1850–1920	Third French Republic 8 Second and third reform bills in Great Britain 8 Meiji Restoration 10 European imperialism 10 U.S. Civil War 8 Establishment of Germany, Italy, and Austria-Hungary 9 Franco-Prussian War 8 Spanish-American War 10 Boer War 10 Russo-Japanese War 9	Bessemer steel process 6 Darwin 7 Pasteur 7 Transatlantic cable 6 Bell's telephone 7 Suez Canal 8, 10 Edison's light bulb 7 Wright brothers 7 Planck and Einstein 7 Panama Canal 10	Realism 7 Dickens 6 Impressionism 7 Nationalism 9, 10 Nihilism 9 Universal education 7 *Principles of Sociology* 7 *Kulturkampf* 9 Socialism 6 Social Darwinism 7 American football 7 Freud 7

*Indicates chapter in which development is discussed

Industrialism and Nationalism

CHAPTER 6

The Industrial Revolution

A revolution quite different from the Scientific Revolution of the 1500s or the political revolutions of the 1600s, 1700s, and 1800s began in Great Britain in the 1700s. This revolution—the Industrial Revolution—transformed the ways goods were produced and completely transformed the world.

The Origins of the Industrial Revolution

Before the Industrial Revolution began, Great Britain experienced a revolution in agriculture. This revolution started when British farmers began to fence off, or enclose, common lands into individual holdings efficient for large-scale farming. By the 1800s, because of improvements in agriculture, farmers needed fewer farm laborers. Many unemployed farmworkers moved to the cities, where they created a large labor force.

The Industrial Revolution began in Great Britain because of a combination of conditions. Great Britain

James Ward painting of a farm family before the Industrial Revolution

had what economists call the factors of production, or the basic resources necessary for industrialization: land, capital, and labor.

The cotton textile industry was the first industry in Great Britain to undergo mechanization—the use of automatic machinery to increase production. Other developments there included the steam engine, which improved transportation, and electricity, which revolutionized communications.

The Factory System

The steam engine could be used to power machinery as well as boats and trains. Steam-powered machinery made work easier to do and made it possible to produce a wide array of products in a relatively short time. Most of these goods were manufactured in factories rather than in people's homes.

Life in the mines and factories of the early Industrial Revolution was hard and monotonous, and life in the workers' homes was not much better. Working people lived in cramped and poorly maintained apartment houses called tenements. At the same time, the middle class grew and enjoyed many luxuries unknown before the industrial age. For middle-class women, this meant expanded opportunities for education and employment.

New Methods and Business Organizations

The factory system introduced a new phase in the development of capitalism—the economic system in which individuals rather than governments control the factors of production. Before the Industrial Revolution, most capitalists were merchants who bought, sold, and exchanged goods. This is called commercial capitalism. The capitalists of the Industrial Revolution, however, became more involved in producing and manufacturing goods using mechanization and industrialization. Thus the capitalism of this period is often referred to as industrial capitalism.

Industrialization changed the methods of production and depended on division of labor, interchangeable parts, and the assembly line. It gave rise to a different form of business organization—the corporation.

Living and Working Conditions

During the Enlightenment of the 1700s, a group of economists attacked the ideas of mercantilism. These economists believed that natural laws governed economic life, and that any attempt to interfere with these natural economic laws was certain to bring disaster. Adam Smith best stated the views of these economists. Smith wrote that every person should be free to go into any business and to operate it for the greatest advantage. The result, Smith said, would benefit everyone. This system of complete free enterprise became known as laissez-faire.

As time went on, more people realized that things could not be left entirely alone. Many people, such as John Stuart Mill, felt that government needed to intervene to protect working children and improve housing and factory conditions. These people argued that laws regulating working conditions would not interfere with the natural workings of the economy. Over time, governments began to agree with these social reformers.

Many workers, however, felt that governments were not moving fast enough. Sometimes these workers called a strike and refused to work until demands were met.

In order to strengthen their position, workers sought ways to organize permanently into associations called unions. These organizations gradually became legal.

Calls for Reform

Some reformers of the 1800s advocated a political and economic system called socialism. In this system, the government owns the means of production and operates them for the good of all the people.

Some thinkers grew impatient with early socialism, which advocated peaceful methods to attain goals. Karl Marx, the most important of these critics, believed that all the great changes in history came from changes in economic conditions. Under capitalism, he said, labor receives only a small fraction of the wealth it creates. Most of the wealth goes to the owners in the form of profits. This unequal distribution of wealth would ultimately lead to a revolution led by the working class, or proletariat.

Marxist, or radical, socialists generally believed in the necessity of revolution to overthrow the capitalist system. They wanted to establish a system in which the government owned almost all the means of production and controlled economic planning. Two forms of Marxism that later developed are communism and democratic socialism. Marx's ideas had profound effects in Russia.

Life in the Industrial Age

In addition to changing the economy and society, the Industrial Revolution had a profound effect on science, art, music, and literature.

Advances in Technology and Communication

Beginning in the early 1800s, manufacturers increasingly applied the findings of pure science to their businesses, generating a new wave of industrial growth. Electricity, a tremendous new source of power, was developed and used to run generators, lights, the telephone, and the telegraph. The invention of the internal combustion engine led to the development of both the automobile and the airplane.

Advances in Science and Medicine

Scientists during the 1800s and early 1900s investigated the biological sciences—those dealing with living organisms. Many explored the structure of cells, the tiny units of living matter, in an attempt to better understand organic matter and thereby improve human life. Disease prevention was one of the breakthroughs accomplished by this knowledge.

Joseph Nash lithograph of Machinery Hall in British section of Great Exhibition, 1851

The most significant developments in the physical sciences—those that deal with the properties of energy and nonliving matter—centered on atomic theory. This theory states that all matter in the universe consists of very small particles called atoms. The arrangement and structure of these atoms and their chemical combinations with each other account for the different characteristics of the materials that make up our world.

Social Sciences in the Industrial Age

During the 1800s, interest in the social sciences, those branches of knowledge that scientifically study people as members of society, grew rapidly. These subjects include political science, economics, history, archaeology, anthropology, sociology, and psychology.

Society and Culture in the Industrial Age

The progress made possible by science and technology helped produce rapid population growth in industrialized countries. As the population grew, it became more mobile. Large numbers of people emigrated to other countries. Others moved to cities to find jobs in factories. Education became more accessible to a larger part of the population. The number and availability of leisure activities grew along with the population.

Literature, Music, and Art in the Industrial Age

Literature, music, and art reflected the social and economic developments of the industrial age. Artists portrayed a sense of the rapidly changing times and the influences of scientific ideas in their works.

Many writers, musicians, and other artists of the early 1800s belonged to the artistic movement known as romanticism. Their work appealed to sentiment and imagination and dealt with the "romance" of life—life as they thought it should be rather than as it actually was. In the mid-1800s, writers and artists began to abandon romanticism and turn to realism, which emphasized the realities of everyday life.

CHAPTER 8

The Age of Reform

During the late 1800s, people throughout the world clamored for reform. These appeals, based on the

philosophy of liberalism, met with varying degrees of success.

Liberal Reforms in Great Britain and Its Empire

Although Great Britain was a limited constitutional monarchy with executive power vested in a cabinet headed by the prime minister, not everyone had a voice in government. In the 1800s, however, a series of reforms extended rights to more of the population. At the same time, vital social and economic reforms took place. Two notable prime ministers—Benjamin Disraeli and William Gladstone—helped promote many of these reforms.

As Great Britain instituted social and political reforms, other changes occurred within the British Empire. The British colonies of Canada, Australia, and New Zealand won self-government. Nevertheless, each maintained close ties with Great Britain.

Expansion and Reform in the United States

The United States expanded across North America, creating a number of new states from these lands. It also acquired foreign territories, especially in the Caribbean region and the Pacific Ocean.

Despite tremendous growth, the United States had one significant problem—the unresolved issue of slavery. This issue, along with the issue of states' rights, led to a brutal civil war that raged between 1861 and 1865 and left much of the nation—particularly the South—in ruins. Nevertheless, the Union was preserved and slavery was abolished. After the Civil War, the United States experienced phenomenal growth primarily as a result of industrialization and immigration.

Revolution and Reform in France

For many years after the Congress of Vienna, the Bourbons continued to rule France. Then in 1830, a revolt forced King Charles X to abdicate. The leaders of the French revolt chose a new king—Louis Philippe, duke of Orléans, who belonged to a branch of the Bourbon family but had a record of liberal beliefs.

In 1848, however, opposition to the regime of Louis Philippe erupted in violence. A new government—a republic—under the leadership of Louis Napoleon was soon proclaimed. Louis Napoleon, however, had imperial ambitions similar to those of his illustrious uncle, Napoleon Bonaparte, and soon established the Second French Empire. The Second Empire lasted until a humiliating defeat by Prussia toppled it in 1871. France was once again proclaimed a republic.

Independence Movements in Latin America

Originally, the Spanish and Portuguese colonies in Latin America were organized primarily by mercantilist principles. Nevertheless, the revolutionary events in British North America and France in the late 1700s aroused interest, particularly among discontented creoles, as upper-class Latin Americans were known. By the mid-1800s this discontent had become full-scale revolution, and the nations of Latin America had won their independence. Leaders such as Simón Bolívar, Toussaint-Louverture, and Miguel Hidalgo y Costilla led these movements.

Portrait of Giuseppe Garibaldi in 1849

CHAPTER 9

Nationalism in Europe

In the late 1800s, the political situation in Europe changed significantly. Nationalism fueled successful efforts to make Italy and Germany unified nations. Russia remained a rigid autocracy, and Austria and Hungary formed the Dual Monarchy.

The Unification of Italy

Italian nationalism became a strong force in the 1800s. Under the leadership of fiery patriots such as Giuseppe Mazzini, people in many parts of Italy clamored for national unity. Although the nationalists made some gains, they could not agree on what type of government the united Italy should have.

One group favored union under the leadership of Sardinia. There, the chief minister or premier, Count Camillo Benso di Cavour, provided the major impetus for Italian unification. Throughout the 1850s and the 1860s, Cavour used diplomacy, war, and persuasion to achieve unity. Finally, in 1870 unification was completed when the Italians claimed Rome.

The Unification of Germany

Like Italy, Germany remained fragmented in the early 1800s. But during the 1860s and 1870s, the long-delayed process of centralization and consolidation under the leadership of Prussia began to pick up speed.

Prussian prime minister Otto von Bismarck used clever diplomacy and wars against Denmark, Austria, and France to achieve unification in 1871. The new German Empire was a federal union under the leadership of the Prussian kaiser, or emperor. The federal government controlled all common matters, such as national defense, foreign affairs, and commerce.

Opposition to Bismarck

In spite of rigid control by the aristocratic Prussians, the new German federal government soon ran into problems. Dissatisfied groups formed political parties that opposed Bismarck's policies. Relations with the Roman Catholic Church proved difficult, and socialists clamored for government ownership of businesses. Despite this opposition, however, Bismarck was able to transform Germany into an industrial power.

Bismarck resigned under the reign of William II. William worked to build up Germany's military strength to an even greater degree and signed new agreements with neighboring nations.

Reform and Revolution in Russia

Ruled by autocratic czars, Russia steadfastly opposed reform. Nevertheless, liberal ideals became popular among discontented Russians—particularly among intellectuals. Faced with problems caused by liberal ideas and restless nationalities, the czars took harsh measures.

Although the late 1800s witnessed reforms such as the freeing of the serfs during the reign of Alexander II, most reform efforts failed. The czars continued to use repression to combat any erosion of their powers. Then in 1904 and 1905 the Russians fought a disastrous war with Japan. Defeat at the hands of the Japanese spurred discontented groups in the country to action and led to revolution. Although Czar Nicholas II granted a few reforms, he later reneged on his promises and resumed his policies of repression.

Unrest in Austria-Hungary

The Habsburgs in Austria also had to confront the rising tide of liberalism in the late 1800s. To combat nationalist demands in the empire, the Austrians formed the Dual Monarchy, in which both Austrians and Hungarians played a vital role in the policies and functions of government.

The formation of the Dual Monarchy failed, however, to solve the problem of nationalities. The Austrians and Hungarians dominated the population in each of their separate national states but national minorities—the Czechs, Serbs, Croats, Romanians, Poles, and Italians—existed in both Austria and Hungary. These people benefited very little from the Dual Monarchy and continued to agitate for self-government.

In addition to internal problems, the Dual Monarchy also faced problems abroad. In the late 1800s, the Habsburgs clashed with the autocratic government of the Ottoman Empire over the Balkans. Although the Ottomans had ruled the Balkans for centuries, their influence steadily weakened as the power of their empire declined. Many parts of the empire were claimed by different European powers.

CHAPTER 10

The Age of Imperialism

Beginning in about 1870, several factors rekindled interest in establishing colonies. During the next 40 years, many nations became involved in imperialism—the domination of a powerful nation over the political, economic, and cultural affairs of another nation or region.

The Roots of Imperialism

Imperialism arose out of a complex mixture of political, economic, and social forces. These forces included a desire for self-sufficiency, the need for new markets, the search for national pride and prestige, the need for places where people could settle and still remain loyal to the home country, the desire to convert people to Christianity, and the desire to transmit Western culture and ideas.

Imperialism created bitter rivalries among the imperial powers and hatred among the colonized peoples. As European powers took over more and more of the world, these rivalries and hatreds intensified.

European Claims in North Africa and the Sudan

In the 1800s most of North Africa belonged to the Ottoman Empire. Because Turkish control in many areas was weak, the Europeans scrambled to claim new colonies. The French claimed Algiers, Tunis, and Morocco. The British established dominance in Egypt and the Sudan, and the Italians took Tripoli, renaming it Libya.

European Claims in Sub-Saharan Africa

The Europeans repeated their colonial ambitions in Sub-Saharan Africa. During the empire building of the 1500s and the 1600s, the Europeans had established settlements on the coasts. In the late 1800s, however, the Europeans moved inland. By 1900 Europeans claimed all land in Sub-Saharan Africa except Liberia and Ethiopia.

Imperialism was a harsh experience for all of Africa. The costs and the benefits resulting from European expansion were unevenly distributed across the continent.

The first voyage through the Suez Canal on November 17, 1869

European Expansion in South and East Asia

The strong forces of imperialism that swept Africa in the 1800s brought important and fateful changes to South and East Asia, although the changes were not as abrupt as they were in so many parts of Africa. In India, for example, the British expanded their imperial rule.

Although European influence in Japan became strong after the overthrow of the Tokugawa shogunate in 1868, Europeans did not dominate Japan as they did India. Rather, the Japanese under the rule of the Meiji emperors managed to keep control of their own affairs and promoted industrialization. At the same time, China came increasingly under European domination, though it remained nominally independent.

Foreign Influence in Southeast Asia and the Pacific

The tide of imperialism did not stop in South and East Asia. It affected Southeast Asia and the islands of the Pacific as well. The British, French, and Dutch claimed parts of Southeast Asia and several islands in the Pacific. The United States claimed part of Samoa, Hawaii, the Philippines, Guam, and Wake Island.

Imperialism in Latin America

Imperialism in Latin America differed from that in the Pacific. The Monroe Doctrine of the United States, along with European attention to other matters, prevented Latin American nations from being recolonized. Nevertheless, the countries of Latin America experienced economic interference as they attracted European and American investment.

In two areas, Cuba and Puerto Rico, however, a foreign government took political control. These islands had been a part of the Spanish Empire for centuries. But in 1898 the United States defeated Spain in the Spanish-American War and claimed the islands. Cuba later became independent, while Puerto Rico became a commonwealth of the United States. And in Panama, the United States built a canal and controlled the territory known as the Canal Zone.

The greatest upheaval in Latin America during the age of imperialism was the Mexican Revolution. A civil war dragged on for a decade among various factions. The United States, which had sent troops in 1914, withdrew in 1917 to focus on the world war in Europe.

Synthesis Review

1. **Understanding Ideas** Why did the Industrial Revolution begin in Great Britain?
2. **Determining Cause and Effect** How did the Industrial Revolution alter population patterns?
3. **Comparing Ideas** How did political developments in France and Great Britain differ in the late 1800s?
4. **Interpreting Ideas** How did Bismarck deal with the socialists?
5. **Analyzing Ideas** What factors led Europeans to found colonies in the late 1800s?
6. **Synthesizing Ideas** Why do you think democracy triumphed in Great Britain and the United States but failed in Russia?

POLITICS AND GOVERNMENT

1882   1892   1902

1882
Triple Alliance upsets European balance of power

1888
William II becomes kaiser of Germany

1899
First arms limitation talks at the Hague in Switzerland

1900
Boxer Rebellion is put down in China

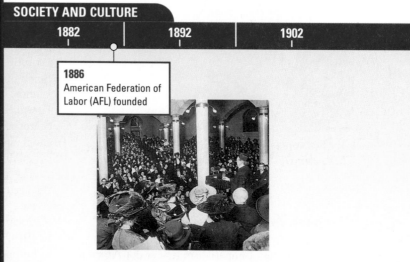

Boxer Rebellion

SOCIETY AND CULTURE

1882   1892   1902

1886
American Federation of Labor (AFL) founded

SCIENCE AND TECHNOLOGY

1882   1892   1902

1884
Modern machine gun invented

1895
Röntgen discovers X rays

1903
Marie and Pierre Curie share Nobel Prize for discovery of radioactivity

Marie Curie

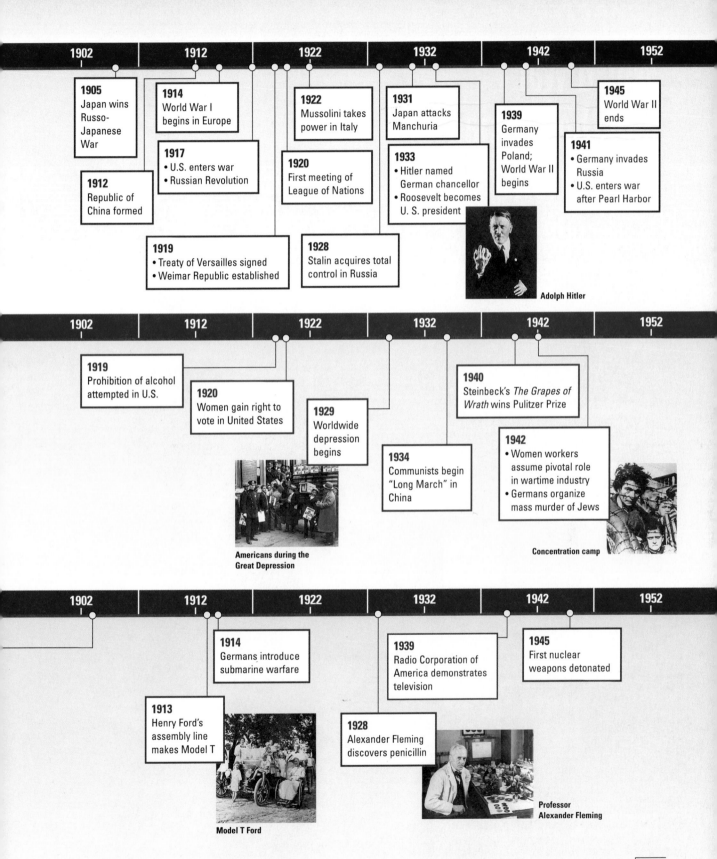

1902 **1912** **1922** **1932** **1942** **1952**

1905
Japan wins Russo-Japanese War

1914
World War I begins in Europe

1917
• U.S. enters war
• Russian Revolution

1912
Republic of China formed

1922
Mussolini takes power in Italy

1920
First meeting of League of Nations

1931
Japan attacks Manchuria

1933
• Hitler named German chancellor
• Roosevelt becomes U. S. president

1939
Germany invades Poland; World War II begins

1945
World War II ends

1941
• Germany invades Russia
• U.S. enters war after Pearl Harbor

1919
• Treaty of Versailles signed
• Weimar Republic established

1928
Stalin acquires total control in Russia

Adolph Hitler

1902 **1912** **1922** **1932** **1942** **1952**

1919
Prohibition of alcohol attempted in U.S.

1920
Women gain right to vote in United States

1929
Worldwide depression begins

1934
Communists begin "Long March" in China

1940
Steinbeck's *The Grapes of Wrath* wins Pulitzer Prize

1942
• Women workers assume pivotal role in wartime industry
• Germans organize mass murder of Jews

Americans during the Great Depression

Concentration camp

1902 **1912** **1922** **1932** **1942** **1952**

1914
Germans introduce submarine warfare

1913
Henry Ford's assembly line makes Model T

1939
Radio Corporation of America demonstrates television

1928
Alexander Fleming discovers penicillin

1945
First nuclear weapons detonated

Model T Ford

Professor Alexander Fleming

World War I and the Russian Revolution

TIME

A.D. **1882–1920**

3.7 million B.C. | 4000 B.C. | A.D. 2100 | A.D. 1882–1920

PLACE

Europe, Africa, and the Middle East

Europe

Africa

Middle East

A Letter from the German Trenches, plate 30 from *The Great War: A Neutral's Indictment*

Significance

In 1899 and again in 1907 in an effort to limit armaments and establish rules of war, representatives of several nations met at The Hague, in the Netherlands. Even as these nations discussed peace, however, some of them prepared for war. In the summer of 1914, a war began that involved nearly all the major nations of the world and was so destructive that people of the time called it the Great War. Today we call it World War I.

Terms to Define

militarism	war of attrition
mobilized	contraband
Triple Alliance	atrocities
Triple Entente	Fourteen Points
Pan-Slavism	armistice
Balkan "powder keg"	Paris Peace Conference
ultimatum	reparations
belligerents	League of Nations
Central Powers	Treaty of Versailles
Allied Powers	World Court
U-boats	economic sanctions
propaganda	mandate

People to Identify

Archduke Francis Ferdinand	V. I. Lenin
Woodrow Wilson	Communists
Arthur Zimmermann	Ferdinand Foch
Mensheviks	Big Four
Bolsheviks	Sudeten Germans

Places to Locate

Serbia	Soviet Union
Bosnia	Château-Thierry
Sarajevo	Saint-Mihiel
Marne River	Rhineland
Danzig	Saar River valley
Gallipoli Peninsula	Polish Corridor
Verdun	Czechoslovakia
Brest-Litovsk	Yugoslavia

Chapter Theme Questions

■ **War and Diplomacy** How might the conflicting interests of nations help set the stage for war?

■ **Technology** In what ways might technology affect warfare?

■ **Politics and Law** What might be the effects of a war on a country's internal political system?

The soldiers of World War I came to realize that terror and death stalk both sides. The following excerpt from Erich Maria Remarque's novel *All Quiet on the Western Front* describes a German soldier's feelings upon the death of an enemy soldier.

❝ *The rattle of machine-guns becomes an unbroken chain. Just as I am about to turn around a little, something heavy stumbles, and with a crash a body falls over me into the shell-hole, slips down, and lies across me. . . .*

The silence spreads. I talk and must talk. So I speak to him and say to him: 'Comrade, I did not want to kill you. . . . You were only an idea to me before. . . . But now, for the first time, I see you are a man like me. . . . Forgive me, comrade. We always see it too late. Why do they never tell us that you are . . . like us, that your mothers are just as anxious as ours, and that we have the same fear of death, and the same dying and the same agony— Forgive me, comrade; how could you be my enemy? If we threw away these rifles and this uniform you could be my brother.' ❞

The events that ended in the horror soldiers experienced on battlefields during World War I began with conflicting national interests among European nations.

Section 1

Setting the Stage for War

Focus Questions

- **What factors led to World War I?**
- **Why were the Balkans called a powder keg?**
- **How were the countries of Europe aligned at the beginning of the war?**

In the decades before 1914, many European nations pursued interests and policies without regard for the wishes or interests of their neighbors. These conflicting interests set the stage for war.

For a time after the Congress of Vienna in 1815, relations among European powers had been more or less harmonious. Beginning in the late 1800s, however, cooperation among the European nations broke down and rivalries increased. These rivalries grew both within Europe, especially in the Balkan region, and overseas as a result of imperialism.

In her book *The Guns of August*, Barbara Tuchman describes an event in England that temporarily brought the European nations together and marked the transition between an old and a new historical era.

"So gorgeous was the spectacle on the May morning of 1910 when nine kings rode in the funeral of Edward VII of England that the crowd, waiting in hushed and black-clad awe, could not keep back gasps of admiration. In scarlet and blue and green and purple, three by three the sovereigns rode through the palace gates, with plumed helmets, gold braid, crimson sashes, and jeweled orders [military decorations] flashing in the sun. After them came . . . heirs . . . queens . . . and a scattering of special ambassadors from uncrowned countries. Together they represented seventy nations in the greatest assemblage of royalty and rank ever gathered in one place and, of its kind, the last. The muffled tongue of Big Ben tolled nine by the clock as the cortege left the palace, but on history's clock it was sunset, and the sun of the old world was setting in a dying blaze of splendor never to be seen again."

As rivalries intensified in the early 1900s, the great powers plunged toward war, pressed forward by at least four factors: nationalism, imperialism, militarism, and the system of alliances.

Nationalism and Imperialism

Spurred by the nationalism that developed after the French Revolution and the Napoleonic Wars, throughout the 1800s, nationalities tried to unite under governments controlled by their own people. This desire to unite all the people of a nation under a single government, however, had explosive possibilities in a Europe where a single government often ruled many national groups.

The European imperialist states came to the brink of war several times as they scrambled to partition Africa, Asia, and the rest of the world. Germany and France, for example, narrowly avoided war over their rival claims to Morocco on two occasions, in 1905 and 1911. They managed to settle the incidents with makeshift compromises that failed to resolve the overall problem.

Militarism

The glorification of armed strength, or **militarism**, dominated the thinking of many European leaders before World War I. These leaders believed that only the use of force could solve problems among nations. It seemed to them that a militarily strong nation usually got what it wanted, as Prussia had proved in its wars with Austria and France. Weaker nations lost out, as Italy had learned from its imperialistic ventures in Africa.

In the late 1800s, European nations built large armies of men who were drafted and given military training. If one nation **mobilized**, or readied its army and other resources for combat, other nations would also mobilize to protect themselves. In a chain reaction, this would force all nations in Europe to mobilize, or else risk being caught unprepared.

As international rivalries intensified, each European nation believed that it was necessary to keep its armed forces stronger than those of any potential enemy. Armies grew larger as spending for such things as new weapons and for the fortification of national boundaries multiplied. In the 1890s, Germany began to build a large navy to rival that of Great Britain. Great Britain, especially dependent on sea power, responded by expanding the size of its navy. In 1906 Great Britain launched the *Dreadnought*, the world's first modern battleship. Germany rushed to build similar ships.

The System of Alliances

In the period from 1864 to 1871, the unification of Germany and that of Italy had changed the balance of power in Europe. The unification of Germany, especially, created an entirely new situation. In place of a group of relatively weak states, a powerful German Empire, under the leadership of Prussia, emerged. Otto von Bismarck, the skillful and strong-willed German chancellor, shaped its ambitious foreign policy.

Three Emperors' League and the Triple Alliance. Bismarck feared that France would seek revenge for its 1871 defeat in the Franco-Prussian War by trying to regain Alsace-Lorraine, the region it had lost to Germany. He therefore set his foreign policy to keeping France diplomatically isolated and without allies. Bismarck particularly wanted to prevent a

In 1906 the British launched the *Dreadnought,* a new type of battleship that featured turbine power and rotating batteries of guns.

Franco-Russian alliance because it would isolate Germany diplomatically and, at worst, mean that Germany would have to fight a war on both its eastern and western borders.

In 1879 Bismarck formed a defensive alliance with Austria-Hungary. Then in 1881 the chancellor set up the Three Emperors' League, a secret agreement among the emperors of Germany, Russia, and Austria-Hungary, who agreed to remain neutral if any of the others went to war with another country.

In 1882 Bismarck persuaded Italy to join in the alliance he had made with Austria-Hungary, thereby creating the **Triple Alliance**. Although Bismarck considered Italy a weak link, the formation of the Triple Alliance had isolated France, accomplishing his primary foreign policy goal. The Triple Alliance completely upset the balance of power in Europe.

The Reinsurance Treaty. In 1887 the Three Emperors' League ended. Russia and Austria-Hungary were rivals in the Balkans, where the Ottoman Empire had lost control over several territories. Russia resented Germany's support of Austria-Hungary in the region, but Bismarck made a new agreement with Russia, the Reinsurance Treaty of 1887. This treaty provided that each nation would be neutral if the other became involved in a defensive war.

The Triple Entente. In 1888 the unstable William II became kaiser of Germany. Before very long, he dismissed Bismarck as chancellor and abandoned Bismarck's careful policies.

France, meanwhile, had been trying to gain allies to break out of the diplomatic isolation in which Bismarck had placed it. The opportunity arose after William II allowed the Reinsurance Treaty to lapse. Because of an economic crisis in Russia, the czar sought a loan. France hurried to lend the money and took other steps to win Russia's friendship. In 1894 Russia and France formed an alliance, making a reality of Bismarck's fear that Germany would face enemies to the east and the west.

As the second-greatest industrial power in Europe, Germany increasingly competed with Britain economically. After 1888 Germany energetically entered the race for overseas territories, demanding its "place in the sun" as a great power. William II also began Germany's naval buildup. The rapid growth of the German navy troubled the British.

Great Britain started its own search for allies. In 1904 the British and the French settled their differences in Africa and reached an agreement, the Entente Cordiale—French for "friendly understanding." In 1907 Great Britain and Russia tried to come to an agreement as well. Reaching such an agreement proved difficult because of the two nations' rivalry from the Middle East to the Pacific. Nevertheless, they now agreed to recognize each other's spheres of influence in Asia. The resulting alignment of France, Russia, and Great Britain was called the **Triple Entente**. Both France and Russia also had secret understandings with Italy, which meant that the Italians had a foot in both camps.

Dangers of the alliance system. By 1907 the rival alliances threatened world peace because they divided Europe into two armed camps. Should hostilities develop between any two rival powers, all six nations might become involved in the fighting, regardless of whether the original dispute concerned all of them. A minor quarrel had the potential to lead to serious consequences, as events in 1914 would prove.

The Balkan "Powder Keg"

Nationalists in Serbia, whose independence from the Ottoman Empire had been recognized by the Congress of Berlin in 1878, hoped to make their country the center of a large Slavic state. The Serbian nationalists especially wanted the provinces of Bosnia and Herzegovina because Serbia was landlocked and these two provinces would provide an outlet on the Adriatic Sea.

The decision of the Congress of Berlin in 1878 to make the two provinces protectorates of Austria-Hungary (see Chapter 22) severely disappointed the Serbs. After Austria-Hungary annexed Bosnia and Herzegovina in 1908, infuriated Serbian nationalists increased their agitation against Austria-Hungary.

Russia, the largest Slavic country, saw itself as the protector of the Balkan Slavs and supported Serbia's goals. The nationalist movement that pressed for the political and cultural unity of all Slavs under Russian leadership was called **Pan-Slavism**. The British distrusted Russian influence in the Balkans, however. They were very concerned with Russian access to the Mediterranean, and the Ottoman Empire seemed too weak to block Russian aggression.

Instead of taking advantage of the Anglo-Russian rivalry, Germany's Kaiser William II pursued policies that created shared interests between the British and the Russians. To reinforce the Triple Alliance and make up for the weakness of Italy, the kaiser began negotiating to bring the Ottoman Empire, an old enemy of Russia, into the Triple Alliance and thereby extend German influence into the Balkans.

Germany also planned to build a railroad from Berlin through the Balkans to Constantinople and on to Baghdad, near the Persian Gulf. This plan aroused many fears. The British regarded the proposed railroad as a threat to the sea route through the Suez Canal, their Mediterranean-Red Sea "lifeline" to India. It also seemed to endanger British interests in the Persian Gulf. The Russians feared that Germany would become a strong protector of the Ottoman Empire. This would diminish Russia's chances of securing access to the Mediterranean through the Dardanelles.

Germany's actions in the Balkans worsened an already dangerous situation. They resulted in what Bismarck had tried to avoid—the strengthening of ties between Great Britain and Russia. Both countries wanted to resist German expansion in the Balkans. Austria-Hungary, on the other hand, feared Pan-Slavism and gained Germany's support in its opposition to Slavic nationalism.

Assassination at Sarajevo

The spark that touched off the explosion of the **Balkan "powder keg"** and led to war came on June 28, 1914. The heir to the Austro-Hungarian throne, Archduke Francis Ferdinand, and his wife were visiting Sarajevo, the capital of Bosnia and Herzegovina. As they rode in an open automobile, a young man fired a revolver at them, killing both the archduke and his wife.

The assassin, Gavrilo Princip, belonged to the Black Hand, one of the many secret societies of Serbian nationalists opposed to Austro-Hungarian rule. Although Princip had acted without the authority of the Serbian government, some Serbian leaders were aware of his plans and had furnished arms and ammunition to Serbian terrorists.

The assassination brought to a head the bitterness between Serbia and Austria-Hungary. The Austro-Hungarian government was determined to use it as a reason to punish the Serbs. Before Austria-Hungary acted, however, it wanted to make sure of German support in case the Russians should try to help Serbia. Germany promised to back Austria-Hungary in anything the nation did. Encouraged by this so-called blank check, the Austro-Hungarians presented an **ultimatum** to the Serbian government. In an ultimatum, one party threatens harmful action to another if the other party rejects its proposals.

War Between Austria-Hungary and Serbia

In its ultimatum, Austria-Hungary made the following demands: (1) The Serbian government would

Gavrilo Princip, a Serbian terrorist, assassinated Archduke Francis Ferdinand. Here he is being taken to prison by police and soldiers.

condemn all propaganda against Austria-Hungary and suppress publications and societies that opposed Austria-Hungary. (2) Serbia would ban from its schools books and teachers who did not favor Austria-Hungary. (3) Serbia would dismiss any officials who had promoted propaganda against Austria-Hungary. (4) Austro-Hungarian officials would participate in the proceedings against those accused of the crime at Sarajevo. If Serbia did not agree to these terms, Austria-Hungary would resort to military action.

The Serbian government replied by accepting the first three terms and rejecting the last, but it offered to submit the fourth point to the International Court at The Hague. Assuming, however, that Austria-Hungary would not accept this offer, the Serbian government ordered mobilization of their troops. Ignoring the positive aspects of Serbia's reply, Austria-Hungary, assuming that it could quickly achieve victory, declared war on Serbia on July 28, after the time limit of the ultimatum had expired.

Mobilization of Europe

Attempts to persuade Austria-Hungary to continue negotiations proved futile. Germany continued to support Austria-Hungary. Russia prepared to defend Serbia by mobilizing troops along the Russian-Austro-Hungarian border. Expecting Germany to join Austria-Hungary, Russia also sent troops to the German border.

Germany immediately demanded that Russia cancel its mobilization or face war. When Russia ignored this ultimatum, on August 1, 1914, Germany declared war on Russia. Convinced that France was prepared to side with Russia and hoping to gain a military advantage by swift action, Germany declared war on France two days later.

Great Britain Enters the War

The great powers had guaranteed Belgian neutrality in 1839, shortly after Belgium gained its independence. Under the terms of this guarantee, Belgium agreed to stay out of any European war and not to help any **belligerents**, or warring nations. In turn, the other powers agreed not to attack Belgium. However, Belgium's location and flat terrain was of great importance to Germany's military plans. The German strategy called for the German army to mobilize, strike, and knock France out of the war before the Russians could attack from the east. Because the Franco-German border was hilly and well fortified, the Germans planned to attack through Belgium on the coastal plain between France and Germany. This attack through Belgium by Germany was in direct defiance of the 1839 guarantee. (See map on page 364.)

After the German government declared war on France, it sent an ultimatum to Belgium, demanding that German troops be allowed to cross Belgian territory. The British protested, insisting that Germany observe Belgian neutrality. The German foreign minister, referring to the 1839 guarantee, replied that surely Great Britain would not fight over "a scrap of paper." German soldiers marched into Belgium on August 4, 1914. The kaiser had promised them, "You will be home before the leaves have fallen from the trees." As a result of the invasion of Belgium, Great Britain declared war on Germany later that day.

The War Expands

Later in August, Japan entered the war on the side of Great Britain and France. Japan hoped to gain German possessions in China and the Pacific.

In Europe all the nations of the Triple Alliance and the Triple Entente except Italy were now at war. The Italian government took the position that the

Europe on the Eve of World War I, 1914

Triple Alliance
Triple Entente
Neutral countries
⊛ **National capital**

ATLANTIC OCEAN

NORWAY

SWEDEN

FINLAND

⊛ Petrograd

RUSSIA

Volga River

GREAT BRITAIN

NORTH SEA

DENMARK

BALTIC SEA

London ⊛

English Channel

NETHERLANDS

BELGIUM

⊛ Berlin

GERMAN EMPIRE

Vistula River

Dnieper R.

CASPIAN SEA

Paris ⊛

LUXEMBOURG

ALSACE-LORRAINE

Rhine R.

Danube R.

⊛ Vienna

AUSTRIA-HUNGARY

FRANCE

SWITZERLAND

Bay of Biscay

PORTUGAL

SPAIN

ITALY

ADRIATIC SEA

BOSNIA AND HERZEGOVINA

Sarajevo•

SERBIA

Danube R.

ROMANIA

BLACK SEA

BULGARIA

⊛ Constantinople

OTTOMAN EMPIRE

Tigris R.

CORSICA (French)

Rome ⊛

MONTENEGRO

ALBANIA

Balkan Peninsula

SARDINIA (Italian)

GREECE

Euphrates R.

Baghdad•

BALEARIC ISLANDS (Spanish)

SICILY (Italian)

MEDITERRANEAN SEA

CRETE (Greek)

CYPRUS (British)

AFRICA

0   200   400 Miles
0   200   400 Kilometers
Azimuthal Equal-Area Projection

Learning from Maps Defensive alliances polarized Europe into two armed camps before the fighting actually began.

? Region What nations belonged to the Triple Entente?

Austro-Hungarians had acted as aggressors when they declared war on Serbia. Thus, the Triple Alliance, which was a defensive treaty, did not require Italy to give aid to its allies.

Italy remained neutral for nine months. Finally, it signed secret treaties with Great Britain, France, and Russia that guaranteed Italy a share of the spoils after the defeat of Germany and Austria-Hungary. In May 1915, Italy entered the war against Germany and Austria-Hungary, which had been its former allies under the Triple Alliance.

In the meantime, Germany had been trying to gain other allies. In November 1914 the Ottoman Empire entered the war on the side of Germany and Austria-Hungary. The Turks, although not a strong military power, occupied a strategic position. Their control of Constantinople and the Dardanelles bottled up Russia's Black Sea fleet. It also prevented Russia's allies from sending supplies to Russia through the Mediterranean and Black Seas. Germany also persuaded Bulgaria, a rival of Serbia, to enter the war in October 1915.

1. **Define** militarism, mobilized, Triple Alliance, Triple Entente, Pan-Slavism, Balkan "powder keg", ultimatum, belligerents
2. **Identify** Archduke Francis Ferdinand
3. **Locate and Explain the Significance** Serbia, Bosnia, Sarajevo
4. **Understanding Ideas** List the factors that contributed to World War I.
5. **Summarizing Ideas** (a) What event can be said to have "lit the fuse" in 1914? (b) What made the area involved so important?
6. **Evaluating Ideas** How did the events that took place on June 28, 1914, develop into full-scale war, and how did the nations involved in these events align themselves?

World War I: A New Kind of War

Focus Questions

- **Who was involved in the war by the beginning of 1916?**
- **What innovations were introduced into warfare during World War I?**
- **What course did the war take from the beginning through 1916?**
- **How did the war affect the United States?**

The soldiers who marched enthusiastically off to war in the summer of 1914 thought they would win a quick and decisive victory and come home as heroes in time to celebrate the New Year. They were wrong—tragically wrong. This war would in fact go on to last for four years.

The Belligerents

Germany, Austria-Hungary, Bulgaria, and the Ottoman Empire became known as the **Central Powers**. Notice on the map on this page that the Central Powers formed an almost solid block of territory extending from the North Sea to the Middle East. This geographical proximity gave the Central Powers the advantages of easy communication and

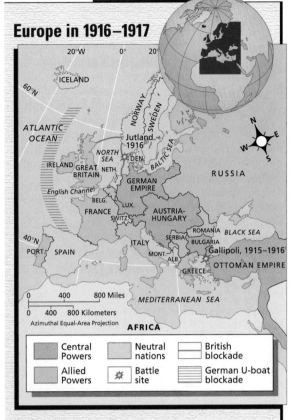

Europe in 1916–1917

ICELAND
NORWAY
SWEDEN
ATLANTIC OCEAN
Jutland 1916
NORTH SEA
IRELAND
GREAT BRITAIN
DEN.
NETH.
BALTIC SEA
English Channel
BELG.
LUX.
FRANCE
SWITZ.
GERMAN EMPIRE
RUSSIA
AUSTRIA-HUNGARY
ROMANIA
BLACK SEA
ITALY
SERBIA
BULGARIA
SPAIN
MONT.
ALB.
Gallipoli, 1915–1916
GREECE
OTTOMAN EMPIRE
MEDITERRANEAN SEA
AFRICA
PORT.

0   400   800 Miles
0   400   800 Kilometers
Azimuthal Equal-Area Projection

Central Powers	Neutral nations	British blockade
Allied Powers	Battle site	German U-boat blockade

Learning from Maps While Britain set up a naval blockade in the North Sea to cut off Germany's sea routes, Germany organized a counterblockade of U-boats off the west coast of Britain.

Place What North Sea battle was fought in 1916 to break through the blockades?

rapid troop movements. Another advantage that the Central Powers enjoyed was Germany's very well-trained and well-equipped army.

Great Britain, France, Russia, and their partners in the war became known as the **Allied Powers**, or the Allies. Although they did not have the geographic unity of the Central Powers, they had more soldiers and a greater industrial potential. The British also had the world's largest navy. Therefore, the Allies could obtain food and raw materials more easily and could blockade and attempt to starve the Central Powers.

As a result of diplomatic maneuvers, Greece and Romania joined the Allies in 1916. Eventually, 32 countries made up the Allied side. Many of them, however, joined late in the war and made only token contributions to the war effort.

Weapons That Changed History

Wars have been fought throughout history. What has determined the outcomes of these wars? One answer is the bravery—or cowardice—of the individual soldier. Another factor that determines the outcomes of these wars is the skill of the commander.

The outcomes of battles and wars, however, have often been decided by the kinds of weapons used by one side or the other. On some occasions, weapons have given an advantage to the attacker. At other times, the advantage has rested with the defensive side.

The first weapons were muscle powered—from rocks or spears thrown from the hands of Cro-Magnon men to swords in the hands of Roman legionnaires to lances and longbows in the hands of medieval knights and archers. Innovative generals added mechanical devices. The ancient Assyrians and Egyptians, for example, put sharp blades on the wheels of their chariots. Many ancient and medieval civilizations used catapults to hurl pieces of rock or metal over city or castle walls.

Animal power augmented human power. For instance, in 217 B.C. Hannibal invaded Italy with elephants.

Trojan horse

The Romans learned the value of cavalry when fierce Goth invaders on horseback crushed the Roman infantry at Adrianople in A.D. 378.

Horses were effective, however, only in the open field. They were useless against the last line of defense—the wall. Cities became self-contained fortresses when surrounded by high walls. Ramparts allowed defenders to fight from above. The Byzantines, for example, sprayed "Greek fire"—an early form of the burning liquid of the flame-thrower—on attackers from the walls of Constantinople and also used it in naval battles.

Gunpowder made war even more destructive. Gunpowder was first used in the West in about 1320, although it had been invented in China centuries earlier. By 1500 any army worth its salt had muskets and cannons. At first, the cannon seemed to be the ideal offensive weapon. Kings such as Louis XI of France used cannons to destroy the castles of upstart nobles and to help create powerful and centralized national states. But, cannons could also be put to defensive use, such as to

Medieval catapult

English longbows

German tank corps

destroy attacking armies as easily as they were able to destroy fortifications.

At the start of the 1800s, Napoleon Bonaparte used combinations of attacking artillery, infantry, and cavalry with dazzling success. He battered the enemy lines with heavy guns, sent his infantry charging in to break the foe, then crushed the retreating troops with his cavalry.

Later in the 1800s, railroads, though not weapons, became a powerful factor in how war was fought. First used extensively in the American Civil War (1861–1865), fought between the North (Union) and the South (Confederacy), railroads made it possible for reinforcements and supplies to reach battling armies quickly. At the Battle of Bull Run (July 1861), for example, reinforcements brought by rail enabled the Confederates to turn defeat into victory.

The American Civil War was one of the first great conflicts fought in the Industrial Age. Factories mass-produced guns, bullets, and other necessary goods such as uniforms, shoes, and blankets. The

Atomic explosion

Union's greater industrial capacity was an important factor in its 1865 victory.

World War I was directed by generals who at first tried to imitate Napoleon. There were long artillery barrages to soften up the enemy, followed by mass infantry charges. However, the machine gun, combined with barbed wire barriers and trenches, gave the advantage to the defenders. Huge infantry attacks resulted in unprecedented slaughter. World War I ended only when one side collapsed from exhaustion.

World War II (1939–1945) brought a shift back to the offensive. Using large numbers of tanks and airplanes, Hitler's German war machine quickly crushed Poland (September 1939) and France (May–June 1940). The tide of war turned against Germany not so much because of new defenses against the tank and the plane, although radar did help. The Allies won the war in large part because they were able to produce more offensive firepower than the Germans. Against such force, the Axis Powers were doomed.

World War II in the Pacific ended with the use of the most fearsome weapon ever developed—the atomic bomb. In August 1945, the United States dropped atomic bombs on two Japanese cities, Hiroshima and Nagasaki. For a few years, only the United States had the atomic bomb. Today a number of other nations have also developed nuclear arms.

The existence of nuclear weapons throughout the world is an unsettling development. Their destructive power would seem to give the ultimate advantage to the attacking side. Yet, as history since 1945 has shown us, nuclear weapons have become the ultimate defense by deterring either side from attacking. By their potential to kill, these weapons have helped keep peace.

American aircraft carrier

F-16 fighters

Innovations in Warfare

World War I was an industrialized war. Industry produced weapons with the same efficient mass production methods that it had applied to other products.

One of the most important new weapons of World War I was the machine gun. Its sweeping, rapid-fire spray of bullets was deadly and often made infantry advances terribly costly. To protect themselves from the machine gun's raking fire and from artillery bombardments, soldiers dug systems of trenches.

Both sides used weapons that had never been tried before. In 1916 the British introduced the tank, an armored vehicle on which guns were mounted. Tanks enabled troops to tear through barbed wire and cross enemy lines.

Another new weapon was the recently invented airplane. Airplanes were primarily used for observing troop movements. Although early military airplanes were not very maneuverable or fast, they sometimes engaged in air battles called dogfights and dropped bombs.

Germany became the first nation to make effective use of submarines. Its **U-boats** (from the German word *Unterseebooten,* meaning "underwater boats") caused extensive losses to Allied shipping. The Germans also introduced poison gas.

Previously in Europe, most wars were fought by professional soldiers whose only source of income was their military pay and rations. In contrast, armies of drafted civilians fought the battles of World War I. Those who could not fight worked at home to help the war effort. Many women participated by working in factories. A war in which nations turn all their resources to the war effort became known as "total war."

To stir the patriotism of their people and support for the war effort, governments made wide use of **propaganda**—ideas, facts, or rumors spread deliberately to further one's cause or to damage an opposing cause. Governments set up agencies to handle the flow of information about the war. Newspapers and popular magazines, especially those of the Allies, portrayed the enemy as brutal and subhuman, while praising their own national aims and achievements.

The War from 1914 to 1916

Germany's attack on France was launched across neutral Belgium. By September 1914, German troops had reached the Marne River near Paris. However, the French and British armies managed to hold the line, and Paris was saved.

France's success in the Battle of the Marne changed the entire nature of the war. Germany's hope of swift victory ended. Both sides now dug trenches on the western front, which stretched from Switzerland to the shores of the North Sea.

On the eastern front, the Russians were still completing mobilization. Responding to a plea by the French to divert German forces from the western front, the Russian army launched an attack toward the important German seaport of Danzig.

In late August, the Russians met a German force in the Battle of Tannenberg, which is located in East Prussia. (See map on this page.) The Russians suffered a

The Eastern Front, 1914–1918

0 200 400 Miles
0 200 400 Kilometers
Azimuthal Equal-Area Projection

Central Powers		Farthest Russian advance, February 1915
Allied Powers		Farthest German advance, May 1918
Neutral nation		Boundary according to the Treaty of Brest-Litovsk, March 3, 1918
✹ German victory		
✹ Russian victory	Marsh	⊛ National capital

Learning from Maps With Russian forces threatening the German port of Danzig, the Germans retaliated by driving the Russians back eastward.

? Movement What battle on the Baltic Sea did the Germans win in 1917?

humiliating defeat. Soon afterward the Germans launched an offensive in the east and crossed into Russian Poland.

The war was fought outside of Europe also. Fighting took place in the Middle East, Africa, and in the Pacific.

Fighting on Gallipoli. Although Russia had a huge army, it lacked enough guns and ammunition to equip its soldiers properly. In 1915 Great Britain and France decided to attempt to force their way through the Dardanelles so that they could capture Constantinople. They had hoped that this would remove the Ottoman Empire from the war and allow supplies to reach the Russians.

The British and French had hoped that bombardment from their heavily armed battleships alone would destroy the Ottoman artillery on the Gallipoli Peninsula.

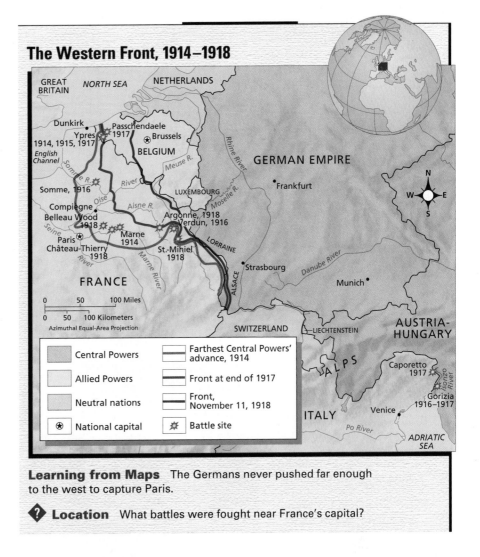

The Western Front, 1914–1918

Learning from Maps The Germans never pushed far enough to the west to capture Paris.

❓ **Location** What battles were fought near France's capital?

When the bombardment failed after several days, however, they decided to land troops on the Gallipoli Peninsula. The Turks resisted stubbornly and the fighting became a stalemate. After eight months of fighting and the loss of hundreds of thousands of lives on both sides, the Allies abandoned their plans to capture Constantinople and withdrew from Gallipoli.

Naval warfare. The British decided to blockade the North Sea to keep merchant ships from reaching Germany. Originally, they set up the blockade to prevent the Germans from getting raw materials to manufacture war equipment. Gradually, however, the blockade became an attempt to ruin the German economy and starve the German people.

Germany also set up a blockade. Employing its fleet of U-boats, it attempted to win the war by sinking ships carrying food and munitions to the British.

In May 1915, without warning, a German submarine sank the British passenger liner *Lusitania* off the coast of Ireland. The sinking of the *Lusitania*, which was carrying passengers as well as a cargo of war materials to England, killed nearly 1,200 people, including more than 100 Americans. Woodrow Wilson, the U.S. president, warned Germany that the United States would not tolerate another such incident. For the next year and a half, Germany used submarine warfare only sparingly. It did not wish to provoke the neutral Americans into entering the war.

In May 1916, the only large naval battle of the war was fought by Germany and Britain in the North Sea off the coast of Jutland, Denmark. Although both sides claimed they had won a victory, the German navy did, however, retire to port, where it remained for the rest of the war.

Women in Wartime

In August 1914, Europe plunged into World War I. European countries found themselves in desperate need of war matériel (equipment and supplies). Many of their former factory workers, however, were men who were now serving as soldiers. In Europe and the United States (which entered the war in 1917), women took on jobs formerly held almost exclusively by men. Women's participation in the war effort would have dramatic social consequences.

With men off at war, women augmented or gave up their traditional roles as homemakers and domestic workers to manage farms or stores or to become factory workers (see top photo), mail carriers, and bank tellers. They served in medical positions on the front lines.

After the war ended in 1918, many women left their jobs to make way for the men returning home from war. In the meanwhile, however, women had gained a new sense of independence that they did not want to lose. This economic independence often led to independence in other areas. For example, some women began to cut their hair short and wear shorter skirts, breaking centuries-old traditions. (See center photo.) Women gained the right to vote and so had a voice in the political process. Aviator Amelia Earhart symbolized the new attitude of many women in the 1920s and 1930s—strong, independent, willing to take the same risks that men took.

When World War II began in 1939, women once again made important contributions to the war effort. As members of the armed forces, women served as nurses and clerical workers. They entered the workforce in record numbers, with some 4 million women working in defense plants. These women were exemplified by "Rosie the Riveter," often seen on posters—the prototype of the able, independent young woman who worked in a factory building tanks, airplanes, or guns. (See bottom photo.)

At the close of the war in 1945, women once again were expected to return to the home. By now, however, their role had permanently taken a new direction. Today women are an established part of the workforce. Female soldiers now train in boot camp alongside men. Although women do not serve as front line infantry, they serve in almost every other military role, including as fighter pilots.

The Stalemate

By 1916 the war in the west had become a stalemate on land as well as on sea. However, military leaders on both sides were slow to realize they could not break through the other's line of trenches. As both armies continued to launch attacks, small areas of land changed hands again and again, costing each side thousands of lives. The conflict had become a **war of attrition**—a slow wearing-down process in which each side tries to outlast the other.

One horrifying example of such warfare occurred in northeastern France. (See map on page 369.) The Germans massed their forces and attacked Verdun in February 1916, hoping to bleed the French army to death. After months of fighting and bombardment, the Germans finally gave up in December. At Verdun each side lost more than 400,000 soldiers.

The United States and World War I

When World War I began in 1914, President Wilson said the United States would be neutral. Most Americans viewed the war as a European affair in which the United States should not become involved.

Trade with the belligerents. Nevertheless, the war soon affected the United States. As the most highly industrialized neutral nation, the United States became a supplier of food, raw materials, and munitions to both sides. The U.S. government insisted on the right of American businesses to trade freely with either side. According to international law, however, if a ship carried **contraband**—war materials supplied by a neutral to a belligerent nation—the goods could be seized. The United States also insisted on the right of its citizens to travel safely on ships of any nation.

The United States government also permitted banks, corporations, and private citizens to buy bonds of foreign governments and sell them goods on credit. At the beginning of the war, American investors and businesspeople dealt with both sides. As the British blockade of Germany tightened, however, American trade became more one-sided toward the Allies.

America enters the war. Britain's propaganda impressed Americans far more than did Germany's. Graphic stories spread by the British of German **atrocities**—brutal crimes of war, often said to have been committed against defenseless civilians—angered Americans, although many of these stories were exaggerated or untrue.

Early in 1917, circumstances pushed the United States into the war. In January the German foreign minister, Arthur Zimmermann, sent a secret telegram to the German ambassador in Mexico. It instructed him to draw Mexico into the war on Germany's side. In exchange, Germany promised Mexico the return of parts of the southwestern United States that Mexico had lost in 1848. The British intercepted the telegram, decoded it, and had it published in American newspapers. Americans were enraged.

Faced with serious food and munitions shortages, the Germans decided to resume unrestricted submarine warfare. They realized this might bring the United States into the conflict, but they hoped the submarine war would force Britain to give up before that could happen. German submarines began attacking any ship found in what Germany declared a "war zone" around Britain. Once again, Americans were killed in some of these attacks. The costly renewed submarine attacks did not force Britain to ask for peace.

Meanwhile, in March 1917, revolutionaries overthrew the autocratic czarist government of Russia. Now all the major Allied countries had democratic governments while none of the Central Powers did. Americans could more readily participate in a war between democratic and nondemocratic countries.

On April 2, 1917, President Wilson addressed Congress. Proclaiming that "the world must be made safe for democracy," he asked for a declaration of war against Germany. On April 6, Congress voted to comply with that request. The United States now joined the war on the side of the Allies.

Section 2 Review

1. **Define** Central Powers, Allied Powers, U-boats, propaganda, war of attrition, contraband, atrocities
2. **Identify** Woodrow Wilson, Arthur Zimmermann
3. **Locate and Explain the Significance** Marne River, Danzig, Gallipoli Peninsula, Verdun
4. **Analyzing Ideas** What countries belonged to the Central Powers and the Allied Powers by the beginning of 1916?
5. **Understanding Ideas** Name some important new weapons and military techniques introduced in World War I.
6. **Summarizing Ideas** Describe the progress of the war from 1914 through 1916.
7. **Analyzing Ideas** (a) How was the United States as a neutral power affected by World War I? (b) What factors led to the United States entry into the war?

The Russian Revolution

Focus Questions

- **What internal problems did Russia face during World War I, and how did they lead to the Russian Revolution?**
- **How did Lenin come to power in Russia?**
- **What steps did the Communists take to cement their control of the Russian government?**

Russia, torn by revolutionary disturbances throughout the 1800s, faced continuing problems in the early 1900s. Russians had long been denied democratic rights and civil liberties, but the Revolution of 1905 had brought about no real changes. The elected legislative body, the Duma, had little power. The czar, Nicholas II, did not trust the Duma and remained a nearly absolute ruler. Some Russians, especially university students, joined secret societies that committed assassinations of government officials.

Grave economic problems also confronted the country. Although Russia had been industrializing rapidly in recent decades, it still was the most backward of the major European powers. Debts, taxes, and rents still kept most Russian peasants in poverty even though serfdom had been abolished in 1861.

Czar Nicholas II was the last Russian emperor. Unable to maintain his people's support, he abdicated in March 1917. He and his family were imprisoned and executed in July 1918.

Russia in World War I

World War I exposed Russia's weaknesses. The country lacked enough railroads and good roads, and its industry could not adequately equip or supply its army. The Ottoman Empire's entrance into the war on the side of the Central Powers helped cut Russia off from outside supplies.

The Allies had counted on the great number of soldiers in the Russian army. When war came, however, Russian troops proved to be poorly equipped and badly led. The inefficient and corrupt government was unfit to deal with the problems of modern warfare. Russian losses in the war were enormous: 1.7 million soldiers were killed, nearly 5 million were wounded or disabled, and some 2 million civilians died.

The spring of 1917 found the Russian people weary of hardships and disheartened by the appalling casualties their army had suffered in the war. They had lost faith in their government and in Czar Nicholas II. Strikes and street demonstrations broke out in Petrograd, as St. Petersburg had been called since 1914. When the Duma demanded reforms in the government, Nicholas dissolved it.

In the past, the government had always been able to use the army against disturbances such as those in Petrograd. Now, however, the soldiers joined the rioters. The Duma, encouraged by the army's disobedience, refused the czar's order to disband.

In March 1917, unable to control either his subjects or his army, Nicholas II abdicated. He and his family were arrested and the next year they were murdered by the Bolsheviks, who were ruling Russia at that time. The monarchy and the Romanov dynasty that had maintained Russian autocracy for 300 years were both ended.

Lenin and the Bolsheviks

A liberal provisional government was set up to rule Russia until a constitutional assembly could be elected to establish a new permanent system of government. While the provisional government tried to restore order, however, another body worked for more radical change in Russia.

This body, known as the Petrograd Soviet of Workers' and Soldiers' Deputies (*soviet* is the Russian word for council), had been quickly organized when disorders began in Russia. The Petrograd Soviet's leaders modeled it on similar organizations that had participated in the Revolution of 1905. Some members of the Petrograd Soviet were socialists called

Mensheviks. The organization also contained a group of more radical socialists, known as Bolsheviks.

Other soviets similar to the one in Petrograd sprang up elsewhere in Russia. Many people throughout the country supported their program. The soviets called for immediate peace, land reforms, and the turning over of factories to the workers. The provisional government, in contrast, pledged to continue the war and was much more cautious about reforms.

The leader of the Bolsheviks was V. I. Lenin. He was born Vladimir Ilyich Ulyanov in 1870, but after becoming a revolutionary he assumed the name Lenin. Lenin was an intelligent and forceful man. He came from the middle class and had studied law. After his older brother was executed by the czarist police as a revolutionary terrorist, Lenin became a revolutionary himself.

On April 16, 1917, Lenin, with German help, returned to Russia from Switzerland, where he had been living, and urged that all governing power be turned over to the soviets. He called for "peace, land and bread," a slogan with great popular appeal.

Lenin was a Marxist. Partly because of the conditions existing in Russia, however, he developed his own version of Marxism. Lenin believed that because Russia had comparatively little industry and only a small working class, the forces of history in the country might not move precisely as Marx had predicted. Therefore, he said, it was necessary for a small group of devoted Marxists to train the workers to become a revolutionary force. Lenin's adaptation of Marxism formed the basis of what became communism.

On November 7, 1917, the Bolsheviks overthrew the provisional government under Alexander Kerensky and seized control of Russia. This revolution is sometimes called the October Revolution (for the month in which it occurred, according to the calendar then used in Russia), or the Bolshevik Revolution, to differentiate it from the March Revolution that ousted Nicholas. In 1918 the Bolsheviks renamed themselves the Communist Party.

Peace and Civil War

Despite the losses Russia had suffered, the provisional government had kept Russia in the war. Now at Lenin's direction, a peace treaty was signed with the Central Powers in March 1918 at the city of Brest-Litovsk, taking Russia out of the war. Desperate for peace, the Communists accepted the very harsh terms dictated by Germany and agreed to give up a sizable amount of territory.

Vladimir Ilyich Lenin, founder of the Communist Party in Russia, led the Bolshevik Revolution.

The new regime then turned its attention to internal problems. The Communists faced much opposition within Russia. Their opponents included liberals, Mensheviks and other socialist factions, and right-wing groups that wanted to restore the monarchy. A civil war broke out in Russia.

The Communists had adopted red, the symbolic color of European revolutionary socialism, as their color. For this reason, they became known as Reds. Right-wing opponents of the Communists were called Whites. The Red Army—as the forces of the new government were called—fought many battles with the White forces, leaving an appalling trail of destruction. The civil war, which began in early 1918, lasted almost three years, adding to the devastation begun by World War I.

The Allies had been angered by the new Russian government's signing of a separate peace with the Central Powers. They wanted to prevent aid they had sent Russia from falling into the hands of the Germans. They also feared that if the Communists gained control of Russia, revolution would spread to their countries. The Communists had been calling for such a revolution. Thus the Allies aided some of the White forces with arms and money. Several nations, including Britain, France, and the United States, even sent small numbers of troops to oppose the communist government. These efforts were half-hearted, however, and had little effect. By 1921 the Communists had completely defeated the White forces. In 1922 the Communists renamed the lands they ruled the Union of Soviet Socialist Republics, or the Soviet Union.

Section 3 Review

1. **Identify** Mensheviks, Bolsheviks, V. I. Lenin, Communists
2. **Locate and Explain the Significance** Brest-Litovsk
3. **Understanding Cause and Effect** How did internal problems in Russia during World War I affect the course of the revolution in Russia in 1917?
4. **Explaining Ideas** How did Lenin and the Bolsheviks come to power in Russia?
5. **Analyzing Ideas** (a) How did the signing of the peace treaty by the Communists in 1918 help the new regime maintain power? (b) Why did it anger the Allied Powers?

Section 4

The Terms of Peace

Focus Questions

- **What were the Fourteen Points?**
- **How did World War I come to an end?**
- **What problems faced the leaders at the Paris Peace Conference?**

President Woodrow Wilson's statement of America's aim in entering the war—to make the world "safe for democracy"—established an idealistic reason for the war. But the Bolshevik Revolution in Russia and Russia's signing of a separate peace treaty with the Central Powers at Brest-Litovsk dampened Allied morale. The bloody stalemate on the western front continued. To many people, the war seemed likely to last years longer.

The Fourteen Points

In January 1918, about 10 months before World War I ended, President Wilson, in a speech to Congress, set forth a set of ideas for a just world after the war.

Wilson's plan became known as the **Fourteen Points**. Six of the points (points 1–5 and 14) contained plans of a general nature. The eight remaining points dealt with specific countries and regions, such as Russia, Belgium, Alsace-Lorraine, and the Balkans.

The six general points may be summarized as follows: (1) no secret treaties; (2) freedom of the seas for all nations; (3) removal of all economic barriers or tariffs; (4) reduction of national armaments; (5) fair adjustment of all colonial claims, with equal consideration given to the interests of the colonial powers and the people of the colonies; and (14) establishment of "a general association of nations" to guarantee political independence and protection to large and small states alike.

The Fourteen Points caught the imagination of people everywhere. Even in Germany, where the population was tired of the hardships of the war, people were impressed by Wilson's proposals.

Defeat of the Central Powers

The Treaty of Brest-Litovsk with Russia allowed the Germans to withdraw troops from the eastern front and concentrate their efforts on a huge offensive in the west during the spring and summer of 1918. This offensive, which lasted until mid-July, represented a last attempt to break through the Allied lines, capture Paris, and end the war before the Americans could arrive in strength and turn the tide.

At the end of May, the Germans again reached the Marne River, only 37 miles from Paris. By this time, however, thousands of American troops were landing in France every month.

Under a newly organized joint command, headed by the French marshal Ferdinand Foch (FAWSH), the Allied forces stopped the Germans in June at Château-Thierry. In July the Allies began to counterattack. A major Allied offensive in September at Saint-Mihiel and in the Argonne Forest forced the German armies back to the borders of Germany. (See map on page 369.)

At the same time, conditions worsened for the Central Powers elsewhere in the war. Bulgaria, seeing little hope for victory or for help from its allies, surrendered on September 30, 1918. The Turks soon asked for peace. By October a revolution in Austria-Hungary had brought the old Habsburg Empire to an end. Austria and Hungary then formed separate governments and stopped fighting.

In Germany the government of Kaiser William II soon collapsed. President Wilson had told German

Costs of the War

The costs of World War I stagger the imagination. Each of the belligerent nations suffered enormous losses that had lasting consequences. It is estimated that the war left some 10 million soldiers dead and around 20 million more wounded—many of them crippled for life.

Militarily, Germany suffered most severely, losing more than 1.8 million soldiers. Russia lost almost as many, and France and its colonies lost nearly 1.4 million. Austria and Hungary counted nearly 1 million dead in the war, and Great Britain lost almost 1 million. The United States lost some 50,000 in battle.

Civilian casualties were also very high. Naval blockades, artillery and aerial bombardments, famine, disease, and political violence all took their toll. The destruction of property was appalling. One historian has estimated that the total cost was more than $300 billion, an enormous figure for the time.

The Paris Peace Conference

After the armistice in November 1918, the Allies faced the task of arranging peace terms. President Wilson had written and spoken of a peace conference that would write a treaty that was fair to all. However, the war had caused so much bitterness and had cost so much in terms of human lives and property that the European Allied governments were determined to dictate the terms of peace.

Delegates of the victorious nations met in Paris in January 1919. This meeting is referred to as the **Paris Peace Conference** or the Versailles Conference. Almost all the Allied Powers sent representatives. Russia, having left the war and now in the midst of a civil war, was not invited.

Representatives of the defeated Central Powers played no role in writing the terms of the treaties. The conference was dominated by the leaders of the four most powerful Allies—Great Britain, France, the

These victorious American soldiers are marching through the Arc de Triomphe (Arch of Triumph), where today an eternal flame burns to honor France's World War I Tomb of the Unknown Soldier.

leaders he would deal only with a government that truly represented the German people. Many Germans, wishing to end the war, looked upon the kaiser as an obstacle to peace. On November 9, the kaiser's abdication was announced, and the German Republic was proclaimed.

In November 1918, the new German leaders signed an **armistice**, an agreement to stop fighting. The armistice provided that at the eleventh hour on the eleventh day of 1918 all fighting would cease. The Germans grimly signed the armistice in a railroad car in the forest of Compiègne in France.

According to the severe terms of the armistice, the Treaty of Brest-Litovsk was canceled. Germany also had to surrender its submarines and a large part of its surface fleet. In addition, it had to release all war prisoners and turn over munitions that might make additional fighting possible. The Allies reserved the right to occupy all German territory west of the Rhine River.

What If?

Nations at War
How do you think world history would have been different if the United States had not entered World War I?

Duchamp and the Dadaists

World War I raged violently for four years. When it ended, more than 10 million soldiers and millions more civilians had lost their lives. Such devastation did not go unnoticed in the art world. Artists expressed their anger and bitterness over the war by producing anti-art, works that mocked the values of a society that could have produced such a war. This school of art was called Dada.* Dada art showed objects and ideas that seemed to have no relation to each other. Some critics refer to Dadaist works as nonart.

Man Ray was one of the most famous of the Dada artists. Born in Philadelphia, he moved to Paris in 1921. Ray worked in a wide variety of media,

including painting, photography, and motion pictures. He experimented endlessly with techniques such as superimposing shapes onto photographs to create strange, nonsensical images. The piece shown to the right, "Aviary," combines paint, pencil, and ink on cardboard.

United States, and Italy. Known as the Big Four, these leaders were Prime Minister David Lloyd George of Great Britain, Premier Georges Clemenceau (kleˈmahnˈSOH) of France, President Woodrow Wilson of the United States, and Premier Vittorio Orlando of Italy.

Problems Facing the Peacemakers

After the end of World War I, Europe faced a confusing political situation. Republics had replaced hereditary monarchies in the three great former empires of Germany, Austria-Hungary, and Russia. A fourth empire, that of the Ottoman Turks, tottered on the brink of collapse. Ethnic groups in Russia and the defeated empires pressed their claims for independence. These groups wanted independence, self-government, and unity within the borders of a single nation. The spirit of nationalism also began to grow in overseas colonies as well.

Territorial claims. The victorious nations had many conflicting territorial demands that they found difficult to reconcile. France wanted, above all, security against

---

*Dada is a French word for wooden horse or hobbyhorse. A sculptor and a German writer accidentally discovered the word in a dictionary. They liked the sound of the word and its whimsical, nonsensical quality. To them, of course, the violence of World War I made no sense either.

another German attack. It insisted on the return of the former provinces of Alsace and Lorraine. This had been guaranteed in the Fourteen Points. In addition, France demanded that its border be moved eastward to the Rhine River so that France would possess the more militarily defensible Rhineland, the German territory located on the west bank of the Rhine River. France also demanded the Saar River valley, with its valuable deposits of coal, as reparation.

Italy claimed the Tirol region and the city of Trieste in accordance with the secret treaties it had made in 1915. It also claimed the port city of Fiume, although Fiume had not been promised in the secret treaties. Lloyd George, Wilson, and Clemenceau agreed to the Tirol region. However, they steadfastly opposed giving Fiume to Italy. The controversy became so bitter that Orlando for a time left the conference and went home in disgust.

Belgium, which had suffered under wartime German occupation, requested two small portions of German territory along the border. Great Britain wanted Germany's African colonies. It also insisted that the German navy be destroyed and that Germany be prohibited from building warships.

During the war, Japan had occupied the previously German-held Marshall, Caroline, and Mariana Islands, as well as Qingdao and most of the

Shandong Peninsula. Now that the war was over, Japan wanted to keep all these regions. Another bitter quarrel followed.

Reparations and peacekeeping. The destruction caused by the war prompted the question of **reparations**—payment for war damages. Who should pay for the damages and how much?

Finally, the conference considered the question of a world organization to maintain peace, an idea dear to Wilson's heart. The formation of a **League of Nations** had widespread appeal, but many European leaders doubted its practical usefulness.

The Peace: Justice or Vengeance?

Early in the conference, two conflicting viewpoints had surfaced. The British, French, and Italian governments claimed to support the Fourteen Points. Yet they had never really given up the aims stated in the secret treaties—to divide the territories taken from the Central Powers among themselves after the war. The Fourteen Points represented a "peace of justice," whereas the terms of the secret treaties represented a "peace of vengeance."

Wilson believed that the conference must write a "peace of justice," as the Fourteen Points outlined, so that the settlement would be fair and lasting and not create a basis for new wars. However, the war had left bitterness, hatred, and a longing for revenge. Many of the victors believed the Central Powers, and especially Germany, had been responsible for the war. They demanded that the defeated be taught a stern lesson.

Section 4 Review

1. **Define** Fourteen Points, armistice, Paris Peace Conference, reparations, League of Nations
2. **Identify** Ferdinand Foch, Big Four
3. **Locate and Explain the Significance** Château-Thierry, Saint-Mihiel, Rhineland, Saar River valley
4. **Summarizing Ideas** (a) What were the six general proposals of Wilson's Fourteen Points? (b) What effect did the Fourteen Points have?
5. **Understanding Ideas** What events led to the end of World War I?
6. **Evaluating Ideas** (a) Why did Wilson believe in a "peace of justice"? (b) Why did others oppose this belief?

Creating a "New Europe"

Focus Questions

- **What were the specific provisions of the Treaty of Versailles?**
- **What issues emerged as the victors dealt with various nations and national minorities?**
- **What were the aims of the League of Nations?**

The victorious Allied Powers made separate treaties with each of the five Central Powers. Because Austria and Hungary now had separate governments, five treaties had to be drawn up—with Germany, Austria, Hungary, Bulgaria, and the Ottoman Empire. The treaty with Germany is called the **Treaty of Versailles** because it was signed at the Palace of Versailles, outside Paris.

The Versailles Treaty

In May 1919 representatives of the new German Republic were called in, presented with a peace treaty, and told to sign it. The Germans complained bitterly that the treaty did not follow the Fourteen Points. They objected especially to two parts. First, the treaty made Germany, the sole surviving Central Power, admit that it alone was guilty of starting the war and therefore must pay reparations. Second, the treaty did not specify the total amount of the reparations. Nevertheless, the Germans had no choice but to sign the treaty. In late June 1919, Germany, still bitterly protesting, signed the treaty.

The Versailles Treaty provided for the formation of the League of Nations, which will be discussed later in this section. It also made numerous territorial adjustments and placed various restrictions on Germany.

Germany lost considerable land along its northern, western, and eastern borders (see map on page 379) as well as its overseas colonies. Alsace-Lorraine was returned to France. Belgium gained some small territories along its border. Germany agreed not to fortify the Rhineland, which Allied troops would occupy for an unspecified period of time. The Saar Valley would fall under the administration of the League of Nations for 15 years. During that time, all the coal mined in the area would go to France in partial payment of reparations. At the end of 15 years, the people of the Saar Valley region would go to the polls to vote.

Building History Study Skills

READ
WRITE
INTERPRET
CONNECT
THINK

Interpreting Visuals: Using a Map as a Historical Document

The Congress of Vienna in 1815 resulted in border changes in Europe (see maps entitled "Napoleonic Empire, 1805–1815," and "Europe After the Congress of Vienna, 1815," in Chapter 4). Studying changes in the map of Europe before and after the Congress of Vienna helps you understand the political and historical development of Europe before World War I.

A major goal of the participants at the Congress of Vienna was to prevent France from again acting aggressively as Napoleon had acted. Consequently, the Austrian Netherlands (Belgium) was united with Holland (the Dutch Netherlands) to act as a buffer state against France. The Rhineland became the border of Prussia. Savoy and Genoa were added to Sardinia to make Sardinia a larger state along the border of France. The changes made by the Congress of Vienna did not allow for self-determination; the overall principle of the changes focused on the balance of power. Do you notice any other balance-of-power provisions indicated by the changes shown on the two maps? What consequences did they have for the historical development of Europe?

How to Use a Map as a Historical Document
To use a map as a historical document, follow these steps.
1. Identify the subject of the map.
2. Identify the historical context of the map.
3. Explain the information about the subject included on the map.
4. Connect the information on the map to the historical context of the subject.
5. Compare the map with other maps.

Developing the Skill
World War I created new borders in Europe. The Treaty of Versailles and the other peace agreements changed the nature of Europe's geography, economy, and politics. Studying maps of Europe before and after World War I, just as you have studied maps of Europe before and after the Congress of Vienna, helps you understand the political and historical development of Europe. Look at the maps entitled "Europe on the Eve of World War I, 1914," on page 364 and "Europe After the Versailles Settlements, 1919–1920," on page 379. How did Europe change? How did these changes affect European history?

The historical context is the impact that World War I had on Europe. The maps give information about the consequences of World War I for European history. Large empires broke up, and a number of smaller countries were created. Germany lost Alsace-Lorraine to France; Serbia became part of Yugoslavia; Austria-Hungary was divided into Austria, Hungary, Czechoslovakia, and Yugoslavia. Poland reappeared, and Russia became the Soviet Union. The Polish Corridor was created out of part of Germany. There were other changes as well. As the Congress of Vienna attempted to prevent French aggression, the World War I settlements attempted to prevent German aggression. The loss of Alsace-Lorraine and the Polish Corridor, for example, weakened Germany. However, the changes also contained the seeds of a future war because of German resentment to the loss of this land and new and continuing nationality problems.

Practicing the Skill
Look at a map that shows the European colonies that are located in Africa in the early 1900s. Then look at a recent map of Africa. What generalizations can you make about shifts in power in Africa since the early 1900s?

To apply this skill, see Applying History Study Skills on page 383.

The Big Four at Versailles

Europe After the Versailles Settlements, 1919–1920

Learning from Maps Many new countries were added to the continent of Europe after World War I.

? Place What city became the capital of Yugoslavia? Of Czechoslovakia? Of Finland? Of Poland?

They could choose to remain under League control, to become part of France, or to rejoin Germany.

Poland was restored as an independent nation and received a large area of formerly German land. This region included the so-called Polish Corridor, which cut off East Prussia from the rest of Germany and gave Poland an outlet to the Baltic Sea. The port of Danzig became a free city administered by the League of Nations.

Germany had to abolish conscription and could not maintain an army of more than 100,000 men. It was not allowed to manufacture heavy artillery, tanks, military airplanes, or poison gas. In addition, Germany could have no submarines and only a small number of warships. These measures were intended to ensure that Germany would not be able to wage aggressive war, but the Allies lacked effective means for enforcing them.

Former Austro-Hungarian Territories

Austria-Hungary's Dual Monarchy had split in two as the war ended. The victors wrote one treaty with Austria in September 1919 and a separate treaty with Hungary in June 1920. Austria, now an independent republic, lost the southern Tirol and the city of Trieste to Italy. The new republic could not grow enough food for its people or supply its industries with adequate raw materials. As a result, Austria soon sank into financial crisis and poverty.

Hungary lost a great deal of the territory it had governed under the Dual Monarchy to the newly created nation of Czechoslovakia, which included Czech, Slovak, and Ruthenian peoples. In the western Balkans, the new nation of Yugoslavia united the former independent kingdoms of Serbia and Montenegro, the former Habsburg provinces of Bosnia and Herzogovina, and a section of the Adriatic coast.

Bulgaria and the Ottoman Empire

The victors also penalized Bulgaria. In its treaty, signed in 1919, Bulgaria lost territory, including its outlet to the Aegean Sea, which went to Greece.

The Ottoman Empire paid an even higher price for being on the losing side. Its treaty, which was signed in 1920, resulted in a great loss of territory. The Dardanelles and Bosporus remained in Turkish hands; however, these areas had to be kept unfortified and controlled by an international commission.

Several new states—Palestine, Transjordan, and Syria (including present-day Lebanon)—emerged from former Turkish territory in the eastern Mediterranean area. Turkish territory farther east became the country of Iraq. These territories were administered by Great Britain or France under the supervision of the League of Nations.

Former Russian Territories

In 1918 four new nations—Finland, Estonia, Latvia, and Lithuania—along the Baltic Sea had declared their independence from Russia. The victorious Allies recognized their independent sovereignty. Much of the territory of restored Poland also came from Russia, as well as from Germany and Austria-Hungary. In addition, Russia lost the province of Bessarabia, in the southwest, to a greatly enlarged Romania.

Dissatisfied Minorities

The peace treaties solved many problems but also created new ones. One of the most difficult problems was that of national self-determination.

President Wilson had held out the promise of independent nationhood for all national or ethnic groups, most of whom had belonged to one or another of the great empires that disappeared at the end of the war. However, not every ethnic group could be united under its own government. For example, there were thousands of German-speaking Austrians in the Tirol, which came partly under Italian rule. Germans lived in Danzig and the Polish Corridor. Some 3 million German-speaking former Austrian subjects—known as Sudeten Germans—now lived in Czechoslovakia.

These national minorities—people of one nationality living under a government controlled by another nationality—were unhappy. Some minorities, such as the Armenians and Kurds, many of whom lived in the Ottoman Empire, were brutally oppressed. Although each minority group was guaranteed certain rights that were to be protected by the League of Nations, the nationalities problem remained.

The League of Nations

During the negotiations among the Allied leaders over the peace settlements, President Wilson made several compromises with the ideals of his Fourteen Points. He realized that the treaties failed in many respects to provide a "peace of justice." He consoled himself, however, with the thought that the new League of Nations would be able to remedy any injustices caused by the treaties.

A special commission, which included Wilson, wrote the Covenant of the League of Nations. This Covenant, adopted by the Paris Peace Conference, became part of the Versailles Treaty, which the United States did not ratify.

Organization. According to the Covenant, the League of Nations had two main aims: (1) to promote international cooperation and (2) to maintain peace by settling disputes among nations and by reducing armaments. The League was to include all independent European sovereign nations. Three main agencies—an assembly, a council, and a secretariat—would conduct League business. The League was to work closely with a related but independent body, the Permanent Court of International Justice, or **World Court**, which is located at The Hague in the Netherlands.

The Assembly would be composed of representatives of all member nations. Regardless of size, each nation was to have one vote. The Council, the main peacekeeping body, was to be composed of 9 member nations (later increased to 14). It would consist of 5 permanent members—Great Britain, France, Italy,

Despite a lack of support from the United States, 42 member countries established the League of Nations in January 1920. This photograph was taken later in 1920 at the League's first public session.

Japan, and the United States—the victorious powers of the war. The remaining seats on the Council were to be filled by rotation from among the other nations.

Maintaining the peace. The members of the League of Nations agreed not to resort to war and promised to submit their disputes to the World Court or specially convened commissions for arbitration. The League of Nations Covenant provided that if a member nation broke this agreement, the League could impose penalties. Possible penalties included breaking diplomatic relations, imposing **economic sanctions**—the refusal to trade with the offending member nation—or blockades. Military force would be considered only as a last resort.

Mandates. The League of Nations provided a way to deal with the colonies of the defeated Central Powers. Until the people of such a colony were considered ready for independence, the League agreed to hold the area in trust and to assume responsibility for it. The League designated the area a **mandate** to be administered by the government of an "advanced" nation. The administering nation pledged that it would prepare the people of the area for self-government and make annual reports to the League concerning the area's progress. German possessions in Africa and the Pacific and Ottoman territories in the Middle East were assigned as mandates either to Britain, France, Australia, New Zealand, or Japan. The mandate for South-West Africa was assigned to South Africa.

The Start of the League. Although the League of Nations had been a favorite idea of Wilson's, the United States itself never became a member of the organization. Some Americans disapproved of the League's powers, while others wanted changes in the

Versailles Treaty, which included the League Covenant. After fighting in a bloody European war, Americans were fearful of being dragged into another war by commitments to League peacekeeping. As a result of this opposition, the U.S. Senate refused to ratify the Versailles Treaty. Instead, the United States eventually signed a separate peace treaty with Germany.

Despite the absence of the United States, the 42 member nations represented at the League of Nations' first meeting in Geneva in November 1920 held an optimistic view of the future. Germany could not join the League until 1926, and Russia did not become a member until 1934. Ultimately, however, 59 countries became members of the League of Nations.

Section 5 Review

1. **Define** Treaty of Versailles, World Court, economic sanctions, mandate
2. **Identify** Sudeten Germans
3. **Locate and Explain the Significance** Polish Corridor, Czechoslovakia, Yugoslavia
4. **Understanding Ideas** Explain the provisions of the Treaty of Versailles concerning **(a)** reparations; **(b)** Germany's colonies; **(c)** German military power.
5. **Analyzing Ideas** How did the Treaty of Versailles create problems with regard to national minorities?
6. **Summarizing Ideas** What was the League of Nations, and what were its aims?
7. **Evaluating Ideas** Do you consider World War I a major turning point in world history? Why?

Chapter 11 Review

| A.D. 1880 | A.D. 1884 | A.D. 1888 | A.D. 1892 | A.D. 1896 | A.D. 1900 |

A.D. 1882
Triple Alliance forms.

A.D. 1888
William II ascends throne of Germany.

A.D. 1899
First arms limitation talks are held at The Hague.

Chapter Summary

The following list contains the key concepts that you have learned about World War I and the Russian Revolution.

1. Suspicions and rivalries among European nations intensified beginning in the late 1800s. This was caused by strong national feelings, the spread of imperialism, military buildups, and a system of rival alliances.
2. The 1914 assassination of Archduke Francis Ferdinand in Sarajevo sparked World War I.
3. Within a few months, almost all the nations of Europe, plus Japan, were at war.
4. Most people expected the conflict to be over quickly and decisively. Instead, the struggle dragged on for four terribly bloody years.
5. In Russia a revolution toppled the 300-year rule of the Romanov dynasty and ended in a Communist-ruled state.
6. In 1917 the United States entered the world war, providing the fresh troops and new resources that helped defeat the Central Powers.
7. In early 1918, Russia signed a peace treaty with the Central Powers that took it out of the war. Germany mounted an offensive to break the military deadlock on the western front but failed.
8. Although the war ended in 1918, it left problems that continued to plague governments for years. Many lives had been lost, much property had been destroyed, and great bitterness remained. Many problems remained unresolved.
9. Woodrow Wilson's Fourteen Points offered idealistic goals that might have created a lasting framework for peace after World War I. At the Paris Peace Conference, however, many of these goals were forgotten as the Allies sought to punish the losers and collect reparations for their wartime losses.
10. After the war, national groups demanded recognition, especially in eastern Europe.
11. Many hoped the League of Nations would help keep the peace and settle disputes among countries. The United States did not join the League.

Reviewing Important Terms

On a separate sheet of paper, match each of the following terms with the correct definition below.

a. mobilize
b. contraband
c. militarism
d. belligerent
e. atrocities
f. reparations
g. armistice
h. ultimatum
i. propaganda

_____ 1. Brutal crimes of war
_____ 2. Payment for war damages
_____ 3. To ready an army and other resources for combat
_____ 4. Threat by one side of harmful action if the other side rejects its proposals
_____ 5. Agreement to stop fighting
_____ 6. War materials supplied by a neutral nation to a belligerent nation
_____ 7. Ideas, facts, or rumors deliberately spread to further a cause
_____ 8. Warring nation
_____ 9. Glorification of armed strength

Developing Critical Thinking Skills

1. **Classifying Ideas** (a) What was the immediate cause of World War I? (b) What were the underlying causes?
2. **Contrasting Ideas** President Wilson believed the war could be settled with a "peace of justice." (a) What ideals in the Fourteen Points worked toward this goal? (b) What obstacles blocked Wilson's efforts to carry out his plan?
3. **Interpreting Ideas** How did the Allies view the Russian Revolution and civil war?
4. **Evaluating Ideas** (a) How did the peace settlements after World War I readjust the balance of power in the world? (b) Did the peace settlements correct the causes of World War I or ignore them? Explain.
5. **Using Maps** Study the maps on pages 364 and 379. (a) What happened to the Central Powers as a result of World War I? (b) What happened to the Russian Empire?
6. **Using Pictures** As you learned in this chapter, governments used propaganda to encourage citizens to support the war effort. Locate a copy of a propaganda

A.D. **1908**
Austria-Hungary annexes Bosnia and Herzegovina.

A.D. **1915**
• Italy enters World War I.
• *Lusitania* is sunk.

A.D. **1918**
• Central Powers are defeated.
• Armistice is signed.

A.D. **1920**
League of Nations meets for first time.

A.D. **1908**   A.D. **1912**   A.D. **1916**   A.D. **1920**

A.D. **1907**
• Second arms limitation talks are held at The Hague.
• Triple Entente forms.

A.D. **1914**
• Archduke Francis Ferdinand is assassinated.
• World War I begins.

A.D. **1917**
• United States enters World War I.
• Russian Revolution begins.

A.D. **1919**
• Paris Peace Conference is held.
• Treaty of Versailles is signed.

poster from the era. **(a)** What techniques or symbols used in the poster might arouse a sense of patriotism? **(b)** To what emotions does this poster seem to appeal?

Relating Geography to History

Using information from this chapter and Chapters 8 and 10, answer the following questions. **(a)** Why did Britain's geographical situation make it very concerned around 1900 about Germany's decision to build a large fleet? **(b)** How did geography work both to keep the United States out of World War I and to contribute a reason for it to enter the war?

Relating Past to Present

1. Review the following causes of World War I: nationalism, militarism, imperialism, and international alliances. Which of these forces are still present in the world? Clip newspaper or magazine articles that support your answer.
2. Before World War I, the Balkan region was known as a "powder keg." **(a)** Why was it given this name? **(b)** Are there any similarities between the Balkans in the early 1900s and the Balkans today? **(c)** If so, what actions might be taken to prevent the start of a war there?
3. In 1899 and again in 1907, several nations participated in arms limitation and laws of war conferences held at The Hague. Using library resources, locate books and articles about disarmament efforts in recent years. You might consider efforts to control nuclear weapons, chemical and biological warfare, and land mines. Are any of the obstacles to disarmament today the same as those faced in the late 1800s and early 1900s? Are any unique to the present? Explain.

Applying History Study Skills

Before completing this activity, review Building History Study Skills on page 378.

Study the maps entitled "Europe in 1916–1917" on page 365; "The Eastern Front, 1914–1918," on page 368; and "The Western Front, 1914–1918," on page 369, in conjunction with the text of the chapter. Then answer the following questions to help you use the maps as historical documents.

1. Where did most of the fighting on the western front take place?
2. Describe the location of the Brest-Litovsk line. What did it mean for the war on the eastern front?
3. Which side do you think had the greater strategic advantage? Why?
4. At the time of the armistice on the western front, had Germany lost much territory?
5. What may have been a reason why Switzerland was a neutral country?
6. Explain why these referenced maps can be described as historical documents.

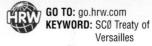
internet connect

Search the Internet through the HRW Web site for additional information on the Treaty of Versailles. Then list three of the most important decisions made in the treaty.

GO TO: go.hrw.com
KEYWORD: SC0 Treaty of Versailles

Building Your Portfolio

1. **Writing a Report** While troops bogged down in the muddy trenches of Europe, other battles were taking place in the skies. Using your school or public library as a source for information, write a short report on developments in air warfare during World War I. Also investigate the pilots who flew these missions, such as Baron von Richthofen (the "Red Baron"), Eddie Rickenbacker, or members of the Lafayette Escadrille. Place your report in your portfolio.

Book Report Read one of the following novels, and present a book report to the class: Ernest Hemingway's *A Farewell to Arms* (Scribner's); Erich Maria Remarque's *All Quiet on the Western Front* (Fawcett); or Willa Cather's *One of Ours* (Random House). Note the author's point of view on war. How does it compare with the idealism expressed by President Wilson at the start of World War I? Place your book report in your portfolio.

The Great Depression and the Rise of Totalitarianism

TIME
A.D. 1919–1936

| 3.7 million B.C. | 4000 B.C. | A.D. 1919–1936 A.D. 2100 |

A.D. 1919–1936

PLACE
Europe and
the United States

Europe

United States

Hitler rally, 1935, Nuremberg

Significance

Disgusted by the death and waste in World War I, writers and painters began reacting against traditional forms of literature and art. The tremendous economic prosperity that appeared immediately after the war soon crumbled into a terrible economic depression.

Totalitarian regimes—highly centralized governments that allowed no opposition and held total control—claimed to offer Europeans security amid the instability and uncertainty of the period. Tragically, this era served only as a prelude to an even more devastating war.

Terms to Define

totalitarian regimes	Maginot Line
surrealism	Locarno Pact
The Waste Land	general strike
cubism	Popular Front
functionalism	nationalized
international style	Easter Rising
economic boom	fascism
Roaring Twenties	corporatist state
Prohibition	*Mein Kampf*
economic nationalism	Third Reich
market speculations	Rome-Berlin Axis
on margin	Union of Soviet Socialist
Great Depression	Republics
Social Security Act	collective farms
Tennessee Valley	command economy
Authority	Politburo
Johnson Act	purge
planned economy	Comintern

People to Identify

Thomas Mann	Éamon De Valera
James Joyce	Józef Pilsudski
Ernest Hemingway	Black Shirts
Igor Stravinsky	*il Duce*
Pablo Picasso	storm troopers
Frank Lloyd Wright	*der Führer*
Herbert Hoover	Gestapo
Ramsay MacDonald	Leon Trotsky

Chapter Theme Questions

- **The Arts** In what ways might the questioning of traditional values and beliefs be reflected in the arts?
- **Economic Organization** How might worldwide depression lead to changes in government?
- **Politics and Law** What conditions might help to encourage the formation of authoritarian forms of government?

During the 1930s a natural disaster overtook the American farmer as a prolonged drought destroyed farmland from Texas to the Dakotas. As the drought continued, wind blew the dry topsoil into swirling dust clouds, turning the region into what became known as the Dust Bowl. These conditions forced many farm families to leave their homes. In this excerpt from his novel *The Grapes of Wrath*, John Steinbeck describes the hardships of Dust Bowl families as they prepare to leave Oklahoma for California.

❝In the little houses the tenant people sifted their belongings and the belongings of their fathers and of their grandfathers. Picked over their possessions for the journey to the west. The men were ruthless because the past had been spoiled, but the women knew how the past would cry to them in the coming days. . . . How can we live without our lives? How will we know it's us without our past? No. Leave it. Burn it. . . . And they piled up the goods in the yards and set fire to them. They stood and watched them burning, and then frantically they loaded up the cars and drove away, drove in the dust. The dust hung in the air for a long time after the loaded cars had passed.❞

Just as these families experienced hardships, so, too, did many millions struggle during the years between the two world wars.

Section 1

The Postwar Era

Focus Questions

- In what ways did Europeans change their way of thinking about society after World War I?
- What developments in sciences and arts contributed to or demonstrated these changes?

World War I profoundly disrupted European and American society. Ideas about nations and people were changed by the mass destruction. A journalist writing in 1938 offered an impression of these times:

> "Marx, Freud, Einstein all conveyed the same message to the 1920s: the world was not what it seemed. The senses, whose . . . perceptions shaped our ideas of time and distance, right and wrong, law and justice, and the nature of man's behaviour in society, were not to be trusted. . . .
>
> The impression people derived from Einstein, of a universe in which all measurements of value were relative, served to confirm this vision."

The work of leading thinkers, writers, and artists of the time reflected and heightened this sense of disquiet and uncertainty.

The Effects of New Scientific Ideas

Following World War I, many people rejected the belief in continual human progress first expressed during the Enlightenment. Instead they felt a sense of alienation and cynicism. Scientists, who since the 1600s had been proving that human beings could solve almost any problem, began to suggest something else in the early 1900s. Some people interpreted the ideas of psychologist Sigmund Freud, for example, to mean that people could no longer be quite so confident about the powers of rational thought.

Freudian psychology. Sigmund Freud had developed theories of the unconscious (see Chapter 7). He believed that the unconscious mind governs human behavior. In Freud's opinion people are generally unaware of the mental processes of the unconscious. Freud had begun writing in the early 1900s, but his ideas about the unconscious mind and irrationality did not gain popularity until after World War I. If people believed that the unconscious and not the rational mind were controlling people's actions, then much that seemed bewildering could be explained. These ideas seemed to help people understand why the dreadful devastation of World War I had taken place, why things had not turned out as they had hoped, and why uneasiness in human life continued.

Einstein's physics. The theory of relativity made Albert Einstein famous (see Chapter 7). In this theory he had argued that even such seemingly absolute and definite concepts as space, motion, and time had to be seen as relative, or dependent on one another. This concept encouraged those who had come to believe that social standards, whether of morality or of artistic taste, were not absolute. The philosophy of ethical relativism argues that values are

relative to societies, and that there is no objective way of justifying one set of principles for all groups. The work of Werner Heisenberg made certainty in basic scientific measurements no longer seem possible, and Einstein's physics seemed to support the relativist's view, though Einstein himself had a "passionate sense of social justice and social responsibility."

After World War I, science itself thus seemed to intensify rather than to relieve doubts about the basic nature of human beings and society. These shifts in understanding caused some people to doubt that science would solve humanity's problems. Distrust in human progress added to uncertainty and lack of confidence in the future.

New Directions in Literature

The major writings of World War I and the postwar years revealed dissatisfaction with traditional ideas, and tried to assert a new vision. The German historian and philosopher, Oswald Spengler, expressed a mood for the era with *The Decline of the West*. Spengler believed that civilizations pass from youth to maturity, and from maturity to old age and death. In his book Spengler predicted that European civilization would disintegrate, a view matching the disillusionment of the era. In literature, writers experimented with form, and influenced by Freud, began to probe unconscious motivations.

Novels. The French novelist Marcel Proust rejected the idea of literature as a pursuit of intellect. Proust believed that reality is a world of memory and sensation lost in daily life. In a minutely-detailed account of a man's search for meaning, Proust vividly brought to life the sensory impressions of a disappeared past. The first part of *Remembrance of Things Past*, a multi-volume novel, appeared in 1913, but most of it was published after World War I. Proust became world famous, and respect for his work continued beyond his death in 1922.

Among the themes of Thomas Mann, Proust's German contemporary, were the constant presence of death amid life and the alienation of the writer from society. An atmosphere of decadence and sadness pervades many of his novels—reflecting moods of the 1920s and 1930s. The somber atmosphere is notable in *The Magic Mountain* (1924), which, set in a hospital, deals symbolically with the moral state of Europe.

The works of Franz Kafka, a Czech writer, pleased those who liked **surrealism** in literature after World War I. Surrealism attempts to merge conscious and unconscious ideas to portray and interpret life in a dreamlike way.

Charlie Chaplin in *Modern Times*

Mechanization created feelings of uneasiness in many people. One of these people was the brilliant comedian Charlie Chaplin. Characterizing the human spirit in its loneliness and humor, he used the new invention, the movie, as the vehicle for his satire. One of his most famous films was *Modern Times,* which was released in 1936. The movie depicts him, in his usual role as a gentle tramp, at work in a huge factory. Here he is shown tightening bolts on an endless assembly line. In pursuit of one neglected bolt, he knocks other workers over, upsets the entire factory routine, and ends as a captive of the machinery.

The Museum of Modern Art/Film Stills Archives

Most of Kafka's works were unknown before his death in 1924, but a friend refused to follow a request to destroy them. In *The Trial* (1925), the main character is tried in a hostile atmosphere for a crime about which he knows nothing. In *The Castle* (1926), a man seeks an authority in a castle, but never finds the official, despite searching through endless corridors and dealing with many other people. These stories of struggle to find meaning and Kafka's unique way of telling them later influenced many writers.

Ireland's James Joyce caused a great stir during this period. In his sometimes bewildering masterpiece, *Ulysses* (1922), Joyce tried to convey everything that happened to a man and everything the man thought, both consciously and unconsciously, in a single day. Joyce used a technique called "stream of consciousness." Influenced by psychoanalysis, the technique attempts to record everything that comes into a character's mind in all experience. *Ulysses* is difficult to understand because it lacks normal punctuation and skips about seemingly at random. *Ulysses* was a revolutionary work that broke away from many of the traditions of the novel. Joyce's

experimentation with language and form was characteristic of post-World War I artists.

American Ernest Hemingway wrote in clear, simple prose. His aim, apparent in *A Farewell to Arms* (1929), was to express the stark disillusionment with life so common in the years after World War I.

Poetry. The American-born poet T. S. Eliot, who spent most of his life in England, expressed the deep pessimism of the postwar years through poetry that altered traditional forms. In his famous poem **The Waste Land** (1922), Eliot gives a despairing description of a world without faith, incapable of restoring spiritual and moral values. Many poets of this period also abandoned traditional rhyme and meter. Instead they wrote poetry without rhyme that had lines of varying lengths. They also experimented with punctuation and even with the physical appearance of their poems.

New Directions in Music and Painting

Musicians and painters cast aside traditional forms and styles with the same creativity as did writers of this period. Some new ideas of musicians and painters originated before World War I, but did not take hold until the unsettled postwar years.

Music. One of the pioneers of a new direction in music was Igor Stravinsky. Born in Russia, he lived most of his life in western Europe and the United States. Stravinsky's ballet *The Rite of Spring* (1913) caused a major uproar at its first performance because it broke so completely with traditional music composition. This composition featured different instruments playing in different keys at the same time, creating a sound that many people found distressing.

Three Austrians, Arnold Schoenberg and his students Alban Berg and Anton von Webern, were even more revolutionary. They wrote what is called atonal music. In Schoenberg's atonal compositions, he abandoned the conventional eight-tone musical scale and instead used a twelve-tone scale. Schoenberg and his followers avoided such traditional forms as the symphony and the concerto. They wrote pieces for unusual collaborations of instruments, such as Webern's *Quartet for Violin, Clarinet, Tenor Saxophone, and Piano*. Their melodies were not developed in a traditional way, and their music sounded strange and unfamiliar to audiences.

Painting. Similar experimentation with forms and styles occurred in the field of painting. Artists of the early 1900s sought new ways to portray the world around them, and dramatically altered traditional representations of humanity and nature.

Pioneers of a new style of art were Spain's Pablo Picasso and the French artist Georges Braque, who worked in Paris. They created a new style called **cubism**, which emphasized geometric forms, shapes, and designs. Using shapes such as cones, cylinders, spheres, flat planes, and especially cubes, they showed the abstract structures of the objects they painted, not their surface appearances. In fact, Picasso and Braque often depicted objects from several different perspectives at the same time. Thus, for example, one might see half a face in profile and half from the front.

Picasso explained nontraditional depictions of reality in his artwork by saying that painting is "a mediator between this strange hostile world and us, a way of seizing the power by giving form to our terrors as well as our desires." Thus Picasso suggested that although he knew his work disturbed people, doing so was part of his purpose. He expressed the anxiety of the era in unsettling forms.

Other painters moved beyond traditional forms in various ways. Surrealistic painters attempted to symbolize the unconscious. Their works featured perfectly painted objects that did not seem to relate to one another. The Spanish surrealist Salvador Dali painted *The Persistence of Memory* (1931), which depicts a dreamlike landscape with what looks like liquid clocks draped over a tree branch and the edge of a shelf. Other artists, notably Russian Wassily Kandinsky and Dutch Piet Mondrian, painted purely abstract designs.

Writers, musicians, and painters of the post-World War I era broke dramatically with the attitudes and styles of the past. They created works reflecting apprehension and cynicism in their views of modern life in the late 1920s and the 1930s—views shared by many people.

Popular Culture

Novelists such as Franz Kafka and composers such as Arnold Schoenberg appealed only to a small audience. Many people found entertainment and escape in other new forms of entertainment.

Popular music. One favorite diversion of many people was listening to music on phonograph records or on the radio. More and more households had radios in the 1920s and 1930s, and music aimed at a mass audience filled the air waves. This was the dawn of the era of the "Big Bands." These "Big Bands" played dance music with catchy melodies written by composers such as Cole Porter and Hoagy Carmichael. In addition, the musical, a type of play featuring song and dance, became a major attraction in the theater. Irving Berlin and George Gershwin composed songs for a golden age of musical theater.

Gershwin and Berlin were also composers of jazz, an innovative popular music borrowed from African Americans. Jazz began in the southern United States in the late 1800s. Performed primarily by African American musicians, jazz developed especially in New Orleans, a city of many cultures. Using African as well as American music as inspiration, jazz emphasizes individual experimentation. One of its major forms, the blues, centers on themes of heartache and sadness, popular during the depressed 1930s.

Film. The chief entertainment for popular audiences of the 1920s and 1930s came from another new art form, the film, or motion picture. Invented around the year 1900, motion pictures swept through Europe and the United States. The first public showings occurred around 1910, and by the 1920s millions of moviegoers routinely waited in long lines to see their favorite films.

The Development of Radio

Up to the end of World War I, radio had been used mainly to send messages by Morse code. David Sarnoff, who became general manager of Radio Corporation of America (RCA), first had the idea of broadcasting music over the radio. RCA began manufacturing "radio music boxes" in 1920. Almost overnight, the radio became a wildly popular consumer item. In just two years, more than 2 million families owned radios.

As radios became popular, the number of broadcasting stations increased dramatically. The first commercial broadcasting station, KDKA in Pittsburgh, went on the air on November 2, 1920, to broadcast the results of the presidential election. Exactly two years later, 564 stations were operating. Soon networks of radio stations were formed: NBC in 1926, CBS in 1927.

Radio became an important source of information and entertainment. News events were broadcast almost as they happened. "Soap operas" (so named because they were often sponsored by soap companies) were popular with homemakers. Shows such as "The Lone Ranger" and "Superman" were aimed at children. In the evening, families listened to the situation comedy "Amos 'n' Andy," a show so popular that many movie theaters interrupted their film to turn on radios so that the audience could hear it. The radio had clearly become an important part of American life.

Films, too, reflected the feelings of the postwar era. Although slapstick comedies were a prevalent form in early movies, some also carried disturbing messages. The greatest film directors—D. W. Griffith in the United States and Sergei Eisenstein in the Soviet Union—made powerful films about human intolerance and cruelty. Most movies, however, offered viewers escape and entertainment.

Architecture

Architecture also underwent great change during the postwar years. New technical advances, such as the use of structural steel, made a remarkable transformation in this area possible.

American Louis Sullivan pioneered the new architecture. Not only did he help to develop the skyscraper, but he also developed a style called **functionalism**. The fundamental principle of functionalism is that a building should be designed for its specific use rather than according to any predetermined style.

Louis Sullivan's pupil Frank Lloyd Wright adopted Sullivan's ideas and added his own. One of Wright's major theories stressed that buildings should be appropriate to their environment. For example, Wright's prairie houses in the Midwest were low buildings with long horizontal lines. In the 1920s Wright built the Imperial Hotel in Tokyo. Adapting the hotel to its location, he floated the foundation on a cushion of mud instead of anchoring it rigidly to rock. Because of this adaptive construction, it was the only large structure in Tokyo to survive the severe earthquake of 1923.

European architects also developed a new style of architecture. Influenced by American architects Sullivan and Wright, a group of architects including the Frenchman Le Corbusier and the German Walter Gropius developed a functional architecture called the **international style**. This style made use of uninterrupted expanses of steel and glass.

The new art forms showed a radical change—a break as dramatic as the one between medieval and Renaissance styles. It was as if nothing—neither music, books, paintings, nor architecture—could be the same again after World War I.

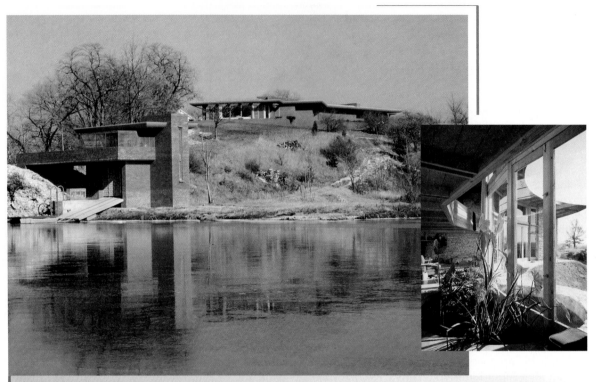

Between 1900 and 1910, Frank Lloyd Wright designed many prairie houses in the Midwest that blended with the flat landscape around them. Subsequent commissions included the Imperial Hotel in Tokyo and the Guggenheim Museum in New York City. Shown above are examples of exterior and interior views of Wright's prairie house design.

Section 1 Review

1. **Define** totalitarian regimes, surrealism, *The Waste Land*, cubism, functionalism, international style
2. **Identify** Thomas Mann, James Joyce, Ernest Hemingway, Igor Stravinsky, Pablo Picasso, Frank Lloyd Wright
3. **Analyzing Ideas** Describe the ways in which the arts and popular entertainment reflected an atmosphere of social uncertainty after World War I in Europe.
4. **Interpreting Ideas** The 1920s and 1930s witnessed much experimentation in art forms. Give an example of this experimentation in each of the following categories: (a) literature, (b) music, (c) painting, (d) film, and (e) architecture.
5. **Explaining Ideas** Describe the theories of Freud and Einstein related to the new scientific ideas of the postwar period.

Section 2

Postwar Prosperity Crumbles

Focus Questions

- How did social life change in the United States after World War I?
- What were the causes of the worldwide Great Depression that began in 1929?
- What were the effects of the Great Depression in Europe and the United States?
- What was the New Deal, and how was it a dramatic change for the government of the United States?

Like France and Great Britain, the United States had fought on the victorious Allied side in World War I. Unlike the Europeans, however, the Americans had fought in the war for less than a year. The Atlantic Ocean had separated the United States from the battle-fields, and no American land had been devastated. The United States emerged much stronger economically at the end of the war. By 1918 the economy had expanded tremendously, resulting in an **economic boom**, or sudden increase in prosperity.

Postwar Prosperity

The United States emerged from the war as an apparent successor to Great Britain in world leadership. American involvement in the war had been decisive in the Allied victory, and the United States had also played a strong role in the peace settlement.

The United States' financial status most dramati-cally indicated its potential leadership. The economy of Europe was badly weakened by the devastation of war, forcing Europeans to purchase many products from the United States. Profits for American busi-nesses resulted in a huge increase in overseas investment after 1914. Meanwhile, Europeans struggled to pay their debts to each other and to the United States after the war.

However, the refusal of the United States to join the League of Nations indicated that the United States did not want the responsibility of world leadership. Americans seemed to want to enjoy their newfound prosperity and avoid further entanglement in European affairs.

The Roaring Twenties

Historians have dubbed the decade of the 1920s the **Roaring Twenties** because of the booming economy that brought a fast pace of life and a sometimes frantic pursuit of pleasure to the era. Some have attributed that atmosphere to American exposure to European attitudes during World War I, or to a disillusioned rebel-lion against traditions that had failed. Other factors also contributed to social change.

During the 1920s many changes affected people's lives. Automobiles became a popular means of trans-portation. Commercial airlines began carrying mail (regular passenger service did not begin until the 1930s, and even then remained uncommon). Telephones linked millions of homes, and movies became a favorite form of entertainment. Jazz became popular, new fast dances like the Charleston gained acceptance, and movie stars became public idols. Charles Lindbergh gained immediate worldwide fame for his 1927 solo flight across the Atlantic Ocean, a feat that had never before been accomplished.

This era of enormous confidence also prompted a revolt against traditional morality and standards. Women gained more freedom as they won the right to vote and joined the work force in greater numbers than ever before. **Prohibition**—the Eighteenth Amendment—forbidding the manufacture, sale, and transportation of alcoholic beverages was widely evaded. Smuggling and bootlegging—the illegal manufacture and sale of liquor—made Prohibition ineffective, and the amendment was repealed in 1933.

The Economy

Although the United States prospered during this period, some economic flaws existed. For example, wages paid to laborers did not keep pace with inflation. In other words, not enough money ended up in the hands of consumers so that they could buy all the goods being produced. Instead, profits went either to stock-holders or toward reinvestment in new machinery and additional factories. Increased use of labor-saving machinery stimulated production but at the same time increased unemployment, as fewer employees were needed to produce more and more goods.

Agriculture suffered as well. During the war, European demand for grain had driven prices up, and many American farmers had taken out loans to buy modern machinery and cultivate new land. In the 1920s European demand fell, and world grain prices dropped. Farmers were forced to produce as much as they could to try to pay off their debts. Serious over-production was the result.

Another problem occurred because of **economic nationalism**. This is the policy a nation uses to improve its economic well-being by establishing protective tariffs and similar restrictions on the import and export of goods. In the 1920s many countries set up tariffs to protect their own expanding industries from foreign competition. However, the home markets of each country could not consume what was produced, and high tariffs made it difficult to market the surplus abroad.

High American tariffs made it hard for European countries to sell their goods in the United States. Because they could not sell goods to the United States, they could not acquire dollars to purchase goods from the United States, or to pay off their war debts. Banks and businesspeople in the United States willingly lent money to Europeans so that they could buy American goods. But this practice merely created more indebtedness.

Speculation, Panic, and Crash

Throughout the 1920s millions of Americans made **market speculations**, or risky investments, in the stock market, hoping for quick, high profits. The stock market is the organization through which stock certificates are bought and sold. A company issues shares of stock to raise capital for its business. Investors buy shares to earn income from the company's earnings called dividends, or to resell the shares for profit if their value rises. During the 1920s prices of stocks sold on the New York Stock Exchange soared, and many investors did make large profits. Everyone expected stock prices to rise indefinitely.

Trouble loomed, however, with the growing practice of buying **on margin**. Investors borrowed money to buy stock using only the value of the stock or its expected profit as security. They often put down as little as 10 percent of the full price. When the stock's value rose, the stock could be sold at the higher value, and profit made to cover the cost. If the value of the stock fell, however, the investor had no means to repay the original amount borrowed, and the lender had no way to recover the money.

On October 29, 1929, panic swept investors in the New York Stock Exchange. Stock prices sank to an all-time low when more than 16 million shares of stock were suddenly dumped on the market. With prices falling, no one would buy. As a result, most of the stocks on the exchange became virtually worthless. Vast fortunes vanished. Banks called in loans, which could not be repaid, and thousands of banks and their customers—businesses, factories, farms, mining companies, and individuals—went bankrupt.

The Great Depression

The collapse of the New York Stock Exchange marked the beginning of a worldwide depression called the **Great Depression**. Some of the effects of this economic crisis included falling wages and prices, a slowdown of business activity, and a high rate of unemployment. Many of the most reliable European banks closed their doors. By 1932 more than 30 million workers in countries throughout the industrialized world could not find jobs. Germany stopped paying reparations, and the Allied nations ceased payments of war debts to the United States.

Strangely, poverty during the Depression occurred in the midst of abundant productivity. Prices fell to very low levels, but goods could not be sold because people simply did not have the money to buy them. Some countries tried to force prices to rise by

What If?

The Great Depression
What if the crash of 1929 had not occurred? Would there have been a Great Depression? Explain.

destroying agricultural surpluses—Brazil burned excess coffee for a decade. The world economy sank. By 1932, the total value of international trade had fallen by more than half.

Responses to the Great Depression

The United States responded to the Great Depression by continuing its policy of economic nationalism. It raised tariffs even higher and cut off American loans to Europe. Germany and Austria had wanted to establish a customs union to aid their economies. However, several European nations opposed the project, and the World Court banned it. In many cases, it appeared, the immediate response to the Great Depression made recovery more difficult.

In 1933 a world economic conference met in London, but it failed to promote greater financial cooperation among the industrial nations. Most of these countries had already decided upon economic nationalism to protect themselves in the Great Depression.

Great Britain tried to induce full employment and stimulate production by granting low-interest loans to its industries. In addition to raising its tariffs against foreign goods in 1931, Great Britain formed a system for economic cooperation within its empire. In 1932 at a conference in Ottawa, Canada, Great Britain devised a system of imperial preference. Through this system the dominions and possessions within the British Empire agreed to levy low tariffs on one another's products. In a period of international economic uncertainty, they were attempting to become economically self-sufficient.

France, less industrialized than Great Britain, did not suffer as badly during the Great Depression. However, French trade declined, unemployment increased, and industrial production dropped sharply. The uncertainty of the Depression years caused greater political instability in France than troubles following the war had created. In 1933 alone there were three changes of government.

Elsewhere in the world, the Great Depression caused unrest and violence. In Germany it helped destroy the Weimar Republic established at the end of the war. The representative governments that did survive the severe shock of the Great Depression had strong democratic traditions.

The New Deal

The United States was behind most other industrial nations in creating social legislation. Unemployment insurance and government relief programs did not exist. As a result, when the Great Depression hit, American workers had to rely on their savings, if any, and on charity provided by private organizations. People stood in breadlines in America to receive a bowl of soup or a plate of stew. Some earned money by selling apples in the streets.

Under President Herbert Hoover, the federal government tried to remedy these severe conditions, but the measures adopted were not extensive. Hoover believed that prosperity was "just around the corner." Americans in great numbers disagreed with Hoover, and elected a new president, Franklin D. Roosevelt, who took office in 1933.

Roosevelt immediately embarked upon a program of relief and reform called the New Deal. Under the provisions of the New Deal program, the government granted money to each state for food, shelter, and clothing for the needy. The government also began a program of public works to provide employment through the construction of various public buildings, roads, and other projects.

Following Roosevelt's emergency relief program, Congress enacted sweeping reform of the economic system. Banks and stock exchanges were placed under stricter regulation. The **Social Security Act** of 1935 provided for unemployment and old-age benefits. A 40-hour workweek and minimum wage levels were established. The federal government guaranteed workers the long fought-for right to form unions.

The federal government also tried to relieve the desperate situation of farmers by paying them to take land out of production and to plant crops that would revitalize the soil. Later the government adopted a program of buying surplus farm crops to prevent the prices of farm goods from plunging.

Another federal program of far-reaching economic and social significance established the **Tennessee Valley Authority**, or TVA, in the valley of the Tennessee River and its tributaries. The TVA built a series of multipurpose dams in this area to generate cheap electricity, help prevent floods and soil erosion, and improve navigation along the river. The project proved remarkably successful.

Occupied primarily with domestic problems, the administration made some effort to revive world trade.

In this scene from the Great Depression, women and children receive food from the New Hope Mission in New York City.

During his nearly four full terms as president of the United States, Franklin Roosevelt developed many government agencies to provide farmers and the unemployed with financial assistance.

Specific efforts were made by the Roosevelt administration to revive trade in Latin America. A series of treaties and laws called the Good Neighbor policy both helped Western economies and at the same time enhanced the image of the United States. However, the United States also passed the **Johnson Act** of 1934, which prohibited loans, even private ones, to countries that had not paid their war debts. Many European nations could not pay their debts, and this act of economic nationalism further hurt foreign trade and European economies.

Under the New Deal, the United States government became more deeply involved than ever before in the welfare of its own citizens. The government attempted in many ways to restore prosperity. However, the impact of the Great Depression was too great to be cured completely by programs, even those as ambitious as the New Deal. Only when the United States mobilized its industrial sector for war did the Great Depression end.

Section 2 Review

1. **Define** economic boom, Roaring Twenties, Prohibition, economic nationalism, market speculations, on margin, Great Depression, Social Security Act, Tennessee Valley Authority, Johnson Act
2. **Identify** Herbert Hoover
3. **Evaluating Ideas** What new inventions and art forms became popular in the 1920s, and how did they change American society?
4. **Organizing Ideas** What conditions helped to bring about the Great Depression?
5. **Summarizing Ideas** (a) How did the Great Depression and attempts to respond to it affect the United States? (b) How did the Great Depression affect Europe?
6. **Explaining Ideas** (a) How was the New Deal supposed to end the Great Depression? (b) Was it successful? Give reasons for your answer.

Section 3

Political Tensions After World War I

Focus Questions

- What were conditions like in France after World War I?
- Why were times difficult in Great Britain after World War I?
- How did the countries created from the former Austria-Hungary fare in postwar Europe?

The events of the postwar years strained older and more experienced European democracies such as France and Great Britain. The economies of these nations had been harmed by the war, and recovery was made difficult by debt and the lack of good markets in the weakened nations. Unemployment rose because production had expanded to fill wartime needs, and now an overabundance existed.

Many Europeans believed that governments needed to take a more active role in economic matters. Before World War I, many people had believed that governments should not interfere in business matters.

However, wartime needs had led several nations to adopt a **planned economy**—an economy in which government directs the use of national resources and regulates the economy to achieve both goals and stability. As the system had worked in wartime, why not use it to solve peacetime economic problems?

In some European nations, such as Poland and Austria, different problems arose. These countries set up republics after World War I. Their societies lacked experienced leaders, as well as a history of democratic institutions solving problems. When problems arose, such as the crisis of the Great Depression, political and social unrest rose rapidly, and serious signs of governmental weakness appeared.

France's Postwar Difficulties

During the four years of World War I, northern France had been a major battleground. At war's end, farmland and even entire cities lay in ruins, and trenches and shell holes scarred the land. The most modern parts of France's agriculture and industry had been destroyed. Most tragic of all, a high percentage of the young men of France had been killed.

Thus France emerged from World War I victorious but unstable. It still owed money that it had borrowed from its citizens and from the United States during and after the war. Its industry was weak and production had declined. Inflation also took its toll. The burden of higher prices fell mostly on industrial workers and the lower middle class—those least able to pay.

The expenses of the French government soared for several reasons. The government embarked on a massive reconstruction of war-damaged areas. Inflation soared and France still had its heavy debt, as well as interest on that debt, for war material. But most important, perhaps, it had to pay for military security.

The Maginot Line. Twice in less than 50 years, Germany had invaded France. To prevent invasion from happening again, France rebuilt its army. It also constructed a series of steel and concrete fortifications called the **Maginot** (MA·zhuh·noh) **Line**. Named after its planner, this extensive defense system stretched nearly 200 miles (320 kilometers) along the borders of Germany and Luxembourg.

Construction of the Maginot Line cost enormous sums of money. Haunted by the experience of World War I, the French planned to make their defenses so strong that the country could never again be invaded overland from the east.

International affairs. In the beginning of 1923, struggling Germany informed the Allies that it could not continue to pay war reparations on schedule. Despite British objections, France and Belgium marched troops into Germany's coal- and iron-rich Ruhr Valley in January 1923. France intended to force payment, even seizing industry, until it collected the money Germany owed. German workers resisted by halting production, and the French withdrew after a renegotiated payment schedule was agreed upon.

By 1925 the political situation in Europe seemed to be improving. In that year, representatives from Great Britain, France, Germany, Belgium, Italy, Czechoslovakia, and Poland met at Locarno, Switzerland. There they signed a number of treaties known together as the **Locarno Pact**. Delegates to the conference pledged that their countries would peacefully settle all future disputes, guaranteed the existing Franco-German boundaries, and negotiated outstanding issues. In addition, France signed mutual assistance treaties with Poland and Czechoslovakia.

However, France's protective alliances began to weaken. By the mid-1930s Belgium canceled its defensive alliance with France and declared itself neutral in any future war. France formed a shaky alliance with its prewar ally Russia, now under a Communist government. Wartime ally Italy, now under the rule of a militaristic dictatorship, resumed its old opposition to France. In keeping with its aim of encircling Germany, France developed postwar alliances with Yugoslavia and Romania as well as the alliances already made with Poland and Czechoslovakia. However, these nations, although they shared France's mistrust of Germany, were relatively weak allies.

Political unrest. In early 1934 a scandal occurred in the French government that touched off huge riots in Paris. Anti-parliamentary rioters demanded an end to the republican form of government. Some advocated fascist regimes that they felt would protect the nation and combat instability.

Trade unions responded to the threat from the right-wing conservatives by calling a **general strike**—a refusal by laborers in various industries to work until demands are met. Shortly thereafter, parties of the left-wing organized a coalition government called the **Popular Front**. Its leader, Léon Blum, a socialist, became premier of France in 1936. United for the moment against the threat of a coup d'état (seizure of power by force), Blum's government carried out reforms.

The Popular Front first persuaded leaders of industry to grant pay increases to end the strike. The government then established a 40-hour workweek and granted workers the right to paid vacations. It also set up a system for the arbitration of labor disputes. The Bank of France came under government control and the armaments industry was partially **nationalized**— put under government control or ownership.

Prices, however, continued to rise to such levels that increased wages did little to help. Industrialists refused to cooperate. Continuing hostility from the right wing, who believed "Better Hitler than Blum," and divisions in his own Popular Front ended Blum's ministry after only one year. Through his leadership in this brief period, however, France's government enacted important reforms.

After the fall of the Popular Front, French workers suffered severe setbacks. Most of the pro-labor reforms of Blum's ministry were canceled, and the working class came to oppose the government harshly. Many political and social groups, some with extreme approaches, developed. Traditional French systems of government and society were questioned.

France remained a democracy, but bitter divisions existed among the people. France also feared German military power, which began recovering strength at an alarming rate.

Great Britain After World War I

Like France, Great Britain faced grave economic difficulties after World War I. Great Britain had become a debtor nation, and the capital it had used to finance industrial expansion was gone.

British industry and trade suffered. As in other countries, disarmament had left many factory workers unemployed. Coal, long a mainstay of British industry, was being surpassed by other forms of power. The United States and Japan had taken many of Great Britain's world markets during the war. After the war Britain's outdated factories and machinery made competition with newer American or Japanese technology difficult. In addition, the high tariffs of economic nationalism damaged British trade because Great Britain needed to sell abroad in order to pay for imports of food and raw materials.

Labor troubles. By 1921, nearly a quarter of Great Britain's work force was unemployed. This high unemployment rate meant labor unrest. Labor unions fought to maintain the high wages and full employment rate of the war years, while industrialists fought to resist the unions' demands. Meanwhile, government had to pay unemployment benefits.

World War I brought death and destruction to millions of people across the world. Here a café in postwar Paris bustles as the French try to regain a sense of normalcy in their lives.

In the Easter Rising, a Citizen Army parades outside Liberty Hall.

In 1926 coal miners called a strike. Workers in iron and steel, transportation, building, and printing industries left their jobs as well, creating one of the largest general strikes in British history. The general strike ended after nine days, and the miners returned to work months later in defeat. Later the government passed legislation that controlled unions and outlawed general strikes.

A spokesman for workers was Ramsay MacDonald, leader of the Labour Party. Although the Labour Party grew stronger, it lacked a majority in the House of Commons. Therefore, MacDonald formed a coalition with the Liberal Party, which had declined in strength because it could not attract working-class members. Coalition government determined British policy for all of the 1930s, with MacDonald, Stanley Baldwin, and then Neville Chamberlain at its head. Through strict government economy, protectionist policies, and help for the construction industry, the British economy slowly recovered. Thus Great Britain avoided the deep social unrest that toppled democratic governments elsewhere in Europe.

Ireland. In the 1920s Great Britain faced more problems in a country it had ruled for centuries. During the 1800s the British government and Irish nationalists struggled over the issue of home rule for

Ireland. The matter of limited self-government was unresolved by 1914, and most Irish people still yearned for complete independence.

During World War I, Irish nationalists revolted in the **Easter Rising** on Easter Monday, April 24, 1916. The British harshly suppressed the rebellion and executed its leaders. Fighting broke out again in 1918. For years the Irish Republican Army and British troops were engaged in a series of violent and bitter struggles.

The British lost what support of the Irish people it had, and with Ireland virtually ungovernable, Great Britain was pressed for settlement. A treaty divided Ireland in 1922, with Catholic southern Ireland becoming the Irish Free State, a self-governing dominion with loose ties to Great Britain. Six northern counties with a Protestant majority chose to remain in the United Kingdom, with representatives in British Parliament, as Northern Ireland.

Many Irish nationalists refused to accept the arrangement, and civil war raged again in 1922. Eventually, Irish nationalists came to power politically. In 1937 the Irish Free State adopted a new constitution and the name Eire (AR·uh). Éamon De Valera (dev·uh·LER·uh) was elected its first prime minister. In 1949 Eire became completely independent, calling itself the Republic of Ireland.

Many of the issues that divided the island for centuries trouble it still. Religious and political factions in Northern Ireland and the Republic of Ireland remain hostile to each other, and the relations between Great Britain and Ireland are still troubled.

Eastern Europe

As western European powers struggled politically and economically to recover in the aftermath of World War I, new nations in eastern Europe struggled to form governments and identities. Instability in eastern Europe had led to the outbreak of World War I, and after the Treaty of Versailles, boundaries had been redrawn. The cultural tensions that sparked the first world war had not disappeared, however. These problems resurfaced in the political situations that existed in eastern European nations, both internally and externally.

As nations with little democratic experience struggled to maintain governments, economic problems added to their difficulties. The breakup of the Russian and Austro-Hungarian empires disrupted old patterns of trade. With the Great Depression devastating economies throughout the industrialized world, policies of economic nationalism offered little prospect of help to the countries of eastern Europe.

Finland, Czechoslovakia, and the Baltic countries of Latvia, Estonia, and Lithuania managed to sustain democratic regimes, but few other nations in eastern Europe succeeded in doing so. Three examples help illustrate what happened.

Austria. The Austria created after the war was a small poverty-stricken nation. Many Austrians would have preferred *Anschluss* (union) with Germany, but peace treaties forbade it. Austria's economic weakness and a continuing struggle between urban socialists and rural conservatives weakened the attempt at democracy. A third of the country's population lived in Vienna, once the capital of a large empire, and they contended for control against the rest of the country, who saw the nation's needs differently. The result was paralysis. Factions set up private armies in the streets, and the desire for order made authoritarian rule more appealing. The country became progressively less democratic.

Hungary. Hungary was declared a republic in November 1918. In March 1919, Béla Kun, a Hungarian Communist who had participated in the Russian Revolution, replaced a weak republic and tried to establish a system modeled on Russia's new government. He succeeded in ousting most of the Romanian troops that were then occupying Hungary, but he also nationalized the land, which antagonized the people. The distribution of food failed. Russia did not help as promised, Kun's government fell, and Romanians entered Budapest in August that same year.

By 1920 the Allies had persuaded Romania to withdraw and Hungarian Admiral Miklós Horthy, a representative of the military class, ruled. Under Admiral Horthy's reactionary rule, postwar reconstruction was impossible. Parts of Hungary's prewar territory had been given to Austria, Romania, Poland, and Italy, and new boundaries cut off factories from supplies and markets. As the wheat market collapsed and the Great Depression deepened, Hungary sought help first from the League of Nations, then Italy and Germany. Thus the nation found itself with less and less control of its destiny.

Poland. The new Polish democratic constitution of 1921 was closely modeled on that of France's Third Republic (see Chapter 8). However, bitter opposition from many groups prevented the new government from operating effectively. High German tariffs crippled the Polish economy, and the country became more and more unstable. In 1926 Marshal Józef Pilsudski (peel·soot·skee) installed a military dictatorship. Economically distressed and located between Germany and Russia, democracy in Poland had little chance.

Section 3 Review

1. **Define** planned economy, Maginot Line, Locarno Pact, general strike, Popular Front, nationalized, Easter Rising

2. **Identify** Ramsay MacDonald, Éamon De Valera, Józef Pilsudski

3. **Organizing Ideas** What internal problems did France experience during the period after World War I?

4. **Analyzing Ideas** In many European countries democracy was replaced by authoritarian rule in the years following World War I. Great Britain, however, avoided this fate. Explain why this was possible.

5. **Explaining Ideas** Why were the eastern European countries less able than their western counterparts to deal with the problems resulting from the Great Depression?

Fascist Dictatorships in Italy and Germany

Focus Questions

- **What common conditions did totalitarian regimes in Europe seek to address?**
- **What were the characteristics of Mussolini's rise to power?**
- **How did provisions of the Treaty of Versailles lead to Hitler's rise to power?**

As it did elsewhere, the war and its aftermath took their toll in Italy and Germany. Heavy loss of life, a crushing burden of debt, high unemployment, and runaway inflation plagued these countries. In Italy labor troubles resulted in violent strikes. The Italian government, a constitutional monarchy, seemed unable to respond effectively to these problems.

The Rise of Fascism in Italy

One person who did offer a clear response was Benito Mussolini. The son of a blacksmith, he had been a socialist as a young man and had edited a socialist newspaper. His writing had brought him several terms in jail and a period in exile. During World War I his views changed. Mussolini became an extreme nationalist, and the Italian Socialist Party expelled him. After Italy joined the Allies, he enlisted in the army and was wounded in battle.

When Mussolini returned from the war, he began to organize his own political party. He called it the Fascist Party and called its doctrine **fascism** (FASH·iz·uhm). The words *fascist* and *fascism* come from the Latin word *fasces*. In ancient Rome a *fasces* was a bundle of rods bound tightly around an ax, symbolizing governmental authority. Mussolini adopted this symbol, referring to a *Fasci di Combattimento*, fighters bound as tightly as the rods around the ax. Thus his nationalist movement gained a name.

In his book *Delivered from Evil*, Robert Leckie describes Benito Mussolini's physical features and the imposing personality that brought him and the Fascist Party to power in Italy in the 1920s:

❝At . . . his full height . . . [he was] . . . remarkable for his commanding head and his broad low brow, piercing black eyes, wide mouth and jutting square jaw. Because of his great head, he gave the impression of physical strength. Yet, if he were to remove his outer garments, it would be seen that his shoulders were thin, his arching chest a pouting pigeon's breast and his arms and legs spindly. However, like Napoleon, he could strike fear into men twice his size with a direct glance from those astonishing eyes.**❞**

Fascism, like communism, relies on dictatorial rule and a totalitarian regime, in which the state maintains rigid control of the people through force and censorship. All authority belongs to the state, with individual rights subordinate to it. However, important differences exist between communism and fascism. Communism seeks a socialist economy and international revolution. It appeals to workers and promises a classless society. Fascism, on the other hand, is extremely nationalistic, and appeals to the middle class while promising to preserve existing social classes. Fascism defends ownership of private property. Each system violently opposes the other.

Mussolini Gains Power

Mussolini found his first followers among demobilized soldiers and discontented nationalists. Gradually, however, the Fascists attracted professionals, wealthy landowners, and businesspeople, especially large manufacturers who were interested in blocking communist gains among workers. These new supporters provided financial assistance to the Fascists. Fascists also developed strong support among the lower middle classes, who had been severely hurt by inflation, and among the unemployed.

Recognizing the appeal of anticommunism, Mussolini emphasized it in his program. He promised to prevent a proletarian revolution. Fascism began to stand for the protection of private property and the middle class. At the same time, he proposed a collaboration between labor and management to restore and protect the economy. He also stressed national prestige, pledging that Italy would return to the military glories of the Roman Empire.

The Fascists began a violent campaign against opponents, especially socialists and communists. Rowdy groups broke up strikes and political meetings and drove properly elected socialist officials from office. Fascists became known as the Black Shirts for the shirt they wore as a uniform.

In October 1922 Black Shirt groups from all over Italy converged on Rome, claiming they were coming to defend Italy against a communist revolution.

Liberal members of the Italian parliament insisted that the king declare martial law. When he refused, the cabinet resigned. Conservative advisers then persuaded the king to appoint Mussolini premier and to ask him to head a coalition government.

Mussolini had often criticized democracy as a weak and ineffective form of government. Once in office, he began to destroy democracy in Italy and set up a dictatorship. He appointed Fascists to all official positions both in the central government and in the provinces. He pushed through parliament a new election law providing that the party receiving the most votes would automatically gain two thirds of the seats in the Chamber of Deputies, the lower house of parliament. The Fascists won the election in 1924, and in 1925, Mussolini was made "head of the government," accountable to no one. He took the title *il Duce* (DOO·chay), Italian for "the leader."

Italy as a Police State

Now all of the outward signs of a dictatorship appeared. Opposition parties were disbanded. The government suspended freedom of speech, freedom of the press, freedom of assembly, and trial by jury. Labor unions came under government control, and strikes were outlawed. Uniformed and secret police spied on everyone.

Mussolini became commander in chief of the army, navy, and air force and head of the police. Although he allowed the king to reign as a figurehead, real power lay in the hands of the Grand Council of the Fascist Party. Mussolini headed the Council.

The Corporatist State

Mussolini argued that in a modern industrial society, representation according to geographic location was outdated. Instead, he introduced a new and complicated system of government called corporatism in which representation was according to profession or occupation. The country's major economic activities, such as agriculture, transportation, manufacturing, and commerce, were formed into syndicates that resembled corporations. Thus Italy became known as a **corporatist state**.

By the 1930s, Italy had 22 of these "corporations." In each corporation representatives of government, management, and labor met to establish wages and prices and to agree upon working conditions. Private property remained in the hands of its owners, and profits were allowed. Labor unions and capitalists alike had to submit to the will of Mussolini's government. All parts of society had to cooperate with one another for the goals of the state.

In addition to reshaping the government, Mussolini strengthened the army and navy and increased armaments. These two additional changes

Mussolini's "Sons of the Wolf"

in Italy had a double purpose: to reduce unemployment and to increase military strength. Thus a new form of linkage between public and private sectors appeared in Italian government. The Fascist dictator, Mussolini, sat at the top of the entire system.

The Weimar Republic

As in Italy, difficulties in Germany gave rise to political change after World War I. In November 1918 Germany was declared a republic. The following year, an assembly met in the city of Weimar (VY·mahr) and drafted a constitution that made Germany a federal republic, known as the Weimar Republic.

Germany's new government had a president and a two-house parliament elected by universal suffrage. The parliament included the Reichsrat (RYKS·raht) and the Reichstag. The president appointed the chancellor, Germany's prime minister.

The Weimar Republic was not popular with the German people. The republic had been born in the desire to end the war and to avoid a revolution in Germany as had occurred in Russia. Many Germans opposed republican government, and because Weimar representatives signed the humiliating Versailles Treaty, the German people came to see the Weimar Republic as a traitorous government.

Many of the difficulties of the Weimar Republic reflected the economic, social, and political problems that faced all of Europe after the war. Unemployment was high and inflation soared, ruining German currency. In 1923 it took more than 1 trillion marks to equal 25 cents, and money devalued so rapidly printers quit putting numbers on bills.

Within its first year, two attempted revolutions threatened the Weimar Republic. In Berlin, a right-wing group tried to overthrow the republic and briefly controlled the city. The attempted overthrow in Berlin was defeated by a general strike. Socialist and communist workers paralyzed Berlin and made it impossible for the right-wing rebels to set up their own government. In 1923, a Communist government took over Munich, the capital of the state of Bavaria, and attempted to withdraw from the federal union. The revolt was crushed by army units and private right-wing armies that began a reign of right-wing terror of their own. Though the rebellions failed, they demonstrated the extreme weakness of the Weimar Republic.

The Nazis and Hitler

One of the many political parties that formed in Germany after World War I was the German Workers'

Inflation soared in Germany during the early 1920s. The value of the mark fell so low that people could get more value out of the marks by baling and selling them by weight as waste paper than they could by using marks as currency.

Party. In 1920 the German Workers' Party, attempting to broaden its appeal, changed its name to the National Socialist German Workers' Party, or Nazi Party. The party did not represent the working class, as its name might indicate. The Nazi Party was extremely nationalistic and violently anticommunist. Promising to protect Germany from communism, the party eventually attracted the support of wealthy business leaders and landowners in Germany.

One of the first Nazi recruits, an ex-soldier named Adolf Hitler, was born in Austria in 1889. He was the son of a minor government official. As a young man, Hitler had gone to Vienna, where he failed as an artist and was therefore forced to work at various odd jobs. It was there in Vienna, where Jews contributed to the city's rich cultural life and also had risen to respected positions, that Hitler became resentful of the Jews and violently anti-Semitic.

Hitler served in the German army in World War I and later moved to the city of Munich in the state of Bavaria, where he joined the German Workers Party. Head of the Nazis by 1921, he took part in the uprising in Munich in 1923. The uprising failed, and Hitler was sentenced to prison. While there, he wrote **Mein Kampf** (*My Struggle*), a rambling book that expressed the spirit of the Nazi movement. In

Hitler (left) and Mussolini (right) review German troops in Berlin on one of Mussolini's many state visits to Germany.

Mein Kampf, Hitler left no doubt about his goals for the German nation. He wrote:

❝If the National Socialist [Nazi] movement really wants to be consecrated [honored] by history with a great mission for our nation . . . it must find the courage to gather our people and their strength for an advance along the road that will lead this people from its present restricted living space to new land and soil.❞

Hitler possessed hypnotic talent as an orator, and after his release from prison, he took advantage of radio to spread his message. In the confused situation of the postwar years, his emotional speeches attracted enthusiastic listeners. The frustration, bitterness, and patriotism Hitler expressed reflected the feelings of many Germans who felt humiliated by the Treaty of Versailles. The unfair war reparations and loss of territory made some eager to follow a leader that might restore Germany's lost glory.

Hitler's program found appeal in Germany. Facing economic and social disaster, Germans responded to the charismatic speaker, and Nazi popularity rose in each election. Hitler promised to repeal the Versailles Treaty, especially the "war-guilt" clause. He said that he would restore Germany to equality in armaments and regain all its lost territory and colonies to build a "Greater Germany." Like Mussolini, he promised protection against communism.

To these promises Hitler added his garbled racial doctrine. According to this doctrine, the Germans, as "Aryans" (a misapplied use of the word), were a "master race." All other races were inferior. As Hitler's power increased, his personal traits of intolerance, hatred, and contempt for non-Germanic people became the policies of the government.

Hitler's Rise to Power

The Nazis had few followers* until the Great Depression. In the election of 1930, however, many middle-class voters turned to the Nazi Party. These voters had experienced economic hardships and had lost their savings because of inflation. In addition, many of them feared a Communist revolution. Two years later the Nazi Party won 230 seats in the Reichstag. Although their party was the largest single party there, the Nazis still did not have enough votes to form a government.

In January 1933, when it appeared that no other party could successfully form a government, the president of the republic, Paul von Hindenburg, appointed Hitler as chancellor.

Because the Nazis still lacked a majority, Hitler used the Nazis' private army—the storm troopers, or Brown Shirts—to intimidate the Reichstag. When someone set fire to the Reichstag building in February 1933, Hitler was granted emergency powers to deal with this alleged Communist revolt. Hitler expertly used these powers to make himself a dictator.

The Nazi Program in Action

Once in power, Hitler, who regarded Mussolini's totalitarian state to be a natural ally, took the title *der Führer* (FYOOR·ur), German for "the leader." Quickly turning Germany into a police state, Hitler banned opposition parties, labor unions, and opposition newspapers. To enforce these policies, Hitler gave the Gestapo, a secret-police force, wide-ranging powers. Former allies in the march to power were executed.

Liberals, socialists, and Communists often ended up dead or in large prisons that were called concentration camps. Members of the so-called inferior races increasingly suffered severe persecutions. Jews became particular targets of the Nazi attacks. They were deprived of their civil rights, publicly humiliated, and murdered by storm troopers. In some places the Nazis forced the Jews to live in segregated neighborhoods called ghettos.

---

*In 1925 the growing Nazi Party had 25,000 members; four years later it had 180,000 members.

Building History Study Skills

READ
WRITE
INTERPRET
CONNECT
THINK

Thinking About History: Analyzing Documents

Documents are basic sources for historians. They are used to answer a question, to develop a theory, or to support a view of a historical event. Documents can be any information written on a particular subject and may consist of essays, books, charts, and graphs, to name a few. Reading and analyzing documents helps you to formulate your own view of events based on the evidence and your analysis. Using documents helps you to integrate information and form conclusions.

How to Analyze Documents
To analyze documents, follow these steps.
1. Explain the question, theory, or point of view being researched in the documents.
2. Classify the documents. Determine whether they deal with political, economic, or social issues.
3. Identify the source of the documents.
4. Determine the validity and bias of the documents being analyzed.
5. Connect the documents to each other.
6. Formulate a thesis statement based on the connection found in the documents.

Developing the Skill
The following documents deal with Hitler's rise to power in Germany. The question the documents focus on is "How did Hitler destroy parliamentary democracy in Germany?"

The Election Results

	November 1932	March 1933
National Socialists	196	233
Nationalists	51	53
People's Party & Bavarian Peoples Party	31	21
Catholic Center	70	73
Socialists	121	120
Communists	100	81

❝The following is decreed as a defensive measure against Communist acts of violence, endangering the state: Sections 114, 115, 117, 118, 123, 124, and 153 of the Constitution of the German Reich are suspended until further notice. Thus, restrictions on personal liberty, on the right of free expression of opinion, including freedom of the press, on the right of assembly . . . association, . . . warrants for house-searches, . . . are also permissible beyond the legal limits otherwise prescribed.❞

The documents should be classified as political because the subject of each is government. The source of the documents is Tony Edwards' *History Broadsheets, Hitler & Germany 1919–1939*. The documents are unbiased because they merely state facts.

The chart of the election results tells us that there was a multiparty system in Germany's Weimar Republic after World War I. The parties are listed from extreme right-wing National Socialists (Nazis) to extreme left-wing Communists. In order to rule, a party had to have most of the seats, or a majority, in the Reichstag. No party was ever strong enough to have a majority without combining their votes with those of at least one other party. As the chart indicates, the Nazis won the most seats in the Reichstag in the election of 1932, but did not have a majority. Their major competitors were the Communists and the Socialists at the other end of the political spectrum. However, following the election of 1933 the Nationalists formed a coalition with the Nazis, giving them a majority in the Reichstag.

The second document helps explain how the Nazis were able to consolidate their power by destroying the opposition. The Emergency Decree was based on the burning of the Reichstag, which the Nazis unjustly blamed on the Communists. This decree played on the fear of disorder and revolution that people believed was caused by the Communists. The Emergency Decree also put restrictions on the Communists, who were the Nazis' biggest rivals and to whom they had lost seats in the Reichstag in the election of 1933.

Practicing the Skill
Read the excerpt from *Mein Kampf* on page 402. What bias does the document show? What can you learn about Hitler's plans for Germany by studying the document?

To apply this skill, see Applying History Study Skills on page 409.

Nazis and German students here carry books and pamphlets to be burned during a demonstration against un-Germanic literature.

Some Jews were forced to wear yellow Stars of David, the six-pointed star that is a symbol of Judaism, on their clothing. Hitler later carried this policy to monstrous extremes resulting in the extermination of millions of Jews. (See Chapter 14.)

Like Mussolini, Hitler promised to restore the glories of Germany's past and to bring Germany to full economic recovery. He called his regime the **Third Reich** and promised the Germans that it would last 1,000 years. *Reich* is the German word for "empire." (The first empire in Germany had been the Holy Roman Empire, and the second was the German Empire of the Hohenzollerns.)

Hitler claimed that German racial superiority justified taking land from the Slavs of eastern Europe in order to provide living space for Germany's expanding population. Such expansion would necessitate a large, well-equipped army. Germany began secretly rearming in the early 1930s, and then in 1935 openly defied the terms of the Versailles Treaty.

According to the Versailles Treaty, the Rhineland was to be left unfortified. However, in the spring of 1936, Hitler ordered troops into the area. Due to the fact that France underestimated Hitler's force and

Great Britain felt that the event was not worth going to war, neither country acted.

Encouraged by his easy success in the Rhineland, Hitler sought alliance with Mussolini, isolated from the rest of Europe because of his invasion of Abyssinia. In the fall of 1936, the two dictators signed a treaty forming the **Rome-Berlin Axis**.

Section 4 Review

1. **Define** fascism, corporatist state, *Mein Kampf*, Third Reich, Rome-Berlin Axis
2. **Identify** Black Shirts, *il Duce*, storm troopers, *der Führer*, Gestapo
3. **Summarizing Ideas** Describe the common conditions that Italian and German forms of fascism sought to address.
4. **Understanding Ideas** How did Mussolini gain and maintain power?
5. **Analyzing Ideas** "The Treaty of Versailles created the atmosphere that made nazism possible." Do you agree or disagree? Give reasons for your answer.

Dictatorship in the Soviet Union

Focus Questions

- How did Lenin deal with the grave problems that were facing the Soviet Union following the successful revolution?
- What was collectivization, and how was it instituted under Lenin and Stalin?
- How did Stalin bring the Soviet Union to a state of totalitarianism?

As soon as the Communists seized power in 1917, they reorganized Russia's government. They sought a settlement of the war. They moved the capital from Petrograd to Moscow, and they tried to resolve internal disagreements. Lenin became the head of the cabinet, the Council of People's Commissars. The Congress of Soviets was established, a national legislative body made up of more than 1,000 representatives. Real power, however, rested with the People's Commissars.

Russia Under Lenin

In 1922 the Communist leaders gave Russia a new name, the **Union of Soviet Socialist Republics** (USSR). This change indicated that power had been transferred to the soviets, or revolutionary councils. After 1922 the people of Russia became known as the Soviet people.

Politically the country was divided into separate republics joined in a federal union. Eventually the USSR was composed of 15 of these republics.

Between 1918 and 1921, Soviet leaders had followed a policy known as War Communism. They nationalized Russian industries. However, social and economic measures were not based on a long-range plan. Communist leaders had to develop a program to build their new society in Russia.

Faced with economic collapse in 1921, Lenin announced the New Economic Policy (NEP) that allowed some free enterprise. The NEP permitted individuals to buy, sell, and trade farm products. The major industries—oil, mining, steel, and the railroads—remained under government ownership and management. Smaller businesses and home industries could be privately owned and operated for profit. A new class of small businessmen, the Nepmen, arose, and the economy made gains.

Soviet agriculture remained a problem. The government tried to persuade the peasants to form **collective farms**—land pooled into large farms on which people could work together as a group. During the revolution farmlands had been seized from the wealthy landlords and divided among the peasants. On a collective farm, peasants could share the scarce modern farm machinery. The policy eventually became mandatory.

A Power Struggle

When Lenin died in 1924, a power struggle erupted in the Communist Party. The main contenders were Leon Trotsky and Joseph Stalin. Trotsky, a talented party organizer, had almost single-handedly created the Red Army that defended the Bolshevik Revolution. Stalin was general secretary, or leader, of the party.

One issue in the power struggle concerned the future of the revolution. Trotsky followed the strict Marxist belief that revolution should take place all over the world. Stalin, however, broke with the doctrine and advocated "socialism in one country." Stalin argued that after socialism succeeded in the Soviet Union, revolution would spread to the rest of the world.

A bitter, savage, and merciless struggle between the two factions began. By 1928, however, Stalin emerged securely as leader. Trotsky went into exile and was later murdered in Mexico, reportedly on Stalin's orders.

The Five-Year Plan

In 1928 Stalin ended the NEP and returned to a controlled **command economy**, in which government planners make all economic decisions. Economic controls from 1918 to 1921 had been emergency measures. Now Stalin's goal was to make the planned economy a permanent feature in the Soviet Union.

A plan for economic growth, the first Five-Year Plan, was published in 1928. It set industrial, agricultural, and social goals for the next five years. Stalin insisted on ambitious targets for the plan.

The Five-Year Plan stretched the resources of the Soviet Union to the breaking point in an attempt to turn the country into a modern, industrialized society. Expansion of heavy industries occurred at the expense of industries producing consumer goods.

After Lenin's death, Stalin gained political power in the Soviet Union, ruling as dictator from 1929 until 1953.

The planners hoped that collective farming would produce enough food for the Soviet people as well as a surplus for export. Money received from farm exports would help pay for modern machinery, which would in turn advance the drive toward industrialization. Efforts to encourage voluntary collectivism had produced inadequate results. Therefore, collectivism was mandated, and all farms were to be merged into collectives. Peasants had to join or suffer severe consequences. Those who attempted to retain their lands faced execution, imprisonment, or exile. Collectivization went poorly, and famine resulted. Millions of people died.

The first Five-Year Plan actually succeeded in most industries. The government turned about 90 percent of the productive farmland into collective farms. A second Five-Year Plan, even more comprehensive than the first, went into effect in 1933. This second program called for production increases in heavy industries, with a particular emphasis on military production. Those who expected an increase in consumer goods or food supply as a reward for hard work and sacrifice were disappointed. In fact, production of consumer goods decreased as the Soviet government placed all of its efforts on the expansion of heavy industry. Rather than receiving a reward, the Soviet people faced harder times as consumer goods and food became more scarce.

Stalin's Dictatorship

Stalin's control of the Communist Party had been his most effective means of blocking his rival Trotsky. Now, as control of government centralized, more control than ever was applied to society at large.

A police state. The czars had used secret police and spies to maintain their absolute rule. Stalin began to use similar tactics. Under Stalin the Soviet people still experienced rule by fear. People had to conform without dissent to the dictates of the Communist Party or face punishment such as imprisonment.

The Soviets disestablished the Orthodox Church and seized its property. They discouraged religious worship and taught atheism in schools. Artists, writers, and musicians were ordered to produce "socialist realism" as an indication of their service to the state, with their works subject to rigid control and censorship by the government.

Government under Stalin. In 1936 Stalin proclaimed a new constitution for the Soviet Union. The Stalin Constitution, as it was called, preserved the essential framework within the Soviet government that had existed under Lenin. The parliamentary body, which was called the Supreme Soviet, met twice a year. The Council of People's Commissars, which was later renamed the Council of Ministers, held executive and administrative authority.

On paper the Soviet government appeared to be democratic. In reality, however, most power lay in the hands of the **Politburo** (Political Bureau) of the Communist Party, which was a small committee that was elected by the Supreme Soviet. As head of the Communist Party, Stalin controlled the Politburo. In other words, he held dictatorial power, with virtually complete authority.

The Soviet Union's totalitarian dictatorship under Stalin grew harsher. In 1934, following the assassination of a high party official, Stalin began a **purge** of party members supposedly disloyal to him. Through intimidation, brutality, and public trials which were staged for show, Stalin began to rid the party of all members who might not submit to his will. This practice of purging extended into the general population, and often occurred without a trial for the accused. Scholars estimate that by 1939 more than 5 million people had been arrested, deported, imprisoned in forced labor camps, or executed.

The Comintern

The Soviet Union's foreign policy during the 1920s and 1930s contained contradictions. On the one

The Soviet Union in 1936

| Trans-Siberian Railroad |

ATLANTIC OCEAN
ICELAND (Den.)
GREENLAND (Den.)
GREAT BRITAIN
NORWAY
SWEDEN
GERMANY
BALTIC SEA
LITHUANIA
FINLAND
GER.
ESTONIA
POLAND
BELORUSSIAN S.S.R.
Minsk
Leningrad
Archangel
Murmansk
ROMANIA
MOLDAVIA
Kiev
UKRAINIAN S.S.R.
Odessa
Kharkov
Rostov
Sevastopol
BLACK SEA
Stalingrad
TURKEY
GEORGIAN S.S.R.
ARMENIAN S.S.R.
AZERBAIJAN S.S.R.
Baku
Moscow
Gorki
Kazan
Samara
Magnitogorsk
Tobolsk
Omsk
Novosibirsk
URAL MOUNTAINS
Siberia
RUSSIAN SOVIET FEDERATED SOCIALIST REPUBLIC
Yenisei
Ob River
Lena
Amur River
SVALBARD (Nor.)
North Pole
ARCTIC OCEAN
ALASKA (U.S.)
Bering Strait
PACIFIC OCEAN
Kamchatka Peninsula
SEA OF OKHOTSK
SAKHALIN ISLAND
Lake Baikal
Irkutsk
TANNU-TUVA
MANCHURIA
Vladivostok
KAZAKH S.S.R.
Aral Sea
Lake Balkhash
CASPIAN SEA
TURKMEN S.S.R.
Ashkhabad
Tashkent
UZBEK S.S.R.
KIRGHIZ S.S.R.
Stalinabad
TADZHIK S.S.R.
AFGHANISTAN
IRAN
CHINA
MONGOLIA
KOREA
JAPAN
INDIA

0   500   1,000 Miles
0   500   1,000 Kilometers
Modified Oblique Conic Conformal Projection

Learning from Maps During his rule, Stalin deported many people to labor camps and killed those who posed a threat to him.

? Place What city is located at the eastern end of the Trans-Siberian Railroad?

hand, the new Communist government wanted to be accepted by the established nations of the world. On the other hand, however, its support of the Third International, also called the Communist International or the **Comintern**, alienated many countries. Lenin had founded this organization in 1919 to help spread the revolution throughout the world. The Comintern continued to agitate for the overthrow of capitalist democracies.

Communist parties existed in many countries outside Russia. The Comintern worked through these parties to arouse workers and urge rebellion. These open calls for revolution caused fear, suspicion, and hostility in the outside world.

Section 5 Review

1. **Define** Union of Soviet Socialist Republics, collective farms, command economy, Politburo, purge, Comintern
2. **Identify** Leon Trotsky
3. **Explaining Ideas** Describe the New Economic Policy of Russia.
4. **Comparing Ideas** (a) How was the idea of a collective farm different from previous agricultural policy? (b) How was collectivization instituted under Lenin and Stalin?
5. **Summarizing Ideas** Describe the growth of totalitarianism under Stalin in the Soviet Union.

Chapter 12 Review

1923
France occupies Ruhr Valley.

1925
Locarno Pact is signed.

A.D. **1918** | A.D. **1920** | A.D. **1922** | A.D. **1924** | A.D. **1926** | A.D. **1928**

1919
• Weimar Republic is established.
• Comintern is founded.

1922
• Mussolini begins rule in Italy.
• Irish Free State is founded.

1928
• Stalin assumes full power in the Soviet Union.
• First Soviet Five-Year Plan begins.

Chapter Summary

The following list contains the key concepts you have learned about political, social, and economic conditions in the United States and Europe following World War I.

1. The period following World War I was a time of major stresses and uncertainties.

2. The literature, music, art, architecture, and science of the time reflected the new outlook and the uncertainties of the period. James Joyce and Pablo Picasso abandoned traditional forms and created works that had disturbing implications. Even new popular art forms, films and jazz, had pessimistic overtones. The Western world entered an unsettled and less optimistic era.

3. Following victory in World War I, people in the United States realized that their country was the richest nation in the world. A sense of optimism and the influence of European contact brought about rapid change. The pace of life quickened during the decade appropriately called the Roaring Twenties.

4. The economic bubble burst with the stock market crash and the beginning of the Great Depression

in 1929. In 1933 President Roosevelt enacted policies for recovery known as the New Deal.

5. In Europe instability was widespread. The British and the French maintained their democratic traditions despite labor unrest and the problems of unemployment caused by the Great Depression. In eastern Europe, a number of the new nations abandoned democracy for dictatorships.

6. In Italy and Germany, dissatisfaction with the weakness and hesitations of democratic governments led to an extreme form of dictatorship that was called fascism. Mussolini in Italy and Hitler in Germany established totalitarian regimes, and both had expansionist foreign ambitions that further undermined Europe's stability.

7. Following its civil war, Russia became the Union of Soviet Socialist Republics, with a government based on the principles of Marx and communism. However, when its first leader, Lenin, died, his successor, Stalin, maintained control of the country only by brutally crushing his opponents and setting up a totalitarian dictatorship.

Reviewing Important Terms

On a separate sheet of paper, supply the term that correctly completes each statement.

1. _____ _____ are formed when land is pooled into large farms on which people can work together.

2. Governmental regulation and direction of national resources to achieve economic stability occurs in a(n) _____ _____.

3. A(n) _____ _____ occurs when workers in several industries refuse to continue working until their demands are met.

4. When a country tries to improve its own economic well-being through protective tariffs and similar restrictions, it is adopting the policy of _____ _____.

5. _____ was the doctrine of Mussolini.

6. A sudden increase in prosperity is called a(n) _____ _____.

7. When people make _____ _____, they are investing in stocks in the hope of attaining quick, huge profits.

Developing Critical Thinking Skills

1. **Interpreting Ideas** How did the arts and popular culture reflect the disillusionment of the postwar era?

2. **Analyzing Ideas** (a) Why did the demobilization of troops put economic pressures on the nations of Europe? (b) Why were Great Britain and France better able to deal with these problems than the new nations of eastern Europe?

3. **Organizing Ideas** Explain how each of the following contributed to the rise of nazism in Germany: (a) creation of the Weimar Republic; (b) signing of the Versailles Treaty; (c) high unemployment and soaring inflation.

4. **Summarizing Ideas** (a) What was War Communism? (b) What was Russia's New Economic Policy? (c) How did each program attempt to stimulate the Russian economy?

5. **Explaining Ideas** Explain the similarities and differences between fascism and communism.

Timeline

| 1929 Great Depression begins. | A.D. 1930 | A.D. 1932 | A.D. 1934 | A.D. 1936 | A.D. 1938 |

1933
- Franklin D. Roosevelt becomes president of the United States.
- Hitler is appointed chancellor of Germany.

1936
- Germany reoccupies the Rhineland.
- Blum's Popular Front government comes to power in France.

Relating Geography to History

Turn to the map of the Soviet Union on page 407 and to the map of Europe after the Congress of Vienna in Chapter 4, page 166. Then complete the following. **(a)** List the republics in the Soviet Union in 1936. **(b)** List the countries bordering the Soviet Union that were part of Russia in 1815. **(c)** Why did the Soviet Union lose a sizable amount of its territory after pulling out of World War I?

Relating Past to Present

1. **(a)** What did the leaders of the Easter Rising in 1916 hope to accomplish? **(b)** Based on what you know about events in Northern Ireland today, have these goals been achieved? **(c)** Explain the goals of the citizens of Northern Ireland today. **(d)** Are these goals the same as those of the Easter Rising?
2. **(a)** List the programs that President Roosevelt instituted during the New Deal. **(b)** Which of these programs are still in existence? **(c)** Choose one of these and find out why this program has continued. **(d)** What is its main purpose? **(e)** Do any groups of people think the program should be discontinued? If so, why?

Applying History Study Skills

Before completing this activity, review Building History Study Skills on page 403.

Study the following documents. The first document gives Stalin's justification of his methods in industrializing the Soviet Union. The second document is a chart summarizing the results of the Five-Year Plans. Decide how each document helps answer the question "How was Stalin able to industrialize the Soviet Union?"

"It is sometimes asked whether it is not possible to slow down the tempo a bit, to put a check on the movement. No, comrades, it is not possible! The tempo must not be reduced! On the contrary, we must increase it as much as is within our powers and possibilities. . . .

To slacken the tempo would mean falling behind. And those who fall behind get beaten. . . . No, we refuse to be beaten! One feature of the history of old Russia was the continual beatings she suffered for falling behind, for her backwardness. She was beaten by the Mongol Khans. She was beaten by the Turkish beys. She was beaten by the Swedish feudal lords. She was beaten by the Polish and Lithuanian gentry. She was beaten by the British and French capitalists. . . . All beat her—for her backwardness."

The Five-Year Plans and Beyond

Economic Growth Rates in the Soviet Union (in percent)		
	First Five-Year Plan, 1928–1932	Second Five-Year Plan, 1932–1937
Industrial Output	10.6	10.1
Electric Power	26.3	21.8
Ferrous Metals	11.0	22.0
Agricultural Output	–5.5	1.0
Crops	2.1	6.5
Livestock	–11.4	–2.1

internet connect

Search the Internet through the HRW Web site for information about the Great Depression. Then write several journal entries as if you were a teenager living then.

GO TO: go.hrw.com
KEYWORD: SC0 Great Depression

Building Your Portfolio

1. **Writing a Report** Using resource books for your research, prepare a brief biographical sketch of Benito Mussolini. Place the report in your portfolio.
2. **Presenting an Oral Report** Prepare a report on the response of the United States and European nations to the Great Depression, explaining why the policy of economic nationalism created more problems than it solved. Place your notes and other research materials in your portfolio.

New Political Forces in Africa, Asia, and Latin America

TIME

A.D. 1898–1938

A.D. 1898–1938

3.7 million B.C. | 4000 B.C. | A.D. 2100

PLACE

Africa, Asia, and Latin America

Latin America

Africa

Asia

Diego Rivera mural

Significance

Europe and the United States faced social, political, and economic challenges during the early decades of the 1900s. In other parts of the world, however, people's main concern was political change. Of the countries of the British Empire, India set out on a path toward independence, and other countries developed new relationships with Great Britain. The two major independent countries of the Middle East, Turkey and Persia, also began rapid political transformation, and new political forces stirred throughout Africa.

Profound changes transformed the great civilizations of China and Japan. In China the ancient dynastic cycle was broken, and the long and difficult process of creating new political structures began. Neighboring Japan set its course for economic growth and foreign expansion.

The countries of Latin America faced economic and social change as well as an uncertain relationship with the United States. Many Latin American countries, like others in the 1920s and 1930s, developed governments with strong centralized power.

Terms to Define

Zionism	Guomindang
passive resistance	Long March
Statute of Westminster	Treaty of Portsmouth
Open Door Policy	Good Neighbor Policy

People to Identify

Arthur Balfour	Leopold Senghor
Mohandas Gandhi	Sun Yixian
Kemal Atatürk	warlords
Reza Shah Pahlavi	Chiang Kaishek
Nnamdi Azikiwe	Mao Zedong
Jomo Kenyatta	

Places to Locate

Egypt	Shaanxi
Iraq	Mexico City
India	Buenos Aires
Ankara	
Iran	
Jiangxi	

Chapter Theme Questions

- **Social Relations** What changes might nationalist groups demand?
- **Politics and Law** What might happen when the military takes an active role in government?
- **Economic Organization** How might economic crises sometimes lead to political crises?

In the early 1900s, dynastic rule in China came to an end. A large nationalistic movement spread across China, led by Sun Yixian, who described the necessity of nationalism to his fellow Chinese.

> **❝Considering the law of survival of ancient and modern races, if we want to save China and to preserve the Chinese race, we must certainly promote nationalism. . . .**
>
> In comparison with other nations we have the greatest population and the oldest culture, of four thousand years' duration. . . . But the Chinese people have only family and clan groups; there is no national spirit. Consequently, . . . we are the poorest and weakest state in the world, occupying the lowest position in international affairs; the rest of mankind is the carving knife and the serving dish, while we are the fish and the meat. . . . If we do not earnestly promote nationalism and weld together . . . we face a tragedy—the loss of our country and the destruction of our race.❞

China was only one area of the world convulsed in change after World War I.

The British Empire in the Postwar Era

Focus Questions

- Why did British rule in Egypt and the Middle East come to an end?
- How did the people of India pursue their desire for self-rule?
- How did the British respond to calls for change in other parts of their empire?

Although the British Empire had grown larger as a result of the Paris peace conference, its continued existence was nonetheless threatened. People in all parts of this vast British empire voiced demands for more freedom, for self-government, and even for their complete independence.

Independence for Egypt

Officially, the Ottoman Empire ruled Egypt, but since 1882 the British had controlled the country. In 1914, when the Ottomans joined the Central Powers, the British declared Egypt a protectorate. Although the protectorate formally ended in 1922, Britain reserved the right to defend Egypt and the Suez Canal and administered part of the country to protect its interests.

During the 1920s and early 1930s, a strong independence movement grew in Egypt. In 1935 Italy invaded Egypt's neighbor Ethiopia. To ward off further Italian aggression, Egypt and Britain signed the Anglo-Egyptian Treaty of 1936. Reached after intense negotiation, the treaty gave Egypt independence and Britain military control of the Suez Canal for 20 years. The two nations pledged to support each other in the event of war in the Middle East, and Britain sponsored Egypt's membership in the League of Nations. Many Egyptians were unsatisfied, however, for British troops remained garrisoned throughout Egypt. Genuine independence did not come until after World War II.

The Palestine Issue

Peace settlements after World War I gave Great Britain mandates for what would become Transjordan, Iraq, and Palestine. These lands were all formerly part of the Ottoman Empire.

A spirit of nationalism had arisen among Arabs during the last years of the Ottoman Empire. In that spirit, Arabs had helped the British against the Ottoman Empire during World War I. When, after the war, France and Britain imposed their control in the Middle East, many Arabs felt betrayed. Some rebelled. To placate angry Arabs, a section of Palestine called Transjordan was separated from the Palestinian mandate in 1921. Although the British recognized Transjordan as an independent state in 1928, they retained considerable control through a strong military presence. In 1932 Great Britain also recognized Iraq as an independent kingdom but again retained authority in military and financial matters.

Of the three Middle Eastern mandates, only Palestine remained under complete British control. Palestine was important because of its strategic location and because a vital oil pipeline from Iraq ended at the port of Haifa. However, the British faced a difficult problem in Palestine.

Since the late 1800s, Jews from Europe had been establishing small colonies in Palestine. These colonists supported a nationalist movement called **Zionism**, which aimed to build a Palestinian homeland for Jews.* In 1917 the British foreign secretary, Arthur Balfour, eager for Jewish support in the Allies' war effort, told Zionist leaders that the British would "view with favour" the creation of a Jewish "national home" in Palestine. The Balfour Declaration, as it came to be called, also stated that the establishment of such a homeland should not threaten civil and religious rights of non-Jews, who made up almost all of Palestine's population.

Earlier, however, the British also had promised to help form an independent Arab state that might include parts of Palestine. After World War I, both Jews and Arabs wanted Great Britain to fulfill its promises. Arabs viewed the number of Jews settling in Palestine as especially alarming. While Britain sought a solution to the problem, tensions between Arabs and Jews intensified, and violence occurred.

Hoping to calm the fears of Arabs, the British placed limitations on the number of Jews allowed to immigrate to Palestine. Jewish settlers bitterly resented this policy, especially when Nazi persecution of European Jews increased. During the 1930s, many Jews fled Europe to avoid Nazi persecution. Immigration to Palestine increased. Arabs demanded that immigration cease and rebelled in 1936. The Peel Commission in 1937 declared the Zionist desire for a homeland and the Arab desire for independence irreconcilable and recommended dividing the area. World War II stalled further action on the controversial plan.

Independence Movements in India

As Great Britain's largest colony, India commanded more British attention than did the Middle Eastern mandates. India had contributed both troops and money to the Allies in World War I. In return Great Britain had promised India more self-government.

Some in Britain felt that giving up control of the colonies would render Britain a "third-rate power." Others believed that the principles of self-rule applied to other parts of the British Empire should govern Indian policy. Indian society itself was split many ways. Some Western-educated Indians remained in favor of continued rule of their country by Great Britain.

*Theodor Herzl, an Austrian Jew, is considered the founder of the Zionist movement. Zion, one of the hills of ancient Jerusalem, came to be a synonym for the Jewish people of their dream for a homeland.

Building History Study Skills

READ
WRITE
INTERPRET
CONNECT
THINK

Writing About History: Writing a Problem-Solution Essay

Writing a problem-solution essay includes analyzing a problem in order to provide a solution to the problem. For example, assume that a city's crime rates are increasing. Consequently, a problem can be identified—it is not safe to walk alone on city streets at night. The problem also has a logical solution—the mayor of the city and the city council could approve more funds so that the police could patrol the high-crime areas more frequently at night.

How to Write a Problem-Solution Essay

To write a problem-solution essay, follow these three steps.
1. Identify the problem.
2. Describe the problem.
3. State a solution and relate it to the problem.

Developing the Skill

Mohandas Gandhi lived for a time in South Africa, where he formulated many of his theories about nonviolence. Gandhi believed that practicing satyagraha would help end the injustice he witnessed in South Africa. *Satya* means truth. *Agraha* means firmness or force. Satyagraha is therefore translated as "truth force," a firm devotion to truth in a spirit of peace and love. If you were to write an essay on the problem of injustice that Gandhi first faced in South Africa and the solution that he formulated, it might appear as follows.

❝In 1906 the Transvaal government of South Africa published an ordinance requiring the official registration of its Indian population. The Indians held a mass protest meeting in September 1906 in Johannesburg. Gandhi, speaking to the large crowd, told the people to pledge defiance of the ordinance and go to jail if necessary. Gandhi believed the people should protest rather than forfeit their right to free movement.

Gandhi's solution to the problem was to develop the idea of satyagraha, which he said is 'the vindication of truth, not by the infliction of suffering on the opponent, but on one's self.' According to Gandhi, 'the opponent must be weaned from error by patience and sympathy.' Satyagraha reverses the 'eye for an eye' policy, which ends in making everyone blind. It returns good for evil until the evildoer tires of evil. This was Gandhi's plan for dealing with South African injustice.❞

The first paragraph identifies and defines the problem—the injustice of the South African government, which requires the Indian people to submit to official registration that monitors their movement and creates racial distinctions. The solution that Gandhi developed was satyagraha, or truth force. That is, if a person resists the law nonviolently and is willing to suffer the consequences, ultimately that person will change the opposition. Gandhi's method, which was not to allow the protestor to adopt the method of the oppressor, was designed to appeal to the conscience of the opposition.

Practicing the Skill

Research the effects of Gandhi's solution and explain how they might be incorporated into the model problem-solution essay.

To apply this skill, see Applying History Study Skills on page 429.

Mohandas Gandhi (left), 1930

In contrast, Indian nationalists wanted complete independence, though they did not agree on how to achieve it. Any settlement in India had to accommodate the diversity and tension present in Indian society. Regional interests varied widely, as did religious thought. An uneasy truce reigned between Hindus and Muslims, and large gulfs existed between upper-caste and lower-caste Hindus.

The leading advocate of Indian nationalism was Mohandas K. Gandhi, who became leader of the Indian National Congress—India's most important political party. Many Indians revered Gandhi as a spiritual force as well as a political leader, calling him Mahatma, or "Great Soul." Educated in England, Gandhi sought complete independence for India. He urged Indians to give up Western ways and return to their ancient culture and religions.

Gandhi opposed any use of force or violence. In 1920 he explained his reasons for favoring nonviolence as a means of achieving independence.

"As soon as India accepts the doctrine of the sword, my life as an Indian is finished. . . . I tell you that whilst my friend . . . has adopted the doctrine of non-violence as a weapon of the weak, I believe in the doctrine of non-violence as a weapon of the strongest. I believe that a man is the strongest soldier for daring to die unarmed with his breast bare before the enemy."

Drawing on ideas from Hindu scriptures and the New Testament, Gandhi developed a political approach known as nonviolent noncooperation. This technique of **passive resistance**, a form of civil disobedience, called for citizens to peacefully refuse to cooperate with the government in order to win concessions from it.

Gandhi's program of nonviolent noncooperation included a boycott of British goods and a refusal to pay taxes. Gandhi and his followers were imprisoned numerous times. Trying to control the nationalist movement, British authorities restricted the civil liberties of many leaders, and British soldiers repeatedly used force to break up nationalist political gatherings. Many moderate Indians turned against British rule.

In 1935, after years of reports and conferences, Great Britain granted India a new constitution that provided for elected representation. However, the British still controlled India's defense, revenue, and foreign policy and could veto legislation. Committed to total self-government, the nationalists opposed the new constitution, but agreed to work within it, and gained greater power after the elections. Efforts for complete independence continued.

The Statute of Westminster

Even in those parts of the British Empire where a degree of self-government already existed, people sought greater independence. In Canada, Australia, New Zealand, and the Union of South Africa, Great Britain still appointed a governor-general, who could veto laws (though they did so rarely). Great Britain also controlled the foreign policy of these areas.

After World War I, these dominions wanted complete self-government. Showing readiness to accommodate, Great Britain agreed without a struggle.

In 1931 an act of Parliament, the **Statute of Westminster**, recognized Canada, Australia, New Zealand, and South Africa as completely independent. The four nations joined with Great Britain as equal partners in a loose organization called the British Commonwealth of Nations. The British Parliament had no power either to make laws for or interfere with Great Britain's Commonwealth partners. However, each member agreed to declare loyalty to the British monarch.

Over the years, other British colonies became independent and joined the Commonwealth. Like other nations, Britain faced economic depression after World War I and needed increased trade to stimulate its economy. British trade abroad was hurt by nationalism, and favorable trade arrangements among Commonwealth nations made membership attractive. The Commonwealth worked well economically for both Great Britain and its former colonies.

Politically, however, the vast British empire had proved burdensome. In the Middle East and India especially, more colonies demanded independence.

Section 1 Review

1. **Define** Zionism, passive resistance, Statute of Westminster
2. **Identify** Arthur Balfour, Mahatma Gandhi
3. **Locate and Explain the Significance** Egypt, Iraq, India
4. **Understanding Ideas** How were Egypt and the Middle East mandates given independence from Great Britain?
5. **Analyzing Ideas** What methods did Gandhi use to gain independence for India?
6. **Evaluating Ideas** How did the Commonwealth of Nations benefit both Great Britain and its former colonies?

Turkey, Persia, and Africa

Focus Questions
- How did ideas about modern nationalism manifest themselves in Turkey and Persia?
- In what way did World War I change the attitude of Africans toward colonial governments?

The nationalist ideas that swept the Middle East after World War I also affected Turkey and Persia in Southwest Asia and the whole of Africa. As a result, new political forces began to stir.

Turkey Under Mustafa Kemal

The Treaty of Sèvres stripped the Ottoman Empire of all its territories except Turkey. In 1919 Greek troops arrived to impose those terms on Turkey and began expanding their control. Pockets of Turkish resistance, officially opposed by the weak Ottoman government, grew.

Under the able and energetic leader Mustafa Kemal, a hero of the fighting at Gallipoli, young nationalists pressed the government to respond and eventually took control of the assembly. Declaring the sultan to be under the control of the nation's enemies, the assembly appointed an executive council, headed by Kemal, to run the country. Defeating the Greeks near Ankara in 1921, Kemal's forces drove them from Turkey in 1922. That same year, the assembly abolished the sultanate and in 1923 established the Republic of Turkey. The nationalists then moved the capital from Constantinople to Ankara.

Initially, the assembly included various factions, but later assemblies seated few who opposed the first president, Mustafa Kemal. The government became a one-party system led by the chief executive.

Kemal sought to modernize and westernize Turkey because he believed that the war had shown the superiority of Western technology. He viewed Islam as a roadblock to modernization and drew up a new constitution that ended the long unity of Islam and the government. He abolished the position of caliph and attacked Islam's influence by shifting the weekly holiday from Friday to Sunday and abandoning the Islamic calendar.

Kemal ordered the Turkish people to adopt Western ways. He prohibited the wearing of traditional clothing such as the fez, the traditional Turkish hat. In addition, he insisted that all Turks adopt family surnames, as Europeans did. He himself took the name Atatürk, meaning "father of the Turks." He also supported laws that gave women the right to vote and hold office, and he abolished polygamy—the practice of having more than one wife.

In further efforts to modernize, Atatürk's country adopted a secular court system, metric weights and measures, and the Roman alphabet. Atatürk also instituted a program of economic development, including state-run industry and subsidized farming.

Modernizing Persia

Turkey's neighbor Persia had never come under Ottoman control. Since the late 1700s, it had been ruled by shahs of the Qajar dynasty. In the early 1900s, however, both Great Britain and Russia established spheres of influence in Persia and increasingly influenced the Persian government.

In 1921 Reza Khan, a Persian army officer with strong nationalist sentiments, seized control of the government in a coup d'état. Some four years later, he deposed the ruling shah and assumed the throne,

The Shah of Persia (right) and Kemal Atatürk (left) met in 1934 in the city of Ankara, Turkey.

taking the title Reza Shah Pahlavi. Like Kemal Atatürk, Reza Shah wanted to modernize his country and free it from foreign domination. He therefore embarked on a massive reform program. He strengthened the army, broke the power of contentious tribes, built roads and hospitals, established a university, and gave women more rights. Reza Shah also introduced an ambitious economic development plan that improved transportation and communication systems and established new industries. In 1935 he announced that the country would be called officially what its people called it—Iran.

Although Iran's constitution called for a limited monarchy, most of the power remained in Reza Shah's hands. He strictly controlled the press and suppressed political parties. The Shah's secret police force ruthlessly put down any opposition to his government. His foreign policy of balancing British and Russian interests led him to seek closer ties to Germany, which would eventually cause his downfall.

Africa After World War I

The many Africans who fought in the armies of Great Britain and France during World War I expected to be rewarded with greater political freedom after the war. Like the Indians, they were disappointed.

Increased political activity. The years after World War I saw an increase in political activity among Africans. The war itself had served as a broadening experience for many. Military service took them away from their homes. For the first time, they experienced the world beyond their immediate villages and families. When these former soldiers returned home, they brought with them new ideas about freedom and nationalism. In time they put these ideas to work organizing anticolonial protest movements.

Colonial education also influenced many Africans to become politically involved. Missionary and government schools taught African students the Western ideals of equality and self-improvement. Yet colonial governments denied these same Africans opportunities for self-determination and economic advancement. As more and more Africans personally experienced the contradiction between Western teaching and the reality of colonialism as it existed in Africa, they became determined that change must come. Racism and political repression awakened in many Africans a desire to work for reform and even independence.

New political associations. Alarmed at the growing spirit of dissent among Africans, many colonial governments considered reform. However, Africans had begun to organize. In Tanganyika, a former German colony whose mandate had been assigned to Great Britain, Africans from the lower ranks of the civil service formed a civil servants' association. Because the association was open to all Africans, it overcame traditional ethnic barriers and was soon at the center of anticolonial protest in Tanganyika. Similarly, other labor unions and workers' associations became important forums for the expression of African grievances.

In response to the formation of these new political associations, colonial governments strengthened the authority of tribal chiefs who favored colonial rule. At the same time, the colonial authorities agreed to institute some reforms. A few cooperative chiefs and piecemeal reform, however, could not stem the rising tide of the opposition of Africans to colonialism and the desire for independence.

New leaders. By the 1930s, Africans increasingly were calling for independence rather than reform. The most insistent of these calls came from the group of young, Western-educated men—among them Nnamdi Azikiwe (ah-ZEEK-wah) of Nigeria, Jomo Kenyatta of Kenya, and Leopold Senghor of Senegal—who had assumed the leadership of the anticolonial movement. Following Gandhi's example, they organized demonstrations, strikes, and boycotts against their colonial rulers. They also employed Western methods of political organization to attract more support for their cause. By the end of the 1930s, these men led a growing movement dedicated to ending colonial rule.

Section 2 Review

1. **Identify** Kemal Atatürk, Reza Shah Pahlavi, Nnamdi Azikiwe, Jomo Kenyatta, Leopold Senghor

2. **Locate and Explain the Significance** Ankara, Iran

3. **Understanding Ideas** Why did the Ottoman Empire finally end after World War I?

4. **Comparing Ideas** (a) How were the reform programs of Kemal Atatürk and Reza Shah alike? (b) How were the reform programs of both different?

5. **Analyzing Ideas** Why did participation in World War I increase Africans' hopes and expectations for independence?

Unrest in China

Focus Questions

- How did resentment of foreign interests lead to the downfall of the Qing dynasty?
- How did the nationalist movement grow and change under the leadership of both Sun Yixian and Chiang Kaishek?
- How did communism develop in China?

Some historians believe that changes occurring in China in the 1920s were rooted in events that took place around 1900. Until then the imperialist powers of France, Germany, Great Britain, Japan, and Russia had maintained spheres of influence mainly along the Chinese coast and up the Chang Jiang. At the turn of the century, however, they began to move into China's interior, pursuing wealth there as well.

The United States, a new world power, watched these developments with some concern. It did not want American merchants excluded from Chinese trade. In 1899 the American government therefore appealed to nations with interests in China to recognize what it called the **Open Door Policy**. Under this policy, all nations would have equal rights to trade anywhere in China. Nations contacted by the United States responded evasively. The United States interpreted the responses as agreement. In practice the scramble for trade and privileges continued as before.

The Boxer Rebellion

By the end of the 1800s, China's fate as a subordinate nation seemed sealed. Foreign powers had won numerous concessions and privileges from the Chinese. Traders and missionaries traveled the country at will. Foreign interests dominated the economy and government through Chinese intermediaries.

In 1898, hoping to stem foreign interference by revitalizing his government, the young Qing emperor attempted a series of reforms to modernize administration, education, law, military affairs, and technology. The drastic cultural changes called for by these reforms offended China's conservative leaders, and the emperor's aunt, the aging empress dowager (widow of an earlier ruler) Cixi (TSOO·SHEE), took action. The emperor was imprisoned, and for the next 10 years Cixi ruled China.

The empress dowager's officials encouraged antiforeign movements breaking out in the provinces. A growing group called the Society of the Harmonious Fists began to attack Chinese converts to Christianity, then foreign missionaries. In English the members of this society were called simply Boxers. In what became known as the Boxer Rebellion, the Boxers attacked foreigners throughout China, destroying churches, railways, and mines—anything connected with outsiders. Seeking protection, many foreigners fled to embassies in Beijing. There they came under siege by an army of angry Boxers.

Despite rivalries, the imperialist nations were determined to protect their common interests in China. They acted jointly against the Boxers, sending to Beijing an army comprising soldiers from Great Britain, France, Germany, Russia, Japan, and the United States. This army relieved the besieged embassies and put down the rebellion in 1900. The foreign powers then imposed heavy penalties on the Chinese, including a demand for payment of a large indemnity. In addition, the foreign powers claimed the right to maintain troops at Beijing and along the Chinese Eastern Railway to the coast.

The crushing of the Boxer Rebellion brought China completely under foreign domination. Partition of China into colonies was avoided because other powers realized that Russia and Japan, because of their location, would benefit most from any division of China. To protect its interests, the United States reasserted the Open Door Policy to include maintaining China's territorial integrity. Still, foreign armies were stationed in the northern provinces of China.

Overthrow of the Qing Dynasty

The Boxer Rebellion failed to fulfill its major aim—to drive foreigners from Chinese soil. However, it did foster nationalistic sentiment among the Chinese people, especially the young and well educated. These nationalists advocated true reform of China itself. A new political party, the **Guomindang**, or Chinese Nationalist Party, grew out of this reform movement. The party's director, Sun Yixian (also known as Sun Yatsen), lived for many years in the United States, attended school in Hawaii, and studied medicine at a British college in Hong Kong.

Influenced by Western ideas gathered by Sun Yixian and others, the nationalists wanted a constitutional government with civil liberties guaranteed by a bill of rights. They also wanted industrialization to defend China economically against imperialist powers. In the nationalists' view, China could protect itself against foreign domination only if it became a modern nation.

The Qing rulers, under pressure from the nationalists, tried to carry out reforms, including outlining a constitution in 1908 and promising its implementation in nine years. Nationalists, merchants, and gentry, however, wanted a complete break with the "Old China" and an end to the Qing dynasty.

In 1911 a series of revolts, led mostly by army officers who supported Sun Yixian, spread throughout southern China. Yuan Shikai, the leader of an imperial army, did not respond with force but negotiated, hoping for a smooth transition to a new dynasty, with himself in a position of power. No agreement was reached, however, and the 268-year Qing dynasty ended.

Forming the Chinese Republic

In February 1912, the Guomindang forced the last Qing emperor, a young boy, to abdicate. The Guomindang then proclaimed China a republic. Sun Yixian had described the Guomindang philosophy as the "Three Principles of the People": the people's government, the people's rights, and the people's livelihood. These principles called for (1) political unification and the end of foreign influence; (2) a gradual change to democratic government, with full personal liberties and rights for all Chinese people; and (3) economic improvements, including industrialization and the provision of more equitable distribution of land.

Problems with the warlords. Proclaiming revolutionary change proved to be easier than accomplishing it. At first the Republic of China hardly existed, as revolution and assassination marked its early years. Yuan Shikai became president, and Sun Yixian fled to Japan. Yuan attempted to restart an imperial dynasty with himself on the throne. His effort failed, but the country was in turmoil. Warlords, who had acquired power during the last years of the Qing dynasty, ruled most of the country and refused to surrender power.

The Nationalists—as members of the Guomindang called themselves—hoped to defeat the warlords and establish the Republic of China with a strong central government. To fulfill this aim, they asked for help from foreign powers. Only the Soviet Union responded. In the early 1920s, the Soviets sent technical, political, and military advisers to help reorganize the Guomindang and build a modern Chinese army.

A split in the Guomindang. When Sun Yixian died in 1925, Chiang Kaishek (chang ky·SHEK), a military commander who had studied the Soviet Red Army in Moscow, assumed leadership of the Nationalists. Under Chiang's command the Nationalist army grew stronger. In 1926 Chiang began a military campaign—called the Northern Expedition—against the warlords of the north. Warlord resistance collapsed when confronted by the efficient, highly motivated Nationalist troops. In quick succession, the Nationalists gained control of Hunan province and the cities of Wuhan (which include Hankou and Wuchang).

Disagreements, however, divided the membership of the Guomindang. The left wing of the party, composed of socialists and Communists, wanted to put more power into the hands of peasants and workers. The conservative right wing opposed such radical change, especially any reforms designed to redistribute land and give it to peasants. Chiang Kaishek became the leader of this right wing.

In 1927, before the Guomindang completed the Northern Expedition, Chiang expelled all Soviet advisers from the country and moved against the party's left-wing members. Troops loyal to Chiang attacked the communist stronghold of Shanghai, arresting thousands of Communists and executing them on the spot. Secure in the belief that the Communists no longer

Sun Yixian (Sun Yatsen), pictured here with his wife, worked to unite China under one government.

P'u-i, the Last Emperor of China

For thousands of years, the Chinese people were ruled by emperors. Imperial rule came to an end in 1912, when the last emperor, a boy of six, gave up the ancient throne.

Ironically, the last emperor of China was not Chinese but Manchu. In the 1600s, the Manchu people invaded and conquered China, establishing the Qing dynasty. Two hundred years later, the Manchu government had become weak and corrupt. During the 1800s, Europeans forced China to open its ports to European trade, and China was in danger of being divided among foreign powers. The Chinese blamed the Manchus for their humiliating situation. In 1911 Nationalist revolutionaries overthrew the Qing dynasty, establishing the Republic of China. The boy Henry P'u-i (also known as Pu Yi), the last Qing emperor, formally abdicated on February 12, 1912.

Former Emperor P'u-i was imprisoned for 14 years by the Chinese as a war criminal. He is shown signing his confession before being released from prison.

The end of imperial rule did not bring peace and prosperity as the revolutionaries had hoped, however. Instead, the country was left weak and disunited. For nearly four decades following the fall of the Qing, China suffered the effects of instability.

posed a threat to his leadership, Chiang established a Nationalist government in Nanjing.

The Nanjing Government

Chiang and his followers wanted a strong, efficient government, but not a democratic one. Eventually, they set up a one-party system with Chiang as virtual dictator.

Chiang tried to promote economic development, but a lack of capital hindered his efforts to industrialize. Defense expenditures took much government revenue that could have been used for industrialization. Foreign control of many of China's natural resources also slowed economic development.

Even so, the areas of China under Nationalist control made notable progress. The Nationalists began a massive road construction program and started to repair, rebuild, and extend the railroad system. In addition, they strengthened the financial system by establishing a national bank. All levels of the educational system also improved.

However, the Nationalists failed to deal with two crucial problems. Because they needed the support of landowners and merchants, they made no changes in the oppressive system of land ownership, nor did they change methods of tax collection in the countryside.

In short, they did little to eliminate the causes of suffering and discontent among Chinese peasants—the country's vast majority.

The Growth of Chinese Communism

In July 1921, a small group of Chinese intellectuals met in Shanghai and founded the Chinese Communist Party. Inspired by the example of the Russian Revolution and the ideologies of Marx and Lenin, the founders of Chinese communism hoped to free their country from foreign domination and economic backwardness. They first set about building strong party organizations and labor unions in the cities. They also cooperated with the Guomindang in efforts to defeat the regional warlords.

At first, when the Guomindang was weak and in need of support, the Nationalists welcomed Communists. As the Communist Party grew stronger, however, conservative Nationalists became alarmed. Chiang Kaishek purged the Communists from the Guomindang in 1927 and executed many of them. In the early 1930s, when Chiang realized that he had failed to destroy the Communist Party, he undertook several large-scale military campaigns to "annihilate" communism once and for all.

Civil War in China, 1925–1935

Learning from Maps It took Communists more than a year to march from the southeastern province of Jiangxi to the northwestern province of Shaanxi.

Place What river did the group cross in the middle of their journey?

The Long March. Those Communists who escaped the purge of 1927 fled first to Jiangxi province in southeastern China. There they set up their own government—modeled after the Russian communist regime—called the Chinese Soviet Republic. Nationalist forces repeatedly attacked, then besieged the soviet in 1934. A few months later, Communists broke through the siege lines and evacuated Jiangxi.

In the famous **Long March**, which lasted more than a year, about 100,000 Communists made their way on foot to Shaanxi province in northwestern China.

Pursued by Nationalist troops and strafed by aircraft, they crossed 18 mountain ranges and 24 rivers, a distance of about 6,000 miles, under incredibly arduous conditions. A few deserted, but many more died on the journey. Those who survived, along with Communists already in Shaanxi, established their headquarters in the isolated mountain town of Yenan. (See map on this page.) On the march, a charismatic young man named Mao Zedong (MAOOH ZUH·DUHNG) had established himself as a leader.

Mao Zedong. Born in the countryside of southeastern Hunan province, Mao had long argued that Chinese peasants, not the urban proletariat, could provide the best basis for a communist revolution in China. In a rural province far from the major cities of China, he had a chance to prove his argument.

In Shaanxi province, Mao and his followers practiced the programs of land and tax reform always advocated by the Communists. To ensure success, they met with the peasants and listened to their problems. The Communists also explained China's problems to the peasants and urged them to support the revolution.

Suspicious of outsiders, the peasants of Shaanxi did not trust the Communists at first. However, when they found that the Communists were trying to understand and help them solve their problems, the peasants rallied to the cause. Many volunteered to

Throughout the Long March, Mao Zedong (shown on horseback) and his group fought Chiang Kaishek's army in a series of military engagements.

serve in the communist army, called the Red Army. Others provided useful information about the location and movement of Nationalist troops.

With the aid of the local peasant population, the Communists managed to rebuild their strength and resist efforts of the Nationalists to destroy them. The Nationalists, under Chiang Kaishek, had chosen to attack communism rather than face the growing threat from Japanese militarism. Many Chinese disliked this policy, believing that "Chinese don't fight Chinese" and that Japan was the true enemy. Support for the Communists grew.

Section 3 Review

1. **Define** Open Door Policy, Guomindang, Long March
2. **Identify** Sun Yixian, warlords, Chiang Kaishek, Mao Zedong
3. **Locate and Explain the Significance** Jiangxi, Shaanxi
4. **Analyzing Ideas** (a) What was the Boxer Rebellion? (b) What were its results?
5. **Classifying Ideas** (a) Describe Sun Yixian's three goals for the Chinese republic. (b) With what problems did the Nanjing government fail to deal?
6. **Evaluating Ideas** What factors helped communism take hold in China?

Section 4

Japan Between the Wars

Focus Questions

- How and why did Japan pursue a policy of expansionism in the late 1800s?
- What caused the Russo-Japanese War, and what were its results?
- What changes in Japanese life were caused by rapid modernization?

Japan had begun to modernize in the late 1800s. However, the economic, social, and political reforms achieved during that time created problems. Japan's desire for territory on the Asian continent intensified these problems.

Japanese Expansion

The reforms introduced by the leaders of the Meiji Restoration transformed Japan into a modern industrial and military power. This newly acquired status enabled Japan to embark on a policy of expansionism in the late 1800s. Extending Japanese influence would serve two purposes. First, it would provide both new sources of raw materials for the country's growing industries and new markets for the products of those industries. Second, it would show the nations of the West just how far Japan had progressed. Other parts of Asia, especially weak China, seemed to provide opportunity for expansion.

Korea and Manchuria. Korea had long interested Japan. The Treaty of Shimonoseki that ended the Sino-Japanese War in 1895 forced China to cede Taiwan and the Pescadores to Japan and provided for Korean independence. Soon, however, Japan dominated the Korean government.

Japan's relationship to China indirectly caused another Japanese conflict, this conflict with Russia. After the Boxer Rebellion, most foreign powers withdrew their troops from China. However, a force of 100,000 Russian soldiers lingered in Manchuria. Despite protests by the Japanese government, Russia maintained the troops and had forced a lease from China for a railway line to extend across Manchuria. The Russians now had a port leased from China in 1898, and they looked set to dominate Manchuria.

Believing that war with Russia was likely, in 1902 Japan signed an alliance with Great Britain. Each nation agreed that the other had the right to defend special interests in China, Manchuria, and Korea against any third power. The two nations agreed that if either one became involved in a war with a single power, the other would remain neutral. If a third power joined the conflict, they would aid each other. The obvious target of the alliance was Russia.

The Anglo-Japanese alliance meant great prestige for Japan. The nation no longer stood alone but now had the support of one of the most powerful countries in the world. The alliance also increased pressure on Russia to withdraw from Manchuria. Diplomatic attempts failed, and finally in January 1904, Japan issued an ultimatum to Russia. Russia refused to answer Japan's demands.

The Russo-Japanese War. In February 1904, without a declaration of war, the Japanese attacked and badly damaged the Russian fleet at Port Arthur in Manchuria. In March Japanese troops overran Korea and pushed the Russians back through Manchuria in a series of battles throughout the summer. Another

Japanese force landed on the Liaodong Peninsula in Manchuria and, with the help of the navy, lay siege to Port Arthur. In February and March of 1905, 330,000 Russian and 270,000 Japanese troops fought a great battle at Mukden. Losses were heavy on both sides, and the Russians pulled back. Then in May 1905, the Japanese navy stunned the world at the Battle of Tsushima with the complete destruction of the Russian Baltic fleet.

Shorter supply lines and a better-prepared military helped Japan in the war against Russia. However, the Japanese army suffered heavy casualties, and the cost of the war strained the Japanese economy. As a result, the Japanese asked United States president Theodore Roosevelt to mediate the conflict. Roosevelt reluctantly agreed, and in 1905 invited representatives from Japan and Russia to negotiations at Portsmouth, New Hampshire. Later that year an agreement ended the Russo-Japanese War.

The Treaty of Portsmouth. Under the agreement known as the **Treaty of Portsmouth**, Russia ceded to Japan its lease on the Liaodong Peninsula, including Port Arthur, and the southern half of the Russian island of Sakhalin, north of Japan. Russia also gave up control of the southern branch of the Chinese Eastern Railway and recognized Japan as the dominant power in Korea. In addition, Russia agreed to withdraw all troops, except for railway guards, from Manchuria.

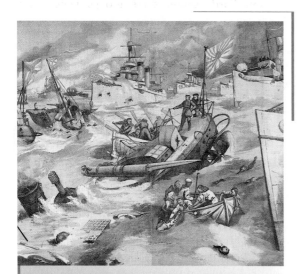

In this painting, the Japanese navy attacks Russian forces at Port Arthur. The Treaty of Portsmouth ended the Russo-Japanese War with the cession of Port Arthur to Japan.

The Treaty of Portsmouth—which won Roosevelt the Nobel Peace Prize in 1906—eliminated any competition in Manchuria. It also signaled that other countries respected Japan's growing strength. When Japan proclaimed the annexation of Korea in 1910, none of the other imperialist powers protested.

Problems of Modernization

In less than 50 years, Japan had advanced from a feudal agrarian nation to one of the world's leading industrial nations. Victories over China and Russia had established Japan as a military power. However, these considerable achievements also created new problems for the island nation.

Industrialization and scientific development brought higher standards of living and improved medical care to Japan, spurring population growth. Cities grew rapidly, and every inch of suitable land was placed under cultivation. Even so, the increased food supply could not match the rapid population growth.

Japanese people began to emigrate to Korea and Taiwan, as well as to Hawaii and other islands of the Pacific. Thousands more left for the United States. In time the United States prohibited the immigration of Asians while still admitting Europeans. The Japanese deeply resented such discrimination.

Japanese industrialization created yet another problem. Japan had to import raw materials because it lacked almost all those needed in modern industry. To pay for these raw materials, it had to sell goods abroad. As purchasers of both food and raw materials, Japan had to export effectively to survive.

In trying to export its goods, Japan met with restrictions in the rough world of international trade. Many countries passed tariff laws to protect their home markets against Japanese competition. These countries argued that Japanese goods had an unfair advantage because cheap labor enabled Japanese manufacturers to

What If?

The Russo-Japanese War
Japan's startling victory in the Russo-Japanese War made it the equal of other imperialist powers competing in the Pacific. How might the course of history have been different if Russia, not Japan, had won the Russo-Japanese War in 1905?

charge lower prices. For the island nation, a modernizing economy had to expand or collapse.

Social Tensions in the 1920s

Social and political stability had marked the Meiji era. During that time, there was a gradual movement toward constitutionalism, but customs and law allowed for little dissent. By the 1920s, however, the situation had changed. Economic development, universal education, and new ideas from the West all contributed to changes in attitudes among the Japanese people. Many believed that the time had come for the people to benefit from Japan's economic advances.

Industrial workers organized labor unions and called strikes for higher wages and better working conditions. Tenant farmers organized unions, too, and demanded lower agricultural rents. Urban intellectuals and university students, inspired by the victory of the Western democracies over Germany in World War I, argued that democracy was the wave of the future. They organized a movement for universal manhood suffrage, which they saw as an essential first step toward promoting democracy in Japan. Women, however, were not given the right to vote until 1945. Other Japanese became interested in socialism and communism. These people protested the government's expansionist policies and tried to organize a revolutionary political movement in Japan.

Some young Japanese also began to question the traditional values of their society. As an educated class grew, its tastes changed from purely Japanese pursuits. New ideas and arts entered Japan from the West along with economic prosperity. The center of Japanese society, formerly an agricultural one, became the modern city. After World War I, Japanese enthusiastically greeted new forms of entertainment. They enjoyed Western dance, listened to jazz, and played baseball. The first modern Japanese novel had appeared in 1889, and the decade after the Russo-Japanese War produced a number of important Japanese writers. Many of their novels dealt with the struggles of individuals in a changing society.

Factories found a source of labor from farm villages, and women took jobs in manufacturing and textile work. Women also began to participate in office work, and a feminist movement, though unsuccessful, began.

These changes did not come without reaction. When markets collapsed in the worldwide depression of 1929, many felt that the country had been subverted economically and morally by focusing on international rather than traditional Japanese interests.

Growing Influence of the Military

Japanese political leaders of the 1920s had difficulty finding answers to all the concerns of the Japanese people. They granted universal manhood suffrage in 1925, yet they could not agree on what to do about other demands. In addition, there seemed to be no clear remedy to the country's precarious economic position. Furthermore, some groups vehemently

Kabuki, a form of Japanese theater incorporating song, dance, and mime, portrays historical and contemporary events during performances that can last an entire day. This is an exterior view of a Japanese Kabuki theater.

opposed increasing westernization. In this atmosphere of discord and dissatisfaction, the influence of the Japanese military grew steadily stronger.

The constitution of 1889 had charged top-ranking officers with carrying out the emperor's commands and recommending to him what those commands should be. Senior officers, who were subject to no civilian control, recommended who should serve as the government's minister of war and minister of the navy. Because only members of the military could hold these two posts, civilian authorities had almost no control over military affairs.

Until the late 1920s, military ministers generally cooperated with civilian members of the government. After that, however, military leaders began to assert their powers in order to influence government policy. They had seen in World War I a new kind of war in which victory had depended on total mobilization, not only of troops but also of the entire spiritual and material resources of the nation. Believing that victory in any future war would require the same kind of mobilization, the military ministers saw discontent in Japan as a serious problem. Dissatisfaction indicated weakness in Japanese society and constituted a threat to the nation's security in the event that there was war. To preserve the nation, the military ministers felt that they must do everything in their power to eliminate this discontent.

The economic problems that Japan faced in the late 1920s also influenced military officers to take a more active role in government. Officers in the army and navy believed that the Western nations would never treat Japan as an equal. As proof of this, they pointed to the restrictions many Western countries had imposed on Japanese immigration and exports. Young officers, particularly, were influenced by groups that believed in the "purity" of Japanese culture and expansionism. Japan should pursue a more independent course, they argued, especially in Asia.

In time the military began to insist that the Japanese people pay greater attention to traditional values. Military leaders also called for a larger army and a stronger navy. In addition, they advocated a Japanese "Monroe Doctrine" that would reserve special powers in East Asia similar to those exercised by the United States in the Western Hemisphere. In particular, military leaders saw Manchuria as a target for future expansion. The growing influence of the military ultimately would have far-reaching consequences for all of Japanese society and for the rest of the world as well.

Section 5

Latin America Between the Wars

Focus Questions

- How did the economies of Latin American nations change after World War I?
- Why did authoritarian regimes come to power in many Latin American nations?
- What kind of relationship did Latin America have with the United States?

As the 1920s began, Latin America appeared to be headed for prosperity. However, the region soon would suffer the effects of the worldwide economic crisis of the 1930s.

Economic Developments

Agricultural products such as beef, wheat, sugar, coffee, and fruits continued to dominate the economies of Latin American nations. However, during the early 1900s, Mexico became a leading exporter of oil. Oil was also discovered in Venezuela, Peru, Bolivia, and Colombia. The mining of other resources, such as copper in Chile and Peru, tin in Bolivia, and bauxite in Guiana, also grew rapidly during this period. For the most part, British and American companies owned the oil and mining operations.

In addition, the 1920s saw a great expansion in the generation of electric and hydroelectric power, financed mainly by foreign investors. The energy that was produced enabled many Latin American countries

History Through the Arts

Rivera's *Fruits of Labor*

After World War I, life in Mexico changed dramatically. Diego Rivera, one of Mexico's finest artists, recorded these changes. As a youth, Rivera studied in Spain and France and was befriended by Pablo Picasso. He settled in Paris and later traveled extensively throughout Europe. In Italy Rivera studied fresco painting. In 1921, he returned to Mexico where the clamor for social reform changed the direction of his work.

As a member of the art movement known as social realism, Rivera produced many paintings that dealt with current problems. Of particular interest are his works that show the plight of the peasants of Mexico. The Mexican government liked Rivera's art and commissioned him to paint murals for many schools and government buildings in Mexico. On the left is a detail from his fresco *Fruits of Labor,* commissioned by the Ministry of Education in Mexico City. In it he honors working people and their children. This impressive fresco took Rivera and a crew of assistants from 1923 to 1929 to complete.

to industrialize during the 1920s. For example, the larger countries in the region began to produce textiles, construction materials, machinery, and automobiles. Oil refining and food processing also became important industries at this time. Heavy industrialization in Latin America, however, would come after World War II.

Changes in Society

Industrialization contributed to the growth of cities. By 1935 Mexico City, Rio de Janeiro, São Paulo, and Buenos Aires all had 1 million or more inhabitants. These and other major cities in the region extended their transportation, sewer, and utilities systems to accommodate the influx of people and industries.

Industrialization also contributed to a change in Latin America's social structure. To provide labor for growing industries, many countries—particularly Argentina, Brazil, and Chile—had encouraged immigration from Europe since the late 1800s. New arrivals from across the Atlantic swelled the ranks of Latin America's working classes.

With growth came an increase in labor union activity. Although Latin American workers first began to organize in the late 1800s, the 1920s saw a surge in labor union membership. Latin American unions, which were largely socialist or anarchist in outlook, employed the strike as the primary way to achieve

their ends. As a result, by the late 1920s, practically every major city in Latin America had been hit by general strikes. Many governments mobilized police and troops to put down these strikes violently. Some governments outlawed both strikes and labor unions.

The middle class also began to grow as new jobs opened up in the professions, government service, and commerce. The increasing numbers of merchants, shopkeepers, and small-business owners added to this growth. The military was professionalized as the sons of the middle class became its officers. Moreover, changes in university programs created opportunities for middle-class youth in engineering, business, and public administration. Such developments gave the middle class potential access to greater power.

Political Changes

Political life in Latin America underwent sweeping change in the early 1900s. In Chile, Argentina, Peru, and Brazil, for example, political parties backed by the middle class emerged. Mexico, wracked by regional factionalism, went to a single-party political system. Mexico's leaders hoped to guarantee stability and solidify the changes that had taken place after the revolution, in spite of assassinations and divisions. In Uruguay reformers led by President José Batlle y Ordóñez (BAHT·yay ee awr·THOHN·yays) enacted a broad reform program that included free elections, a social security system, and nationalization of railroads and public utilities.

Democracy still eluded most Latin American governments. The nature of the groups in power, though, shifted. As countries industrialized, the concerns of the growing number of workers could not be ignored, and urban political movements made these concerns their agenda. Middle-class politicians, struggling for control with the upper-class landowners, turned also to the new working class for support in elections. Elections did not necessarily transfer power smoothly, however. In some countries, forcible overthrow remained the method of changing governments.

The Effects of the Great Depression

As the 1920s drew to a close, prices for Latin America's major agricultural exports, such as sugar and coffee, began to fall. Chile's export economy suffered a crippling blow when German scientists developed a process for making synthetic nitrates which are used in fertilizers and explosives. As a result of this new process, the market plunged for Chile's major export, nitrates.

The worldwide economic depression caused the prices of Latin America's exports to fall even farther. Because they received such a small return on their exports, many Latin American nations found it impossible to import any but the most essential goods. Some countries stopped making payments on foreign debts. As the region's economies continued to falter, unemployment spread, causing worker unrest.

Authoritarian Regimes

Economic crisis soon led to political crisis. Coups d'état overthrew many Latin American governments in the 1930s. In some cases, these coups toppled constitutional systems that had existed for 30 to 40 years. Only Uruguay, which experienced a minor crisis between 1933 and 1935, and Mexico, which had undergone a revolution from 1911 to 1917, avoided major political upheaval.

Planters and exporters, whose fortunes had been wiped out during the Great Depression, lost much of their power as middle classes rebelled. The military strongly influenced or controlled many new governments. In some countries, American-trained military leaders sought to rule. In Nicaragua, for example, General Anastasio Somoza seized power in 1936, two years after assassinating his chief rival, nationalist guerrilla leader Augusto César Sandino. In the Dominican Republic, General Rafael Trujillo

Molina (troo·HEE·yoh moh·LEE·nah) began a 31-year dictatorship in 1930.

In some countries, the new military officers considered upper-class landowners and exporters corrupt, accusing them of having conducted dishonest elections and of allowing foreigners to take control of national resources. Consequently, the military leaders limited the landowners' political influence. At the same time, some new governments broke the power of labor unions and other worker and peasant organizations. Many governments simply abolished these groups and jailed their leaders. In Brazil power became increasingly concentrated in the hands of President Getúlio Vargas, who suppressed any expression of dissent and dismantled any framework of democracy. Sometimes the military governments reacted more violently. In El Salvador, for example, the army massacred more than 10,000 peasants in an effort to destroy a popular movement led by Agustín Farabundo Martí, a onetime follower of Sandino in Nicaragua.

Some military leaders, however, saw that they could curb popular movements through persuasion rather than terror. A number of governments controlled the labor movements by recognizing and giving favors only to those unions loyal to the military. At the same time, many military governments tried to limit the appeal of left-wing movements by responding to some of the needs of ordinary people. These governments enacted some land reforms and passed laws giving workers benefits such as pensions and minimum wages.

Relations with the United States

In U.S. relations with Latin America, President Franklin D. Roosevelt's administration tried to undo the ill will and suspicion created by the earlier United States policy of intervention. During the 1930s, Roosevelt fostered a program he called the **Good Neighbor Policy**. This policy stressed cooperation among the American nations and noninterference by the United States in Latin American affairs.

In 1933 the United States joined other American nations at the Pan American Conference in Montevideo, pledging not to intervene in the internal or external affairs of Latin American nations. As proof of its intentions, the United States recalled the army units that had occupied Haiti since 1915. It also surrendered its right to interfere in the affairs of Panama in the Hull-Alfaro Treaty of 1936.

A situation in Cuba, however, sorely tested the Roosevelt administration's commitment to the Montevideo agreement. In 1933 a group of radical

Disorder was widespread in Cuba in 1933. Here police open fire on Cubans in Havana as they are celebrating the rumor that President Machado has resigned.

reformers overthrew the Cuban dictator Gerardo Machado. The new government immediately declared a socialist revolution and nationalized a number of companies owned by investors from the United States. In response the Roosevelt administration refused to grant diplomatic recognition to the new government. Once again it appeared that the United States would intervene, as was its privilege under the Platt Amendment. (See Chapter 10.)

The United States did not interfere directly, but when Cuban army sergeant Fulgencio Batista decided to overthrow the reformers, Roosevelt's envoy to Cuba encouraged him. Even though the United States no longer intervened directly in Latin American affairs, it still had considerable influence over Latin American nations such as Cuba. Batista remained the power in the background while a series of civilian governments nominally ruled Cuba. In recognition of the stability that Batista brought to Cuba, the United States canceled the Platt Amendment in 1934.

Economic Nationalism

During the 1930s, most governments of industrialized Latin American nations followed a policy of economic nationalism. They reacted to the decline in markets for their exports by encouraging industry. In this way, they hoped to become more self-sufficient. The Vargas regime in Brazil achieved considerable

success in this effort. By the time the army ousted Vargas in 1945, Brazil was producing many of its own consumer goods.

In some ways, economic nationalism was a product of the world's Great Depression. With international markets gone and exchange rates unfavorable for what little was imported, many Latin American nations had no choice but to develop their own industries for manufactured goods. The necessity of economic nationalism coincided with growing feelings of political nationalism, encouraged by the middle class, who wanted to be dependent on neither Europe nor the United States.

The most significant act of economic nationalism occurred in Mexico in 1938. American- and British-owned oil companies in Mexico became involved in a wage dispute with their workers. When the Mexican Supreme Court ruled in favor of the workers, the foreign-owned oil companies refused to accept the decision of the court. As a result, President Lázaro Cárdenas intervened and nationalized the oil industry.

The British angrily broke diplomatic relations. The Americans hesitated, then took a more subtle approach, attempting to preserve the Good Neighbor Policy. The Roosevelt administration applied various indirect pressures, trying to force the Mexican government to pay the oil companies what they claimed their holdings were worth. Finally, the two governments reached a compromise. Mexicans regard March 13, 1938, when President Cárdenas nationalized the oil companies, as the birth date of Mexican economic independence.

Section 5 Review

1. **Define** Good Neighbor Policy
2. **Locate and Explain the Significance** Mexico City, Buenos Aires
3. **Analyzing Ideas** (a) What economic problems did Latin America experience during the late 1920s and the 1930s? (b) What impact did these economic problems have on political life in Latin America?
4. **Understanding Ideas** Why did authoritarian governments come to power in many parts of Latin America?
5. **Evaluating Ideas** How did the Good Neighbor Policy affect the relationship between Latin America and the United States?

Chapter 13 Review

1902 Anglo-Japanese alliance is signed.

1912 Republic of China is formed.

A.D. **1895** | A.D. **1900** | A.D. **1905** | A.D. **1910** | A.D. **1915**

1898 Empress Dowager Cixi begins rule of China.

1900 Boxer Rebellion is suppressed.

1904–1905 Russo-Japanese War occurs.

1910 Japan annexes Korea.

1917 Balfour Declaration is issued.

Chapter Summary

The following list contains the key concepts you have learned about the political forces that emerged in Africa, Asia, and Latin America in the early 1900s.

1. During the 1920s and 1930s, Egypt, Transjordan, and Iraq appeared to become independent countries. However, Great Britain continued to exert control in these countries. At the same time, Palestine's future remained in doubt, but India moved toward independence.

2. Great Britain and its former colonies organized the Commonwealth of Nations.

3. Political and social reforms were attempted in Turkey and in Persia. Africa witnessed the stirrings of political activity that were to lead to major transformations in the years ahead.

4. The Chinese began the long and difficult process of making adjustments to the modern world.

Revolution brought imperial rule to an end in China; however, the Guomindang had trouble establishing its power in the new republic.

5. Dramatic change took place in Japan. This change was witnessed as Japan defeated first China and then Russia at the turn of the century. The Japanese faced economic and social pressures after the end of World War I.

6. Developments in Latin America reflected the worldwide economic crisis. The 1920s and 1930s were also a time of rapid social change, and, in a number of countries, governments became more authoritarian in nature.

7. Latin American relations with the United States improved as a result of the Good Neighbor Policy; however, economic nationalism led to a degree of tension between the countries.

Reviewing Important Terms

On a separate sheet of paper, supply the term that correctly completes each statement.

1. Many Jews supported _____, which aimed to build a Palestinian homeland for the Jews.

2. Gandhi's technique of _____ _____ called for citizens to peacefully refuse to cooperate with their government in order to win concessions from it.

Developing Critical Thinking Skills

1. **Analyzing a Primary Source** The verse below is from a poem entitled "Reproach" by Muhammad Iqbal, an Indian poet and a fervent nationalist who wanted independence for India. Read these lines, and answer the questions that follow.

"Your fate, poor hapless India, there's no telling—
Always the brightest jewel in someone's crown;
Mortgaged to the alien, soul and body too,
Alas—the dweller vanished with the dwelling—,
Enslaved to Britain you have kissed the rod:
It is not Britain I reproach, but you."

(a) What does Iqbal think India's fate will be?
(b) Whom does he blame for this situation? (c) Why?

(d) What actions do you think Iqbal might want the Indian people to take?

2. **Comparing Ideas** After World War I, many colonies wanted independence. Compare the British reaction to demands for Indian independence with the reaction to similar demands from Canada, Australia, New Zealand, and the Union of South Africa.

3. **Interpreting Ideas** (a) How did Sun Yixian hope to bring democracy to China? (b) What obstacles prevented him from succeeding?

4. **Summarizing Ideas** (a) What changes did the Nationalists initiate in China? (b) What problems did they fail to solve?

5. **Determining Cause and Effect** What economic and social problems did Japan face as a result of its rapid modernization and industrialization?

6. **Analyzing Ideas** Why did President Roosevelt introduce the Good Neighbor Policy during his administration as president?

7. **Classifying Ideas** Name the country in which each of the following people played vital leadership roles: (a) Anastasio Somoza; (b) Kemal Atatürk; (c) Chiang Kaishek; (d) Mohandas Gandhi; (e) Fulgencio Batista; (f) Reza Shah Pahlavi.

1922
Mustafa Kemal reforms Turkey.

1928
Transjordan gains independence.

1930
Trujillo Molina regime begins in the Dominican Republic.

1934
• Platt Amendment is canceled.
• Long March occurs in China.

1936
• Somoza regime begins in Nicaragua.
• Egypt achieves independence; Britain retains control of Suez Canal.

A.D. 1920   A.D. 1925   A.D. 1930   A.D. 1935   A.D. 1940

1921
Reza Khan takes control of Persia.

1925
Universal manhood suffrage is granted in Japan.

1931
Statute of Westminster is enacted.

1935
Great Britain grants India a constitution.

1938
Oil companies in Mexico are nationalized.

Relating Geography to History

Study the map of the Guomindang military operations on page 420. (a) Near what cities did the Guomindang victories over the warlords take place? (b) Near what cities did the Guomindang strikes against the Communists take place?

Relating Past to Present

1. Examine a historical atlas containing a map of the Middle East in the 1930s. (a) How does this map compare with a map of the Middle East today? (b) What recent problems in the Middle East date to the days of the British and French mandates? Explain how the mandates contributed to these problems.
2. (a) What issue strained relations between the United States and Mexico in the 1930s? (b) Does this issue still cause difficulties between the two nations? Explain.
3. Review the information in this chapter on the importance of the military in Japan, Persia (Iran), and Latin America. Choose one of these areas. Use newspapers and magazines to determine what role the military plays in this area today. Is the military stronger or weaker than it was in the 1920s and 1930s?

Applying History Study Skills

Before completing this activity, review Building History Study Skills on page 413.

Mohandas Gandhi organized the "Salt March" in India in 1930 to protest the British tax on salt. Read the following excerpt on the march from *I Found No Peace* by journalist Webb Miller.

"The salt deposits were surrounded by ditches filled with water and guarded by four hundred native Surat police. . . . Half a dozen British officials commanded them. The police carried lathis—five-foot clubs tipped with steel. Inside the stockade twenty-five native riflemen were drawn up.

In complete silence the Gandhi men drew up and halted a hundred yards from the stockade. A picked column advanced from the crowd, waded the ditches, and approached the barbed-wire stockade, which the Surat police surrounded, holding their clubs at the ready. Police officials ordered the marchers to disperse under a recently imposed regulation which prohibited gatherings of more than five persons in any one place.

The column silently ignored the warning and slowly walked forward. . . .

Suddenly, at a word of command, scores of native police rushed upon the advancing marchers and rained blows on their heads with their steel-shod lathis. Not one of the marchers even raised an arm to fend off the blows. They went down like tenpins. . . .

The survivors without breaking ranks silently and doggedly marched on until struck down."

1. What problem does the excerpt describe?
2. What is the solution to the problem?
3. How is the solution related to satyagraha?
4. (a) How would you evaluate the method? (b) Can nonviolence triumph over violence? (c) Why or why not?
5. Write a conclusion analyzing the method of nonviolence in response to the salt tax. Use your answers to question 4 to support your conclusion.

internet connect

Search the Internet through the HRW Web site for information on Mustafa Kemal and the reforms that occurred in Turkey under his rule. Be sure to include specifics on such reforms as women's rights and the separation of church and state. Be prepared to discuss your findings with the class.

GO TO: go.hrw.com
KEYWORD: SCØ Mustafa Kemal

Building Your Portfolio

1. **Preparing an Oral Presentation** Empress Dowager Cixi was a power in China from 1861 until her death in 1908. Using research materials, prepare a brief report on the life of this leader. In your report, note reasons why her policies might have helped bring about the end of the Qing dynasty. Place your research materials in your portfolio.
2. **Constructing a Chart** Make a list of the major changes that took place in Latin America during the 1920s and 1930s. Then prepare a chart in which you classify each of the items on your list under one of the following headings: economic, social, or political. Place the chart in your portfolio.

World War II

TIME

A.D. **1921–1945**

A.D. **1921–1945**

| 3.7 million B.C. | 4000 B.C. | A.D. 2100 |

PLACE

Asia and the Pacific, Europe and the Mediterranean

Europe and the Mediterranean

ARCTIC OCEAN

NORTH AMERICA
EUROPE
ASIA
PACIFIC OCEAN
AFRICA
Equator
SOUTH AMERICA
ATLANTIC OCEAN
INDIAN OCEAN
AUSTRALIA
PACIFIC OCEAN
ANTARCTICA

Asia and the Pacific

U.S. troops land on Normandy Beach, June 10, 1944

Significance

By the mid-1930s, most European nations once more claimed loyalty to one of two opposing camps. One group included those nations generally satisfied with the World War I peace settlement. The other group consisted of dissatisfied nations. International relations between the two groups grew strained. In 1939 Japanese aggression in Asia and German aggression in Europe erupted into World War II.

Terms to Define

Kellogg-Briand Pact	Neutrality Acts
Lytton Commission	isolationists
Falange	Lend-Lease Act
Axis Powers	Atlantic Charter
Anti-Comintern Treaty	"New Order"
Munich Conference	"Final Solution"
appeasement	Auschwitz
German-Soviet	Holocaust
nonaggression pact	"soft underbelly of the
blitzkrieg	Axis"
"phony war"	island hopping
collaborators	Operation Overlord
Luftwaffe	V-E Day
Battle of Britain	V-J Day

People to Identify

Yuko Hamaguchi	Charles de Gaulle
Francisco Franco	Franklin D. Roosevelt
Neville Chamberlain	Erwin Rommel
Edouard Daladier	Hideki Tojo
Winston Churchill	Dwight Eisenhower
Philippe Pétain	Douglas MacArthur

Places to Locate

Beijing	El Alamein
Ethiopia	Munich
Italian Somaliland	Stalingrad
Sudetenland	Pearl Harbor
Albania	Guadalcanal
Tinian	Normandy
Iwo Jima	Okinawa
Dunkirk	Hiroshima

Chapter Theme Questions

- **War and Diplomacy** How might regional conflicts grow to involve many nations?
- **Social Relations** How might racial prejudice be used as a political weapon?
- **Technology** When technology is developed in response to war, how can it be both beneficial and destructive?

A colonel in the American Thirty-ninth Infantry Regiment wrote a longing letter to his fiancée from Germany on October 12, 1944. A portion of his letter read:

Well darling, I am growing older as the days go by, why in two more days I'll be twenty-five. Bet I'll be an old grey-headed man by the time all of this is over and the countries have decided to do away with the Army of Occupation. Every now and then I get to see an American paper and it seems to me that everybody is so worried about what is to happen after the War that they do not give very much thought to the fact that there is a long road ahead of us before the War is over.

It would indeed be seven months before the Allies would declare victory in Europe. It would be nearly a year until the Japanese surrendered unconditionally and World War II was over. The Allied victory came about 6 years after the beginning of World War II, but concern about world peace had arisen as much as 20 years earlier, during the 1920s.

Threats to World Peace

Focus Questions

- **What aggressive territorial policies did Japan and Italy carry out beginning in the early 1920s?**
- **Why was the League of Nations ineffective in trying to stop aggression in Asia and Europe during this period?**
- **How did civil war in Spain lead to a fascist dictatorship there?**

The League of Nations had limited effectiveness, and the major powers held diplomatic conferences outside the organization. The first of these conferences was held in 1921 and 1922 in Washington, D.C. Nine powers that had interests in East Asia (excluding the Soviet Union, which was not invited to the meeting) attended the Washington Conference.

Several treaties resulted from the conference. The Five-Power Treaty, for example, provided for a 10-year "naval holiday," during which no major warships would be built. The participating nations also signed the Nine-Power Pact, agreeing to take no additional territory from China and to maintain the existing Open Door Policy. As a result of the Washington Naval Conference and other diplomatic settlements, peace was preserved throughout the 1920s.

The most optimistic of the international conferences took place in 1928 in Paris. The American secretary of state, Frank B. Kellogg, and the French foreign minister, Aristide Briand, drafted a treaty condemning war. Eventually, 62 nations signed the **Kellogg-Briand Pact**, which made war "illegal," though it did not specify how to prevent war. In the 1930s, it became clear that such imprecise and unenforceable measures would no longer be adequate.

Japanese Aggression in Asia

Beginning in the late 1920s, the military gained increasing power in Japan. In 1930 Japan's liberal prime minister, Yuko Hamaguchi, was fatally shot. Political disorder followed. Within two years, militarists controlled the Japanese government.

Attack on Manchuria. In September 1931 a group of Japanese soldiers set off an explosion on a Japanese-controlled railroad near the city of Mukden, Manchuria. The Japanese government blamed China, as the soldiers had hoped. Japanese troops occupied Mukden and, within several months, all of Manchuria. The Republic of China appealed to the League of Nations for help. This incident sparked a conflict between Japan and China that was to continue, intermittently, until 1945.

The League of Nations sent an investigating commission, headed by Lord Lytton of Great Britain, to Manchuria. At the same time, Japan continued its conquest. In 1932 Japan declared Manchuria to be an independent nation, under the name Manchukuo (MAN·CHOO·KWOH), and installed a puppet government.

The **Lytton Commission** advised the League not to recognize Manchukuo's independence and recommended that the region be restored to China. When the League voted on this recommendation, only Japan opposed it. The recommendation was thus defeated, but Japan withdrew from the League of Nations in protest of what it called unfair treatment.

Although the major nations joined in condemning Japan's aggression, no nation was willing to take military action on China's behalf. Japanese aggression unleashed a chain reaction that led to the collapse of peace in the West and in the East.

War in China. Confidently, Japan made further demands on China. It announced its intention to extend its influence not only to all of China but also throughout East and Southeast Asia and the western Pacific. In July 1937, Japanese and Chinese troops clashed near Beijing. Japanese armies captured the city and at once began to move southward. Though the Chinese armies engaged Japanese forces in a costly and damaging war, the Chinese gradually lost ground to Japan.

By 1939 the Japanese occupied about one fourth of China, including all its seaports, the Chang Jiang Valley as far as Hankou, and many cities in the interior. (See map on opposite page.) Still the Chinese stubbornly resisted. This resistance proved an enormous strain on the resources of both nations.

Italy's Conquest of Ethiopia

Italy was a one-party state under the fascist premier Benito Mussolini, who had assumed power in 1922. Mussolini focused on improving the nation's economy through increased taxation, reduced government spending, and suppression of strikes. Mussolini also sought to solve his country's economic problems by overseas expansion. Ethiopia, one of the few independent nations in Africa, became the object of his ambitions.

A border incident provided the pretext for aggression. In December 1934 an Italian border patrol in Italian Somaliland clashed with an Ethiopian border patrol. Ethiopia, unprepared to resist aggression from a power such as Italy, asked the League of Nations for protection. The League could not help in a military sense; it maintained no armed forces. It did bring the dispute to arbitration, but the results were inconclusive. After nearly a year of tension, Mussolini, using Italian forces from Eritrea and Italian Somaliland, invaded Ethiopia. (See map on page 437.) The poorly equipped Ethiopian army was no match for the Italians.

The League then declared Italy an aggressor and applied economic sanctions—a boycott on trade with Italy. The sanctions, however, were too weak to undermine Italy. For example, they did not include oil, iron, or steel. Italians triumphantly entered the Ethiopian capital, Addis Ababa (AHD·dis AH·bah·bah), in spring 1936. Mussolini declared Ethiopia a part of the Italian

The Expansion of Japan, 1928–1941

Learning from Maps Over a 10-year period, Japan occupied about one fourth of China.

? Place What four groups of American islands did Japan attack in 1941?

Empire and proclaimed the Italian king, Victor Emmanuel III, emperor of Ethiopia.

Despite almost universal disapproval of Italy's actions, no major power was willing to use force to uphold the League's sanctions. In Great Britain and the United States, people still remembered the horror of World War I. They did not want to risk another war. France, where the loss of men in the war had been great, adopted a defensive policy and built elaborate fortifications along the Maginot (MA·zhuh·noh) Line.

In addition, many nations were preoccupied with the effects of the Great Depression. In 1937 Italy withdrew from the League. In light of the world's failure to act, it was easy for Japan and Italy to conclude that they could continue their acts of aggression unopposed.

Civil War in Spain

Economically, Spain lagged far behind the rest of western Europe during the 1800s. Although some industry existed, the economy remained primarily agricultural. The nobility owned large estates that included much of the nation's land. The educational system was controlled by the church.

In 1876 the Spanish government had become a constitutional monarchy. An elected parliament called the Cortes limited the king's power. Politically, the country was unstable. Throughout the early 1900s, violent strikes, political assassinations, military plots, and separatist movements in the provinces plagued the nation.

After World War I, the chaos in Spain grew worse. In 1923 General Miguel Primo de Rivera y Orbaneja, known as Primo, led a revolt and established a military dictatorship. King Alfonso XIII remained as a figurehead and supported the military leader insofar as he allowed him to enact political and economic reforms. Primo, backed by the army, held power until he lost the support of both the army and the king in 1930. King Alfonso forced Primo to resign, but the king had lost the public's respect through his initial support of Primo's dictatorship. In 1931 King Alfonso abdicated, and Spain became a republic.

The Spanish Republic. Spain's new leaders planned to establish freedom of religion, to separate church and state issues, and to place education under government control. The government took land from the Catholic Church and the nobility and gave it to landless peasants. Members of the clergy were barred from teaching in schools, and the Catholic Church now had to pay its clergy. Workers received many benefits—shorter hours, better wages, the right to organize, and a voice in the management of business.

These sweeping reforms antagonized Spanish conservatives, who quickly lent their support to a fascist party called the **Falange**.* The Falange was determined to preserve the power of the army, landowners, and the church, regardless of whom the voters might elect to office.

Nationalists versus Loyalists. In February 1936, a Popular Front government that included Socialists and Communists won a major election. The Spanish Popular Front, like the Popular Front in France, represented a coalition of left-wing working-class parties united in their opposition to fascism. Prominent fascists were jailed, and the Falange responded with terrorist acts. In July a Falange leader was assassinated. Following his murder, army uprisings, led by Falangists, erupted in the Canary Islands and in Spain itself. The bitter civil war that followed lasted for almost three years.

The Falangist rebels, who were led by General Francisco Franco, called themselves Nationalists. Those who supported the republic were known as Loyalists, or Republicans. By the end of 1936, the Nationalists controlled most of northern and western Spain. The Loyalists controlled the east and southeast, most of the northern coastline, and the capital city of Madrid.

Foreign Assistance to Spain

The Spanish Civil War soon became a small European war. Germany and Italy saw a fascist Spain as a part of

---

Falange is the Spanish word for "phalanx."

This Spanish woman is assembling a fuselage in an airplane factory during the Spanish Civil War.

Guernica by Pablo Picasso

Although Pablo Picasso lived in France, he was born in Spain and was keenly sympathetic to the Loyalist cause during the Spanish Civil War. His painting *Guernica* expressed his outrage over the bombing of the town of Guernica, which had no strategic value. Using only blacks, grays, and whites, Picasso evoked anguish and horror with his distorted figures writhing in agony under a stark electric light. The painting was on tour in New York City in 1939 when World War II began. Picasso directed that it stay in the United States until democracy had returned to Spain. *Guernica* was returned to Spain in 1981 and was placed in a museum in Madrid.

their plan to surround France with unfriendly powers and threaten Great Britain. They sent fully equipped military units to bolster Nationalist forces.

Sympathetic to the republican government, the Soviet Union sent planes, technicians, and military advisers. Soviet help to the Loyalists, however, was not nearly as extensive as the support Franco received from his fascist allies.

Volunteers from France, Great Britain, the United States, and other nations also clamored to help the Spanish Republic. These antifascist volunteers became known as the International Brigades. The number of brigade volunteers may have been as high as 70,000, though there were only about 20,000 on the field at any given time. On the other hand, Italy sent more than 50,000 trained troops to assist the Nationalists.

The Spanish Civil War brought into the open the seething struggle between fascism and socialism in Europe during the 1930s. It also became a testing ground for new weapons and tactics such as improved aircraft and strategic bombing missions.

The French and the British feared that the Spanish Civil War might spread to the rest of Europe. In September 1936, at the suggestion of the French government, a nonintervention committee representing the major European nations was established. These nations unanimously agreed to a policy of nonintervention in Spain that included a blockade intended to halt the flow of volunteers and supplies to both sides. The blockade cut off most aid to the Loyalists, but it did not hinder German and Italian assistance to Franco.

Spain Under Franco

By the spring of 1938, the Nationalist forces in Spain had grown strong enough for a large-scale offensive. They defeated the Loyalist troops in March 1939, with the capture of Barcelona and Madrid. During the Madrid campaign, one of Franco's generals claimed he had four columns—long, narrow lines of troops—marching on the city and a fifth column within Madrid that would rise against the defenders at the appropriate time. The term *fifth column* has come to mean traitors within a country who assist its enemies.

Franco then set up a fascist government modeled loosely on Mussolini's dictatorship in Italy and became head of the state with unlimited power. He assumed the title *el Caudillo* (cow·THEE·yoh)—Spanish for "the leader." Franco's political party, the Falange, was the only one permitted. Its national council, chosen by Franco, advised him on legislation, though the council held no real power.

The economic organization of Spain resembled that of fascist Italy, with syndicates, or corporations, organized according to occupations and economic activities. In other respects, however, Spain was clearly under the domination of a militaristic leader. The government abolished free elections and most civil rights. Under Franco's regime, the old ruling groups— the army, the landowners, and the Roman Catholic Church—continued to hold positions of power.

Although Spain had become a fascist dictatorship, Franco did not join the Rome-Berlin Axis. The civil war had devastated the country, and many years were to pass before economic recovery took place and hatred among Spaniards waned.

Section 1 Review

1. **Define** Kellogg-Briand Pact, Lytton Commission, Falange
2. **Identify** Yuko Hamaguchi, Francisco Franco, Nationalist, Loyalist, International Brigades
3. **Locate and Explain the Significance** Mukden, Manchukuo, Beijing, Chang Jiang Valley, Ethiopia, Italian Somaliland
4. **Summarizing Ideas** Describe the aggression of Japan and Italy that began in the early 1920s.
5. **Analyzing Ideas** What factors contributed to the ineffectiveness of the League of Nations in dealing with the aggression of Japan and Italy?
6. **Determining Cause and Effect** How did a fascist dictatorship develop in Spain?

Section 2

Hitler's Aggressions

Focus Questions
- **How was Hitler able to acquire Austria and Czechoslovakia?**
- **In what ways did Great Britain and France try to avoid war, and how did they prepare for war when it became inevitable?**
- **How did the major powers of Europe respond to the Nazi-Soviet Pact, and how did they respond to Hitler's invasion of Poland?**

As Germany grew stronger, Adolf Hitler's foreign policy became more aggressive. In 1933 he had taken Germany out of the League of Nations and announced his intention to rearm the country. In March 1936, German troops marched into the Rhineland, violating the Treaty of Versailles. In October 1936, following the outbreak of the Spanish Civil War, Hitler and Mussolini formed a military alliance called the Rome-Berlin Axis and began referring to themselves as the **Axis Powers**.* Shortly afterward Japan and Germany pledged to work together to prevent the spread of Russian communism. They signed an agreement called the **Anti-Comintern Treaty**, which Italy soon endorsed. Thus by the end of 1936, the nations that would eventually enter World War II as the Axis Powers— Germany, Italy, and Japan—had camouflaged their aggressive intentions under the pretense of resisting communism. Hitler became convinced that he could do as he pleased, and for a time he seemed right. The democratic nations had done very little to halt the spread of fascism in Ethiopia and Spain.

Annexing Austria
A Nazi Party had been formed in Austria in the late 1920s. By the early 1930s, the extremely conservative Austrian government was doing little to resist Nazi inroads. By 1938 threats from both Hitler and Mussolini forced the Austrian government to include Nazi members in its cabinet.

Though the Austrian chancellor had made an agreement with Hitler on *Anschluss* (union) with Germany, he regretted the agreement and suggested that the Austrian people be allowed to vote on the issue. Hitler refused to permit it, preferring instead to overcome Austria with a show of strength. The chancellor resigned, and a German army marched into Austria unopposed. In March 1938, Hitler proclaimed Austria a part of the Third Reich. (See map on opposite page.) Even though *Anschluss* was specifically forbidden by the Treaty of Versailles, Great Britain and France did nothing more than send protests to Hitler, which he ignored. The League of Nations took no action.

The addition of Austria enlarged Germany's population, territory, and resources. It also increased Hitler's influence in Europe. Strategically, Germany had now penetrated the heart of central Europe and reached a common border with its ally Italy. The annexation of Austria threatened Czechoslovakia,

---

*Mussolini originated the term *Axis Powers*. He claimed that an imaginary line drawn from Rome to Berlin formed the "axis" on which the world would turn from that time forward.

which Hitler had designated as the next objective in his expansion program. Germany now almost completely encircled Czechoslovakia. Nazi propaganda, however, claimed that Czechoslovakia had become a "dagger pointed at the heart of Germany."

Czechoslovakia and the Sudeten Crisis

Around the western rim of Czechoslovakia, in a region known as the Sudetenland (soo·DAYT·uhn·land), lived more than 3 million Germans. This territory, once part of the huge Habsburg Empire, had been included in Czechoslovakia after World War I. A chain of mountains, which gave the new state a natural and defensible frontier, separated the Sudetenland from Germany and Austria. Czechoslovakia had fortified these mountains heavily. Now they had become a defensive line—second in importance in Europe only to France's Maginot Line.

German and Italian Expansion, 1935–1941

Legend:
- Germany, 1935
- Acquired by Germany, 1935–1939
- German protectorates and Vichy France
- Italy and possessions, 1935
- Acquired by Italy, 1935–1939
- Minor Axis powers, 1941
- Axis advances
- Controlled by Axis, December 1941
- Controlled by Allies, December 1941
- Area of the Battle of Britain
- Neutral countries
- Farthest Soviet advance, 1940

Ethiopia, 1935–1941

Learning from Maps Within six years of expansion, the Axis Powers controlled much of Europe and North Africa.

? Region What countries remained neutral during this period?

The Czech government tried to protect the rights of the Sudeten Germans. It allowed the people to use the German language in their schools and to be represented according to population in the parliament, civil service, and army. Still, many Sudeten Germans wanted union with Germany. Also, a strong Nazi Party grew in the Sudetenland.

After Germany's annexation of Austria, Sudeten Nazis demanded a completely self-governing Sudetenland. Hitler took up their cause. Riots broke out in the Sudetenland, and in September 1938, the situation became so critical that the Czech government placed the country under martial law.

Hitler, representing his actions as protective of fellow Germans, announced that Germany would invade and then annex the Sudetenland. This would mean disaster for Czechoslovakia. The loss of its heavily fortified mountain region would leave the country defenseless against Germany. When Germany sent troops to the frontier, the world waited tensely to see what action Czechoslovakia's allies would take.

The Czechs had defensive alliances with both France and the Soviet Union. The Soviet alliance provided for assistance to the Czechs only if France did likewise. France turned to Great Britain for support. Great Britain, however, urged France to be patient and advised the Czechs to make every possible concession to avoid war. The Czech government then granted increased independence for the Sudetens.

Still dissatisfied, Hitler began to increase Germany's military preparations. On September 22, 1938, he demanded that the Sudetenland be turned over to Germany. If it were not, he said, he would invade it and take it by force.

Appeasement at Munich

As tensions mounted in Europe, Hitler invited the British prime minister, Neville Chamberlain, and

German soldiers enter Prague as residents of the city stand somberly on the sidewalks.

Edouard Daladier (dah·lahd·yay), the premier of France, to attend a meeting in Munich (referred to as the **Munich Conference**). Also in attendance would be Italy's Mussolini. The conference was to begin on September 29, and the four participants would attempt to settle the Czech problem peaceably. Conspicuously not invited to send representatives were the Soviet Union, which, along with France, had pledged to defend Czechoslovakia, and Czechoslovakia itself.

Fearful of German military might and knowing how ill-prepared their own countries were, Chamberlain and Daladier accepted Hitler's demand that the Sudetenland be annexed to Germany. The policy they followed—attempting to preserve peace by yielding to the demands of the aggressor—is known as **appeasement**. Upon his return to London, Chamberlain triumphantly addressed a cheering crowd, announcing that he believed he had achieved "peace in our time."

Soon after the Munich Conference, France announced that it would neither honor its alliance with Czechoslovakia nor provide any assistance. Germany began to occupy the Sudetenland. The small country of Czechoslovakia, deserted by its allies, was now rendered defenseless. The rule of force in international affairs marked yet another victory.

In speaking of the Sudetenland, Hitler stated that it was the last territorial claim he would make in Europe. In March 1939, however, Hitler sent his

What If?

The League of Nations

If the League of Nations had taken stronger actions against Hitler and protected the independence of European countries such as Czechoslovakia, how might the course of world history have been different?

troops throughout the Czech area of Czechoslovakia and made it a German protectorate. He then declared the remainder of the country an independent state called Slovakia, which he soon seized.

Czechoslovakia had been the last democracy in Central Europe. Yet within six months, this independent republic was erased completely from the map. Once again the League of Nations had failed to be effective; its complete helplessness was now obvious. In the meantime, the political situation in Europe headed rapidly toward chaos.

Unchecked Fascist Aggression

Not satisfied with Czechoslovakia, Hitler next moved toward Lithuania. His quarrel with that nation involved the former East Prussian port city of Memel. (See map on page 437.) Germany had surrendered Memel to the Allies under the Versailles Treaty. In 1923 Lithuania took the city.

After Hitler came to power, a Nazi Party formed by the Germans in Memel demanded that Germany annex the city. Hitler echoed these demands. By March 1939, Lithuania could not withstand the pressure and ceded Memel and adjacent territory to Germany.

Still another nation lost its independence in the spring of 1939. Mussolini, once a model for other dictators, had by now become Hitler's imitator. In April 1939, Mussolini invaded Albania, on the east coast of the Adriatic Sea. (See map on page 437.) The Italians took the country in only a few days. King Zog and Queen Geraldine fled the country, and the king of Italy, who had recently become emperor of Ethiopia, gained an additional title—king of Albania.

Preparations for War

After Hitler took over Czechoslovakia, British and French leaders could no longer maintain their illusions about the intentions of the fascist dictators. Britain and France therefore began to prepare for war. In Great Britain, Neville Chamberlain ordered that Britain's rearmament program be stepped up and rushed a draft law through Parliament. France already had a defensive alliance with Poland. Great Britain announced that it, too, would help Poland if Germany attacked.

France also had a nonaggression treaty with the Soviet Union. Now Great Britain and France approached the Soviet leader, Joseph Stalin, suggesting a mutual alliance against Germany. Even though the Soviet Union had joined the League of Nations, while Japan, Germany, and Italy had dropped out, Soviet leaders remained suspicious of the Western democracies. Until this time, the Western nations—fearful of communism—had excluded the Soviet Union from all major decisions affecting Europe and the rest of the world. The Soviet leaders in turn feared that the Western powers would welcome a chance to turn Hitler loose on them.

The Soviets insisted that any mutual assistance pact they might sign with Great Britain and France guarantee the independence of Poland, Finland, and the Baltic countries of Estonia, Latvia, and Lithuania. The Soviets also wanted a military alliance with all of these countries to ensure immediate response in the event of a German attack. This suggestion brought instant protests from the nations involved. All but Lithuania had common borders with the Soviet Union. A military agreement would mean that, in case of a German attack, Soviet armies would have the right to move into their countries to meet the Germans. The negotiations dragged on, resulting in a stalemate.

The Nazi-Soviet Pact

At the same time that Stalin was negotiating with Great Britain and France, he was carrying on secret negotiations with Germany. In August 1939, the Western democracies received a tremendous shock. Hitler proudly announced a **German-Soviet nonaggression pact**. Soviet leaders in Moscow soon confirmed the announcement.

This cartoon satirizes Stalin's pact with Hitler; together they agreed to carve eastern Europe into new territory for the Soviet Union and Germany.

The reasons for such an agreement between openly declared enemies were not immediately apparent. However, many historians believe that neither the Germans nor the Soviets expected the treaty to be a lasting one. Both Hitler and Stalin may simply have been playing for time. Hitler wanted to assure himself of Soviet neutrality in the event that Britain and France took action against Germany. Stalin apparently hoped that Hitler would find himself bogged down in the West. This would give the Soviet Union adequate time to prepare for its eventual, inevitable encounter with Germany.

Publicly the German-Soviet nonaggression pact, also called the Nazi-Soviet Pact, pledged that Germany and the Soviet Union would never attack each other. Each would remain neutral if the other became involved in war. Secretly, however, the two dictators agreed to divide eastern Europe into spheres of influence. Germany was to take western Poland. The Soviet Union was to have a free hand in the Baltic countries, in eastern Poland, and in the province of Bessarabia, which it had lost to Romania in 1918.

Little doubt existed as to the meaning of the pact. The Western nations had lost a possible ally in the East, and Germany had secured a pledge of the Soviet Union's neutrality, a tremendous military advantage.

Danzig and the Polish Corridor

The crisis that finally touched off World War II began in Poland. Hitler's dispute with that country involved the Polish Corridor, the strip of territory cut through Germany to allow Poland access to the seaport of Danzig. (See map on page 437.) Danzig was a free city, protected by the League of Nations. Both Germany and Poland had rights to use the port.

Because Danzig had a large German population, Hitler claimed it for Germany. A strong Nazi Party, encouraged by propaganda and financial help from Berlin, developed in Danzig. By 1937 it controlled the city government. It took actions and issued demands that made relations with Poland increasingly difficult. The city commissioner appointed by the League was powerless to do anything.

After securing Austria and Czechoslovakia, Hitler intensified his campaign against Poland. Within a week after signing the nonaggression pact with the Soviet Union, Hitler demanded that Danzig be returned to Germany and that the Germans be allowed to occupy a strip running through the Polish Corridor.

On the morning of September 1, 1939, Hitler declared the annexation of Danzig to the Reich.

At the same time, without warning, his air force launched a massive attack on Poland. Nazi troops, led by tank columns, penetrated the border. Two days later Great Britain and France decided that they would not tolerate any further Nazi aggression. They kept their promises to Poland and declared war on Germany. Within 48 hours the unannounced attack on Poland had become the beginning of World War II.

Section 2 Review

1. **Define** Axis Powers, Anti-Comintern Treaty, Munich Conference, appeasement, German-Soviet nonaggression pact
2. **Identify** Neville Chamberlain, Edouard Daladier
3. **Locate and Explain the Significance** Sudetenland, Munich, Memel, Albania, Polish Corridor, Danzig
4. **Evaluating Ideas** How did Hitler's annexation of Austria benefit Germany?
5. **Sequencing Ideas** Describe the steps by which Hitler took over Czechoslovakia.
6. **Understanding Ideas (a)** How and why did Great Britain and France try to appease Hitler? **(b)** What preparations did these two countries make for war when Hitler's intentions became clear to them?
7. **Summarizing Ideas** How did the German-Soviet pact and Hitler's aggression in Poland lead to World War II?

Section 3

Axis Gains

Focus Questions

- How did control of Norway, Denmark, and the Low Countries benefit Hitler?
- What success did Hitler have in France?
- What was the Battle of Britain, and why were the Germans unable to prevail?
- What role did the United States play at the outset of the war, and how did that role change?

Hitler's invasion of Poland introduced the world to a new kind of warfare. The attack was a **blitzkrieg**

(German for "lightning war"); that is, it was conducted with great speed and force. Dive-bombers screamed from the skies, dropping explosives on cities. Panzer* units—tanks and armored trucks—advanced swiftly. Poland was unprepared for this kind of mechanized warfare. After a month of resistance, Poland surrendered to Hitler.

The "Phony War"

While Germany attacked Poland, France moved its army up to the Maginot Line, the chain of fortifications guarding France's eastern frontier. British forces landed on the northern coast of France. The British navy blockaded Germany's ports. The Germans massed troops behind the Siegfried Line, the system of fortifications they had built in the Rhineland. Although German submarines had begun to sink merchant ships, there was little action on the western front. Despite the increase in mobilization and arms production, newspapers began to speak of the **"phony war"** in western Europe. Many people referred to this war as a "sitzkrieg," or sitting war, instead of a blitzkrieg. Some still hoped that an all-out war could be avoided.

As the Germans marched into Poland from the west, the Soviet army massed on the Soviet-Polish border. Then, in accordance with the secret provisions of the Nazi-Soviet Pact, the Soviets invaded eastern Poland on September 17. Once again Poland disappeared from the map of Europe. The Soviets also seized control of Estonia, Latvia, and Lithuania.

On November 30, 1939, the Soviet Union attacked Finland. The Finns appealed to the League of Nations, which did little but expel the Soviet Union for its aggression against a fellow member nation. Although the Finns fought bravely, their resistance crumbled in March 1940.

Scandinavia and the Low Countries

On April 9, 1940, the "phony war" ended with a sudden German invasion of Denmark and Norway. The Germans could sometimes rely on help from **collaborators,** people who were willing to assist their country's enemies. In Norway a critical collaborator was a Norwegian Fascist Party leader named Quisling, whose name is now used as a synonym for the word *traitor.* He gave significant aid to the occupying forces, even providing information prior to the invasion. In a single day, German troops seized several of Norway's strategic North Sea ports. Both Denmark and Norway fell to German control.

*Panzer comes from the German word for armor.

The reasons for Hitler's invasion of these countries soon became clear. By seizing them, Germany had secured an outlet to the Atlantic. Thus Hitler made certain that his country's navy would not be bottled up in the Baltic Sea as it had in World War I. The long, irregular Scandinavian coastline gave Germany excellent submarine bases. The terrain also provided many good sites for airfields. Thus shipping to France and Great Britain was put in grave danger.

The British realized that Hitler now posed an immediate threat to their safety. Neville Chamberlain, who symbolized the policy of appeasement, was forced to resign as prime minister in May 1940. He was succeeded by Winston Churchill, one of the few prominent politicians to attack appeasement and to warn against the Nazi menace in the 1930s.

Hitler, meanwhile, continued to attack. On May 10, 1940, German armored units invaded the Low Countries—the Netherlands, Belgium, and Luxembourg. Luxembourg fell in one day, the Netherlands in five. When the Dutch city of Rotterdam resisted the German army, Hitler ordered his air force to attack it. Even while a surrender was being negotiated, Nazi bombers leveled the heart of the city. At the end of May, Belgium also surrendered.

Hitler's forces were now in a position to outflank France's Maginot Line. German panzers drove westward toward the English Channel. Reaching the coast, they cut off a large number of British,

A blitzkrieg or "lightning war," such as the one Germany used against Poland, included military tactics of speed and surprise. Germany's motorized army is shown speeding into Poland.

Belgian, and French troops from the main French force to the south. Outnumbered and with no room to maneuver, the encircled Allied troops attempted to evacuate from the French seaport of Dunkirk.

Evacuation of Dunkirk. The British air force, badly outnumbered, struggled to assist the trapped forces in Dunkirk. Fortunately, the German ground forces stopped their advance. Every available ship and boat—even fishing craft and rowboats—in Britain was ordered to Dunkirk. They were subject to attacks by aircraft, submarines, and artillery as they picked up troops from the beaches. Between May 27 and June 4, about 338,000 men were safely transported across the channel to England, although all their heavy equipment was lost.

The reason why Hitler did not attack the retreating Allies is not known for certain. For three days, he held back his tanks, probably believing his air force could finish off the Allied forces. This decision would later be considered a costly mistake because it allowed Britain to rally.

Although Dunkirk represented a military defeat for the Allies, the success of the rescue operation helped raise British morale considerably. On June 4, Prime Minister Churchill addressed the British people in one of his most stirring speeches. His forceful and engaging voice boomed over the airwaves:

> "We shall go on to the end, we shall fight in France, we shall fight on the seas and oceans, we shall fight with growing confidence and growing strength in the air, we shall defend our island, whatever the cost may be, we shall fight on the beaches, we shall fight on the landing grounds, we shall fight in the fields and in the streets, we shall fight in the hills; we shall never surrender, and even if, which I do not for a moment believe, this island or a large part of it were subjugated and starving, then our Empire beyond the seas, armed and guarded by the British fleet, would carry on the struggle, until, in God's good time, the New World, with all its power and might, steps forth to the rescue and the liberation of the old."

The Fall of France

After the evacuation of Dunkirk, the French were left to fight alone on the European continent. The Maginot Line was useless. Having taken Belgium, the Germans were in a position to attack France from the north, where few fortifications existed.

Germany turned southward to attack the heart of France early in June 1940. The French fought a desperate, losing battle. Their army, anticipating the static fighting of World War I, was neither trained nor equipped for this new kind of war. Northern France was a scene of utter confusion. Civilians, carrying whatever possessions they could, blocked roads in their attempt to flee southward. German planes bombed and machine-gunned the refugees, causing further panic and disorder.

Mussolini, taking advantage of France's weakness, declared war on France and Great Britain on June 10, and Italian forces attacked southern France. On June 14, the Germans entered Paris, and the French armed resistance in the north collapsed. Rather than surrender, the French cabinet resigned.

Some French leaders, however, were willing to surrender. The aged Marshal Philippe Pétain (PAY·tan), a hero of World War I, formed a government and assumed dictatorial powers. Late in June, Hitler forced the Pétain government to sign an armistice with Germany and Italy. Hitler insisted it be signed in the same railroad car where the Germans had signed the armistice to end World War I in November 1918.

The terms of the armistice were severe. German troops were to occupy northern France, including Paris, and a strip of territory along the Atlantic coast southward to Spain. France had to pay the costs of this occupation. The French navy was to be disarmed and confined to French ports. Pétain's government moved to the city of Vichy (VISH·ee), in the south. Thus France was divided into occupied France, administered by the Germans, and Vichy France, which collaborated with the Germans. The Vichy government also controlled most French possessions in North Africa and the Middle East.

The French Resistance. Some of the French who wanted to continue to fight against Germany escaped to Africa or to Britain. Under the leadership of General Charles de Gaulle (duh GOHL), they formed the Free French government, with its headquarters in London. As the war went on, the Free French army, equipped by the Americans and British, played a part in several campaigns.

Within France itself, an underground movement, the resistance, flourished. Its members worked secretly to oppose the occupying German forces. Similar resistance movements developed in other German-occupied countries as well. Members of some of these resistance groups were called *maquis* (mah·KEE)—a French term for scrubby undergrowth, common in the areas where resistance fighters hid.

Resistance to Nazi Occupation

Tens of thousands of ordinary people chose to act with extraordinary courage and resist Nazi domination in Europe by forming underground resistance organizations. In many countries, small bands of guerrilla fighters lived in the countryside, harassing German troops and destroying military trains and communication lines. In urban areas, resistance members published underground newspapers, passed information about the Nazis on to the Allied forces, provided safe houses for people hunted by the Nazis, and performed acts of sabotage.

No group in Europe was more at risk from Nazi tyranny than the Jews. Many European

U.S. Postal Stamp honoring Raoul Wallenberg

citizens risked their lives to protect their Jewish neighbors from being deported to the Nazi camps, where death was almost certain. Jews were hidden in secret rooms, in attics, and in barns. Many individuals also helped Jews escape Nazi-occupied Europe to other countries.

One such person was the Swedish diplomat Raoul Wallenberg, who helped save as many as 100,000 Hungarian Jews. He issued Swedish passports to Jews, which allowed them to claim protection from neutral Sweden. He hid many in houses he had bought or rented himself, and toward the end of the war, he persuaded the Nazis to spare the lives of 70,000 Jews living in a ghetto in Budapest.

To cripple the Germans, the *maquis* engaged in sabotage. They blew up bridges, wrecked trains, and cut telephone and telegraph lines.

The Battle of Britain

After France fell, French generals predicted that Britain, which they considered a weaker country, would "in three weeks . . . have her neck wrung like a chicken." (Churchill later commented: "Some chicken! Some neck!")

Hitler began scattered bombing raids on Great Britain, gradually increasing them in intensity. He then offered to negotiate a peace settlement, but Churchill rebuffed him.

At the end of June 1940, Churchill braced the British people for the dangerous battle that he was certain would soon come.

❝Hitler knows that he will have to break us in this island or lose the war. If we can stand up to him, all Europe may be free and the life of the world may move forward into broad, sunlit uplands. But if we fail, then the whole world, including the United States, including all that we have known and cared for, will sink into the abyss of a new Dark Age. . . . Let us therefore brace ourselves to our duties, and so bear ourselves that, if the British Empire and its Commonwealth last for a thousand years, men will say, 'This was their finest hour.'❞

Hitler ordered his air force, the **Luftwaffe**, to soften up Britain for invasion. He shifted the *Luftwaffe* squadrons to airfields closer to Britain, in occupied France and Belgium. Germany first focused its devastating air attacks on British military targets. Later the Germans struck at railroads and civilian and industrial targets. This period of Germany's air raids on Britain is known as the **Battle of Britain**.

German bombers blasted British cities with explosives and firebombs. The *Luftwaffe* bombed London continually during September and October. In November the city of Coventry burned almost to the ground. The Germans wanted to lower morale and destroy the people's will to fight, but the undaunted British resolutely dug out of the ruins and carried on. Essential to their resistance was the more and more

The Battle of Britain, lasting 10 months, involved a series of German air attacks against Great Britain. Here a mother and daughter prepare homemade wooden shutters for protection.

United States Involvement

In a series of **Neutrality Acts** passed between 1935 and 1937, the United States had expressed its determination to remain neutral in future wars. This legislation forbade Americans to sell war equipment to belligerent nations, prohibited loans to belligerents, prohibited Americans from sailing on ships of belligerents, and restricted the entry of American ships into war zones.

When war in Europe broke out in 1939, many people believed that Nazi Germany threatened not only Europe but civilization itself. The majority of Americans, however, believed that Europe's wars were of no concern to the United States. These **isolationists**, as they were called, had risen to power at the end of World War I and were responsible, in part, for keeping the United States out of the League of Nations. Now, however, their power began to fade as fear of a Nazi conquest of the world increased.

In 1939 a revised Neutrality Act allowed American firms to sell munitions to belligerent nations on a cash-and-carry basis. In spite of German submarine attacks, Great Britain still controlled the sea routes between the United States and Great Britain. Thus, in effect this law permitted the sale of arms only to Great Britain.

After the evacuation from Dunkirk and the fall of France, American sympathy for the British increased. President Franklin D. Roosevelt was convinced that Britain was the front line of a war that would involve the United States sooner or later. In September 1940, President Roosevelt, by executive order, transferred 50 old American naval destroyers to Great Britain. In exchange Great Britain gave the United States long-term leases on naval and air bases in Newfoundland, the West Indies, and British Guiana. In that same month, Congress passed the first national draft law ever adopted by the United States during peacetime.

Early in 1941, Churchill appealed to the United States: "Give us the tools, and we will finish the job." In March, Congress passed the **Lend-Lease Act**, authorizing the president to supply war materials to Great Britain on credit. Now the direction of America's involvement became clear.

The Atlantic Charter

To avoid the criticism that the secret treaties of World War I had raised, President Roosevelt and Prime Minister Churchill publicly announced the national policies of the two democracies. In August 1941, they met on board a British battleship off the

successful defense by fighter planes of the Royal Air Force, or the RAF.

British planes, though fewer in number, were more maneuverable than the German planes. British pilots flew combat missions day after day, night after night. The RAF also had radar, a new electronic tracking device that helped detect the approach of enemy aircraft or ships. This prevented the Germans from making surprise attacks. Without the element of surprise, the *Luftwaffe* was not able to dominate. The RAF's control of the air prevented German invasion across the English Channel. Of the British fighter pilots, Churchill said, "Never in the field of human conflict was so much owed by so many to so few."

The Germans continued their night bombing raids for almost two years. At the same time, British bombers made increasingly heavy raids on German cities. By the middle of 1941, air warfare had leveled off, partly because Germany had begun directing some of its war resources to the east. However, because of Germany's effective blockade of British shipping from European ports, there was a chance that Great Britain could be starved into surrendering. This might have happened had it not been for the United States.

coast of Newfoundland and drew up a statement that became known as the **Atlantic Charter**.

Among its provisions and in the spirit of Wilson's Fourteen Points, the charter stated that Britain and the United States (1) sought no territorial gain, (2) would allow no territorial changes without the consent of the people concerned, (3) respected the right of all people to choose their own form of government, (4) believed that all nations should have equal rights to trade and to raw materials, (5) wanted nations to cooperate on economic matters to ensure everyone a decent standard of living, (6) believed people everywhere should have the right to security and freedom from want and fear, (7) believed freedom of the seas should be guaranteed, and (8) believed that nations must abolish the use of force and establish a system of general security, implying the formation of an international organization.

By autumn 1941, the United States Navy was waging an undeclared war on German submarines. American warships escorted convoys in the western Atlantic, allowing the British to concentrate in the eastern Atlantic. Isolationist opinion remained strong in the United States, although the bombing of British cities had aroused American sympathy. Now the only remaining restrictions prohibited American merchant ships from being armed or entering war zones. In November 1941, Congress abolished even these restrictions. The United States now gave the British all aid short of joining in the war.

Section 3 Review

1. **Define** blitzkrieg, "phony war," collaborators, *Luftwaffe*, Battle of Britain, Neutrality Acts, isolationists, Lend-Lease Act, Atlantic Charter

2. **Identify** Winston Churchill, Philippe Pétain, Charles de Gaulle, *maquis*, Franklin D. Roosevelt

3. **Locate and Explain the Significance** Maginot Line, Siegfried Line, Rotterdam, Dunkirk, Vichy France, occupied France, Coventry

4. **Summarizing Ideas** Summarize German progress in the war through the first half of 1941.

5. **Evaluating Ideas** How was British airpower able to prevent a German invasion across the English Channel?

6. **Sequencing Ideas** Describe the progression of United States involvement in World War II from the Neutrality Acts to giving Great Britain all aid short of entering the war.

The Soviet Union and the United States

Focus Questions

- **What steps did the Axis Powers take in an effort to control eastern Europe, the Middle East, and the Soviet Union?**
- **What did Hitler hope to accomplish with his "New Order" and his "Final Solution"?**
- **How did Japan's goals in the Pacific lead to war with Britain and the United States?**

In the fall of 1940, Germany held almost all of western Europe. It controlled the Atlantic coastline from the tip of Norway to southern France. (Spain, under Franco's fascist rule, remained neutral but allowed German submarines to use its ports.) Italy and Germany also controlled much of the western Mediterranean coastline, an important advantage.

Great Britain still held Gibraltar, on the southern coast of Spain; the islands of Malta and Cyprus, in the Mediterranean; and Alexandria, in Egypt. British troops were stationed in Palestine and in Egypt, protecting the Suez Canal. In September Japan joined the Rome-Berlin Axis, allying itself with Hitler and Mussolini.

Eastern Europe and the Mediterranean

Mussolini, hoping to build a Mediterranean empire for Italy, sent his troops into Egypt and Greece in the fall of 1940. The decision proved to be unwise. The attack on Greece quickly bogged down. The British stopped the Italian army's advance into Egypt. In their counterattack, the British took Tobruk, a port city of Libya. (See map on page 437.) An Italian invasion of British Somaliland at the same time also failed, and a counterattack by the British drove the Italians out of Ethiopia as well.

When Hitler turned his attention to the Balkans, Axis fortunes in eastern Europe improved. Germany seized Romania, needed for its rich oil fields. In March 1941, pressure on Bulgaria resulted in German occupation. By November, Romania, Bulgaria, and Hungary had allied themselves with Germany.

In April 1941, Hitler invaded Yugoslavia, having failed to persuade its government to allow German

World War II in Europe and North Africa, 1939–1945

Major battles:
- �֍ — Britain, July–Oct. 1940
- ✷ — Leningrad, Sept. 1941–Jan. 1944
- ✷ — El Alamein, Oct. 1942
- ✷ — Stalingrad, Sept. 1942–Feb. 1943
- ✷ — Kursk, July 1943
- ✷ — Anzio, Jan.–Mar. 1944
- ✷ — D-Day, June 6, 1944
- ✷ — Minsk, July 1944
- ✷ — The Bulge, Dec. 1944–Jan. 1945
- ✷ — Warsaw, Aug.–Oct. 1944
- ✷ — Berlin, Apr.–May 1945

Allied countries	
Axis countries	
Axis-controlled territory, 1942	
Neutral countries	
→ Allied advance	
→ Axis advance	
✳ National capital	
• Other city	

Nonaggression pact with Germany, Aug. 23, 1939

Learning from Maps   World War II transformed Europe and North Africa into one huge battlefield.

 Location   What two battles took place along the 50°N parallel in Europe?

troops to march through to Greece. Although the Germans crushed the Yugoslav army in less than two weeks, Yugoslavs waged an effective guerrilla campaign for the rest of the war.

Next came Greece. Despite fierce resistance by the Greeks, assisted by British troops, the German forces quickly prevailed. The British withdrew to the island of Crete, which the Germans captured in May with a parachute assault. Thus Germany controlled the Balkan Peninsula except for European Turkey. (See map on this page.) In June, Germany and Turkey signed a treaty ensuring Turkish neutrality.

The German victories in the Balkans set the stage for Hitler's more basic goal, the invasion of the Soviet Union. Axis forces were also in a position to threaten the Middle East. The rich oil fields of the region would have given Hitler a considerable advantage, and the loss of the Suez Canal would have endangered the British position in India, Southeast Asia, and the Pacific. The French mandates, Lebanon and Syria, were controlled by the Vichy government, and many citizens of Iraq and Egypt, eager to be rid of their British occupiers, leaned toward the Axis.

A pro-Axis coup d'etat in Iraq in the spring of 1941 sharpened Allied fears. British and Indian troops moved in and crushed the coup in May, while Free French forces drove the Vichy French out of Lebanon and Syria in July. Now the Allies turned their attention to North Africa, where the situation had grown worse.

German troops, commanded by General Erwin Rommel—soon to be nicknamed the Desert Fox—had moved across the Mediterranean to Libya in early 1941. These forces quickly inflicted several defeats on the British, driving them back into Egypt. Fighting raged back and forth through 1941 and 1942.

However, by the summer of 1942 the British were achieving success in the naval and air war in the Mediterranean, allowing them to build up troops and equipment in North Africa while increasingly cutting off Axis supplies. In October, Rommel's forces were soundly beaten at the Battle of El Alamein. (See map on page 446.) Now the Axis forces, unable to make up their losses, retreated to Tunisia.

Germany's Attack on the Soviet Union

The Soviet Union regarded the German victories in the Balkans with alarm and anger. It considered the Balkans, especially Romania and Bulgaria, to be within its own sphere of influence.

At a Soviet-German conference in Berlin in November 1940, the Soviets demanded that Bulgaria, Istanbul, the Dardanelles, and the Bosporus be retained in their sphere of influence. Hitler suggested instead that Germany should have Europe and that the Soviet Union should establish a sphere in Asia. The Soviets rejected this suggestion.

On June 22, 1941, the war entered a new phase. Without declaring war, German armies invaded the Soviet Union. Hitler had opened a massive new front in the east, 2,000 miles long from north to south. Churchill offered aid to the Soviet Union, and the United States also declared its willingness to help.

Sending aid to the Soviets, however, was extremely difficult. Ships could not sail the route across the Mediterranean and through the Dardanelles, the Bosporus, and the Black Sea without risking submarine and air attacks from bases in Italy and the Balkans. The route through the Baltic Sea was impossible. Convoys to two Soviet ports, Murmansk and Archangel in the Arctic, had to pass the long, German-held coast of Norway. To avoid these dangers, the Allies developed a new route from the Persian Gulf across Iran by train and truck to the southern part of the Soviet Union.

The Soviet Defense

The initial thrust of the Nazis into the Soviet Union was devastating. Everywhere the Soviet armies were driven back. Soon Moscow and Leningrad were under siege. There, however, the attack bogged down.

The Soviet defenders used the same scorched-earth tactics against Hitler that their ancestors had used against Napoleon. The retreating soldiers and civilians carried away what they could and destroyed everything else. Thus the territory the Germans gained was more a hindrance than a help. In addition, many Soviet soldiers remained hidden in swamps and forests, making daring guerrilla attacks on railroads, bridges, and trains.

Hitler had expected the Soviet Union to surrender quickly. The long sieges at Leningrad and Moscow disrupted his timetable, however. When the short Russian autumn came, Hitler faced the same decision Napoleon had had to make: Should he retreat or should he stand? Hitler chose to stand.

Soon the Germans had to face a new enemy—the bitterly cold Russian winter. The Soviets chose the winter for a counterattack, which was intended primarily to relieve pressure on Moscow. The Germans were forced to retreat.

The year 1941 ended with the Germans deep inside the Soviet Union. In the spring of 1942 Hitler ordered a new offensive to the south. The strategic objective was the oil-producing area around Baku, on the shore of the Caspian Sea. To protect the flank of that main attack, a part of the German army was to capture the city of Stalingrad on the Volga River. (See map on page 446.) German troops pushed into Stalingrad on September 12, 1942, but there Soviet resistance grew stronger. Hitler now made capture of Stalingrad the main objective of the offensive, while Stalin ordered that the city be held at all costs. The Battle of Stalingrad had begun.

"New Order" and "Final Solution"

The invasion of the Soviet Union was part of Hitler's master plan for a European **"New Order."**

Geopolitics

Early on the morning of September 1, 1939, German tanks, troop carriers, and dive-bombers poured over the Polish border. The Polish army, outnumbered perhaps two to one, fought valiantly, but it was no match for the overwhelming surprise attack. In just a few weeks, Poland was utterly defeated by Hitler's blitzkrieg. World War II had begun.

Theories of geopolitics current at the time helped inspire Hitler's aggressive policies. In the decades before World War II, Englishman Sir Halford J. Mackinder and German Karl Haushofer had attempted to develop geopolitics into a science. Both had developed theories that attempted to "prove" that world domination in the future would be based on the control of Europe, Asia, and Africa. These theories treated these three continents as a single landmass, called the World Island. The World Island held the majority of the world's population and natural resources, so control of it by any single nation would inevitably allow control of the rest of the world. The key to controlling the World Island, according to these theorists, was control of the region Mackinder named the Heartland, which included eastern Europe and the western Soviet Union. A nation that controlled this strategic area would be self-sufficient in food and natural resources, and would be in a position to conquer the rest of the World Island.

Historians are not certain to what extent Hitler was directly influenced by the writings of Mackinder and Haushofer. However, even before the Nazis came to power in Germany their political agenda included the need for *Lebensraum*, "living space" in which the German people could expand. Hitler rejected overseas colonies as the solution to this problem, and insisted that the necessary territory was to be found in eastern Europe. Of course, since this territory was already populated, this would require military invasion.

In Hitler's view, people and nations were locked in a constant struggle for existence. Therefore, the German people were perfectly justified in conquering land that was populated by Slavic peoples, who were, according to Hitler, biologically inferior. This view, in turn, fit perfectly with another of Hitler's motivations, his hatred of communism and the Soviet Union.

Nazi troops in Warsaw, Poland

Hitler's racist ideas helped convince him that the Soviets would be easily defeated by the soldiers of the German "master race."

Germany was not alone in its aggressive expansionism. Japan also had too many people and too few resources, and it was heavily dependent on imports of raw materials. Following the worldwide economic collapse in 1929, Japan developed a policy of expansionism. In 1931 Japan seized the Chinese territory of Manchuria, which had plentiful natural resources. In 1937 the Japanese attacked China, and by 1939 they controlled a large portion of eastern China. Japanese military leaders began plans for a Pacific empire that would include all of eastern Asia.

The struggle for territory by both Germany and Japan ultimately failed, but not before it brought a war in which millions of lives were lost. In the end, expansionist policies brought devastation to Germany and Japan, as well as to much of Europe and Asia.

Geopolitics are still an influence on international relations today. However, they are no longer considered as important as they were in the past. Technological advances such as improved communications and transportation have helped nations overcome geographical factors that once limited them. The ability of bombers and, above all, long-range missiles to attack from one continent to another with nuclear weapons means that no geographical barrier or strategic territory can ensure military security.

Hitler wanted to organize the European continent into a single political and economic system ruled from Berlin and dominated by the "Aryan race." According to this plan, the Soviet Union would supply Germany with food and raw materials. Any problems this would cause the Russians were not of concern to Hitler. According to Nazi ideology, all Slavs were "racially inferior."

Another aspect of Hitler's "New Order" went into effect as the Germans continued their offensives. In 1941 Hitler ordered the annihilation of the entire Jewish population of Europe. The Nazis referred to this program as the **"Final Solution"** of the "Jewish question." This unbelievably barbaric goal was possible in Hitler's Germany because of the zeal of the minority who accepted Nazi theories about Aryan superiority and because of the passivity of the majority of Germans.

Jews were transported to Germany and Poland by the hundreds of thousands. There they were held in "protective custody" in concentration camps. Among the most infamous of these camps were Dachau and Buchenwald in Germany. In Poland there were Treblinka and **Auschwitz**, which were extermination camps. Those Jews who were not shot or murdered by poison gas lived in unspeakable conditions. The combination of forced labor, brutal treatment, starvation, squalor, and disease killed thousands of other camp residents.

In his book *Never to Forget*, Milton Meltzer quotes an SS* officer sent to a Polish death camp to deliver poison gas. There he witnessed the mass extermination of Polish Jews. The following excerpt is from the officer's handwritten account.

"They all walked along the path . . . and entered the death chambers. A sturdy SS man stood in the corner and told the wretched people in a clerical tone of voice: 'Nothing at all is going to happen to you! You must take a deep breath in the chambers. That expands the lungs. This inhalation is necessary because of illness and infection. . . .'

This gave some of these poor people a glimmer of hope that lasted long enough for them to take the few steps into the chambers without resisting. The majority realized—the smell told them—what their fate was to be. So they climbed the steps and then they saw everything. . . . They hesitated, but they went into the gas chambers, pushed on by those behind them, or driven by the leather whips of the SS. . . . Many people were praying. . . .

The SS forced as many in together as was physically possible. The doors closed. . . . After 28 minutes only a few were still alive. At last, after 32 minutes everyone was dead.

Men of the work squad opened the wooden doors from the other side. . . . The dead were standing upright . . . pressed together in the chambers. . . . One could see the families even in death. They were still holding hands. . . . Two dozen dentists opened the mouths with hooks and looked for gold. . . . The . . . corpses were carried in wooden barrows just a few meters away to pits."

During the war, people in some western European countries, especially Denmark, tried to protect Jewish citizens. In eastern Europe, however, a long tradition of anti-Semitism made the Nazi program easier to carry out and its results more devastating.

By the time the Nazi government fell, its leaders and its followers had murdered an estimated 6 million European Jews. This systematic Nazi destruction of almost an entire race is referred to as the **Holocaust**. The Nazis also murdered millions of Slavs, Gypsies, homosexuals, and others who did not fit the perfect "Aryan mold."

Japanese Aggressions in the Pacific

The struggle against the Axis Powers took another important turn in December 1941, when events in the Pacific drew the United States into the war. Japanese militarism and aggression had increased throughout the 1930s. Japanese armies pushed farther and farther into China, although the Chinese continued to resist. Early in 1939, with the situation in Europe growing increasingly tense, Japan saw a chance to extend its control over Southeast Asia. Japan first captured several small islands off the coast of French Indochina. (See map on page 453.) Thus Japan severed the British sea route from Hong Kong to Singapore. Neither France nor Great Britain had a chance to prevent this move.

After both the Netherlands and France fell, Japan made further aggressive moves in East Asia. The Japanese government declared the Netherlands East Indies to be under Japanese "protective custody." The Japanese forced the Vichy government to allow French Indochina to become a Japanese protectorate.

---

*Hitler's SS (*Schutzstaffel*) was the military arm of the Nazi Party, sworn to absolute obedience. Members served as Hitler's bodyguards and later took charge of intelligence, central security, and the extermination of people in concentration camps.

In September 1940, Japan formed an alliance with Germany and Italy. The United States disapproved but did nothing. In April 1941, Japan and the Soviet Union signed a five-year nonaggression treaty. In July Japan, knowing it was taking a risk, moved farther south to occupy lands in French Indochina. The United States responded to this action in three ways: by protesting violations of the Nine-Power Pact of 1922, by providing assistance to the Chinese Nationalists, and by placing an embargo on the sale of oil and scrap iron to Japan. Japan thus became even more intent on securing oil reserves in the Netherlands East Indies. Now only the American-held Philippines and the Hawaiian Islands threatened Japanese supremacy in the Pacific. The United States, meanwhile, had already moved a large part of its Pacific Fleet to Hawaii.

Relations between the United States and Japan steadily deteriorated. An even more militaristic government came to power in Japan under Premier Hideki Tojo. Early in 1941, the Japanese government had decided that war could not be avoided. They began to plan a surprise attack on the U.S. Pacific Fleet. In spite of that plan, the Japanese government sent special "peace" mission representatives to Washington, D.C., in November.

American Entry into the War

On December 7, 1941, while Tojo's representatives were still in Washington, the Japanese launched a surprise bombing raid on the American naval base at Pearl Harbor, Hawaii. They intended to strike such a severe blow that the United States would be unable to resist the Japanese in the Pacific. Several American battleships were sunk; others were badly damaged. American dead totaled more than 2,300. By luck, the three American aircraft carriers escaped the attack. These vessels were vital to U.S. efforts later.

In an excerpt from his book *At Dawn We Slept*, historian Gordon Prange relates an eyewitness account of the attack on Pearl Harbor.

❝When the attack began, . . . the explosion of bombs, the whine of bullets, the roar of planes, the belching guns of aroused defenders, the acrid smell of fire and smoke—all blended into a nerve-racking cacophony [sound] of chaos. . . . Bombardiers still dropped their torpedoes, while dive bombers pounced like hawks. . . . Far above, high-level bombers rained their deadly missiles as fighters shuttled in and out, weaving together the fearful tapestry of destruction.**❞**

"THE GIRL HE LEFT BEHIND" IS STILL BEHIND HIM
She's a **WOW**
WOMAN ORDNANCE WORKER

During World War II, the warring nations used posters, cartoons, and radio announcements as propaganda to encourage civilians to take part in the war effort.

On December 8, 1941, Congress declared war on Japan, as did the British Parliament. Three days later, Germany and Italy declared war on the United States, and Congress replied with its own declaration of war. The United States became a full-fledged belligerent in World War II.

The Japanese quickly took advantage of American unreadiness. On the same day as the attack on Pearl Harbor, Japan captured the American island outpost of Guam and began aerial attacks on the Philippines. Soon afterward the Japanese landed on the island of Luzon. In less than three months, mainland areas of Burma, Thailand, and Malaya, including the mighty British fortress of Singapore, fell to Japan. (See map on page 453.)

The Japanese went on to conquer what became a vast island empire: most of the Netherlands East Indies (Indonesia), the Philippines, and the Gilbert Islands. Australia remained the last stronghold of resistance in the southwest Pacific. The landing of the Japanese on New Guinea and the Solomon Islands, however, threatened to cut off Australia's critical supply routes from Hawaii.

Section 4 Review

1. **Define** "New Order," "Final Solution," Auschwitz, the Holocaust
2. **Identify** Erwin Rommel, Hideki Tojo
3. **Locate and Explain the Significance** El Alamein, Murmansk, Stalingrad, Pearl Harbor, Gilbert Islands, Solomon Islands
4. **Summarizing Ideas** Describe the success of the Axis attacks on eastern Europe, the Middle East, and the Soviet Union.
5. **Interpreting Ideas** (a) What were Hitler's plans for a "New Order" in Europe? (b) How did his "Final Solution" fit into this plan?
6. **Analyzing Ideas** (a) What did the Japanese hope to gain by their attack on Pearl Harbor? (b) Did they succeed? Explain your answer.

Section 5

The End of the War

Focus Questions

- What success did the Allies experience in North Africa, Italy, and at sea?
- How did the Allies achieve victory in Europe?
- What steps did the Allies take to end the war with Japan?

Representatives of 26 nations met in Washington, D.C., in January 1942 to unite in the common purpose of defeating the Axis. Chief among these Allies were Great Britain, the Soviet Union, and the United States. Other nations in Europe, Asia, and the Americas contributed as well. Each nation pledged to use all its resources to defeat the Axis, not to sign any separate peace treaties, and to abide by the provisions of the Atlantic Charter.

Important Offensives

The German offensive in the summer of 1942 had pushed the Soviets back to Stalingrad. (See map on page 446.) There what may have been the most decisive battle of the war went on for six months. The Germans penetrated the city, suffering terrible losses in the process. Instead of retreating, the determined Soviets defended the city street by street and house by house.

In November 1942, the Soviets began a counterattack, encircling the German troops in Stalingrad. Although Hitler ordered his trapped forces to fight to the death, what was left of his army in the city surrendered in January 1943. The Battle of Stalingrad was a crucial point in the war. The Germans never entirely recovered from this defeat.

North Africa. The Allies also made progress in North Africa during 1942. British troops under General Bernard Montgomery were pursuing Rommel's forces westward across Libya into Tunisia. In November 1942, American and British forces under General Dwight Eisenhower of the United States landed in Morocco and Algeria. They pushed eastward into Tunisia as Montgomery's army moved westward. Rommel's army was trapped between the two Allied forces. By the middle of May 1943, the Axis forces in North Africa were forced to surrender.

As a result of Rommel's defeat, North Africa was securely under Allied control. Italy's African empire disappeared, and control of the French colonies in Africa passed to the Free French government. The Allies had maintained control of the Suez Canal and had made the Mediterranean more secure for Allied naval operations.

The Invasion of Italy

Throughout 1942 Stalin demanded that the British and Americans open a second front in Europe to relieve the German pressure on the Soviet Union. The Allies argued that an attack before they were fully prepared would be too risky. Stalin suspected the Allies hoped that Germany and the Soviet Union would destroy each other.

When the Allies secured North Africa, Stalin renewed his demands for a landing in Europe. American leaders proposed an invasion of France, the most direct route to Germany. Churchill, however, insisted on attacking what he called the **"soft underbelly of the Axis"**—through Italy and the Balkans. In July 1943, American and British armies landed on the island of Sicily. The American and British took the island in little more than a month. Then they prepared to invade the Italian mainland.

Many Italian leaders were ready to make peace with the Allies as a result of the Axis defeats in North Africa. With the Allied landing on Sicily, Mussolini was forced to resign, and Marshal Pietro Badoglio (bah·DOHL·yoh) became premier. Badoglio's first act was to dissolve the Fascist Party. His government also began secret negotiations with the Allies. When the

Allied army landed on the southwestern tip of Italy in September 1943, the Italians agreed to cease aggression against the Allies. In fact Italy declared war on Germany. German troops still present in Italy, however, continued to resist Allied troops.

The War at Sea and in the Air

Meanwhile, the Allies were winning the Battle of the Atlantic. This conflict between German and Allied ships had begun in 1939. For a time, German submarines sank an enormous number of Allied ships. In the spring of 1943, however, destroyers and other armed ships effectively escorted convoys of troop and supply ships sailing from the United States. Planes based both on land and on aircraft carriers also protected the convoys. Improved sonar technology located submarines, eliminating much of their advantage.

American and British bombing attacks against Germany and the occupied countries intensified. The Allies bombed strategic military sites as well as industrial areas. The Allies bombed nearly every German city, and many were severely damaged.

The War in the Pacific

The Japanese advance in the Pacific suffered its first setback in May 1942. In the Battle of the Coral Sea, American and Australian air and naval forces defeated a Japanese fleet steaming toward Australia. Soon afterward an American fleet met a larger Japanese fleet pushing eastward to try to capture Midway Island, northwest of Hawaii. (See map on opposite page.) The Americans defeated the Japanese in the crucial Battle of Midway in June. With these two victories, the United States Navy began to turn the tide in the war against Japan.

Early in August 1942, to protect the Australian supply line, American marines landed on the Solomon Islands, seizing the airfield on Guadalcanal. This was the first invasion of Japanese-held territory and an important morale booster for the United States. Four times in the next three months the Japanese launched savage attacks on the American forces. All were repulsed, with horrendous losses on both sides.

In 1943 the Allies took the offensive in the Pacific. Forces from Australia and New Zealand assisted those from the United States. Together they waged a long series of battles aimed at driving the Japanese out of the Solomon Islands. Then they adopted a strategy called **island hopping**. Only certain Japanese-held islands were captured; others were bypassed and left without supplies.

During 1944 the Americans cleared the Japanese from the Marshall Islands, New Guinea, and the Marianas. Saipan and Tinian, in the Marianas, became bases for bombing attacks on Japan. In October 1944, an American army under General Douglas MacArthur landed at Leyte in the central Philippines. Shortly after the landing, the Japanese fleet suffered a crushing defeat in a great air and sea fight, the Battle of Leyte Gulf. After six months, the Allies had secured the Philippine Islands; small, fierce battles continued there, however, until the end of the war.

At the same time, British forces (actually mostly troops from India, West Africa, and other British colonies), with increasing American support, were fighting the Japanese in the jungles and mountains of Burma. The main Allied goal was to open a supply line to the Nationalist Chinese, since the Japanese occupied the Chinese coast. In late 1944 and early 1945 the Allied armies pushed into Burma, although Japanese forces there continued to hold out until the end of the war.

Victory in Europe

As British and American troops slowly fought their way up the Italian Peninsula, the bulk of German forces were still locked in savage battles with the Soviet Union. It was clear that another, larger invasion of Europe was needed to create the hoped-for "second front." Plans were drawn up for **Operation Overlord**, the invasion of northwest France. It would be the largest amphibious invasion in history.

On June 6, 1944—D-Day as the military called it—the long-awaited landing began. Thousands of landing craft brought soldiers to the beaches of a narrow, heavily wooded peninsula on France's Normandy coast. (See map on page 446.) The Germans had expected a landing in France but could not predict the exact location of the assault. When they did find out, German forces rushed to meet the Allied invasion. Allied air power, however, hindered their progress. Within a month, more than 1 million Allied troops had landed.

After heavy fighting, Allied troops broke out of Normandy and into northern France. At the same time, Allied forces landed on the Mediterranean coast of France and fought their way northward. On August 25, 1944, Allied troops entered Paris. By September they faced the strongly fortified Siegfried Line along Germany's western frontier.

World War II in the Pacific, 1941–1945

Learning from Maps In 1943 the Allies waged a series of battles against the Japanese in the Pacific.

? Place Over what two cities did the Allies drop the atomic bombs just three days apart?

The drive from the east. Several weeks after D-Day, the Soviets began a major drive against Germany from the east. By the end of 1944, the Red Army had taken Finland, Estonia, Lithuania, Latvia, Romania, and Bulgaria. The British assisted in driving the Germans out of Greece. Yugoslavia had been liberated earlier with the help of resistance fighters under Marshal Tito. By July 1944, Soviet troops were approaching the eastern outskirts of Warsaw, Poland.

The drive from the west. The Americans pierced the Siegfried Line in October after five weeks of fighting. The Allies captured port cities in France and Belgium, easing their supply problems. The Allies also cleared Alsace and Lorraine of German troops.

The Germans still had enough strength for one desperate counterattack. Just before Christmas in 1944, they drove a 50-mile wedge into Allied lines in Belgium. After a costly 10-day battle—the Battle of the Bulge—the Allies turned back the German drive.

Finally, in early spring 1945, German defenses collapsed. At the end of April, the German army in Italy surrendered unconditionally. Italian guerrillas pursued and captured Mussolini, shot him, hung his body upside down by the heels, and displayed it in Milan.

The Soviet and American armies made their first contact at Torgau, in eastern Germany, on April 25, 1945. It was agreed that the Soviets would take Berlin. On April 30, as the Soviets closed in, Hitler committed suicide. Two days later, the Soviets captured the devastated city. Within a week the German high command surrendered unconditionally. May 8, 1945 was **V-E Day**, the day of victory in Europe.

Attacks on Japan

Though the war had ended in Europe, it continued in the Pacific. Long-range bombers from the Marianas could now reach the main islands of Japan. Systematic raids on Japanese industrial cities had begun in November 1944. However, the Allies needed still closer islands to use as fighter bases and emergency landing fields.

American marines landed on the small volcanic island of Iwo Jima, about 650 miles southeast of Tokyo, and captured it after a month of the most bitter fighting of the war. (See map on page 453.) The Japanese resisted even more strongly as their home islands were approached. Okinawa, the largest of the Ryukyu Islands, was taken by the Allies after more desperate fighting.

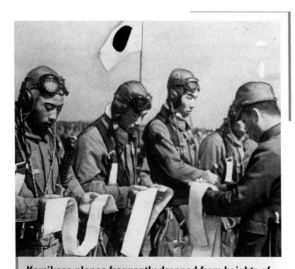

Kamikaze planes frequently dropped from heights of 25,000 feet and achieved speeds of over 600 miles per hour by the time of impact. Ceremonial headbands were given to kamikaze pilots before takeoff.

At Okinawa 263 Allied ships were sunk or damaged by suicide attacks of Japanese pilots who crashed their planes into the ships. These were called kamikaze attacks, meaning "divine wind." The Japanese believed that pilots who pledged to die for the emperor would save the empire, just as the divine wind had saved Japan from Chinese-Mongol attack in 1281.

The kamikaze pilots were young volunteers. Their only mission was to select an appropriate target and dive onto it. An excerpt from a diary kept by a sailor includes a kamikaze pilot's last letter to his girlfriend.

> ❝Do not weep because I am about to die. If I were to live and one of my dear ones to die, I would do all in my power to cheer those who remain behind. I would try to be brave. . . .
>
> I pray for the happiness of you all, and I beg your forgiveness for my lack of piety.
>
> I leave for the attack with a smile on my face. The moon will be full tonight. As I fly over the open sea off Okinawa I will choose the enemy ship that is to be my target.
>
> I will show you that I know how to die bravely.❞

Despite such determined resistance, the Allies continued their intensive bombing of Japan. Japanese ports were effectively blockaded and the Japanese navy was immobilized. Nevertheless, the Japanese government refused to surrender. The Allies began to prepare for a massive invasion of the Japanese home islands.

Yalta and Potsdam

Roosevelt and Churchill had long hoped to persuade Stalin to enter the war against Japan. Before the defeat of Germany, however, the Soviet Union had been completely occupied in defending itself.

In February 1945, Roosevelt and Churchill met with Stalin at Yalta, in the Soviet Union. The Big Three, as these Allied leaders were called, agreed that, once defeated, Germany would be temporarily divided and occupied by Allied troops, including those of France. The liberated areas of Europe would be allowed to democratically elect their governments. The Soviet Union was to enter the war against Japan. As compensation it was to receive several Japanese territories.

Another conference began on July 17, 1945, at Potsdam, near Berlin. Roosevelt had died in April, and Harry Truman was now president of the United States. He scheduled a meeting with the other members of the Big Three—Churchill and Stalin. But, before the Potsdam meeting ended on August 2, Churchill had been replaced at the conference.

Building History Study Skills

READ
WRITE
INTERPRET
CONNECT
THINK

Reading About History: Understanding a Biographical Account

History is more than the factual study of events and the analysis of important issues. People, and the decisions they make, have a significant impact on history. One way to understand the role of people from a historical perspective is to study biographical accounts—secondary sources about a person's life that are based on primary sources. Biographical accounts help establish a person's place and significance in regard to a historical event.

How to Understand a Biographical Account

To understand a biographical account, follow these steps.

1. Explain the historical context of the subject of the account. For example, what events led up to the events that occurred during the person's life?
2. List the major events of the person's life.
3. Identify the person's beliefs.
4. Explain the person's responses to historical events during his or her life.
5. Identify how other people have tended to view the person.
6. Assess the historical significance of the individual. For example, what role did he or she play in the causes or the effects of certain events?

Developing the Skill

Prime Minister Winston Churchill's leadership abilities in government and his influence as the author of such books as *The Second World War* and *A History of the English-Speaking Peoples* affected not only British history but world history as well.

The following excerpt from the prime minister's speech to the House of Commons in May 1940, as well as the wartime conferences listed in the next column, illustrate Churchill's place in history. What do the excerpt and the list suggest about Churchill's ideas and actions?

❝I have nothing to offer but blood, toil, tears, and sweat. . . .

You ask what is our policy? I will say: It is to wage war, by sea, land and air, with all our might and with all the strength that God can give us: to wage war against a monstrous tyranny, never surpassed in the dark, lamentable catalogue of human crime. That is our policy. You ask, What is our aim? I can

answer in one word: Victory—victory at all costs, victory in spite of all terror, victory, however long and hard the road may be; for without victory, there is no survival.❞

The following list contains several of the wartime conferences Churchill attended during World War II.

- August 1941: Churchill and Roosevelt meet on a battleship off the coast of Newfoundland to issue the Atlantic Charter on postwar aims.
- December 1941: Churchill and Roosevelt meet in Washington, D.C., to confirm that the defeat of Germany will take precedence over the defeat of Japan.
- August 1942: Churchill confers with Stalin in Moscow and informs the Soviet leader that there can be no second front in Europe in 1942.
- August 1943: Churchill and Roosevelt meet in Quebec to confirm the Allied landings at Normandy, and they also agree to landings in southern France.
- September 1944: Churchill and Roosevelt meet in Quebec to discuss victory plans.
- October 1944: Churchill and Stalin meet in Moscow to discuss eastern Europe's future.
- July–August 1945: Churchill, Truman, and Stalin meet at Potsdam to hammer out peace treaties.

Churchill became prime minister at a moment of disaster. The German armies occupied Holland, the Belgian king surrendered, and the French army was driven back to Paris. Although the outlook for Europe appeared dim, the inspiring words of Churchill's "blood, sweat, toil, and tears" speech rallied the British people and encouraged them to persevere. His unwavering leadership at the wartime conferences contributed to the Allied victory, thus having an impact on world history.

Practicing the Skill

Locate two of Franklin Roosevelt's speeches to Americans during World War II and identify significant excerpts from each. How do these excerpts help you determine Roosevelt's significance in world history?

To apply this skill, see Applying History Study Skills on page 459.

Clement Attlee of the Labour Party had become Britain's new prime minister. The leaders planned for the control and occupation of Germany and issued an ultimatum to Japan, demanding unconditional surrender. Japan rejected the ultimatum.

However, the Americans now had a secret weapon, an atomic bomb. Scientists from many nations—including refugees from fascist-controlled countries—had worked to harness the enormous energy released by splitting atoms. They had succeeded in creating the most destructive weapon yet known. By using this weapon, the Allies would not need to invade Japan.

Japanese Surrender

When the Japanese government refused to surrender, President Truman made an important decision—to use the atomic bomb against Japan. On August 6, 1945, an American B-29 bomber dropped the deadly weapon on Hiroshima.

The impact of the bomb pulverized everything in the vicinity and generated a spontaneous fire that destroyed the city. At least 80,000 people were killed instantly, with many more injured. Subsequent deaths and illness from radiation sickness are uncounted. In Tokyo, government officials had difficulty comprehending the scale of the damage. On August 9, the Soviet Union declared war on Japan. Soviet armies swept into Manchuria, where they met little resistance. On the same day, an American plane dropped a second atomic bomb on the city of Nagasaki.

On August 14, the Japanese surrendered unconditionally, asking only that the emperor be allowed to retain his title and authority as emperor. The Allies agreed, on the condition that he accept the orders of the supreme allied commander in the Pacific, General Douglas MacArthur. On September 2, 1945 (known as **V-J Day**), representatives of both sides signed the Japanese surrender documents aboard the American battleship *Missouri* anchored in Tokyo Bay.

Costs of the War

World War II, to a much greater extent than World War I, was a war of movement and of machines. These factors helped make it the most destructive war in history. More than 22 million military personnel died, and more than 34 million were wounded. Battle losses of the Soviet Union alone have been estimated at anywhere from 7 million to 11 million lives, although an

The Big Three meet in Yalta to decide the fate of postwar Europe. Seated from left to right: Churchill, Roosevelt, and Stalin.

These Coast Guardsmen on board their ship celebrate V-J Day. Although Japan agreed to end the war on August 14, 1945, the statement of surrender was not signed until September 2, 1945, thus making that date the official V-J Day.

accurate count has never been made. Germany lost about 3.5 million military personnel. Japan's total loss—civilian and military—was nearly 2 million. Great Britain, France, and the United States each lost several hundred thousand in battle. Six million Jews and millions of other people died or were killed in German concentration camps and gas chambers. Upward of 16 million civilians were killed in Europe and Asia. Millions more were uprooted as the war moved across the countryside.

As the war progressed, weapons and tactics became more devastating. More shocking, people even in the Western democracies came to feel that killing civilians was acceptable if it weakened the enemy. By 1943 Allied air attacks on Axis civilian centers were accepted as simply part of modern warfare. The destruction of Hamburg and Dresden and the atomic bombings of Hiroshima and Nagasaki did not immediately bring any great public protest. By 1945 the bombing of cities was seen as a normal practice of war.

Section 5 Review

1. **Define** "soft underbelly of the Axis," island hopping, Operation Overlord, V-E Day, V-J Day

2. **Identify** Dwight Eisenhower, Douglas MacArthur

3. **Locate and Explain the Significance** Guadalcanal, Saipan, Tinian, Normandy, Iwo Jima, Okinawa, Hiroshima

4. **Understanding Ideas** What did the Allies gain as a result of their victories in North Africa, in Italy, and in the Atlantic?

5. **Analyzing Ideas** (a) What was the importance of D-Day? (b) How did Germany try to counterattack Allied forces in France?

6. **Evaluating Ideas** (a) What role did the atomic bomb play in the surrender of Japan? (b) Were the Allies right to use the atom bomb on Japan? Why or why not?

Chapter 14 Review

A.D. 1920   A.D. 1922   A.D. 1931   A.D. 1933   A.D. 1935

1921–1922
Washington Naval Conference is held.

1931
Japanese attack Manchuria.

1936
Spanish Civil War begins.

Chapter Summary

The following list contains the key concepts you have learned about World War II.

1. In the 1930s, a series of acts of aggression by the Japanese, Italians, and Germans brought about World War II. At first the democracies were reluctant to resist these acts, preferring instead to follow a policy of appeasement.

2. The Japanese made gains in Manchuria and China. Italy captured Ethiopia, fascists took over Spain following the country's civil war, and the Germans seized Austria and Czechoslovakia. The League of Nations proved incapable of halting these advances.

3. Only when Hitler invaded Poland in September 1939 did his principal opponents, Great Britain and France, decide to stand firm. They were at a severe disadvantage because the Soviet Union had signed a nonaggression pact with Germany. Nevertheless, Great Britain and France declared war on Germany in 1939.

4. By the fall of 1940, the Axis Powers had conquered most of Scandinavia, defeated France, and forced British troops off the continent of Europe. They also had formed an alliance with Japan. During the next year, their battle successes reached a peak and then began to decline.

5. Despite isolationist opposition, the United States began to send supplies to Great Britain in 1940.

During the same year, Great Britain's air force turned back German air attacks and prevented an invasion of England.

6. In 1941, after considerable successes in the Balkans, Germany suddenly attacked the Soviet Union. In addition, the Japanese attacked the American fleet at Pearl Harbor in Hawaii. This assault brought the United States into the war.

7. Within German-occupied Europe a vicious and barbaric policy of exterminating all Jews, known as the Holocaust, was put into effect.

8. The Soviets counterattacked, and the German army was forced to engage in heavy fighting on the eastern front.

9. In 1943 the Allies invaded Sicily from North Africa. At the same time, they began an offensive to drive the Japanese out of the Pacific islands.

10. In 1944 the Allies invaded France. Finally, in 1945, they conquered Germany.

11. The dropping of atomic bombs on Hiroshima and Nagasaki forced Japan to surrender.

12. The cost of the war, in terms of suffering and death, was worse by far than that of any other war in history.

13. The end of the war brought hope that the aims proclaimed in the Atlantic Charter of 1941—including an end to wars, self-determination, and decent living conditions for all people—might at last be realized.

Reviewing Important Terms

On a separate sheet of paper, match each of the following terms with the correct definition below.

a. appeasement
b. Holocaust
c. blitzkrieg
d. isolationists
e. collaborators

_____ 1. Those who oppose involvement in the affairs of other nations
_____ 2. Systematic destruction of Jews by the Nazis
_____ 3. People who cooperate with the enemies of their country
_____ 4. Lightning war
_____ 5. Attempt to preserve peace by giving in to an aggressor's demands

Developing Critical Thinking Skills

1. **Analyzing Ideas** (a) Japanese aggression in Asia started a chain reaction that eventually led to war. Why? (b) At what point do you think world war became inevitable? Explain.

2. **Evaluating Ideas** (a) In certain respects, the Spanish Civil War was a preview of the global war that was to come. Why? (b) What role did Spain play once World War II started?

3. **Classifying Ideas** (a) What nations participated in the conference at Munich? (b) What did each of these nations hope to achieve? (c) How did the decisions that were reached at Munich affect the future of Czechoslovakia?

1938 • Munich Conference takes place. • Germany annexes the Sudetenland.	**1940** • Evacuation from Dunkirk occurs. • France surrenders. • Battle of Britain begins.	**1942** • Battle of the Coral Sea is fought. • Battle of Midway occurs.	**1944** • Allies invade Normandy. • Battle of the Bulge occurs.	

A.D. 1937   A.D. 1939   A.D. 1941   A.D. 1943   A.D. 1945

1939 Germany invades Poland.	**1941** • Germany invades the Soviet Union. • Japan attacks Pearl Harbor.	**1943** • Allied victory in North Africa occurs. • Italy surrenders.	**1945** Germany and Japan surrender.

Relating Geography to History

Turn to the map on page 446. **(a)** What nations did the Axis Powers hold at the height of their power? **(b)** What nations remained neutral or nonaligned? **(c)** Based on information on this map, why might Churchill have considered Italy the "soft underbelly of the Axis"?

Relating Past to Present

1. "The next World War," declared Albert Einstein after the bombing of Japan, "will be fought with stones." **(a)** What might he have meant by this comment? **(b)** What efforts are being made today to limit the production and sale of nuclear weapons?
2. Prior to American entry into the war, President Roosevelt called the United States the "arsenal of democracy." **(a)** What did he mean by this phrase? **(b)** Does the United States still play this role in world affairs? **(c)** Why or why not? If possible, clip current newspaper or magazine articles that illustrate your answer.
3. Review the failure of the League of Nations to end Italian aggression in Ethiopia during the 1930s. Then find information on Soviet intervention in Afghanistan and Poland during the 1980s. **(a)** What actions did the United Nations take? **(b)** Were any of the problems faced by the United Nations similar to those experienced by the League? Explain.

Applying History Study Skills

Before completing this activity, review Building History Study Skills on page 455.

Read Mussolini's description of the nature of fascism. Then answer the questions that follow his description.

"The foundation of Fascism is the conception of the state—its character, its duty, and its aim. Fascism conceives of the State as an absolute, in comparison with which all individuals or groups are relative, only to be conceived of in their relation to the State. The conception of the Liberal State is not that of a directing force . . . but merely a force limited to the function of recording results: on the other hand, the Fascist State is itself conscious and has itself a will and a personality. . . .

The [individual] is deprived of all useless and possibly harmful freedom, but retains what is essential; the deciding power in this question cannot be in the individual, but the State alone."

1. How did Mussolini define fascism?
2. **(a)** What do you think Mussolini meant when he said the state was an absolute? **(b)** That freedom could be "useless" or "harmful"?
3. Use information in the chapter to determine whether Mussolini's ideas coincided with his actions.
4. **(a)** What is Mussolini's place in Italian history? **(b)** In world history?

internetconnect

Search the Internet through the HRW Web site to gather information on some of the battles of World War II that are not mentioned in the text. Research one land battle, one sea battle, and one air battle. Who was involved in each of these battles? What was the outcome of each? **GO TO:** go.hrw.com **KEYWORD:** SC0 World War II Battles

Building Your Portfolio

1. **Writing a Report** Prepare a report on one of the following books about the Holocaust: Anne Frank's *The Diary of a Young Girl* (Doubleday), John Hersey's *The Wall* (Random House), Ilse Koehn's *Mischling, Second Degree* (Puffin), Arnost Lustig's *Night and Hope* (Northwestern University Press), or Elie Wiesel's *Night* (Bantam). In your report, note whether the story is fiction or nonfiction. Briefly discuss the background of the author. Then describe the way each of the central characters responds to Nazi persecution. Place your report in your portfolio.
2. **Conducting an Interview** Interview a friend or relative who remembers the World War II years. Ask this person to explain the meaning of the following words or phrases: *victory garden, ration books, blackouts, dog tags, Rosie the Riveter, war bonds, C-rations, black market*. During your interview, try to discover other World War II terms that you might add to the list. Place your notes in your portfolio.

Unit Summary

The following list contains the key concepts you have learned about world war in the twentieth century.

1. The rivalries among European nations intensified in the late 1800s and early 1900s.

2. The 1914 assassination of Archduke Ferdinand and his wife in Sarajevo sparked World War I and within a few months almost all the nations of Europe, and Japan, were at war. Italy entered the war in 1915, and the United States entered in 1917, both on the side of the Allies.

3. A dramatic upheaval took place in Russia, where in 1917 a revolution abolished the monarchy. Following the civil war in Russia, a government based on the principles of Karl Marx and communism was created.

4. Although World War I ended in 1918, the problems it caused continued to plague governments.

5. Woodrow Wilson's Fourteen Points offered idealistic goals, but as the Allies sought to collect reparations for their wartime losses and to gain additional territory, many of his goals were forgotten.

6. In 1920, 42 nations founded the League of Nations. The United States, however, did not join.

7. The new outlook and the uncertainties of the stressful period following World War I were reflected by the science, literature, music, and art of the time.

8. In the United States, a sense of optimism and the influence of European contact brought about rapid change during the decade called the Roaring Twenties.

9. The stock market crash in 1929 marked the beginning of the Great Depression. In Europe the depression caused widespread political instability.

10. In Italy and Germany dissatisfaction with the weakness and hesitations of democratic governments led to an extreme form of dictatorship called fascism.

11. In territories controlled by Great Britain, major political changes took place during the 1920s and 1930s. Political and social reforms also took place in Turkey, Persia, China, Japan, and Africa.

12. Developments in Latin America reflected the worldwide economic crisis.

13. In the 1930s the League of Nations failed to halt a series of aggressions by the imperial government of Japan and the Fascists, which brought about World War II. In 1945 the Allies conquered Germany and Japan.

Reviewing Concepts

On a separate sheet of paper, match each item at the left with its description at the right.

a. Kellogg-Briand Pact
b. Balfour Declaration
c. Nazi-Soviet Pact
d. Atlantic Charter
e. Zimmermann telegram
f. Fourteen Points
g. Yalta Conference
h. *Mein Kampf*
i. Treaty of Portsmouth
j. Versailles Treaty

1. Called for "peace of justice"
2. Stated principles underlying Nazi movement
3. Settled Russo-Japanese War
4. Levied heavy reparations on Germany
5. Outlawed war
6. Announced war aims of the democracies
7. Pledged Soviet Union's neutrality
8. Temporarily divided Germany
9. Favored creation of Jewish "national home"
10. Invited Mexico to join the Central Powers

Applying Critical Thinking Skills

1. **Summarizing Ideas** (a) How did World War I help bring about a boom period in the United States? (b) What conditions brought this boom period to an end?

2. **Classifying Ideas** Choose two of the following areas and discuss how they reflected the uncertainties of the period following World War I: (a) literature, (b) music, (c) painting, (d) architecture, (e) film.

3. **Contrasting Ideas** How did Sun Yixian, Chiang Kaishek, and Mao Zedong differ in their plans for China's future? Include the following topics in your answer: (a) the role of the people; (b) foreign interference in China; (c) economic reforms; (d) constitutional government; and (e) the need for modernization.

4. **Evaluating Ideas** (a) What were the foreign policy objectives of Italy, Germany, and Japan in the 1930s? (b) How did these nations achieve their objectives?

5. **Determining Cause and Effect** (a) Compare the causes of World War I with the causes of World War II. (b) Why might the Versailles Treaty be considered a cause of World War II?

6. **Comparing Ideas** (a) Compare the principles expressed in the Atlantic Charter with those presented in the Fourteen Points. (b) How did each of these documents seek to establish "peace of justice"?

7. **Analyzing Ideas** (a) How did the United States assist the Allies before December 1941? (b) Why did the United States move away from its neutral status?

8. **Determining Cause and Effect** (a) How did the bombings of Hiroshima and Nagasaki change the nature of warfare? (b) What other technological developments grew out of World War II?

Relating Geography to History
Refer to maps in Chapter 11 and Chapter 14. How did the map of Europe change after the Treaty of Versailles? How did it change during World War II?

Writing About History
President Truman once declared, "Men make history and not the other way around." Use three of the following leaders as examples to explain Truman's statement: (a) Woodrow Wilson, (b) Sun Yixian, (c) Mustafa Kemal, (d) Mohandas Gandhi, (e) Winston Churchill.

Further Reading
Achebe, Chinua. *Things Fall Apart*. Knopf, 1995. Discusses the effects of Western customs and values on traditional Nigerian culture, set in an Ibo village during the height of European imperialism.

Horne, Alistair. *The Price of Glory: Verdun 1916*. Viking Penguin, 1994. A vivid narrative account of the battle of Verdun.

Remarque, Erich Maria. *All Quiet on the Western Front*. Fawcett, 1987. A reprinting of the famous 1929 novel describing World War I through the eyes of a group of German soldiers.

Richter, Hans P. *I Was There*. Puffin Books, 1987. Gives an eyewitness account of a boy who participated in the Hitler Youth.

Salisbury, Harrison E. *The New Emperors: China in the Era of Mao and Deng*. Avon, 1993. An account of Chinese leadership from the time of Mao forward.

Steinbeck, John. *The Grapes of Wrath*. Viking Penguin, 1992. A reprinting of the classic 1939 novel, recounting the struggle of Dust Bowl families during the Great Depression.

UNIT 3 CHRONOLOGY

Date	Politics	Science and Technology	Society and Culture
1880–1910	Zionism **13*** Triple Alliance and Triple Entente **11** Boxer Rebellion **13** Russo-Japanese War **13**	Louis Sullivan **12** Einstein **12**	Freudian psychology **12** Picasso and cubism **12** Motion pictures **12**
1910–1920	Chinese Republic **13** Assassination of Archduke Ferdinand **11** World War I **11** *Lusitania* sunk **11** Russian Revolution **11** Treaties of Brest-Litovsk and Versailles **11** Weimar Republic **12**	U-boats **11** Machine guns **11** Military airplanes **11** Tanks **11**	Proust **12** Stravinsky, Schoenberg, Berg, Webern **12** Spengler's *The Decline of the West* **12**
1920–1930	Mohandas Gandhi **13** Lenin's NEP **12** Chiang Kaishek **13** Mussolini **12** Stalin **12** Atatürk **13** Fascism **12**	Frank Lloyd Wright **12** Automobile, telephone, radio **12**	Jazz **12** Joyce's *Ulysses* **12** T. S. Eliot **12** Mann **12** Kafka and surrealism **12** Hemingway's *A Farewell to Arms* **12**
1930–1939	Great Depression **12** Rise of Hitler **12** Azikiwe, Kenyatta, Senghor **13** FDR's New Deal **12** Soviet purges **12** Long March **13**	TVA **12**	big band era **12** Steinbeck's *The Grapes of Wrath* **12** Dali **12**
1939–1945	Germany invades Poland **14** Pearl Harbor **14** Yalta and Potsdam **14**	Hiroshima and Nagasaki **14** Blitzkrieg **14** Panzer units **14** Radar **14**	Atomic bomb **14** Meltzer's *Never to Forget* **14**

*Indicates chapter in which development is discussed

World War in the Twentieth Century

CHAPTER 11

World War I and the Russian Revolution

In the summer of 1914, a war began that resembled no previous conflict. Industrial technology had produced weapons far more destructive than any used in previous wars. This horrifying war dragged on for more than four years, taking a devastating toll in lives and property.

Setting the Stage for War

In the last half of the 1800s cooperation among nations broke down and rivalries increased. As these rivalries intensified in the early 1900s, the major powers plunged toward war, pressed forward by at least four factors: nationalism, imperialism, militarism, and the system of alliances. By 1907 rival alliances, divided into two armed camps, threatened world peace.

A Letter from the German Trenches, plate 30 from The Great War: A Neutral's Indictment

The incident that provoked Europe to go to war occurred in the Balkans on June 28, 1914, when Archduke Francis Ferdinand and his wife were assassinated. The assassin belonged to a secret society of Serbian nationalists who strongly opposed Austro-Hungarian rule.

The murders brought to a head the bitterness between Serbia and Austria-Hungary. When Serbia did not accept all of the terms of an ultimatum issued by Austria-Hungary, its leaders declared war on Serbia. Then on August 1, 1914, Germany declared war on Russia. Convinced that France was prepared to side with Russia and hoping to gain a military advantage by swift action, Germany declared war on France. When German troops passed through neutral Belgium on their way to France, Great Britain declared war on Germany. Other European and Asian nations soon entered the war.

A New Kind of War

Germany, Austria-Hungary, Bulgaria, and the Ottoman Empire became known as the Central Powers. Great Britain, France, Russia, and their partners in the war joined together as the Allied Powers, or the Allies. Eventually 32 countries made up the Allied forces. Many of them, however, joined late in the war and made only token contributions to the war effort.

Previously in Europe, most wars were fought by professional soldiers whose only source of income was their military pay and rations. In contrast, armies of drafted civilians fought the battles of World War I. Those people who could not fight worked at home to help the war effort. Many women participated by working in factories.

Both sides dug trenches on the western front, which stretched from Switzerland to the North Sea. On the eastern front, the Germans forced the Russians eastward into Poland. By 1916 the war in the west had become a stalemate on land as well as at sea.

As the most highly industrialized neutral nation, the United States became a supplier of food, raw materials, and munitions to both sides. When the Germans began attacking any ship, enemy or neutral, the United States joined the war on the side of the Allies.

The Russian Revolution

The spring of 1917 found the Russian people weary of hardships and disheartened by the appalling casualties that they had been suffering in the war. They had lost faith in the government and Czar Nicholas II. Strikes and street demonstrations broke out in Petrograd, as St. Petersburg had been called since 1914. In March 1917, unable to control either his subjects or his army, Nicholas abdicated. He and his family were arrested, and they were murdered the following year.

A liberal provisional government was set up to rule Russia until a constitutional assembly could be elected to establish a new permanent system of government. While the provisional government tried to restore order, another group worked for more radical change in Russia. By November the Bolsheviks, or Communists, under the leadership of V. I. Lenin, had seized control of the Russian government.

At Lenin's direction, a peace treaty was signed with the Central Powers in March 1918. The new regime then turned its attention to internal problems. Civil war lasted almost three years, with the Communists ultimately gaining control of Russia.

The Terms of Peace

In January 1918, about 10 months before World War I ended, President Wilson of the United States announced his ideas for a just world after the war. His plan became known as the Fourteen Points. After the armistice in November 1918, the Allies faced the task of arranging peace terms. The Paris Peace Conference, or Versailles Conference, considered territorial claims and payments for damage. While the Allies believed that the settlement should be fair and lasting, the war had left a feeling of bitterness and hatred among many of the victors. They thought that the Central Powers, especially Germany, had been responsible for the war.

Creating a "New Europe"

In a series of peace treaties with each of the five Central Powers, the Allies redrew the boundaries of Europe. The Versailles Treaty forced Germany to pay reparations, surrender territory, and limit the number of men in its army. In addition, the Allies made provisions to form the League of Nations. According to its Covenant, the League had two aims: (1) to promote international cooperation and (2) to maintain peace by settling disputes among nations by reducing armaments. Although the League of Nations had

been a favorite idea of Wilson's, the United States itself never became a member of the organization.

CHAPTER 12

The Great Depression and the Rise of Totalitarianism

For a time immediately following World War I, it appeared that the world had indeed been made "safe for democracy." However, the war changed how people viewed the world. Many nations struggled to survive politically and economically.

The Postwar Era

Following World War I, many people rejected the belief in continual human progress first expressed during the Enlightenment. Instead, scientists, writers, and artists expressed a sense of alienation and cynicism.

Many of these intellectuals, however, appealed to a small audience. Most people found escape from the disillusionment of troubled times in new forms of entertainment such as popular music and motion pictures. Architecture also underwent great change during the postwar years. New technical advances, such as the use of structural steel, made skyscrapers and bold new architectural designs possible.

Postwar Prosperity in Ruins

The United States emerged from the war as an apparent successor to Great Britain in world leadership. However, the refusal of the United States to join the League of Nations indicated that the United States did not want this responsibility. Americans preferred to enjoy their newfound prosperity during the Roaring Twenties and avoid further entanglement in European affairs.

This prosperity, however, was short-lived. The collapse of the New York Stock Exchange plunged the United States and the rest of the industrial world into a severe economic recession, known simply as the Great Depression.

In response to the hardships of the Great Depression, voters in the United States elected Franklin D. Roosevelt president. Roosevelt embarked on a program of relief and reform, called the New

Deal, to combat the depression. However, only when the United States mobilized for war once again in the late 1930s, did the economy improve.

Political Tensions After World War I

The events of the postwar years strained the older and more experienced European democracies of France and Great Britain. The economies of these nations had been harmed by the war, and recovery was made difficult by debt and lack of good markets.

France emerged from World War I victorious but unstable. The country still owed money that it had borrowed from French citizens and the United States during and after the war. Its industry was faltering, production was declining, and inflation was soaring. Although a socialist government took power in 1936, bitter divisions still existed.

Like France, Great Britain faced grave economic difficulties after World War I. By 1921 nearly one fourth of Great Britain's work force was unemployed and workers from many industries began striking. The British and Irish governments also struggled over control of Ireland.

As western European powers attempted to recover from World War I, the nations of eastern Europe struggled to form governments and identities. While Finland, Czechoslovakia, and the Baltic countries managed to sustain democratic regimes, other countries, such as Austria, Hungary, and Poland, were less successful.

Fascist Dictatorships in Italy and Germany

The war and its aftermath also took their toll in Italy and Germany. Heavy loss of life, the burden of debt, high unemployment, and runaway inflation plagued these countries. In Italy the problems led to the rise of Benito Mussolini, whose Fascist Party set up a military dictatorship. In Germany Adolf Hitler became dictator and leader of the Nazi Party. The new leaders of both countries established totalitarian regimes.

Dictatorship in The Soviet Union

Similar developments occurred in the Soviet Union. Although Lenin had allowed free enterprise to exist under his New Economic Policy (NEP), his successor Joseph Stalin announced the end of the NEP and the return to a controlled command economy. Through a series of Five-Year Plans, the Soviets tried to create an industrialized nation. These plans, however, con-

Hitler rally, 1935, Nuremberg

centrated on the expansion of heavy industry and defense at the expense of producing consumer goods, creating shortages of basic necessities. Like the Fascists in Italy and the Nazis in Germany, Stalin created a totalitarian regime that deprived the people of human rights.

CHAPTER 13

New Political Forces in Africa, Asia, and Latin America

The postwar years also witnessed profound changes outside Europe. When India set out on a path toward independence, other countries followed suit; Turkey, Persia, and Africa began political transformations. Likewise, the civilizations of China, Japan, and South America faced political, social, and economic change.

The British Empire

Although the British Empire had grown larger as a result of the Paris Peace Conference, its continued existence was nonetheless threatened. People in all parts of the empire voiced demands for more freedom, for self-government, and even for complete independence.

In the Middle East, the British recognized the independence of Transjordan and Iraq. Only Palestine remained under British control. While the British and Egyptian governments agreed that Egypt would be granted independence, Great Britain would control the Suez Canal for 20 years.

As Great Britain's largest colony, India commanded more British attention than did the Middle Eastern mandates. Some Western-educated Indians favored continued rule by Great Britain. In contrast, Indian nationalists wanted complete independence. Mohandas K. Gandhi became a great advocate of Indian nationalism. In 1935, after years of reports and conferences, Great Britain granted India a new constitution with provisions for elected representation. However, the British still controlled India's national defense, revenue, and foreign policy and could veto legislation. Committed to total self-government, the nationalists opposed the new constitution, but they agreed to work within it to gain power after the elections.

Even in those other parts of the British Empire where a degree of self-government already existed, people sought greater independence. In Canada, Australia, New Zealand, and the Union of South Africa, Great Britain still appointed a governor-general who could veto laws. After World War I, these dominions sought complete self-government. Showing remarkable willingness to accommodate and adjust to political reality, Great Britain readily agreed to their demands.

Turkey, Persia, and Africa

The nationalist ideas that swept the Middle East after World War I also affected Turkey, Persia, and Africa. In Turkey, an able and energetic leader, Mustafa Kemal, emerged as president and worked to modernize the nation.

In Persia, Reza Khan, an army officer with strong nationalist sentiments, seized control of the government in a coup d'état. Some four years later, he deposed the ruling shah, took the title Reza Shah Pahlavi and assumed the throne. Like Kemal, Reza Shah wanted to modernize his country and free it from foreign domination.

The years after World War I also saw an increase in political activity among Africans. Many leaders such as Nnamdi Azikiwe (AH·ZEEK·WAH) of Nigeria,

Jomo Kenyatta of Kenya, and Leopold Senghor of Senegal worked for independence in their countries.

China

In the 1800s the Western powers carved out spheres of influence in China. When the Chinese attempted to oust foreigners during the Boxer Rebellion, the imperialist nations crushed the revolt and imposed heavy penalties on the Chinese. Although the rebellion failed to drive foreigners from Chinese soil, it fostered nationalistic sentiment among the Chinese people.

In 1911 a series of revolts, led mostly by army officers who supported Sun Yixian, spread throughout southern China. Although the leader of the imperial army hoped to negotiate with these rebels, no agreement was reached and the Qing dynasty ended. In 1912 the emperor abdicated and a republic was proclaimed.

However, China's problems were far from over; the ruling political party, the Guomindang, soon split into rival factions. On one side were the Nationalists, led by Chiang Kaishek (chang ky·SHEK). Opposing the Nationalists were the Communists, led by Mao Zedong (MAOOH ZUH·DUHNG).

Japan

By the early 1900s, Japan had advanced from a feudal agrarian society to a leading industrial and military power. Although the Japanese economy grew rapidly, it could not provide food for everyone. As a result, many Japanese people began emigrating to Korea, Taiwan, Hawaii, and other islands of the Pacific Ocean. Thousands more left for the United States.

Japan also had to import raw materials, since it lacked much of those needed in modern industry. To pay for these raw materials, it had to sell goods abroad. Many countries, however, placed tariffs on Japanese goods. For the island nation, a modernizing economy had to expand or collapse. Many Japanese, dissatisfied with the economy, began to accept the arguments of military leaders that Japan needed to become an imperialist power in order to survive.

Latin America

The 1920s brought a period of prosperity to Latin America. Industrialization contributed to the growth of cities and the expansion of the middle class. Many Latin American countries became leading exporters of agricultural products and mining resources.

Diego Rivera mural

However, the Great Depression caused the prices of these exports to fall. Because they received such a small return on their exports, many Latin American nations found it impossible to import any but the most essential goods. Economic crisis soon led to political crisis. Coups d'état overthrew many Latin American governments in the 1930s. In some cases, these coups toppled constitutional systems that had existed for 30 to 40 years.

President Roosevelt fostered a program called the Good Neighbor Policy. This policy stressed mutual cooperation among the American nations and restricted interference by the United States in Latin American affairs.

CHAPTER 14

World War II

During the 1930s most European nations once more claimed loyalty to one of two opposing camps. One group included those nations that were generally satisfied with the World War I peace settlement. The other group consisted of dissatisfied nations. With each passing year, relations between the two groups grew more strained.

Threats to World Peace

Although many international conferences in the 1920s worked to maintain peace, several local conflicts erupted. The Japanese military, having gained control of the government, invaded Manchuria. Japan soon occupied about one fourth of China. In Africa, Mussolini and his Italian forces waged a campaign to conquer and colonize Ethiopia. In Spain, a bitter civil war resulted in the establishment of a fascist government under the leadership of Francisco Franco.

Hitler's Aggressions

Germany also embarked on a program of conquest in the 1930s. In March 1936 German troops marched into the Rhineland, violating the Treaty of Versailles. Then in October 1936, following the outbreak of the Spanish Civil War, Mussolini and Hitler formed a military alliance called the Rome-Berlin Axis and began referring to themselves as the Axis Powers. Shortly afterward, Japan and Germany pledged to work together to prevent the spread of communism in Russia.

In March 1938 Hitler's troops marched unopposed into Austria and the Sudetenland in Czechoslovakia. In 1939 Germany occupied all of Czechoslovakia, the last democracy in Central Europe. The Axis Powers wanted still more territory, and in the spring of 1939, Hitler took Lithuania, and Mussolini conquered Albania.

Faced with this aggression, Great Britain and France prepared for war. Although the two countries tried to forge a mutual alliance with Joseph Stalin of the Soviet Union, their negotiations failed. Instead, the Western democracies received a tremendous shock when Hitler announced a German-Soviet nonaggression pact. Publicly this pact pledged that Germany and the Soviet Union would never attack each other; each would remain neutral if the other became involved in war. Secretly, however, the two dictators agreed to divide eastern Europe into spheres of influence. Germany was to take western Poland and the Soviet Union was to have eastern Poland and the Baltic countries.

The crisis that finally began World War II was Hitler's attack on Poland. Great Britain and France stood by Poland and declared war on Germany.

Axis Gains

Hitler's attack was conducted with great speed and force; Poland was unprepared and after a brief but devastating war, it surrendered to Germany. Next, Hitler invaded Scandinavia, the Netherlands, Belgium, and Luxembourg. By June 1940, the Axis Powers had launched attacks in both northern and southern France. Hitler tried to conquer Great Britain as well, but the British held their own. Although the United States remained officially neutral, it gave assistance to Great Britain in the form of war supplies.

The Soviet Union and the United States

By late 1940 it appeared that the Axis Powers were winning the war. They controlled the Atlantic coastline from the tip of Norway to southern France and also much of the Mediterranean coastline. Hitler also sent forces into the Middle East and North Africa.

On June 22, 1941, the war entered a new phase. Without declaring war, German armies invaded the Soviet Union. British Prime Minister Winston Churchill offered aid to the Soviet Union, and the United States also declared its willingness to help. This assistance helped the Soviets stall the Nazi offensive.

The invasion of the Soviet Union was part of Hitler's master plan for the creation of a "New Order" in Europe. Hitler wanted to organize the entire continent into a single political and economic system ruled by the "Aryan race." To reach this goal, the Nazis mercilessly murdered millions of Jews, Gypsies, Slavs, homosexuals, and other groups whom they considered inferior.

The struggle against the Axis Powers received a major boost in December 1941 when conflict in the Pacific Ocean drew the United States into the war. Japan, having formed an alliance with Germany and Italy, launched a surprise attack on the American naval base at Pearl Harbor, Hawaii. As a result, the United States declared war on the Axis Powers.

The End of the War

Throughout 1942 and 1943 the Axis Powers experienced defeats in Europe and the Pacific. The war reached its final phase with the Allied invasion of France on June 6, 1944.

Before the end of the war, Allied leaders Franklin Roosevelt of the United States, Winston Churchill of Great Britain, and Joseph Stalin of the Soviet Union met at Yalta in February 1945. The Big Three, as these Allied leaders were called, agreed that Germany should be temporarily divided and occupied by Allied troops, including those of France. Germany surrendered on May 8, 1945.

Another conference began on July 17, 1945, at Potsdam, near Berlin. At this conference the leaders planned for the control and occupation of Germany and issued an ultimatum to Japan demanding unconditional surrender. Japan surrendered in August after the United States dropped atomic bombs on Hiroshima and Nagasaki.

U.S. troops land on Normandy Beach, June 10, 1944

Synthesis Review

1. **Comparing Ideas** How did World War I differ from earlier wars?
2. **Interpreting Ideas** Why did the Great Depression lead to political instability in Europe?
3. **Evaluating Ideas** What factors led many countries in Asia, the Middle East, and Africa to seek independence?
4. **Analyzing Ideas** What event precipitated Japan's surrender?
5. **Synthesizing Ideas** How did disillusionment with the World War I peace settlements lead to World War II?

POLITICS AND GOVERNMENT

1945   **1953**   **1961**

1945
United Nations is established

1947
India gains independence

1948
Soviet blockade of Berlin and U.S. airlift occur

1949
Communists win control of China

1950
Outbreak of Korean War

1959
Castro overthrows Batista in Cuba

1961
Building of Berlin Wall

Berlin Wall

Fighting the Korean War along the 38th parallel

SOCIETY AND CULTURE

1945   **1953**   **1961**

1946
Nuremburg trials end

1948
Marshall Plan goes into effect

1953
The term *rock 'n' roll* gains wide usage in U.S.

1950
Mother Teresa founds religious order in Calcutta

1954
U.S. Supreme Court bans school segregation

Mother Teresa

SCIENCE AND TECHNOLOGY

1945   **1953**   **1961**

1946
ENIAC computer built in U.S.

1949
USSR detonates its first atomic bomb

1957
USSR launches *Sputnik* satellite

1961
Soviets put first human in space

ENIAC computer

1954
Salk polio vaccine released

Child being immunized

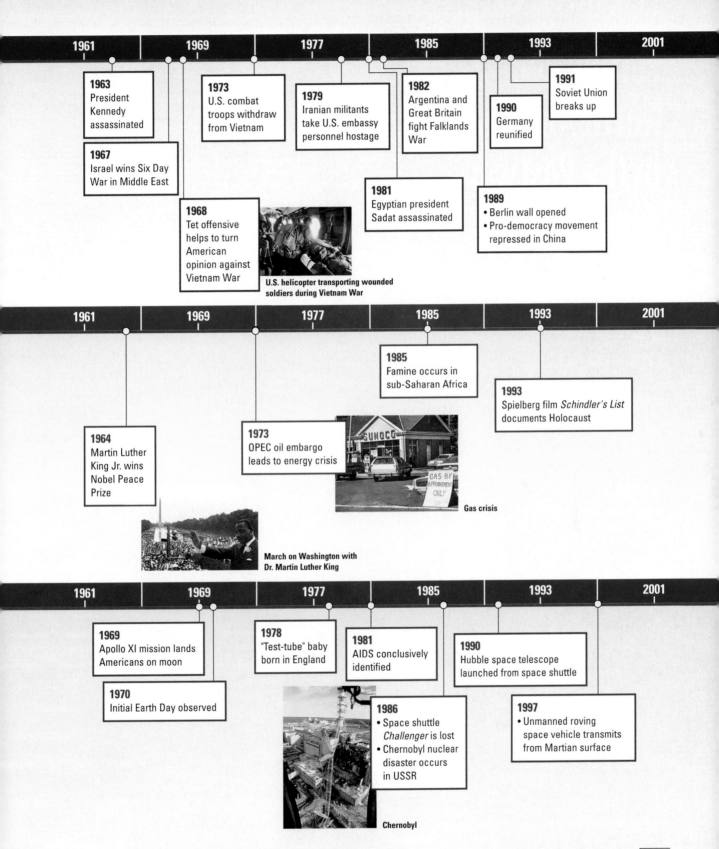

1961

1969

1977

1985

1993

2001

1963
President Kennedy assassinated

1967
Israel wins Six Day War in Middle East

1968
Tet offensive helps to turn American opinion against Vietnam War

1973
U.S. combat troops withdraw from Vietnam

1979
Iranian militants take U.S. embassy personnel hostage

1981
Egyptian president Sadat assassinated

1982
Argentina and Great Britain fight Falklands War

1990
Germany reunified

1991
Soviet Union breaks up

1989
• Berlin wall opened
• Pro-democracy movement repressed in China

U.S. helicopter transporting wounded soldiers during Vietnam War

1961

1969

1977

1985

1993

2001

1985
Famine occurs in sub-Saharan Africa

1993
Spielberg film *Schindler's List* documents Holocaust

1964
Martin Luther King Jr. wins Nobel Peace Prize

1973
OPEC oil embargo leads to energy crisis

Gas crisis

March on Washington with Dr. Martin Luther King

1961

1969

1977

1985

1993

2001

1969
Apollo XI mission lands Americans on moon

1970
Initial Earth Day observed

1978
"Test-tube" baby born in England

1981
AIDS conclusively identified

1990
Hubble space telescope launched from space shuttle

1986
• Space shuttle *Challenger* is lost
• Chernobyl nuclear disaster occurs in USSR

1997
• Unmanned roving space vehicle transmits from Martian surface

Chernobyl

Europe and North America in the Postwar Years

TIME

A.D. **1945–1968**

A.D. **1945–1968**

3.7 million B.C. | 4000 B.C. | A.D. 2100

PLACE

Europe, the United States, and Canada

Canada

Europe

United States

United Nations General Assembly in session

Significance

During World War II, Allied leaders met several times to discuss what the future of Europe would be after the war. Once the war ended, however, prewar differences that had divided the Western European democracies from the communism of the Soviet Union re-emerged. The Soviet Union moved to ensure its future security by establishing communist-controlled governments in the countries occupied by its troops. Alarmed by such apparent Soviet expansionism, the Western democratic nations and many other noncommunist countries rallied behind U.S. leadership to contain the threat of communist expansion.

Suspicion and hostility between the communist and Western nations led to the **Cold War**, a conflict waged primarily by economic and political means, as each side sought to extend its influence among the other nations of the world.

Terms to Define

Cold War	welfare state
Nuremberg trials	Great Society
denazification	recessions
veto power	civil rights
containment	NAACP
Cominform	DEW Line
market economy	St. Lawrence Seaway
command economy	

People to Identify

Big Three	Charles de Gaulle
Allied Control Council	Nikita Khrushchev
Council of Foreign	Alexander Dubcek
Ministers	Joseph McCarthy
Security Council	Martin Luther King Jr.
General Assembly	Fidel Castro
Konrad Adenauer	

Places to Locate

Yalta	East Prussia
Oder-Neisse line	

Chapter Theme Questions

- **War and Diplomacy** How might strategic decisions made during a war affect the conduct of diplomacy during peace?
- **Cross-Cultural Interaction** What kinds of groups might nations form in order to solve their common problems?
- **Economic Organization** How might economic organizations affect a country's ability to recover from the devastation of war?

In 1946 Sir Winston Churchill, the former prime minister of Great Britain, visited Westminster College in Fulton, Missouri. His address to an audience of students, faculty, and their distinguished guest, President Harry Truman, became one of the most memorable speeches of his career. The recent takeovers by Soviet-backed communist regimes in Eastern Europe had deeply disturbed the Western nations. The following excerpt from Churchill's speech describes the sense of uncertainty that darkened postwar Europe—and the world.

A shadow has fallen upon the scenes so lately lighted by the Allied victory. . . . From Stettin in the Baltic to Trieste in the Adriatic, an iron curtain has descended across the Continent. Behind that line lie all the capitals of the ancient states of central and eastern Europe. . . . All these famous cities and the populations around them lie in what I must call the Soviet sphere, and all are subject in one form or another, not only to Soviet influence, but to a very high and, in many cases, increasing measure of control from Moscow. . . . I have felt bound to portray the shadow which, alike in the west and in the east, falls upon the world.

This standoff between East and West colored world events during the postwar era.

Section 1

Aftermath of the War in Europe

Focus Questions

- What were the basic provisions of the postwar settlement in Europe?
- How did the Allies respond to the Nazi atrocities that became public knowledge after the war?
- How and why was the United Nations organization established?

Victory over the Axis powers brought on a whole new set of problems for Allied leaders. To a certain extent these problems were the result of strategic decisions made during the war. In November and December 1943, for example, the three main leaders of the Allied powers—Roosevelt, Churchill, and Stalin—met at Tehran, the capital of Iran. They decided to defeat Germany by forcing a war on two fronts: Western Allied forces, led by the United States and Britain, would launch an invasion of the European continent across the English Channel and attack Germany from the west, while Soviet forces would attack Germany from the east. This decision was fateful, for it meant that the Western forces would meet their Soviet allies somewhere in the middle of Germany, with Soviet troops occupying most of Eastern Europe.

In February 1945, Roosevelt, Churchill, and Stalin met again in the Black Sea resort town of Yalta. The three leaders reached agreements in several areas. With victory now clearly in sight, they agreed to divide both Germany and Austria into zones of military occupation based on the territories their respective armed forces were liberating from the Nazis. Berlin, which would lie wholly within the Soviet zone, was also to be divided into four parts, with the Soviets in charge of East Berlin and the Western Allies establishing their own zones in West Berlin. Vienna was to be similarly divided. The division of Germany was supposed to be only a temporary measure, however, until a final settlement could be arranged at a general peace conference.

The Allies also seemed to reach an agreement on Poland and the territories the Soviets had already taken in Eastern Europe. Roosevelt and Churchill believed that these countries should be allowed to determine their own futures. Consequently, they obtained promises from Stalin that he would allow free elections and the establishment of democratic governments in accordance with the terms of the Atlantic Charter. In return they agreed with Stalin that the governments in these eastern countries must be friendly to the Soviet Union. Each side left the conference with the impression that its own viewpoint had won the day. For Stalin, however, friendly governments meant governments under Soviet control. Moreover, he believed that free elections and democracy could really only occur after the peoples of Eastern Europe had been properly educated in socialist principles. In short, from a Western perspective, his promise of free elections would eventually prove meaningless.

The three leaders also considered the larger question of how to prevent another war from occurring.

There was considerable disagreement. Both Churchill and Stalin believed that the best way to insure peace was for the victorious Allies to divide the world into spheres of influence. President Roosevelt, however, advocated the internationalist approach that had been the basis of the League of Nations after World War I. He proposed a new United Nations Organization that would succeed (where the old League of Nations had failed) in keeping the peace through collective security arrangements. The initial plans for such an organization had already been worked out in a conference attended by representatives of the United States, Britain, the Soviet Union, and China in the summer of 1944 at Dumbarton Oaks, near Washington, D.C. At Yalta the three leaders discussed the proposed charter and agreed on voting procedures to be followed in the United Nations.

The Occupation of Germany

After Germany's surrender in May 1945, the Allies completed the occupation of their respective zones and established temporary military governments. (See map on opposite page.) In July the Big Three met at Potsdam, outside Berlin, to establish the groundwork for a postwar settlement. The Soviet Union was represented by Stalin and the United States by Truman (who had become president of the United States upon Roosevelt's death in April). Churchill, and later Clement Attlee (who had replaced Churchill as British prime minister), represented Great Britain. The three powers agreed on several basic principles. Germany must be demilitarized; the Nazi Party must be disbanded and outlawed; German political life should be reconstructed on a democratic basis; and those responsible for the atrocities of the war should be brought to trial. The Allied leaders also agreed that Germany should remain a single state though decentralized and under the rule of occupation governments for the moment.

To oversee the various occupation governments, the Allies had established the Allied Control Council. They also agreed at Potsdam that a Council of Foreign Ministers, representing the Soviet Union, Great Britain, the United States, France, and China, should write the peace treaties. As the two councils began their work, however, it soon became clear that the Western democracies and the Soviet Union had very different plans for a postwar settlement. The major disagreements occurred over two questions: reparations and the boundaries of postwar Germany.

Territorial adjustments. Stalin insisted that the Soviet Union would retain the Polish territories and territories on the Baltic Sea gained as a result of the Nazi-Soviet Pact. Poland, he suggested, should be compensated for this loss of its eastern territories with a gift of territory in the west—German territory up to the line of the Oder and Neisse Rivers. At Potsdam, the Western Allies agreed to the Oder-Neisse boundary line. Poland also took part of East Prussia, and the Soviet Union took the rest. This transfer of territory to Poland and the Soviet Union stripped Germany of one fourth of its land.

One of the consequences of these territorial adjustments was a large increase in Germany's postwar population. The Soviets, for example, evicted the Germans from East Prussia and from the Soviet-controlled Baltic countries. Poland followed suit, expelling Germans from the area of prewar Poland as well as from the new territory they had just gained at Potsdam. Czechoslovakia, too, insisted that Sudeten Germans who had supported Hitler's invasion of Czechoslovakia must leave the country. These moves, though not surprising in view of the prewar troubles with ethnically German minorities, created a serious problem. The burden of housing, feeding, and employing these refugees fell on a shrunken and divided postwar Germany.

Demilitarization and reparations. The Allied Control Council solved the immediate problem of keeping Germany peaceful by swiftly disbanding all German land, air, and sea forces. The Allies demanded that all industrial plants and equipment that had been used in the war industry be dismantled. This plan proved difficult to enforce, however, since the Allies first had to answer the complex question of what constituted a war industry. A factory that manufactures tractors, for example, may easily be converted to produce tanks.

In addition, the Allies disagreed on the question of German economic revival. The United States and Britain concluded that a revival of German industry was essential to the general prosperity of postwar Europe as a whole. France initially preferred to keep Germany weak industrially to prevent any possibility of future rearmament. To the Soviets, reparations were more important than a revival of German industrial and economic prosperity. They demanded that Germany pay them the staggering sum of $10 billion in reparations.

Western leaders haggled with the Soviets, but in the end, they agreed that the Soviets might claim

Occupied Germany, 1945–1955

National capital ⊛

Zones:
- U.S.
- Soviet
- British
- French

0   100   200 Miles
0   100   200 Kilometers
Azimuthal Equal-Area Projection

Occupied Berlin

West Berlin
East Berlin

Azimuthal Equal-Area Projection

Learning from Maps After the war, the Allies decided to divide Germany into zones of military occupation.

? Place How was the city of Berlin divided?

reparations, mostly in the form of industrial equipment, not only from their own zone of occupation but from the Western zones as well. Under this agreement, the Soviets dismantled and moved hundreds of manufacturing and industrial plants from Germany to the Soviet Union. The removal of so many factories and industrial materials severely damaged the prospects for German industrial revival. Eventually, the Western Allies halted the flow of reparations from their zones to the Soviet Union.

Confronted by such controversial issues and disagreements, the Allied Control Council found it increasingly difficult to reach decisions. With the council in almost constant deadlock, the Allied occupation administrations soon began to ignore it altogether and to administer their own zones as they saw fit.

Nuremberg trials and denazification. The military occupation of Germany revealed to the world the full extent of the horrors of German concentration camps and the terrible consequences of the Nazi policy of racial purification. Although Hitler was dead and some of his highest-ranking officers had escaped to Spain and Latin America, many Nazi leaders had been captured. The victorious Allies were determined that those responsible for the war and all of its horrors should be held accountable. In 1945 and 1946, a special international court met at Nuremberg, Germany. The Nuremberg court charged 22 of the principal Nazi leaders with crimes against peace and crimes against humanity as well as conspiracy in the extermination camps, the slave labor camps, and the conquered countries. In a series of trials, referred to as the **Nuremberg trials**, 12 of the defendants were sentenced to death, 7 were sentenced to life imprisonment, and 3 were acquitted. At the same time, the court declared the Nazi Party a criminal organization. Trials of other war criminals continued for many years in postwar Germany.

In addition to trying Nazi leaders, the Allies also pursued a policy of **denazification**, which included removing former Nazis from positions of authority in government, industry, and education. However, difficulties soon developed. The German economy had broken down almost completely. Its rebuilding required technically skilled leaders, many of whom had been Nazis.

Peacemaking Problems

In addition to deciding what to do with the defeated powers, the Allies confronted the daunting task of reconstructing Europe itself. The governments of the United States, the Soviet Union, and Great Britain had survived the test of war. Elsewhere, however, the destruction unleashed by the Nazis had undermined or destroyed many prewar governments. As many of the European states emerged from the shambles of the war, they established new forms of government in place of the old.

This October 1946 photo was taken at the Nuremberg trial of Nazi leaders.

In 1946, for example, a plebiscite, or a direct vote by the people on a national issue, abolished the monarchy in Italy and established a republican form of government. In France a provisional government, headed by General Charles de Gaulle, ran the country until 1946, when a new constitution was adopted and the Fourth Republic was proclaimed.

Much of the rest of Europe also faced major changes. In Eastern Europe, the Soviets had established temporary governments in the countries they had liberated. These governments were heavily dominated—in most cases controlled outright—by Communists, despite the anticommunist feelings of the majority of the population. Greece had a tottering monarchy and was in the throes of a civil war, and the political futures of both Germany and Austria remained uncertain. Allied efforts to achieve a final postwar settlement in all of these areas proved extremely difficult. It soon became clear that the Soviet Union and the Western Allies had fundamentally conflicting goals for postwar Europe.

In February 1947, after nearly a year and a half of heated debate, the Council of Foreign Ministers reached agreement on peace treaties with Italy, Romania, Bulgaria, Hungary, and Finland. Italy renounced all claims to countries that it had invaded during the war. It also lost some territory to France, Yugoslavia, and Greece; its colonies were placed under a trusteeship of the United Nations. Romania, Hungary, Bulgaria, and Finland also had to return territory they had taken and accept changes in their prewar boundaries. Furthermore, they had to reduce their armed forces and pay reparations to nations that their armies had invaded.

The negotiations over the treaties exposed a growing rift between the Soviet Union and the Western Allies. The Soviets were determined to ensure that Communists controlled the governments of the Eastern European countries that were occupied by the Red Army. Only in this way, they insisted, would they be safe from future invasion. The Western Allies objected, insisting that there must be free elections and governments that were generally representative of all democratic elements in the population. In the end, a compromise was reached when the Soviet Union agreed to allow a few representatives of noncommunist political parties to participate in the new governments of Eastern Europe.

The Allies were unable to achieve agreement on the most important treaties. The four-way occupation of Austria, for example, continued for years without any agreement as to peace terms. Finally, in 1955, a treaty with Austria was negotiated and signed. The treaty restored Austria as a sovereign, independent republic within its 1938 boundaries. Austria, however, had to agree to be permanently neutral. It had taken the Allies 10 years to reach an agreement over Austria. In the case of Germany, the Allies never agreed to a final settlement. The division of Germany into eastern and western parts eventually became a formal division into two countries.

The United Nations

Despite their disagreements over the status of Eastern Europe, Germany, and Austria, after the war the Allies continued with their plans for a new international organization to be known as the United Nations, which would replace the old League of Nations.

In April 1945, representatives from 51 nations met in San Francisco. After two months, this General Assembly agreed to a final version of the charter, which was then submitted to the government of each representative for ratification. By October 1945, the required number of nations had ratified the charter, and the United Nations (UN) was established. Its primary purpose was to maintain international peace and security and to act as a deterrent to aggressors. As a part of this mission, it was also designed to foster cooperation among the nations of the world in solving international social, cultural, and economic problems.

In many ways the structure of the United Nations represented a compromise between those who still thought that great powers deserved more influence, and those who preferred a more idealistic approach to maintaining world peace on the basis of collective security. Consequently, the two most important bodies of the UN were the Security Council and the General Assembly.

The Security Council. The Security Council was the body charged primarily with maintaining international peace and security. It was to act as a mediator in international disputes and seek to prevent aggression by any nation. The Council was composed of 10 temporary members, elected from the General Assembly for two-year rotating terms, and 5 permanent members. The permanent members were the five major powers that had formed the core of the Allied powers—the United States, Britain, France, the Soviet Union, and China. Each of these countries could prevent the Council from taking an important action by using its **veto power**—the power to defeat a measure with a single vote. In this way the

Security Council was designed to satisfy those who felt that some nations should have more influence than others.

The General Assembly. The General Assembly, on the other hand, was designed to appeal to those who felt that all nations deserved equal status. Ultimately, any nation that wished to join would be admitted to the General Assembly, including those that had been defeated in the war. Each member nation in the Assembly, regardless of size or power, would have the same rights and voting power as any other. The Assembly was responsible for drawing up the UN budget and assessing each member nation's share of the cost. The General Assembly also elected the secretary-general and the judges of the International Court of Justice.

In addition to these two main bodies, the UN is also composed of four other major organizations. Sustaining and supporting the entire organization is the Secretariat, a staff of clerical and administrative workers, technical experts, and advisors, all working under the secretary-general. The International Court of Justice at The Hague, in the Netherlands, presides over questions of international law. The new Trusteeship Council replaced the old mandate system of the League of Nations. Finally, the Economic and Social Council sponsors a host of specialized agencies including the World Health Organization (WHO), the UN Educational, Scientific and Cultural Organization (UNESCO), the International Bank for Reconstruction and Development (also called the World Bank), and the International Monetary Fund (IMF), among others.

Section 1 Review

1. **Define** Cold War, Nuremberg trials, denazification, veto power
2. **Identify** Big Three, Allied Control Council, Council of Foreign Ministers, Security Council, General Assembly
3. **Locate and Explain the Significance** Yalta, Oder-Neisse line, East Prussia
4. **Understanding Ideas** Describe the principal terms of the postwar settlement of Europe.
5. **Summarizing Ideas** What action did the Allies take to deal with the atrocities committed during the war?
6. **Analyzing Ideas** What are the goals of the United Nations?

What If?

The United Nations
One of the main purposes of the United Nations is to maintain world peace. How might peace have been maintained in the postwar world if the UN General Assembly had had the power to enforce decisions and the Big Five did not have veto power?

Origins of the Cold War

Focus Questions
* How did the Western Allies respond to Soviet policies in Eastern Europe immediately after World War II?
* What long-range measures did the United States take to deal with Europe's economic plight and the apparent threat of Soviet expansion?

With the Red Army occupying all of Eastern and part of Central Europe at the war's end, and the United States in sole possession of the atomic bomb, each side increasingly came to fear the other. Although the struggle between democracy and communism occasionally led to bloody local wars, for the most part the Cold War was a war of ideas and differing worldviews waged by the two great superpowers, as they came to be called. Political and economic means were used instead of weapons, partly because the development of atomic bombs and later nuclear weapons that could destroy the world made another world war unthinkable.

The End of the Alliance

As the Soviet Union and the Western Allies continued to disagree over fundamental questions after the end of World War II, the alliance that had defeated the Axis powers finally dissolved. In its place, a new rivalry emerged between two armed camps supporting the two superpowers. On one side was the Soviet Union, supported by the communist nations of the world. The Soviet Union and its communist allies were sometimes called the Eastern bloc. On the other side was the United

States, supported by the Western democracies and other noncommunist nations. The two sides were distinguished by completely different political and economic systems.

Partly as a consequence of these political and economic differences, after the war the Soviet Union and the Western Allies also came to have vastly different ideas about how to reconstruct Europe. Each side naturally believed that its own system should be the model. In addition, each side was worried about its future security. The Soviet Union was determined to protect itself from any future attack from the West—as the Germans had attacked Russia twice in a generation. With this in mind, as the Red Army rolled across Eastern and Central Europe, Stalin insisted on placing governments that would be friendly to Soviet interests in power in the liberated states. This would create a buffer zone of communist countries along the western frontier of the Soviet Union.

Disagreement over Poland. The first sign of trouble came in Poland, whose invasion by Hitler had been the trigger for the war in the first place. Although a free Polish government-in-exile had been established in London, Stalin refused to recognize it. Instead, he installed a pro-Soviet Polish government that was dominated by Communists. In addition, he insisted that the Soviet Union would retain the territories in Poland and the Baltic states that it had taken at the time of the Nazi-Soviet Pact. To the Americans and British, however, this policy seemed to violate his agreement at Yalta to allow free elections in the countries that had been liberated by the Red Army. The Western Allies became increasingly suspicious that Stalin's real goal was to dominate all of Europe.

Soviet expansion. Other Soviet actions fueled Western fears. In the summer of 1945, for example, Stalin massed troops along the border of Turkey. He demanded the return of territory in Caucasia that had once been annexed by the czars. He also insisted on joint Soviet-Turkish control over the straits connecting the Black Sea to the Aegean and Mediterranean Seas. Such control would guarantee the Soviet Union an outlet for its Black Sea fleet into the Mediterranean. Then, in February 1946, Stalin suddenly announced that the communist struggle for worldwide revolution would continue. In March, Soviet forces that had occupied northern Iran during the war refused to withdraw as scheduled. Instead they supported the establishment of the communist Tudeh Party in Iran.

Winston Churchill delivered his "iron curtain" speech at Fulton, Missouri, in early March 1946.

Under intense pressure from the United States and Britain, the Soviets eventually backed down from their position in Turkey and Iran. Nevertheless, other Soviet actions seemed to indicate a policy of expansionism, not mere self-defense. When a further crisis broke out in Greece in early 1947, the United States finally decided to openly oppose the expansion of communism around the world.

The Truman Doctrine

In 1944, after the Nazis had withdrawn from Greece, civil war broke out between conservative members of the Greek resistance movement, loyal to the monarchy, and the communist partisans. Britain, supporting the royalists, negotiated a truce in 1945. In the summer of 1946, however, the Communists renewed the civil war. They were aided and supplied by the new communist governments of Albania, Bulgaria, and Yugoslavia. The Greek government turned once again to the British for help.

Exhausted and practically bankrupted by the war, the British decided that they could no longer afford to defend states like Iran, Turkey, and Greece against Soviet expansion. In February 1947, the British informed the United States that they were ending financial aid to Greece and Turkey and would withdraw their troops from Greece. They hoped that the United States would provide the necessary assistance to prevent communist domination in the region.

Building History Study Skills

READ
WRITE
INTERPRET
CONNECT
THINK

Reading About History: Identifying an Argument

When we hear the word *argument,* we often think of a disagreement or a dispute. However, when historians use this word, they are speaking of a thesis or main point supported by reasons and examples. Identifying an argument is the first step in determining its validity.

How to Identify an Argument

To identify an argument, follow these steps.

1. Explain the author's thesis or main point. Ask what the author is attempting to prove. You can look for key words and phrases such as *therefore, in conclusion, consequently,* or *I support.*
2. Identify the reasons given to support the main thesis. How does each reason elaborate on the main point?
3. Find the examples that support the reasons.
4. Connect the thesis of the argument with the reasons and examples.

Developing the Skill

Read the following selection from Thomas G. Paterson's *On Every Front: The Making and Unmaking of the Cold War.*

"[T]he Cold War derived from three closely intertwined sources: the conflict-ridden international system; the divergent fundamental needs, ideas, and power of the major antagonists, the United States and the Soviet Union; and the diplomatic conduct . . . —the tactics—of American and Soviet leaders. . . . International, national, and individual elements intersected to produce a world divided into competing spheres of influence. . . . Two nations . . . emerged from the rubble of World War II to claim high rank. . . . The competitive interaction between the United States and the Soviet Union . . . shaped the bipolarism . . . of the immediate postwar years. . . . The major powers, in short, intervened abroad to exploit the political opportunities created by the destructive scythe of World War II. The stakes seemed high. A change in a nation's political orientation might presage [predict] a change in its international alignment. The great powers tended to ignore local conditions . . . which might and often did mitigate against alignment with an outside power. Americans . . . feared that a . . . Communist Greece would look to the East and permit menacing Soviet bases on Greek territory or open the door to a Soviet naval presence in the Mediterranean. Moscow dreaded a conservative

President Truman making his first speech to Congress

anti-Soviet Polish government . . ., for it might prove so weak and so hostile to Moscow as to permit a revived Germany to send storm troopers once again through the Polish corridor into the heart of Russia. . . . A Communist China . . . might align with the Soviet Union; a Nationalist China would remain in the American camp. All in all, the rearranging of political structures within nations drew the major powers into competition, accentuating the conflict inherent in the postwar international system."

The author's main point or thesis is that the origin of the Cold War lies in the goals of the United States and the Soviet Union. Both nations, in their efforts to protect their superpower status and their national security, engaged in tactics that reinforced mutual suspicion. The competing ideologies were a basis for mutual mistrust.

The writer supports his thesis with details about the political situation at the end of World War II. He contends that the Soviet Union and the United States interfered in local conflicts because they saw their power interests at stake. The examples that Paterson cites are the situations in Greece, Poland, and China.

The author's argument is based upon his thesis that both powers, the United States and the Soviet Union, share responsibility for the development of the Cold War.

Practicing the Skill

Read a recent newspaper or magazine article that states a thesis or argument on a political point. Identify the argument, using the skill you have just learned.

To apply this skill, see Applying History Study Skills on page 493.

On March 12, 1947, President Truman, speaking before Congress, announced what came to be called the Truman Doctrine. The United States, he said, considered the continued spread of communism to be a threat to democracy. It must be the policy of the United States, he went on, to support free peoples who are resisting attempted takeovers by armed minorities or by outside pressures. He asked Congress to appropriate $400 million to help defend Greece and Turkey from communist aggression. Congress agreed, and with American financial and technical assistance, the Greek government put down the rebellion.

Over the next several months, Truman's advisors developed a full-scale strategy to carry out the president's new policy. The United States would not try to stamp out communism in countries where it already existed, or in any country that freely chose communism. However, it would use its money, materials, technical knowledge, and influence to help countries that were threatened by communist takeover if they asked for help. In short, the United States would contain, or restrict, the spread of communism wherever possible, a policy known as **containment**.

The Marshall Plan
Disagreement over German economic recovery also contributed to the Cold War. Western leaders interpreted Stalin's reluctance to rebuild the German economy as an effort to keep Western Europe economically weak and depressed. Continuing poverty and economic hardship, they feared, would cause people to turn to local communist parties and communist-dominated labor unions.

In 1947, United States secretary of state George Marshall announced a new plan for massive American economic assistance to help Europe recover from the war. The European Recovery Program, often called the Marshall Plan, stipulated that the United States was prepared to assist Europe on certain terms. For example, European countries were encouraged to work together to determine their needs. They were also to try to remove trade barriers so that goods could flow freely throughout the continent. In this way, prosperity was to be restored. The United States included the Soviet Union and its satellites in its offer of aid, but those nations found the conditions unacceptable and rejected it. Eventually, however, 17 European nations participated in the European Recovery Program.

Between 1948 and 1952, the United States spent over $13 billion on the Marshall Plan with tremendous success. By 1952 both industrial production and agricultural production in Europe had risen considerably above prewar levels, and the continent was once again on the road to prosperity. The United States also benefited from the plan, as it supplied export goods for the recovering European economies.

The Cold War in Central Europe
From the Soviet point of view, both the Truman Doctrine and the Marshall Plan seemed like Western efforts to encircle and undermine the Soviet Union. In September 1947, the Soviet government established the Communist Information Bureau, or **Cominform**, an organization that included all European communist parties. Its purpose was to oppose Marshall Plan aid, which was denounced as an American capitalist effort to dominate Europe economically. The Cominform was unsuccessful in opposing Marshall Plan aid. Its major effect was simply to create tension between communist and noncommunist political parties in Europe.

As the West put its new containment policy into place, the Soviets also tightened their grip on the countries of Eastern and Central Europe. In February 1948, for example, the communist members of Czechoslovakia's still-democratic government staged a coup. Taking complete control of the government, they turned Czechoslovakia into a tightly controlled one-party communist state. Thus, Czechoslovakia joined the Soviet-dominated Communist bloc.

Only one break appeared in the iron curtain that divided East and West. During the spring of 1948, a disagreement developed between Stalin and Marshall Tito of Yugoslavia. Although a devoted Communist, Tito objected to Soviet domination. He announced that Yugoslavia would follow an independent course. By June 1948, the split had become definite, and Yugoslavia was expelled from Cominform.

The Division of Germany
By 1948 it was clear that joint government in Germany by the four former Allies was impossible. In late 1947 and early 1948, anxious to achieve economic recovery, the three Western occupying powers took steps to reunite their zones economically and to revive democratic German political life. It became obvious that they were moving toward the establishment of a unified West German state—a move that the Soviets bitterly opposed.

The Berlin blockade. In response, in June 1948 the Soviets blockaded the East German border to all land and water traffic into Berlin from the west. They refused to allow trucks, barges, or trains to pass the checkpoints at the borders, thus threatening the people of West Berlin with starvation. The Western nations acted swiftly during the Berlin blockade. The United States and Great Britain organized an airlift to supply West Berlin. They flew food and supplies in daily to the inhabitants of the Western sectors of the city. The airlift operated so efficiently that raw materials were also supplied to West Berlin factories. To send the message that the Western Allies would not be intimidated, the United States sent strategic bombers to Great Britain. The Soviets made no serious attempts to stop the airlift, and in May 1949, they lifted the blockade.

East and West Germany. In the long term, the Berlin blockade might be seen as the official beginning of the Cold War. In the short term, it had an immediate and important consequence: the division of Germany. With the approval of the Western Allies, in May 1949 a constitutional assembly proclaimed the

The top photo shows supplies being airlifted into West Berlin by the United States and Great Britain. The bottom photo shows a German airlift worker's wife feeding children. Each child's ration is a slice of dark bread and margarine.

Federal Republic of Germany (popularly known as West Germany), with its capital in Bonn. The Soviet Union followed suit. In October 1949 the German Democratic Republic (popularly known as East Germany) was established in the Soviet zone of Germany. The formal division of Germany became a major symbol of the East-West division that was the Cold War.

Cold War Alliances

The division of Germany was but one of a series of events in 1949 and 1950 that made clear the extent of the split between East and West. As the former Allies divided Europe, the Cold War also seemed to spread to the rest of the world. It also became more dangerous as other powers besides the United States learned the secrets of atomic power. In the summer of 1949, for example, the Soviets detonated their first atomic bomb. In October the West was further alarmed when armies of the Chinese Communist Party defeated the Chinese Nationalist government and forced it off the mainland to the island of Taiwan. Not least, the outbreak of the Korean War in 1950, when the communist forces of North Korea invaded South Korea, reminded many people that the Cold War could all too easily become hot. Perhaps the clearest indication of the split, however, came in the form of new political and military alliances.

The North Atlantic Treaty Organization. In April 1949 a mutual defense pact provided for creation of the North Atlantic Treaty Organization (NATO). Twelve nations originally signed the North Atlantic Treaty: the United States, Great Britain, France, Italy, Portugal, Norway, Denmark, Iceland, Canada, Belgium, the Netherlands, and Luxembourg. Greece and Turkey joined NATO in 1952, and West Germany followed in 1955. (See map on opposite page.) The signers agreed that if one member nation were attacked, all members would take united action against the aggressor. Although a detailed defense plan called for a large standing NATO force drawn from all member nations, eventually the organization came to rely heavily on American nuclear weapons to act as a deterrent to any Soviet invasion of Western Europe.

The Warsaw Pact. The Soviet Union responded to the inclusion of West Germany in NATO by establishing a formal, unified alliance of its own. In May 1955 in Warsaw, Poland, the Soviet government held a meeting of representatives of the European Communist bloc—the Soviet Union,

European Alliances, 1955

Legend:
- NATO nations
- Warsaw Pact nations
- Other Communist nations
- Neutral nations
- Iron Curtain
- National capital
- Other cities

The United States and Canada are the North American members of NATO.

Learning from Maps NATO and the Warsaw Pact divided European allegiances.

? Region Which countries remained neutral in 1955?

Poland, East Germany, Czechoslovakia, Hungary, Romania, Bulgaria, and Albania. These nations adopted a 20-year mutual defense agreement called the Warsaw Pact. The combined troop strength contributed by member countries along with Soviet troops already stationed throughout the region meant that the Warsaw Pact greatly outnumbered NATO in terms of ground troops. This overwhelming difference in ground troops between NATO and the Warsaw Pact only reinforced the Western reliance on the nuclear deterrent.

Section 2 Review

1. **Define** containment, Cominform
2. **Understanding Ideas** What was the purpose of the Truman Doctrine?
3. **Summarizing Ideas** What were the basic features of the Marshall Plan?
4. **Analyzing Ideas** (a) What were the functions of NATO and the Warsaw Pact? (b) Why were these alliances formed?

Reconstruction, Reform, and Reaction in Europe

Focus Questions

- **How did Western European countries respond to the challenges of postwar reconstruction?**
- **What actions did Western European leaders take to integrate their economies?**
- **How did the Eastern European experience of postwar reconstruction differ from that of the West? Why?**

Thanks to the Marshall Plan and the resolve of the European people, postwar Western Europe experienced a remarkable economic and political recovery. After the war, the Western Allies remained committed to democracy and the principle of majority rule. In economic terms, they also continued to accept the basic principles of capitalism and at least some form of **market economy**. A market economy is one in which competition among private businesses and individuals generally determines what goods and services will be produced, how they will be produced, and what they will cost. The Communist bloc, on the other hand, accepted the Marxist-Leninist doctrine that ordinary people did not always know what was in their own best interests or the interests of society as a whole. Consequently, only the elite Communist Party was believed capable of organizing society properly. In keeping with this principle, communist countries practiced a **command economy**, in which the government made all economic decisions. The market economies of Western Europe helped those nations achieve a higher standard of living than that of Eastern Europe. In a relatively short time, Western Europeans cleared away the rubble of bombed cities and rebuilt roads, rail lines, and bridges. Industries rapidly returned to full production. Eastern Europe also revived after the war, but not nearly as quickly or successfully as the West.

The West German "Miracle"

As the Western Allies encouraged the revival of democratic political parties in West Germany, two main parties emerged that would dominate West German politics in the 1950s and 1960s, the Christian Democrats and the Social Democrats.

The first West German chancellor, Konrad Adenauer, was a Christian Democrat. Under Adenauer's free-market policies, the reconstruction and industrial development of West Germany progressed at a remarkable rate. Many people referred to it as the "German miracle."

During the postwar years, the West German government managed to provide housing and jobs for the many refugees from East Germany and other Eastern European nations. The labor of these refugees contributed to West Germany's rapidly growing economy. German industry flourished, thanks to technological innovation, a commitment to quality, and the absence of strikes and other labor troubles. The West German unit of currency, the *Deutsche mark*, became one of the most stable in the world.

In his book *Germany and the East-West Crisis*, William S. Schlamm describes how one West German built a successful business after the war.

" . . . [A] young friend of mine, a former Sudeten-German, . . . in 1948—when he was thirty-two—crossed the border of the German Soviet Zone and started to manufacture nylon stockings in West Germany. At the end of 1957, nine years later, . . . [H]is plant would be the pride of any United States chamber of commerce. Beautifully remodeled in 1957, it is an authentic example of shrewd rationalization techniques, of mechanical perfection, of tidiness and profitability. **"**

By 1958, West Germany was the leading industrial nation in Western Europe. Under Adenauer's guidance, especially through his commitment to establishing the rule of law as the fundamental principle of the German state, West Germany had also become one of the world's most stable democracies.

Staunchly anticommunist, and especially anti-Soviet, Adenauer also followed a policy of close alignment with the Western Allies. Under his guidance, Germany joined NATO in 1955. He also encouraged Germans in the Soviet bloc to escape to the West. Many did so, particularly in Berlin, where the Western Allies continued to administer the western half of the city. Indeed, so many refugees fled East Germany through Berlin that in 1961 the East German government, almost overnight, erected a wall separating the two halves of the city. Anyone who was caught trying to escape over the wall was shot. The Berlin Wall, with its cap of barbed wire, became a major symbol of the Cold War.

The German government founded the Volkswagen company in 1937, with its headquarters in Wolfsburg. The "Beetle" and "Rabbit" models became very popular in the United States during the 1960s and 1970s.

Although Adenauer retired in 1963, he was followed by a fellow Christian Democrat, Ludwig Erhard, who had been in many ways the architect of the free-market policies that had produced the "miracle." Under Erhard, Germany continued to prosper, although its rate of growth slowed during the 1960s. A mild recession or slowdown in economic activity occurred in 1966. Worries over the economy and the Christian Democrats' foreign policy of complete alignment with the United States eventually caused many Germans to turn to the Social Democrats. Throughout the 1960s the Social Democrats gained ground in local elections and even in the federal parliament. Not until 1969, however, did the Social Democrats win a national majority in the Federal Republic of Germany under their leader, Willy Brandt.

Great Britain After the War

Ironically, perhaps, at the same time that Germany was pursuing free-market policies, Britain was going in the opposite direction. In 1945, British voters rejected Winston Churchill's Conservative Party at the polls. Winning a substantial majority in Parliament, the Labour Party formed Britain's postwar government under Clement Attlee. The Labour Party, a moderate socialist party, made many changes in the British economic and social systems. The government nationalized railroads, utilities, coal mines, and the Bank of England, but did not interfere with four fifths of industry, which remained privately owned. Many welfare measures were passed, including free medical care for everyone. Great Britain became a **welfare state**—a state in which the government undertakes primary responsibility for the social welfare of its citizens.

Great Britain also faced many severe economic problems after the war. Its industrial equipment was outdated and inefficient. Many workers had been killed in the war. Some scientists and managers had emigrated to Canada, Australia, and the United States. After the war, Great Britain lost valuable colonies and possessions, and the cost of the nation's remaining overseas commitments was a heavy burden. The nation struggled to overcome its nagging economic difficulties.

A new Conservative government was elected in 1951. As prime minister once again, Churchill reversed some of the Labour government's nationalization policies. The government reduced unemployment, raised wages, and allowed industry to thrive. However, the general outlines of the welfare state remained intact even under the Conservatives.

Moreover, Britain continued to lag behind the rest of Europe in economic recovery. Although industrial growth occurred, it was much slower than that of other countries, especially Germany and France. In the 1960s, Great Britain's industrial productivity fell to one of the lowest national levels in the industrialized world. One important reason for this decline was the shift in the world economy from coal as an energy source to oil and nuclear power. Britain's strength traditionally had been its large coal reserves. The Labour Party blamed the Conservatives for the poor economy but did no better when back in office during the 1960s and 1970s.

Inflation began in the late 1960s and escalated in the 1970s. British labor unions fought to maintain high wages, but without also increasing the productivity of British workers. This meant that British goods cost more to make—and to sell—than goods produced by their competitors. Consequently, Britain was unable to develop a favorable balance of trade—in which more goods are exported than imported—and real prosperity remained elusive.

New Republics in France

Postwar France also faced serious problems. After the war, the voters adopted a new constitution and proclaimed the Fourth Republic, but this government was almost as unstable politically as its predecessor. Economically, France had suffered considerable damage during the war, with many towns and cities destroyed and valuable farmlands ravaged. After the war, inflation caused great hardship for the French people. Economic revival began under the policies of French economist Jean Monnet, however, and especially with the help of the Marshall Plan, French agriculture and industry slowly began to recover and even to modernize.

As economic recovery proceeded slowly and painfully at home, France also faced challenges in its overseas empire. Anxious to restore its own prestige as well as France's after the defeat of 1940, the French army conducted bitter and costly wars to re-establish French authority in Indochina and North Africa. In the late 1950s, a crisis over Algeria brought France to the brink of civil war.

Algeria was considered an integral part of France, with more than a million European settlers, many of whose families had been there for a century. In 1954, however, Arab nationalists began a bitter and bloody war for independence. After several years of extreme violence, many people in France were prepared to let Algeria go. Others, including leading elements in the army, violently opposed such a course. In 1958, as crisis engulfed the nation, the French legislature—under pressure from army leaders—turned to General Charles de Gaulle to save the nation from civil war. He was authorized to write a new constitution and to rule by decree until its ratification.

The new constitution created France's Fifth Republic. The constitution gave the president a great deal of power. He appointed the prime minister and could dissolve the legislature and assume dictatorial powers in a national emergency. Through the prime minister, the president could enact laws unless a majority of the National Assembly opposed them.

De Gaulle became the first president of the Fifth Republic. To the surprise of the army, he ended the war in Algeria by accepting Algerian independence. He also moved to peacefully transform the French empire into a voluntary association of self-governing nations known as the French Community.

In foreign policy, de Gaulle was a nationalist. He believed that Europe could prosper only as a close alliance of national states that would retain their individual identity and freedom of action. He opposed British and American influence in Europe because he feared that a rise of imperialism would threaten the individuality of every nation. He feared the Soviet Union less, although he was wary of Soviet expansion into Europe. Balancing these factors, de Gaulle withdrew French forces from NATO command and insisted on developing an independent nuclear force for France, although France remained a political member of NATO.

To further counter Anglo-American influence in Europe, de Gaulle pursued a policy of French and German cooperation. He established close relations with West German Chancellor Adenauer. Together, he believed, the French and Germans could prevent Europe from being dominated too much by Britain and the United States, while at the same time acting as a deterrent to Russian expansion.

In the late 1960s, political conditions within France became unstable. Violent riots shook the nation in 1968. Militant students demanded reforms in the educational system, and strikes for higher wages and better working conditions spread rapidly throughout industrial areas. To meet the crisis, de Gaulle dissolved the National Assembly and called for a general election.

To win a favorable vote, de Gaulle acknowledged the need for social improvements in France. However, soon afterward his popularity declined. In April 1969, in a direct vote, the French people rejected his proposals for reform, and the 79-year-old president resigned.

Other Western European Nations

Recovery in the other nations of Western Europe took many different paths. Denmark, Norway, and Sweden, for example, had experienced relatively little dislocation as a result of the war. Sweden had remained neutral, and although occupied by the Nazis, Norway and Denmark had not been the scenes of any major fighting. After the war, Social Democratic parties that had first been elected in the 1930s remained in power until the 1970s. With strongly entrenched democracies and greater political stability than in other countries in Western Europe,

ARCHITECTURE

Chapel by Le Corbusier

World War II, so devastating to people in Europe and elsewhere, also had among its casualties many great works of art. Numerous old and beautiful churches were damaged or destroyed. It was with great joy, then, that Europeans hailed the construction of this new place of worship. Built between 1950 and 1955 by the great architect Le Corbusier, the chapel stands proudly in the green fields of Ronchamp, in France.

Called Notre Dame du Haut, this was one of Le Corbusier's most famous works. The chapel appears large, although it is quite small. It holds only about 200 people. The walls are made of concrete sprayed over metal mesh; the finished walls were then painted white. The roof is also concrete but was left unpainted. Some say that

Le Corbusier's soaring chapel design was inspired by an image of praying hands or the wings of an angel.

throughout the 1950s and 1960s their economies prospered. This prosperity allowed them to establish extensive welfare states, though at the cost of extremely high taxes.

In Italy the Christian Democratic Party dominated the political arena during the 1950s and 1960s. Under Alcide de Gasperi, prime minister from 1945 to 1953, Italy established a capitalist economy, and the country experienced major industrial and agricultural growth.

By the 1960s, the Socialist and Communist Parties had gained considerable strength as labor unrest increased. At the end of the decade, Italy's economic growth declined sharply. This decline contributed to the undermining of political stability.

Economic programs in Greece, Spain, and Portugal met with varying degrees of success. Of all the Western European countries, only Portugal and Spain did not establish full democratic government after the war, but remained authoritarian. All three nations, however, were able to develop free-enterprise systems.

Western European Integration

In the 1950s the French proposed that the nations that produced most of Western Europe's steel and coal

unite their facilities. In 1952, France, West Germany, Italy, and the Low Countries (Belgium, the Netherlands, and Luxembourg) formed the European Coal and Steel Community (ECSC). A central authority regulated production and prices, and members did not charge each other tariffs on coal or steel. A remarkable feature of the ECSC was its freedom from national control.

The Common Market. In 1957 the same six nations took another important step toward economic union by establishing the European Economic Community (EEC)—usually called the Common Market. The Treaty of Rome provided for the gradual abolition of tariffs and import quotas among the six member nations. A common tariff would be placed on goods coming into the Common Market from nonmember nations.

The European Community. The Common Market made steady progress toward European economic unity in the 1960s. In 1967 it adopted a five-year plan to provide greater price and wage stability and more uniform tax levels among member countries. Also in 1967, the EEC merged with the European Coal and Steel Community and the Atomic Energy Community, which the six nations had created to share information on the peaceful uses of atomic energy, to form the European Communities, later the European Community, or EC. The European Community set up a single European commission with headquarters in Belgium.

Although Britain could have joined the EEC in the 1950s, British leaders decided against such a course. They still saw their future as tied to the British Commonwealth, rather than to Europe. In the 1960s, however, the EEC prospered economically while Britain lagged behind. Eventually, the British changed their minds and applied for admission. Still worried about undue British influence in Europe, French president Charles de Gaulle vetoed the application. Not until after de Gaulle's retirement and death did Britain finally gain admission to the EEC in 1973.

The Soviet Union After Stalin

In March 1953 Joseph Stalin, who had ruled the Soviet Union with an iron hand for three decades, died. Stalin's death led to a power struggle within the Soviet government. Eventually, Nikita Khrushchev (kroosh·CHAWF), former secretary of the Communist Party in the Ukraine, emerged as Stalin's successor.

After consolidating his position, in February 1956 Khrushchev shocked the leadership of the Soviet Union. In a speech to the 20th Congress of the Communist Party he denounced the policies of his predecessor, condemning Stalin for creating a "cult of personality," for murdering thousands of innocent Soviet citizens and loyal Communist Party members, and for committing a host of other crimes against the Soviet people.

Khrushchev's speech marked the beginning of his new policy of destalinization. Reversing a number of Stalin's policies, Khrushchev lifted restrictions on intellectuals and artists, freed many political prisoners, and ended some of the terrorism of the secret police. He also loosened the central government's tight grip on the economy. Incentives were offered to increase agricultural production. Local factory and farm managers were given more control to help them meet production quotas.

Khrushchev's primary goal was to increase the availability of consumer goods to the Soviet people. Even under his reforms, however, a continuing emphasis on heavy industry, and especially military spending, prevented substantial advances in the production of consumer goods. In addition, although Soviet industry had been rebuilt after the war, it was rebuilt largely with prewar technology. With the limitations imposed

President Dwight D. Eisenhower (left) welcomed Premier Nikita S. Khrushchev to the United States in 1959.

by centralized planning, the only real innovations achieved by the Soviet Union were in military and space technology. To the surprise of the world, the Soviets began the space age when they launched the first orbiting satellite, *Sputnik*, in 1957.

Despite these problems, over the next several decades the Soviet economy did expand, and living standards rose considerably. The Soviet Union gradually became a modern industrial society. By the 1970s, for example, it was producing more coal, steel, cement, cotton, natural gas, and oil than any other country in the world.

For a time, Khrushchev also seemed anxious to improve relations with the Western powers. He adopted a policy known as peaceful coexistence. However, this temporary thaw in East-West relations lasted only until 1960, when an American U-2 spy airplane was shot down over the Soviet Union, leading to the cancellation of a summit talk planned between Khrushchev and U.S. president Dwight Eisenhower. Diplomatic relations further deteriorated with the building of the Berlin Wall in 1961 and a crisis over Cuba in 1962 that brought the Soviet Union and the United States to the brink of nuclear war. After Khrushchev's economic policies also failed to produce the desired results, in 1964 he was forced to resign from office. Under his successor, Leonid Brezhnev, both domestic and foreign policies were tightened once more.

Economic Recovery in Eastern Europe

Like the rest of Europe, the new satellite countries of the Eastern bloc also had to rebuild after the end of World War II. To do so under the thumb of Soviet rule, however, proved difficult. Like the Soviet Union itself, the Eastern European countries lagged behind the West in recovering from the war. Under the new Soviet-controlled governments, efforts were made to collectivize agriculture, with varying results. In Hungary, for example, local resistance resulted in the collectivization of only about a third of the land. Bulgaria, on the other hand, collectivized over half of its available farmland. The Poles resisted collectivization so forcefully that most land remained in private hands. All these efforts at collectivization of agriculture along Soviet lines simply delayed economic recovery in the Eastern European countries.

Under Soviet-style Five-Year Plans and central planning, industrialization of Eastern Europe was more successful. East Germany and Czechoslovakia had industrialized before World War II. Under the new policies these countries expanded their industrial bases. East Germany, which had suffered considerably from having to pay reparations to the Soviet Union in the form of factories and industrial goods, eventually became the major industrial power in Eastern Europe. Hungary and Poland, although still agrarian countries before the war, now also became industrialized. Despite industrialization, however, under Soviet domination consumer goods remained a low priority. Consequently, living standards in Eastern Europe, though they improved, also remained low in comparison with the West.

Upheavals in Eastern Europe

During the early postwar years, the Communist bloc seemed a solid, firmly knit group of nations united by common beliefs, policies, and goals. However, the satellite countries had once been independent nations, some with long-standing antagonisms toward the Soviet Union.

Yugoslavia's growing independence from the Soviet Union after 1948 aroused envy and also inspired some people in the satellite countries. In 1953, Soviet tanks and troops put down a revolt by East German workers. In 1956, Poland threatened to revolt, and as a result, gained a small amount of independence in domestic policy-making. Hungary, too, revolted against Soviet domination in 1956. At first Soviet troops withdrew, but they later returned and violently suppressed the revolt.

Dissatisfaction with communism, and especially with Soviet domination, continued in much of Eastern Europe throughout the 1960s. In 1968, Czechoslovakia, under Alexander Dubcek (DOOB·chek), began a program of reforms. Dubcek promised civil liberties, democratic political reforms, and a more independent political system. This short-lived period of freedom became known as the Prague Spring. Within six months, Warsaw Pact troops, chiefly from the Soviet Union, invaded Czechoslovakia. They seized the reform leaders and replaced them with pro-Soviet people.

Section 3 Review

1. **Define** market economy, command economy, welfare state

2. **Identify** Konrad Adenauer, Charles de Gaulle, Nikita Khrushchev, Alexander Dubcek

3. **Explaining Ideas (a)** Why did the West German economy experience tremendous growth after the war? **(b)** How did this differ from what happened in Great Britain?

4. **Summarizing Ideas (a)** What changes did the Labour Party bring about in Great Britain? **(b)** What problems did Great Britain begin to experience in the 1960s?

5. **Analyzing Ideas** What efforts did Western European countries make to integrate their economies after 1945?

6. **Interpreting Ideas** What factors made economic recovery in Eastern Europe different from that in Western Europe?

Section 4

The United States and Canada

Focus Questions

- What kinds of domestic problems did American presidents confront after World War II?
- What were the most pressing foreign-policy issues in the United States after World War II?
- How did Canada develop after World War II?

Despite flourishing economies and powerful roles in world affairs, the United States and Canada faced a number of problems in the postwar years. These difficulties included internal conflicts, political problems, and a gradual realization that economic growth has its limits. Both nations, however, remained committed to maintaining positions of great influence.

Challenges Facing the United States

Between 1945 and 1968, three Democratic presidential administrations and one Republican administration represented the American people. Although these four presidents often had similar goals, they just as often differed on policies for carrying out their goals. Some of the problems that arose during this period proved extremely trying for the men who held the highest office in the land. Their decisions set precedents and shaped the way in which the American people viewed both the world and themselves during a critical period in their country's history.

Domestic policy. At home the United States presidents consistently aimed to resolve social and political problems and maintain a flourishing economy. Following the example of the New Deal, later presidents created new programs to address social problems. Many social programs were launched during the Kennedy and Johnson administrations. President John F. Kennedy introduced a broad program of domestic reforms, highlighted by legislation to reduce social inequalities. He was assassinated in November 1963, however, before Congress had passed much of his proposed legislation.

Vice President Lyndon B. Johnson succeeded Kennedy and attempted to implement an even more sweeping vision of reform. He was determined to create what he called the **Great Society**. His program included major social reform legislation, along with important new civil rights programs.

The economy. Efforts at social reform were underpinned by a booming American economy. After World War II the American economy reached new peaks of productivity, with huge new industries and rapid growth of new construction. Several minor **recessions**—periods of temporary business slowdown and increased unemployment—occurred in the 1940s and 1950s, but the 1960s were a period of continuous growth. Only toward the end of the decade did rising inflation seem to foreshadow problems to come.

McCarthyism. Although economic prosperity led to a rising standard of living, the Cold War contributed to feelings of continuing insecurity for many Americans. In the immediate postwar period, for example, many people did not understand why the

United States had allowed the Soviet Union to spread its sphere of influence throughout Eastern Europe and into other parts of the world. A number of people tried to explain these events by using a conspiracy theory. They believed that Soviet gains had occurred because certain people in the United States government were sympathetic to communism.

Senator Joseph McCarthy of Wisconsin became the most dramatic spokesman for the conspiracy theory. Between 1950 and 1954, he questioned the loyalty of many government officials and built up a large following. In the process he damaged the reputations of many Americans. In 1954 a Senate committee investigated McCarthy's conduct and found his charges groundless, and his influence collapsed. Nevertheless, ongoing crises between East and West, and especially the ever-present threat of nuclear war, left many people feeling uneasy.

The civil rights movement. As the United States grew more affluent, many minorities who had earlier missed out on such opportunities now began to demand equal **civil rights** with the majority of the nation. African Americans, for example, had been freed from slavery during the Civil War and had officially been granted their rights as citizens but, in fact, still lived under many social, political, and economic restrictions. In many regions, in both the North and the South, black people were prevented from voting and from obtaining decent educations, jobs, and housing. Dissatisfaction grew, especially after World War II. Organizations such as the Urban League and the National Association for the Advancement of Colored People **(NAACP)** worked to find employment and to secure civil rights for black Americans.

A turning point in the civil rights movement came in 1954. In the landmark case of *Brown v. Board of Education of Topeka*, the United States Supreme Court unanimously declared that state laws requiring black children to attend separate schools were unconstitutional. States that had such laws were ordered to integrate their schools. This important decision encouraged the growing civil rights movement of the late 1950s and 1960s. In the 1960s, Congress passed several civil rights and voting rights acts that promised political equality for African Americans and other minorities.

The most prominent civil rights leader was Dr. Martin Luther King, Jr., a Baptist minister. He advocated the use of nonviolent methods, such as boycotts, marches, and sit-ins to bring about change. African Americans held peaceful demonstrations and

In an unusual occurrence, four U.S. presidents appear together in this 1961 photograph taken at the funeral of Sam Rayburn. From left to right, they are: John F. Kennedy, Lyndon B. Johnson (who was vice-president at the time this photo was taken but later served as president), Dwight D. Eisenhower, and Harry S Truman.

mass protests against discrimination. For his efforts in furthering the cause of civil rights through nonviolent means, Dr. King was awarded the Nobel Peace Prize in 1964. However, in spite of Dr. King's efforts, many of these protests attracted violent reactions. Dr. King himself died violently at the hands of an assassin. His murder in 1968 dealt a severe blow to the civil rights movement and sparked a wave of riots in cities across the country.

Foreign Policy and the Cold War

For the most part, United States foreign policy during the postwar period revolved around the containment of communism. Following the example of the Truman Doctrine, the Marshall Plan, and NATO, American leaders in the 1950s and 1960s remained determined to prevent Soviet expansion. In Asia, the United States sent troops to South Korea in a "police action" to stop Communists from North Korea from taking over the country. Truman's successor, Dwight D. Eisenhower, brought the Korean War to an end and

created the Southeast Asia Treaty Organization (SEATO) in an attempt to halt further communist advances in that region. He also announced the Eisenhower Doctrine, which provided economic and military assistance to anticommunist countries in the Middle East.

Although there were some efforts to ease Cold War tensions, none lasted. In 1960, for example, a proposed summit between Eisenhower and Khrushchev was scuttled when the Soviets shot down an American U-2 spy plane over the Soviet Union. The following year, the construction of the Berlin Wall made it clear that the Cold War continued in full force.

The Cuban missile crisis. In 1959 the government of Cuba, a corrupt dictatorship, fell to Marxist rebel forces led by Fidel Castro. As Castro began to implement a full communist revolution in Cuba, the Eisenhower administration feared that the island would become a base of Soviet operations. In April 1961, the newly-elected President Kennedy authorized an invasion of Cuba by anti-Castro

Cubans, trained and equipped by the Central Intelligence Agency. The landings, known as the Bay of Pigs invasion, failed to spark the expected anticommunist uprising. American air support was cancelled, and the invaders were killed or captured. Castro now turned to the Soviet Union for support against the United States.

The Bay of Pigs operation convinced Khrushchev that Kennedy was indecisive, and he decided he could strengthen Soviet military power by building nuclear missile sites in Cuba. In October 1962 an American spyplane discovered these missile sites. Alarmed, Kennedy demanded that the Soviet Union withdraw the missiles and blockaded Cuba to prevent any further weapons from entering the island. NATO and Warsaw Pact military forces were placed on full alert. For 13 days the world stood on the brink of nuclear war. Finally, the Soviet Union backed down and agreed to remove the missiles—in exchange for a commitment from the United States not to invade Cuba. Kennedy also indicated privately that he would remove U.S. missiles that had been stationed in Turkey.

The Vietnam War. If the Cuban missile crisis was the most dangerous moment in the Cold War, from an American perspective the Vietnam War was even more damaging internally. American military advisers had been sent to South Vietnam in the 1950s as the French were being forced to withdraw from the country by Vietnamese nationalists. American involvement increased under President Kennedy, and under President Johnson the United States began to commit large numbers of American troops to helping noncommunist South Vietnam defend itself against the communist government of North Vietnam, which was supported by the Soviet Union.

As the war dragged on during the 1960s, however, it soon caused major unrest within the United States. Many antiwar protesters, particularly college students and civil rights supporters, expressed their discontent by staging demonstrations on university campuses. The protesters argued that United States involvement in Vietnam caused needless loss of life. The antiwar protests reached their height in 1968. President Johnson announced that he would not seek re-election, and a violent confrontation broke out between antiwar protesters and the police in the streets of Chicago during the Democratic Party Convention. A shocked nation watched the violence on television. Such scenes did much to undermine the nation's self-confidence.

Canadian Challenges

Active participation in two world wars ended the isolation policy that Canada had maintained for many years. After World War II, Canada became a vigorous supporter of the United Nations and an important member of NATO; loaned billions of dollars to other countries; and welcomed thousands of refugees from Europe.

Economic growth. Canada experienced considerable economic development after World War II. Much of the country remained basically agricultural, producing wheat, corn, and feed grains. Canada's industries also grew after World War II. The large Canadian forest areas provided many wood products. The wood pulp and paper industries expanded. Development of electric power and improvement of transportation stimulated the mining of iron, coal, and uranium, and greater production of oil and gas. Aircraft, electrical, and automobile industries developed in the provinces of Quebec and Ontario. The United States furnished much of the capital for this industrial development.

Relations with the United States. For more than a century, Canada has had a close relationship with the United States. During and after World War II this relationship strengthened, especially with regard to military and economic affairs.

Canadian national defense relied heavily on the United States. Together the two nations built a line of radar installations, called the Distant Early Warning **(DEW) Line**, which extended along the Arctic Circle, to furnish early warnings of air attacks. Together they also established the North American Air Defense Command.

In 1959 the close economic cooperation between Canada and the United States produced the **St. Lawrence Seaway**, a 2,300-mile waterway linking the Great Lakes with the Atlantic Ocean. The seaway enables oceangoing ships to reach every port on the Great Lakes. Another important cooperative venture was the development of the Columbia River basin. This project doubled the water-storage capacity of the Pacific Northwest.

The rise of separatism in Quebec. While Canada prospered in most respects after the war, by the 1960s a new challenge had appeared internally. This new challenge was the growing desire of many French-speaking Canadians, particularly those living in the province of Quebec, to separate from the rest of Canada. Feelings of French nationalism, however, had begun to develop in Canada even before World War II.

Through various lakes, canals, and locks, the St. Lawrence Seaway links the Great Lakes to the Atlantic Ocean.

In the 1960s the desire for separation grew even more intense. In 1967 this movement was fueled by French president Charles de Gaulle. During a visit to Quebec he ended a speech with the slogan of the French nationalists in the province, "Vive le Québec Libre!" which means "Long Live Free Quebec!". By 1970, a new political party, the Parti Quebecois, was able to gain 24 percent of the popular vote in the province of Quebec. Their platform was a call for secession from the Canadian Confederation. Although this was not enough to give them much power, it did serve as an indication that there would be future challenges to Canadian unity by many of its French-speaking citizens.

Section 4 Review

1. **Define** Great Society, recessions, civil rights, NAACP, DEW Line, St. Lawrence Seaway
2. **Identify** Joseph McCarthy, Martin Luther King Jr., Fidel Castro
3. **Understanding Ideas** Describe the domestic policy concerns of the United States from 1945 to 1968.
4. **Explaining Ideas** What foreign-policy issues confronted the United States after World War II?
5. **Interpreting Ideas** What kinds of changes took place in Canada in the postwar years?

Chapter 15 Review

A.D. 1947 Truman Doctrine is announced.

A.D. 1949 NATO is created.

A.D. 1955 Warsaw Pact is established.

A.D. 1946

A.D. 1948

A.D. 1954

A.D. 1945 United Nations is established.

A.D. 1945–1946 Nuremberg trials are held.

A.D. 1948
• Marshall Plan passes in Congress.
• Berlin blockade begins.
• Berlin airlift begins.

A.D. 1954 *Brown* v. *Board of Education of Topeka* is decided.

Chapter Summary

The following list contains the key concepts you have learned about Europe, the United States, and Canada from 1945 to 1968.

1. After World War II, disagreements between the Soviet Union and the United States resulted in the Cold War. Germany was divided into four zones and occupied by France, Great Britain, the United States, and the Soviet Union. Many Nazi leaders were brought to trial.

2. Following World War II, the United Nations (UN) was established to help maintain world peace. The UN also assumed an important humanitarian role in the promotion of human rights and world health.

3. The creation of satellite nations and establishment of Cominform convinced the West that the Soviet Union planned to spread communism throughout the world. The Truman Doctrine and the Marshall Plan were attempts by the United States to contain communism.

4. The Soviet threat in Europe resulted in the formation of the North American Treaty Organization, which most Western European nations joined. The Soviet Union responded with the Warsaw Pact.

5. West Germany recovered quickly after the war. Great Britain faced difficult economic conditions while maintaining political stability. France experienced economic prosperity despite the political uncertainties of the postwar period.

6. A major source of the growing wealth of Western Europe was the European Economic Community, which was founded in 1957. The organization attempted to eliminate trade barriers that existed between nations.

7. The Communist bloc nations experienced discontent throughout the 1950s and 1960s. In 1956 the Hungarians unsuccessfully revolted, and Czechoslovakia attempted reforms in 1968.

8. When the Soviets placed nuclear missiles in Cuba, the United States blockaded the island. The crisis was the most dangerous moment in the Cold War.

9. The civil rights movement and opposition to the war in Vietnam confronted the United States during the Johnson administration.

10. Canada enjoyed an economic boom after 1945, but it also experienced a separatist movement. Relations with the United States remained close.

Reviewing Important Terms

On a separate sheet of paper, supply the term that correctly completes each statement.

1. The _____ _____ was waged by political and economic means rather than with weapons.

2. The United States policy that attempted to restrict the spread of communism during the postwar era was called _____.

3. A state in which the government undertakes primary responsibility for the social welfare of its citizens is called a(n) _____ _____.

4. A period of slowdown in economic activity is called a(n) _____.

5. _____ was a post-World War II policy of removing Nazis from power in Germany.

Developing Critical Thinking Skills

1. **Explaining Ideas (a)** Why did the Cold War develop?

(b) How did it affect the postwar foreign policies of the major world powers?

2. **Summarizing Ideas** What postwar developments increased tensions between the Soviet Union and Western nations?

3. **Comparing Ideas** Compare the UN General Assembly with the UN Security Council.

4. **Interpreting Ideas** How were the Marshall Plan and the Truman Doctrine designed in an effort to carry out the containment policy?

5. **Organizing Ideas** What were the purposes of the alliance systems set up by the Western nations and by the Communist bloc after 1945?

6. **Understanding Ideas** Why did the countries of Western Europe establish the Common Market?

7. **Synthesizing Ideas** How did the work of civil rights leaders such as Dr. Martin Luther King Jr. lead to changes in United States policy toward equal rights for all citizens?

A.D. 1957
Common Market
is established.

A.D. 1958

A.D. 1962

A.D. 1966

A.D. 1956
Hungary revolts.

A.D. 1961
Berlin Wall is built.

A.D. 1964
Martin Luther King Jr.
is awarded the Nobel
Peace Prize.

A.D. 1968
Antiwar protesters
clash with police
in Chicago.

Relating Geography to History

Turn to the map on page 481. **(a)** Which European nations belonged to NATO? **(b)** Which nations belonged to the Warsaw Pact? **(c)** Which nations remained neutral? **(d)** How was this system of alliances different from the one in operation during the war? **(e)** What accounts for this change?

Relating Past to Present

1. The policies of containment and economic aid were used after World War II to stem the spread of communism. **(a)** What policies has the United States used in recent years to contain communism? **(b)** Did these policies prove successful? **(c)** Are containment policies necessary today? Explain your answer.
2. In the 1950s several Eastern bloc nations tried to free themselves from Soviet control, with little success. In 1989, however, these same nations broke away from the Soviet Union with relative ease. What changes in the communist world made this possible?
3. Cooperation between the United States and Canada has continued since 1945. Using information in the textbook and recent articles in the news, identify some of the ways in which Canada and the United States work together today. What actions might be taken to strengthen our ties with Canada?

Applying History Study Skills

Before completing this activity, review Building History Study Skills on page 478.

On March 12, 1947, President Truman addressed the Congress of the United States with a justification for containment as a basis for American foreign policy. Read the following excerpt from his speech, and then answer the questions to help you identify his argument.

"At the present moment in world history nearly every nation must choose between alternative ways of life. The choice is too often not a free one.

One way of life is based upon the will of the majority, and is distinguished by free institutions, representative government, free elections . . . and freedom from political oppression.

The second way of life is based upon the will of a minority forcibly imposed upon the majority. It relies upon terror and oppression, a controlled press . . . and the suppression of personal freedoms.

I believe that it must be the policy of the United States to support free peoples who are resisting attempted subjugation. . . . I believe that our help should be primarily through economic and financial aid which is essential to economic stability and orderly political processes."

1. How is containment illustrated in this excerpt from President Truman's speech?
2. What reasons does President Truman use to support his main point?
3. How does the president feel about the Soviet Union? Does he give examples to support his position?
4. How would you define the Truman Doctrine?

internetconnect

Search the Internet through the HRW Web site for more information about the McCarthy era and its effects on the United States. If possible, locate some first-person accounts of people whose reputations were damaged during this time. Discuss your findings in class.

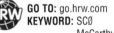

GO TO: go.hrw.com
KEYWORD: SCØ
McCarthyism

Building Your Portfolio

1. **Presenting an Oral Report** After Franklin Roosevelt's death, his widow, Eleanor Roosevelt, became the United States ambassador to the United Nations in New York City. Using the *Dictionary of American Biography* or the most recent edition of *Notable American Women*, research Eleanor Roosevelt's public life, beginning with her years as first lady and ending with her career as a diplomat of the United States. Present your findings to the class.
2. **Writing a Report** The position of secretary-general of the United Nations is a demanding and sometimes controversial job. Prepare a written report to find out more about each of the following secretaries-general: Trygve Lie, Dag Hammarskjöld, U Thant, Javier Pérez de Cuéllar, and Boutros Boutros-Ghali.

Asia Since 1945

TIME

A.D. **1945–the present**

A.D. **1945–the present**

3.7 million B.C.   4000 B.C.   A.D. 2100

PLACE

Asia

Asia

ARCTIC OCEAN

NORTH
AMERICA

EUROPE

ASIA

PACIFIC
OCEAN

AFRICA

Equator

AUSTRALIA

SOUTH
AMERICA

ATLANTIC
OCEAN

INDIAN
OCEAN

PACIFIC
OCEAN

ANTARCTICA

Ho Chi Minh City

Significance

The years after World War II saw major political, economic, and social changes in Asia. The movements for self-rule in Asia that had begun decades earlier came to fulfillment in the postwar period. However, this transition from domination to independence was not always achieved peacefully. A number of newly independent Asian nations became the focus of armed conflicts arising out of the Cold War.

As the 1900s drew to a close, other Asian nations attempted to imitate Japan's "economic miracle." In time, nearly all of these nations began to take an independent, active role in world economic and political affairs.

Terms to Define

nonalignment	Geneva Accords
mixed economy	domino theory
Awami League	Tet Offensive
Great Leap Forward	Paris Peace Accords
Cultural Revolution	ASEAN
"MacArthur Constitution"	"Four Tigers"
Diet	

People to Identify

Jawaharlal Nehru	Toshiki Kaifu
Lord Louis Mountbatten	Ferdinand Marcos
Indira Gandhi	Sukarno
Benazir Bhutto	Viet Minh
Nawaz Sharif	Ho Chi Minh
Mao Zedong	Viet Cong
Deng Xiaoping	Norodom Sihanouk
Syngman Rhee	Khmer Rouge
Park Chung Hee	Pol Pot

Places to Locate

Pakistan	38th parallel
Kashmir	Seoul
Tibet	Phnom Penh
Bangladesh	Hanoi
Taiwan	

Chapter Theme Questions

- **War and Diplomacy** How might conflicting religions and cultures affect the growth of nations?
- **Politics and Law** What problems might nations possibly face as they make the transition from colonial possession to independent statehood?
- **Economic Organization** What factors might aid, and what factors might hinder, the economic development of a country?

The hopes and aspirations of all peoples who seek freedom from colonial rulers were eloquently summed up by Jawaharlal Nehru in a speech announcing Indian independence that he rose to give as midnight approached on August 14, 1947:

" *Long years ago we made a tryst [appointment] with destiny, and now the time comes when we shall redeem our pledge, not wholly or in full measure, but very substantially. At the stroke of the midnight hour, when the world sleeps, India will awake to life and freedom. A moment comes, which comes but rarely in history, when we step out from the old to the new, when an age ends, and when the soul of the nation, long suppressed, finds utterance. . . .*

At the dawn of history India started on her unending quest, and trackless centuries are filled with her striving and the grandeur of her success and her failures. Through good and ill fortune alike she has never lost sight of that quest or forgotten the ideals which gave her strength. We end today a period of ill fortune and India discovers herself again. The achievement we celebrate today is but a step, an opening of opportunity, to the greater triumphs and achievements that await us. **"**

Within 20 years of this speech made by Nehru, almost every Asian nation had, like India, redeemed the pledge of self-determination.

Section 1

South Asia After Empire

Focus Questions

- **How did differences between Hindus and Muslims lead to a divided India?**
- **What problems did India face after achieving its independence?**
- **How did Pakistan and Bangladesh develop after the partition of the Indian subcontinent?**

In the years following World War II, the peoples of South Asia moved from colonial rule to independence.

The transition was not an easy one, however. As India and Pakistan emerged from the British Empire to become independent nations, violent clashes between Muslims and Hindus caused turmoil and bloodshed in the region.

The End of British Rule

A movement for independence from Great Britain had developed in India after World War I. Indian nationalists continued to make strong demands for independence throughout World War II. Because of the British government's reluctance to give in to these demands, Indians gave Britain only limited support in the war effort. Furthermore, the Indian National Congress resented the fact that Great Britain had declared India at war with Germany without even consulting with the Congress. Indeed, the government's unilateral action caused the Congress's angry ministers to resign in October 1939 and call for immediate self-government. Subsequent resistance to Great Britain's war effort by leaders of the Congress and others opposed to British rule led to arrest and imprisonment for many Indians.

Wartime developments. With Japan entering the war on the side of Germany, India took on greater importance as an Allied base. Pressure on Britain to reach a settlement with India increased. In March 1942, Britain sent Sir Stafford Cripps on a mission to negotiate terms for India's independence once the war ended. However, the Indian National Congress rejected the government's proposal, as did the Muslim League. Nationalist leader Mohandas Gandhi angrily asked Cripps why he had even come if the British had nothing more to offer.

Soon after the Cripps mission failed, Gandhi launched the "Quit India" movement. Gandhi insisted that Britain's complete separation from India was the only answer to their differences, and he demanded that the British leave India. With Japan posing a growing threat in Southeast Asia, the British government was in no mood for further internal resistance. Britain treated the Quit India campaign as a rebellion and arrested some 60,000 Congress supporters by the end of the year.

While the Indian National Congress continued to resist the British, the Muslim League was more willing to support the war effort. Led by Muhammad 'Ali Jinnah, the Muslim League demanded that a separate Muslim state be formed. The creation of an independent country would ensure that the interests of the Muslim minority would not be lost in a nation with a Hindu majority. As the Indian National Congress pressed its demand that Britain "Quit India", the Muslim League called on Britain to "Divide and Quit."

Despite repeated attempts, talks between Gandhi and Jinnah failed to resolve long-standing differences between Hindus and Muslims. Even after World War II ended, when Great Britain was ready to grant India independence, representatives of the Indian National Congress and the Muslim League could not reach an agreement.

In 1946, Britain's desire to transfer its power to a single Indian administration led to the proposal of a new plan. Under this plan, India would be divided into a federation of provinces. The federation would have a central government, but Muslims would retain control of those provinces in which they formed a majority. This plan also failed, however, when the Indian National Congress and the Muslim League once again could not agree on terms.

After this collapse in negotiations, violence erupted between Muslims and Hindus. Bloody riots first broke out in Calcutta and then spread throughout India. Thousands were killed and injured.

The partition of India. In March 1947, Lord Louis Mountbatten took over as British viceroy. India had by now become such a burden to Britain that the British government had decided to transfer its power to Indian authority no later than June 1948. However, India's raging civil war convinced Mountbatten that even a year was too long to wait to resolve the bloody and dangerous situation. Despite Gandhi's urging to keep India unified, Mountbatten decided to divide India and to do it quickly. The subsequent partitioning of the Indian subcontinent took place along religious lines. (See map on opposite page.)

The process of partition caused tremendous upheaval and resulted in an explosion of violence and bloodshed. As the day of independence approached, millions of Hindus, Muslims, and Sikhs rushed to cross the borders into the newly created nations. Violent clashes left as many as 1 million people dead.

The stroke of midnight on August 15, 1947, marked the official birth of the two nations of India and Pakistan. Their first task involved the integration of the princely states. Over the next two years, these states decided which nation to join. Only Kashmir, which had a Hindu ruler and a predominantly Muslim population, at first joined neither.

Less than six months after the partitioning of India, Mohandas Gandhi, one of the key figures in India's years of struggle for independence, was assassinated.

Religious Divisions and the Partition of India, 1947

India and West Pakistan fought for control of this area.

In 1971 East Pakistan became the independent nation of Bangladesh.

Major religious areas:

- Over 90% Muslim
- 70%–90% Muslim
- Over 90% Hindu
- 60%–90% Hindu
- 30%–40% Sikhs
- 80%–100% Buddhist
- Over 30% Christian
- National boundary
- Disputed border
- Cease-fire line
- National capital

SOVIET UNION · AFGHANISTAN · IRAN · Rawalpindi · Lahore · Amritsar · JAMMU AND KASHMIR · WEST PAKISTAN · EAST PUNJAB · CHINA · TIBET · Indus River · Delhi · New Delhi · NEPAL · Katmandu · SIKKIM · BHUTAN · Thimbu · Jaipur · Agra · Brahmaputra River · Hyderabad · Karachi · Allahabad · Ganges River · Varanasi · INDIA · Dhaka · Calcutta · EAST PAKISTAN · BURMA (Br.) · Narmada River · 20°N · Bombay · Poona · Hyderabad · Bay of Bengal · ARABIAN SEA · Bangalore · Mysore · Madras · 10°N · CEYLON (SRI LANKA) (Br.) · Colombo

0   250   500 Miles
0   250   500 Kilometers
Mercator Projection

60°E   70°E   80°E   90°E

Learning from Maps The partitioning of India created conflicts among the country's main religious groups.

❓ **Region** Which two religious groups were fighting for the control of Kashmir?

The assassin was a Hindu fanatic who resented Gandhi for his tolerant attitude toward Muslims.

Independent India

In 1950 India's new constitution went into effect. It established the Indian government as a federal republic with an elected president and parliament. Although the president is the official head of state, the prime minister and cabinet wield the power.

Government leaders and policies. Jawaharlal Nehru served as India's first prime minister until his death in 1964. Unlike Gandhi, who wanted independent India to return to its traditional way of life, Nehru emphasized modernization.

As prime minister, Nehru had several goals. For one thing, he wanted to unify India by overcoming the dividing forces of religion, language, caste, and regional interests. Having seen religious passions stirred by partition, he wanted India's government to be free of religious interference. He also hoped to strengthen democracy in India. Regarding the economy, Nehru was influenced by Marxism and the socialist model. The government developed a series of Five-Year Plans in an effort to build economic strength. Finally, in foreign affairs he chose to follow a policy of **nonalignment**, refusing to ally India with either the United States or the Soviet Union. Nehru's views on this last matter influenced the leaders of other developing nations, many of whom also adopted a policy of nonalignment.

Two years after Nehru's death, his daughter, Indira Gandhi, became the prime minister of India and attempted to carry out his policies. A controversial figure, Indira Gandhi dominated Indian politics for nearly two decades.

In 1971, after Indira Gandhi's reelection as prime minister, her opponents charged that she had rigged the voting. In 1975, when the courts found her guilty of election fraud, opposition leaders called for her immediate resignation. Gandhi then declared a constitutional state of emergency, which gave her the power to arrest anyone who she thought might threaten internal security. During the state of emergency, which lasted two years, Gandhi enacted a number of unpopular laws. Many Indians turned against her, and in 1977 they voted her out of office. However, she was elected prime minister again in 1980.

This photo shows Indira Gandhi, the only child of Jawaharlal Nehru, campaigning to become prime minister of India. She held office from 1966 to 1977 and from 1980 until 1984.

The most pressing problem that Gandhi faced on her return involved a religious minority, the Sikhs. A group of Sikh separatists, in a campaign to win independence for the province of Punjab, had attacked a number of government officials. In 1984 Gandhi ordered the Indian army to storm the separatists' base, the Golden Temple—the Sikhs' holiest place of worship—in Amritsar. Between 500 and 1,000 people died in the attack. The Sikhs, incensed by this act of sacrilege, vowed revenge. A few months later, two of Gandhi's Sikh bodyguards assassinated her. Her son, Rajiv Gandhi, succeeded her.

In 1989 Gandhi's Indian Congress Party lost the national elections, and V. P. Singh of the National Front Coalition became the new prime minister. Singh championed minority rights, especially rights of the lower castes, but widespread caste and religious violence led to his resignation in 1990. Most observers expected voters to return Rajiv Gandhi to power. However, Gandhi was assassinated, and P. V. Narasimha Rao, who succeeded Gandhi as head of the Congress Party, became prime minister.

In the 1996 elections, the Congress Party was heavily defeated, and Rao resigned. More turmoil followed these elections. H. D. Deve Gowda became prime minister of a coalition government, but the Congress Party withdrew its support of this coalition government in March 1997. I. K. Gujral became prime minister in April. Among the key goals that Gujral set for his coalition government was an improved relationship with Pakistan. Still, with nearly two dozen parties competing for power in parliament, India's political future remained uncertain.

Social and economic problems. Indians speak with great pride of the social and cultural diversity of their country. This very diversity, however, has hindered attempts at unification and thus created problems. India's great variety of languages provides but one example of this. The country has 16 major languages and more than 1,000 minor languages and dialects. In newly independent India, government officials from different regions often found that they could not understand one another. (Although Hindi is the official language of India, English often serves as an auxiliary official language.)

By the end of the 1980s, India's economy had made considerable progress. Under Nehru the country had developed a **mixed economy**, in which private companies owned some industries and the government owned the rest. Through a series of Five-Year Plans, the government charted the way in

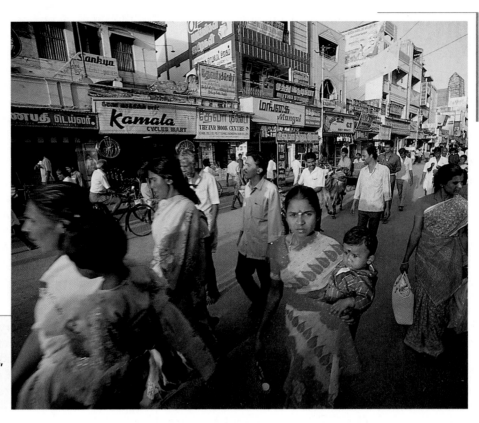

Overcrowding has been a major problem in Indian cities, such as Madurai, for many years.

which it wanted the economy to grow. These plans proved quite successful. The country's agricultural output increased, and its textile and steel industries experienced considerable growth. Exports of finished manufactured products, such as clothing and bicycles, showed a marked increase.

Despite such progress, problems remained, many of them stemming from India's ever-growing population. In 1950 the population stood at about 360 million. A little over 30 years later, the population had increased to about 684 million. By the mid-1980s, India had 16 percent of the world's population but only 2 percent of the world's land area. The nation's economic growth could not keep pace with the population increase. Consequently, by the late 1980s, annual per capita income averaged below $300, and the unemployment rate had reached 20 percent. Millions of Indians lived in poverty.

In the 1990s, the government made new efforts to deal with the country's economic problems. With the adoption of a more open policy toward foreign investment and trade, India's economic growth accelerated to an annual rate of almost 7 percent. Nevertheless, serious problems remain. The population continues to grow. Indeed, according to current projections, India—with over 950 million people in 1998—will become the most populous country in the world by 2050, surpassing China.

Foreign relations. In world affairs, India tried to cultivate friendships with both the Communist bloc and the West. As a result, it soon assumed a leadership role in the Non-Aligned Movement among African and Asian nations.

However, India's commitment to nonalignment was strained by tensions with China. In 1950 the Chinese occupied Tibet. Tibetans attempted a rebellion, which the Chinese violently put down. For a long time, India had supported the Dalai Lama, Tibet's religious and political leader. After the Chinese invasion, the Dalai Lama and some of his followers fled to India, where they formed a government in exile. India's relations with China became even more strained in the next few years.

During the 1970s India moved away from its nonaligned stance, establishing close ties with the Soviet Union. Then, in the 1980s, India sought to improve relations with the United States. Even so, the country avoided making a complete commitment to either side in the Cold War. In the 1990s, reforms in India's economic policies led the nation to take a more open approach to foreign affairs and to seek a greater role in the global economy.

The Continuing Problem of Kashmir. Partition in 1947 had left India and Pakistan with a difficult problem in the northern state of Kashmir. (See map on page 497.) Kashmir's ruling prince, a Hindu, at first tried to avoid joining either country. However, Pakistan claimed Kashmir because at least three quarters of its people were Muslim. Jawaharlal Nehru, himself a Kashmiri, supported the Hindu prince with Indian troops.

Clashes between Muslims and Hindus in Kashmir soon led to fighting between Indian and Pakistani soldiers. When the fighting began, the prince declared Kashmir part of India. Sporadic fighting between the two countries continued until 1949. At that time, the United Nations established a cease-fire line. At the point of the establishment of the cease-fire line, India occupied two thirds of Kashmir.

In 1957 India officially annexed part of Kashmir. Pakistan protested, and after sporadic fighting, a full-scale war erupted between the two countries in 1965. Eventually the prime ministers of India and Pakistan agreed to withdraw their troops behind the cease-fire line that had been established in 1949 by the United Nations and to negotiate a settlement. However, the issue of Kashmir nationality remained unsettled, and violence occasionally erupted in the region.

In the late 1980s, Muslim Kashmiris began to demand complete separation from India. Blaming Pakistan for orchestrating these demonstrations, the Indian authorities sent troops to the area. In response, Pakistan put its army on war alert. Border clashes and other violence between warring militant groups became increasingly common. Despite the fact that more than 20,000 people had been killed by 1997, fighting went on. Muslim militants persisted in their demands for independence; insurgents battled against counterinsurgents; and Indian and Pakistani forces continued to exchange gunfire. No immediate prospects for peace in Kashmir were in sight.

The Division of Pakistan

The fate of Kashmir was not the only problem in Indian-Pakistani relations. The issue of independence for Bangladesh also brought India and Pakistan into conflict.

When colonial rule ended, Pakistan was divided into two parts—West Pakistan and East Pakistan—separated by a huge wedge of Indian territory some 1,000 miles wide. The divided nation faced problems similar to those that plagued India—a rapidly growing population, widespread poverty and illiteracy, and cultural and linguistic differences. In addition, a lack of natural resources and its peculiar geographic situation hindered Pakistan's economic development.

At first a dominion of the British Commonwealth, Pakistan became a parliamentary republic in 1956. Soon, however, a succession of military leaders took control of the government.

Independence for Bangladesh. In the elections held in 1970, the **Awami League**—a political party dedicated to independence for East Pakistan—won the majority of the East Pakistani seats in the national assembly. The central government refused to accept the election results. Riots erupted in East Pakistan. The new president of Pakistan, General Agha Muhammad Yahya Khan, sent troops to quell the riots and to arrest the leaders of the Awami League. The situation soon developed into a civil war. Ten million East Pakistanis fled to India. During the civil war, India came to the aid of the East Pakistani rebels, first by sending arms to them and then by providing troops. Late in 1971 the Pakistani troops were defeated. East Pakistan then became the new nation of Bangladesh.

Bangladesh and Pakistan today. Both Bangladesh and Pakistan faced major problems after the division. Bangladesh, ravaged by war, also suffered recurrent famines, floods, and devastating tropical storms. The new government proved unequal to the huge task of rebuilding the country, and in the mid-1970s, it was toppled by a military coup.

In elections held in 1991, the conservative Bangladesh National Party (BNP) won a victory over the left-wing Awami League. BNP leader Khalida Zia became Bangladesh's first woman prime minister. In subsequent years, however, Zia faced mounting attack by Awami League-led opponents, who accused her of mismanagement. Zia was finally forced out in 1996, and new elections brought an Awami League government into power, under Prime Minister Sheikh Hasina Wazed. Although disturbances eased, frequent natural disasters, economic instability, and a legacy of political ill will between the Awami League and the BNP made the future of this desperately poor country very uncertain.

Pakistan, too, faced political instability. For the first half of the 1970s, a civilian government led by Zulfikar Ali Bhutto ruled Pakistan. However, General

When Benazir Bhutto was sworn in as the prime minister of Pakistan, she became the first woman to govern a Muslim country.

Mohammed Zia ul-Haq seized control of the government in 1977 and, two years later, had Bhutto executed. Zia imposed martial law, banned political parties, and reformed the legal system so that it followed Islamic teachings more closely.

Zia answered a growing clamor for a return to democratic rule by promising to hold free elections in 1988. Although Zia was killed in an airplane crash, the elections still took place, and Benazir Bhutto, the daughter of Ali Bhutto, emerged as the winner. She became the first woman to serve as head of state of a Muslim nation. However, charges of corruption and misconduct against members of her administration and growing discontent among the military led to Bhutto's ouster in 1990. She was reelected in 1993, but three years later she was soundly defeated by Nawaz Sharif, after more charges of corruption and incompetence. Like his counterpart in India, Prime Minister Sharif sought to improve relations with his neighbor. However, the history of distrust and violence between India and Pakistan continued to make peace an elusive goal. The development of nuclear weapons by both countries has made the stakes of their rivalry even higher.

Section 1 Review

1. **Define** nonalignment, mixed economy, Awami League
2. **Identify** Jawaharlal Nehru, Lord Louis Mountbatten, Indira Gandhi, Benazir Bhutto, Nawaz Sharif
3. **Locate and Explain the Significance** Pakistan, Kashmir, Tibet, Bangladesh
4. **Determining Cause and Effect** How did differences between Hindus and Muslims lead to a divided India?
5. **Classifying Ideas** List the main political, social, and economic problems faced by India in the last two decades.
6. **Synthesizing Ideas** How did Pakistan and Bangladesh develop after the partition of the Indian subcontinent?

The Rise of Communist China and Taiwan

Focus Questions

- **How did Mao Zedong's Communist Chinese government try to rebuild China in the years after World War II?**
- **What changes occurred in China after the death of Mao?**
- **What occurred at Tiananmen Square, and what were the consequences for China?**
- **Why was Korea divided, and how have the two Koreas developed since 1953?**

During World War II, the Nationalist and communist Chinese agreed to halt their civil war and form a united front against their common enemy, the Japanese. However, even though both did fight against Japan, conflict between Nationalist and communist forces soon resumed, each side hoping to gain an advantage over the other.

The Communists effectively used the war as an opportunity to expand both their political and military influence in China. By the time World War II ended, the Communists had significantly increased the size of their army as well as the territory under their control. In time, the Communists won the upper hand in the civil war, and by 1949 they had driven the Nationalists from power.

In 1949 Chiang Kaishek, the Nationalist leader, fled with his supporters to the island of Taiwan and established a government there. (See map on opposite page.) On the Chinese mainland the Communists, led by Mao Zedong, established the People's Republic of China. The United States government, which had aided the Nationalists, refused to recognize this new communist government on the mainland.

China Under Mao Zedong

The Communists wanted to create a modern, industrialized nation dominated by the Communist Party. To achieve this goal, the Communists took administrative control. By a combination of elections and appointments, they placed Communist Party members in all the key government and military offices. The

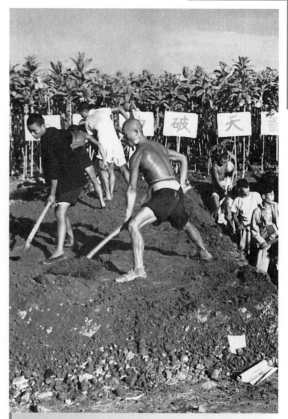

China embarked on its first Five-Year Plan for economic growth in 1953.

new constitution gave executive power to the party's Central Committee and its Political Bureau, headed by Mao Zedong. Zhou Enlai became premier and foreign minister and was a spokesman for China in world affairs.

An overwhelming task faced this new communist government. Years of war had devastated China. Farms lay destroyed, and industry and transportation had almost ceased to function. The Chinese people had fared little better than their country. Miserably poor, they had been decimated by epidemics and famines.

The Communists acted to restore order, bring inflation under control, and eliminate various forms of corruption. They also took violent action against their opponents. About 1 million people lost their lives in Communist Party purges.

In 1953 the Communists began the process of rebuilding China by issuing their first Five-Year Plan for economic growth. The Soviet Union provided part of the capital for this plan—which was modeled

Revolution in China, 1945–1949

Map labels:
SOVIET UNION
MONGOLIA
Ulaanbaatar
The People's Republic of China is proclaimed on October 1, 1949.
Harbin
MANCHURIA
XINJIANG
Shenyang
NORTH KOREA
40°N
Beijing
Tianjin
Lüshun (Port Arthur)
SOUTH KOREA
WEST PAKISTAN
Yenan
Zibo
Huang He (Yellow R.)
YELLOW SEA
JAPAN
CHINA
Xi'an
Nanjing 1946–Apr. 1949
TIBET
Chengdu Nov. 1949–Dec. 1949
Wuhan
Shanghai
30°N
Chang Jiang (Yangzi R.)
Chongqing 1938–1946 Oct. 1949–Nov. 1949
EAST CHINA SEA
NEPAL
SIKKIM
BHUTAN
INDIA
Kunming
Taipei
EAST PAKISTAN
Guangzhou Apr. 1949–Oct. 1949
TAIWAN
Xi Jiang
BURMA
MACAO (Port.)
HONG KONG (Br.)
In late 1949, Chiang Kaishek's Nationalist government flees to Taiwan, where it re-establishes the Republic of China.
20°N
HAINAN
SOUTH CHINA SEA
FRENCH INDOCHINA
PHILIPPINES
80°E 90°E 100°E 110°E 120°E 130°E

Areas occupied by Communists:
- By 1945
- 1945–June 1946
- July 1946–June 1948
- July 1948–June 1949
- July–Sept. 1949
- After October 1949

- National boundary
- ◉ Communist capital until 1949
- ✳ National capital since 1949
- ★ Nationalist capitals
- • Other city

0   250   500 Miles
0   250   500 Kilometers
Robinson Projection

Learning from Maps Communists gained control of China over a four-year period.

Place Which city was a communist capital until 1949?

on similar Soviet plans—but most of the financing was Chinese. Although the plan stressed the rapid buildup of heavy industry, it also focused on land reform. The Communists seized farmland from landlords and redistributed it to the peasants. Thousands—some estimates are in the millions—of landlords were killed in the course of this land redistribution program. The peasants organized their newly acquired land into collective farms, while the government operated state farms on much of the land that remained.

Despite periodic droughts and floods, some peasant resistance to collective farming, and inefficient planning by government officials, the first Five-Year Plan was a success. Both agricultural and industrial output increased.

Building History Study Skills

READ
WRITE
INTERPRET
CONNECT
THINK

Reading About History: Identifying Fallacies in Reasoning

In order to prove a point, an author uses logic, or reasoning. Logic is the process of reaching a conclusion based on the available evidence. One way of determining the strength of an argument is to identify fallacies in reasoning. A fallacy is an error in logic.

One type of fallacy in reasoning is to make overgeneralizations, vague or indefinite statements made without supporting evidence. Another example of a fallacy in reasoning would be the stacking of an argument—in other words, carefully choosing only those facts that support one's argument and ignoring others. For example, one might argue for the superiority of the Republican party by pointing out that Republican presidents have negotiated the ends to our wars. While a Republican indeed negotiated the end to both the Korean War and the Vietnam War, Democratic presidents also negotiated the ends to wars. Even if only Republican presidents had negotiated such treaties, this fact alone would not prove one party superior to the other.

How to Identify Fallacies in Reasoning

To identify a fallacy in reasoning, follow these steps.

1. Identify the author's conclusion.
2. Explain the author's reasoning that supports the conclusion.
3. Decide whether the author is making overgeneralizations or stacking the argument.
4. Evaluate the argument. Are the connections valid? Is only one cause identified? Are other causes or issues hidden or ignored? Has a connection between the cause and the effect been proven?

Developing the Skill

Read the following justification of the shooting of landlords from the political writings of Mao Zedong. Can you spot fallacies in Mao's reasoning?

Mao Zedong

"The execution of one such big local bully [landlord] or one member of the evil gentry has its repercussions . . . and is very effective in eradicating any remnant of feudalism. . . . [T]he only effective way of suppressing the reactionaries is to execute at least one or two guilty of the most serious crimes and wrongdoing. . . . When the local bullies and evil gentry were at the height of their power, they killed peasants without batting an eyelid. . . . In view of these atrocities . . . how can one say that the peasant should not now rise and shoot one or two of them . . . ?"

What Mao is seeking to establish is that the shooting of landlords is justified. His main argument is that it is justified because it has a strong effect; in fact, he moves from saying that it has a strong effect to saying that it is the *only* effective means of suppressing reactionaries. Even if it is true that killing has a strong effect, this does not prove that killing is necessary to effect a revolution. He stacks his argument by adding that in the past, landlords shot peasants. Even if landlords did shoot peasants in the past—and he gives no statistical information or proof to support this claim—this does not constitute a justification for such extreme action against a particular landlord now.

Practicing the Skill

Reread the steps in identifying fallacies in reasoning. Then read an editorial in a newspaper and identify any generalizations or fallacies in the editor's reasoning.

To apply this skill, see Applying History Study Skills on page 531.

The Great Leap Forward. Impatient to accelerate progress, Mao's government announced a second Five-Year Plan in 1958. Known as the **Great Leap Forward**, this plan was more ambitious than the first Five-Year Plan. It aimed to speed up economic development while simultaneously developing a completely socialist society.

Under the Great Leap Forward, the Chinese government hoped to increase industrial output to the point where it matched or exceeded that of many Western European countries. To reach this goal, China purchased modern machinery and tried to increase output by running this machinery almost continuously in factories. The government even encouraged the Chinese people to make their own iron and steel in small backyard blast furnaces.

The Great Leap Forward also established huge collective communities, called people's communes, that incorporated agricultural activities and small industries. Life on a commune bore a strong resemblance to life in the military, with dormitories and communal dining halls. Often, children were taken from parents to be raised in separate dormitories. People worked long hours in the fields or factories under strict supervision, and everyone received the same pay, regardless of how much he or she produced.

Many of the changes made under the Great Leap Forward reflected Mao's rejection of individualism. The Communist Party controlled almost every aspect of people's lives on the communes. Furthermore, the Communists stressed loyalty to the Communist Party and to the state, moving away from the Chinese people's traditionally strong ties of family loyalty.

The Great Leap Forward failed dismally. Industrial output decreased, and there were food shortages. In fact, it has been estimated that more than 20 million people starved between 1958 and 1960. The failure of the program also led to disagreements within the Communist Party. Faced with falling productivity and constant criticism from workers and peasants, the government abandoned the Great Leap Forward.

The Cultural Revolution. Since assuming power in 1949, Chinese Communist Party officials have had two basic goals: economic development and creation of a classless society. However, there has often been disagreement within the party on policies to achieve these goals.

In the early 1960s, after the failure of the Great Leap Forward, Mao's prestige within the Communist Party hierarchy was seriously damaged. Liu Shaoqi, Mao's eventual successor as chairman of the People's Republic, implemented his own economic development policies. (Mao had given up the day-to-day administrative tasks of running the country to Liu, but he remained in his position as Communist Party chairman.) For example, although peasants still had to work on the communal farmland, they also had small private plots of land, on which they could raise their own crops. They were also given monetary incentives to raise more crops. Mao was highly critical of these policies.

In 1966 Mao launched the Great Proletarian Cultural Revolution, best known as the **Cultural Revolution**, a violent attempt at social change. Mao aimed to rid China of the "Four Olds"—old customs, old habits, old thoughts, and old culture—replacing them with a new socialist culture. Mao chose China's young people to lead this revolution. These radical high school and college students soon became known as the Red Guards. They went on a rampage throughout China, vandalizing historic buildings, ruining ancient works of art, burning books, and destroying anything they considered part of what they called the "old way." However, they saved their greatest zeal for those people who did not comply fully with Mao's teachings. The Red Guards denounced these people, publicly humiliated them—and sometimes beat, tortured, or even killed them. Those who survived punishment by the Red Guards lost their jobs and their Communist Party membership. Liu himself suffered denunciation and died in jail.

The Cultural Revolution had a disastrous effect on the Chinese economy. Agricultural and industrial production fell dramatically, and the country's economic development plans suffered a severe setback. In 1968 and 1969, Mao and his successor, Lin Biao, tightened the grip of the military over the country, dispersing the Red Guards.

China After Mao

Mao Zedong died in 1976. Upon his death, a struggle began between moderate Communists and a radical group led by Mao's widow, Jiang Qing (jee·AHNG CHING). The moderates wanted to restore order and economic growth, while Jiang Qing's group—later known as the "Gang of Four"—wanted to continue the Cultural Revolution and rid China of all vestiges of the past.

In time, the moderates won control of the major party and government offices, and in an attempt to crush the threat posed by the radicals, they placed the Gang of Four on trial for treason. Found guilty, Jiang

Qing and her three compatriots received life sentences. The moderates then began to reinstate many of those who had been purged from government offices and from the Communist Party during the Cultural Revolution. Over time, the moderates offered some criticism of Mao's radical ideas, denouncing the idea that his policies should invariably be followed.

By the late 1970s, Deng Xiaoping (DUHNG SHOW·PING) had emerged as the leader of the moderates. Although Deng had helped to found the Chinese Communist Party, during the Cultural Revolution his career had been severely damaged. His economic development plan, known as the Four Modernizations, aimed to improve agriculture, industry, science and technology, and national defense. He also fostered greater social openness by encouraging cultural and scientific exchanges with Western countries.

Economic progress and problems. The Four Modernizations plan was intended to improve and update four important areas of the economy. The plan softened the model of state centralized planning, allowing a market economy to develop. In addition, the Four Modernizations encouraged the import of technology from the West.

Through a series of Five-Year Plans, the Chinese government encouraged farmers to increase agricultural production. For example, this merchant sells produce from his own government-allotted farm plot.

Over time, China reformed the areas of banking, finance, city planning, and agriculture. In addition, it encouraged a degree of free enterprise. This new direction in policy led to major economic gains in the mid-1980s and early 1990s. China's economy during this time grew faster than any other major nation's. These gains, however, masked serious economic problems. The rapid growth of the economy fueled inflation, which by 1989 was running at an annual rate of close to 20 percent.

Many Chinese believed that their economic woes were partly the result of government mismanagement and corruption. Their dissatisfaction with the government's handling of the economy helped to create a massive popular movement for political and economic reform in the spring of 1989—a movement that had violent and bloody consequences.

Massacre in Tiananmen Square. In the late 1980s, Deng Xiaoping gave up his government and Communist Party positions, leaving the country in the hands of a younger generation of leaders. The new openness Deng had fostered encouraged many Chinese, especially students, to voice their opinions publicly. Some charged that the government's economic reforms had not brought the promised prosperity, while others called for a "fifth modernization"—democracy. Such views had supporters in high places, including Hu Yaobang, the Communist Party general secretary. Hu was removed from this office in 1987 because of his liberal views.

Hu's views won him a vast following among the reform-minded students of Beijing, however, and when he died in the spring of 1989, thousands took to the streets to mourn his loss. Soon, students were demonstrating daily, calling for the democratic reforms Hu had advocated, such as freedom of the press and free and open elections.

In the spring of 1989, hundreds of thousands of pro-democracy demonstrators occupied Tiananmen Square, Beijing's central gathering place. They demanded an end to corruption in the ruling party, more participation in government, and better conditions at the universities.

Thousands of the students staged a hunger strike. Government orders for them to leave the square were ignored. On May 20 the government imposed martial law. Even so, the demonstrations continued, and large numbers of workers joined the students in Tiananmen Square.

Fearing for the survival of their regime, Chinese leaders ordered the army to use any means necessary

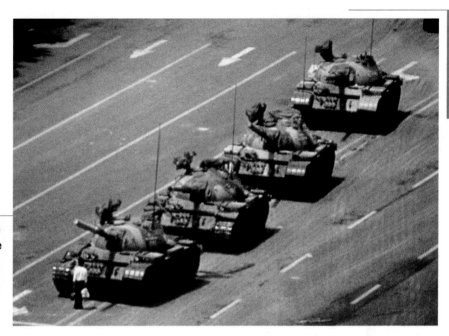

A lone man stands before a line of tanks as Chinese troops move to end student demonstrations in Tiananmen Square on June 3 and 4, 1989.

to end the demonstrations. On June 3 and 4, government troops began to move toward Tiananmen Square, shooting at anyone they saw on the streets. The following morning, soldiers—not students—occupied the square. China's democracy movement had been crushed under the tracks of the army's tanks.

After the crackdown. The exact toll of this brutal suppression remains uncertain, but it is estimated that after several days, up to 500 people were dead and another 3,000 wounded. In addition, thousands of suspected "counterrevolutionaries" were rounded up throughout China. Some were promptly executed, but many remained in jail awaiting trial. Most were eventually sentenced to long prison terms.

World reaction was immediate and stern. The United States, Japan, and the European Community (the European Union since 1993) imposed economic sanctions and demanded that the Chinese government end the crackdown. In response, Chinese officials protested what they called interference in China's internal affairs. Although they eventually lifted martial law, Communist Party leaders maintained a tight hold on Chinese society.

Economic consequences. Stunned by the communist regime's actions, most Western nations and international aid agencies suspended or restricted China's loans. Foreign private investors, too, drastically cut back on their financial activities in China. Tourism, which had become a major source of income for China, dwindled to almost nothing. With most of its sources of capital now cut off, the already fragile Chinese economy began to founder.

In response, the Chinese government took steps to transform China into a market economy while keeping a communist system. Over time, the government has alternately made greater moves toward market economy reforms and advocated a return to more traditional communist economic policies, including central control.

Despite the fact that many of China's economic and social problems remained unresolved, China's economy grew rapidly in the 1990s. Moreover, the government was able to cut the inflation rate from between 30 and 20 percent in the 1980s to just over 10 percent in 1995, and then to just 7 percent in 1996. Still, unemployment exceeded 30 percent in some cities, labor unrest was widespread, and some 65 million Chinese people lived in poverty.

Jiang Zemin, chosen by Deng Xiaoping as his successor in 1989, became China's president in 1993. In 1997, Jiang proposed a radical new plan to cope with China's persistent socioeconomic problems. Jiang's strategy called for the government to relinquish control of thousands of unprofitable state-owned enterprises. These firms have been experimenting with ways to increase profits, but they have so far been only partially successful in orienting themselves to a market economy.

Foreign Relations Since 1949

While Mao Zedong's government endeavored to reorganize the newly established People's Republic of China, the Chinese Communists were also engaged in worldwide efforts toward an international socialist revolution. In the early 1950s, the Soviet Union and the People's Republic of China were allies, united by political ideology and common economic interests. However, the two nations soon diverged.

Soviet leaders believed that world communism could be achieved through scientific and economic successes rather than through military conquests. Therefore, they felt that they could have "peaceful coexistence" with the West. Chinese leaders, on the other hand, claimed that communist nations had an obligation to support "national wars of liberation." They also argued that nations could never live in peaceful coexistence while capitalism existed. The Chinese insisted that by rejecting revolution as the means of social change, the Soviets had abandoned true Marxism. The Chinese also doubted that the Soviet model of economic development, which stressed heavy industry, would work in China, with its large farming population.

Changing relations. At first the Chinese and the Soviets confined their differences to bitter public speeches as they struggled for leadership in the Communist bloc and in the developing regions of the world. However, during the 1960s both countries began to station troops along their common border. As a result, a number of clashes occurred.

These border skirmishes helped bring about a change in Chinese foreign policy. In the past, Mao Zedong and his advisers had made foreign policy decisions based on which nation they believed posed the greatest threat to China's security. For 20 years no one doubted that that nation was the United States. As Chinese-Soviet relations worsened, however, China became more willing to come to terms with the United States.

The first major sign of change came in 1972, when President Richard Nixon visited China. Soon after, the two nations began to permit the exchange of sports teams, journalists, educators, artists, and business leaders. Finally, in 1979, the United States gave full diplomatic recognition to the People's Republic of China. At about the same time, the United States withdrew its recognition of the Nationalist Chinese government in Taiwan.

Throughout the 1980s China continued to improve its relations with the West. It signed financial aid, technical assistance, and trade agreements with the United States and other Western countries. Further, Chinese leaders negotiated for the return in 1997 of neighboring Hong Kong, which had been a British colony since the 1840s. Over time, Chinese-Soviet relations began to thaw, and Soviet leaders pulled their troops back from the border. Following the dissolution of the Soviet Union, China sought to develop relations with the former Soviet Central Asian republics.

After Tiananmen. Events in Tiananmen Square dramatically changed China's foreign relations. Most Western nations reconsidered their financial and political ties with China. They insisted that they would continue normal relations with China only if the government ended suppression of Chinese citizens' civil and human rights. To bolster their country's tarnished international image, China's leaders turned to the Third World. They forged links with developing countries in Asia and throughout the world. They even developed relations with countries, such as South Korea, that China did not officially recognize.

By 1992, China had largely mended its damaged relationships with most foreign nations except for the United States. By the mid-1990s, however, the two countries enjoyed improved relations. In 1997, President Jiang came to the United States for talks with President Clinton, although China's refusal to meet international standards in regard to human rights continued to cast a shadow over U.S.-Chinese relations.

Korea

Much of the tension between the People's Republic of China and the United States during the 1950s and 1960s grew out of events that took place in Korea after World War II. Agreements made at the end of the war divided Korea at the 38th parallel. The Soviet Union occupied Korea north of this line, while the United States moved troops into the southern part of Korea. The two occupying powers agreed that elections should be held to form a government that

---

What If?

China and the United States
What if China had not been in conflict with the Soviet Union? Would relations between the United States and China have been different?

The Transfer of Hong Kong

At exactly midnight on June 30, 1997, the Union Jack, Britain's national flag, was lowered for the last time over the territory of Hong Kong. In its place, the red-and-gold flag of China was raised. After 156 years of British control, Hong Kong returned to Chinese rule. For Chinese people around the world, it was a time of great national pride.

For many citizens of Hong Kong, however, the transfer was a time of anxiety. Some were worried that Communist China would try to limit Hong Kong's freedoms, such as freedom of the press or freedom of religion. Others were afraid that Hong Kong's economy, which had been one of the strongest in the region, would falter.

Despite the fears, daily life in Hong Kong remained relatively unchanged for the first several months after the handover. The new government did not interfere with religious freedom or freedom of the press. On the other hand, since the transfer, China has made changes in the Hong Kong legislature that many residents say reduce participation and allow Hong Kong lawmakers less power.

In addition, the widespread problems with Asian economies that occurred at the end of 1997 have affected Hong Kong along with other Asian countries. The effects of this and of decreased tourism—an important industry in Hong Kong—remain to be seen.

would rule the entire country. However, in 1947 the Soviet Union prevented the United Nations commission that was sent to supervise these elections from entering the north.

The Korean War. Elections held in the south resulted in the creation of the Republic of Korea, known as South Korea, with Syngman Rhee as its president and the city of Seoul (SOHL) as its capital. At the same time, the Democratic People's Republic, or North Korea, led by Kim Il Sung, was created in the north. The United Nations recognized South Korea as the legal government, and the Soviet Union recognized only North Korea.

In June 1950 the North Korean army invaded South Korea, quickly taking Seoul. The United Nations Security Council, meeting in emergency session, declared the invasion an unwarranted aggression. It called on UN members to furnish troops and supplies to resist the invasion. (See map on next page.)

Most of the UN troops, as well as their commander, General Douglas MacArthur, came from the United States. In September 1950, MacArthur launched an attack at Inchon, on the coast near Seoul. The North Koreans fell back behind their border, with the UN forces in hot pursuit. As the UN troops approached the Yalu River, the border between Korea and China, several hundred thousand Chinese soldiers joined those of North Korea. This combined force drove MacArthur and his army south of the 38th parallel.

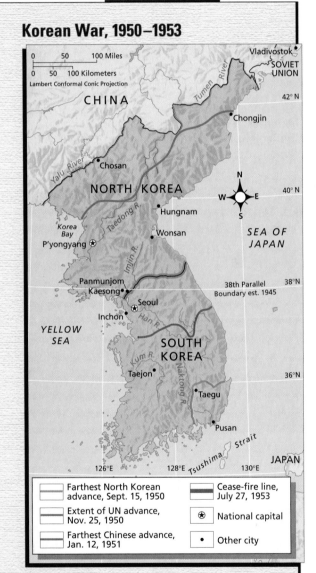

Korean War, 1950–1953

Learning from Maps The Korean War began in June 1950, when North Korea invaded South Korea.

Location Along which degree of latitude was a cease-fire line established?

A controversy then arose over MacArthur's desire to bomb China's bases in Manchuria and to blockade the Chinese coast. President Harry Truman and the UN General Assembly opposed these actions, fearing that they might lead to a third world war. When MacArthur continued to publicly urge bombing attacks on China, Truman removed him from his post.

Under MacArthur's successor, General Matthew B. Ridgway, the UN forces pushed the Chinese and North Koreans back across the 38th parallel. In July 1951, with the situation at a stalemate, talks to end the hostilities began. After two years of negotiations, the two sides signed an armistice in July 1953 at Panmunjom. It fixed the boundary line between the two Koreas near the 38th parallel. It also established a demilitarized zone of 1.25 miles on either side of the boundary. The armistice also called for a political conference to be held within three months. This conference never took place, however, and no peace treaty was ever signed.

Postwar South Korea. Despite South Korea's small size, various antagonisms divided the country. These conflicts—between provinces, between Buddhists and Christians, between rural and urban people—had existed for years. Despite their differences, however, South Koreans were united in their fear of North Korea. After 1953, President Syngman Rhee used this fear to justify moves that would increase his power and curb criticism of his policies. Therefore, although it had been established as a democracy in 1948, South Korea virtually became a dictatorship.

Violent protests followed Rhee's election to a fourth term as president in 1960, and he resigned. In 1961, army officers led by General Park Chung Hee staged a coup. For the next 18 years, Park ruled with an iron fist, imposing strict censorship on the press and using a powerful secret police force to suppress opposition.

However, President Park also used his power to promote economic development. South Korea's economy expanded very rapidly under his leadership. His government developed industry and increased foreign trade. Although Park's program gave South Korea one of the fastest-growing economies in the world, it was undemocratic and gave South Koreans little political freedom.

Park was assassinated in 1979 by a member of his own Korean Central Intelligence Agency. Almost immediately, a military strongman, Chun Doo Hwan, took control. Chun ruled as an authoritarian, but he continued to support the nation's economic growth. By 1987, however, demonstrations against Chun's govern-

General Douglas MacArthur was commander of the UN forces at the beginning of the Korean War; however, President Truman removed him from his post after MacArthur expressed a desire to bomb Chinese bases in Manchuria.

ment resulted in his resignation. Roh Tae Woo, Chun's handpicked successor, won the election that followed.

Roh promised democratic reforms, some of which he delivered. A new constitution was drafted, allowing the direct election of the president by popular vote. In foreign affairs, Roh promoted contacts with the Soviet Union (later Russia) and China. In 1991 he obtained South Korea's admission to the United Nations and worked to reduce tensions with North Korea. However, both Roh and former president Chun Doo Hwan were tried and convicted in 1996 for having plotted the 1979 government coup through which Chun had come to power. Chun was sentenced to death, and Roh was sentenced to more than 20 years in prison. In sparing him from a death sentence, the court took into account Roh's democratic reforms. These reforms made it possible for Kim Young Sam to succeed Roh as South Korea's next president.

The two Koreas. One of the most notable changes made by Roh's administration was an effort to develop relations with the communist world and to open a dialogue on reunification with North Korea. The idea of reconciliation between North and South Korea gained momentum after the changes in Eastern Europe and the reunification of East and West Germany. (See Chapter 19.) In 1991 the two Koreas signed a pact of reconciliation and nonaggression. However, concern about North Korea's capacity to produce nuclear weapons remained a troubling point.

North Korea's internal problems contributed to continuing unstable relations between North and South Korea. North Korea's centralized, state-owned economy was unable to provide enough food to feed its people. Worsening food shortages plagued the nation so much that many peasants were forced to eat the leaves and bark of trees. The United States and other nations sent millions of dollars in food aid to North Korea. Nevertheless, concerns grew in the mid-1990s that North Korea's famine might possibly cause the government to launch a desperate attack on South Korea. Even though North Korea finally agreed in June 1997 to attend peace talks, the possibility of armed conflict on the Korean peninsula continued to be a cause for great international concern.

Supporters of Roh Tae Woo gathered in Seoul for a campaign rally. He was elected to a five-year term as president of South Korea on February 25, 1988.

In February of 1998, former dissident Kim Dae-jung was sworn in as president of South Korea. Once imprisoned and under a death sentence for leading the fight against South Korea's dictatorship, Kim has been described as "Asia's Mandela." He has placed great importance on reviving South Korea's economy and has stated that democracy will go hand in hand with economic growth.

The Nationalists in Taiwan

After the Communists took control of China in 1949, the Chinese Nationalists established themselves on the island of Taiwan, about 100 miles from the Chinese mainland. Their government, called the Republic of China, appeared to be democratic. In reality, however, it operated more like a one-party system, with Chiang Kaishek and other Guomindang (Chinese Nationalist Party) officials holding all the power. Nevertheless, the Republic of China's free enterprise system boosted productivity, and the people enjoyed a relatively high standard of living.

The Republic of China, or Nationalist China, occupied China's permanent seat on the United Nations Security Council until 1971. In that year, the UN expelled the Nationalists and admitted the People's Republic.

The United States had given aid to Chiang Kaishek for many years and had maintained army and navy bases on Taiwan. Agreements reached during President Nixon's visit to the People's Republic, however, led to the renewal of diplomatic ties between the United States and the People's Republic of China. Nevertheless, the United States continued to maintain its social and economic ties with Taiwan. Although it ended diplomatic and military ties, the United States asserted that it would continue to sell defensive arms to Taiwan.

Diplomatic isolation did not prevent Taiwan from developing into a leading economic power in Asia. Even though it had few natural resources, Taiwan developed into one of the world's major producers of manufactured goods. Cheap but skilled labor and efficient management made these goods highly competitive in terms of price and quality. Thus Taiwan soon became a leading exporter, with a large percentage of those exports going to the United States. Over time, the government introduced measures to diversify trade and make the economy less dependent on the export of manufactured goods. Taiwan continued to prosper in the 1990s, achieving one of Asia's highest gross national products.

Moving to democracy. In the political sphere, fundamental changes took place during the 1980s. For the first time, a native Taiwanese held the presidency and the leadership of the Guomindang. Furthermore, Taiwan's leaders encouraged the formation of opposition political parties, promising that future elections would be completely open. In 1989, for the first time, parties other than the Guomindang were able to participate in an election.

Significant political changes continued in the 1990s. Pressure increased for democratic reforms that had been promised in the mid-1980s but were not yet in operation. Finally, in 1996, Taiwan held its first direct presidential election. Incumbent president Lee Teng-hui, the Guomindang candidate, won the election with a landslide victory.

Taiwan and China. Talk of reuniting China and Taiwan has led to little real progress. Although Taiwan has never formally proclaimed its independence, the nation has been self-governing since 1949. In the 1990s the movement for official independence drew increasing support from Taiwan's people. However, while Taiwan demanded to be recognized as China's equal, China insisted that Taiwan was a "renegade province" and warned that a declaration of independence could provoke war. Indeed, in 1995 and 1996, China carried out military exercises and

Since World War II, Taiwan has become a leading nation in the shipbuilding industry.

missile launches off the coast of Taiwan in an attempt at intimidation. The United States sent aircraft carriers to the area in a show of support for Taiwan.

Section 2 Review

1. **Define** Great Leap Forward, Cultural Revolution
2. **Identify** Mao Zedong, Deng Xiaoping, Syngman Rhee, Park Chung Hee
3. **Locate and Explain the Significance** Taiwan, 38th parallel, Seoul
4. **Understanding Ideas** What methods did the Chinese Communists use to rebuild China after World War II?
5. **Contrasting Ideas** Contrast life in China under Mao with life after his death.
6. **Analyzing Ideas** How did the events that occurred in Tiananmen Square affect China's foreign relations?
7. **Synthesizing Ideas** What problems have troubled the two Koreas?

Section 3

The Japanese Miracle

Focus Questions

- What factors allowed Japan to recover as effectively as it did after World War II?
- How has the relationship between Japan and the United States changed in the years since World War II?
- What political difficulties has Japan faced in the past decade?

After World War II, Japan lost all the territory that it had gained during its period of expansion. Its population, now confined to the home islands, faced very severe shortages of food, clothing, fuel, and other necessities. Japan's economy was ruined. The country desperately needed to increase imports to satisfy its people's needs. Unfortunately, most of the industries that had produced export goods to pay for imports had been damaged or destroyed during World War II.

The devastating effects of the war were apparent throughout the country. Japan's cities lay in ruins. Factories, homes, and the country's infrastructure were damaged or destroyed. The Japanese people were shocked and demoralized.

The Occupation of Japan

After the war, American troops occupied Japan under the command of General Douglas MacArthur. As Supreme Commander of the Allied Powers (SCAP) in Japan, MacArthur became the country's virtual ruler. His first task was to demilitarize Japan. He acted to remove the individuals who had been powerful in the Japanese war machine. Some top war leaders were executed, and more than 5 million troops were disarmed and released from military service. In addition, MacArthur planned to confiscate as reparations the war industries that remained in Japan. By taking factories as reparations, however, he would have created the same difficulties in Japan as were evident in Germany. Unless the Allied Powers wished to support them indefinitely, the Japanese had to be given the opportunity to provide for themselves. To do this, the Japanese needed to keep their factories and convert them to peacetime activities. The United States therefore suggested that the payment of reparations be postponed indefinitely.

MacArthur's second task involved the creation of a nonmilitary and democratic government. Under his supervision the Japanese adopted a new constitution in 1947. The **"MacArthur Constitution"** established Japan as a parliamentary democracy. It called for direct election of the Diet, or parliament, with all adults given the right to vote. The emperor, having renounced his divine status, remained only as a symbol of state. He had little power. Finally, the constitution ended Japan's militarism and included a clause in which the Japanese renounced war as a political tool.

Postwar Developments

Before World War II, Japan had been the most completely industrialized of the Asian nations. Although the destruction of many factories and the loss of its Asian possessions had hurt its economy, Japan made a rapid and impressive recovery after the war.

Economic development. Several postwar SCAP policies aided Japanese economic development. A major program of land reform allowed farmers to own their own land. Mechanization and improved strains of crops also had a positive impact on Japanese agriculture. Farm output increased dramatically.

Before and during the war, powerful industrial and banking firms called *zaibatsu* had controlled industry. The American occupation leaders worked to break up some of these firms, enforce fair trading practices, and prevent the return of monopolies. The large banks were not broken up, however, and they became a positive force in Japan's economic recovery.

In addition, Japan changed the structure of its economy. Instead of concentrating on providing inexpensive textile products, mainly for Asian markets, Japan began to produce advanced technology for a world market. The modern technology that Japan had imported after the war was operated by a skilled and highly motivated workforce. In addition, government cooperation and support for industry fueled Japan's industrial gains.

As a result, by the 1980s, Japan had emerged as Asia's leading economic power. In the 1990s, however, Japan became mired in a stubborn recession, caused partly by financial problems created during the rapid growth of the 1980s and partly by intensifying global competition. Economic growth slowed—to a near standstill from 1992 to 1994—and unemployment rose, reaching a record high 3.5 percent in 1996. As the government came under increasing pressure, its efforts to revive growth met with only limited success.

Japan-U.S. trade. Japan's remarkable economic growth depended on the country finding markets for its rapidly expanding volume of production. For many years the United States was Japan's best customer and its principal supplier of raw materials and agricultural products. In this trade relationship, Japan bought more from the United States than the United States purchased from Japan. Thus the trade balance favored the United States for many years.

Beginning in the late 1960s, however, the balance of trade swung heavily in favor of Japan. Within two decades, Japan's exports to the United States were worth millions of dollars more than the goods the country imported from the United States. In response to this situation, many American politicians pressured their government to limit Japanese imports, such as automobiles. They also wanted Japan to remove controls that restricted the entry of American imports into Japan. The Japanese government agreed to buy more goods from the United States and loosened some restrictions on foreign imports, and by the early 1990s the trade balance between the two countries had improved.

By the mid-1990s, however, the trade imbalance had once again become a significant issue. Talks in April 1997 between President Bill Clinton and Japanese Prime Minister Ryutaro Hashimoto were in part aimed at resolving issues that pertained to this continuing trade imbalance. Other large industrialized countries shared the United States' hope that Japan would increase its imports and take other actions to balance international trade and foster a healthy world economy.

Economic and social changes. Postwar economic growth did not benefit everyone in Japan, but it did bring prosperity to a large part of the population. This prosperity led to an increase in consumerism. For example, many families who had lived more simply before the war acquired labor-saving household appliances and new automobiles.

Economic growth, however, did not necessarily bring an improvement in the quality of life. The Japanese worked longer hours than their Western counterparts, and the cost of living was much higher in Japan than in other industrialized nations. The differences in prices were most marked in land and housing. Rapid industrialization and population growth put land for building at a premium. Consequently, from the 1960s onward, prices for land and housing soared. Industrialization also created another serious problem—environmental pollution. In recent years, many Japanese have called on their government to pay more attention to improving the quality of life and less to promoting further development.

Postwar economic developments brought about far-reaching social changes. As more and more women joined the workforce, their status in Japanese society began to change. In time, they won greater legal, political, and social freedoms. Changing roles within the family and changes in housing arrangements began to cause a decline in the importance of the family, traditionally the center of all Japanese life. As a result, young people began to make decisions and choices for themselves—about marriage partners and work, for example—that their parents would once have made for them.

Foreign Relations and Political Life

The Cold War between the Soviet Union and the West led to a reversal of Japan's international position. The 1947 constitution had limited Japanese armed forces and military production. In addition, the Japanese had signed a treaty agreeing to renounce war as a political tactic. The communist victory in China

Japanese youth during the post-World War II years began to make decisions and choices for themselves.

and the stalemate in Korea changed Western policy toward Japan. The Western nations now felt that Japan should be able to defend itself and also to aid them in case of war in Asia. These nations, therefore, urged Japan to increase its armed forces.

Fearing a return of the militaristic governments of prewar days, the Japanese had little desire to rearm. They preferred to spend their money building peacetime industries, expanding exports, and raising living standards. As a result, Japan's military expenditures remained low. In 1997 the United States and Japan reached an agreement under which Japan would provide the United States with noncombative support and assistance in case of a conflict near Japan.

A more independent stance. Over the past several decades, Japan and the United States have maintained friendly ties. Still, relations between the nations have showed some signs of stress over the years. The Japanese have expressed resentment over the economic and defense pressures put upon them by the United States and other nations during the 1970s and 1980s. The issue of U.S. troops stationed in Japan—especially the forces on the island of Okinawa—has been a sore point since the 1960s. At the same time, many Americans have felt apprehensive about the United States's growing trade deficit with Japan and Japan's increasing stature as a world economic power.

As the 1980s drew to a close, Japan began to pursue a more independent course in international affairs. Japanese leaders moved to consolidate their country's position as an economic and political leader in Asia. They also increased the level of Japan's financial and technical aid to developing countries. By the end of the 1980s, Japan had become the world's leading donor of economic aid. Also, with the growth of democracy in Eastern Europe, Japan's leaders reassessed their country's relations with the nations of the former Soviet Union. For example, in 1996 the leaders of Japan and Russia met for talks. However, relations between the two countries continued to be strained by an ongoing dispute over the Kuril Islands, which the Soviet Union occupied after World

Independent Nations in Southeast Asia, 1945–1984

Learning from Maps Many of the colonies in Southeast Asia became independent countries after World War II.

❓ **Place** In what year did the Philippines gain their independence?

Toshiki Kaifu and Mikhail Gorbachev signed a joint declaration in April 1991.

Section 3 Review

1. **Define** "MacArthur Constitution," Diet
2. **Identify** Toshiki Kaifu
3. **Evaluating Ideas** What factors allowed Japan to recover as successfully as it did after World War II?
4. **Analyzing Ideas** What role has trade played in the changing relationship between Japan and the United States since 1945?
5. **Summarizing Ideas** Describe Japan's growing independence in world affairs as well as its internal political difficulties.

War II, and which now belong to Russia. Japan still claims several islands in the southern part of the chain of Kuril Islands.

Politics in Japan. Japan's conservative Liberal Democratic Party (LDP) controlled the **Diet**, which is Japan's national legislature and therefore its government. But the Socialists and other opposition parties voiced strong criticism of its policies. These parties especially condemned the ongoing security pact with the United States and the presence of American military bases on Japanese soil.

The ruling party's greatest troubles, however, were self-made. A 1989 financial scandal, involving many top party members, stunned the country. The LDP's image was temporarily rescued by Toshiki Kaifu, who became prime minister some months after the scandal broke. However, Kaifu was forced out of office in 1991, and two years later another political scandal brought down the government of his successor. In the 1993 elections, the LDP lost its majority in the Diet, ending the party's almost 40-year rule. In subsequent years, various coalition governments endeavored to bring about political reforms as well as economic changes for Japan. It was in 1996 that Ryutaro Hashimoto, president of the LDP, became Japan's prime minister.

Section 4

Independence Struggles in Southeast Asia

Focus Questions

- What were the causes and effects of authoritarian rule in the Philippines and Indonesia?
- What types of struggles did nations in Southeast Asia face as they sought stability and prosperity?
- How did the Vietnam War affect Vietnam, Cambodia, and Laos?
- How have events in Thailand followed a different path from that of events in many other Southeast Asian countries?

Southeast Asia consists of 10 countries: the Philippines, Indonesia, Malaysia, Singapore, Brunei, Vietnam, Thailand, Laos, Burma (renamed Myanmar in 1989), and Cambodia (renamed Kampuchea for a time). With the exception of Thailand, all were once colonies. After World War II, these countries gained independence. Some did so peacefully, while others resorted to violent means. After achieving independence each began the long and difficult process of political and economic development. (See map on page 516.)

The Philippines

Spain ceded the Philippines to the United States in 1898. In 1934 the United States Congress passed an act granting autonomy to the Philippines. This legislation also provided for the Philippines to become independent on July 4, 1946, when the country became the Republic of the Philippines. After that date, however, the United States continued to maintain military bases in the Philippines. As compensation, it contributed large sums of money to repair war damage and rebuild the Philippine economy. These close ties to the United States led the Philippine government to adopt a strongly pro-Western foreign policy.

In the 1970s, Marxist guerrillas began to threaten the peace in the Philippines. A revolt by Muslim separatists further strained the country's stability. To deal with this internal disorder, Philippine president Ferdinand Marcos declared martial law and arrested hundreds of his political opponents. In 1973, Marcos extended his power by proclaiming a new constitution that gave him an almost unlimited term in office.

Under the Marcos regime the country made little progress toward democracy, and economic conditions worsened. Opposition to the regime began to grow, however. Then, in 1983, the assassination of opposition leader Benigno Aquino sparked widespread rioting. In 1986 Aquino's widow, Corazon Aquino, ran against Marcos in a special presidential election. Marcos claimed victory, but when it became obvious that he had rigged the election, he was forced to flee the country.

On taking office, Aquino pledged to recover the billions of dollars that she said Marcos and his family had embezzled from the treasury. Aquino did make some gains. She restored constitutional democracy after years of dictatorial rule, and she promoted free enterprise. However, many of the changes she promised—land reform, for instance—were never enacted, and poverty and official corruption persisted.

Fidel Ramos succeeded Aquino as president in 1992. Under Ramos, the economy continued to strengthen. Ramos made an effort to reduce restrictions on business, break up monopolies, and encourage foreign investment in the Philippines. Ramos also made progress in talks with Muslim opposition groups. The economy experienced solid growth in the mid-1990s, but internal problems persisted.

Indonesia

During World War II, the Japanese occupied the East Indies, a group of islands including Sumatra and Java. When the war ended, the Dutch, who had ruled the East Indies since the 1600s, expected to regain control. An Indonesian civil engineer named Sukarno, however, led an independence movement against them. (Many Indonesians have only one

name or are known by only one name.) After a year of bitter fighting, the United Nations intervened to secure a cease-fire. Then, after further struggle and lengthy negotiations, in 1949 the Netherlands granted independence to the East Indies. The East Indies became the Republic of Indonesia, with Sukarno as its first president. West Irian, part of the island of New Guinea, was not included in the Dutch settlement with Indonesia.

Indonesia faced problems similar to those of many other newly independent countries. It had few trained civil servants or administrators and a chaotic political system. However, the country made some significant gains in health and education. Sukarno was also successful in developing a sense of national identity among the Indonesian people.

In the early 1960s, Sukarno's rule became much more authoritarian. In a move that established what he called a guided democracy, Sukarno dissolved the elected parliament and appointed a new one. This appointed legislature proclaimed him President for Life. At about this time, Sukarno also gained control of West Irian from the Dutch.

Sukarno found, however, that Indonesia's problems were multiplying. The economy slowed almost to a standstill. Exports decreased, and inflation and debts rose. Reckless spending brought the nation close to bankruptcy. In 1965, General Suharto, the conservative head of the Indonesian army strategic command, took advantage of a communist insurrection to seize control of the government.

As president, Suharto emphasized economic reforms and worked to build closer ties with the West. Using Western aid, he began an ambitious industrial development program. The slump in oil prices in the early 1980s had a devastating effect on the Indonesian economy, however. As a result, the pace of industrial development in Indonesia again slowed. Suharto continued Sukarno's interest in West Irian. In 1969 he managed to force West Irian to unite with Indonesia. However, opposition to the Indonesian government in this region, today known as Irian Jaya, continued through the 1990s. Unrest also continued in East Timor, an island territory invaded by Indonesia in 1975.

In the late 1980s and through the 1990s, Suharto's authoritarian government came under criticism from people both within and outside the country. Many Indonesians complained about the growing gap between the country's rich and poor, the continued mismanagement, and the corruption of many government officials. Also, a number of Western countries voiced concern

Ikat Cloth

The woven cloth shown in this feature, from Bali, Indonesia, was made by an ancient method of dyeing and weaving known as ikat. The ikat method can be found in several parts of Southeast Asia, including Indonesia and Cambodia, and may have originated in India.

Cotton and silk are the most common fibers used for ikat. Before the thread is woven, bundles of threads are tied tightly at carefully calculated points. Then the bundles are dyed. Most of the thread will absorb the dye, but the places where the strands are tied together do not absorb color. Sometimes the process is repeated to include additional colors.

After it is dyed, the yarn is woven on a loom. As the weaving progresses, complex designs begin to appear. Often only the threads running one way—the threads extended lengthwise on the loom—are pre-dyed. In the southern part of Sumatra, however, the threads going both ways are also dyed. Beautiful designs, with figures such as birds and animals, can be created during this process. Although the process is extremely difficult and laborious, the finished cloths are stunning.

Decorated textiles such as these ikat cloths have been an important part of Indonesian culture for centuries. Ikat cloths are sometimes given as wedding gifts between families. Because of the long time needed to produce them and the high quality of the weaving, however, the cloths were used mostly in ceremonies. Many are considered to represent works of art.

over human rights abuses allegedly committed by the Indonesian military and police forces. Nevertheless, Indonesia continued to make economic progress in the 1990s, and its political and economic importance in the world grew.

President Suharto remained in power until May 1998. After a worsening economic crisis and widespread demonstrations paralyzed the country, Suharto finally resigned, handing over power to his vice-president, B.J. Habibie. People were hopeful that democratizing reforms would follow.

Malaysia, Singapore, and Brunei

In 1963 Malaya (now West Malaysia), Singapore, Sarawak, and Sabah (North Borneo), which had all become independent from Great Britain, united to form the Federation of Malaysia. The new nation faced both external and internal difficulties. To begin with, the Philippines claimed part of Sabah. Also, Indonesia's President Sukarno tried to block the formation of the new federation, saying that it was nothing more than a move by the British to encircle his country. In addition, Sarawak and Sabah had come under heavy attack from Indonesian communist guerrillas.

Internally, a clash of cultures threatened the federation. The nation's population consisted of Malays, Chinese, and a small percentage of Indians and other ethnic groups. The greatest proportion of the people—about half—were Malays; Singapore, however, had a large majority of Chinese. Most Malays were farmers, while the Chinese were mainly city dwellers, technically trained and experienced in commerce. Malays controlled the government of the federation, but the Chinese controlled most of the business and the wealth.

The Malays forced Singapore to secede from the federation in 1965. Tensions continued to grow between the Malays and the Chinese who remained in Malaysia. Then, in 1969, the tensions exploded in racial riots. As a result, the government declared a state of emergency and suspended parliamentary rule.

After these riots, the government began to seek ways to raise the living standard of the Malay population. By improving the status of the Malay majority, the government hoped to eliminate the educational and economic differences between Malays and other ethnic groups.

Racial tensions erupted once again in 1979 with the arrival of thousands of Vietnamese refugees in Malaysia. Since many of these refugees were ethnically Chinese, the Malays feared that the Chinese faction would gain power. As a result, the Malaysian government denied entry to the refugees. Racial friction continued throughout the 1980s, causing considerable political instability.

In the 1990s, tensions caused by ethnic differences began to ease somewhat. Political difficulties were moderated by Malaysia's impressive economic growth in this period. Indeed, by 1996 Malaysia's economy had become one of the strongest and fastest-growing in the Asia-Pacific region. Still, while sustained economic progress had a positive effect on overall conditions in Malaysia, serious problems remained, such as poor living conditions for many people, pollution, and continued racial and ethnic friction.

The Republic of Singapore. Singapore, a cluster of one major island and more than 50 smaller islands, measures less than 240 square miles in area. For nearly all of the time since it seceded from the Federation of Malaysia in 1965, Singapore has been dominated by one man and one political party—Prime Minister Lee Kuan Yew and his People's Action Party. Throughout his time in office, Lee created a regulated society, imposing strict controls on labor unions, political activity, and the media. When Lee stepped down in

November 1990, however, Singapore was one of the world's most politically stable and economically prosperous countries. The People's Action Party remained in control of Singapore's authoritarian government through the mid-1990s, with Lee retaining a role in affairs as Senior Minister.

Singapore began its march to prosperity after it seceded from the Federation of Malaysia. Since the 1970s the economy has grown at an annual rate often reaching 10 percent. This spectacular growth rate was based on a program of industrial development that emphasized, at first, shipbuilding and petroleum refining, and later, electronics and computer software. By the mid-1990s, Singapore had become the center of economic activity in Southeast Asia, and the country's 3 million people enjoyed one of the highest standards of living in Asia.

Brunei. The small sultanate of Brunei on the northern coast of Malaysian Borneo decided against joining the Federation of Malaysia. Its leaders feared that it would be overwhelmed by the larger states of Malaya and Singapore. This oil-rich land remained a protectorate of Great Britain until it achieved full independence in 1984.

Burma (Myanmar)
Since medieval times the area known as Burma has been a strategically important region, an area of important trade routes. During World War II, the country, held by the British, was the starting point of

This view of skyscrapers shows the modernization and the westernization of Singapore.

the Burma Road, over which supplies moved to China for the war against Japan. Japanese armies invaded Burma in 1942 and held it until 1945, when British rule resumed. In 1948, Great Britain recognized Burma's independence.

The new nation faced difficulties that included the lack of a strong central government, a scarcity of trained civil servants, tribal and political dissension, and communist attempts to seize the country. The first premier, U Nu, headed a coalition government that brought the nation some degree of order. However, the coalition soon broke into rival factions, and in 1962 the army, led by General Ne Win, seized control of the government.

Ne Win wanted to make Burma a socialist nation. His repressive government took strict control of the economy, a move that led to economic ruin. Farm production fell, and consumer goods became scarce.

In 1974 a new constitution under Ne Win proclaimed Burma the Socialist Republic of the Union of Burma. In 1988, violent demonstrations forced Ne Win to resign, although the military remained in control. Signaling that they intended to make a fresh start, the leaders of the new military junta renamed the country Myanmar in 1989. They promised to establish a new economic order and enact political reforms, including free elections in 1990. However, when the major opposition party swept the elections, the junta refused to step down. Instead it cracked down on everyone it considered a challenge to its power. One famous dissident, Aung San Suu Kyi, won a Nobel Peace Prize in 1991, while she was under house arrest, for her efforts to bring democratic reform to her country. She was released in 1995. The military's brutal repression added to the nation's unrest. Although antigovernment opposition continued into the mid-1990s, the junta still dominates the country.

Myanmar has had some success in attracting foreign investments, but relationships with the United States and other Western nations have been limited. Myanmar's poor record in human rights as well as its role as a leading producer of illegal narcotics has earned the country growing criticism.

Vietnam

In the late 1800s, the French became the dominant power in the eastern part of the peninsula of Indochina, an area roughly equivalent to the present-day countries of Vietnam, Laos, and Cambodia. However, during World War II, the Japanese took control of the area. When the French tried to return

after the war, the Viet Minh, a communist-led guerrilla group that had fought the Japanese, now began to resist the French. The group's leader, Ho Chi Minh, declared the country independent in September 1945. No major governments recognized Ho's declaration, however, and by the end of 1945 the French had regained control of much of Vietnam.

Ho hoped to negotiate a quick settlement of the independence question. However, the French would agree only to recognize Vietnam as a free state within the French Union, or empire. In 1946 fighting broke out between the French and the Viet Minh in the northern cities of Hanoi and Haiphong. The war dragged on for years. After a major defeat in 1954 at Dien Bien Phu (dyen byen FOO), in which the Viet Minh captured some 13,000 French troops, French leaders were finally ready to negotiate an end to the war.

Vietnam divided. The **Geneva Accords**, signed in 1954, called for the withdrawal of all foreign troops from the area. They also divided Vietnam into two zones at the 17th parallel. (See map on page 523.) For the time being, Ho Chi Minh would remain in control of the north. But an election, set for 1956, would allow the Vietnamese to select a government to reunite the country.

The Geneva Accords left the Viet Minh in a better situation than that of the government in the south. The north began a program of industrialization and collectivization of agriculture, and it experienced steady economic progress for the next decade. With Chinese and Soviet assistance, the Viet Minh began to consolidate their economic and political strength, building a communist state in the north.

In contrast, the south experienced political chaos. Its war-torn economy, a flood of refugees from the north, and fighting among political and religious groups all posed problems for the newly formed government of Ngo Dinh Diem.

Guerrilla war in Vietnam. Under Diem, South Vietnam returned to some semblance of order, but at a price. Diem ruled by totalitarian methods, attempting to suppress all opposition to his government. He showed little interest in reforms or in eliminating government corruption. He refused to hold the proposed elections in 1956.

As Diem's government became increasingly repressive, opposition grew. By the late 1950s the Viet Minh were taking advantage of the situation, forming the National Liberation Front (NLF) with the goal of overthrowing Diem and reuniting Vietnam. The NLF, a mixture of Viet Minh members and dissidents from the south, soon became known as the Viet Cong, or Vietnamese Communists.

With weapons and military expertise from the north, the Viet Cong infiltrated the rural areas of South Vietnam. Their goals were to "neutralize" the south, force the withdrawal of all foreign troops, and finally reunite the two regions under the government of the north. Their tactics, however, included assassination and sabotage as well as more traditional methods of persuasion.

Ngo Dinh Diem responded to both internal dissent and Viet Cong guerrilla activity by becoming increasingly repressive. With conditions in the south growing more and more chaotic, a group of army officers assassinated Diem and took control of the government in 1963. Over the next three years, several different military groups ruled South Vietnam.

American involvement. United States involvement in Vietnam began almost unnoticed. It grew slowly, without either a declaration of war by Congress or an announcement by the government to the American people. President Dwight D. Eisenhower sent financial and military aid as well as a few hundred military advisers to South Vietnam. President John F. Kennedy continued this policy, sending military advisers and supplies to help the South Vietnamese army. As the guerrilla war increased in intensity, so did the American commitment.

American troop strength began to reach significant numbers in the mid-1960s under President Lyndon Johnson. In March 1965, Marines landed on the beaches near Da Nang, marking the beginning of direct United States military involvement in the war. The Johnson administration explained the increased American military presence in a number of ways. First, communism had to be contained. Second, the administration cited the **domino theory**, the belief that if South Vietnam fell to communism, all of Southeast Asia would follow. Third, the North Vietnamese were aggressors in the conflict and had to be stopped. In January 1965 President Johnson expanded the war by ordering air attacks on North Vietnam.

At the beginning of 1968, North Vietnamese troops and the Viet Cong launched a major offensive. American and South Vietnamese forces drove back the attackers, inflicting heavy casualties. Even so, the Viet Cong considered the **Tet Offensive**—named for the Vietnamese New Year celebration, during which the attack began—a psychological victory. Many Americans, after seeing television pictures of the fierce fighting, openly questioned United States involvement in the war.

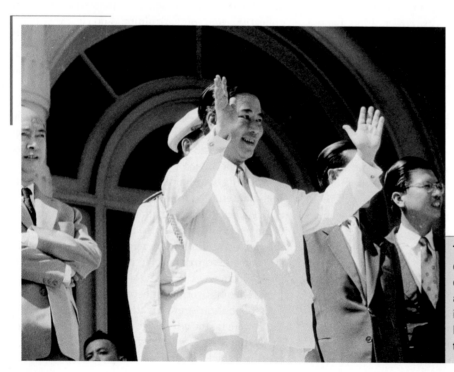

The fourth agreement of the Geneva Accord called for independence and presidential elections in Vietnam. Ngo Dinh Diem became president of the Republic of Vietnam.

In March 1968, President Johnson announced a temporary halt to the bombing of North Vietnam. An agreement with North Vietnam to begin negotiating an end to the war soon followed. However, these peace negotiations quickly became deadlocked. During 1969, the first year of Richard Nixon's presidency, there were 540,000 U.S. troops in Vietnam. Nixon announced a policy of "Vietnamization." This involved allowing the South Vietnamese gradually to take over fighting the war while the United States supplied them with arms, equipment, air support, and economic aid. As a first step in this process, he announced the gradual withdrawal of American troops—but at the same time, he escalated the war. In 1970 Nixon ordered an invasion of Cambodia, long used by the Viet Cong as a refuge, and in 1972 he resumed the bombing of North Vietnam.

Ending the war. In 1973 the major parties in the Vietnam War reached a cease-fire agreement. Under this agreement, known as the **Paris Peace Accords**, the United States withdrew its remaining troops from South Vietnam. In return the North Vietnamese were to release American prisoners of war. However, fighting continued in Vietnam in violation of the accords. The South Vietnamese army, without American support, could not hold back the enemy advance, and in April 1975, North Vietnamese troops entered Saigon. Within 24 hours the South Vietnamese government surrendered.

The Vietnam War caused widespread devastation. Estimates of civilian and military casualties for both North and South Vietnam range from 1.3 million to more than 2 million. American combat casualties totaled more than 58,000 killed and some 300,000 wounded. The neighboring countries of Laos and Cambodia also suffered their share of death and destruction. Long-standing rivalries between these two countries and Vietnam complicated efforts to recover and rebuild after the war.

A reunited Vietnam. After the war, North Vietnamese officials controlled and administered all of South Vietnam. Then, in July 1976, the two Vietnams united as one country—the Socialist Republic of Vietnam—with Hanoi, in the north, as the capital. The former southern capital, Saigon, was renamed Ho Chi Minh City, after the North Vietnamese president, who died in 1969.

Even before unification, the North Vietnamese had begun to reform the south along northern lines. Economically, this reform involved nationalizing property, imposing controls on private enterprise, and moving the population from cities to rural areas.

War in Southeast Asia, 1954–1975

Learning from Maps As in Korea, a war occurred in Vietnam between the northern and southern sections of the country.

? **Movement** Through how many countries could a traveler journey along the Ho Chi Minh Trail?

In the years after the fall of Saigon, more than 1 million South Vietnamese fled their country. Some left because they feared punishment by the North Vietnamese. Others left because of food shortages. However, most people moved on because they did not want to live under a communist government.

Sometimes these refugees had to bribe government officials just to leave Vietnam. Then they faced a dangerous sea voyage to Malaysia, Thailand, or some other

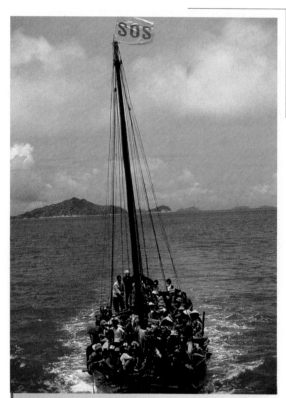

After the Vietnam War, over a million people left Vietnam by boat as refugees.

Vietnam's economy boomed. Foreign trade expanded, foreign investment in Vietnam increased, inflation was brought under control, and even diplomatic relations with the United States were restored. By 1996, Vietnam's economy was growing at a rate of more than 9 percent.

Cambodia

Cambodia, which had gained independence from France in 1953, attempted to remain neutral in the Vietnam War. The country's leader, Norodom Sihanouk, found neutrality a difficult path to follow, however. North Vietnamese and Viet Cong troops frequently fled into Cambodia to escape capture, and their chief supply route—the Ho Chi Minh Trail—ran through the eastern part of the country.

In 1970, Lon Nol, a pro-American army general, overthrew Sihanouk in a military coup. Lon Nol promised to take a firmer stand against the Vietnamese Communists who used Cambodia as a refuge.

The Khmer Rouge. During the war in Vietnam, the Vietnamese Communists had helped to arm and train a group of Cambodian insurgents called the Khmer Rouge. With this assistance, the Khmer Rouge rapidly grew in strength. Sihanouk, who had gone into exile in China, voiced his support for this group. In 1975, just before Saigon fell, the Khmer Rouge seized Phnom Penh, the Cambodian capital, and established a new Marxist regime under the leadership of Pol Pot.

This new government mounted a brutal campaign to resettle Cambodia's population, sending most city residents into the countryside to create new agricultural villages. Lacking tools and farming experience, many of these former city dwellers died of starvation. The Khmer Rouge also undertook a systematic program to eliminate almost all of Cambodia's government officials, army officers, teachers, and intellectuals. Between 1975 and 1977, well over 1 million Cambodians—about one fifth of the country's people—met their deaths by execution or starvation under Pol Pot's regime. Thousands more fled to makeshift refugee camps in neighboring Thailand.

The Vietnamese invasion. Border disputes and rivalries that were centuries old soon brought the Khmer Rouge into conflict with its Vietnamese neighbors. The Vietnamese invaded Cambodia in 1978. As the Vietnamese advanced toward Phnom Penh, the Chinese threw their support to the Khmer Rouge. Even so, by early 1979 the Vietnamese had overthrown Pol Pot and established a pro-Vietnamese government in Phnom Penh, led by Hun Sen. Throughout the 1980s,

Southeast Asian country. Many of these "boat people," as the refugees were called, died at sea. Those who survived spent months in crowded camps, waiting for permission to settle permanently in another country. Many eventually made their way to Western countries. The largest number of immigrants came to the United States. In the late 1980s, the troubles of the boat people grew. Some Southeast Asian countries, already overrun with refugees from Indochina, refused to accept any more boat people.

Economic progress. After 1975, Vietnam struggled to make ends meet economically. Burdened by huge debts from fighting the Vietnam War, the country took on more debt in an effort to rebuild after hostilities ended. Military action in Cambodia put further strain on the economy in the 1980s. By the late 1980s, inflation was wildly out of control in Vietnam, and the nation was mired in poverty.

Following the example of other communist countries, Vietnam began to restructure its economy, adding elements of free enterprise. At first, progress under this program of renovation was slow, but, in the 1990s, fighting between the Chinese-backed Khmer Rouge and Hun Sen's troops with their Vietnamese allies was almost constant. Once again the refugee camps in Thailand became a haven for fearful Cambodians.

In the late 1980s, under pressure from the UN, Vietnam withdrew its troops from Cambodia, and China cut military aid to the Khmer Rouge. The UN sponsored talks on the future of Cambodia to which all affected parties—including Sihanouk's followers, the Khmer Rouge, and the Vietnamese-backed government—were invited. After much discussion, all of these factions agreed in late 1991 to back a UN-sponsored government that would rule until free elections were held.

The UN-sponsored elections finally took place in May 1993 and resulted in a coalition government, with Norodom Sihanouk as king and two co-prime ministers: Norodom Ranariddh, son of Norodom Sihanouk, and Hun Sen. However, conflict between the two prime ministers and their supporters, as well as ongoing Khmer Rouge opposition to the government, left Cambodia's political situation in the mid-1990s increasingly unstable.

Still, there were some positive developments in Cambodia. In 1996 the Khmer Rouge showed clear signs of weakening, and in 1998 the notorious Pol Pot died.

Laos

Like Cambodia, Laos gained independence from France in 1954. Almost immediately, civil war broke out among the country's political factions. This turmoil continued for the next 20 years.

In the meantime Laos, although neutral, became increasingly involved in the Vietnam War. The Ho Chi Minh Trail, the Viet Cong's major supply route, wound through the mountain valleys of eastern Laos into Cambodia and South Vietnam. To break this supply line, the United States began bombing the Laotian countryside, causing heavy damage and many civilian casualties.

By 1975 the internal strife in Laos had ended. The communist faction, the Pathet Lao, had set up a communist regime, the Lao People's Democratic Republic. This new government tried to follow a nonaligned course in the complicated politics of Asia. Ultimately, however, nonalignment proved impossible. Laos had to call on the Vietnamese for help in controlling anticommunist forces in its northern provinces. In return it allowed Vietnam to station 50,000 troops on Laotian soil. As a result, relations

between Laos and its neighbors continued to be tense throughout the 1980s.

As the new decade began, this situation gradually changed. Vietnam withdrew its troops from Laos in 1989. Laotian leaders made efforts to improve relations with Thailand and China. They also signed trade and financial aid agreements with the United States, Japan, and the Soviet Union. By the mid-1990s, Laos had attracted a significant amount of foreign investment. Although still one of the world's poorest countries, Laos saw its economy grow at an average annual rate of 6.5 percent between 1990 and 1996.

Thailand

Thailand, formerly called Siam, had never been a European colony. During World War II, however, Thailand became an ally of Japan. Under Japanese pressure Thailand joined the Axis and declared war on Great Britain and the United States.

In the late 1950s, the Thai army took control of the government, establishing a military dictatorship. Strongly pro-Western, this government received military and economic aid from the United States. During the Vietnam War, this close relationship continued. The United States used bases in Thailand as a staging area for bombing raids on North Vietnam, Laos, and Cambodia.

Throughout the 1970s, Thailand was deluged with refugees from war-torn Vietnam, Laos, and Cambodia. The Thai government, along with international relief agencies, set up refugee camps along its border with Cambodia. Communist victories in Vietnam, Laos, and Cambodia during the mid-1970s forced Thailand to reconsider its relationship with the United States. The Thai government began to work to better its ties with its communist neighbors.

Although Thailand has experienced a slow but steady democratization of its political system in recent years, control has shifted back and forth between civilian and military leadership. The nation's various uneasy coalition governments have been unstable and often ineffective. Moreover, political corruption has been all too common.

While Thailand struggled politically, however, the nation developed economically. As foreign investments poured into the country, the Thai economy grew at a rate averaging more than 8 percent annually between 1985 and 1994—one of the world's fastest-growing economies. In 1996, however, the economy weakened. Exports declined, bad debts began to mount, and investors lost confidence.

Thailand also experienced environmental problems, such as erosion caused by the overharvesting of timber. By 1997 the nation was in the grip of a severe financial crisis, and in November of that year, the prime minister (in office less than a year) was forced to resign. The worsening crisis left Thailand's political and economic future uncertain.

Section 4 Review

1. **Define** Geneva Accords, domino theory, Tet Offensive, Paris Peace Accords
2. **Identify** Ferdinand Marcos, Sukarno, Viet Minh, Ho Chi Minh, Viet Cong, Norodom Sihanouk, Khmer Rouge, Pol Pot
3. **Locate and Explain the Significance** Phnom Penh, Hanoi
4. **Comparing Ideas** Compare the causes and aftermaths of authoritarian rule in the Philippines and in Indonesia.
5. **Contrasting Ideas** Describe the differences between the movements toward prosperity in Malaysia and in Singapore.
6. **Summarizing Ideas** How did the struggle in Vietnam affect nations in other parts of the world as well as those in Southeast Asia?
7. **Analyzing Ideas** How has Thailand's history differed from that of its Southeast Asian neighbors since the 1950s?

Section 5

Asian Paths to Prosperity and Security

Focus Questions
- **What factors led to the development of authoritarianism in many parts of Asia?**
- **What problems did Asian countries face as they developed economically, and how did they solve these problems?**
- **In what ways have Asian cultures and economies had an effect on the West?**

Asia is a continent of great diversity, composed of many nations that differ significantly from one another.

However, a closer look at these nations reveals a number of experiences nearly all have shared.

Political Development

Most countries of Asia were once colonies. After achieving independence, most new Asian nations set up representative governments and attempted to build democratic societies. As time passed, however, democracy faded. Violent revolutions established communist governments in China, Vietnam, Cambodia, and Laos. Elsewhere—in the Philippines, Indonesia, and Burma (Myanmar), for example—civil rights came under attack, and authoritarian rule emerged. During the 1980s some Asian countries, such as the Philippines, actually established democratic political systems, while others, like China, flirted with democratization. However, a return to authoritarian rule remained a real and almost constant threat for these fledgling democratic movements.

By and large, three factors gave rise to and helped sustain authoritarianism in Asia. The first factor was the ethnic and cultural diversity within Asian nations. In India, Malaysia, and the Philippines, for example, age-old antagonisms existed among groups with different heritages or religions. From time to time these antagonisms erupted into violence. In such cases government leaders often relied on their military and police forces to maintain domestic peace. To make their work easier, these forces frequently argued for the imposition of strict controls on civil rights. Occasionally, the military forces themselves took over the government when civilian leaders seemed reluctant to impose such controls.

The second factor that helped the development of authoritarianism was fear about national security. For example, because of the communist movements on the Indochina Peninsula, leaders in the Philippines and Indonesia feared the spread of revolutionary ideas to their own countries. As a result, these leaders cracked down on leftist groups and granted sweeping powers to the military whenever the slightest signs of communist influence arose. Similarly, communist countries feared the anticommunist policies of the free world. They also feared each other's intentions. For these communist countries too, fear led to a desire for strong central government and a lack of tolerance for debate and dissent.

The third factor was the desire for economic growth. Many Asian leaders perceived democratic government as wasteful, inefficient, and a hindrance to the speedy development of industrializing policies and programs.

Therefore, the desire of these leaders for rapid economic growth contributed to the emergence of authoritarian regimes. To understand this development, it is necessary to examine economic growth in Asia.

Economic Development

By the 1990s roughly 3 billion people, more than half the world's total population, lived in Asia. A significant number of Asia's people lived in poverty and suffered its consequences—malnutrition, illiteracy, and sharply reduced life expectancy. At the same time, Asia was home to some of the fastest-growing economies in the world.

Attempts at economic development. To help create more prosperous and stable societies, in the 1950s most Asian governments began to foster economic development. The approaches of these governments varied. Some used capitalist means, encouraging private enterprise. Others followed socialist principles, with the central government taking control of the economy. Still others pursued a middle course, combining government planning with private enterprise. Whatever the approach, most governments experienced the same result. With a few exceptions, economic development proceeded slowly, if at all.

Generally, most Asian countries experienced slow economic growth because they had little wealth in the first place. Industrialization required huge investments of money in machinery, factories, and distribution networks. Also, the later a country began the process of industrialization, the greater the investment had to be to bring that country up to the level of the more advanced nations.

In order to get the investment funds they needed, Asian countries depended either on loans or on the export of agricultural goods or natural resources: cocoa, tea, spices, timber, rubber, and copper and other minerals. Throughout most of the 1950s and 1960s, however, the prices of these items in world markets remained relatively low. In addition, periodic economic recessions in the West reduced the demand for these goods.

A shortage of experienced managers and trained workers also slowed economic development in much

Corazon Aquino, elected in 1986, was the first female president of the Philippines.

of Asia. To combat this problem, many Asian governments reformed their educational systems and established vocational schools and industrial training programs. Even so, time was needed for these changes to take effect.

Cooperating for development. In the 1970s, Asian countries began to find ways of dealing with their economic problems. For example, to ensure higher and more stable prices for their exports, many countries combined to form loose economic associations. In addition, Asian countries joined with other developing nations to work for greater concessions from such international loan agencies as the World Bank and the International Monetary Fund (IMF).

Also, Asian countries followed the example of such bodies as the European Union (EU), cooperating to develop common trade and economic policies. For example, the Association of Southeast Asian Nations **(ASEAN)** was organized in 1967 by the governments of Indonesia, Malaysia, the Philippines, Singapore, and Thailand. Its goals were to promote economic growth, social progress, and cultural development in the region as well as to encourage peace and security.

Brunei became a member of ASEAN in 1984 and Vietnam in 1995.

The organization holds regular summit meetings to discuss ways to encourage trade and to handle the problems associated with economic development. In 1996 three more nations—Myanmar, Laos, and Cambodia—joined ASEAN as observer nations. This was a first step toward their full membership in the organization.

Many Asian nations, however, have attempted to spur economic growth through greater government control. Some Asian governments have nationalized certain key industries—oil in Indonesia, for example. By such actions they hoped to ensure the reinvestment of profits in the country's development. Many governments, to prevent interruptions in production, have passed laws limiting the organization of labor unions, or prohibiting strikes and other industrial actions. Such authoritarian measures, in some cases, have led to more rapid economic growth, but at the expense of individual rights and freedoms.

Economic expansion. By the 1990s, Asia's economic situation remained a mixed picture.

The containers stacked on the deck of this Japanese freighter hold just a fraction of the billions of dollars' worth of goods that the United States imports every year from Asian countries.

While some Asian countries had made only limited advances toward economic development, others had made significant progress. Indeed, some countries—most notably those that gave strong support to free enterprise—enjoyed remarkable success. Japan, for example, ranked as one of the world's major economic powers, with Japanese trade and investment contributing significantly to the economic growth of the whole Asian region. South Korea, Taiwan, Singapore, and Hong Kong—known collectively as the **"Four Tigers"**—also played an increasingly important role in the region as well as in the global economy.

In fact, by the mid-1990s, Asia in general had become a region of such powerful economic expansion that observers frequently referred to "the Asian miracle." Many Asian nations were growing at annual rates of 6 to 10 percent. China, an especially dramatic example, has quadrupled its gross national product in the past two decades. Furthermore, although millions of Asia's people still lived in poverty, the number of poor people in East and Southeast Asia had decreased by more than 50 percent between 1975 and 1995.

Nevertheless, there are significant problems in the region, including political instability, overpopulation, and a growing gap between rich and poor. In 1997 the financial crisis in Thailand began to spread to neighboring nations, raising concerns that the Asian miracle was coming to an end.

How quickly Asia will recover from this financial crisis, and how widespread its effects will be, is open to question. However, there seems to be no question about the Pacific region's continuing—and increasingly important—role in the world economy. Indeed, many observers feel that, just as the 1900s were called the American Century, the next 100 years will be the Asian Century. The full impact of Asia's economic growth and development on the global economy is still yet to be seen.

Asian Cultural Diffusion

For hundreds of years, Asia has exercised an incredibly powerful influence on the West. The ancient religions, philosophies, and martial arts of China and Japan have long fascinated many Westerners. Exhibits of Asian porcelain, carpets, manuscripts, and other arts and crafts have drawn huge crowds to Western art galleries. More recently, Asia has exerted an economic influence on Western life by bringing about a change in the buying habits of Western consumers. For example, Asian-made radios, computers, cameras, video equipment, and automobiles, by and large, have dominated world markets over the past decade. Further, many "Western-made" appliances were indeed constructed in the West—but from Asian components.

This economic competition from Asia has both alarmed and intrigued Western business leaders. Since the late 1970s, Western economists have traveled throughout Japan, trying to discover why Japanese goods compete so well in world markets. Many economists have suggested that the answer lies in the cooperative relationship between management and workers. Others have noted that government assistance and low-interest business development loans enable Japanese companies to buy the latest machinery. Still others have pointed out that the Japanese educational system emphasizes the study of science and math. This focus has helped produce a force of scientists and engineers who have been able to develop better, more competitive products. Whatever the answer, most American business schools have deemed that the Japanese approach to management is worthy of extensive study.

Asian thought has also influenced the West, especially since the end of World War II. For example, Mohandas Gandhi's ideas about nonviolent resistance had a powerful impact on the leaders of the civil rights movement in the United States during the 1960s.

At one time, many people believed that because of the significant cultural differences between East and West, mutual understanding was all but impossible. Asians would never understand western society, nor would Westerners ever comprehend the ways of Asian society. However, in the 1980s and 1990s, greater understanding has developed. This understanding certainly will continue to improve as Pacific economic powers such as Japan, South Korea, Singapore, Hong Kong, and Taiwan play an even greater role in the world economy.

Section 5 Review

1. **Define** ASEAN, "Four Tigers"
2. **Classifying Ideas** List three factors that contributed to the development of authoritarian government in Asia.
3. **Analyzing Ideas** What problems have Asian nations faced in bringing about industrial development?
4. **Interpreting Ideas** How have Asian ideas influenced life in the West?

Chapter 16 Review

A.D. 1949
• Communists take over China.
• Indonesia gains independence.

A.D. 1950–1964
Nehru serves as prime minister of India.

A.D. 1942 A.D. 1946 A.D. 1950 A.D. 1954 A.D. 1958 A.D. 1962

A.D. 1946
The U.S. grants independence to the Philippines.

A.D. 1947
India gains independence.

A.D. 1950–1953
Korean War is fought.

A.D. 1954
Geneva Accords divide Vietnam at the 17th parallel.

A.D. 1958
Great Leap Forward begins.

Chapter Summary

The following list contains the key concepts you have learned about the nations of Asia between the end of World War II and the present.

1. The period following World War II was a time of conflict and tension for many Asian nations.
2. As India became independent of British rule, the subcontinent was partitioned. The nation continued to face internal conflict and economic problems.
3. Pakistan faced problems similar to India's. In addition, Pakistan was divided into two parts. After a civil war, East Pakistan became Bangladesh.
4. The victory of Mao Zedong in 1949 brought the Communist Party to power in China. The Chinese Nationalists, led by Chiang Kaishek, fled to the island of Taiwan, off the coast of China.
5. The Communists implemented several plans to modernize their vast nation, including the Great Leap Forward. After Mao's death, more moderate leaders took over.
6. Korea was divided after World War II. When the communist state of North Korea invaded South Korea in 1950, it was repulsed by UN forces, and an armistice was eventually signed.
7. Japan achieved economic success in the postwar period. Trade imbalances with the United States have caused friction between the two nations.
8. Japan has experienced internal political problems caused by political scandals in the last decade.
9. In the Philippines, Indonesia, Malaysia, and Singapore, economic development was fostered by strong central governments. Despite social problems, these nations began a process of industrialization and economic growth.
10. Decades of conflict in Vietnam involved the United States as well as the Asian nations of Laos and Cambodia. North Vietnam conquered South Vietnam and united the nation in the mid-1970s.
11. Thailand struggled politically and grew economically, but in recent years the country has experienced economic troubles.
12. The difficulties of economic development led many Asian nations to rely on strong central governments. However, in the last decades Asian nations have begun to cooperate for the sake of economic development. Asia has been a continuing economic influence on the West.

Reviewing Important Terms

On a separate sheet of paper, supply the term that correctly completes each statement.

1. A(n) _____ _____ is an economic system in which private companies own some industries while the government owns the rest.
2. India followed a policy of _____, refusing to ally itself with either the United States or the Soviet Union.
3. According to the _____ _____, if South Vietnam fell to communism, other nations of Southeast Asia would follow.

Developing Critical Thinking Skills

1. **Understanding Ideas** What economic and social problems did India face after achieving independence?
2. **Analyzing Primary Sources** Below is the preamble to the Indian Constitution. Read this selection, and answer the questions that follow:

"We, the people of India, having solemnly resolved to constitute India into a sovereign democratic republic and to secure to all its citizens:
JUSTICE—social, economic, and political;
LIBERTY of thought, expression, belief, faith, and worship;
EQUALITY of status and of opportunity; and to promote . . .
FRATERNITY assuring the dignity of the individual and the unity of the Nation,
. . . do HEREBY ADOPT, ENACT AND GIVE TO OURSELVES THIS CONSTITUTION."

(a) What type of government does the constitution promise to the Indian people? (b) What ideals does it swear to uphold? (c) How do these ideals compare with those stated in the preamble to the United States Constitution?

A.D. 1966–1969
Cultural Revolution takes place.

A.D. 1976
• Mao Zedong dies.
• Vietnam is unified.

A.D. 1984
Indian troops storm the Golden Temple.

A.D. 1966   A.D. 1970   A.D. 1974   A.D. 1978   A.D. 1982   A.D. 1986

A.D. 1965
Pakistan and India go to war.

A.D. 1967
ASEAN is formed.

A.D. 1971
Bangladesh becomes independent from Pakistan.

A.D. 1979
United States gives mainland China diplomatic recognition.

A.D. 1986
Corazon Aquino is elected president of the Philippines.

3. **Summarizing Ideas** What political and economic policies did the Communists bring about in China after they took over the government?
4. **Analyzing Ideas** How did events in Tiananmen Square affect China's foreign relations?
5. **Evaluating Ideas** (a) Explain how Japan became a powerful industrial nation. (b) What changes and problems came about as a result of this industrialization of Japan?
6. **Determining Cause and Effect** (a) What were the causes of the Vietnam War? (b) How did the United States become involved in the Vietnam War? (c) What were the results, both for Southeast Asian nations and for the United States?
7. **Classifying Ideas** List reasons for past hostilities between the following countries: (a) the Soviet Union and China; (b) India and Pakistan; (c) Pakistan and Bangladesh.
8. **Comparing Ideas** (a) How did the Korean War differ from the Vietnam War in causes and results? (b) How were the two conflicts similar? (c) What roles did the United States and the People's Republic of China play in each of these wars?

Relating Geography to History
Turn to the map of Asia on page 503. (a) How many miles separate Taiwan from the People's Republic of China? (b) How many kilometers? (c) Why is Japan a strategic location for defense of American interests in the Pacific?

Relating Past to Present
1. On a sheet of paper, list evidence that your community has contact with the nations of Asia. For example, observe the cars on a busy street. How many of them are Japanese? Can you buy a shirt made of Indian cotton or a book of Chinese or Japanese poetry? Using this information, write a short essay discussing Asia's influence on the Western world.
2. Use your school or public library to find articles on China today. Then prepare a report that explains how the Communists have changed traditional Chinese society, what economic problems still exist in China, and what modern life is like in China.

Applying History Study Skills
Before completing this activity, review Building History Study Skills on page 504.

Read the following statement from the writings of Mao Zedong. After reading the statement, identify any fallacies in reasoning.

"This leadership of the poor peasants is extremely necessary. Without the poor peasants there can be no revolution. To reject them is to reject the revolution. To attack them is to attack the revolution. From beginning to end, the general direction they have given the revolution has never been wrong. They have hurt the dignity of the local bullies and evil gentry. They have knocked down the big and small local bullies and evil gentry and trampled them underfoot. Many of their deeds in the period of revolution, described as 'going too far,' were in fact dictated by the very needs of the revolution."

▶ internet**connect**

Search the Internet through the HRW Web site for more information on the major urban centers of Southeast Asia. Construct a chart to compare these cities. Include information on population, places of interest, and major economic activities.

GO TO: go.hrw.com
KEYWORD: SC0 SE Asia

Building Your Portfolio
1. **Writing a Report** Conduct research on the Vietnam War and answer the following questions: (a) What were the goals of Ho Chi Minh between 1945 and 1954? (b) Why did the peasants support the Viet Cong? (c) What was the final outcome of the war? Place the report in your portfolio.
2. **Analyzing Literature** One way to gain insight into a culture is to read its literature. Present a short report to the class on a modern novel by a Chinese, Japanese, or Indian author. Tell the class how the book helped you understand the culture of China, Japan, or India. Place your notes or an audiotape of your report in your portfolio.

Africa and the Middle East Since 1945

A.D. **1945–the present**

A.D. **1945–the present**

3.7 million B.C.   4000 B.C.   A.D. 2100

PLACE

Africa and the Middle East

ARCTIC OCEAN

NORTH
AMERICA

EUROPE

ASIA

PACIFIC
OCEAN

AFRICA

Equator

SOUTH
AMERICA

INDIAN
OCEAN

AUSTRALIA

PACIFIC
OCEAN

ATLANTIC
OCEAN

ANTARCTICA

Africa

Middle
East

African National Congress rally

Significance

Like World War I, World War II was a watershed in the history of Africa and the Middle East. After the war, nationalism grew at a faster pace than ever. In Africa more radical younger leaders came to the fore, demanding complete self-government and eventually independence from the European colonial powers. The Middle East also saw the emergence of new leaders determined to break free from European domination once and for all. Many of the new nations, however, remained tied economically to the former colonial powers.

Terms to Define

Pan-Africanism	*colons*
CPP	FLN
Mau Mau	*kibbutz*
apartheid	PLO
MPLA	shuttle diplomacy
UNITA	Camp David Accords
desertification	*intifada*
negritude	petrodollars

People to Identify

Kwame Nkrumah	David Ben-Gurion
Jomo Kenyatta	Chaim Weizmann
Robert Mugabe	King Farouk
Sékou Touré	Gamal Abdel Nasser
Nelson Mandela	Adnan Menderes
F.W. de Klerk	Anwar Sadat
Jerry Rawlings	Ayatollah Khomeini
Ibrahim Babangida	Hafiz Asad
Laurent Kabila	Saddam Hussein
Wole Soyinka	

Places to Locate

Ghana	Persian Gulf
Kenya	Beirut
Zimbabwe	Bahrain
South Africa	Qatar
Horn of Africa	United Arab Emirates
Rwanda	Oman
Aswan High Dam	Tehran

Chapter Theme Questions

- **Politics and Law** How might the process used by a country to achieve its independence affect its subsequent history?
- **Social Relations** How might the presence of different ethnic groups within a country affect the political history of that country?
- **Economics** How might the discovery of an important resource in a region affect that area's history?

D uring the 1960s, Obafemi Awolowo, a political leader from western Nigeria, reflected on how his newly independent homeland should view human rights:

   Every member of any human association has rights, intangible though they are, which are sacred and inalienable, and which must be protected against any invasion, at all costs. In a State, such rights are more carefully and elaborately spelt out, and are termed fundamental human rights. These rights are also regarded as inalienable because they are inherent in, not acquired by, man. Only acquired rights are alienable. . . .

   It is, therefore, of exceeding importance that in every written constitution, fundamental human rights should be entrenched, and provisions for their inviolable protection and impartial enforcement should also be clearly set out and entrenched.

Awolowo was only one of many African and Middle Eastern leaders who worked to lead newly independent nations after 1945.

African Independence After World War II

Focus Questions

- What were the characteristics of African nationalism after World War II?
- How did colonial rule end in Ghana, Kenya, and British central Africa?
- How did the end of colonial rule in the French and Belgian colonies differ from what occurred in the British colonies?
- How did South Africa's experience of colonialism and independence differ from that of other nations of Africa?

World War II was a turning point in the history of Africa. During the war, thousands of Africans served in the armies of the European colonial powers, both inside and outside Africa. The continent itself became a supply route between the Allies and the rest of the world. During the war, the Allied powers also seemed to imply the end of colonial rule in declarations such as the Atlantic Charter. When the war ended, many Africans were no longer satisfied with the status quo, and a new wave of nationalism began to gain strength throughout the continent. Exhausted and nearly bankrupted by the war, most of the old colonial powers soon realized that independence was inevitable. Within a few short decades, the political map of Africa was transformed as colony after colony achieved independence. By the 1990s, all Africa was free from colonial rule.

African Nationalism

Before 1945, talk of nationalism in Africa was largely confined to a few Africans who had been particularly affected by their interaction with Europeans. In the British colonies of West Africa, for example, families of African merchants, along with chiefs from the interior, had long engaged in trade and other business relationships with Europeans. Among these few, many had received an education in Europe or the United States. Some of these individuals worked as missionaries, spreading Christianity in Africa. Others became civil servants. Through such contacts, some became convinced that only by forming modern nations, like those of Europe, could African peoples become free and join in the life of the modern world.

As members of a privileged group, however, many of these Western-educated Africans did not always feel at ease with their own people and did not seek broad popular support. Nor were their demands very great. Generally, they called simply for wider participation in the colonial governments. At the same time, because of their African heritage, they were excluded from European society. Consequently, before the war, these Africans had little influence on colonial policy.

In the 1930s, however, a new brand of African nationalism emerged. During the Great Depression, most colonial governments cut back on wages for African civil servants. This angered many and fueled anticolonial sentiment. The 1936 Italian invasion and conquest of Ethiopia, which had been the last great independent African state, also shocked and angered Africans throughout the continent. A younger, more radical generation of African nationalists began to call for complete self-government, if not yet complete independence.

This second generation of African nationalists was also heavily influenced by the Pan-African movement. **Pan-Africanism** promoted the cultural unity of people of African heritage in their mutual struggle for freedom. The Pan-African movement began among people of African descent in North America and the West Indies. It gained strength particularly in the first half of the 1900s under Marcus Garvey of Jamaica and African American educator W. E. B. Du Bois. Their aim was to win equality for black people in all parts of the world. Ending colonial rule in Africa was central to this aim.

Garvey's cry of "Africa for the Africans at Home and Abroad" alarmed colonial powers. It also drew many young Africans to the cause. For example, delegates to the 1945 Pan-African Congress in Manchester, England, included Kwame Nkrumah (en·KROO·muh) of the Gold Coast, Jomo Kenyatta of Kenya, and Hastings Banda of Nyasaland (now Malawi). They all became leaders of independence movements in their countries.

The events of World War II also contributed to the growth of a more popular African nationalism. During the war, Africa once again became a major supplier of men and matériel for the Allied war effort. Some 80,000 Africans, for example, served in France's armies in Europe, while Great Britain recruited or drafted hundreds of thousands of Africans from its colonies to help the Allies win the war. These Africans, many of whom served outside of Africa, were introduced to a larger world and new ideas. At the same time, declarations such as the Atlantic Charter seemed to promise self-determination for all peoples after the war. Such declarations or statements raised expectations among many Africans that their demands for greater freedom would soon be met.

Despite the expectations of African nationalists immediately after World War II, the colonial powers did not plan to give up their empires in Africa any time soon. Consequently, the struggle for national independence in Africa took many forms. Some colonies followed a sometimes slow constitutional process, with popular elections and a peaceful transfer of power. Other colonies suffered lengthy "wars of national liberation." The specific form of the independence effort depended on the particular experience of imperialism in that part of Africa.

Winds of Change in British Africa

In February 1960, British prime minister Harold Macmillan addressed the South African Parliament.

African Independence, 1946–1993

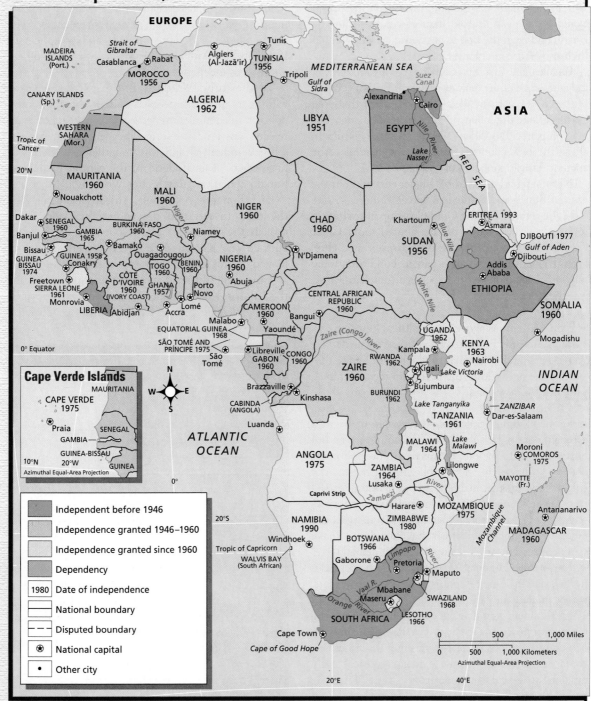

Map Legend

- Independent before 1946
- Independence granted 1946–1960
- Independence granted since 1960
- Dependency
- 1980 — Date of independence
- National boundary
- --- Disputed boundary
- ⊛ National capital
- • Other city

Cape Verde Islands
MAURITANIA
CAPE VERDE 1975
Praia
GAMBIA
SENEGAL
GUINEA-BISSAU
GUINEA
10°N 20°W
Azimuthal Equal-Area Projection

Learning from Maps Many former African colonies have become independent nations since 1946.

❓ **Region** What country remained a dependency in 1993?

Somewhat to the dismay of his listeners who represented both houses of Parliament, he warned that a "wind of change" was sweeping through Africa that would blow away the old days of colonialism. The British had been the first to acknowledge this wind in their own African colonies.

Ghana. The first Sub-Saharan colony to achieve independence under majority rule was Britain's colony of the Gold Coast, in West Africa. In 1957 the Gold Coast became the independent nation of Ghana. (See map on page 535.) Ghana's leader, Kwame Nkrumah, chose the new country's name to commemorate the ancient African kingdom of Ghana.

Nkrumah had received his higher education in the United States and worked in Great Britain. In late 1947, he returned to the Gold Coast upon invitation to be general secretary of the United Gold Coast Convention, a political party of the westernized elite. From this post, Nkrumah began to build a national following. He believed that political unity in Africa was the key to success.

❝African unity is above all a political kingdom, which can only be gained by political means. The social and economic development of Africa will come only within the political kingdom, not the other way around.❞

Soon Nkrumah called on the people to begin a campaign of civil disobedience, including strikes and boycotts of British goods. In this new, more politically charged atmosphere, riots broke out in Accra, the colony's capital city, in 1948. Soon the rioting spread to other towns, and it took the colonial authorities several days to restore order. The Accra riots did much to convince the British that they should make some concessions to African nationalist demands.

Meanwhile, Nkrumah's radical tactics and demands had alarmed the more conservative African leaders, who expelled him from his post. Consequently, in 1949 Nkrumah founded his own political party, the Convention People's Party **(CPP)**, dedicated to achieving immediate self-government. Under his guidance, the CPP became a major political party designed to appeal to the masses.

Under almost constant pressure from the CPP, in 1951 the British colonial authorities agreed to hold a national election in the Gold Coast. Nkrumah's party won a huge victory, but Nkrumah continued to pressure the British for complete independence. Britain finally granted Ghana full sovereignty in 1957.

Kenya. The example of Ghana became an inspiration to African nationalists in other colonies. In some, however, particularly those with significant numbers of white settlers, the movement toward independence was more difficult and complicated. Kenya in East Africa, for example, took a very different road to independence.

By the early 1950s, the British government was willing to give the peoples of East Africa limited political freedom. White settlers in the area, however, rejected any kind of reform. They feared that African self-government would threaten their ownership of huge tracts of fertile land in the central highlands. Rapid population growth after World War II had led to land shortages. As a result, Africans had demanded the right to settle in the central highlands even though they were not allowed to own land there. Further, the Kikuyu, Kenya's largest ethnic group, looked on this area as their ancestral homeland.

Land ownership had an almost mystical quality for the Kikuyu. Kikuyu leader Jomo Kenyatta described the Kikuyu feeling about land this way:

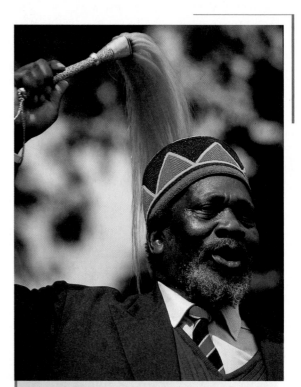

Jomo Kenyatta, who was jailed on charges of leading the Kenyan Mau Mau rebellion of 1952, became the prime minister of Kenya in 1963 and president a year later.

"It is the key to the people's life; it secures them that peaceful tillage [cultivation] of the soil which supplies their material needs and enables them to perform their magic and traditional ceremonies in undisturbed serenity."

The continued exclusion of the Kikuyu from the central highlands soon became a source of tension. Then, in the early 1950s, this tension actually exploded into violence.

In a four-year guerrilla campaign, the "Land and Freedom" army, a secret Kikuyu organization that became popularly known as the **Mau Mau**, caused terror and destruction in the central highlands. During the campaign, the Mau Mau killed about 100 Europeans and some 2,000 Africans loyal to the British government. The British took military actions to suppress the movement. More than 11,500 Kikuyu were killed during or as a result of the war. Thousands were jailed in detention camps. Eventually, the British succeeded in suppressing the Mau Mau and restoring order in Kenya, but they could not put down the drive for Kenyan independence.

In 1961 Kenyatta, who had been jailed as a suspected leader of the Mau Mau, was released. He emerged from prison as the leader of the independence movement. His popularity and forceful leadership helped overcome ethnic rivalries and brought about a shared sense of Kenyan nationalism. Kenyatta won an easy victory in national elections held in May 1963. Later that year, Kenya gained its independence, and Kenyatta became the first prime minister of the new nation. In 1964 he became president, a position he held until his death in 1978.

British central Africa. Developments in Britain's colonies in central Africa—Southern Rhodesia (present-day Zimbabwe), Northern Rhodesia (present-day Zambia), and Nyasaland (present-day Malawi)—also represented an unusual example of both guerrilla warfare and constitutional change. Southern Rhodesia's large white population had achieved internal self-government in the 1920s. The other two territories were governed by Britain.

After World War II, the settlers of Southern Rhodesia combined efforts with the much smaller settler population of Northern Rhodesia to convince the British government to allow the creation of a Central African federation. The British included the small protectorate of Nyasaland, but the Africans who lived there strongly opposed it. As in their other colonies, the British hoped to create a multiracial state. This

policy, however, was opposed by the white settlers, who were favored by imperial policies in the 1950s.

Established as a 10-year experiment in 1953, the Federation of Rhodesia and Nyasaland was always bitterly opposed by African nationalist leaders. They saw the Federation as a means by which the white settlers could maintain their control over the black majority populations of the three territories. Throughout the life of the Federation, African nationalism continued to develop. At the end of the 10-year trial period, in 1963, the African majorities in Northern Rhodesia and Nyasaland voted to withdraw from the Federation. In 1964 the two colonies became the independent states of Zambia and Malawi under majority African rule. Britain also tried to force progress toward majority rule on Southern Rhodesia, but the white population led by Prime Minister Ian Smith refused to cooperate.

In 1965 Smith issued the Unilateral Declaration of Independence (UDI) and proclaimed the independent state of Rhodesia. Great Britain and the rest of the world refused to accept Smith's act, insisting that it was illegal, and reduced or cut off trade relations. Although the Smith government was isolated internationally, it still refused to initiate reforms. Consequently, as happened in the neighboring Portuguese colonies, a guerrilla war began.

Little success was achieved in the early years of fighting. However, when Angola and Mozambique became independent from Portugal in 1975, the liberation forces gained a military advantage. They now had countries that were friendly to their cause located in southern Africa. Under the leadership of Robert Mugabe and Joshua Nkomo, the African forces intensified their attacks and succeeded in disrupting the economy of Rhodesia.

As the war became increasingly unpopular among the white population, Smith was forced to seek a solution. Eventually, he worked with moderate African leaders to form a new government under African leadership that would continue to guarantee the privileged status of whites. Even this was not enough to stop the ongoing guerrilla war. Still under enormous pressure, the Rhodesian government finally agreed to hold free elections open to all parties, including the liberation leaders. In these 1980 elections, Robert Mugabe, considered the most radical of the candidates, was the victor.

In April 1980, Rhodesia became the new nation of Zimbabwe—a name taken from the ancient southern African kingdom of Great Zimbabwe. After years of civil war, Zimbabwe's future seemed settled, and the government turned its energies to economic recovery.

The French Colonies

While the British decided to compromise with the demands of African nationalists fairly quickly and easily, in French colonial territories a different pattern emerged. As with other parts of Africa, World War II marked a turning point in France's African colonies.

Before World War II, most of France's African colonies had been organized in two administrative units, French West Africa and French Equatorial Africa. The colonial governors of French West Africa remained loyal to Vichy during the war. French Equatorial Africa, however, led by the governor of Chad, Felix Eboué, the first black man to become a colonial governor, declared its support for the Free French forces of General de Gaulle. In 1944, with de Gaulle's approval, the governors of French Equatorial Africa met in Brazzaville to announce more liberal policies. The Brazzaville Declaration, which outlined these reforms, however, also made it clear that the French Empire would continue and that the colonies could not expect independence.

Following the Allied victory, France itself adopted a new constitution. Under this constitution, the French Empire was transformed into the French Union. The vote was extended to more Africans, who were now eligible to elect some 20 African representatives to the French National Assembly in Paris. Other Africans were also elected to the Assembly of the French Union.

Although this system provided many Africans with political experience, it fell short of real independence. Many Africans felt that their interests were second to those of France. In response, African leaders such as Léopold Senghor of Senegal, Felix Houphouet-Boigny (oo·FWAY BWAH·nyuh) of the Côte d'Ivoire, and Sékou Touré (too·RAY) of Guinea, began to develop the same kind of popular parties that were emerging in British colonies. At first the new political parties only sought self-government within the French Union. As it became increasingly clear that France was not interested in granting anything but limited control over the colonies, however, many African nationalists became more radical in their demands.

In 1958 Charles de Gaulle, the new French president, offered the African colonies a choice. They could remain independent within the French Community (the newly transformed French Union), subject to French control of their foreign affairs, or they could become totally independent. Those colonies that chose to remain within the French Community would continue to receive aid from France. Those that chose independence would be immediately cut off from all aid and contacts with France.

Only Guinea, under Sékou Touré, chose complete independence. The others accepted de Gaulle's new French Community. As de Gaulle had warned, Guinea was immediately isolated from the rest of the French Community, both politically and economically. However, in 1960 those African colonies that accepted membership in the French Community were granted the very independence that Touré had insisted on, but without sacrificing their close economic and political ties to France.

The Belgian Congo

Perhaps the most traumatic transition to independence occurred in the Belgian Congo. (The Belgian Congo later became Zaire, which was renamed the Democratic Republic of the Congo in 1997.) Belgium, which opposed independence because of the colony's great wealth in timber and mineral resources, provided few opportunities for Africans to develop their skills in government.

The Congo was home to many different groups of people, speaking different languages and with different customs. Under Belgian rule, these differences did not diminish but were reinforced. During World War II,

The Congo was a Belgian colony from 1908 until 1960. Violence broke out across the country after independence. Here UN troops arrive in the Congo in 1961.

however, as the local economy worked harder to produce goods for the war effort, many Congolese began to leave their villages and flock to the cities. There they came in contact with other Congolese and began to establish cultural clubs. In the 1950s, events in neighboring British and French colonies finally introduced ideas of nationalism into the Congo. After 1955 the Belgian authorities even allowed the development of new political parties. Most of the new parties remained committed to their local regions, but a few had programs of national unity for all the Congo.

At first the Belgian government resisted nationalist demands. They proposed a gradual 30-year timetable to prepare the Congo for independence. In 1959, however, the pressures of new national ideas and dissatisfaction with Belgian colonial rule resulted in rioting in the capital city of Léopoldville. Alarmed by the violence and aware of developments in the rest of colonial Africa, Belgian authorities reversed their former policy. In January 1960, they announced that the Congo would become independent in six months—on June 30, 1960.

African leaders were not prepared for independence to come so quickly. Many different political parties, all representing different ethnic communities, geographical regions, or political beliefs, participated in the first elections. Patrice Lumumba (luh·MUHM·buh), an outspoken critic of European influence, became premier. Joseph Kasavubu (kah·sah·VOO·boo), the leader of the second-largest party and Lumumba's chief political rival, became president. Fearful of Lumumba's anti-European stance, the vast majority of Belgian technicians and experts left the country almost immediately. With few trained Africans to replace them, the Congo soon descended into chaos.

In July 1960, Congolese soldiers mutinied against their Belgian officers. A period of violence aimed mostly at white people followed. To make matters worse, the copper-rich province of Katanga, led by Moise Tshombe (CHAWM·be), seceded from the Congo. As civil war broke out, first Belgium and then the United Nations intervened. On the invitation of Kasavubu, the Congolese army, under Colonel Joseph Mobutu, overthrew Lumumba, who was assassinated in 1961. Katanga was also brought back into the republic. Fighting wracked the country until 1965, however, when Mobutu himself took full control. Mobutu gradually established a ruthless military dictatorship that lasted into the 1990s. The length of his rule was partly due to the effects of the Cold War, in which Mobutu was supported by the Western

powers as a counterbalance to African countries that leaned toward the Eastern bloc. In the 1970s, he pursued a policy of Africanization, changing the name of the country to Zaire and himself taking the African name Mobutu Sese Seko.

The Portuguese Colonies

While many African nations were winning their independence, the Portuguese government continued to oppose independence for its colonies. In desperation, African leaders in Portuguese West Africa, Portuguese Guinea, and Portuguese East Africa organized "liberation armies" to fight for freedom. In a series of long, bloody wars, they gained control of much of the countryside.

These wars continued until 1974, when the military staged a coup in Portugal and announced that Portugal would withdraw from Africa. Within months of the announcement, in 1974 and 1975, Portuguese Guinea, Portuguese West Africa, and Portuguese East Africa—present-day Guinea-Bissau, Angola, and Mozambique, respectively—became independent. The establishment of African nationalist governments in these countries also put enormous pressure on the last holdout of minority white rule in Africa, the Republic of South Africa.

South Africa

South Africa's experience differed from that of any other African nation. In 1910 four territories had come together to form the Union of South Africa: the British territories of Cape Colony and Natal and the former Boer republics of the Transvaal and the Orange Free State, which had been defeated in the recent Boer War and brought under British rule. The new Union of South Africa was a white-ruled nation with dominion status. Although linked to Great Britain in foreign affairs, the dominion ruled itself internally as it saw fit.

Relying on its resources of gold, diamonds, and cheap labor, South Africa experienced an industrial revolution in the early 1900s. Its industrialization was based on the labor of black Africans, who vastly outnumbered whites. Even so, blacks were excluded almost totally from the benefits of South Africa's economic success.

Apartheid. Before World War II, English-speaking whites had dominated the government. By custom, whites and nonwhites were segregated socially. Over time, an unofficial system of separate public facilities for whites and nonwhites developed. Moreover, nonwhites were given few educational opportunities and were kept out of better jobs. Since 1911 employment opportunities for the nonwhite populations had been restricted by law to low-paying manual labor. In addition, the Land Act of 1913 and subsequent amendments restricted Africans, who made up approximately 75 percent of the population, to only 10 percent of the land. Then in 1948, the National Party, which was dominated by the white, Afrikaans-speaking descendants of the original Dutch settlers, came to power in South Africa. The Afrikaners quickly transformed this unofficial system of social segregation and economic exploitation into government policy.

This policy became known as **apartheid**—the Afrikaans word for apartness. It consisted of a number of laws that separated the races in every aspect of life. These laws were a way to legally establish white supremacy in the country. One law called for all people to be classified by race: Bantu (black), Colored (mixed race), Asian, or White. Another law established where each of the four races could live. A third law banned intermarriage between the races. A fourth required all nonwhites to carry an identity pass when traveling outside their designated areas. Other laws established different pay scales for whites and nonwhites.

Apartheid also involved the founding of separate tribal states, known as homelands or Bantustans, for Africans. After a brief period of self-government, these homelands would become completely independent. Afrikaner leaders cited the homelands program to support their claim that the intent of apartheid was that each race would prosper if developed separately. However, the homelands were located in the most barren areas of the country and had few natural resources. Even after independence, the homelands would remain completely dependent on South Africa.

Protests against apartheid. Some organizations had fought racial discrimination in South Africa long before apartheid was established. The African National Congress (ANC)—the best-known antiapartheid group—was founded in 1912. In the 1950s, the ANC launched a campaign of civil disobedience in which ANC members openly violated apartheid laws. The response of the South African government to this campaign of civil disobedience was swift and brutal. In 1960 police opened fire on a peaceful demonstration in the town of Sharpeville, leaving more than 60 dead and hundreds wounded. As world opinion condemned the Sharpeville massacre, in 1961 Prime Minister Hendrik Verwoerd, one of the primary architects of apartheid, decided to proclaim South Africa a republic and to withdraw from the British Commonwealth.

After Sharpeville some ANC leaders, the black lawyer Nelson Mandela among them, felt that in self-defense they would have to confront violence with violence. In response the government banned the ANC in 1960. Then in 1962, Mandela and other ANC leaders were arrested. Charged with treason and found guilty, they all received life jail terms.

Despite the ban and the loss of its leaders, the ANC continued to operate, primarily from bases outside South Africa. In addition, Desmond Tutu, Steve Biko, and other black leaders continued to speak out against the repressive apartheid laws. Some, such as Biko, paid with their lives. An increasing number of white South Africans, too, became involved in the antiapartheid movement. Helen Suzman, for example, used her position as a member of parliament to criticize the government's policies. However, hers was very much a lone voice in the legislature.

In the meantime, the government proceeded with its policy of repression. In 1976, schoolchildren in Soweto, a black township near Johannesburg, marched peacefully in protest against a new law enforcing the use of Afrikaans in all South African schools. They were met by police who opened fire, killing many. Over the next months, outraged Africans rioted all over the country. About 600 people, most of them black, were killed in the violence. After the Soweto riots, many in South Africa were no longer willing to wait peacefully for change.

In the 1980s, faced with growing protests both inside South Africa and from abroad, the South African government began to retreat from its strict apartheid policies. Constitutional reforms gave some political voice to Colored and Asian South Africans. Black Africans, however, were still denied any political participation, and civil strife continued. Meanwhile, the international community imposed economic sanctions on South Africa, pressuring the country to change its racist policies.

A change of direction. In September 1989, the pace of change in South Africa quickened with the election of F. W. de Klerk as president. De Klerk lifted a 30-year ban on antiapartheid rallies and legalized the ANC and other banned organizations. He also ordered the release of Nelson Mandela in February 1990. In a speech at Capetown celebrating his freedom, Mandela repeated the words he had spoken during his trial:

South Africans stood in long lines as the first all-race South African election took place in April 1994.

Section 1 Review

1. **Define** Pan-Africanism, CPP, Mau Mau, apartheid
2. **Identify** Kwame Nkrumah, Jomo Kenyatta, Robert Mugabe, Sékou Touré, Nelson Mandela, F. W. de Klerk
3. **Locate and Explain the Significance** Ghana, Kenya, Zimbabwe, South Africa
4. **Understanding Ideas** Describe how African nationalism began to emerge after World War II.
5. **Summarizing Ideas** Summarize the changes that occurred in Ghana, Kenya, and British central Africa after World War II.
6. **Analyzing Ideas** What factors led to the differing experiences of independence between the British colonies and those of the French and Belgians?
7. **Interpreting Ideas** How did apartheid shape South African history?

"I have fought against white domination, and I have fought against black domination. I have cherished the ideal of a democratic and free society in which all persons live together in harmony and with equal opportunities. It is an ideal which I hope to live for, and to see realized. But . . . if needs be, it is an ideal for which I am prepared to die.**"**

De Klerk expressed the hope that Mandela and other opposition leaders would meet with him to discuss ways to build a new South Africa. The promise of reform, however, did not end the violence and dissension. A fight for leadership of the black population erupted between the ANC and the largely Zulu Inkatha Freedom Party, led by Mangosuthu Gatsha Buthelezi. This fight resulted in the deaths of thousands of black South Africans in the 15 months following the legalization of the ANC. Moreover, not all whites supported de Klerk. Many Afrikaners left de Klerk's National Party and joined the much more right wing Conservatives.

Despite all these challenges, however, in 1994 South Africa held its first all-race elections. Nelson Mandela was elected by an overwhelming majority as the new president of a multiracial South Africa. Pursuing conciliatory policies, Mandela called on people to "heal the wounds of the past." As South Africa moved toward the end of the century, a new era of partnership and cooperation seemed to have replaced the dark era of apartheid.

Section 2

Africa Since Independence

Focus Questions

- **What challenges did newly independent African countries face?**
- **How did rivalry between the superpowers of the Cold War affect Africa?**
- **How did ethnic diversity contribute to political instability in independent African nations?**
- **In what ways did Africa experience a revival of African culture?**

After gaining independence, the new nations of Africa still faced many serious problems. While specific geographical and historical factors made each nation's problems unique, some common experiences also existed. Practically all the new nations struggled with economic difficulties. Ethnic tensions also racked some of the new countries. In addition, drought, disease, and the Cold War all took their toll on these new nations. Despite these problems, however, the independence that these nations experienced stimulated a revival and development of new cultural expressions throughout much of Africa.

Political and Economic Challenges

Despite the high hopes with which many Africans greeted independence, the years following the end of colonial rule were not easy ones. The new African leaders were inexperienced in politics and in running the new states they had inherited from the colonial rulers. As they failed to improve the lot of their peoples rapidly enough, in many countries, the military began to intervene. Soon most African countries were being ruled by military dictatorships. The case of Ghana provides a good example of the pattern that emerged in many African states after independence.

Ghana. The early years of Kwame Nkrumah's rule coincided with high prices on world markets for Ghana's main cash crop—cocoa. The prosperity that Ghana enjoyed at this time helped make Nkrumah very popular among the people. He exploited this popularity, however, building up a cult of personality around himself. Nkrumah's drive for absolute power resulted in a new constitution in 1964, which established Ghana as a one-party state. Any challenge to Nkrumah was the equivalent of treason. Yet people continued to criticize, especially after the fall of world prices for cocoa. This price drop, combined with government debt and corruption, caused the Ghanaian economy to collapse. Nkrumah responded by becoming more and more ruthless. His popularity declined rapidly, and in 1966, while on a visit to another country, he was ousted in a military coup.

Although few people in Ghana mourned Nkrumah's departure, the situation did not improve. Over the next 12 years, Ghana went back and forth between civilian and military rule. This political instability was matched by fluctuations in the economy, which remained tied to cocoa.

In 1979, just before an election designed to return the government to civilian rule, the military stepped in yet again. This takeover was led by Jerry Rawlings, a young air force pilot. Rawlings stated that the present military leaders were corrupt and inefficient and had to go. After public trials, a number of leading military officers were executed. Rawlings then allowed the elections to take place, and the country returned to civilian rule.

A little over a year later, however, Rawlings stepped in once again. He dissolved the civilian government, claiming that it was worse than the military junta it had replaced. Rawlings felt that Ghana should follow socialist policies. After two years of ever-worsening economic reports, he changed his opinion. In 1983 he put the country's economy on a course toward free enterprise. By 1990 Ghana's annual rate of economic growth was one of the highest in Africa.

This improvement in the economy, however, came at great cost to the Ghanaian people. They had to endure high taxes on imports, a sales tax, and an income tax. Subsidies on food and fuel were reduced, and the currency was devalued to stimulate exports. Ghanaians grew weary of continued economic measures and Rawlings' rigid government style. Demands for a return to civilian rule increased. In 1992 a new constitution was adopted, and civilian rule was established. Resigning from the military, Rawlings ran for the presidency and won.

Nigeria. While Ghana's experience following independence was similar to that of many African nations, some had to deal with special problems. Many of these problems were left over from the days of colonial rule. For example, new national boundaries often were artificial, drawn by the imperialist powers for their own convenience. In some cases, people of similar racial or cultural backgrounds were separated, while people of different heritages were grouped together. In some places, such as Nigeria, these problems soon led to civil war.

At the time of independence in 1960, Nigeria was a federation of three regions, each of which retained a large degree of local independence. A fourth region was created in 1963. Although this situation resulted in strong ethnic and regional differences in the country, the government hoped that this loose federation would prevent warfare among the various groups. It did not, however, prevent conflict.

In 1966 the military took over the government, but it could not overcome the tensions created by the ethnic and regional distrust. After independence, for example, the federal government's exploitation of major oil deposits, discovered in the late 1950s in the Niger Delta, had increased regional tensions. In 1967 the Eastern Region, home of the Ibo-speaking people, seceded from the federation and declared itself the independent Republic of Biafra. Nigeria plunged into civil war. After more than two years of war and the deaths of as many as several million Biafrans from starvation and disease, Biafra surrendered. Pursuing a policy of conciliation, the Nigerian government gradually restored stability to the country. Nevertheless, ethnicity and regionalism continued to be sensitive issues in Nigeria.

A democratically elected civilian government returned to Nigeria in 1979. At the same time, the country's oil wealth provided Nigerians with the opportunity to escape the poverty that threatened most other African nations. It also appeared that Nigeria might be the first African nation other than South Africa to achieve a high degree of industrialization.

In the 1980s, however, a drop in the international price of oil—the commodity that accounted for 95 percent of Nigeria's export revenues—caused Nigeria's economy to falter. In late 1983, military officers overthrew the civilian government and introduced strict new measures to turn the economy around. In 1983 and again in 1985, the government forced foreigners living illegally in Nigeria, many of them from Ghana, to leave the country.

This government proved very unpopular. In 1985, another military coup, this one led by Major General Ibrahim Babangida, had taken place. Babangida immediately introduced bold new reforms to restore economic and political stability. He renegotiated the country's foreign loans, applying for assistance from international financial organizations.

In 1992 Babangida fulfilled a promise to return the country to civilian rule. In the elections that followed, Moshood Abiola was elected president. Before he

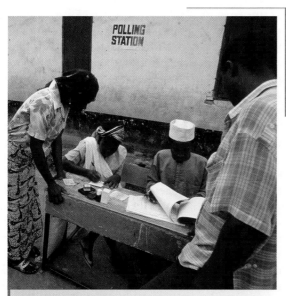

During the late 1980s, the government of President Ibrahim Babangida supported a return to civilian rule in Nigeria, leading to local elections in 1991, national legislative elections in 1992, and presidential elections in 1993. Nigerians are shown above voting in a 1992 election.

could be inaugurated, however, the military again intervened and declared the election results invalid. When Abiola declared himself president anyway, he was imprisoned. Nevertheless, pressures remained strong to return to civilian rule. In 1997 General Sani Abacha, the current military leader, scheduled elections for sometime in 1998. In mid-1998, however, both Abacha and Abiola died of natural causes. A new military strongman, General Abdulsalam Abubakar, took power, pledging to return the country to civilian rule in the near future.

Superpower Rivalries

Superpower rivalry complicated the efforts of new African nations to achieve peace and stability. As these nations sought financial and technical assistance from both the Soviet Union and the United States, they often found themselves caught up in the Cold War.

Angola. When civil war broke out in Angola after independence in 1975, the United States and the Soviet Union rushed arms and support to the rival factions. Soviet military advisers and Cuban troops supported the Marxist Popular Movement for the Liberation of Angola **(MPLA)**. The National Union for the Total Independence of Angola **(UNITA)** received aid from the United States. Fearing that the MPLA might assist Marxist rebels in Namibia, South Africa also supported UNITA. The MPLA eventually gained control, but about 50,000 Cuban troops stayed in Angola to help fight off continued attacks by UNITA.

For the next 12 years, Angola became a battleground for the Cold War between the United States and the Soviet Union. When tensions between the two superpowers eased, moves were made to end the civil war in Angola. A regional agreement that linked independence for Namibia with the withdrawal of Cuban troops from Angola was reached in 1988. In May 1991, the MPLA and UNITA hammered out a peace treaty that also called for free elections late in 1992. The continued hostility between MPLA and UNITA leaders, however, left the success of the treaty in question.

The Horn of Africa. Soviet-American rivalry was even more complex in the Horn of Africa, a strategic area that includes Ethiopia and Somalia. The Horn overlooks the Red Sea as well as the Indian Ocean sea-lanes to the oil-rich Persian Gulf. It is also an area of relative instability, characterized by frequent border disputes and local independence movements.

Although the United States had established a military base in Ethiopia in the 1950s, when the Ethiopian emperor Haile Selassie was overthrown in 1974, a Marxist regime came to power. To support the socialist governments in Ethiopia and in nearby Somalia, the Soviet Union provided military aid and advisers. Cuban troops were stationed in Ethiopia. Although the Soviet Union gained a temporary advantage, it had provided arms to two traditionally hostile neighbors. When Somalia invaded Ethiopia in 1977, the Soviets supported Ethiopia. Somalia was defeated in 1978 by Cuban troops with Soviet weapons, but guerrilla fighting in the region continued until 1988.

The topsy-turvy situation created by superpower rivalry demonstrated that African nations often preferred practical assistance to ideological commitments. This became even clearer in the 1980s and early 1990s, after the end of the Cold War. In 1984 a worldwide relief effort was initiated to help Ethiopia during a severe drought. Somalia, also devastated by drought, called on its Arab neighbors and the United States for aid. Despite financial support, in 1991 the military dictatorships in both Somalia and Ethiopia collapsed. Their overthrow, however, only brought more problems.

Somalia descended into civil war as different clans and rival warlords fought for power. The fighting prevented humanitarian aid from reaching victims of the drought. Consequently, at the urging of the United States, in 1992 an international force, under the authority of the United Nations, intervened in Somalia. Unable to stop the bloodshed, the American-led force withdrew from the country in frustration in 1994.

Meanwhile Eritrea, a northern region of Ethiopia, won its independence after a long guerrilla war against the Ethiopian government.

Ethnic Violence

As Africa moved toward the new millennium, ethnic violence also remained a major problem in many regions. The Nigerian civil war had shown what could happen within a single country. Similar problems existed throughout Africa. In the 1990s, such problems also spilled over national borders, threatening whole regions with conflict.

Rwanda. In Rwanda tensions between the two major ethnic groups, the Tutsi and the Hutu, exploded into violence. In 1994 an estimated 200,000 or more people, mainly Tutsi, had died in massacres.

An estimated 2 million Tutsi and Hutu fled to refugee camps in neighboring Zaire and other countries. Since that time, an additional 100,000 Hutu have been killed by the Tutsi. Many refugees have also died as a result of disease and other natural causes.

Zaire. The presence of so many Rwandan refugees proved a destabilizing factor in Zaire. Partly in response to the problems presented by the refugees, in 1995 the government announced a policy of forced expulsion from the country of the Banyamulenge, ethnic Tutsi who had settled in the eastern Congo as early as the eighteenth century. The Banyamulenge responded by arming to defend themselves and capturing the town of Bukavu. Many observers feared that the Hutu-Tutsi conflict was about to engulf the entire central African lake region. Eventually, however, the Tutsi rebels were joined by other anti-Mobutu forces led by Laurent Kabila. Kabila had been fighting the autocratic and corrupt Mobutu regime for many years. With his new allies, Kabila marched on Kinshasa and in May 1997 forced Mobutu to flee the country. After taking power, Kabila renamed Zaire the Democratic Republic of the Congo and promised to rebuild the country and halt the interference of foreign powers.

Economic and Environmental Challenges

In addition to political challenges, the new African nations faced economic uncertainty. As colonies, they had been part of the economic system of imperialism. In most cases, upon receiving their independence, the new nations lacked the balance between agriculture and industry required for economic growth. Many of them depended on a single crop or mineral resource for most of their income. For example, Ghana depended on cocoa and gold, Zambia on copper, Sudan on cotton, Zaire on cobalt, and Nigeria on oil. All these products were subject to large price swings in world markets.

As they sought to improve their national economies, many African countries turned to international organizations such as the World Bank for loans. However, bad planning, mismanagement, and corruption frequently left them worse off than ever. In addition, African economies were highly vulnerable to changes in the global economy. A worldwide rise in oil prices in the early 1970s, for example, led to huge increases in the prices Africans had to pay for imported goods, which in turn deeply affected their internal economies. Soon most African countries were deeply in debt.

Other problems also plagued Africa. Under colonial rule, improvements in health care, disease control, and nutrition had led to population growth. As the population of Africa continued to expand, however, many farmers overused the land. To grow more food and to produce cash crops for the global economy, farmers planted in dry areas or on hills, where fierce winds often stripped away the topsoil. In addition, people in many parts of Africa cut down trees for firewood. As a result of these practices, **desertification**, or the spread of the desert, became common.

The weather too has not been kind to Africa. Beginning in the late 1960s, a series of droughts struck northeastern Africa, bringing starvation to millions in the Sudan, Somalia, and Ethiopia. International aid in the form of food supplies has helped people survive, but it has not provided a permanent solution to the problem of famine. Further, foreign governments and voluntary agencies have found that providing assistance of any kind is very difficult because of the ongoing civil wars in these countries.

Not the least of Africa's problems has stemmed from the emergence of new diseases. New strains of viruses appeared on the scene in the 1970s and 1980s. AIDS, for example, spread rapidly through many regions of the continent. In 1995 the deadly Ebola virus struck in Zaire, causing the government to close its borders in an effort to halt the disease's spread.

Revival of African Culture

Despite the economic and political disappointments that followed independence, the people of Africa made great strides in one very important area. They experienced a rebirth of cultural self-confidence.

During the colonial era, many Africans lost faith in their own culture as they adopted European attitudes toward Africa. African art and music were considered primitive and crude by Western standards. The literature of Africa—a treasury of oral traditions including myths, proverbs, and folktales—was largely unknown to Europeans, who had no desire to learn about them. Seeing these attitudes, most Africans turned away from their own history and cultural heritage.

Not all Africans, however, followed the European example. In East Africa, Swahili poetry and tales continued to be studied as they had been for hundreds of years. The written records of this Bantu language go back to the 1600s. The language itself has continued to evolve. The acknowledged father of modern Swahili literature is Shaaban Robert, who is best known as a poet but also writes essays and novels.

Miriam Makeba, a prominent South African singer, performs at a concert celebrating Nelson Mandela's 70th birthday.

Many plays and novels have been written in Swahili, the national language of Tanzania and Kenya.

In West Africa, a new literary tradition developed, one using the colonial languages of English and French. Many African authors, especially those from French-speaking areas, first achieved international recognition through works of protest against colonial oppression. In a very intense and personal style, the poems of Léopold Senghor, who later became president of independent Senegal, described the hardships of colonialism. Senghor also celebrated his sense of the deep pride and dignity of being a black African, a concept he called **negritude**, or "blackness." Senghor's works, and the novels of Camara Laye, an exile in Senegal, proudly pointed to the deep, spiritual traditions of Africa and its sense of social community. In 1986 the Nigerian playwright and poet Wole Soyinka won the Nobel Prize in literature, becoming the first African to win the coveted award.

These African writers created a new artistic tradition. The result was a remarkable and varied artistic outpouring. Similar achievements were made in reawakening an interest in African music. In addition, a film industry was begun.

The creativity of Africa's contemporary literature, music, and films was also seen in sculpture. In workshops in Nigeria, Zimbabwe, and elsewhere, African artists employed age-old techniques to give shape to wood and copper. Others were more clearly influenced by Western art. Throughout Africa, this mixture of African and outside influences gave an unusual vitality to the arts. More and more westerners began to appreciate the achievements of African art. Africans themselves found a new pride in their ancient heritage and its unique contribution to world culture.

Section 2 Review

1. **Define** MPLA, UNITA, desertification, negritude
2. **Identify** Jerry Rawlings, Ibrahim Babangida, Laurent Kabila, Wole Soyinka
3. **Locate and Explain the Significance** Horn of Africa, Rwanda
4. **Understanding Ideas** List three problems that African nations faced after independence.
5. **Summarizing Ideas** How did superpower rivalries affect the nations of Angola and Ethiopia?
6. **Determining Cause and Effect** How did ethnic diversity contribute to problems in the independent countries of Africa?
7. **Analyzing Ideas** How has African culture revived in the last half of the 1900's?

Section 3

Nationalism in North Africa and the Middle East

Focus Questions

- How did the rise of Arab nationalism in Algeria affect France's position elsewhere in North Africa and the Middle East after World War II?
- How did conflict in Palestine between Arabs and Zionists affect developments in the Middle East in the postwar period?
- What major issues confronted Turkey and Iran after World War II?

As in Africa below the Sahara, World War II was a turning point for North Africa and the Middle East.

During the war, the British in particular had reestablished their control over strategic countries such as Egypt and Iran. Such control angered many and led to an even more intensive development of nationalism in the region after the war. In addition, the United Nations decision to grant independence to Italy's former colony of Libya raised expectations and demands among the French North African peoples that they, too, should be free from colonial rule. Not least, the discovery of the extent of the Holocaust, which had almost destroyed the Jewish population of Europe, led to renewed conflict in Palestine and eventually the emergence of the new state of Israel.

French North Africa and the Middle East
Like Great Britain, France was exhausted by World War II. Yet also like the British, the French did not immediately expect to have to give up their colonies. The first successful challenge to French colonialism came in the Middle East, in Syria and Lebanon.

Syria and Lebanon. France had first gained control of Syria and Lebanon as a mandate after World War I. In the 1920s, French policy had encouraged the development of a separate state in Lebanon, where there was a slight Christian majority. During World War II, Free French and British troops had taken control of both countries from the Vichy government. After the war, however, despite promises of independence, French troops remained in Syria and Lebanon. Only under British pressure and several brief but bloody battles with Arab nationalists did France finally agree to withdraw. In the mid-1940s both Lebanon and Syria became fully independent republics.

Algeria. The success of Arab nationalism in Syria in particular proved an inspiration to Arab nationalists in French North Africa. The heart of the French colonial empire in North Africa was Algeria. Like South Africa within the British Empire, Algeria had a large European settler community, people known as *colons*, accounting for about 10 percent of the population. These settlers, many of whose families had lived in Algeria since the 1800s, owned most of the colony's industry and its best land. Algeria was not just a colony, however, but had been legally absorbed into France. Algerian voters elected representatives to the French National Assembly in Paris, although voting restrictions limited the participation of the large majority of Muslim Arabs.

As nationalism emerged in other parts of the Middle East after World War II, the Algerians also began to demand independence. When both the *colons* and the French authorities resisted these demands, Algerian nationalists formed an organization in 1954 to fight for independence. The Algerian National Liberation Front, or **FLN** (its French initials), launched its revolution on November 1, 1954.

The Algerian war became extremely brutal as both sides committed atrocities to gain their goals. The FLN waged a terror campaign not only against the French but also against less radical Algerian Arabs who opposed independence. Torture was used by both sides in the conflict. So severe was the war that in 1958 an uprising among the *colons* in Algiers, supported by many army leaders, contributed to the downfall of the French Fourth Republic and the return of General Charles de Gaulle to power in France. The military and the settlers expected de Gaulle to pursue the war against the FLN. Instead, he decided to negotiate a settlement, even if it meant granting Algeria independence. Despite resistance from the army and the settlers, including attempts on his own life, in 1962 de Gaulle did indeed grant Algeria independence.

French police troops occupied streets in Algiers during a 1961 demonstration. The Algerian Revolution ended with the 1962 referendum on independence.

Morocco and Tunisia. The Algerian war had a devastating impact on French colonialism everywhere. The war was an important factor in influencing de Gaulle to offer his terms for independence to the African territories south of the Sahara. It was also partly responsible for independence in Morocco and Tunisia. Neighbors of Algeria, these two Muslim states were French protectorates. French rule in Morocco, in fact, had only been established relatively recently—in the 1920s—and Moroccan resistance remained strong. In 1954 both Moroccan and Tunisian nationalists also launched guerrilla campaigns designed to drive the French from their countries. In 1956, as the war raged in Algeria, France finally gave in. Morocco became a constitutional monarchy under the sultan Sidi Muhammad ben Yusuf, who became King Muhammad V. Tunisia became a republic under Tunisian nationalist leader Habib Bourguiba.

British Withdrawal from the Middle East

Like the French, the British also faced major challenges to their influence and position in the Middle East after World War II. During the war, Britain had stationed huge numbers of troops in Egypt to protect its interests. As in World War I, the British, supported by the United States and the Soviet Union, had also occupied much of Iran in order to keep supply lines to the Soviet Union open. To ensure a pro-Allied government, they had also forced the abdication of Reza Shah and placed his son, Mohammad Reza Shah, on the throne. British troops had occupied Syria along with the Free French government. British troops had also established control over Iraq in order to prevent a pro-German government from seizing power during the war. Not least, the British still held their mandate for Palestine, despite opposition from both Jews and Arabs. In short, at the end of World War II, Britain seemed to be even more firmly in control of the Middle East than ever before. In fact, however, Britain's control over the region was about to slip away.

Creation of Israel. The first major challenge to Britain's position in the Middle East came in Palestine. Once the war in Europe was over, the semi-official Jewish Agency in Palestine withdrew its support for the British mandate in Palestine. The agency conducted an active campaign against the terms of the 1939 White Paper, which had promised an end to Jewish immigration and the establishment of an independent Palestinian state. The Jewish Agency actively supported a massive wave of illegal immigration, as its agents in Europe recruited the displaced Jewish survivors of the Nazi Holocaust for the new Jewish state they hoped to build in Palestine. Meanwhile, extremist Zionist groups, such as the Stern Gang and the Irgun, waged a terrorist campaign against British authorities. In 1946, for example, the Irgun, headed by Menachem Begin (BAY·guhn), blew up the King David Hotel in Jerusalem. Eventually, a virtual state of war existed between the British and the Zionists.

In 1946 the British tried to obtain the help of the United States government to resolve the situation through a joint Anglo-American Committee of Inquiry. The British expected the United States to understand the impossibility of giving the Zionists an independent state of their own in the face of opposition by the Arab majority in Palestine. The committee did recommend against creating a Zionist state. Instead, it recommended continuation of the mandate to give Jews and Arabs a further chance to cooperate economically, as a first step toward creating a binational, bilingual state. Such recommendations were rejected by Arabs and Zionists alike.

Unable to obtain support from the United States or to get the Arabs and Zionists to agree on a settlement, in 1947 Britain announced that it was giving up the mandate and referred the entire problem to the United Nations. In November 1947, the UN voted to partition Palestine into separate Jewish and Arab states, with Jerusalem as an international city. When the last British troops left Palestine in May 1948, Zionist leaders proclaimed the Republic of Israel. Chaim Weizmann became its first president and David Ben-Gurion its first prime minister.

The establishment of a Jewish nation infuriated the Palestinian Arabs. As soon as British troops withdrew from the area, armies from neighboring Arab countries moved against Israel. Although outnumbered by the Arabs, the determined Israelis triumphed. When the war ended in early 1949, Israel had won more territory than it had been allotted in the UN partition plan. The Arab nations accepted a cease-fire, but UN-sponsored efforts to negotiate permanent peace failed. Moreover, hundreds of thousands of Palestinians had been uprooted by the conflict and were living as refugees in neighboring Arab lands. Attempts to work out either the return or the resettlement of these Palestinian refugees also failed.

From 1948 to 1970, Israel absorbed about 1.3 million immigrants, almost tripling the Jewish population of the new country. Impressive social and economic programs were also developed. Collective farms (the best-known form of which is called the **kibbutz**) proved successful in turning former desert areas into productive land.

Among the Arab nations, one emerged from the 1948 war with territorial gains. What remained of the proposed Palestinian state was officially annexed by Transjordan in 1950. (Around the same time, Transjordan changed its name to Jordan.) Other Arabs, including many Palestinians, bitterly opposed this action.

Egypt. At the same time that the British were grappling with the problem of Palestine, they also faced challenges from the growth of nationalism in Egypt. During World War II, British troops had used Egypt as a base of operations. After the war, the continuing presence of large numbers of troops, especially in the vast Suez base, angered many Egyptian nationalists. So too did Britain's continuing control of the Sudan, which many Egyptians considered an Egyptian province. After 1945 Egyptian nationalists expressed their desire for the complete evacuation of the British troops and the ending of British control. Between 1945 and 1952, however, all efforts to negotiate a settlement on either issue failed.

Meanwhile, the corrupt and inefficient government of King Farouk was also coming under fire from both nationalists and reformers. After Egypt's defeat by Israel and partly due to the diversion of funds from the war effort to enrich some of the king's relatives, a group of army leaders decided to overthrow the government. In 1952 the Free Officers Movement led a coup that toppled the monarchy and transformed Egypt into a republic. Eventually, a young charismatic colonel, Gamal Abdel Nasser, emerged as Egypt's new leader.

In foreign affairs, Nasser decided to rid Egypt of foreign domination once and for all. In 1954, after intense negotiations, Great Britain had agreed to evacuate the Suez base and to allow free elections in the Sudan. Despite Egyptian expectations, the Sudan chose independence rather than union with Egypt.

Meanwhile, in domestic affairs, Nasser emphasized land reform, industrialization, greater government control over the economy, and expanded rights for women. He also sought to modernize Egypt through major development projects. His ambitious plans were expensive, however, and he soon decided to seek aid from both East and West. In 1956 these efforts led to a crisis in the Middle East over the Suez Canal.

STAINED GLASS

Windows in Jerusalem

At the beginning of World War II, almost 9.5 million Jews lived in Europe. Then, during the Nazi terrorism that engulfed Europe, as many as 6 million Jews, about two-thirds of all European Jews, lost their lives. In 1948, when the state of Israel was proclaimed, many Jews went to live there to join earlier settlers in developing land.

During the early years when Israel experienced tremendous growth, the Israelis constructed houses, schools, and other facilities for the growing population. One of these was a hospital in Jerusalem. Shown in the photo to the right are brilliantly colored stained-glass windows from the hospital's chapel, or synagogue. These are six of a series of 12 windows, each devoted to one of Jacob's 12 sons, believed to be the founders of the tribes of ancient Israel.

The windows were designed by Marc Chagall, a Russian Jewish artist who spent much of his

time in France, settling there permanently in the 1920s. There are no figures of human beings in any of these windows because, by Jewish law, images of people are not permitted to appear in synagogues. The artist cleverly used symbols and abstractions of animals, birds, plants, and fish to tell the stories of the Old Testament. An intensely devout man, Chagall conveyed his love for his faith as well as his sense of history in these beautiful windows.

The Suez Crisis

In 1955 Nasser had announced the signing of an arms agreement between Egypt and Czechoslovakia (acting for the Soviet Union). Alarmed by the possibility of an alliance between Egypt and the Eastern bloc, the United States and Britain offered to help fund the most ambitious of Nasser's development projects for Egypt, the construction of a new dam at Aswan on the Nile. The Aswan High Dam would irrigate new lands for agricultural expansion and produce hydroelectric

power. American and British leaders hoped this would keep Egypt from slipping further into the sphere of Soviet influence. Nasser hesitated, however, hoping for a better offer of aid from the Soviets. He also recognized the communist government of the People's Republic of China. When he did finally accept the Western offer to finance the dam, he was told abruptly that the offer had been withdrawn.

Viewing the withdrawal as an insult to Egyptian national dignity, Nasser suddenly nationalized the Suez Canal, which was still controlled primarily by British and French shareholders. The revenues from the canal would help pay for the Aswan High Dam. Nationalizing the canal was also a public way of asserting Egypt's independence from continuing efforts at European domination of the country.

For Arabs and anticolonial nationalists everywhere, Nasser became a great hero. To the West and especially to Britain, however, he became a demon. His nationalization of the Suez Canal eventually led to confrontation with the old colonial powers.

The countries that felt most directly threatened by the move were Britain, France, and Israel. Israel was

What If?

The Birth of Israel
What if the Holocaust had not occurred? Do you think the United Nations would have supported the creation of Israel?

especially alarmed because the Egyptians refused to allow Israeli ships to pass through the canal. Britain and France also were outraged by the maneuver because they both had a stake in the company that had built the canal. The British in particular worried about the strategic implications of an independent Egypt, friendly to the Soviet Union, controlling such a strategic waterway, through which much of the world's trade passed. The French were also angry that Nasser was encouraging anti-French movements in North Africa.

With careful, secret planning, Israel, Britain, and France conspired to overthrow Nasser and take control of the canal. They agreed that Israel should launch a lightning attack across the canal into Egypt. Britain and France would then intervene, supposedly to separate the Israelis and Egyptians, but in reality to help destroy the Egyptian armed forces, especially the air force, and reestablish European control over Suez.

At first all went well with the plan. In 1956 Israel launched a sudden invasion, seizing the Gaza Strip— an Egyptian-administered coastal district adjoining Israel's southern border. The Israelis then defeated the

Aswan, on the east bank of the Nile River, is one of the most important commercial and resort cities in the Nile Valley.

Egyptians in the Sinai Peninsula and advanced toward the canal. Great Britain and France sent an ultimatum to Egypt demanding a cease-fire. They also insisted on temporary British-French occupation of the canal. When Egypt refused, British and French troops seized the Mediterranean end of the canal. Both sides placed ships in the canal and sank them to block it.

Worried that the Soviets would be drawn into the crisis, the United States, under President Eisenhower, decided to intervene. Privately, Eisenhower threatened to cut off all American aid to Britain unless the invasion ended and the Anglo-French forces withdrew. Unable to withstand such a threat, the British agreed and the invasion collapsed.

In a settlement negotiated at the United Nations, Britain and France withdrew their forces. The Israelis gained a vague guarantee to allow Israeli ships in the canal, which Egypt later blockaded. Then they also withdrew. A UN force was sent to patrol the cease-fire line between the Israelis and the Egyptians in the Sinai Desert. As Egypt emerged from the war still in control of the canal, Nasser claimed victory over the European imperialists and Israel. Throughout the world, the Suez Crisis was seen as the final defeat of European imperialism. Nasser himself became the most popular leader in the Arab world. In the aftermath of the Suez Crisis, many Middle Eastern countries began to pursue new courses of political and social development.

Political and Social Change

As the countries of the Middle East became independent, they also confronted more clearly than ever the challenges of modernization. Unlike Africa, where most states had been led to independence by younger, Western-educated leaders, most of the new Middle Eastern states had been granted independence under an older generation of traditional elites. Iraq and Jordan, for example, had become Arab kingdoms under the sons of Sharif Husayn (Husayn ibn 'Ali) of Mecca. Saudi Arabia too was a traditional Arab kingdom ruled by the house of Ibn Saud. Syria and Lebanon were both ruled by wealthy landowning and merchant elites who had prospered under French rule. Only in Egypt did revolution precede real independence, when officers of the army deposed King Farouk and then negotiated Britain's withdrawal.

The Egyptian revolution began as a reaction to the corruption of the monarchy. Under Nasser it also developed a political ideology designed to bind together not only Egypt but all of the Arab world. Although Nasser always made his appeal for support in Islamic terms that would appeal to his listeners, he insisted that modernization along socialist lines was the key to independence:

"Revolution is the way in which the Arab nation can free itself of its shackles, and rid itself of the dark heritage which has burdened it. . . . [It] is the only way to overcome underdevelopment which has been forced on it by suppression and exploitation . . . and to face the challenge awaiting the Arab and other underdeveloped nations: the challenge offered by the astounding scientific discoveries which help to widen the gap between the advanced and backward countries. . . . Freedom today means that of the country and of the citizen. Socialism has become both a means and an end: sufficiency and justice."

Under Nasser the Egyptian government put an end to the practice of absentee landownership, in which wealthy landowners living in the cities made enormous profits from overworked laborers and tenants who actually worked the land. As the government took control of most industry and businesses such as banks and insurance companies, it also proclaimed laws limiting the hours of work, establishing a minimum wage, and creating a whole host of social services. Education was extended even further, and the government tried to improve the status of women.

Similar plans were embraced by members of the Ba'ath Party, which first emerged in Syria. Although at first the Ba'athists had emphasized a kind of Pan-Arab nationalism, by the mid-1950s they had also adopted socialism as a basis for bringing about major reforms in Arab society. The Ba'athists appealed primarily to the new generation of Western-educated intellectuals who had begun to emerge in the Middle East under colonial rule. Ba'athism soon spread to neighboring countries, especially Iraq and Lebanon. In 1958 a Ba'athist-inspired revolution broke out in Iraq, and a Ba'athist government took over in Syria. There also emerged a new generation of leaders who similarly believed in socialism as the best model for further modernization. Socialism, however, whether exercised by the various civilian or military governments that came to power in the 1960s in several Middle Eastern and North African countries, proved to be but the first step toward dictatorship.

Meanwhile, the old ideal of Pan-Arabism also resurfaced to complicate political developments in the Middle East. Nasser in particular began to preach a new brand of Pan-Arabism combined with socialism. In 1958, partly to coordinate efforts against Israel, Nasser convinced Syria to merge with Egypt in what became the United Arab Republic, or UAR. As new Arab leaders began to emerge in Syria and Iraq, however, so too did their own fears of Egyptian domination. In 1961, despite all the talk of Pan-Arabism, Syria broke away from the UAR once again. Perhaps the only point of agreement among all Arab leaders was their ongoing opposition to the state of Israel.

Iran

At the end of World War II, Great Britain and the Soviet Union still occupied Iran. Although American and British pressure eventually forced the withdrawal of Soviet forces from northern Iran, the country remained under heavy British influence. In particular, Britain owned the majority of the Anglo-Iranian Oil Company, which controlled Iran's oil industry. Many Iranian nationalists resented this continuing British domination of their country. At the same time, they believed that political reform along truly democratic, constitutional lines was the key to Iranian development.

In 1951, the popular Iranian nationalist leader Mohammad Mosaddeq (MOHS·ad·dek), became prime minister of Iran. Dr. Mosaddeq had two goals: to firmly establish constitutional government in Iran and to free Iran from foreign interference. Consequently, he tried to limit the power of the shah and to strengthen the power of the *Majlis*, the Iranian parliament. He also decided to establish Iran's sovereignty over the country's primary source of income, the oil industry. Shortly after coming to power, he therefore nationalized the Anglo-Iranian Oil Company. These moves outraged both the British government and the Iranian conservatives who supported a strong monarchy.

The British denounced nationalization as illegal and organized a worldwide boycott of Iranian oil. American officials were alarmed not only by the nationalization but by Mosaddeq's acceptance of political support from Iranian communists. The United States feared that under communist influence, the Soviet Union might gain control of Iran. For this reason, in 1953 the U.S. Central Intelligence Agency helped Mosaddeq's opponents engineer a coup that overthrew his government. The United States then supported the restoration of full power to the young shah of Iran.

Thereafter, the shah worked to establish his power and to impose rapid modernization upon his country. He relied on close ties with the United States and on his army and secret police. By the early 1960s, the shah was firmly in control of Iran.

Turkey

While the Arab Middle East struggled to throw off the last traces of Western imperialism, Turkey, too, faced significant challenges after World War II. Following the war, the secularist and modernist policies of Atatürk continued under his successor Ismet Inönü (i·nuh·NOO). By careful diplomacy, Inönü managed to keep Turkey neutral throughout World War II, only declaring war on Germany and the other Axis Powers once it became clear they were going to lose. Consequently, Turkey avoided the destruction that would certainly have come with war.

After World War II, however, Turkey came under increasing pressure from the Soviet Union, which continued to push south just as imperial Russia had once done. Turkish leaders responded to this threat by allying themselves more closely with the United States and the Western world. In 1952 Turkey joined NATO.

Meanwhile, Inönü also moved away from Atatürk's autocratic rule toward a more democratic government. In 1945 he announced the end of the one-party state and allowed the formation of other political parties. In May 1950, the first free elections brought the opposition party to power under their leader Adnan Menderes. When Menderes began to lose support in the late 1950s, however, he began to impose restrictions on his opposition rather than give up control. He also threatened to undo some of the reforms imposed by Atatürk. Alarmed at these innovations, in 1960 the Turkish army intervened and deposed Menderes, who was later executed. The army soon restored civilian rule but made it clear that future efforts to stray from the path laid down under Atatürk and Inönü might also be met with intervention.

Throughout this political turmoil, Turkey continued to industrialize and to look toward Europe for its model. Education continued to increase, and the Turkish economy generally prospered. On the other hand, many Turks also began to be privately irritated at continuing restrictions on religion. Eventually, some Turks organized themselves in an effort to lift the restrictions on Islam and restore it to a central role in national life.

> **Section 3 Review**

1. **Define** *colons*, FLN, kibbutz
2. **Identify** David Ben-Gurion, Chaim Weizmann, King Farouk, Gamal Abdel Nasser, Adnan Menderes
3. **Locate and Explain the Significance** Aswan High Dam
4. **Understanding Ideas** How did events in Algeria affect the French in other areas of North Africa and the Middle East?
5. **Summarizing Ideas** Describe what occurred in Palestine in the postwar years.
6. **Determining Cause and Effect** How did past history affect events in Turkey and Iran after World War II?

> **Section 4**

War, Oil, and Revolution in North Africa and the Middle East

Focus Questions

- **How did conflicts between Arabs and Israelis shape the history of North Africa and the Middle East?**
- **How did the presence of oil fields in the Middle East affect political stability in the region?**
- **What types of new leadership emerged in the Arab world in the 1960s and after?**

By 1962 most countries in North Africa and the Middle East had achieved independence. The remaining British protectorates in the Persian Gulf area gained full independence in the early 1970s. The major issues during the final decades of the 1900s concerned the Arab-Israeli confrontation, oil, and political instability within the nations of North Africa and the Middle East.

The Arab-Israeli Confrontation

After the breakup of the union between Egypt and Syria in 1961, Nasser became more cautious about Pan-Arabism. Yet Egypt's president did not want to forfeit his country's leadership role in the Arabic-speaking world. He therefore faced a difficult choice when tension rose along Israel's border with Syria and Jordan in the late 1960s. Nasser could support his Arab neighbors at the risk of war with a militarily strong Israel, or he could hold back at the risk of losing his standing as leader of the Arabic-speaking world. Nasser decided to act.

In May 1967, Nasser demanded the withdrawal of the UN troops that had been policing the border between Egypt and Israel since the end of the Suez crisis in 1956. He also announced a blockade of the Gulf of Aqaba to cut Israel's direct sea route to Africa and Asia. (See map on this page.)

The Six-Day War. Realizing the danger of delay, Israel launched a lightning attack on June 5, 1967. In six days of fighting, Israel captured the Sinai Peninsula and the Gaza Strip from Egypt, seized the Golan Heights from Syria, and took from Jordan the entire west bank of the Jordan River. The so-called West Bank, part of the original Palestine mandate, had remained in Arab hands after the Arab-Israeli war of 1948. Israel also captured the Jordanian section of Jerusalem. Israel then annexed Jerusalem, despite a UN ruling making it an international city.

The Six-Day War, as the brief hostilities came to be called, radically changed Middle Eastern politics. Israel confirmed its military superiority over its neighbors, but peace remained elusive. Many displaced Palestinians lost faith in the Arab governments' ability to recapture what had been Palestine. As a result, they increasingly relied on their own guerrilla organization, the Palestine Liberation Organization **(PLO)**, led by Yasir Arafat.

All parties involved on the international level had reason to seek a compromise settlement after 1967. Realizing that they might be drawn into an Arab-Israeli war, the United States and the Soviet Union became interested in arranging a permanent peace settlement in the area. Egypt, Jordan, and Syria wished to regain lost territory. Mutual suspicions and fears, however, doomed many efforts to work out a peace.

Egypt Under Sadat

Nasser died in September 1970 and was succeeded by Anwar Sadat. Under Sadat's leadership, Egypt and Syria secretly planned a war against Israel that began on October 6, 1973. Although the Arabs were successful at first, Israeli troops pushed them back and crossed the Suez Canal to occupy Egyptian land. The Israelis, however, suffered severe losses during their drive into Egypt.

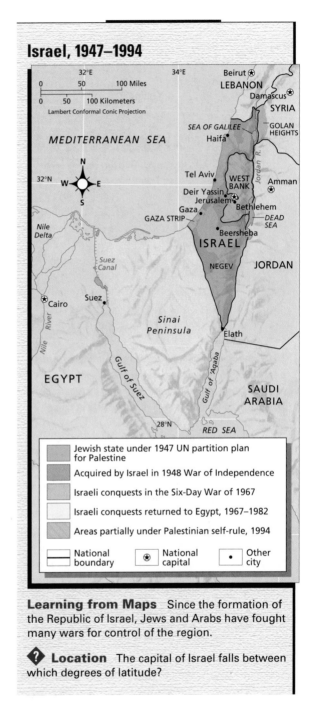

Israel, 1947–1994

	Jewish state under 1947 UN partition plan for Palestine
	Acquired by Israel in 1948 War of Independence
	Israeli conquests in the Six-Day War of 1967
	Israeli conquests returned to Egypt, 1967–1982
	Areas partially under Palestinian self-rule, 1994
	National boundary
	National capital
	Other city

Learning from Maps Since the formation of the Republic of Israel, Jews and Arabs have fought many wars for control of the region.

? Location The capital of Israel falls between which degrees of latitude?

As had been true after the Six-Day War, all sides had reason to seek a compromise settlement. U.S. secretary of state Henry Kissinger began an intensive campaign of **shuttle diplomacy**—moving back and forth from Israel to Egypt and Syria to try to obtain an agreement. He eventually achieved two settlements, one between Israel and Egypt and one between Israel

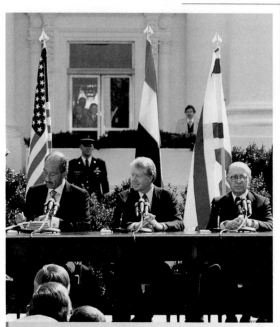

The Camp David Accords, agreements between Israeli prime minister Menachem Begin and Egyptian president Anwar Sadat, were mediated by American president Jimmy Carter in September 1978 at Camp David, Maryland.

and Syria. Thereafter, the movement toward peace seemed to run out of steam. In November 1977, however, Sadat surprised the world. He went to Israel to speak in person to the Israeli parliament and to Israeli prime minister Menachem Begin.

Sadat's action opened a new dialogue between Egypt and Israel, which the United States openly supported. Many months of delicate negotiations followed, aided by the direct support of President Jimmy Carter. In September 1978, Carter invited the two leaders to Camp David, the presidential retreat in Maryland. After meetings and negotiations there, Sadat and Begin agreed on the framework for a peace settlement. The **Camp David Accords** were followed by a peace treaty that Egypt and Israel signed in March 1979.

Egypt and Israel had achieved a great breakthrough, but many people doubted it would end the Arab-Israeli confrontation. Most Israelis supported the peace with Egypt, but many resisted the idea of a process that might lead to a Palestinian state. The Camp David Accords led to division within the Arab world as well. While Sadat had many supporters, his

opponents claimed that the Egyptian leader had sold out the Palestinians to regain Egyptian territory. In 1981 a group of Egyptian radicals assassinated Sadat, darkening hopes for peace in the Middle East.

Continued Arab-Israeli Conflict

After the Camp David Accords, the PLO and other Palestinian guerrilla organizations stepped up their operations. From camps in neighboring Lebanon, the PLO launched attacks that spread terror throughout northern Israel. Determined to end the PLO threat for good, the Israelis invaded Lebanon in 1982. For two months, they bombed Lebanon's capital, Beirut, where the PLO had its headquarters. Eventually, a settlement was reached whereby the PLO withdrew its forces to Tunisia.

Even though the Israelis finally withdrew from Lebanon in 1985, their invasion had a lasting impact on the region. Rather than destroying the PLO, the invasion had helped strengthen the organization's standing among Palestinians. Moreover, the Israeli intrusion into Lebanon intensified an already bitter civil war being fought there, and many Israelis, including some prominent military commanders, had been opposed to the invasion. This caused a deep split within Israeli society.

Israelis also disagreed about how to handle problems in the occupied territories, the zones Israel had acquired during the Six-Day War. (See map on page 553.) Since the 1970s, Israelis had been moving into these zones, where they were establishing settlements. Palestinians living in these territories started demonstrating against the Israeli presence. In December 1987, the demonstrations turned violent, in an uprising the Palestinians called the *intifada*, an Arabic word meaning "shaking." Day after day, young Palestinians threw rocks and bottles at army patrols and other symbols of Israeli authority. The Israeli army responded with armed military suppression. During the first year alone, the *intifada* claimed the lives of more than 300 Palestinians. Thousands more were wounded, and another 20,000 were imprisoned.

Many Israelis supported the harsh measures the authorities used to put down the *intifada*. Others, however, believed that it might be time to withdraw from the occupied zones, exchanging land for a peace settlement with the Palestinians. Unfortunately, events in 1990 seemed to dash any hope for peace.

Under the leadership of Mikhail Gorbachev, the Soviet Union had relaxed restrictions on the emigration of Jews. As a result, Soviet Jews began to move to Israel in huge numbers—200,000 in 1990 alone. Much to the anger of the Palestinians, the Israeli government seemed determined to settle most of these new arrivals in the occupied zones. As a result, violence exploded in the occupied zones once again in October 1990.

The specific incident involved the Temple Mount in Jerusalem, one of Judaism's most holy places. It is also holy to Muslims, who know it as al-Haram ash-Sharif, or "the Noble Holy Place." On October 8, 1990, responding to rumors that their mosques were going to be attacked, hundreds of Palestinians gathered at the Temple Mount. They threw rocks, and Israeli police answered with volleys of rifle fire. At least 20 Palestinians were killed and some 150 were wounded.

New Moves Toward Peace

Despite the continuing *intifada*, not all hope for peace was lost. A growing Israeli peace movement combined with the Israeli general election of 1992 reoriented the situation. Israel's Labor Party won control of the government from the Likud bloc, an alliance of several conservative parties. Yitzhak Rabin (rah·BEEN), a former army chief of staff who had led Israeli forces to their spectacular victory in the Six-Day War, became prime minister. Committed to reaching a settlement with the Palestinians, Rabin authorized secret negotiations with Palestinian leaders.

Israeli and Palestinian representatives met in Oslo, Norway, during 1993. Eventually, the Israeli foreign minister, Shimon Peres, met with PLO Chairman Arafat. Israel agreed to Palestinian autonomy—or self-government—in the West Bank and Gaza Strip, while the PLO officially recognized Israel's right to exist. On September 13, 1993, as a surprised world looked on, Rabin, Peres, and Arafat met in Washington, D.C., to sign a preliminary agreement. The three leaders jointly received the 1994 Nobel Peace Prize for their efforts.

Not everyone was satisfied with the new move toward peace, however. Extremists on both sides opposed aspects of the peace process. As the Israeli army prepared to withdraw from parts of the occupied territories, many Israelis who had settled on the West Bank feared harassment and violence at the hands of the new self-governing Palestinian Authority. In 1994 one radical Israeli settler with an automatic rifle killed 29 Palestinians in the West Bank city of Hebron. At the same time, a radical Palestinian organization known as Hamas, which opposed recognition of Israel

and Arafat's leadership, launched a campaign of terrorism within Israel.

By the end of 1995, the peace process had begun to falter yet again. In November an Israeli radical who opposed handing over any territory to Palestinian control assassinated Prime Minister Rabin. Although Rabin's successor, Shimon Peres, remained committed to the settlement with the Palestinians, Israelis grew increasingly skeptical of the peace process as Hamas continued to wage its terror attacks. In 1996 Israeli voters returned the conservative Likud bloc to power. While the new prime minister, Benjamin Netanyahu, pledged his support of the peace process, he stressed that henceforth Israel would move more cautiously.

As the century drew to a close, the Arab-Israeli confrontation remained unsettled and the future uncertain. Although Israel had reached an agreement with neighboring Jordan in 1995, conflict over the border with Syria remained an ominous possibility as of 1998. While implementation of Palestinian self-government in some areas of the West Bank and in the Gaza Strip went forward, personal friction between Israeli and Palestinian leaders combined with sporadic outbreaks of violence continued to put the peace process under enormous strain.

Oil and World Energy Needs

The development of ships, automobiles, and aircraft fueled by petroleum products greatly increased the demand for oil during the early 1900s. As the growing demand threatened to outstrip the production from existing oil fields, a search for new sources of oil began. One area that attracted attention was the Middle East. In 1901 the shah of Persia (present-day Iran) granted a concession, or land-use lease, to a British prospector. Seven years later, the prospector struck oil. Other countries in the region soon granted oil concessions to foreign prospecting companies, mostly from Britain and the United States. Over the next 30 years, these companies discovered major oil fields in Iraq, Saudi Arabia, Kuwait, Bahrain, and elsewhere in the region around the Persian Gulf as well as in Libya in North Africa.

The rulers of these countries, many of whom were absolute monarchs, received a share of the profits from the oil companies' operations. As the oil fields of the Persian Gulf were increasingly developed after World War II, these rulers and many of their citizens became very rich. While critics pointed out that the profits from oil—sometimes called **petrodollars**—

served largely to expand the personal fortunes of local rulers, much of the money went to improve the lives of their citizens. Petrodollars laid the foundation for social welfare systems and giant economic development projects throughout the Persian Gulf. They provided the funds to build roads, schools, and plants to supply precious fresh water to the desert region by desalinating seawater.

With the rising tide of nationalism following World War II, many of the oil-producing countries began to demand that the western oil companies grant them a larger share of the profits. Often the foreign companies were unwilling to grant these demands. In Iran, for example, the Anglo-Iranian Oil Company and the government were unable to reach any kind of agreement. As a result, the Iranian government, as mentioned earlier, nationalized the country's oil industry in 1951. Iran, however, gained little from this action. The Anglo-Iranian Oil Company managed to organize an international boycott of Iranian oil. Because oil was easily bought from other countries, the boycott of Iranian oil sales had little impact on the world market.

Iran's experience showed that, individually, oil-producing countries had little power when negotiating with the oil companies. Together, however, they could bargain from a position of strength. Therefore, in 1960 Iran, Iraq, Kuwait, Saudi Arabia, and the Latin American oil-producing nation of Venezuela created the Organization of Petroleum Exporting Countries (OPEC). Other oil-producing nations joined the organization later.

As the bargaining agent of the oil-producing nations, OPEC worked to set oil production levels and world oil prices. OPEC's power soon became apparent. During the Arab-Israeli War of 1973, the Arab members of OPEC used their oil as an economic weapon. They temporarily cut off shipments of oil to the United States as punishment for supporting Israel. Although this embargo was later eased, not least because the boycott of oil sales to the West harmed the finances of OPEC members, the price of oil rose sharply, from about $3 to more than $12 per barrel.

The discovery and development of new oil fields, especially in Alaska and the North Sea, helped Western nations reduce their dependency on Middle Eastern oil in the years after 1973. The oil fields of the Persian Gulf, however, remain the world's largest. They still constitute a critical source of energy for the industrialized world, and particularly for the rapidly developing economies along Asia's Pacific Rim. Experts predict that as production declines in oil fields outside the Middle East early in the next century, oil produced in the five nations of Iran, Iraq, Kuwait, Saudi Arabia, and the United Arab Emirates will become more important than ever to the world economy. Consequently, the Persian Gulf is likely to remain a principal focus of international attention in the future.

Political Instability

Despite the wealth generated by oil, the Middle East has seen considerable political instability.

Under severe financial strain late in the 1960s, Britain announced plans to withdraw most of its remaining military forces from the Persian Gulf and to grant full independence to Qatar (KAH·tuhr), Bahrain, and the Trucial States (today called the United Arab Emirates). By 1971 each of these former protectorates was fully independent, although British advisers remained influential in their affairs. In neighboring Oman, British troops remained active into the 1970s. They helped successfully put down a communist rebellion in Oman, which is located astride the vital route for the shipment of oil out of the Persian Gulf through the Strait of Hormuz.

As a result of Britain's withdrawal from the Persian Gulf, Iran emerged as the leading power in the region. Western nations, including the United States, looked to the shah of Iran as the main guarantor of the region's security. To many observers in the mid-1970s, the shah's regime appeared militarily strong and politically stable. Discontent was growing within Iran, however.

The Iranian Revolution

Many Iranians continued to oppose Mohammad Reza Shah Pahlavi even after the ouster of Mosaddeq in the 1950s. Some were socialists, while others were Islamic traditionalists eager to rid the country of Western influences. By the late 1970s, social forces at work in Iran had reached an explosive stage.

Throughout the 1960s, the Iranian government had carried out ambitious modernization programs. These included land distribution to the peasants, a campaign against illiteracy, and increased industrialization. As a result, millions had left the countryside for Iran's cities. When an economic slump hit Iran in the 1970s, these uprooted masses rapidly grew anxious. As their prospects for prosperity seemed to vanish, many of these Iranians became ready to support the call for revolution.

Interpreting Visuals: Reading a Special-Purpose Map

Historians use many different types of special-purpose maps. A special-purpose map relates data to the geographic setting shown on the map.

How to Read a Special-Purpose Map
To read a special-purpose map, follow these steps.
1. Determine the purpose of the map. Is it designed to give you information on troop movements? Resources? Land use?
2. Formulate conclusions about the information presented on the map. For example, if the map shows troop movements, can you learn why the troops took the particular routes they did?

Developing the Skill
Study the map entitled "Oil Deposits in the Middle East and North Africa, 1990," below. The map shows the oil reserves of countries in the region. The purpose of the map, then, is to show which countries in North Africa and the Middle East contain major deposits of oil. The map also shows the oil reserves of North Africa as well as of each of the major producers in the Middle East. It further shows which of the major producers are OPEC members. One conclusion that you can draw from the map is that the Persian Gulf is a vital source of oil.

Practicing the Skill
What other conclusions can you formulate from the information shown on the map of oil deposits in the Middle East and North Africa shown on this page?

To apply this skill, see Applying History Study Skills on page 563.

Oil Deposits in the Middle East and North Africa, 1990

OPEC member

95.3 Oil reserves, in billions of barrels (1990)

Compounding the problem, the shah had failed to win loyalty even from those Iranians who had directly benefited from the modernization programs. The shah's government had paid for thousands of young Iranians to go abroad for higher education, but many of these same Iranians feared and detested the shah's rule. They pointed to the atrocities believed to have been committed by the SAVAK, the Iranian secret police, as a symbol of the shah's tyranny. Moreover, the shah tried to keep all control and power in his hands. As a result, not even his own ministers felt strong loyalty to him.

Much of the opposition to the shah found expression in a revived interest in Islam. Conservative Islamic leaders who had long opposed the modernization programs of the shah began to attract wide support in their calls to rid Iran of Western influences. The Ayatollah Ruhollah Khomeini (koh·MAY·nee) soon emerged as the leader of religiously based opposition to the shah. Banished from Iran since 1964, the 76-year-old religious leader had directed a propaganda campaign against the shah from exile in France. By 1978, as the shah's regime entered its final phase, Khomeini's supporters prepared for his return to Iran.

Iran's Islamic republic. In 1978 discontent with the shah's rule erupted in demonstrations and riots throughout Iran. The shah was unable to contain the unrest. Finally, in January 1979, he left the country, appointing a prime minister to preside over Iran in his absence.

Khomeini returned to Iran in February. He demanded abolition of the monarchy and its replacement by an Islamic republic that would govern Iran according to strict Islamic principles. By mid-February Khomeini's revolution had triumphed. Iranians overwhelmingly voted to establish an Islamic republic, and they elected a president in January 1980. Real power, however, remained with Khomeini. His supporters rapidly eliminated other political forces, such as the socialists, who had helped overthrow the shah.

On November 4, 1979, Iranian militants captured the American embassy in Tehran, seizing more than 60 American hostages. The militants were protesting the American decision to let the ailing shah enter the United States for medical treatment. They demanded that the shah be returned to Iran to stand trial. The shah left the United States in December 1979 and died in Egypt in July 1980. Even though the Iranian militants faced worldwide condemnation, they continued to hold the hostages. The United States

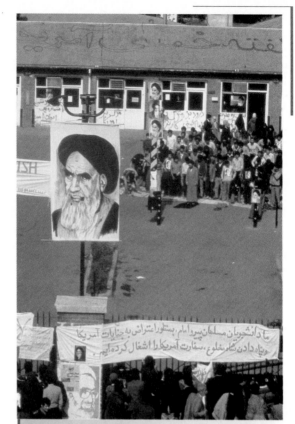

On November 4, 1979, Iranian revolutionaries seized the American embassy in Tehran and held more than 50 people hostage until January of 1981.

launched a military operation to rescue the hostages, but the mission was recalled when several aircraft involved collided with each other on the way into Tehran. The militants finally released the American hostages in January 1981.

Iran's situation worsened in September 1980, when neighboring Iraq launched an attack to take control of the waterway that divided the two countries in the south. A bitter war raged for eight years, with both sides suffering heavy casualties but making few territorial gains. The war also posed a serious threat to the stability of the oil-rich Persian Gulf region, worrying many world leaders. Under enormous economic strain from damage caused by the war, Iran finally agreed to a cease-fire in 1988.

Iran's road to recovery proved difficult, even after Khomeini's death in 1989. Although somewhat more moderate leaders took control of the government, many Western nations, including the United States, remained reluctant to do business with the Islamic republic. Iran's continued support of terrorism around the world and calls for Islamic revolution in the Middle East undermined the country's efforts to win international aid.

By the late 1990s, Iran's situation finally seemed to be improving. Foreign oil companies were eagerly seeking deals with Iran, and the gains made by comparatively liberal Iranian leaders in the election of 1997 appeared to hold the promise of improved relations with the United States. However, with traditionalist, anti-Western elements still extremely powerful in the government, Iran's future remained uncertain.

New Leadership in the Arab World

When Anwar Sadat succeeded Nasser, he assumed two roles—leader of Egypt and symbolic leader of the Arab world. After he signed the Camp David Accords, however, most Arabs rejected Sadat's and Egypt's leadership. Thereafter, a struggle over which country would lead the Arab world began. Two major contenders were Syria and Iraq.

Syria. In 1961 Syria seceded from the United Arab Republic and was reestablished as an independent state by a military coup. The government changed hands a number of times in the next few years. This process ended in 1970, when General Hafiz Asad took control. He quickly consolidated his power, ruthlessly putting down any challenge to his authority.

Like other Arab leaders, Asad's foreign policy was driven by the Arab-Israeli conflict. After a devastating defeat at the hands of the Israelis in 1973, however, Asad turned his attention to building his influence in the Arab world. He offered assistance, training, and safe haven to a number of Palestinian guerrilla groups. Yet his great opportunity came in 1975 with the outbreak of civil war in neighboring Lebanon. He first acted as a mediator, trying to bring the warring factions to the peace table. Then, in early 1976, he sent a large peacekeeping force to Lebanon. Nevertheless, many observers felt that Asad was more interested in gaining control of Lebanon than in bringing peace to that nation. That certainly seemed to be the opinion of the Israelis. When they invaded Lebanon in 1982, Syrian positions outside Beirut were among their early targets.

When Israel withdrew from Lebanon in 1985, at least 30,000 Syrian troops remained. In 1990 these troops played a major role in defeating the forces of General Michel Aoun, the last faction opposing the Lebanese government. This gave the Lebanese people real hope for a lasting peace. However, many observers feared that in return for Asad's assistance, the Lebanese authorities might allow him to play a major role in Lebanon's future.

Asad played a leading role in other regional issues. In 1980 he supported Iran in the Iran-Iraq War. In 1990 he condemned Iraq once again for its invasion of Kuwait. In addition, he sent troops to join the coalition forces in the Gulf War against Iraq.

Iraq. In 1968 the radical, nationalist Ba'ath Party seized power in Iraq. A driving force behind the Ba'ath Party was Saddam Hussein. The deputy leader of the government, Saddam was in charge of internal security. Using assassination, execution, imprisonment, and terror tactics he removed threats to the party with brutal efficiency. Saddam continued this approach when he took control of the government in 1979. One of his most ruthless acts was the use of chemical weapons against the Kurds, a minority group in northern Iraq. They had angered Saddam by calling for a degree of self-government.

Saddam began a march to power in the region by laying claim to Iranian territory that had once been part of Iraq—the Shatt al Arab waterway. This resulted in the war between the two countries in 1980. Badly disorganized after the revolution of 1979, the Iranian army was caught by surprise. In the first few months of the war, Iraq made major territorial gains. The Iranians rallied, however, and by 1982 the Iraqis had been pushed back and were on the defensive.

At this point, the Iraqis were faced with the possibility of an internal uprising. About 55 percent of the Iraqi population are Shi'ah Muslims, as are the vast majority of Iranians. Iranian Shi'ah leaders called on the Muslim faithful in Iraq to overthrow their government.

As the war went on, the destruction increased. Both sides shelled, bombed, and fired missiles against each other's major cities. Huge frontal assaults cost the lives of tens of thousands of soldiers. Iraq even resorted to chemical warfare. Eventually, the Iraqi army regained the advantage. The Iranians, devastated by eight years of war, agreed to make peace.

The Iran-Iraq War left Saddam Hussein in a strong position. He began a program of reconstruction and negotiations with neighboring countries. Further, he had built up the country's armed forces. Iraq now had the largest and best-equipped army in the Arab world. However, the country faced terrible economic problems. Iran had targeted Iraq's oil facilities during the war, leaving them in ruins, and Iraq had to pay off huge war debts.

The Gulf War. In mid-1990, Saddam Hussein charged that the small neighboring state of Kuwait was waging economic warfare against Iraq by pumping Iraq's share of oil from a jointly owned oil field. Kuwait's high level of production was driving down the price of oil. Attempts by the Kuwaitis to negotiate a settlement of these and other issues failed, and on August 2, Iraq launched a surprise invasion of Kuwait. Iraq quickly took possession of the smaller country and formally annexed Kuwait on August 8.

Although the leaders of most Arab countries denounced Saddam's actions, the region's poor and dispossessed—especially the Palestinians—looked on him as a hero. Huge demonstrations in support of Saddam spread across North Africa and the Middle East.

World opinion was solidly against the Iraqi invasion. When Iraq seemed poised to invade Saudi Arabia, opinion was backed up by action. Led by the United States, a coalition of about 30 nations launched Operation Desert Shield, sending more than 600,000 troops to defend Saudi Arabia. The United Nations also took action. The General Assembly passed resolutions imposing economic sanctions on Iraq if it did not withdraw from Kuwait. A later resolution set January 15, 1991, as the date for Iraqi withdrawal. After that date, UN members were authorized to use military force to oust Iraq from Kuwait.

The deadline passed with Iraq still occupying Kuwait. The following day, Desert Shield became Desert Storm as coalition forces, led by the United States, launched an air attack. Unable to challenge the coalition for control of the skies, the Iraqis made little response. Their only retaliation was to launch missile attacks against Saudi Arabia. They also made good on an earlier threat to fire missiles against Israel.

The coalition forces kept up an almost constant air barrage against Iraq for nearly 40 days. Then ground forces began to move into Kuwait and southern Iraq. Worn down by weeks of bombing, the Iraqi troops had no heart for a fight. The war ended in 4 days, and Kuwait was liberated.

With his army destroyed and economic sanctions against Iraq remaining in place, Saddam's ambitions seemed checked. Yet he continued to survive, defying international law and opinion throughout the 1990s. In the first days after the war, Shi'ah Muslims in Iraq's south and Kurds in the north attempted to overthrow Saddam's government. Both uprisings failed, leaving Saddam in control. Later UN inspectors arrived in Iraq to ensure Saddam's compliance with UN orders that he dismantle his programs to develop weapons of mass destruction. However, on several occasions the Iraqis deliberately hindered UN inspections, finally expelling the American members of the inspection team. The American inspectors were later allowed to return, but Iraq continued to make UN inspections difficult.

An Uncertain Future

People throughout the world hoped that the end of the Persian Gulf War would create opportunities for a lasting peace in North Africa and the Middle East. U.S. secretary of state James Baker shuttled between Israel and various Arab nations in an effort to get them to agree to a peace conference. However, no major breakthroughs occurred.

The war had left deep divisions between Arab nations. Relations between Saudi Arabia and Kuwait, on one side, and nations such as Jordan that had sided with Iraq on the other, were icy at best. Further, the Saudis and Kuwaitis had been among the PLO's major financial supporters. Because PLO head Yasir Arafat favored Saddam Hussein, however, the Saudis and Kuwaitis reexamined their support of the PLO.

Problems also existed within Saudi Arabia and Kuwait. The ordinary people of these countries had few political rights. After their efforts in the Persian Gulf War, many expected to play a greater role in governing their countries. Islamic radicals in Saudi Arabia, who opposed the country's monarchy and its cooperation with Western nations such as the United States, resorted to terrorism. During the 1990s, they set off bombs in Riyadh (ree·AHD), the Saudi capital, and outside an American military barracks in the city of Dhahran. The attack in Dhahran killed several American personnel.

Terrorism remained a major problem in many parts of the Middle East and North Africa. The use of terror by fanatics on both sides posed an ongoing threat to the peace process between Israel and the Arab world. In Egypt, Islamic radicals repeatedly attacked Egyptian Christians, government officials, and Western tourists. In Algeria, Islamic revolutionaries retaliated against government efforts to suppress their movement by launching attacks on high-ranking officials, security forces, foreigners, and others. The bombing of the World Trade Center in New York City in 1993 highlighted the potential of Middle Eastern terrorism to reach the West.

A major concern of world leaders in the 1990s was the sponsorship of terrorism by various governments in the Middle East and North Africa. The nations of Iran, Iraq, Syria, and Sudan were suspected of supporting terrorist organizations with money, arms, and advice. The government of Libya was linked to several terrorist attacks during the 1980s, including the mid-air destruction of an American airliner over Lockerbie, Scotland, in 1989.

The danger of major war in the Middle East also remained high in the late 1990s. Considerable tensions continued to exist between Israel and Syria. In the Persian Gulf, Saddam Hussein remained entrenched in power and apparently committed to the development of weapons. As of early 1998, his continued interference with UN inspectors in Iraq still threatened to reignite military conflict between Iraq and the United States, Britain, and their Middle Eastern allies.

In addition to these political and military problems, the nations of North Africa and the Middle East confronted a number of other issues. As they experienced modernization, many people sought a greater sense of security by reasserting traditional values. Perhaps the most important movement in this regard was a revival of traditional Islamic values and a rejection of Western culture. This resurgence of Islamic fundamentalism, however, raised other issues. For example, one issue concerned the status of women. During the 1900s and especially after World War II, women in many countries of North Africa and the Middle East won new rights and social freedoms, including education for girls and professional employment. The resurgence of traditional Islam seemed to many to reverse some of the strides that had been made and drew criticism from the West. On the other hand, many women in the region identified with their Islamic heritage and embraced Islamic values and the social restrictions that accompanied these Islamic values.

Serious economic problems also persisted at century's end in much of North Africa and the Middle East. Poverty and the lack of resources, combined with ballooning populations, placed many national economies under great strain. The unequal distribution of wealth between the oil-rich states of the Persian Gulf and poor, heavily populated countries such as Egypt, Sudan, and Yemen created resentments and laid a foundation for conflict. All in all, the nations of North Africa and the Middle East faced an uncertain future.

While many women in the Middle East today wear traditional clothing, others have adopted Western-style clothes.

Section 4 Review

1. **Define** PLO, shuttle diplomacy, Camp David Accords, *intifada*, petrodollars

2. **Identify** Anwar Sadat, Ayatollah Khomeini, Hafiz Asad, Saddam Hussein

3. **Locate and Explain the Significance** Persian Gulf, Beirut, Bahrain, Qatar, United Arab Emirates, Oman, Tehran

4. **Summarizing Ideas** Describe the efforts to attain peace in North Africa and the Middle East after the Arab-Israeli war of October 1973.

5. **Analyzing Ideas** (a) How has OPEC demonstrated its power in world affairs? (b) Has it succeeded in fulfilling its goals? Explain.

6. **Interpreting Ideas** (a) What factors led to the Iranian revolution of 1979? (b) Why did Iranian militants seize American hostages in 1979?

7. **Evaluating Ideas** (a) Why has there been a struggle for the leadership of the Arab world since 1979? (b) Do you think the Gulf War helped or hindered the leadership struggle? Why?

Chapter 17 Review

A.D. 1976
Violence in Soweto erupts.

A.D. 1979
• Revolution in Iran occurs.
• Hostage crisis in Iran begins.

A.D. 1980
Rhodesia is renamed Zimbabwe.

A.D. 1967

A.D. 1971

A.D. 1975

A.D. 1979

A.D. 1965
Joseph Mobutu takes full control of the Congo.

A.D. 1967
• Civil war erupts in Nigeria.
• Israel fights Six-Day War against its Arab neighbors.

A.D. 1975
• Civil war in Angola begins.
• Angola and Mozambique become independent.

A.D. 1979
Israel and Egypt sign Camp David Accords.

Chapter Summary

The following list contains the key concepts you have learned about Africa and the Middle East since 1945.

1. Independence came rapidly to the African nations after World War II. Most African countries achieved independence peacefully, but a few resorted to violence.
2. South Africa and Rhodesia resisted any efforts to give the black majority of their populations a real voice in government. The South African government instituted the apartheid system that separated the races.
3. Africa's new nations faced a number of difficulties. There was often hostility among the groups within a country. This led to violence in Nigeria. In Angola the superpowers intervened, as they did in the conflict between Ethiopia and Somalia in the Horn of Africa.
4. Africans also faced economic difficulties, ethnic violence, and environmental challenges.
5. African culture experienced a revival after independence. African writers, musicians, and sculptors allowed westerners to appreciate the achievements of African arts.
6. Many nations in the Middle East also gained independence after 1945. Nations that had gained independence earlier reduced the influence of foreign governments.
7. A continuing problem in the Middle East was the relationship between Israel and its Arab neighbors. Several Arab-Israeli wars were fought between 1948 and 1973. An offer of peace by Egypt led to the signing of a peace treaty in 1979, but the other Arab nations rejected the pact.
8. The nations of the Middle East vary enormously in size, population, and wealth. A number of them gained considerable power as a result of the rise in oil prices in the 1970s.
9. A revolution in Iran resulted in the overthrow of the shah and the establishment of an Islamic republic.
10. In 1991 Iraq occupied and annexed the country of Kuwait. A coalition of about 30 countries opposed Iraq and liberated Kuwait. Saddam Hussein, the leader of Iraq, continued to cause problems for UN forces after his defeat in the Persian Gulf War.
11. The rapid changes of the period after World War II led to upheaval and a revival of Islam. The region faced continuing uncertainties and tension in the 1990s. The use and support of terrorism by certain Middle Eastern and North African governments continues to undermine efforts for peace.

Reviewing Important Terms

On a separate sheet of paper, supply the term that correctly completes each statement.

1. The South African policy based on the principle of racial separation became known as _____, the Afrikaans word for apartness.
2. The movement that promotes the cultural unity of people of African heritage in order to struggle for freedom together is known as _____.
3. Unwise land use patterns have led to _____, or the spread of the desert in Africa.
4. A form of collective farm in Israel is known as a(n) _____.
5. In the 1970s, Secretary of State Henry Kissinger began an intensive campaign of _____ _____, in which he moved back and forth from Israel to Egypt to Syria to try to reach a peace agreement.
6. Profits made from oil are often called _____.

Developing Critical Thinking Skills

1. **Comparing Ideas** (a) How did nationalists after 1945 differ from earlier African leaders? How did each of the following contribute to the rise of nationalism in Africa? (b) Kwame Nkrumah; (c) Jomo Kenyatta; (d) Robert Mugabe
2. **Analyzing Ideas** (a) Which African nations achieved independence with relatively little opposition? (b) Which did not? (c) What reasons might account for these different experiences?
3. **Interpreting Ideas** How is the history of Ghana representative of the postindependence experience of most African nations?
4. **Determining Cause and Effect** What were the causes and results of the Arab-Israeli War of 1948–1949?
5. **Interpreting Ideas** Of the changes that occurred in the Middle East after 1945, which do you think has had the most impact on the rest of the world? Why?

A.D. **1980–1988**
Iran-Iraq War is fought.

A.D. **1990**
Nelson Mandela is released from prison.

A.D. **1991**
Persian Gulf War occurs.

A.D. **1983**

A.D. **1987**

A.D. **1991**

A.D. **1995**

A.D. **1981**
Islamic extremists assassinate Anwar Sadat.

A.D. **1988**
Cuban troops withdraw from Angola.

A.D. **1989**
African National Congress is legalized.

A.D. **1997**
Mobutu Sese Seko is forced out of power in Zaire.

6. **Classifying Ideas** Name the country that each of the following political and cultural leaders considered their home country; **(a)** Robert Mugabe; **(b)** Kwame Nkrumah; **(c)** Chaim Weizmann; **(d)** Anwar Sadat; **(e)** Jomo Kenyatta; **(f)** Gamal Abdel Nasser; **(g)** Ayatollah Khomeini; **(h)** Hafiz Asad; **(i)** Menachem Begin; **(j)** Saddam Hussein.

Relating Geography to History
Study the map on page 557. **(a)** How do the oil reserves of Africa compare with the oil reserves of the Middle East? **(b)** How might this affect the history and politics of the nations of Africa and the Middle East?

Relating Past to Present
1. In the 1990s, the situation in the Middle East has remained unsettled. Do library research to locate recent articles on events in one of the following nations: Egypt, Israel, Saudi Arabia, Iran, Iraq, Syria, Jordan, or Lebanon. **(a)** How have conditions in this country changed in recent years? **(b)** How have other nations responded to these changing conditions in the Middle East?
2. Examine the pictures of African art in Chapter 13 of this textbook. Then find examples of contemporary African art in sources such as *National Geographic* or general histories of Africa. On the basis of evidence in these pictures that you examine, support or challenge the following statement: Modern African art reflects a pride in the cultural achievements of earlier African civilizations.

Applying History Study Skills
Before completing this activity, review Building History Study Skills on page 557.

Study the map entitled "The World: Land Use and Economic Activity" on pages R8–R9 and answer the following questions.
1. In what countries outside the Middle East is drilling for oil a major economic activity?
2. How is most of the land on Madagascar used?

Building Your Portfolio
1. **Preparing an Oral Report** The novels of Chinua Achebe give westerners a glimpse into Nigerian society and

internet connect

Search the Internet through the HRW Web site for information on President Clinton's 1998 trip to Africa. Find and be prepared to discuss what countries he visited, what the purpose of the visit was, and what agreements or changes came about as a result of his trip.

HRW GO TO: go.hrw.com
KEYWORD: SC0
President Clinton

a changing Africa. Read one of these novels and prepare an oral report on the effects of modernization and the struggle to save or adapt old ways. Possible works include *Man of the People* (Doubleday), *No Longer at Ease* (Doubleday), and *Things Fall Apart* (Doubleday). Place your notes in your portfolio.
2. **Preparing a Panel Discussion** Work with a group of your classmates to find information on the capture of the American embassy in Tehran and the seizure of more than 50 American hostages by Iranian militants on November 4, 1979. Find information that describes the effects of the incident on the Iranians, the hostages, the United States, and the world. Then use the information you have collected to prepare a panel discussion on the effects of the incident. Place the information you collect in your portfolio.
3. **Dramatizing History** In recent decades, the Organization of Petroleum Exporting Countries (OPEC) has been prominent in world affairs. Work with several of your classmates to find out how OPEC conducts its meetings. Then conduct a mock OPEC meeting in which the ministers discuss how to raise the price of oil and how to enforce their decisions. Place a report of the panel meeting in your portfolio.
4. **Conducting a Debate** Prepare a debate on the following topic to present to the class.

Resolved: The world community of nations should agree never to meet any terrorist demands.

As you and other students prepare your debate, you might find it useful to research some of the terrorist incidents that have taken place in the world in recent years. Place notes from the debate in your portfolio.

Latin America Since 1945

TIME

A.D. **1945–the present**

A.D. **1945–the present**

3.7 million B.C. | 4000 B.C. | A.D. 2100

PLACE

Latin America

Latin America

The Andes Mountains

Significance

Latin America, rich in human and natural resources, persists in working for political, economic, and social progress.

For many years Latin America was overshadowed by the colossus to the north—the United States. The region's governments and economies, particularly of those countries bordering the Caribbean, depended on the United States. However, this situation is fast changing as the 1900s draw to a close. These developing nations have begun to steer their own courses.

Terms to Define

multinational corporations	PRI
monoculture	campesinos
import substitution	Contras
hyperinflation	FMLN
North American Free Trade Agreement	Contadora Principles
demographic transition	dissidents
Organization of American States	Operation Bootstrap
geopolitical region	*desaparecidos*
	Sendero Luminoso
	Medellín cartel

People to Identify

Carlos Salinas de Gortari	Jean-Bertrand Aristide
Daniel Ortega	Eva Perón
José Napoleón Duarte	Fernando Collor
Manuel Noriega	Salvador Allende
Oscar Arias	Patricio Aylwin
Fidel Castro	Alberto Fujimori
Luis Muñoz Marín	

Places to Locate

Mexico	Cuba
Nicaragua	Puerto Rico
El Salvador	Dominican Republic
Panama	Haiti

Chapter Theme Questions

- **Economic Organization** In what ways might economic factors affect the political development of a nation?
- **Social Relations** How might rapid population growth and urbanization affect a society?
- **Politics and Law** What challenges might occur when countries make the transition from authoritarian to democratic forms of government?

The death in 1952 of Eva ("Evita") Perón, first lady of Argentina, sparked an outpouring of national grief. In Evita, the former stage and radio actress, the lower economic classes believed that they had found their champion. Whether she truly had their interests at heart remains a matter for conjecture. The following is a description of the flamboyant Evita as she declined the nomination for vice president in 1951.

The woman who mounted the steps and looked out upon the frenzied crowd was a far cry from the fledgling first lady of 1946, or the glamour queen of the Rainbow Tour. The blonde curls and gaudy attire had long since given way to what one scholar has called 'the streamlined, eternally classic style which was to be hers—and uniquely hers at that time—until her death.' Her hair was pulled back severely, accentuating the growing gauntness of her features. Tears flooded her eyes. She raised her arms in response to the delirium, and a look of uncertainty clouded her expression.

Like Argentina, other nations of Latin America have witnessed dramatic changes in government during the recent chapters of their history.

Section 1

Facing New Challenges

Focus Questions

- **What economic challenges did Latin America face after World War II?**
- **What challenges has the region faced in terms of population, urbanization, poverty, and the environment?**
- **What social and political forces have emerged in Latin America?**

The countries of Latin America underwent enormous changes after World War II. Once largely rural and agricultural, and with a secondary role in world affairs, Latin America became a focus of world attention. Its growing population, the discovery of its petroleum deposits and other resources, and its rapid industrialization increased Latin America's presence in the world.

Since achieving independence in the early 1800s, most Latin American societies had followed traditional social and economic patterns. After 1945, however, Latin America seemed to be not merely catching up with the industrialized world, but creating its own patterns.

Economic Development

During World War II, Latin America had provided vast quantities of raw materials and food to the Allies. After the war, Latin American nations found economic stability difficult to achieve. There was, however, increased demand for their raw materials and agricultural products.

Most political leaders in Latin America saw internal economic development as the key to resolving the region's problems. Economic development would provide jobs for the increasing population. Industrialization would lessen these countries' dependence on foreign sources for vital manufactured goods and would provide consumer goods for everyone. Throughout the region, the drive for economic development became a major government-driven project. To finance these projects, Latin American nations sought economic aid from foreign governments and took out loans from commercial banks.

Latin American leaders also invited foreign corporations and manufacturers to establish businesses in their countries. They hoped that the foreign corporations' investments and technology would help spur industrialization. Since foreign participation would bring in machinery and capital, it seemed like an inexpensive and rapid way to promote economic development.

Relations between foreign-owned businesses, known as **multinational corporations**, and their host countries developed into a major political issue. Many Latin Americans resented the foreign ownership of important factories. In addition, factory owners often took their profits out of the country instead of reinvesting the funds.

The problem of monoculture. Among the serious economic challenges facing Latin America was the region's reliance on a limited number of crops. The dependence of a region or country on one crop is known as **monoculture**. Monoculture contributed to Latin America's considerable economic instability. Almost every country in the region depended on one or two crops or minerals for the bulk of its export income. For example, Venezuela and Mexico relied on oil; the major cash export of Colombia and many of the Central American countries was coffee. The economic fortunes of countries with one or two cash crops rise and fall with the prices of those products on the world markets. Thus, when world prices of various commodities rose sharply in the 1970s, for instance, only to plunge in the 1980s, Latin American countries were caught on an economic roller coaster.

Patterns of industrialization. In Chapter 13, you read that most Latin American countries followed a policy of economic nationalism during the 1930s. They took action to encourage industry, promote economic self-sufficiency, and reduce dependency on foreign imports. One policy designed to accomplish these goals was known as **import substitution**, or import-substituting industrialization (ISI). Under import substitution, governments chose to replace certain imported manufactured products with goods produced by industries inside the country. Various kinds of favors were granted to encourage manufacturers to produce these items. At the same time, tariffs or quotas would be set to discourage or prevent importation of similar goods, giving the local industries a chance to develop.

Import substitution worked fairly well in the largest countries—Brazil, Mexico, and Argentina—because they had large markets and enough of their own resources to accomplish the task. Starting in the 1950s, these countries produced steel, heavy machinery, automobiles, pharmaceuticals, and many consumer goods. Between 1950 and 1978, the manufacturing sector in Latin America grew at an annual rate of 6.5 percent. Some other Latin American countries, such as Chile, Colombia, and Guatemala, experienced lower, but still significant, rates of development.

By the mid-1980s, all of the easier substitutions of imports had been made. Further growth was obstructed by the fact that the majority of people in many Latin American countries could not afford to purchase consumer products in great volume. The market for the goods, therefore, was sharply limited. In addition, a worldwide recession had begun to affect Latin American economies.

International debt crisis. Adding to Latin America's economic difficulties was the huge burden of foreign debt.

Making Connections with History: Linking Economics to History

All societies have access to limited amounts of resources that can be used to produce goods and services to satisfy people's wants and needs. Specifically, at any one time, each society has a given amount of labor, capital, and natural resources. In every society, people's wants seem to exceed what can possibly be produced. This condition is called scarcity, and it creates a basic economic problem. Because we cannot have everything we want, we make choices. Much of economics involves the ways and reasons why institutions, people, and societies make the choices that they do.

Opportunity cost, another key economic concept, deals with the economic choices that are made in relation to the sacrifices involved. For example, if you are given a choice of going to a play or to a concert, and you choose the play, the concert becomes your opportunity cost because you sacrificed it when you chose the play.

Economic systems determine the manner in which people decide what to produce, how to produce it, and for whom to produce it. These are the basic economic decisions that every society must make. They are based upon scarcity and opportunity cost. The economic system of a society affects people's relationships with one another, the kind of government they create, and the history of the society.

How to Link Economics to History
To link economics to history, follow these steps.
1. Identify and define the economic concept being discussed. It is either scarcity, opportunity cost, or an economic system.
2. Describe the effects of the economic concept on government or society.

Developing the Skill
Read the following excerpt. How does the description of a hacienda in Latin America help us to understand the development of the society there?
"The hacienda as a society may be described by saying that it was—and is—an economic and social system that seeks to achieve self-sufficiency . . . on a local scale. . . . Each unit

Highland farming in Peru

expands until it has within its own borders all that it needs—salt from the sea, *panela* (black, unrefined sugar) from its own cane fields, corn, barley, wheat, coconuts, bananas, apples, and pears. All of this depends upon where the hacienda is located. . . . [I]t can run from the seacoast to the mountain top. . . . Not all haciendas . . . satisfy this ideal completely, but that is the aim of hacienda organization: to buy nothing; to raise and make everything within the limits of its own boundaries. The big house is built from the timbers found on the land. . . . [T]he furniture is made at home. The cloth is woven there from wool shorn off home-grown sheep. The llamas that graze in the hills, the oxen and the horses are raised and broken where they were born. . . . The wooden plow, the wagon, the windmill for the grinding of the corn, or the water mill for the grinding of the cane are all fabricated [made] locally."

The passage describes an economic system. The decisions about what to produce, how to produce it, and for whom to produce it are made by the owner of the hacienda. The goal of the owner is to make and keep this economic unit self-sufficient and self-governing. The problem of scarcity is solved by the planned use of natural resources. The opportunity cost comes in when the owner makes the choice of what is to be produced on the hacienda.

Practicing the Skill
In the free enterprise system of the United States, who answers the three basic economic questions?
To apply this skill, see Applying History Study Skills on page 591.

Foreign debt plagued most of the nations of Latin America. To finance their industrialization and modernization plans, most Latin American governments borrowed enormous sums of money from foreign countries and commercial banks. Between 1970 and 1980, the region's total foreign debt rose by more than 1,000 percent.

Many of Latin America's loans were made in the late 1970s, when interest rates were high. By the early 1980s, with their economies in decline, most Latin American governments had difficulty meeting their loan payments. Many made only token payments. To prevent the debtor nations from completely defaulting on their loans, the lenders agreed to renegotiate repayment schedules. Some nations were also forgiven on a part of their principal—the original amount they had borrowed. Other nations were granted lower interest rates. Still others were allowed a longer time to repay. Even with this help, the Latin American foreign debt still amounted to hundreds of billions of dollars.

This foreign debt greatly contributed to another economic problem—inflation. During the late 1980s, most Latin American countries spent a huge percentage of their revenues on interest payments. At the same time, these countries continued to fund government programs, state-run industries, and bureaucracies to administer them. They did this simply by printing more and more paper money. With so much money in circulation, the value of Latin American currencies plunged, and prices soared. By the 1980s, many Latin American countries were experiencing extremely high rates of inflation, or **hyperinflation**. Several countries had annual inflation rates of over 1,000 percent.

To combat hyperinflation, most Latin American governments raised taxes, cut spending, and eliminated most subsidies to industries. In addition, they drastically reduced the numbers of government workers and strictly controlled the wages of those who remained. In most cases, these measures worked. However, inflation rates remained high compared to those of Western industrial nations. Furthermore, to cut inflation most governments had brought their economies almost to the point of recession. Hardest hit by the burden of these government measures were the people of the working class, who sometimes responded with demonstrations and strikes. It appeared that in the years ahead, Latin America would continue to face significant economic hurdles: limited growth, burdensome foreign debt, high inflation, and widespread unemployment.

Regional economic alliances. In the postwar years, Latin American countries tried new forms of economic relations in an effort to lessen their dependence on industrialized countries and to cooperate in areas of production, tariffs, and trade. The Andean Pact, enacted in 1969, restricted foreign investment and encouraged both lower tariffs and economic cooperation among the Andean nations—Colombia, Ecuador, Peru, Bolivia, and Chile.

Many Latin American countries have strengthened economic links in the 1990s by making agreements with the United States and establishing regional free-trade agreements with one another. For example, the **North American Free Trade Agreement** (NAFTA), which became effective in 1994, brought together Mexico, Canada, and the United States into one of the largest free-trade zones in the world. Argentina, Brazil, Paraguay, and Uruguay formed a free-trade alliance under the Mercosur Treaty, which took effect in 1995. The Mercosur group subsequently negotiated free-trade agreements with Chile and other Andean nations.

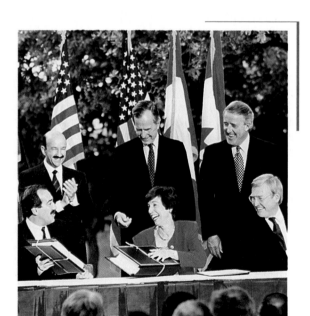

NAFTA, a trade pact signed by leaders of Mexico, Canada, and the United States in 1992, went into effect on January 1, 1994. Standing from left to right are Mexican president Carlos Salinas de Gortari, U.S. president George Bush, and Canadian prime minister Brian Mulroney.

Changes and Challenges

With Latin America's industrialization came many benefits, including economic growth, higher standards of living, and improved health care. However, industrialization created problems, too.

Population growth. In 1950 the population of Latin America totaled about 160 million. This figure had nearly tripled by the mid-1990s, reaching 470 million. Today the region's population continues to grow. The graph on this page shows how the population in selected Latin American countries is expected to grow by the year 2025.

A decline in the death rate—especially the infant mortality rate—spurred this population explosion. Public health measures reduced the number of deaths from disease each year. For example, the spraying of insecticides to kill the mosquitoes that carry malaria and yellow fever, the chlorination of water, and expanded programs of vaccination had a great effect. In addition, improved health care and technology have enabled people to live longer. Since the 1960s, improved socioeconomic conditions have also boosted population growth.

Latin America's population surge was typical of the kind of **demographic transition**—change in the characteristics of a population—that occurs when a nation gradually becomes industrialized. Typically, before industrialization takes place in a country, both birthrates and death rates are high. Industrialization decreases death rates by improving standards of living, including sanitation, nutrition, and medical care. Over time, birthrates also decline; women have fewer babies, knowing that their children will probably survive. During the period of transition, however—when birthrates continue to be high while death rates have declined—a population boom occurs. At present, Latin American countries are at varying points in this period of transition.

The growth of cities. Latin American cities, like cities all over the world, exercise a powerful attraction because they contain a concentration of social services, schools, and popular entertainments. Hospitals, universities, and secondary schools are mostly found in the region's cities. Even more important, however, cities in Latin America grew because large numbers of people migrated from rural areas to the cities in search of work.

Over the past several decades, the populations of Latin America's cities have grown much faster than the general population. Population growth in the cities is often twice that of Latin American nations as

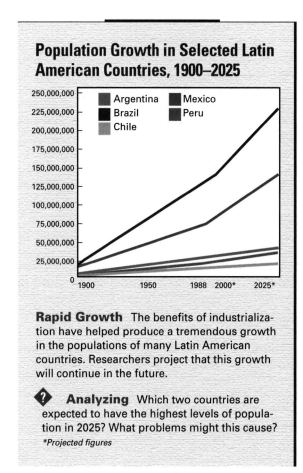

Population Growth in Selected Latin American Countries, 1900–2025

Legend: Argentina, Brazil, Chile, Mexico, Peru

Rapid Growth The benefits of industrialization have helped produce a tremendous growth in the populations of many Latin American countries. Researchers project that this growth will continue in the future.

? Analyzing Which two countries are expected to have the highest levels of population in 2025? What problems might this cause?

*Projected figures

a whole. The region's largest cities showed the greatest rate of growth.

City and national governments have had to deal with complex administrative problems. For example, sewer lines, water mains, and electric lines have had to be installed. Large investments have had to be made in road building, public buses, and subway systems. The heavy machinery and other equipment for all of these projects could not be found in most Latin American countries. The need to import these items often created a financial burden.

Many other problems arose in connection with the growth of cities. Most cities faced severe shortages of both housing and jobs. The governments, with so many other new expenses, could not afford to build public housing for the expanding city population. In addition, most of the rural migrants who could find work did not earn enough money to pay for housing. They therefore squatted—took up living space without permission—on whatever empty land they could find, throwing together shacks of scrap metal and other cast-off materials. In recent years many newcomers to Latin American cities have ended up in these shantytown slums, known as *favelas* in Brazil, *barriadas* in Peru, and *colonias* in Mexico.

When large numbers of people live in areas with inadequate sewage systems and no clean running water, a perfect environment is created for the spread of disease. About half the population of Central America lacks safe drinking water, and the situation is similar in other parts of Latin America. In 1991 a cholera outbreak occurred in the slums of Lima, Peru. The outbreak soon became an epidemic and spread to Brazil, Chile, Colombia, and Ecuador. In its first three months, the epidemic killed more than 1,000 people and infected 150,000 others.

Rapidly growing city populations also add to environmental problems. The pollution caused by Mexico City's thousands of factories and 3 million cars is a major hazard to life and health in the city. Half of all infants in Mexico City, for example, have harmful levels of toxins in their blood.

Poverty and frustration. Even though Latin America's economies generally grew during the 1990s, the region's social problems have shown little improvement in recent years. In 1997 almost half of Latin America's people were poor—an increase of 60 million in about 10 years. Rising unemployment made a difficult situation worse. By the mid-1990s, the average unemployment rate for Latin America was almost 8 percent, and five nations had unemployment rates of more than 15 percent. Meanwhile, the gap between Latin America's wealthy people and its poor continued to grow. Social discontent was widespread as people became increasingly frustrated. Many Latin Americans, particularly those in the northern part of the region, migrated to California, Florida, Texas, and other parts of the United States, seeking better-paying jobs and more secure lives.

Environmental problems. Latin America's environment paid a high price for industrialization and the development of natural resources. Millions of acres of land were cleared to make room for buildings, roads, factories, and farms. In Central America alone, more than two thirds of the rain forests have been destroyed. Many plant and animal species have become extinct, and there has been significant soil erosion.

Dangerous pesticides, many of which have been banned in the United States, are still being used in Latin America.

Much of Latin America's rain forest has been destroyed by logging, industrialization, and the development of land for agriculture.

New Political and Social Forces

Events in the last several decades have given rise to new political and social pressures in Latin American society. By the early 1990s, most of the countries of Latin America were moving toward constitutional government.

Women are one emerging political force. The struggle for women's right to vote began in Latin America around World War I. However, not until 1961 did women win the right to vote throughout the region. Their votes increased their influence in government. Even though Latin American women continue to struggle for full equality with men, they have had some political successes. In several of the southern Latin American countries—such as Chile, Uruguay, and Argentina—women were leaders in the struggle against military dictatorships.

Labor also gained political clout in postwar Latin America. As employment in factories increased, labor organizing spread and the union movement grew stronger. Today there are about 40 million union members in Latin America, making up about 20 percent of the workforce. The labor movement has experienced success with strikes and other actions to achieve better conditions.

The Roman Catholic Church represents another emerging political force. In the past, the Catholic Church had supported conservative ideas in Latin American society and politics, which usually translated to church support of those already in power. Historically, however, the church has maintained a concern for the poor and the powerless. Following a meeting of the Catholic bishops of the region in 1968, the church's leaders began to take more liberal stands on the political issues of welfare and human rights.

A theology of liberation emerged, in which many church leaders committed themselves to the struggle for social justice and pledged to change oppressive economic and political systems. Grassroots organizations emerged, often led by priests, and combined religious study with efforts to solve practical social problems.

Although the majority of Latin Americans remained Catholic, Protestantism expanded rapidly in the late 1900s. The emphasis of Protestants on individual spiritual improvement and a close relationship between the clergy and laity differed from Catholicism and appealed to many people.

Political Alliances

During and just after World War II, the nations of the Western Hemisphere entered into several mutual defense pacts. Many political leaders viewed such pacts as necessary steps to contain communism.

Inter-American cooperation went a step further in 1948, when delegates from the nations of the Western Hemisphere met at Bogotá, Colombia, and founded the **Organization of American States** (OAS). The goal of the organization was economic, military, and cultural cooperation among the nations of the Western Hemisphere. The group still exists today and aims to prevent outside states from intervening in the Western Hemisphere and to maintain peace among member nations.

The founding of the OAS represented a continuation of the Good Neighbor Policy, through which the United States sought cooperation with its southern neighbors. This ideal, however, proved difficult to achieve. Although the OAS supported American intervention in the revolution in the Dominican Republic in 1965, the situation soured United States-Latin American relations. Today the OAS has 35 members, including nearly all of the independent countries in the Western Hemisphere.

> ### Section 1 Review
>
> 1. **Define** multinational corporations, monoculture, import substitution, hyperinflation, North American Free Trade Agreement, demographic transition, Organization of American States
> 2. **Interpreting Ideas** How did the drive to industrialize cause economic difficulties in Latin America after World War II?
> 3. **Analyzing Ideas** What challenges are presented by population growth, the growth of cities, and environmental damage?
> 4. **Evaluating Ideas (a)** Briefly describe three new political forces that emerged in Latin America in the years after World War II. **(b)** Explain the impact of each on the region.

Section 2

Mexico and Central America

Focus Questions

- **What crises has Mexico faced since World War II?**
- **How did Nicaragua, El Salvador, and Panama move from political instability to the possibility of peace?**
- **What efforts have been made to bring peace to Central America?**

Mexico and Central America are part of what cultural geographers sometimes call Middle America, an area that also includes the Caribbean islands. Geographers also refer to the area as Central America and the Caribbean. (See map on page 574.) This area forms a single **geopolitical region**, one whose communities share similar political and geographic features.

The importance of this region lies in its location at a commercial and military crossroads. The region connects the north-south routes of the hemisphere as well as the routes between the Atlantic and Pacific Oceans via the Panama Canal. Although the largest modern aircraft carriers and supertankers cannot pass through the canal, it is still a major artery for commercial shipping. Such heavy traffic in the waterway results in its continued strategic and commercial importance.

Political and economic turmoil has rocked Central America and the Caribbean in recent decades. As a result, the United States and other nations have focused much attention on this region.

Mexico

Immediately after World War II, Mexico appeared to be one of the most stable countries in Latin America. By 1946, Mexico's Institutional Revolutionary Party, or **PRI**, had a firmly established civilian government. Thereafter, under the policies of a succession of PRI presidents, Mexico made great economic progress, building up its infrastructure and promoting industry. Despite these advances, however, the PRI allowed little opposition. As the party remained entrenched in power, it also became resistant to demands for political reform.

In the late 1960s, student protests racked Mexico, just as they had done in many other nations. This led to numerous confrontations between protesters and police. In 1971 a guerrilla campaign began against the government, further undermining its stability. The government took a hard line, hunting down and capturing or killing the guerrillas. By the mid-1970s, the threat had faded, and Mexico faced very little guerrilla or terrorist activity for some 20 years.

Economic instability. Throughout the three decades following World War II, Mexico experienced economic problems. To remedy these difficulties, the government lowered the value of the currency several times and cut back its spending.

Mexico's economic picture improved greatly with the discovery of huge oil reserves in the 1970s. Mexico's oil earnings soared from $500 million in 1976 to over $13 billion by 1981, and it looked as though the country might finally overcome its economic difficulties. Anticipating these oil revenues, the government borrowed heavily in order to undertake massive development projects.

In the 1980s, however, new problems arose. Corruption in the state-owned oil company, PEMEX, reduced the profits available for government spending. Even more discouragingly, a worldwide slump in oil prices proved devastating for the Mexican economy. Government borrowing during the 1970s had driven up the foreign debt to almost $80 billion. The annual rate of inflation soared; by 1986 it was almost 106 percent. A tremendous earthquake ravaged Mexico City in late 1985, putting additional strain on the nation's economy. The government faced the prospect of rebuilding the shattered capital and providing for the many thousands who were left homeless.

The Mexican economy continued to face challenges through the rest of the decade. By 1988 the annual inflation rate had jumped to 143 percent, and the foreign debt by the end of the decade was approaching $100 billion.

President Carlos Salinas de Gortari, who took office in 1988, attempted to deal with this economic crisis. He loosened controls on the Mexican economy. The government sold some of its business holdings to encourage foreign investors to play a greater role in the economy. Salinas also moved toward establishing free-trade arrangements with Mexico's major trading partners. For example, he pushed hard for approval of the North American Free Trade Agreement (NAFTA), which he hoped would result in heavy investment in Mexico by its northern neighbors.

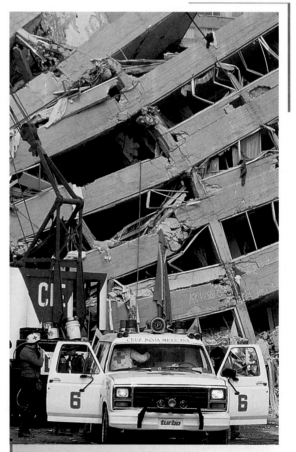

The earthquake that struck Mexico City in September 1985 killed approximately 9,500 people.

Such investment would further stimulate economic growth and create thousands of new jobs.

Monetary crisis. Despite the government's efforts, however, economic pressures led the next president, Ernesto Zedillo Ponce de León to order the devaluation of the Mexican peso in December 1994. Confidence in the Mexican economy plunged, stifling foreign investment, which had been on the rise. By early 1995, Mexico was caught in a severe monetary and investment crisis. U.S. President Bill Clinton managed to pull together a multibillion-dollar financial aid package, but Mexico's economic woes continued. Inflation rose again, reaching nearly 50 percent, and the country suffered the worst recession in its history. Not until 1996, with the help of government-implemented austerity measures, did the Mexican economy begin to recover.

Emigration problems. New jobs were a constant concern for the Mexican government because of rapid population growth. The economy did not grow nearly as fast as the population, so there were not as many jobs as there were people looking for work. To find employment, tens of thousands of Mexicans slipped illegally into the United States each year. The problem of illegal immigrants troubled United States-Mexican relations.

In 1986 the United States Congress passed the Immigration Reform and Control Act in an attempt to reduce tension between the two countries. The law granted legal status to persons who had entered the United States illegally before January 1, 1982, and had been living in the country continuously since then. The law also required employers to check the residency status of all job applicants, and it established penalties for hiring illegal aliens.

Both the Mexican and U.S. governments hoped that Mexico's economic growth and the creation of new jobs would reduce the number of illegal immigrants crossing the border. However, Mexico's subsequent economic troubles made both unemployment and illegal immigration persistent problems in the 1990s.

Political consequences. The PRI, by now one of the world's longest-ruling parties, had been in power since 1929. However, Mexico's problems in the 1980s and 1990s increased opposition to the PRI. In 1988, for example, the party's candidate for the presidency, Carlos Salinas de Gortari, was—according to many observers—guaranteed election only by resorting to widespread voter fraud. During Salinas's presidency, apparent corruption within the president's own family further rocked confidence in the PRI.

There has been rapid population growth in Mexico since 1915; the number of Mexican immigrants to the United States has also increased drastically. Shown in the photo is a border checkpoint between the United States and Mexico.

Adding to the PRI's problems was an uprising of Maya peasant farmers in the southern state of Chiapas in 1994. After violent clashes between revolutionary guerrillas and Mexican soldiers, the government and the rebels eventually reached an agreement. Additional signs of political unrest were clear, however. These included the assassination later the same year of the PRI presidential candidate.

The PRI's long-standing hold on Mexican politics continued to weaken in 1995 and 1996. For the first time, elections held in 1997 gave control of Mexico's congress to opposition parties rather than to the PRI. Nevertheless, the popularity of President Zedillo, a member of the PRI, was higher than ever, thanks largely to Mexico's improving economy and well-received electoral reforms.

Postwar Conditions in Central America

Following World War II, Central America experienced economic growth. Between 1950 and 1970, cooperation among countries allowed industry to grow and important trade routes, such as highways, to be built. People moved to the cities in great numbers. Between 1970 and 1988, urban populations grew steadily in nearly every country in Central America.

However, only a certain sector of the population benefited from economic growth. The peasants, known as the **campesinos**, did not share in this prosperity. Often the best land in rural areas remained in the hands of the rich. As rents rose, more peasants joined a growing class of landless farm workers.

In addition, earthquakes in Guatemala and Nicaragua in the 1970s, as well as devastating hurricanes that decade and the next, left many already poor citizens homeless. Throughout the 1970s and 1980s, the countries of Central America remained some of the poorest in the world, due in part to inequality in the distribution of wealth.

A lack of sufficient medical help, sanitation facilities, and educational services plagued the countries of Central America. The population increased at a high rate. In the late 1970s and early 1980s, skyrocketing inflation slowed the economies of the region to a standstill. Faced with almost constant political upheaval, social and economic inequalities, and the threat of natural disasters, thousands of people fled the region. Most entered the United States, often illegally, hoping to find a better life there. Many of those who remained began to demand reforms.

The Nicaraguan Revolution

Following a meeting held by the Catholic bishops of Latin America in 1968, members of the clergy throughout Latin America began to withdraw their support for military dictatorships and other powerful groups. The Latin American Catholic Church began

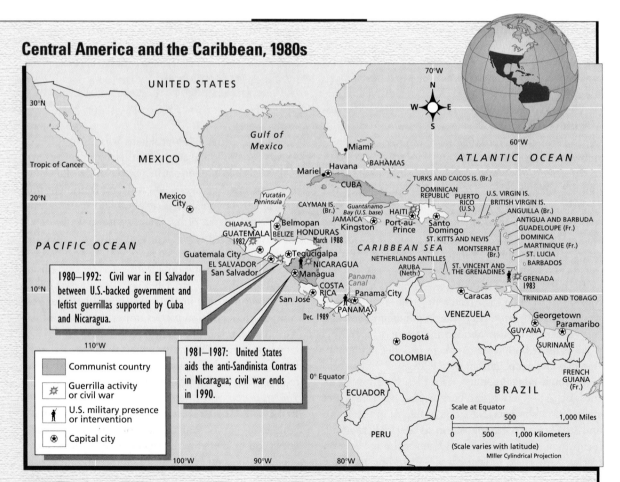

Central America and the Caribbean, 1980s

1980–1992: Civil war in El Salvador between U.S.-backed government and leftist guerrillas supported by Cuba and Nicaragua.

1981–1987: United States aids the anti-Sandinista Contras in Nicaragua; civil war ends in 1990.

Communist country
Guerrilla activity or civil war
U.S. military presence or intervention
Capital city

Scale at Equator
0   500   1,000 Miles
0   500   1,000 Kilometers
(Scale varies with latitude)
Miller Cylindrical Projection

Learning from Maps The countries of Central America and the Caribbean experienced many political upheavals in the 1980s.

? Region In which areas did the United States maintain a military presence in the 1980s?

to believe that it must commit itself to the struggle for social justice, fighting for the oppressed.

In addition, a growing class of educated people joined the ranks of those who opposed corrupt dictators. Both of these factors bolstered the revolutionary movement against the corrupt and oppressive dictator Anastasio Somoza in Nicaragua. Almost the entire population had risen up against his regime by 1979.

A Marxist-inspired revolutionary organization, the Sandinistas, gained control of the anti-Somoza revolution by promising a better life and political pluralism. The Sandinistas took their name from a Nicaraguan nationalist guerrilla leader of the 1920s, Augusto César Sandino. After taking control of Nicaragua, the Sandinistas established a ruling council, or junta, with Daniel Ortega as its head. The junta forged close ties with the Communist governments in Cuba and the Soviet Union. It also began to build a Marxist dictatorship in Nicaragua.

Opposition to the Sandinistas' economic and political policies developed in the early 1980s. In time, the opposition adopted the Sandinistas' approach to political change—armed rebellion. A rebel group called the **Contras** began a guerrilla war to overthrow the Sandinista government. The United States supported the Contras with financial and military aid, while the Sandinista government received support from the Soviet Union and Cuba.

With a civil war raging, survival became the major aim of the Sandinistas. They spent more and more of the national budget on the military, causing severe economic problems. Shortages of manufactured goods were common. As the 1980s wore on, the fighting between government forces and the Contras cost many lives.

El Salvador

The Central American country of El Salvador, located northwest of Nicaragua, was ruled either by wealthy civilians or by military dictatorships from the 1940s to the late 1970s. (See map on opposite page.) Guerrilla groups began to form in the 1970s to fight the inequities imposed by the government. These organizations managed to mobilize people into antigovernment demonstrations.

José Napoleón Duarte of the moderate Christian Democrats led the civilian reform movement and was president through most of the 1980s. During this time, the U.S. government sent military advisers and financial aid to El Salvador to help the government. However, violence marred much of Duarte's administration. The Farabundo Martí National Liberation

Front (**FMLN**), a leftist guerrilla group, undertook a terror campaign of kidnappings, assassinations, and attacks on government buildings. In response, right-wing death squads—many of them backed by the army—hit out at anyone who expressed any kind of support for the FMLN's aims. Their most notorious acts included the 1980 assassination of Oscar Romero, the Catholic archbishop of San Salvador, and the murders of three American nuns and an American volunteer later that year.

In the late 1980s, the government took a turn to the right when the conservative ARENA Party won control of the legislature and the presidency. This spurred the FMLN forces to further violence. In 1989 they attacked a number of large army bases and launched a major offensive against the country's capital, San Salvador, and other urban centers. The message FMLN leaders seemed to be sending was that they could strike anywhere at any time. Right-wing violence increased as well. In November 1989, for example, a death squad murdered six Catholic priests who had expressed anti-ARENA sentiments.

By the end of the decade, the violence had claimed the lives of thousands of Salvadorans. Tired of the killing and the constant turmoil, most people simply wanted peace.

Panama

The country of Panama experienced a political and economic situation similar to that of its Central American neighbors. The only major difference was that the United States controlled the Panama Canal and 10 miles of territory on either side, known as the Canal Zone, that was once part of Panama. American-Panamanian negotiations over control of the canal continued throughout the postwar period. The two nations finally ratified a treaty in 1979. This treaty, which called for the gradual transfer of the canal to Panama by December 31, 1999, caused much controversy in the United States. Many Americans believed that United States security would be in danger when Panama gained control of the canal.

In the late 1980s, relations between Panama and the United States deteriorated. United States officials accused the Panamanian dictator, General Manuel Noriega, of helping South American narcotics dealers send illegal drugs into the United States. President Ronald Reagan attempted to pressure Noriega into resigning. When this failed, Reagan stopped all United States military and economic aid to Panama. Then, in December 1989, after Panamanian forces

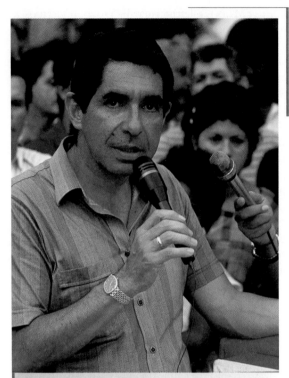

Oscar Arias, president of Costa Rica from 1986 until 1990, received the Nobel Peace Prize in 1987 for the plan he proposed and signed with leaders of Guatemala, El Salvador, Honduras, and Nicaragua.

ative economic and political stability—proposed a peace plan for Central America. The plan called for an end to all fighting in the region, a halt to foreign aid to rebels, and economic reforms. The following excerpt from a speech by Arias underscores his belief in the connection between peace and democracy:

"The democracy in which many American nations live today cannot be consolidated without economic development and social justice. Before any political or economic conditions can be imposed on the democracies of the Americas, there must be a commitment from the Western world to strengthen democracy in all our nations. In the Americas, peace must be democratic, pluralistic, tolerant, and free. While dogmatism [stubborn opinions] and intransigence [stubbornness] persist and there is no dialogue, peace will be impossible. Working together for democracy, freedom, and development is working together for peace."

Five Central American countries—Costa Rica, El Salvador, Guatemala, Honduras, and Nicaragua—and the United States endorsed Arias's proposal. For his work, Arias received the Nobel Peace Prize in 1987. Not until the early 1990s, however, did peace seem possible in Central America.

Recent Developments in Central America

As in several other parts of the world, the 1990s brought new hope for peace and democratic change.

Nicaragua. Fighting between the Sandinistas and the Contras finally ended in 1990. In free elections held that year, Violeta Barrios de Chamorro, a candidate who opposed the Sandinistas, was elected president of Nicaragua. Against expectations, the Sandinistas handed over power peacefully. Almost immediately the United States government lifted the trade embargo that it had imposed on Nicaragua in 1985. In addition, the United States and a number of Western European nations provided aid to the new government.

Under Chamorro, the country faced ongoing political instability and severe economic problems, including hyperinflation, massive foreign debt, and 50 percent unemployment. In 1996, Arnoldo Alemán succeeded Chamorro, defeating former Sandinista president Daniel Ortega and many other candidates. Like his predecessor, President Alemán had to deal with Nicaragua's continuing difficulties, including high rates of unemployment and inflation.

killed one American soldier and detained and severely beat another one, U.S. President George Bush sent troops to Panama to restore order and capture Noriega. Noriega was taken to Florida, where he was later convicted and sentenced to 40 years in prison for drug trafficking.

Peace Proposals for Central America

A number of Latin American countries made attempts to find a peaceful settlement to problems in Central America. In 1983, for example, political leaders of Colombia, Mexico, Panama, and Venezuela agreed to the **Contadora Principles**. This document, named for the island where the leaders met, called for a freeze on arms sales and a reduction of foreign military bases and personnel in the area. It also promoted negotiations rather than violence as the only way to settle regional differences.

In 1987, representatives from throughout Central America met in Guatemala City, Guatemala, for a regional peace conference. At this conference Oscar Arias, the president of Costa Rica—a country with rel-

With a series of three lakes and locks—the Gatun, the Pedro Miguel, and the Miraflores—ships can be raised and lowered from one sea level to the next through the Panama Canal.

Section 2 Review

1. **Define** geopolitical region, PRI, campesinos, Contras, FMLN, Contadora Principles
2. **Identify** Carlos Salinas de Gortari, Daniel Ortega, José Napoleón Duarte, Manuel Noriega, Oscar Arias, Violeta Barrios de Chamorro
3. **Locate and Explain the Significance** Mexico, Nicaragua, El Salvador, Panama
4. **Understanding Ideas** Describe the problems faced and the gains made by Mexico since 1945.
5. **Analyzing Ideas** Nicaragua, El Salvador, and Panama moved from political instability to the possibility of peace by the 1990s. Do you agree or disagree with this statement? Why?
6. **Interpreting Ideas** Why do you think some people consider the 1990s a decade of hope for Central America? Do you agree with them? Why or why not?

El Salvador. In El Salvador, President Alfredo Cristiani—who succeeded José Napoleón Duarte in 1989—and FMLN leaders made tentative steps toward peace for their country. By 1992, with the aid of UN mediation, opposing sides had signed a peace treaty. This peace treaty finally brought the costly 12-year civil war to an end. In the first postwar elections, which were held in 1994, Armando Calderón Sol, the ARENA candidate, was elected president of El Salvador. ARENA retained control of the legislature in the 1997 elections, although the FMLN showed considerable strength.

Panama. After the United States intervention in 1989, Panama began the new decade with its first democratically elected government in years. During the early and mid-1990s, the people of Panama seemed determined to hold on to democracy and avoid a return to military dictatorship. However, the country struggled with deep economic and social problems.

With 1999 approaching, preparations were under way for transfer of control of the Panama Canal to Panama. American and Panamanian officials were working to resolve issues concerning future administration of the vital waterway.

Section 3

Nations of the Caribbean

Focus Questions

- **How did the revolution in Cuba affect life on the island and its relations with the rest of the world?**
- **How has the Puerto Rican economy and identity developed since the 1950s?**
- **What troubles have the Dominican Republic and Haiti experienced?**

The islands of the Caribbean Sea, sometimes called the West Indies, stretch from the Bahamas, off the tip of Florida, to the island nations within sight of Venezuela in the south. (See map on page 574.) Of these, Cuba, Puerto Rico, the Dominican Republic, Haiti, and Jamaica are sometimes called the Greater Antilles. The Lesser Antilles are the chain of smaller islands that includes the U.S. Virgin Islands and extends down to Trinidad and Tobago. While some Caribbean islands are independent nations, others remain politically tied to European countries or to the United States.

Revolution in Cuba

In 1959 a revolution in Cuba overthrew Fulgencio Batista, the army officer who had ruled Cuba through puppet regimes from 1934 to 1944, and then as president beginning in 1952. Led by Fidel Castro, the Cuban Revolution was the greatest political upheaval Latin Americans had experienced since the Mexican Revolution of the early 1900s.

Fidel Castro began his campaign to overthrow the Cuban government in 1953 with an attack on a military barracks in Santiago de Cuba. Jailed for his role in this attack, Castro later went into exile in Mexico, where he trained a group of revolutionaries. He returned to Cuba with a band of men in 1956. For the next three years, Castro, with his brother Raúl and a young Argentine revolutionary named Ernesto ("Ché") Guevara, led guerrilla operations against the Batista government.

Batista answered with brutal, repressive measures. As a result, the Cuban people began to shift their support to the revolutionaries. By 1958 the United States government had reassessed its backing of the Batista regime and suspended arms shipments to his government. Realizing that he faced almost certain defeat, Batista fled, and Fidel Castro's revolutionaries took over the Cuban government.

Cuba under Castro. At first, most Cubans welcomed the revolution. Castro's promises of the reinstatement of civil liberties and agrarian reform were very attractive, as were his pledges to improve education and health care.

Both the lower and middle classes welcomed the change in government. Castro's promise of speedy, open elections seemed to assure a return to democracy. His statement that he would build a new Cuba, independent of United States influence, was welcomed by many. In a relatively short time, however, the new Cuban government began its swing toward the Soviet bloc. By the end of 1959, Cuba clearly stood on the path to communism.

Castro's now openly communist regime became dictatorial, suppressing the free press. The revolutionaries held public trials of Batista supporters and executed many. The government began to enact a program of Marxist reforms, including land reform and redistribution of income. The government took over the operation of many businesses and agricultural estates owned by Americans.

Castro did enact many of his promised social reforms. His educational reforms concentrated on a literacy campaign. As a result, Cuba's literacy rate has risen to 96 percent, the highest in Latin America. Other social reforms were also enacted. At the same time, however, Castro continued his authoritarian style of rule, maintaining strict censorship on the press and suppressing all dissent.

Although he enjoyed a reasonably high level of support among the poor, Castro lost the backing of many middle- and upper-class Cubans. Businesspeople and landowners were angered by the seizure of their property. Middle-class intellectuals and liberal politicians were shocked by Castro's turn toward authoritarian communism. In time, increasing numbers of Cubans from all classes and walks of life began to flee the island. Many settled in Florida, not far from their homeland.

The population of the West Indies is heterogenous in terms of nationality, language, religion, age, and culture.

Through a guerrilla revolution in 1959, Fidel Castro seized political power in Cuba and pursued a series of Communist reforms.

The Bay of Pigs. In 1960 the Cuban government ordered U.S. owned oil companies on the island to process fuel supplied by the Soviet Union. When the companies refused, Cuba seized their refineries. The United States responded by refusing to import sugar from Cuba. Castro fought back by seizing other U.S. properties in Cuba.

The United States government viewed this situation and the developing relationship between Castro and the Soviets as threats to U.S. national security. The Central Intelligence Agency (CIA) began to funnel money to exiles for the training of anti-Castro troops in Guatemala. In April 1961, a United States-approved rebel landing was made in Cuba. This invasion, which took place on the southern coast at the Bay of Pigs, failed utterly. The expected anti-Castro uprisings did not take place, and the U.S. air support that had been promised was withdrawn. Castro's forces, better armed than the rebels, killed or captured the invasion forces.

The Bay of Pigs invasion was a foreign-policy disaster for the Kennedy administration. Because the rebels had included quite a number of Batista supporters, it appeared to many people that the United States was trying to re-establish a dictatorship in Cuba. Furthermore, the move drove Castro into even closer ties with the Soviet Union.

The Cuban missile crisis. Fearing that the United States would attempt another invasion, Fidel Castro quickly complied with a Soviet request to be allowed to construct nuclear missile sites in Cuba. The resulting crisis (as discussed in Chapter 15) brought the world to the brink of nuclear war in 1962. The agreement reached by the Soviet Union and the United States included a promise that the United States would not invade Cuba.

What If?

The Bay of Pigs
What might have happened if the Bay of Pigs invasion had been successful? Would the Cuban missile crisis have occurred? How might the history of Cuba be different?

Ché Guevara served in various posts under Fidel Castro's leadership. He was later captured and killed while leading a guerrilla attack near Santa Cruz, Bolivia.

Exporting revolution. In the mid-1960s, Castro launched a program to support communist revolutions in other developing nations, particularly in Latin America and Africa. The Cuban government sent arms, troops, and military advisers to Latin American nations such as the Dominican Republic and Nicaragua and to African nations such as Angola and Ethiopia.

Ché Guevara carried out some of the guerrilla activity associated with this effort. A former physician from Argentina, Guevara had become a revolutionary after witnessing the U.S.-sponsored overthrow of President Arbenz of Guatemala in 1954. Guevara personally led a band of guerrillas into the mountains of Bolivia in 1967. Shortly after, he was killed by a troop of U.S.-trained Bolivian rangers.

The United States persuaded the OAS to expel Cuba because of its efforts to export revolution. The American government also called on other nations in the region to join in an economic boycott of Cuba. The island nation thus began a long period of political and economic isolation from its neighbors in the Western Hemisphere.

Economic and social difficulties. This isolation added to Castro's problems in trying to boost the Cuban economy. Industrialization did not proceed as planned, and sugar production declined. As a result, during the 1970s, Cuba became more and more dependent on economic assistance from the Soviet Union.

The failure of Cuba's centrally planned command economy and a lack of consumer goods created social unrest in Cuba. In 1980 this dissatisfaction with the government led many Cubans to seek political asylum in other countries. These people first sought refuge at the Peruvian embassy in Havana. When the Castro government realized how many **dissidents**, or people who disagreed with the government, were among its citizens, it allowed anyone to emigrate, as long as he or she informed the authorities. The total reached 125,000, and most left Cuba from the port of Mariel, in boats provided by Cuban exiles in Miami. However, Castro did more than rid Cuba of dissidents. He also opened the gates of Cuba's prisons and mental hospitals, forcing criminals and mentally ill people onto boats that carried other refugees to the United States.

Throughout the 1980s, Cuba continued its policy of exporting the means for revolution. In addition, it provided support to communist regimes that were already established in African countries such as Angola and Ethiopia. Cuba also maintained its strongly anti-U.S. position in foreign affairs.

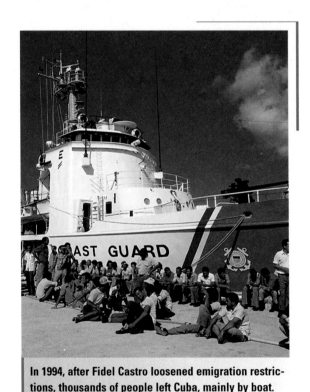

In 1994, after Fidel Castro loosened emigration restrictions, thousands of people left Cuba, mainly by boat.

Economically, Cuba remained dependent on the Soviet Union, which in fact subsidized the Cuban economy for many years. However, the Soviet government began to reassess its relations with Cuba after Premier Mikhail Gorbachev's reform programs took effect. (See Chapter 19.) In the late 1980s the Soviets, short of funds themselves, drastically reduced aid to Cuba. Both the Soviet Union and some Eastern European countries also established trade agreements that were less favorable to the Caribbean nation.

Without huge amounts of Soviet aid, and with the continued pressure of the U.S. trade and financial embargo that had been in effect for more than three decades, the Cuban economy came close to collapse in the early 1990s. Nearly every commodity was in short supply, and the government began rationing food and gasoline.

Nevertheless, Castro insisted that the country would continue on the path of communism. By the mid-1990's, however, Castro had allowed some limited private enterprise and had implemented various other economic reforms. The Cuban economy slowly began to show signs of recovery, further benefited by rising tourism and increased foreign investment. In 1997, Cuba also intensified its efforts to improve relations with other Caribbean countries.

Puerto Rico

The United States took control of Puerto Rico in 1898, after the Spanish-American War. The Jones Act, passed by Congress in 1917, established Puerto Rico as a territory of the United States and gave all Puerto Ricans U.S. citizenship. In the early 1930s, however, Puerto Ricans led by Luis Muñoz Marín began to lobby for increased autonomy from the United States. Under pressure from the United Nations, the United States finally permitted Puerto Rico a degree of self-government in 1947. The following year, Muñoz Marín became Puerto Rico's first elected governor.

The forceful Muñoz Marín at first pushed for even greater freedom from the United States. A 1950 act of Congress permitted Puerto Rico to write its own

Although Luis Muñoz Marín (shown with his hands raised) initially advocated Puerto Rico's independence from the United States, he was later elected governor of the U.S. commonwealth and supported social and economic reforms on the island.

constitution, which Puerto Rican voters ratified in 1952. That same year another congressional resolution granted Puerto Rico commonwealth status within the United States.

During the 1940s, Muñoz Marín had drawn up a plan to modernize the Puerto Rican economy. This program, called **Operation Bootstrap**, encouraged outside investment and industrialization of the economy. With the help of the United States government, which gave tax breaks and other special advantages to those who invested in Puerto Rican enterprises, the program made great progress. The Puerto Rican economy thrived over the next two decades. Economic development changed life for Puerto Rico's people. By the 1970s, Puerto Rico—once very poor—had raised its per capita income dramatically.

However, population growth outstripped economic growth, as it did elsewhere in Latin America, and there were not enough jobs for Puerto Rico's growing labor force. As a result, during the 1960s and 1970s, many Puerto Ricans went to the United States in search of work. Today, several million Puerto Ricans live in the United States. Many people believe that this has created two Puerto Rican cultures—a mainland culture strongly influenced by the U.S. way of life and an island culture dominated by the Hispanic heritage.

Puerto Rico's political status has been a constant source of debate on the island and in the United States. However, while public sentiment remains split over the question of commonwealth status versus statehood, only a small but vocal group has called for complete independence from the United States. In 1967, when Puerto Ricans were asked to vote on the matter, 60 percent chose to continue as a commonwealth. In a nonbinding vote taken in 1993, 48.4 percent preferred commonwealth status and 46.2 percent favored statehood, while a small percentage—less than 6 percent—voted for independence. The debate over Puerto Rico's future political status continued into the late 1990s.

Other Caribbean Nations

Cuba was not the only troubled island nation in Latin America in the 1960s. Many countries experienced a shift toward the political left and were disrupted by a series of coups and assassinations.

The Dominican Republic. The Dominican dictator Rafael Trujillo, assassinated in 1961, was succeeded by Juan Bosch, the first president to be democratically elected in the Dominican Republic in more than 30 years. After a coup toppled Bosch in 1963, his

followers, some of whom were Communists, started an uprising to return him to power. Hoping to prevent a communist takeover like the one in Cuba, President Lyndon Johnson of the United States in 1965 sent tens of thousands of marines to support the Dominican Republic's military regime.

After 1965 the Dominican Republic made much political and economic progress. Throughout much of the 1970s and 1980s, the island was stable. Although the economy remained heavily dependent on the export of sugar, efforts to diversify the economy through the development of light industry and tourism met with some success.

In the 1990s, however, the Dominican Republic faced considerable political and economic upheaval. An energy shortage—the nation's utilities were able to meet only 50 percent of demand—disrupted business and industry. Both unemployment and inflation soared.

By the mid-1990s, conditions had improved somewhat. Tourism was up, and inflation—once as high as 100 percent annually—was down to 9.5 percent in 1995. However, the unemployment rate was still about 30 percent, and millions of people lived in poverty. Democratic elections held in 1996 proceeded without incident, but the government faced continuing economic problems and antigovernment unrest.

Haiti. In 1986 the 30-year reign of the Duvalier family ended when "President for Life" Jean-Claude Duvalier was forced into exile. The people of Haiti, the poorest country in the Western Hemisphere, hoped

Armed troops patrol the streets of Port-au-Prince, Haiti, in January 1988.

that they would soon have a democratic government. The military regime that first took control of the government reluctantly allowed an election to be held in 1987. However, this election was canceled because of the violence that erupted among the rival political parties. Another election, held in 1988, brought a civilian government to power, but the military soon seized control again.

The government remained in the hands of the military until 1990, when Jean-Bertrand Aristide, a populist Catholic priest, won, becoming Haiti's first democratically elected president. In September of 1991, however, the military again seized power, forcing Aristide to flee the country. Three years later, mainly through the efforts of the United States, Aristide was able to return to Haiti and once again take office. In 1996 he was succeeded by René Préval—the first time that one elected Haitian civilian had completed his term in office and peacefully passed power to another. Aristide, however, continued to play an important role in Haitian politics, and observers believed that he would again seek the presidency. Meanwhile, Haiti continued to suffer dire economic and social problems, ranging from extreme poverty and widespread illiteracy to rampant crime and corruption.

The Smaller Caribbean Nations

European powers colonized the islands of the West Indies more than two centuries ago. Today, most of these islands have their own governments, and many are independent nations.

In 1958 most of the British islands were joined into a country called the West Indies Federation. The federation was dissolved in 1962, after Jamaica seceded; Jamaica, Trinidad and Tobago, and Barbados soon became independent nations. A number of other small islands have gained their independence relatively recently. For example, Grenada became independent in 1974, Antigua in 1981, and St. Kitts and Nevis in 1983. In response to a request from neighboring Caribbean countries in 1983, President Reagan sent U.S. forces to Grenada to overthrow a communist regime there.

Despite certain physical, historical, and economic similarities, little cohesiveness developed among these Caribbean islands. However, in the mid-1990s, regional groups and associations such as the Caribbean Community and Common Market (Caricom) took on increasing importance as a means of advancing the islands' trade and economic interests.

Section 3 Review

1. **Define** dissidents, Operation Bootstrap
2. **Identify** Fidel Castro, Luis Muñoz Marín, Jean-Bertrand Aristide
3. **Locate and Explain the Significance** Cuba, Puerto Rico, Dominican Republic, Haiti
4. **Analyzing Ideas (a)** Why was Fidel Castro's revolution initially welcomed by many Cubans? **(b)** What caused large numbers of Cubans to lose faith in the revolution?
5. **Contrasting Ideas** How has the experience of Puerto Rico since World War II been different from that of Cuba?
6. **Summarizing Ideas** Describe political developments in the Dominican Republic and Haiti in the past several decades.

Section 4

South America

Focus Questions

- **What political and economic problems have the South American countries of Argentina, Brazil, Chile, Peru, and Colombia had in the years since 1945?**
- **What signs of hope are there for these countries, and what struggles do they continue to face?**

Many of the nations of South America experienced turbulent political development in the decades following World War II. Revolutions swept the continent, leaving very few governments and individuals untouched.

Argentina

General Juan Perón rose to power in Argentina in the 1940s, gaining support from lower-class workers and the growing middle class. Elected president by a huge majority in 1946, Perón depended greatly on the advice of his wife, Eva or "Evita," a former film and radio actress. Through the skillful political use of the mass media, Evita built up a huge following, especially among the country's working class. Although Perón held the title of president, his wife was the one loved by the people of Argentina.

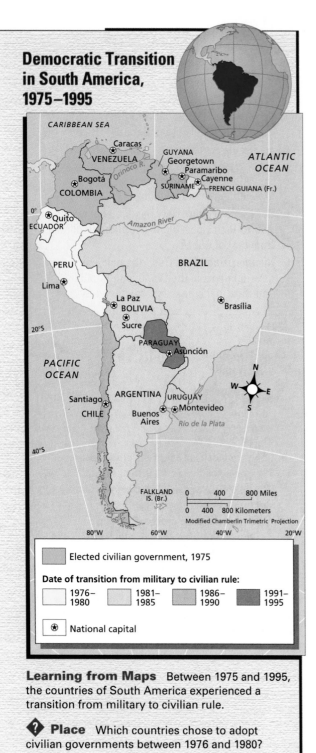

Democratic Transition in South America, 1975–1995

CARIBBEAN SEA

Caracas
VENEZUELA
GUYANA
Georgetown
Paramaribo
Cayenne
SURINAME
FRENCH GUIANA (Fr.)
ATLANTIC OCEAN

Bogotá
COLOMBIA

Orinoco R.

Quito
ECUADOR

Amazon River

PERU

BRAZIL

Lima

La Paz
BOLIVIA
Sucre

Brasília

PACIFIC OCEAN

PARAGUAY
Asunción

ARGENTINA
URUGUAY
Santiago
CHILE
Buenos Aires
Montevideo
Río de la Plata

N
W E
S

FALKLAND IS. (Br.)

0   400   800 Miles
0   400   800 Kilometers
Modified Chamberlin Trimetric Projection

80°W   60°W   40°W   20°W

Elected civilian government, 1975

Date of transition from military to civilian rule:

| 1976–1980 | 1981–1985 | 1986–1990 | 1991–1995 |

⊛ National capital

Learning from Maps Between 1975 and 1995, the countries of South America experienced a transition from military to civilian rule.

❓ **Place** Which countries chose to adopt civilian governments between 1976 and 1980?

---

slowly created an authoritarian regime that suppressed political dissent.

During World War II, Argentina had profited from selling beef and grain to the Allies. Although the Perón regime controlled inflation, other attempted reforms did not improve the economy. By the early 1950s, Argentina had many economic troubles.

When Eva Perón died of cancer in 1952, her husband lost his greatest political asset. In death, Evita took on mythical qualities. Juan Perón's popularity, in contrast, plunged. His rule came to an end in 1955, when a military coup forced him into exile.

Over the next 18 years, a succession of military and civilian governments struggled against political and economic instability. A violent terror campaign, begun by leftist guerrillas in the late 1960s, added to the chaos. By 1972 the Argentine people had begun to look back fondly on the Perón years as a time of peace and prosperity. The following year, Perón returned from exile and, in a landslide election victory, again became president. His new wife, Isabel, won election as vice president.

Perón immediately launched an offensive against the left-wing guerrilla groups and made efforts to bring the unruly economy under control. However, he died in 1974, before he could make any progress. His widow succeeded him, becoming the first woman president in the Americas. Incapable of dealing with Argentina's many problems, Isabel was overthrown in 1976 when the military seized control once again.

The dirty war. To put an end to the guerrilla insurrection once and for all, the military regime launched what it called a holy war. Army and police units arrested and imprisoned opposition leaders and anyone else who expressed antigovernment sentiments. Some, perhaps as many as 20,000, were spirited away during the night and never seen again. Most of these *desaparecidos*—disappeared persons—were tortured before being killed. For this reason, the military's campaign against the guerrillas became known as the "dirty war."

The dirty war and continuing economic problems caused support for the military junta to dwindle. To bolster its popularity, the junta ordered an invasion of the British-held Falkland Islands. Argentina had long laid claim to this territory, which the Argentines called the Malvinas. The junta believed that Britain would not bother to defend these desolate islands, and a quick military victory against a major power would be very popular among Argentines.

The junta's judgment proved disastrously wrong. British prime minister Margaret Thatcher in 1982

By promising—and delivering—much to the working class, the Peróns soon had the support of much of the country. Facing little opposition, they

Earlier Battles for the Falklands

On April 2, 1982, a tiny garrison of British Royal Marines was attacked by Argentine soldiers on the Falkland Islands. After two hours of fighting, the marines gave up. The Argentine victory, however, was short-lived. In the brief but bloody war that followed, Britain regained the islands.

The first settlers in the Falklands seem to have been neither Argentine nor British, but French. In 1764 these

Port Howard Settlement, East Falkland Island

French settlers, lured by the prospect of a rich supply of whales and seals—whose oils were in high demand—established a fort on what is now East Falkland. In 1765 the British claimed the islands, establishing Port Egmont on West Falkland. Spain, nervous at having two rivals perched so close to the edge of South America, demanded that both groups of foreigners leave the islands, which it called Las Islas Malvinas. The French left easily after Spain offered them a cash payment. The British were not so easy to dislodge. Spain and Great Britain came to the edge of war in 1770, but Spain backed down and returned Port Egmont to Britain in 1771. By 1774, however, British priorities had changed, and British troops simply withdrew from the islands, leaving them to the Spanish. They were abandoned by Spain in 1811.

In 1820 the new Argentine nation took possession of the islands, and they once again became a focus of dispute. The new government developed an increasingly strict stance against foreign fishermen, considering them to be intruders and an economic threat. In 1831, ships from the United States were seized off the islands' coast for illegal fishing. The United States attempted to have the islands declared free of government, but by 1833 the British had restored their control of the area. Ever since that time, the Argentines have considered the British action as illegal and imperialist. These disputed claims of ownership set the stage for the Falklands War of 1982.

sent an armada of ships and thousands of soldiers to reclaim the territory. The Argentine military was totally mismatched against the well-trained, professional British forces. In a matter of weeks, the British won a decisive victory. This humiliation at the hands of the British greatly angered most Argentines.

A return to democracy. Argentina's defeat in the Falklands led to the downfall of the military government. (See map on opposite page.) Free elections followed in 1983, won by Raúl Alfonsín of the Radical Union Party. Alfonsín had promised to put on trial those military and government officials who had been involved in the dirty war. The promise proved difficult to keep, however. Those who were guilty of crimes probably numbered in the thousands, but only three former presidents and some high-ranking officers went on trial. This situation, along with continuing economic problems, undermined Alfonsín's popularity. He decided not to run for another term, and in the 1989 elections, Carlos Menem of the Perónist Party became president.

On taking office, Menem faced massive economic problems. Inflation was high. The government had difficulty making its foreign debt payments. Menem also faced difficulties with the armed forces, and the threat of military takeover seemed constant.

Through strict wage and price controls and the privatization of many state monopolies, Menem managed to bring some stability to the economy. To soothe the military, Menem pardoned all but a few of those found guilty of crimes in the dirty war. However, many Argentines resented this action.

Rio de Janeiro stands as a major commercial and financial city with access to Brazil's eastern coast.

In the early 1990s, Argentina's economy continued to improve under the programs of President Menem. Gross national product and annual per capita income both rose sharply, while the rate of inflation declined. Despite a slowdown in the economy, Menem was reelected in 1995. His economic measures helped return Argentina to growth, although the rate of unemployment remained at about 15 percent in 1997.

Brazil

Political unrest and economic chaos characterized Brazil from the postwar period to the early 1990s. Often governments in Brazil were overthrown in an effort to save the economy. Such a situation occurred in the early 1960s, when João Goulart, with the support of a growing labor movement, became president of Brazil. Under Goulart's leadership, inflation worsened and industry declined. Various groups within the society became polarized.

To counter what they viewed as a threat to the economy as well as a political threat from the left, the army overthrew Goulart in 1964. The military government forced wages down by setting a low minimum wage and by pressuring the labor unions. Foreign corporations were also urged to invest in Brazil.

The economy grew so fast that it was widely hailed as the "Brazilian Miracle." People migrated to the cities, where jobs were available. At the same time,

the government suppressed dissent and dissolved political parties. It also went heavily into debt. Brazil emerged from the 1980s with the highest foreign debt among developing countries.

In 1990 a civilian government took office, led by Fernando Collor. Collor's major concern was Brazil's dire economic situation. He attacked inflation, which had risen steadily. To reduce government spending, he drastically cut the government labor force and sold a number of state-owned industries to private concerns. To control private spending, he froze most savings and checking accounts.

Collor's economic program pushed the Brazilian economy into recession. The economy shrank, and inflation jumped. In late 1992 Collor resigned and was succeeded by his vice president Itamar Franco. For most of Franco's 27 months as president, Brazil's problems worsened, with inflation soaring while corruption and crime flourished.

In 1994 Franco's finance minister, Fernando Henrique Cardoso, devised economic reforms which proved so successful that the increasingly popular Cardoso himself went on to become president in 1995. Under Cardoso, Brazil's economy regained some stability. In 1996, inflation fell below 14 percent, and the nation's GDP—the largest in the region by far—grew about 3 percent, in its fourth consecutive year of growth. In 1997, however, volatile financial markets challenged Brazil's ability to maintain the economic progress made in recent years.

Chile

Chile, once the oldest continuing democracy in Latin America, underwent important governmental changes in the 1970s and 1980s. In 1970 an alliance of the Socialist and Communist Parties resulted in the election of Salvador Allende. With Allende as president, a Marxist government had come to power through peaceful means, the first to do so in the Western Hemisphere.

Allende's administration nationalized copper mines and other industries, forced the breakup of many large estates, and implemented an across-the-board wage increase. At the same time, radical supporters seized many farms and factories. Before long the economy was in turmoil. Economic output declined, and food shortages spread. Hard pressed for funds, Allende's treasury printed more money to meet its needs. By 1972 rampant inflation had created hardships for all segments of the population.

As the economy worsened, unrest and disillusionment spread. Meanwhile, the U.S. government supported military leaders who opposed Allende. Finally, in 1973, the army overthrew the government and took power. Allende died in the bloody coup. Once in control, the military swiftly eliminated all forms of opposition.

The new military government executed people who had opposed their coup. Fearing for their lives, thousands of others fled into exile. The military leader, General Augusto Pinochet, dissolved the legislature and outlawed all political parties. He also placed tight controls on the press and cut back many civil liberties.

In addition, he ended all government interference in the economy, allowing it to operate by the forces of supply and demand. This action had a dramatic impact on inflation, which had run wild in the last years of the Allende government. By the end of the 1970s, inflation had fallen to about 30 percent annually, and it ran at about 20 percent a year through most of the 1980s. Such success came at a cost. Unemployment soared. Twenty-one percent of workers had no jobs in the early 1980s. However, Pinochet's economic program, reinforced by a huge inflow of foreign capital, began to work. By the late 1980s, Chile had become one of Latin America's most prosperous countries.

Even so, civil unrest continued to plague the country. Pinochet responded with repressive measures. To strengthen his hold on power, in 1988 Pinochet called for a plebiscite, or special vote, to determine whether he should remain in power. He expected to win, but nearly 55 percent of the electorate said that he should step down. Accepting defeat, Pinochet set free elections for 1989. In that vote, Patricio Aylwin, the candidate of a coalition of parties, was elected president.

Under Aylwin, Chile continued to prosper, the country's economic growth helped by free trade and billions of dollars in foreign investment. Chile's GDP grew by 11 percent in 1992 and 6 percent in 1993, while inflation remained at about 12 percent a year. In December 1993, voters chose Eduardo Frei to succeed Aylwin as president. Chile's stability and economic strength continued into the mid-1990s, even as the government grappled with such problems as widespread poverty and increasing pollution. By 1997, Chile's economy had grown for 14 consecutive years, and Chile had one of the most prosperous economies in Latin America.

To keep its economy growing, the Frei government continued to pursue international trade agreements as a key part of its foreign policy. In 1996, Chile signed free trade agreements with Canada and with the Mercosur group (Argentina, Brazil, Paraguay, and Uruguay). Chile also has agreements with Mexico, Venezuela, Colombia, and other nations.

Peru

In the decades following World War II, Peru's government was run by either military dictators or conservative civilians. Like so many other Latin American nations, Peru faced serious economic problems, including hyperinflation, unemployment, crushing poverty, and mounting foreign debt.

In the 1980s, Peru suffered an economic depression. In addition to its economic crisis, the country faced growing political problems. The greatest challenge to democracy in Peru was the war waged against the government by communist-inspired guerrillas. This war involved two major guerrilla groups.

In the cities, the Tupac Amarú Revolutionary Movement (MRTA) bombed public buildings and utility companies and assassinated police and government officials. Another group, **Sendero Luminoso**, or "Shining Path," carried out a similar terror campaign in the rural highland areas. Shining Path followed a Maoist ideology, believing that the present society had to be destroyed and a new socialist society built on its ruins. Illegal drugs, one of the major problems of the late 1900s, prompted further terrorist activity. Peru is Latin America's leading producer of coca, the plant from which cocaine is obtained. Drug trafficking provided a quick and easy way for the guerrillas to raise funds. The MRTA and Shining Path accepted arms and money in exchange for protecting the profitable cocaine business.

In 1990 a surprise election victory by Alberto Fujimori, son of a Japanese immigrant, set the stage for significant change. The new president took over a country in chaos, with surging hyperinflation (2,800 percent in 1989), huge foreign debt, and a deadly guerrilla war in progress. Austerity measures soon brought inflation down to a manageable level. By the end of 1994, terrorism and violence in Peru had decreased, and the economy was growing. Fujimori easily won re-election in 1995 with 64 percent of the vote, despite criticism of his autocratic approach to government.

By mid-1996, however, slowing economic growth and charges of government corruption had caused Fujimori's popularity to decline. Then, in December 1996, a small group of heavily armed MRTA guerrillas invaded the Japanese embassy in Lima, Peru, taking numerous hostages. The crisis did not end until April 1997, when Fujimori ordered Peruvian soldiers to storm the embassy. All of the guerrillas were killed in the raid, along with one hostage and two soldiers. Popular approval of Fujimori rose again, but not for long.

In subsequent months the president's political position became uncertain. Both Fujimori's power and his popularity appeared to be on the decline. At the same time, Peru's military, which had always played a key role in Fujimori's government, seemed to be taking an ever-increasing share of control. As observers looked ahead to the next election, scheduled for the year 2000, they wondered whether Peru's future would bring democracy or dictatorship.

Colombia

The years immediately following World War II were a time of severe turmoil in Colombia. From 1946 to 1958, both military and civilian dictators came to power amid civil and economic strife. However, by the mid-1960s, Colombia's future appeared brighter. The economy stabilized, and Colombia became known as one of the models of democracy in Latin America.

Unfortunately, the demand for illegal drugs increased in Europe and the United States during the late 1960s and early 1970s. The fertile land of Colombia became a prime region for growing marijuana as well as the coca plant that is used to make narcotics. Huge profits resulting from trade in these illegal products led to an increase in their production. Crime soared, as those who wanted to control this trade jockeyed for power and position. Medellín, once a flourishing industrial city in Colombia, became a headquarters for the **Medellín cartel** that ran the Colombian drug trade.

The Medellín cartel used assassinations and other means of intimidation to gain control of law enforcement agencies. Many officials, especially those at the lower levels of government, were either bribed or threatened by the drug lords until they cooperated with the cartel.

The terror campaigns of many left-wing guerrilla groups added to the violence. The most notorious of these groups, M-19, targeted officials of the justice system for assassination. During the 1980s, actions by M-19 took the lives of hundreds of judges and prosecutors. Right-wing death squads, many connected with the army, added to the death toll by assassinating people who expressed left-wing sympathies. Often dozens of murders would occur in Colombia in one day. Behind all this political violence stood the drug lords, who willingly financed terror groups.

In the late 1980s, the Colombian authorities declared war on the drug cartels. They called on United States law officers and military to assist in this offensive. They also promised to turn over to the United States any drug traffickers they captured. The result was open warfare on the streets of Medellín and Cali, headquarters of the other large drug cartel. The elections of 1990 proved particularly bloody.

Alberto Fujimori, the son of a Japanese immigrant, won the 1990 Peruvian presidential election; he was reelected in 1995.

Magic Realism

In the spellbinding fictional worlds of many Latin American writers of the 1900s—such as Gabriel García Márquez, Isabel Allende, and Nélida Piñon—a character may ascend to heaven while clutching bed linens from the clothesline, play the piano without lifting the lid, or be followed everywhere by yellow butterflies. In such a landscape and amidst such characters, real and surreal elements join forces to create the literary style known as magic realism.

Millions of readers around the world have been enchanted in recent decades with the imaginary and marvelous images, settings, and characters that writers of magic realism create. While these elements may seem new and unique, the themes explored are rooted in Latin American everyday town and village life, history, religion, superstition, and myth. As the

Gabriel García Márquez

Brazilian novelist Nélida Piñon says, "The myths eat with us at our table." Colombian novelist and short-story writer Gabriel García Márquez explains magic realism's lens in this way:

"I have the character Ulises make glass change color every time he touches it. Now, that can't be true. But so much has already been said about love that I had to find a new way of saying that this boy is in love. So I have the colors of the glass change, and I have his mother say, 'Those things happen only because of love.'**"**

In his best-selling, award-winning novel *One Hundred Years of Solitude*, García Márquez tells the story of Macondo, a small Colombian village. At the same time, he also uses his novel to cry out for his troubled region: where forests are destroyed, political power is abused, and massacres can be covered up and forgotten.

In the early 1990s, Columbian government leaders pledged to continue the fight against the drug cartels. However, corruption funded by drug money was very extensive in this country. Drug trafficking continued into the mid-1990s, as did murder, terrorism, and guerrilla violence.

By 1995 the Cali cartel was thought to control as much as 70 percent of the world trade in cocaine. Moreover, Colombian president Ernesto Samper was himself widely believed to have accepted millions of dollars from the cartel to finance his 1994 election campaign.

The nation struggled with economic difficulties, too. In 1996, inflation in Colombia rose, gross domestic product declined, and unemployment hit an eight-year high. Colombia's political and economic problems continued into 1997. Guerrilla groups, financed by drug money, took more lives, while President Samper expressed the government's hope for peace talks to end the violence.

> ### Section 4 Review
>
> 1. **Define** *desaparecidos, Sendero Luminoso,* Medellín cartel
> 2. **Identify** Eva Perón, Fernando Collor, Salvador Allende, Patricio Aylwin, Alberto Fujimori
> 3. **Summarizing Ideas** What occurred during the administration of the Peróns in Argentina?
> 4. **Synthesizing Ideas** What problems are shared by all of the countries discussed in this section?
> 5. **Understanding Cause and Effect (a)** What caused the growth of the drug trade in Colombia? **(b)** How did this growth affect the government and economy of Colombia?

Chapter 18 Review

1962 Cuban missile crisis occurs.

1965 U.S. Marines are sent to the Dominican Republic.

A.D. 1945　　A.D. 1950　　A.D. 1960　　A.D. 1965　　A.D. 1970

A.D. 1946 Juan Perón is elected president of Argentina.

1952
• Eva Perón dies.
• Puerto Rico becomes a commonwealth within the United States.

1948 OAS is founded.

1961 Bay of Pigs invasion takes place.

1959 Fidel Castro's revolutionaries take control of Cuba.

1967 Ché Guevara dies.

1970 Allende is elected president of Chile.

Chapter Summary

The following list contains the key concepts you have learned about the countries of Latin America from the postwar period to the present.

1. Economic problems faced by nations of Latin America were caused in part by monoculture, import substitution, and large foreign debt. Population growth, rapid urbanization, continued poverty, and environmental problems were major challenges for the region.

2. Women, labor unions, and the Catholic church all emerged as powerful political forces in the Latin American countries.

3. The Organization of American States (OAS) was founded to promote cooperation among the nations of the Western Hemisphere.

4. Revolution in Nicaragua in 1979 brought a Marxist regime to power. A civil war broke out in that country between the government, run by the Sandinistas, and guerrillas called Contras. The United States aided the Contras; Cuba and the Soviet Union aided the Nicaraguan government.

5. The Contadora Principles, along with other Latin American efforts, are bringing hope for peace to Central America.

6. Revolution in Cuba in 1959 brought a communist dictatorship under Fidel Castro to power. Confrontations with the United States occurred with the Bay of Pigs invasion in 1961 and the Cuban missile crisis in 1962. Cuba went through economic difficulties in the early 1990s but has recovered slightly in recent years.

7. Both the Dominican Republic and Haiti overthrew dictators. As the 1990s began, both tentatively established democratic governments.

8. In Argentina, Juan Perón established a dictatorship but was ousted in 1952. In 1976, the military overthrew the government led by his wife, Isabel. After the disastrous Falklands conflict, Argentina returned to civilian government.

9. Political unrest and economic chaos have characterized Brazil in the postwar period. By the 1990s, the country faced massive foreign debt. The economy showed signs of recovery in the late 1900s.

10. Chile's government was a military dictatorship from 1973 to 1988. Chile began to prosper in the 1990s. Both Peru and Colombia faced political unrest through the 1980s. The drug trade has caused problems throughout South America.

Reviewing Important Terms

On a separate sheet of paper, supply the term that correctly completes each statement.

1. A foreign-owned business is called a(n) _____ _____ .
2. _____ _____ is an economic policy in which a country encourages the internal production of goods that the country had been importing.
3. An area whose countries or regions have common geographical and political features is called a(n) _____ _____ .
4. _____ are Central American peasants.
5. The dependence of a country or region on one crop is _____.
6. People who disagree with the government of a country are called _____.

Developing Critical Thinking Skills

1. **Understanding Cause and Effect (a)** What were the causes of the population increase in Latin America? **(b)** What were the consequences?
2. **Interpreting Ideas (a)** What benefits did Latin American leaders envision from economic development? **(b)** What efforts did they make to achieve it?
3. **Synthesizing Ideas** How would economic prosperity in Latin America help establish greater political stability?
4. **Understanding Relationships** What were the results of the United States involvement in **(a)** Nicaragua; **(b)** Cuba; **(c)** the Dominican Republic?
5. **Analyzing Ideas** "Demand, not supply, needs to be brought under control." Do you agree that this

1973
Juan Perón returns to power.

1982
Falklands conflict begins.

1986
Duvalier regime is overthrown in Haiti.

1989
Chile holds free elections.

1994
North American Free Trade Agreement (NAFTA) goes into effect.

A.D. **1975**   A.D. **1980**   A.D. **1985**   A.D. **1990**   A.D. **1995**

1976
Isabel Perón is overthrown.

1979
• Somoza regime is overthrown in Nicaragua.
• U.S. Senate ratifies Panama Canal treaty.

1983
Contadora Principles are adopted.

1990
• Violeta Barrios de Chamorro is elected president of Nicaragua.
• Jean-Bertrand Aristide comes to power in Haiti.
• Alberto Fujimori is elected in Peru.

approach will end the Latin American drug trafficking problem? Explain your answer.

6. **Comparing Ideas** (a) How were the revolutions in Cuba and Nicaragua different? (b) How were they similar?

Relating Geography to History

Turn to the map of Central America and the Caribbean on page 574. (a) How many of these nations have communist governments? (b) How many miles are they from the United States? (c) What effect might the presence of communist governments throughout this region have on United States security?

Relating Past to Present

1. Political affairs in many Latin American countries remain unsettled. Choose one Latin American country and do research to find articles on recent developments there. How have changes in Central America affected U.S. foreign policy?

2. Find out how many governments in Latin America today came to power by either a coup or a revolution. Are these governments secure? How many are dictatorships?

Applying History Study Skills

Before completing this activity, review Building History Study Skills on page 567.

Read the following paragraph describing what takes place on a hacienda during a revolution.

"[W]hat we call social revolutions have all occurred in agricultural countries where the mass of the people lived on what they themselves raised from the soil. In such a society, a revolution is a simple thing. First, you cut off the head of the *hacendado,* then you divide the wheat, corn, and barley stored in the barn and the *hacendado*'s cows, horses, sheep, and chickens. Similarly the plows, digging sticks, and other tools are distributed. The land is taken by the peasants and the revolution is over. What really happens is that the stored consumer goods are divided up among the sur-

rounding peasants, and the limited producers' goods, in the form of seed, animals, tools, and the land itself, fall into the hands of those who have used the tools and animals and worked the land."

1. What economic questions are raised by the passage?
2. How is scarcity dealt with after a revolution?
3. What does the passage imply might be some of the causes of the revolution?

🖅 internet**connect**

Search the Internet through the HRW Web site for recent statistics on per capita gross domestic product, major exports, and major imports of these countries: Mexico, Guatemala, El Salvador, Honduras, Belize, Nicaragua, Costa Rica, Panama, Cuba, the Dominican Republic, Haiti, Colombia, Venezuela, Bolivia, Peru, Chile, Brazil, Paraguay, Uruguay, and Argentina. Then assemble the information you have gathered into a chart to display.

GO TO: go.hrw.com
KEYWORD: SCØ LA Stats

Building Your Portfolio

1. **Presenting an Oral Report** Although the Brazilian economy grew rapidly in the 1960s and 1970s, many Brazilians still lived in poverty. Find out about living conditions in the slums, and present an oral report to the class. Place your notes in your portfolio.

2. **Preparing a Panel Discussion** Work with a group of your classmates to find more information on how the nations of Latin America are dealing with low rates of economic growth, high rates of unemployment and population growth, and burgeoning foreign debts. Then use the information you have collected to prepare a panel discussion detailing possible solutions to these problems. Place your notes or an audiotape of the discussion in your portfolio.

The Superpowers in the Modern Era

TIME

A.D. **1969–the present**

A.D. **1969–the present**

3.7 million B.C.   4000 B.C.   A.D. 2100

PLACE

Africa, Asia, Europe, the Americas, and Australia

Europe

Australia

The Americas

Africa

Asia

The fall of communism in Russia

Significance

The final decades of the 1900s marked a period of transition among the industrialized nations of North America and Europe.

Indeed, the late 1900s were also a period of contrasts. The United States remained a leading power in world affairs, while the Soviet Union as one nation disappeared. As the Soviet Union unraveled, the nations of Western Europe moved toward closer union as the fall of communism reawakened old ethnic divisions in Eastern Europe. At the same time, Canada survived challenges to its unity, notably from separatists in Quebec.

Terms to Define

Vietnamization
Watergate scandal
stagflation
trade deficit
détente
Carter Doctrine
weapons of mass
  destruction
Meech Lake Accord
IRA
Ostpolitik

Helsinki Accords
Maastricht Treaty
Brezhnev Doctrine
perestroika
glasnost
CIS
ethnic cleansing
Dayton Accord
IFOR

People to Identify

Jimmy Carter
Ronald Reagan
Bill Clinton
Margaret Thatcher
François Mitterrand
Jacques Chirac
Helmut Schmidt

Helmut Kohl
Juan Carlos
Mikhail Gorbachev
Boris Yeltsin
Lech Walesa
Vaclav Havel
Nicolae Ceausescu

Places to Locate

Estonia
Latvia
Lithuania
Republic of Georgia
Caspian Basin

Czech Republic
Slovakia
Bosnia and
  Herzegovina

Chapter Theme Questions

- **War and Diplomacy** How and why might international conflict continue after the end of the Cold War?
- **Economic Organization** How might nations benefit from pursuing free trade and free enterprise?
- **Cross-Cultural Interaction** How might cultural differences within societies in Europe and North America give rise to conflict?

On Christmas Day 1991, Soviet leader Mikhail Gorbachev appeared on television to make an extraordinary announcement. The Soviet Union, he said, would in a few days cease to exist. Less than a week later the world watched with amazement as one of the century's mightiest totalitarian powers officially ceased to exist.

For more than seven decades, the Soviet Union had been a primary force in international politics. Now it had crumbled under the weight of its own economic inefficiency and the spread of democratic ideals. Across the vast stretch of Eurasia, to the borders of the Middle East in the south and to the Pacific in the east, 19 independent republics, with Russia the largest, eventually emerged in its place.

Challenges remained, however. Would democracy and free enterprise take hold? As the appeal of communism faded, the strength of nationalism resurged—sometimes with bloody consequences. At the dawn of a new millennium, a new set of international relationships took shape.

Section 1

The Industrial Powers of North America

Focus Questions

- **How did the Vietnam War and the Watergate scandal affect political attitudes in the United States in the late 1900s?**
- **What changes have occurred in the United States's economy since 1970?**
- **What major changes did American foreign policy undergo in the 1970s, 1980s, and 1990s?**
- **What major challenges did Canada face in the late 1900s?**

During the late 1900s, the United States confronted a number of challenges. Defeat in Vietnam created doubts about America's military power, but the Persian Gulf War appeared to relieve those doubts. The U.S. economy fluctuated through the 1970s, but recovered in the mid-1980s and generally grew through the 1990s. Canada similarly grappled with serious political and economic problems, somewhat reluctantly moving toward closer relations with its neighbor to the south.

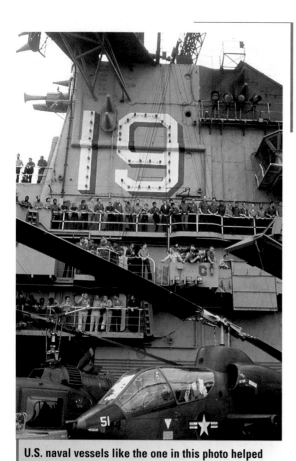

U.S. naval vessels like the one in this photo helped evacuate South Vietnamese citizens in 1975.

Ending the Vietnam War

In 1969, Richard M. Nixon became president of the United States. Foremost among the challenges that he faced was the increasingly unpopular and economically burdensome war in Vietnam. Hoping to avoid outright defeat, Nixon sought a way to end American involvement in Vietnam "with honor."

American withdrawal. Nixon first began the process of **Vietnamization**, preparing the South Vietnamese to take over the fighting while gradually withdrawing American forces. By January 1973 the number of American troops in Vietnam had decreased from well over 540,000 (in 1969) to some 24,000.

At the same time, Nixon increased military pressure against the communists in order to compel their leaders to negotiate on American terms. He ordered the invasion of Cambodia in 1970 and subsequently stepped up the bombing of North Vietnam. On January 27, 1973, Communist negotiators finally accepted a comprehensive agreement, known as the Paris Peace Accords, to end the Vietnam War. The accords provided for the withdrawal of all U.S. and allied forces from Vietnam in exchange for the return of all prisoners. Within two months the last major U.S. combat units in Vietnam had returned home, although some troops remained until 1975.

The impact of the Vietnam War. President Nixon managed to extract the United States from Vietnam, but the effects of the war on American society persisted. The war left particularly deep scars on the American national identity. It had inflicted a heavy human toll and placed a substantial burden on the nation's economy. Moreover, with the fall of South Vietnam to the Communists in April 1975, the war seemed an utter failure of U.S. power. As a result, many Americans began to doubt the wisdom of the United States continuing to play a leading role on the world stage.

The Vietnam War bitterly divided the American people. Although Nixon had appealed to what he called a "silent majority" of Americans in 1970 to support the Vietnam War, the antiwar movement that had begun in the mid-1960s continued to gain strength through the Nixon administration. Actions such as the invasion of Cambodia appeared to contradict Nixon's promise to end the war. Demonstrations on college campuses became routine. Some turned violent, and a few turned deadly. At Kent State University in Ohio, four students were killed during a demonstration on May 4, 1970. Ten days later, two students were killed in another protest at Jackson State College in Mississippi. In the end, as the government's estimations of success in Vietnam proved exaggerated, growing numbers of Americans began to question the trustworthiness of their leaders.

Watergate and Its Legacy

A major scandal involving President Nixon added to the disillusionment with government that many Americans experienced after Vietnam. In 1972, burglars were caught breaking into the headquarters of the Democratic National Committee in the Watergate complex in Washington, D.C. In 1972, journalists from the *Washington Post* charged that officials of Nixon's re-election campaign had planned the break-in. An investigation by the Senate followed and found that Nixon's White House staff had used money from an illegal secret fund to conceal the incident's connection to the president. It soon became clear that Nixon himself had known about the cover-up. Facing impeachment by Congress, Nixon chose to

Maya Ying Lin

Among the 1,421 people who entered the competition to design a memorial to the veterans of the Vietnam War was Maya Ying Lin, a 21-year-old senior at Yale University. Her design for the memorial, shown at right, was simple: two long black granite walls, rising out of the earth and meeting at an angle. Written on these walls would be the names of the more than 58,000 soldiers declared killed or missing in action in Vietnam.

What drew the judges to the work of this young sculptor and architect? Like all great architecture, Lin's design was uniquely suited to its location, the sweeping lawns of the Constitution Gardens on the Mall in Washington, D.C. The design inspired contemplation and reflection; it was dignified and eloquent.

Lin chose a design that entered the earth and came back out again, feeling that such a design suitably symbolized death and remembrance. She also considered the symbolism of a scar—a painful reminder of loss that can heal but never really disappear.

Carved into the walls are the names of the dead and missing. They are arranged chronologically on each wall by the date of death or disappearance. On the east wall, the names begin at the center and travel toward the end. On the west wall, the names begin at the end and travel toward the center. In this way, at the intersection of the walls the first and last deaths meet.

Lin chose black granite rather than white marble for several reasons. Black is, after all, a traditional color of sorrow in the American culture. In a practical sense, the names would be easier to read on black than on white. Also, black granite could be highly polished, allowing it to reflect the Mall and the people who were reading the names. In this way, finally, the dead and those who wished to remember them could once again be brought together.

---

resign his office in August of 1974. He was succeeded by his vice president, Gerald R. Ford.

The **Watergate scandal** shook the faith of many Americans in their political system. People began to sense that politicians generally lacked integrity. President Ford's decision to pardon Nixon did not help to restore public confidence in government. In the minds of many people, as a result of Watergate, Washington politics increasingly became synonymous with dishonesty and corruption. As a result, several post-Watergate candidates for the presidency campaigned as outsiders with no ties to Washington. They vowed to clean up corruption in the political system. In 1976, James Earl ("Jimmy") Carter, a former governor of Georgia, was elected president. Carter proved to be a man of high integrity, but his presidency suffered from some serious problems. Carter upset many people by announcing his belief that the United States had lapsed into a "national malaise." Despite all efforts, the economy remained sluggish. Several reversals in foreign policy also afflicted Carter's presidency. Not least among these was the seizure in 1979 of the American embassy in Iran by Muslim militants, followed by a disastrous rescue attempt and a hostage crisis that Carter was unable to resolve.

In 1980, President Carter lost his bid for re-election to another outsider: Ronald Reagan, a former governor of California. Reagan's abiding optimism in the United States inspired many Americans and helped him to win reelection in 1984. During Reagan's second term, however, scandal once again captured public attention. Members of the National Security Council staff had become involved in illegal transactions involving the sale of arms to Iran in order to win the release of U.S. hostages in Lebanon. Proceeds of the arms sales were diverted and used to support anticommunist rebels—known as Contras—in Nicaragua. Some observers compared the situation to Watergate, dubbing the new scandal "Irangate." President Reagan's public image was tarnished, yet he remained popular.

Although Reagan's vice president, George Bush, a longtime Washington insider, won the presidency in 1988, the appeal of outsiders to American voters remained strong. In 1992, Bill Clinton, the governor of Arkansas, ran as an outsider and defeated President Bush. Accusations of questionable financial dealings and sexual misconduct dogged Clinton even before he took office. In the mid-1990s, an investigation into these accusations turned up evidence of possible crimes. In late 1998, the House of Representatives voted to begin an inquiry into possible grounds for the impeachment of President Clinton.

The U.S. Economy

During the late 1960s, government spending had skyrocketed as President Johnson tried to finance both his Great Society programs and the Vietnam War at the same time. This dramatic increase in government spending, combined with rising energy costs and higher prices for other commodities due to the devaluation of the dollar, led to inflation—a general increase in prices and a decline in the buying power of the dollar. Instability of the U.S. economy became an issue of some concern in the 1970s. It was not until the mid-1980s that the economy began a recovery, and the United States entered a period of general growth and renewed prosperity.

Attempts to stabilize the economy. Attempts to stabilize the U.S. economy in the 1970s proved unsuccessful. President Nixon tried to stimulate the economy by proposing tax changes. His policies, however, had little effect on inflation and actually helped to trigger a recession. The resulting combination of decreased economic activity, high unemployment, and rising prices, known as **stagflation**, remained a problem through the rest of the decade. Presidents Ford and Carter tried to fight stagflation through tight controls on federal spending, tax cuts, and voluntary price and wage freezes, but the economy showed little improvement.

The 1980s saw the return of economic growth. President Reagan took office in 1981, promising to improve the economy. He proposed new reductions in government spending, but it was largely a recession in the early 1980s that finally brought inflation down. To increase economic activity, Reagan called for tax cuts that would encourage spending by consumers and investment by business. This spending in turn would generate economic growth. By the mid-1980s, unemployment had dropped significantly as the economy entered a period of sustained growth. Despite a brief downturn in the early 1990s, the economy would continue its upward trend into the mid-1990s.

Not all was well, however. During the 1980s, the debts of the United States government ballooned. Although Congress had approved Ronald Reagan's proposed tax cuts and increased military expenditures, his proposed reductions in the growth of spending on various government social programs proved harder to implement. As a result, until the late 1980s, the government ran at increasingly larger annual deficits as it spent more than it took in from taxes. To make up the difference, the government borrowed money—much of it from foreign lenders.

As the debt and the interest on it grew, many American leaders became increasingly concerned. In 1985, Congress ordered across-the-board cuts in federal spending if the government failed to meet targeted yearly reductions in the deficit. The debt continued to grow, though at a slower rate. In 1994 the Republicans won majorities in both houses of Congress for the first time since the 1950s. They promised to reform expensive social programs and to press for reductions in the growth of spending to balance the budget. President Clinton, a Democrat, stated his agreement in principle, winning congressional passage of a $500 billion deal in taxes and spending cuts in 1993. The process of balancing the budget, however, proved politically contentious. In the late-1990s, overall growth of the economy made it possible to balance the budget for the first time in almost 30 years. However, the national debt remained a major challenge for the United States.

Changes in the U.S. economy. In many ways the economy lay beyond the control and influence of the government. Changes in the world economy, for example, significantly affected the U.S. economy. During the 1970s and 1980s, the United States began to lose its long-standing lead in heavy industry to other nations. American steel companies, shipbuilders, and automakers found it increasingly difficult to compete with their counterparts in countries like Japan and Germany. As a result, many Americans lost their jobs through the closing of steel mills, shipyards, and automobile plants in the 1980s.

The decline of American heavy industry contributed to the creation of a **trade deficit**. Beginning in the 1970s, the United States imported more goods than it exported. Still, even as Americans began to buy more from abroad and some U.S. businesses had difficulty selling their products overseas, many U.S. enterprises proved very successful in the world marketplace. Through the 1980s and 1990s, U.S. products dominated such important industries as aerospace engineering and pharmaceuticals. U.S. companies pioneered the revolution in computers and information technology during the 1980s, and these same companies remained the leaders in that field in the 1990s.

In fact, during the 1980s and 1990s, the creation of new jobs outpaced the loss of jobs in heavy industry. Many of the new jobs were in advanced technology and the so-called service industries, such as banking, retail, and restaurants. Economists suggested that this development reflected a transition to a more modern economy, much as heavy industry had replaced agriculture as the basis of the American economy a century earlier. They pointed out that the new economy would demand higher levels of education and more advanced skills than most people had needed in the past. Some worried that while educated people would do well, unskilled and low-skilled workers would fare poorly. Then American society would consist of a small group of extremely wealthy people, a shrinking middle class, and a large class of extremely poor people. On the whole, however, Americans in the mid-1990s enjoyed a comparatively high level of prosperity, and their country still boasted the world's largest economy.

Energy. The cost and availability of energy was one of the determining factors in the performance of the U.S. economy. Fossil fuels such as coal, natural gas, and especially oil were the most important sources of energy for the United States in the late 1900s. The fact that by the 1970s the United States was importing much of its oil, particularly from the Middle East, posed a serious problem. Shortages and price hikes

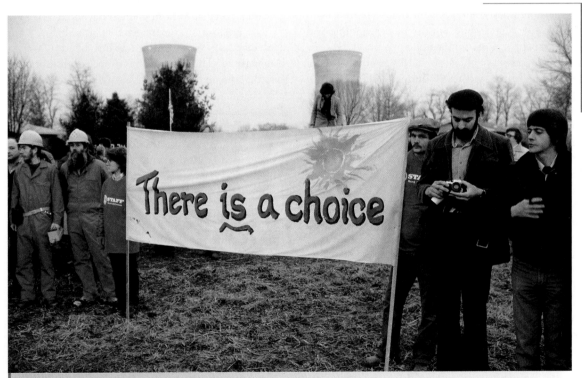

The accident on March 28, 1979, at the nuclear power station on Three Mile Island led to new health and safety concerns regarding this source of power. Protestors like these called for alternative sources of energy.

stemming from the OPEC oil embargo of 1973 and the Iranian revolution of 1979 added significantly to the instability of the U.S. economy in the years following Vietnam.

Worried about future supplies of oil, Americans began to consider alternative sources of energy. A greater emphasis on the use of coal was one possibility, but many people found the option unattractive because of the pollution created by coal. Some Americans began to demand the development of solar and wind power as clean and renewable sources of energy. President Carter called for research into such alternatives, combined with measures to conserve fossil fuels. The Reagan administration, however, discontinued many of these programs in the early 1980s.

Nuclear power attracted considerable interest as an economical alternative to fossil fuels. Critics worried, however, about the safety of nuclear energy. In 1979, an accident at the Three Mile Island nuclear power plant in Pennsylvania brought widespread attention to these worries. In 1986 the much more serious accident at the Chernobyl nuclear power plant in the Soviet Union further reinforced the growing popular dissatisfaction with nuclear energy.

In the meantime, oil companies had begun to develop previously untapped oil fields, many within the United States. The most notable example was in Alaska. New and significant discoveries of oil continued to be made in such places as the Gulf of Mexico and the Caspian Sea into the 1990s. By the mid-1990s, oil remained the single most important source of energy for the United States and the world.

But even as fears of severe oil depletion in the near future began to diminish, many Americans expressed other concerns about dependence on oil, particularly as fuel for automobiles. One such concern was the pollution caused by heavy oil usage. Other observers noted the strategic danger posed by continued reliance on imported oil. Many of the world's major oil fields lay in politically unstable regions. The Persian Gulf War of 1991 underscored these concerns.

Changes in Foreign Policy

American foreign policy underwent several changes in the late 1900s. In the 1970s, American leaders sought to ease the tensions behind the Cold War through improved relations with the communist world. Responding to continued Soviet expansion, however, the United States increased pressure on the Soviet Union in the 1980s. In the 1990s, U.S. foreign policy confronted a host of new problems that emerged in the wake of the Cold War's end and the collapse of the Soviet Union.

Relations with the Soviet Union. Efforts to improve relations with the Soviet Union began under President Nixon. In 1972, Nixon became the first U.S. president to visit Moscow. During his visit, President Nixon and Soviet leader Leonid Brezhnev signed the Strategic Arms Limitation Treaty, or SALT. This agreement limited each country's production and deployment of certain nuclear weapons. Nixon and Brezhnev also signed several accords related to environmental, health-related, and technological cooperation. The general improvement in Soviet-American relations that followed became known as **détente** (day·TAHNT), a French word meaning an easing of strain.

Presidents Ford and Carter continued the policy of détente throughout much of the 1970s. By the end of the decade, however, renewed tensions between the United States and the Soviet Union began to show. President Carter, insisting that human rights be made a major factor in U.S. foreign policy, began to speak out against Soviet treatment of dissidents—opponents of government policies. He also criticized Soviet and Cuban intervention in Africa, specifically in the Angolan and Ethiopian civil wars.

The most serious break in the relationship came in December 1979, when the Soviet Union invaded Afghanistan. The invasion threatened the security of the oil-rich and economically vital Persian Gulf. In what became known as the **Carter Doctrine**, President Carter declared in his 1980 State of the Union Address that the United States would regard any attempts by outside forces to gain control of the Persian Gulf region as an assault on the vital interests of the United States—an assault that might be answered by military force. He restricted U.S. trade with the Soviet Union and called for an international boycott of the 1980 Olympic Games in Moscow. Carter also called for a delay in ratifying a second Strategic Arms Limitation Treaty—SALT II—that was pending at the time.

By the early 1980s, détente had come to an end. Some Americans believed that the reduction of the U.S. military after Vietnam had served to encourage the aggressive actions of the Soviet Union. On taking office in 1981, President Reagan consequently called for substantially increased defense spending. Congress approved his request, and the United States soon began to build up its conventional forces, modernize its nuclear arsenal, and provide new aid to anticommunist forces that existed overseas.

Looking Beyond Planet Earth

The successful mission of the space shuttle *Discovery* in October 1988 reaffirmed the American commitment to space exploration that had faltered some two years before with the loss of the *Challenger* and its crew of seven. President Ronald Reagan underscored this rekindled commitment when he declared that the United States fully intended to expand human activity beyond Earth into the solar system. In the 1990s, progress toward cooperation with Russia in reaching these goals has been impressive.

The National Aeronautics and Space Administration (NASA) has already begun planning journeys to the farther reaches of the solar system. The first step involved the construction of a space station, a permanently manned outpost in orbit. The space station is designed to serve as a base for scientific observation and experimentation, a refueling station, and a base for launching other satellites or spacecraft.

Earth, as viewed from the space shuttle

The first successful experimental space station was launched by the United States in May 1973. Called *Skylab,* it remained in orbit for nearly a year. During that time, the astronauts made observations of the Sun and conducted experiments on how the body responds to zero-gravity conditions on extended missions. From 1974 to 1982, the Soviet Union also orbited a series of smaller space stations. In 1986 the Soviets launched a new space station called *Mir,* designed to be the core of a permanent manned orbiting facility. Between 1995 and 1998, in a sign of Russian-American cooperation, *Mir* hosted a series of NASA astronauts as crew members.

Both American and Russian scientists also want to explore other parts of the solar system, however. Throughout the 1960s and 1970s, both nations sent out deep-space probes. It was during this period that the Viking landings on Mars; the Voyager fly-bys of Jupiter, Saturn, and Uranus; and the Venera explorations of the surface of Venus were accomplished.

In July 1997 the Mars *Pathfinder* descended to the surface of Mars. Fascinating photographs of the Martian surface were transmitted back to Earth, and a rover vehicle called *Sojourner* moved over the Martian surface.

In the past, historical events and the personalities engaged in them were confined to the surface of Earth. However, the plans of the space programs of both the United States and Russia ensure that a new history will soon unfold in a new geography—that of the planets that lie in the vastness of space far beyond our own world.

Many feared that the United States was now pushing the Soviet Union too hard. The administration, however, maintained the pressure, believing it would ultimately force a more conciliatory policy from the Soviets.

By the mid-1980s, Soviet-American tensions had begun to ease. Recognizing the burden of the Cold War on his country's economy, the new Soviet leader, Mikhail Gorbachev, decided to pursue a friendlier relationship with the United States. In 1985, Reagan and Gorbachev held a summit meeting in Geneva, Switzerland. The two leaders met again in 1986 in Reykjavik (RAY·kyah·veek), Iceland. In 1987, Gorbachev visited Washington, D.C., where he and Reagan signed a new arms agreement eliminating short- and medium-range nuclear weapons.

By the end of the decade, Soviet-American relations had improved significantly. The Soviets began to reduce their military presence around the world, and in 1989 they finally withdrew their forces from Afghanistan. When democratic movements swept communist governments from power in Eastern Europe, the Soviets did not try to stop them. With its satellite states gone, racked by ethnic discord, and still straining under economic inefficiency, the Soviet Union itself faced imminent demise by the early 1990s. In December 1991, the Soviet Union formally ceased to exist. It was replaced by a loose association of many of its former republics, now independent nations.

The "new world order." Numerous threats to world stability, however, persisted after the Cold War ended. Ambitious regional powers represented a major concern of U.S. leaders in the 1990s. In 1990, for example, Iraq invaded Kuwait. In 1991 the United States launched its largest military operation since Vietnam, leading an international coalition in the Persian Gulf that succeeded in expelling Iraq from Kuwait. Iraq's continued efforts to acquire **weapons of mass destruction**—nuclear, chemical, and biological weapons—remained a major concern in the mid-1990s. American officials also worried about the proliferation of such weapons, which might spread from producers like Russia and China to potentially hostile regimes in countries like Iran and North Korea. During the Persian Gulf crisis, President Bush suggested to the United Nations that it was time for all nations to work toward a "new world order" based on peace and mutual cooperation and to defend weaker countries against aggressors. However, some suggested that the international community might defend only those weaker countries that possessed a valuable commodity, like the oil in Kuwait.

Another major concern was the resurgence of militant nationalism and ethnic conflict after the end of the Cold War. The disintegration of Yugoslavia in the early 1990s attracted particular attention. Worried that the ensuing civil war in the province of Bosnia and Herzegovina threatened the stability of Europe, American diplomats mediated a settlement between the Republic of Croatia, Bosnia's Muslim-led government, and Serbian separatists in 1995. To enforce the agreement, President Clinton ordered American troops to Bosnia and Herzegovina, often called Bosnia, as part of a multinational peacekeeping force. Clinton also dispatched American forces to support multinational peacekeeping missions in Somalia and Haiti.

Despite reductions in its military forces after the Cold War ended, the United States seemed to be playing an increased role in world politics in the mid-1990s. In addition to regional conflicts and civil strife, issues such as trade, terrorism, narcotics, and the environment loomed large in American foreign policy. Presidents Bush and Clinton focused on settling the Arab-Israeli dispute. In addition, some observers cautioned that Russia, heir to most of the Soviets' vast nuclear arsenal, still represented a potentially serious threat. China, too, might pose a significant danger, especially as the countries of Asia were growing in importance to the world's economy as the 1900s drew to a close.

Relations with China. American relations with China improved steadily through the 1970s and 1980s. In 1972, President Nixon visited China, beginning a period of diplomacy that culminated in full diplomatic relations with the People's Republic of China starting on January 1, 1979. While many Americans saw opportunities for investment and trade in China's rapidly growing economy, mutual distrust of the Soviet Union provided much of the basis for the improvement of Sino-American relations.

With the end of the Cold War, however, differences between China and the United States began to surface once again. Following China's crackdown on pro-democracy demonstrators in Tiananmen Square in 1989, many Americans expressed misgivings about China's record on human rights. Others worried about China's export of advanced weapons to potentially hostile states like Iran—and about China's own military buildup. By the mid-1990s, the question of how to deal with China—through incentives, such as trading advantages, or through stepped-up economic and military pressure—had become a major issue of debate among American policymakers.

Although the Meech Lake Accord failed to become part of the Canadian constitution, many Quebécois continue to favor separation from Canada.

Canada

Canada is the world's second-largest country in terms of geographic area and possesses a vast wealth of raw materials. Although much of its territory—especially in the north—is unsuitable for habitation, Canada is also one of the world's most highly developed countries. In general, Canadians enjoy a relatively high standard of living and a quality of life envied by many people around the world. Nonetheless, Canada confronted difficult political and economic challenges during the late 1900s.

Led by Prime Minister Pierre Trudeau, Canada's Liberal Party controlled the government throughout the 1970s. Trudeau was committed to preserving Canada's federal union, and he emphasized constitutional issues during his years in office. A recession led many Canadians to call for significant economic reform in the early 1980s. In 1984 the Progressive Conservative Party won a general election. To improve the economy, the new government under Prime Minister Brian Mulroney pursued the privatization of various industries, the deregulation of business, and reform of the tax structure. But if economic problems had led to the rise of the Conservative Party in the 1980s, they contributed to its downfall in the 1990s.

A deepening recession in the early 1990s contributed to a major shake-up in Canadian politics. Facing a crisis of confidence, the Conservatives decided to replace Mulroney as their party leader. They chose Kim Campbell to take his place, and she became Canada's first woman prime minister in mid-1993. Within a few months, however, the Conservatives suffered catastrophic defeat in a general election. The Liberal Party won control of the government for the first time since 1984. In late 1993, Jean Chrétien, who was the leader of the Liberal Party, took office as prime minister.

Chrétien faced many of the same problems that had confronted his predecessors. Many Canadians called for constitutional reform at the federal level. French Canadian separatism and relations with the United States were two of the most important issues.

Separatism. Although the majority of Canadians are of English-speaking descent, people of many cultural backgrounds make Canada their home. Native Americans make up one important segment of Canada's population. Many immigrants have come to Canada from South and East Asia as well as from Europe. In one of Canada's 12 provinces, Quebec, French-speaking Canadians form the majority of the population. Approximately 80 percent of Quebec's inhabitants claim French as their first language.

Throughout Canada's history, Quebec's French-speaking population has struggled to preserve its distinctiveness, both in its language and in its French-based traditions. During the 1960s a separatist movement gained strength among the French-speaking population of Quebec. French Canadians sought special recognition for their language and heritage. They also demanded a greater role in both provincial and national government and protections against discrimination. French Canadians gained a notable victory in 1969 with the passage of the Official Languages Act. This act made both French and English official languages of Canada.

Many French Canadians remained unsatisfied, however. The Parti Quebécois favored the complete separation of Quebec from Canada. In 1976 it won control of the provincial government. Four years later, in 1980, it held a referendum on separation, but the people of Quebec voted by a majority of 60 percent to remain a part of Canada. Nonetheless, French Canadian demands for special status for Quebec persisted through the 1980s and into the 1990s.

In 1987, Canadian leaders met at the resort of Meech Lake. There they agreed to accept Quebec as a "distinct society" within Canada. Had Parliament and all of Canada's provincial legislatures ratified the **Meech Lake Accord** by 1990, it would have become part of the Canadian constitution. Many Canadians, however, believed that the accord gave too much power to Quebec. The agreement failed to win the unanimous endorsement necessary for implementation.

The failure of the Meech Lake Accord reinvigorated separatist sentiments. In 1995 the issue of separation for Quebec was once again put to a referendum. Once again the separatists lost—but only by the narrowest margin. Quebec remained part of Canada, but with 49.4 percent of the vote in favor of separation, the issue was far from settled.

Relations with the United States. Most Canadians live within several hundred miles of the border with the United States. This border is the longest undefended international frontier in the world. Indeed, relations between Canada and the United States have become very close during the 1900s. As the century drew to a close, the flow of trade across the Canadian-U.S. border remained the heaviest bilateral trade traffic in the world.

Despite the general friendliness between the two countries, however, Canada and the United States have experienced periodic friction. Disputes over fishing rights in the Atlantic and the Pacific continued to occasionally afflict their relations into the 1990s. By far the greatest strains have resulted from Canada's uneasiness over American involvement in its economy.

Many Canadians were especially unsure about free trade. They voiced particular concern after the announcement of the United States-Canada Free Trade Agreement in 1988. The agreement proposed to eliminate almost all tariff barriers between Canada and the United States. Opponents feared that the agreement would reduce Canada to the status of an economic colony of the United States. The debate over free trade grew even more heated in the early 1990s, when the possibility of adding Mexico to the 1988 agreement was raised just as the Canadian economy went into a major recession. In the end, however, Canada joined with the United States and Mexico in 1992 to sign the North American Free Trade Agreement, or **NAFTA**. This agreement went into effect on January 1, 1994.

Section 1 Review

1. **Define** Vietnamization, Watergate scandal, stagflation, trade deficit, détente, Carter Doctrine, weapons of mass destruction, Meech Lake Accord

2. **Identify** Jimmy Carter, Ronald Reagan, Bill Clinton

3. **Understanding Ideas** What events caused many Americans to lose confidence in their government after 1970?

4. **Summarizing Ideas** Describe the U.S. economy from 1970 through 1990.

5. **Contrasting Ideas** How did the foreign-policy challenges facing the United States after the end of the Cold War contrast with President Bush's concept of a "new world order"?

6. **Synthesizing Ideas** What have been the main issues in Canadian politics since the 1970s?

Section 2

Europe

Focus Questions

- **How did the British and French governments respond to economic problems in the late 1900s?**
- **What changes have taken place in Germany since 1960?**
- **How have the nations of southern Europe changed politically in the late 1900s?**
- **What strides were made toward greater unity among the nations of Western Europe?**

During the late 1900s, many countries in Western Europe tried to consolidate the economic gains they had made in the early postwar period. Other countries made political advances, turning from dictatorships and military governments toward democracy. Although progress was far from smooth, Western Europe in general made significant strides toward political and economic integration.

Great Britain

By the mid-1960s, Britain's postwar recovery seemed uncertain. By the end of the decade, the country faced severe economic problems and had decided to pull back from major defense commitments overseas. Outdated factories, low productivity, and worker apathy made it difficult for Britain to compete with other industrial nations. The economy came under even greater stress as the government raised taxes and increased borrowing. The 1980s would witness a turn-around for British productivity, but unemployment and inflation would continue.

Margaret Thatcher. In a decisive victory in the general election of 1979, Britain's Conservative Party came to power. The party's leader, Margaret Thatcher, became prime minister—the first woman to hold that office. She argued that the government regulated business and industry too closely and that it taxed the British people too heavily. She planned to start Britain on the road back to prosperity by substantially reducing the government's role in the economy.

Over the next few years, Thatcher began to implement her ideas. She oversaw cuts in social spending, including the complete elimination of some programs. Her opponents charged that Thatcher's real intention was to dismantle the welfare state completely. Thatcher pressed ahead nonetheless, leading successful efforts to reduce taxes and to ease government regulation of business. She also began to privatize Britain's many government-owned industries. Not least, Thatcher managed finally to break the overwhelming influence that Britain's labor unions had exercised over the economy since the 1970s.

Aided by the development of new oil fields in the North Sea, the economy had begun to rebound by the mid-1980s, most notably in southern England. The country's northern areas did not fare as well, however. In this predominantly industrial region, unemployment remained very high. This was partly the result of a general shift in Britain's economy, like that in the United States, from heavy industry to services. Although Thatcher pointed to an overall improvement in the economy, critics charged that her policies favored the wealthy and created an unequal society.

One reason for the harmonious relationship between the United States and Great Britain was the personal friendship between Prime Minister Margaret Thatcher and President Ronald Reagan.

Thatcher brought a tough, no-nonsense approach to Britain's foreign policy as well as to economic affairs. In 1982 she ordered British troops and naval forces to retake the Falklands after Argentina's invasion of the British-held islands in the South Atlantic. The maintenance of strong ties with the United States represented a consistent theme of Thatcher's approach to foreign policy. In 1990 she played an important role in the formation of the international coalition that ultimately forced Iraq to withdraw from Kuwait in 1991.

Changes in leadership. With a downturn in the British economy during the late 1980s, Thatcher began to lose popularity. Even her support within the Conservative Party began to weaken. Her situation became critical following her implementation of the so-called poll tax. This tax, which replaced property taxes as the source of funds for local government, charged all taxpayers the same rate, or percentage, regardless of their income level. The tax proved extremely unpopular with the British people. Many Conservatives began to realize that they would have to reverse the tax if their party was to win the next election. Thatcher, however, continued to support the poll tax as the most fair and efficient way of financing local government.

As Thatcher's popularity continued to fall, her opponents in the Conservative Party challenged her leadership. Convinced by her closest advisers that she could not win the fight for leadership of the party, she stepped down in November 1990. When she left, more than a decade after first taking office, Margaret Thatcher had served longer than any British prime minister in this century.

In her place the Conservatives chose John Major, a leading member of Thatcher's cabinet. Major was generally considered more moderate than Thatcher in many of his views, especially on closer union with Europe, but he shared Thatcher's belief in free-enterprise economics and her support for especially close relations with the United States. Major was a strong supporter of the United States in the Persian Gulf crisis of 1991. During his term of office, Britain's economy began to pick up once again.

After nearly 18 years of Conservative government, however, the British electorate decided on a change, prompted by scandals and incompetence in the government. In 1997 the Labour Party, led by the young moderate Tony Blair, won control of the government for the first time since 1979. Although Labour promised a number of changes, they did not propose to restore the British welfare state to the level it had reached in the 1970s. Many of Thatcher's political and economic ideas had taken hold. A number of challenges faced Blair nonetheless. Among them was the lingering problem of Northern Ireland.

Northern Ireland. After the creation of an independent Republic of Ireland in 1922, Northern Ireland had remained part of Britain. Many people hoped that the old antagonism between Britain and Ireland would finally diminish, but new disagreements soon emerged. Over the years, the Protestant majority in Northern Ireland gained control of the government and dominated the country's economy. The lack of political power and the limited economic opportunities among Northern Ireland's Catholic minority increasingly produced resentment and ultimately erupted in violence.

In the late 1960s, Catholics in Northern Ireland began to demonstrate for an end to discrimination in areas such as employment and housing. At first peaceful, these demonstrations soon turned violent. To keep the peace, in 1969 the British government sent troops to Northern Ireland, and these troops were seen by the Catholics as representatives of a foreign power. This stationing of soldiers in Northern Ireland

A series of bombings and assassinations occurred in Northern Ireland during the 1970s. IRA gunmen are shown here in Londonderry in 1973.

became a permanent policy. Large numbers of British troops remained garrisoned there into the mid-1990s.

Throughout the 1970s, the violence in Northern Ireland escalated as Catholic and Protestant extremists alike took advantage of the situation. Assassinations, car bombings, and attacks on British troops became an almost daily occurrence. The most active extremist group was the **Irish Republican Army (IRA)**. Almost entirely Catholic, the IRA wanted to drive the British out of the north and unite all of Ireland. The IRA took its "war of liberation" far beyond Irish borders, bombing public sites in a number of British cities and attacking British soldiers in other parts of Europe.

In addition to taking strong military measures, the British government tried to end the violence in Northern Ireland through political means. Progress came in the Anglo-Irish Agreement of 1985, which gave the Republic of Ireland a voice in the affairs of Northern Ireland. In time, however, both Catholics and Protestants denounced the agreement. In the early 1990s, generally improving relations between Britain and the Republic of Ireland—combined with growing pressure from Europe and the United States—brought new hope for a settlement in Northern Ireland. In 1993 the British and Irish prime ministers jointly pledged their commitment to the principle of self-determination in Northern Ireland. The IRA declared a cease-fire the following year, but the British insisted that the IRA would have to disarm before talks could begin. The IRA refused and in 1996 renewed its campaign of terror. Peace talks resumed, however, following the Labour Party's victory in the British elections of 1997. A major breakthrough seemed to come with the Good Friday peace accords, signed in 1998. Hopes were high that a lasting peace might soon become a reality.

France

After Charles de Gaulle resigned in 1969, his prime minister, Georges Pompidou, replaced him as president. Although the two men had worked together for many years, they viewed French interests differently. De Gaulle saw France as a major player on the world stage. In contrast, Pompidou believed that France should limit its overseas involvement and focus instead on domestic issues.

Pompidou and Giscard d'Estaing. Pompidou believed that changes in the international situation had made de Gaulle's nationalist approach to foreign affairs impractical. A more realistic strategy, Pompidou argued, would seek close cooperative relations with traditional allies. He therefore worked to strengthen ties with the United States and ended French opposition to British membership in the European Economic Community, or EEC. Within the EEC, Pompidou pursued cooperation rather than French leadership.

Pompidou focused on domestic issues for much of his time in office. He introduced a number of social programs, which he hoped would ease the problems that had given rise to the political upheavals of the late 1960s. He also embarked on an ambitious plan to renovate much of Paris, which was not only France's capital but a major tourist attraction. Pompidou had to curtail many of his plans, however, in the face of an economic crisis that was largely brought on by the OPEC oil embargo and price increases of 1973.

On Pompidou's sudden death in 1974, Valéry Giscard d'Estaing became president. Giscard d'Estaing wanted to improve French standing abroad and encourage social change at home. He continued Pompidou's foreign policy, moving toward fuller cooperation with other countries. On the domestic front, he reduced state controls in the economy. However, high rates of unemployment and inflation undermined Giscard d'Estaing's plans for social change, making his programs virtually impossible to implement.

From Mitterrand to Chirac. Disappointed with Giscard d'Estaing's failure to fulfill his promises of prosperity and social change, in 1981 French voters elected a socialist president, François Mitterrand. Mitterrand faced severe economic problems, including high inflation, growing trade deficits, and rising unem-

ployment. In contrast to Margaret Thatcher in Britain, Mitterrand sought to bolster his country's economy by expanding the government's role. Several industries and banks were nationalized, and taxes were raised for people with high incomes. Mitterrand expanded government programs for the unemployed. In the wake of further economic reversals in the mid-1980s, however, Mitterrand was forced to pursue a more conservative approach to economics.

Under Mitterrand, France once again adopted an assertive foreign policy. French troops were especially active in Africa, frequently operating in support of former French colonies. For example, France assisted Chad in its border war with Libya during the 1980s. France also made major military contributions to multinational peacekeeping operations in Lebanon and Bosnia and participated in the international coalition against Iraq in 1990 and 1991.

Although Mitterrand had moved away from traditional socialist policies by the 1990s, support for his Socialist Party's policies wavered when Mitterrand's popularity waned. In 1993 Mitterrand's party lost significant ground in midterm elections. Economic problems, such as unemployment and recession, persisted. Immigration of Arabs from North Africa into

François Mitterrand, the first socialist president of France, served two terms between 1981 and 1995.

France was an increasing source of substantial social tension. Many people voiced concern about France's ability to balance the economic and political power of a reunified Germany. A deep sense of uncertainty over the future afflicted France in the mid-1990s.

In 1995, French voters elected a new president. They chose Jacques Chirac, mayor of Paris and a member of the conservative Gaullist Party, or RPR. Chirac promised reforms and a fresh approach to France's economic problems. Chirac's government, however, soon encountered difficulties, including disruptive protests by various groups of laborers, farmers, and truckers who feared the loss of jobs and income as France dropped barriers to trade with its European neighbors. Chirac provoked controversy abroad by ordering a new round of nuclear weapons tests in the South Pacific during 1996, though he stopped the testing after international protests. In 1997, Chirac's political future appeared uncertain as his party suffered a setback at the polls.

Germany

By the late 1960s, West Germany had become a major economic power in Western Europe. Even so, the country still faced certain political problems. Access to West Berlin and relations with East Germany, the Soviet Union, and other communist countries posed difficult foreign policy challenges.

Ostpolitik. After his election in 1969, Chancellor Willy Brandt, a member of the liberal Social Democratic Party, tried to meet these challenges. Brandt believed that West Germany had to remain firmly allied with the rest of Western Europe and the United States. At the same time, however, he concluded that tensions between his country and the communist countries of Eastern Europe had to be reduced. Brandt's effort to improve relations between East and West, known as **Ostpolitik** (German for "Eastern Policy") resulted in West German treaties with the Soviet Union and Poland in 1970. *Ostpolitik* eventually led to the mutual recognition of East and West Germany in 1973, and ultimately to the Helsinki Accords in 1975 (see page 609).

In 1974, Helmut Schmidt became chancellor of West Germany after Brandt resigned following the revelation that a member of his staff was an East German spy. Schmidt admired and continued Brandt's *Ostpolitik*. He also pursued closer economic and political cooperation with Western Europe. In the early 1980s, however, recession hit the West German economy. For the first time since the early postwar period, West Germans faced the prospect of rising unemployment coupled with widespread inflation.

Helmut Kohl. As in both Britain and France, economic troubles led to political change in the early 1980s. In 1982 the Christian Democrats regained control of the government after more than a dozen years out of power. Helmut Kohl, the new chancellor, charged that Schmidt and the Social Democrats had brought on the recession through high levels of government spending. The conservative Kohl promised to return the country to prosperity through policies similar to those of Prime Minister Thatcher in Britain and President Reagan in the United States.

Chancellor Kohl also made changes in West German foreign policy. He strongly reaffirmed West Germany's commitment to the NATO alliance, though he criticized the deployment of American intermediate-range nuclear missiles in West Germany. Kohl worked to improve relations between West Germany and the United States. This relationship remained generally strong into the 1990s, although the reunification of Germany early in the decade created new anxieties among some of Germany's neighbors in Europe.

Reunification. The reunification of Germany was perhaps Kohl's greatest challenge. The process of reunification began almost immediately after the fall of the Berlin Wall in 1989. Talks involving the two Germanies and the four victorious Allies of World War II—Britain, France, the Soviet Union, and the United States—set October 1990 as the date for reunification. Two months later Helmut Kohl, benefiting

Chancellor from 1982 until 1998, Helmut Kohl witnessed the unification of West and East Germany in 1990.

from the goodwill created by this great change, was elected as chancellor of a reunified Germany.

Although initially seen as a hero, Kohl soon began to lose popularity. By the summer of 1991, unemployment was widespread in the former East Germany, and much of the promised investment and reindustrialization was yet to be seen. Germans in the western part of the country also became disillusioned as the enormous costs of reunification became apparent. The reintegration of East Germany became an increasing burden on the German economy through the mid-1990s. Helmut Kohl, however, remained in office until 1998, when he was defeated in September by Gerhard Schroeder and his Social Democratic Party. Schroeder pledged to reduce unemployment and stimulate the economy.

Northern Europe

The smaller but still highly developed nations of northern Europe enjoyed a general period of prosperity during the late 1900s. The small principalities of Monaco and Liechtenstein managed to maintain their sovereignty, while Belgium, Luxembourg, and the Netherlands worked to foster European unity.

Denmark, Iceland, and Norway, members of the NATO alliance, contributed vitally to Western Europe's defense during the Cold War. Despite a sometimes heated dispute with Britain over fishing rights, the island nation of Iceland played a key role in the protection of the Atlantic shipping lanes. So did Norway, which benefited greatly from the discovery and development of North Sea oil in the 1980s.

Although Finland, Sweden, Austria, and Switzerland maintained good relations with the rest of Western Europe, each country remained neutral throughout the Cold War. Recession in the early 1990s, however, offered a strong incentive for these countries to strengthen political and economic ties with Western Europe. Finland, Sweden, and Austria all chose to join the new European Union, while Swiss voters narrowly decided to maintain their country's traditional neutrality. On the domestic front, Sweden implemented free-enterprise reforms, steering away from its socialist policies of the past.

Southern Europe

During the 1970s and 1980s, the nations of southern Europe underwent major political changes. Italy, once one of the more stable European nations, experienced almost constant political turmoil. At the same time, Spain, Portugal, and Greece returned to democratic forms of government.

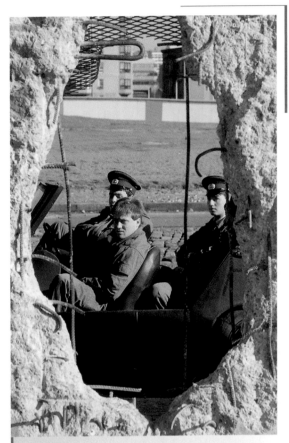

In August 1961, East Germany sought to restrict travel to and from West Berlin by erecting a wall to separate East Berlin from West Berlin. This photo shows remnants of the Berlin Wall, which came down in 1989.

Italy. The world economic recession of the early 1970s hit Italy especially hard. For much of the decade, unemployment levels soared and inflation was rampant. During the same period, the country's political system experienced a great deal of turmoil. None of the more than 14 political parties could gain a majority in the Italian parliament, so governments had to be formed through coalitions. Since few of these coalitions lasted very long, little could be done to lessen the country's severe political and economic problems. Late in the decade, Italy experienced a wave of terrorism. These acts of terrorism only added to Italy's problems.

Italy's situation improved greatly during the 1980s. By the mid-1980s, the power of the terrorist cells had largely been broken. The economy took off after the introduction of a number of free-enterprise reforms.

By 1994, Italy ranked eighth among all industrialized nations and fourth among the countries of the European Economic Community. Its economy, however, remained burdened by a huge national debt. Moreover, a marked social division existed between Italy's prosperous, industrialized north and the poor, mostly rural south.

In the mid-1990s, however, Italy continued to face serious political instability. Corruption scandals, particularly some that involved organized crime, racked the government. By 1997, the implementation of reforms, begun in 1994 concerning the allotment of seats in parliament, had lent Italy at least some measure of stability.

Spain. During the 1970s, Spain made the transition from dictatorship to democracy. On the death of Spanish dictator Francisco Franco in 1975, Juan Carlos became king. Juan Carlos immediately set about the task of returning Spain to democracy. In 1977, Spain held its first free elections in more than 40 years. In those elections, moderate political parties led by socialists won the majority of the seats in the Cortes, or parliament. Spain's new democracy was not yet secure, however. In 1981 a group of army officers tried to seize control of the government. Although the attempt failed, it demonstrated the fragility of democratic government.

Other challenges to Spain's new democracy included the questions of Basque separatism and of economic development. The Basque people, who possess a distinct language and culture and inhabit a region in Spain's mountainous northwest, have long sought independence from Spain. In 1980, they won self-government within Spain, but some remained unsatisfied. The Basque separatist group, ETA, demanded complete independence and resorted to the use of terrorism throughout the 1980s.

Spain also faced the same economic problems that confronted many other European nations: high levels of unemployment and inflation. One way in which Spanish leaders sought to improve the economy was through trade. In 1986, Spain joined the European Economic Community. Although the issue of Basque separatism lingered and economic problems persisted, in the mid-1990s Spain remained democratic and numbered among the leading economic powers of Western Europe.

Portugal. Like its Spanish neighbor, Portugal also made the transition from dictatorship to democracy in the late 1900s. Ironically, the process began with a military coup. In 1974, army officers led by General Antonio de Spinola ousted the dictator Marcello Caetano. Spinola quickly granted independence to most of Portugal's remaining colonies, including Angola and Mozambique. Spinola then resigned, after calling for elections. Portugal grappled with serious economic and political instability over the next several years. In 1986, Portugal joined the European Economic Community. At the same time, the government introduced a series of free-enterprise reforms. These measures helped spur economic growth and reinforce the stability of Portugal's democracy into the 1990s.

Greece. During the late 1900s, Greece entered a period of political uncertainty. From 1967 to 1974, a repressive military junta ruled Greece. Its interference in the affairs of Cyprus led to its downfall. In 1974, Greek voters chose to make Greece a republic rather than restore the monarchy. In 1981 they elected a socialist government, which implemented various social reforms. Although a more conservative government in the 1990s promised closer cooperation with the West, Greece remained at odds with many Western governments.

European Cooperation

The spirit of cooperation among the nations of Western Europe that had developed in the years after World War II continued to grow during the later part of the 1900s. Formal institutions, such as NATO and the European Economic Community, grew in both strength and membership. The collapse of communism

Living in the Pyrenees Mountains on both sides of the French-Spanish border, the Basques maintain their own culture and government.

in Eastern Europe left the structure and purpose of some of these organizations open to question. At the same time, however, it opened the possibility of an even wider union of European nations.

The Helsinki Accords. In 1975, representatives of 35 nations, including the United States and the Soviet Union, met in Helsinki, Finland, to discuss the topics of security and cooperation in Europe. The meeting resulted in a series of agreements known as the **Helsinki Accords**. These agreements specified ways of improving economic and technological cooperation between East and West, endorsing the use of peaceful means rather than force to settle disputes between nations. The accords also settled a major Cold War issue by recognizing the legitimacy of certain boundaries in Eastern Europe that were established after World War II but were disputed by some countries. Perhaps the most important part of the accords, however, concerned the protection of human rights, including freedom of speech and freedom of worship. The Helsinki Accords called on all nations to respect the basic human rights of their citizens.

Although the Helsinki Accords provided for no real means of enforcement, they proved to be an important symbolic step. By showing little interest in complying with the human rights aspects of the accords, the Soviets and other Communist bloc countries undermined their own credibility in the international community. The accords also formed an important foundation for the democratic movement that ultimately swept across Eastern Europe in the late 1980s. In the 1990s, following the collapse of communism, European nations worked to reaffirm their commitment to the principles set forth in the Helsinki Accords.

NATO. Although the North Atlantic Treaty Organization (NATO) remained the cornerstone of Western European security as the 1900s drew to a close, its policies and future role increasingly came into question. Friction between Greece and Turkey, both members of NATO, led to Greece's withdrawal from the alliance in 1974. Greece eventually rejoined, but its relations with other NATO countries remained strained. The deployment of American nuclear weapons in Europe during the Cold War proved especially controversial. Some member countries refused to allow American nuclear weapons on their soil; others expressed serious reservations. At the same time, the United States demanded that other members agree to take on a larger share of the burden of defending Europe.

NATO's future grew increasingly uncertain following the collapse of the Soviet Union in the early 1990s. With the military threat from the Eastern bloc diminished, NATO seemed to many people to have outlived its usefulness. Others pointed out that threats to European security still existed, and that NATO provided a framework to deal with problems like containing the civil war in the countries of what had been Yugoslavia, or a possible revival of Russian military power. Many countries of Eastern Europe sought to join NATO. Critics argued that any expansion of NATO eastward would require a burdensome commitment from current members and might provoke Russian hostility. In 1997, despite Russian objections, NATO leaders agreed to invite Poland, Hungary, and the Czech Republic to join the alliance.

From EEC to EU. The late 1990s saw the evolution of the European Economic Community (EEC) into the even more closely knit European Union (EU). A general expansion of the EEC preceded this transformation.

After the Maastricht Treaty, the European Economic Community became the European Union, continuing the quest for economic and political cooperation among countries. New "Euro" European currency shown here.

During the 1970s and 1980s, the EEC grew from 6 members to 12. After lengthy negotiations, Britain finally joined in 1973. Ireland and Denmark also joined in that year. In 1981 Greece became a full member, followed by Spain and Portugal in 1986. In the early 1990s, Austria, Finland, and Sweden joined.

As the EEC grew, it made headway toward setting common practices for its members in taxation, credit, and labor and monetary policies. In 1993 the EEC countries implemented the **Maastricht Treaty**, creating the European Union (EU). Under the terms of the treaty, they dropped trade barriers among themselves, agreed to pursue closer cooperation in defense and foreign relations, and accepted the idea of a common currency.

The implementation of the Maastricht Treaty had not come easily, however, and many problems remained unresolved in the mid-1990s. Several members of the EEC worried that the EU would undermine their sovereignty. British leaders in particular voiced misgivings. In Denmark, voters barely chose to ratify the Maastricht Treaty, but in Norway they rejected membership in the EU. As the century drew to a close, the future of the EU remained unclear. Aligning the economies of Western Europe was proving especially difficult, and the EU remained divided over whether or not to admit Turkey and various Eastern European countries. The nations of Western Europe had nonetheless achieved a real degree of unity in a century marked by two world wars.

Section 2 Review

1. **Define** IRA, *Ostpolitik*, Helsinki Accords, Maastricht Treaty
2. **Identify** Margaret Thatcher, François Mitterrand, Jacques Chirac, Helmut Schmidt, Helmut Kohl, Juan Carlos
3. **Understanding Ideas** How did the leaders of Great Britain and France respond to economic challenges after 1970?
4. **Explaining Ideas** When did Germany reunify, and what challenges followed its reunification?
5. **Summarizing Ideas** What major political changes took place in southern Europe during the late 1900s?
6. **Evaluating Ideas (a)** How have the nations of Western Europe moved toward greater unity? **(b)** What are some potential points of conflict among members of the EU?

Section 3

The Fall of Communism

Focus Questions

- How did Mikhail Gorbachev attempt to reform the Soviet Union?
- What happened in Russia after the collapse of the Soviet Union?
- What major problems faced Russia, the other republics of the former Soviet Union, and the nations of Eastern Europe in the aftermath of communism?

By the early 1980s, the division of Europe between the communist East and the free West appeared permanent. However, the 1980s and 1990s witnessed the total breakdown of communist rule in Eastern Europe. Although some countries looked forward to a prosperous future, political and economic instability prevailed throughout much of Eastern Europe and the former Soviet Union.

The Soviet Union and Its Successors

At the end of the 1970s, the power of the Soviet Union appeared unshakable to many outside observers. Soviet leaders, however, faced a huge and rapidly growing problem in their country's inefficient economy. The 1980s brought an attempt at fundamental reform, but the Soviet predicament proved overwhelming. After losing its Eastern European satellites to a wave of democratic reform in the late 1980s, the Soviet Union itself finally disintegrated in 1991.

The Brezhnev years. Leonid Brezhnev led the Soviet Union throughout the 1970s. He proved to be a forceful leader. With the invasion of Czechoslovakia in 1968, Brezhnev demonstrated that the Soviet government would tolerate no dissent among its satellite nations in Eastern Europe. He subsequently announced the **Brezhnev Doctrine**, declaring that the Soviet Union would intervene in any satellite nation that seemed to be moving away from communism. As a result, no satellite government attempted reforms on the scale of the Prague Spring during the Brezhnev years. Brezhnev also cracked down on dissent at home. Basic human rights such as the freedoms of speech, worship, and movement were seriously curtailed in the Soviet Union.

While seeking to crush all opposition both domestically and in the Soviet satellites of Eastern Europe,

Brezhnev worked to strengthen his country's position in the balance of world power. Through détente, he tried to stabilize relations with the United States. The Soviet Union's continued military buildup and support for anti-Western forces during the Brezhnev years, however, called into question the sincerity of Soviet commitments to peace. The Soviet invasion of Afghanistan in 1979 proved to be the last straw. Relations with the United States had substantially deteriorated by the time Brezhnev died in 1982.

Gorbachev and reform. Many Soviets experienced a decline in their standard of living during the Brezhnev years, and the Soviet economy remained extremely inefficient. Agricultural failures, an inadequate transportation infrastructure, and outmoded factories all contributed to the dire state of the Soviet economy. Heavy military spending compounded the problem severely. The critical need for reform became increasingly apparent and helped to prompt a struggle for power in the Soviet Union following Brezhnev's death.

At first the old guard—made up of Soviet leaders born before the revolution of 1917—held out. Many of them recognized the need for reform but worried that it might lead to the weakening of the Soviet state. Hoping to improve the economy without endangering the political survival of communism, they named Yuri Andropov, a former head of the secret police, as Brezhnev's successor. Andropov was in poor health, however, and held office only 15 months. His elderly successor, Konstantin Chernenko, lasted little more than a year. On Chernenko's death a younger generation of Communist Party leaders finally gained control of the Soviet government.

In 1985 a rising young star in the Politburo, Mikhail Gorbachev, became the new leader of the Soviet Union. Gorbachev came to office with a background in agricultural and economic affairs. He planned nothing less than a complete overhaul of Soviet political and economic systems. He pledged himself to a course of dramatic reforms known as **perestroika** (per·uh·STROY·kuh), or restructuring, and **glasnost** (GLAZ·nohst), or openness. Gorbachev relaxed government controls on the economy and eased restrictions on dissent, allowing Soviet citizens a greater freedom to speak their minds and to read whatever they liked. Recognizing the burden that military spending put on the Soviet Union, Gorbachev planned to reduce the armed forces and increase their efficiency. He also sought a way to end the bloody, protracted, and increasingly unpopular Soviet occupation of Afghanistan.

Gorbachev's reform-minded attitude won wide acclaim abroad. Relations between the Soviet Union and the United States soon began to improve. Gorbachev met several times with President Reagan, and in 1987 the two men signed agreements to keep fewer nuclear weapons of certain types and to limit the production of others. In 1988, Gorbachev told the United Nations that the Soviet Union would soon begin reducing the number of troops it deployed in Eastern Europe, and in the following year he oversaw the full withdrawal of Soviet forces from Afghanistan.

At home, however, Gorbachev's program of reform ran into problems. Results came slowly and were often ineffective. Liberal supporters complained that Gorbachev was proceeding too cautiously. Despite perestroika, consumer goods remained in short supply, and there were shortages in basic necessities, including bread. In 1990, Gorbachev introduced a program to establish a mixed economy—one combining private ownership with government control—in the Soviet

Mikhail Gorbachev, leader of the Soviet Union from 1985 to 1991, received the Nobel Peace Prize in 1990. He is shown here with his wife, Raisa.

Union, but he soon had to abandon it under pressure from hard-line Communists.

Gorbachev also faced intense criticism from people who worried that he was moving too fast. Many Soviet citizens became discouraged as reforms designed to increase efficiency on the national level seemed only to impose personal hardship. Perestroika represented a drastic change in the way of life to which Soviet citizens were accustomed. No longer did they enjoy guaranteed lifetime employment and secure incomes. As a result, many Soviet citizens questioned the wisdom of Gorbachev's new policies.

The most serious challenge came in the summer of 1991, when some strictly conservative members of the government and military attempted a coup. They arrested Gorbachev, but Boris Yeltsin, the liberal-minded president of Russia, rallied popular opposition to the coup. The coup ultimately failed after Soviet soldiers refused to carry out orders to eliminate the opposition. Gorbachev's popularity never recovered, however. Boris Yeltsin emerged from the crisis as the new champion of reform.

The collapse of the Soviet Union.

As Gorbachev's reforms took effect, holding the Soviet Union together became one of the primary challenges facing the Soviet leader. Glasnost helped to fuel tensions among the various nationalities and ethnic groups of the Soviet Union as people began to express opinions that they would previously have kept to themselves. In the late 1980s, ethnic fighting erupted in the predominantly Muslim Soviet republic of Azerbaijan following a territorial dispute with the neighboring and predominantly Christian Soviet republic of Armenia.

After democratic movements swept communist governments in Eastern Europe from power in 1989, some Soviet republics began to demand their own independence. In an attempt to hasten reform, all three Baltic republics—Estonia, Latvia, and Lithuania—legalized non-communist parties, and in 1990 they called for secession from the Soviet Union. Gorbachev responded by deploying troops and threatening the republics with economic boycotts. The attempted crackdown backfired, however, prompting angry demonstrations across the Soviet Union and condemnation from abroad.

The dissolution of the Soviet Union soon became a foregone conclusion. Throughout 1991, one republic after another demanded independence. This trend began to move even faster after the failed coup in August 1991. In December, Gorbachev stepped down as president of the Soviet Union. While an amazed world looked on, the Soviet Union ceased to exist at the end of 1991.

Russia under Yeltsin.

Led by President Boris Yeltsin, the Russian Federation—generally referred to simply as Russia—emerged as the largest and most powerful of the newly independent states. During the 1990s, Russia began to make the transition to democracy and an economy based on free enterprise. Many observers believed that the success of that transition depended on the political survival of the reform-minded Yeltsin. Both frequently seemed in doubt in the mid-1990s.

Yeltsin faced numerous challenges. First among them was the state of the economy. During the early 1990s, inflation soared and industrial output plummeted. High unemployment and shortages of food and housing persisted across Russia.

Throughout the 1990s, Yeltsin expressed his personal commitment to liberalization of the Russian economy. Under his leadership, many industries were privatized. Russia increasingly opened its doors to foreign investment. Yeltsin also sought financial assistance from the West, but political disagreements over issues such as Russian arms sales to aggressive states in the Middle East jeopardized such aid.

Economic improvement was slow in coming for Russia. By the late 1990s the Russian economy remained in poor condition. Although a growing class of entrepreneurs enjoyed newfound wealth in Russia, many Russians still suffered severe deprivations as the 1900s drew to a close.

Russia's persistent economic troubles contributed to political uncertainty. Yeltsin faced several political challenges throughout the 1990s. Early on, he encountered strong hostility in the Russian legislature, which still included many Communists. When Yeltsin tried to dissolve the legislature in 1993, defiant members denounced the move as unconstitutional and declared a new government under Alexander Rutskoi. Yeltsin had the army surround the legislature building in Moscow with tanks, but Rutskoi refused to surrender. Hoping to rally public sympathy and turn the army to his side, Rutskoi called on supporters to seize Moscow's television station. Yeltsin then ordered the army to open fire. Rutskoi gave up and was arrested.

Yeltsin's position, however, remained shaky. Ultranationalists and Communists who were opposed to democratic and free-enterprise reform began to win growing support by the mid-1990s. There was also the danger of a coup as the military grew increasingly

In June 1990, Boris Yeltsin became the first popularly elected leader in the history of Russia.

resentful over low pay and poor living conditions. To appease the growing number of critics, Yeltsin began to appoint conservative leaders to key government positions in place of reformers. Amid questions about his health, Yeltsin faced a formidable challenge in the presidential elections of 1996 from Communists led by Gennady Zyuganov. Only by offering a government post with broad powers to a charismatic former general named Alexander Lebed did Yeltsin manage to cement his re-election.

Groups outside the government also wielded considerable influence in the new Russia. The Orthodox church experienced a general revival. It enjoyed a restoration of property and power that had been lost over several decades of communist rule—not always to the liking of democratic reformers. In 1997 the Orthodox church won special status under a new religious law that restricted the activity of non-Orthodox groups such as evangelical Christians in Russia.

A particularly harmful influence on Russian life was the growth of organized crime in the wake of communism's fall. By 1993, observers estimated that between 3,000 and 4,000 crime gangs dealing in drugs, prostitution, and black-market goods operated in Russia.

Although ethnic Russians make up about 80 percent of the population of the Russian Federation, another pressing problem was separatism among various non-Russian minorities. The most serious case involved a small region in southern Russia called Chechnya. A largely Muslim group, the Chechens had long fought their Russian conquerors. Under the Soviet regime, Stalin had deported the Chechens to Central Asia. With the disintegration of the Soviet Union in 1991, Chechnya saw an opportunity to gain freedom and declared its independence.

President Yeltsin, however, soon made it clear that Chechnya—a region with rich oil resources—would not be allowed to break away. In 1994, Yeltsin ordered the Russian army to capture the capital city and put down Chechen resistance. Russia's brutal war on

What If?

Gorbachev

What might have happened if Gorbachev had been more successful in achieving his goals and had not been forced to resign in 1991? Would the history of the Soviet Union and Eastern Europe be any different?

Chechnya brought international criticism, and Russian forces took heavy casualties. Eventually a compromise was reached, keeping Chechnya within the Russian Republic but granting the region almost complete self-government.

Russia and the world. Russia was not the only successor state to the Soviet Union. The dissolution of the Soviet Union created 14 other independent republics. To coordinate economic and defense policies among the newly-created states, Russia engineered the establishment of the **Commonwealth of Independent States (CIS).** (See map on opposite page.) Eventually, 12 of the republics joined the CIS. In 1992 the members of the CIS agreed to a mutual security treaty, under which they largely entrusted their defense to Russia. In 1997, except for the three Baltic states, the Russian army had troops deployed in all of the former Soviet republics.

Despite the formation of the CIS, however, relations between Russia and the other republics were often strained in the 1990s. In particular, several points of conflict emerged between Russia and the second largest republic, Ukraine. One such conflict involved the division of former Soviet military resources between Russia and Ukraine. Another matter of conflict concerned the status of predominantly Russian-speaking regions in Ukraine, including the Crimea and the economically vital Don River basin.

In the Caucasus region, where Russia remained particularly active, Russian tactics often appeared heavy-handed. In 1992, Russia incited a rebellion in a northeastern region of the Republic of Georgia. The Georgian government had previously been reluctant to join the Russian-dominated CIS. The rebellion forced Georgia to appeal to Russia for assistance, to join the CIS, and to permit the stationing of Russian troops on its soil.

In the mid-1990s, observers began to express concern that Russia was pursuing an aggressive policy in the former Soviet republics surrounding the oil-rich Caspian basin. These concerns gave rise to suggestions that the eight new nations comprising the Caucasus and former Soviet Central Asia were still effectively dominated by Moscow.

Although Yeltsin's government, in critical need of economic aid, generally pursued cooperative relations with the West, a number of differences emerged. Considerable progress was made between Russia and the United States in the area of arms limitation and reduction, but disagreements erupted over issues such as expansion of the NATO alliance into Eastern Europe. Many Western leaders expressed concern over the future of the demoralized but still extensive Russian military—especially about the security of Russia's vast arsenal of nuclear weapons.

Eastern Europe

During the 1970s, although dissent continued, the threat of Soviet intervention under the Brezhnev Doctrine prevented any real liberalization in the nations of Eastern Europe. The reforms implemented by Gorbachev, however, gave new encouragement to democratic forces in the region. In 1989 a tide of democratic reform swept communist governments from power across Eastern Europe. The fall of communism, however, left new and serious problems in its wake.

The growth of dissent. During the 1970s the communist governments of Eastern Europe followed the Soviet lead and imposed repressive measures to end internal dissent. Even so, many people in Eastern Europe continued to voice their opposition to totalitarian rule. Anticommunist writers skirted government censors by issuing *samizdat,* or self-published editions of their work. Following the announcement of the Helsinki Accords in the late 1970s, dissidents in Czechoslovakia called on their government to abide by the human rights articles of the accords. Dissidents throughout Eastern Europe subsequently began to make similar demands.

In Poland, economic troubles during the 1970s fueled the growth of dissent. In 1980 huge price increases spawned a series of labor strikes. Led by an unemployed electrician named Lech Walesa (LEK vah·LEN·suh) and a group of shipyard workers, the strikers demanded political and economic reforms. In response the government agreed to allow labor unions to organize outside of the Communist Party. An independent trade union, known as Solidarity, was then formed. Under Walesa's leadership, Solidarity pressed for further concessions from the Polish government. Fearing Soviet invasion, however, the government refused and imposed martial law. Demonstrations in support of Solidarity continued nonetheless through the 1980s; these demonstrations eventually culminated in the downfall of the communist government following the spread of glasnost and perestroika into Eastern Europe.

Initially, both communist governments and dissidents in Eastern Europe were skeptical of Gorbachev's reforms. Although they faced tremendous economic

The Breakup of the Soviet Sphere

Learning from Maps In 1989, Soviet republics began to demand their independence.

? Region Which former Soviet republics did not become part of the Commonwealth of Independent States?

difficulties of their own, many Eastern European governments, controlled by old-guard communists, were uneasy about restructuring along Soviet lines. In Hungary, however, the government believed that Gorbachev's economic reforms did not go far enough. Reaction among dissidents was also mixed at first. Many expressed outright disbelief, but in the end they overwhelmingly threw their support behind the new policies as the best hope of winning freedom. By 1988 the citizens of Eastern Europe were widely citing glasnost and perestroika as they demanded democratic reform.

The revolutions of 1989. In 1989 the growing pressure on the communist governments of Eastern Europe reached a critical level as demands for democratic reform swept uncontrollably across the entire region. Poland led the way. In April 1989 the Polish government legalized Solidarity. The result of this action was the election of Poland's first noncommunist prime minister in more than 40 years. In 1990 the Communist Party was dissolved in Poland and replaced by two social democratic parties.

Other nations soon followed Poland's example. In Czechoslovakia, people took to the streets of the capital to demand reform. The government tried to break up the demonstration by force, but the police began to join the demonstrators. Having lost the backing of its security forces, the Czech government quickly gave in to demands for reform. In December, only six weeks after the first demonstrations had begun, the national legislature selected Vaclav Havel, a playwright and former dissident leader, as the country's new president. So smooth was the transition from communism in Czechoslovakia that people dubbed it the "Velvet Revolution."

The transition to a non-communist government proved less peaceful in Romania. Ruled by the ruthless dictator Nicolae Ceausescu (chow·SHES·koo), the people of Romania suffered one of the most repressive regimes in Eastern Europe. Ceausescu tried to crush pro-reform demonstrations with a brutal crackdown by Romania's secret police, but the demonstrators fought back. A brief civil war followed. By the end of the year, pro-democracy forces had captured Ceausescu, whom they executed for treason.

In East Germany the government came under increasing pressure throughout 1989 to open its borders. As communist governments in Czechoslovakia and Hungary loosened restrictions on their own borders with Western countries, many East Germans obtained permission to visit Czechoslovakia and Hungary. Once there, they fled to West Germany. Amid growing protest, the East German government agreed to open East Germany's borders at midnight on November 9, 1989. That night thousands of Berliners from East and West Germany alike assembled on either side of the infamous Berlin Wall—perhaps the most powerful symbol of the Iron Curtain. On the stroke of midnight, they raced to break holes in the wall or to climb over it. More than any other event, the fall of the Berlin Wall came to symbolize the triumph over communist tyranny.

The aftermath of communism. The end of communist rule in Eastern Europe held the promise of greater prosperity but also left many problems in its wake. The new governments of Eastern Europe soon set about the task of implementing democratic reform. Many adopted free-enterprise reforms to boost their economies. In March 1991 the member countries of the Warsaw Pact voted to disband the

The Berlin Wall came down in November of 1989 after dividing East and West Germany for nearly 30 years.

alliance. Some governments hoped for closer cooperation with the West, and in 1997, Poland, Hungary, and the Czech Republic were invited to become members of NATO.

At the same time, serious problems afflicted many countries. Eastern Europe lost its largest trading partner with the fall of the Soviet Union, and inefficient industries and outmoded factories rendered many regional economies uncompetitive with the West. Rising energy costs added to the economic problems of Eastern Europe as the region also lost its cheap supply of fuel with the fall of the Soviet Union. On top of these problems, decades of communist rule had taken an especially heavy toll on the environment. By the late 1990s, Eastern Europe remained among the world's most polluted regions.

Finally, the new freedoms that had been gained in Eastern Europe released old ethnic tensions. In 1992, Czechoslovakia split in two following the rise of a Slovak nationalist party in the eastern portion of the country. The result was the creation of the more prosperous Czech Republic and the poorer country of Slovakia. The breakup of Czechoslovakia came peacefully through the ballot box. Other areas were less fortunate. Massive civil unrest gripped Albania in the mid-1990s. In Yugoslavia, ethnic divisions produced one of the most hostile civil wars in the history of modern times.

Yugoslavia comprised a patchwork of ethnic groups, including Serbs, Croats, Slovenians, Macedonians, and Albanians. Many Yugoslavs shared a mutually comprehensible language; the main distinctions ran along religious lines. The Serbs were predominantly Eastern Orthodox; the Croats and Slovenians were predominantly Roman Catholic. The single largest segment of the population in the central province of Bosnia and Herzegovina, which had once formed part of the Ottoman Empire, adhered to Islam. These divisions erupted in bloody conflict as anticommunist reform took hold in Yugoslavia.

Yugoslavia began to unravel with the fall of communist governments across Eastern Europe. Serbia tried to exert dominance over the other groups, but the effect instead was to encourage Croatian and Slovenian nationalism. In 1991, Croatia and Slovenia declared their independence. As a result, bitter fighting broke out between Serbia and Croatia, ending in a truce that was mediated by the EEC and the United States. A UN peacekeeping force soon arrived to monitor the cease-fire. Though Croatia

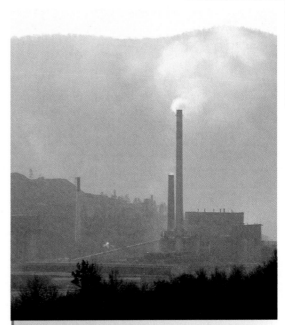

Eastern European countries such as Poland, the former East Germany, the Czech Republic, Slovakia, and Hungary became some of the most polluted regions in the world.

paid a high price for its demand for freedom, Slovenia had managed to escape the fighting. Both had secured independence, however. In 1992, Bosnia followed suit and declared its independence.

In Bosnia's case, the greatest problem was the ethnic mix within the province. Muslims formed the single largest group, but they did not represent a majority. Nearly a third of Bosnia's population identified themselves as Serbian, while 17 percent claimed Croatian descent. Led by Radovan Karadzic, many Bosnian Serbs wished to remain part of Serbian-dominated Yugoslavia. Receiving aid from the Yugoslavian government in Belgrade, Bosnian Serb military units engaged in a program of **ethnic cleansing**—a campaign of terror and murder to drive Muslims out of those parts of Bosnia that the Bosnian Serbs claimed for themselves.

The United Nations imposed an arms embargo in an effort to end the fighting. The result harmed the Muslim-controlled Bosnian government's ability to resist the better-armed Serbs. In response to repeated Serb attacks, the UN declared certain areas of Bosnia to be "safe havens" under the protection of UN forces. The UN then began an investigation of Serbian atrocities.

Building History Study Skills

READ
WRITE
INTERPRET
CONNECT
THINK

Thinking About History: Conducting a Debate

A debate is a formal competition between two teams to determine which team has the greater skill in speaking and reasoning. The two sides publicly dispute an issue in a systematic way, appealing to logic and reason rather than to emotion.

How to Conduct a Debate
To conduct a debate, follow these steps.
1. Select the teams. There should be two teams, each composed of two or three members, although the size of the team may vary depending on the debate topic or the format used.
2. State the proposition. A proposition is a thesis statement or conclusion that the teams research and then discuss in the debate. The proposition is often stated as a resolution.
3. Prepare for the debate. Assign members of each team research on the proposition. Team members should organize the information into an orderly and logical outline called a brief. Arrange the points of the brief on index cards that may be used during the debate.
4. Conduct the debate. The debate itself should consist of two parts separated by an intermission. In the first part—the constructive speeches—each team presents its arguments. Members of each team speak alternately, beginning with the affirmative team. Each constructive speech is limited to eight minutes. Intermission follows. After the intermission, each team refutes the arguments of the opposing team in four-minute speeches called rebuttals.

Developing the Skill
Read the following proposition, the constructive speech of the affirmative side, and the rebuttal of the negative side.

Resolved: As a leading power in the Western alliance, the United States should contribute troops to the NATO Implementation Force (IFOR) deployed in Bosnia and Herzegovina to maintain the peace established by the Dayton Accord in 1995.

Affirmative Speech: The Dayton Accord has brought an end to the brutal civil war that gripped Bosnia between 1992 and 1995. The United States played a key role in mediating the agreement and must now play a key role in its implementation.

The dispatch of well-equipped American troops is critical to the effectiveness of the NATO IFOR in Bosnia. With advanced air power on hand, some question the need to send ground forces. Although modern air power offers a powerful means of retaliation, it cannot, however, hold territory.

Finally, the credibility of the United States as a world leader depends on a willingness to share in the danger and popular criticism of missions it expects allied governments to undertake.

Negative Rebuttal: While the United States should certainly use its diplomacy to re-establish peace in Bosnia, the deployment of American troops as part of IFOR is a flawed policy.

American leaders should have learned from the disastrous peacekeeping mission to Somalia in the early 1990s that troops cannot *impose* a lasting peace. Fighting is likely to resume once the troops are withdrawn. Aggressors will simply wait out the presence of peacekeeping forces. The alternative will be a permanent and unpopular stationing of troops in Bosnia.

Finally, throughout the postwar era the United States has carried the largest burden for European defense—not least because the Soviet Union posed a direct threat to the United States as well as to Europe. Bosnia, however, is essentially a European problem. Primary responsibility for its resolution should fall to our European allies.

Practicing the Skill
In a recent issue of your local newspaper or a news magazine, find an article that deals with a controversial issue. Use the article to write a proposition, and from this, develop and conduct a debate.

To apply this skill, see Applying History Study Skills on page 621.

American troops in a Bosnian village

This photo shows children playing at a new playground in a suburb of Dobrinja, Sarajevo. This same area had been totally surrounded by Serb forces for six months as part of their ethnic cleansing campaign.

Serbian aggression continued nonetheless. Continued shelling of Sarajevo, the Bosnian capital, combined with Serbian attacks on UN "safe havens," eventually prompted NATO to carry out extensive air strikes on Serbian targets in 1995.

The Bosnian Serbs agreed to enter peace talks mediated by the United States in Dayton, Ohio. The resulting agreement, known as the **Dayton Accord**, gave the Bosnian Serbs a degree of autonomy in certain areas, at the same time recognizing the overall sovereignty of Bosnia's Muslim-led government. In December 1995, NATO sent a joint military **Implementation Force**, or **IFOR**, to Bosnia to enforce the new peace. IFOR included large numbers of American troops.

At first the peace established in Bosnia by the Dayton Accord seemed to be holding. Its survival, however, seemed to depend on the continued presence of foreign troops. The future of Bosnia, like that of much of Eastern Europe, remained uncertain as the 1900s drew to a close.

Section 3 Review

1. **Define** Brezhnev Doctrine, perestroika, glasnost, CIS, ethnic cleansing, Dayton Accord, IFOR
2. **Identify** Mikhail Gorbachev, Boris Yeltsin, Lech Walesa, Vaclav Havel, Nicolae Ceausescu
3. **Locate and Explain the Significance** Estonia, Latvia, Lithuania, Republic of Georgia, Caspian Basin, Czech Republic, Slovakia, Bosnia and Herzegovina
4. **Understanding Ideas (a)** What kinds of reforms did Gorbachev introduce in the Soviet Union? **(b)** What role did these reforms play in the breakup of the Soviet Union?
5. **Synthesizing Ideas** How did the fall of communism affect the people of the former Soviet Union?
6. **Determining Cause and Effect** How did the fall of communism contribute to the resurgence of ethnic tensions in Eastern Europe?

Chapter 19 Review

A.D. 1974
Valéry Giscard d'Estaing becomes president of France.

A.D. 1975
Helsinki Accords are signed.

A.D. 1977
Free elections are held in Spain.

A.D. 1970   **A.D. 1972**   **A.D. 1974**   **A.D. 1976**   **A.D. 1978**

A.D. 1969
West Germany's *Ostpolitik* begins.

A.D. 1972
Watergate break-in occurs.

A.D. 1973
• OPEC oil embargo occurs.
• American troops are withdrawn from Vietnam.

A.D. 1976
Jimmy Carter is elected president of the United States.

A.D. 1979
• Full diplomatic relations begin between People's Republic of China and the United States.
• Soviet Union invades Afghanistan.
• Margaret Thatcher becomes prime minister of Great Britain.

Chapter Summary

The following list contains the key concepts you have learned about North America and Europe from 1969 to the present.

1. The Vietnam War had a long-lasting impact on the United States.
2. Many Americans lost faith in their government when the Watergate scandal was brought to the attention of the public in 1973.
3. Inflation and unemployment were among the economic problems that plagued the United States throughout the 1970s and into the mid-1980s. After a recovery during President Reagan's administration, the economy generally grew in the 1990s.
4. The nature of the American economy changed significantly during the 1970s and 1980s.
5. Efforts were made during the 1970s to ease tensions between the United States and the Soviet Union. The invasion of Afghanistan by the Soviet Union ended these efforts. However, by the mid-1980s, the two countries once again sought to establish better relations.
6. A separatist movement in Quebec threatened Canadian unity in the 1970s and again in the 1990s.
7. Relations between Canada and the United States have been close despite periodic friction.
8. During the 1970s many Western European nations turned to conservative governments to solve their economic problems.
9. The purpose and policies of NATO came under close scrutiny after the collapse of communism in Eastern Europe in 1989 and 1990.
10. The European Economic Community (EEC) grew in membership during the 1970s and 1980s; in 1993, with the Maastricht Treaty, it became the European Union (EU).
11. During the 1970s the Soviet Union repressed dissent both at home and in its satellite nations. At the same time, it sought to improve its relations with the West.
12. Mikhail Gorbachev introduced a number of reforms in the Soviet Union through the policies of glasnost and perestroika.
13. The nations of Eastern Europe moved from communism to democracy but continued to face economic and political problems.
14. Late in 1991 Gorbachev resigned, and the Soviet Union ceased to exist. Russia, one of the 15 independent nations created from this dissolution, engineered the Commonwealth of Independent States (CIS). Twelve of these nations joined the CIS.

Reviewing Important Terms

On a separate sheet of paper, supply the term that correctly completes each statement.

1. _____ is the name given to the improvement in relations between the United States and the Soviet Union during the 1970s.
2. West German chancellor Willy Brandt's efforts to create better relations between East and West became known as _____ .
3. Mikhail Gorbachev's policy of _____ loosened the reins of censorship and eased the repression of the Brezhnev years.
4. Through _____ , or restructuring, Mikhail Gorbachev planned to overhaul the political and economic systems of the Soviet Union.
5. _____ _____ is the name for a campaign of terror and murder to drive Muslims out of those parts of Bosnia that the Bosnian Serbs claimed for themselves.

Developing Critical Thinking Skills

1. **Analyzing Ideas (a)** What economic problems faced the United States in the 1970s and 1980s? **(b)** What policies did Presidents Ford, Carter, Reagan, Bush, and Clinton use to try to solve these problems?
2. **Comparing Ideas** What similarities and differences are there between the political changes that took place in Great Britain and those that took place in West Germany during the 1970s and 1980s?

A.D. 1982
Helmut Kohl becomes chancellor of West Germany.

A.D. 1985
Mikhail Gorbachev becomes leader of Soviet Union.

A.D. 1988
George Bush is elected president of the United States.

A.D. 1990
• Communism falls in Eastern Europe.
• East and West Germany reunite.

A.D. 1980 | A.D. 1982 | A.D. 1984 | A.D. 1986 | A.D. 1988 | A.D. 1990

A.D. 1980
• Separatist referendum in Quebec is defeated.
• Ronald Reagan is elected president of the United States.

A.D. 1986
• Reagan and Gorbachev meet in Reykjavik.
• Disaster at Chernobyl occurs.

A.D. 1989
Berlin Wall is opened.

A.D. 1991
• Persian Gulf War occurs.
• Soviet Union breaks up.

3. **Understanding Ideas** Why were the purpose and policies of NATO reassessed after the fall of communism in Eastern Europe?
4. **Summarizing Ideas** What progress has the EU made toward political unity in Western Europe?
5. **Organizing Ideas** How did glasnost and perestroika change life in the Soviet Union?
6. **Evaluating Ideas** The Nissan plant in Tennessee (below) is an example of Japan's economic expansion. Why did it become increasingly difficult for the United States to compete economically with Japan?

Relating Geography to History
Turn to the map on page 615. **(a)** Which former Soviet republics have not joined the Commonwealth of Independent States? **(b)** Which members of the Commonwealth of Independent States border Europe? **(c)** What benefits and disadvantages do you think are associated with joining the Commonwealth of Independent States?

Relating Past to Present
1. Canada's uneasiness about its relationship with the United States is not new. Using information in this textbook and in encyclopedias, trace the development of this feeling among Canadians, describing when such feelings have surfaced in the past.
2. Many political scientists have noted similarities between the reforms introduced in Czechoslovakia during the Prague Spring and Mikhail Gorbachev's policies

of glasnost and perestroika. **(a)** What similarities do you see between the two? **(b)** Explain your answer.

Applying History Study Skills
Before completing this activity, review Building History Study Skills on page 618.

Conduct a debate, using the following steps and proposition or thesis statement.

Resolved: The nations of Western Europe should achieve political as well as economic unity.
1. Select teams.
2. State the proposition.
3. Prepare for the debate.
4. Conduct the debate.

internet**connect**

Search the Internet through the HRW Web site for recent events in one of the countries discussed in this chapter. Find out about major events in that country, and either create a time line of recent events or write a paragraph that could be added to the existing text about that country.

GO TO: go.hrw.com
KEYWORD: SC0 Current Events

Building Your Portfolio
1. **Presenting an Oral Report** Relations between Canadians who speak English and Canadians who speak French have occasionally been tense. Present an oral report on the differences between these two cultural groups. Your report should include a discussion of recent trends toward separatism and away from it. Place your notes and other research materials in your portfolio.
2. **Constructing a Chart** Use resources in the library to gather information on the economies of the nations of Eastern Europe. Note each nation's major industries, leading imports and exports, and chief trading partners. Construct a chart showing your findings. Place the chart in your portfolio.

The World in the Twenty-First Century

TIME
A.D. **1945–the present**

A.D. **1945–the present**

3.7 million B.C. | 4000 B.C. | A.D. 2100

PLACE
The world and beyond

ARCTIC OCEAN
NORTH AMERICA
EUROPE
ASIA
PACIFIC OCEAN
AFRICA
Equator
SOUTH AMERICA
ATLANTIC OCEAN
INDIAN OCEAN
AUSTRALIA
PACIFIC OCEAN
ANTARCTICA

Lunar landing

Significance

The emotional scars of World War II remained, but people rebuilt their lives. Advances in technology and communication unified the world community. Satellites made it possible for millions of television viewers, otherwise separated by distance and ideas, to witness historic events as they occurred. Although it was a U.S. spacecraft that first achieved a manned lunar landing, astronaut Neil Armstrong represented all people on Earth when in 1969 he became the first human being to set foot on the moon.

In the 1970s and 1980s the United States embarked on an ambitious space exploration program. Television coverage of successful launches became almost routine. Then on January 28, 1986, millions of horrified television viewers watched in disbelief as the space shuttle *Challenger* disintegrated into a ball of flame shortly after liftoff.

Terms to Define

Discovery	acid rain
Spacelab	greenhouse effect
miniaturization	abstract
supercomputers	expressionism
laser	pop art
antibiotics	op art
DNA	conceptual art
genetic code	performance art
cloning	

People to Identify

Yuri Gagarin	Lina Wërtmuller
Alan Shepard	Steven Spielberg
Neil Armstrong	Arthur Miller
Jackson Pollock	Ralph Ellison
Louise Nevelson	Alice Walker
George Balanchine	Salman Rushdie
Martha Graham	

Place to Locate

Chernobyl

Chapter Theme Questions

- **Technology** How might technological change affect ideas and behavior?
- **Social Relations** What challenges to well-being can people expect in the future?
- **The Arts** What direction did the arts and literature follow after World War II?

Throughout history the lure of the unknown has challenged people's courage, tested their ingenuity, and inspired them to embark on dangerous quests. Many individuals and groups of people have blazed the trail of human progress. Each era of history has provided unique challenges to its people.

We live in a time of rapid change—a time of promise and possibility. Many ideas that existed only in dreams and science fiction 50 years ago have become reality in the 1990s. Children in the 1940s could only imagine what it would be like to travel in space. Today children can watch the massive space shuttle slice through the clouds on its way to dock with an orbiting space station. Robot spaceships have even journeyed to Mars and beyond, gathering information about the universe.

Other frontiers remain on Earth—in science labs where researchers are discovering new treatments and cures for disease; in industry and business, where advancing technology is changing our lives; in the oceans, where scientists and engineers are exploring and tapping mineral resources on the ocean bottoms; and in classrooms, where traditional knowledge and fresh ideas are sparking a new generation to meet today's challenges, explore tomorrow's frontiers, and strive to enhance the quality of human life.

Section 1

Science and Technology

Focus Questions

- **What advances in travel and in space exploration have occurred since 1945?**
- **What impact have miniaturization and computerization had on modern life?**
- **What technological improvements have been made in medical science?**

Dramatic advances in science and technology after World War II affected all the nations of the world. Although industrialized societies felt the effects most directly, inventions, discoveries, and new technological devices also brought changes to developing nations. It is impossible to list all the discoveries and applications of new ideas that affected the way people thought and lived after 1945. However, a look at some spectacular developments illustrates the broad range and sweeping significance of the advances that have taken place in these decades of rapid change.

Faster Travel

Improvements in airplanes transformed travel throughout the world. Advances in air travel were a direct result of World War II. In the United States and Germany, for example, the search for better weapons led to the development of jet airplanes. After the war was over, these designs were adapted for civilian travel.

The first jetliner, the Boeing 707, began passenger service between the United States and Europe in 1958. By the mid-1960s, jetliner travel had become commonplace. The first commercial jumbo jet, the Boeing 747, began service in 1970. At speeds of more than 400 miles per hour, jets like the 747 could allow travel to nearly anywhere in the world in a matter of hours. Supersonic transport is a more recent development in air travel. The Concorde, a sleek airliner developed by the British and the French, travels at speeds of more than 1,000 miles per hour. It slashed travel time from Europe to the United States to three hours, though traveling on it was too expensive for most people. Meanwhile, complex traffic-control systems powered by sophisticated computers helped airports deal with ever-increasing air traffic.

While air travel became the most popular and convenient way to reach distant places, other means of transportation also advanced rapidly. Trains in Japan and Europe sped through the countryside at more than 150 miles per hour. Automobile use increased around the world. From 1950 to 1995, annual world production of motor vehicles jumped from about 10.5 million to nearly 50 million. And in 1994 Europeans welcomed a new link between Great Britain and France with the completion of the Channel Tunnel under the English Channel.

Space Exploration

Although Canada, Japan, and several Western European nations have developed space exploration programs, the United States and the Soviet Union have dominated the space race. The Soviets achieved the earliest successes. As the 1960s progressed, however, the United States stepped up its program.

Early successes. The Space Age began on October 4, 1957, when the Soviet Union launched *Sputnik*, the world's first space satellite, into orbit around Earth. Then in 1961 the Soviets built a rocket with enough power to put a person into orbit around Earth, and Soviet astronaut Yuri Gagarin became the first person to orbit Earth.

The United States had already begun its own ambitious program for space exploration. Now, however, the United States space program expanded rapidly. In 1958 the United States successfully launched an unmanned satellite into space, and in 1961 Alan Shepard became the first American to travel in space. In March 1965 the first Soviet astronaut walked in space, and by August the United States had responded with the 20-minute space walk of Edward White.

Lunar landing. On July 20, 1969, the United States won the intense race to put the first person on the moon. The Apollo XI mission transported three American astronauts—Neil Armstrong, Edwin E. Aldrin, Jr., and Michael Collins—to the moon aboard the spaceship *Columbia*. While Collins stayed behind on the *Columbia* to help coordinate the mission, Armstrong and Aldrin descended to the surface of the moon aboard the lunar module, the *Eagle*. The following excerpt from the transmission between *Eagle* at Tranquility Base on the moon, the orbiting spacecraft *Columbia*, and two control teams—Apollo XI Control and Mission Control—in Houston, Texas, illustrates the triumph of this historic event.

> **"EAGLE:** Houston, Tranquility Base here. The *Eagle* has landed. . . .
> HOUSTON: Roger, Tranquility. Be advised there are lots of smiling faces in this room and all over the world. . . .
> HOUSTON (10:37): Neil, this is Houston. What's your status on hatch opening?
> TRANQUILITY BASE: Everything is go here. . . . We're going to try it. The hatch is coming open. . . .
> ARMSTRONG: Okay, Houston, I'm on the porch. . . .
> HOUSTON: We're getting a picture on the TV. . . .
> ARMSTRONG: I'm at the foot of the ladder. . . . the surface appears to be very, very fine-grained. . . . I'm going to step off the LM [lunar module] now.
> That's one small step for a man, one giant leap for mankind.**"**

Edwin Aldrin joined Neil Armstrong on the moon's surface and for the next two hours the astronauts took photographs, collected lunar soil and rocks, planted a U.S. flag on the moon's surface, and conducted experiments. About 22 hours after the *Eagle* had landed, the astronauts left the moon and returned to the command module. On July 24, 1969, they returned to Earth.

The world watched, listened, and followed the quest for knowledge about space into the 1970s, when the main results of space exploration came from unmanned spacecraft.

Unmanned spacecraft. After a series of manned moon landings from 1969 to 1972, the U.S. space program shifted its emphasis to unmanned spacecraft that explored deep into our solar system. Late in 1973, 21 months after its launch, *Pioneer 10* became the first spacecraft to fly by Jupiter. Then in mid-1976, *Viking 1* and *Viking 2* landed on Mars, the "red planet." For several years they sent information back to Earth that provided a vivid picture of the planet's makeup.

Voyager 1 and *Voyager 2*, launched in 1977, explored the more distant planets of the solar system. Both made flybys of Jupiter and Saturn between 1979 and 1981, sending back spectacular photographs. Then *Voyager 2* continued to the outer reaches of the solar system. It encountered the planet Uranus in 1986 and by 1989 had reached Neptune.

After a break of some years, the United States restarted its unmanned space exploration program in 1989 with the *Magellan* and *Galileo* missions. *Magellan* began orbiting and sending back information from Venus in 1990, mapping nearly the entire surface of the planet. *Galileo* went into orbit around Jupiter in December 1995, transmitting data about the planet and its moons. In 1997 the *Cassini* spacecraft was launched on a mission to Saturn.

One of the most dramatic accomplishments in the mid-1990s was the landing of another U.S. spacecraft on Mars. The *Pathfinder*, which touched down on July 4, 1997, provided scientists with strong evidence that there had once been water on Mars—the key ingredient for creating and sustaining life.

Satellites. The United States, the Soviet Union, and other countries have launched satellites into

Viking II photo of Mars (above). Viking II view of Mars ice cap (right).

orbit around Earth. These satellites are divided into several types: communications, weather, Earth observation, navigation, and military.

Communications satellites act as relay stations, receiving radio signals from one location and transmitting them to another. Weather satellites help scientists study and forecast the weather. Earth observation satellites locate resources—such as minerals and water—on Earth. They also allow scientists to study the sources and effects of pollution. Navigation satellites allow people operating aircraft, ships, and land vehicles to determine their locations. Military satellites track movements of military equipment and determine where weapons are placed.

New frontiers in space. The 1980s and 1990s brought even greater American and Soviet advances in manned space flight. A new phase of space exploration began in 1981 with the launch of the first U.S. space shuttle, *Columbia*. By 1986 these reusable shuttles, which incorporated elements of both the traditional space capsule and the airplane, had completed two dozen successful missions. Everyone thought that the launch of the *Challenger* on January 28, 1986, would be another routine success. However, 73 seconds after liftoff the shuttle broke apart, disintegrating into a ball of flame. The *Challenger* and its crew of seven were lost. The disaster halted the United States' manned exploration of space until the successful launch of the shuttle *Discovery* in 1988. That same year, the Soviet Union successfully launched an unmanned space shuttle.

The United States and the Soviet Union also challenged each other in the development of space stations, which are orbiting observation centers. The Soviets led the way with the launch of *Salyut 1* in 1971. Two years later, the United States followed with *Skylab*. These two craft provided an opportunity to do experimental work in geography, engineering, medicine, and many other fields of study. They also allowed scientists to test the effects of long-term space travel on humans. The Soviets launched several more space stations, including *Mir* in 1986, but the United States ended its space station program and focused on the development of the shuttle. *Spacelab*, a joint venture of several European nations, took the place of a permanent space station. This module, carried in the space shuttle's cargo bay, provided the facilities needed to carry out large-scale experiments in space. In 1990, the crew of the shuttle *Discovery* placed into orbit the Hubble Space Telescope, a sophisticated orbiting observatory.

Science experiments were performed in a weightless environment during the Life and Microgravity Mission aboard *Columbia* in 1996. This photograph shows an earlier launch of the reusable shuttle.

What If?

We Are Not Alone
What if a spaceship from Earth discovers intelligent creatures on another planet? How will this affect the way people view their place on Earth and in the universe?

Although for many years the United States and the Soviet Union raced against each other in the conquest of space, the end of the Cold War has brought about a greater spirit of cooperation. In 1975, for example, the Soviet *Soyuz* craft docked in orbit with the U.S. *Apollo*. The Soviet cosmonauts and U.S. astronauts then worked together on experiments for two days. In 1995 the United States space shuttle *Atlantis* docked with Russia's space station *Mir*. However, by 1997, *Mir* was experiencing increasing problems, and the station's continued operation was called into question.

Miniaturization

Possibly the most important influence on the design of aircraft and spacecraft is weight. Researchers are always looking for ways to decrease the weight of equipment without making it weaker or less effective. Therefore, inventing ways to make machines, especially electrical equipment, smaller and lighter was a significant consequence of air and space travel. This process is known as **miniaturization**.

The best-known device that resulted from miniaturization is the transistor. This tiny electronic device, invented in 1947, came to replace the much larger vacuum tube. In fact, one transistor could do the work of many vacuum tubes more efficiently. Within 25 years, numerous transistors and other components could be placed on an integrated circuit—a tiny wafer of material, usually silicon.

Miniaturization made possible dozens of new products that affect the activities of people around the world. Portable radios, pocket calculators, digital watches, and automatic cameras were developed as part of this process. Initially, these products were expensive and not widely available. However, costs fell rapidly as technology advanced and the demand for such products increased.

Computerization

The most remarkable product of miniaturization was the modern computer. In the 1600s the French scientist Blaise Pascal invented the first automatic calculator, which worked by means of wheels linked to each other by gears. The idea intrigued scientists and engineers over the next 300 years. In the 1830s Charles Babbage designed a mechanical calculating machine that he called the "analytical engine." His machine is often seen as the forerunner of the modern computer, since it included all of a computer's basic elements: data storage, memory, a system for moving between the memory and storage components, and an input device. Babbage was not, however, able to construct the device he had designed.

ENIAC (Electronic Numerical Integrator and Calculator) was an enormous computer built in 1946. It took up an entire room at the University of Pennsylvania, where it was constructed. The discovery of transistors and later development of integrated circuits made possible much smaller machines capable of storing and rapidly processing information. These computers, which scientists improved year after year, quickly

Computer chips, such as this one, seem astoundingly small considering the extensive amount of information they contain.

made an impact on society. They advanced in both speed and efficiency, while requiring less and less space to store gigantic amounts of information. Integrated circuits opened the door to wider application of computer power. They found their way into machines and appliances of all shapes and sizes, from automobiles to self-focusing cameras to microwave ovens.

By the 1990s computers were performing a multitude of functions and affecting people's lives in dramatic ways. For example, computers make it possible for doctors to diagnose diseases and treat patients more effectively than ever before. CAT (computerized axial tomography) scanners, MRI (magnetic resonance imaging) machines, and other complex devices allow doctors and technicians to view the human body in incredible detail. As a result, many medical problems that once would have required exploratory surgery can now be diagnosed with little risk or discomfort to the patient. Outside the medical field, computers serve to guide spacecraft, operate manufacturing equipment, record airline reservations, print newspapers, construct maps, diagnose automotive problems, and perform a broad range of other functions.

In addition, large and powerful **supercomputers** help provide solutions to complex scientific and engineering problems that not long ago would have been all but impossible to solve. Because supercomputers have more than one processing unit, they can perform billions of computations per second. Supercomputers have revolutionized methods of research, development, and experimentation. For instance, scientists and engineers use supercomputers in the aerospace, petroleum, and automotive industries. They allow engineers to create exact models of what they are studying. Supercomputers are now used widely in weather forecasting, where numerical models are part of the forecasting process.

Today computers increasingly affect people's daily lives. Desktop and lightweight laptop computers are common in offices, homes, schools, and libraries. Businesses use computers to process and store enormous amounts of financial and administrative information—everything from customers' credit-card transactions to employees' retirement benefits. The range of activities controlled or facilitated by computers is growing daily. Meanwhile, computers continue to increase in power and speed while shrinking in size and cost.

Communications

In the decades after World War II, technological advances made radio and then television affordable to more people. Radio and television made it possible to transmit ideas and information more rapidly and widely than ever before.

Computers and the Internet. The advent of computers added a dramatically new dimension to the information revolution. The Internet, a vast global network that connects many computer networks, allows computer users to communicate with one another over telephone lines. Through the Internet, people all over the world can exchange information—words, pictures, and sound—nearly instantaneously. By the mid-1990s, the Internet linked millions of computers all over the globe.

The impact of computer communications is profound. In the comfort of their homes or offices, computer users have worldwide electronic access to stunning amounts of information. In addition, individuals can communicate with one another through e-mail—electronic messages transmitted almost instantaneously. Furthermore, companies can use the Internet to transact business, carry out research, and market their products.

Other innovations. Besides desktop computers, many other important communications innovations came into use over the past several decades. In the 1970s photocopiers established themselves as essential business machines. In the 1980s and 1990s fax machines became affordable and widespread. By the mid-1990s, cellular phones were common. Fiber-optic cables, which use light instead of electricity or radio waves to send signals, offered a faster and better alternative to other types of cables for telecommunications.

The thick layer covering this statue in Venice, Italy, was built up through hundreds of years of rain and air pollution, and was removed by laser cleaning.

Lasers

In 1960 a U.S. scientist built the first laser, although the idea of the laser had been conceived during the 1950s. A **laser** concentrates light and releases it in an intense beam that travels in a straight line. The laser's uses are extraordinarily varied, including applications in medicine, industry, and communications.

Doctors use lasers to repair damaged tissue in the eye and to burn away unhealthy tissue. Lasers help manufacturers cut precisely into hard substances, such as metal or diamonds. Lasers also transmit radio, television, and telephone signals. They can even be used to clean delicate pieces of art. Scientists are continuing to find new uses for this versatile invention.

Medical Science

Not all the advances that followed World War II involved physics or electronics. Biologists and other scientists made significant breakthroughs in their battle against disease.

Antibiotics. In 1928 the British scientist Alexander Fleming discovered a substance he called penicillin, noting that it stopped the growth of many types of bacteria. Thus it could help cure illnesses caused by those bacteria. In the years after Fleming's discovery, other substances were found to have similar effects. Streptomycin, which was discovered in 1944, attacked some bacteria that could resist penicillin. Substances that destroy or limit bacterial growth are called **antibiotics**, and after 1945 these "wonder drugs" transformed the fight against disease. They cured certain illnesses, such as tuberculosis, that previously had had no cure, and they lessened the risk of infection following surgery. Although some bacteria came to resist antibiotics, these medicines became essential in reducing sicknesses and preventing the contamination of food.

Vaccines. Medical researchers also made remarkable progress in preventing disease. Jonas Salk's polio vaccine was released for general use in 1954. In 1960, Albert Sabin produced an oral polio vaccine, which began to be used in 1961. As a consequence, polio has been all but eliminated in developed countries. Similarly, a worldwide campaign against smallpox virtually eliminated the disease by the 1980s. The last known naturally occurring cases of smallpox occurred in 1977.

AIDS. The first cases of AIDS (acquired immunodeficiency syndrome) in the United States were reported in the early 1980s. From the beginning of the epidemic to the middle of 1996, the United Nations

Medical researchers, such as this one, continue studying HIV, the virus that causes AIDS.

UNAIDS program had recorded 30 million cases of HIV/AIDS around the world.

While there is as yet no known cure for the disease and no vaccine to prevent it, researchers have had increasing success in fighting the progress of the disease with combinations of powerful new drugs. Research continues, but until a cure is found or a vaccine developed, efforts to combat the disease rely on education programs that teach people how HIV, the virus that causes AIDS, is spread and how it can be prevented.

Genetic Research and Biotechnology

In 1962 the Nobel Prize for medicine, the most prestigious scientific award in the world, was given to an American, James D. Watson, and two British scientists, Maurice Wilkins and Francis Crick, who had discovered the structure of **DNA** (deoxyribonucleic acid) in 1953. DNA is an essential component of genes—the small units of chromosomes that convey characteristics, such as color of hair and eyes, from parent to child. By understanding DNA, one can understand how a gene is structured—what scientists call the **genetic code**.

By unraveling the genetic code, the DNA experimenters came closer to explaining how different life forms are created. This breakthrough made possible new research into viruses, bacteria, human cells, and diseases such as cancer.

Cloning. The process of manipulating a cell from an animal so as to produce a genetically identical duplicate of that animal is referred to as **cloning**.

The Global Economy

In one day, traders on Wall Street buy and sell a record number of shares as confidence in the market soars. The next day, stock markets in London, Paris, and Tokyo rally. A month later, discouraging economic trends in Japan cause Asian markets to dive sharply. Within minutes, investors across the globe are selling stocks in record numbers. Both scenarios are possible in today's global economy. Modern digital communication allows information to spread almost instantaneously. One result is a global economy in which many economic entities are linked and react to one another's activities. Though the nature of today's global economy is historically unprecedented, economic interdependence has existed for thousands of years.

By the second millennium B.C., the Phoenicians dominated the world trade scene. By about 1100 B.C., Phoenician colonies which bordered the Mediterranean Sea in present-day Spain, northern Africa, and Sicily connected commerce throughout the entire region. Purple-dyed garments were instantly recognizable as the work of Phoenician craftspeople, and the glass, cedar, wine, metalwork, and ivory of Phoenicians could be found in virtually any major trade center located along the Mediterranean Sea.

Unlike the sea routes of the Mediterranean, the Silk Road served as an overland link between east and west. Established between about 300 B.C. and 200 B.C., the 4,000 mile trade route stretched from China to a point in Southwest Asia. Goods were then transferred to ports located along the Mediterranean, where they eventually found their way to western markets. The Chinese traded their valuable silks for western wools, gold, and silver.

Sea and river routes determined the trade landscape of the Middle Ages. Generally, the northern trade routes dealt in common bulk goods, and southern traders specialized in luxury items from the east, such as spices and silks. These separate European trading contingents occasionally overlapped. At large-scale international fairs in Flanders and Champagne, goods from virtually anyplace in the known world could be bought and sold.

In the 1200's, a group of about 150 north German merchants formed the Hanseatic League. For several hundred years, the trade association dominated economic exchanges in northern Europe. They obtained trading rights in the Baltics, Flanders, England, and Scandinavia. Traders might start with goods from the Baltics, exchange those goods in transactions from Norway to England to Flanders, and return to the Baltics with items that would normally be unavailable in the region. Goods that were traded included everyday staples, such as English wool, Baltic

Left: Medieval Port of Venice

Above: Phoenician trading ship (c. 700 B.C.)
Right: The Steelyard-Depot of the Hanseatic Merchants in London

Above: Medieval Arab traders in dhows

grains, Flanders cloth, and Scandinavian fish. The trading partners of the Hanseatic League benefited from guidelines that promoted independence while at the same time encouraging cooperation among the trading partners.

In the southern European trading sphere, Asian spices and luxurious fabrics traveled from the eastern Mediterranean to central and northern European centers, where nobles purchased them. Favorably situated between the Byzantine Empire to the east and European states to the north and west, Venice became a dominant international trade force of the Middle Ages and was a key mover of exotic goods.

In the 1600's and the 1700's, European conquest and colonization on the Indian subcontinent and in the Americas radicalized the character of the global economy. Through special charters, Britain, France, Spain, and the Netherlands gained nearly exclusive trade rights and authority over the inhabitants of certain regions.

However, the growing number of western trade routes had the greatest impact on the global economy. Interests in sugar plantations in the Caribbean—and slave laborers from Africa to work them—soon made trade routes across the Atlantic the most lucrative in the world.

Today, the largest trade organization in the modern Western world is the European Union (EU). The EU boasts 15 member nations that engage in tariff-free trade, bolstering their own economies while enjoying the benefits of trade with other members. In addition to trading with member countries, EU nations also trade with nations across the globe.

In 1992, the North American Free Trade Agreement (NAFTA) eliminated all existing tariffs and trade barriers among Canada, the United States, and Mexico. Such trading partnerships can foster interdependence of nations by creating a larger, unified market of people buying and selling goods and services. However, economic interdependence can create inequities, as well. Opponents of NAFTA have argued that for the

Signing of NAFTA agreement

United States, for instance, the enticement of lower manufacturing costs in Mexico might lead to lost jobs in the United States. Such perceived imbalances must be negotiated in a global economy.

In the past, the international economy was often dominated by one trading power that was virtually unaffected by its trading partners. Today, this scenario is unlikely. Modern nations have forged economic links in which every partner feels the effects of the others' actions. In the early 1990s, for example, when many Asian countries experienced phenomenal economic growth, nations around the globe saw investment opportunities and sank money into the region. In the late 1990's, when markets in Japan, Hong Kong, and other Asian countries suffered serious financial setbacks, the global economy reeled. Markets in North America, Europe, and Latin America experienced losses of varying degrees.

Meeting of the New European Commission

English dignitary of the East India Company being transported by elephant

Genetic Engineering

Since the dawn of humanity, our ancestors have struggled to alter their environment in order to survive. Prehistoric people shaped the natural resources around them into tools, weapons, clothing, and shelter. Through thousands of years of human history, we have learned to effectively control our environment through new developments in food production, housing, travel, and communication. We have learned to control the microscopic environment around us by stopping the spread of infectious diseases, curing infections with antibiotics, and preventing disease with vaccination. Today we are on the edge of being able to control our "internal environment"—the genes that determine our physical heredity—the color of our eyes, our height, and our susceptibility to colon cancer or heart disease.

In the 1980s, scientists began to use genetic engineering to alter genes in plants and animals to produce bigger or better food sources. Today, scientists are involved in perhaps the most dramatic project since the development of the atomic bomb—the Human Genome Project, which is mapping all the genes of the human body. As scientists discover the location and function of individual genes, they have identified genes that cause or contribute to certain diseases: Alzheimer's disease,

Dr. Ian Wilmut and his cloned ewe Dolly

breast cancer, and skin cancer. Scientists are also learning how to use gene therapy—replacing defective genes with normal ones.

This new knowledge and ability has raised some thorny ethical questions: Will insurance companies be able to refuse coverage based on genetic information? Can criminals claim their gene for excessive aggression is responsible for their criminal behavior? Should people be allowed to create "designer babies" by selecting specific characteristics such as hair color, eye color, or musical ability? Bioethicists are still struggling with such questions as our ability to control our genetic structures continues to grow.

In 1997 researchers at the Roslin Institute in Edinburgh, Scotland, successfully cloned a sheep. This was the first mammal ever cloned from a single cell of an adult animal. Some experts believe that within the next decade scientists might have the ability to clone humans.

The Atom

Just as biologists were able to probe inside the cell, physical scientists became more knowledgeable about the smallest of nature's building blocks, the atom. With increasingly powerful instruments, scientists could examine the tiny particles within the atom. They soon learned how to use the energy released when the structure of the atom is altered.

Atomic energy was first used to build more powerful bombs. Later it was used to develop efficient generators to produce electricity for a growing population. Whenever atomic energy is tapped, dangerous radiation, known as radioactivity, is released. When carefully controlled, radioactivity can have extremely beneficial medical uses—for example, in the treatment of cancer. Extensive uncontrolled exposure to radioactivity, however, can alter genes and kill life forms.

The disastrous explosion at the Chernobyl nuclear power plant in the Soviet Union in 1986 provided a vivid illustration of radiation's dangers. (See Chapter 19.) The explosion spread significant amounts of radioactive material over parts of Europe. Tens of thousands of people living near Chernobyl had to be evacuated. Numerous people subsequently died of radiation-related illnesses. Cancer rates jumped, as did the frequency of birth defects, a trend that doctors anticipated would continue for decades.

The explosion at Chernobyl was the world's worst nuclear accident, and it brought into focus people's doubts about the safety of nuclear energy. Consequently, opposition to nuclear power increased in many countries. Nevertheless, by 1995, there were 437 nuclear power plants in 31 countries. And even though disenchantment with nuclear power had grown, advances in the understanding of the atom continued to offer benefits. For example, researchers in nuclear physics developed new methods for diagnosing and treating disease. Other scientists devised new approaches to preserving food.

Plastics

The first synthetic substances—substances that do not occur in nature—were developed by chemists in laboratories in the 1800s. A few of these substances began to have wide applications. For example, celluloid was used to make movie films, and Bakelite was used for telephones, pot handles, and electrical equipment. It was not until the 1940s, however, that these synthetic substances, called plastics, began to appear in every area of life.

Plastics became an essential part of daily existence. They completely altered the appearance as well as the manufacture of most of the products people use, from toothbrushes to telephones. Synthetic fibers were woven into easy-care fabrics for clothing and upholstery. By the mid-1990s, plastics were being used to make everything from automobiles and household appliances to desktop computers and disposable medical products. Many plastics are made from petroleum products. Therefore, the petroleum industry became increasingly important as the demand for plastics grew.

Technology's Continuing Impact

Since 1945 technological advances have virtually transformed the world. Devices such as telephones, radios, refrigerators, and cameras existed before 1945. However, only after 1945 were they manufactured inexpensively enough for millions of people to buy them. These products are more common in the industrialized nations, but they have also had an enormous impact on life in the developing nations of the world.

What was so remarkable in the period after 1945 was the widespread application of these modern products. New industries, such as television and computer manufacturing, sprang up. Millions of people were employed in new kinds of jobs, and world markets flourished as nations traded the products of the new technological age.

Scientists working for the military also found applications for these advances in technology. Some of their developments were used in battle for the first time during the Persian Gulf War of 1991. Computer guidance systems directed Tomahawk cruise missiles toward targets hundreds of miles away. Computer-operated Patriot missiles intercepted and destroyed Iraqi SCUD missiles. Radar guidance warned the Patriots' computers of the SCUDs' approach.

These "smart" weapons systems and such everyday consumer items as portable computers, video recorders, microwave ovens, and laser printers represent extraordinary advances in the field of technology. Yet, these technological advances are only a hint of technological developments still to come.

Section 1 Review

1. **Define** *Discovery, Spacelab,* miniaturization, supercomputers, laser, antibiotics, DNA, genetic code, cloning
2. **Identify** Yuri Gagarin, Alan Shepard, Neil Armstrong
3. **Locate and Explain the Significance** Chernobyl
4. **Summarizing Ideas** Describe how exploration of space has moved from competition between major powers to cooperation.
5. **Classifying Ideas** List three technological or scientific advances that have taken place since 1945. Explain the importance of each.
6. **Analyzing Ideas** Explain how technology can be both a benefit and a burden.

Section 2

Health and Human Rights

Focus Questions

- How do population pressures affect the well-being of the people of the world today?
- What types of environmental problems are the people of the world trying to solve?
- What are human rights abuses, and how are the nations of the world dealing with them?

The second half of the 1900s was a time of significant political, economic, and social change. In industrialized nations, standards of living generally improved and opportunities multiplied. Change in developing nations was less dramatic, but there, too, most people's lives benefited from technological and scientific advances. Still, progress brought new challenges, and global cooperation became more important than ever as a means of dealing with the world's problems.

Population Pressures

One of the most noteworthy—and startling—developments to occur during the postwar decades was the rapid growth in world population. Between 1930 and 1950, world population increased by about 23 percent. In the next four decades, however, population increased by 112 percent, reaching 5.3 billion people in 1990. And by mid-1997, the world population had soared to 5.8 billion. The U.S. Census Bureau projects it will reach 7.6 billion by 2020 and 9.3 billion by 2050.

This explosive growth resulted from a combination of factors. Medical advances and improvements in health and sanitation practices caused a striking decline in death rates, both in infants and adults.

While better medical care helped keep people alive, scientific research helped feed them. In the 1960s scientists developed seeds that yielded much more rice and wheat than ever before. The use of chemical fertilizers and advances in irrigation methods and farming techniques further improved crop yields. This Green Revolution, as it came to be known, increased food production in many poor countries, helping people to lead longer, healthier lives.

Most of the world's population growth occurred in developing nations, such as those in Asia and Latin America. The most rapidly growing region of all, however, was Africa. As the number of people on Earth continued to multiply, scientists and economists became increasingly concerned with the consequences of overpopulation.

Although populations are increasing in developing countries, increases have been slowing throughout the century in North America and Europe. Many economists are concerned that the rapidly growing populations in developing countries will cancel the economic advances of these areas. Moreover, rapid population growth in some of the world's poorer nations has contributed to political instability and social discontent, particularly when there is a great gap between the rich and the poor.

Human migration. Adding to the challenges of population growth are the effects of large-scale migrations. After World War II, some 400,000 refugees came to the United States. Since the 1960s, the United States has experienced an influx of immigrants from Asia and Latin America. This is a change from the historical immigration pattern of the United States, in which most immigrants came from Europe.

Large-scale migrations occur for many reasons, including war, famine, political changes, a search for fertile soil, and ethnic rivalries. In the Middle East in the early 1990s, as many as 5 million people sought safety in Turkey, Iran, and other countries during the 1991 Persian Gulf War. In Rwanda in the mid-1990s a bloody civil war between the country's two major ethnic groups caused the movement of large numbers of people.

Urban growth. Migration from rural areas to urban areas—a trend known as urbanization—has swelled city populations around the world. Indeed, urban populations in many countries are increasing much more rapidly than rural populations.

Thirty years ago, about 25 percent of the world's population lived in cities of 20,000 or more. By 1980, this figure had increased to about 40 percent. By 2000, that number is estimated to approach 50 percent. Such explosive urban growth has severely challenged the resources of cities.

From Mexico City to Cairo to Calcutta, overcrowding has strained governments' ability to provide adequate health and human services. As cities have expanded, both jobs and housing have become scarce. Some cities have experienced water shortages.

Positive steps. Various efforts are under way to deal with problems related to world population growth. Some governments have promoted programs to limit the birth rate. The Chinese government, for example, undertook a campaign in the 1970s to persuade families to have no more than one child. Still, in many parts of the world, large families continue to be common.

Scientists are working to develop further agricultural methods and technology in order to increase world food production. For example, they are exploring ways to make deserts fertile and to farm the oceans. In addition, using genetic engineering, they are trying to produce food crops that can grow in Earth's driest regions.

While researchers work to produce more food for the world's hungry, the Red Cross, United Nations agencies, and other groups try to help those in need. For example, after the famine and severe economic problems in Nigeria in the 1960s and 1970s and the destruction in Cambodia in the 1970s, relief organizations fed millions of starving people. Governments and organizations are also trying to improve food distribution so that available food reaches victims of famine and malnutrition.

Environmental Concerns

Technological and scientific advances, while improving the quality of life for many people in the world, did not come without cost. As industries grew and as developing countries struggled to build their own industries, industrial waste products polluted Earth's air, water, and land. Moreover, pollution and land development posed a growing danger to animal and plant life. People around the world came to realize that cooperative efforts were essential to clean up, preserve, and protect the environment.

Acid rain. One of the most devastating kinds of pollution is **acid rain**. Acid rain forms when precipitation falls through air polluted by toxins produced by the burning of fossil fuels. Acid rain pollutes water, kills fish, and ravages forests. It can also damage buildings. The destructive effects of acid rain have been felt in North America, Europe, and other parts of the world. In recent years many nations have cooperated to reduce emissions from motor vehicles and factories. Unfortunately, according to studies in 1996, the acidity of waters in Europe had not yet decreased.

Pesticides. Industrialization was not the only cause of pollution. Farming methods of the Green Revolution relied in part on the use of pesticides. Pesticides increase crop production, but they can be dangerous. As biologist Rachel Carson pointed out in her 1962 book *Silent Spring*, pesticides are not selective; they poison all living things with which they come into contact.

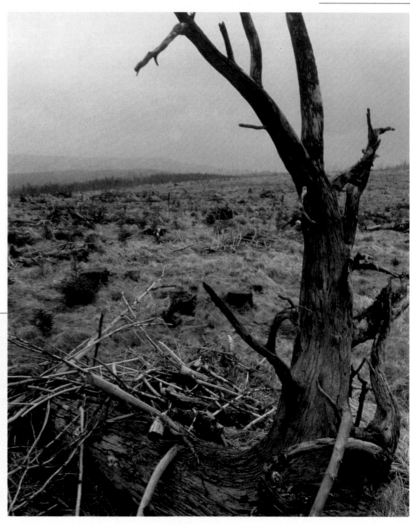

When sulfur dioxide and nitrogen oxide are released into the atmosphere, they combine with water vapor to produce sulfuric and nitric acids. This highly acidic precipitation is particularly damaging to aquatic organisms and plant life. Shown in the photo is the Giant Mountains National Park in northeast Bohemia. The park is dying from acid rain.

Waste disposal. Industrialization and population growth increased the amount of waste produced. National and local governments looked for ways to handle both toxic and nontoxic waste. Some governments wanted to export their waste elsewhere, but environmentalists objected that one city or country should not become the waste dump for another. Government and industry leaders in many nations are working to reduce waste products, encourage recycling, and find safe ways to dispose of hazardous wastes.

Endangered species. World population growth and industrialization increases the need for land and other natural resources, leading to the destruction of forests, wetlands, and other areas. Losing these natural habitats threatens the survival of numerous plant and animal species. Rain forests, for example, are being destroyed so quickly that thousands of species are being lost each year. Scientists are concerned about this reduction of biodiversity, the natural variety of plants and animals that naturally occurs in the environment. This loss of biodiversity could have damaging effects on humans as well as the environment.

Ozone depletion. Some scientists warn that pollution is depleting the ozone layer of the stratosphere. Ozone is a gas that shields Earth against the Sun's ultraviolet rays, which can cause skin cancer in humans and damage animal and plant life. Some scientists believe that a leading cause of ozone depletion is the use of chemicals called chlorofluorocarbons (CFCs), used in aerosol sprays, coolants, and the manufacture of electronic parts and plastics. Although scientists did not agree on the cause of ozone depletion, during the 1980s and 1990s many countries began to phase out or ban the use of CFCs.

Global warming. Carbon dioxide and other gases in Earth's atmosphere allow the Sun's rays to warm the planet but do not let the heat radiating from Earth to escape. This **greenhouse effect** helps keep Earth's temperature at levels suitable for life. According to many scientists, the burning of oil, coal, and natural gas has increased the amounts of these gases in the atmosphere, trapping more heat and contributing to a rise in global temperatures. While scientists do not agree on just how great a danger global warming represents, many warn that temperatures may rise by as much as 6°F by 2100. Such an increase could have devastating consequences. For example, if portions of the polar ice caps were to melt, sea levels would rise, and low-lying areas of the world would be flooded.

Global responses. People around the world are making an increasing effort to deal with environmental concerns. Numerous organizations have been established to meet challenges to the environment. For example, Greenpeace, an international organization, has fought against various practices that they believe are dangerous to the environment, such as offshore oil drilling, dumping of radioactive wastes into the oceans, and whaling.

In the past several decades, the United Nations has sponsored international meetings on environmental matters. During this time, several international agreements have addressed such issues as endangered species, the ozone layer, and hazardous wastes. In 1992, delegates from 178 nations attended the United Nations environmental conference, nicknamed the "Earth Summit," in Brazil. Several significant agreements emerged from this conference, including one on the prevention of climate change and one on the preservation of biodiversity.

Human Rights Issues

The horrors of World War II underscored the need to protect human rights around the world. In the preamble to its 1945 charter, the newly formed United Nations (UN) declared:

> "We the peoples of the United Nations, determined . . . to reaffirm faith in fundamental human rights, in the dignity and worth of the human person, in the equal rights of men and women and of nations large and small, . . . have resolved to combine our efforts to accomplish these aims."

In 1948, the UN adopted the Universal Declaration of Human Rights, outlining basic human rights to which every person is entitled.

However, while the Declaration and subsequent UN agreements demonstrated the international community's concern for human rights, they were not binding on all nations, and they provided no means of enforcement. Indeed, most countries insisted that any attempt at enforcement would violate their national sovereignty. This opposition to external interference in internal affairs persists as a major obstacle to international human rights protection.

The pursuit of human rights. Even though the United Nations continues to address human rights abuses around the world, such abuses remain all too common. Human rights violations often have political, ethnic, racial, or religious roots. For example, brutal "ethnic cleansing" during the civil war in Bosnia resulted in thousands of deaths. Terrorist violence carried out by extremists in Northern Ireland has killed or injured many innocent people. In many parts

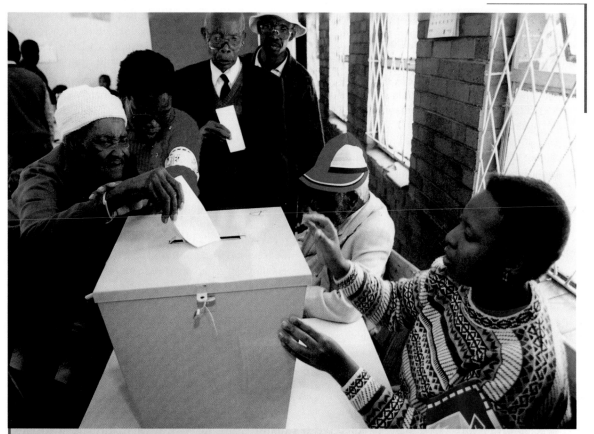

South Africa held its first free presidential election in April 1994. Millions of people waited patiently in line to cast their votes. Nelson Mandela won by a landslide.

of the world, repressive governments have imprisoned, tortured, and executed people who have spoken out against them.

Still, there has been significant progress. For instance, international pressure helped bring an end to apartheid in South Africa, and in 1994 that nation held its first truly democratic election. Political changes in the Soviet Union, both before and after the collapse of the Soviet system, also led to improved human rights.

Besides the United Nations, various other organizations work in pursuit of human rights. For example, Amnesty International, a private organization, investigates and reports on human rights abuses around the world. Numerous regional organizations, such as the Council of Europe, also try to advance the cause of human rights.

In addition to human rights in general, people in many countries have actively supported the rights of specific groups. The women's liberation movement, for example, sought to eliminate barriers to women's equality with men. In the United States, various groups, including the American Association of Retired Persons, work to protect the rights of elderly people.

Differing perspectives. The concept of human rights does not have a single, universal meaning. Different cultures have different perspectives. For example, some people, especially in non-Western countries, place greater emphasis on the interests of the community than on the rights of the individual. Many of these people criticize Western nations for trying to impose their ideals and values on other nations.

Similarly, such concepts as women's rights have different meanings in different societies. In the Islamic world, for instance, women's rights are viewed within the context of the Qur'an, the holy book of Islam. Thus, while the world's many nations may be able to agree on certain basic human rights, all nations must try to understand cultures and values that are different from their own.

Section 3

The Arts and Literature

Focus Questions

- **What trends occurred in painting, sculpture, and architecture after World War II?**
- **What innovations appeared in music, dance, film, and drama since 1945?**
- **How did poetry and novels express the mood of the times?**

In the decades after World War II, the arts and literature reflected the political turbulence and social changes of the times. Artists and writers moved beyond past methods and attitudes, exploring different perspectives and new means of self-expression. Two trends became particularly noticeable after 1945. One trend was the commitment to experimentation, which had been evident since the early 1900s. The other trend was the enormous popular interest in artistic and intellectual developments.

Painting and Sculpture

After 1945 New York City became one of the liveliest centers of new ideas and painting styles. The dominant style of painting became known as **abstract expressionism**. The leading abstract expressionist was an American, Jackson Pollock. Pollock believed that art comes from a person's unconscious mind. A painting is a personal expression, he thought, and should be judged by how authentically it reflects the nature of the artist. Pollock chose to express himself by randomly dripping different colors of paint onto a canvas that was spread out on the floor. Other abstract expressionists used

different techniques. Mark Rothko, a Russian-born American, placed large areas of color next to each other, blurring them together and creating a dazzling effect.

In the 1950s painters moved away from abstract expressionism to experiment in other ways. It was no longer possible to speak of one dominant style. In Great Britain and the United States, a number of artists returned to showing reality—but a special kind of reality. Developing a style called **pop art**, these artists chose as their subjects common objects such as soup cans, comic strips, or road signs. Experimentation also occurred in sculpture. The U.S. sculptor Louise Nevelson, for example, created large wooden sculptures. Many are wall units, like her sculpture *Black Chord*, filled with objects placed within boxed compartments.

New styles of painting arose in the late 1950s and 1960s. One group of artists concentrated on **op art**—a type of art that used optical illusions. These artists rejected reality as the subject of paintings, instead concentrating on the manipulation of brilliant colors and shapes for visual effect. Another type of painting, called hard-edge painting, used geometric areas of bright color with precisely defined contours.

The 1970s and 1980s saw some return to realism in paintings of scenes, objects, and people. Some European and U.S. painters, such as the neo-expressionist German artist Anselm Kiefer, turned away from abstract painting and returned to portraying recognizable objects. Often Kiefer, in particular, dealt with the moral problems posed by Nazism in his painting. Experiments continued, however, and many styles of art seemed acceptable.

The modern age has led artists to incorporate futuristic technology into their work. Today the title "artist" has come to include photographers, filmmakers, ceramists, glassblowers, and many others. The artist's materials range from the traditional canvas, paint, marble, and bronze to materials such as plastic and scrap metal. Modern art forms may be welded, wired, glued, sewn, or lighted. Some artists even construct and paint images from sand, create artistic patterns in plowed fields, or—like the contemporary artist Christo—wrap islands or buildings in fabric. Indeed, the line between sculpture and other art forms is not nearly as clear as it once was.

Another art trend of the modern age is **conceptual art**. Often conceptual art reduces the emphasis on isolated art objects and focuses instead on the arrangement of "environments" composed of both objects and people. Conceptual artists believe that the act of creating the art is more important than the actual art object.

History Through the Arts

Sydney Opera House

The Sydney Opera House, which dominates the harbor in Sydney, Australia, in appearance resembles a ship with its sails set for the future. Built on a peninsula, the building consists of a series of concrete shells that house a center for the performing arts.

Australia, despite its geographical isolation from Europe, has continued to maintain a strong British heritage. After World War II many European refugees settled in this island continent. They have helped to make the nation's culture more international.

When the Australian government decided to build a center to celebrate the arts, it sponsored a worldwide competition to choose an architect. Joern Utzon, a Dane, was the winner. His building rests on a high platform, and the shells rise more than 200 feet above sea level. Utzon's structure contains four theaters—a concert hall, an opera theater, a drama theater, and a playhouse that was originally designed for chamber music—each acoustically perfect for the type of performance it holds. Opened in 1973, the Sydney Opera House is among the most recognizable buildings in the world and is considered by many to represent a masterpiece of modern architecture.

Another trend that arose in a new form in the 1970s is **performance art**. In performance art, the artist himself or herself becomes a kind of living work of art. The German artist Joseph Beuys, for example, spent a week caged in a New York gallery with a coyote. In another example of performance art, by Nam June Paik, a Buddha contemplates himself on television.

Architecture

The search for new ideas and techniques dominated architecture, as it had since the invention of the skyscraper in the early 1900s. Since 1945 materials have changed frequently. One popular material was reinforced concrete, which was used by French architect Charles-Édouard Jeanneret, known as Le Corbusier, one of the most influential architects of the century. He admired the clean, precise shapes of machinery, and his buildings reflect this preference.

Smoothness and polish also interested architects, who created this smoother look mainly by using huge walls of glass. Le Corbusier himself took this approach when he, along with a committee of other designers, designed the headquarters of the United Nations in New York City.

Architects also experimented with new ways of building houses. Some houses were cast in concrete in standard units and then shipped to the building site. Others made use of new plastic materials.

New shapes appeared in architectural designs. Notable among these unusually shaped buildings is the group of concrete shells that make up the Sydney Opera House in Australia. Another new architectural design is the spiral-shaped form of the Guggenheim Museum in New York City. This was designed by the U.S. architect Frank Lloyd Wright, a leader in the use of unconventional shapes.

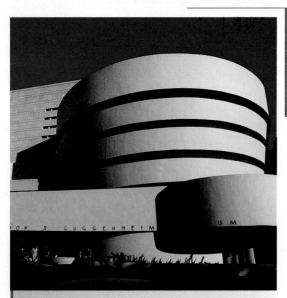

The Guggenheim Museum in New York City, designed by Frank Lloyd Wright to display Solomon R. Guggenheim's modern art collection, contains a spiral ramp that encircles the inside of the building for six stories.

Throughout the 1970s and 1980s, architectural designs assumed more contemporary lines. The rapid development of new engineering techniques prompted the construction of domed stadiums such as the Astrodome in Houston, Texas. Designs of the late 1980s emphasized spaciousness and employed innovative features. Some modern homes combined attractive and practical design with solar energy or other devices to save fuel. Many cities had buildings with unique designs, large expanses of glass, or gleaming mirrored tiles.

However, no single design or method of building has dominated architecture in the years since 1945. Experimentation has led to a wide variety in architectural styles, which often are found side by side in city centers. Some observers criticize such mixture of styles, particularly when modern additions are made to historic buildings.

Music and Dance

Experimentation has been equally apparent in the world of music. New uses of instruments, rhythm, harmony, and melody were introduced. Some composers, however, did write traditional types of music. The British composer Benjamin Britten, for example, wrote operas. The later work of Russian composer Dmitry Shostakovich included symphonies built on Baroque structures.

After 1945 new kinds of sound entered the world of serious music. Experimenters found that computers could produce sounds. Innovative composers wrote pieces for synthesizers or for combinations of traditional instruments and synthesizers. Composers also began to write music that gave performers—and even the audience—a major role in determining how a piece would sound. The unorthodox ideas of U.S. composer John Cage, for example, had a profound influence on the music of his time.

The determination to break new ground and to leave the past behind was especially obvious in popular music. During the 1950s, a form of music known as rock 'n' roll emerged in the United States. It had roots in many different places, including African American rhythms and the blues of the rural southern United States. Rock had a heavy, accented beat and a simple, repetitive melody. During the 1960s, the Beatles, a group from Liverpool, England, became one of the most popular and influential rock bands in history. A number of different styles, with such names as folk rock, hard rock, punk rock, and disco, developed. Another form of popular music, country-western, usually consisted of sentimental ballads, and African American musicians developed popular styles such as soul music, rhythm-and-blues, and rap.

In the 1980s and 1990s music videos became increasingly popular, helping to spread popular music and win worldwide fans for many musicians. At the same time, interest grew in the music of other cultures, and artists drew inspiration from the music of Africa, the Caribbean, South America, and other parts of the world.

The world of dance also followed new directions after 1945. Artists who had left Russia after its revolution were especially influential in ballet. The most influential was George Balanchine. Balanchine was founder, artistic director, and chief choreographer/director of the New York City Ballet. In the 1960s and 1970s, young ballet stars such as Rudolf Nureyev, Mikhail Baryshnikov, and Natalia Makarova defected from the Soviet Union to make their careers in the West.

After 1945 the freer and looser forms of modern dance began to influence ballet. As in all the performing arts, the tendency was to leave uniformity behind, to experiment, and to allow more individual expression. Martha Graham, an American, was a very influential teacher of modern dance. Her work expressed powerful emotions.

Building History Study Skills

READ
WRITE
INTERPRET
CONNECT
THINK

Making Connections with History: Linking Architecture to History

Architecture often reflects the values of a culture. The skyscraper is both the triumphant symbol of—and at the same time, an unwelcome intruder into—the city. It shatters scale and steals light, yet it suggests the personality of the city of which it is a part. It has also made the city's character a reflection of its own quality. For example, the Sears Tower in Chicago and the Empire State Building in New York City are the symbols of these metropolitan areas just as the Cathedral of Notre Dame is a symbol of Paris. Linking architecture to history helps historians explain how the environment affects a society, determine the individual's reaction to the environment, and visualize the society's values.

How to Link Architecture to History

To link architecture to history, follow these steps.

1. Establish the historical context of the piece of architecture.
2. Identify the society that built the structure.
3. Identify the major characteristics of the piece of architecture.
4. Describe characteristics of the environment.
5. Relate the environmental characteristics to the historical context.
6. Identify the values expressed by linking the historical context of the piece of architecture and the environmental characteristics.

Developing the Skill

Analyzing the skyscraper's architecture helps you link architecture to modern history. The skyscraper has become the symbol of the U.S. city of the 1900s. It defines life in the metropolis.

Skyscrapers began to rise above 40 stories by 1907. These towering symbols of urbanization housed more than offices—they also included stores and restaurants. Their lobbies became so large that they became gathering places.

One example of the skyscraper is the Woolworth Building in New York City. Completed in 1913, it gracefully extends 792 feet above the ground. Although the building is perceived as a sheer tower, its base consists of a 30-story

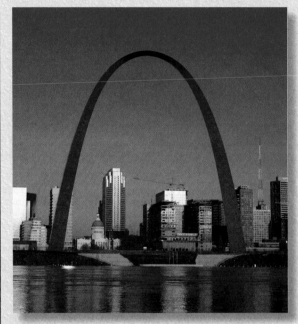

The Gateway Arch, St. Louis, Missouri

U-shaped mass. Rising from the center front of the structure is a square tower that culminates in an ornate crown at the top. The vertical lines of the base shoot up into the tower, melding the upper and lower masses together.

The architecture of a particular society also reveals more than cultural values—it reveals information about the economic characteristics of a society. An impressive building is a symbol of a successful corporation. The visual effect of massive buildings suggests corporate glory and represents human ability and technical achievement. In the modern age, skyscrapers have become the cathedrals of commerce.

Practicing the Skill

The Gateway Arch in St. Louis, Missouri, is shown on this page. Research this piece of architecture. Link this piece of architecture to the city where it was built as well as the history of the United States.

To apply this skill, see Applying History Study Skills on page 647.

In recent decades U.S. choreographers such as Alvin Ailey, Jr., Twyla Tharp, Paul Taylor, and Alwin Nikolais have been especially influential in dance.

Film

Traditional subjects—adventures, comedies, and social dramas—dominated most filmmaking after 1945. Spectacular productions, costing millions of dollars, continued to be popular. Other films tried to break free of traditional restrictions.

In the 1940s and 1950s, Italian directors such as Federico Fellini produced shattering and sometimes bizarre commentary on social and political injustice. At the end of the 1950s, a group of young French directors known as the "New Wave" further revolutionized film. These directors, including Louis Malle and Jean-Luc Godard, believed that the director should act as the *auteur*, or author, of a film. That is, a film should be the conception of one person—the director—not a commercial package put together by a movie studio. The "New Wave" directors often rejected traditional filmmaking techniques. They used hand-held cameras and often edited their works in new ways. They believed that the visual style of a film—not necessarily the storyline—was what was most important.

Some of the most interesting but disturbing films made in the 1960s and 1970s came from Japan. Akira Kurosawa and other Japanese directors used violence and a melancholic atmosphere to create startling and frightening new effects. Meanwhile, director Lina Wertmüller was making deeply satirical films concerning Italian politics and society as well as the relations between men and women.

Technical mastery was increasingly evident in American films from the 1970s on. George Lucas's *Star Wars* series, Steven Spielberg's *E.T.—The Extraterrestrial* (1982), and James Cameron's *Titanic* (1997), for example, depended heavily on visual effects. The creative application of advanced computer technology dazzled viewers in *Jurassic Park* (1993), *Toy Story* (1995), and *Twister* (1996).

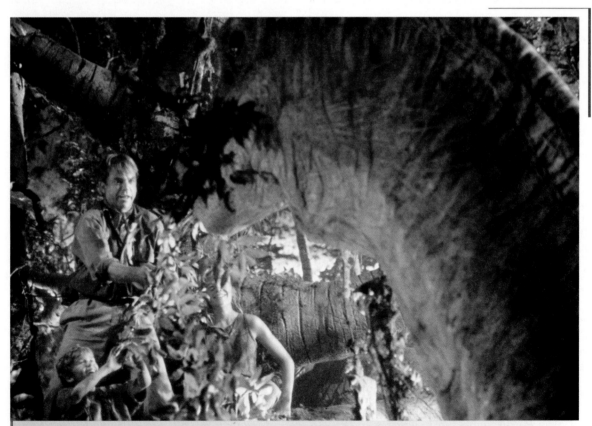

Computers can be used to generate spectacular effects in movies today. This movie still is from *Jurassic Park*.

Meanwhile, independent moviemakers took film in a new direction. Largely free of ties to the big studios, they made films with strong social commentary. Director Spike Lee, for example, made such provocative movies as *Do the Right Thing* (1989) about the experiences of African Americans in urban America. Despite numerous multimillion-dollar successes, the American filmmaking industry had financial setbacks. Although the explosion of videotapes and VCRs in the homes of the 1980s stimulated interest in films of all kinds and from many countries, some large studios lost huge amounts of money on unsuccessful big-budget movies. The widespread use of cable television in American homes also gave movie theaters increasing competition. In the 1990s economic considerations led many movie studios to become part of large entertainment conglomerates.

Drama

In the theater, too, important new techniques developed. In East Germany the company founded by playwright Bertolt Brecht staged plays with an emphasis on artificiality. Audience members were not to be drawn in but were to be constantly reminded that they were watching a play.

Perhaps the most powerful new vision of the modern age was the biting social commentary of the playwrights of the so-called theater of the absurd. Its leaders were Samuel Beckett and Eugène Ionesco, an Irishman and a Romanian, respectively, who lived in France. Bewilderment and absurdity run throughout Beckett's works, including his most famous play, *Waiting for Godot* (1953).

More realistic but no less biting attacks on modern society were apparent in the works of other playwrights of this period. The most notable of these dramatists were John Osborne, an Englishman, and Arthur Miller, an American. Osborne addressed the bleakness of the lives of the British working class, and Miller's powerful dramas, particularly *Death of a Salesman* (1949), explored human weaknesses and the tensions in families. Another American, Tennessee Williams, explored similar themes concerning the American South.

Social analysis and comment even entered the boisterous world of U.S. musical theater. Perhaps the most remarkable musical of the post-1945 period was *West Side Story* (1957), based on Shakespeare's *Romeo and Juliet*. Composer and conductor Leonard Bernstein wrote the score, and Jerome Robbins handled choreography for the musical.

During the 1980s and 1990s, many musicals, such as *The Phantom of the Opera* (shown above) and *Les Misérables,* became dramatic successes.

The 1980s and 1990s saw the production of "blockbuster" musicals in theaters all over the world. These musicals involved spectacular stage sets and lavish musical arrangements and often had unusual themes or settings. *The Phantom of the Opera* (1986), by British composer Andrew Lloyd Webber, told of the fascination between a young opera singer and a "ghost" that haunted an opera house located in Paris. A novel written by French author Victor Hugo inspired the hit musical *Les Misérables*. In 1996, *Cats*, based on the work of British poet T.S. Eliot, became the longest-running Broadway show in history.

Poetry and Novels

Many poets and novelists took a stand against the comfortable self-satisfaction they saw in the world around them. For example, society's most prosperous citizens and their values became the target of a group of writers who made up what was called the Beat Generation. These writers, most of them living in San Francisco, Los Angeles, and New York City, began writing in the 1950s. Beat novelist Jack Kerouac and poet Allen Ginsberg attacked the conventions of the American way of life, such as commercialism, materialism, and insensitivity. They thought writing should be completely spontaneous and rejected the traditional forms of the novel and the poem.

Protest was a major theme of the leading writers of the postwar years. Among the most powerful African American writers were Ralph Ellison and James Baldwin. Each explored, with dismay and anger, the life of African Americans in the United States. Nigerian novelist Chinua Achebe examined the effects of colonial rule on his native land. West German novelists Günter Grass and Heinrich Böll explored Hitler's impact on Germany. Boris Pasternak and Alexander Solzhenitsyn wrote of the repressions of the Soviet system. The dissident writers of Eastern Europe, too, wrote about the hardships of life under communism. In fact, these "underground" works were the only source of truth for many Eastern Europeans.

Scientific and technological advances after World War II boosted interest in science fiction, making it one of the most popular forms of literature. Writers such as Ray Bradbury, Robert Heinlein, and Isaac Asimov stimulated the imaginations of millions of readers with tales of space travel, robots, and distant planets.

Naguib Mahfouz became the first Arab writer to be awarded the Nobel Prize for Literature in 1988; his collection of work includes novels, short stories, and plays.

A related theme of literature written during the postwar period was escape from an increasingly hostile and confusing world. Writers such as the American Kurt Vonnegut, Jr., created fantasies about imaginary worlds. The writers of this period used these fantasies to suggest pessimistic and satirical alternatives to what they saw as the dehumanizing attitudes of the times.

Prominent Latin American writers chose a similar approach. Nobel Prize winner Octavio Paz, a Mexican author, used contrasting images of the inevitable loneliness of people and their desire for companionship in surrealistic, dreamlike poems. The Colombian Gabriel García Márquez, also a Nobel Prize winner, wrote haunting, mystical novels and stories about ordinary subjects.

Not all authors and poets wrote of protest or other worlds. Some writers, like American poet Wallace Stevens, explored the interaction of reality and what one can make of that reality in one's own mind. Another American poet, Marianne Moore, used subjects from nature to write about, often as symbols of steadfastness and honesty.

In recent years the voices of minority women have become increasingly powerful in the United States, and their novels and poems have often been best-sellers. Pulitzer Prize winners Alice Walker (*The Color Purple*) and Toni Morrison (*Beloved*) confronted the issues of African American life from the period of slavery through contemporary times. Maya Angelou's poetry explored the black experience in the South. And in her novels Laura Esquivel similarly explored the Hispanic experience of feminism in repressed countries like her native Mexico.

Some writers provoked controversy. For example, in 1988 Western critics acclaimed Anglo-Indian author Salman Rushdie's satirical novel *The Satanic Verses*. Many Muslims, however, called it blasphemous. Some governments banned the book, and violent demonstrations against it occurred in Pakistan and other countries. Then Ayatollah Ruhollah Khomeini of Iran issued a death sentence against Rushdie, forcing the writer into hiding. In 1994 Egyptian author Naguib Mahfouz, the first Arab writer to win the Nobel Prize, was attacked by an assailant who objected to Mahfouz's treatment of Islam in his works.

In the 1990s novelists and poets continued to share their unique insights and personal experiences with readers around the world. Notable writers of this decade included Japanese novelist

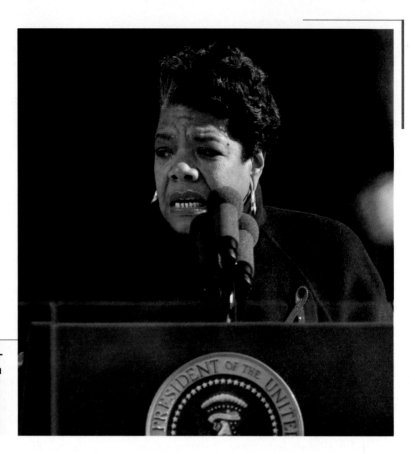

Maya Angelou, known for her autobiographical works, read her poem "On the Pulse of Morning" during President Clinton's inauguration ceremony in 1993.

Kenzaburo Oe, American novelist John Updike, and Irish poet Seamus Heaney.

The Audience for the Arts

The excitement of postwar artistic and literary activity generated enormous public appeal, particularly in the United States. After World War II, museums responded to a better-educated society. Of the existing museums in 1988, 75 percent were founded after 1950 and 40 percent since 1970. More Americans paid to go to museums, concerts, operas, ballets, and theaters each year than to attend sporting events.

Around the world, more people are completing the equivalent of a high school education, and more people are attending college. People have more time for leisure activities, particularly in the industrialized nations. Television exposes millions of viewers to films, plays, concerts, and a wide range of other cultural activities. Many people continue to pursue similar entertainment outside the home. Thus education, increased leisure time, and expanding cultural awareness have combined to give the arts and literature greater exposure and support than ever before.

Section 3 Review

1. **Define** abstract expressionism, pop art, op art, conceptual art, performance art
2. **Identify** Jackson Pollock, Louise Nevelson, George Balanchine, Martha Graham, Lina Wërtmuller, Steven Spielberg, Arthur Miller, Ralph Ellison, Alice Walker, Salman Rushdie
3. **Summarizing Ideas** Describe some of the changes in artistic and architectural styles since 1945.
4. **Interpreting Ideas** How did new trends in music and dance reflect some of the same themes as painting and sculpture since 1945?
5. **Analyzing Ideas** Using specific examples, describe how film and theater reflected new techniques and themes.
6. **Interpreting Ideas** Do you agree or disagree with the statement that novels, films, and poetry often give a truer picture of the condition of a country than news reports or other nonfiction? Explain.

Chapter 20 Review

A.D. 1957
Sputnik
is launched.

A.D. 1961
Yuri Gagarin
becomes first person
to travel in space.

A.D. 1945   A.D. 1950   A.D. 1955   A.D. 1960

A.D. 1947
The transistor
is invented.

A.D. 1950s
• Computers are developed.
• Pop art develops.
• Rock 'n' roll begins.

A.D. 1954
Salk's polio vaccine is
released for general use.

A.D. 1960
First laser is built.

Chapter Summary

The following list contains the key concepts you have learned about the modern age.

1. Major technological advances brought about changes in ideas and behavior after 1945. Advances in air travel and space exploration changed the way people thought about their world. Miniaturization, computers, and advances in communication changed the ways people lived and worked. Medical knowledge grew and expanded rapidly. Scientists' growing understanding of the power of the atom had both positive and negative effects.

2. Population grew rapidly in the years after 1945. Most of the world's growth occurred in the developing nations. Rapid population growth can lead to a number of problems. When urban populations increase, for example, city resources are strained.

3. Environmental concerns of recent decades include acid rain, the effects of pesticide use, waste disposal, endangered species, ozone depletion, and global warming. Countries are working together to solve many of these problems.

4. Human rights issues became important in the postwar years. Human rights violations often have political, ethnic, racial, or religious roots. Differing cultural views of human rights sometimes made consensus difficult.

5. The arts and literature continued the experimentation that had marked their development since the early 1900s. New forms of painting, notably abstract expressionism, pop art, and op art, transformed the visual arts. Sculpture and architecture also took new forms.

6. Musicians experimented with new kinds of sounds, both in serious compositions and in popular forms. New styles of creativity were also evident in dance and filmmaking. Drama moved in new directions as traditional plays were transformed by the theater of the absurd.

7. Writers after 1945 expressed many different ideas, including a stand against complacency and various forms of protest. Science and technological advances promoted an interest in science fiction. Other writers focused on an escape from a hostile and confusing world. The voices of minorities, including women, have been heard in greater numbers.

Reviewing Important Terms

On a separate sheet of paper, supply the term that correctly completes each statement.

1. The process of making machines, especially electrical equipment, smaller is called _____ .
2. _____ are medicines used to treat bacterial infections.
3. The style of art dominant after 1945 and demonstrated by Jackson Pollock is called _____ _____ .
4. Paintings of common objects such as soup cans are examples of an art style called _____ _____ .
5. _____ _____ forms when precipitation falls through air polluted by toxins produced by the burning of fossil fuels.
6. The trapping of heat by a layer of gases in the atmosphere is called the _____ _____ .
7. The manipulation of a cell from an animal so as to produce a genetically identical duplicate of the animal is called _____ .

Developing Critical Thinking Skills

1. **Comparing Ideas** (a) How were the early successes of the space exploration programs of the United States and the Soviet Union similar? (b) Compare more recent advances in manned space flight and space stations of these two countries.
2. **Debating Ideas** (a) What are some of the benefits and the dangers of atomic power? (b) What other technological advances of the 1900s have both positive and negative impacts?
3. **Evaluating Ideas** How might rapid population growth in a developing country slow down other types of growth and development?
4. **Analyzing Ideas** How did changes in the arts during the modern age reflect other changes in society?
5. **Determining Cause and Effect** (a) How did lifestyles in America change after World War II? (b) What factors account for these changes?

A.D. 1975
Apollo and *Soyuz* spacecraft dock in orbit.

A.D. 1986
Challenger space shuttle explodes.

A.D. 1995
U.S. space shuttle *Atlantis* docks with Russian space station *Mir*.

A.D. 1970 A.D. 1975 A.D. 1980 A.D. 1985 A.D. 1990 A.D. 1995

A.D. 1969
Apollo XI mission lands on the moon.

A.D. 1970s
Performance art develops.

A.D. 1992
Earth Summit is held in Brazil.

A.D. 1997
Researchers in Scotland successfully clone a sheep.

Relating Geography to History

Select a writer, a composer, or an artist from the United States or a foreign country. Write a short biographical essay and describe how that person's environment influenced his or her contribution to the arts.

Relating Past to Present

1. In 1970 Alvin Toffler wrote a book about the effect of rapid change, about people facing the future too soon. Read the passage below from Toffler's *Future Shock* and then answer the questions that follow.

   "The high velocity [rapid rate] of change can be traced to many factors. Population growth, urbanization, the shifting proportions of young and old—all play their part. Yet technological advance is clearly a critical node in that network of causes; indeed, it may be the node that activates the entire net. One powerful strategy in the battle to prevent mass future shock, therefore, involves the conscious regulation of technological advance."

   a. According to Toffler, what factors bring about rapid change?
   b. Which of these factors is most important?
   c. Based on what you learned in this chapter and on your knowledge of current events, do you agree with Toffler? Explain your answer.

2. (a) Using a tape recorder, prepare a program of popular music of the 1990s. Then prepare a similar tape for a previous decade. Possible sources of recordings include friends, relatives, and your school or local library. (b) What do the tapes reveal about each period? (c) How have popular tastes changed? (d) What, if any, new instruments are used today? (e) How might musical recordings contribute to an understanding of history?

Applying History Study Skills

Before completing this activity, review Building History Study Skills on page 641.

Locate and compare photographs of the medieval cathedral located at Salisbury in England and the Trump Tower building located in New York City. Then answer the following questions.

1. (a) What characteristics of Gothic architecture can you find in the photographs? (b) How are these characteristics similar? (c) How are they different?
2. Which values of medieval society did Gothic architecture tend to reflect?
3. Which values of modern society do skyscraper architecture tend to reflect?
4. Write a brief essay that compares the cathedral to the skyscraper.

Search the Internet through the HRW Web site for information about one of the writers or artists mentioned in this chapter or about another contemporary individual working in the arts or literature. Locate an interview or other information about the person. Prepare a short oral report that tells what you learned about the person and his or her art or writings.

GO TO: go.hrw.com
KEYWORD: SCØ Artists

Building Your Portfolio

1. **Writing a Report** The Space Age began in 1957 with the launching of the Soviet satellite *Sputnik 1*. Using reference materials, prepare a report on why the United States has emerged as the world leader in space exploration. Based on your research, what are some reasons for the success of the United States space program? Place the report in your portfolio.

2. **Preparing an Oral Presentation** Technological advances have had an impact not only on developed nations but also on developing nations. Select one area of scientific or technological progress, and present information to the class on how advances in this area have changed life in the developing nations of Asia, Africa, and Latin America. Place your notes and other research materials in your portfolio.

Unit Summary
The following list contains the key concepts you have learned about the challenges that faced the world from 1945 to the present.

1. After World War II, conflicts between Communist and Western nations resulted in the Cold War that threatened world peace.
2. When communist North Korea invaded South Korea in 1950, its troops were repulsed by UN forces, and an armistice was eventually signed.
3. In Southeast Asia, the United States became heavily involved in fighting in Vietnam.
4. Independence came rapidly to the African nations after World War II. Until 1994 the white government of South Africa resisted giving the country's black majority any significant power in government.
5. North Africa and the Middle East experienced several wars after 1945. Arab-Israeli conflicts, civil

war in Lebanon, and wars in the Persian Gulf took place during this period.
6. Many countries of Latin America were racked by military upheaval after World War II. However, these developing nations are beginning to work for peace and economic growth as the 1900s come to an end.
7. After Mikhail Gorbachev instituted his policies of glasnost and perestroika, United States–Soviet relations began to improve.
8. The future of NATO grew increasingly uncertain after the collapse of communism in Eastern Europe and the former Soviet Union.
9. After 1945 technological changes transformed communications, the understanding of the universe, the processing of information, the products people used every day, economic activities, medicine, and food production.

Reviewing Concepts
On a separate sheet of paper, supply the term that correctly completes each statement.

1. _____ is a term used to describe the communist nations that supported the Soviet Union.
2. The South African policy based on the principle of racial separation became known as _____, the Afrikaans word for "apartness."
3. _____ is the name given to the improvement in relations between the United States and the Soviet Union during the 1970s.
4. Through _____, or restructuring, Mikhail Gorbachev planned to overhaul the political and economic systems of the Soviet Union.

Applying Critical Thinking Skills
1. **Organizing Ideas** What was the purpose of the alliance systems set up by the Western nations and by the Communist bloc after 1945?
2. **Synthesizing Ideas** How did the work of civil rights leaders such as Dr. Martin Luther King lead to changes in the United States government's policy toward equal rights for all of its citizens?
3. **Comparing Ideas** How did the Korean War and the Vietnam War differ in terms of causes and effects?
4. **Evaluating Ideas** How did each of the following individuals contribute to the rise of nationalism in Africa? (a) Kwame Nkrumah; (b) Jomo Kenyatta; (c) Gamal Abdel Nasser.
5. **Summarizing Ideas** What changes occurred in the nations of the Middle East after 1945?
6. **Analyzing Ideas** How might economic prosperity in Latin America help bring political stability?

7. **Understanding Relationships** What were the results of the United States involvement in each of the following countries: (a) Panama, (b) Puerto Rico, (c) Cuba, (d) the Dominican Republic.
8. **Synthesizing Ideas** Should there be a set time period after which war crimes and violations of human rights cannot be punished? Why or why not?
9. **Interpreting Ideas** (a) What are some of the many reasons that people study history? (b) How can a knowledge of the past help people understand the present?

Relating Geography to History
Refer to the maps in Chapter 14 and Chapter 15. How did the spread of communism affect the map of Europe after the end of World War II?

Writing About History
Write a report that summarizes three major areas of disagreement between the United States and the Soviet Union between 1945 and 1991. Which was the most threatening to world peace? Why?

Further Readings
Allende, Isabel. *The House of the Spirits*. Bantam, 1986. Uses magic realism to explore the importance of family and political allegiance in Latin America.

Fitzgerald, Frances. *Fire in the Lake: The Vietnamese and the Americans in Vietnam*. Random House, 1989. Describes the Vietnam War.

Yergin, Daniel, and Thane Gustafson. *Russia 2010: And What It Means for the World*. Random House, 1995. Offers a clear and concise assessment of the key problems facing Russia and other former Soviet republics and their possible outcomes.

UNIT 4 CHRONOLOGY

Date	Politics	Science and Technology	Society and Culture
1945–1955	Formation of UN 15,* OAS 18, NATO 15, Warsaw Pact 15 Filipino 16, Indian 16, and Israeli 17 independence Egyptian 17, Chinese 16, and Viet Minh 16 revolutions Nuremburg trials 15 Truman Doctrine and Marshall Plan 15 Berlin blockade 15 Korean War 15 *Brown v. Board of Ed.* 15 Suez Crisis 17	Synthetics and plastics 20 Nuclear power 19 Computer revolution 20 Transistor 20 DNA research 20 Television 20	Léopold Senghor 17 Le Corbusier 20 Abstract expressionism 20 Mark Rothko 20 Science fiction 20 Britten and Shostakovich 20 Baldwin and Ellison 20 Beat Generation 20 John Cage 20
1955–1965	United States in Vietnam 16 Martin Luther King Jr. and civil rights 15 OPEC 17 Berlin Wall built 15 Cuban revolution and missile crisis 15, 18	St. Lawrence Seaway 15 *Sputnik 1* 20 Laser technology 20 Green Revolution 20	Pop and op art 20 French "New Wave" movies 20 Miller and Williams 20 *West Side Story* 20 Pasternak and Solzhenitsyn 20 The Beatles 20
1965–1975	Six-Day War 17 Soviet invasion of Czechoslovakia 15 Arab-Israeli War of 1973 17, PLO 17 SALT, détente 19 Watergate 19 OPEC embargo 19 Helsinki Accords 19 Pol Pot executes intellectuals 16	Lunar landing 20 Japanese industrialization 16 Asian economic revolution 16 Jumbo jets 20	Chinese Cultural Rev. 16 Vonnegut and García Márquez 20 *Samizdat* 19 Objection to Vietnam War 15, 19
1975–1997	Camp David Accords 17 Solidarity 19 Assassinations of Sadat 17, Indira and Rajiv Gandhi 16 Perestroika, glasnost 19 Gorbachev and Reagan summit 19 Berlin Wall torn down 19 Persian Gulf War 17 Breakup of Soviet Union 19 NAFTA 18, 19 Transfer of Hong Kong to China 16	Three Mile Island 19 *Columbia, Challenger* shuttles 20 Chernobyl 19, 20 *Mir* space station 20 AIDS research and education 20 Channel Tunnel 20 Cloning 20	Protests against apartheid 17 Steven Spielberg and Spike Lee 20 Wole Soyinka 17 Webber's *The Phantom of the Opera* 20 Rushdie's *The Satanic Verses* 20

*Indicates chapter in which development is discussed

The World Since 1945

CHAPTER 15

Europe and North America in the Postwar Years

The Soviet Union was one of the Allied Powers in World War II, and at the end of the war the Allies had seemed to reach agreements about Germany and Eastern Europe. However, differences dividing the Western democracies and the communist Soviet Union re-emerged. Suspicions between communist and Western nations led to the so-called Cold War, a conflict waged primarily by political and economic means.

Aftermath of the War in Europe

As postwar hostility between the Western democracies and the Soviet Union grew, Allied decisions about Eastern Europe, Germany, and Austria became more and more difficult to reach. For example, it took 10 years to reach an agreement about Austria, and no final agreement was ever reached on Germany. Instead, Germany remained occupied by American, British, French, and Soviet troops. Despite disagreements, however, the United Nations was founded as a body dedicated to preserving peace.

Origins of the Cold War

As the war was ending, Stalin placed governments friendly to Soviet interests in Eastern and Central Europe. Other Soviet actions seemed to indicate a policy of expansionism. In response, early in 1947 President Truman, announcing what came to be called the Truman Doctrine, dedicated the United States to helping countries threatened by communism. With a policy known as containment, the United States would contain, or restrict, the spread of communism.

The United States also instituted the European Recovery Program, often called the Marshall Plan, to help Europe recover from the war. Between 1948 and 1952, the United States spent more than $13 billion with tremendous success. Industrial and agricultural production in Europe rose above prewar levels.

New alliances made clear the extent of the split between East and West. In April 1949 the nations of Western Europe founded the North Atlantic Treaty Organization (NATO), a mutual defense pact. The Soviets and other countries of the European communist bloc responded by founding the Warsaw Pact. The Warsaw Pact greatly outnumbered NATO in terms of ground troops, which reinforced a Western reliance on nuclear deterrents.

Reconstruction, Reform, and Reaction in Europe

In a relatively short time, postwar Western Europe experienced a remarkable economic and political recovery. Eastern Europe also revived, but not nearly as quickly or successfully as the West did.

In 1957 the European Economic Community (EEC)—usually called the Common Market—was founded. It provided for the gradual abolition of tariffs and import quotas among the six member nations.

Stalin's successor, Khrushchev, began a policy of destalinization, loosening some of the government's control on the economy. His economic policies, however, failed to produce desired results.

Immediately after the war, the communist bloc seemed to be a solid group, but dissatisfaction with Soviet domination soon became apparent. In 1956 there was a revolt in Hungary, and in 1968 Czechoslovakia tried to institute reforms. The Soviets crushed the rebels in both countries.

The United States and Canada

At home, the United States aimed to resolve social and political problems and to maintain a flourishing economy. In response to the civil rights movement, in the 1960s Congress passed several acts that promised political equality for African Americans and other minorities. The United States's foreign policy revolved around containment. For example, the United States committed large numbers of troops to help noncommunist South Vietnam defend itself against communist North Vietnam.

After World War II, Canada became a vigorous supporter of the United Nations and an important member of NATO. It loaned billions of dollars to other countries and welcomed thousands of refugees from Europe. Canada also experienced considerable economic development.

Asia Since 1945

The years after World War II saw major political, economic, and social changes in Asia.

South Asia After Empire

In 1947, the British granted independence to India, but violence erupted between Muslims and Hindus when Britain partitioned the subcontinent along religious lines. The governments of India and East and West Pakistan struggled to cope with several problems: rapidly growing populations, poverty, illiteracy, and great cultural and linguistic differences.

By the 1980s, India's economy had made considerable progress, but economic growth had difficulty keeping pace with the ever-growing population. In 1971 civil war between East and West Pakistan resulted in the formation of the new nation of Bangladesh. Frequent natural disasters, economic instability, and a legacy of ill will between the major political parties made Bangladesh's future uncertain. Pakistan, too, faced political instability. India and Pakistan sought to improve relations, but a history of distrust and violence between them made peace an elusive goal.

The Rise of Communist China and Taiwan

By 1949 the Communists took control of the Chinese mainland and forced the Nationalists to flee to Taiwan. In 1966, Mao Zedong launched a Cultural Revolution, a violent attempt at social change that had disastrous effects on the economy. In time, the moderates won control and instituted more liberal economic policies and some political reforms. Calls for more political reforms in 1989, however, were brutally suppressed. Chinese leaders continue to maintain a tight hold on Chinese society.

After World War II China was first closely aligned with the Soviet Union, but Chinese-Soviet relations worsened and China's relations with the United States improved. In 1979 the United States formally recognized the People's Republic of China, but China's refusal to meet international human rights standards continued to cast a shadow over foreign relations in the mid-1990s.

Korea. Korea was divided at the end of World War II. North Korea's attempt to conquer South Korea in 1950 was prevented by the intervention of the United Nations. However, concern grew in the mid-1990s that a famine in North Korea could cause the government to launch new attacks on South Korea. In 1998, the president of South Korea pledged that democratic reforms in his country would go hand-in-hand with economic growth.

Taiwan. Run by a one-party system until the 1990s, Taiwan nevertheless enjoyed economic success under its free enterprise economy. In the 1990s a move toward official independence was viewed in a negative light by the People's Republic of China.

The Japanese Miracle

Japan made rapid economic progress after the war by producing highly advanced technology for a world market. By the end of the 1980s Japan was Asia's leading economic power. Postwar economic developments brought about far-reaching social changes in Japan. In the 1990s, however, Japan became mired in a stubborn recession, and political scandals caused governmental changes.

Ho Chi Minh City

Independence Struggles in Southeast Asia

Southeast Asia consists of 10 countries: the Philippines, Indonesia, Malaysia, Singapore, Brunei, Vietnam, Thailand, Laos, Myanmar (formerly Burma), and Cambodia. Except for Thailand, all of these countries were once colonies. After the war, they gained independence. For some, it was a peaceful transition. In others, violence occurred.

In the Philippines, Fidel Ramos, who became president in 1992, made efforts to strengthen the economy and encourage foreign investment. Indonesia continued to make economic progress in the 1990s, and its political and economic importance in the world grew.

By 1996, Malaysia's economy had become one of the strongest in the Asia-Pacific region, although the country still faced serious problems. Singapore had become the center of economic activity in Southeast Asia, and the country's people enjoyed one of the highest standards of living in Asia. Myanmar had some success in attracting foreign investment, but relations with the United States remained troubled.

Communist North Vietnam and pro-Western South Vietnam were at war more than 20 years. The United States intervened on behalf of South Vietnam. The Communists prevailed and united the country in 1976. The years of war drained the nation's resources, and many people have fled the country since 1976. The Communist government added some elements of free enterprise to the economy, which boomed in the 1990s.

The Communist Khmer Rouge, under the leadership of Pol Pot, captured the government of Cambodia in 1975. Between 1975 and 1977, 1.2 million Cambodians met their deaths by execution or starvation. Thousands fled to Thailand. In 1996, the Khmer Rouge showed signs of weakening, and in 1998 the notorious Pol Pot died of natural causes.

In recent years control of the government of Thailand has shifted back and forth between civilian and military leaders. Between 1985 and 1994 Thailand had one of the world's fastest growing economies. However, by 1997 a severe economic crisis made its future uncertain.

Asian Paths to Prosperity and Security

After independence, most new Asian nations attempted to build democratic societies. However, three factors gave rise to and helped sustain authoritarianism in Asia: (1) ethnic and cultural diversity that sometimes caused violent conflicts; (2) fear about national security; and (3) the desire for economic growth.

In the 1990s, roughly 3 billion people, more than half of the total population of the world, lived in Asia. A significant number of Asia's people lived in poverty and suffered its consequences—malnutrition, illiteracy, and reduced life expectancy.

By the mid-1990s, many parts of Asia had experienced economic expansion. China was an especially dramatic example, and there was no question about the Pacific region's continuing—and increasingly important—role in the world economy.

CHAPTER 17

Africa and the Middle East Since 1945

The African and Middle Eastern nations that became independent in the years after World War II faced problems of economic development, drought, famine, and disease. As the colonial era faded, ethnic and political divisions throughout Africa and the Middle East re-emerged.

Independence for African Nations

The struggle for independence in Africa took many forms. Some colonies followed a constitutional process while others suffered lengthy wars of national liberation. Eventually, even the most reluctant colonial powers had to grant independence. South Africa's experience differed from that of any other African nation. The white minority continued to rule and impose apartheid, a system of complete separation of races that oppressed nonwhites. In 1994, however, Nelson Mandela became president of South Africa, and a new era of multiracial cooperation began.

Africa Since Independence

Having achieved independence, African nations still faced serious problems. Practically all the new nations struggled with economic difficulties. Ethnic tensions also plagued most of them. In addition, drought, disease, and superpower rivalries took their toll. Despite

African National Congress rally

these problems, independence stimulated a revival and development of new cultural expressions. Africans found a new pride in their ancient heritage and its unique contribution to world culture. A mixture of African and outside influences gave an unusual vitality to the arts on the continent.

Nationalism in North Africa and the Middle East

World War II was a turning point for North Africa and the Middle East. During the war, the British had reestablished their control over strategic countries such as Egypt and Iran. Such control angered these countries and fueled the development of nationalism in the region. French North Africans also fought to be free of colonial rule. The establishment of the Jewish nation of Israel angered Palestinian Arabs and neighboring Arab countries. It has been a source of continuing conflict.

War, Oil, and Revolution

By 1962 most countries in North Africa and the Middle East had achieved independence. The remaining British protectorates in the Persian Gulf area gained full independence in the early 1970s. The major issues concerning the nations of the area during the final decades of the 1900s were oil, political instability, and the Arab-Israeli conflict, which continued despite the peace process begun with signing of the Camp David Accords by Egypt and Israel in 1979. Experts predict that after production peaks in oil fields outside

the Middle East early in the next century, oil produced in the nations of Iran, Iraq, Kuwait, Saudi Arabia, and the United Arab Emirates will become more important than ever to the world economy. Consequently, the Persian Gulf is likely to remain a principal focus of international attention in the future.

A revolution in Iran and the growing aggression of Iraq drew the world's attention to this strategically important region. The danger of a major war in the Middle East remained high in the final years of the 1900s. In 1991 the Persian Gulf War drew many nations into conflict. In addition to political and military problems, the nations of North Africa and the Middle East confronted social and economic issues.

CHAPTER 18

Latin America Since 1945

Latin America, rich in human and natural resources, stands on the threshold of dynamic change and development, although countries in this region continue to suffer political and economic instability.

Facing New Challenges

A growing population, petroleum deposits and other resources, and rapid industrialization increased Latin America's presence in the world after World War II. With industrialization came many benefits, including higher standards of living, improved health care, and economic growth. However, economic hurdles remained.

Mexico and Central America

By the late 1980s, a huge foreign debt had nearly crippled Mexico's economy. Not until 1996, with the help of government-implemented austerity measures, did the economy begin to recover. The Marxist-inspired Sandinistas took control of the Nicaraguan government in 1979. Opposition to their policies led to a civil war that finally ended in 1990, when free elections were held. In El Salvador, violence from left-wing and right-wing groups claimed thousands of lives in the 1980s. In 1992 opposing sides signed a peace treaty, and the first postwar elections were held. In December 1989, after Panamanian forces killed an American soldier, United States' troops restored order and captured Manuel

Noriega, the country's dictator. Noriega, tried and convicted in Florida of drug trafficking, was sent to prison.

The Nations of the Caribbean

The presence of a communist government led by Fidel Castro in Cuba, a country in close proximity to the United States, alarmed American leaders. Clashes such as the Bay of Pigs invasion and the Cuban missile crisis occurred in 1960 and 1961. Later, an uneasy peace typified relations between the two countries. By the mid-1990s, to boost an economy close to collapse, Castro allowed limited private enterprise.

The people of Haiti overthrew the ruling Duvalier regime in 1986. Jean-Bertrand Aristide, the country's first democratically elected president, was succeeded in 1996—the first time that one elected Haitian civilian had peacefully passed power to another.

South America

In Argentina a succession of military and civilian governments characterized the postwar period. Carlos Menem was elected president in 1989 and again in 1995, and the economy improved. In Brazil political unrest and economic chaos marked the postwar period into the early 1990s. Under Cardoso, who was elected president in 1995, Brazil's economy regained some stability, but in 1997 volatile financial markets challenged the country's ability to maintain economic progress. In Chile, once the oldest continuing democracy in Latin America, a peacefully elected communist regime was overthrown by a military dictatorship, but a civilian government was elected in 1989 and again in 1993. The country enjoyed economic growth. In Peru there were political problems and the government teetered between dictatorship and democracy. In Colombia, growing cocaine traffic threatened to tear the nation apart.

CHAPTER 19

The Superpowers in the Modern Era

The final decades of the 1900s marked a period of transition—the Cold War ended and a "new world order" emerged. Free enterprise and democracy advanced as communism declined. The United States

remained a leading power, while the Soviet Union as an entity disappeared.

The Industrial Powers of North America

The Vietnam War left deep scars on America's national identity and placed a substantial burden on the American economy. Also, the Watergate scandal shook the faith of many Americans in their political system and helped to make Washington, D.C., a symbol of corruption. As a result, several post-Watergate presidential candidates campaigned successfully as outsiders to Washington.

High inflation rates and unemployment plagued the nation in the 1970s. Both, however, had been brought under control by the 1980s. Despite a brief downturn in the early 1990s, the economy continued an upward trend into the mid-1990s.

Responding to continued Soviet expansion, the United States increased pressure on the Soviet Union in the 1980s. In the 1990s, American foreign policy confronted a host of new problems, such as the resurgence of militant nationalism and ethnic conflict. These problems emerged in the wake of the Cold War's end and the collapse of the Soviet Union.

Challenges also faced Canada in this period. The nation struggled with a determined French Canadian separatist movement but maintained close, although at times strained, relations with the United States.

Europe

Western Europe in general made significant strides toward political and economic integration, although

The fall of communism in Russia

the reunification of East and West Germany proved an increasing burden on the German economy through the mid-1990s. In the last decades of the century, formal institutions such as NATO and the European Economic Community—which evolved into the European Union in 1993—grew in strength and membership. The collapse of communism in Eastern Europe made possible an even wider union of European nations.

The Fall of Communism

By the early 1980s, the division of Europe between the Communist East and the free West appeared permanent. However, by the 1990s all the former satellites had broken off from the Soviet Union and had thrown out their Communist governments. Finally, the Soviet Union itself broke up into 15 nations. Although some countries looked forward to a prosperous future, political and economic instability prevailed throughout much of Eastern Europe and the former Soviet Union in the wake of communism.

CHAPTER 20

The World in the Twenty-First Century

Vast changes in people's lifestyles and attitudes marked the years following 1945.

Science and Technology

Dramatic advances in science and technology affected all the nations of the world. The United States and the Soviet Union dominated the space race. An important consequence of space exploration was the shift toward smaller and lighter machines. The most remarkable product of miniaturization was the modern computer. Today computers increasingly affect people's lives, and the range of activities controlled or facilitated by them grows daily. The Internet, a vast global network that connects many computer networks, allows computer users around the world to communicate with one another over telephone lines.

Biologists and other scientists made significant breakthroughs in their battle against disease with the development of vaccines, antibiotics, and other powerful new drugs.

Health and Human Rights

The second half of the 1900s was a time of significant political, economic, and social change. In industrialized nations, standards of living generally improved and opportunities continued to multiply. Change in developing nations was less dramatic, but in most areas of the world people's lives benefited from technological and scientific advances. One of the most noteworthy developments during the postwar decades was the rapid growth in world population. Rapid population growth in some of the world's poorer nations has contributed to political instability and social discontent. People around the world are continuously making an effort to deal with environmental concerns brought about by world population growth and industrialization.

The Arts and Literature

In the decades after the war, arts and literature reflected the political turbulence and social changes of the times. Artists and writers moved beyond earlier methods and attitudes, exploring different perspectives and new means of self-expression. Two trends became particularly noticeable after 1945. One was the commitment to experimentation, which had been evident since the early 1900s. The other was the enormous popular interest in artistic and intellectual developments.

Synthesis Review

1. **Understanding Ideas** What was the Cold War and what effect did it have on world events?
2. **Summarizing Ideas** In what ways did Asia change since 1945?
3. **Interpreting Ideas** Why is the Persian Gulf likely to play a part in world affairs in the future?
4. **Determining Cause and Effect** What types of problems have been caused by population growth in Latin America?
5. **Seeing Relationships** What were the results of the breakup of the Soviet Union?
6. **Analyzing Ideas** How did scientific and technological breakthroughs affect ordinary people's lives?
7. **Synthesizing Ideas** How are events in Latin America since 1945 like those in Asia? How are they different?